Connectivity and Standards

Connectivity and Standards

BY THE EDITORS OF DATA COMMUNICATIONS MAGAZINE

Data Communications
BOOK SERIES

McGraw-Hill Information Services Company
1221 Avenue of the Americas
New York, NY 10020

Cover Photograph by Walter Wick

Library of Congress Cataloging-in-Publication Data

Connectivity & standards / edited by the staff of Data communications
    magazine.
       p.   cm. — (The Data communications book series)
     ISBN 0-07-607020-4 (v. 3) : $39.95
     1. Computer networks — Standards — United States.   2. Computer
network protocols.   I. Data communications.   II. Title:
Connectivity and standards.   III. Series: McGraw-Hill data
communications book series.
TK5105.5.C663 1990
004.6'2'0973 — dc20   90-5511
                                                     CIP

McGraw-Hill Information Services Company
1221 Avenue of the Americas
New York, NY 10020

- **Basic Guide to Data Communications, Edition 2**
- **Cases in Network Design**
- **Connectivity and Standards, Volume 3**
- **Data Communications: A Comprehensive Approach, Edition II**
- **Data Communications: Beyond the Basics**
- **Data Network Design Strategies, Volume 4**
- **Inside X.25: A Manager's Guide**
- **Integrating Voice and Data, Volume 3**
- **Linking Microcomputers**
- **The Local Area Network Handbook, Volume 3**
- **Network Management and Maintenance, Volume 4**
- **Networking Software**
- **Telecommunications and Data Communications Factbook**

Table of Contents

Preface

The information industry, according to researchers at the Massachusetts Institute of Technology, "improves its fundamental technological cost performance at 30% to 40% compounded annually and has been doing so for three decades—with more to come." For communications managers and network planners, this is a mixed blessing. Because standards makers cannot keep pace, assuring connectivity of equipment—across generations as well as across networks—can be of vital importance.

This was clearly the case in the late 1980s. In the U.S. alone, the market for data-communications equipment grew from $57-million in 1985 to an estimated $104-million in 1989. With regulation loosening and global competition heating up, the problems of connecting disparate equipment were increasingly exacerbated by the need to bridge political boundaries.

As the U.S. Telecommunications & Information Administration saw it: "The challenge is to plan and implement efficient multivendor networks in a competitive market environment. For users, the challenge is to make cost-effective choices among a growing array of competing equipment and service alternatives. A similar trend towards competitive market conditions, and a similar set of challenges, are emerging in other countries and, increasingly, in international telecommunications as well."

This volume chronicles how those challenges were being met in the late 1980s, and how leading industry and experts planned to meet them in the coming decade. Feature articles edited by the staff of McGraw-HIll's Data Communications Magazine deal not only with the latest equipment advances but also with the innovative techniques being developed to connect disparate equipment, operating systems and even networks themselves.

Bolstered with in-depth case histories as well as reports on evolving protocols and standards, this collection is intended to serve as a handbook for information managers charged with steering their networks through the 1990s and into the 21st Century.

Section 1
Equipment

Menachem E. Abraham, ChipCom Corp., Needham, Mass.

Running Ethernet modems over broadband cable

Broadband promises bigger, better Ethernets that use controllers now installed in many computers. This tutorial shows how the modems that run these new networks operate.

Many local area networks in place today are fashioned after the Ethernet CSMA/CD (carrier-sense multiple access with collision detection) specifications designed by Xerox Corp. Newer networks are built using the variation of these specifications put forward by the IEEE 802.3 standards committee. Until recently, such networks could only be implemented on baseband coaxial cables dedicated to a single data channel. While these networks provide high communications speed and performance, they can lead to expensive recabling when nondata network applications become necessary.

However, a new IEEE standard and recently developed products bring significant enhancements to users of local area networks (LANs). For the first time, users of Ethernet networks can easily "change the channels" by using a broadband cable, which can support additional LANs (such as token bus) on different frequency bands. Other services—such as video (for security, teleconferencing, or robotics), voice, and various point-to-point links—can share the same cable (DATA COMMUNICATIONS, "Video and voice communications join Ethernet on broadband cable," March 1985, p. 293). Specifications for this broadband version of Ethernet have been approved by the IEEE 802.3 standards committee and the IEEE standards board recently, making it the first and only industry-standard broadband CSMA/CD network (see "Broadband CSMA/CD standards: A status report").

Central to this standard is a device that lets the Ethernet controller (typically a board in an attached computer) access a broadband medium, such as simple CATV-type wire. The IEEE 802 specification describes a new radio frequency (RF) transceiver that modulates the Ethernet signals and places them on one channel of a multichannel network.

The new IEEE broadband Ethernet specification provides a relatively easy upgrade for users who already have a baseband Ethernet. The transceivers (modems) and the network cable must be replaced. But since all Ethernet protocol instructions reside on the controller boards in the node computers, the same connectors and attachment cables can be used. Also, all existing controller hardware and software can be used without change. Moving to broadband is as simple as unplugging the node's attachment cable from the baseband transceiver and hooking it into the broadband Ethernet modem.

LAN users benefit today from the maturity of IEEE 802.3 and Ethernet networking products. Without sacrificing performance and while protecting their investment in all previously developed or purchased hardware and software, they can take a convenient upgrade path to a shared broadband medium that provides full area coverage of more than 23 square kilometers (km), or approximately 8.9 square miles. High-performance 10-Mbit/s broadband Ethernet/802.3 products were shipped for the first time by a number of vendors in June 1985.

Distance- and area-coverage advantages
Besides the benefits of a shared physical medium, broadband Ethernet networks can cover a wider distance and area than the baseband version. This is due to a fundamental difference in the way the two networks are laid out. Baseband Ethernet runs along a single cable bus, which can be as long as 500 meters (0.3 miles) without repeaters. In order to cover a circle or a square area, a single baseband cable would have to hit every node in that area, reducing the coverage of that segment to a circle much smaller than 500 meters in diameter.

Broadband CSMA/CD standards: A status report

Although a first edition of the ANSI/IEEE standard for CSMA/CD (carrier-sense multiple access with collision detection) local area networks has been in print since early 1985, the IEEE 802.3 committee is currently developing a number of variants. The process of developing a standard consists of eight major phases:

Proposal. A scheme that is believed to merit standardization is proposed by an individual or a relatively small interested group.

Study. A task force is formed to evaluate and further develop the proposal. Should the task force determine that the scheme (or a similar one) merits standardization, it recommends so to the 802.3 committee.

Project. The 802.3 committee votes on the standard recommended by the task force. If the vote is affirmative, the task force is allowed to proceed with the drafting of specifications.

Draft specifications. After a number of reviews internal to the task force and the 802.3 committee, the document that results from the process is ready for letter balloting.

802.3 ballot. 802.3 voting members and observers are given a 30-day review period, after which they respond through a letter ballot.

TCCC ballot. After an affirmative and unanimous vote by 802.3 (all comments and negative votes having been resolved to the satisfaction of the voters), the revised draft specifications are reviewed by voting members of the IEEE technical committee on computer communications (TCCC). They are given the opportunity to respond through a letter ballot after a 30-day review cycle.

IEEE standards board approval. After affirmative and unanimous vote by TCCC, the revised document is forwarded to the IEEE standards office for approval.

Published standard. The IEEE publishes a supplement to the existing 802.3 standard or reprints the complete 802.3 standard.

Two broadband variants of the original baseband CSMA/CD specifications have been considered by the committee:

■ A 2-Mbit/s version with no exposed baseband interface would be incompatible with existing baseband hardware (since the controller and the modem would reside in one closed box).

■ A 10-Mbit/s version with an exposed interface identical to the one used on baseband transceivers would be compatible with the baseband version's attachment unit interface (AUI).

On July 11, 1985, the IEEE 802.3 committee decided that the 2-Mbit/s scheme does not merit standardization and that, therefore, the committee will not promote the 2-Mbit/s effort from the study phase up to the project phase. This means the termination of all related activities within IEEE 802.3. However, the committee decided that the 10-Mbit/s broadband specifications will be forwarded to the IEEE standards board for final approval as an IEEE standard. The IEEE standards board met on September 19, 1985, and approved the 10-Mbit/s broadband CSMA/CD specifications.

For distances longer than 500 meters or for better area coverage, the baseband version of the network uses digital repeaters. According to the Ethernet standard, a network can use three segments of 500 meters each and a 1-km (0.6-mile) lightwave segment, connected in series with repeaters in between. Thus a full-size Ethernet network is 2.5 km (1.5 miles) long. However, since no tapping mechanism is provided into the lightwave link, 40 percent of the maximum distance is unavailable for network user connections.

A broadband Ethernet network, like cable TV plant, uses a branching-tree topology. In this case, the specified maximum distance of the network is also the diameter of a circle (or sphere), the area (or volume) of which is fully covered by the network. A tap can be brought near any station without affecting the maximum usable distance. By using a standard IEEE 802.3 broadband Ethernet, the complete area of a circle having a diameter of 3.75 km (about 2.3 miles) can be covered. This coverage, of approximately 11 square km (4.2 square miles), should be more than enough for many buildings and campuses. If it is not, a 5.5-km (3.4-mile) diameter (about 23.5 square km or 9 square miles) is practically achievable (though not part of the IEEE standard).

The broadband Ethernet transceiver performs transmission, reception, and collision detection functions on Ethernet data packets. While totally transparent to the Ethernet controller hardware and all the software layers above it, the broadband transceiver operates differently from its baseband equivalent. Baseband and broadband transceivers exchange messages with the Ethernet controllers they are attached to on three separate two-wire circuits in an attachment cable (Fig. 1): two for data (transmit and receive) and one for collision.

Different techniques for equivalent function

On the collision circuit, the presence of a 10-MHz square wave signals a collision. The signals on the transmit and receive circuits are Manchester encoded. Under Manchester encoding, transitions between low and high are made in the middle of each bit. These transitions help the receiving controller synchronize and recover bit-boundary information from the incoming signal.

The data passing between the transceiver and the controller takes the form of 10-Mbit/s packets consisting of a preamble of alternating ones and zeroes, a start-of-frame delimiter, the destination and source addresses, a data field, and a frame-check sequence (Fig. 2). The baseband Ethernet scheme allows these Manchester-encoded packets to continue through the transceiver onto the network; in the broadband case, the preamble is modified and a postamble added.

The baseband transceiver must massage or "clean up" the data before sending it out. This typically includes some filtering of the Manchester waveform. Filtering prevents the signal from changing state too fast and radiating energy out of the cable, which could cause RF interference.

How the transmitter works

The transmitter component in the baseband transceiver is essentially a digital circuit with current source characteristics, meaning that it forces a fixed amount of current out onto the cable. Since the transceiver is attached at a driving point somewhere along the backbone network, it sees two pieces of coaxial cable: one to the left and one to the right of it. Since each side of the cable presents a 50-ohm resistance to current, the transceiver must drive a 25-ohm load.

The signal on the coaxial cable is approximately 2 volts peak-to-peak (from the top to the bottom of the waveform). Also, its harmonic content is very rich. Even with filtering, there is power at frequencies up to nearly 80 MHz, since the signal changes state quickly.

A baseband cable carries only one signal, so it does not matter if its power distribution is all over the spectrum. The network can use the coaxial cable's entire bandwidth, since data runs as a dedicated application. In a broadband network, however, an attempt must be made to limit signals to a narrow band, since the data channel is supposed to be only one of the occupants on the cable.

An unadulterated baseband Ethernet signal would occupy about 80 MHz out of a total of 400 MHz on a broadband cable. The signal, therefore, must be modified to take up less bandwidth for broadband Ethernet. The techniques used in the broadband IEEE 802.3/ Ethernet transmitter differ from their baseband functional equivalents in two areas: framing (the signaling method used to mark

__1. Attachment.__ Nodes link to a broadband Ethernet network by three pairs of wires, two for Manchester-encoded data and one for a 10-MHz collision signal.

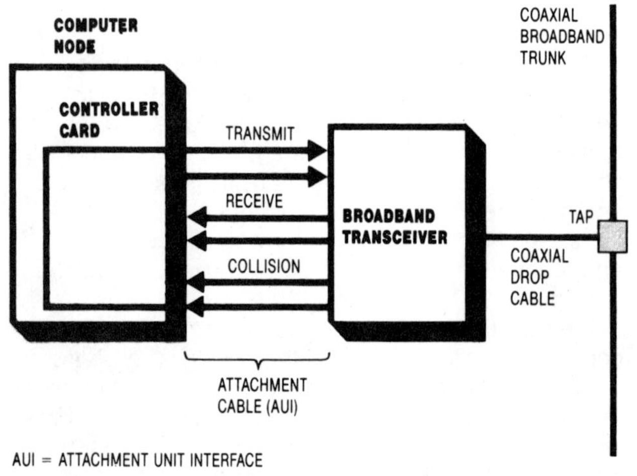

4

__2. Packet framing.__ To use baseband Ethernet packets on broadband, the preamble is modified for scrambling. A new postamble helps detect the end-of-frame.

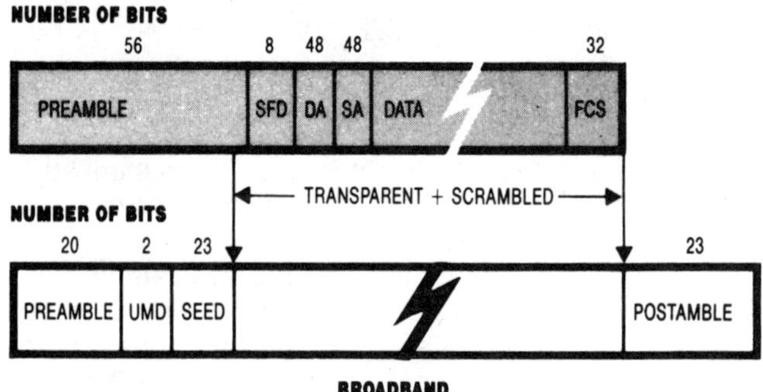

SFD = START-OF-FRAME DELIMITER
DA = DESTINATION ADDRESS
SA = SOURCE ADDRESS
FCS = FRAME-CHECK SEQUENCE
UMD = UNSCRAMBLED-MODE DELIMITER
SEED = FIRST 23 PREAMBLE BITS (ALSO SENT SCRAMBLED—USED FOR DESCRAMBLER SELF-SYNCHRONIZATION)

packet boundaries) and spectral shaping and placement of the transmitted signal. Shaping is an attempt to confine the signal to a narrow band, while placement refers to the selection of a carrier frequency around which to center the signal.

Narrowing the signal's band

No spectral placement is done in baseband, since no carrier frequency is used by a signal that takes up the entire wire. However, on a broadband coaxial cable shared by multiple frequency-division multiplexed services, the transmitted signal can only be allowed to occupy a limited bandwidth centered around a given VHF (very high frequency) carrier, as high as 400 MHz. The transmitted spectrum is confined by using a different encoding method and a special filtering technique.

Ethernet uses Manchester encoding between the controller and the transceiver, but this method takes up 80 MHz, due to harmonics caused by the rapid and frequent transitions. Therefore, nonreturn-to-zero (NRZ) encoding is used on the broadband cable. (In NRZ, the low condition is used to represent a "zero" and the high to represent a "one.")

The broadband specification also calls for raised-cosine filtering. The problem with simply throwing away the power at the higher frequencies, as a simple low-pass filter does, is that it introduces distortion that prevents the bits from being recovered. If the filtering is performed incorrectly, a bit could be rendered indecipherable by the bits that came before it.

Such intersymbol interference (ISI) can be avoided by using raised-cosine filtering, a technique originally developed to transmit telegraphs between the United States and Europe. An ISI-free signal is characteristic of all filters in the raised cosine family. After being encoded and filtered, the signal is modulated via phase-shift keying and sent out.

The need to change the framing technique is a result

of the timing uncertainty associated with the RF carrier-detect signal deassertion (lowering). Since Ethernet is packet-based, it is important to be able to delineate the beginning and ending of a packet. The circuit tends to add a "tail" to a packet, which may result in extraneous bits being presented by the modem to the attached station. This is avoided by means of the postamble that the receiving broadband modem uses to figure out the location of the bits. After stripping the postamble off the packet, the modem forwards the data bits to the controller.

Encoding

The broadband modem decodes the Manchester waveform presented to it by the controller and encodes it for the broadband cable using NRZ in conjunction with two enhancements: scrambling and differential encoding. Scrambling the data before transmission gives it a pseudorandom nature, which helps the receiver extract bit-timing information from data transitions. It also improves the spectral characteristics in terms of uniform power distribution, as opposed to the potentially strong discrete spectral lines in non-scrambled data.

To further enhance clock extractability, a periodic waveform is transmitted at the beginning of the packet so that the receivers may be synchronized quickly. Although the whole packet is scrambled, the first 20 (preamble) bits are transmitted unscrambled as they occur in the Ethernet packet. The alternating ones and zeroes are followed by a delimiter (the UMD, or unscrambled-mode delimiter) that indicates the beginning of the scrambled part of the packet.

The UMD is followed by the "seed," a 23-bit pattern that helps prepare the receiver to descramble the signal. After 11 more bits of preamble, the start-of-frame delimiter sent by the station is transmitted in the scrambled part of the packet. The broadband transceiver is totally transparent to the rest of the original packet, merely scrambling it and passing it along without modification. Everything after the seed can be unscrambled by the receiver and used as data.

Modulation and filtering

In order to simplify the demodulating circuitry in the receiver, the scrambled NRZ data undergoes a differential encoding modulation. Rather than make one phase a "one" and the other a "zero," this PSK (phase-shift keying) technique shifts the phase of the carrier 180 degrees only when a zero occurs. Thus a differential decoder always compares the phase of the received bit with that of the previous bit in order to distinguish between ones and zeroes.

The signal on the broadband side of the transceiver, representing the baseband packet, can be obtained by multiplying the waveform of an RF-carrier oscillator inside the modem with the differentially encoded binary data (assume for example -1 for a "low" and 1 for a "high"). This multiplication is, in fact, the modulation process, resulting in two opposite phases of the carrier for the two possible data values. As shown in Fig. 3a, the points at which the envelope goes through zero are the phase reversal points.

This, according to the differential-encoding scheme, means that the phase-changing zero-bit has been transmitted.

Two band-limiting techniques are commonly used for filtering. One could be applied to the signal before the modulation process and one after. The first limits bandwidth by slowing down the transitions between one and zero. (Note that the filtered signals from the broadband cable shown in Fig. 3 do not resemble square waves, which they would without filtering.) This case, in which a low-pass filter significantly narrows the spectrum of the digital binary data prior to modulation, is referred to as baseband or premodulation filtering. Alternately, the major band-limiting element may be a bandpass filter, which cuts off the frequencies above and below a certain range (in this case, the range surrounding the carrier). With such a filter located after the modulator, the situation is referred to as passband or postmodulation filtering.

Both techniques are applicable in the IEEE 802.3/ Ethernet broadband modem. Simple band-limiting results in a distorted waveform. However, if the signal is treated with raised-cosine filtering, the identity of the transmitted bits can be detected just as easily as it is on the original.

Framing

The IEEE 802.3 broadband specifications require that the band-limiting devices have certain amplitude and phase characteristics. Specifically, raised-cosine filtering must have a 0.4 rolloff (a measure of how much power "rolls off" to frequencies outside the assigned band). If this type of filtering is used, previously sent or subsequent bits cannot interfere with the present bit, provided that the received data waveform is sampled at the correct instant. Also, the modulated form of the 10-Mbit/s signal occupies a mere 14-MHz band on the cable centered around the carrier frequency.

Figure 3 shows framing. In Figure 3a, the beginning of a radio-frequency packet is being transmitted onto the coaxial cable. During the first 20 nonscrambled bits of the preamble, the phase is reversed every two bits. The first two consecutive phase reversals within a one-bit interval represent the UMD. A typical pattern in the middle of an RF packet is shown in Figure 3b.

In the baseband case, end-of-frame delimiting is accomplished through the lack of a signal on the wire after the last bit has been received. With broadband, however, the end of a frame is signaled through the addition of a postamble after the last bit of the baseband packet. The 23-bit postamble on the broadband side of the transmitter is shown in Figure 3c.

The receive function

The postamble consists of a carrier phase change after the last bit of the packet followed by a constant-phase carrier for 22-bit intervals, after which the carrier is turned off (denoting the end of the packet). It is followed by a collision-detect self-test, as explained below. The receiver uses the postamble in conjunction with the dropping of carrier to ensure that no extraneous bits are sent to the attached controller.

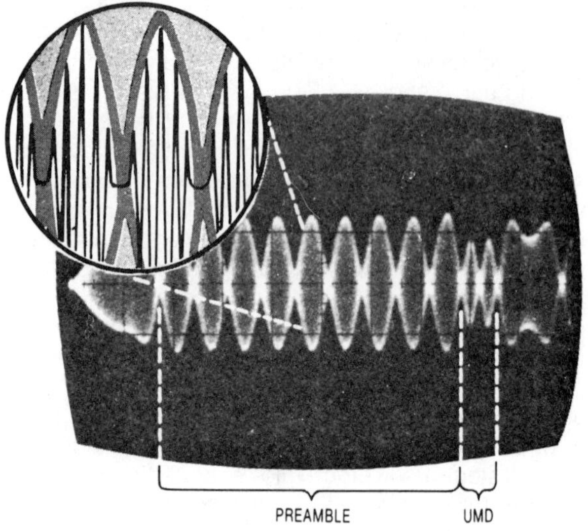

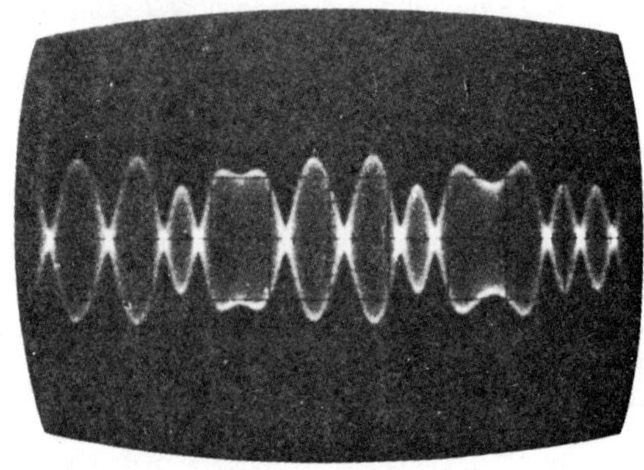

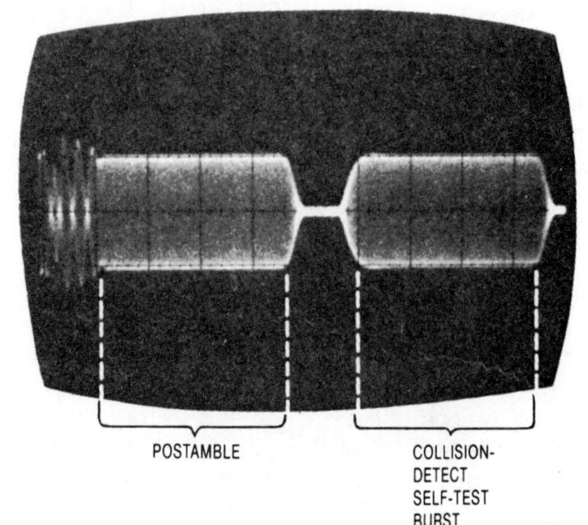

3. The look of broadband. *Three views of a typical packet—beginning (A), middle (B), and end (C)—show the envelope around the modulated carrier.*

In a baseband network, the receiver does a limited amount of filtering. After traveling along the cable, the signal may have deteriorated somewhat, so the baseband receiver amplifies and shapes it to give it a cleaner waveform. The receiver then presents the signal to the controller with the appropriate level and impedance characteristics.

The receiving function can be implemented with simple circuitry for two reasons. First, since the baseband signal is the only user of the coaxial cable, it can be transmitted at a relatively high level (approximately two volts, peak-to-peak). Second, the cable loss is relatively small because of the signal's low frequency (cables tend to attenuate more when the frequency is high) and the short cable run (500 meters between repeaters).

In broadband networks, the high-frequency carrier signals are attenuated by the long coaxial cables used. Therefore, wide-band amplifiers and equalizers are placed in the network, with spacing dependent on the type of cable used and the number of taps and splitters attached to the cable. Amplifiers used in broadband networks are required to uniformly amplify signals in all bands while maintaining very good linearity. That is, all channels on the cable must be amplified the same amount without distortion. Lack of linearity might induce cross-modulation, causing the signals in different bands to affect and interfere with each other. Cross-modulation can result in quality degradation of video signals or bit errors in data channels.

In order to keep these amplifiers in their linear region, the signals on the broadband coaxial trunk are relatively small, ranging from 10 millivolts (mv) to 100 mv. Also, to minimize loading of the trunk by the stations attached, the broadband modems are connected to the coaxial cable through a tap that further attenuates this signal to a level typically between 0.5 and 5 mv. The receiving section of the broadband transceiver is, therefore, required to do carrier detection and demodulation on small signals in a relatively wide amplitude range and at very high frequencies. The receiver first amplifies the signal and then converts it down to an intermediate frequency (IF), where it filters out signals from the other bands. Then demodulation and carrier detection functions are performed, also at the IF.

Two different techniques can be used for the demodulation process: synchronous detection and delay-line detection. In the synchronous case, a reference IF carrier is recovered and used to determine the data content of the received phase-modulated IF signal. Delay-line detectors use the phase of the IF carrier in the previous bit to determine the data content of the present bit. Synchronous detectors provide superior performance (lower error rate) in the presence of noise and transmission impairments.

Bit-timing information is typically extracted from the demodulated data waveform by processing the low-to-high or high-to-low signal transitions. The recovered clock is used for sampling of the demodulated waveform to extract the data. Since differential encoding is used by the transmitter, the opposite process has to occur in the receiver. This, in fact, happens as part of the delay-line detection, if that demodulation technique is used. With synchronous detection, differential decoding is performed digitally on the received data.

The modem uses a descrambler to recover the original data, and it Manchester-encodes the packet before presenting it to the baseband attachment unit interface (AUI, the IEEE term for the controller interface). The postamble pattern, designed to ensure that no extraneous bits are added by the modem at the end of a packet, is detected by the receiver. Then, in conjunction with deassertion of the carrier-detect signal, the position of the last bit in the packet is determined.

This end-of-frame detection technique requires that the receiver make a decision on where the last bit of a packet occurred. However, no such decision can be made until the end of the postamble. Therefore, a delay of at least 23 bits is introduced between the receiver and the controller interface.

Collision detection

An attempted transmission by more than one station simultaneously is referred to as a collision. Collision detection in baseband transceivers is typically accomplished by sensing the d.c. voltage on the coaxial cable or by an analog subtraction of the transmitted waveform from the received waveform. Collision detection based on d.c. level sensing is possible in baseband networks due to the following:

■ Manchester-encoded waveform has a fixed, pattern-independent d.c. content.

■ The d.c. voltage drop on a 500-meter coaxial cable is relatively low.

Therefore, d.c. levels about two or more times those of a single transmitter are interpreted by the baseband transceivers as collisions, the presence of which are then signaled to the controller by means of a 10-MHz square wave.

Collision-detection techniques used in baseband transceivers are not applicable in the broadband case. Since CATV-type equipment was designed to pass only RF signals, which are alternating current (a.c.), the possibility of d.c. sensing is eliminated. In addition, two colliding broadband signals could be received at two significantly different levels, with the stronger one received error free in spite of the other's presence. To ensure reliable collision detection by all transceivers and fairness of access to the network (preventing those stations received more strongly from capturing the medium during a collision), a combination of digital and analog techniques are used, including an out-of-band collision-enforcement signaling mechanism.

Three different events that can be detected digitally by transmitting modems are indications of a collision:

■ A bit error in the station's unique source address (if a packet with another address is received concurrently, the transmitting modem knows that someone else is talking at the same time).

■ An attempt by the controller to transmit while the modem attached to it is already receiving a packet from the coaxial cable (in which case the collision occurs first in the modem box, after which it spills outward onto the broadband cable).

■ Failure to detect the unscrambled mode delimiter in the packet received from the coaxial cable at the proper time. Such detection is supposed to occur after the non-scrambled portion of the broadband preamble.

At least one of the modems participating in the collision will detect it through one of the three mechanisms described above. The modem that detects the collision transmits a collision-enforcement RF signal on a dedicated band to notify all modems on the network.

A time-space diagram showing one possible collision scenario is shown in Figure 4. In the case shown, nodes A and B are separated by the maximum distance; node B starts transmitting just before it receives node A's transmission. The 3.75-km (2.3-mile) distance includes a 3.6-km (2.2-mile) trunk, two 25-meter (82-foot) coaxial drop cables, and two 50-meter (164-foot) attachment cables.

The 30-bit interval shown between the beginning of A's transmission and the beginning of its propagation onto the network is the total delay allocated for hardware and the AUI cable. The Ethernet modem at node B detects the collision by finding bit errors in the source address field (of course, the collision could be sensed by A as well). The transit delay of the packet across the network is 140 bits.

In this worst-case scenario, node B finds the error in the last bit of the source address (the 160th bit in the packet) and only activates the collision-enforcement signal after an additional hardware delay of 34 bits. All nodes, including A, are notified through this out-of-band mechanism. Notification is followed by some hardware delay (36 bits allowed) and a short "jamming" time, during which the controller continues to dump another 32 bits onto the line after it learns of a collision. (Delaying the end-of-transmission by jamming lets all the other stations detect the collision.)

As the collision-detection circuitry in the modem is essential to high-performance network operation, a self-test of this function is performed after every successfully transmitted packet. Figure 3c, described earlier, shows the postamble at the end of an RF packet followed by the collision-enforcement self-test burst. The power spectrum of these RF packets is shown in Figure 5. The collision-enforcement band is the slender, 4 MHz-wide tower to the right. The 14-MHz hill to its left is the data band. Thus the bandwidth allocated for collision enforcement consumes a significant part of the total bandwidth used by this scheme; without such enforcement, however, severe performance degradation would result.

The problems with non-802.3 broadband

Traditionally, broadband CSMA/CD networks did not perform reliable collision detection. Also, collision enforcement or notification in these older designs was nonexistent. As a result, two problems plagued those networks:

■ Packets were lost by the physical layer.

■ The network did not allow fair access to all stations, since priority was given to the stations received most strongly.

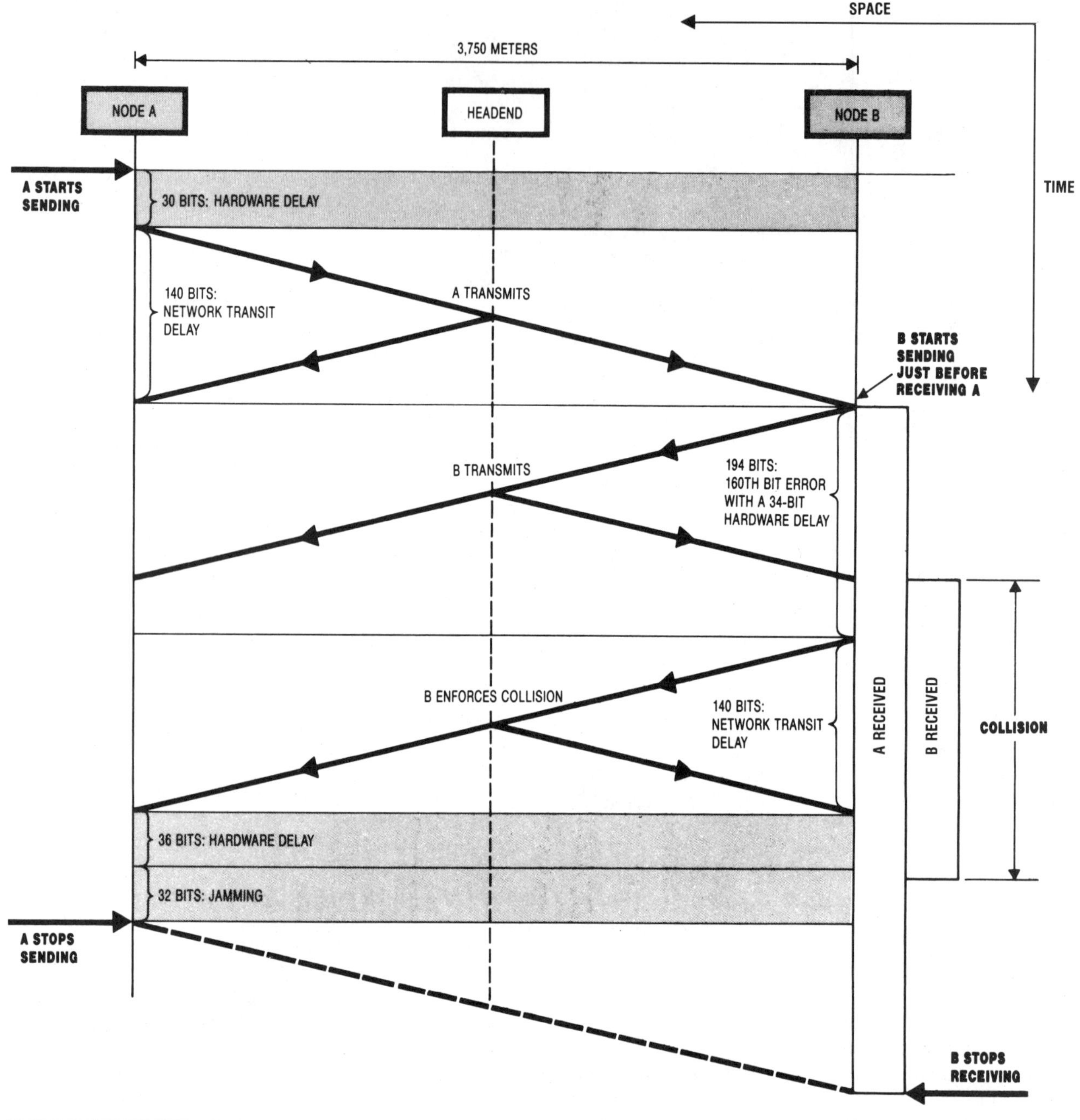

These problems resulted in frequent need for intervention by higher-layer software (requesting retransmission). The resulting performance degradation in such networks was significant.

To see how severe the problems could be when the reliable collision-detection scheme specified by IEEE 802.3 is not implemented, consider the following example. On a two-node network, node A sends a packet to node B. The packet collides with node B's transmission of a packet to node A. Assume that A's signals are received with a significant level advantage relative to those of node B so that, at both receiving modems, the packet sent by A is demodulated error free.

Modem A does not detect the collision and, therefore, assumes that its packet reached the destination. Modem B detects the collision (the bits it received are not identical to the ones it sent); however, without a collision-enforcement mechanism, it cannot notify A. Since node B was transmitting while a packet intended for it arrived, it could not receive the packet due to the half-duplex characteristics of Ethernet-controller chips. This packet from node A, although correctly demodulated by the modem at node B,

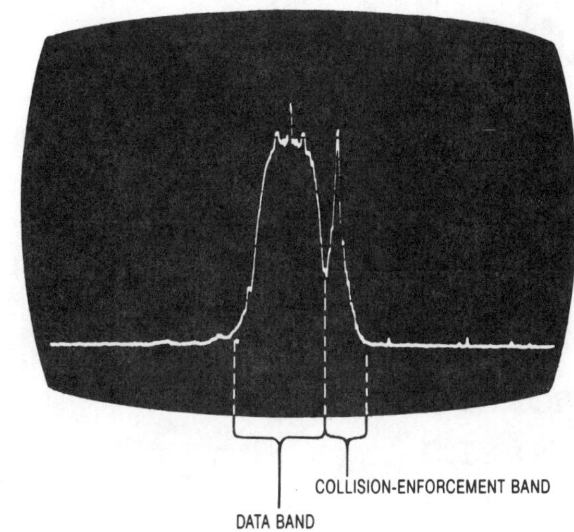

5. Power spectrum. *Broadband Ethernet packets use 18 MHz of bandwidth: 14 for the data and 4 as a separate collision-notification band.*

was lost by that node.

The IEEE 802.3 broadband Ethernet approach ensures collision detection and enforcement, so no packets will be lost by the physical layer. In the scenario discussed above, an IEEE 802.3 Ethernet modem at node B would notify A about the collision through the collision-enforcement mechanism. This would cause immediate backoff and retry (retransmission) by A and B with no need for higher-layer software intervention.

In order to demonstrate unfairness of access in networks that do not implement the IEEE 802.3 broadband Ethernet scheme, consider the following example. In a three-node network, node A sends long and frequent packets to nodes B and C. Meanwhile, B and C attempt to respond simultaneously and collide. Assume that B's signal is received significantly stronger than C's so that all three modems receive the packet sent by B error free. Modem C detects the collision and backs off while modem B transmits its entire message. This will happen every time. Therefore, node C is not given fair access to the medium.

The IEEE 802.3 broadband Ethernet approach eliminates this problem by reliable collision detection and enforcement. In the three-node scenario above, the Ethernet modem at C will enforce the collision on the network so that A and B will know about it and both B and C will retry following the fair backoff algorithm. ■

Menachem E. Abraham is vice president of product development at ChipCom Corp., Needham, Mass. Within the IEEE 802.3 working group he is the chairman of the task force that developed the broadband standard. He holds M. S. E. E. and B. S. E. E. degrees, both summa cum laude, from Technion, Israel's Institute of Technology. Over the last 16 years he has held various engineering positions at Digital Equipment Corp., Fibronics, Technion, the Israeli Defense Force, and Tel Aviv University.

Stevan Eidson and David Taylor, Zoran Corp., San Jose, Calif., and
Christopher Moore, Advanced Micro Devices Inc., Sunnyvale, Calif.

An inside look at on-board modem design

Single chips allow on-board modems to handle routine signal processing and autodialing while connecting directly to a PC processor bus.

With the advent of dial-up databases, the number of modem users has increased dramatically. As a result, prices have plummeted, even as many of these devices have gained the ability to perform more and more "intelligent" functions. Not only is it becoming increasingly popular to sell personal computers with modems already built in, but modems are also being sold as add-on plug-in upgrade cards.

While the modem on a printed circuit card has begun to replace the traditional standalone modem, the actual modulation and demodulation circuits still tend to be hybrids of analog and digital components. Modem manufacturers are looking toward very-large-scale integrated circuit (VLSI) modem chips as replacements for the present modem circuit card technology. These single-chip modems have become available from many semiconductor manufacturers over the past three years. Typically such modems-on-a-chip integrate filtering, modulation, and demodulation processes that are usually associated with an external or standalone modem.

However, all these integrated modems lack a parallel microprocessor interface as well as the automatic dialing and answering functions that users associate with intelligent modems. It would be advantageous, therefore, to integrate automatic calling functions, modem chip control, and the personal computer interface into another chip. Fortunately, most single-chip microprocessors available today are powerful enough to accommodate this integration.

The block diagram of the modem chip in Figure 1 has a standard RS-232-C connection, pins for connection to the telephone network, and a port for selecting the modem type (see "Modem types"). The analog portion of the modem is connected through the telephone line interface to the network. The telephone line interface — the data access arrangement, or DAA — provides on-hook/off-hook control and ringing indication (RI) as well as analog input and output. The dual tone multifrequency (DTMF) generator accepts parallel digital data from the autodialer and generates the associated analog tone for each dialed digit. The communications control unit (CCU) interface circuitry controls the interrupt structure between the host central processor unit (CPU) and the CCU.

The CCU has several subsystems. The command processor acts on parallel command data from the host CPU, returns status to the host on request, and controls the state of the modem. The universal asynchronous receiver/transmitter (UART) converts parallel to serial data for the modem and vice versa. The UART also appends and deletes start, stop, and parity bits to each transmitted character or data byte. The autodialer determines the digits to dial, the interdigit dialing delay, and the method of dialing (pulse or tone). Finally, the progress tone detector indicates to the command processor when dial tone, busy tone, or ringback signals are present.

Smart card

Using a modem chip and a single-chip microprocessor as a CCU, the authors designed an intelligent modem card for the IBM PC. Associated with this fully integrated modem circuit card is a sophisticated software package. The software to drive the intelligent modem card was developed as part of the IBM PC project and is written in a combination of IBM Basic and 8088 Macro Assembler.

The entire intelligent modem card was developed using a handful of transistor-to-transistor logic (TTL) devices and a half dozen VLSI parts (Fig. 2). The two

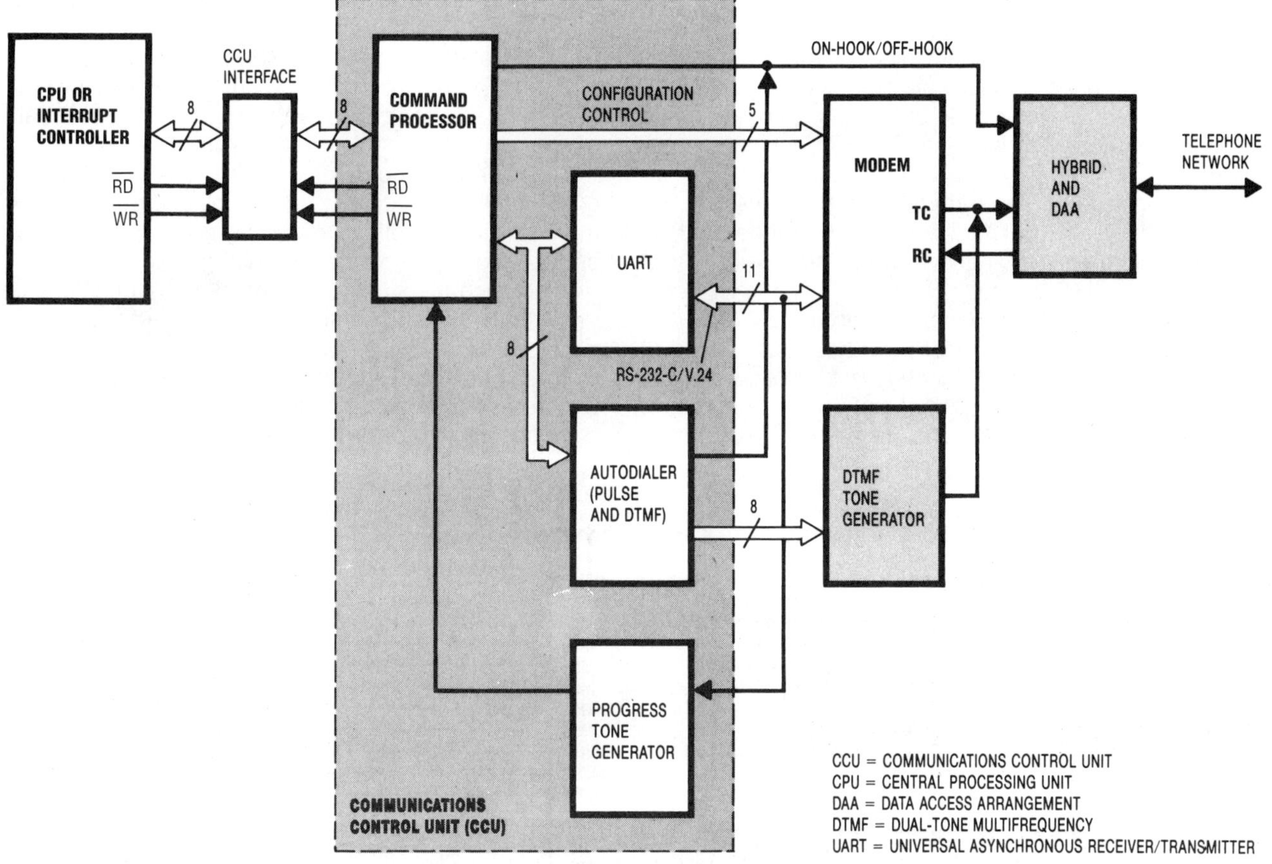

1. Block modem. *The command processor, universal asynchronous transmit and receive device, autodialer, and progress-tone detector are all integrated into a single-chip microcomputer. The modem, DTMF communications interface, and 2- to 4-wire hybrid are also highly integrated components.*

main components in the design of the card are the CCU and the single-chip modem.

The VLSI modem (Am7910) is a frequency-shift keying (FSK) modem using digital signal processing throughout. The chip has nine basic modem types built into it, and analog loopback test modes are provided for each. Modem selection is made through the modem's five mode-control pins, which are MC0 through MC4. Standard RS-232-C serial control pins are provided for the CCU interface.

Convert serial to parallel
The Am8051 is a single-chip microprocessor with a built-in UART, a standard microprocessor data bus, and two other 8-bit programmable input/output ports. In the project considered here, the chip was programmed to provide the required automatic calling/answering, progress-tone detection, UART, and loopback test functions.

The Am8051 UART converts the serial modem data to a parallel format for the microprocessor in the IBM PC. The UART has a programmable character word length of 10 or 11 bits per character. Note that 10 or 11 character bits provide 1 start bit, 8 or 9 data bits, and 1 stop bit. The eighth or ninth data bit may be a parity bit calculated in software. It is possible for two stop bits to be included by making the last data bit a binary 1.

The International Telegraph and Telephone Consultative Committee V.23 back-channel filter (600 bit/s and 1.2 kbit/s) can be used for detecting all of the progress tones. In progress-tone detection mode, the CCU sets the modem into a V.23 back-channel loopback mode and prepares to receive the progress-tone cadence (busy, fast-busy, for example) on the modem's back-channel carrier detect pin. Energy present in the progress-tone frequency band will cause the back-channel carrier detect (BCD) pin to go low and to remain at that low level for as long as energy is present.

No ambiguity
Dedicated pins located on the CCU control the modem configuration port and RS-232-C pins. Clear-to-send (CTS), back-channel clear-to-send (BCTS), carrier detect (CD), and BCD are combined because their meaning is unambiguous to the CCU. When request-to-send (RTS) or back-channel request-to-send (BRTS) are asserted, the CCU is aware of the main or back-channel source of clear-to-send and carrier detect. Because of this clarity, the need for two CCU pins for these functions is eliminated. The CCU crystal fre-

quency of 9.8304 MHz is four times the required 2.4576-MHz input clock of the Am7910. The U10 section provides the divide-by-four clock to the modem chip.

The IBM PC backplane interface to the intelligent modem card consists of an eight-bit bidirectional data port (D0-D7), two interrupt request lines, address lines, a reset line, plus a read and a write line. The Am2950 command processor has a bidirectional I/O port that controls the interface between the IBM PC backplane and the CCU.

The backplane read, write, interrupt, and address lines control the status of U2. The command processor has two internal registers, R and S, which are oriented in a feedback loop (R output to S input, R input to S output). When data is read to the CCU or the IBM PC,

the R- and S-register outputs are enabled, respectively. A write signal clocks information into the R and S registers. When the CCU writes to the system through the command processor, an interrupt request (IRQ7) is sent to the IBM PC interrupt controller.

The interrupt request is similar to a receiver ready (RxRDY) interrupt from a UART. Another interrupt request (IRQ6) similar to a transmit ready (TxRDY) is generated when the CCU reads data from the command processor.

An address comparator, U4, decodes the location of the intelligent modem circuit card in the IBM PC memory map. All of the remaining components on the circuit card are dedicated to analog and telephone-line interface functions. Generation of the dual tone multifrequency is accomplished by U6, a Mostek

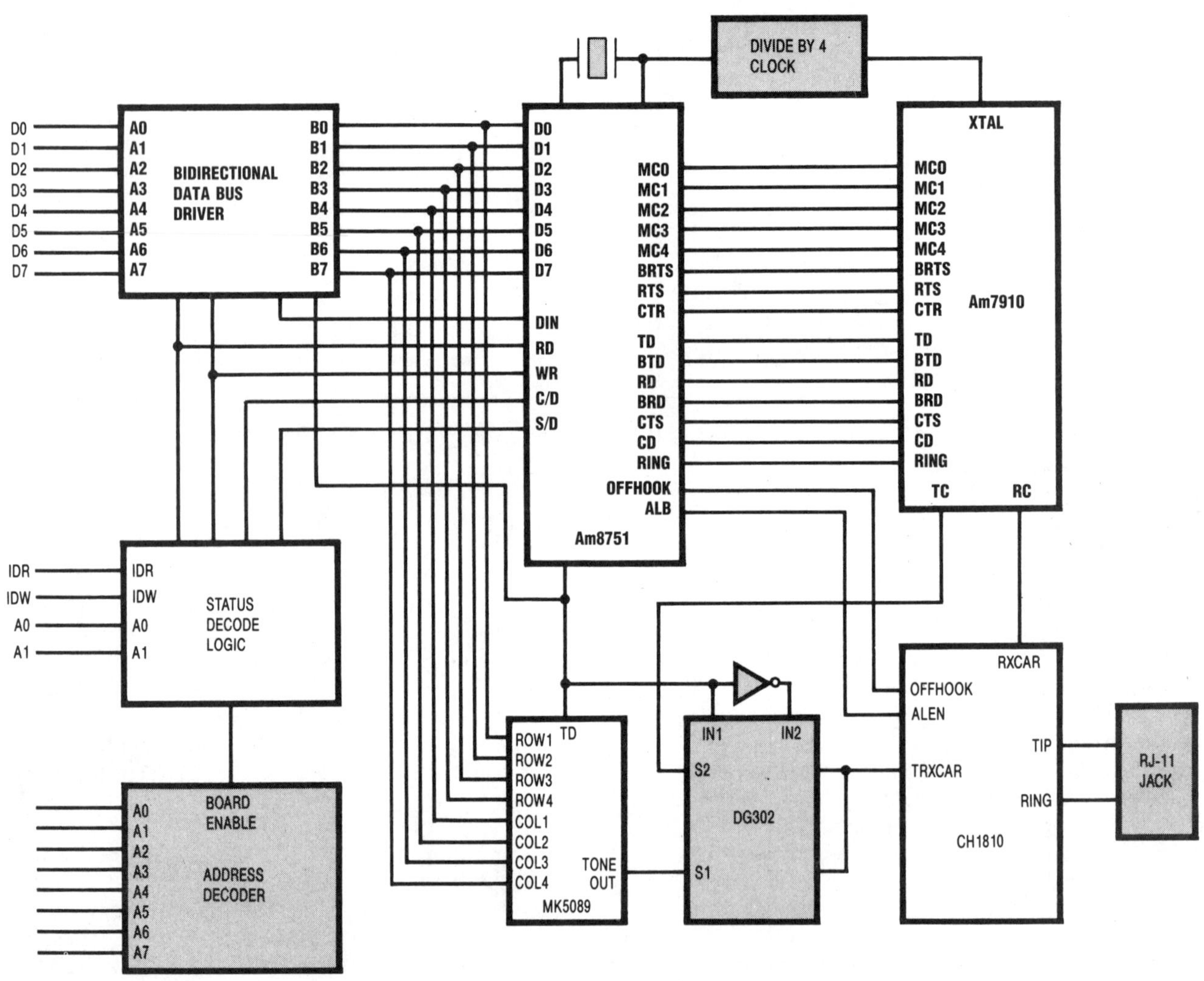

2. IBM Personal Computer. *This simplified schematic of an intelligent modem circuit card shows the component connections following directly from the block diagram in*

Figure 1. The entire modem can be implemented using only six large-scale integrated and very large-scale integrated components.

A = ADDRESS
ALB = ANALOG LOOPBACK
BRTS = BACK REQUEST TO SEND
C/O = CONTROL OR DATA
DIW = DATA IW
IOR = I/O READ
IOW = I/O WRITE
MC = MODE CONTROL
S/D = STATUS OR DATA
S1 = SIGNAL 1
S2 = SIGNAL 2
TRXCAR = TRANSMIT CARRIER
RXCAR = RECEIVE CARRIER

Modem types

A modem allows digital data to be sent over the telephone network, which is designed primarily for carrying analog voice signals. The telephone company multiplexes many separate lines onto a single pair of wires to reduce costs and, by doing so, must modulate conversations into different 4-kHz frequency bands. This technique, known as frequency-division multiplexing (FDM), along with other network distortions, generally limits the usable data communications frequency band to the 300-to-3,200-Hz range. The most familiar 1.2-kbit/s full-duplex modems are commonly known as Bell 212A compatible or CCITT V.22 compatible. The 300-bit/s modems use frequency-shift keying (FSK) to modulate data, while the 1.2-kbit/s modems use differential-quarternary phase-shift keying (DQPSK).

Frequency-shift keying is a method of modulation whereby a logical "one" is assigned to a frequency called a mark and a logical "zero" is assigned to another frequency, called a space. The frequency assignments for Bell 103 modem types are shown in Figure A. As the data switches between the two logic values, the modulated signal switches between the two frequencies. This frequency shifting produces a spectrum that covers about one Hertz (cycle) for every bit per second of modem speed. For example, a 300-bit/s modem generates a frequency spectrum that is about 300 Hz wide. Note that there must be adequate channel separation to eliminate interference in full-duplex transmission. Since the modulating frequencies are mapped directly from the digital data without regard to a timing or synchronization signal, data can be transmitted by an FSK modem at any speed up to the maximum data rate. Hence, a 300-bit/s FSK modem can really transmit at any data rate from zero to 300 bit/s. Worldwide FSK modem standards allow a maximum of 1.2-kbit/s transmission on the dial-up telephone network.

FSK modem standards are generally accepted worldwide. At 300 bit/s full duplex, the Bell 103 in North America and the CCITT V.21 in Europe are the standards. The North American Bell 202 and the European CCITT V.23 are the 1.2-kbit/s half-duplex standards. The frequency assignments for the Bell 202 type are shown in Figure C. The full-duplex modems are assigned as either originate or answer — depending on whether the modem is calling or being called.

Unfortunately, DQPSK and FSK are incompatible modulation techniques. DQPSK encodes two bits as one of four discrete signal phase shifts at a single modulation frequency. Each packet of two bits is called a dibit and takes one baud interval to transmit. Thus the 1.2-kbit/s Bell 212A modem transmits dibits at 600 baud. Figure B shows the frequency assignments of a Bell 212A modem and the associated phase shifts for each dibit.

DQPSK generates a frequency-spectrum width that is approximately equal to the baud rate of transmission. Because DQPSK transmits at 600 baud and generates a 600-Hz wide spectrum per channel, it is possible to communicate full duplex. Since FSK transmission creates a 1,200-Hz-wide spectrum at 1,200 baud, communications must be half duplex. To complement 1.2-kbit/s half-duplex communications, FSK split-speed modems add back channels of up to 150 bit/s.

Half-duplex or split-speed data transfer can be more difficult to implement since high-speed data communications can occur in only one direction at a time. Line turnaround, the protocol for changing the direction of communications, may be desired in some applications. Turnaround requires a low-speed backward or secondary channel from the receiving modem to the transmitting modem. Both the Bell 202 and the CCITT V.23 have backward channels. The Bell 202 back channel is a 5-bit/s on/off keyed channel used for signaling, while the CCITT V.23 back channel is a 75-bit/s FSK data channel that can be used for both data and signaling.

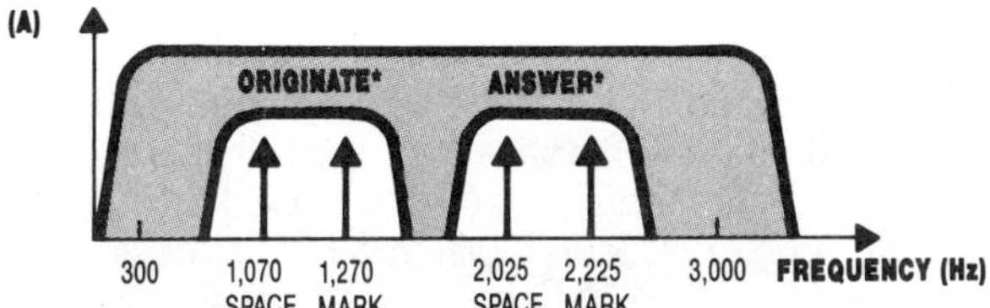

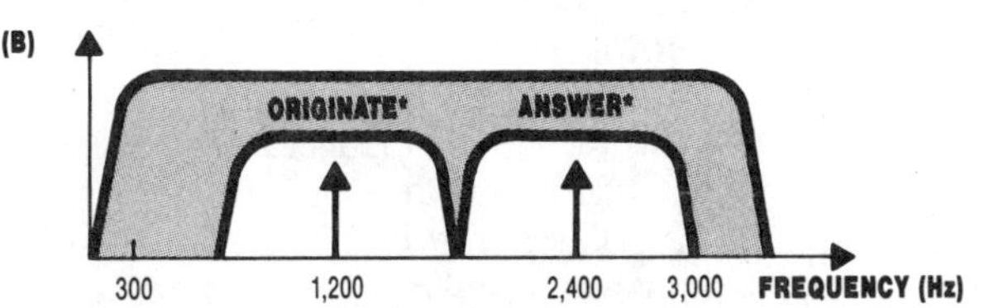

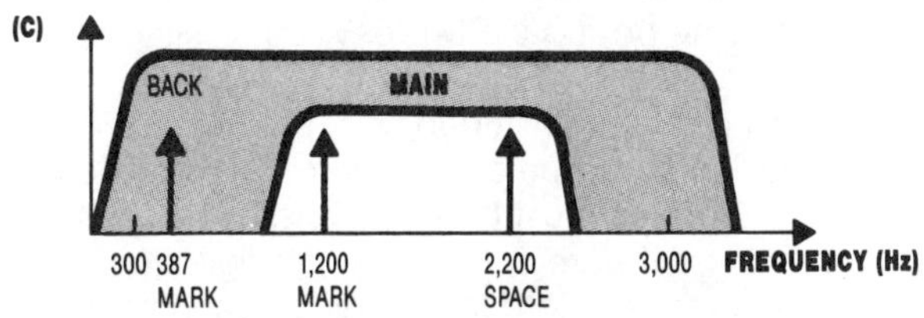

*ANSWER AND ORIGINATE FREQUENCIES REFER TO TRANSMIT BAND.

**PHASE-SHIFT DATA ENCODING IS DIFFERENTIAL, ASSUMING THE PAST BAUD INTERVAL PHASE SHIFT WAS 45°.

Δ = DELTA, OR CHANGE

DTMF-tone dialing matrix

LOW-GROUP FREQUENCY (Hz)	HIGH-GROUP FREQUENCY (Hz)			
	1,209	1,336	1,477	1,633
697	1	2	3	A[1]
770	4	5	6	B[1]
852	7	8	9	C[1]
941	*	0	#	D[1]

[1] CURRENTLY NOT USED   DTMF = DUAL-TONE MULTIFREQUENCY

MK5089. This tone dialer chip anticipates an eight-bit row and column input corresponding to the low-group and high-group frequencies that can be found in the dual tone multifrequency matrix, respectively (see table).

The analog output is attenuated by a resistor network before being passed to the analog multiplexer. The analog multiplexer, U5, is a Siliconix DG302 analog multiplexer under the control of the CCU. The CCU chooses between the transmit carrier output of the modem and the DTMF tone dialer output of U6. The final piece of important hardware on the circuit card is U7, the telephone line interface module. This is a Cermetek CH1810 module containing a two- to four-wire hybrid and an FCC preregistered data access arrangement.

Communications software

In addition to the modem circuit card, software is needed to control IBM PC communications. The most basic data communications software must be able to sense characters typed at the keyboard for transmission to the modem, as well as interpret the characters received by the modem for display on the screen. Besides offering these basic "dumb terminal" functions, many software packages include functions for bidirectional file transfers with other computers, automatic telephone dialing, and automatic telephone answering for the modem.

The transfer of characters from keyboard to modem and from modem to screen is a relatively simple process. The most common method is known as polled I/O. In this mode, the computer is continually checking both the modem board and the keyboard to see if something needs to be done. The computer spends a majority of its time polling the two devices, waiting for something to happen.

Before data can be transferred from modem to keyboard and from keyboard to modem, a connection to the remote devices must be established. It is at this juncture that the software controls the intelligence that is built into the modem card. An intelligent modem is able to dial a number, determine whether or not the call was answered, and take the appropriate action. If the call was answered by the remote computer, the communications routine is then called to handle data transfer.

If a call is unanswered, an intelligent modem will recognize this condition and will redial the call. The communications software must then tell the modem whether or not to redial the call and how many times it should try before giving up. The software also must tell the modem what number to dial.

Very often an intelligent modem can store several telephone numbers. Modems with the ability to store telephone numbers on-board, such as the IBM PC intelligent modem, allow the user to program frequently called numbers and then to recall them as need be. The communications software has the task of telling the modem which numbers to store where, and which number to dial.

Solving file-transfer problems

Once the connection is established, the software also oversees the interchange of computer files. The simplest form of transfer is to copy everything that appears on the screen onto a disk file. There are cases where this type of file transfer, or logging, is not adequate. In the case of a binary file transfer, it would be meaningless for the contents of the file to appear on the screen. Also, should an error occur during file transfer (for example, someone picking up an extension telephone while a call is in progress), the entire file would have to be retransmitted—assuming the error was even noticed by the operator.

To solve such problems, several protocols have been developed, one of the more common being the Xmodem or Christensen protocol. This protocol allows two computers to transfer blocks of information using a few special characters as block synchronization and error-correction codes. When a block is received correctly, the receiving equipment tells the transmitting party to continue. If an error occurs in the block, the receiving device requests the sending device to retransmit the block. This assures error-free transmission without echoing the transferred file on the display screen.

The Xmodem protocol uses a checksum to detect errors. This means that the transmitted characters are added together as they are transferred, with the sum being the last character sent. The receiving portion of Xmodem adds up all the characters and compares the calculated sum with the transmitted sum. If the two additions do not match, there has been an error in the block. In this case the receiving program must request a retransmission. ∎

Stevan Eidson, a senior software engineer at Zoran Corp., was formerly system development engineer at Advanced Micro Devices. Eidson has bachelor of science degrees in electrical engineering and computer science from the University of California at Irvine and an M. S. E. E. from UCLA. David Taylor, a senior marketing engineer at Zoran, was section manager at Advanced Micro. He has a B. S. E. E. from California Polytechnic Institute at San Luis Obispo and is pursuing a master's in computer science at Santa Clara University. Christopher Moore, senior technician in Advanced Micro's data communications group, attended DeAnza College in Cupertino, Calif.

Arielle Emmett and David Gabel,
Special to DATA COMMUNICATIONS

Modem connections: Practical, quick check

In this, the second part of a two-part article, the authors offer 11 points to aid in sending data between micros.

Implementing modem communications between microcomputers no longer requires the specialized training of a network operator, but the task can still be quite complex and fraught with errors. This article, the second of two parts, provides a quick checklist for modem connections.

1. Check pins, protocols, and control characters, in that order.

Before attempting to transmit, check hardware, communications protocols available for use in software, and special control codes your computer may use to perform transmission functions or formatting. Even if standard Bell-compatible modems are used (both modems must implement the same hardware protocol), you must assure yourself that you've chosen the correct RS-232-C cable.

Check your cable selection with a dealer and have him try it out for you before buying the cable. Otherwise you may get a garbled transmission or no transmission at all. Problems with hardware handshaking may also destroy the tail end of transmission buffers.

Communications settings or parameters are also crucial. If you are transmitting one-on-one to another computer, choose the highest-level protocol common to sender and receiver. If it doesn't work, proceed downward on the ladder until you find a common protocol that does work. For example, buffered terminal mode will enable virtually all dissimilar computers to communicate ASCII text files, as long as communications settings match and hardware handshaking is working properly. However, buffered terminal mode does not do error checking.

Control characters are used differently in different computers. They let either the computer or the user control some transmission tasks and formatting. Review your list of control characters in your documentation or software. Learn the idiosyncracies of your communicating computers: It may be necessary not only to rely on the control codes automatically sent back and forth by the software, but also to separately enter control characters from the keyboard to open and close files.

2. Files are best converted into as simple a format as possible.

Start with ASCII text files and the simplest communications settings possible: for example, seven bits, even parity, one stop bit, 300 bit/s. Ignore the parity bit, if necessary. Avoid using an eight-bit setting because eight bits correspond to ASCII codes above 128. These are nonstandard, control, formatting, and graphics characters.

3. Type back and forth in terminal mode before beginning a file transfer.

Once you are hooked up, access terminal mode and type a few words to test the accuracy of the data bits coming across the line. Never attempt a file transfer until you have ironed out garbles or nonmatched communications settings in your software.

4. Choose the highest-level error-checking protocol implemented in both sender and receiver communications software.

Always try a protected or error-free protocol before you resort to straight, unprotected, buffered terminal transmission. Protected transfers are vital if you're sending computer programs, numerical data, or binary files. But be forewarned: Some protocols are actually subsets or reinterpretations of standard protocols.

Also, dissimilar computers running packages implementing the same protocol may nevertheless misread incoming characters. The only way to know for sure is to experiment; you can always crank down to a simple X-On/X-Off (or no protocol) if the other schemes don't work.

5. Try modem communications first, direct connect second.

Modem communications are almost always easier to set up and troubleshoot than a direct serial transfer. By con-

trast, serial and null modem cables pose the problem of hard-wire connection, a complex matter. Take our advice, try a modem connection first. It's comparatively easy.

6. Pay attention to parity bits if you use them.

A screenful of mixed garbage and legible characters often signals a discrepancy in parity checking. Make sure parity is matched before pulling the panic button. Try each parity setting methodically (even, odd, ignore, no parity) on both sending and receiving ends and record the results.

7. Learn how to open and close data files.

Some telecommunications packages don't help an operator call up and survey a file that has just been transmitted. A case in point is PC to Mac and Back (Dilithium Press)—otherwise an excellent telecommunications program. Its conventions demand that the user first store a file on disk, then call it up with the MacWrite word processing program. Other programs don't tell a user exactly how to save a file once it's been stored in the capture buffer. Just to play safe, familiarize yourself with file saving and loading operations before you attempt a transmission.

8. Read your manuals.

Most contain troubleshooting checklists breaking out characteristic symptoms, possible causes, and cures. Modems generally come with checklists, as do programs. Often solutions are buried in the back of the manual under a heading like "Advanced Topics." You may also get some help by purchasing additional books geared toward your particular computer and its operating system.

9. Experiment with file conversion formats.

Some telecommunications software, as well as spreadsheets, database, and word processing programs, offer special file conversion utilities that enable you to convert data files into a neutral or virtual format. These files are then suitable for transmission to other computers. Programs such as VisiCalc and 1-2-3 offer a file format called DIF (Data Interchange Format) enabling the receiving com-

puter to read the data and reconvert it to a form that its own version of the program can use. Other neutral file formats are also available. Some telecommunications programs geared toward specific machines (PC to Mac and Back, for instance) offer conversion utilities for data files from WordStar and Multiplan.

10. Transmit in half duplex when possible.

Remember, half duplex affects local echo settings. Full-duplex settings can cause echo-back problems. Sometimes an operator may transmit to another computer in full-duplex terminal mode, finding that his own words, entered from the keyboard or from a disk file, don't appear on his own screen. The remedy is almost invariably a switch to half-duplex setting. Half duplex echoes characters both to the screen and the communications line; full duplex sends characters out the communications line, then waits for the receiving computer to echo back the characters. In some cases, though, the echoed characters are misinterpreted as a control code.

11. If your files are overtyped . . .

Some communications programs don't send line feeds after carriage returns. Some computers' screen controllers will send line feeds, while others will screen out the line-feed codes so that the type is overwritten on the receiving end. The ASCII codes for line feeds may be stored in the receiving computer's memory. Off-line, the receiver's own word processing program may be able to read these codes and format the document accordingly. If that fails, the operator may need to write a small program to insert line feeds in the transmitted text when needed. ■

(This is the second part of a two-part article excerpted from the upcoming book Direct Connections: Making your Personal Computer Communicate. *Copyright © 1986 by Arielle Emmett and David Gabel. Published by New American Library.)*

Modem marks remain high

Users are generally satisfied with the performance of their modems, according to a recent survey by Datapro Research Corp. The survey is divided into dial-up and leased-line modems as well as fiber optic and limited-distance modems.

Of the vendors that received more than 25 responses, IBM had the best score (3.6) for Overall Performance of

Table 1: User ratings of dial-up and leased-line modems

MANUFACTURER/ MODEL	NUMBER OF USER RESPONSES	NUMBER OF MODEMS INSTALLED	EASE OF INSTALLATION					DIAGNOSTIC CAPABILITIES					HARDWARE RELIABILITY					MAINTENANCE SERVICE/TECHNICAL SUPPORT					OVERALL PERFORMANCE				
			WA	E	G	F	P	WA	E	G	F	P	WA	E	G	F	P	WA	E	G	F	P	WA	E	G	F	P
ANCHOR AUTOMATION— ALL MODELS	4	7	3.8	3	1	0	0	3.0	1	2	1	0	3.8	3	1	0	0	3.3	1	3	0	0	3.5	2	2	0	0
ANDERSON JACOBSON— ALL MODELS	7	131	2.9	1	4	2	0	2.3	0	3	3	1	3.3	2	5	0	0	3.0	0	5	0	0	3.1	1	6	0	0
ARK ELECTRONIC— 24K/PLUS	4	28	3.5	2	2	0	0	3.3	1	3	0	0	3.3	1	3	0	0	3.3	1	3	0	0	3.3	1	3	0	0
AT&T— 201C	8	151	3.0	1	6	1	0	2.5	2	0	6	0	3.9	7	1	0	0	2.6	2	2	3	1	3.3	3	4	1	0
202T	3	558	3.3	2	0	1	0	2.0	1	0	0	2	3.7	2	1	0	0	3.0	0	3	0	0	3.3	2	0	1	0
208B	14	182	3.1	3	10	0	1	2.6	3	6	1	4	3.6	9	5	0	0	2.9	4	6	3	1	3.3	4	10	0	0
212A	18	539	2.9	3	12	2	1	2.6	1	10	5	2	3.6	10	8	0	0	3.1	6	8	4	0	3.2	6	10	2	0
DATAPHONE II	68	2,241	3.2	27	29	11	1	3.0	21	29	14	4	3.5	39	25	3	1	2.9	15	31	20	1	3.2	22	40	5	1
2224A/B	3	78	3.7	2	1	0	0	3.7	2	1	0	0	3.7	2	1	0	0	3.7	2	1	0	0	3.7	2	1	0	0
2500-DSU	3	78	3.0	0	3	0	0	3.7	2	1	0	0	3.7	2	1	0	0	3.0	0	3	0	0	3.7	2	1	0	0
2600-DSU	6	431	3.5	3	3	0	0	2.7	1	3	1	1	3.7	4	2	0	0	3.2	2	3	1	0	3.5	4	1	1	0
OTHERS & UNSPECIFIED	17	1,283	3.4	9	6	1	1	3.3	7	9	0	1	3.5	9	7	1	0	3.1	5	8	3	0	3.4	8	8	1	0
SUBTOTAL	140	5,541	3.2	50	70	16	4	2.9	40	59	27	14	3.6	84	51	4	1	3.0	36	65	34	3	3.3	53	75	11	1
BLACK BOX CATALOG— ALL MODELS	3	10	3.7	2	1	0	0	2.7	1	0	2	0	3.0	1	1	1	0	3.7	2	1	0	0	3.3	1	2	0	0
CASE— 212A	7	293	3.0	1	5	1	0	2.9	1	4	2	0	3.3	3	3	1	0	3.0	1	4	1	0	3.1	2	4	1	0
R212A	3	7	3.3	1	2	0	0	3.0	1	1	1	0	3.7	2	1	0	0	3.0	1	1	1	0	3.3	1	2	0	0
TA208A/B	4	277	2.0	0	1	2	1	1.8	0	2	0	2	2.0	0	2	0	2	2.0	0	1	2	1	2.0	0	2	0	2
1224	3	40	3.7	2	1	0	0	2.0	0	1	1	1	2.0	0	1	1	1	2.0	0	1	0	1	2.3	0	2	0	1
4096	3	93	1.7	0	1	0	2	2.0	0	1	0	2	1.7	0	1	0	2	2.0	0	1	1	1	1.7	0	1	0	2
96FP	3	29	2.7	1	1	0	1	2.7	2	0	0	1	3.0	2	0	0	1	2.7	1	1	0	1	2.7	1	1	0	1
OTHERS & UNSPECIFIED	13	487	3.1	6	3	3	1	2.6	2	5	3	2	3.2	5	6	2	0	2.4	1	6	2	3	2.8	1	10	1	1
SUBTOTAL	36	1,226	2.9	11	14	6	5	2.5	6	12	9	7	2.9	12	14	4	6	2.5	4	15	7	7	2.7	5	22	2	7
CERMETEK— ALL MODELS	3	511	3.0	1	1	1	0	1.7	0	1	0	2	2.3	0	1	2	0	2.0	0	1	1	1	2.7	0	2	1	0
CODEX— CS 48 FP	7	312	2.9	2	2	3	0	3.1	3	2	2	0	3.1	2	4	1	0	2.9	1	4	2	0	3.3	3	3	1	0
CS 9600	5	337	2.8	1	2	2	0	3.4	2	3	0	0	3.0	1	3	1	0	2.4	1	2	0	2	3.2	1	4	0	0
LSI 48 FP	4	107	3.3	2	1	1	0	3.0	1	2	1	0	3.5	2	2	0	0	2.3	0	2	1	1	3.0	1	2	1	0
LSI 4800	5	154	3.8	4	1	0	0	3.4	3	1	1	0	3.6	4	0	1	0	3.4	2	3	0	0	3.6	3	2	0	0
LSI 96	5	275	3.4	2	3	0	0	3.0	1	3	1	0	3.6	3	2	0	0	3.0	1	3	1	0	3.6	3	2	0	0
LSI 9600	11	331	3.6	7	4	0	0	3.1	5	3	2	1	3.9	10	1	0	0	3.5	5	6	0	0	3.5	5	6	0	0
UNSPECIFIED LSI SERIES	5	2,282	3.0	1	3	1	0	2.2	1	1	1	2	3.0	2	2	0	1	2.6	1	2	1	1	2.8	1	3	0	1
MX 2400	8	2,186	3.4	3	4	0	0	3.1	2	5	1	0	3.6	6	1	1	0	3.3	2	6	0	0	3.4	3	4	0	0
2232	4	13	3.0	0	4	0	0	3.8	3	1	0	0	3.8	3	1	0	0	3.8	3	1	0	0	3.5	2	2	0	0
2600	12	2,437	3.5	8	2	2	0	3.8	10	1	1	0	3.2	5	5	1	1	3.3	6	3	3	0	3.3	4	7	1	0
2640	12	2,934	3.4	5	7	0	0	3.8	9	3	0	0	3.7	8	4	0	0	3.5	5	6	0	0	3.5	6	6	0	0
2660	17	2,351	3.5	9	8	0	0	3.8	13	4	0	0	3.6	10	7	0	0	3.3	7	7	2	0	3.6	10	6	0	0
5201R	3	228	3.3	1	2	0	0	2.7	1	0	2	0	3.7	2	1	0	0	3.7	2	1	0	0	3.7	2	1	0	0
5208R	6	169	3.7	5	0	1	0	2.8	2	1	3	0	3.2	3	2	0	1	3.0	2	3	0	1	3.5	4	1	1	0
OTHERS & UNSPECIFIED	21	1,470	3.5	11	9	1	0	2.9	8	5	6	2	3.2	9	9	2	1	2.9	6	8	6	1	3.3	7	13	1	0
SUBTOTAL	125	15,586	3.4	61	52	11	0	3.3	64	35	21	5	3.4	70	44	7	4	3.1	44	57	16	6	3.4	55	62	5	1
COMDATA— ALL MODELS	5	56	3.8	4	1	0	0	3.0	2	1	2	0	3.6	3	2	0	0	3.4	2	3	0	0	3.6	3	2	0	0

WEIGHTED AVERAGE (WA) IS BASED ON 4 FOR EXCELLENT (E), 3 FOR GOOD (G), 2 FOR FAIR (F), AND 1 FOR POOR (P).
WEIGHTED AVERAGE IS INVALID FOR FEWER THAN 3 RESPONSES.

User survey exclusive

dial-up and leased-line modems (Table 1). This is based on a weighted average of 1.0 (poor) to 4.0 (excellent). Of the vendors that received more than 15 responses for fiber optic and limited-distance modems, Codex, and Racal-Milgo tied for best Overall Performance (3.4). Other vendors scored just as high but had fewer responses. The categories of Ease of Installation and Hardware Reliability received the highest overall weighted averages, while Diagnostic Capabilities received the lowest.

This survey is based on 1,388 responses — all from DATA COMMUNICATIONS magazine subscribers — representing 151,348 modems. For further information on this and other related surveys, contact Datapro, 1805 Underwood Blvd., Delran, N. J. 08705 (Telephone: 609-764-0100).

Table 1: User ratings of dial-up and leased-line modems (continued)

MANUFACTURER/ MODEL	NUMBER OF USER RESPONSES	NUMBER OF MODEMS INSTALLED	EASE OF INSTALLATION					DIAGNOSTIC CAPABILITIES					HARDWARE RELIABILITY					MAINTENANCE SERVICE/TECHNICAL SUPPORT					OVERALL PERFORMANCE				
			WA	E	G	F	P	WA	E	G	F	P	WA	E	G	F	P	WA	E	G	F	P	WA	E	G	F	P
CONCORD DATA SYSTEMS—																											
CDS 224	18	590	3.2	6	9	3	0	2.7	4	6	6	2	3.0	7	5	5	1	2.8	4	6	8	0	3.1	6	7	5	0
OTHERS & UNSPECIFIED	6	616	2.5	0	4	1	1	2.5	0	4	1	1	2.2	0	2	3	1	2.2	0	2	3	1	2.3	0	3	2	1
SUBTOTAL	24	1,206	3.0	6	13	4	1	2.6	4	10	7	3	2.8	7	7	8	2	2.6	4	8	11	1	2.9	6	10	7	1
DATEC—																											
212	3	53	3.3	1	2	0	0	2.0	0	1	1	1	3.3	1	2	0	0	2.3	0	1	2	0	3.3	1	2	0	0
DIGITAL EQUIPMENT CORP.—																											
DF112	4	19	4.0	4	0	0	0	3.5	2	2	0	0	3.8	3	1	0	0	3.7	2	1	0	0	3.5	2	2	0	0
OTHERS & UNSPECIFIED	4	56	3.0	1	2	1	0	2.5	1	0	3	0	3.3	2	1	1	0	3.3	2	1	1	0	3.0	1	2	1	0
SUBTOTAL	8	75	3.5	5	2	1	0	3.0	3	2	3	0	3.5	5	2	1	0	3.4	4	2	1	0	3.3	3	4	1	0
GANDALF—																											
LDS 309A	5	670	3.4	2	3	0	0	3.2	1	4	0	0	3.8	4	1	0	0	3.3	1	3	0	0	3.4	2	3	0	0
SM9600	4	32	3.8	3	1	0	0	3.5	2	2	0	0	3.8	3	1	0	0	3.5	2	2	0	0	3.8	3	1	0	0
LDM SERIES	4	105	3.8	3	1	0	0	3.3	2	1	1	0	4.0	4	0	0	0	3.5	2	2	0	0	3.7	2	1	0	0
OTHERS & UNSPECIFIED	4	285	3.3	2	1	1	0	2.3	0	2	1	1	3.0	1	2	1	0	2.3	1	1	0	2	2.8	0	3	1	0
SUBTOTAL	17	1,092	3.5	10	6	1	0	3.1	5	9	2	1	3.6	12	4	1	0	3.1	6	8	0	2	3.4	7	8	1	0
GENERAL DATACOMM—																											
201 SERIES	5	282	3.0	2	1	2	0	2.0	1	1	0	3	2.8	1	3	0	1	2.4	0	3	1	1	2.6	1	1	3	0
208A/B	4	66	2.8	0	3	1	0	2.5	1	1	1	1	2.5	1	1	1	1	2.0	0	1	2	1	2.5	0	3	0	1
2400 ASM	3	53	3.7	2	1	0	0	1.7	0	1	0	2	3.3	1	2	0	0	2.3	0	1	2	0	3.0	0	3	0	0
4800 SERIES	3	23	3.7	2	1	0	0	3.0	0	3	0	0	4.0	3	0	0	0	3.0	1	1	1	0	3.7	2	1	0	0
9600 SERIES	10	131	2.5	1	3	6	0	2.2	0	4	4	2	2.3	1	2	6	1	1.8	0	2	4	4	2.3	1	2	6	1
500 SERIES (DSU)	7	175	3.0	2	3	2	0	2.6	0	4	3	0	2.9	1	5	0	1	2.6	0	5	1	1	2.8	1	4	0	1
OTHERS & UNSPECIFIED	19	1,052	3.1	7	7	5	0	2.8	4	9	2	3	3.1	8	6	4	1	2.8	4	8	5	1	3.1	7	8	3	1
SUBTOTAL	51	1,782	3.0	16	19	16	0	2.5	6	23	10	11	2.9	16	19	11	5	2.5	5	21	16	8	2.8	12	22	12	4
HAYES—																											
SMARTMODEM 300	8	121	3.4	3	5	0	0	2.1	0	3	2	2	3.3	4	3	0	1	2.6	1	3	2	1	3.0	2	5	0	1
SMARTMODEM 1200	100	14,422	3.6	61	36	2	0	2.8	19	45	25	8	3.5	60	32	7	0	3.1	28	43	19	2	3.3	38	54	7	0
SMARTMODEM 1200B	6	17	3.2	2	3	1	0	2.8	1	3	2	0	3.3	3	2	1	0	2.8	1	3	0	1	3.2	1	5	0	0
SMARTMODEM 2400	14	181	3.6	10	3	0	1	3.0	5	5	3	1	3.3	7	5	1	1	3.0	5	5	3	1	3.2	5	8	0	1
SMARTCOM I	4	213	3.5	2	2	0	0	3.3	1	3	0	0	3.8	3	1	0	0	3.0	0	3	0	0	3.3	1	3	0	0
212A	3	67	4.0	3	0	0	0	3.0	1	1	1	0	4.0	3	0	0	0	3.7	2	1	0	0	3.7	2	1	0	0
OTHERS & UNSPECIFIED	6	1,018	3.7	4	2	0	0	2.5	1	2	2	1	3.5	3	3	0	0	2.8	1	3	2	0	3.5	3	3	0	0
SUBTOTAL	141	16,039	3.6	85	51	3	1	2.8	28	62	35	12	3.5	83	46	9	2	3.0	38	61	26	5	3.3	52	79	7	2
IBM—																											
3863	3	122	3.7	2	1	0	0	3.0	1	1	1	0	4.0	3	0	0	0	3.3	2	0	1	0	3.7	2	1	0	0
3864	6	122	3.7	4	2	0	0	3.0	2	2	2	0	3.8	5	1	0	0	3.3	3	2	1	0	3.7	4	2	0	0
3865	10	328	3.6	7	2	1	0	3.0	3	4	3	0	3.9	9	1	0	0	3.7	7	3	0	0	3.7	7	3	0	0
OTHER 386X MODELS	7	607	3.3	3	3	1	0	3.1	1	6	0	0	3.7	5	2	0	0	3.4	4	2	1	0	3.6	4	3	0	0
5865	5	292	4.0	5	0	0	0	4.0	5	0	0	0	4.0	5	0	0	0	3.6	3	2	0	0	4.0	5	0	0	0
OTHER 586X MODELS	4	8	3.3	1	3	0	0	2.8	1	1	2	0	3.3	1	3	0	0	3.3	1	3	0	0	3.3	1	3	0	0
OTHERS & UNSPECIFIED	8	392	3.3	3	4	1	0	2.8	2	4	0	2	3.4	4	3	1	0	3.1	3	3	2	0	3.1	3	3	2	0
SUBTOTAL	43	1,871	3.5	25	15	3	0	3.1	15	18	8	2	3.7	32	10	1	0	3.4	23	15	5	0	3.6	26	15	2	0
INFINET—																											
DMX SERIES	5	540	3.2	3	1	0	1	3.2	3	1	0	1	2.6	1	2	1	1	2.2	0	1	4	0	2.6	1	2	1	1
OTHERS & UNSPECIFIED	4	2,143	3.0	1	2	1	0	2.8	0	3	1	0	3.0	2	0	0	1	2.3	0	2	1	1	2.8	1	1	2	0
SUBTOTAL	9	2,683	3.1	4	3	1	1	3.0	3	4	1	1	2.8	3	2	1	2	2.2	0	3	5	1	2.7	2	3	3	1
MICOM—																											
4095	3	32	3.7	2	1	0	0	3.7	2	1	0	0	3.3	2	0	1	0	3.0	1	1	1	0	3.3	2	0	1	0
OTHERS & UNSPECIFIED	12	582	3.4	5	7	0	0	2.8	2	6	4	0	3.1	3	7	2	0	3.0	4	4	4	0	3.1	2	9	1	0
SUBTOTAL	15	614	3.5	7	8	0	0	3.0	4	7	4	0	3.1	5	7	3	0	3.0	5	5	5	0	3.1	4	9	2	0

Table 1: User ratings of dial-up and leased-line modems (continued)

MANUFACTURER/ MODEL	NUMBER OF USER RESPONSES	NUMBER OF MODEMS INSTALLED	EASE OF INSTALLATION					DIAGNOSTIC CAPABILITIES					HARDWARE RELIABILITY					MAINTENANCE SERVICE/TECHNICAL SUPPORT					OVERALL PERFORMANCE				
			WA	E	G	F	P	WA	E	G	F	P	WA	E	G	F	P	WA	E	G	F	P	WA	E	G	F	P
MICROCOM—																											
SX/2400	5	229	2.8	0	4	1	0	2.6	1	1	3	0	2.2	0	1	4	0	3.0	1	3	1	0	2.8	0	4	1	0
OTHERS & UNSPECIFIED	7	73	3.0	1	5	1	0	3.1	2	4	1	0	2.9	1	4	2	0	2.9	3	1	2	1	3.0	2	3	2	0
SUBTOTAL	12	302	2.9	1	9	2	0	2.9	3	5	4	0	2.6	1	5	6	0	2.9	4	4	3	1	2.9	2	7	3	0
MULTITECH—																											
MT 212	5	164	3.4	2	3	0	0	2.6	1	1	3	0	3.4	2	3	0	0	2.8	1	2	2	0	2.8	1	2	2	0
MT 224	6	366	3.7	4	2	0	0	3.2	2	3	1	0	3.7	4	2	0	0	3.5	3	3	0	0	3.5	3	3	0	0
OTHERS & UNSPECIFIED	5	128	3.4	2	3	0	0	2.4	0	2	3	0	3.2	1	4	0	0	3.0	0	5	0	0	3.2	1	4	0	0
SUBTOTAL	16	658	3.5	8	8	0	0	2.8	3	6	7	0	3.4	7	9	0	0	3.1	4	10	2	0	3.2	5	9	2	0
NEC—																											
DSP SERIES	3	78	4.0	3	0	0	0	4.0	3	0	0	0	3.7	2	1	0	0	3.7	2	1	0	0	4.0	3	0	0	0
OTHERS & UNSPECIFIED	15	17,348	3.3	6	8	1	0	2.7	4	6	2	3	3.2	7	5	2	1	3.1	8	1	5	1	3.1	6	6	2	1
SUBTOTAL	18	17,426	3.4	9	8	1	0	2.9	7	6	2	3	3.3	9	6	2	1	3.2	10	2	5	1	3.3	9	6	2	1
NOVATION—																											
SMART-CAT	5	7	3.2	2	2	1	0	2.4	0	3	1	1	2.8	2	1	1	1	2.3	0	2	1	1	2.4	0	2	3	0
PARADYNE—																											
CHALLENGER SERIES	5	10,014	3.6	3	2	0	0	2.6	1	1	3	0	2.8	1	2	2	0	2.8	1	1	2	0	3.0	1	3	1	0
MPX 2400	3	1,045	3.0	1	1	1	0	3.0	1	1	1	0	2.7	1	1	0	1	2.3	0	1	2	0	2.7	0	2	1	0
MPX 4800	10	484	3.1	3	5	2	0	3.3	5	3	2	0	2.8	1	7	1	1	2.6	2	3	4	1	3.1	2	7	1	0
MPX 9600	18	1,383	3.2	5	11	2	0	3.2	8	5	5	0	2.6	3	7	6	2	2.5	3	5	9	1	2.7	2	10	5	1
OTHER MPX MODELS	4	1,531	2.8	0	3	1	0	2.5	0	2	2	0	2.3	0	1	3	0	2.5	0	2	2	0	2.5	0	2	2	0
T-96	11	1,974	3.6	7	4	0	0	2.9	2	6	3	0	3.6	8	2	1	0	3.1	3	7	0	1	3.5	6	5	0	0
UNSPECIFIED 14.4 MODELS	4	280	2.3	1	0	2	1	2.8	0	3	1	0	2.5	0	3	0	1	2.0	0	2	0	2	2.3	0	2	1	1
UNSPECIFIED 9600 MODELS	6	61	3.0	1	4	1	0	2.8	0	5	1	0	3.2	2	3	1	0	3.2	2	3	1	0	3.0	1	4	1	0
OTHERS & UNSPECIFIED	26	12,381	3.1	7	14	5	0	2.7	2	16	4	3	3.1	10	11	2	3	2.7	3	13	8	1	2.9	3	19	3	1
SUBTOTAL	87	29,156	3.1	28	44	14	1	2.9	19	42	22	3	2.9	26	37	16	8	2.7	14	37	28	6	2.9	15	54	15	3
PENRIL—																											
300/1200 SERIES	3	2,320	3.7	2	1	0	0	2.3	1	0	1	1	3.0	1	1	1	0	3.0	0	3	0	0	3.3	1	2	0	0
OTHERS & UNSPECIFIED	8	438	3.1	3	3	2	0	2.3	0	4	2	2	2.9	2	3	3	0	2.4	0	5	1	2	2.6	1	4	2	1
SUBTOTAL	11	2,758	3.3	5	4	2	0	2.3	1	4	3	3	2.9	3	4	4	0	2.5	0	8	1	2	2.8	2	6	2	1
PRENTICE—																											
P-212	3	255	4.0	3	0	0	0	2.7	1	0	2	0	3.3	1	2	0	0	2.7	0	2	1	0	3.3	1	2	0	0
OTHERS & UNSPECIFIED	4	70	3.8	3	1	0	0	3.3	1	3	0	0	2.8	1	2	0	1	3.3	1	3	0	0	3.3	2	1	1	0
SUBTOTAL	7	325	3.9	6	1	0	0	3.0	2	3	2	0	3.0	2	4	0	1	3.0	1	5	1	0	3.3	3	3	1	0
PROMETHEUS—																											
PROMODEM 1200	4	10	3.5	2	2	0	0	3.5	2	2	0	0	3.8	3	1	0	0	3.8	3	1	0	0	3.5	2	2	0	0
RACAL-MILGO—																											
CMS SERIES	4	5,130	3.5	2	2	0	0	3.8	3	1	0	0	3.8	3	1	0	0	3.3	1	3	0	0	3.8	3	1	0	0
MPS 48	3	96	3.0	0	3	0	0	2.3	0	2	0	1	2.7	0	2	1	0	3.0	1	1	1	0	2.7	0	2	1	0
MPS 9600	7	265	3.6	4	3	0	0	2.4	0	4	2	1	3.4	3	4	0	0	3.1	2	4	1	0	3.3	2	5	0	0
OMNIMODE 48	7	115	3.3	2	5	0	0	3.3	3	3	1	0	3.6	4	3	0	0	3.1	2	4	1	0	3.4	3	4	0	0
OMNIMODE 96	25	2,441	3.5	12	13	0	0	3.7	18	7	0	0	3.6	16	9	0	0	3.2	8	14	3	0	3.6	14	11	0	0
OTHER OMNIMODE MODELS	11	3,159	3.2	3	7	1	0	3.5	6	4	1	0	3.1	5	2	4	0	3.1	5	3	2	1	3.2	4	5	2	0
COM-LINK 3	5	127	3.4	2	3	0	0	2.8	0	4	1	0	3.6	3	2	0	0	3.0	1	3	1	0	3.2	1	4	0	0
2400 LSI	8	834	3.4	3	5	0	0	2.5	1	3	3	1	3.3	3	4	1	0	3.0	2	4	2	0	3.1	2	5	1	0
9601	3	13	2.0	0	1	1	1	3.0	0	3	0	0	3.0	0	3	0	0	2.3	0	1	2	0	3.0	0	3	0	0
OTHERS & UNSPECIFIED	13	2,411	3.4	5	8	0	0	2.8	1	8	4	0	3.5	8	3	2	0	3.0	4	6	2	1	3.2	5	6	2	0
SUBTOTAL	86	14,591	3.3	33	50	2	1	3.2	32	39	12	3	3.4	45	33	8	0	3.1	26	43	15	2	3.3	34	46	6	0
RACAL-VADIC—																											
VA212	14	653	3.4	7	6	1	0	3.0	4	6	4	0	3.4	6	7	1	0	3.0	3	8	3	0	3.3	5	8	1	0
VA212-LC	8	277	3.8	6	2	0	0	2.0	1	1	3	3	3.4	4	3	1	0	3.0	2	3	2	0	3.4	4	3	1	0
VA2400 SERIES	9	481	3.3	4	4	1	0	2.6	0	5	4	0	3.0	2	5	0	1	2.8	0	7	2	0	3.0	1	7	1	0
VA3450 SERIES	16	623	3.3	6	9	1	0	2.1	0	5	7	4	3.3	7	6	3	0	2.7	0	11	3	1	3.1	3	11	2	0
VA348X SERIES	3	44	2.3	0	2	0	1	2.0	0	1	1	1	3.7	2	1	0	0	2.7	0	2	1	0	3.3	1	2	0	0
VA3467	17	5,862	3.3	5	12	0	0	2.8	4	6	7	0	3.3	9	5	2	1	2.8	3	9	3	2	3.1	5	9	3	0
1200 SERIES	9	106	3.2	3	5	1	0	2.6	2	2	4	1	3.1	3	4	2	0	2.4	0	4	5	0	2.9	2	4	3	0
2400PA	4	217	3.0	1	2	1	0	2.8	1	1	2	0	3.0	1	2	1	0	2.8	0	3	1	0	2.8	0	3	1	0
OTHERS & UNSPECIFIED	32	2,320	3.4	14	17	1	0	2.9	8	14	9	1	3.2	12	15	5	0	3.0	7	16	7	0	3.2	10	18	4	0
SUBTOTAL	112	10,583	3.3	46	59	6	1	2.6	20	41	41	10	3.2	46	48	15	2	2.8	15	63	27	3	3.1	31	65	16	0
TIMEPLEX—																											
AIM 9600	5	153	3.4	2	3	0	0	3.2	2	2	1	0	3.8	4	1	0	0	3.2	2	2	1	0	3.4	2	3	0	0

WEIGHTED AVERAGE (WA) IS BASED ON 4 FOR EXCELLENT (E), 3 FOR GOOD (G), 2 FOR FAIR (F), AND 1 FOR POOR (P).
WEIGHTED AVERAGE IS INVALID FOR FEWER THAN 3 RESPONSES.

Table 1: User ratings of dial-up and leased-line modems (continued)

WEIGHTED AVERAGES AND RESPONSE COUNTS

MANUFACTURER/ MODEL	NUMBER OF USER RESPONSES	NUMBER OF MODEMS INSTALLED	EASE OF INSTALLATION					DIAGNOSTIC CAPABILITIES					HARDWARE RELIABILITY					MAINTENANCE SERVICE/TECHNICAL SUPPORT					OVERALL PERFORMANCE				
			WA	E	G	F	P	WA	E	G	F	P	WA	E	G	F	P	WA	E	G	F	P	WA	E	G	F	P
UNIVERSAL DATA SYSTEMS—																											
201C	7	127	3.4	3	4	0	0	3.1	2	4	1	0	3.9	6	1	0	0	3.3	3	3	1	0	3.6	4	3	0	0
208A/B	12	486	3.5	6	6	0	0	2.6	3	3	4	2	3.3	6	4	2	0	3.3	6	4	1	1	3.3	4	7	1	0
212A	11	4,492	3.5	6	4	1	0	2.5	0	7	2	2	3.0	3	6	1	1	2.8	1	6	3	0	2.8	0	9	0	1
212LP	5	206	3.2	1	4	0	0	2.4	0	3	1	1	3.2	2	2	1	0	3.0	0	4	0	0	3.0	0	5	0	0
9600	8	752	3.5	4	4	0	0	2.4	0	5	1	2	3.4	5	1	2	0	3.1	3	3	2	0	3.4	3	5	0	0
9600A/B	4	29	3.3	1	3	0	0	3.3	2	1	1	0	3.8	3	1	0	0	3.8	3	1	0	0	3.5	2	2	0	0
OTHERS & UNSPECIFIED	19	4,607	3.4	9	8	2	0	2.9	6	7	4	2	3.5	11	7	1	0	3.1	4	11	3	0	3.4	8	11	0	0
SUBTOTAL	66	10,699	3.4	30	33	3	0	2.7	13	30	14	9	3.4	36	22	7	1	3.1	20	32	10	1	3.3	21	42	1	1
U.S. ROBOTICS—																											
PASSWORD	7	69	3.6	4	3	0	0	1.9	0	2	2	3	3.0	2	3	2	0	2.7	1	3	1	1	3.3	3	3	1	0
OTHERS & UNSPECIFIED	6	16	3.5	4	1	1	0	2.5	2	1	1	2	2.8	2	1	3	0	3.2	2	2	1	0	3.0	2	2	2	0
SUBTOTAL	13	85	3.5	8	4	1	0	2.2	2	3	3	5	2.9	4	4	5	0	2.9	3	5	2	1	3.2	5	5	3	0
VEN-TEL—																											
PC MODEM HALF CARD	4	9	2.8	0	3	1	0	2.8	0	3	1	0	3.5	2	2	0	0	2.5	0	2	2	0	3.3	1	3	0	0
EC1200	6	1,402	3.5	3	3	0	0	2.8	2	1	3	0	3.2	2	3	1	0	2.5	1	3	0	2	3.0	2	2	2	0
MD212	3	68	3.7	2	1	0	0	2.3	0	2	0	1	2.7	1	0	2	0	1.7	0	0	2	1	3.0	1	1	1	0
OTHERS & UNSPECIFIED	5	21	3.4	2	3	0	0	3.2	2	2	1	0	3.0	2	2	0	1	2.8	2	1	1	1	3.0	2	2	0	1
SUBTOTAL	18	1,500	3.3	7	10	1	0	2.8	4	8	5	1	3.1	7	7	3	1	2.4	3	6	5	4	3.1	6	8	3	1
ALL OTHERS	46	1,870	3.4	23	18	5	0	2.6	9	16	14	6	3.2	19	18	8	1	3.0	14	19	9	2	3.1	11	29	6	0
GRAND TOTAL	1,144	138,634	3.3	504	520	103	15	2.8	302	462	267	104	3.3	554	421	128	38	2.9	294	516	239	58	3.2	382	615	117	24

Table 2: User ratings of fiber optic and limited-distance modems

WEIGHTED AVERAGES AND RESPONSE COUNTS

MANUFACTURER/ MODEL	NUMBER OF USER RESPONSES	NUMBER OF MODEMS INSTALLED	EASE OF INSTALLATON					DIAGNOSTIC CAPABILITIES					HARDWARE RELIABILITY					MAINTENANCE SERVICE/TECHNICAL SUPPORT					OVERALL PERFORMANCE				
			WA	E	G	F	P	WA	E	G	F	P	WA	E	G	F	P	WA	E	G	F	P	WA	E	G	F	P
AMDAHL— ALL MODELS	3	108	3.3	1	2	0	0	3.0	0	3	0	0	3.7	2	1	0	0	2.3	0	1	2	0	3.0	0	3	0	0
AREA NETWORK PRODUCTS— ALL MODELS	4	164	2.5	0	2	2	0	2.8	0	3	1	0	3.3	1	3	0	0	2.5	0	2	2	0	3.0	0	4	0	0
ARK ELECTRONIC—																											
LDM-5	4	148	3.5	2	2	0	0	2.8	1	2	0	1	3.5	2	2	0	0	2.5	0	2	2	0	2.8	0	3	1	0
OTHERS & UNSPECIFIED	3	25	3.0	0	3	0	0	2.3	0	2	0	1	3.7	2	1	0	0	2.7	0	2	1	0	3.3	1	2	0	0
SUBTOTAL	7	173	3.3	2	5	0	0	2.6	1	4	0	2	3.6	4	3	0	0	2.6	0	4	3	0	3.0	1	5	1	0
ASTROCOM—																											
MOS/2	3	450	3.7	2	1	0	0	2.0	0	1	1	1	3.3	1	2	0	0	2.3	0	1	2	0	3.0	0	3	0	0
OTHERS & UNSPECIFIED	4	470	3.3	2	1	1	0	2.0	0	1	2	1	3.0	2	0	2	0	2.5	1	1	1	1	3.0	1	2	1	0
SUBTOTAL	7	920	3.4	4	2	1	0	2.0	0	2	3	2	3.1	3	2	2	0	2.4	1	2	3	1	3.0	1	5	1	0
AT&T— LADS	3	50	3.3	1	2	0	0	2.3	0	1	2	0	3.0	1	1	1	0	2.3	0	2	0	1	2.7	0	2	1	0
AVANTI— ALL MODELS	10	237	2.9	3	5	0	2	2.0	0	2	6	2	3.4	5	4	1	0	2.7	0	6	3	0	3.2	4	4	2	0
BLACK BOX CATALOG—																											
LDM SERIES	4	66	4.0	4	0	0	0	2.0	0	2	0	2	4.0	4	0	0	0	4.0	4	0	0	0	4.0	4	0	0	0
OTHERS & UNSPECIFIED	9	85	2.8	2	4	2	1	1.8	0	2	3	4	3.4	4	5	0	0	2.9	2	3	3	0	3.1	2	6	1	0
SUBTOTAL	13	151	3.2	6	4	2	1	1.8	0	4	3	6	3.6	8	5	0	0	3.3	6	3	3	0	3.4	6	6	1	0

WEIGHTED AVERAGE (WA) IS BASED ON 4 FOR EXCELLENT (E), 3 FOR GOOD (G), 2 FOR FAIR (F), AND 1 FOR POOR (P).
WEIGHTED AVERAGE IS INVALID FOR FEWER THAN 3 RESPONSES.

Table 2: User ratings of fiber optic and limited-distance modems (continued)

WEIGHTED AVERAGES AND RESPONSE COUNTS

Manufacturer/Model	Number of User Responses	Number of Modems Installed	Ease of Installation WA	E	G	F	P	Diagnostic Capabilities WA	E	G	F	P	Hardware Reliability WA	E	G	F	P	Maintenance Service/Technical Support WA	E	G	F	P	Overall Performance WA	E	G	F	P
CANOGA DATA SYSTEMS— ALL MODELS	7	304	3.3	4	1	2	0	2.7	2	1	4	0	3.4	4	2	1	0	3.2	2	3	1	0	3.3	3	3	1	0
CASE— LDM 720	5	104	3.0	1	3	1	0	3.0	1	3	1	0	3.2	1	4	0	0	3.3	1	3	0	0	3.4	2	3	0	0
CODEX— LDM 8250	3	280	3.0	0	3	0	0	1.7	0	0	2	1	3.7	2	1	0	0	3.0	1	1	1	0	3.0	0	3	0	0
2100 SERIES	6	170	3.3	2	4	0	0	3.2	1	5	0	0	3.2	1	5	0	0	3.2	1	4	0	0	3.2	1	5	0	0
8200 LDSU	7	304	3.6	4	3	0	0	2.6	2	1	3	1	3.9	6	1	0	0	3.0	3	2	1	1	3.7	5	2	0	0
8250 LDSU	12	634	3.7	8	4	0	0	2.8	4	4	2	2	3.5	7	4	1	0	3.3	6	4	1	1	3.5	7	4	1	0
OTHERS & UNSPECIFIED	10	1,094	3.4	5	4	1	0	3.0	4	3	2	1	3.3	5	3	2	0	3.3	5	3	2	0	3.4	5	4	1	0
SUBTOTAL	38	2,482	3.5	19	18	1	0	2.8	11	13	9	5	3.5	21	14	3	0	3.2	16	14	5	2	3.4	18	18	2	0
DATATEL— DCP SERIES	6	99	3.2	1	5	0	0	2.2	0	2	3	1	3.2	1	5	0	0	3.0	1	4	1	0	3.2	1	5	0	0
DEI TELEPRODUCTS— ALL MODELS	3	110	3.0	1	1	1	0	1.3	0	0	1	2	3.0	1	1	1	0	3.0	0	3	0	0	3.0	1	1	1	0
GANDALF— LDS SERIES	12	2,392	3.0	2	8	2	0	2.4	0	6	5	1	3.1	4	6	1	1	3.0	4	5	2	1	2.8	1	8	2	1
mLDS 122	3	188	3.7	2	1	0	0	2.3	0	2	0	1	3.7	2	1	0	0	3.7	2	1	0	0	3.7	2	1	0	0
OTHERS & UNSPECIFIED	11	355	3.2	4	5	2	0	2.0	0	4	3	4	3.2	4	5	2	0	2.5	1	5	2	2	2.9	2	6	3	0
SUBTOTAL	26	2,935	3.2	8	14	4	0	2.2	0	12	8	6	3.2	10	12	3	1	2.9	7	11	4	3	2.9	5	15	5	1
GENERAL DATACOMM— NMS-2020	6	184	3.0	0	6	0	0	3.5	4	1	1	0	3.5	4	1	1	0	3.2	2	3	1	0	3.3	3	2	1	0
NMS-2030	5	197	3.2	1	4	0	0	3.2	3	1	0	1	3.8	4	1	0	0	3.2	1	4	0	0	3.6	3	2	0	0
OTHERS & UNSPECIFIED	3	151	3.0	1	1	1	0	1.7	0	0	2	1	3.0	0	3	0	0	2.0	0	1	1	1	2.7	1	0	2	0
SUBTOTAL	14	532	3.1	2	11	1	0	3.0	7	2	3	2	3.5	8	5	1	0	2.9	3	8	2	1	3.3	7	4	3	0
IBM— 3044	3	11	3.7	2	1	0	0	2.5	0	1	1	0	3.5	1	1	0	0	3.0	1	1	1	0	3.3	1	2	0	0
OTHERS & UNSPECIFIED	4	46	3.3	2	1	1	0	3.3	2	1	1	0	3.3	2	1	1	0	3.8	3	1	0	0	3.3	2	1	1	0
SUBTOTAL	7	57	3.4	4	2	1	0	3.0	2	2	2	0	3.3	3	2	1	0	3.4	4	2	1	0	3.3	3	3	1	0
MICOM— MICRO400 SERIES	8	304	3.6	5	3	0	0	2.5	1	3	3	1	3.5	5	2	1	0	2.8	2	3	2	1	3.0	3	2	3	0
OTHERS & UNSPECIFIED	3	20	3.3	1	2	0	0	2.7	0	2	1	0	3.3	1	2	0	0	2.3	0	1	2	0	3.3	1	2	0	0
SUBTOTAL	11	324	3.5	6	5	0	0	2.5	1	5	4	1	3.5	6	4	1	0	2.6	2	4	4	1	3.1	4	4	3	0
PARADYNE— ALL MODELS	5	220	3.4	2	3	0	0	2.8	1	2	2	0	3.4	2	3	0	0	3.2	1	4	0	0	3.4	2	3	0	0
PENRIL— PSH 96A	3	525	3.3	2	0	1	0	2.3	1	0	1	1	3.7	2	1	0	0	2.3	0	1	2	0	3.3	1	2	0	0
PILKINGTON— ALL MODELS	4	12	3.3	1	3	0	0	2.3	1	0	2	1	2.8	1	1	2	0	2.3	0	1	3	0	2.5	1	0	3	0
PRENTICE— ALD/1	3	62	3.3	1	2	0	0	2.3	0	1	2	0	3.0	0	3	0	0	3.0	0	3	0	0	3.3	1	2	0	0
SLDMK/2	4	272	3.3	1	3	0	0	2.8	1	1	2	0	3.0	1	2	1	0	3.0	1	2	1	0	3.3	1	3	0	0
OTHERS & UNSPECIFIED	3	225	3.7	2	1	0	0	3.3	1	2	0	0	3.3	2	0	1	0	2.7	1	1	0	1	3.3	1	2	0	0
SUBTOTAL	10	559	3.4	4	6	0	0	2.8	2	4	4	0	3.1	3	5	2	0	2.9	2	6	1	1	3.3	3	7	0	0
RACAL-MILGO— COMLINK 3	16	801	3.2	4	11	1	0	2.8	2	10	3	1	3.4	8	7	1	0	3.1	3	11	2	0	3.2	4	11	1	0
COMLINK 7	3	42	4.0	3	0	0	0	3.7	2	1	0	0	4.0	3	0	0	0	3.7	2	1	0	0	4.0	3	0	0	0
UNSPECIFIED COMLINK SERIES	4	52	3.3	1	3	0	0	2.0	0	1	2	1	3.8	3	1	0	0	3.3	1	3	0	0	3.5	2	2	0	0
OTHERS & UNSPECIFIED	3	453	3.7	2	1	0	0	2.7	0	2	1	0	3.7	2	1	0	0	3.3	1	2	0	0	3.7	2	1	0	0
SUBTOTAL	26	1,348	3.3	10	15	1	0	2.8	4	14	6	2	3.6	16	9	1	0	3.2	7	17	2	0	3.4	11	14	1	0
RAD DATA COMMUNICATIONS— SRM-6	3	26	3.3	2	0	1	0	2.0	1	0	0	2	3.7	2	1	0	0	3.5	1	1	0	0	3.3	1	2	0	0
ALL OTHERS	29	1,274	3.6	17	10	1	0	2.5	3	10	13	2	3.4	16	9	4	0	3.1	8	14	4	1	3.2	9	16	3	0
GRAND TOTAL	244	12,714	3.3	101	119	20	3	2.5	38	89	78	37	3.4	121	97	24	1	3.0	62	116	46	11	3.2	84	129	29	1

WEIGHTED AVERAGE (WA) IS BASED ON 4 FOR EXCELLENT (E), 3 FOR GOOD (G), 2 FOR FAIR (F), AND 1 FOR POOR (P).
WEIGHTED AVERAGE IS INVALID FOR FEWER THAN 3 RESPONSES.

Brian Laughlin, Damac Products Inc., Santa Fe Springs, Calif.

Data wiring, or learning to live with spaghetti

A survey shows how networkers copewith the computer-generated tangle of twisted-pair and coaxial cable: Most just grimace and bear it.

Beneath the streamlined veneer of today's paperless office sprawls a proliferating mess of wire. The clutter accompanying computer power and data communications cabling is epidemic, to be sure. But it is also a problem that many users simply sweep under the rug. What's more, one recent survey indicates that this path of least resistance is not only the most popular but also, possibly, the most efficient.

A survey of 2,000 DATA COMMUNICATIONS readers, whose names were supplied to the survey group, reveals that over 80 percent of the respondents consider their workplace wiring to be a shambles (see "The question is wiring"). Even so, only 38 percent of survey participants said that they would consider enlisting a consultant for help.

Why not? Most of those surveyed (44 percent) cited cost as the main reason they weren't interested in trying to solve cable clutter; 38 percent said they were concerned it would cause equipment downtime. Other reasons cited for not disturbing the status quo included personnel downtime, space considerations, uncertainty about future plans, the "if it ain't broke, don't fix it" syndrome, company politics, and plans to relocate.

In the context of the survey, equipment downtime referred to that period between the unpatching and repatching of terminal devices that would be affected. Computer equipment and its power supply would likely not be shut down during this time. Personnel downtime was defined as users' temporary lack of access to their regular terminals.

Typical comments from respondents include, for example: "The spaghetti is a mess, but it takes too much time to clean it up." "Since this situation arises from lack of or poor planning, we handle it as the problem hits us." "Shall we call in a consultant or louse it up ourselves?" "Is there one easy way to control wiring confusion?"

In sum, the data processing manager, facilities manager,

or communications manager faced with the tangle of computer-to-terminal wiring would just as soon ignore the disorder. Perhaps, the study indicates, this kind of thinking may be the most constructive.

In the past few years, computer terminals have become commonplace in virtually every department throughout companies of all sizes. Along with the obvious advantages of computer technology, however, has come a wiring nightmare for building managers. To address this, several manufacturers have designed an assortment of "data wiring systems." These encompass a host of different approaches to organizing the flow of data between computers and terminals. Such schemes have ranged from simple patch panels to elaborate and complicated data switches and local area networks (LANs).

But unless a company is buying a new computer, moving into a new facility, or rearranging an existing plant, there is little motivation to make major revisions in wire management. Simply cleaning up the clutter does not seem to warrant the cost of ripping out one set of wiring and replacing it with another. As long as users can get along with things the way they are, common sense says to leave well enough alone.

While sound planning could prevent cable disarray in most cases, usually very little attention is paid to it before it becomes a problem. Not until it is time to move into a building is the task of wiring given much thought. This lack of vision occurs despite the fact that the typical installed cost of data wiring is $200 to $300 per terminal. And while an average number of terminals might be in the 100 to 200 range, there could be as many as 1,000 or more.

Understandably, the many problems facing users can breed procrastination when it comes to wiring. As the number of terminals in a particular environment increases, such problems multiply. What's more, there is no single standard for connecting terminals to a computer within a

The question is wiring

The following are selected questions and responses from a survey of user plans and attitudes regarding data network wiring. Of the 2,000 data communications professionals queried about their data wiring, 163 (8.15 percent) responded by the cutoff date.

Not all the respondents answered all the questions, which accounts for fewer than 163 answers in questions 1 and 2. Other questions, such as number 5, allowed for multiple answers and therefore received more than 163 responses.

Question 1: Do you experience problems with data wiring disarray or clutter within your facility?
Answers: Yes, 81 percent. No, 19 percent.

Question 2: If data wiring clutter became a problem at your present site, would you consider turning to a wire management consultant for help?
Answers: Yes, 37.5 percent. No, 62.5 percent.

Question 3: What are the inhibiting factors to solving a cable clutter problem within your facility? (If more than one answer is applicable, please list in order of importance.)
Answers: Cost: 44 percent. System Downtime: 38 percent. Other: 18 percent.

Question 4: Who else in your company becomes involved in computer-to-terminal wiring? (If more than one answer is applicable, please list in order of importance.)
Answers: Data Processing Manager: 27 percent. Facilities Manager: 23.5 percent. Facilities Engineer: 16 percent. Telecommunications Manager: 22 percent. Wire Management Consultant: 0.6 percent. Other: 11 percent.

Question 5: What products presently on the market do you feel offer the best solution to cable clutter? (If more than one answer, please list in order of importance.)
Answers: Point-to-Point Wiring: 8.5 percent. Coax Eliminator/Twisted-Pair Wiring: 19.5 percent. Multiplexing: 22.5 percent. Data Switches: 20 percent. Local Area Networking: 23 percent. Other: 6.5 percent.

Fifty-seven respondents said that they use in-house staff to solve data wiring clutter. About one-third of this number said they handled such problems themselves. One respondent was unaware that wiring consultants existed.

When respondents were asked who would be their first choice for help in resolving wiring problems, the positions most often named first were: Data Processing Manager: 23; Facilities Manager: 7; Facilities Engineer: 5; Telecommunications Manager: 12; and Wire Management Consultant: 1.

When asked their first choice of wiring option, respondents answered: Point-to-Point Wiring: 3; Coax Eliminator/Twisted-Pair Wiring: 16; Multiplexing: 12; Data Switches: 13; and Local Area Networking: 16.

---

1. Distribution center. At the heart of this wiring plan, computer ports and terminal ports home in on a single, central distribution center. Patching between computers and terminals can therefore be accomplished quickly, and connections can easily be changed in order to accomplish the addition or rerouting of terminals.

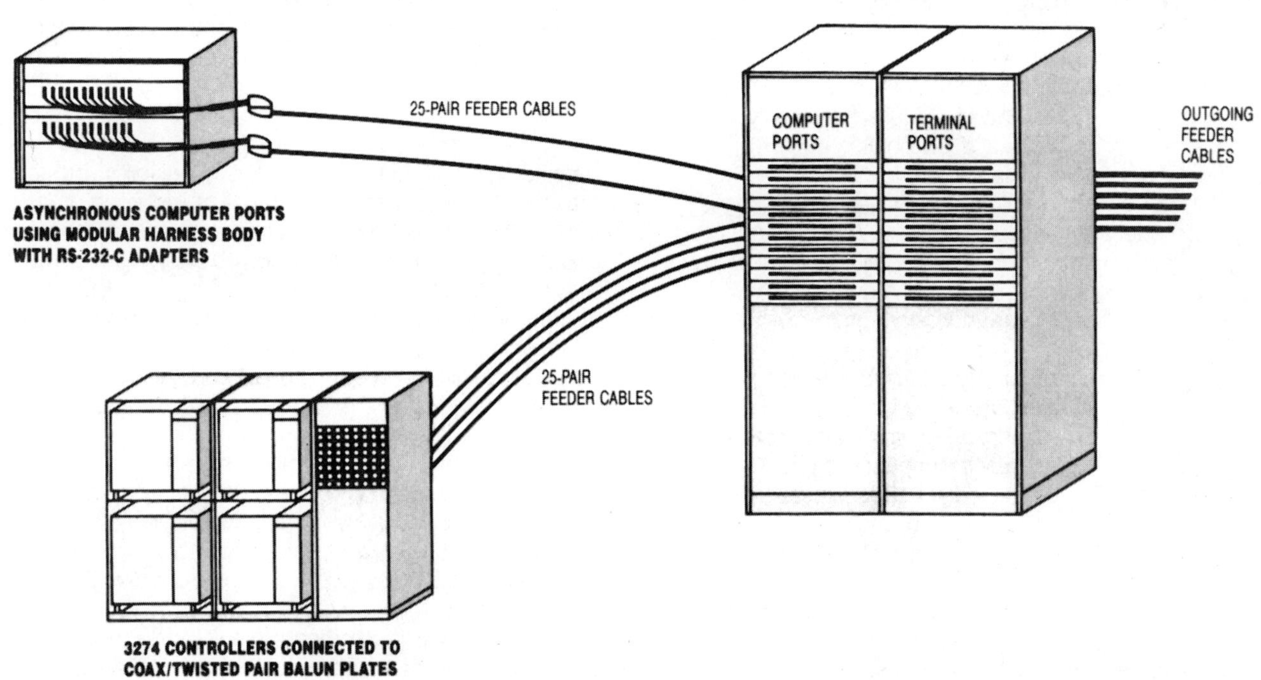

building. To a great extent, suppliers of data wiring schemes are driven by manufacturers of data communications hardware.

The IBM 3270 terminal family, for example, operates at signal speeds close to 2.4 Mbit/s. The company now has a LAN that runs at 4 Mbit/s, and it is predicting a network in the next few years that will operate at 16 Mbit/s. Most other local terminal connections and configurations support lower-speed transmission rates, the most common being 1.2, 9.6, and 19.2 kbit/s.

The wiring industry must accommodate vast differences in device signaling rates—and signal speed has a great deal to do with the type of wiring the user chooses. The wiring problem is compounded when a decision is made to substitute one brand of mainframe computer for another. Changing from an IBM computer to one from Digital Equipment Corp., for instance, requires complete rewiring because the two types of machines support very different transmission specifications.

Coaxial maze

Many user facilities contain miles of bulky, expensive coaxial cable because traditional IBM terminal networks mandated a point-to-point wiring scheme that could use only coaxial cable. For every terminal, a separate cable would be run from a computer through the floor, up the ceiling, down into the wall, and out into an office. And every time a terminal was added, the same process would be repeated. Before long, cabling would be strung throughout the building.

Recently, more attention has been given to using multipair wiring, where a single cable contains many discrete wire pairs, allowing it to accommodate many different terminals and speeds. With this cabling, an office can be wired once with passive components from the work site, back to a distribution center, and from there to the computer.

A multipair approach gives wiring managers much more flexibility in retaining existing wiring when computer equipment is changed. Also, it obviates running cable all the way back to the computer or disrupting the office workplace when more terminals are added. (Figure 1 shows typical changes that can be made at a distribution center.)

Much reluctance to cleaning up cable clutter stems from uncertainty. No one, it seems, is sure that existing wiring is going to be adequate five years hence. With continual change in data communications and computer technology, users have little confidence that what they plan now will accommodate their computer hardware and networking needs in the future.

Devoting the resources to designing an effective wire management program runs counter to most users' thinking. Nevertheless, it can, and should, be done. A wiring plan should be based on the computer hardware purchased today, not five years from now. And communications managers should buy wiring that can handle their present equipment, because they have no way of knowing what will be available in 1992.

Postponing the purchase of, say, a personal computer in hopes of buying a better model at lower cost may be a wise decision. Selecting a data wiring scheme, however, does not allow that luxury. The choice is this: To spend two to three times the amount on a cabling plan that, with luck, takes into account every parameter of possible change (but which still might not be workable in the future); or to spend much less on a cabling configuration that handles present requirements and offers reasonable prospects for growth. In short, plans need to be put into effect based on an assessment of hardware needs for the next year or two— five or 10 years from now.

Options

In setting up a wire management plan, there are plenty of alternatives. In addition to point-to-point wiring—which in general is bulky, hard to manage, expensive to run, and particularly difficult to rearrange—users today can choose from alternatives that include twisted-pair, multipair wiring, multiplexing, data switches, LANs, and fiber optics.

The "wireless" options of LANs and data switches can greatly increase communications flexibility, but they still need to be supported by some type of wiring. (Figure 2 shows a typical twisted-pair wire layout.)

Twisted-pair, multipair wiring provides fully discrete, point-to-point connections that don't require programming or hardware changes. It is lightweight, inexpensive, and flexible. The basic 25-pair trunk cable is only one-half inch in diameter and serves up to 25 terminals for about half the cost of coaxial cable. While twisted pair cannot support the distances that coaxial cable can, or provide the noise immunity of optical fiber, it still is a viable alternative for distances up to 1,000 feet.

Twisted-pair wiring can carry both synchronous and asynchronous signals and can, therefore, support hardware from many different manufacturers. In certain situations, however, twisted pair has limitations—such as when wide bandwidth, or broadband, video channels are required.

As the high-end capabilities of twisted pair are becoming better understood, and as more effective transmitters and receivers are being designed, the range of applications supported by twisted-pair cabling continues to expand. Its low cost and ease of connectivity make it the medium of choice today in many inside-building wiring plans.

The decision to add multiplexing or data switching as part of one's cabling plan adds from $100 to $400 per terminal. Both options offer increased flexibility, but this may not always be necessary. Many multiplexing products and data switches have operational restrictions and cannot, for example, handle both high- and low-speed signals.

A big advantage, however, to adding a multiplexing capability, compared with plain old twisted-pair wiring, is the significant increase in transmission distance that can be obtained. Multiplexers can be a particularly good choice if a group of terminals is located several thousand feet away from the computer.

Data switching provides instant reconfigurability, but at a relatively high cost. Many users do not require such a high degree of versatility. What's more, many users are discovering that LANs are not always compatible with different kinds of computers. For example, an IBM Token Ring may be ideal for linking certain IBM networks, but it generally cannot accommodate multivendor networks.

Optical fiber has the advantage of being able to support very high data rates while offering virtual immunity to noise.

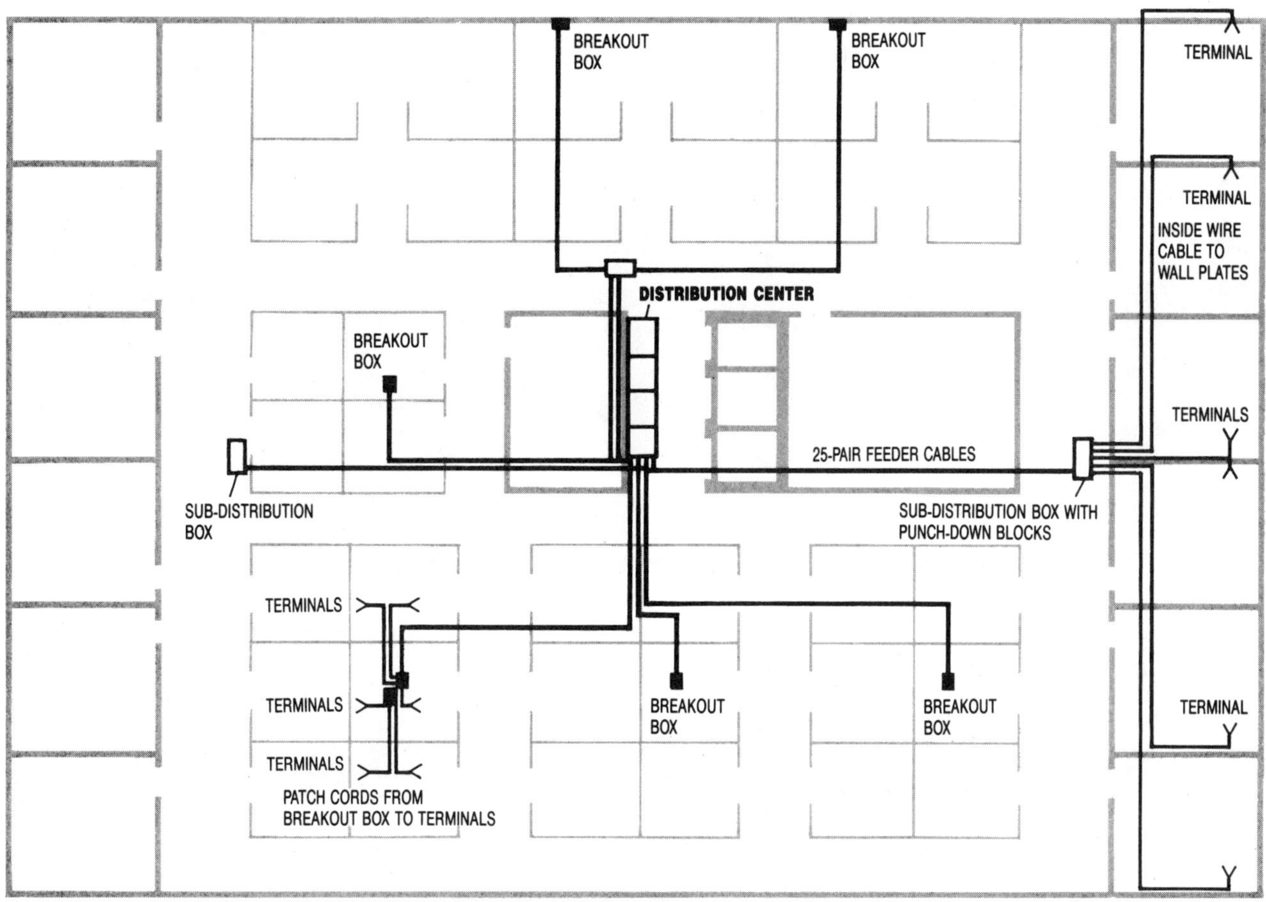

However, this medium demands greater skill for installing connectors and splices. It also requires more expensive interface devices, which are necessary to convert the signals from optical to electrical.

In specifying a wiring scheme, it is important to take into account such special requirements as video transmission. Video uses up a large amounts of bandwidth, which mandates very high-speed, expensive cabling. For video, a completely separate wiring subnetwork is recommended.

Many data processing and communications managers are unaware of the wide range of wiring options available today. (Some may not even realize that they have a cable clutter problem.) There is, however, a trend toward enlisting the aid of a consultant who specializes in this increasingly complex field. Similarly, more and more contractors who specialize in data wiring installation are assuming the role of consultant.

A few years ago, companies devoted exclusively to the provision and installation of data wiring were impossible to find. There are a few today, and their number is growing, but it still takes a little effort to locate them. One way is to ask the manufacturer of the computer hardware.

Network and data processing managers will generally devote considerable resources to studying their computer configurations. But many tend to overlook wiring until the consequences demand attention. Because the cost of wiring—which can be as high as $250,000—is still a relatively small amount compared with $5 million or more for mainframe computers, the wiring issue is neglected.

Another reason that wiring receives last-minute treatment is that computer manufacturers, more concerned with selling mainframes, have traditionally avoided this aspect of the installation. Vendors selling terminals or peripherals also rarely participate in this area. In short, data wiring has been the poor stepchild that has received very little attention from those who should be more concerned.

After acknowledging that they do, in fact, have a problem with data wiring clutter, managers must decide whether it is worth solving. A relocation of an office or a comprehensive reorganizing of an existing plant are two good opportunities to try to fix the problem. In many cases, simply replacing point-to-point coaxial wiring with a more flexible and less costly twisted-pair distribution network will result in a dramatic untangling of the web. ∎

Brian Laughlin has been vice president of Damac Products Inc. for three years. Prior to that he was a consultant for 10 years in the design and construction of office buildings. He earned a B. A. in business from Loyola University, Los Angeles, and an M. B. A. from the University of California, Irvine.

Robert A. Heath, NCR Corp., West Columbia, S. C.

Synchronous dialing modems are advancing at full tilt

Not even the standards bugaboo can hold back the new modems. Trends in dialing capabilities and a look at CCITT recommendations follow.

On the modem frontier, devices are appearing that handle synchronous signals with an ease previously reserved for asynchronous communications. Autodialing, for example, is no longer an asynchronous-only capability. How do asynchronous and synchronous autodialing modems differ? What trends are emerging in dialing capabilities? What standards are evolving for synchronous dialing interfaces? These questions are increasingly important to network managers.

Synchronous autodialing modems have recently appeared in the wake of asynchronous units. Like their predecessors, the synchronous devices accept dialing commands within the data stream until a connection is made. Then they transfer to data mode and pass the signals—transparently—to the dialed end.

Unlike their predecessors, however, synchronous modems have no recognized industry standard. Where asynchronous devices follow the de facto standard established by the Hayes AT command set, the synchronous modems must get along with standards that remain in flux.

Since the early 1980s, intelligent modems have brought affordable dial-up asynchronous communications to all levels of processing, from simple terminals to expensive mainframes. Known as autodialing modems, they replaced earlier schemes that required automatic dialing equipment separate from the modem itself.

Both synchronous and asynchronous modems operate similarly in that they accept commands for dialing via the same interface through which they pass data. They divide modem activity into a command mode and a data mode. During command mode prior to dialing, the intelligent modem interacts with the local user or software to accept commands and parameters. On completion of a dialing command, the modem switches to data mode, during which it passes all data.

An escape sequence in the data stream allows the user to return to command mode to disconnect the call. With the widespread acceptance of microcomputers in offices and homes, the asynchronous dialing modem has become a commonplace peripheral.

The family of high-speed (2.4- to 56-kbit/s) message-oriented computer protocols that govern synchronous communications includes the following: binary synchronous communications (BSC), synchronous data link control (SDLC), and high-level data link control (HDLC). Although they have been available in the world of microcomputers for years, they have generally been used in concentrator-to-mainframe and mainframe-to-mainframe operations. Unlike asynchronous communications, where all of the data originates at the user's keyboard and is displayed on the user's screen, synchronous protocols require more complex hardware and software and the generation of characters for synchronization, framing, error-checking, and headers. This complexity has delayed support for synchronous dialing modems.

In contrast, asynchronous dialing modems quickly gained popularity because of the simultaneous appearance of the microcomputer and an abundance of communications software that drives the smart asynchronous modems. Synchronous modem manufacturers were challenged with architecting dialing interfaces that would coexist with the link level software that had been in place for years.

The classic protocol for dial-up synchronous communications is IBM 2780/3780 BSC. This recognized communications protocol, which dates from the 1960s, is still used because it has a simple data stream and peer-to-peer capability. Since IBM 2780/3780 is basically a two-way alternate, contention protocol, it is compatible with half-duplex modems for 2.4- and 4.8-kbit/s service (types 201 and 208B, respectively). The other BSC protocol widely recognized in the data communications industry is IBM

Making the electrical connection

Computers must somehow dial telephone numbers. The way they do it is defined by an Electronic Industries Association standard called RS-366, the counterpart of the CCITT's V.25.

RS-366 describes the electrical and signaling interface between data terminal equipment (DTE), which wishes to place a call in order to send some information, and automatic calling equipment (ACE), which controls the switched telephone network to place a call. The automatic calling equipment is sometimes referred to as an 801 automatic calling unit (ACU), named after the industry standard Bell implementation.

The RS-366 interface is composed of 13 signals, as shown in the figure. To make a call, the DTE turns on the Call Request signal. The DTE may check the Power Indication signal and the Data Line Occupied signal from the ACU to be certain that the calling attempt can proceed.

On detecting the ACU's Present Next Digit signal, the DTE places a digit value on the four parallel digit signals and turns on the Digit Present signal. On accepting the digit, the ACU turns off Present Next Digit, and then the DTE turns off Digit Present. This digit-passing handshaking sequence continues until all the digits have been passed.

The ACU determines that the calling process is complete when it either receives an end-of-number code within the digit stream or detects the answer tone from the remote modem. If the call fails, the ACU turns on Abandon Call & Retry. If the call is successful, the ACU turns on Call Origination Status and transfers control to the associated modem.

From this point on, the ACU is not involved during ordinary data transfer. When data transfer is complete, the modem is responsible for disconnecting the call.

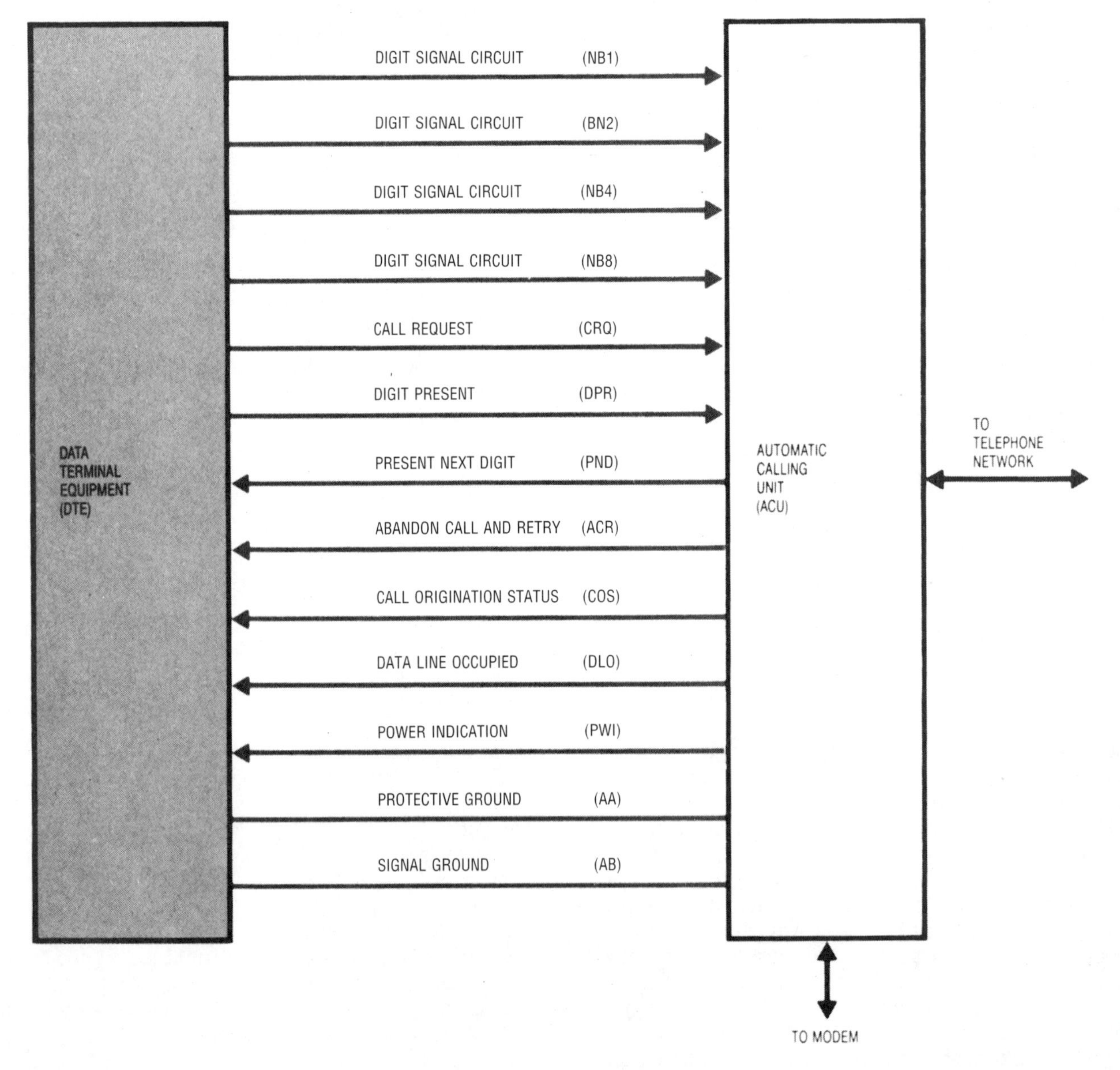

3270. But it is found predominately on private leased networks rather than on dial-up lines. Thus the IBM 2780/3780 variation of BSC has been targeted as a dialing protocol for intelligent synchronous modems.

SDLC, as commonly used between mainframes and less-powerful processors, is a polling, two-way alternate protocol that readily lends itself to leased, multipoint networks. When used in a dial-up network, it relies on polling rather than the contention technique that IBM 2780/3780 BSC employs. The same modems that are used for dial-up BSC can be reused for SDLC.

Until recently, SDLC's network layer SNA (Synchronous Network Architecture) has dictated hierarchical rather than peer-to-peer networks. However, new forms of SNA such as Physical Unit Type 2.1 have evolved that allow peer-level networking. This new architecture opens the possibility for low-level products to interwork, ultimately increasing the need for modems that can alternately dial and answer. For example, a microcomputer would use the same hardware and software to call either a mainframe or another microcomputer. In turn, the remote configuration would use the same modem to call the personal computer.

In contrast to the BSC and SDLC protocols, HDLC (used with X.25) is a two-way simultaneous protocol, requiring full-duplex modems. Traditionally, X.25 networks have required leased, point-to-point connections between the data terminal equipment and the public data network itself. In the past two years networks have added dial-in capability. At 1.2, 2.4, and 4.8 kbit/s, Telenet requires the following modems, respectively: 212A-types, V.22*bis*-types, and the Anderson-Jacobson 4048-2. In addition to X.25 service, many public data networks now offer dial-in protocol conversion for BSC and SDLC services.

Synchronous autodialing

Figure 1a shows the configuration that was first to be widely recognized in the industry for automatic dialing in both start/stop and synchronous communications. The commonly used term for the computer or terminal hardware that wishes to place a call is Data Terminal Equipment (DTE). An external piece of hardware called the Automatic Call Unit (ACU), controlled by the DTE through an RS-366 interface (see "Making the electrical connection"), dials the telephone number. On completion it hands off the call to the modem. The modem itself is referred to as data circuit-terminating equipment, or DCE. This configuration requires the expense of hardware and software in the DTE to control the RS-366 interface.

In a more recently developed alternative a serial auto-dialer replaces the RS-366 interface with an RS-232-C port carrying asynchronous dial data (Fig. 1b). This approach saves costs in medium- to large-sized installations with multiple ports because the price per port of an RS-232-C connection is usually lower than that of an RS-366 port. An additional, one-time expense will occur in programming the RS-232-C to issue the dial data.

The RS-366 interface can be merged into the modem itself, thus reducing the cost of hardware (Fig. 1c). Between the DTE and modem the RS-232-C interface carries data while the RS-366 carries dial control. This scheme has the advantage of being software compatible with the external autodialer configuration shown in Figure 1a.

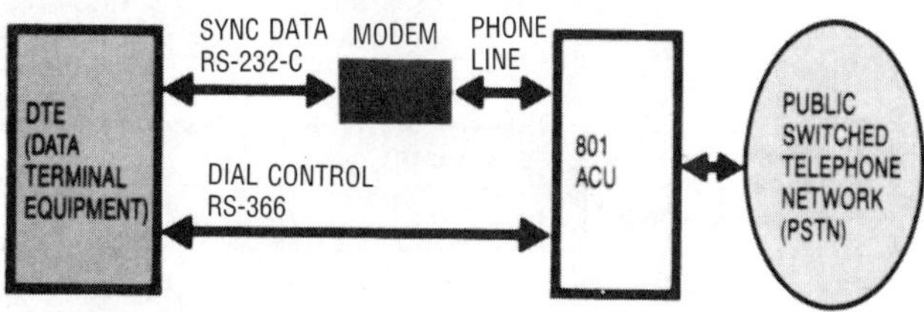

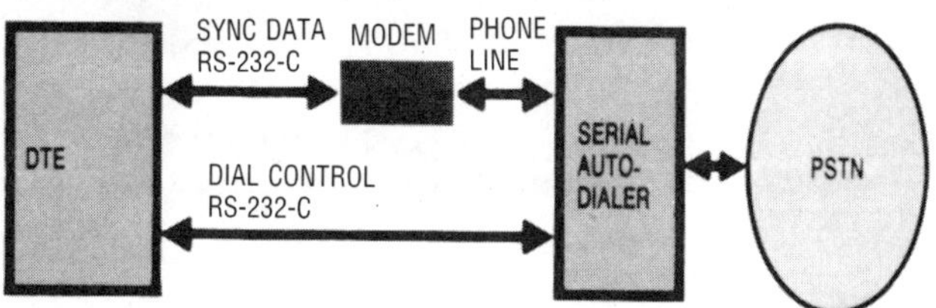

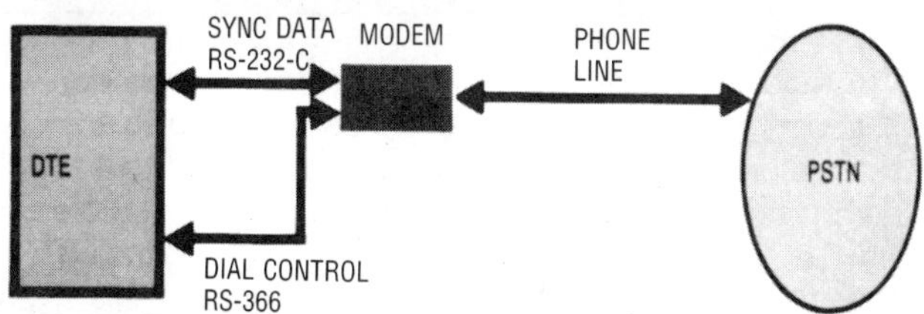

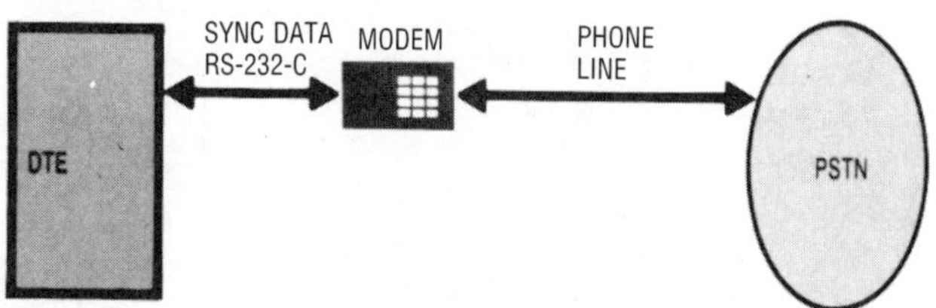

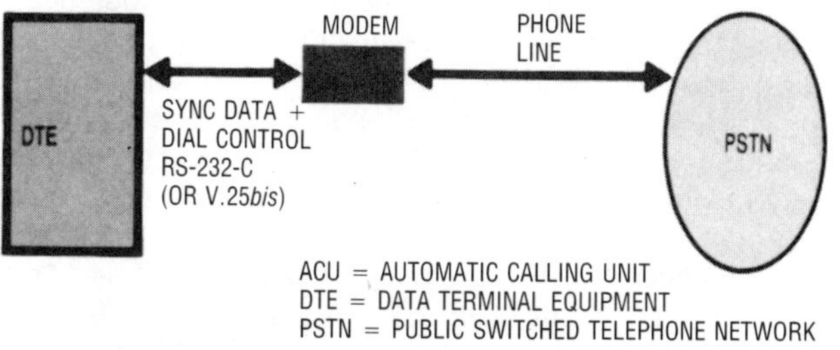

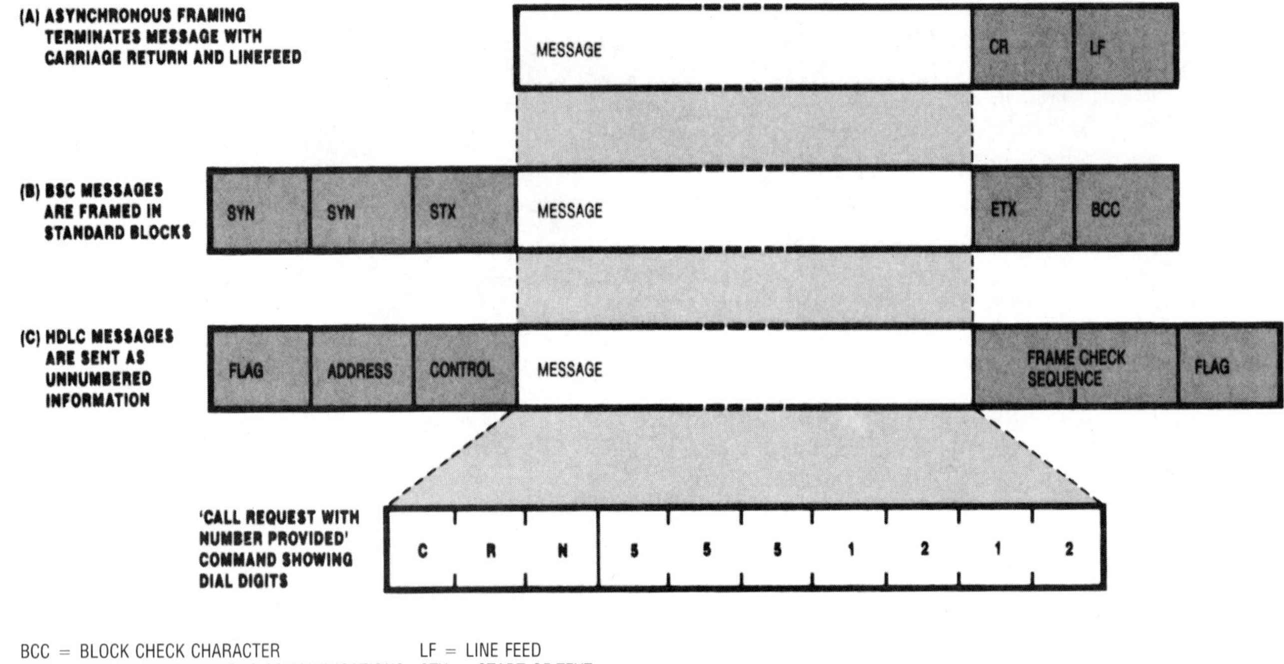

A recent trend in synchronous dialing modems is depicted in Figure 1d, where the modem incorporates an external keypad through which an operator can store dialing sequences. In this arrangement, called Dial Stored Number Mode, the modem initiates dialing when the DTE raises the modem signal Data Terminal Ready. This scheme is effective when the DTE usually dials only one number, or the number does not have to be changed often. It does not require new programming in the DTE, and it can be easily adopted where manual dialing was formerly required.

The configuration that depicts the best trade-off in terms of hardware cost and dialing flexibility is shown in Figure 1e, where the dialing functions have been integrated into the modem. The figure shows a synchronous modem to which the dialing commands are delivered by way of standard synchronous protocols. The products described in this article follow this technique. Although this method offers flexible dialing and hardware savings, an initial software expense may be required to program the DTE to adapt to these new interfaces.

In a given modem the various dialing techniques of Figure 1 need not be mutually exclusive. Intelligent synchronous modems may combine keypad dialing, an external RS-366 interface, or the acceptance of dial commands within the data stream. Many products also incorporate manual dialing using an attached telephone handset.

Autodialing on an international scale has its own set of requirements. In 1984 the CCITT (International Telegraph and Telephone Consultative Committee) approved V.25bis. This recommendation specifies how the electrical signals of V.24 are used for automatic dialing and answering. (CCITT V.24 defines the signaling counterpart of Electrical Industries Association, or EIA, standard RS-232-C.) Three main operations are defined by V.25bis:

■ Automatic dialing by passing dial control messages through the interface signals.
■ Automatic dialing of a prestored number.
■ Automatic answering.

Automatic dialing is the most significant of the three operations since the latter two were technically feasible in some manner before V.25bis was introduced. For example, the well-known dialing scheme shown in Figure 1d is known in V.25bis as Direct Call controlled by DTE circuit 108/1. V.25bis combines both an electrical-interface protocol and a message-oriented protocol to effect serial dialing and answering.

Two strong points of V.25bis are that it standardizes message framing in start-stop, character-oriented, and bit-oriented protocols; and that it defines a common message syntax regardless of the framing. Figure 2 shows how the command to dial a given phone number is framed in each of the three types of protocols. The specified character set is International Alphabet No. 5 (IA5), which is the international equivalent of ASCII. In start/stop arrangements, the message is terminated with a carriage return and line feed sequence. Character-oriented protocols send the message as a nontransparent text block, begun by a start of text (STX) character and ended by an end of text (ETX) character. In HDLC the frames carry both the "global address," which is a wild-card address value, and the value of the "unnumbered information control field," which means that the regular sequence numbering is not active.

Figure 3 shows a sample of V.25*bis* messages. There are 22 messages in all, but the six shown are the ones most relevant to automatic dialing. When the DTE sends a message, it is called a command; when the DCE sends a message, it is called an indication. A command called Call Request with Number Provided (CRN) directs the modem to dial an included number. The number itself can contain:

■ The usual dial digits from the set 0,1 . . . 9; 2).

■ The colon ":" to wait for a tone.

■ Other separators—"<," "=," and ">"—which are reserved for national use.

Spaces or periods may be inserted for readability. The Program Number (PRN) command allows the DTE to store a number at a memory address in the modem for later reference. The memory address is passed as a string of IA5 digits from the set 0,1 . . . 9. A semicolon separates the memory address from the number. The DTE sends the CRN command to direct the modem to dial a number stored by a previous PRN command. The modem sends a Valid (VAL) indication to reply to a command that it accepts. To reject a command on the basis of content or format, the modem sends an Invalid (INV) indication. No indication is sent for a command received with framing or check sequence errors. The Call Failure Indication (CFI) returns on an unsuccessful call and contains a two-character code that diagnoses the failure.

Under V.25*bis*

Figure 4 shows how V.25*bis* automatic dialing and clearing works (dashes indicate optional steps in the process). To initiate a call, the DTE turns on signal Data Terminal Ready. The DCE indicates recognition by turning on the signal CleartoSend. The presence of CleartoSend also implies that the DCE is in command mode and will recognize commands within the data stream. The DTE sends a CRN command containing either the actual phone number or a reference to a prestored number. If the DCE accepts the command, it optionally returns the message: VAL. At that point the DCE dials the phone number. When the DCE detects the remote modem's answer tone, it turns off Clear to Send. After a carrier handshake, it turns on the signal Data Set Ready.

If the call fails, the DCE optionally returns a CFI message to the DTE with a two-character diagnostic code, describing the nature of the failure. An additional implementation option is that the modem may transmit a message to the answering party, identifying the calling party. The decision to implement the identification message depends on if the telephone network administration requires it.

Clearing a call dialed via V.25*bis* is easy; the DTE simply turns off Data Terminal Ready. The DCE responds by turning off Data Set Ready. Alternatively, the DCE may indicate that the call has been cleared by turning off Data Set Ready, to which the DTE must respond by turning off Data Terminal Ready.

V.25*bis* provides a protocol for storing a number in the DCE and referencing it by a shorthand value known as its memory address. Figure 3 shows the format of the PRN message, which contains both the number to dial and the memory address at which to store the number. Once the number is stored, dialing proceeds much the same way as

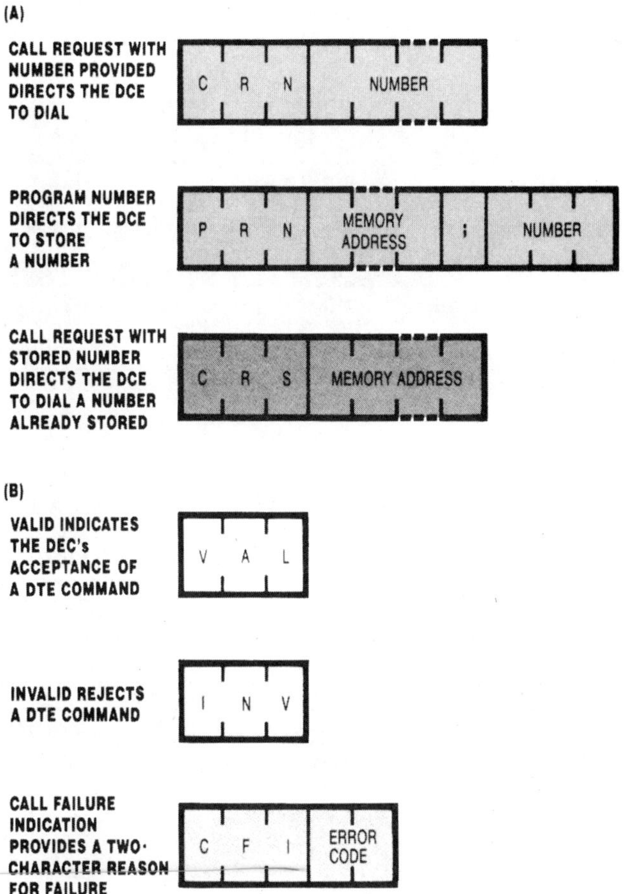

*3. V.25bis **sample.** Encoded in ASCII V.25bis command messages are sent by DTEs to initiate calls or to store numbers (A), indications are sent by the DCEs (B).*

in Figure 4. The DTE directs the modem to dial that number by referencing its memory address in a CRN command. If the call succeeds, the modem raises Data Set Ready. If the call fails, the modem may send CFI.

In general, a synchronous dialing modem's need to store phone numbers is an overrated feature. Storing phone numbers in the DTE rather than in the modem is a better trade-off when the DTE has sufficient disk capacity. This frees the DTE from having to recover either when a modem loses the stored number or when the maximum numbers it can store is exceeded. This trade-off is further justified when the time to transfer the entire number to the modem is short compared with the overall time to complete the call.

The chief advantage of V.25*bis* compared with other proposed dialing standards is that it has CCITT sponsorship. Another advantage is that V.25*bis* requires only a minimal protocol interchange to initiate a call.

Some criticisms of V.25*bis* are:

■ It does not define progress signals during calling.

■ It does not call out the minimum set of commands and indications that a DCE must implement to be considered in conformance.

■ It requires the DTE to send data before Data Set Ready goes active. (The DTE usually waits for Data Set Ready to become active first. It is possible that this may be a draw-

Sampling of synchronous autodialing modems

	ANALOG COMPATIBILITY	BIT RATES	CLOCKING		DIALING PROTOCOLS			DIALING COMPATIBILITY	KEYPAD DIALING
			SYNCHRONOUS	ASYNCHRONOUS	ASYNCHRONOUS	BISYNCHRONOUS	BIT-ORIENTED		
ANDERSON JACOBSON 4048-2	FOX PROPRIETARY	2400, 4800	YES	YES	YES	YES	YES	V.25*bis*	YES
ANDERSON JACOBSON 9631-S	V.32TCM	4800, 9600	YES	NO	NO	YES	YES	V.25*bis*	YES
CODEX 2233	V.22, V.22*bis*, 103, 212A	300, 1200, 2400	YES	YES	YES	YES	YES	V.25*bis*, AT	NO
CODEX 2238	V.22, V.22*bis*, 103, 212A	300, 1200, 2400	YES	YES	YES	YES	YES	V.25*bis*, AT	NO
CDS 224 AUTODIAL PLUS	212A, 224, 103, V.22*bis*	300, 1200, 2400	YES	YES	YES	NO	YES	AT, CDSCS, V.25*bis*	NO
CDS 224 AUTODIAL PLUS E	212A, 224, 103, V.22*bis*	300, 1200, 2400	YES	YES	YES	NO	YES	AT, CDSCS, V.25*bis*	NO
CDS 224 SERIES II	212A, 224, 103, V.22*bis*	300, 1200, 2400	YES	YES	YES	NO	YES	AT, CDSCS, V.25*bis*	NO
CDS 296 TRELLIS	V.32	4800, 9600	YES	YES	YES	NO	YES	AT, CDSCS, V.25*bis*	NO
GENERAL DATACOMM 208BT/SD	208B	4800	YES	NO	NO	NO	YES	V.25*bis*	NO
NEC 2428/38Y	V.22*bis*	300, 1200, 2400	YES	YES	NO	YES	YES	V.25*bis*	NO
PHILIPS 4821	V.27*bis*, V.27*ter*	2400, 4800	YES	–	–	YES	YES	V.25*bis*	NO
PHILIPS 9636	V.32TCM	4800, 9600	YES	YES	YES	YES	YES	V.25*bis*, AT	NO
RACAL-VADIC 2400 PA-2	V.22*bis*	300, 1200, 2400	YES	NO	NO	YES	YES	SADL, AT, RVCS	NO
RACAL-VADIC 4850 PA	208B, V.27	2400, 4800	YES	NO	NO	YES	YES	SADL	YES
RACAL-VADIC 9650 PA	V.29, V.27*ter*	4800, 7200, 9600	YES	NO	NO	YES	YES	SADL	YES
RACAL-VADIC VA 4891	208A/B, V.27*bis*, V.27*ter*	2400, 4800	YES	NO	NO	YES	YES	SADL	NO
UDS 208 B/D	208B	4800	YES	NO	NO	YES	NO	2780/3780	NO
UDS 201 C/D	201	2400	YES	NO	NO	YES	NO	2780/3780	NO

AT = HAYES AT COMMAND SET
CDSCS = CONCORD DATA SYSTEMS COMMAND SET
FDX = FULL DUPLEX
RVCS = RACAL-VADIC COMMAND SET
SADL = SYNCHRONOUS AUTODIALING LANGUAGE
TCM = TRELLIS CODED MODULATION

back at the hardware level for some DTEs.)

In spite of its apparent weaknesses, V.25*bis* is implemented by no less than six manufacturers of synchronous modems (see table). As an example of how manufacturers regard the new international standard, Concord Data Systems' (Marlborough, Mass.) director of product marketing, Lynn Faust-Burger, states: "Support for V.25*bis* dialing is highly important for modem manufacturers competing in the international marketplace."

In 1984, Racal-Vadic introduced the first synchronous autodialing modem. Since then the company has extended the dialing interface used in that product to become the standard that it implements in a line of dialing modems.

The proper name for this standard is the Synchronous AutoDialing Language, or, SADL (pronounced "saddle"). Racal-Vadic fully documents SADL in a designer's guide that it provides to potential users.

During dialing, SADL generally follows the strategy found in many smart asynchronous modems. The modem initially appears connected at the electrical interface to satisfy the lowest levels of hardware logic; then it undertakes connection via a dialog at the data-link control level.

In contrast to V.25*bis*, the outcome of end-to-end connection is visible entirely at the message level rather than partially at the electrical level and partially at the protocol level. Figure 5a illustrates a typical SADL protocol ex-

TELEPHONE HANDSET DIALING	MAXIMUM NUMBERS STORED	DTR-CONTROLLED DIALING	RS-366 PORT	MOUNTING
YES	8	YES	YES	STANDALONE, RACKMOUNT
YES	8	YES	-	STANDALONE, RACKMOUNT
YES	0	NO	NO	STANDALONE
YES	0	NO	NO	RACKMOUNT
YES	10	YES	NO	STANDALONE
YES	10	YES	NO	STANDALONE
YES	10	YES	NO	STANDALONE RACKMOUNT, INTEGRATED PC
YES	10	YES	NO	STANDALONE, RACKMOUNT
YES	0	NO	NO	STANDALONE, SHELF-MOUNT
YES	40	NO	NO	STANDALONE, RACKMOUNT
-	0	-	NO	STANDALONE, RACKMOUNT
-	0	-	NO	STANDALONE, RACKMOUNT
YES	0	NO	NO	STANDALONE
YES	15	NO	YES	STANDALONE
YES	15	NO	YES	STANDALONE
NO	0	NO	NO	RACKMOUNT
YES	0	NO	NO	STANDALONE
YES	0	NO	NO	STANDALONE

2780/3780 = USES PROPRIETARY 2780/3780 DIALING INTERFACE

change in BSC mode. (The particular flavor of BSC shown here is industry standard IBM 2780/3780.) The DTE initiates a call by sending an ENQ (enquiry) sequence to contact the modem, which accepts by sending ACK0 (the proper BSC acknowledgment sequence). Next the DTE sends a standard data block, carrying the dial data. The modem acknowledges the dial data, and then the DTE relinquishes the conversation by sending EOT (end of transmission). As the modem begins to dial, it in turn alerts the DTE with ENQ and sends a dialing status within the data. Successive data messages indicate the dialing progress as follows:

■ Ringing, at the remote number.

■ Answer Tone detected at the remote site.

■ On Line, to show that the connection has been completely established.

At the protocol level this handshaking follows pure IBM 2780/3780 BSC, which should ease the integration of SADL modems into existing dial-up BSC environments. SADL also defines a bit-oriented mode. As in V.25*bis*, the frames carry both the HDLC global address and the value in the unnumbered information control field. SADL defines two forms of bit-oriented mode: SDLC and HDLC. At the data-link control level the frame formats and handshaking sequences are identical; the only difference is that SDLC frames carry EBCDIC data, and HDLC frames carry ASCII data.

Figure 5b shows the same dialing sequence found in Figure 5a but uses the case of data being transmitted with bit-oriented framing. The order in which messages are exchanged is very similar to that used in BSC. Though the framing for bit-oriented SADL is compatible with the SDLC and HDLC protocols, the frame contents and sequences are different from those provided by the respective networking layers: SNA and X.25. Thus it would require a somewhat greater programming effort to integrate bit-oriented SADL into existing SDLC and HDLC DTEs than it would to integrate BSC SADL into existing BSC products.

Racal-Vadic, says its product manager William Eggleston, has a corporate commitment to include SADL in all its high-speed synchronous products. To encourage support for SADL among modem users and software developers, the company has placed SADL in the public domain and has initiated a SADL development program. Eggleston states that Racal-Vadic is actively pursuing other manufacturers to add SADL to their modem lines.

Dialing async, talking sync

User acceptance of the microcomputer boosted sales of 1.2-kbit/s modems; but it has also created a demand for even higher data transmission rates. A current trend in asynchronous communications is to upgrade from 212A-type 1.2-kbit/s modems to the increasingly more affordable V.22*bis* 2.4-kbit/s modems. V.22*bis*, which, like V.25*bis*, is a 1984 CCITT recommendation, calls out 2.4-kbit/s full-duplex operation with a fall-back rate of 1.2 kbit/s. Although the analog interface V.22*bis* is new, manufacturers are retaining the standard dialing interfaces so that DTE software that works for 1.2-kbit/s modems will also work for 2.4-kbit/s modems.

The V.22*bis* standard specifies both asynchronous and synchronous operation, but its synchronous capability, for the most part, is underutilized by the data communications industry. Modem manufacturers are aware of this omission and would like to expand the sales of V.22*bis* modems in the area of synchronous dial-up communications.

One drawback to a more widespread acceptance of V.22*bis* for synchronous dial-up gear has been the absence of a synchronous dialing standard. For asynchronous use, the dialing standard is the AT command set, named for the first two characters that Hayes modems require in dialing commands. Most V.22*bis* modems implement the AT command set for asynchronous dialing, but the AT command set cannot be easily adapted to synchronous operation. A few manufacturers of V.22*bis* modems are adding synchronous dialing, but many are

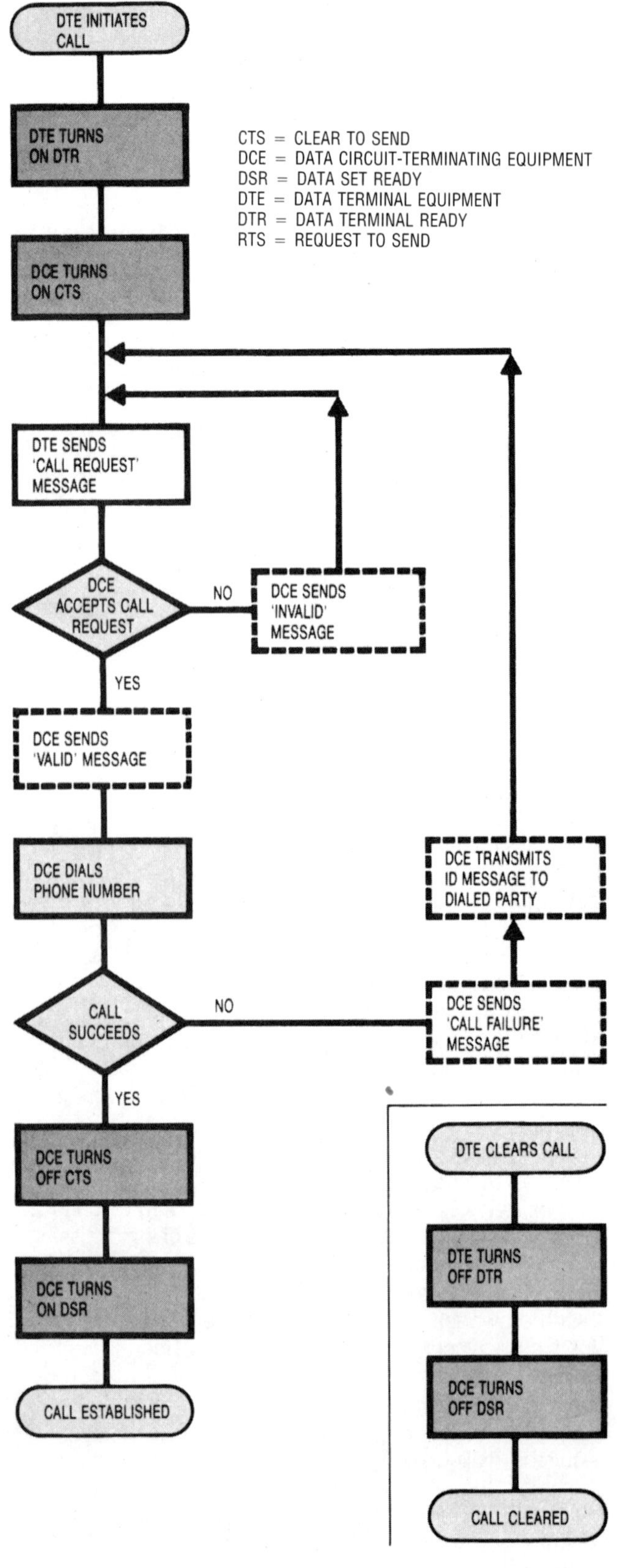

4. Making V.25bis work. *V.25*bis *dialing combines electrical interface protocol with message level protocol. How it operates is shown here with optional steps.*

developing alternatives to synchronous dialing. Some of these alternatives require the DTE to:

■ Store a number during asynchronous mode, reconfigure the modem to synchronous mode, and then dial the number by raising Data Terminal Ready.

■ Issue dial commands in start/stop mode that direct the modem to dial then automatically switch to synchronous mode on connection.

■ Contrive sequences of synchronous data that appear to the modem as the asynchronous dialing commands of case 2. The most popular technique is dialing asynchronously and then talking synchronously.

Integrated solutions for PCs

Although asynchronous communications hardware in the world of microcomputers is fairly standardized, synchronous communications hardware interfaces for microcomputers vary. A current trend in synchronous communications is to provide an all-in-one solution by combining link level firmware, DTE hardware, and a dialing modem onto a single board.

In this scheme the RS-232-C interface disappears because the link level hardware closely couples with the modem. A disk-based application is usually packaged to drive the all-in-one hardware. One example of an integrated synchronous solution is the Universal Data Systems Sync-Up series, which allows any combination of 3270 or remote job entry emulation over SNA or BSC network protocols using either 201, 212, or 208-compatible integrated modems. CLEO Software (Rockford, Ill.) offers similar products based on its SYNCmodem series.

Proposed synchronous standard

As part of its strategy in the market of microcomputer-based synchronous communications, Hayes Microcomputer Products (Norcross, Ga.) has proposed a standard: the Hayes Synchronous Interface (HSI). It outlines a hardware-independent interface between a user's application program and a synchronous communications driver (the software that directly controls the hardware); a standard Hayes Synchronous Driver, which supports Hayes communications products; and support of Hayes V.22*bis* modems.

The Hayes solution for V.22*bis* in synchronous dial-up networks is to issue in asynchronous mode dialing commands that direct the modem to change over to synchronous mode once connection has been established. In the DTE this technique relies on standard universal synchronous/asynchronous receiver transmitter chips that handle both modes of operation. The Hayes plan implies that DTEs that can flexibly switch between start/stop, character-oriented, and bit-oriented operation will be able to interwork with the greatest variety of dialing modems.

To encourage support of HSI, Hayes Microcomputer Products has published a technical reference document that Hayes includes in an information package for potential HSI developers. Garry Betty, vice president of sales at Hayes, states that Hayes has placed HSI in the public domain. He adds that over 100 developers have taken advantage of the HSI development package.

Providing a brief product overview, the accompanying table includes profiles of a number of standalone modems that can automatically dial using V.25*bis* or proprietary synchronous protocols. The dialing protocols listed are defined between the local DTE and its modem. Modems from different manufacturers can interconnect when their analog interface is compatible, for example, with V.22*bis*. Racal-Vadic offers a family of three synchronous dialing modems covering rates from 1.2 to 9.6 kbit/s. The Racal-Vadic devices are distinguished by their low profile, liquid crystal display, and integrated keypad, which allows the user to enter both parameters and phone numbers.

The Anderson-Jacobson 4048-2 is the only modem specified by Telenet for its 4.8-kbit/s X.25 dial-in service. With its keypad and external RS-366 interface, it offers the widest range of dialing capabilities of those modems sampled. The NEC 2420/30Y is the synchronous autodialing member of NEC's large family of V.22*bis* modems. Although it lacks a flashy exterior, the NEC's 40 internal option switches let users set the parameters for just about any part of its digital or analog interface. The UDS 208B/D is a 4.8-kbit/s, 208B-compatible device whose proprietary dialing protocol is based on IBM 2780/3780 BSC. Another 208B-compatible is the GDC 208B/SD, which dials using a subset of V.25*bis* in HDLC mode. The Codex 2233 is a 2.4-kbit/s V.22*bis* modem that provides synchronous dialing using V.25*bis* commands and asynchronous dialing using the Hayes command set.

The spread of new synchronous services such as peer-level SNA and dial-in public data networks is creating new demands for dialing modems. Modem manufacturers are finding ways for low-cost V.22*bis* modems to cross over from asynchronous to synchronous markets. New dialing standards, such as V.25*bis* and SADL, are coming into popularity to accommodate the growing number of synchronous DTEs. ∎

Consulting analyst Robert A. Heath has been developing networking software with NCR since 1975. A former member of ANSI committee X3S34, he has edited a number of NCR corporate engineering standards in data communications. He holds a B. S. in electrical engineering from Georgia Tech and an M. S. in electrical engineering from the University of South Carolina. Since 1982 he has developed communications software used in the NCR Tower product.

Further reading

Carlson, A. A., and Scharen-Guivel, James. "How intelligent
    autodial modems vary—and the best ways to apply
    them." DATA COMMUNICATIONS, Sept. 1985, p. 217.
Kemezis, Paul. "The problems and promise of synchronous
    autodialing." DATA COMMUNICATIONS, April 1987,
    pp. 72-73.
*SADL, The 24-Hour Protocol: A Designer's Guide for
    Remote Micro-to-Mainframe Synchronous Autodialing.* Racal-Vadic.
Recommendation V.25*bis*, "Automatic Calling and/or
    Answering Equipment in the General Switched
    Telephone Network (GSTN) Using the 100-Series
    Interchange Circuits." *CCITT Red Book,* Fascicle
    VII.1. Geneva, 1984.
Technical Reference: Hayes Synchronous Interface for
    Applications Software, Release 1.0. Hayes Micro-
    Computer Products, Inc. Norcross, Ga., 1986.

5. The SADL approach. *In BSC mode, SADL uses the 2780/3780 dialing protocol (A); in bit-oriented modes, the modems use unnumbered information frames (B).*

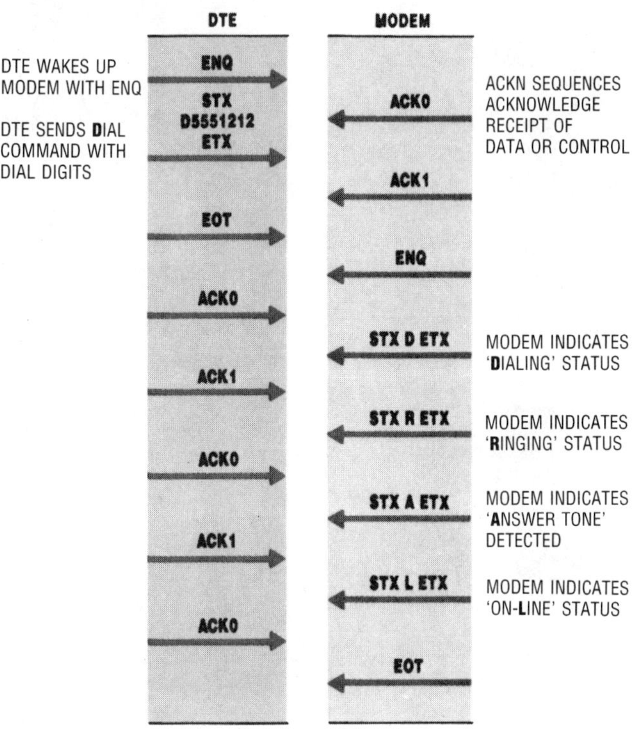

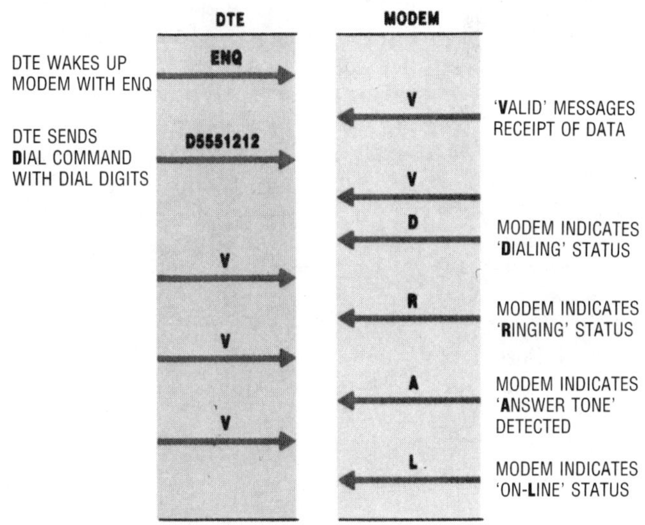

ACK = ACKNOWLEDGMENT
BSC = BINARY SYNCHRONOUS COMMUNICATIONS
DTE = DATA TERMINAL EQUIPMENT
ENQ = ENQUIRY
EOT = END OF TRANSMISSION
STX = START OF TEXT
ETX = END OF TEXT

William Sheridan, Telecomputing Strategies Ltd., Rancocas, N. J.

How to make and use null modem cables

To link two computers or a computer to a terminal over a short distance requires nothing more than a cable — with some of its wires crossed. Here's how to build your own.

Modem cables are used to connect a terminal, printer, or computer (the data terminal equipment, or DTE) to a modem (the data circuit-terminating equipment, or DCE). Such cables typically conform to the Electronic Industries Association's (EIA) Recommended Standard RS-232. Since all 25 leads on the interface are connected end-to-end, the modem cables ensure success in linking DTE to DCE.

However, some applications call for the direct connection of two DTEs without intervening modems and data transmission facilities. For example, a user may wish to connect a terminal to a computer in the same room or building. Compensating for the absence of modems and transmission lines requires a special cable, terminated into RS-232-type connectors, that is variously called a "null modem cable," a "dummy modem," or a "modem eliminator." Null modem cables simulate interface signals, making the DTEs think the signals are coming from modems, when they are actually coming from themselves or from the attached DTE.

In many cases, users can purchase the needed cable from such suppliers as Black Box Corp. (Pittsburgh, Pa.), Micom Systems Inc. (Simi Valley, Calif.), or RAD Data Communications (Englewood, N. J.). In other cases, however, it may be more economical, expedient, or appropriate to devise one's own cables. To understand the construction of a null modem cable, it is helpful to know something about the RS-232 standard. (Unless otherwise noted, RS-232 refers, throughout this article, to the latest revision, RS-232-D.)

At first glance, the subject of electrical and physical interface hardware appears straightforward. However, it harbors many misconceptions that need clarification. One of the most common is that RS-232, the widely known interface standard, specifies a protocol for error-protected and flow-controlled communications. Actually, RS-232 is merely a set of rules, agreed to by members of the EIA, that govern the physical and electrical properties of connections between the DTE and the DCE.

Another common misconception is that RS-232 is a single, unchanging standard. In fact, RS-232-C, the old workhorse of data communications interfaces, is being replaced by RS-232-D, one of several more or less successful offspring of Revision C (see "Standards update").

Crossover

Essentially, a null modem cable takes the place of a circuit with modems on each end by transposing certain control leads. To understand why this is required, consider the Transmit Data signal on pin 2 of the RS-232 interface cable. If the cable is standard, all wires run straight through, and the terminal's Transmit Data lead is connected to the computer's Transmit Data lead (that is, pin 2 at one end is connected to pin 2 at the other). Obviously, the Transmit Data lead of the terminal should be connected to the Receive Data lead of the computer and vice versa.

When two DTEs are connected through modems, this transposition takes place in the modems. This is because the modems (or, in the less automated case, their users) assign one modem as the call originator and the other as the call recipient. Transmit and receive frequencies are specified for the originating modem and reversed for the receiving modem. Without modems, the transposition must be made in the interconnecting cable.

In addition to the crossing of Transmit Data and Receive Data, most setups other than very simple terminals require that some of the control leads be modified to make the interface work properly. Figure 1 shows a null modem configuration for connecting a common type of asynchronous terminal to a computer. In this example, at each DTE, two DTE-originated signals, Request To Send (pin 4) and DTE Ready (pin 20), are jumpered at the connector to their

Standards Update

Officially, RS-232-C was to be gradually replaced by three standards beginning in 1977: RS-449 (using 37-pin and 9-pin connectors) supplemented by the RS-422 and RS-423 electrical specifications. These standards were to provide higher data rates and additional functionality. However, RS-449 never succeeded in finding its niche. The Electronic Industries Association (EIA) issued RS-232-D (Revision D) in January 1987 and RS-530 in March 1987.

Both of these standards include a specification of the familiar D-shaped 25-pin interface connector. RS-232-C, on the other hand, merely made reference to the connector in an appendix, explicitly stating that the connector was not part of the standard.

RS-232-D provides new functions (see "RS-232-D signal summary") that support testing of both local and remote DCEs, while RS-530, which also provides the test functions, achieves higher data rates than RS-232 (greater than 20 kbit/s). It does this by specifying the use of balanced signals at the expense of several secondary signals and of the Ring Indicator signal provided in RS-232 (see "RS-530 signal summary"). To say that the signals are balanced means that each signal, such as Transmit Data or Receive Data, uses two wires with opposite polarities, which minimizes distortion. The elimination of Ring Indicator suggests that RS-530 is not intended for use in dial-up applications.

The foreword of the RS-530 standard states that it is intended to gradually replace RS-449. In the author's opinion, RS-449 never caught on because it specifies two different connectors, neither of which is the nearly universal 25-pin connector. Both RS-422 and RS-423, however, survive. They specify the electrical characteristics of the interface and are referenced by RS-530 as well as by other EIA standards.

In addition to the differences noted above, RS-232-D changed some signal names (for example, Data Terminal Ready, DTR, became DTE Ready and Data Set Ready, DSR, became DCE Ready). It also modified the use of Protective Ground to provide shielding, added signals to support modem testing, and generally brought the standard up to date and in line with the international standards. One can safely assume that EIA expects to continue the use of the already ubiquitous RS-232 into the foreseeable future.

The international standards that deal with comparable interfaces are CCITT V.24, CCITT V.28 and ISO International Standard IS2110, issued by the International Telegraph and Telephone Consultative Committee (CCITT) and the International Organization for Standardization (ISO). Generally, devices built to one standard are compatible with devices built to another. However, in accordance with Murphy's Law, slight but problematic differences can sometimes arise.

A word of caution: Null modems for use with RS-530 will certainly differ from those for RS-232. Users should refer to RS-422 and RS-423 as well as RS-485, a standard that provides guidance for connecting multiple drivers and receivers to the same pair of wires. This standard will be applicable in most null modem designs. —WS

Table 1: RS-232-D signal summary

PIN NO.	CIRCUIT	SIGNAL DESCRIPTION
1	–	SHIELD
2	BA	TRANSMITTED DATA
3	BB	RECEIVED DATA
4	CA	REQUEST TO SEND
5	CB	CLEAR TO SEND
6	CC	DCE READY
7	AB	SIGNAL GROUND
8	CF	RECEIVED LINE SIGNAL DETECTOR
9	–	RESERVED FOR TESTING
10	–	RESERVED FOR TESTING
11	–	UNASSIGNED
12	SCF/CI	SECONDARY RECEIVED LINE SIGNAL DETECTOR/ DATA SIGNAL RATE SELECT (DCE SOURCE)
13	SCB	SECONDARY CLEAR TO SEND
14	SBA	SECONDARY TRANSMITTED DATA
15	DB	TRANSMITTER SIGNAL ELEMENT TIMING (DCE SOURCE)
16	SBB	SECONDARY RECEIVED DATA
17	DD	RECEIVER SIGNAL ELEMENT TIMING (DCE SOURCE)
18	LL	LOCAL LOOPBACK
19	SCA	SECONDARY REQUEST TO SEND
20	CD	DTE READY
21	RL/CG	REMOTE LOOPBACK/SIGNAL QUALITY DETECTOR
22	CE	RING INDICATOR
23	CH/CI	DATA SIGNAL RATE SELECT (DTE/DCE SOURCE)
24	DA	TRANSMIT SIGNAL ELEMENT TIMING (DTE SOURCE)
25	TM	TEST MODE

Table 2: RS-530 signal summary

PIN NO.	CIRCUIT	SIGNAL DESCRIPTION
1	–	SHIELD
2	BA	TRANSMITTED DATA
3	BB	RECEIVED DATA
4	CA	REQUEST TO SEND
5	CB	CLEAR TO SEND
6	CC	DCE READY
7	AB	SIGNAL GROUND
8	CF	RECEIVED LINE SIGNAL DETECTOR
9	DD	RECEIVER SIGNAL ELEMENT TIMING (DCE SOURCE)
10	CF	RECEIVED LINE SIGNAL DETECTOR
11	DA	TRANSMIT SIGNAL ELEMENT TIMING (DTE SOURCE)
12	DB	TRANSMIT SIGNAL ELEMENT TIMING (DCE SOURCE)
13	CB	CLEAR TO SEND
14	BA	TRANSMITTED DATA
15	DB	TRANSMITTER SIGNAL ELEMENT TIMING (DCE SOURCE)
16	BB	RECEIVED DATA
17	DD	RECEIVER SIGNAL ELEMENT TIMING (DCE SOURCE)
18	LL	LOCAL LOOPBACK
19	CA	REQUEST TO SEND
20	CD	DTE READY
21	RL	REMOTE LOOPBACK
22	CC	DCE READY
23	CD	DTE READY
24	DA	TRANSMIT SIGNAL ELEMENT TIMING (DTE SOURCE)
25	TM	TEST MODE

1. Asynchronous. *One possible asynchronous null modem cable crosses the Data leads, passes the Shield and Ground leads through, and jumpers several other leads, an arrangement that allows the DTEs to present signals to themselves that they think are coming from the remote DTE and thus save on the number of wires used.*

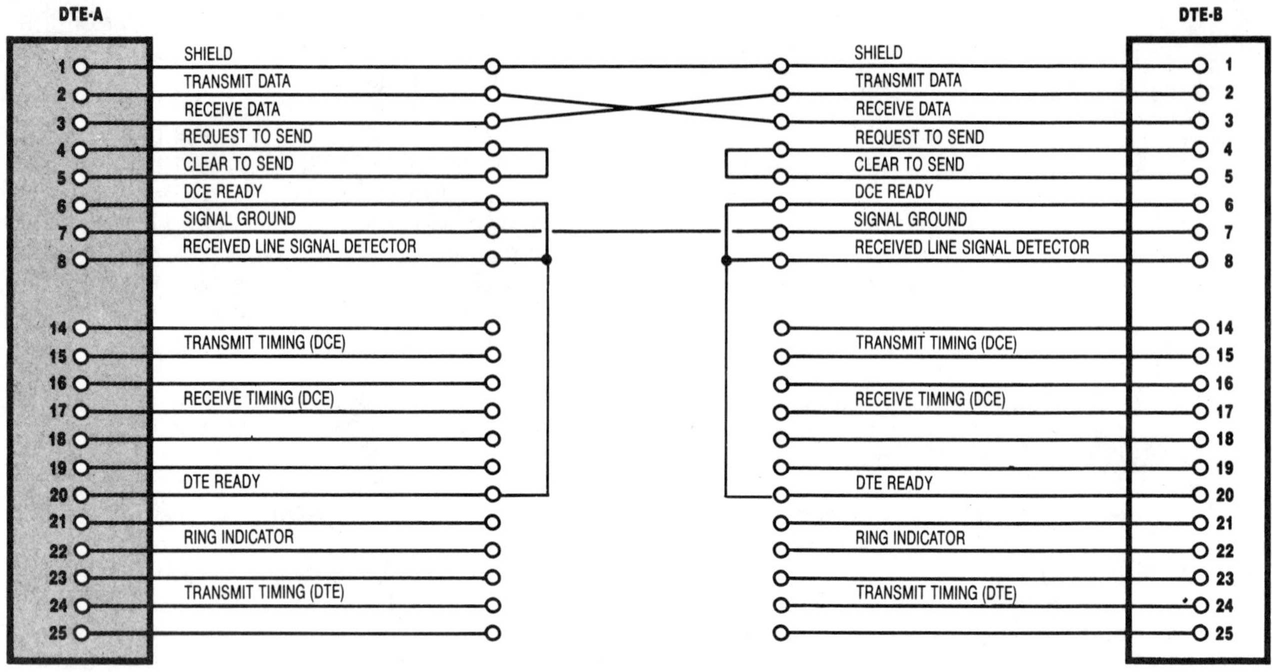

2. Synchronous. *This case differs from asynchronous in that certain control leads must be run across the cable while timing leads are hooked to an external source. As before, the transmit and receive data leads are crossed, —he shield and ground pass through, and the Clear and Request To Send leads are jumpered at the connector.*

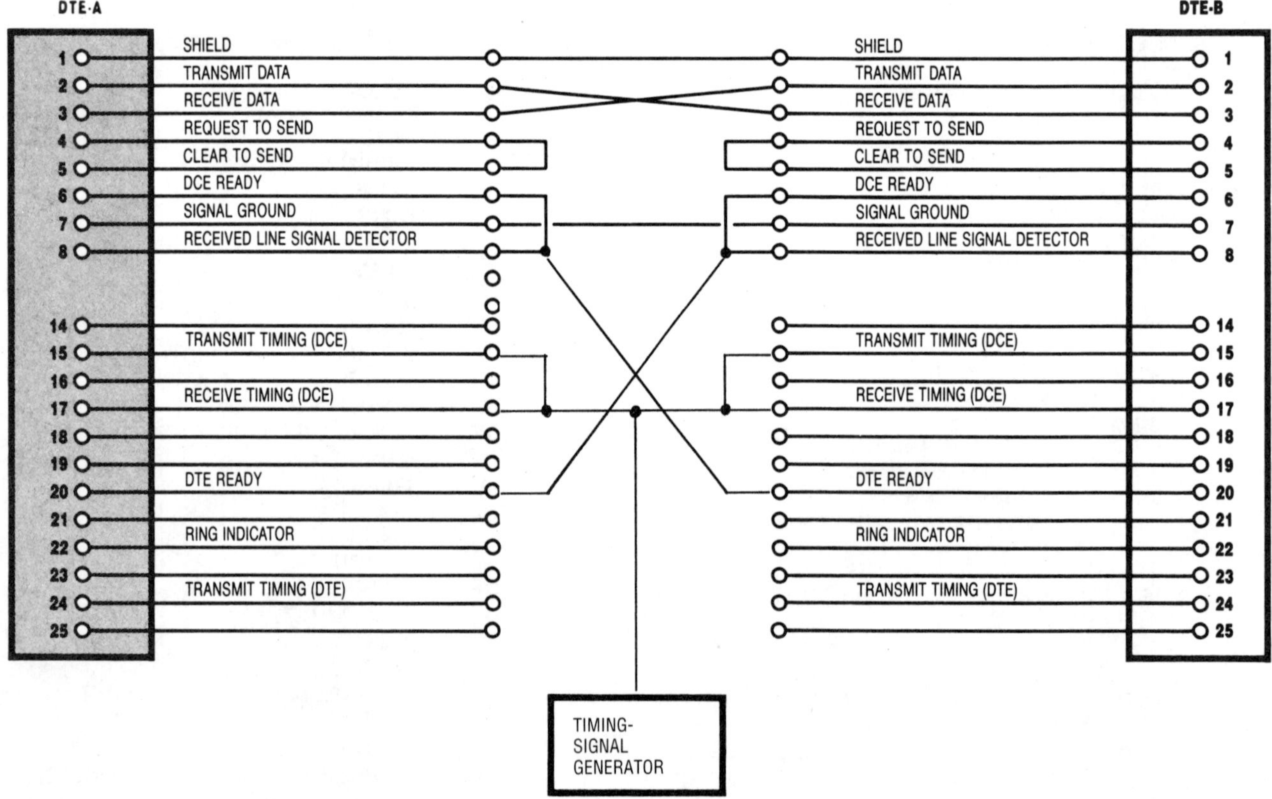

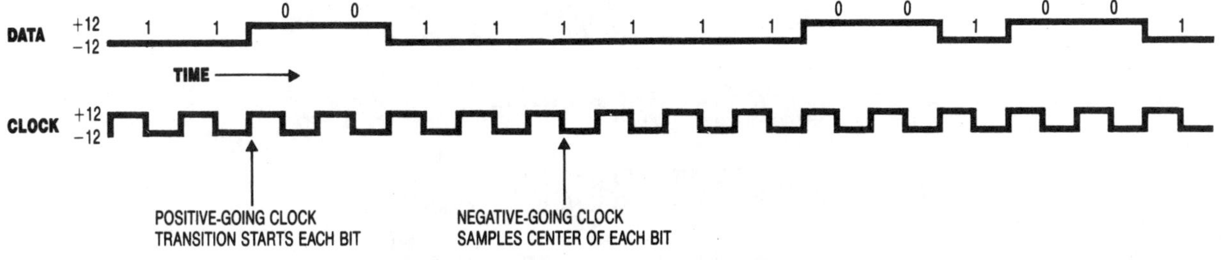

3. Tick, tock. *This figure shows the timing relationship between the clock signals and the data passing over a synchronous communications interface. The bits begin when the clocks go positive, as from 12 to 12 volts, and are sampled at their midpoint when the clock signal goes from positive to negative.*

counterpart modem-originated signals, Clear To Send (pin 5) and DCE Ready (pin 6).

Received Line Signal Detect (pin 8, formerly Carrier Detect) is also jumpered to DTE Ready at both ends because the DTE is usually informed when the modem is ready and an end-to-end connection is in place. When a DTE turns on Request To Send and DTE Ready, this arrangement makes that DTE think it is connected to a modem that is ready to send or receive data, even though the other DTE may not be connected.

Synchronous null modems

Synchronous terminals need clock signals for the timing of data transmission and reception, adding another degree of complexity to the interface. In a null modem connecting synchronous terminals, all clock signals must be supplied from an external timing-signal generator (Fig. 2). Most synchronous terminals require that an external source (usually a modem) supply clock signals on pins 15, Transmitter Signal Element Timing (DCE source), and 17, Receiver Signal Element Timing (DCE source). Pin 15 normally is driven by an oscillator in the modem, which tells the DTE when to transmit the next bit. Pin 17, which tells the DTE to look for a new data bit on the Receive Data line, is kept in harmony with the remote modem by being adjusted on the basis of the incoming signal. Unlike in the asynchronous null modem cable, DTE Ready is here transposed with DCE Ready and Receive Line Signal Detect and run across the cable. This is because synchronous DTEs must know that the DTE on the other end is up and running before attempting to exchange data.

Moreover, it is extremely important that the clock signal used as the Transmit Timing for DTE A also be used as the Receive Timing for DTE B and vice versa, otherwise numerous garbled transmissions can be expected. As shown in Figure 3, each bit is started when the clock signal changes from negative to positive. Since each bit lasts a full clock cycle, the clock transition from positive to negative can be used to sample the center of each bit in the data stream.

In cases where one or both DTEs supply transmit clock, an external source is not required, but the Transmit Clock signal (pin 24) of a DTE supplying clock must be connected to the Receive Clock (pin 17) of the other DTE. Such terminals are rarely encountered.

One of the most important signals on the interface is ground, especially for applications involving synchronous transmission. The result of careless ground connections can be numerous transmission errors or, in some cases, the inability to communicate at all. Two separate wires were specified by RS-232-C, Protective Ground (pin 1) and Signal Ground (pin 7). Protective Ground was replaced in RS-232-D by the Shield lead, which specifies that pin 1 be a common connection point for the shield of a shielded cable used to suppress electromagnetic interference (EMI). The standard recommends that pin 1 not be connected at the DCE but only at the DTE end, so that the shield does not form a circuit that might give off EMI.

The frame of both devices (the DTE and either the DCE or the other DTE) should have a solid grounding connection. Typically, a DTE or DCE gets alternating-current power through a three-wire connector, the third wire being the common Protective Ground. If a three-wire connector is not used, the user should investigate how best to get a proper ground. The Signal Ground is usually connected to Protective Ground internally (RS-232-D specifies connection through a 100-ohm resistor) and is also connected with the remote device's Signal Ground via the interface wire specified for that purpose.

Operation without modems has led to diverse interpretations of the RS-232 standard. Some asynchronous terminals (especially printers) use one of the control signals, either Request To Send, Clear To Send, or DTE Ready, for flow control. This allows the terminal to tell the other DTE, typically a computer, that it is or is not ready to receive data. It is not unusual to connect the DTE Ready and DCE Ready signals at one DTE while leaving them unconnected at the other DTE.

Some terminals require Received Line Signal Detect, while Ring Indicator, used for automatic answering of phone lines, is inappropriate for a null modem. To reduce cost, some DTEs are designed to use less than the full complement of RS-232 interface signal wires. In such cases, the DTE may require jumper wires or specific switch settings. ∎

William Sheridan entered the computer field in 1955 at the Eckert-Mauchly Computer Corporation (now Burroughs/Sperry Univac), where he worked while attending Pennsylvania State University. He received training in electronics in the U. S. Army during the Korean War, a B. A. in math from Penn State, and an M. S. E. E. from the University of Pennsylvania. Since then, he has worked as a logic design and software engineer and in various management positions. He is currently an independent consultant.

Jack Douglas, Universal Data Systems, Huntsville, Ala.

V.32 modems are breaking through the echo barrier

Knowing the ins and outs of high-speed modem technology takes the worry out of shopping for the new dial-up equipment.

Until recently, making a full-duplex dial-up modem that ran faster than 2.4 kbit/s was impractical. Despite the fact that the International Telegraph and Telephone Consultative Committee (CCITT) V.32 recommendation for 9.6-kbit/s, full-duplex modems had been specified since 1984, the high cost of implementing the technology tended to price the gear out of the market (see "Speed limits"). However, advances in signal-processing techniques have brought manufacturing costs down, and the market has begun to take off.

Currently, there are over a dozen companies with V.32 modems on the market. But the performance of these devices varies greatly from manufacturer to manufacturer. Specifically, how well these modems implement a signal-processing technique called echo cancellation is a primary factor in how well they operate overall. If potential buyers are to make intelligent purchasing decisions, they must have a good understanding of what causes echoes on telephone channels, how echoes are removed (so that they won't interfere with data transmission), and why some echo cancellers produce lower data-error rates than others.

Echoes are telephone-channel impairments caused by signal reflections at points in the transmission path where circuit impedances are dissimilar. There are several types of echoes, including near-end, far-end, talker, and listener echoes (Fig. 1). Reflections occur in the "hybrids" located in modems and in telephone lines. Hybrids are used to make telephone-line connections between two-wire circuits and four-wire circuits on the transmission path. A hybrid in the modem permits the transmitter and the receiver to be connected to the telephone line at the same time.

In the telephone network, a hybrid connects the two-wire circuit of the local telephone loop to the four-wire circuit used to bridge the telephone company central offices (COs) together. Four-wire circuits are always used between COs so that signal amplifiers, analog carrier setups, and digital carrier setups may all be used on the same network.

In the United States, telephone line echoes fall into two distinct categories: near-end and far-end. Near-end echoes occur at the hybrid at the local telephone company's CO; far-end echoes occur at the receiving end of the channel. Occasionally, the signal contains intermediate echoes, which occur at hybrids in the four-wire CO network.

Near-end echoes, which are predominant, have time delays of less than 10 milliseconds (ms). Far-end echoes and intermediate echoes have delays varying from 20 ms to 110 ms on terrestrial circuits and up to 700 ms on satellite circuits. Echoes that originate at the local modem and are heard by the local modem are called talker echoes, while echoes that originate at the local modem but are heard by the far-end modem, are called listener echoes.

Echo busters

Basically, there are two classes of echo cancellers. One class is located within the telephone network; the other is located at the ends of the network in echo-cancelling modems. Both types cancel echoes by subtracting an estimated replica of the echo from the signal containing the true echo.

The heart of all echo cancellers is the adaptive tapped delay-line circuit (Fig. 2). This circuit dynamically forms a signal, an echo replica, that is approximately the same amplitude and phase as the true echo signal. The echo replica and the incoming signal—the true echo plus the desired signal impaired by noise and other channel disturbances—are then fed into a summation circuit, where the echo replica is subtracted from the true echo and the desired signal is passed undisturbed.

Telephone-line echo cancellers, as shown in the figure, use this combination of circuits. They are implemented

Speed limits

Over the years, data communications equipment manufacturers have had to overcome many hurdles in their attempts to transfer data at increasingly high speeds over dial-up lines. Until now, full-duplex dial-up operation was limited to 2.4 kbits/s (V.22*bis*) and was accomplished by frequency-division multiplexing (FDM) techniques. With FDM, half the available bandwidth is used for transmitting data and half for receiving data. The relatively narrow 3-kHz bandwidth of the telephone line (300 Hz to 3.3 kHz, of which only 2.4 kHz is consistently usable) is the main factor limiting the maximum possible data rate.

The new CCITT V.32 echo-cancelling modem requires only a two-wire dial-up line to operate at 9.6 kbit/s, in synchronous or asynchronous full-duplex operation. This is because the V.32 modem transmits and receives simultaneously over the same frequency band. V.32 modems rely on trellis-coded modultation (see "Trellis encoding: What it is and how it affects data transmission," DATA COMMUNICATIONS, May 1985, p. 143) and echo-cancellation techniques to achieve the performance levels needed to run effectively on the public switched telephone network. (PSTN).

The CCITT released the V.32 recommendation in November 1984, but only recently has its implementation become widespread. This recommendation defines a family of two-wire duplex modems operating at data rates of up to 9.6 kbit/s for use on the dial-up PSTN and on point-to-point leased telephone-type circuits. The V.32 recommendation is divided into six sections and an appendix, delineated as follows:

■ Line signals. This section recommends the following: a carrier frequency of 1.8 kHz to operate with received frequency offsets of as much as plus-or-minus 7 Hz; the transmitted power spectrum must conform to CCITT Recommendation V.2; a modulation rate of 2.4 kbaud (signal elements); signal-element coding for 9.6 kbits/, with two alternatives—nonredundant encoding and trellis encoding (specified in the recommendation); 32-point signal structure with trellis-coded 9.6-kbit/s and 4.8-kbit/s operation (A); 16-point signal structure with nonredundant coding for 9.6-kbit/s and 4.8-kbit/s operation (B).

■ Interchange signals. This section recommends CCITT V.24 and CCITT V.28 signal specifications that apply to V.32.

■ Scrambler/descrambler allocation. This section recommends the type of scrambler and descrambler that should be used for originating and answering stations for public and private line operation.

■ Operating procedures. This section recommends the following: a V.25 auto-answering sequence; a receiver-conditioning signal that consists of an optional time period of at least 650 milliseconds used for echo-canceller training (technique is unspecified) and three distinct signal segments used for training the modem receiver; a rate-signal generator and detector consisting of repeated 16-bit binary sequences (this determines the speed and mode of operation); start-up answer-modem and calling-modem procedures and timing sequences.

■ Testing facilities. This section recommends the provision of test loops two (remote digital loopback) and three (local analog loopback), as defined in Recommendation V.54.

■ Appendix 1 indicates that there may be a need for a multimode V.32 modem compatible with V.25*ter* (which specifies a full-duplex echo-cancelling modem at 2.4 kbit/s). This modem should operate at rates of 9.6 kbit/s, 4.8 kbit/s, and 2.4 kbit/s.

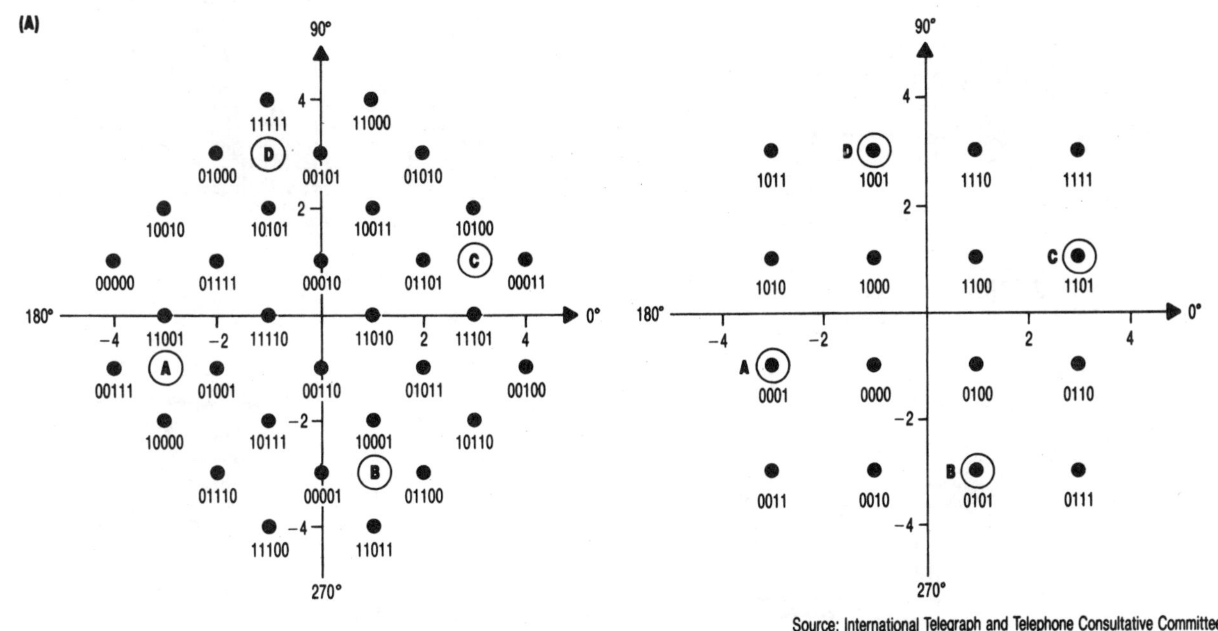

Source: International Telegraph and Telephone Consultative Committee

1. Echoes. Near-end echoes occur at the local modem's hybrid and at the central office hybrid (A); far-end echoes occur at the far-end hybrid (B); talker echoes originate at the local modem and are heard by that modem (C); listener echoes originate at the local modem but are heard by the far-end modem (D).

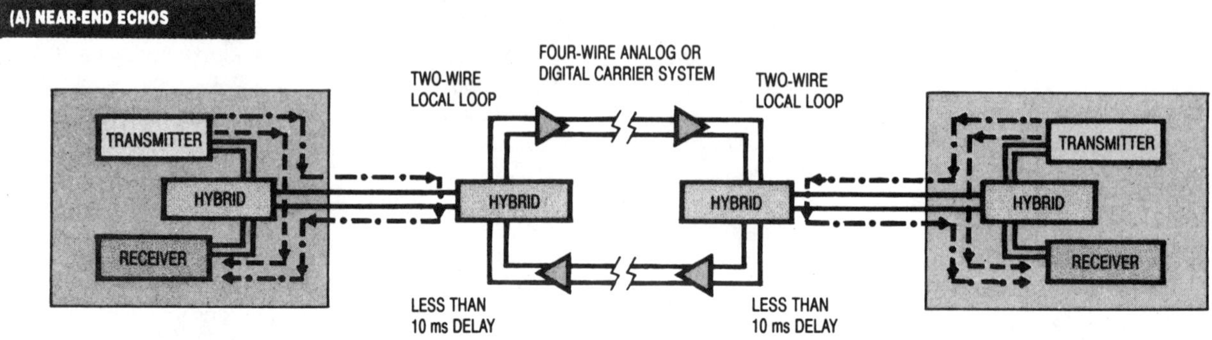

(A) NEAR-END ECHOS
TWO-WIRE LOCAL LOOP
FOUR-WIRE ANALOG OR DIGITAL CARRIER SYSTEM
TWO-WIRE LOCAL LOOP
TRANSMITTER
HYBRID
RECEIVER
HYBRID
HYBRID
TRANSMITTER
HYBRID
RECEIVER
LESS THAN 10 ms DELAY
LESS THAN 10 ms DELAY

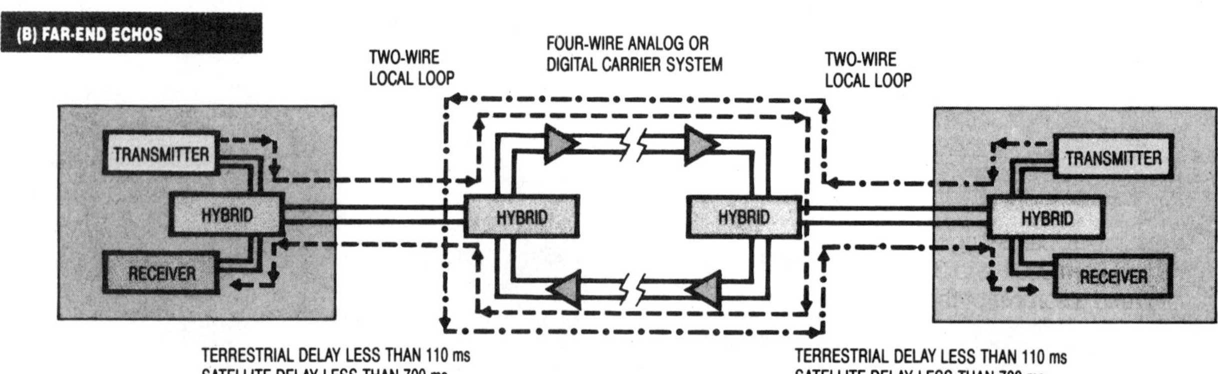

(B) FAR-END ECHOS
TWO-WIRE LOCAL LOOP
FOUR-WIRE ANALOG OR DIGITAL CARRIER SYSTEM
TWO-WIRE LOCAL LOOP
TRANSMITTER
HYBRID
RECEIVER
HYBRID
HYBRID
TRANSMITTER
HYBRID
RECEIVER
TERRESTRIAL DELAY LESS THAN 110 ms
SATELLITE DELAY LESS THAN 700 ms
TERRESTRIAL DELAY LESS THAN 110 ms
SATELLITE DELAY LESS THAN 700 ms

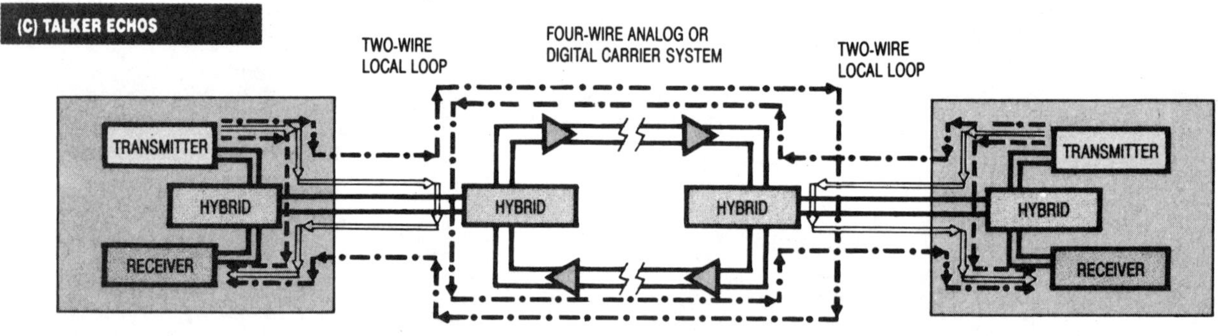

(C) TALKER ECHOS
TWO-WIRE LOCAL LOOP
FOUR-WIRE ANALOG OR DIGITAL CARRIER SYSTEM
TWO-WIRE LOCAL LOOP
TRANSMITTER
HYBRID
RECEIVER
HYBRID
HYBRID
TRANSMITTER
HYBRID
RECEIVER

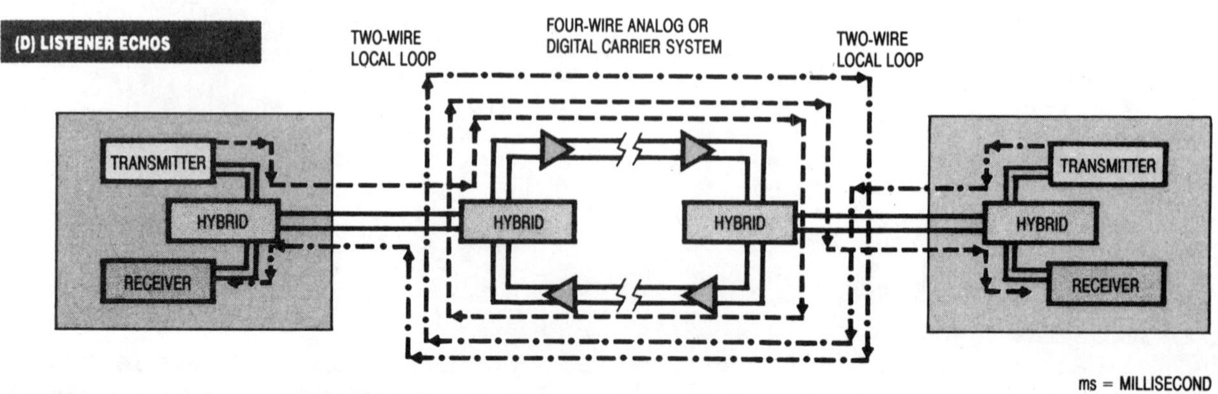

(D) LISTENER ECHOS
TWO-WIRE LOCAL LOOP
FOUR-WIRE ANALOG OR DIGITAL CARRIER SYSTEM
TWO-WIRE LOCAL LOOP
TRANSMITTER
HYBRID
RECEIVER
HYBRID
HYBRID
TRANSMITTER
HYBRID
RECEIVER
ms = MILLISECOND

2. Cancellers. *Telephone-line echo cancellers feed a sample of the received signal into an adaptive tapped delay line and summation circuit.*

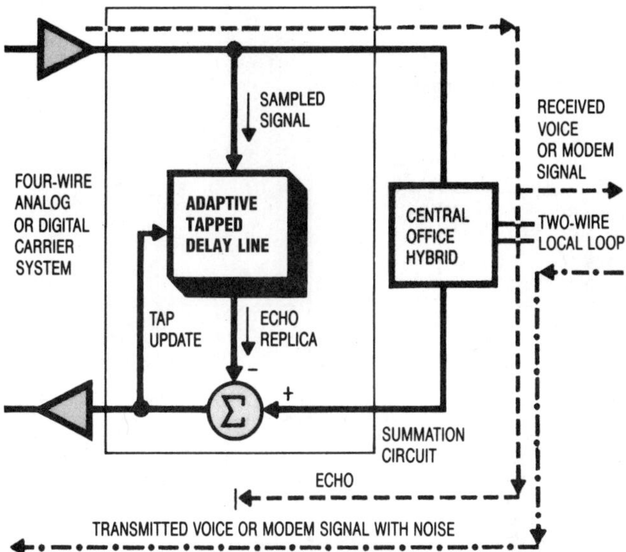

1. The near-end echo generated in the modem's hybrid.
2. The near-end echo reflected from the local CO hybrid.
3. The replica of the near-end echoes.
4. The desired far-end modem signal.
5. The far-end (or intermediate) echo.

At the output of the near-end summation circuit, only the far-end echo and the desired far-end modem signal are present. The far-end echo replica—generated in the far-end echo-canceller tapped delay line—is then subtracted from the far-end modem signal and far-end echo in a summation circuit. The result is that only the desired far-end signal reaches the modem's receiver.

Although all echo cancellers work on the same principle, there can be vast differences in the techniques used to implement them. Factors such as the ability to accurately detect the presence of echoes, the ability to cancel those echoes in the presence of impairments, and the accuracy of the adaptive tapped delay lines greatly affect the eventual performance of the echo canceller. Since there is no standard echo-cancelling technique defined by the CCITT or used in the industry, each modem manufacturer must develop its own. Hence, the design of the echo canceller is a compromise of price, performance, and available hardware.

Training time

Accurately detecting the presence and time delay of echoes is one of the most difficult tasks that must be done during echo cancellation. The modem's echo cancellers are initially trained to locate and estimate echo characteristics during a half-duplex-mode training period that is provided for in the V.32 recommendation. During this 2.5-second training time, the modem sends out a training signal (not specified in V.32) that is used to detect the presence, delay, and characteristics of the echoes. The cancellers are also trained to replicate the echoes. If only the near-end echo is cancelled or the echoes are falsely or inaccurately detected, the modem will perform poorly. This is because uncancelled or incorrectly cancelled echoes appear as impairments to the modem.

A second factor in effectively cancelling echoes—especially far-end echoes—is the modem's ability to nullify the effects of any impairments that may have affected the echo as it passed through the telephone line. Impairments such as noise, frequency translation, envelope distortion, and attenuation distortion (see "Coming to terms") can distort the echo and cause it to be falsely or inadequately cancelled.

Often, the most difficult to deal with of these impairments is frequency translation. Unless the V.32 modem possesses an adequate frequency-translation tracker, the far-end echo will generally be improperly or incompletely cancelled. For the modem to provide quality performance, it must be able to deal with these impairments.

The accuracy of the echo canceller's adaptive tapped delay-line and tap-update registers is a critical factor in accomplishing effective echo cancellation. Any echo can be effectively cancelled if its presence and characteristics are properly identified, the tapped delay line is long enough

as passband circuits, cancelling echoes in the voice-frequency band from 300 Hz to 3.3 kHz. Telephone-line cancellers feed a sample of the received signal into an adaptive tapped delay line before the received signal enters the hybrid. The output of the delay line is then fed into a summation circuit that sums the echo replica, the transmitted signal, the echo generated in the hybrid, and any noise or other impairments present on the telephone line. The output of the summation circuit is the transmitted signal plus any line noise; the echo is cancelled out.

In the modem, the echo canceller may also be implemented as a passband circuit, cancelling the echo before the signal is demodulated. However, echo cancellers can also be implemented as baseband circuits, cancelling the echo after the signal is demodulated. A good echo-cancelling modem will have two stages of echo cancelling (Fig. 3). One stage cancels the near-end echo and the other cancels the intermediate or far-end echo, whichever is greater.

The near-end canceller contains an adaptive tapped delay-line circuit and a summation circuit. The far-end canceller contains an adjustable bulk delay in addition to the adaptive tapped delay-line and summation circuits. The purpose of the bulk delay is to delay the far-end echo replica in time to coincide with the reception of the far-end echo. This bulk delay is typically adjustable between 20 ms and 700 ms. Both the near-end and far-end echo-canceller tapped delay lines are continuously updated, based on the signal at the output of the canceller. This ensures that the maximum amount of echo cancellation is achieved. The near-end and far-end canceller circuits are driven by the local modem's transmitter.

Five signals reach the summation circuit of the near-end canceller:

3. Stages. *Modem echo cancellers have two stages: one for near-end echo cancellation and one for intermediate or far-end echo cancellation, whichever is greater. In addition to an adaptive tapped delay-line circuit, the near end has a summation circuit and the far end has a summation circuit and an adjustable bulk delay.*

ECHO-CANCELLING MODEM

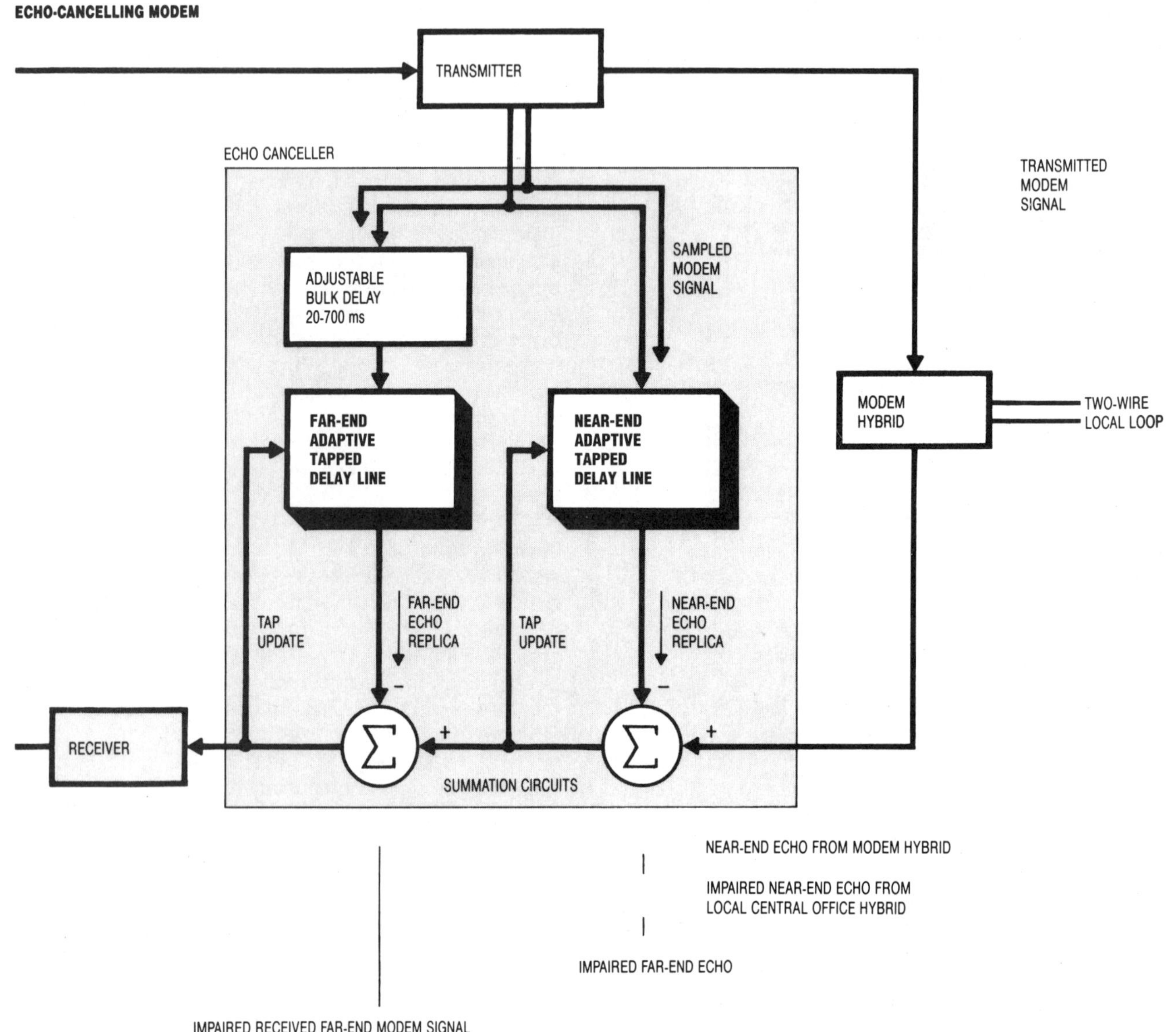

to span the echo, and the delay-line and tap-update registers have sufficient precision to accommodate the extremely precise numbers necessary for highly discriminate echo cancellation. (The more precise the number, the more information available to characterize the echo, so the better the cancellation.)

Therefore, in the competitive environment of V.32 echo-cancelling modems, the manufacturer must carefully select hardware adequate to accomplish the difficult task of echo cancellation but not so elaborate as to be cost-prohibitive. In addition, the modem's architecture and hardware must be flexible enough to permit it to readily adapt to new and better cancellation techniques as they develop.

Most modem designs use a set of custom very large-scale integration (VLSI) chips, a set of digital signal processor (DSP) chips, or a combination of VLSI and DSP chips. Designs that use only custom VLSI chips are usually more difficult and costly to update. On the other hand, designs that use DSP chips generally may be updated more quickly and economically.

Finally, the modem's ability to effectively equalize and demodulate the high-speed modem signal in the presence of impairments is key to good performance. The public switched telephone network (PSTN) contains many of the previously mentioned impairments that negatively affect the modem signal as well as producing an unacceptable echo.

These include attenuation distortion, envelope-delay distortion, white noise, impulse noise, quantization effects, phase jitter, amplitude jitter, intermodulation distortion, and frequency translation. The higher the speed, the more the modem is affected by these impairments.

A modem may have the best echo canceller in the world, but if it is unable to perform in the presence of any or all of the above signal impairments, it will not perform on the public switched telephone network. Designing and effectively implementing a low-speed, full-duplex modem (either a 1.2-kbit/s 212A or a 2.4-kbit/s V.22*bis*) is a relatively simple task compared with designing a 9.6-kbit/s V.32 modem. The 212A and V.22*bis* modems are, by comparison, only slightly affected by the above impairments. This is because these modems are much slower and use frequency-division multiplexing rather than echo cancelling to accomplish full-duplex operation. Frequency-division multiplexing divides the available bandwidth in half, using one half of the bandwidth for transmitted data and the other half for received data. ■

Jack Douglas is a senior manager at Universal Data Systems. He is chairman of the EIA TR30.3 technical subcommittee on telecommunications network interfaces and also serves on three Federal Communications Commission working groups. He has authored two books on data communications and teaches courses on that subject at the University of Alabama in Huntsville and at Athens State College, Athens, Ala. Douglas received his B. S. E. E. from the University of Alabama in Huntsville.

Breaking the Throughput Barrier: Which High-Speed Modems Test Best

Let the word get out that your company is thinking of buying an unspecified quantity of high-speed, 9.6-kbit/s, dial-up modems, and you are apt to find yourself inundated with reams of glossy product literature and calls from an army of sales reps just aching to close a deal.

Vendor claims—some documented, some not—can range anywhere from a modest 9.6-kbit/s data rate to a blistering 19.2 kbit/s, error-free. With potentially tens of thousands of dollars hanging in the balance, whom are you to believe?

In order to make buying decisions a little easier, DATA COMMUNICATIONS magazine decided to put these products to the test.

The magazine contracted with Telequality Associates, a Golden, Colo.-based test laboratory and consultancy specializing in modem testing, to run some characterization tests to determine how well a sampling of the leading high-speed, dial-up modems fared under line conditions users are likely to encounter on the public switched telephone network (see Table 1).

The modems that were selected for testing represent a variety of asynchronous 9.6-kbit/s, dial-up modem technologies. Five of those modems employ the now standard International Consultative Committee for Telephone and Telegraph (CCITT) V.32 recom-

mendation for full-duplex, 9.6-kbit/s, dial-up transmission. Seven other 9.6-kbit/s modems, representing non-standard "pseudo-duplex" technology, were also tested (see "A high-speed modem primer").

The tests yielded some interesting findings. Among them:

■ Of the pseudo-duplex modems, the U S Robotics Courier HST outperformed all the other nonstandard modems under simulations of frequently encountered line conditions. The Courier HST yielded an average throughput in excess of 9 kbit/s over tests simulating short- and long-haul line conditions.

■ In terms of reliability, the Racal-Vadic 9600 VP gave the most consistent performance of all line-simulation tests. In fact, data throughput (average 4.3 kbit/s) varied little over all conditions, including the worst-case scenario.

■ Of the modems that were able to establish connections under worst-case conditions, the Telebit Trailblazer Plus came out on top with an average data throughput of over 6 kbit/s under the most severe conditions.

The Racal 9600 VP, the Microcom AX/9624c, and the Data Race BMX VM-24 were also able to connect under worst-case conditions. The Data Race VM-24I, the Hayes 9600 V Series, and the U S Robotics Courier HST were not, however.

■ As it turned out, the higher-priced V.32 modems outperformed all the modems tested. And it seems there is little difference in their performance, except under severe, atypical line conditions. Of the V.32 modems, only the Concord Data Systems V.32 modem was unable to establish a connection under the worst-case scenario.

Since the V.32 modems are true full-duplex modems, they were tested for simultaneous two-way file transfer. Table 2 reflects average throughputs for file transfer in both forward and reverse directions. (The values shown are an average of the forward and reverse channels' performance, as are the standard deviations.) For on-line applications demanding simultaneous two-way file transfer, the V.32 modems are clearly efficient performers.

For the most part, the V.32 modems turned in fairly uniform performances, although the Concord 296 Trellis modem experienced some trouble with its reverse data path. Even running an MNP error-correction protocol, the Concord modem was unable to transmit 100 percent error-free data in the reverse direction. This was probably due to a single faulty modem, however, since the problem followed the errant modem when the transmission direction was reversed.

The overall hardy V.32 performances come as no surprise, since these modems have both a transmit and receive path of 9.6 kbit/s and can accept DTE data at 9.6 kbit/s in either direction or in both directions at the same time. The circuitry to accomplish such robust performance is highly complex, however, and has not yet made its way into inexpensive silicon. As a result, these modems tend to be relatively expensive (see Table 1).

Jack Humphrey, general partner of Telequality Associates, says there is no single modem test that can give an absolute characterization of a modem's performance (in part because customer traffic patterns, which vary widely, will also yield greatly varying performance levels). Still, says Humphrey, tests can prove a useful guideline to the modems' overall and relative performance.

■ **Pseudo duplex.** For the most part, the pseudo-duplex modems using asymmetrical operation and Ping-Pong technology are based on well-established techniques that have been around for years in one form or another. As a result, the core processing needed to implement these techniques is widely available in relatively inexpensive chips. For this reason, there is a considerable price/performance difference between the pseudo-duplex modems and the standard V.32s.

Since the pseudo-duplex modems have to turn the high-speed transmission path around each time they transfer a file, they do not do as well as the V.32 modems with two-way file transfers and interactive, or on-line, host queries and transaction traffic. But the manufacturers of the devices do not promote them for those applications, so DATA COMMUNICATIONS tested the pseudo-duplex modems for one-way file transfer only.

The accepted threshold for interactive keyboard delay—that is, from the time a character is sent from a remote keyboard until it is echoed back from the host—is less than 250 milliseconds. Delays exceeding 250 ms are perceived as particularity annoy-

ing to users. A recent high-speed dial-up modem study conducted by Concord Data, however, shows that some of the pseudo-duplex modems can echo characters in less than 250 ms.

Just how much of a price/performance trade-off a customer is willing to accept depends largely on the user's application. And this is made difficult because there is little information available comparing the actual performance efficiency of the modems.

The DATA COMMUNICATIONS-sponsored tests revealed that, unlike the V.32s', the performance of the pseudo-duplex modems varied widely. Nevertheless, the tests showed that among the nonstandard pseudo-duplex modems, the variations in their prices were not directly related to performance (see Table 3).

The U S Robotics Courier HST modem, the least expensive of all the modems tested, outperformed all the other pseudo-duplex modems on all line-simulation tests, except the one simulating the worst possible line conditions. In that test, the U S Robotics modem was unable to establish a connection.

The Telebit Trailblazer Plus finished a respectable second in tests simulating transmission over a relatively short-distance (intraLATA, though still interoffice) connection and an average long-distance call. And it placed first in the test simulating a worst-case dial-up connection.

Also noteworthy was the fact that the Racal-Vadic 9600 VP offered consistently the same throughput under all line conditions—from best to worst.

In no case, however, did any of the pseudo-duplex modems, or for that matter the V.32 modems, even approach the 19.2-kbit/s data rate that some of the vendors boast of in their marketing materials.

■ **The compression factor.** Vendor claims of 19.2-kbit/s throughput are largely based on their modems' application of data compression to the bit stream. For example, although Telebit

Table 1: Modem testing lineup

V.32 MODEMS:

ANDERSON JACOBSON 9631/-SA
$3,095 (QUANTITY ONE PRICE)
ANDERSON JACOBSON INC.
SAN JOSE, CALIF.

AT&T 2296A
$1,995-$2,495
(DEPENDING ON CONFIGURATION)
AT&T
BASKING RIDGE, N.J.

CODEX 2260
$1,995
CODEX CORP.
CANTON, MASS.

CONCORD 296 TRELLIS
$1,995
CONCORD DATA SYSTEMS INC.
MARLBOROUGH, MASS.

UDS V.32
$1,595
UNIVERSAL DATA SYSTEMS INC.
HUNTSVILLE, ALA.

PSEUDO-DUPLEX MODEMS:

DATA RACE BMX VM-24
$1,245
DATA RACE VM-24I
$1,345
DATA RACE
SAN ANTONIO, TEX.

HAYES V-SERIES
SMARTMODEM 9600
$1,299
HAYES MICROCOMPUTER PRODUCTS
NORCROSS, GA.

RACAL-VADIC 9600 VP
$1,495
RACAL-VADIC
MILPITAS, CALIF.

US ROBOTICS COURIER HST
$995
US ROBOTICS INC.
SKOKIE, ILL.

MICROCOM AX/9624c
$1,399
MICROCOM INC.
NORWOOD, MASS.

TELEBIT TRAILBLAZER PLUS
$1,395
TELEBIT CORP.
CUPERTINO, CALIF.

A high-speed modem primer

V.32 modems are based on the International Consultative Committee for Telephone and Telegraph (CCITT)-specified, full-duplex, V.32 dial-up modem technology. V.32 is a state-of-the-art and still fairly expensive technolgy that uses quadrature amplitude modulation (QAM).

QAM is a combined modulation of signal phase and amplitude. V.32 also uses Trellis encoding, a method of forward error correction whereby each signaling element is assigned a binary value representing that element's phase and amplitude. This value allows the receiving modem to determine — based on the values of preceding signal elements — whether or not a signal was received in error.

The V.32 modems are true full-duplex modems, allowing signals to travel in both directions at the same 9.6kbit/s speed by splitting the allotted bandwidth in half. True V.32 modems also require echo cancellers: complex circuits that cancel the vestiges of transmitted signals echoed back from the phone network.

■ **Multicarrier.** The Telebit Trailblazer is equally complex, though not quite as high-priced, as the V.32 modem. The Trailblazer uses Telebit's proprietary multicarrier modulation technique, which splits the available bandwidth into separate narrow channels.

At start-up, each modem "trains" with the other to determine which channels have significant impairments and which do not. The modems select only those channels data can pass over. The advantage of doing this is that the modems reserve power for only "good" portions of the bandwidth. They do not waste power trying to transmit data on portions of the bandwidth that are unable to pass data.

The Trailblazer is full duplex only in the sense that it presents the data terminal equipment (DTE) with a full-duplex asynchronous interface. Like other modems that use this so-called Ping-Pong technology, the Trailblazer modems use data buffers, on the data circuit-terminating equipment (DCE) side, to send and receive data in one direction only.

■ **V.29.** The Microcom AX9624C uses standard CCITT V.29 technology in half-duplex mode internally; that is, like the Trailblazer, it buffers data on the modem side in order to present the DTE with a full-duplex RTS/CTS convention. Between the two modems, the full bandwidth is used in one direction at a time.

Designed for the facsimile industry, the CCITT V.29 technology uses a modified QAM signaling scheme to achieve the same data rate as the V.32. However, since V.29 uses no Trellis encoding or forward error correction, and is designed to send data in one direction at a time, V.29 is much simpler to implement than either V.32 or Telebit's multicarrier technologies.

■ **Ping-Pong.** The Hayes V-Series Smartmodem 9600 uses a Ping-Pong operation like the Microcom AX9624C Plus and the Trailblazer. However, the Hayes 9600 uses a V.32 QAM Trellis-encoded signaling scheme like the Concord Trellis 296. But since the Hayes modem only transmits in one direction at a time, it does not require the expensive echo cancellation circuitry that the Concord modem does.

The Racal-Vadic 9600 VP uses V.29 line signaling combined with a mix of full-duplex and half-duplex technology called dynamic duplex. Like other pseudo-duplex modems, the Racal modem uses buffers to simulate full-duplex RTS/CTS interface conventions. However, on the modem or DCE side, call setup information and interactive keystrokes are sent in true full duplex using the CCITT V.22*bis* specification for 2.4-kbit/s full-duplex operation. (Like V.32, V22*bis* also uses QAM, but without Trellis encoding.)

When the modems begin sending bulk files, they switch to V.29-based 9.6 kbit/s for file transfer. Conversely, when frame acknowledgements (ACKs) are sent, the Racal modems drop back to full-duplex V.22*bis* in order to ensure that the ACKs are received correctly. Acording to the manufacturer, the slower V.22*bis* full-duplex channel used for ACKs ensures greater data throughput. If an ACK is lost, the entire lot of unacknowledged transmitted frames must be retransmitted.

■ **Asymmetrical.** The U S Robotics Courier HST uses what is known as an asymmetrical transmission scheme. That is, the modem uses most of the available bandwidth for high-speed forward file transfer. But it reserves a low-speed 300 bit/s channel for interactive keyboard operation and line turnaround signaling.

For the high-speed forward channel, the U S Robotics modem uses a version of V.32 QAM with Trellis encoding. Like the Hayes modem, which transmits V.32 in only one direction, the Courier HST does not require expensive echo-cancellation circuitry.

■ **Half duplex.** The Data Race BMX VM-24 uses Rockwell V.29 chip sets and operates in a true half-duplex scheme. That is, it transmits at the same speed but in only one direction at a time. Using proprietary technology, the modems claim to be able to turn the line around in less than 140 milliseconds.

The Data Race VM-24I splits the bandwidth asymmetrically using a 200-bit/s backward channel and a fast forward channel based on standardized V.27 (4.8k-bit/s) technology.

The modem sends data in various-size blocks and compresses data in a 2-kbit buffer. Then it sends a big block (1 kbit or 2 kbits). After initial training, the modems store up data pertaining to the line conditions. If line conditions are determined to be good, the modem transmits blocks of up to 2 kbits. If line quality is bad, the modem transmits in smaller blocks, thus optimizing throughput under bad conditions. —*J.B.*

claims at least an 18-kbit/s throughput for the Trailblazer Plus, even without compression, our tests were unable to substantiate that claim.

Many of the compression algorithms are designed to be most effective with 7-bit ASCII data streams, as is typical of many word processing documents and spreadsheet files. The Telequality testers, however, used a pseudo-random (binary) bit stream as the transmitted test data. Certain graphics or software object-code (but usually not source-code) files are similarly transferred as binary bit streams.

Where the modem manufacturer stated that compression should be disabled for 8-bit non-ASCII data, the modem's compression feature was disabled for the testing. Also, if no mention was made of which type of data the modem could compress, Telequality performed preliminary tests to determine whether a modem worked better or worse with compression. Where these tests showed the modem running poorer with compression, the feature was disabled, if possible.

Compression could not be disabled with the Hayes and the Racal modems. In Concord Data's own recent in-house testing, where ASCII test data was run, the Hayes modem did appreciably better than it did with the pseudo-random 8-bit data used in the Telequality/ DATA COMMUNICATIONS tests.

Likewise, the Racal modem did slightly better in the tests run by Concord Data with ASCII data. Telequality's Humphrey acknowledges that certain modems tested would likely have done better if the test data had been ASCII data. Still, he questions whether many users are willing to lock themselves into a specific type of data traffic (say, 7-bit ASCII) when selecting modem equipment costing thousands of dollars.

■ **Test setup.** Telequality Associates used a proprietary testing apparatus to simulate a variety of line conditions. According to Humphrey, the simula-

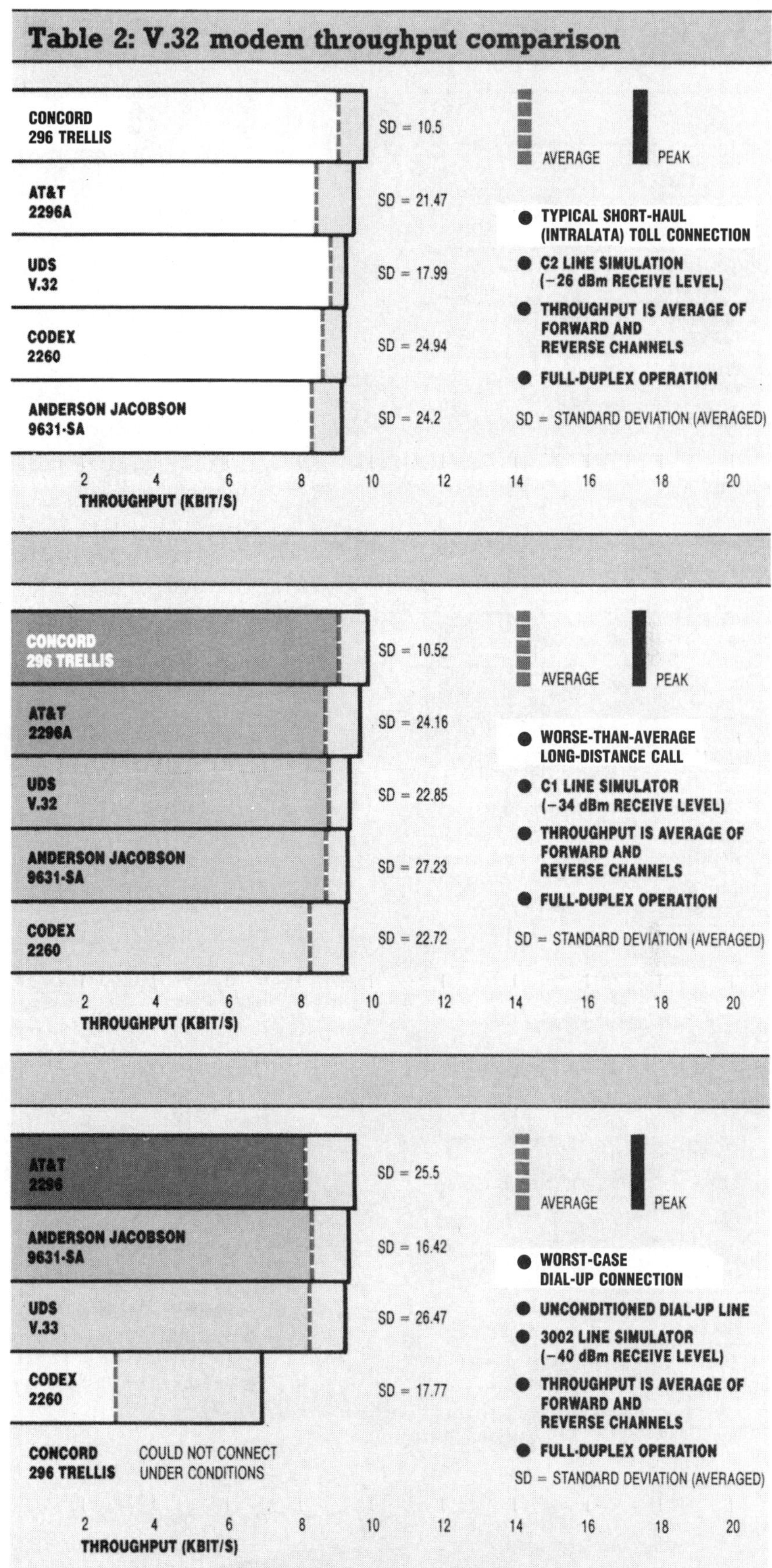

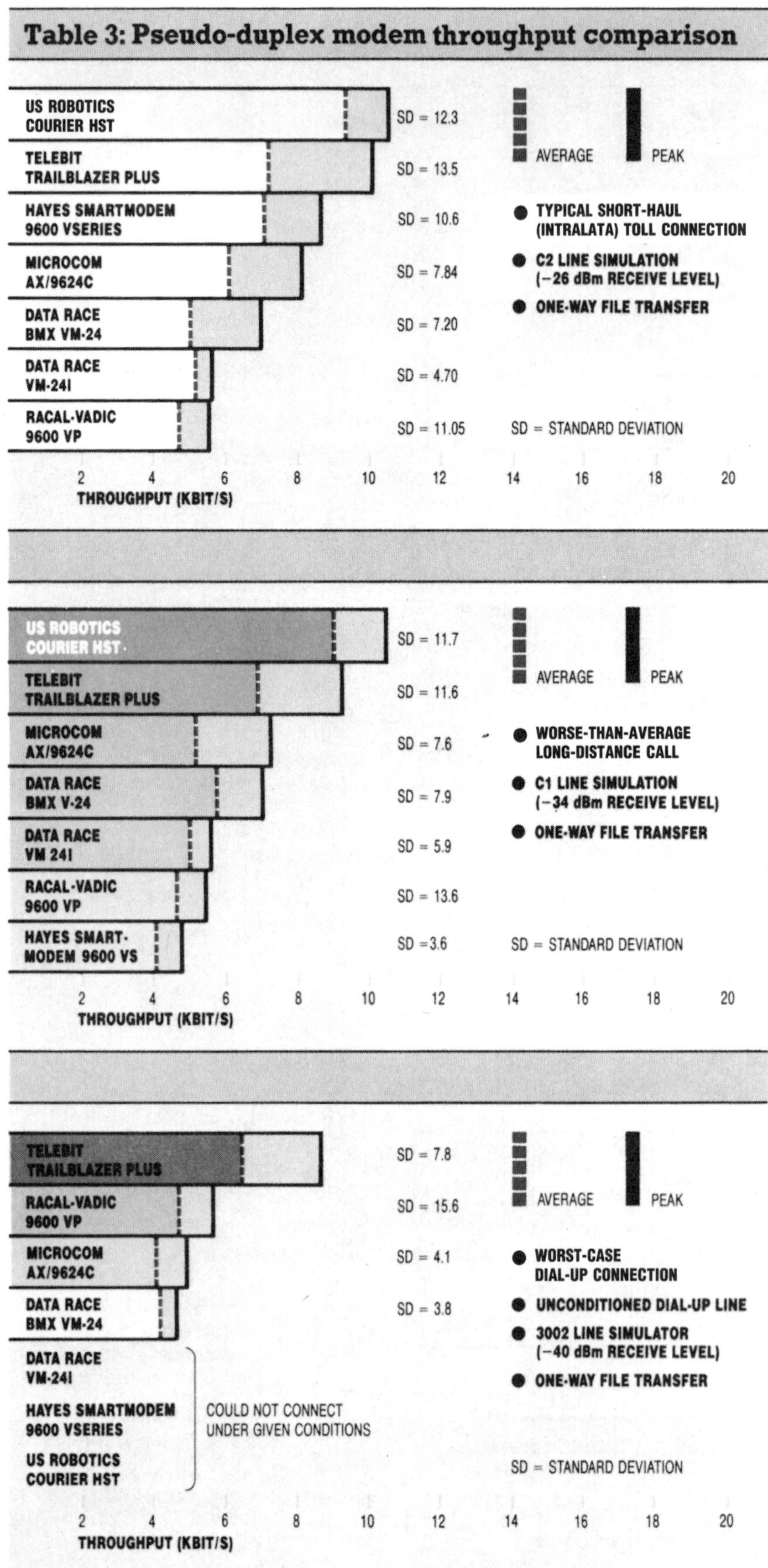

tions used for DATA COMMUNICATIONS' tests were roughly equivalent to conditions of an average call "to the suburbs" (a relatively short-haul dial connection, such as across town), a worse-than-average long-distance call, and a worst-case scenario that users are unlikely to encounter on the switched telephone network.

The respective simulations are based on AT&T tariffs for line-quality conditions: C2 for short-haul calls exhibiting minor levels of amplitude distortion and envelope delay; C1 for a worse-than-average long-distance call with substantial amplitude and envelope delay distortion; and 3002 for a plain dial-up connection with a high degree of line impairment and substantial amplitude and envelope delay distortion.

For each test, a measurement was taken of the modem's transmit level after the signal had passed through the line simulator. The transmit signal was then attenuated to ensure a specific receive signal level. For DATA COMMUNICATIONS' tests, receive signals of -26 dBm, -34 dBm, and -40 dBm were chosen for the C2, C1, and 3002 tests, respectively.

■ **The modem killer.** While under test, noise was added to the receive signal to decrease the signal-to-noise ratio (SNR) by 1 dB for each test point. The SNR was gradually decreased until the modem being tested ceased to operate. The point at which the modem fails is important because it represents the device's performance range under gradually degrading lines. Says Humphrey: "The grace with which the modem croaks is useful information."

A fixed SNR of 35 dB was chosen as the line impediment for the reverse path. This level was derived from AT&T's 1982/83 end-office connection survey (*AT&T Bell Labs Technical Journal;* Vol. 63, No. 9). DATA COMMUNICATIONS chose to leave the reverse-path SNR constant rather than vary it proportionally with the forward path.

Under actual conditions, the two

paths on a four-wire interoffice connection could have entirely different noise impairments. One path could be particularly noisy, while the reverse path could be relatively noise-free and vice versa. Anyone who has received a long-distance call where the person at the far end can hear fine, but the near-end talker can barely hear, is familiar with this phenomenon.

Since the pseudo-duplex modems, especially, use error correction to ensure error-free transmission, it was decided to insert some noise in the reverse path to test the modems' ability to acknowledge outstanding frames via the reverse channel. Ultimately, the modems' ability to do this is reflected in its throughput.

■ **Test reliability.** At each test point, the Telequality tester fed the modem being tested enough data to ensure a specified confidence limit. In the DATA COMMUNICATIONS tests, we specified a 90 percent confidence limit, with a 4 percent margin of error.

The sample size was figured in terms of blocks. Each block was 2,048 characters long. Each test terminated when the modem was operating at less than 10 percent efficiency after 32 blocks had been transmitted (again, 2,048 characters per block).

An efficiency coefficient for each modem was determined by multiply-ing the number of good blocks received times the number of bits per block (16,384). That number was multiplied by the time it took to receive the blocks. The result was then divided by the theoretical time it should take to transmit the data, as specified by the DTE port speed.

Data throughput was determined by multiplying the efficiency coefficient by the DTE port speed. The tabulated throughputs (Tables 2 and 3) are accompanied by the standard deviation for each test. Standard deviation is a reasonable index of the modem's consistency of performance. The smaller the standard deviation, the closer each sample throughput is to the test average.

■ **Port speed.** Manufacturers specify varying DTE port speeds that their modems can handle. In each case, DATA COMMUNICATIONS chose to set the port speed at the maximum data rate allowed by the manufacturer. For the pseudo-duplex modems, the DTE port speed was set to 19.2 kbit/s, except for the Racal-Vadic 9600 VP, where the manufacturer specified 9.6 kbit/s as the maximum allowable DTE port speed.

Port speeds for all the V.32 modems were set to 9.6 kbit/s, except for the Concord modem, which was set to 19.2 kbit/s.

Potential buyers, however, should keep in mind that the port speed does not equate to the modem's actual data throughput. As our tests show, that is clearly not the case.

In many cases, setting the DTE port speed to 19.2 kbit/s merely establishes the rate at which data is transferred from the DTE buffer to the modem's buffer.

So-called power users may find this capability useful for offloading a file to the modem's buffer before returning to another job. However, this does not cut down on the modem's transmit time. And higher transmit time ultimately translates to higher telephone bills.

Clearly, buying decisions are based on applications, budget, and performance demands. As the test results show, when price, performance, and reliability are factored in, there is no clear-cut winner.

If, for example, buyers are willing to spend $1,700 to $2,200 per modem, and two-way file transfer is a must, then the V.32 modems have a clear-cut advantage over the pseudo-duplex devices. If, on the other hand, users are willing to settle for slower data rates and only require one-way file transfer, some of the nonstandard pseudo-duplex modems are an excellent buy.

—*John Bush*

Report card's out: Modem grades are generally high

Modem marketplace
Response share by vendor

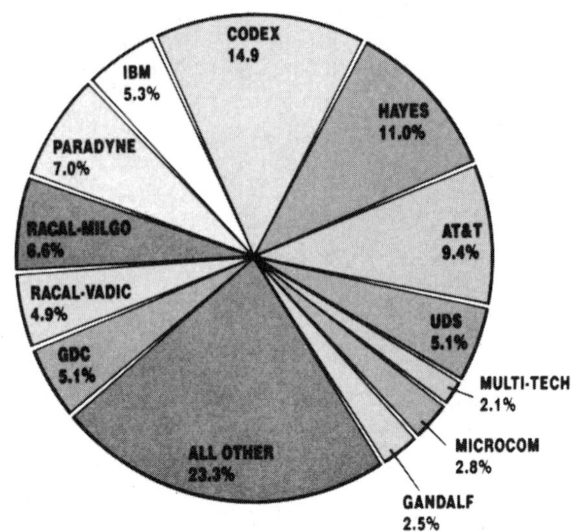

GDC = GENERAL DATACOMM
UDS = UNIVERSAL DATA SYSTEMS

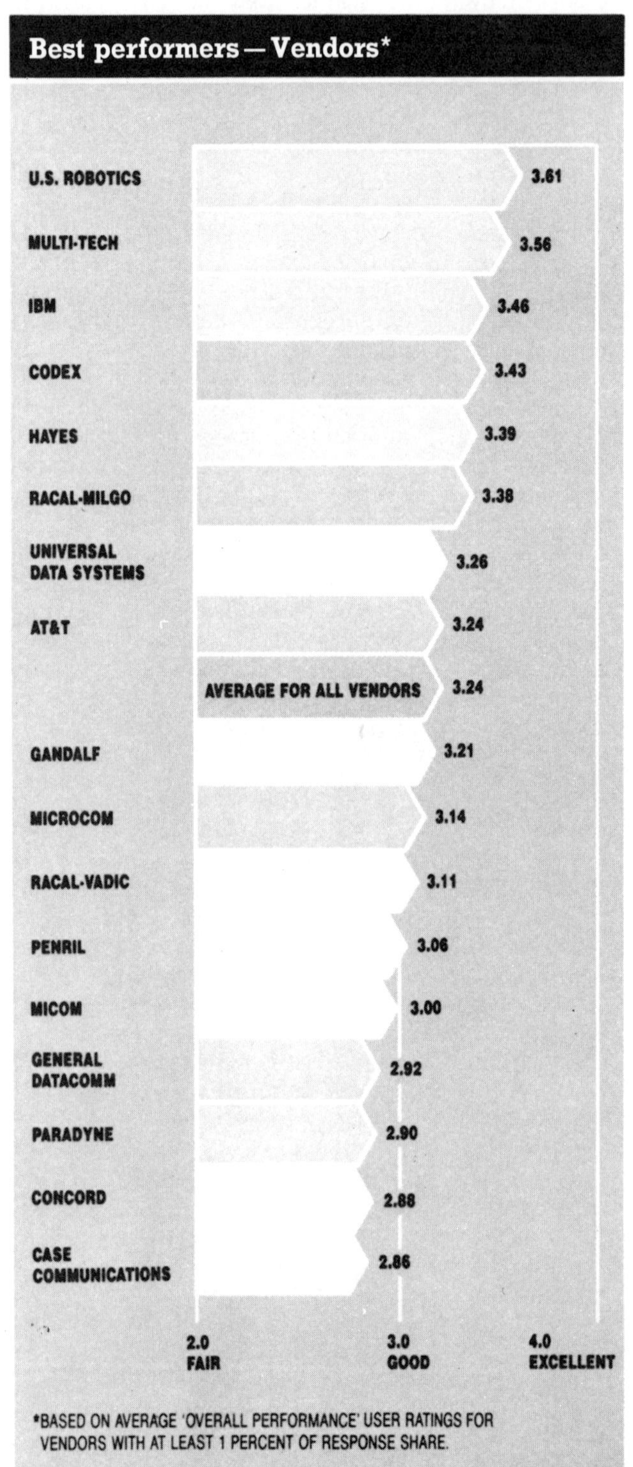

*BASED ON AVERAGE 'OVERALL PERFORMANCE' USER RATINGS FOR VENDORS WITH AT LEAST 1 PERCENT OF RESPONSE SHARE.

As in other sectors of the computer and communications equipment marketplace, AT&T's share of the modem market appears to be on the decline—this according to Datapro Research Corp.'s soon-to-be-published annual survey of modem users.

Of the more than 1,300 individual responses and modem ratings that were tabulated as part of the survey (after screening and eliminating invalid responses), AT&T's response share (see pie chart) amounted to 9.4 percent of the total. While this still is impressive, it is down from the 12 percent share AT&T garnered in last year's survey. On the upside, Codex Corp., which had the largest response share last year with 12.5 percent, has climbed into a clear lead position with 14.9 percent of this year's responses.

While a vendor's response share in the Datapro survey tends to be fairly well representative of the percent of all industry users with that particular vendor's products, it does not necessarily equate to installed base, however. This is especially true for modems, where one vendor's customers may only have a handful of modems, on average, while another's may have hundreds of units.

The modem market has apparently not undergone dramatic change in recent years, since the same dozen or so vendors still dominate more than three-fourths of the marketplace. And as before, literally dozens of other modem makers are vying for the remainder. This year's survey does, however, indicate increased market penetration by Multi-Tech, Microcom, and Gandalf, with a corresponding decrease for Case Communications.

Users were asked to rate their modems and their modem vendors on five criteria: Ease of Installation; Diagnostic Capabilities; Hardware Reliability; Quality of Manufacturer's Maintenance Service/Technical Support; and Overall Performance. A comparison of the average Overall Perfor-

User ratings of dial-up and leased-line modems

MANUFACTURER/ MODEL	NUMBER OF USER RESPONSES	EASE OF INSTALLATION					DIAGNOSTIC CAPABILITIES					HARDWARE RELIABILITY					QUALITY OF MANUFACTURER'S MAINTENANCE SERVICE/TECHNICAL SUPPORT					OVERALL PERFORMANCE				
		WA	E	G	F	P	WA	E	G	F	P	WA	E	G	F	P	WA	E	G	F	P	WA	E	G	F	P
ANCHOR AUTOMATION—																										
VOLKSMODEM	3	3.67	2	1	0	0	2.33	0	1	2	0	3.67	2	1	0	0	3.00	0	3	0	0	3.00	0	3	0	0
OTHER	3	3.50	1	1	0	0	3.00	0	1	0	0	3.00	1	0	1	0	2.00	0	0	1	0	3.00	1	0	1	0
SUBTOTAL	6	3.60	3	2	0	0	2.50	0	2	2	0	3.40	3	1	1	0	2.75	0	3	1	0	3.00	1	3	1	0
ANDERSON-JACOBSON—																										
ALL MODELS	7	2.86	1	5	0	1	2.57	1	3	2	1	2.57	1	4	0	2	2.71	1	3	3	0	2.57	0	5	1	1
ASTROCOM—																										
MOS/2	5	3.60	3	2	0	0	2.60	0	3	2	0	2.60	1	2	1	1	2.50	1	1	1	1	3.20	1	4	0	0
OTHER	1	4.00	1	0	0	0	3.00	0	1	0	0	4.00	1	0	0	0	4.00	1	0	0	0	4.00	1	0	0	0
SUBTOTAL	6	3.67	4	2	0	0	2.67	0	4	2	0	2.83	2	2	1	1	2.80	2	1	1	1	3.33	2	4	0	0
AT&T—																										
208	4	3.00	2	0	2	0	2.25	0	1	3	0	4.00	4	0	0	0	3.00	1	2	1	0	3.00	1	2	1	0
2200 SERIES	8	2.88	3	2	2	1	3.00	2	4	2	0	3.38	5	2	0	1	2.71	2	2	2	1	3.25	4	3	0	1
DATAPHONE	5	3.40	2	3	0	0	3.60	3	2	0	0	3.60	3	2	0	0	3.40	2	3	0	0	3.60	3	2	0	0
DATAPHONE I	3	3.33	1	2	0	0	3.33	2	0	1	0	3.67	2	1	0	0	3.00	1	0	1	0	3.33	1	2	0	0
DATAPHONE II	41	3.41	21	17	2	1	3.27	21	12	6	2	3.51	25	13	2	1	2.98	12	17	9	2	3.39	20	18	2	1
DATAPHONE II 2048	5	3.20	2	2	1	0	3.20	2	2	1	0	3.20	1	4	0	0	3.20	1	4	0	0	3.00	1	3	1	0
DATAPHONE II 2096	26	2.92	7	11	7	1	3.27	9	15	2	0	3.46	15	9	1	1	3.15	6	18	2	0	3.08	5	18	3	0
DSU	3	3.33	1	2	0	0	2.33	0	1	2	0	3.67	2	1	0	0	3.00	1	1	1	0	3.33	1	2	0	0
OTHER	28	3.29	10	16	2	0	3.04	8	14	5	1	3.43	13	14	1	0	3.04	7	14	6	0	3.18	7	19	2	0
SUBTOTAL	123	3.22	49	55	16	3	3.15	47	51	22	3	3.49	70	46	4	3	3.04	33	61	22	3	3.24	43	69	9	2
CASE COMMUNICATIONS—																										
R212	3	3.67	2	1	0	0	3.00	1	1	1	0	3.67	2	1	0	0	3.33	1	2	0	0	3.33	1	2	0	0
OTHER	18	3.00	3	12	3	0	2.83	2	11	5	0	2.89	5	8	3	2	2.60	0	11	2	2	2.78	2	12	2	2
SUBTOTAL	21	3.10	5	13	3	0	2.86	3	12	6	0	3.00	7	9	3	2	2.72	1	13	2	2	2.86	3	14	2	2
CODEX—																										
2100 SERIES	10	3.90	9	1	0	0	3.30	4	5	1	0	3.70	7	3	0	0	3.50	5	5	0	0	3.70	7	3	0	0
2200 SERIES	21	3.33	11	7	2	1	3.29	10	7	4	0	3.71	15	6	0	0	3.38	10	10	0	1	3.52	11	10	0	0
2300 SERIES	18	3.35	8	7	2	0	3.35	7	9	1	0	3.59	10	7	0	0	3.47	8	9	0	0	3.47	8	9	0	0
2400 SERIES	3	3.67	2	1	0	0	3.33	1	2	0	0	3.67	2	1	0	0	3.33	1	2	0	0	3.33	1	2	0	0
2500 SERIES	4	3.75	3	1	0	0	4.00	4	0	0	0	4.00	4	0	0	0	4.00	4	0	0	0	3.75	3	1	0	0
2600 SERIES	76	3.55	44	28	3	0	3.53	42	32	0	1	3.65	51	22	2	0	3.28	32	35	5	3	3.56	44	29	2	0
5200 SERIES	3	2.67	0	2	1	0	1.00	0	0	0	2	2.00	0	0	3	0	2.00	0	0	3	0	2.00	0	0	3	0
CS SERIES	5	3.20	1	4	0	0	2.40	0	2	3	0	3.60	3	2	0	0	2.80	1	3	0	1	3.00	1	3	1	0
LSI 9600	7	3.00	1	4	1	0	2.67	1	2	3	0	3.33	3	2	1	0	3.00	2	2	2	0	3.33	2	4	0	0
LSI ALL OTHER MODELS	5	3.20	2	2	1	0	2.80	1	2	2	0	3.60	3	2	0	0	2.60	1	2	1	1	3.20	1	4	0	0
MX SERIES	3	4.00	3	0	0	0	3.67	2	1	0	0	3.67	2	1	0	0	4.00	3	0	0	0	4.00	3	0	0	0
OTHER	40	3.13	11	24	4	1	3.08	11	21	6	1	3.30	19	17	1	3	3.13	14	18	3	3	3.20	16	18	4	2
SUBTOTAL	195	3.40	95	81	14	2	3.29	83	83	20	4	3.55	119	63	7	3	3.26	81	86	14	9	4.43	97	83	10	2
CONCORD DATA SYSTEMS—																										
224	8	3.13	3	3	2	0	2.50	1	2	5	0	3.13	4	2	1	1	2.50	0	5	2	1	3.13	2	5	1	0
OTHER	8	2.38	0	4	3	1	2.25	1	2	3	2	2.50	1	3	3	1	2.13	1	1	4	2	2.63	1	4	2	1
SUBTOTAL	16	2.75	3	7	5	1	2.38	2	4	8	2	2.81	5	5	4	2	2.31	1	6	6	3	2.88	3	9	3	1
CTS DATACOMM—																										
2400	5	3.20	1	4	0	0	2.40	0	3	1	1	2.80	1	3	0	1	2.60	0	4	0	1	2.50	0	4	0	1
OTHER	2	3.00	0	2	0	0	2.50	0	1	1	0	3.00	1	0	1	0	3.00	0	2	0	0	3.00	0	2	0	0
SUBTOTAL	7	3.14	1	6	0	0	2.43	0	4	2	1	2.86	2	3	1	1	2.71	0	6	0	1	2.71	0	6	0	1
DATARACE—																										
OTHER	4	3.00	0	4	0	0	2.50	0	2	2	0	2.75	0	3	1	0	3.00	1	2	1	0	3.00	0	4	0	0
DATATEL—																										
DCP 3080	3	3.67	2	1	0	0	2.50	0	1	1	0	4.00	3	0	0	0	3.67	2	1	0	0	3.67	2	1	0	0
OTHER	8	3.38	3	5	0	0	3.13	1	7	0	0	3.25	2	6	0	0	3.13	1	7	0	0	3.13	1	7	0	0
SUBTOTAL	11	3.45	5	6	0	0	3.00	1	8	1	0	3.45	5	6	0	0	3.27	3	8	0	0	3.27	3	8	0	0
DIGITAL EQUIPMENT CORP.—																										
ALL MODELS	4	3.75	3	1	0	0	3.25	2	1	1	0	3.50	2	2	0	0	3.75	3	1	0	0	3.50	2	2	0	0
EVEREX—																										
ALL MODELS	8	3.38	3	5	0	0	2.38	0	4	3	1	3.13	3	4	0	1	2.50	0	4	1	1	3.00	1	6	1	0

WEIGHTED AVERAGE (WA) IS BASED ON ASSIGNING A WEIGHT OF 4 TO EACH USER RATING OF EXCELLENT (E), 3 TO GOOD (G), 2 TO FAIR (F), AND 1 TO POOR (P).

User ratings of dial-up and leased-line modems (continued)

WEIGHTED AVERAGES AND RESPONSE COUNTS

Manufacturer/Model	Number of user responses	Ease of installation — WA	E	G	F	P	Diagnostic capabilities — WA	E	G	F	P	Hardware reliability — WA	E	G	F	P	Quality of manufacturer's maintenance service/technical support — WA	E	G	F	P	Overall performance — WA	E	G	F	P
FUJITSU—																									
1921L	3	3.67	2	1	0	0	3.33	1	2	0	0	4.00	3	0	0	0	3.33	1	2	0	0	3.67	2	1	0	0
M192 XL	3	3.33	2	0	1	0	3.33	2	0	1	0	4.00	3	0	0	0	3.33	1	2	0	0	3.67	2	1	0	0
OTHER	3	4.00	3	0	0	0	4.00	3	0	0	0	4.00	3	0	0	0	3.67	2	1	0	0	4.00	3	0	0	0
SUBTOTAL	9	3.67	7	1	1	0	3.56	6	2	1	0	4.00	9	0	0	0	3.44	4	5	0	0	3.78	7	2	0	0
GANDALF—																									
LDM SERIES	4	3.25	1	3	0	0	2.75	1	1	2	0	3.50	2	2	0	0	3.25	1	3	0	0	3.25	1	3	0	0
LDS SERIES	6	3.33	2	4	0	0	3.00	1	4	1	0	3.50	3	3	0	0	3.00	0	6	0	0	3.00	0	6	0	0
OTHER	23	3.22	8	12	3	0	2.87	3	16	2	2	3.55	13	8	1	0	3.00	3	16	3	0	3.26	7	15	1	0
SUBTOTAL	33	3.24	11	19	3	0	2.88	5	21	5	2	3.53	18	13	1	0	3.03	4	25	3	0	3.21	8	24	1	0
GENERAL DATACOMM—																									
201 MODELS	3	4.00	3	0	0	0	2.67	0	2	1	0	2.67	1	0	2	0	2.00	0	1	1	1	2.67	0	2	1	0
212 MODELS	4	2.75	0	3	1	0	2.75	1	1	2	0	3.00	2	0	2	0	2.25	0	1	3	0	2.50	0	2	2	0
9600	8	2.75	0	6	2	0	2.63	1	4	2	1	2.75	1	4	3	0	2.13	0	2	5	1	2.86	0	7	1	0
DC SERIES	6	3.67	4	2	0	0	3.00	2	2	2	0	3.50	3	3	0	0	3.33	2	4	0	0	3.50	3	3	0	0
DSU	3	3.33	1	2	0	0	3.00	1	1	1	0	2.33	0	1	2	0	1.67	0	1	0	2	2.67	0	2	1	0
GSU 500A	2	3.50	1	1	0	0	3.00	0	2	0	0	3.00	1	0	1	0	2.50	0	1	1	0	3.00	0	2	0	0
NMS SERIES	7	3.14	1	6	0	0	3.43	4	2	1	0	3.14	3	2	2	0	2.43	0	3	4	0	2.71	0	5	2	0
OTHER	33	3.06	11	14	7	1	2.63	6	12	10	4	2.97	9	15	8	1	2.58	5	14	9	5	2.76	5	16	11	1
SUBTOTAL	66	3.14	21	34	10	1	2.78	15	26	19	5	2.97	20	25	20	1	2.48	7	27	23	9	2.82	8	39	18	1
HAYES—																									
9600 V SERIES	4	3.75	3	1	0	0	3.75	3	1	0	0	3.75	3	1	0	0	3.50	2	2	0	0	3.75	3	1	0	0
SMARTMODEM 1200	69	3.44	32	34	2	0	2.90	15	34	16	3	3.49	37	27	4	0	3.10	18	39	9	1	3.35	25	42	1	0
SMARTMODEM 1200B	16	3.40	8	6	0	1	2.67	4	5	3	3	3.20	7	4	4	0	2.86	4	5	4	1	3.20	7	4	4	0
SMARTMODEM 2400	32	3.61	19	12	0	0	3.00	8	16	6	1	3.65	20	11	0	0	3.10	10	14	5	1	3.52	17	13	1	0
SMARTMODEM 2400B	5	3.75	3	1	0	0	3.50	2	2	0	0	3.50	2	2	0	0	3.25	2	1	1	0	3.50	2	2	0	0
OTHER	17	3.47	10	5	2	0	3.00	5	7	5	0	3.53	9	8	0	0	2.87	4	5	6	0	3.35	7	9	1	0
SUBTOTAL	143	3.50	75	59	4	1	2.95	37	65	30	7	3.50	78	53	8	0	3.07	40	66	25	3	3.39	61	71	7	0
IBM—																									
3800	21	3.14	5	14	2	0	2.95	4	12	5	0	3.52	11	10	0	0	3.35	9	11	1	0	3.29	6	15	0	0
5800	35	3.35	18	12	2	2	3.44	21	9	2	2	3.56	23	9	0	2	3.18	15	13	3	2	3.50	22	10	2	0
OTHER	13	3.58	8	3	1	0	3.25	5	5	2	0	3.67	8	4	0	0	3.42	7	3	2	0	3.50	7	4	1	0
SUBTOTAL	69	3.33	31	29	5	2	3.25	30	26	9	2	3.57	42	23	0	2	3.28	31	27	6	3	3.48	35	29	3	0
INFINET—																									
IDM SERIES	4	3.75	3	1	0	0	4.00	4	0	0	0	4.00	4	0	0	0	3.25	1	3	0	0	3.50	2	2	0	0
NCM SERIES	4	2.75	0	3	1	0	3.50	2	2	0	0	2.50	1	0	3	0	2.50	0	2	2	0	3.00	0	4	0	0
OTHER	4	2.75	0	3	1	0	3.00	1	2	1	0	2.25	0	2	1	1	2.75	0	3	1	0	2.25	0	2	1	1
SUBTOTAL	12	3.08	3	7	2	0	3.50	7	4	1	0	2.92	5	2	4	1	2.83	1	8	3	0	2.92	2	8	1	1
KINEX—																									
ALL MODELS	3	3.33	1	2	0	0	2.67	1	0	2	0	3.67	2	1	0	0	3.33	1	2	0	0	3.33	1	2	0	0
LEADING EDGE—																									
ALL MODELS	3	4.00	3	0	0	0	2.67	0	2	1	0	3.33	2	0	1	0	4.00	2	0	0	0	3.00	1	1	1	0
MICOM—																									
ALL MODELS	19	3.16	4	14	1	0	2.58	1	10	7	1	2.89	5	8	3	2	2.67	2	9	6	1	3.00	4	11	4	0
MICROCOM—																									
AX/2400	13	3.09	3	6	2	0	3.00	3	6	1	0	3.18	3	7	1	0	3.00	3	6	1	1	3.18	3	7	1	0
AX/9624C	6	2.50	1	2	2	1	3.17	2	3	1	0	3.17	1	5	0	0	2.50	1	2	2	1	3.00	1	4	1	0
AX SERIES	4	3.00	1	2	1	0	3.50	2	2	0	0	3.25	2	1	1	0	3.00	1	2	1	0	3.00	0	4	0	0
OTHER	14	3.21	3	11	0	0	2.92	2	8	1	1	3.29	7	5	1	1	3.08	4	7	1	1	3.21	5	7	2	0
SUBTOTAL	37	3.03	8	21	5	1	3.06	9	19	3	2	3.23	13	18	3	1	2.94	9	17	5	3	3.14	9	22	4	0
MULTI-TECH—																									
MT 212	3	4.00	3	0	0	0	3.67	2	1	0	0	3.67	2	1	0	0	3.67	2	1	0	0	3.67	2	1	0	0
MT 224	19	3.58	11	8	0	0	3.16	6	10	3	0	3.84	16	3	0	0	3.63	12	7	0	0	3.63	12	7	0	0
OTHER	5	2.80	0	4	1	0	3.00	1	3	1	0	3.20	2	2	1	0	3.00	1	3	1	0	3.20	1	4	0	0
SUBTOTAL	27	3.48	14	12	1	0	3.19	9	14	4	0	3.70	20	6	1	0	3.52	15	11	1	0	3.56	15	12	0	0
NEC—																									
ALL MODELS	7	3.57	5	1	1	0	3.67	4	2	0	0	3.83	5	1	0	0	3.43	4	2	1	0	3.43	4	2	1	0
NOVATION—																									
ALL MODELS	4	3.50	2	2	0	0	3.25	1	3	0	0	3.00	2	1	0	1	3.25	3	0	0	1	3.00	2	1	0	1

User ratings of dial-up and leased-line modems (continued)

MANUFACTURER/ MODEL	NUMBER OF USER RESPONSES	EASE OF INSTALLATION					DIAGNOSTIC CAPABILITIES					HARDWARE RELIABILITY					QUALITY OF MANUFACTURER'S MAINTENANCE SERVICE/TECHNICAL SUPPORT					OVERALL PERFORMANCE				
		WA	E	G	F	P	WA	E	G	F	P	WA	E	G	F	P	WA	E	G	F	P	WA	E	G	F	P
PARADYNE—																										
3400 SERIES	6	4.00	6	0	0	0	4.00	6	0	0	0	4.00	6	0	0	0	4.00	5	0	0	0	4.00	6	0	0	0
CHALLENGER 9600	9	3.11	2	6	1	0	3.00	2	5	2	0	3.00	3	3	3	0	2.89	2	4	3	0	2.89	2	4	3	0
FDX 2400	4	3.25	1	3	0	0	2.75	0	3	1	0	3.00	1	2	1	0	2.50	0	2	2	0	2.75	0	3	1	0
MPX 4800	11	2.73	1	6	4	0	3.00	3	6	1	1	3.09	4	5	1	1	2.56	1	4	3	1	2.82	1	8	1	1
MPX 9600	15	2.87	3	8	3	1	3.33	5	10	0	0	3.07	4	9	1	1	2.87	2	9	4	0	2.93	2	11	1	1
MPX 14.4	4	2.50	0	2	2	0	2.75	0	3	1	0	2.75	1	1	2	0	2.25	1	0	2	1	2.50	0	2	2	0
OTHER	40	3.05	10	22	6	1	2.85	9	18	9	3	2.92	14	13	7	5	2.77	13	7	16	3	2.79	6	22	8	3
SUBTOTAL	89	3.03	23	47	16	2	3.03	25	45	14	4	3.05	33	33	15	7	2.81	24	26	30	5	2.90	17	50	16	5
PENRIL DATA COMM—																										
1800 DED	3	4.00	3	0	0	0	2.00	0	0	3	0	3.67	2	1	0	0	2.67	0	2	1	0	3.00	0	3	0	0
DATALINK SERIES	3	3.67	2	1	0	0	3.67	2	1	0	0	3.67	2	1	0	0	3.00	0	3	0	0	3.67	2	1	0	0
OTHER	11	3.45	5	6	0	0	3.00	3	6	1	1	3.00	4	4	2	1	2.73	2	5	3	1	2.91	2	6	3	0
SUBTOTAL	17	3.59	10	7	0	0	2.94	5	7	4	1	3.24	8	6	2	1	2.76	2	10	4	1	3.06	4	10	3	0
PRACTICAL PERIPHERALS—																										
ALL MODELS	3	4.00	3	0	0	0	4.00	3	0	0	0	4.00	3	0	0	0	3.67	2	1	0	0	4.00	3	0	0	0
PRENTICE—																										
ALL MODELS	6	3.50	3	3	0	0	2.33	0	3	2	1	2.83	1	3	2	0	2.67	2	0	4	0	2.83	1	3	2	0
RACAL MILGO—																										
9600 SERIES	11	3.09	2	8	1	0	3.00	0	11	0	0	3.09	1	10	0	0	3.00	1	9	1	0	3.18	3	7	1	0
CMS SERIES	6	3.00	0	6	0	0	3.33	2	4	0	0	3.00	2	3	0	1	3.33	4	0	2	0	3.17	2	3	1	0
COMLINK SERIES	9	3.78	7	2	0	0	2.67	0	6	3	0	3.56	6	2	1	0	3.67	6	3	0	0	3.67	6	3	0	0
MPS SERIES	3	3.67	2	1	0	0	3.33	1	2	0	0	3.67	2	1	0	0	3.67	2	1	0	0	3.67	2	1	0	0
OMNIMODE SERIES	24	3.21	6	17	1	0	3.50	13	10	1	0	3.71	17	7	0	0	3.25	11	8	5	0	3.50	12	12	0	0
OTHER	32	3.28	11	19	2	0	3.06	8	19	4	1	3.29	10	20	1	0	3.09	9	17	6	0	3.25	10	20	2	0
SUBTOTAL	85	3.28	28	53	4	0	3.16	24	52	8	1	3.40	38	43	2	1	3.22	33	38	14	0	3.36	35	46	4	0
RACAL VADIC—																										
1200 SERIES	3	3.33	1	2	0	0	3.00	1	1	1	0	3.33	1	2	0	0	3.33	1	2	0	0	3.33	1	2	0	0
2400 PA	5	2.8	1	2	2	0	3.00	1	3	1	0	3.80	4	1	0	0	3.00	1	2	1	0	3.00	1	2	1	0
2400 SERIES	9	2.89	1	7	0	1	2.22	0	4	3	2	3.22	3	5	1	0	2.78	1	5	3	0	3.00	1	7	1	0
3400 SERIES	9	3.22	3	5	1	0	2.56	1	5	1	2	3.00	2	5	2	0	2.75	2	3	2	1	3.11	2	6	1	0
VA 212	9	3.44	4	5	0	0	3.00	2	5	2	0	3.44	4	5	0	0	3.33	3	6	0	0	3.33	3	6	0	0
OTHER	29	3.21	9	17	3	0	2.79	5	14	9	1	3.31	12	15	1	1	3.00	6	18	4	1	3.07	8	16	4	1
SUBTOTAL	64	3.17	19	38	6	1	2.73	10	32	17	5	3.31	26	33	4	1	3.00	14	36	10	2	3.11	16	39	7	1
TELEBIT—																										
TRAILBLAZER	8	3.50	4	4	0	0	3.50	4	4	0	0	3.75	6	2	0	0	3.38	4	3	1	0	3.50	4	4	0	0
TIMEPLEX—																										
ALL MODELS	4	3.75	3	1	0	0	3.75	3	1	0	0	4.00	4	0	0	0	3.25	3	0	0	1	4.00	4	0	0	0
U.S. ROBOTICS—																										
COURIER 2400	15	3.87	13	2	0	0	3.60	11	2	2	0	3.80	12	3	0	0	3.53	9	5	1	0	3.80	12	3	0	0
PASSWORD	3	4.00	3	0	0	0	3.00	1	1	1	0	3.33	2	0	1	0	3.33	2	0	1	0	4.00	3	0	0	0
OTHER	4	3.40	3	1	1	0	2.40	1	0	4	0	2.80	2	1	1	1	2.20	1	1	1	2	2.80	1	2	2	0
SUBTOTAL	23	3.78	19	3	1	0	3.26	13	3	7	0	3.52	16	4	2	1	3.22	12	6	3	2	3.61	16	5	2	0
UNIVERSAL DATA SYSTEMS—																										
201/BC	6	3.20	1	4	0	0	2.40	0	2	3	0	3.20	1	4	0	0	3.20	1	4	0	0	3.20	1	4	0	0
208 A/B	17	3.50	9	6	1	0	2.88	2	11	2	1	3.50	9	6	1	0	3.38	7	8	1	0	3.44	8	7	1	0
212 A/D	8	3.50	4	4	0	0	2.63	1	4	2	1	3.38	4	3	1	0	3.13	1	7	0	0	3.38	3	5	0	0
224 A/D	3	3.33	1	2	0	0	3.00	0	3	0	0	3.33	1	2	0	0	3.00	0	3	0	0	3.00	0	3	0	0
9600 A/B	11	3.18	3	7	1	0	2.91	2	6	3	0	3.36	4	7	0	0	3.27	4	6	1	0	3.27	3	8	0	0
OTHER	22	3.09	8	8	6	0	2.64	3	11	5	3	3.41	11	9	2	0	3.05	5	12	4	0	3.14	5	15	2	0
SUBTOTAL	67	3.28	26	31	8	0	2.74	8	37	15	5	3.40	30	31	4	0	3.19	18	40	6	0	3.26	20	42	3	0
VENTEL—																										
ALL MODELS	12	3.25	4	7	1	0	2.33	1	3	7	1	3.17	4	6	2	0	2.73	2	4	5	0	2.92	2	7	3	0
ZENITH—																										
ALL MODELS	6	3.83	5	1	0	0	3.33	3	2	1	0	4.00	6	0	0	0	3.67	5	0	1	0	3.83	5	1	0	0
OTHERS & UNSPECIFIED	80	3.40	40	33	6	1	2.88	22	32	17	7	3.33	35	37	5	2	3.07	25	31	14	3	3.21	28	37	10	1
GRAND TOTAL	1,304	3.31	544	616	113	16	3.02	385	593	245	56	3.37	650	497	101	36	3.05	395	588	216	54	3.24	467	681	117	19

WEIGHTED AVERAGE (WA) IS BASED ON ASSIGNING A WEIGHT OF 4 TO EACH USER RATING OF EXCELLENT (E), 3 TO GOOD (G), 2 TO FAIR (F), AND 1 TO POOR (P).

Methodology

A questionnaire was designed and produced by Datapro's senior data communications editors and mailed in January to a selected group of subscribers to DATA COMMUNICATIONS magazine, all of whom were identified as domestic users of data communications equipment.

The subscribers were asked to fill out the forms, providing ratings and other information, and return them in a postage-paid envelope to Datapro.

Responses were disqualified whenever the vendor/model identity was omitted, user ratings were not assigned, an obvious vested interest on the part of the respondent was judged to exist, or incomprehensible or unreasonable answers were given. The remainder was shipped to DataVision Research of Princeton, N. J., for key entry and computer tabulation. Summary information was prepared in the form of totals, percentages, or weighted averages as appropriate.

Weighted averages were used to determine the ratings given by users. These were computed in the following manner. "Excellent" was weighted as 4; "Good" as 3; "Fair" as 2; and "Poor" as 1. The tallied numbers for each value were then multiplied by the corresponding weight, and the average taken by dividing the sum of the products by the total number of responses for that category.

Datapro strongly suggests that the reader use the information presented with discretion. The individual equipment ratings should not be the major consideration in making an acquisition decision. Rather, the ratings and other information should be used as guides to potential strengths and weaknesses, which may warrant further investigation in selecting the most suitable equipment for the reader's needs.

mance ratings is shown in the figure. Included are all modem vendors that garnered at least 1 percent (more than 13) of the responses.

While U.S. Robotics had earned a healthy 3.2 Overall Performance rating last year, it climbed to the top of the charts in this year's survey with 3.61. Multitech's performance also improved significantly in users' eyes, from 3.0 last year to a second-place 3.56 this year.

The individual ratings, by vendor and by specific modem model, are summarized in the table. It should be noted that the Overall Performance rating for a particular vendor is a composite average (see "Methodology") for all that vendor's modem products' ratings—leased line, dial-up, and so on. Where enough users specified a particular modem model, those ratings are included individually as well. Users seeking, say, high-speed, V.32-based, dial-up Trellis-encoding modems should compare the different vendors' ratings for that particular modem type.

For more information on the modem survey, or to obtain a copy, contact Datapro Research Corp., 1805 Underwood Blvd., Delran, N. J. 08075; telephone 609-764-0100.

David McNamara, Codex Corp., Canton, Mass.; Warren L. Henderson Jr., Henderson Communications Corp., Moreno Valley, Calif.; and C. Kenneth Miller, Concord Data Systems, Marlboro, Mass.

Measuring modems' moxie

V.32 and other high-speed modems require a special test methodology to accurately gauge their performance in a real-world environment.

Modem evaluation and testing is growing ever more complex, just as networking technology itself evolves. V.32 modems are a case in point. V.32s use echo-canceling techniques to achieve full-duplex transmission at 9.6 kbit/s over standard two-wire telephone lines. Understanding the relationship between modems and network impairments is useful because it offers insights into proper test methods and test criteria that can be applied to modem evaluations. Moreover, standardized test methods provide users with sound comparative evaluation criteria they need to select a modem to meet their application needs.

Ever since the first non-Bell modems were introduced, manufacturers have been contending with gremlins in the switched telephone network. For example, in the early 1970s, when modem manufacturers began using quadrature amplitude modulation (QAM) techniques, they discovered that a network phenomenon called phase jitter could degrade modem performance (see "Network impairments: The dark side of the force"). Phase jitter had little effect on older, less sophisticated modulation technologies such as phase-shift keying and differential phase-shift keying, but QAM was much less forgiving. Later, techniques were developed to overcome phase jitter in the recivers of QAM modems, but the solution took time.

Since the early 1970s, increased knowledge of telephone network impairments—what causes them, their statistical likelihood, and the severity of occurrences—has become a valuable tool for manufacturers in developing high-speed modems. The ability of any particular vendor's modems to perform better on actual telephone network circuits depends on the amount of real-world knowledge that was applied to the implementation of the design.

When evaluating any modem destined for operation in the PSTN, it is critical for the user to simulate the actual network as closely as possible. Otherwise, the test results may be invalid and misleading. One problem in doing this simulation is that dial lines are not controlled in the same way that leased telephone circuits are. Leased telephone circuits offer predictable bandwidth and limit the frequency and severity of major impairments. Dial lines are intended for voice communications and impairments are not controlled to levels that guarantee successful data transfer. On a dial-up line, circuit integrity changes from connection to connection with wide variations and combinations of impairments. Connection routing, too, can vary widely—depending on time of day, day of week, and end-point locations. Often a connection is routed through concatenated carriers and local loops; each has imperfections that contribute to the overall line degradation.

What are network-induced impairments, and where do they come from? How do they affect a modem's data transmission? Can the powerful digital signal processing (DSP) engines used in modern high-speed modems overcome them?

There is no simple answer to such questions. There are many types of impairments present on the switched network that can affect the echo-cancellation technology used in modern modems. Modem manufacturers are only beginning to learn about some of them. This whole problem is reminiscent of the education manufacturers received when phase jitter struck QAM modems.

Phase roll, for example, is an impairment that does not affect performance of non-echo-canceling modems, but it can strike a death blow to V.32s. Some modem vendors have incorporated phase-roll compensation capabilities in their V.32 modems to eliminate the effect phase roll has on the modem's receiver.

Dynamic range issues are also very important in echo-canceling modems. Near-end echo, in particular, can be

Network impairments: The dark side of the force

What is the relationship between modem performance and network impairments? While there are no simple answers, a user armed with an understanding of telephone network impairments can readily design modem tests that simulate real-world network conditions. Therein lies the surest way to finding the modem that works best for the user's application.

■ **Noise:** Also called white noise or Gaussian noise, it is a random, broadband interference signal often heard as a hiss or hum on the telephone line.

Cause: Telephone network digitizing electronics (quantization), circuit-to-circuit radiated interference (cross talk), and active amplifier (thermal) noise enhancement.

Effect: Though modem receivers do their best to minimize it by using optimized filter and equalizer schemes, there is no getting it out once it is in the received signal.

■ **Attenuation and delay distortion:** A linear distortion that causes nonuniform levels of signal loss and signal delay across the transmission frequency band.

Cause: N-carrier channel bank filters, transmission cable frequency characteristics, and local-loop frequency characteristics. It's the combination of these concatenated transmission elements that results in the end-to-end distortion.

Effect: Primary cause of signal dispersion, otherwise referred to as intersymbol interference. It causes the modem received signal and the echoes that need to be canceled to be dispersed in time. The primary function of the automatic adaptive equalizer in high-speed modems is to compensate for this impairment in the modem's receiver. The echo canceler must also compensate for these impairments so that it can optimally cancel the echoes.

■ **Frequency offset:** A nonlinear distortion that causes a shift in frequency of the received signal.

Cause: Carrier-system timing errors that are continuous in nature. Most prominent in N-carrier and radio microwave systems.

Effect: Modem's receiver has an offset in the resulting demodulated signal, reducing the margin of error on all signal points. Most high-speed modems have the ability to detect and compensate for this distortion.

■ **Phase jitter:** A nonlinear distortion that causes the phase of the received signal to be modulated by a periodic interference signal, often some harmonic of the local power utility a.c. frequency.

Cause: Power supply noise feed-through in active carrier system electronics. Most prominent in radio microwave carrier systems.

Effect: Modem received signal varies or wobbles around the ideal signal point. Some high-speed modem receivers implement signal processing algorithms that remove periodic phase jitter. These modems are virtually insensitive to phase jitter. Modems that do not implement such algorithms experience a reduced margin of error in the presence of phase jitter.

■ **Intermodulation distortion:** Sometimes referred to as harmonic or nonlinear distortion, intermodulation distortion causes the received signal to appear distorted at the extremes of its voltage swing and around its zero crossing.

Cause: Primarily caused by the nonuniform operation of N-carrier companders. The electronics of these systems cause a reconstruction of a compressed signal to expand nonuniformly, greater than or less than the original (precompressed) signal.

Effect: Modem receivers generally cannot compensate for this type of distortion. Some modems are less susceptible than others, depending on the modulation type and transmission bandwidth. The narrower the bandwidth, the less susceptible the modem is to this distortion.

■ **Amplitude jitter:** Also called amplitude modulation, it causes the received signal to have a periodic, time-varying amplitude level.

Cause: Residual amplitude modulation after demodulation of single-sideband amplitude modulation in carrier

---

far larger in amplitude than the received signal. For this reason, V.32 modems need to be tested with a wide range of combinations of transmit level, receive level, and local loop characteristics in order to model the varied signal-to-echo ratios met in the real world.

Dial-line surveys

But just knowing what these key impairments are and how they affect a modem is not enough. Equally important is a clear understanding of the severity and statistical rate of occurrence of each impairment on the actual switched network. How bad is "bad," and what should be the acceptable performance level? How much phase roll and noise should a modem be able to handle to be acceptable? And how does one select the proper combinations and levels when evaluating these modems?

The answers to these questions can be found in two documents: *Characterization of Subscriber Loops* for Voice and ISDN Services (1983 Subscriber Loop Survey Results), Bell Communications Research, and *1982/83 End Office Connection Study,* published under the old Bell Laboratories imprint. These two technical reports present statistical and analytical results of Bell impairment surveys of the PSTN in the continental United States. The studies provide the information that makes it possible to determine what impairment levels constitute an average line or one of poor quality.

Characterization of Subscriber Loops focuses on the local loop, which is the part of the telephone network that starts at the customer premises and ends at the local central switching office. The second document, the *End Office Connection Study,* addresses the remainder of the systems. N-carrier systems are the most common source.

Effect: Some modem receivers can adapt to and cancel this impairment. Although generally not very prevalent, amplitude jitter can significantly reduce receiver error margin.

■ **Echo:** Also referred to as reflection, this impairment occurs at multiple points in the network and causes the modem receiver to see multiple, attenuated, delayed, and distorted versions of its own transmitted and received signal.

Cause: Echo is caused by any analog impedance mismatch in the network. The largest echo with which a modem must deal is the result of imperfect impedance matching between the modem and the local loop.

Effect: Most non-echo-canceling modems experience few adverse effects from this. Echo-canceling modem performance is heavily dependent on how effectively the modem cancels the various echoes present in its received signal.

■ **Phase roll:** A recently defined impairment that causes the received echo of the modem's transmitted signal to have a time-varying phase relationship with the actual transmitted signal from which it originated.

Cause: Timing offsets between two concatenated analog systems on a connection. Very common on international and satellite links.

Effect: Some vendors of V.32 echo-canceling modems have implemented receiver algorithms that correct for this phenomenon. Without such compensation, the modem will periodically lose synchronization and require a retrain to resynchronize.

■ **Loss:** Overall signal attenuation, often referred to as 1,004-Hz loss or link loss. This impairment is not time-variable or frequency-dependent.

Cause: All analog transmission elements of the network (for example, local loop, N-carrier, radio microwave, and satellite) will introduce some loss in the end-to-end channel.

Effect: Most modems implement automatic gain-control circuitry to compensate for this impairment. However, operating performance in the presence of high loss is dependent on the modem's receive dynamic range. Although a simple impairment to describe, proper network simulation is critical to modem testing.

■ **Timing slips:** A sudden timing-delay change that can occur periodically during a call.

Cause: In telephone networks with digital backbones (T-carriers), a master clock controls the timing. When there is a call that crosses between networks, the master clocks differ and there is data buffering between the two. If a buffer over- or underflows during the time of a call, the result is a sudden time-delay change. This is most common on international calls. But it can also occur on calls within the country if, for example, the routing of the call traverses digital trunks of different carriers.

Effect: It will typically cause the modem's timing-recovery circuit to lose lock. Some modems can recover timing locks and others need to retrain to gain synchronization. Similar in effect to a massive phase hit but more likely to require retraining to recover synchronization.

■ **Transients:** Phase hits, gain hits, impulse hits, and dropouts are all forms of transient distortion. These impairments are short-term, random, and generally of large magnitude.

Cause: The sources of this class of distortion are varied. For example, phase hits are often nothing more than timing slips between two concatenated carrier systems with independent system timing sources, and impulse hits are often the result of radiated noise from older electromechanical relays and appear as clicks and pops on the telephone.

Effect: Modem receivers cannot cancel these impairments because of the unpredictable nature of their occurrence and characteristics. Transients cause bursts of errors, the duration of which is dependent on how well a modem's receiver is designed to recover from them.

network primarily comprised of the varied end-office-to-end-office transmission media such as N-carrier, radio microwave, and T-carrier sections.

Such a bifurcated model of the network has not traditionally been applied to modem testing. In the past, most modem test methods made assumptions that combined (and in some cases eliminated) the local and long-haul elements in what was perceived to be an accurate model of the network for evaluation purposes. Prior to the emergence of echo-canceling modems, such an assumption was reasonable. However, applying the bifurcated model is necessary to obtain test results that reflect actual network performance of echo-canceling modems.

So, the evaluation of high-speed dial modems is quite complex. Previously undefined impairments affecting new modem technology, the effects of combinations of impair-

ments, proper network modeling, and concrete benchmarks of measure are all crucial to obtaining credible modem performance test results. The bottom line is that any test methods employed in evaluating the performance of new high-speed dial modems must accurately model the actual public switched network. Some vendors of off-the-shelf test equipment are making progress toward this end. But the leaders of this crusade are the members of the Electronics Industry Association (EIA) technical subcommittee TR-30.3.

EIA TR-30.3 is a group representing manufacturers of modems, computers, and terminal and test equipment as well as independent consultants, representatives of government agencies, and users. The TR-30.3 subcommittee is charged by its parent committee, EIA TR-30, with the development of standards for data transmission equipment

Table 1: Network impairment combinations: The industry standard

IMPAIRMENT COMBINA-TIONS	ATTENUATION CURVE[1]	ENVELOPE DELAY DISTORTION[2]	PEAK-PEAK PHASE JITTER		INTERMODULATION DISTORTION (dB)		1,004 Hz LOSS (dB)[3]	FREQUENCY OFFSET (Hz)	NOISE LEVEL (dBrnC)[4]	32 KBIT/S CODE C (ADPCM TECHNIQUE)	ECHO[6]
			DEGREE	Hz	2ND	3RD					
1	A	1	15	20	42	40	15		40		
2	C	2	5	60	42	40	20		36		
3	B	3	10	120	40	38	26		32		
4	B	4	5	120	42	40	30	−1	30		
5	B	5	10	60	42	40	22	+1	36		
6	B	2	5	120	53	53	16		38		[5]

1. SEE INSET "A." 2. SEE INSET "B."

3. THE INPUT TO THE SIMULATOR IS A PROGRAMMED ARRANGEMENT WHERE THE RESISTOR IS SET FOR NOMINAL SIGNAL LEVEL OF −4dBm. ASSUMING −4dBm MODEM TRANSMIT LEVEL, RECEIVE 1,004 Hz SIGNAL LEVEL IS COMPUTED BY: LEVEL RECEIVED = 1,004 Hz LINE LOSS −4. THE 1,004 Hz RECEIVE SIGNAL LEVELS FOR IMPAIRMENT COMBINATIONS 1 TO 6 ARE −19, −24, −30, −34, −26, −20 dBm, RESPECTIVELY.

4. NOISE INSERTED IN ACCORDANCE WITH EIA-496-A, SECTION 5.4.2.1 SHALL BE MEASURED WITH A C-NOTCHED WEIGHTED FILTER. SIGNAL-TO-NOISE RATIO (SNR) AS RELATED TO THIS TABLE IS DEFINED AS THE 1,004 Hz TONE TO C-NOTCHED NOISE RATIO. ASSUMING −4dBm TRANSMIT LEVEL, SNR MAY BE COMPUTED BY: SNR = (90 NOISE LEVEL −1,004 Hz LOSS −4) dB. THE SNRs FOR IMPAIRMENT COMBINATIONS 1 TO 6 ARE 31, 30, 28, 26, 28, AND 32 dB, RESPECTIVELY.

5. THIS TEST CHANNEL IS UNDER STUDY AT THIS TIME. IF IT BECOMES NECESSARY TO ENSURE OPERATION IN THE PRESENCE OF ADPCMs, THE TEST SETUP SHALL REQUIRE THAT ADPCMs BE INSERTED IN THE TEST CIRCUIT AFTER THE IMPAIRMENTS SPECIFIED IN THE TABLE. THE ADPCMs USED SHOULD BE IN CONFORMANCE WITH THE STANDARD DEVELOPED IN ANSI COMMITTEE T1. THIS WILL ONLY APPLY TO CATEGORY 1 SERVICE AS DEFINED IN THE AMERICAN NATIONAL STANDARD 32 KBIT/S ADPCM TANDEM CODING LIMITS.

6. THE SPECIFICATION OF THE PARAMETER IS UNDER STUDY.

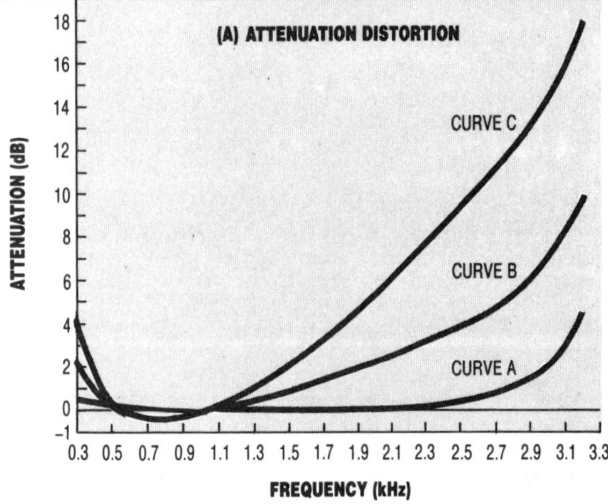

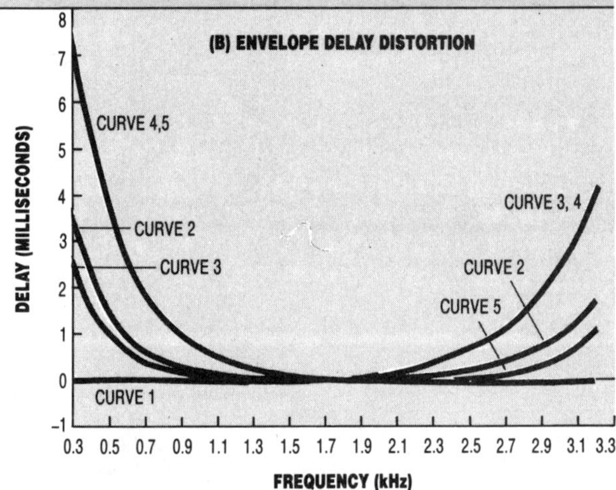

at the telecommunication network interface. At the request of the American National Standards Institute (ANSI) and the Federal Communications Commission (FCC), the TR-30.3 technical subcommittee has been working on the development of a modem interface and performance criteria standard since early 1984.

EIA has recently published the second release in a series of technical standards on modem interface and performance: EIA-496-A. The standard covers the technical requirements of Part 68 of the FCC rules, relating to the switched network interface as well as data transmission evaluation criteria for modems intended for operation over the PSTN. The latter set of criteria specifies a series of test channels that can provide a prediction of the potential performance of a modem on the PSTN.

EIA-496-A is the first step on the road to realizing an industry-accepted test methodology that addresses the problems of impairments on the PSTN. While it does not now solve all problems, it does provide a solid foundation that one day will yield common, comparative test results indicative of a modem's true performance over the PSTN. At a minimum, EIA-496-A is an industry-accepted test methodology for impairments such as noise, phase jitter, amplitude and delay distortion, intermodulation distortion, loss, and frequency offset. Work is still needed to define formats for simulated data transmission as well as methods for evaluating modems employing internal error correction and data compression schemes.

Table 1 details the impairment combinations chart used in this standard. Table 2 is a summary of the severity of impairment levels of Table 1 when compared to the statistical data in the Bell surveys. The data in Table 2 is expressed as the percent of lines that will exhibit a given level of impairment or less. Thus a 97 percent noise level used in impairment combination 3 indicates that no more than 3 percent of all lines will exhibit noise worse than that level. Hence, that level of impairment covers 97 percent of the lines. Generally, the higher the percentage, the worse the impairment.

Notice that in Table 2 each impairment combination stresses one key impairment while applying moderate to average levels in the other impairment areas. This is intentionally done to provide a broad coverage of worst-

496-A and are currently under study in EIA TR-30.3. These include 32-kbit/s adaptive differential pulse code modulation (ADPCM) coding, echo distortion, transients, local-loop simulation, and phase roll. The study group is targeting a third release of EIA-496 that will address part or all of these impairments in the same fashion as EIA-496-A.

Performance criteria

Now that the industry experts have established a baseline of accepted standard test methodology and work is progressing to address the outstanding performance criteria, how can users translate baseline studies into measures of performance to test modems? What is meant by measure of performance? Should such measures be used to determine how well a modem performs in the presence of any one of the established test conditions?

The answer is that there is no single correct measure to use. However, the measure employed must appropriately

Table 2: Impairment combinations: How they affect the network

IMPAIRMENT COMBINA-TIONS	ATTENUATION CURVE[1] LOW/HIGH	ENVELOPE DELAY DISTORTION[1] LOW/HIGH	PEAK-PEAK PHASE JITTER		INTERMODULATION DISTORTION (dB)		1,004 Hz LOSS (dB)	FREQUENCY OFFSET (Hz)	NOISE LEVEL (dBrnC)	32 KBIT/S CODE C (ADPCM TECHNIQUE)	ECHO[2]
			DEGREE	Hz	2ND	3RD					
1	5%	NONE	99%	20	90%	90%	MEAN		90%		
2	95/99%	MEAN	85%	60	90%	90%	75%		95%		
3	MEAN	23/99%	98%	120	97%	95%	99%		97%		
4	MEAN	99%	85%	120	90%	90%	95.5%	99.5%	99.5%		
5	MEAN	99/20%	98%	60	90%	90%	90%	99.5%	97%		
6	MEAN	MEAN	85%	120	MEAN	MEAN	MEAN		85%		2

1. LOW/HIGH REFERS TO THE LOW-BAND/HIGH-BAND DISTORTION FOR THAT PARTICULAR TEST LINE.
2. THIS TEST CHANNEL IS UNDER STUDY.
3. THE SPECIFICATION FOR THIS PARAMETER IS UNDER STUDY.

case conditions of each impairment in the presence of otherwise average line conditions and thereby identify the weaknesses a particular modem implementation may exhibit. Since not all modems are created equal, presenting the data in this way enables the evaluator to identify the potential problem areas a modem will experience on the actual switched network in the United States (see: "V.32 modems are breaking through the echo barrier," DATA COMMUNICATIONS, April 1988, p. 187).

Users that want to make best use of the impairment combinations charts must be familiar with their own application and be able to duplicate the environment for their own tests. The values and percentages quoted in the Table 1 insets are actual voice-frequency measurements. Throughput or error-rate effects on transmitted data are not specified for any of the EIA impairment combinations. This leaves the evaluator in a very subjective position, thus reinforcing the need for in-depth knowledge of application-specific testing needs.

Several of the key impairments are not covered in EIA-

reflect the application for which the test is being performed.

Accurate modeling is the key to sound test results. To obtain a credible measure of performance, it is critical to model the application as closely as possible. Ideally, users would run the actual application under a variety of test cases and determine how well it meets their needs. Often, though, this is not possible. In such situations, models must be used to simulate the characteristics of the user's applications. There are four useful measures typically employed in modeling performance: bit error rate, block error rate, throughput/file transfer, and turnaround time. Each of these measures has value when applied correctly.

Bit error rate information has traditionally been used in evaluating older modems, but it is not a sufficient test value in modern modems. This is true because modern modems use multidimensional modulation schemes. Trellis coding, for example, while improving overall performance, exhibits an error-multiplication phenomenon. This phenomenon causes singular telephone-line bit errors to result in multiple errors at the output of the modem's receiver. Since most communications applications run some form of block-mode error correction, a single bit error has the same effect on performance as do several bit errors in a short string. Hence, the multiplication of errors does not severely affect the application performance, and is not a good representation of the expected performance. For this reason, bit-error-rate performance measurements are seldom used in evaluating modems that employ Trellis-coded modulation, as do V.32 units.

Block error rate, however, is a representative measure of performance for the modern modem environment since it results in a measure of the percentage of blocks transmitted and received error free. This measure can be related directly to the percent efficiency of the link under test when the block size employed in the test is the same or close to that used in the application being modeled. In order to obtain true block-transfer efficiency, this test should be performed without employing any form of error correction.

Throughput is the best measure of performance for applications employing modems with integral error-correction schemes. Because this is a relatively new performance measure for modems, it reflects the importance of recent popular error-protection protocols such as MNP (Microcom Networking Protocol).

The recent passage of V.42, a CCITT recommendation for error correction in modems, further enhances the importance of throughput. No errors will occur in error-protected modems, though throughput, expressed as bits per second or characters per second, declines under adverse network conditions.

Turnaround time is also a useful measure of performance. It is used to determine how quickly a modem can return a response from the remote end of the communications link. This measure is valuable in determining how well the modem will perform in interactive user applications. It is particularly important when evaluating modems intended for deployment in an asynchronous application where the link-error control, such as V.42 or MNP, is used and the host echoes each character.

Each measure of performance—bit error rate, block error rate, throughput, and turnaround time—is useful to measure modem performance. The EIA, ANSI, and FCC representatives, as well as major equipment manufacturers, recognize the value of standardizing modem evaluation methodology. Repeatability and consistency in the measurement of performance are necessary to provide users with data representing true modem performance. Standardization of the test methods and criteria is the only means that users have to ensure that the data used in their decisions is accurate, comparable, and representative of real-world conditions. ■

David McNamara is senior product planning manager for high-speed dial modems at the Codex Corp., Canton, Mass. C. Kenneth Miller is the chairman and chief technology officer of Concord Data Systems, Marlboro, Mass., a firm he founded in 1981. Warren L. Henderson Jr. is president of Henderson Communications Corp., Moreno Valley, Calif., a firm specializing in modem evaluation and testing.

Andres Llana Jr., Vermont Studies Group Inc., Westover, Vt.

The pluses and minuses of the high-end FEPs

A consultant compares the networking capabilities and technological advances of front-end processors from IBM, NCR Comten, and Amdahl.

Communications processors have been evolving more slowly than other networking devices, but they are catching up. Improvements in front-end communications processors have extended the ability of network managers to augment the performance of their networks: interconnecting larger user populations with greater numbers of communications lines and integrating multiple computers and diverse networks into a single viable network. Indeed, technology advances are increasingly making the front-end processor (FEP) the focus of network management.

Three of the most mentioned players in the FEP marketplace are IBM, NCR Comten (St. Paul, Minn.), and Amdahl (Sunnyvale, Calif.). Comten pioneered the programmable FEP with its 1972 version of the 3670, which was followed by the 3690. The most recent products to emerge in this rapid evolution in communications processor technology have been Comten's 56X5 series, IBM's 3745, and Amdahl's 4745. Among their prominent features (detailed later): IBM's 3745 Model 410 contains two redundant Model 210s; Comten's 5675 supports up to 1,024 lines; Amdahl's 4745 provides multilevel component backup. All offer performance levels above the IBM 3705 and 3725 (see "The complexities of choosing a front-end processor," DATA COMMUNICATIONS, January 1984). IBM has announced the lower-end 3745 Model 130, 150, and 170, which compare more closely to Amdahl's offerings. (Where pertinent, Amdahl 4745 features are included in this FEP comparison. For a summary of its configuration and capacity, see "The Amdahl 4745.")

Performance characteristics

The performance characteristics of a front-end processor become critical as the network expands in size and complexity. Using the Comten 3695 as a benchmark with a relative performance value of 1.0, the Comten 5675 has a relative performance value of 4.5, while the IBM 3745 Models 210/410 have a relative performance value of 2.0. Architectural differences among the processors affect their performance. The Amdahl 4745-210 has a relative performance of 1.4 compared to the IBM 3745. (Relative performance values are based on the results of Comten and Amdahl benchmark programs.) The relative performance figures are based on a maximum number of Network Control Program/Synchronous Data Link Control (NCP/SDLC) transactions for a given time period and a common workload. Actual performance characteristics in a specific user network will depend on such factors as configuration, traffic type, and backup requirements.

The 3745 Model 410 is essentially two independent computers that function as two Model 210s. The two independent central control units (CCUs) are viewed by mainframe-resident Virtual Telecommunications Access Method software as two distinct subareas. The Model 410 has an upper limit of 256 lines, which is scheduled to grow to 448 by the end of 1989.

Although the configuration of a Model 410 consists of two 210s, its performance is not enhanced beyond that of a single 210. Therefore, the evaluation of the 410 must be based upon the performance of the 210.

The design of the 410 is such that the processors function with one CCU on standby and one on active. Thus, each CCU in a Model 410 has a predefined upper limit of 256 lines.

In contrast, the Comten 5675 is architecturally a single processor providing more resources, such as larger memory, greater cache memory, and more lines, translating into more network options (such as increased sharing of line-termination communications—discussed later). Specific design characteristics of the Comten 5675 contribute directly to its relative performance advantage. For example, the Comten 56X5 series separates its CPU physically and logically from the I/O control subsystem (see the later discussion of the Universal Communications Adapter). The Comten FEP can be configured with up to 16 Mbytes of memory, while the IBM 3745 is limited to 8 Mbytes (per CCU) on-line at a time. The Comten 5675 can support multiple NCPs, which would contain the size of a multinode network by reducing the communications complexity between nodes and enhancing the routing capabilities. In this case, the number of routes between nodes would be lowered, making switching more efficient.

The IBM 3745 supports multiple NCPs by having each 210 unit loaded with a different NCP version. The Amdahl 4745 can load more than one NCP version. The efficiency of supporting multiple NCPs is apparent when considering the case of an NCP release that falls. With the earlier NCP release (as backup) loaded, switching to it promptly — rather than having to load it — saves production time.

Communications with hosts

The IBM 3745 can effectively support up to 256 lines (per on-line CCU, with the other CCU as backup); the Comten 5575, up to 1,024 lines; the Amdahl 4745, up to 256 lines. In addition, the line-configuration rules for the IBM 3745 limit various line permutations potentially important to the network planner. For example, to support the attachment of a token ring LAN, the IBM 3745 must be configured at the factory with special token ring LAN adapters, which are used in conjunction with the Line Interface Coupler (LIC) units. These are plug-in cards that are communications interfaces (refer to Fig. 2). However, the rules for the 3745 state that if token ring adapters are configured, the user is limited to only four additional scanners (rather than eight) to support the LICs. (The scanner is the interface between the CCU and the LIC — refer to Fig. 2.) In such a configuration, up to 64 lines (9.6 kbit/s each) could be lost to the network planner — one token ring adapter replaces two scanners or 16 lines.

The IBM 3745 scanner architecture has limitations dependent upon the "weight" of active lines. For example, any combination of 56-kbit/s LIC 3 and 256-kbit/s LIC 4b lines can be placed on a scanner; however, only one 256-kbit/s line can operate at a time. (LIC 3 and LIC 4b are IBM product names for its Line Interface Couplers that operate at 56 and 256 kbit/s, respectively.) The Comten 5675 has the capability, through its Universal Communications Adapter (UCA) technology, to support multiple eight simplex (or four duplex) 256-kbit/s lines operating at the same time.

Although the IBM 3745-410 can connect up to 16 (channel-attached) hosts, only eight are operational at a time (the capacity of each of the 3745-210s). In comparison, the Comten 5675 can link up to 16 hosts and, the Amdahl 4745, eight.

Both the Comten 5675 and the Amdahl can support host-attachment through a 3-Mbyte/s multiplexer that has a distance limitation of about 200 feet. However, a recent 4.5-Mbyte/s multiplexer attachment for the IBM 3745 extends the distance of the FEP from 200 feet to 400 feet (61 meters to 122 meters). IBM's higher distance limit, rather than the higher data rate, is the significant point here.

The IBM 3745 can link up to eight token ring LANs, but not as a field upgrade. Amdahl says that its 4745 should have token ring adapters by May 1990. The Comten 5675 provides direct connection to token rings through the release of its Advanced Communications Function/Network Control Program (ACF/NCP) 4.2 software and two new LAN "platforms" (hardware modules), which are its Network Interface Adapter and the Token Ring Interface Module (TRIM). (IBM has the equivalent with its token ring adapter.) The Comten 5675 can connect up to 64 token rings and the TRIMs, like other line interface units, can be installed in the field. The Comten token ring connection enables diagnostic data and network statistics to reach an IBM NetView operator; the ACF/NCP 4.2 software is compatible with NetView Releases 1.0 and 2.0.

The IBM 3745 has NetView support. Amdahl says it plans to offer NetView support for its 4745.

The IBM, Comten, and Amdahl units can all work with X.25 equivalently. (IBM's and Comten's X.25 support is especially notable in Europe.) The 3745 uses the NCP Packet Switching Interface (NPSI), a series of programs supported under ACF/NCP that provides an X.25 interface to non-SNA terminals. The 5675 X.25 Version 2 software offers a package similar to NPSI. In addition, the Comten

---

The Amdahl 4745

The IBM 3745 and the Comten 5675 typify high-end front-end processors (FEPs). However, the preponderance of networks are still supported by a single FEP or two smaller FEPs. The Amdahl 4745 is in many ways similar to the IBM 3745 or Comten 56X5 machines, but is targeted at the midrange 3725 and 3705 markets. To compete in this market, Amdahl has looked to a different set of features than either IBM or Comten. While the Amdahl 4745 is price-competitive with the lower- and midrange IBM FEPs, the device is also meant to compete against 3745-like processors.

Amdahl's Control Program Migration feature can run native Network Control Program (NCP) Version 4 and Version 5, whereas the 3745 will run only NCP Version 5. This capability allows the FEP to keep two program generations operating, so that users can fall back to NCP Version 4 if a problem arises with NCP Version 5.

Amdahl's Integrated Switching Architecture (ISA) provides multilevel component backup as well as multiprocessor backup. ISA backs up the FEP's Central Control Unit and main storage, Line Interface Couplers, scanners, channel adapters, buses, and power supplies. In addition, a line-switching capability operates similar to a matrix switch: Lines can be switched from on-line to standby by the maintenance and operation subsystem operator.

The Amdahl 4745 can support up to 16 lines at 256 kbit/s operating at 80 percent utilization while the IBM 3745 supports up to 36 lines at 56 kbit/s, also operating at 80 percent utilization.

software includes Advanced X.25 Connection Services (AXCS), which provides this XI (X.25 Interconnection) capability and allows users to interconnect diverse types of equipment in a multivendor network. Further, Comten's X.25 Version 2 software offers support for 14 different packet-switching networks, among them Canada's Datapac, West Germany's Datex-P, the Netherlands' DN-1, France's Transpac, the U.K.'s UKPSS, and the U.S.'s Telenet and Tymnet. The Amdahl 4745 can run native NCP software, supporting both NPSI and XI.

Interconnecting non-SNA terminals has traditionally been unsupported in an SNA network (such flexibility is apparently contrary to IBM's marketing strategy). However, the IBM 3745, operating with XI Version 2 as a resident module running in the CCU, will support some non-SNA data terminal equipment (DTE) via an X.25 interface.

The Comten unit supports the connection of non-SNA terminals to IBM hosts, the connection of SNA terminals to non-IBM hosts, or a combination of both.

In recent years many large-scale SNA users have overcome the non-SNA terminal problem by employing protocol converters in conjunction with their LICs. The Comten 5675 provides an Integrated Protocol Converter (IPC) as one of the interface cards supported by the UCA subsystem. The IPC interface on the UCA permits direct attachment of asynchronous terminals and microcomputers. To the host computer, the IPC appears as an IBM 3274 cluster controller, enabling any number of non-SNA DTEs to be connected to an SNA network. Amdahl has no equivalent integrated device.

Migration from the IBM 3705/3725 presents an additional problem to the configuration planner. Since the IBM 3745 has been designed as a totally new product with no upward migration from the earlier IBM 3705/25, the user cannot use LICs and cabling from the older units. By comparison, the Comten 5675 is upwardly compatible from the company's 3690 line, with complete interchangeability between the communications components, including line-termination equipment such as Modem Interface Modules (MIMs).

As for Amdahl, there is some limited upward-migration capability among the low-end FEP models.

High-speed carrier

The IBM 3745 can accept T1 (the 1.544-Mbit/s rate is sometimes called the aggregate) through its scanners: up to 16 lines, with eight active at any one time. Fractional T1 support is possible through third-party T1 multiplexers. Warning to network managers: Be aware that T1-carrier buffer sizing and its memory demands can lower overall machine performance. For each high-speed scanner configured, 16 lines (9.6 kbit/s each) are lost from the configuration.

The Comten 5675 currently supports direct attachment of T1 through a user-supplied T1 multiplexer. Comten has announced the capability of direct termination of 24 T1

lines. The Amdahl 4745 is expected to have T1 adapters by May 1990.

T1 support via scanners, multiplexers, or adapters is all basically the same technique. The differences are in the vendors' terminology.

NCR Comten, IBM, and Amdahl all have announced plans to develop ISDN interfaces.

The IBM 3745 is configured with two sets of buses: Group 1 and Group 2. These serve as the main route to the CCU, attaching channel adapters and communications line adapters. The bus group forms the connection between the host and any attached remote users. An IBM 3745 Model 410, running a single NCP, with one CCU active and another acting as a hot standby, can switch only bus groups; individual lines cannot be switched between CCUs. Isolation of a group of lines from the rest, and enabling operation of both the switched and unswitched lines (as done with the Comten 5675), facilitates troubleshooting for the network manager.

In the hot-standby mode, the alternate processor is loaded and running. When the maintenance and operation subsystem (MOSS) detects a hardware or software failure in the active CCU, the bus group is switched to the backup CCU. However, sessions can be lost in this process, and users will have to reestablish their applications sessions. (With either the IBM 3725 or 3705, backup necessitates an additional, physically separate unit. Neither is supported by an equivalent of a MOSS. Therefore, backup is more primitive than with the 3745.)

The Comten 5675 provides flexible backup and switching capabilities through the physical and logical separation between the CPU and communications controllers. This approach allows two communications processors to share the same UCA with up to eight communications controllers, so that, for example, there can be two active and two backup paths between communications processors.

Communications Base (CB) line adapters support the termination of 16 lines, so that groups of 16 or fewer lines can be switched between communications processors. In the event of a communications processor failure, more options are available for line reconfiguration. If an active computer goes down, communications lines in multiples of 16 can be switched to a backup computer via the UCA. In effect, this provides backup for every component in the network. In addition to providing backup, the model-independence of the communications equipment permits users to test new software and hardware by gradually migrating lines between production and test processors. The Comten unit's line-switching flexibility makes the 5675 superior to the others in backup. The Amdahl 4745 supports twin backup, dual backup, and hot standby.

Network restoral is a critical function in any large and

T1-carrier buffer sizing and its memory demands can lower 3745 performance.

complex network. When the IBM 3745 Model 410 is operating in standby mode, only one NCP is active while the second CCU is waiting as backup. In this scenario, the hard disk contains the NCP program generation (gen) for the second CCU and is used in case of a total failure.

The hard disk on the IBM 3745 is a 45-Mbyte unit, divided into 22.5 Mbytes for each CCU. There is a fixed amount of storage available to support NCP Loads, main-storage dumps, and maintenance files.

In contrast, the Comten 5675 has an 80-Mbyte hard disk, which can support up to 16 load modules as well as three main-storage dumps. In addition, there is a Comten service subsystem, residing on its own hard disk, that provides a function similar to that of the IBM 3745 MOSS. The Comten's larger disk capacity provides the capability to try new gens in a test situation with rapid fallback to the original gen if trouble develops. This expanded capability also makes it possible to readily run several different networks at different times of the day—for example, interactive ones during the day and batch ones at night.

The Amdahl 4745 network recovery operates in a manner similar to IBM 4745's.

Redundancy

Both the IBM 3745 and the Comten 5675 provide a certain level of power backup. The 3745 provides distributed power supplies throughout the device: a redundant backup. The Amdahl 4745 uses similar techniques.

The Comten 5675 manages power backup with redundancy in the principle power components. The 5675 houses multiple power regulators—if there is one component failure, there is sufficient power for the entire unit to continue operation. Such a failure would be detected by the service subsystem and logged for immediate operator intervention. Full network redundancy is established through the application of the Comten UCAs and CBs, allowing multiple communications processors to share the same UCAs. If an active communications processor fails, its CB-attached lines can be switched to backups through a secondary switching path. In effect, this provides for continual backup of the network.

In contrast, switching of line groups is not supported in the 3745. When switching to the standby 210 unit, all the lines must be transferred from the suspect 210.

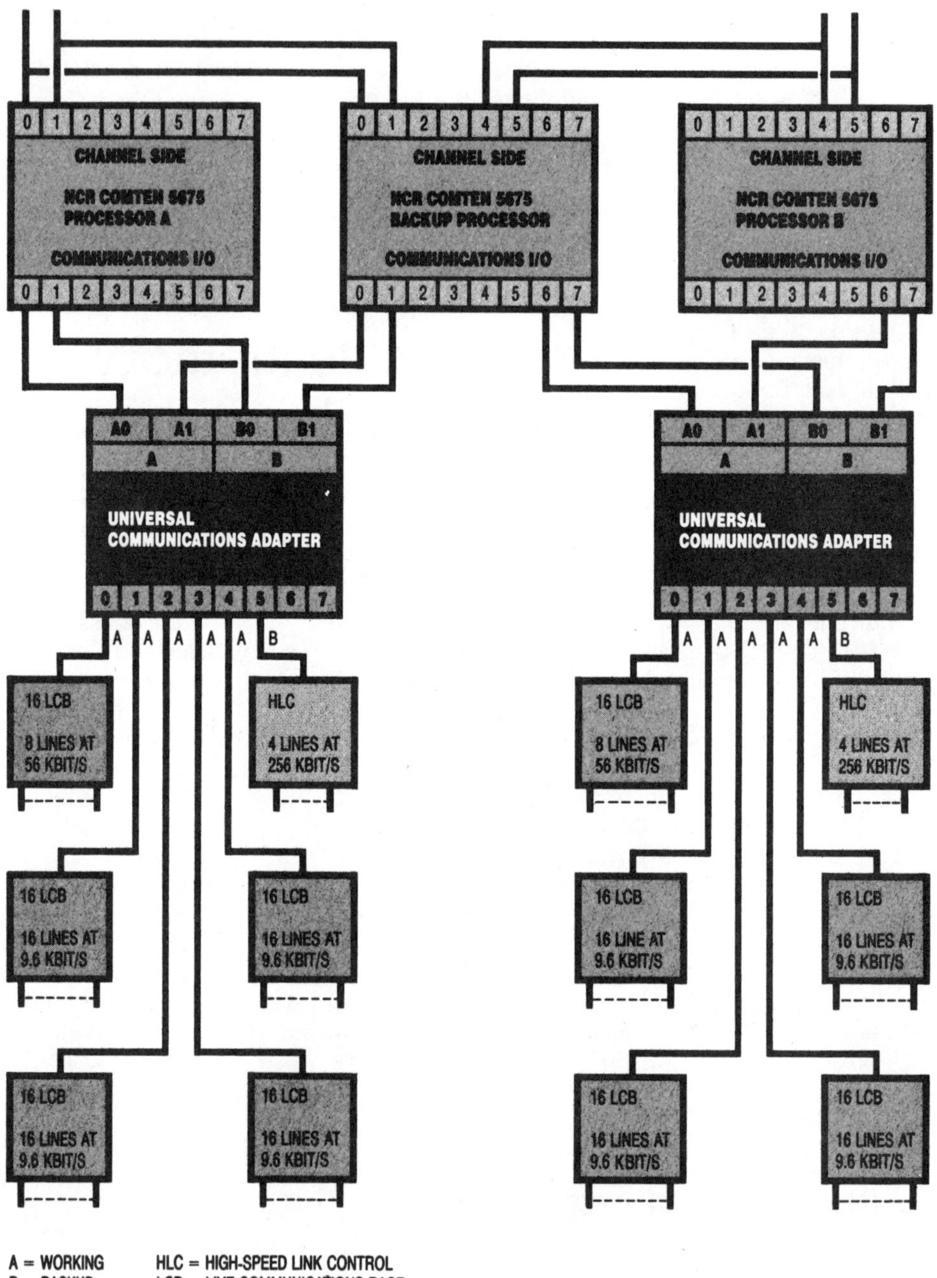

1. Hot standby plus two. *An NCR Comten configuration supporting multiple hosts has three communications processors—two are operational and one is a hot standby for backup. At the processors' channel side there are eight ports, each can support a separate host.*

Figure 1 shows an NCR Comten configuration supporting multiple hosts. Notice the physical separation—up to 100 feet (about 30 meters)—of the communications processors from the UCA, an important element in the redundancy of the Comten communications architecture. This configuration shows two operating processors, with one hot standby as a backup. Note that at the processor's channel side, there are eight ports that can support up to eight separate hosts. Each host channel is attached to an IBM channel adapter (not shown).

At the processor's "COMM I/O" side, the eight communications I/O ports are associated with the shared UCA. Up to 1,024 (8 × 128) lines can be attached through these devices. Aside from its contributing to the FEP's backup capabilities, the UCA provides convenient installation where access to the telecommunications demarcation point is limited.

The UCA can support a backup communications processor through two levels of switching. Typically, the resources of the UCA would be shared across several devices using two active and two backup paths to achieve redundancy and load sharing. Several line-connection strategies can be employed. A high-speed link controller can connect to four 256-kbit/s lines while interfacing to one channel on a UCA. In addition, 16 LCBs can link multiples of up to 16 lines at 9.6 kbit/s or eight at 56 kbit/s. IPCs configured at eight, 16, or 32 lines could also be connected through the UCA.

In this scenario (Fig. 1), if processor A were down,

---

2. Dual backup. *Here, a dual IBM 3745 Model 410 configuration has both units (A and B) provided with equally divided resources. Each Central Control Unit has a complete* bus group with access to and control over four of the eight channel adapters for host connections and four of the eight I/O communications adapters.

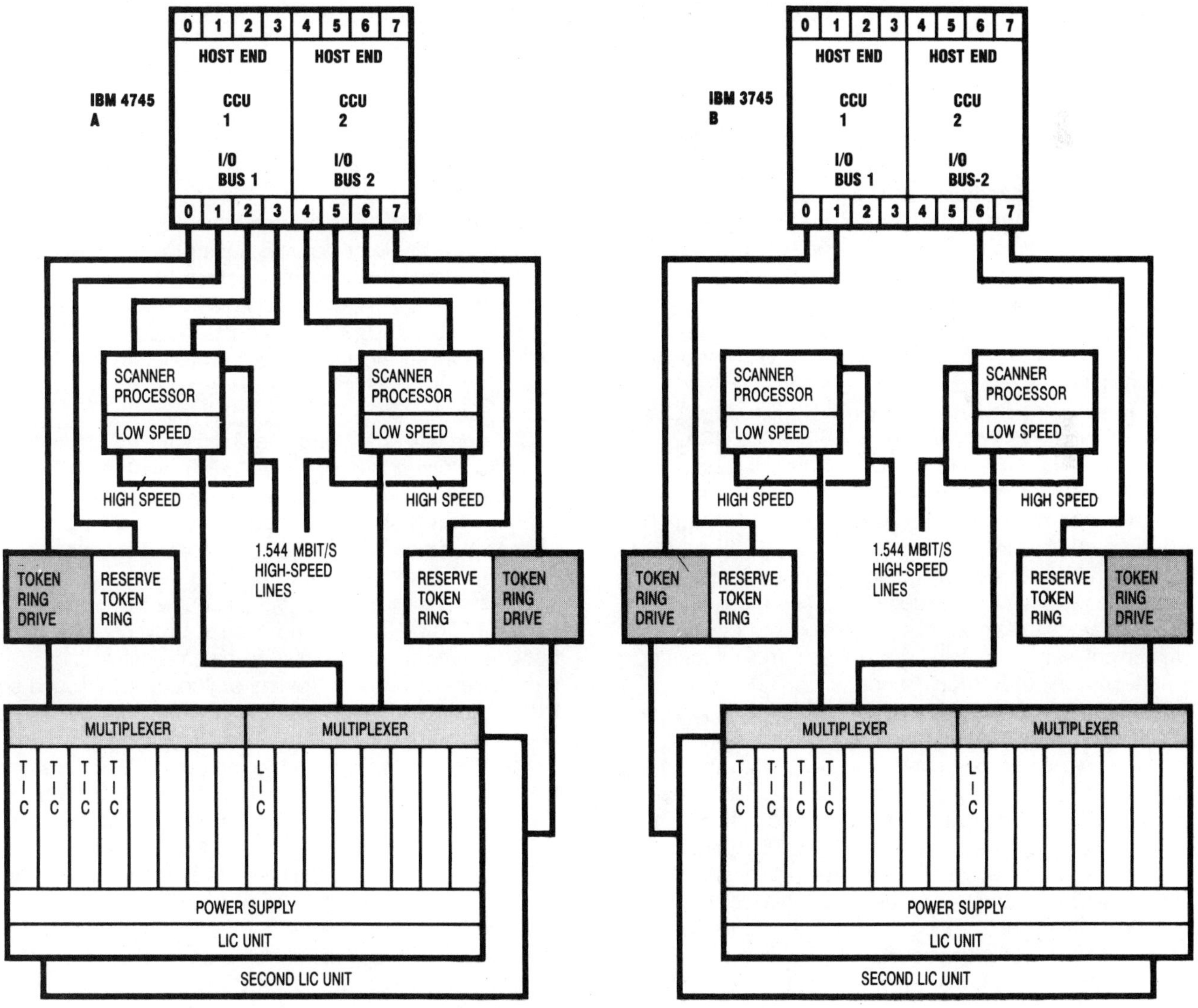

processor B would remain active and the backup would take over for A. Conversely, if B failed, the A unit would remain active and the backup unit would become the B unit. If both A and B were down, then the backup could conceivably assume the loads of A and B.

Figure 2 shows a dual IBM 3745 Model 410. Note that both units A and B have equally divided resources. Each CCU has a complete bus group with access to and control over four of the eight channel adapters for host connections and four of the eight I/O communications adapters. In this example, token ring adapters have been built in, and two LIC units are each configured to support 32 lines at 19.2 kbit/s each, or 64 at 9.6 kbit/s. In addition, there are eight token ring interface couplers (TICs), four in each LIC unit plus spares. These occupy the space for 64 low-speed lines, a limitation that must be taken into account when planning network capacity. Not shown is the LIC unit needed to support a T1 carrier.

More line capacity can be achieved by adding 3746-All, A12, L13, and L14 expansion cabinet units to house additional channel adapters, scanner processors, and LICs. These would bring the line capacity of the 3745-410 up to 512 lines, less the 64 line spaces occupied by the token ring adapters. Hence, line capacity would be limited to 224 ([512 − 64] ÷ 2) lines per CCU.

However, within this 224-line limitation, any number of 256-kbit/s lines can be attached, with the proviso that only one 256-kbit/s line can be active at one time within a scanner. In addition, unlike the shared UCA and the CBs operating within the Comten unit, the IBM 3745 LIC units must be attached directly to a 3745 base cabinet and are not relocatable. What this means in the event of a host failure is that communications lines on the IBM 3745 cannot be individually switched.

An IBM 3745 can be configured to operate in either a twin dual mode or a twin standby mode. As shown (Fig. 2), the CCUs are standalone separate nodes and do not communicate with each other except as remote nodes on an SNA network. In twin dual mode, each CCU runs separate, independent NCPs, with each CCU acting as one SNA subarea. In this mode, one CCU in each of the processors would contain one active NCP, while the second CCU would contain a copy of the first and would assume control in the event of a failure. Upon failure, the MOSS would record the failure and instruct the hard disk to load the other processor. At the same time, lines would be switched to the other CCU, either automatically or by operator intervention, and the second CCU would assume control of the network. The hot-standby backup bus groups—not individual buses—can be switched between CCUs.

Operating both IBM 3745-410s in twin backup mode allows the system programmer to allocate resources supporting critical applications across several active CCUs. In the event of failure, some or all of the critical lines could be assumed by one of the active CCUs. In the example, lines in CCU1 unit A could be transferred to CCU2 unit B while lines in CCU2 unit B could be transferred to CCU1 in unit B. By carefully allocating communications lines across the four CCUs, the network manager could provide backup support. In addition, lines could be manually removed and reconnected to a functioning CCU. With shared communications resources, the process of reallocating lines to a functioning communications processor becomes less cumbersome, with less chance of session loss.

All three examined FEPs support the latest versions of VTAM and NCP. In this writer's opinion, IBM does not have an edge in this market. The IBM 3745, with two processors in the same cabinet, presents the idea of replacing older FEPs on a two-for-one basis. For example, a user with an IBM 3705 and an IBM 3725 could replace both of these machines with one IBM 3745. Such a strategy is attractive since it reduces the costs for equipment, maintenance, and software licensing fees.

However, users contemplating the support of multiple hosts with a single communications processor, which contains internal backup, may actually be at the very limit of their network's backup support. Obviously, the IBM 3745 would be able to support two hosts, as could a Comten 5675. However, the issues are then redundancy and load management, which in turn raise the issue of the capacity to support demand.

Compared to employing dual 3725s, the IBM-stated 1.6 processor-power gain of the IBM 3745 over the 3725 might not be sufficient to support an expanding network. However, the buyer should be made aware of IBM's plans to phase out support of the 3725—similar to what happened to the 3705—in the next two or three years.

Installations equipped with two coupled or cross-connected FEPs could use load-sharing to smooth out traffic between networked processors. In some installations, there might even be a degree of line switching established so that the full performance of both communications processors is required during certain peak traffic periods.

Therefore, for example, replacing two FEPs with a single IBM 3745 is not always advisable. A 3745-410 might not meet the two-for-one replacement needs, since the second CCU would be required for hot standby. This would make it difficult to achieve the same performance level found with two separate communications processors. ∎

Andres Llana Jr. received a BS in biology from Temple University in Philadelphia and is a graduate of the U.S. Army Signal School and of the Command and General Staff College. In his 30-year career he has been a network planner for the U.S. Army, General Electric, and RCA. He serves on the advisory board for Datapro Management of Telecommunications.

> # Installations with coupled or cross-connected FEPs could use load-sharing or smooth traffic.

Edwin E. Mier, editor at large, DATA COMMUNICATIONS

Adding to your net worth with T1-to-LAN devices

Falling T1 prices, LANs sprouting up everywhere — and users carping for connectivity. The bottom line? Consider the wealth of new LAN bridges and routers built just for T1.

When the battery of leased phone lines that linked its dispersed Ethernets in southern California couldn't handle the growing traffic load anymore, communications management at Hughes Aircraft decided to upgrade to 56-kbit/s digital connections. To their surprise, it turned out that 56 kbit/s was not enough for several of the critical LAN-to-LAN junctures.

"The broadcast messages upon start-up would saturate [a 56-kbit/s link], so we didn't have any throughput," says Tom Nakamura, product manager for Hughes's engineering design network. "For some of our sites, 256 kbit/s seemed to be the minimal acceptable," he adds. Now Hughes has four T1s, each spanning 20 to 40 miles, that link four Ethernets at dispersed sites around Los Angeles.

Hughes's experience is typical of what a growing number of communications managers are facing: excessively long user response times across inter-LAN links. This degradation is related to ever-increasing LAN-to-LAN traffic — especially multiple, concurrent file transfers — and to throughput bottlenecks at many points in end-to-end paths. These changing traffic patterns and intractable bottlenecks result in lost packets, retransmissions caused by time-outs, and in some cases, major congestion in wide-area links.

By definition, LANs are geographically restrictive. And when the distance between LANs exceeds the reach of the LAN technology employed (ranging from a few hundred meters for coaxial or twisted-pair baseband transmission to dozens of kilometers using broadband radio-frequency modulation), a mix of data-transmission technologies — local and long-haul — is inevitable.

The demand for equipment to build wide-area connections between similar and dissimilar LANs has fostered a booming industry (see "Connecting nets, a growth business," DATA COMMUNICATIONS, Industry Watch, July 1989). Indeed, the estimated $115 million being spent this year for so-called remote bridges is more than double last year's

sales for such devices, which was double the previous year's. And another doubling, to $230 million in annual sales, is projected within the next three years.

Which LAN-linking technology a user selects — satellite, phone line, or some other — depends on distance and bandwidth requirements. For its ubiquity, however, and because rights-of-way tend to run out before the distance limitations of the LAN are reached, most users have turned to the public telephone network for bridging facilities.

While a number of futuristic metropolitan area network proposals and prototypes have been floated, the choices available to most users are limited to currently tariffed offerings: leased lines and digital services — including T1. In fact, an estimated one-third of remote bridges now shipped are configured for interfacing to a T1 facility (as opposed to other, lower-speed phone-line and digital-service interfaces), and that figure is growing.

Two ways to go

There are two main methods used today to get data from, say, an Ethernet out over a T1 and back onto another, remote, Ethernet. The most prevalent involves a remote bridge that "extends" a LAN out over the T1 in a data-link, Layer 2, sense only. The bridge makes two LANs function as if they were a single LAN. The other approach is to use a "router," which segregates T1-linked LANs according to routing protocols, as well as physically. This significant distinction is discussed more later.

Though many companies have taken the T1   LAN plunge and many more are poised to, establishing high-speed wide-area connections is not trivial. For starters, matching the speed differences between a 1.544-Mbit/s T1 and a 4-, 10-, or even a 16-Mbit/s LAN can be a problem. Then there are thorny issues to resolve involving data integrity and end-to-end control. And where LANs are already linked via fairly low-speed facilities that have become inadequate for the traffic volume (as was the case at Hughes), making a hefty investment in a T1 upgrade may not be necessary.

Addressing these issues is complicated by a marked absence today of good internetwork engineering tools. Indeed, jumping to a higher-speed LAN-to-LAN link may not necessarily be the best long-term solution, though it may be the most expedient.

"You don't want to be running the LAN-to-remote LAN [transmission link] at 100 percent," advises Bob Roman, a product manager with 3Com's Enterprise Systems Division (formerly Bridge Communications). "If you can afford the higher [link] rate, do it." He and others, however, recommend that users first undertake, to the extent possible, a

Matching the speed differences between a TI and a LAN can be a problem

comprehensive study of their LAN-to-LAN traffic.

Ideally, such a study will result in a histogram of LAN-to-LAN traffic, which should help identify:

■ *Percentage of packets that are traveling off-LAN.* The old rule of thumb is the 80/20 rule: No more than 20 percent of the packets should routinely need to be forwarded to a remote LAN (at least 80 percent should be addressed to destinations on the LAN where the packets originate).

The 20 percent optimum may be exceeded at peak times, but ideally stays below 50 percent. The 80/20 mix is nice when you can get it, but certain geographically dispersed companies can have unusually high on-LAN/off-LAN traffic ratios approaching 20/80, requiring complex wide-area connections composed of multiple T1s.

■ *The most frequently accessed remote resources.* It may be possible to relocate a particular resource—a host application, an electronic-mail server, a special plotter or laser printer, for example—to a remote LAN where the attached nodes access it more frequently.

Before relocating resources, though, you need to ensure that the move would not produce as much (or perhaps even more) "reverse" traffic, from the resource's former LAN to the one where it would be relocated. Perhaps replicating the resource, installing a similar device or application on the remote LAN, may be the best solution.

■ *The heavy users of remote resources.* Even if the traffic situation can't be improved by juggling LAN resources and making adjustments, it may yield enough hard data to justify moving an individual or department to the site where the high-demand computing resources reside.

Alternatively, it may be advisable to direct-wire with a dedicated phone line or digital facility individuals or workgroups that need a point-to-point remote connection,

which is not available to other users. This would be a dedicated facility.

At a minimum, determining the heaviest users of an expensive LAN-to-remote LAN transmission facility, by studying the traffic flow over a protracted period of time, can help to more accurately allocate the costs associated with maintaining the link or the expense of adding another or upgrading to a higher-capacity link.

Is T1 enough?

After communications management has explored all the alternatives for reducing LAN-to-remote LAN traffic, if the need for a high-capacity pipeline between LANs seems the only viable choice, then it's probably time to consider a T1 circuit.

Depending on where and how far the link is going, there probably are at least two T1 carriers from which to choose. And as T1 price wars continue to flare, it will pay to comparison shop. Unless your organization already has multiple T1s connecting the two dispersed LAN sites, these will have to be ordered. And depending on local-exchange-carrier and long-distance-carrier lead times, the sooner ordered the better. Hughes Aircraft was fortunate to be able to pull extra T1s out of 45-Mbit/s T3 fiber facilities that the company was already leasing to link several of its Ethernet locations. .

It can generally be said that a single T1 can adequately handle "normal" levels of LAN-to-LAN traffic generated between two dispersed Ethernets—though this depends on how you do it and a few dozen other variables. And, because a given site rarely has only one Ethernet, multiple T1s may be required to provide sufficient bandwidth between two sites or multiple remote sites. Fortunately, today's T1 bridges and routers come in a healthy diversity of configurations.

Because of the inherent inefficiencies in any LAN, the actual throughput between LAN stations is considerably less than the raw data rate of the LAN—4 Mbit/s for token ring, 10 Mbit/s for Ethernet, and so on. Consequently, gauging the relationship between the throughput of the LAN and the speed of the T1 pipe is not as simple as comparing raw bit-speed figures—10 Mbit/s versus 1.54 Mbit/s, for instance. Generally, Ethernet will not use more than 40 percent of its bit-rate capacity, regardless of the number of users or type of traffic. This is the cumulative equivalent of about 4 Mbit/s. There are a number of reasons for this, one of which is that at higher duty cycles an increasing incidence of collisions imposes a point of diminishing returns on the Ethernet's throughput.

This is not the case with token ring LANs, which is good news for token ring users though it poses a real performance challenge for makers of bridges that connect token rings. There are no collisions with token rings, and the overhead per frame can be as low as 21 bytes (compared with 64 bytes per Ethernet). In fact, performance tests generally show that a 4-Mbit/s token ring can operate on a sustained basis at more than 75 percent utilization—delivering more than 3 Mbit/s.

With token ring, the combination of high effective throughputs and less per-packet overhead translates into very high packet rates. Some of the new token ring bridges filter at a rate in excess of 20,000 packets per second. (Ethernet bridges, by comparison, do not need to filter any more than 15,000 packets per second.)

Filtering and forwarding rates are two of the primary performance considerations for routers and bridges. Filtering rate is the speed at which a device can read addresses from the header of LAN packets to determine if they should be further processed. If a device can't filter at the maximum speed and packet density of a given LAN topology, packets will be delayed or missed.

Forwarding is the rate at which a device processes and outputs packets after it has taken them in during the filtering process. Forwarding rates are dependent on the efficiencies of the internal architecture and software algorithms of a bridge or router. Forwarding can be time-consuming if the device must reexamine the packet several times (bridges), or convert a packet's structure (routers). One way manufacturers achieve high forwarding speeds in bridges and routers is to keep the input, processing, and output operations all on the same circuit board.

T1-to-LAN devices can generally fill the full 1.54 Mbit/s of a T1 link, minus a small amount for overhead. This "full-pipe" performance will fall off somewhat if the device supports multiple T1 links in the same box.

One leading vendor, for instance, can support 2,500 packets per second (64-byte packets) for a single T1 line—the equivalant of about 1.3 Mbit/s. With two T1 lines in one box, the same vendor's throughput falls to 2,000 packets per second, or approximately 1 Mbit/s per T1. The aggregate bandwidth for two parallel T1s is over 4 Mbit/s when used for bidirectional traffic over a full-duplex T1 line. This is enough bandwidth to keep up with all but the most extreme wide-area applications, considering some vendors can combine two or more T1 lines using a "load-sharing" feature that makes multiple T1s look like a single data path.

Another mechanism that regulates the amount of data that flows over a LAN (and between LANs linked by a T1) is the particular higher-level protocols employed: TCP/IP, Novell IPX, DECnet, and so on. These protocols effectively throttle the amount of user data that can move over a LAN (some to a much greater degree than others), thus constraining the relative utilization efficiency of the LAN. This imposes limitations on how quickly packets must be delivered to the remote LAN (discussed more later).

According to Mark Strangio, director of systems marketing at Wellfleet Communications (a Bedford, Mass.-based maker of routers that link remote Ethernets via T1 facilities), the protocol stack might limit LAN utilization to perhaps no more than 30 percent.

"Generally speaking, the most common implementations of TCP/IP limit the data [delivery of Ethernet] to about 3 Mbit/s," says Strangio. He says that TCP/IP, of the protocol stacks commonly used on Ethernets, is one of the most throughput-inhibiting, "especially when combined with the [throttling] mechanisms of Berkeley BSD 4.3 Unix." He adds that DECnet, too, imposes a high degree of protocol throttling.

T1 bridges and routers generally come in a modular format that allows high- and low-speed ports to be added by sliding in appropriate circuit boards. The simplest of these devices is configured with a single LAN port and a single synchronous port for T1. On the other end of the spectrum, a fully outfitted router from Cisco Systems Inc. (Menlo Park, Calif.) can support up to eight Ethernet ports, a half dozen or more T1 lines, a 56-kbit/s line, and a token ring connection.

As with the LAN ports, the wide-area ports on a T1-to-LAN device are of many types. Commonly supported interfaces include: CCITT V.35, CCITT X.21, RS449, and RS422. The speeds of these ports accommodate data rates from 56 kbit/s to 2.048 Mbit/s, depending on the vendor.

The manner in which a T1 bridge or router is connected to the T1 line is often flexible. Some devices come with an internal DSU (data service unit); others require the DSU/CSU (channel service unit) externally. Synchronous V.35 ports are provided to connect LANs together through T1 multiplexers. And depending on the bandwidth required for each LAN-to-LAN link, several may be multiplexed over the same T1 to take advantage of unused network bandwidth.

Larse Corp.,Santa Clara, Calif., is a leading manufacturer of DSU/CSU equipment and a supplier of equipment to T1 bridge vendors. Larse's marketing product manager, Alex Dobrushin, says: "Not all internal DSUs [in bridges] have the same capabilities as external equipment." Consequently, T1 bridge buyers should carefully evaluate the capabilities of a T1 bridge's internal DSU for the application at hand.

In addition to simple point-to-point connections, T1 bridge and router vendors sometimes provide sophisticated multipath configurations. For instance, three locations may be connected through three T1 lines in a triangular layout, with dynamic load balancing and fault tolerance between the sites.

As with any emerging technology, there is considerable confusion concerning the proper applications for T1 bridges and routers. Although it is impossible to give a complete list of the appropriate applications for each device, the two topology diagrams—"T1-bridge scenario" and "T1-router scenario"—give some indication of how T1-to-LAN connections are being used today by aggressive communications managers.

Bridging our differences

A bridge, which operates primarily at the media access control (IEEE MAC) layer of LANs, creates a low-level extension of the LAN over the T1 and onto the remote LAN. To LAN users, LAN applications, and the operation of the higher-level protocol stack on the connected LANs, the bridges aren't apparent. The local nodes and protocols do nothing any differently, even though a destination node may be located across the T1 on the other LAN and a thousand miles away.

Bridges look at (filter) all the Ethernet packets or token ring frames passing by on the LAN to which they are attached. Any packets that are addressed to a remote LAN are then forwarded through the wide-area link.

The corresponding remote bridge, located at the other

T1 — bridge scenario

One suitable application for T1 bridges involves more than a dozen small remote sites with one or two token ring LANs (or Ethernets) each. The remote sites connect through T1 bridges, such as those from CrossComm Corp., back to token ring based hosts at company headquarters. The T1 links in this application are made through a fault-tolerant Stratacom T1 backbone, which, along with the bridges, supports dual paths between LANs and satelite backup at 56 kbit/s. Because the bridges are transparent to higher level protocols, any LAN software can be used between workstation and fileservers or hosts.

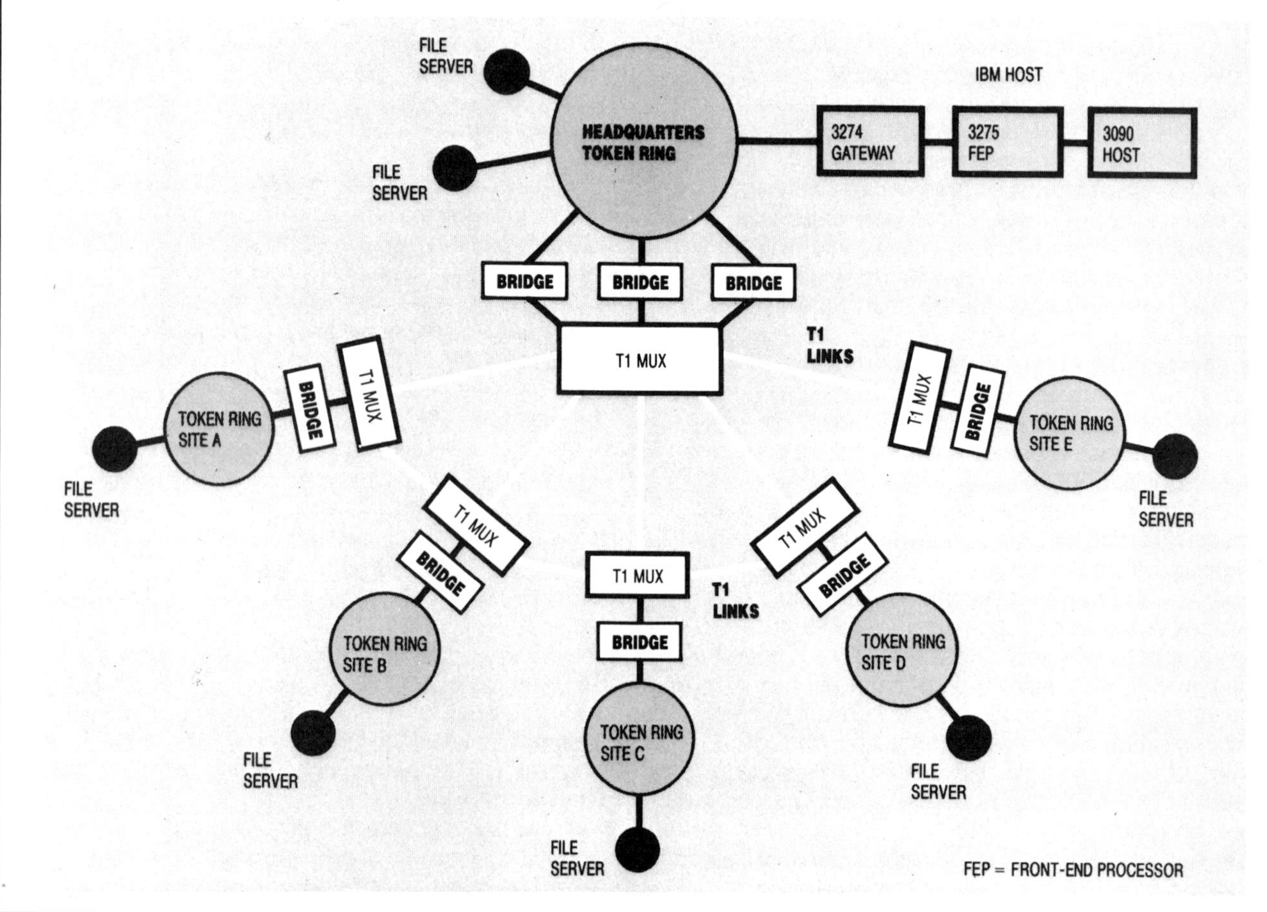

end of the T1 and attached to the remote LAN, examines the forwarded packet and, assuming it agrees with the first bridge's decision, transmits it to the other LAN.

The packet delivered by the destination bridge to the remote LAN is usually a perfect bit-by-bit replica of the original packet plucked off the first LAN by the first bridge. Sometimes, however, there could be a subtle change or two — the result of errors incurred en route.

The different bridge makers differ philosophically over whether it's best always to deliver exactly the same LAN packet with the same frame check sequence (FCS) to the remote LAN.

Some bridge makers insist that it is better to preserve the packet's original FCS throughout the forwarding process, deliver the packet with the original FCS to the destination LAN, and then leave it up to higher-level protocols to check the original FCS against the delivered packet. An error incurred by the packet during processing would then be detected by the receiver (the FCS calculated on receipt wouldn't match the original one attached), and the receiving LAN node would request a corrected copy (usually through retransmission).

The alternative to this process, used by some bridges, is either to recalculate the forwarded packet's FCS en route (and deal with errored packets appropriately — usually by discarding them) or to deliver the packet however it arrives at the destination LAN (without the packet or the FCS having been "preserved" along the way).

Bridges' transparency to LAN nodes (and higher-level protocol stacks) is a mixed blessing to efficient LAN-to-LAN communications. As already pointed out, a LAN node accepts every packet in the belief that it came from another, nearby, node on the same LAN.

LANs tend to be fairly clean (low error rate) communications environments, and the typical LAN node has no inherent reason to mistrust the integrity of a received packet in which the FCS checks out. But some protocol changes might be made (such as switching over from a "datagram" delivery protocol to a more robust connection-oriented one) if receiving nodes knew that an incoming packet was sent by a T1 bridge   connected LAN node a thousand miles away, that the FCS may have been recalculated or changed en route, or that the preceding or following packet might have been discarded somewhere along the way.

The bridge manufacturers who were interviewed acknowledge that, depending on events that can occur with variable frequency, bridges can be overwhelmed—and buffers overloaded. (An example is a bridge that receives many large file-transfer packets over the T1 but can't deliver them because the local LAN is extremely busy.)

What happens in such a case? One of two things: Either packets are discarded or, if they are not lost, they are significantly delayed. When buffers get full, subsequent arriving packets are simply discarded, since bridges are usually in no position at such times to try to retain or regain them. As shown in Table 1, bridge designers have usually allocated between 256 Kbytes and 1 Mbyte for buffer

T1—router scenario

In contrast to the bridge's straightforward star-wired hub of small regional sites, routers can build huge, complex internetworks. In this configuration, there are many LANs on each site and many sites.

Third-party routers, such as those from Cisco Systems, use higher-level protocols to transport packets for all major host and network operating systems. Client workstation support includes: Macintosh, IBM PCs and compatibles, Sun and Apollo workstations, 3Com and Novell stations, TCP/IP nodes, Digital Equipment Corp. terminals, and others.

The highest degree of redundancy and fault tolerance is possible with routers. Unlike the bridge, the routers conduct congestion control in concert with end nodes to ensure that packets traversing huge internets do not experience critical time-out errors.

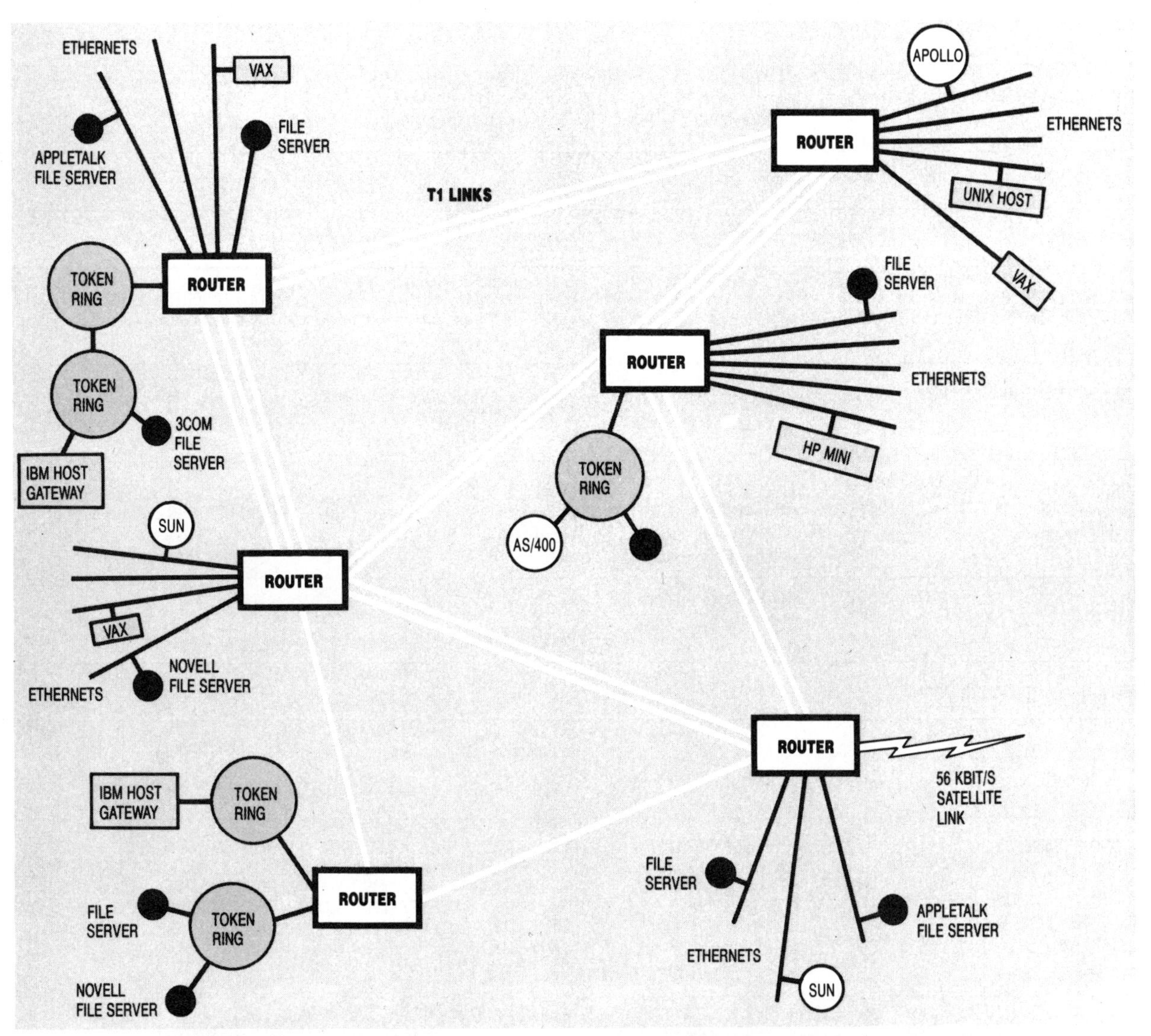

memory to cope with congestion.

And while most vendors say they rarely have to drop packets, it does happen. Adding more buffer memory is not always the answer, though, since this can also add significantly to the processing delay that packets experience en route. And any appreciable delay can be a packet killer.

One may think that a packet delivered after a considerable delay is still better than a packet that is not delivered at all. Unfortunately, all high-level LAN protocol stacks have specified delay time-outs, at which they presume a packet is lost or corrupted and then retransmit it.

This time-out often becomes critical with bridges — because, again, the higher-level protocols do not know

Table 1: LAN-to-LAN T1 bridges: A comparative sampling

VENDOR	CROSSCOMM CORP. MARLBOROUGH, MASS. (508) 481-4060		HALLEY SYSTEMS INC. SAN JOSE, CALIF. (408) 943-2600
BRIDGE	NTB (NOVELL T1 BRIDGE)	ILAN (INTEGRATED LAN)	CONNECTLAN 100
DESCRIPTION	BOARD UNIT, PLUGS INTO PC/AT BUS OF NOVELL SERVER	STANDALONE, LAN-ATTACHED UNIT	STANDALONE, LAN-ATTACHED UNIT
LANs SUPPORTED	LINKS VIA T1 ANY NOVELL LANs RUNNING NETWARE 2.1 OR LATER (INCLUDING ETHERNET, TOKEN RING, ARCNET)	ETHERNET-TO-ETHERNET (INCLUDING CHEAPERNET, STARLAN, IN ANY MIX) AND/OR TOKEN RING-TO-TOKEN RING (MULTIPLEXED ON SAME T1)	ETHERNET-TO-ETHERNET (INCLUDING MIX OF ETHERNET VERSION 2.0 AND IEEE 802.3)
NUMBER T1 LINKS SUPPORTED	1	UP TO 4	1
CPU BASE	ASSORTED 8-BIT	INTEL 80286 (16 MHz)	INTEL 80286 (10 MHz)
BUFFER MEMORY	16 KBYTES	256 KBYTES	256 KBYTES
DATA INTEGRITY/ERROR CHECKING OVER T1	HDLC	HDLC	HDLC (BRIDGES ENSURE THE SAME FCS IS DELIVERED TO THE DESTINATION LAN)
MANAGEMENT/CONTROL ACCESS	–	VIA ANY PC/XT OR AT ATTACHED TO ANY CONNECTED LAN, RUNNING VENDOR'S MANAGEMENT SOFTWARE	TERMINAL ON BRIDGE OR NONDEDICATED PC SERVER ON LAN
INTERFACE TO T1	RS-422 (DB-25 CONNECTOR) OR T1/DSX-1 (VIA RJ-45, UP TO 630 FEET TO EXTERNAL CSU); FRACTIONAL T1 AS AVAILABLE	RS-422 OR T1/DSX-1 (VIA RJ-45, UP TO 630 FEET TO EXTERNAL CSU); FRACTIONAL T1 AS AVAILABLE	RS-422, V.35, T1/DS-1 (DB-15 CONNECTOR TO EXTERNAL DSU/CSU)
FIRST AVAILABLE	6/89	1/88 (ETHERNET BRIDGE) 7/89 (TOKEN RING BRIDGE)	9/88
NUMBER SHIPPED (THROUGH 9/89)	OVER 100	OVER 500 (ETHERNET BRIDGES)	100 (AS OF 9/89)
PRICE	$4,850	$5,000 to $17,000 (VARIES SIGNIFICANTLY, DEPENDING ON CONFIGURATION)	$10,045 (RETAIL)
LIMITATIONS/COMMENTS	PC-BASED NOVELL SERVER CAN DELIVER ONLY ABOUT 40 TO 50 KBYTE/S (300 TO 400 KBIT/S) OVER AT BUS TO T1 BOARD; HENCE, ONLY ABOUT ¼ TO ½ OF T1 LINK CAN BE EFFECTIVELY USED, EVEN AT MAXIMUM DELIVERY RATE.	CANNOT BRIDGE FROM TOKEN RING TO ETHERNET, BUT RING-TO-RING LINKS CAN SHARE SAME T1 WITH ETHERNET-TO-ETHERNET LINKS; ILAN UNIT STATISTICALLY MULTIPLEXES THE TWO TRAFFIC STREAMS WITHIN THE SAME T1 BANDWIDTH.	RECENT SOFTWARE SUPPORTS UP TO 32,000 ADDRESSES IN ROUTING TABLE; PERFORMANCE WILL DEGRADE AS NUMBER OF ADDRESSES IN ROUTING TABLE GROWS.

NOTE: LISTING IS NOT EXHAUSTIVE

CRC = CYCLIC REDUNDANCY CHECK (HDLC)
CSU = CHANNEL SERVICE UNIT

DSU = DATA SERVICE UNIT
FCS = FRAME CHECK SEQUENCE

they may be operating over a bridged connection with added propagation delay, bottlenecks, congestion, and so on.

Filtering and performance
As the bridge comparison table shows (the table, by the way, does not include every vendor with a LAN-to-LAN bridge product), this has become a hot market, which many vendors are attacking with a fury. Within the last year alone, more than a half dozen manufacturers have introduced products that bridge LANs via one or more T1 links.

The move up to T1 for these bridge products (which previously had supported 56-kbit/s links, at best) was made possible through refined designs and streamlined software

RETIX SANTA MONICA, CALIF. (213) 399-2200	3COM CORP. SANTA CLARA, CALIF. (408) 562-6400	VITALINK COMMUNICATIONS CORP. FREMONT, CALIF. (415) 794-1100	
4880 REMOTE LAN BRIDGE	IB/3	TRANSLAN III AND 350	TRANSRING 550
STANDALONE, LAN-ATTACHED UNIT	STANDALONE, LAN-ATTACHED UNIT	STANDALONE, LAN-ATTACHED UNIT	STANDALONE, LAN-ATTACHED UNIT
ETHERNET-TO-ETHERNET (INCLUDING CHEAPERNET)	ETHERNET-TO-ETHERNET (INCLUDING BASEBAND TO REMOTE BROADBAND)	ETHERNET-TO-ETHERNET (CUSTOMER PROVIDES TRANSCEIVER UNIT AND THUS DETERMINES PARTICULAR ETHERNET VARIANT—SUCH AS VERSION 2.0, IEEE 802.3)	TOKEN RING-TO-TOKEN RING (TOKEN-TO-TOKEN TRAFFIC CAN BE CARRIED ALONG WITH ETHERNET-TO-ETHERNET OVER SAME T1 BACKBONE FACILITIES)
1 OR 2	UP TO 4	1 (TRANSLAN III) 1 OR 2 (TRANSLAN 350)	1 OR 2
MOTOROLA 68020 (16 MHz)	68020 (AND 68000s FOR I/O)	DUAL 68010s (III) OR 68020s	DUAL 68020s (16 MHz)
578 KBYTES	512 KBYTES TO 1 MBYTE	1 MBYTE	1 MBYTE
LAPB (WITH EXTENDED SEQUENCING CAPABILITY, NO SELECTIVE REJECT)	HDLC (CRC IS USED, BUT NO ADDRESSING)	HDLC (ALL VITALINK BRIDGES ENCAPSULATE ETHERNET AND/OR TOKEN RING PACKETS, INCLUDING FCS, INTACT WITHIN HDLC, AND DELIVER INTACT TO DESTINATION LAN)	
TERMINAL ON EACH BRIDGE OR DEDICATED 386/PC FOR NETWORK BRIDGE MANAGEMENT	VIA LOCAL CONSOLE OR THROUGH NETWORK CONTROL SERVER	TERMINAL ON EACH BRIDGE OR DEDICATED DEC-BASED LAN SERVER FOR NET MANAGEMENT	TERMINAL ON EACH BRIDGE OR DEDICATED DEC-BASED LAN SERVER FOR NET MANAGEMENT
RS-449, V.35, T1/DSX-1 TO CSU (WITH INTERNAL DSU OPTION)	V.35, RS-422, RS-449	V.35, RS-442, OR T1/DSX-1 (INTERNAL DSU OPTION)	V.35, RS-449, RS-442, T1/DSX-1 (VIA INTEGRAL DSU)
2/89 (INTERNAL DSU OPTION ADDED 8/89)	7/88 (SINGLE T1) 10/88 (TO 4 T1s)	1986 (TRANSLAN III) 7/88 (TRANSLAN 350)	10/88
800 (ESTIMATED, AS OF 9/89)	2,500 (AS OF 9/89)	10,000 (PRIMARILY TRANSLAN IIIs)	NOT AVAILABLE FROM VENDOR
$10,400 TO $15,000 (1 OR 2 T1s); INTERNAL DSU OPTION ADDS ABOUT $2,000	$10,750 TO $18,200 (FROM 1 TO 4 T1s)	$14,500 (TRANSLAN III); $21,250 (TRANSLAN 350, 2 T1s); ADD $1,500 FOR INTERNAL DSU	$23,250 (SINGLE T1); $24,700 (DUAL T1); ADD $1,500 FOR INTERNAL DSU
MAXIMUM ADDRESS CAPACITY FOR ROUTING TABLE IS 2,000; PERFORMANCE MAY DEGRADE WHEN UNIT IS EXPANDED FROM SINGLE- TO DUAL-T1 CONFIGURATION.	ADDRESS CAPACITY FOR ROUTING TABLE IS 8,000; BIT-PATTERN MASKS ARE USED FOR FILTERING; SUPPORTS TO 4 MASKS PER FILTER.	MULTIPROCESSOR ARCHITECTURE MINIMIZES ANY DEGRADATION OF THROUGHPUT PERFORMANCE AS ADDRESS ROUTING TABLE GROWS (MAXIMUM IS 8,000 ADDRESSES); ABILITY TO CONFIGURE UP TO 16 FILTERS PER FRAME.	BRIDGE FORWARDS ONLY TOKEN FRAMES DESTINED FOR REMOTE LAN, CHANGING FRAME STATUS BITS WHEN FORWARDED; BRIDGE IS TRANSPARENT TO SOURCE ROUTING AND FORWARDS REGARDLESS OF WHETHER FRAME IS SOURCE-ROUTED.

HDLC=HIGH-LEVEL DATA LINK CONTROL
LAPB=LINK ACCESS PROCEDURE-BALANCED

written for the latest microprocessors. For example, almost all now employ central microprocessors running at 10 MHz or faster.

But new microprocessors and designs notwithstanding, throughput performance remains a complex issue. Several operational and design differences between products greatly affect performance, and users should fully explore these factors before buying. Two such factors are:

■ *Address-table size and lookups.* A large address-table capacity certainly enables the bridge to handle more network devices and enhances its filtering capacity. But in some bridge designs, especially where a single microprocessor handles all I/O chores as well as filtering functions like address lookups, throughput performance can drop

The more sophisticated software capabilities of routers may make them the better buy

dramatically as the address table fills up.

Mike Graham, product manager for Halley Systems (San Jose, Calif.) acknowledges that, as the ConnectLAN 100's impressive 32,000 address table capacity is filled up, throughput performance fades proportionally. CrossComm's Tad Witkowicz says that its firm's ILAN design, by comparison, segregates the table lookup function. "Our performance does not change for 40,000 addresses," he says, adding that whether there are 1,000 or 40,000 addresses in the table, lookup time is always a constant 12 microseconds.

■ *Levels of filtering.* During the last year or so, bridge vendors have added a host of new filtering capabilities to their products. Most now have many in common. Where destination and source addresses used to be the primary criteria for making a filter/forwarding decision, most bridges can now also filter based, for example, on which high-level protocol stack the packet uses. (Those with multiple-remote-link capabilities can direct, say, TCP/IP traffic onto one link, and Novell IPX onto another.)

While this and similar capabilities have prompted some bridge vendors to apply the term "brouter" to their products, it should be noted that identifying the LAN protocol is not the same as understanding it. Most protocol recognition involves a bridge looking at the 2-byte "protocol type" field right behind the IEEE 802 source address field. (The hexadecimal code 6003, for example, is used to identify the packet as a DECnet message). This is not complicated, but it does involve an additional filtering examination of the packet.

The performance specifications published by most bridge vendors are usually based on minimal filtering (which might involve one, or perhaps two, examinations of each packet). For some of the bridges, any additional levels of filtering (some support up to 16 levels, or passes)

will choke performance and throughput drastically (cutting the forwarding rate in half, for example). In some more sophisticated bridge designs, a single packet examination can be used to read several different fields for making filtering/routing decisions. Users should be sure to get performance data based on the levels and extent of filtering they are going to require.

As mentioned, some of the problems that bridges inherently face, such as transmission time-outs, are avoided through the use of routers rather than bridges. Unlike bridges, routers are fully functional network nodes and are recognized as such by all the other LAN nodes that are running the same higher-level protocol stacks. And packets sent to routers are addressed specifically to the router, whereas a bridge must assume that any packet may need forwarding.

The routing difference

Routers have more time for packet manipulation than bridges because they can conduct flow-control dialogues with on-LAN sources, thus meeting protocol time-out constraints. Routers can throttle sources that could otherwise deluge bridges with high rates of very long packets.

However, where bridges filter and forward packets no matter what or how many higher-level protocol stacks are simultaneously running on the attached LAN, the router must be configured to "speak" as a network-layer node individually for each protocol stack to be supported. Increasingly, router manufacturers can support several different protocol stacks simultaneously.

There are not as many vendors of LAN routers as there are of bridges. A comparison of the capabilities of three of the leaders—Cisco Systems, Proteon Inc. (Westborough, Mass.), and Wellfleet Communications Inc.—is shown in Table 2. All these products offer impressively high performance, support multiple protocol stacks as routers, and two of them can also be configured to run as bridges at the same time.

Routers, unlike bridges, can translate between underlying IEEE 802 topologies. Indeed, Cisco Systems (the products of which are now being incorporated into T1-switch configurations by Network Equipment Technologies as an OEM) supports a number of protocol stacks both as an Ethernet-attached router and a token ring-attached node.

The performance of routers will degrade as the number of protocol stacks supported simultaneously increases, as the size of address tables grows, and so on. But because their operation accommodates protocol time-outs and they are able to throttle individual sending stations, they can be viewed as more robust devices for maintaining data integrity over LAN-to-remote LAN T1 links.

In addition, some router configurations can be expanded to support several different LAN interfaces and perhaps a half-dozen or more remote T1 links, in one box. Consequently, routers also assume important roles as multiplexers of mixed traffic types over T1 backbones, as well as intermediate T1 routing nodes.

Bridges are fairly limited in this. Rerouting and support for more sophisticated "mesh" and "loop" backbone T1

Table 2: LAN-to-LAN routing via T1

VENDOR	CISCO SYSTEMS INC. MENLO PARK, CALIF. (415) 326-1941	WELLFLEET COMMUNICATIONS BEDFORD, MASS. (617) 275-2400	PROTEON INC. WESTBOROUGH, MASS. (508) 898-2800
PROTOCOL STACKS FOR WHICH ROUTING VIA T1 IS SUPPORTED	NOVELL XNS (NETWARE IPX*, CLIENT-SERVER) UNGERMANN-BASS XNS* XEROX XNS* 3COM XNS DECNET* (LAT PROTOCOL ONLY SUPPORTED VIA BRIDGING) TCP/IP* ISO CONNECTIONLESS SERVICE* APPLETALK (PHASE 1) APOLLO DOMAIN (OTHERS INCLUDE XEROX PUP PROTOCOL, CHAOSNET	DECNET (PHASE IV, LEVEL 1 AND 2 ROUTING) TCP/IP (INTERNET OR PRIVATE NETWORK) NOVELL XNS (NETWARE IPX)** 3COM XNS** BANYAN XNS**	NOVELL NETWARE/IPX* XEROX NETWORK SYSTEMS (XNS) TCP/IP* DECNET PHASE IV, LEVEL 1 AND 2* APPLETALK APOLLO DOMAIN** OSI/ISO CONNECTIONLESS SERVICE (AVAILABLE FIRST QUARTER 1990)
SIMULTANEOUS BRIDGE AND ROUTING OPERATION?	YES	YES	NO
HARDWARE TECHNOLOGY	12-MHz 68020 PROCESSOR COMBINED WITH MULTIPLE BIT-SLICE CIRCUITS; MULTIBUS-BASED; 256 TO 512 KBYTES BUFFER MEMORY	MULTIPLE 12- AND 25-MHz 68020 CPUs; VME BUS-BASED; 1 MBYTE BUFFER MEMORY	16.7 MHz 68020 CPU WITH 8 SLOTS FOR NETWORK INTERFACE CARDS; MULTIBUS-BASED; 1-2 MBYTE MEMORY —OR— 286-BASED AT BUS WITH 640 KBYTES MEMORY; 4 SLOTS FOR NETWORK INTERFACE CARDS
CONFIGURATION PRICE (SYSTEM SUPPORTING MULTIPLE ROUTED PROTOCOLS, 1 LAN INTERFACE, 2 T1s)	$11,000 TO $12,000 —MAC-LAYER BRIDGING EXTRA —NO INTERNAL DSU, EXTERNAL CLOCKING	$13,330 —INCLUDES 3 DIFFERENT ROUTING/ BRIDGING APPLICATIONS —OPTIONAL INTERNAL DSU/CSU	$8,000 TO $15,000, DEPENDING ON PLATFORM —NO INTERNAL DSU
ERROR CONTROL VIA T1	SIMPLE HDLC FRAMING (CRC ONLY, NO ADDRESSING, SEQUENCING, RETRANSMISSION).	HDLC ENCAPSULATION; USER CAN ADD LAPB (LLC-2) CAPABILITIES FOR ERROR CORRECTION.	SIMPLE HDLC FRAMING WITH CRC; LINE UP/DOWN PROTOCOL TO ENSURE LINE QUALITY.

NOTE: TABLE IS NOT AN EXHAUSTIVE LISTING OF ROUTER VENDORS.

*ALSO SUPPORTED TO/FROM TOKEN RING

**SCHEDULED FOR SEPTEMBER 1989 AVAILABILITY.

HDLC = HIGH-LEVEL DATA LINK CONTROL
CRC = CYCLIC REDUNDANCY CHECK
LAPB = LINK ACCESS PROCEDURE-BALANCED

topologies is restricted or nonexistent in bridges. Advanced bridges can, as a rule, detect a failed link and then move traffic to another standby. But dynamic load balancing and automatic rerouting if a failed link comes back up are generally not supported. If two links to the same destination exist, a bridge can deactivate one, for example. And if a failed link is restored, manual intervention is usually required to reactivate it to the bridges. This can cause problems for networkers with elaborate backbone topologies.

Token-to-token

The recent take-off of token ring LAN popularity is driving bridge and router manufacturers to invest heavily in developing products for token-to-token bridging and routing. Only a few have already delivered products, however.

Bridging token rings poses some unusual technical and performance problems, not the least of which is source routing.

Currently, most vendors do not support source routing in ring-to-ring communications. Source routing is diametrically opposed to the network-layer routing-node philosophy that all other LAN protocol stacks and vendors employ. In fact, LAN operating system vendors like 3Com and Novell, whose products can also operate over token rings, do not use source routing and instead retain their dynamic-routing-node approach (where routing is a network-layer function, and not a part of the 802.5 frame structure, as is source routing).

Bridge makers, whose products operate below the network level, need to decide whether they will offer "source-routing bridges," or "bridges that are transparent to source routing" (these will filter and forward source-routed packets, but not appear to the ring as a source-routing bridge and not even look at the source-routing information imbedded in packets).

Currently, bridge products from Vitalink Communications Corp. (Fremont, Calif.) and CrossComm support token ring-to-token ring bridging. Both have decided to be transparent to source routing in their current products. However, Halley Systems Inc. (San Jose, Calif.), which is expected to make available this fall its first token ring bridge product, will be a source routing   compliant bridge.

"We do source routing between Halley bridges," says Bob Craven, Halley Systems' vice president of engineering, "even for non-source-routing frames." He explains that, by embracing source routing, the Halley bridge will in fact route between IBM token ring "subnets." Bridges that are transparent to source routing "make interconnected rings look like a single subnet," which he says can lead to problems as rings proliferate and are interconnected.

IBM has announced two source-routing bridge products for connecting token rings: a direct ring-to-ring bridge using a 386-based PS/2; and a remote bridge supporting a single link up to 56-kbit/s. While attachment to the 16-Mbit/s token ring will be supported (the LAN-to-LAN direct bridge was delayed and shipped this spring; the remote bridge, also delayed, hadn't been shipped yet by midsummer), the performance of both bridges is already being questioned.

According to a source who requested anonymity, early analysis of IBM's PS/2-based bridge reveals a forwarding throughput of only about 1,000 frames per second. If true, this represents not even 2 percent of the 16-Mbit/s token ring's delivery capacity. And even if the remote bridge completely fills a 56-kbit/s remote link with forwarded frames, which is unlikely, this still equals only about 2,000 minimal-sized frames. What this means is that IBM has its work cut out for it, and that bridges with much higher throughput will be needed before Big Blue's customers can link high-speed token rings over long-haul distances at anything close to T1 data rates.

To bridge, perchance to route

Although the complexities of T1 bridges and routers make them a challenge to evaluate, the possible gains are well worth the effort. Considering the projected needs for wide-area connection of LANs, T1 bridges and routers are the key building blocks for a highly connected future.

Reminiscent of a medieval theological debate, the question of the relative merits of a router over a bridge, or vice versa, has captivated public relations and advertising agencies—indeed, even some members of the trade press—for over a year. It turns out that the differences between a bridge and a router do have a significant impact on connecting LANs via T1 facilities:

■ Because of the low level they operate on, bridges are generally more susceptible than routers to being overloaded as a result of heavy off-LAN traffic and unexpected traffic surges.

■ Most bridges will perform best in a simple single-link LAN-to-LAN configuration, especially over shorter LAN-to-LAN distances and where forwarding decisions are few and straightforward (based primarily on destination-address filtering, not multiple paths).

■ As network complexity grows, and where the LAN-to-LAN T1 traffic traverses mesh or loop topologies, routers are generally more suitable.

■ In general, where LAN-to-LAN traffic involves three or more remotely connected LANs, multiple T1 links or routes, multiple high-level protocol stacks that operate concurrently over the interconnected LANs (especially where packet routing is based on higher-level protocols), routers are clearly preferred.

■ Price and performance are narrowing between bridges and routers, but there still remain both obvious and subtle differences among current offerings. Because the T1 link is normally the slowest segment in an end-to-end path, forwarding figures for T1 devices are not as critical as they are for local segmentation devices that operate well above T1 speeds.

For comparable forwarding throughput and support for, say, one LAN interface and two T1s, either a bridge or a router will cost between about $10,000 and $14,000. The generally more sophisticated software capabilities of routers may make them the better buy, all else being equal. ■

Edwin E. Mier, editor at large for DATA COMMUNICATIONS, *is also president of Mier Communications Inc., a communications and networking consultancy in Princeton Junction, N.J. Mier, who holds a BA degree from Lehigh University, specializes in connectivity issues and problems.*

Edward R. Teja, special to DATA COMMUNICATIONS

Router roundup: Tools for network net segmentation come of age

A head-to-head comparison of the leading router vendors, and the key issues to keep in mind while you are router shopping.

Today, increased competition, evolving user needs, and corporate mergers are forcing network managers to marry previously independent networks. Their task is not to create a network from the ground up, but to aggregate subnets into a viable internetwork that will equally serve the parts and the whole of the organization. When putting networks together, the challenge is to let data—not network faults—flow across internetwork boundaries.

This sounds great, but in many cases separate networks with vastly different networking strategies have been forced into unnatural relationships, in spite of their installed bases of different hardware and software. Integrating diverse systems into a single network, therefore, means accommodating a variety of protocols and user needs without sacrificing overall integrity.

Under such circumstances, it makes sense to build an internetwork that retains the characteristics and autonomy of the individual subnets, while at the same time allowing users to share resources and data without the restrictions introduced by location or protocol incompatibility. The only way that this can happen is through intelligent network segmentation.

The concept of network segmentation reflects an important reality: On a single LAN, every component is a relatively equal partner in the network address space, but this situation can spell disaster in a relatively large network. A single address space in a large inter- and intracorporate network plays havoc with network reliability, management and planning, and flow control.

Here's why. The fallibility of an electronic system is equal to the combined failure rates of all of its components. The more components, the higher the overall failure rate. Furthermore, the reliability of the system can never be any better than that of its least-reliable element. That's a sobering thought when you are mixing PCs, minicomputers, mainframes, and special-purpose servers on a single network. Common sense dictates that an unlimited number of these devices, unrestricted, on the same wire is not an ideal situation.

The best way to manage the interaction of large numbers of devices on a network and also eliminate the single address space is with routers. Segmenting a network with routers inherently builds fire walls between the subnets. A failure in one subnet might disrupt that LAN but won't bring down the entire network. More important, if you create a high-speed backbone and link subnets to the backbone through routers, you can place critical shared resources on the backbone and not worry about the failure of a subnet gaining access to a critical resource (see figure).

Because of the increased demands on segmentation devices, the networking industry is starting to discover that the router is the correct way to segment a network into independent LANs that can easily share data and resources. A router is the only network element that does this job, and it is the only job that a router does best. Bridges are not routers, no matter how much they look like routers, appear to do router functions, or even cost as much as routers (see "Bridges and routers—different tools for different jobs").

Today, there are not as many routers available as there are bridges and repeaters, though this will likely change as internets grow in size and sophistication. The primary third-party router vendors are Cisco Systems (Menlo Park, Calif.), Proteon Inc. (Westborough, Mass.), and Wellfleet Communications Inc. (Bedford, Mass.). These are the aftermarket vendors whose products are not embedded in host computers or file servers, as they are with DEC and Novell routers.

Each third-party router vendor brings a somewhat different approach to routing. The intent of this article is not

Router Roundup

Router isolated backbone. *Putting critical resources on the Ethernet or token ring backbone and segmenting the network with routers puts a fire wall between the users and the resources that must not be impaired by faults that may develop on local network segments. Data propagates through the internet, but not faults.*

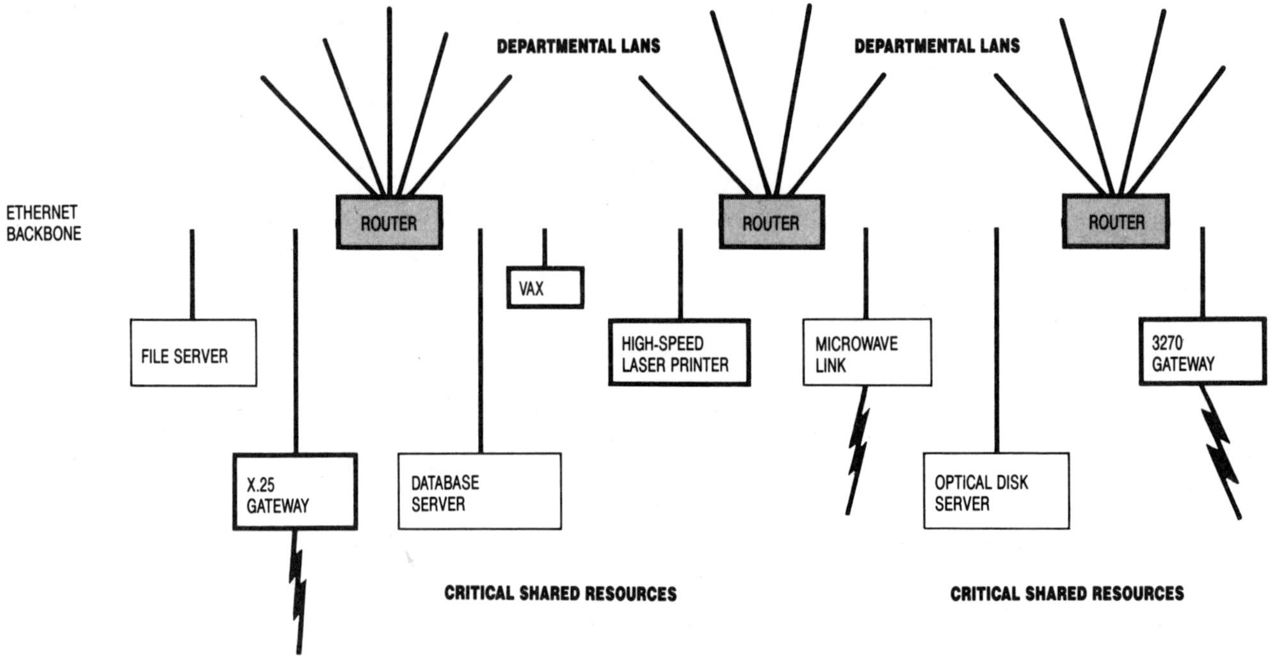

an exhaustive evaluation of all vendor products, but rather an introduction to basic features and functionality available in this emerging industry.

Stacking up the stacks

Each network architecture (SNA, DECnet, NetWare) has its own protocols that define packet formats and the way packets are directed through an internetwork. Many protocols share a single heritage, but there are differences. Each of the third-party router vendors supports one or more network protocols and, in some cases, OSI stack components as well.

Conformance with several network protocols provides interoperability between dissimilar networks. Unlike a bridge, a router can support multiple protocols on multiple protocol layers. This allows interoperability not possible with bridges. For example, a router that has interface and protocol compatibility with both Ethernet and token ring can connect the two, passing messages from one to the other.

Among the well-established protocols are:

■ CLNS, the International Organization for Standardization's Connectionless Network Services (as specified by ISO 8743).

■ TCP/IP, used extensively both commercially and in military networks.

■ XNS (Xerox Network Systems), which is used by many commercial vendors.

■ DECnet, from Digital Equipment Corp. One of DEC's important network protocols is Local Area Transport, or LAT, a terminal server protocol.

■ IPX/SPX (Internet Packet Exchange/Sequenced Packet Exchange), the protocol used by Novell's Advanced NetWare.

■ EGP (Exterior Gateway Protocol), the routing protocol used by gateways on the Defense Data Network (DDN).

■ Chaosnet, developed at MIT for the artificial intelligence community, provides routing plus host functions such as status and uptime services.

Some protocols are more important and relevant than others. For example, while Chaosnet represents a specialized and limited market, XNS, IPX/SPX, and TCP/IP are far more common. Still, if you must aggregate subnets that use specialized protocols, it doesn't matter that they may be arcane. Being multilingual is a plus, and some router vendors are more multilingual than others.

Of course, there are different interpretations of every protocol, and standards do not necessarily define all aspects of the protocol well. Thus, there are differences in the robustness of the implementations. The only way to be certain that an implementation is up to par is to look at the vendor's customer base and see if the company has a fair amount of experience in dealing with a particular protocol.

Increasingly, one well-implemented protocol is not enough for a large organization. Flexibility in aggregating networks requires an ability to use multiple protocols simultaneously. Without this, it becomes impossible to effect dependable internetworks.

Network protocols like XNS and TCP/IP are not the only protocols used by a router. To maintain their internal tables and keep abreast of events on the internet, routers talk among themselves using router management protocols.

When a router receives a packet, it must decode the destination address and determine the best path to route it through the internet. This is known as the "policy routing" and also affects how well a router will enact flow control. There are differences in the ways that routers select the best path for a message. Some routers are configured by the network manager, who establishes the cost of each possible path by entering the speed, number of hops, and path length in the routing table. These are termed "static" routers. Most multiprotocol routers are "dynamic" routers, which automatically configure and reconfigure the routing table as needed.

Even though dynamic routing is widely supported, vendors differ on how to go about it. Those differences reflect their philosophies of routing algorithms and the influence of the established protocols they choose to implement.

Basically, there are two competing internal routing algorithms: distance vector and link state. Cisco, Proteon, and Wellfleet currently make use of distance/vector routing protocols derived from Xerox's Routing Information Protocol (RIP).

RIP is a distance vector (Bellman-Ford) protocol that describes the network in terms of "hop count" metrics. In this system, a number between 1 and 15 represents the number of routers between the current node and the destination node, making no distinction between high-speed paths and slower ones.

Some RIP implementations add to the hop count of slower networks to weight them more accurately. But the maximum value of the metric is 15, seriously limiting the effects of such weighting. A router using RIP propagates its metrics throughout the network as part of update messages. These metrics provide a snapshot of the network routing table and its status.

Wellfleet Communications, for instance, uses RIP for TCP/IP environments but features extensions to it that allow its routers to make better use of the network's resources.

Most vendors offer some proprietary extension to RIP, but there is another alternative. The Internet Engineering Task Force of the Internet Activities Board developed a new-generation protocol called the Open Shortest Path First (OSPF), a link state algorithm. Proteon, an early implementer of OSPF, contends that the algorithm elimi-

---

Bridges and routers — different tools for different jobs

Bridges play an important role in extending networks. They interconnect LANs, passing traffic between them at high rates of speed.

Bridges are Media Access Control (MAC) store-and-forward devices that can run at high packet rates because they ignore network-level (and above) protocols.

Bridges offer more than simple store-and-forward operation, however. They can link dissimilar LANs, for instance. And units such as Vitalink's TransLAN bridges can link local area networks into wide area networks, even interconnecting subnets over T1 links.

Bridges are also significantly less expensive than routers. The price for Proteon's lowest-cost p4100 router, for instance, starts at $3,750, and then one has to buy network interfaces, which range from $500 to $3,900 for a dual-port X.25 interface. CrossComm Corp.'s Integrated Local Area Network (ILAN) bridge costs under $3,000 for token ring networks. And this is not a bargain basement model.

A user gets a great deal of performance from a bridge for less money than the router; what isn't available at that price is intelligent network segmentation and flow control.

Routers provide an intelligent link between networks, using network protocols to examine and then pass only the traffic from one subnet (one side of its interface) that is addressed to a station on the subnet on the other side of the interface. Although bridges such as Vitalink's TransLAN use spanning tree protocols to try to minimize traffic congestion, they are still transparent to network protocols, such as SNA and TCP/IP.

This automatic alternate-path routing by bridges is an invasion of the router's traditional territory. The term for such hybrid status is "brouter." But the router vendors don't take the challenge of brouters seriously. Multiple path-control functions in brouters are proprietary and can only be used with other brouters from the same vendor; it does move bridges into an area of network management. Brouters don't provide the fire wall of segmentation, nor do they reduce cross-network traffic. The functions are different, and what brouters bring to the party is nothing more than a capability of handling higher-peak traffic.

But just when the separation of bridge and router grows crystal clear, along comes Wellfleet. Wellfleet makes both routers and bridges, but rather than offering models of each, the company packages bridging and routing services together. Wellfleet uses its proprietary Communication and Application Protocol Environment to provide both learning bridge and routing services in the same box under selective control of the network manager. Cisco also can bridge and route in the same device. So, with both of these products the answer to the question "What is the difference between a bridge and a router?" for all practical purposes becomes "The configuration you choose."

The advantage of the combined bridge-router approach is that it adapts to any network need. The user pays for all this flexibility, whether all the bridge and router functions are needed or not. Conversely, when a multiple-protocol router is called for, why pay for bridging capability as well? The answer is that some networks don't support Layer 3 (network) protocols, making bridges the only viable solution for interconnection. The combination of bridging and routing in the same chassis supplies the tools to mix and match LANs of all types into a heterogeneous network. —E.R.T.

Router Roundup

nates routing loops and black holes that can crop up with other algorithms.

Rather than broadcasting the entire routing table to all other routers, in OSPF each router transmits a packet with a description of its own links to other routers. Each router receiving the packet acknowledges it to the sender. Routing tables are built from the collected descriptions sent by all the routers. Because link descriptions are small and infrequent, they require little routing traffic, keeping the network free for other messages.

Router selection criteria

Router evaluations must take into account the two protocol touchstones discussed above: router management algorithms and standard network protocols.

In their design process, vendors choose a management protocol, then interpret the routing information contained in the network protocols and use it according to their internal routing algorithms. There is nothing in the packet structure standards that dictates routing policy. So the router can collect routing data from a variety of network routing protocols and send a packet that conforms to yet another protocol. Table 1 shows what network protocols the routers from Cisco, Proteon, and Wellfleet support.

An important criterion in selecting a router is the number and selection of network protocols it supports (TCP/IP, XNS, LAT, and so on). But connecting to a network is more than a question of the right software; it is also a hardware, or physical-level, issue. A router's network interfaces comprise the ports and hardware required for interfacing to existing networks. As with software, there are some obvious standard networks to be accommodated, such as IEEE 802.3 (Ethernet) and 802.5 (token ring). These are so pervasive as to be mandatory, but others, such as wide-area interfaces for X.25, T1, and Dataphone Digital Service, make the router more useful in the average network setting.

In the same vein, it's advisable to find out how many of these interfaces (ports) each vendor's router can accommodate in one box at one time. Much of the router price is in the chassis, power supply, and system intelligence. The more interfaces a single chassis can handle, the more versatile and cost-effective each unit can be. Table 2 lists the maximum number of network interfaces of each type.

Of course, these lists don't tell the entire story. In the case of Cisco, for example, the router chassis has nine slots. Two slots are used by the system CPU card and memory. That leaves seven slots for interfaces, all of which can be used for token ring interfaces. With Ethernet the situation is different.

Cisco supplies two types of Ethernet interface cards: the Multiport Communications Interface (MCI) provides two Ethernet interfaces and two serial (up to 4 Mbit/s) ports; the Serial Communications Interface (SCI) provides four serial and two Ethernet ports. Because of power supply considerations, the chassis accepts only five MCI or SCI cards, limiting a user to 10 Ethernet interfaces per router. With additional "oomph" for the power supply, however, a user can (and several do) use all seven slots for MCI cards, upping the maximum to 14 Ethernet interfaces. This mega-router will route packets between 14 independent LANs from one box.

Another clarification for Table 2 relates to nonstandard interfaces. Proteon, an early innovator in the LAN field, developed its own network interface hardware long ago. So, in addition to the standard IEEE varieties, Proteon provides access to its own LANs, such as the ProNET-80, an 80-Mbit/s token ring network. ProNET-80 allows a user to space adjacent networks 1.24 miles (2 kilometers) apart and use fiber optics for the interconnection. Proteon also offers a complete fiber optic incarnation that lets ProNET-80 systems run over 18.6 miles (30 kilometers). If nonstandard interfaces were included, Table 2 would show a maximum of four ProNET-10 interfaces and three ProNET-80 interfaces.

In general, the fiber optic LAN market is hot. So hot that all three router vendors have wasted no time in promising connections to the Fiber Distributed Data Interface (FDDI). That means, from a practical standpoint, that they'll be available to play with later this year (assuming you are a large customer) and to buy in 1990. The reason for the push is that FDDI provides a 100-Mbit/s network ideal for a backbone in a large system, connection to a high-speed backbone being a major application for routers.

Router roots

Looking at the offerings from Cisco, Proteon, and Wellfleet, a definite pattern emerges, one that points up the heritage of each of three vendors. Including its own implementations, Proteon offers far more LAN interface choices than the other two. A logical circumstance when you consider that Proteon has a history as a LAN interface vendor. Routers were added to the product line to meet the needs of customers building larger networks. This experience in LANs means that Proteon often gets more performance on the LAN side than other vendors, at least with its proprietary products.

In 1986, Wellfleet was founded to develop a product

Table 1: Network protocols supported

Network protocols	Cisco	Proteon	Wellfleet
APPLETALK	YES	YES	NO
APOLLO DOMAIN	YES	Q4-89	NO
CHAOSNET	YES	NO	NO
ISO CLNS	YES	AVAILABLE 2/1/90	NO
DECNET **DECNET (PHASE 5)**	YES FUTURE[1]	YES FUTURE	YES
EGP	YES	YES	YES
HELLO	YES	NO	NO
TCP/IP	YES	YES	YES
IPX	YES	YES	NO
XNS	YES[2]	YES	YES

1. Phase 5 should be compatible with OSI.
2. Xerox, 3Com, and Ungermann-Bass implementations

Interfaces	Cisco	Proteon	Wellfleet Link model	Concentrator model
ETHERNET	10	7	8	26
DDN 1822	7	7	NOT AVAILABLE	
DDN X.25	18	14	NOT AVAILABLE	
DDS	18	14	16	52
PDN X.25	18	14	NOT AVAILABLE	
T1	18	14	8	26
TOKEN RING	7	7	NOT AVAILABLE	

DDN = Defense Data Network
DDS = Dataphone Digital Service
PDN = Public Data Network

that provided both bridge and router functions, on the sound theory that both were needed to solve all networking needs. Coming from Interlan and Codex, the founders brought chip-to-system-software experience to their products, as well as a different way of looking at internetworking. They intended to create a product that would support growth and change. Recently, one customer, testing the success of Wellfleet's intentions, began upgrading a system with four routers to a 24-router network.

Unlike the other two vendors, Cisco started as a router company. Founded in 1984, Cisco came out of Stanford University where its founders had implemented the TCP/IP network under contract to Defense Department's Advanced Research Projects Agency. This work was the basis for Cisco's routers. The firm's experience, therefore, is focused on high-performance, large-scale networks and intercontinental capability. For example, one of Cisco's customers has put together a worldwide network consisting of 300 routers and more than 450 links. A network manager with a similar goal might find comfort in this company's experience.

Router performance: The hard part
Even after a network's protocol and interface requirements are defined, the issue of performance can still make decisions difficult. There are, at present, no viable router performance benchmarks, and a lot of fuzzy spots in the vendor-supplied statistics.

The performance evaluation problem is not limited to routers, by the way. In general, a lack of meaningful performance benchmarks for internetworks is a thorn in the side of the industry. Consider the problem of determining how much traffic a network will support. The network's bandwidth is a measure of the number of bits-per-second the medium will handle. For instance, a token ring interface provides 4-Mbit/s operation.

A more meaningful metric, though, is the number of packets it will handle per second (PPS). This is because there is often a great deal of overhead involved in routing packets. A packet travels at 4 Mbit/s between intermediate

nodes in the routing process but is delayed significantly while it is processed by each router in the path. Consequently, the raw bandwidth of a network is no indication of the actual throughput from end node to end node, taking into account the delays. The PPS indication is far more accurate a measurement of performance but far more difficult to achieve.

Unfortunately, when evaluating routers, it isn't easy to discover this specification by looking at the data sheets. For one thing, the vendors don't all measure throughput the same way. Some router vendors count each interface transition (entrance and exit) as a separate passthrough. In other words, if it passes 1,000 packets through both interfaces in one second, this is considered a throughput rate of 2,000 PPS. Other vendors measure the transfer of a packet through the router once, providing a measurement of 1,000 PPS for the exact same performance. To be sure, it's necessary to ask.

During the preparation of this article, Cisco, Proteon, and Wellfleet were invited to provide their packet performance for two particular situations—Ethernet to Ethernet and token ring to token ring. The results, measured in terms of the filtering rate and the forward rate, are presented in Table 3. Filtering rate indicates how many packets per second the router can take off the line. Forwarding rate is the speed the device processes and transfers packets to the output network.

Note that these specifications won't reveal the dropout rate, packet size, delay, or other important factors. They do, however, provide a starting place for discussions on performance evaluation. A user concerned with restricting access to his LAN from some larger network to which it is connected, should ask the router salesperson: What happens to performance when you invoke enhanced access control? In some cases, the performance will degrade. If access control is needed, then the degraded performance figures are the ones to use for comparison.

Another problem with the performance numbers is that they don't usually indicate whether the rates are for a single interface card with multiple ports or for multiple interface cards (performance will often degrade when transfers involve passing through the router's backplane). Similarly, the numbers can represent a sustained data rate over time or a burst-oriented data-forwarding rate. Is the vendor giving both, or just the best the router can do under the best of circumstances? The numbers Wellfleet provided, for example, are for a sustained data rate, across a single interface card, using 64-byte packets (we asked).

Even the seemingly straightforward filtering rate can be a perplexing specification. Proteon contends that it is a bridge specification, not a router specification. That is reasonably true in that a router has to process only those packets that are addressed directly to it. Bridges, by contrast, must make filtering decisions on every packet that hits the wire. In spite of this, other vendors seem concerned with filtering rates for routers, so it becomes a router specification as well.

This measurement nightmare is aggravated by the fact that no two networks are alike. Traffic patterns or peak

Table 3: Head-to-head performance comparison			
Interfaces	**Cisco**	**Proteon**	**Wellfleet**
ETHERNET TO ETHERNET			
FILTERING (PPS)[1]	15,000	–	15,000
FORWARDING (PPS)	12,000	1,000[2]	7,200[3]
TOKEN RING TO TOKEN RING			INTERFACE NOT AVAILABLE FROM VENDOR
FILTERING (PPS)	15,000	–	
FORWARDING (PPS)	1,500	1,000	

1. Proteon does not consider the filtering rate a router performance specification.
2. Numbers constant with or without access control.
3. Sustained data rate for 64-byte packets.
PPS = Packets per second

loads that present no hardship to one router can overwhelm another. At this stage in the game, the most valid criterion is experience. The vendor's assurances that the problem won't arise mean something only if the vendor has experience with a network of the scale of — and protocols similar to — what is being put together.

The problems grow as the typical network is growing. At Stanford University, for instance, the campus network includes 51 TCP/IP gateways (routers) and 79 subnets — and it is constantly growing. Most organizations face the same situation. Computational power continues to migrate to the work site, and communications needs grow proportionally.

This trend often puts companies on the leading edge of what is known about router performance. There are no simple solutions, but the facts suggest that the canny user should shop for routers by finding a vendor who has sold to customers with network demands comparable to his own. And today that means much more than a number on a data sheet or benchmark. ■

Vendor addresses

Cisco Systems Inc., 1350 Willow Rd., Menlo Park, Calif. 94025 (415) 326-1941

CrossComm Corp., Box 699, Marlborough, Mass. 01752 (508) 481-4060

Proteon Inc., Two Technology Dr., Westborough, Mass. 01581 (508) 898-2800

Wellfleet Communications Inc., 12 DeAngelo Dr., Bedford, Mass. 01730-2204 (617) 275-2400

Vitalink Communications Corp., 6607 Kaiser Dr., Fremont Calif. 94555 (415) 794-1100

Edward R. Teja is a free-lance writer who specializes in electronics and communications subjects. His book PC and PS/2 Graphics will be available this fall from Microtrend Books, San Marcos, Calif.

Richard Boulé and John Moy, Proteon Inc., Westborough, Mass.

Inside routers: A technology guide for network builders

An ambitious router tutorial that climbs to an inspiring view of enterprise networks and then descends to explore the details of the enabling digital technologies.

Corporate planners and workgroups can choose from a wide variety of LAN and WAN technologies today, but the burgeoning need to share data between these networks is driving MIS managers to seek solutions to connect computing environments together. Experience has shown that multiprotocol routers are invaluable for creating enterprise-wide networks that integrate different LAN technologies, such as Ethernet and token ring, together with wide-area technologies, such as dedicated leased lines and public data networks.

Early attempts to build large networks with low-level bridges produced flat architectures with little or no segmentation. The lack of organization and fault-tolerance of bridged networks is a persistent problem. Routers, in contrast, provide the mechanism for organizing traffic on large heterogeneous networks to make multitiered networks with many levels of integration (see Fig. 1).

As with any well-engineered system, a router-segmented network exhibits structured qualities such as proper coupling and span of control. The result of a structured design approach is efficient, dependable service for local workgroups as well as end-to-end transmissions that traverse the entire length of the network.

One way to conceptualize the internetworking abilities of routers is to make an analogy with the process of preparing a letter and mailing it through the U.S. Postal Service. Imagine that Scientist A has written a report to be sent to Scientist B, who is across the country. (This report is like user data that must be sent through a network.) Scientist A gives the report to a secretary, who formats and types it, then puts it in an envelope addressed to Scientist B.

The envelope provides a means to encapsulate or completely contain the report in a protected shell. The address on the envelope conforms to accepted rules of procedure in order to guarantee that all postal employees interpret the information consistently, ensuring delivery in the most efficient manner. A report in an envelope is analogous to packetization of the data in the network context.

After addressing, the secretary gives the envelope to the office delivery person, who puts it in a mailbag and takes it to the nearest post office. A postal worker then takes the envelope out of the mailbag, reads the address, and makes a decision on where to route the envelope—but does not read the letter in the envelope.

In the course of delivery, the envelope is forwarded by a number of intermediate post office facilities before reaching its destination. During each leg of the trip, the envelope is transported between post offices in a mailbag. Each mailbag has addressing information written on it that the Postal Service understands but is never seen by the original sender.

Transportation between post offices can be by various means. These can include truck, airplane, or train—whatever is most appropriate for efficient delivery to the next post office. At the final post office, the envelope is placed in a bag for a specific letter carrier, and it is delivered to Scientist B's location later in the day. At the destination, a mail room employee directs it to the correct floor or department, and a secretary reads the name on the envelope and hands it to Scientist B. Neither the sender nor the receiver knows the path taken by the envelope.

Applying this analogy to the internetwork environment, a host computer sending information to another host computer starts with a packet, formatted with an agreed-upon address. (In this context a host is *any* computer on the network.) The host transfers the packet to a communications interface that conveys the data through the network media to a router (the equivalent of a mail room or the nearest post office). Just as the post office moves envelopes, routers receive data packets and forward them on their journey.

Tutorial

In the analogy, the rules by which the envelope is addressed and by which the mailbags are marked can be thought of as conforming to a communications protocol. The encapsulation of the report into an envelope and then into a mailbag is similar to the process of adding and removing packet headers and trailers by the layers of various communications protocols. In a subsequent section our analogy will be mapped into the relevant layers of a communications protocol.

Each leg of the packet's journey uses a distinct communication medium, the equivalent of the trucks and airplanes in the post office example. Routing at each step is based solely on the address; the packet's user data contents are never examined or modified.

The same is true for internetworks. An organization with many LANs in a circumscribed area, such as a building or campus, can interconnect them with a backbone network such as a token ring or an Ethernet, or with a high- speed fiber network such as the Fiber Distributed Data Interface (FDDI), the emerging 100-Mbit/s network standard. Figure 2 shows a block diagram for both the post office and network form of information delivery.

Real-life internetworks

One example of a well-organized internetwork is the backbone network installed at the University of Illinois's Champaign-Urbana campus. The university owns a huge array of computer resources, including thousands of personal computers, some mainframes, minicomputers, microcomputers, and a supercomputer. Before installing its multitiered network, the university had several local and wide area networks, but their users were unable to transfer files or share information among them, and they could not access the supercomputer.

Now all resources are interconnected via 20 miles of fiber optic cable in an 80-Mbit/s token ring network that provides access to university-wide electronic mail and databases and also provides communications between mainframes,

---

1. Manageable multitiered networks. Large and small organizations are inherently multitiered. Networks should reflect this structure in order to provide good managability for network managers and good access and dependability for network users. Shown is a typical multibuilding, multicampus configuration.

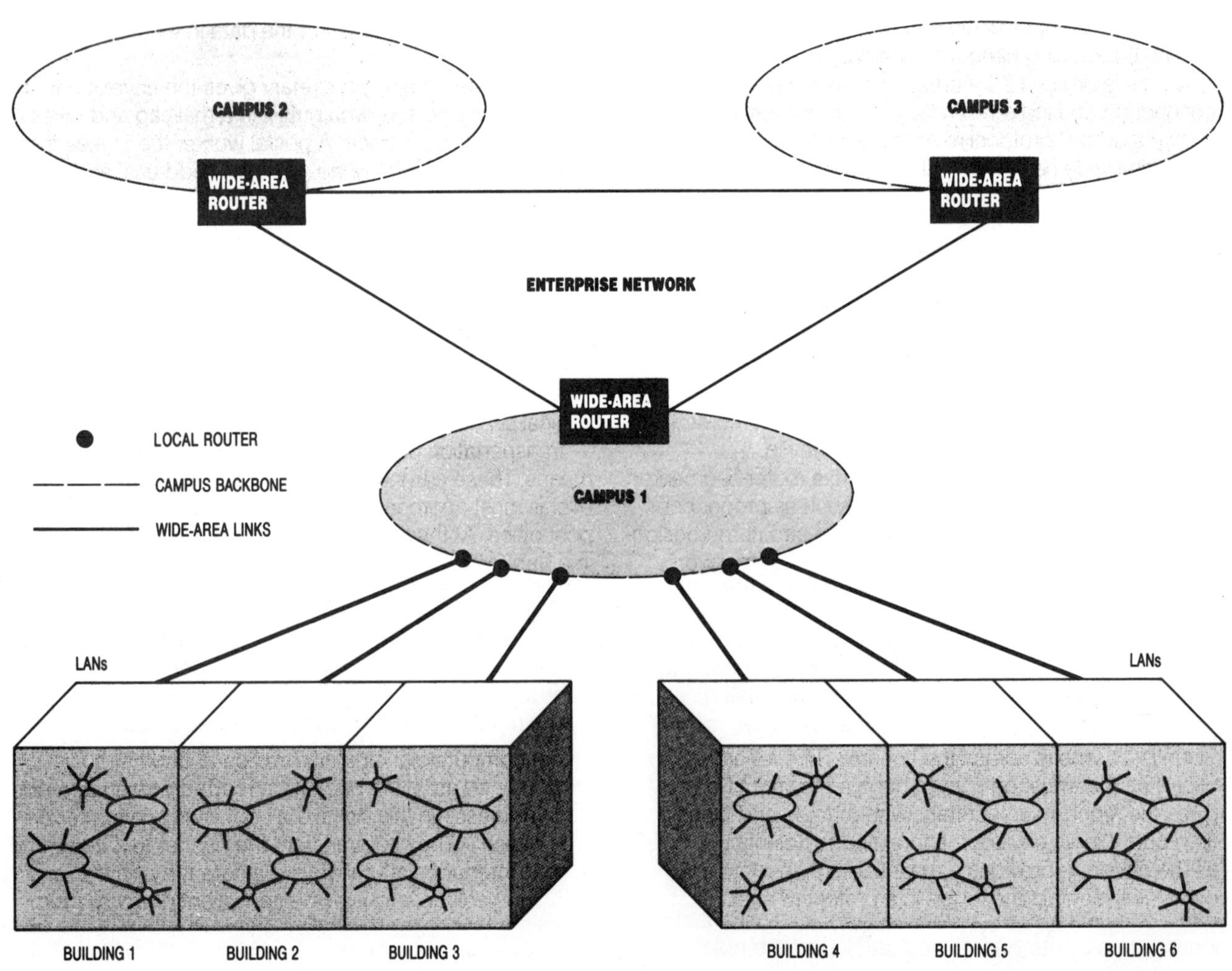

2. Post office delivery analogy. *Much as the U.S. Postal Service forwards mail between its various facilities in mailbags, networks forward user data in packets between* routers. *The post office uses a variety of transportation methods to convey mail; similarly, routers users a variety of local and long-distance transport links.*

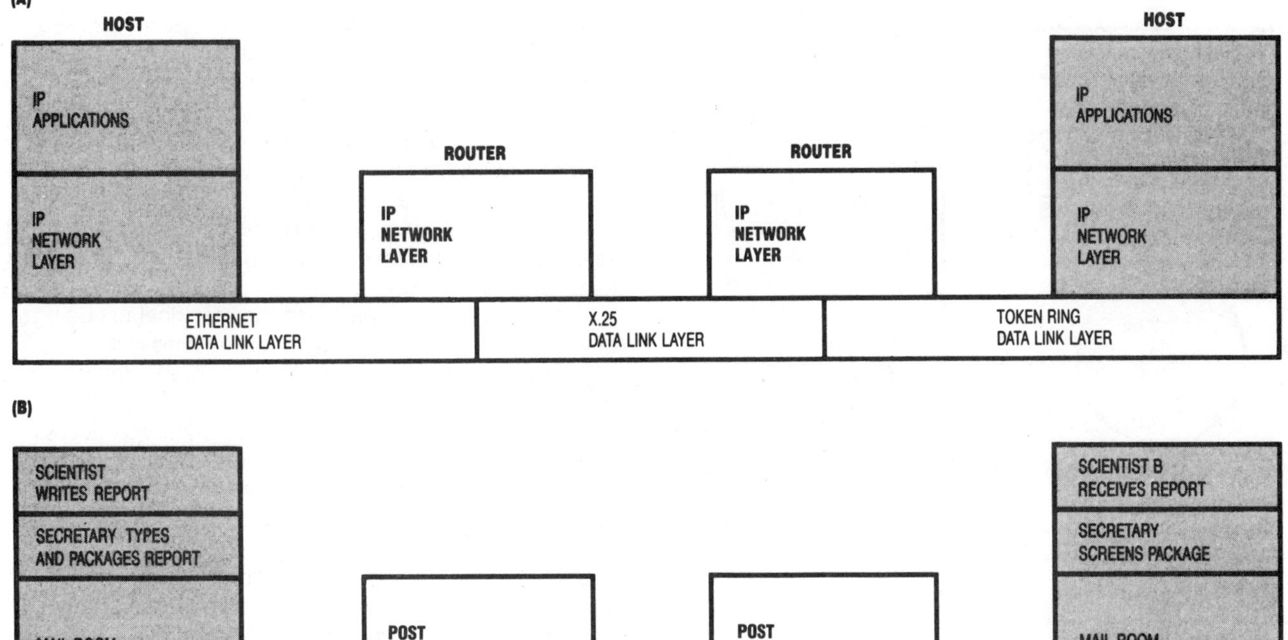

workstations, and personal computers located on more than 150 Ethernets.

The Illinois internetwork has five major divisions, each with smaller building-wide or department-wide subnetworks that provide access to file sharing, print servers, and electronic-mail services.

The network also provides a backbone for smaller LANs in various campus buildings, with routers linking these LANs to the backbone. The resulting system enables students and faculty to access the computer resources of the 16 colleges on campus, as well as the central campus computing facilities, the National Center for Supercomputing Applications's Cray supercomputers, and the Internet.

An alternative form of multitiered network consists of wide-area connections. In our original analogy, the Postal Service had to deliver the scientific report across a long distance using one or more transport means at a variety of speeds. This is also the case for connection of geographically scattered LANs. Such LANs can be interconnected with synchronous or asynchronous long-haul services, such as T1, fractional T1, Dataphone Digital Service, and private bypass methods. LANs also can be connected over X.25 packet-switched public data networks, such as the Defense Data Network, Telenet, and DataPAC.

The Southeastern Universities Research Association network (SURAnet), which is managed from the Computer Center at the University of Maryland, provides a good example of a WAN. SURAnet stretches from Florida to Delaware, joining more than 60 universities and research institutions, including the University of Alabama, the Johns Hopkins University, NASA, the National Institutes of Health, and the Triangle University Computing Center. Routers at internetwork access points are connected in a wide-area ring configuration, with some cross-links, by 56-kbit/s and T1 circuits.

Besides joining separate LANs, SURAnet also provides access to large nationwide networks such as NSFnet, Arpanet, and Milnet. Data from a researcher at the University of Alabama, for example, can originate on the university's LAN, traverse SURAnet, and then access the supercomputer facilities at an NSF supercomputer center, such as the Cornell National Supercomputer Facility at Cornell University in Ithaca, N.Y.

In its most developed form, an internetwork is a combination of both campus and wide-area topologies. Using multiprotocol routers, a complex multitiered network may combine high-speed backbones and WANs in a hierarchy of well-managed networks.

Layered multiprotocols

In the post office analogy, a communications protocol prescribes what can be written on the front of the envelope and on the mailbags.

Similarly, a variety of different data communications

---

3. A network of networks. *Complex internets are kept well-organized with a hierarchical numbering scheme that allows division and subdivision of huge architectures.*

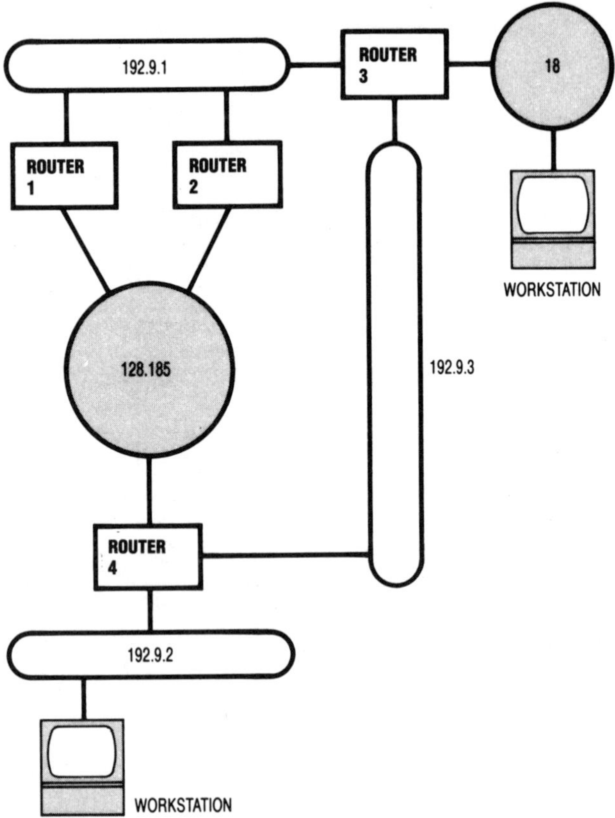

---

protocols are in use today, since there is no one standard. Therefore, modern routers are able to understand multiple protocols. The most widely used communications protocol is TCP/IP, which was developed by the Defense Advanced Research Projects Agency (DARPA). TCP/IP is used in the largest internetwork in operation, the Internet, which connects computing resources supporting the U.S. Common Internet applications, including electronic mail, file transfer, file sharing, remote log-in, and some kinds of remote job entry.

The International Standards Organization (ISO) protocols for OSI, although not yet fully specified, are beginning to receive wide support both in the U.S. and abroad.

In addition to these two standards, there are a number of widely used proprietary communications protocols, such as XNS by Xerox, DECnet by Digital Equipment Corp., SNA by IBM, and NetWare/IPX by Novell. Several of these are published de facto standards.

The ISO seven-layer reference model is particularly helpful in discussing the operation of multiprotocol routers. The layers, in descending order, are: application, presentation, session, transport, network, data link, and physical. The first four deal with establishing contact with the receiving side, sending and receiving data in a common format, and negotiating a method of retransmission in the event that one or more packets are lost.

The network layer provides information that is used primarily by routers along the packet's journey. The most useful information included in the network layer is a general address. This network layer address determines the hops that the packet will make from network to network. A "hop" is made each time a packet crosses to another network through a router. The network layer also provides an array of other services that will be covered later.

The data link layer services know how to put a packet on the network (access) and how to take it off (delivery). This layer contains an address that is useful only on a particular link, for example, a particular Ethernet segment. The layer performs other functions as well, such as a check to ensure data integrity.

The physical layer deals with the electrical encoding of data onto a specific medium for transmission.

Devices that forward packets through an internetwork can operate at different layers. Bridges operate at the data link layer and provide a transparent connection across similar data link layers (for example, Ethernet to Ethernet or token ring to token ring). Because of their transparency, no information can be sent to them since they are not individually addressed.

Unlike bridges, routers are full-fledged network citizens that can provide valuable information to a host, such as advising it of a different route or telling it to slow down because of congestion in the internetwork. A router can translate between different data link types, so it can accommodate heterogeneous internetworks (that is, arbitrary combinations of Ethernets, token rings, and WANs).

With routers, the data link layer addresses for a packet change at each stop along an internetwork. To continue the postal analogy, the data link layer is like the mailbags. Postal employees at each stop, or hop, along the report's journey place it in different mailbags and address each mailbag much differently than the address on the envelope. The mailbags can be viewed as local data links, the intermediate postal facilities as routers.

A third type of device operates at the application layer. These devices are known as protocol converting gateways, or gateways. Suppose in our example Scientist A wishes to distribute a copy of the report to a Japanese colleague. In this case the report could be mailed to an intermediary that is capable of translating English to Japanese. This translation service acts as an application gateway. Unfortunately, some information is lost since not all concepts translate precisely. This application gateway is providing a limited, specialized service; application gateways in fact are most often used to interpret mail messages from one protocol stack to another.

Network layer richness

Much of the viability of an internetwork is determined by the quality of services at the network layer. As previously discussed, routers establish network-to-network links between applications by processing the network layer headers of the packets they are forwarding.

Network layer addresses can be hierarchical, with

multiple levels of addresses corresponding to the zip code, street, and street number of a mailing address (see Fig. 3). Each item in an address list further defines the destination. This means that a router does not have to be concerned with how to reach every LAN in the internetwork, only with how to get to the next address level. As a packet moves through the internetwork, the routers along the way will process more and more of the address. The segmentation capability of network layer addresses will be considered fully in the next section.

Packet fragmentation is a network layer feature that lets the router connect networks with different maximum packet sizes. Most LANs have a maximum packet size dictated by the data link layer of the communications protocol; for Ethernet it is 1,514 bytes, while for satellite transmission, packet size may be restricted to 200 bytes. If the user wishes to transmit a larger packet than the destination network can deal with, the network layer can divide the packet into fragments and transmit them separately over the outgoing link. It is the responsibility of the final destination to take all the fragments and reassemble them.

The various congestion control and nondelivery notification features of the network layer help to improve end-to-end performance and make better use of network bandwidth. Take TCP/IP. If the router cannot send a packet because of congestion, the router will send a signal to the source indicating that the packet cannot be delivered. This will allow the host to reduce its offered load to the internet. Different signals are sent if the header is badly formatted or if the router does not know the address.

The ability to separate data traffic into classes is referred to as "type of service" (TOS) in the network layer header, as shown in Figure 4A. In the Postal Service analogy some mail is air mail, some is certified, and some is first class. This information is encoded on the envelope for the postal employees to inspect and also determines the path, or mailbag, in which the envelope will be placed. The type-of-service indicator in the network layer prescribes the attributes of the link to be taken in terms of delay, throughput, and reliability.

Error-checking at the network layer is enhanced by providing a checksum of the network layer header. Unlike checksumming at the data link layer, which can deal only with errors at the physical layer, checksumming at the network layer ensures that the packet is not corrupted in the router's memory, as the router copies the packet to the interface, or elsewhere in the router.

Intelligent segmentation

Encoded within every source and destination address in the network layer is the logical location of the network and host that have sent (or will receive) the packet. Thus, if an internetwork has five LANs, each is identified by a separate network address. Each host on each LAN also has an individual address. This level of addressing allows routers to perform intelligent network segmentation. Much larger internetworks can be designed and operated because each router only needs to know a portion of the address.

Intelligent segmentation makes it much easier to develop and maintain routing tables for a router than for a bridge. For example, if bridges were used to interconnect 200 LANs, each with 100 hosts, each bridge would need to store 20,000 addresses because all LANs appear as a single LAN to the bridge. If a router interconnects the same 200 LANs, it needs to store only the 200 LAN addresses.

A bridge "listens" to all traffic on the internetwork in what is called a "promiscuous" mode and thus is prone to passing on malformed packets, errors, and faulty transmissions. A router, because it deals with network layer addresses, receives only packets addressed directly to it and passes on little or no erroneous information. If something in the network layer doesn't make sense, a router will discard the packet, while a bridge, which can't check all layers, will pass it on. The router effectively provides a "fire wall" to isolate certain local network problems and prevent them from propagating throughout the internetwork.

Routers are full-fledged network citizens that can provide valuable information to a host.

The network layer also allows routers to form internetworks with mesh topologies, in which more than one path exists from any source to any destination, much like a highway system. In a mesh, all the links are on-line all the time, providing a high level of reliability and availability of network services. The router is able to choose the optimal path from among all those available and can update paths dynamically. In addition, multiple active links can transport data simultaneously.

Failure of a link simply results in traffic being rerouted over a longer path. This mesh topology contrasts sharply with the typical topology allowed by bridges. In the topology of bridged internetworks, redundant lines ordinarily carry no traffic unless a failure occurs in the primary path. A mesh topology allows a much richer, redundantly connected topology, which leads to increased reliability and throughput.

How routers work

A sample router hardware architecture consists of network interfaces plugged into a backplane. The system includes two or more boards plus a CPU that handles coordination of the router's functions, such as setting up receptions and transmissions and the actual forwarding of packets. The system also has a watchdog timer that can restart when the system fails, nonvolatile RAM for storage of configuration information, bootstrap code, and more. In addition,

__4. Network layer fields.__ The rich functionality of the network layer is made possible by fields shown in (A). A typical routing table (B) has three types of fields.

VERSION	HEADER LENGTH	TOS	PACKET LENGTH
IDENTIFICATION			FRAGMENTATION
TTL		PROTOCOL	CHECKSUM
IP SOURCE			
IP DESTINATION			

TOS = TYPE OF SERVICE
TTL = TIME TO LIVE

DESTINATION	COST	NEXT HOP(S)
192.9.1	1	*
128.185	1	*
18	2	192.9.1.3
192.9.2	2	128.185.0.4
192.9.3	2	192.9.1.3, 128.185.0.4

some amount of RAM is used to buffer packets while they are in transit through the router.

The basic building blocks of a router are the network interface cards that can be mixed and matched in various ways. Most network interface boards have a limited amount of RAM and firmware that allows them to send and receive packets. The RAM on the network interface cards serves as a first in, first out (FIFO) buffer. The main CPU board acts as a master, interfacing with slave network interface boards.

In addition to the FIFO buffers on each of the network interface cards, there are other queues and buffers maintained by a router on the main CPU board. Some of these RAM-resident stores are set up at router initialization; others are allocated dynamically. In a typical router, there are input packet queues for each network interface, a queue for each of the protocol forwarders, and an output queue for each of the network interfaces.

A packet is never copied from queue to queue, but rather, a pointer to the location of the packet in RAM is moved from queue to queue. This is done to avoid needless copying of packets in router memory. Different queues are employed to process a packet through the router to provide fairness to all packets and to provide early detection of congestion.

Let's look at a router consisting of a backplane to which an Ethernet and a token ring board are attached. This router includes a protocol forwarder on the main board for the TCP/IP suite.

When the Ethernet interface detects a packet that is addressed to its own physical address, it transfers it off the wire and into its local FIFO buffer. The controller then moves the packet directly to the router's main memory and sets the pointer for this queue to the next available entry. An interrupt is generated to the router's CPU to notify the software of the arrival of the packet. As a result, the appropriate interrupt service routine is executed to process the incoming packet from the Ethernet interface.

The interrupt service routine does a check of the Ethernet interface's error registers to verify that no error that can be detected by the interface has occurred. A typical error that can occur on this level is a cyclic redundancy check error. The interrupt service routine then posts an output completion to the I/O handler for Ethernet interfaces. This handler is a software routine generic to all Ethernet interfaces, and there is only one copy of this software in router memory.

Next, the I/O handler for Ethernet boards reviews the packet and determines that it has valid length and type fields; in other words, the handler analyzes the Ethernet data link layer. If the type field is illegal, the packet is discarded. Otherwise the type field indicates a protocol the router is familiar with, for instance, an IP packet. The I/O handler then adjusts the pointer of the packet to the beginning of the network layer header; this is equivalent to unwrapping or removing the data link header from the packet. Next, the I/O handler enqueues the packet pointer on the IP forwarder queue and initiates the IP forwarder task if it is not already in process.

The IP forwarder task handles the incoming packet. The first check that is performed is to verify that the IP header version number is correct; Figure 4A shows the fields. Only one version number is legal on a given network. The header length is checked to verify that it is at least the minimum; otherwise the packet is discarded. To ensure that the packet has not been corrupted in being copied into the router, the checksum of the header is verified.

Next, the total number of bytes transferred from the device is checked against the packet length field. If the number of bytes transferred is less than the packet length, it was a truncated packet and is discarded. At this point the packet has passed the validity checks and a message is logged showing the source and destination address. Log messages allow network administrators to trace packets and abnormal behavior, if desired. The log messages can be viewed using severity of message or other criteria. The packet is now ready to be considered for forwarding.

At this point in the forwarding process the source and destination addresses are checked to see if they are on an access control list that is configurable by the network administrator. Access control checks every packet to verify that it is one that can be forwarded through (inclusive) or one that should not be forwarded through (exclusive) the router. A packet that is is not to be forwarded is discarded.

Now the routing table lookup is performed (see Fig. 4B). If no route exists to the network number indicated in the destination address, a "network unreachable" message signal is sent to the host that originated the packet. Otherwise, the packet is forwarded to the appropriate upper layer in the router if it is for one of the addresses configured for an interface in this router.

To maximize efficiency of internet usage, the packet is now checked against the maximum packet size allowed for the outgoing network interface; a packet that is too large is submitted to the fragmentation process.

The next step is to verify that this packet has not been in circulation for too long in the internet. This is done by decrementing the time-to-live field in the header. If it goes to zero, the packet is discarded and a signal is sent to the source address notifying the host of nondelivery. The checksum is now recalculated (not the whole checksum — it is done incrementally to save compute cycles).

The only thing left to do is to check the options field. This is checked primarily to see if the record-route option is specified. If it is, this router's address must be added to the variable length options field that records a history of the packet's route. The packet is now handed off to the output queue for the outgoing device.

The I/O handler for the outgoing interface reforms the data link layer header and initiates the transmission of the packet to its next destination.

Dynamic routing protocols

Dynamic routing protocols are special management protocols that are used by routers to build the routing tables used in the packet forwarding process. Every protocol family has a dynamic routing protocol; they are an intrinsic function of the network layer.

Because the network layer of each communications protocol has its own version of a dynamic routing protocol, many different dynamic routing protocols may be used in a multiple-protocol router. Formerly, the network manager would enter static routing information into the configuration tables, but this did not allow the router to react immediately to changes in the network domain.

Dynamic routing protocols automatically detect what destinations in the internetwork are reachable; learn the best route to each destination; detect failures in routers, networks, or media; and route traffic around failures. These route management protocols are transparent to hosts connected anywhere on the network.

There are two basic approaches to developing a dynamic routing protocol. Most are based on the Bellman-Ford algorithm, which uses a distributed calculation model (see Fig. 5A). Bellman-Ford requires that every router periodically broadcast (or advertise) its entire routing table to all neighboring routers. To route a packet, the router compares all the tables it has received and picks the route that will deliver the packet in the fewest number of hops between networks.

When a neighboring router advertises a route of N hops to a destination, the router's cost of transmitting the packet will be, at the most, N + 1 hops — the + 1 being the hop from the router to the neighbor. The cost may be expressed as hops, as a function of delay, or as a function of bandwidth. The advantages of the Bellman-Ford algorithm are that it is simple, easy to implement, and does not require much memory.

A second type of dynamic routing protocol, is link-based or shortest path first (SPF) based (see Fig. 5B). SPF is less prone than Bellman-Ford to developing routing loops, which happen when network topology changes; it converges faster (that is, finds the best new route faster); and generates less network traffic than Bellman-Ford.

5. The dynamic duo of routing. *Two major, competing routing management protocols are the Bellman-Ford (A) and the shortest path first or link-based algorithms (B).*

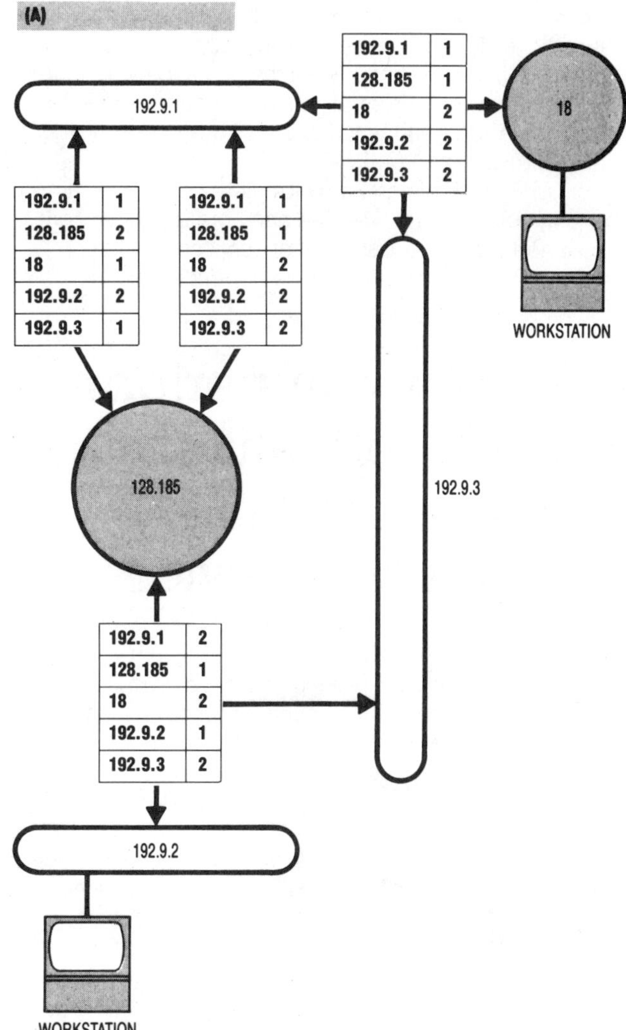

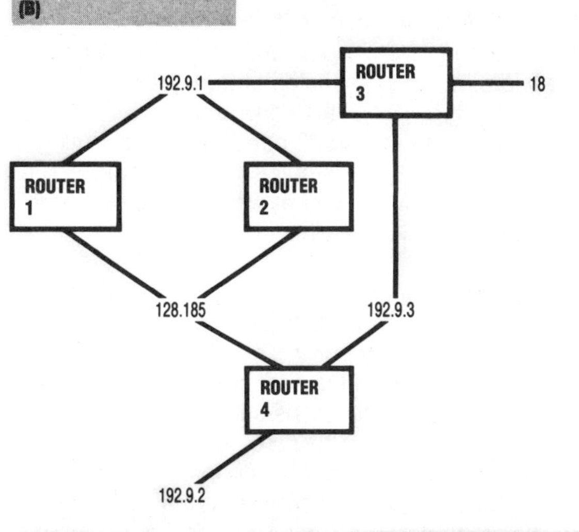

The basic mechanism of SPF is a distributed database. Routers do not broadcast their entire routing tables; they simply flood information on their local LAN connections to all routers in the internetwork on a periodic basis. Every router thus has a database of all other routers' LAN connections. This database is essentially a map of the internetwork, and the map looks the same in every router on the internetwork. From this map the router is able to generate the set of shortest paths to all destinations in the internetwork.

Both SPF and Bellman-Ford ultimately will find the same shortest route for a packet. Bellman-Ford algorithms are simple and provide a basic set of services for small internets. As the internet expands and more complex

Routers can perform lower-level management functions but not high-level services.

requirements appear, SPF algorithms become more attractive. This is the result of their superior responsiveness, lower routing bandwidth, and adaption for services such as type-of-service-based routing. An SPF algorithm called OSPF (for open SPF) has recently been developed for use by the TCP/IP community.

OSPF has been designed to support very large internetworks and incorporates features such as load-sharing, TOS routing, and authentication. OSPF offers a standards-based alternative to RIP and other nonstandard Bellman-Ford protocols, providing significant new features that are far beyond the capabilities of previous routing protocols.

SPF-based routing has also been proposed for use by ISO environments: Digital Equipment Corp. has submitted an SPF-based routing document to the ANSI X3S3.3 committee. For the TCP/IP community, the OSPF working group was formed within the Internet Engineering Task Force in the spring of 1988. This working group was tasked with developing a standard SPF-based dynamic routing protocol tailored to the needs of the TCP/IP protocol. The working group is jointly chaired by John Moy of Proteon and Mike Petry of the University of Maryland.

Internetwork management

The planning, design, installation, and operation of multiprotocol, multivendor internetworks require a sophisticated level of management. While routers can perform certain lower-level management functions such as congestion detection and error control, they are not able to provide higher-level services. Thus, router vendors have recently begun to introduce management systems that can provide an overview of the entire internetwork. Among the basic functions such systems provide are:

■ fault management, to detect and correct abnormal conditions in the internetwork;
■ configuration management, to configure and control the internetwork environment;
■ performance management, to assess and maximize the availability of internetwork services; and
■ event- and error-log management, to keep records of important traffic events and faults on the internet.

Network management systems enable network managers to increase system availability by detecting system faults and performance problems, and by minimizing downtime. System availability is a critical performance criterion, taking into account system component reliability, serviceability, and overall system design. Network management also allows for the identification and monitoring of system bottlenecks, permitting network managers to plan and install needed network extensions.

Some internetwork management systems let the network manager define the internetwork topology in a hierarchy of groups, networks, and nodes, and thus identify problem areas quickly. Using management software and graphics terminals, managers can "zoom" down into the topology to find the exact location of a malfunction.

Industry-standard protocols are being developed to provide internetwork management system functions. The Internet Activities Board last year specified the Simple Network Management Protocol (SNMP) for TCP/IP, while ISO has proposed a new protocol standard called Common Management Information Protocol (CMIP). All vendor devices implementing one of these protocols can be monitored from a single network management station.

The TCP/IP community has defined a Management Information Base (MIB) for network management. This MIB specifies a list of TCP/IP objects that create a sort of abstract version of an actual network to be used during management operations. Examples of particular objects include a router's IP addresses, its routing table, and packet throughput statistics.

SNMP runs over an unguaranteed IP transport mechanism (UDP). A typical network management station polls internet routers by sending SNMP "get request" packets. If these polls are lost because of network congestion, for example, they must be retransmitted.

A combination of multiprotocol routers and internetwork management software such as SNMP or CMIP allows network managers to build and manage very large multitiered networks that can grow to support thousands of hosts with diverse connectivity requirements. The emerging view is that data communications requirements of today and into the future are successfully met using router technology. ■

Rich Boulé is director of software development at Proteon Inc. He holds a BS degree from Western New England College and an MS degree from the University of Vermont.

John Moy is a senior staff engineer at Proteon Inc. He holds a BS from the University of Minnesota and an MA from Princeton University. Moy is the cochairman of the OSPF Working Group formed under the Internet Engineering Task Force (IETF).

Users swear by their modems

Modems are still reliable and easy to install, but diagnostics, support need improvement

Users continue to have an astonishing affection for their modems.

Of 25 modem vendors mentioned by 460 respondents in a recent survey, 20 were said to be offering "good" products, and two of the remaining five were close behind. Users were asked to rate the modems on a scale of 1 to 4, with 4 being excellent. This year's mean overall performance score was 3.2—3.0 is a good score.

The survey, conducted by Datapro Research Corp. (Delran, N.J.), shows that user perceptions of modem quality seem to be narrowing. This is to be expected in a commodity market.

Users, on the average, find modems to be reliable (3.4) and easy to install (3.3). The respondents were slightly less enthusiastic about modems' diagnostic capabilities (3.0) and support (3.1).

Many of the vendors mentioned by the respondents received marks the same as or better than last year's. Those showing improvements in overall performance this year include Telebit (up to 3.7 from 3.5 last year), Gandalf (3.6 from 3.2), Concord (3.3 from 2.88), Penril (3.3 from 3.0), and Paradyne (3.2 from 2.9). Those vendors rated lower than last year include U.S. Robotics (3.4 from 3.6), Multitech (3.0 from 3.56), Case/Datatel (2.5 from 2.86), and Infinet (2.3 from 2.92).

Of the top-rated modem vendors that generated a significant number of responses (eight or more), Gandalf received an especially high mark for hardware reliability (3.9) but received a low score (2.5) for diagnostic capabilities.

Hayes modems were consistently said by users to be reliable (3.5) and easy to install (3.6). Racal-Milgo received uniformly high scores in all categories. U.S. Robotics, Codex, AT&T, IBM, Universal Data Systems, and Paradyne (recently acquired by AT&T) all received high marks for reliability and ease of installation.

The vendors rated the best for diagnostics (with eight or more responses) were Racal-Milgo, Codex, and IBM, each with a rating of 3.3.

Of the vendors that generated more than eight responses, those offering the best service and technical support were U.S. Robotics (3.4), followed by IBM and Racal-Milgo (3.3), and Codex, AT&T, and Hayes (3.2).

The survey information represents the opinions of users. Some rated entire lines of modems (the Codex 26XX series, for example), while others were more specific and rated individual models in that line (such as Codex's 2640).

With such a wide variety of modems available, it is inevitable that a random survey does not gather enough comments from users to represent a statistically meaningful scientific survey. Nevertheless, vendors were included in the chart as long as a minimum of three users indicated they were owners of that vendor's equipment. Remember this when reading the high overall satisfaction scores for vendors like Everex and Telebit, which generated four and three responses respectively, and the low values for Case/Datatel and Infinet, each of which received only four responses.

The responses are somewhat reflective of market share, although as previously stated, they aren't scientifically sampled. It is interesting to note, however, that Codex (13 percent) and Hayes (12 percent) were mentioned by the largest percentage of users. More users had IBM modems (8 percent) than AT&T (7 percent). But with Paradyne's response share thrown in, the AT&T percentage equals Codex's.

Datapro strongly suggests that the reader use the information presented in the survey with discretion. The ratings should be used as guides to potential strengths and weaknesses; further investigation is almost certainly warranted for readers who would select the most suitable equipment for their needs.

For further information and reprints of the survey, contact Datapro Research Corp., 1805 Underwood Blvd., Delran, N.J. 08075; telephone 609-764-1100.

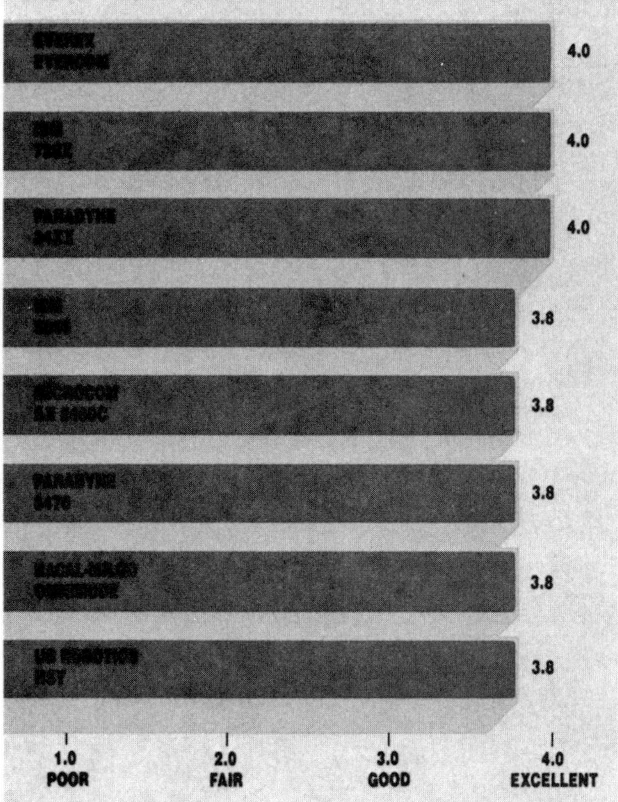

The top-rated modems

Modems

User ratings of modems

VENDOR	OVERALL PERFORMANCE	EASE OF INSTALLATION	DIAGNOSTIC CAPABILITIES	HARDWARE RELIABILITY	MANU-FACTURER'S SERVICE/ TECHNICAL SUPPORT	WOULD RECOMMEND			TOTAL
						YES	NO	DON'T KNOW	
TOTAL RESPONDENTS	3.2	3.3	3.0	3.4	3.1	366	51	43	460
EVEREX									
EVERCOM SERIES	4.0	3.5	3.0	4.0	3.3	4	–	–	4
TELEBIT									
ALL MODELS	3.7	3.7	3.7	3.7	4.0	3	–	–	3
GANDALF	3.6	3.4	2.5	3.9	3.1	7	–	1	8
GANDALF LDM 419	3.7	3.7	1.7	4.0	3.3	3	–	–	3
OTHER MODELS	3.6	3.2	3.0	3.8	3.0	4	–	1	5
HAYES	3.4	3.6	3.0	3.5	3.2	52	1	2	55
HAYES 1200B	3.7	3.0	3.0	3.7	3.7	3	–	–	3
OTHER MODELS	3.7	3.7	3.4	3.8	3.4	9	–	–	9
HAYES 9600	3.6	3.8	3.3	3.9	3.3	8	–	–	8
HAYES 2400	3.5	3.5	3.3	3.6	3.2	13	–	–	13
HAYES SMARTMODEM	3.3	3.9	3.1	3.4	3.0	7	1	–	8
HAYES 1200	2.9	3.4	2.3	3.2	2.9	12	–	2	14
RACAL-MILGO	3.4	3.3	3.3	3.4	3.3	26	2	1	29
RACAL-MILGO OMNIMODE	3.8	3.6	3.8	3.8	3.8	8	–	–	8
OTHER MODELS	3.3	3.1	3.1	3.3	3.2	18	2	1	21
US ROBOTICS	3.4	3.5	3.1	3.4	3.4	13	3	1	17
US ROBOTICS HST	3.8	3.3	3.5	3.5	3.8	4	–	–	4
US ROBOTICS COURIER	3.7	3.7	3.5	3.5	3.7	5	1	–	6
OTHER MODELS	3.0	3.3	2.3	3.3	2.7	2	1	–	3
US ROBOTICS 2400	3.0	3.5	2.8	3.0	3.3	2	1	1	4
CODEX	3.4	3.3	3.3	3.7	3.2	59	1	1	61
CODEX 26XX	3.7	3.6	3.9	3.9	3.6	7	–	–	7
CODEX 2680	3.7	3.7	3.8	4.0	3.2	6	–	–	6
CODEX 23XX	3.6	3.0	3.2	3.8	3.6	5	–	–	5
CODEX 2640	3.6	3.6	3.8	3.9	3.4	8	–	–	8
CODEX 21XX	3.4	3.8	3.0	4.0	3.4	5	–	–	5
CODEX 2660	3.4	3.6	3.6	4.0	3.2	5	–	–	5
CODEX 2600	3.3	2.8	3.3	3.5	3.5	4	–	–	4
CODEX 9600	3.3	3.0	3.0	3.5	2.8	3	–	1	4
OTHER MODELS	3.3	3.1	3.1	3.5	3.3	11	–	–	11
CODEX 22XX	2.7	2.8	2.5	3.3	2.3	5	1	–	6
AT&T	3.3	3.3	3.1	3.6	3.2	23	5	5	33
AT&T DATA PHONE II	3.7	3.7	3.3	3.7	3.7	3	–	–	3
AT&T 2096	3.3	3.4	3.0	3.4	3.1	5	2	–	7
OTHER MODELS	3.2	3.2	3.1	3.7	3.1	15	3	5	23
CONCORD DATA									
ALL MODELS	3.3	3.3	2.8	3.8	3.0	4	–	–	4
CXR ANDERSON									
ALL MODELS	3.3	3.8	3.0	3.3	3.5	3	1	–	4
IBM	3.3	3.5	3.3	3.5	3.3	29	6	1	36
IBM 786X	4.0	3.7	4.0	3.7	4.0	3	–	–	3
IBM 5866	3.8	4.0	3.8	4.0	3.6	5	–	–	5
IBM 5822	3.7	3.7	4.0	3.7	3.7	3	–	–	3
IBM 5865	3.7	3.3	3.7	3.7	4.0	3	–	–	3
OTHER MODELS	3.2	3.3	3.1	3.4	3.0	13	2	1	16
IBM 3864	2.7	4.0	3.0	3.0	3.0	1	2	–	3
IBM 3865	2.7	3.0	2.3	3.3	3.3	1	2	–	3

Modems

VENDOR	OVERALL PERFORMANCE	EASE OF INSTALLATION	DIAGNOSTIC CAPABILITIES	HARDWARE RELIABILITY	MANU-FACTURER'S SERVICE/ TECHNICAL SUPPORT	WOULD RECOMMEND			TOTAL
						YES	NO	DON'T KNOW	
PENRIL									
ALL MODELS	3.3	3.5	3.7	3.3	3.0	3	–	1	4
UNIVERSAL DATA SYSTEMS	3.3	3.4	2.9	3.5	3.1	26	–	3	29
UDS 208 A/B	3.7	3.7	3.3	3.7	3.7	3	–	–	3
UDS V32	3.5	3.5	3.3	3.5	3.0	4	–	–	4
OTHER MODELS	3.3	3.3	2.8	3.4	3.1	15	–	2	17
UDS 9600	3.2	3.4	2.6	3.6	3.0	4	–	1	5
PARADYNE	3.2	3.2	3.1	3.4	3.0	15	5	9	29
PARADYNE 34XX	4.0	3.7	4.0	4.0	3.3	3	–	–	3
PARADYNE 3470	3.8	3.8	3.8	3.5	3.8	4	–	–	4
PARADYNE 9600	3.3	3.2	2.3	3.2	2.8	2	–	3	5
PARADYNE CHALLENGER	3.0	3.0	3.5	4.0	3.0	1	1	1	3
OTHER MODELS	2.8	3.0	2.8	3.2	2.8	5	4	5	14
RACAL-VADIC	3.1	3.3	2.6	3.4	2.8	6	–	4	10
RACAL-VADIC VA212 SER.	3.7	4.0	2.7	3.7	3.3	3	–	–	3
OTHER MODELS	2.7	3.0	2.6	3.3	2.4	3	–	4	7
BYTCOM									
ALL MODELS	3.0	3.7	3.0	3.0	3.0	2	–	1	3
DATARACE									
ALL MODELS	3.0	3.0	3.0	3.3	2.3	3	–	–	3
MULTI-TECH	3.0	3.0	2.6	3.3	2.8	5	2	2	9
MULTITECH 224ER	3.0	3.0	2.8	3.2	3.0	4	1	1	6
OTHER MODELS	3.0	3.0	2.0	3.5	2.0	1	1	1	3
NEC									
ALL MODELS	3.0	3.3	3.0	3.0	3.0	7	2	1	10
VEN-TEL									
ALL MODELS	3.0	3.3	3.3	3.0	2.8	4	–	–	4
GENERAL DATACOMM	2.9	3.1	2.9	3.0	2.6	18	9	1	28
OTHER MODELS	3.2	3.2	3.1	3.4	3.0	10	3	–	13
GDC 4800	2.7	3.0	2.7	3.3	2.3	2	1	1	3
GDC 9600	2.6	3.0	2.8	2.4	2.6	5	4	–	9
GDC 208	2.3	2.7	2.3	2.7	1.7	1	1	1	3
MICOM									
ALL MODELS	2.9	3.0	2.8	2.9	2.9	5	2	2	9
MICROCOM	2.9	3.0	2.3	2.9	2.7	9	2	1	12
MICROCOM AX/2400C	3.8	3.8	3.0	3.8	2.8	4	–	–	4
OTHER MODELS	2.8	2.8	2.2	2.2	2.8	3	1	1	5
MICROCOM AX/9624C	2.0	2.3	1.7	3.0	2.3	2	1	–	3
CASE/DATATEL									
ALL MODELS	2.5	2.8	2.8	3.0	2.8	2	1	1	4
INFINET									
ALL MODELS	2.3	2.8	3.0	2.5	3.0	2	1	1	4
ALL OTHERS	3.1	3.3	2.8	3.2	2.9	36	8	4	48

Section 2
Interconnections

Mauricio J. Mathov, World Bank, Washington, D. C.

The World Bank: Choosing a path to interconnection

This international lender systematically folded thousands of workstations into hundreds of interlocking local area networks and reaped big returns.

The World Bank differs from commercial banks and other institutions in many ways. Lending more than $15 billion a year, it has only 146 potential clients, the member countries that have contributed their share to the bank's capital. The bank was established in 1945 to help raise living standards in developing countries by channeling financial resources into them from more fortunate countries.

And yet, the bank's information needs may seem familiar to corporate networkers. The World Bank is a significant collector, consumer, and producer of information. Its lending activity requires the uninterrupted evaluation of each member country's economy as well as the analysis of each relevant economic sector (agriculture, education, energy, industry, transportation, and water supply, to name but a few). This is because countries, like individuals, present different credit risks in different situations.

For example, if a country requests a loan to mine for tin or to build and operate an aluminum plant, the request must be studied by the bank's experts in that country as well as by experts in mining or mineral markets. The bank also provides its member countries with policy advice, aid coordination, technical assistance, training, development research, etc. Thus, since the bank's employees use information as their raw material, the management of information is central to the institution's effectiveness.

As a first step toward enhancing the productivity of its personnel, the bank adopted the information-resource management (IRM) operating concept about three years ago.

The IRM concept arose partly in response to the fact that information technology had caught on in a big way at the bank. In the late 1970s there had been a rapid and uncontrolled growth in the presence and use of a variety of computers and word processors. During this time, the bank acquired over 750 word processors, 100 micro-computers, and about 1,500 terminals. The mainframes installed in the bank included several Burroughs, IBM, and Digital Equipment Corp. (DEC) computers. By 1983, expenditures on information processing were in excess of $20 million per year, with over $11 million worth of equipment already installed.

The implications of this mushrooming growth were worrisome to the bank: Many databases contained duplicative or inconsistent data; there was no clear and comprehensive picture as to exactly what data was held within the institution; the hardware and software components from different manufacturers that had proliferated were, in general, incompatible with each other. To handle this and implement the IRM strategy, several projects were started under "the Launching Package." One aimed at selecting a family of standard workstations that would be supplied to all bank staff members according to needs for clerical, decision-making, and computational support. The workstations had to be able to function in standalone mode, so they would be microcomputers with data processing and storage (floppy- and/or hard-disk) capacity. Thus, the Launching Package's office automation people began examining alternative microcomputers to use as standardized workstations.

At the same time, the communications team within the Launching Package group had to devise a way to link these workstations to each other as well as to the bank's hosts and to external database and newswire services, such as those used to gather information on interest rates by currency, news about the bond market, and so on. The group carried out this task systematically, following the approach shown in "Step-by-step network selection."

Step-by-step network selection

The procedure followed by the World Bank to link its users may be useful to any organization undertaking a similar project:

- Interview users and determine their basic needs.
- Define geographical distribution and constraints.
- Define the typical "work group" and its major tasks.
- Determine physical restrictions, if any.
- Visit installations in other organizations and try to get a flavor of basic problems and solutions.
- Develop an ideal configuration.
- Select potential vendors.
- Match user requirements against potential products and eliminate those that do not fulfill them.
- Develop a checklist of technical characteristics.
- Pilot test the products still being considered, eval-uating them in terms of the characteristics on the checklist.
- Define a standard configuration for all vendors.
- Start compiling cost figures for each alternative.
- Select the characteristics that are critical.
- Prepare and fill in an evaluation.
- Visit the premises of the best-rated vendor(s).
- Visit installations similar to the one you will implement in your corporation.
- Make a decision.
- Negotiate an agreement with the vendor(s).
- Prepare an implementation plan.
- Have the decision and implementation plan aproved by top management.
- Cross your fingers.
- Good luck. (You're going to need it!)

The Launching Package project began with user interviews to determine their basic needs. In the bank, there are three major complexes: operations (loan granting and managing), finance (money management and accounting), and personnel and administration, which includes such services as data processing, medical, and payroll. Each user group is represented by a data administrator (DA). Naturally, people in the different groups planned to use workstations for different tasks.

These users told their stories in their own terms, often involving a number of staff members who functioned as a sort of work group. The interviews enabled the project group to define the typical work group and its major tasks. It was discovered that the usual size of a work group in the bank is about 20 people, comprising a manager plus secretarial and professional staff members. Most of the work performed has to do with the preparation of reports and financial modeling. Professional staff members prepare spreadsheets and texts that secretarial staff members later use to produce different papers.

For example, a scenario might be as follows: In preparing a report about a loan approval or denial, a professional brings information about the requesting country into a desktop PC. This information is then sent to a secretary who prepares it for presentation. The report then goes to a manager who suggests changes that the secretary implements. Then the professional reviews the final copy, which gets printed out and mailed. Once installed, local area networks should eliminate much of the paperwork by handling this sort of document electronically.

Actually, the professional/secretary/manager setup was the main work group of the operations complex, the foremost of the three complexes in terms of size and importance. (Giving loans is the bank's main business, no matter how well it support programs or accounting routines work.)

Work groups in the other departments differ, it was found. They often need access to mainframes, mostly to transmit files. In the finance complex, instead of sending reports to each other, the users (clerks) have groups of accounts that they check. As an example, in the accounts receivable department of a corporation other than the World Bank, which operates somewhat differently, one clerk may deal with clients whose names begin with the letters A-C, another may handle D-F. At the beginning of the day, the clerks download from the host all the files needed for that day. Then each starts posting applicable transactions. At the end of the day, users transmit the updated files back to the host.

The scenario entails neither secretary nor manager; the basic work group is a number of accountants updating different files. A network to serve these users might need access to only one host, for a database retrieval in the morning and a database update at the close of day.

Based upon the user interviews, certain general characteristics and user requirements started to emerge. Needs, among many others, were for:

- Sharing certain peripherals, mainly disk storage and printers, within the work group;
- Staff to access the bank's electronic resources from outside locations (such as from their homes or from overseas locations when they are on mission, both to retrieve and to send electronic mail and files);
- "User friendliness" or ease of use (a large majority of users are not data processing professionals), including a neat network data-management setup (for instance, one where files backups would be performed automatically by the system without user intervention);
- All workstations to be capable of running in 3270 (synchronous) mode, since everybody in the bank would probably use the institutional database residing on an IBM mainframe;
- Asynchronous communications capability for all workstations, in order to access other mainframes in the bank and those of external vendors; and
- Users to be able to work in spite of the inevitable hardware malfunctions (or at least an environment in which the number of users out of service would be kept to a minimum).

The project group then defined the bank's geographical distribution and constraints, which concerns how much distance there is between users, where sites are located with respect to each other, and so on. Most of the 6,000 employees of the World Bank are located amidst the 19 buildings that the bank owns or leases in downtown Washington, D. C., in a campus-like environment. Less than 10 percent of the staff work in the 76 offices that the bank has outside the United States. Therefore, the need for some sort of local networking was clearly established.

A lot of information is shared within the work group (both text and data files), but it was felt that only 20 percent of the data traffic would require the establishment of communications outside the work group. Thus, with 20 user work groups, linking 6,000 workstations would call for 300 local area networks.

Next, physical restrictions (such as available conduit space, electricity, air conditioning, and so on) were considered. Since the bank premises are in many cases 20 years old or more, there was a desire to keep the wiring requirements to a minimum. Although tempting, the idea of using a digital PBX to transmit both voice and data through the same set of telephone wires was discarded for two reasons: The technology is immature, and most of the traffic would be file transfers, an application not well suited to PBXs. Therefore, it was decided that, if possible, one single wire, preferably not the thick coaxial variety that eliminated broadband networks, should interconnect each workstation with the external world.

As its next step, the group visited installations in other organizations to try to appraise other people's experiences. Group members went to the Massachusetts Institute of Technology's Athena networking project, Dartmouth College's Apple network, and George Mason University's broadband network. These academic networks did not suggest a typical business environment. In

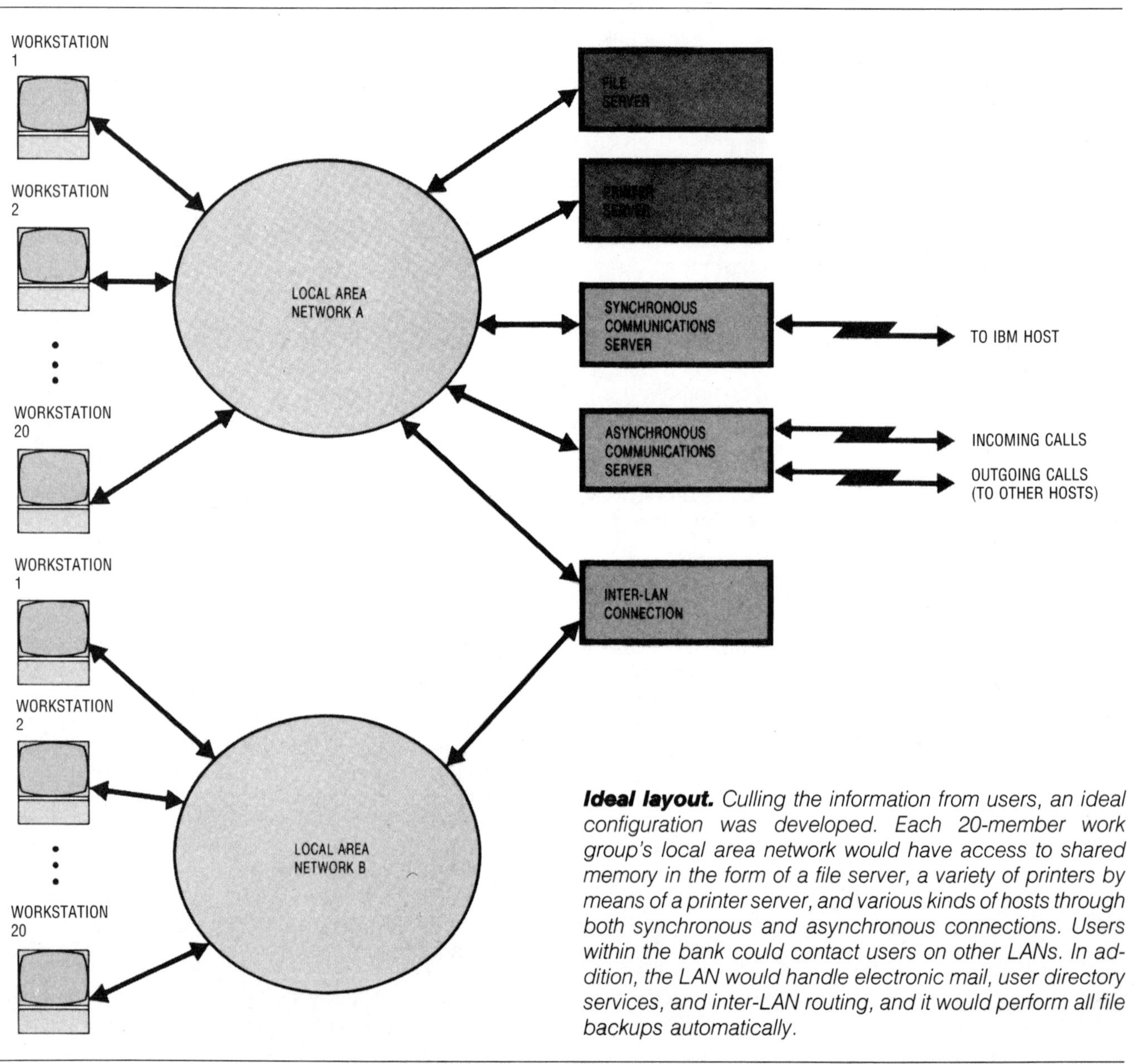

Ideal layout. Culling the information from users, an ideal configuration was developed. Each 20-member work group's local area network would have access to shared memory in the form of a file server, a variety of printers by means of a printer server, and various kinds of hosts through both synchronous and asynchronous connections. Users within the bank could contact users on other LANs. In addition, the LAN would handle electronic mail, user directory services, and inter-LAN routing, and it would perform all file backups automatically.

Table 1: Checklist of network features

	YES ✔	NO ✔
1. USER INTERFACE		
1.1 —MENU-BASED ACCESS TO NETWORK SERVICES	—	—
1.2 —EXPERIENCED USER MAY BYPASS BASIC STEPS	—	—
1.3 —MID-SESSION HELP AVAILABLE	—	—
1.4 —USER MAY TERMINATE ANY ACTIVITY AT ANY POINT	—	—
1.5 —NETWORK DISPLAYS STATUS INFORMATION ON EACH USER S WORKSTATION	—	—
1.6 —USER-DEFINED DEFAULT OPTIONS	—	—
1.7 —ERROR MESSAGES ARE EXPLICIT AND UNDERSTANDABLE	—	—
2. FILE SHARING		
2.1 —ALL USERS CAN SHARE THE SERVER'S HARD DISK(S)	—	—
2.2 —HARD DISK(S) CAN BE PARTITIONED	—	—
2.3 —VOLUME SIZE CAN BE VARIABLE	—	—
2.4 —UPPER LIMIT OF VOLUME SIZE IS USER-DEFINED	—	—
2.5 —DISK DRIVES ARE VIRTUAL TO THE USERS (THAT IS, TO THE USER, THE SERVER DISK SEEMS TO BE CONNECTED DIRECTLY TO THE WORKSTATION)	—	—
2.6 —ONE VOLUME MAY OCCUPY MORE THAN ONE DRIVE	—	—
2.7 —MULTIPLE VIRTUAL DRIVES CAN EXIST	—	—
2.8 —PASSWORD PROTECTION AT VOLUME LEVEL:		
2.8.1 —PRIVATE VOLUME	—	—
2.8.2 —GROUP VOLUME	—	—
2.8.3 —PUBLIC VOLUME	—	—
2.9 —DISK-TO-TAPE BACKUP AVAILABLE:		
2.9.1 —BY VOLUME	—	—
2.9.2 —BY FILE	—	—
2.9.3 —INCREMENTAL	—	—
2.9.4 —AUTOMATIC (PROGRAMMABLE)	—	—
2.10 —RESTORE TAPE-TO-DISK AVAILABLE:		
2.10.1 —BY VOLUME	—	—
2.10.2 —BY FILE	—	—
2.11 —FILE NAMES LOCATED IN A DIRECTORY/SUBDIRECTORY	—	—
2.12 —MULTIPLE FILE SERVERS ALLOWED IN ONE LOCAL AREA NETWORK (LAN)	—	—
2.13 —USAGE STATISTICS AVAILABLE	—	—
2.14 —DIAGNOSTIC TOOLS FOR MAINTENANCE AVAILABLE	—	—
3. PRINTER SERVER		
3.1 —NETWORK PRINTERS CAN BE SHARED BY ALL USERS	—	—
3.2 —TYPES OF PRINTERS SUPPORTED:		
3.2.1 —PARALLEL PRINTERS	—	—
3.2.2 —SERIAL PRINTERS	—	—
3.2.3 —LASER PRINTERS	—	—
3.2.4 —GRAPHICS PLOTTERS	—	—
3.2.5 —HIGH-SPEED (9.6 KBIT/S) PRINTERS	—	—
3.2.6 —LOW-SPEED (300 BIT/S) PRINTERS	—	—
3.3 —PRINT JOB MANIPULATION ALLOWED:		
3.3.1 —PRINT-FILE SPOOL	—	—
3.3.2 —PRINT-FILE QUEUE	—	—
3.3.3 —PRINT-FILE PRIORITY	—	—
3.3.4 —PRINT FILE ABORT/DELETE	—	—
3.3.5 —START/STOP JOBS IN PRINT QUEUE	—	—
3.3.6 —BY THE USER	—	—
3.3.7 —BY THE NETWORK ADMINISTRATOR	—	—
3.4 —DEFAULT PRINTER SETUP	—	—
3.5 —USAGE STATISTICS AVAILABLE	—	—
3.6 —DIAGNOSTIC TOOLS FOR MAINTENANCE AVAILABLE	—	—
4. COMMUNICATIONS SERVER		
4.1 —SHARE COMMUNICATIONS LINKS AMONGST ALL USERS	—	—
4.2 —TYPES OF COMMUNICATIONS LINKS SUPPORTED:		
4.2.1 —3270 BINARY SYNCHRONOUS COMMUNICATIONS	—	—
4.2.2 —3270 SYSTEMS NETWORK ARCHITECTURE	—	—
4.2.3 —ASCII ASYNCHRONOUS DIAL-OUT	—	—
4.2.4 —ASCII ASYNCHRONOUS DIAL-IN	—	—
4.2.5 —ASCII ASYNCHRONOUS DEDICATED LINES	—	—
4.2.6 —X.25	—	—
4.2.7 —VT-100 EMULATION	—	—
4.2.8 —BURROUGHS POLL/SELECT	—	—
4.3 —INTERFACE WITH THE BANK'S CODEX DATA SWITCH	—	—
4.4 —AUTOMATIC DIAL-OUT CAPABILITY	—	—
4.5 —EASY TO USE	—	—
4.6 —USAGE STATISTICS AVAILABLE	—	—
4.7 —DIAGNOSTIC TOOLS FOR MAINTENANCE AVAILABLE	—	—
5. ELECTRONIC MAIL		
5.1 —MENU-DRIVEN	—	—
5.2 —PREFORMATTED SCREENS FOR DIFFERENT TYPES OF DOCUMENTS	—	—
5.3 —SUPPORTS DIRECTORY WITH UP TO 6,000 USERS	—	—
5.4 —WORD PROCESSING-TYPE EDITOR FOR MESSAGE CREATION	—	—
5.5 —RETURN-RECEIPT OPTION AVAILABLE	—	—
5.6 —MESSAGE BROADCAST AVAILABLE	—	—
5.7 —PREDEFINED GROUPS FOR MESSAGE BROADCAST	—	—
5.8 —URGENT-MESSAGE HANDLING	—	—
5.9 —MERGING OF TEXT AND DATA FILES ALLOWED	—	—
5.10 —DISPLAY LIST OF ALL MESSAGES CREATED	—	—
5.11 —DISPLAY LIST OF ALL MESSAGES SENT	—	—
5.12 —DISPLAY LIST OF ALL MESSAGES RECEIVED	—	—
5.13 —AUTOMATIC PRINTING OF MESSAGES FOR NONREGISTERED USERS (TO BE DELIVERED BY HAND)	—	—
5.14 —IF USER IS ON, THE ARRIVAL OF A MESSAGE IS NOTICEABLE TO THE USER	—	—
5.15 —IF USER IS ON, THE ARRIVAL OF A MESSAGE DOES NOT INTERRUPT PROCESS	—	—
5.16 —MESSAGE RECEIVED MAY BE PRINTED ON REQUEST	—	—
5.17 —OLD MESSAGES MAY BE PURGED/DELETED	—	—
5.18 —A USER MAY HAVE MULTIPLE MAILBOXES	—	—
5.19 —REPLY TO CURRENT MESSAGE DEFAULTS TO SENDER'S NAME	—	—
5.20 —MESSAGES CAN BE FORWARDED TO OTHER USERS	—	—
5.21 —MESSAGES CAN BE FILED	—	—
5.22 —USER-GENERATED DISTRIBUTION LISTS ALLOWED	—	—
5.23 —UNREAD MESSAGES HIGHLIGHTED	—	—
5.24 —UNANSWERED MESSAGES HIGHLIGHTED	—	—
5.25 —UNSENT MESSAGES HIGHLIGHTED	—	—
5.26 —DATE/TIME OF MESSAGES AUTOMATICALLY INCLUDED	—	—
5.27 —USER-DEFINED PRIORITY FOR OUTGOING MESSAGES	—	—
5.28 —USER-DEFINED PRIORITY FOR INCOMING MESSAGES	—	—
5.29 —POSSIBILITY TO WITHDRAW MESSAGES ALREADY SENT (BUT NOT YET READ)	—	—
5.30 —USAGE STATISTICS AVAILABLE	—	—

<table>
<tr><td></td><td align="center">YES ✔</td><td align="center">NO ✔</td><td></td><td align="center">YES ✔</td><td align="center">NO ✔</td></tr>
</table>

6. NETWORK CALENDARING

		YES	NO
6.1	—NETWORK CALENDARING AVAILABLE FOR ALL USERS IN A LAN	___	___
6.2	—NETWORK CALENDARING AVAILABLE THROUGHOUT ALL INTERCONNECTED LANs	___	___
6.3	—APPOINTMENT-SCHEDULING PASSWORD PROTECTED	___	___
6.4	—AUTOMATIC SCHEDULING OF MULTIPLE-USER MEETINGS	___	___
6.5	—AUTOMATIC RESOURCE SCHEDULING (SUCH AS MEETING ROOMS)	___	___
6.6	—USAGE STATISTICS AVAILABLE	___	___

7. COMPATIBILITY REQUIRED WITH APPLICATION SOFTWARE

		YES	NO
7.1	—dBASE II	___	___
7.2	—dBASE III	___	___
7.3	—PERSONAL COMPUTER FOCUS	___	___
7.4	—PERSONAL COMPUTER MODEL 204	___	___
7.5	—LOTUS 1-2-3	___	___
7.6	—MULTIPLAN	___	___
7.7	—VISICALC	___	___
7.8	—MULTIMATE	___	___
7.9	—WORDPRO	___	___
7.10	—WORDSTAR	___	___

8. DATA TRANSMISSION WITHIN THE LAN

		YES	NO
8.1	—FILE TRANSFER BETWEEN WORKSTATIONS	___	___
8.2	—FILE TRANSFER BETWEEN FILE SERVER AND WORKSTATIONS	___	___
8.3	—FILE TRANSFER WITH A CENTRALIZED OFFICE ENVIRONMENT, SUCH AS ALL-IN-ONE FROM DIGITAL EQUIPMENT CORP. (DEC)	___	___
8.4	—WORKSTATIONS THAT MAY BE USED IN THE LAN:	___	___
8.4.1	—DATA GENERAL'S DESKTOP	___	___
8.4.2	—DEC'S PROFESSIONAL	___	___
8.4.3	—IBM PERSONAL COMPUTERS (PCs)	___	___

9. LAN-TO-LAN INTERCONNECTION

		YES	NO
9.1	—NEARBY LANs CAN BE INTERCONNECTED	___	___
9.2	—REMOTE LANs CAN BE INTERCONNECTED	___	___
9.3	—USERS ON ONE LAN MAY TRANSPARENTLY ACCESS RESOURCES ON ANOTHER LAN	___	___
9.4	—FILES CAN BE TRANSFERRED BETWEEN LANs	___	___
9.5	—GLOBAL ELECTRONIC MAIL THROUGHOUT LANs	___	___
9.6	—HETEROGENEOUS LANs CAN BE INTERCONNECTED	___	___
9.7	—INTER-LAN TRAFFIC STATISTICS AVAILABLE	___	___

10. IBM PC COMPATIBILITY

		YES	NO
10.1	—IBM PCs MAY COEXIST ON THE SAME LAN	___	___
10.2	—FILES MAY BE TRANSFERRED BETWEEN A USER AND AN IBM PC	___	___
10.3	—ELECTRONIC MAIL MAY BE SENT TO AN IBM PC	___	___
10.4	—COMPATIBILITY AT THE DATA LEVEL	___	___
10.5	—COMPATIBILITY AT THE PROGRAM LEVEL	___	___
10.6	—FILE-FORMAT TRANSLATION REQUIRED AND AVAILABLE	___	___

11. SECURITY

		YES	NO
11.1	—ACCESS TO INDIVIDUAL LANs PASSWORD-PROTECTED	___	___
11.2	—ACCESS TO INTERCONNECTED LANs PASSWORD-PROTECTED	___	___
11.3	—ACCESS TO VOLUMES PASSWORD-PROTECTED	___	___
11.4	—ACCESS TO FILES PASSWORD-PROTECTED	___	___
11.5	—PASSWORD CHANGE EASY TO PERFORM	___	___
11.6	—AUTOMATIC FILE-CLOSING WHEN USER TURNS OFF WORKSTATION	___	___

12. NETWORK ADMINISTRATION

		YES	NO
12.1	—EASY ADD/DELETE OF USERS, PRINTERS, AND SO ON	___	___
12.2	—CONTROL ACCESS TO THE NETWORK	___	___
12.3	—USAGE STATISTICS PROVIDED	___	___
12.4	—SERVICE START/SHUTDOWN CONTROLLED	___	___
12.5	—DISK-TO-TAPE BACKUP:		
12.5.1	—PRESCHEDULED	___	___
12.5.2	—ON DEMAND	___	___
12.5.3	—UNATTENDED	___	___
12.6	—NETWORK MANAGEMENT CONSOLE	___	___
12.7	—NETWORK RECOVERY FROM POWER FAILURES:		
12.7.1	—AUTOMATIC	___	___
12.7.2	—ATTENDED	___	___
12.8	—ADDING/DELETING NETWORK RESOURCES DOES NOT INTERFERE WITH SERVICE	___	___
12.9	—REMOTE MAINTENANCE CAPABILITY:		
12.9.1	—DIAL-IN	___	___
12.9.2	—FROM AN INTERCONNECTED LAN	___	___
12.10	—REMOTE-ADMINISTRATION CAPABILITY	___	___
12.10.1	—DIAL-IN		
12.10.2	—FROM AN INTERCONNECTED LAN	___	___

13. DOCUMENTATION

		YES	NO
13.1	—INSTALLATION GUIDE AVAILABLE	___	___
13.2	—NETWORK ADMINISTRATION GUIDE AVAILABLE	___	___
13.3	—USER'S GUIDE AVAILABLE	___	___
13.4	—PLANNING GUIDE AVAILABLE	___	___
13.5	—MAINTENANCE GUIDE AVAILABLE	___	___
13.6	—TRAINING AIDS AVAILABLE	___	___
13.7	—MID-SESSION HELP AVAILABLE	___	___

14. ENVIRONMENTAL SPECIFICATIONS

		YES	NO
14.1	—AIR CONDITIONING IS REQUIRED	___	___
14.2	—NOISE GENERATED IS LESS THAN 50 dB	___	___
14.3	—SPACE REQUIREMENTS ARE LESS THAN ______ (FILL IN)	___	___
14.4	—HEAT GENERATION IS LESS THAN 400 WATTS	___	___
14.5	—ELECTRICAL POWER CONSUMPTION IS LESS THAN ______ (FILL IN)	___	___

scientific applications, for example, the student enters a few characters and out come a few lines in response. This is because most of the work, such as calculus or matrix crunching, is done by the host, implying low communications with high computing. The bank's case is the opposite: long files transmitted for local processing.

Also, students will get in line to wait for terminals or printers. It would be inappropriate to ask professionals to wait their turn for computer resources. Also, a professional worker should have a dedicated draft-quality printer, as well as access to a higher-quality printer for a document's final version. Thus, traffic patterns and resource needs suggest that network designs should differ between business and academia.

In visits related to wiring examples, the Launching Package group went to AT&T's and IBM's towers on Manhattan's Madison Avenue, but it was somehow discouraged by the wires' large diameters, the need for space-consuming wiring closets, and the number of questions to which these vendors were not able to respond. (Nonetheless, the IBM wiring scheme was eventually installed in the bank.)

At this point, the group was able to develop an ideal configuration or to draw a basic diagram of what it was looking for (see figure). About 20 workstations would be linked, through a single wire, to some sort of LAN. LAN servers would provide the desired functionality to the work group on a LAN. For example, a file server would store the files to be shared by the work group; a printer server would manage the spooling of texts to the printers shared by the work group. A synchronous communications server would perform the protocol conversion needed to make the IBM host believe that each workstation was a 3270 device (and that the server was a 3274 controller), while an asynchronous communications server would concentrate the management of all asynchronous incoming and outgoing calls. Also, an interface or bridge would interconnect all the LANs.

By this time, the team in charge of selecting the workstation had narrowed its choices — through a process that had lasted several months and started with a vast array of potential vendors (more than 70) — to fewer than 10. The elimination process was begun by matching the list of requirements with the specifications of each vendor. For instance, Wang's Professional Computer, which connects to its LAN with one wire, requires a second wire to link with an IBM 3274 controller for synchronous communications. This was clearly undesirable.

(A personal note: Much is being said nowadays about the sales slump in the data processing hardware industry. The author's opinion is that, until now, sales representatives were mainly "order takers." Due to their clients' increased sophistication, however, the situation has changed drastically. What we found in our contacts with the vendors was that salespeople did not know intimately the products they were trying to sell, let alone those of their competitors. When we asked sales representatives questions about the data communications specifications of their products, we mostly received an absurd and wrong answer or a request to hold the question until they could bring in a data communications expert. The author believes that, if the industry wants to increase its slow sales, it needs to upgrade the technical quality of its sales teams.)

With the help of the communications team and the addition of criteria for networking, the list was further reduced to three: Desktop Generation workstation from Data General (DG); DEC's Professional 350 and 380 workstations; and IBM's PC product line. If DG or DEC workstations were selected as the bank's standard, then its proprietary Ethernet LANs would have to be used. If the IBM PC family was chosen, the group decided to initially consider: (1) Banyan (the server finally chosen); (2) IBM's PC Net; (3) Novell's Netware; (4) Proteon's ProNet; (5) Ungermann-Bass's Net/One; and (6) 3Com's Etherseries.

In a pilot test to evaluate these products, each vendor was asked to supply several units on complementary loan or, for a nominal charge, to verify that the products performed as advertised. To test the different alternatives, the bank built a laboratory environment with a capacity for about 20 workstations, into which all the vendors were invited to install their products. Several types of wiring (coaxial cables, twisted pair, RS-232-C) reached each workstation location and ended in a patch panel that allowed the evaluators to interconnect the workstations in different ways and to test alternative configurations.

A checklist of networking features was developed (Table 1). No product ranking was attempted; the checklist was merely meant to inventory their capabilities. (Other corporations going through this selection process may wish to modify these characteristics to more closely resemble their specific needs.) By working in the lab, the group was able to fill in most of the items in the list, but visits to installations and discussions with the vendors were also required.

Ungermann-Bass was eliminated due to its lack of interest in participating in the evaluation process. Later on, IBM's PC Net was also eliminated because it is a peer-to-peer LAN (that is, there are no real file servers; electronic messages sent to nonconnected users are lost). In addition, PC Net required the connection of a telephone line to each workstation to allow for asynchronous communications (instead of concentrating such links in a server).

In order to make a homogeneous comparison of the vendors' offerings, the Launching Package group decided to compute the price from each vendor for one standard configuration (considered typical for the bank). This configuration was composed of:
- Five workstations, each with a 10-Mbyte hard-disk and a floppy-disk drive;
- Fifteen workstations with floppy drives only (the assumption being that the file server made hard disks mostly unnecessary);
- Twenty standard-carriage dot matrix printers (one for each workstation), type Epson FX-80;
- One file server, with a capacity of about 40 Mbytes, with (cartridge) tape backup;
- One printer server, with one wide-carriage dot matrix

printer (type Epson FX-100) and one laser printer (type Hewlett-Packard Laserjet);

■ One synchronous communications server, with a minimum capacity of eight simultaneous 3270 sessions;

■ One asynchronous communications server, with a minimum capacity of four asynchronous lines.

The group compiled cost figures for five alternatives, namely DEC's Decnet, Data General's proprietary network, and IBM PCs with each of the following: the Proteon network with the Banyan server, the Proteon network with Novell software (which uses PCs as servers), and the 3Com network with the Banyan server. Price information was garnered from proposals or price lists. For each of these alternatives, the total costs for workstations, servers, wiring, boards, and so forth were entered into a Lotus spreadsheet (Table 2). Again, corporations going through this process may wish to modify the cost items included in Table 2 according to their particular circumstances.

Due to lack of information, certain cost items were not included. For instance, installation costs were not considered, although it was certain that the solutions requiring thick Ethernet wiring would be more expensive to install. User training was not included either.

The spreadsheet resulted in a total cost for the workstations and the LAN, as well as an average cost per workstation. This last number turned out to be between $4,500 and $5,800 for the alternatives using IBM PCs, and between $9,300 and $15,000 for DG and DEC. The main reason for these differences was that DG and DEC did not have servers to offer and had to use minicomputers to perform that function. Of course, a minicomputer may accomplish other tasks and/or serve a group of more than 20 users, but that did not fit into the bank's strategy.

As the final stage of its selection process, the Launching Package group constructed an evaluation card (Table 3), where it entered its rating of the different characteristics of each of the five alternatives mentioned above. This evaluation card uses a 0-to-4 scale, with 0 being the worst and 4 the best. The group further distinguished between those features considered more important for the bank (critical factors) and those thought less important (noncritical factors). Note that a reader doing this type of evaluation could also weight each factor, not just dividing the world into critical and noncritical, but multiplying each factor's numerical weight by the 0-4 assessment value. The results clearly favored the Banyan server with a Proteon network linking IBM PCs, alternative A in the evaluation. (The various IBM PC alternatives, as well as the DEC and DG single-vendor proposals, are shown on the evaluation card.)

Besides the results of the evaluation, there were a large number of IBM PCs installed at that time (about 1,200; today, there are about 2,000). Therefore, it was decided that PCs (or compatibles) were to be the bank's standard workstation. These would gradually replace the variety of word processors and terminals and eventually be provided to each of the bank's 6,000 employees. The policy does not force users to buy microcomputers now, but rather specifies that, when they wish to replace their present equipment (using funds from their own budgets), users must select machines with IBM PC compatibility in mind.

Proteon, it was felt, has established itself as a LAN vendor. Banyan, however, is a new and relatively small company. Therefore, the bank's main concern had to do with its stability and the lack of sophisticated software available for such functions as calendaring. On the other hand, the selection team liked the product's architecture and was very impressed by the quality of its management and technical personnel.

Another factor favoring Banyan was its responsiveness to special requests as well as the company's willingness to customize its software to the bank's requirements if necessary. On the technical side, Banyan was the only vendor offering true LAN-to-LAN connectivity. That is, each Banyan server may be directly connected to other Banyan servers via a "backbone" LAN. Also, the company's addressing scheme for accessing users and other resources on the network was far superior to those of other vendors (see "Servers: Glue for the bank's networking").

Table 2: Cost analysis spreadsheet

	VENDOR A				VENDOR B
	QTY	DESCRIPTION	UNIT COST	TOTAL COST	QTY
WORKSTATION (WS)					
WITH HARD DISK	—	—	—	—	— ...
FLOPPY DRIVE ONLY	—	—	—	—	— ...
PRINTER	—	—	—	—	— ...
****SUBTOTAL (WS)**	—	—	—	—	— ...
LOCAL AREA NETWORK (LAN)					
FILE SERVER	—	—	—	—	— ...
TAPE BACKUP	—	—	—	—	— ...
PRINTER SERVER	—	—	—	—	— ...
MATRIX PRINTER	—	—	—	—	— ...
LETTER-QUALITY PRINTER	—	—	—	—	— ...
COMMUNICATIONS SERVER	—	—	—	—	— ...
ASYNCHRONOUS	—	—	—	—	— ...
3270	—	—	—	—	— ...
OTHER LAN HARDWARE	—	—	—	—	— ...
TRANSCEIVER CABLE	—	—	—	—	— ...
NETWORK CABLE	—	—	—	—	— ...
ADAPTER CARDS	—	—	—	—	— ...
COMPONENTS	—	—	—	—	— ...
CONSOLE	—	—	—	—	— ...
LAN INTERCONNECTORS	—	—	—	—	— ...
LAN SOFTWARE	—	—	—	—	— ...
LAN-TO-LAN CONNECTION	—	—	—	—	— ...
DISK SHARING	—	—	—	—	— ...
PRINTER SHARING	—	—	—	—	— ...
ELECTRONIC MAIL	—	—	—	—	— ...
ASYNCHRONOUS COMMUNICATIONS SHARING	—	—	—	—	— ...
3270 COMMUNICATIONS SHARING	—	—	—	—	— ...
****SUBTOTAL (LAN)**	—	—	—	—	— ...
TOTAL COST (WS + LAN)	—	—	—	—	— ...
AVERAGE COST PER WS	—	—	—	—	— ...

Table 3: Evaluation card

	VENDOR A	VENDOR B	VENDOR C	VENDOR D	VENDOR E
CRITICAL FACTORS					
USER INTERFACE	4	2	3	3	0
FILE SHARING	3	4	1	3	0
PRINTER SERVER	2	3	2	3	4
COMMUNICATIONS SERVER	2	1	3	1	1
INTER-LAN COMMUNICATIONS	4	0	1	2	1
IBM PC COMPATIBILITY	4	4	4	1	1
WIRING FLEXIBILITY	4	2	1	0	0
SUBTOTAL 1	23	16	15	13	7
NONCRITICAL FACTORS					
INTRA-LAN COMMUNICATIONS	2	2	2	3	3
PERFORMANCE	2	3	3	3	1
SECURITY	3	4	1	3	3
LAN ADMINISTRATION	4	2	2	3	3
DOCUMENTATION	2	2	2	2	2
ENVIRONMENT	3	3	3	2	3
MATURITY RELIABILITY	2	3	4	3	0
SUBTOTAL 2	18	19	17	19	15
TOTAL SCORE	41	35	32	32	22

0 = DOES NOT MEET REQUIREMENTS OR IS NOT AVAILABLE   1 = POOR   2 = FAIR   3 = GOOD   4 = EXCELLENT

Before making a final decision, the Launching Package group visited the manufacturing plants of both Banyan and Proteon and talked with their top executives, getting a first-hand impression of their financial status and future plans, which the group considered satisfactory.

Since the vendors had donated only two or three units each for the bank's laboratory work, and the specified work group has 20 users, the Launching Package group wanted to see how the networks would perform under actual conditions. Thus, the group asked the vendors to demonstrate existing, operational examples of the sort of network they were proposing for the bank. Proteon was able to demonstrate such an installation; Banyan could not, simply because the bank was practically its first major user.

In April of 1985, the Launching Package group made a decision that the bank will probably have to live with for the next 10 to 15 years. On the LAN board side, it decided to combine Banyan with Proteon's ProNet. Although ProNet and 3Com are both supposed to work at 10 Mbit/s, tests determined that the combination of Banyan and ProNet was 10 to 20 percent faster than using Banyan with 3Com. Another advantage for ProNet is that it may use shielded twisted-pair wiring (which not only is easier to install than coaxial cable but also fits with IBM's wiring architecture, which the bank had decided to install). ProNet's LAN organization is a token-passing star-ring architecture, with quite practical and small wire centers, which we believe will simplify the network's management and maintenance. A problem with any

workstation can be indicated by the presence or absence of a light on a wire center, and the workstation can be disconnected from the network with the flick of a switch.

On the software side, the bank plans to realize substantial savings by storing the shared, network-version applications packages purchased under multi-user licenses stored on the server (and not in each workstation). Some software vendors have already defined a rate structure for groups of users sharing their products. Another advantage of this setup is that the update of a software version (or its replacement by a new version) will be done at the LAN level and not at the workstation level. In this case, it meant having to work with only 300 updates, a large number, but still significantly fewer than 6,000.

After negotiating an agreement with the vendors, the group prepared an implementation plan to determine the timetable for installing the LANs. This step-by-step plan laid out the resources (time, money, and people) needed to implement the networking scheme.

One of the problems remaining to be solved was the need for bankwide electronic mail and appointment scheduling. These applications can be implemented throughout the network only after all 6,000 employees are connected to their respective LANs. Since it was clear that the wiring and installation of the 300 LANs would take two to three years, an interim solution was required. The bank was already using DEC's All-in-One software, which runs in VAX minicomputers quite successfully. Therefore, it decided to use All-in-One as a temporary solution.

Access to All-in-One will be provided through dial-in ports in a cluster of VAXes. Users already connected to a LAN will link with All-in-One, to send and receive electronic mail and to schedule appointments, through one of the dial-out asynchronous lines of their Banyan server. Users not yet connected to a LAN will have to dial the All-in-One telephone number from the device they have available today (such as a dumb terminal, a microcomputer, or a word processor).

Finally, the Launching Package group presented its decision and implementation plan for approval to top management. As is the routine at the bank, management had already authorized the group to evaluate and select a network. Then, after it had negotiated a contract with the vendor (but before the agreement was signed), the group knew the exact prices and terms and could present the contract and the plan to management. The contract was approved, signed, and deployment began in May of 1985.

As of this writing, the first 10 LANs of an initial pilot group of 32 are running, thus far without major problems. The other 22 of the eventual 300 are currently being installed. ■

Mauricio J. Mathov, a senior computer specialist at the World Bank, is presently conducting a study to interconnect the bank's 76 overseas locations with the Washington, D. C., headquarters. Mathov has a masters degree in electronic engineering from the University of Buenos Aires in Argentina.

Servers: Glue for the bank's networking

Interviewing users revealed a need to access a number of shared devices, such as memory, paper output, and connections to hosts and other bank users. Banyan integrates these server functions into a single box that includes a hard disk or disks, a tape-cartridge backup, a printer, and communications ports. Since the server uses a bus similar to that in an IBM PC, local area networks think that the Banyan is just another PC. That is, almost any LAN board that runs on an IBM PC may be plugged into the server. By selecting Banyan, the bank was free to combine it with 3Com's Ethernet, Proteon's ProNet, etc.

The Banyan server hardware includes a 32-bit Unix-based processor; up to 8 Mbytes of main memory; a six-slot, IBM PC-type input/output bus; up to four 86-Mbyte hard-disk drives; 60-Mbyte cartridge-tape drive for disk backup; and battery backup. The server's architecture consists of three functional elements (see figure).

The front-end portion, consisting of slots that accommodate PC boards, might be used to let multiple LANs use one server. (In the bank, each LAN has its own server.) The front-end also provides built-in asynchronous links. The "back-end" that connects the server to hosts, supporting such protocols as asynchronous, IBM's 3270 binary synchronous communications (BSC), and Systems Network Architecture (SNA), as well as to public X.25 data networks and to other Banyan servers; and Banyan's "services": proprietary applications for file sharing, printer sharing and spooling, network administration (such as who is attached where, plus failure, performance, and usage statistics), network mail, automatic file backup (by time clock), and restoral (after each crash, if desired),

VT100 terminal emulation, asynchronous file transfers to and from hosts, security (file-access authorization by password), a global naming arrangement, and others.

When a PC is connected to the Banyan server, it gains access to any of the services available on that server, to any connected host, or to resources on other interconnected Banyan servers.

The disadvantage of having all of the server functions in a single box is that, when the server does not work, the LAN dissolves into a set of standalone PCs. However, this drawback is overcome by the fact that each server may be connected to two LANs. Thus, in an emergency, a server would work for 40 users instead of the standard 20. While the server-to-server link interconnects all of the LANs, the slots labeled LAN1 and LAN2 in the front-end portion allow pairs of LANs to back each other up buddy-fashion.

According to the naming scheme used to identify users or resources in the network, a name is independent of its location, so the person or device it refers to can be relocated without changing names. Each name has three parts: user, group, and organization identifiers. User is usually the person's name, and the other identifiers refer to where that person works.

Therefore, all that a user has to do in order to reach someone in this labyrinth of 6,000 people is to enter the name of person and organization and then let the server locate the person. Also, the naming scheme allows PC users to locate and access services and devices independently of their locations on the network. Once the link is established, these resources appear as if they were attached directly to the user's Personal Computer.

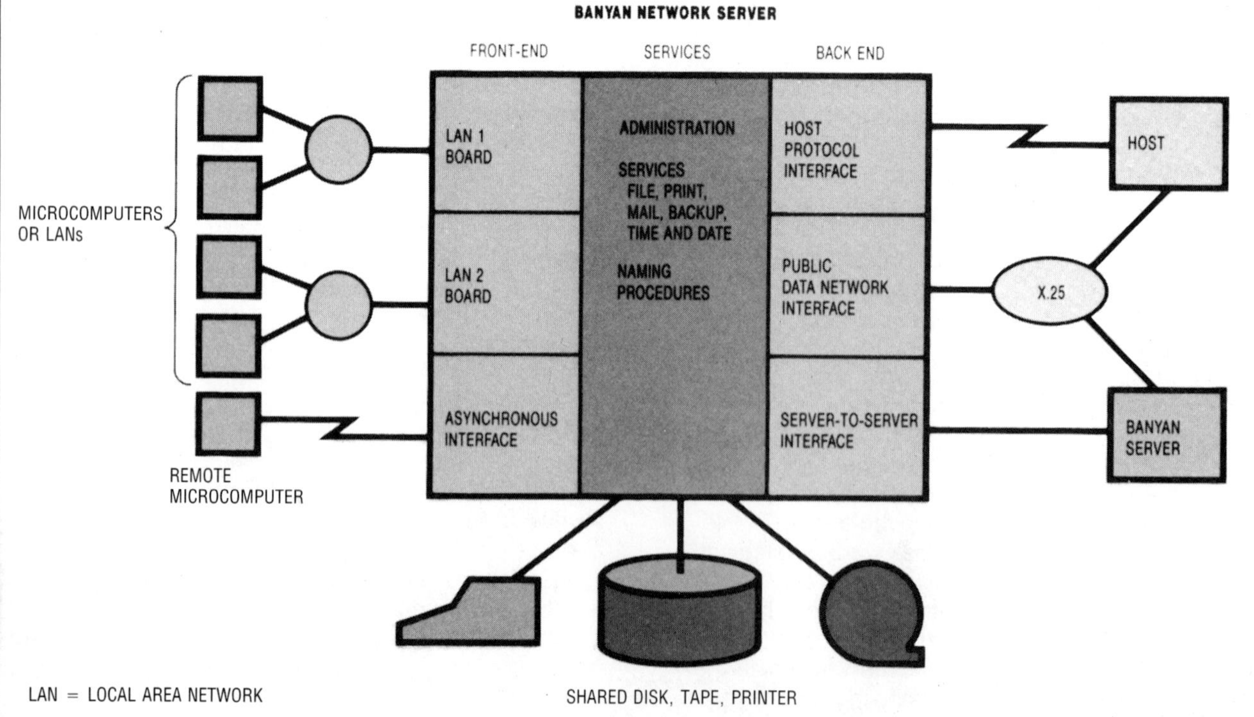

George T. Koshy, Booz, Allen & Hamilton Inc., Lexington, Mass.

Understanding multiple LANs: The why and how of linking up

A consultant argues for the proliferation of multiple LANs in an organization that is bridged at the Data Link Layer.

In the late seventies and early eighties, computer users and vendors realized that they required networks to tie their diverse equipment together and to make their data processing more efficient. Controversy was fervent among vendors regarding the most appropriate single medium as well as the most appropriate single technique to access the medium. Today, such discussions have subsided because vendors and users alike have learned that neither one medium nor one access scheme will satisfy all needs at all times.

The emerging trend is toward the existence of multiple local area networks (LANs) within one organization—each one catering to the needs of a specific operation or a functional group. Multiple LANs within an organization need to be interconnected so that all users can communicate with all others if necessary. The devices that perform the interconnection are called bridges, providing high throughput and low delay so that users do not experience any significant performance degradation when communicating with other users attached to the conglomerate of LANs.

Why have multiple LANs?

This article consists of two parts. In the first part, the need for the existence of multiple LANs is described in detail. The second part deals with one issue of the architectural layer at which the interconnection should take place.

Local area networking products available today do not conform to a single standard. They exist on a variety of media, such as twisted pair, coaxial cable, and optical fiber; use two signaling schemes (baseband and broadband); and work with a variety of media access techniques, such as carrier-sense multiple access with collision detection (CSMA/CD), token passing, time-division multiplexing, and so on. There is wide support among all segments of the computer industry for the Institute of Electrical and Electronics Engineers (IEEE) 802 standards, and it is expected that within the next few years most LAN products will conform to one of these standards.

Currently, IEEE 802 standards support the following schemes:
- CSMA/CD on baseband cable.
- CSMA/CD on broadband cable.
- Token-passing bus on broadband cable.
- Token-passing bus on baseband cable.
- Token-passing ring on baseband cable.

Although they do not offer a single scheme, the IEEE 802 standards have reduced the number of options for new products.

A number of LANs may coexist in a single organization for several reasons:
- Number of stations.
- Security.
- Area of coverage.
- Media access schemes.
- Organizational growth.
- Maintenance.

The following is a detailed description of these reasons.

Number of stations. In any media access scheme the performance deteriorates with an increase in the number of stations. In CSMA/CD, the greater the number of stations, the greater the probability of collisions that reduce the effective throughput. In a token-passing scheme, the effect of the number of stations on the throughput and delay is more straightforward. The token has to pass through more stations. This reduces the time available for transmission of data and increases the time a station needs to wait in order to receive the token. In a token-passing ring network, adding more stations increases the perimeter of the ring that will reduce the throughput and increase the delay.

Security. The establishment of multiple LANs may improve the security of communications. It is desirable to keep different types of traffic that have different security needs on physically separate media. At the same time, the different types of users with different levels of security need to communicate through controlled and monitored mechanisms. Multiple LANs, rather than a single LAN, are necessary under such circumstances. For example, a LAN used by personnel or for in-house financial projections should be separate from one used for customer service or on the factory floor.

Area of coverage. In many situations, one LAN is not capable of covering all areas of a user organization, due to inherent limitations of certain media access schemes, performance, and geographical locations. Certain media access schemes put a limit on the maximum distance of the LAN. The most obvious example is CSMA/CD, which imposes a limit on the maximum distance for a given minimum frame size and transmission speed. This restriction is necessary for the effective detection of collisions. Increasing the minimum packet size increases the maximum distance, but this affects the effective throughput because frames will have to be stuffed with nondata characters. Reducing transmission speed also increases the distance, but this reduces the throughput and the number of stations that may be attached to the LAN. So a CSMA/CD scheme operates on the basis of a set of fixed values for these parameters.

For example, IEEE 802.3 specifies the speed, 10 Mbit/s; the minimum frame size, 512 bits; and the maximum distance, 1.5 kilometers (km), or 0.9 miles. In this LAN, the maximum distance between the coaxial cable and the stations, such as computers or terminal concentrators, is only 50 meters (64 feet).

Broadband LANs also do not cover all areas of large organizations. Even though CATV broadband cable can cover areas of 10s of kilometers, these LANs have restrictions, covering a maximum distance up to only a few kilometers. For example, a standard IEEE 802.3 broadband CSMA/CD LAN covers an area within a radius of 1.4 km (0.87 miles) from the headend.

Media access schemes. The nature of media access schemes makes it necessary in many cases for multiple LANs with different media access schemes to be set up. Each of the common access schemes has its individual merits and demerits that make it suitable for certain environments and unsuitable for others. For example, CSMA/CD performs well under light loading but cannot provide deterministic delays. The token-passing scheme on a bus topology provides deterministic delays but introduces relatively larger delays at low levels of loading. Token-passing rings also provide

deterministic delays but are more vulnerable to failures in cables and stations. They have an advantage in that they can use optical fiber and run up to a few hundred bit/s.

The access scheme chosen for a LAN will depend on these characteristics, and an organization within one local area may have LANs of many different types. A manufacturer might use the General Motors-sponsored Manufacturing Automation Protocol (MAP) for its factory-floor communications, employing a token-passing bus LAN based on a broadband cable. Devices such as programmable contollers and robot controllers, which are directly involved in manufacturing operations, are attached to the broadband cable. The mainframe computers and peripherals at the same company might be tied together on a 10-Mbit/s token-passing ring, and the office computers and peripherals may be on a CSMA/CD bus. In this case, most communications would be confined within one type of LAN, but occasionally the office computers might need to talk to the mainframe or get information from the computers on the factory floor.

Traffic partitioning. Traffic originated at different sources must be partitioned into a number of groups, each with certain dominant characteristics. In most LANs, two major services are terminal-to-host communications and host-to-host communications. Terminal-to-host communications are characterized by small frame sizes and relatively fewer numbers of these frames. Host-to-host communications typically involve large frames and continuous generation of these frames. These two types of traffic should be put on different LANs having different characteristics. For example, terminal-to-host communications may be put on a channel operating at less than 1 Mbit/s, and host-to-host communications may be on a channel operating at 5 to 10 Mbit/s.

There are also administrative reasons for traffic partitioning. Divisions or groups within a large organization may require independence from each other. For example, a LAN for accounting and personnel departments should be separate from a second LAN used for the engineering department. Traffic can be monitored in different departments and users charged for their connect time for billing purposes. With multiple LANs, each department can grow and change its functions without affecting other sections of the company and without being affected by other sections of the company.

Organizational growth. Organizational growth could be the single most important reason for the existence of multiple LANs within an organization. If a department only has a small number of computers and peripherals, and this arrangement does not change significantly, then there is little incentive to create a LAN. If, however, the departmental computing resources are expected to change and grow, there is evey reason to have a LAN: With a LAN, the department's equipment will not have to be reconfigured every time there is a change in hardware or software. In cases like these, the motivation for establishing a LAN becomes a business rather than technological decision. This reason could be useful in convincing nontechnically oriented managers of the value of LANs.

Once a LAN is in place, the changing nature of most businesses results in the procurement of many different types of computers and peripherals for many different reasons. In most large organizations, a stable environment as far as computer networking is concerned is almost nonexistent. There will always be some part of an organization that is putting new computers into service or trying out a new piece of software or hardware. In such an environment it is advisable to divide the network into smaller sections that are independently managed, making it possible to run pilot tests without endangering the company's everyday operations.

Maintenance. Equipment that is modular in structure is easier to maintain. The same is true with networks. Even today's typical small networks of a few mainframes or minicomputers coupled with 10s of terminals are not easy to manage; networks are expected to grow into thousands of computers and terminals in the next few years, and it will be extremely difficult to manage such large networks as single entities. The solution is to divide the network into manageable sizes. Consider as an example an office complex wired with a baseband LAN using bus topology and the CSMA/CD access scheme. When the LAN does not function due to a faulty transceiver or controller on the station, it affects the entire user community. It is then difficult to locate the fault. If, on the other hand, the LAN consists of a number of separate segments, the improper operation due to a faulty component would be confined to that segment only. Such an arrangement also makes it easier to isolate the faulty component.

Mechanisms for interconnection

Having said that most large organizations will probably have multiple LANs within a limited geographical area, let us look at the possible means of providing the required interconnection between different LANs, whether local or remote. The interconnection between distant LANs will be more common than the interconnection between local LANs. The requirements and available means are different in these two situations; consequently, the solutions are also different.

LANs that are separated by long distances (perhaps up to thousands of miles) are typically interconnected using point-to-point lines operating at a few kilobits per second. These lines, which are leased from common carriers, are characterized by high cost and high incidence of bit errors (1 in 10^5).

Another common way to interconnect LANs as well as individual stations is via a Public Packet-Switching Network (PPSN). The PPSNs employ protocols that are different from the LANs, and their effective rate of data transmission is in the range of 10s of kilobits per second.

Private branch exchanges are usually used for long-distance connections and cannot usually handle enough throughput for efficient local communications. For this

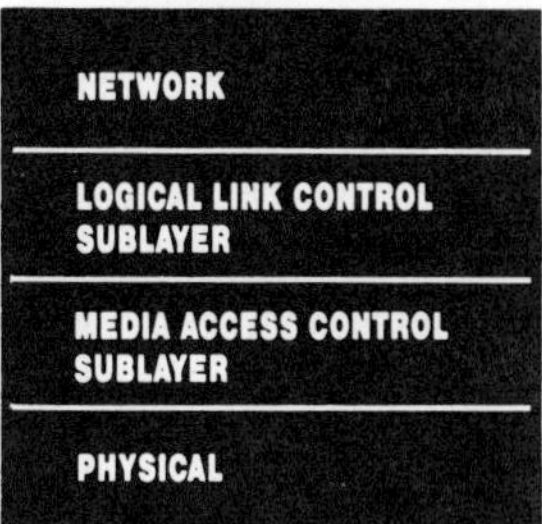

1. OSI and 802. *Two IEEE sublayers correspond to one OSI Data Link Layer. The MAC sublayer handles addressing and identification of station networks.*

reason, such considerations are not relevant to this discussion.

A long-haul network may be required to provide the interconnection of hundreds of host computers and 10s of LANs. In order to guarantee delivery in the event of link outages, there may be alternate paths in the topology. The links may use different speeds and transmission technologies. These factors make the routing of information among the stations and LANs attached to a long-haul network involve complex algorithms.

Local LANs may be interconnected using the same algorithms as those for long-haul interconnection. The Department of Defense's TCP/IP (Transport Control Protocol/Internet Protocol) is a good example. But many significant features of LANs make such complex algorithms unnecessary for interconnection when the LANs are close to each other. If the number of LANs is small and they are geographically close (within a few miles), they need not use expensive, low-speed lines leased from common carriers. Small numbers and geographical proximity can contribute to relatively fewer instances of lost connectivity that is due to hardware failures.

In such cases, interconnecting paths can be of a simple topology and would, therefore, not require an optimal path. Interconnecting devices that are all located within a limited geographical area can be easily managed.

Because the interconnection of local LANs is different from that in long-haul networks, the question arises: At which architectural layer does the interconnection take place?

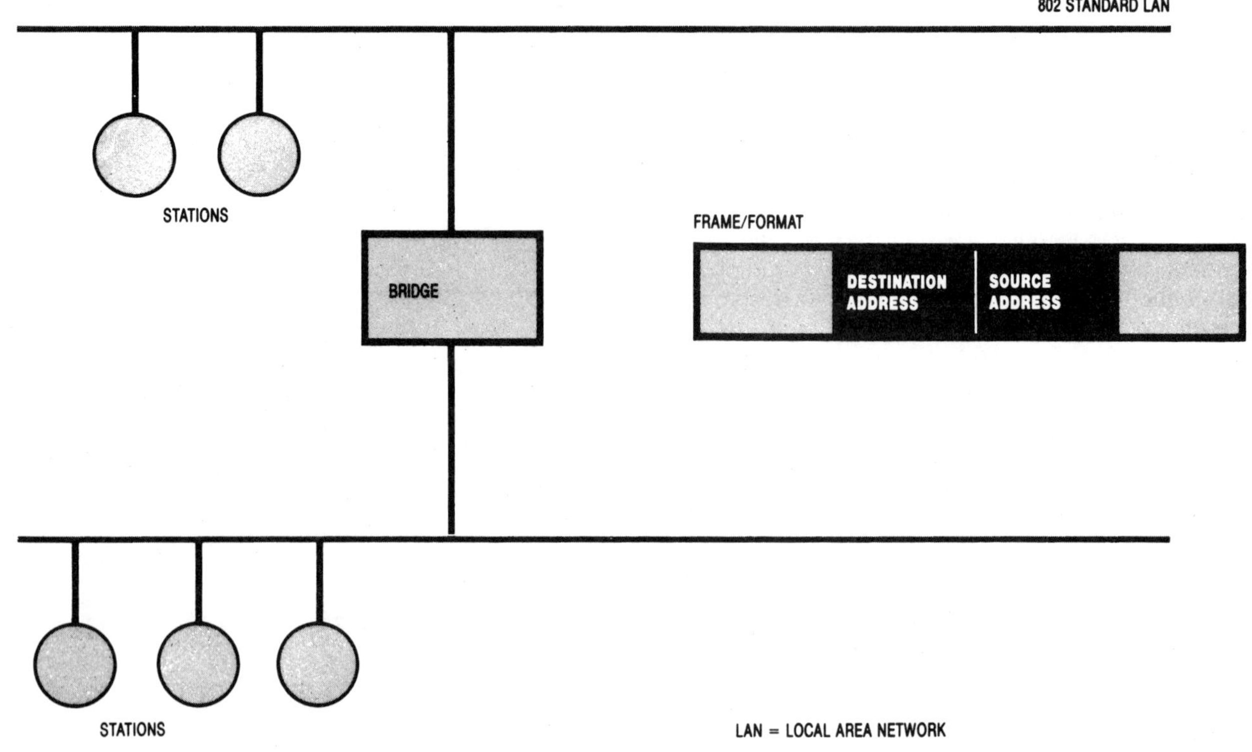

2. Two LANs and a bridge. *A bridge makes decisions about switching frames between local area networks based on the address of a station. It provides the interconnection between LANs. Bridges can use different sorts of algorithms to determine the best method of network interconnection.*

Traditionally, interconnection is at the OSI (Open Systems Interconnection) Network Layer, Layer 3, but the simplicity of algorithms suggests that the interconnection can take place at the Data Link Layer, Layer 2.

Decisions at the Data Link Layer

Figure 1 shows the OSI reference model and IEEE 802 model for LANs. In the IEEE model, the Data Link Layer consists of a logical link control (LLC) sublayer and a media access control (MAC) sublayer. The MAC sublayer involves addresses for stations to be identified in a network. Figure 2 shows two LANs connected through an interconnection device called a bridge. The bridge can make a decision about switching frames between the LANs on the basis of the address of a station. A number of simple algorithms may be used for making this decision. From a practical standpoint, the fact that interconnection between local LANs takes place at the MAC sublayer means that higher throughput will be achieved due to the relative simplicity in decision-making algorithms that are used at the MAC sublayer compared with other layers.

Bridges as defined above are possible between similar LANs. Even though IEEE 802 does not have a single standard, the similarities between the various standards are such that bridging between them is possible.

Figure 3 shows a configuration for a campus. It consists of four separate LANs—two baseband CSMA/CD networks, two broadband token-passing bus networks on one CATV cable, and one token-passing ring network. One 10-Mbit/s CSMA/CD baseband network connects the office machines, and the other 10-Mbit/s CSMA/CD baseband network runs the computer-aided design (CAD) room. A 20-Mbit/s token-passing ring creates the network for the mainframe computers and peripherals in the computer room. One 5-Mbit/s token-passing bus network ties together all data-gathering equipment requiring deterministic delays.

The LAN that is made up of a 10-Mbit/s broadband token-passing bus acts as a backbone interconnecting the other four LANs. Each bridge provides the interconnection between the backbone and one other LAN: thus Bridge 1 connects the backbone and one baseband LAN; Bridge 2 connects the backbone and the other baseband LAN; Bridge 3 connects the backbone and the token-passing ring; and, finally, Bridge 4 connects the backbone and the 5-Mbit/s token-passing bus LAN.

Algorithms for bridges

Among the many possible algorithms for decision making in bridges, two are significant for the present discussion. These two in particular have been proposed to the IEEE 802 committees. One, proposed by Digital Equipment Corp. (DEC), uses a nonsource routing scheme. Alternatively, IBM has proposed a source-routing scheme. Other proposals have been variations on these two methods.

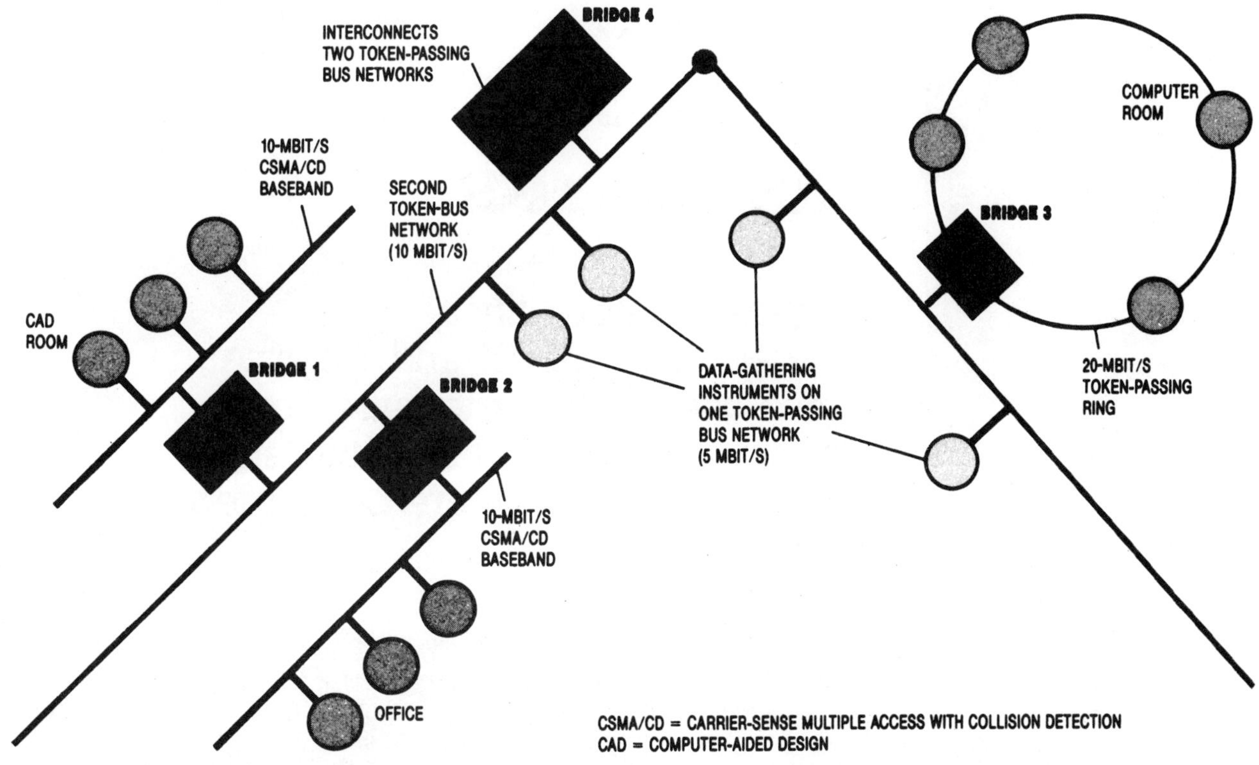

The DEC learn-and-decide scheme is shown in Figure 2. Here, the bridge connecting the two LANs maintains a database of the addresses of stations on each side. This database is empty to begin with and watches all frames that go by on the two LANs, learning the relative locations of the stations. This information is put into the database. When a new frame is picked up by the bridge, it searches the database for the destination address contained in the frame. The forwarding of the frame to the other side is based on the results of this search.

This simple algorithm requires no extra effort by end stations to switch frames through bridges, so that operation of the bridges is transparent. With this method, bridges do need to search the database for every frame before the next frame arrives. This DEC-proposed algorithm raises challenging design issues because the database entries are addresses that are up to 48 bits long.

The IBM algorithm works when the source station originating the frame sends the routing information within the frame itself. This enables the bridge to make the switching decision. For example, the frame might contain an ordered list of the addresses of the LAN segments through which the frame has to travel before it reaches its destination. This algorithm makes it easy for the bridge to make its switching decisions but requires the involvement of the end station. This means that bridge operations are not transparent to end stations.

The terms bridge and gateways are both used to refer to devices that perform the interconnection in networks. They should be treated as two separate types of devices. Both perform the general function of interconnection, but they do so at different levels in the architecture. Bridges, as proposed in this article, interconnect LANs using simple algorithms at the Data Link Layer. Gateways interconnect LANs and hosts in a long-haul network of arbitrary topology and use complex algorithms belonging to the Network Layer.

How is the distinction between gateways and bridges relevant to the user? The algorithmic simplicity of bridges enables them to have better performance characteristics, such as throughput and delay, compared with gateways. Gateways typically have throughput in the 56-kbit/s range, while it is not too difficult to accomplish throughput in the vicinity of 5 to 7 Mbit/s with bridges. Gateways need only be used when LANs are separated geographically or are not of the IEEE 802 type. In order to achieve maximum performance when a number of LANs are interconnected locally, bridges are necessary. ∎

George Koshy has a B. S. in electronics and communications engineering from Kerala University, Trivandrum, India, and an M. S. from Massachusetts Institute of Technology. He has worked for more than 11 years on network hardware, software, protocols, and architecture. Prior to joining Booz, Allen, he worked for Digital Equipment Corp.

R. L. A. Cottrell, Stanford Linear Accelerator Center, Stanford, Calif.

A tale of two networks

At the Stanford linear accelerator, a PBX and Ethernet give users access to subatomic energy data—sophisticated stuff. The two networks are compared.

In the world of elementary particle physics at Stanford Linear Accelerator Center, or SLAC, each breakthrough tends to bring with it a multitude of new questions. These questions, in turn, beg for ever more complex experiments to gather the data needed for a better understanding of the basic building blocks of the universe. Because of this, the pressure at SLAC to add new research tools, increase computer resources, and improve user access to SLAC computers is enormous.

The SLAC network management staff have experienced dramatic growth in interactive computing over the past decade. From supporting a few small pools of terminals, the user network has increased to over 1,000 terminals both on- and off-site. SLAC staff have also expanded the size and capabilities of the terminal pools provided for intermittent users. With more than a tenfold growth in the number of terminals located at SLAC, the center's local data communications requirements have grown exponentially in the last 10 years.

Early on, terminals communicated over dedicated links to host computers. As terminals were added, however, operations grew more complicated. Instead of a few locations, the center began supporting many terminals scattered about the SLAC facility; at the same time, computing capabilities grew, and many users found it necessary to access several computers. Simple cables and line drivers no longer did the job. There emerged a need for a network to support local data communications.

In 1981, we installed a data private branch exchange (PBX) as the hub of a terminal-access network. The PBX controls and coordinates interactive access to SLAC's various computers; and due to its modular design, we've been able to expand the network as new users and computers come on-line. In 1983, we installed an Ethernet and cross-connected it to the PBX network. In addition, using a Digital Equipment Corp. (DEC) PDP-11, we developed sophisticated statistics-gathering, monitoring, and multiplexed control capabilities for the terminal network.

Figure 1 shows the SLAC network. Each month the network handles about 60,000 terminal sessions, totaling 40,000 connect hours. Researchers from the United States and other nations can connect their terminals to the SLAC network via the dial telephone network, over the Tymnet X.25 packet-switched network, or through multiplexed and leased lines. Conversely, terminal users at SLAC use the same channels—dial modems, packet switching, multiplexed private circuits—to access various remote computing resources, in the United States and abroad.

The SLAC facility, located on 480 acres of the Stanford University campus, near Palo Alto, Calif., is operated by Stanford University for the U. S. Department of Energy. It is devoted to experimental and theoretical research in elementary particle physics, and to the development of new techniques in high-energy accelerators and elementary particle detectors.

Today, it has become obvious that the future of subatomic particle physics depends on machines that will produce colliding beams of even higher energy. Yet, for all the focus on physical research, as recently as 1974 SLAC's data communications capability was confined to 60 IBM Selectric typewriter terminals and a few CRTs in pool areas for the physicists.

Since data acquisition and analysis are performed by different computers, many terminal users need access to more than one computer. Initially, this problem was solved by placing a terminal for each computer in common areas. This required extra cabling, terminals, and ports. Eventually, however, SLAC staff found themselves running out of ports, as demand for computer access increased.

With the installation in 1981 of a Micom PBX, the terminal-access shortage began to come under control. The PBX acts as the hub of the terminal network. All cabling extends from this unit to terminals, computers, and other sources in order to have a central point providing monitoring and control of the network. With the PBX, the SLAC network essentially became a private telephone network for data. Instead of a telephone at each extension, there is either a terminal or a computer port. The PBX connects terminals and ports in response to requests entered at the user's keyboard. Once a connection is made, the PBX passes data transparently until it recognizes a terminal's request to disconnect.

The PBX solution

The PBX provides features similar to those in today's newer voice exchanges, but it is adapted to a data-only environment. A basic example of this adaptation is how the user specifies a message destination when asking for a connection: Where the voice user can most easily dial a series of digits, the terminal user can request a resource by "class" name, such as SYSTEMA. The PBX also provides features such as "camp-on-busy" and "call forwarding." Also, the terminal data rate need not be known in advance, since the PBX's autobaud feature provides automatic terminal speed recognition up to 9.6 kbit/s.

Terminals are connected to the PBX in a variety of ways. Terminals can be cabled to the PBX directly at distances of up to 700 feet, although the Electronics Industries Association (EIA) RS-232-C standard only specifies signal integrity for 50 feet. For intermediate distances of up to one or two miles, terminals are connected by line-drivers or local multiplexers. For longer distances, terminals are connected via modems communicating over dial-up, or multiplexed, telephone circuits. Each incoming interface is monitored by the PBX just as a local computer interface would be. Access to the PBX's ports can be restricted for security by entering instructions through the command port.

For managing the network, the PBX has a command port. Using a terminal connected to this port, SLAC network management can redefine class names for ports, enter new security restrictions, or take entire classes of ports out of service for preventive maintenance.

For an on-site user, the PBX makes network access simple: One depresses the terminal's RETURN key. The PBX responds with a request for the class of service the user wants, and the user replies accordingly. The class designations can specify a certain computer, specific ports on a particular computer, or other services that the network offers. Once the user enters the class designation, the PBX makes the connection and displays a GO message on the terminal. If the connection cannot be completed, the PBX displays a message on the user's terminal indicating the reason. If all of the ports in the requested class are in use, the PBX responds with a BUSY message and tells the user how many others are waiting for connection to the class. The user can then opt to get into the queue and be connected automatically when a port becomes available. This puts service contention on an orderly basis, and the interactive communications with the PBX makes the system "friendly" to work with.

Figure 2 shows the terminal dialog for a few common types of sessions. Since terminals are not hard-wired to computer ports, a single terminal has access to all service classes. Experience with about 660 different terminal lines

accessing the switch per month shows that each one selects, on average, 5 (median 3, maximum 32) different service classes. Service classes may be allocated resources based on usage level, provided infrequently used services can be shared by many users.

Also, fewer ports than terminals are required. The PBX has more than 900 terminals and personal computers connected, as well as 425 computer ports. The contention ratio (terminal/ports) would be much higher if the SLAC network did not provide access to over 45 different service classes, including 21 DEC VAXs, an IBM 3033, an IBM 3081 mainframe, front-ended by an IBM 3705 communications controller and an IBM Series/1 performing 3270 emulation. For example, one of the major service classes has 85 computer ports, which are accessed by over 480 different terminal lines each month. The ability for a single terminal to select multiple service classes and the contention feature allowed SLAC network management to cut costs while providing a high service level.

Special features

The PBX also made it easy to provide special service classes for users, such as:

— *Loop-back.* One port on the PBX is wired to loop back to the sending terminal. Thus, if users experience difficulty, they can quickly check to see that their terminal is transmitting correctly. In order to prevent users inadvertently getting stuck on this service, this port times out in two minutes if there is no activity.

■ *Tracing.* When users request the TRACE class their terminal is connected to a port on the PDP-11. This port interrogates the PBX command port and tells the user the address and data rate of the line he or she is using. Thus, if they have problems, they can supply information to aid in troubleshooting.

■ *Help.* When users request the HELP class, they are provided with a listing of the available service classes, important telephone numbers, and instructions for using the network. They can also request the STATUS class, which provides the current status of the main computer services. The HELP and STATUS functions are implemented on the PDP-11.

Special connections

The Lawrence Berkeley Laboratory (LBL), in Berkeley, Calif., does a great deal of work using SLAC facilities. Since LBL and SLAC are in line-of-sight, the connection is made by a microwave link. Further, since LBL's network is built around a data switch too, we are able to make switch-to-switch connections that provide virtually universal access within the two locations. Similarly, Fermi National Accelerator Laboratory, a physics research facility outside Chicago, has a PBX switch that is connected via a 9.6-kbit/s multiplexed satellite link to SLAC's PBX. An additional 11 sites are connected to SLAC by multiplexed leased land lines or satellite links.

SLAC also has a dedicated broadband network to control the accelerator. So that terminal users on either network may access services on the other, we have successfully cross-connected the two networks.

In addition to the asynchronous terminal network that this article explores, SLAC also has a terminal network of some

1. Terminal network. *Each month the network handles roughly 60,000 terminal sessions, totaling 40,000 connect hours. Remote users connect to the SLAC network via the dial-up links, over the Tymnet X.25 network, or through multiplexed and leased lines. SLAC users the same channels to access remote computing resources.*

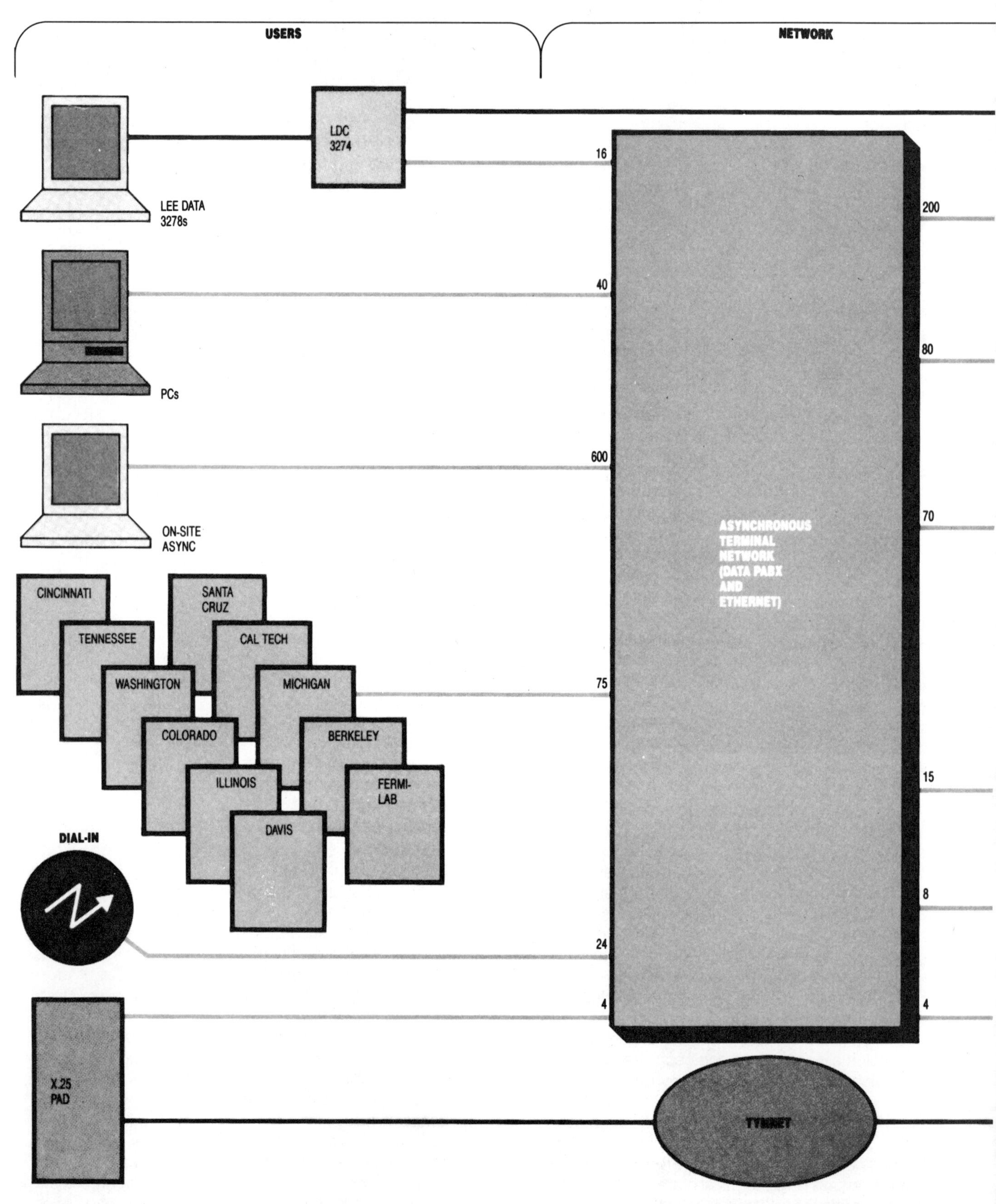

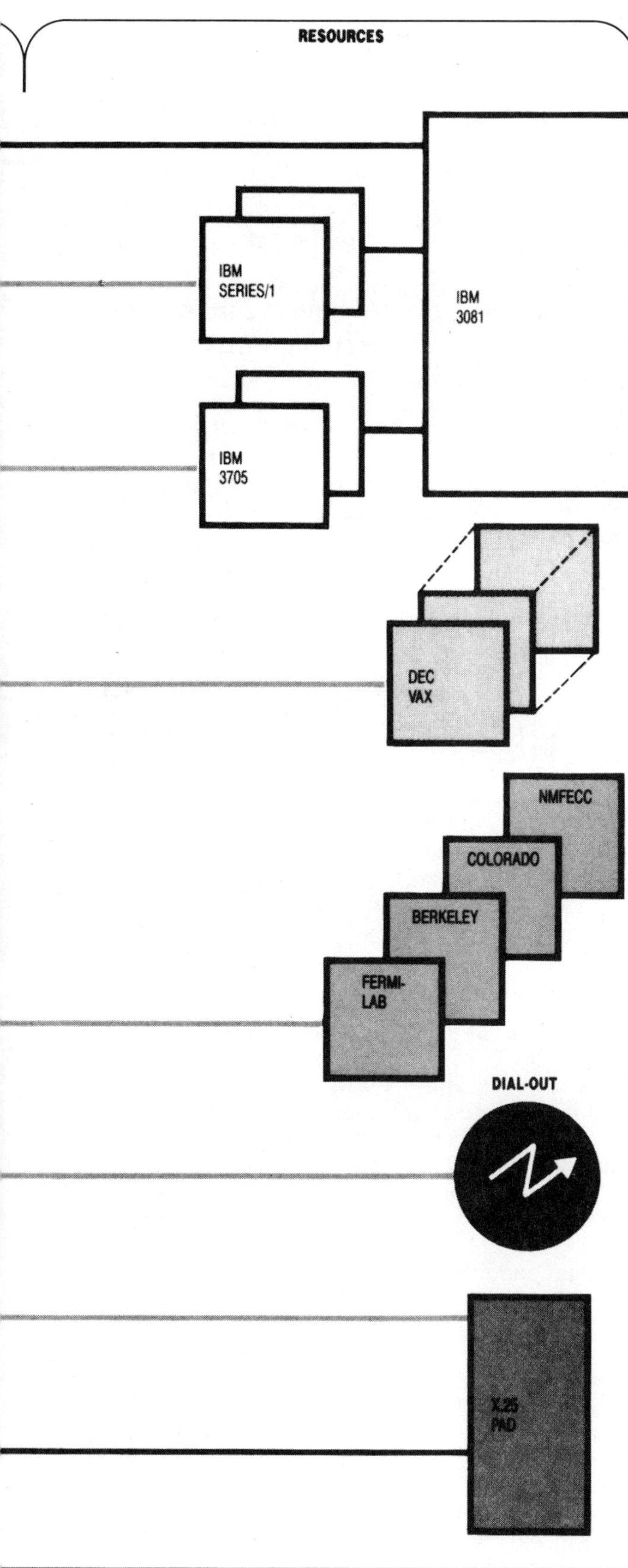

200 Lee Data Corporation IBM 3278 look-alike terminals, connected via coaxial cable links with controllers locally attached to the IBM mainframes. Some terminals have asynchronous capabilities, so we installed a link between their controller and the PBX. Thus users going through the controllers could establish a direct IBM mainframe link, and/or have a simultaneous asynchronous connection through the PBX to the DEC VAX, for example.

Another network

In spring 1983, a study group was formed to explore local area network needs at SLAC. Subsequently, SLAC installed a small Ethernet terminal network. Its aims were:

- To gain experience with the new technology.
- To learn how to connect Ethernet terminal servers to the PBX.
- To compare the Ethernet approach with that of the PBX when both are used for terminal access.
- To find a smooth migration path from PBX to Ethernet technology.
- To make recommendations on how to best serve terminal users in the future.

Initially, we installed about 1,300 meters of cable, transceivers, and a pair of Bridge Communications CS/1 terminal servers, both configured for eight RS-232C connections. Our cost estimates at that time favored the PBX solution. However, we felt the Ethernet approach was more open-ended, and that distributing networking intelligence could provide a network more responsive to its users than the PBX. We also expected rapid price erosion in the Ethernet market.

Based on initial experiences and expectations, we decided to expand the Ethernet network and test its capabilities. We upgraded our two terminal servers to their maximum complement of 32 ports each, and added a third 32-port server. To make it easier for us to diagnose problems, we initially put only experienced users on the network. At the same time we decided to expand the Ethernet installation, we decided to freeze any further acquisition of PBX equipment.

By the summer of 1984, our initial Ethernet experiment spawned two distinct networks. These comprise 11 Ethernet segments, roughly 2,200 meters of coaxial cable, and eight repeaters. One network supports 24 VAX computers running DECnet communications software, and the IBM mainframe running file transfer software written in-house. The other provides PBX-like access, and includes:

- Seven Bridge CS/1 terminal servers, each supporting an aggregate of 32 terminals and computer ports.
- Two Bridge CS/100 and two Bridge CS/200 terminal servers with 10 ports apiece.
- Five additional VAX computers.
- A PDP-11 used for terminal network management.

Figure 1 shows a Bridge terminal-server installation. We use DEC-supplied network interfaces for the VAXs, an Interlan NI1010 for the PDP-11, and an IBM Device Attach Control Unit (DACU) with another Interlan NI1010 controller board to bring the IBM 3081 mainframe onto the Ethernet. Most of the transceivers are from DEC, with three being from Interlan.

There are 127 terminal devices and 72 computer ports on our terminal servers, leaving 45 terminal-server ports for

```
SLAC MICOM SWITCH (Ver 2A-D)                        Welcome message
Common Classes:  VMLINE. VM24. VM43. HELP. STATUS
Enter class:  VM24
*** Type <cr> after GO ***
GO                                                  successful connection
.
Enter class:  TRACE              The user wants to know the terminal's line number
Type:  HELLO TRACE/<cr>                             special class instructions
GO
> HELLO TRACE/
.
sta p256                              The PDP-11 asks the Micom about this line
PO256 C031 S9600 TOO IOOO PTOOO CONN 0091      The terminal is on line 91
>; Make a note of the of the number after CONN
>; on the lines above
SLAC MICOM SWITCH(Ver 2A-D)    The PDP-11 automatically returns to the Data PABX
Common Classes:  VMLINE. VM24. VM43. HELP. STATUS
Enter class:  DIAL                           Attempt to use dial-out class
NOT AUTHORIZED                    Authorization is needed to use this class
Enter class:  VM43
BUSY-WAIT Y/C?003 C          All vm43 class ports busy with 3 people waiting
Enter class:  JUNK                                 Try another class
NO SUCH CLASS
Enter class:  DISCONNECTED             User did not respond within 12 secs
```

expansion. The terminal servers support terminals, auto-answer modems, IBM PCs, VAX ports, microVAXs, an IBM Series/1 computer acting as a channel-attached 3270 terminal emulator, and an IBM 3705 communications controller. Additionally, 32 terminal-server ports attach to the PBX: Eight channels provide access from the PBX to Ethernet services, and 24 channels provide access from the Ethernet to services available through the PBX.

The Ethernet terminal-server network typically has a maximum of 40 simultaneously active terminals. This includes, on average, 16 terminals on the Ethernet accessing resources through the PBX. Our PBX, heart of a network comprising roughly 1,200 devices, typically has seven of its more than 220 peak-use connections going through the Ethernet, and 10 coming from it. These "cross-overs" are due to resource availability: Either the resource does not exist on the originating network, or it exists on both, but all available ports on the originating network are unavailable.

We found that the cross-over requirement was fairly easy to meet. The PBX network was connected to the Ethernet network using RS-232-C cables between PBX interfaces and terminal-server interfaces. However, this approach requires the user to deal with both networks when making a connection. For a PBX terminal, the user accesses the class BRIDGE. The terminal behaves as if it were directly connected to the Ethernet terminal server; the user must then make a final connection request of the terminal server. Conversely, an Ethernet-attached terminal can ask to be connected to the PBX by issuing the command DO MICOM. The user will then complete the connection via the PBX's dialog.

Ethernet experience

During SLAC's first experience with Ethernet, we encountered abundant learning opportunities. For instance, we learned to mark off the coaxial cable at 2.5-meter intervals, so we could more easily comply with the LAN's standard requirement transceiver spacing. It was also important to comply with the Ethernet standard's maximum 500-meter cable length. We checked the lengths of already installed segments using a time-domain reflectometer, a device that can measure cable length by sending a test signal through a circuit, and measuring the time it takes for the signal's echo to return.

Transceivers also need secure mounting. Similarly, cable between transceiver and the supported station should be anchored firmly for strain relief. We replaced the Ethernet-specified slide connectors on the transceiver cables with more secure screw-down connectors. Attaching a transceiver to the cable requires drilling a hole in the coaxial cable to accommodate the "sting" that makes contact with the cable's center conductor. While this is not especially difficult, it requires care, since a faulty installation can bring down the LAN segment or make the device attached to the transceiver inoperative. We tried to standardize on equipment from as few vendors as possible, but we encountered problems between Bridge terminal servers and DEC transceivers. The result was more packet-alignment errors, and consequent multiple error retries.

Diagnosing problems on an Ethernet proved a challenge. A major problem facing the network management team is the current lack of simple-to-use, inexpensive diagnostic devices similar to the line monitors and RS-232-C breakout boxes used on the PBX network. Simply stated, the intellectual effort to run an Ethernet is greater than that required to run a PBX.

Nonetheless, most problems on the SLAC network were due to installation problems and faulty transceiver cables. Transceiver failures usually occur only after the devices have been "played" with. Left undisturbed, they seem to work indefinitely. Moreover, transceiver failure has been fairly easy to find, since the station, terminal server, or computer also fails. Indicator lights on the repeaters help isolate Ethernet faults. For instance, a lit Collision Detect (CD) light usually indicates trouble nearby.

Server problems

We encountered a few problems with the terminal servers we installed at SLAC. Some were such bugs as spontaneous disconnections in mid-session, servers losing some or all of their configuration data, interference between DECnet and Bridge communications over the same Ethernet cable, and occasional long delays—measured in seconds—between the time a key is hit and the time a character is echoed from the computer.

The delay problem turned out to be the Ethernet terminal server network, since the terminals and ports could be ruled out as the time-delaying culprits. Probably the delay is due mainly to retries associated with error recovery. Other shortcomings can be attributed to a lack of features or perhaps, in some cases, design flaws. For instance, when logging off from a computer, characters from the end of the computer dialog are transmitted to the terminal. This bothered some users, since the information often contained accounting data regarding the user's session.

The automatic data-rate detection provided by the original terminal servers is also somewhat awkward. Instead of providing a single autobaud range to 9.6 kbit/s as desired, the Bridge terminal servers provide autobaud in two ranges: below 2.4 kbit/s and 2.4 kbit/s and 9.6 kbit/s. This means services must be fragmented into two classes based upon speed. This limitation also means that it is difficult to connect the new 300/1200/2400 bit/s auto-answer modems to the Bridge terminal servers.

For the first couple of years operating the Ethernet network, no network server was available. Since our terminal servers were scattered over a half-mile radius, installing new software reconfigurations, or entering new welcome messages was a tedious proposition. Also, the time-and-date stamps in each server were not synchronized. Recently, Bridge introduced the NCS/150 network communications server, which enables the above activities to be centralized.

Comparing network service

Using an IBM PC, we measured Ethernet turnaround delay between the time a character is entered and when it is echoed by the host. The round trip takes roughly 1/12 of a second. On terminals sending more than 12 characters per second, users will see the cursor jump if the host echoes the character, since several characters will be buffered into a single packet. This makes positioning the cursor difficult. On the other hand, there are no problems of this type on the PBX, even when the character repeat rate is 30 per second. To minimize jumpiness on the Ethernet, the terminal-server ports are configured to tie off packets and send them with minimal delay. However, the short packets increase the Ethernet loading, as each packet usually contains only a single data character and several dozen bytes of packet overhead.

The X-on/X-off flow control caused considerable consternation. In general, we set our terminal servers to pass X-on/X-off flow-control characters transparently, the conventional way the PBX network does. Thus, it is up to the computer port or terminal to act on the X-on or X-off character. In the case of graphics terminals and other semi-intelligent devices, the terminal server needs to take over the X-on/X-off character supervision. Otherwise, the terminal may send an X-off when its buffers fill to a threshold, but characters coming from buffers in the terminal servers may overflow the receiving server device, unless the terminal server knows to invoke flow control. Since the PBX doesn't buffer data, this is not a problem on that network.

Transparent flow control was needed on terminal server ports supporting IBM PC-to-mainframe file transfers. SLAC network planners found that PC file transfers worked well through the Bridge network. However, the throughput of 700 characters/second for a disk-to-disk file transfer through a 9.6-kbit/s channel was about 7 to 10 percent less through the Etherent terminal servers than through the PBX. This likely is due to packet processing overhead in the terminal servers. If Ethernet's speed-matching capability is used, the problem gets worse, and time-outs in the file transfer code probably need adjustment at the personal computer, the host, or both. Configured as they are, with short tie-offs to best support terminal access, the terminal servers send most packets with only a few data characters, and several dozen bytes of packet overhead. There may be unwanted interference between the long packets (around 1.5 kbytes) used by Ethernet file transfer applications and the short packets (averaging around 75 bytes) used by the terminal servers, resulting in unpredictable response times for interactive terminal users. In other words, Ethernets tailored for terminal access applications may lose some of their effectiveness for file transfers.

The Ethernet terminal network performs speed matching, which means that the user terminal's speed does not need to match that of the port being accessed. However, if the terminal runs much slower than the port, for example a 1.2-kbit/s dial-in user accessing a 9.6-kbit/s service is likely to run into problems: If the computer sends data at 9.6 kbit/s, the terminal cannot accept it, and the network buffers will quickly fill. But flow control still can manage this situation. However, if the user wants to interrupt the computer, then all the data in the network buffers pending delivery must be emitted to the terminal at its slower speed before the terminal can output the response to the user's interruption. In the case of a mismatch of 1.2 kbit/s to 9.6 kbit/s, this is annoying and leads to poor responsiveness; for a 300-bit/s to 9.6-kbit/s mismatch, the service borders on unaccept-able. The PBX does not perform this type of speed match-ing, as it only connects terminals and ports configured for the same speed. While this requires that the terminal speed be preset to that of the port, the improved response more than makes up for any inconvenience.

One of the flexible features of Bridge terminal servers is their ability for the ports to convert X-on/X-off character flow control to the RS-232-C Clear-to-Send (CTS) signal control, without passing a character through the port. Since the on-site IBM 3705 communications controllers are config-ured as half-duplex devices they cannot respond to character input while outputing characters to a terminal. We therefore modified the IBM 3705 software to respond to CTS flow control, hence providing IBM 3705 ports with that function. To do the same things with the PBX we had to build our own special X-on/X-off-to-CTS flow-control con-verters, since the standard PBX interfaces passed the X-on/X-off characters through to the IBM 3705, thus confus-ing the front-end.

While the PBX network adheres to a one-user, one-ses-sion philosophy, the Ethernet terminal server's ability to support multiple simultaneous sessions (one active, the rest suspended) is highly attractive. Although this feature is particularly useful to network management personnel, it has its tradeoffs, since each session ties up a terminal-server port and a computer port. This, in turn, reduces the effec-tive contention ratio of terminals to ports, so extra ports may be needed. To reduce this negative impact, we have limited to two the number of simultaneous sessions allowed for most terminal users, and have not heavily advertised this feature.

Currently, the maximum number of terminals with more than one simultaneous session in progress typically peaks at three of four, and the maximum number of ports tied up by multiple-session users is around six, thus the impact on our contention ratio is relatively small. Bridge provides a unique and useful macro facility for its terminal servers. An authorized network manager can store a lengthy sequence of terminal-server commands for subsequent invocation with a DO command. This facility allows network managers to provide users with a more friendly interface to the network. For instance, we use macros to initiate all connec-tions. Such a macro may, among other things, connect to a port within a named service class, set the speed and parity of the remote port, specify echoing of the local port, and send an autobaud character to the host.

Early on in SLAC network planning we recognized the importance of centralized control and monitoring facilities. Collecting and analyzing network statistics helps in assess-ing the service quality. These analyses also help spot trends and plan future network growth. Two standard features of our PBX address these requirements. The unit has a command port, to which a terminal can be attached to manage the network. At the command port, users can enter commands to redefine resource classes, take classes out of service for maintenance, alter inactivity time-outs, force connections between any two interfaces on the switch, and so forth.

Complementing the command port, a statistics log port on the PBX outputs an audit trail of all switch activity. The statistics log consists of time-and-date stamped records of every connect and disconnect attempt. For unsuccessful connect requests, the log shows the reason. The log also shows queuing activity.

To enhance management capabilities, planners dedi-cated a PDP-11 computer to that task, connecting the command port and statistics log output port to the PDP-11. We've programmed the PDP-11 to provide capabilities the PBX, by itself, does not offer.

Connecting the command port to the PDP-11 allows the networking staff more convenient ways of dealing with the PBX. Where the command port supports only a single terminal, we can have the PDP-11 time-share the command port between several authorized users. Through a link to the IBM mainframe, these users also can be logged on to the IBM virtual machine (VM) operating system on the IBM host, and interactively issue commands to the PBX. We also can store VM macro command sequences for reuse, and we can have the computer automatically issue com-mands to the PBX for such predictable situations as taking a host off-line for preventive maintenance. The PDP-11 can also alter such things as terminal time-outs to the PBX network based on performance changes noted from the statistics log output.

For management reporting, the PDP-11 monitors the statistics log port. Each time a terminal accesses the PBX it causes the PDP-11 to create a session record, with such information as start time, class of call, line I.D., port I.D., number of ports in the class currently in use. When the terminal disconnects the computer adds the disconnect time to the record and logs it in a disk file, which is sent daily to an IBM mainframe.

For the Ethernet, we developed our own software to collect network data activity. We again used the PDP11, bringing network management for both the PBX and Ethernet to a central point.

The PDP-11 connects to the Ethernet via an Interlan controller board. The PDP-11 communicates with the Bridge terminal servers using Interlan's XNS/ITP software. The computer interrogates all network servers every minute the status of each server can be logged. The PDP-11 has been programmed to derive session records from these status snapshots. By watching for status changes, the software deduces where sessions start and finish, and so forth. The software then builds session records that contain the terminal server active port (the terminal end), the terminal server passive port (the computer port end), service class name, start and finish time of the session (resolved to our sampling interval), number of other ses-sions in progress for the terminal, number of ports in use and free for the resource class, and total number of Bridge sessions in progress. We save these records on disk, transmitting them daily to an IBM mainframe. Recently SLAC networking staff acquired a Bridge NCS/150, which can aid in generating these session records.

The IBM mainframe does the actual network statistical analysis of session records—both those captured on the Ethernet and those coming from the PBX. We use a statistical software package to help us identify usage patterns by service class, by terminal server, and by individual ports. Information available includes the maximum number of simultaneous sessions per day per service class, elapsed minutes and total number of sessions by class, the number of different terminals using a given service class, and which ports and terminals are not used. With this information we can spot trends, decide where to add or remove capacity, and uncover strange behavior that may indicate problems.

For users in central SLAC areas, we developed an additional, inexpensive aid for working with the network. The PDP-11 accumulates key information from the PBX and Ethernet session records, on the fly, to arrive at totals for lines in use, ports in use, number of people waiting in queue, and so on. The totals are transmitted to an IBM PC where they are used to periodically update color TV displays distributed over the SLAC site.

Contrary to expectations, the costs for Ethernet terminal connections are still not lower than those for the PBX. This is due in part to a new Micom multiplexing product, which has cut the cost required to add a terminal. The multiplexers have also allowed us to more efficiently use existing twisted-pair wiring. For example, the Micom 32-port time-division multiplexers allow up to 1,600 terminals on a 100 twisted-pair trunk cable, where previously only 33 to 50 terminals could be supported, depending on whether two or three wire pairs were used per terminal.

Today it costs SLAC about $550 to connect a terminal to either the PBX network or the Bridge network. These figures include the cabling and installation costs and assume the terminal will locate beyond the RS-232-C distance from the computer port, and so in the PBX case, will need a line driver (often built into multiplexers). Also, for each terminal connection we add 50 percent of connecting to the computer port so we can maintain a contention ratio of two terminals for each computer port.

Still, it does not pay to install Bridge terminal servers with fewer than 10 ports. This means that for areas with only one or two terminals, one has to run long device cables from the terminal to the nearest Bridge terminal server. The PBX is more flexible in this respect, since one can get four port multiplexers, and one can easily and cheaply attach single terminals. ∎

R. L. A. Cottrell, assistant director of computer services at the Stanford Linear Accelerator Center, received his B. S. and Ph. D. degrees in computer science from Manchester University in Manchester, England.

Ken Sekhon, Radik Gens, and Ken Graham,
Pacific Western Airlines Ltd., Vancouver, B. C.

Private to public messaging: The transparent solution

Building a gateway to a public service was the best way for this airline to rapidly expand the reach of its private messaging scheme.

Confronted by a problem that demands an alteration to their network, users have several choices. Often they wait for a crisis. Wiser solutions include buying new hardware or software or paying a consultant to invent an alternative. Users can, however, opt to meet the problem head on and design new hardware or software schemes.

After Pacific Western Airlines warded off a crisis by inventing its own solution, the company found that the new network configuration offered even more advantages than had been expected.

In January 1985, Pacific Western Airlines began a trial of IBM's Professional Office System (PROFS), an electronic-mail scheme for IBM mainframes. Pacific Western's processing facilities included a central host site in Vancouver, B. C., that consisted of twin IBM 4381s running the Virtual Machine (VM) and Multiple Virtual Storage operating systems. Pacific Western's network was of the Systems Network Architecture variety, and it provided access to the host via dedicated lines from various cities in Canada: Vancouver, Calgary, Edmonton, Winnipeg, and Toronto. Any terminal on the dedicated network could access applications on both the VM and the MVS hosts. To maintain security, circuit-switched access was not provided to the two hosts.

PROFS was received very well by the user community, and the trial evolved, over time, into limited use. Initially, the user community grew slowly. Soon, however, network traffic grew phenomenally in a very short period because of anticipated labor disruptions.

Anticipating a possible strike, Pacific Western management wanted to be able to operate and manage the business with limited personnel. A strike would put a tremendous burden on the existing voice communications network because the management staff would not only be spread out over 45 operational sites but also constantly shuffled from place to place. Management realized that PROFS could serve as a valuable tool for coordinating the operational end of the business. The decision to augment the voice network with additional business communications functions—and to do so immediately and with minimal additional cost—left the network management team few alternatives. PROFS access was required in places where the current dedicated network access was not available.

Expanding the network to these locations would require new dedicated lines. Since this was time-consuming and prohibitively expensive, management looked for other ways to provide PROFS access. Providing switched access to the hosts in Vancouver was rejected because of security concerns and the high direct distance dialing costs of a switched network.

However, at about this time, Telecom Canada's Envoy 100 public electronic messaging facility, which was also on trial at Pacific Western, was becoming more widely known throughout the company. Whereas PROFS provides the functions of a private electronic messaging scheme, Envoy 100 allows subscribers to participate in a public electronic messaging facility.

Management decided that the combination of a private and public electronic messaging facility could allow quick implemention of links to any of the remote locations without sacrificing security requirements. In addition, it would entail only the relatively low communication costs of packet-switching technology.

Although Envoy 100 was a very attractive alternative with which to augment the corporate PROFS service, Pacific Western faced a significant problem. A gateway node was required between PROFS and Envoy 100 so that messages could flow in either direction and the services would appear as a single electronic-mail facility. The question was whether to acquire a prepackaged PROFS-Envoy 100 gateway or to construct one quickly and inexpensively.

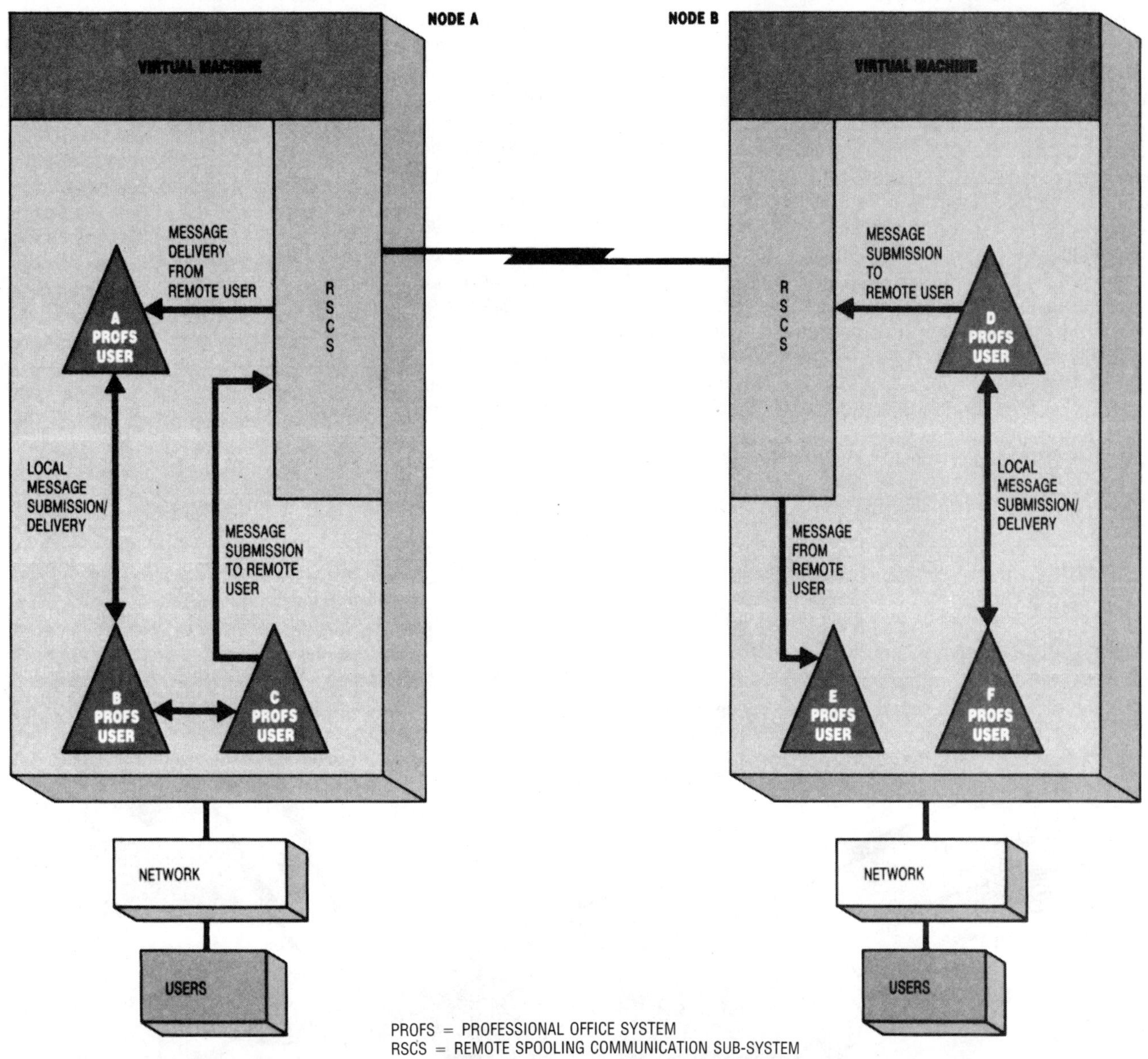

Only two known gateway products were on the market: Telecom Canada's 3780 and Comstar products. Neither was totally transparent to PROFS users, and both required a major reconfiguration of the front-end communications processor.

After considering the various gateway alternatives, Pacific Western decided to construct the gateway so that it could retain all the features of the PROFS electronic-mail component and have the implementation completely transparent to the PROFS users, who would not necessarily be aware of the existence of Envoy 100. Before discussing Pacific Western's implementation of the PROFS-Envoy 100 gateway, it will be helpful to describe in brief the electronic messaging components of IBM's PROFS and Telecom Canada's Envoy 100.

IBM's PROFS offers the capabilities to edit, distribute and receive, file, search, format, and print messages. Users can also manage calendars, keep reminders, schedule facilities, and send and receive messages. The present discussion includes only those features relevant to the electronic-mail component.

(In PROFS terminology, the term "message" has a special connotation within the PROFS implementation. In this discussion, however, the more universally acceptable term "message" will refer to all store-and-forward electronic communications between various electronic-mail users.)

PROFS makes it easy for the user to send and receive mail, and, depending on the type of mail, the user can perform one or more of the following actions on the messages: read, add comments, make changes, file them in a variety of ways, erase, forward, send replies to the sender, print the messages, or leave them in the in-box. Special primitives are also provided to copy messages to individual users, to use distribution lists for groups, and to request acknowledgments of message receipt. Various functions are provided to operate on message logs that are maintained for audit trails and retransmissions.

The PROFS administrator maintains a directory of the various corporate users and their locations. The individual users can further maintain their own subdirectories of nicknames and locations to identify the users with whom they communicate, which gives them very flexible multilevel control of the mail directory. The architecture and implementation make it possible for users to be recognized by mail identification and location. Figure 1 illustrates the mechanism by which PROFS messages are communicated between mainframes. The communications network is transparent to the users, and all message transfers to users on remote facilities are handled by the Remote Spooling Communication Sub-System. RSCS resides under the VM operating system and is the standard mechanism for handling communications between VM hosts.

While PROFS implements private messaging, Envoy 100 is a national store-and-forward messaging service designed for public mail applications. It makes possible an extensive set of customer selectable features and options to allow registered users to prepare, correct, send, distribute, access, and file messages destined within and between subscribing companies. Envoy 100 uses the Datapac network to ensure error-free communications to the user terminal. Users can access Envoy 100 through the regular telephone network, Datapac, TWX, U. S.-based packet-switching networks (for example, GTE Telenet and Tymnet), and the worldwide Telex network (Fig. 2). Some of the functions available include delivery assurance capability, batch entry, user-selectable time zones, and distribution lists.

Two delivery options are available. Mailbox messages can be stored until the intended message recipient signs on and requests the messages. Alternatively, autodelivery messages are delivered to available terminals automatically by Envoy or are distributed at timed intervals throughout the day.

Other value-added services are offered through Envoy 100 and are continually being upgraded. EnvoyPost, for example, uses Envoy 100 to access the national mail network. Subscribers to the Envoy 100 messaging service can send messages to the Canada Post Corp., where they are printed, placed in an envelope, and physically deliv-

---

2. Multipurpose. *Although Pacific Western Airlines originally intended only to link PROFS users to the Envoy service, a logical next step was to provide them access to a wide variety of public communications schemes, including Tymnet and GTE Telenet packet-switching networks in the United States and the switched telephone network.*

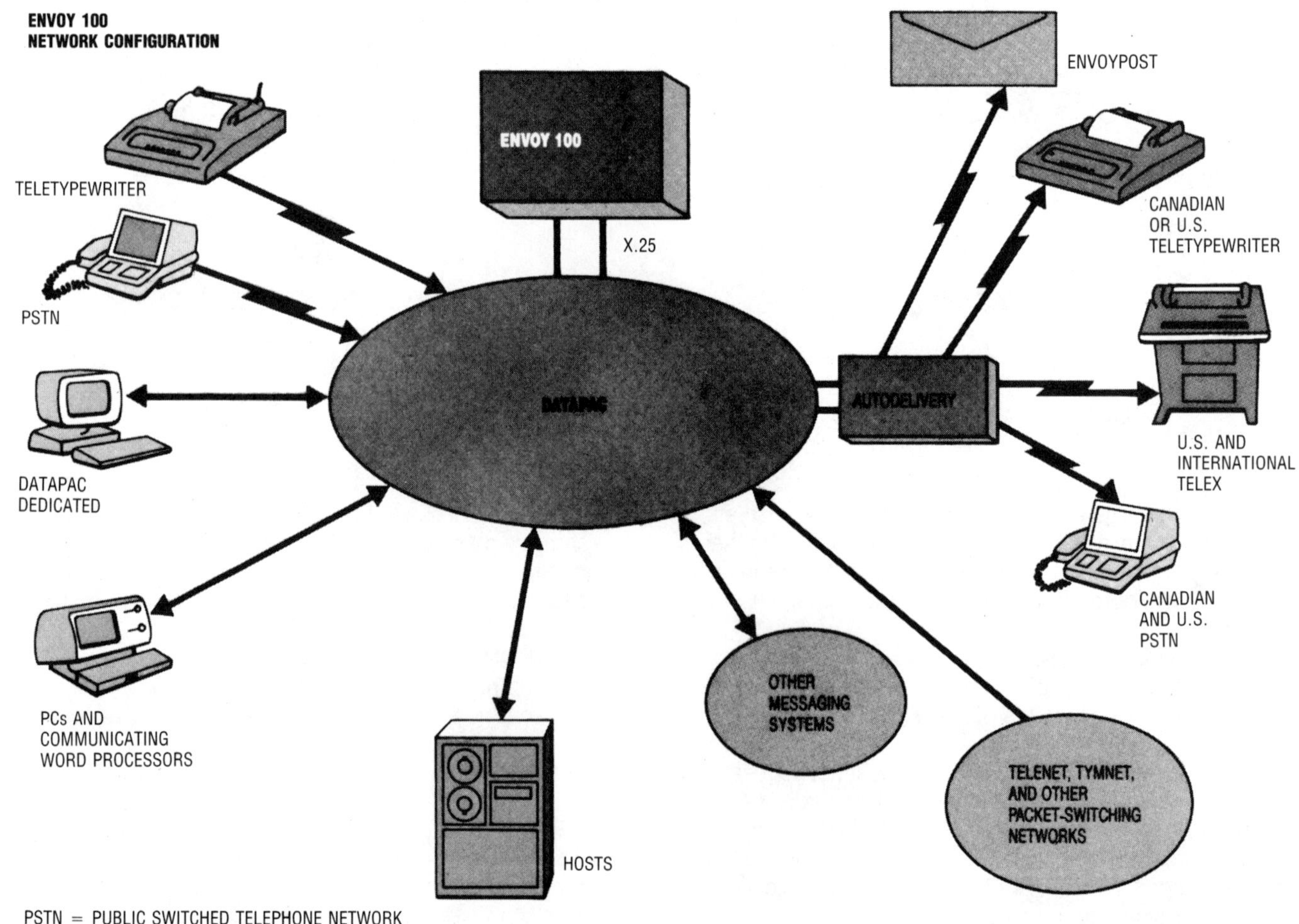

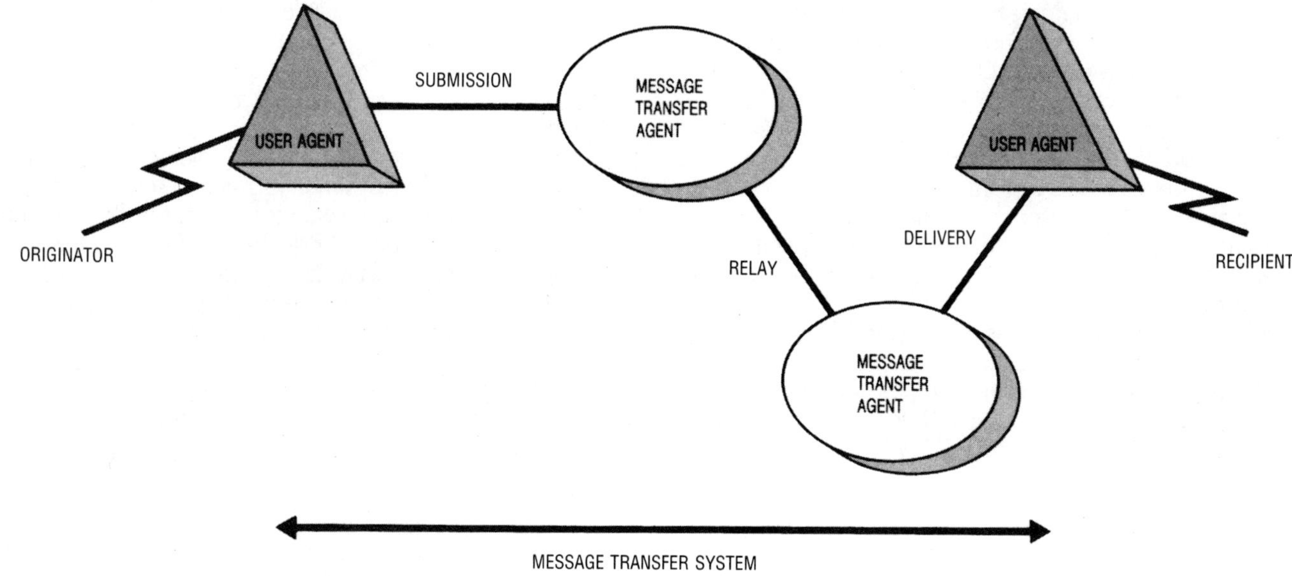

ered by a letter carrier. Another value-added store-and-forward service from Envoy to Telex is called Textran.

Also, Telecom Canada has announced future support for the X.400 messaging standard, which will simplify communications among electronic messaging schemes worldwide. One of the first implementations adhering to this will be between Envoy 100 and GTE Telenet's Telemail service in the United States.

Gateway architecture

The planned gateway provides a completely transparent interface to the public electronic-mail network from the private corporate mail service. Vendor-supplied software (such as PROFS or RSCS) cannot be modified, even if this requires a sacrifice in efficiency or speed of implementation. Moreover, as Pacific Western management requested, the design permits unattended operation to allow automatic scheduling of mail transmission on the basis of a predefined frequency and interval and to be robust in recovering from network-related failures.

The gateway architecture was defined using terminology from the X.400 message-handling standard. X.400 specifies the network architecture, protocol structure, implementation options, message transfer, and interpersonal messaging services for interconnecting electronic-mail networks.

Network users, message originators, and recipients can be people or processes. A function directly under the control of the sender is termed "user agent," because it acts on behalf of the user and assists in preparing, storing, sending, and receiving messages. The PROFS processes running in the user's virtual machine can be seen as the user agent. Once the user prepares the message with the aid of a user agent, a "message transfer agent" is responsible for transferring it. As a group, the message transfer agents are called the "message transfer system" and

provide store-and-forward delivery services between user agents. The Remote Spooling Communication Sub-System can be viewed partially as a message transfer agent (Fig. 3).

Following are important features of the gateway architecture:
- All PROFS users can send messages to all authorized Envoy 100 users just as if they were regular PROFS users.
- All authorized Envoy 100 users can compose and send messages to all PROFS users.
- PROFS and Envoy users can own a mailbox on both of the messaging services. This option is exercised primarily by users who travel frequently and are often away from their regular means of accessing the PROFS network.
- Users can initiate message transfers between the two mailboxes on demand or, in the PROFS environment, automatically.
- The acknowledgment of messages between the mail networks is supported with total transparency.

The architecture of the gateway is depicted in Figure 4. The message transfer agent component of the gateway handles communications with PROFS. When an Envoy-to-PROFS message is destined for a local PROFS user agent, the message transfer agent simply delivers the message to the PROFS user agent. When the PROFS user agent is remote, the RSCS portion of the message transfer agent (not shown in the figure) relays the message to a remote message transfer agent, which will pass it to the destination user agent.

The Envoy user agent thinks the gateway is simply another Envoy user agent, but the gateway ensures that the Envoy-to-PROFS messages are routed to the message transfer agent, which sends them to the correct PROFS user agent. Envoy-to-PROFS messages are sent to a general PROFS mailbox on Envoy. At intervals defined by network management, this mailbox is emptied, and all the messages are routed to the gateway and then to the correct PROFS user. Messages within Envoy are handled by the message transfer agent Envoy 100 component.

About 5 percent of PROFS users also maintain private Envoy mailboxes. The gateway also provides facilities for those PROFS users who want to retrieve their messages from the Envoy environment. On request, the gateway can make a switched connection directly to a particular Envoy user agent, after which the user can download messages from the Envoy mailbox to PROFS.

The standard PROFS implementation provides for a user directory with the following information: user nickname, node identification (where the user resides), system user identification (user identification or user account code), and user's real name.

Multiple levels of directories exist on the PROFS, but they essentially fall into two categories—private, maintained by the user, and public, which is maintained by the PROFS administrator.

The "send" primitive in PROFS searches private directories before searching public ones. If the recipient of the message resides on the same node as the originator, then the message is sent directly to the recipient; otherwise, the message is tagged appropriately and sent to the RSCS to be forwarded to the remote user.

RSCS can be seen as a partial implementation of a transport level service. When registering a new user, the PROFS administrator is aware of the user's node, the user's identification, and the default user nickname. At this time, PROFS determines whether the user's mailbox resides on the public messaging service or on PROFS. At any time, the user can override this attribute by creating an updated

---

*4. **All things to all services.** The gateway appears as a message transfer agent to PROFS and an Envoy user to the Envoy messaging scheme. PROFS users maintaining private Envoy mailboxes can download messages to their PROFS mailbox via a gateway and initiate message transfers between mailboxes on demand.*

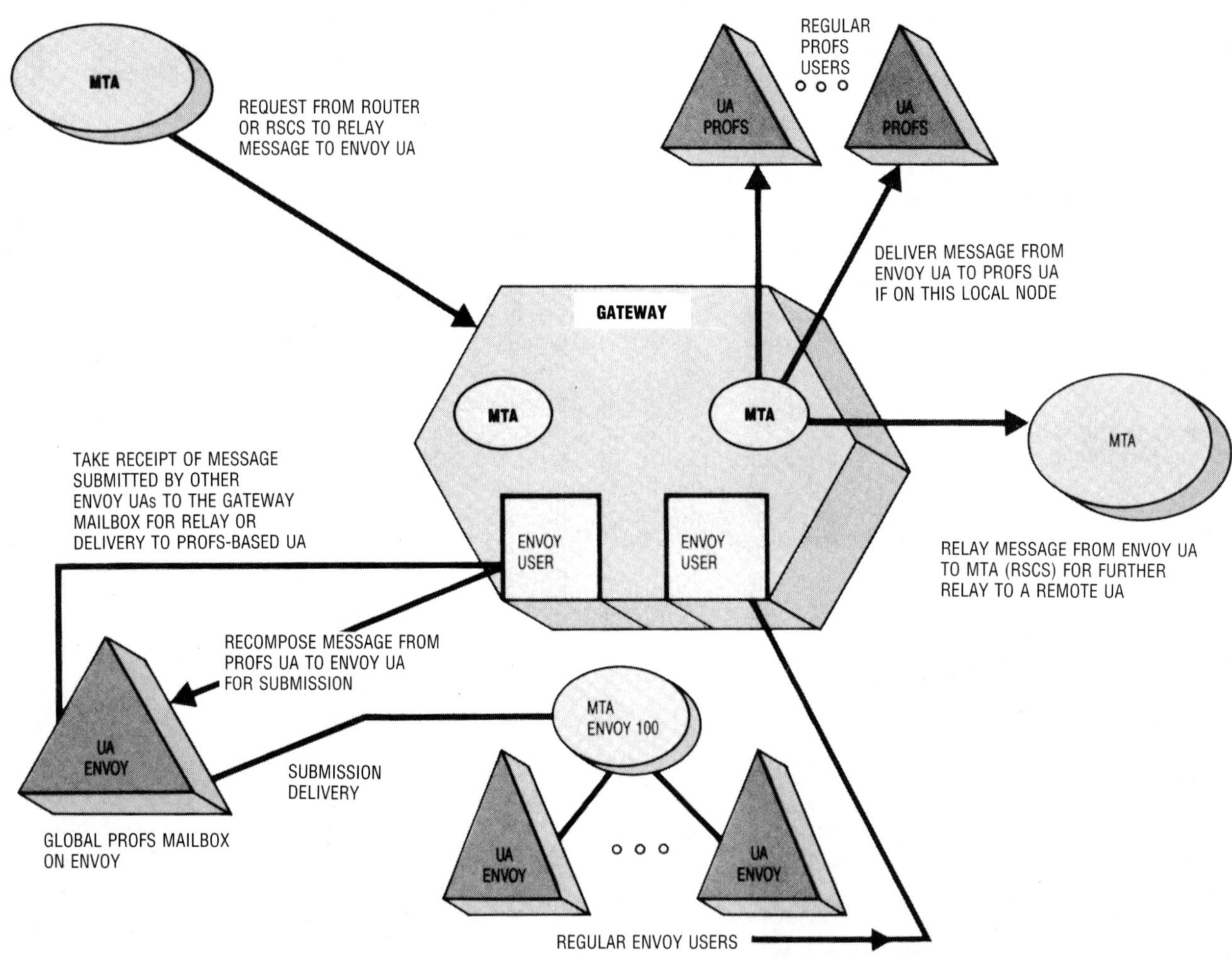

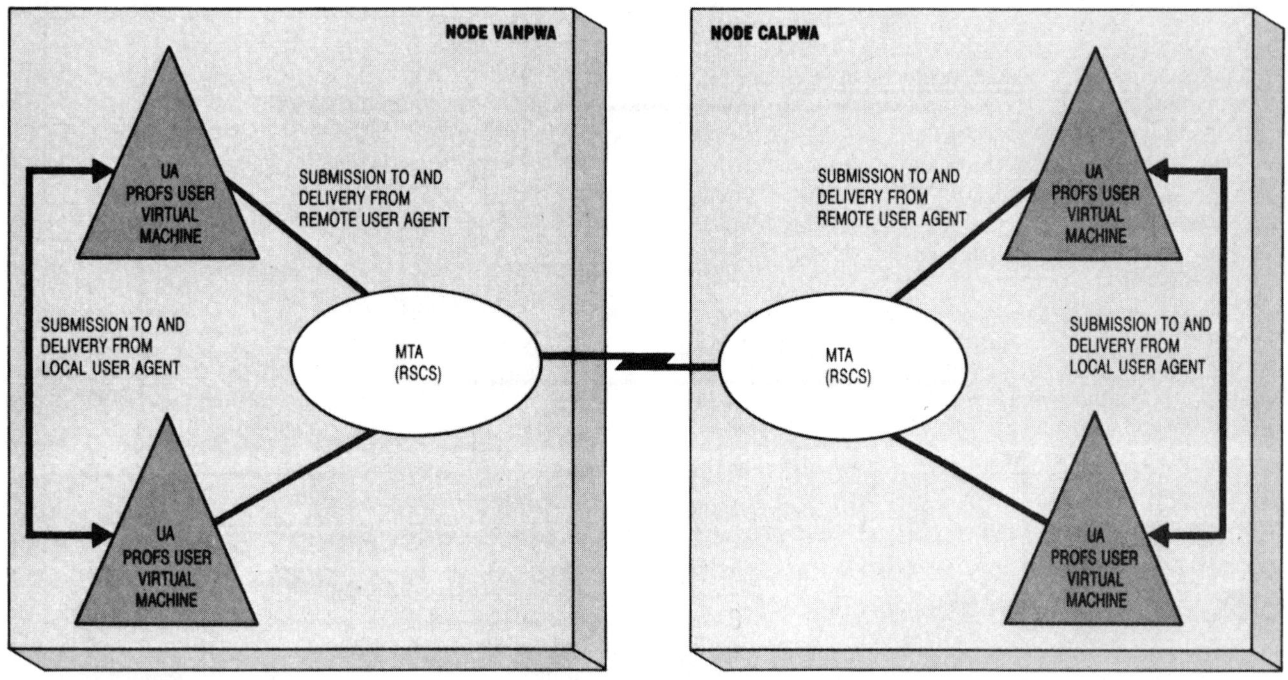

5. Virtual machine communications. *In the usual PROFS configuration, messages go directly between PROFS user agents. For communications to remote hosts, the RSCS acts as a Message Transfer Agent, forwarding messages to, and receiving them from, a comparable RSCS on the other host.*

BEFORE:

AFTER:

MTA = MESSAGE TRANSFER AGENT
PROFS = PROFESSIONAL OFFICE SYSTEM
RSCS = REMOTE SPOOLING COMMUNICATION SUB-SYSTEM
UA = USER AGENT

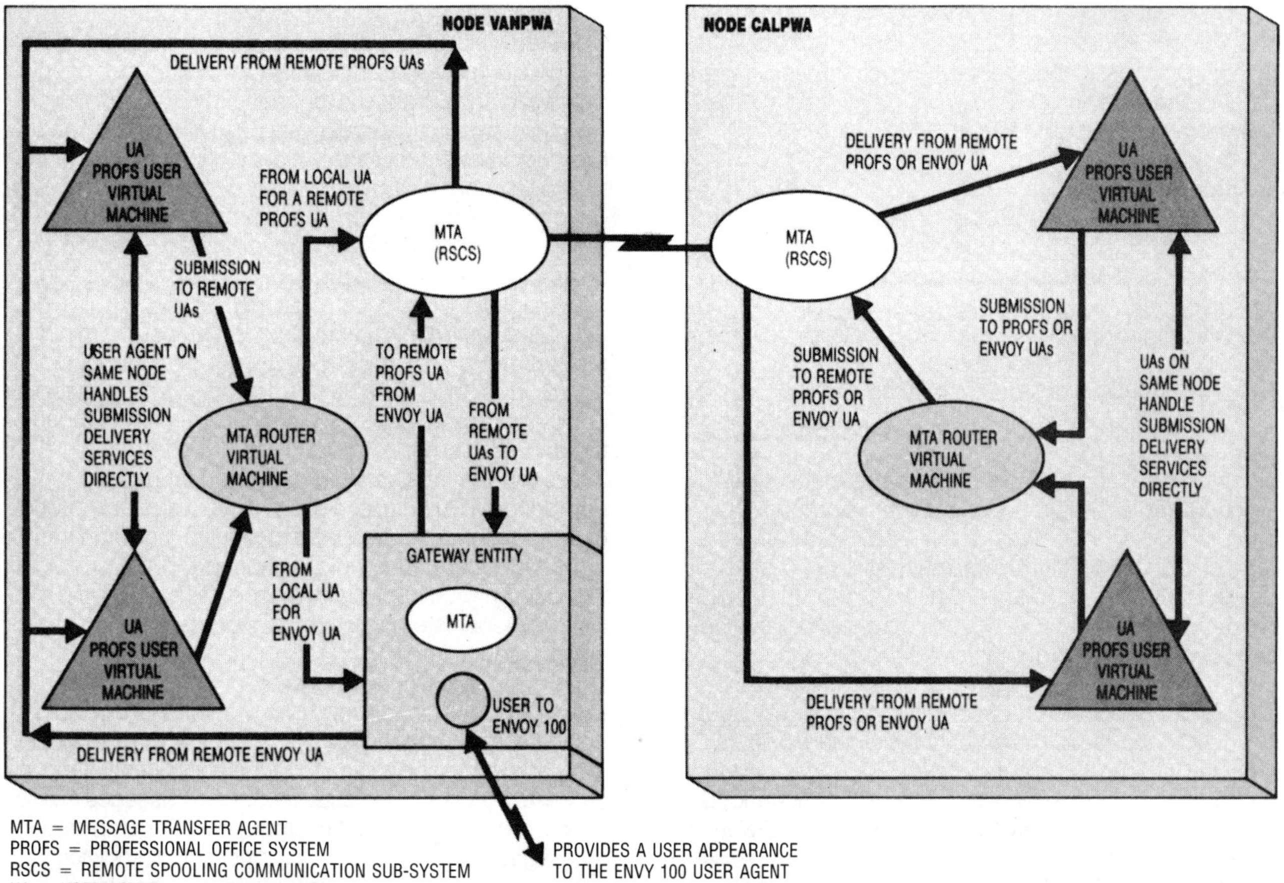

6. Intercepter. *For the implementation of the gateway, the Router acts as an interloper between the user agents and the RSCS. Messages for remote PROFS users are sent to the RSCS, and messages for the Envoy users are routed to the gateway. The Envoy 100 service sees the gateway as a user agent.*

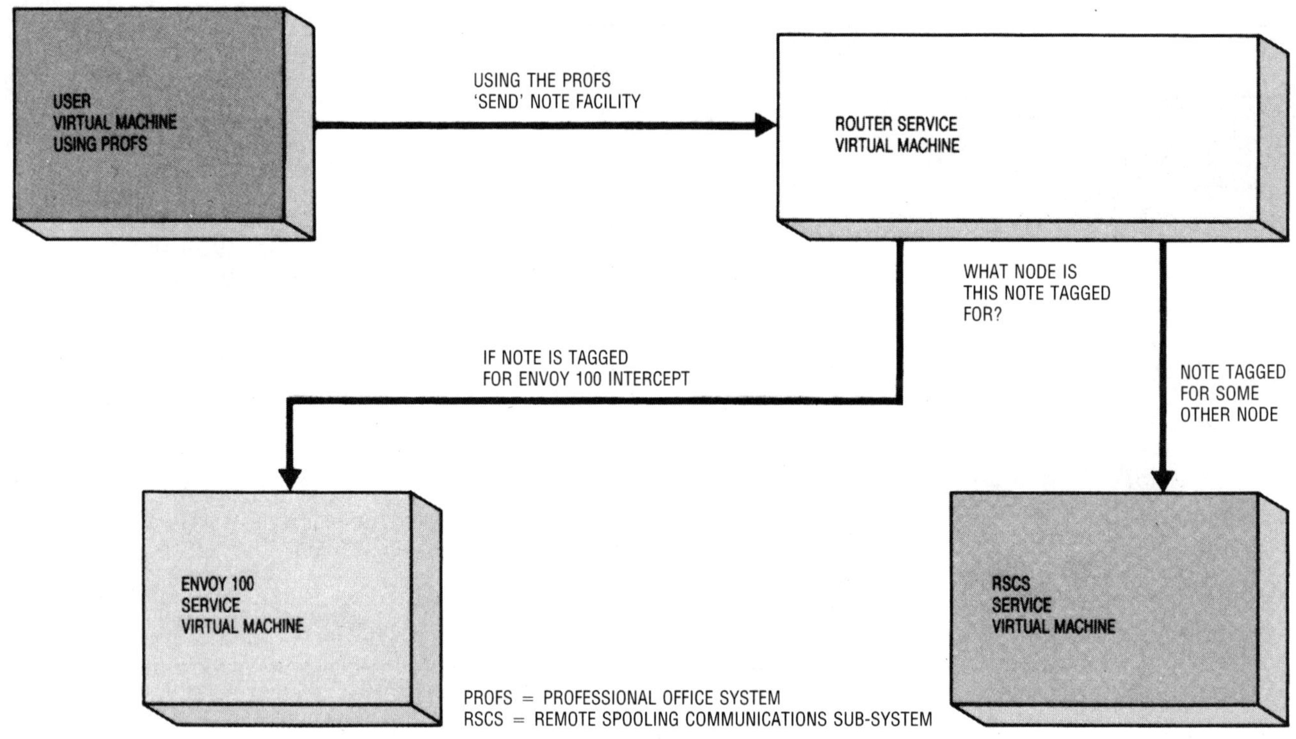

private directory. If the user is on the Envoy 100 public messaging service, a node name of "Envoy" is used in the directory; otherwise, the directory name is the name of the node where the user resides.

Message routing

When PROFS is installed and customized the installer has an opportunity to specify the name of the virtual machine that handles RSCS functions. At this stage, a pseudo-RSCS virtual machine called "Router" is specified instead of the RSCS virtual machine. This fools PROFS into sending all messages destined for remote users to this entity. Upon interception, the "Router" filters out any messages tagged for "Envoy" and transparently passes the remaining messages to the RSCS machine. "Router" further transfers the intercepted message to another service machine called "Envoy100" for further processing (Figs. 5 and 6).

The gateway service virtual machine (Envoy100) is logged on to the VM (virtual machine) host via a PC equipped with a 3270 emulation board (Fig. 7). With the aid of a program developed by Pacific Western that utilizes the High Level Language Application Program Interface (HLLAPI), the 3270-PC monitors and interacts as a console with the virtual machine on one side, and the Envoy 100 user agent on the other. The majority of the gateway logic resides on the virtual machine with the PC performing the role of a protocol converter (ASCII to EBCDIC [Extended Binary Coded Decimal Interchange Code]) and a network connection manager.

The gateway entity can be found in one of four major states:

1. Wait state—the gateway is waiting for a timed interval expiry or a message arrival from a PROFS user agent for delivery to the Envoy service.

2. Message-delivery relay state—a PROFS user agent has submitted a message for delivery to an Envoy-based user agent, or an automatic acknowledgment has been generated for relay from a previous message exchange. If the message for delivery is requesting acknowledgment, an appropriate Envoy message is composed before further relay.

3. Message-receipt relay state—this has two minor sub-states:

a. Timer expiry—when the timer expires, the gateway knows it is time to make a switched connection to a particular Envoy-based user agent to recover any messages on the secondary mailbox and to relay them back to the appropriate PROFS user agent. If a message acknowledgment has been specified, an appropriate message transformation is performed to indicate that the PROFS user agent respond on receipt of the message.

b. Global internetwork mailbox receipt—in this state any messages residing in the global mailbox on the Envoy service are received and relayed to the appropriate PROFS-based user agents. Some of these messages could be acknowledgments of receipt for a previous message submission from a PROFS user agent; others are requests from an Envoy user to transfer messages from the user's secondary PROFS mailbox; still others are regular messages to a PROFS user. If a message acknowledgment has been requested, the appropriate message transformation is performed before delivery to the PROFS user agent

7. Hardware. *A PC equipped with 3270 capability (typically, in the form of an add-on board) serves as the host of some of the software implementing the gateway.*

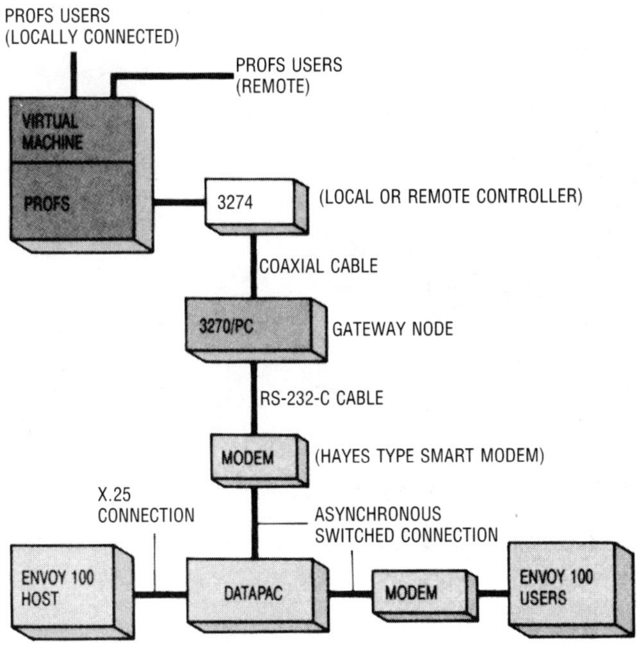

to indicate that the PROFS user agent must respond upon receipt of the message.

4. Error state—if a mail recipient does not exist, the originator is notified by a message and the original message is returned. If a network error occurs in any state, the whole process is started again with no loss of integrity or messages, and an appropriate error message is delivered to the PROFS network operator.

Address header modifications

The gateway service virtual machine is responsible for making appropriate modifications to the address header when relaying messages to users based on the Telex or Post networks. The basic design requirements called for sheltering the PROFS user from the peculiarities of the various messaging networks. All the relevant addressing information for recipients on foreign networks is maintained by the PROFS/Envoy administrator when registering new users and is accessible to the gateway node. When the gateway is in the "message-delivery-relay-state" and processing a message bound for a recipient on "Telex" or "Post," it appends the appropriate addressing information to the message before further relay.

Soon after the initial configuration was placed into production, users began to make requests for further enhancements. For example, some wanted a PROFS-to-Telex facility and wanted EnvoyPost services to be made available to the PROFS user community. Because of architectural decisions made early in the project, these enhancements could be accomplished with a minimal development effort. Users on a Telex network were handled by adding a new node type of "TELEX" in the PROFS

directory. Similarly, users accessible via Canada Post were treated as if on another node type of "POST." As a result, the regular PROFS message submission facilities were used.

The originator of a message in PROFS refers to the recipient by a nickname, and all the special format and addressing changes are handled transparently by the network. A separate user nickname and Telex or home address file is maintained by the administrator on behalf of the users. If a message is destined for a user on a Telex network or Canada Post service, the gateway automatically looks up the relevant addressing information and composes a modified message for delivery.

In addition, two other functional enhancements have been made to PROFS. The Receive feature allows the PROFS users who are maintaining dual mailboxes to request automatic transfer of messages from their Envoy mailbox to their PROFS mailbox. This feature is implemented in a batch timed-delivery process on the gateway. The other new capability, autoforwarding, is a feature similar to call forwarding in telephony. It allows the PROFS user to specify an alternate recipient for messages. The user's redirected mailbox can reside in PROFS, Envoy, Telex, or Canada Post.

Some users employ the autoforwarding feature in combination with Envoy's text-to-voice conversion service. If these users are going to be away from their usual access to PROFS, they can autoforward their messages to their Envoy mailbox before leaving and they will still be able to receive all their messages over the regular voice network. This combined feature is roughly comparable to a number of the voice tele-messaging services that are available.

Additional interfaces to CNCP electronic office system, GTE Telemail, and General Electric Quick-Comm have also been implemented. Moreover, communication between PROFS hosts is supported using a public switched network as a transport medium. Pacific Western is also engaged in a feasibility study of providing for an implementation that would be based on the International Telegraph and Telephone Consultative Committee message-handling standard X.400 series. ■

Ken Sekhon completed his B. S. in computer science from the University of British Columbia in 1975 and received an M. A. in electrical engineering from the University of Ottawa in 1981. He has over 10 years experience in the airline industry and has worked for Bell Northern Research's Datapac packet-switching group. Currently, he is managing the technical services group at Pacific Western.

Radik Gens graduated with an M. A. in mathematics from the Lomonosov Moscow University in 1971. His experience with computers dates back to 1964, when he programmed the earliest Russian-made computers. Gens now works at Pacific Western as a senior systems engineer responsible for the operating systems area in the technical services department.

Ken Graham completed his B. S. in computer science and mathematics from the University of British Columbia in 1975. Graham has more than 10 years experience in the airline industry, specializing in data communications. Today he is a senior systems engineer responsible for the corporate data communications network in the technical services department of Pacific Western.

Nicholas Papadopoulos, President, Thrysos Consulting Inc., San Francisco, Calif.

Combining data and voice network management

Sharing transmission but separating switching are key to optimum integrated operation of mixed voice and data networks.

Increasingly, communications managers are asked to plan and manage both data and voice networks. Some companies have added significant data communications requirements, requesting that their telecommunications managers manage data as well as voice networks. In other cases, voice networks have been handled by the local telephone company. And since divestiture, some companies have brought voice network management inhouse; in these cases, data managers are asked to take on the voice network also.

Integrated Services Digital Network is becoming a key concept (see "ISDN: Users think it's a distant prospect. Wrong," DATA COMMUNICATIONS , December 1985, p. 193). Both ISDN and the underlying similarity in voice and data transmission mean that the telecommunications manager must at least be aware of both data and voice network management. The manager needs this awareness to talk, at the very least, to colleagues who control the other part of the network.

Comparisons and contrasts

ISDN is based on the observation that both data and voice can be represented and transmitted by bit streams. Modems show the converse: Data and voice can be represented and transmitted by analog signals in the voice band. Of course, there are significant differences in the characteristics of data and voice calls. Bandwidth, accuracy, delay requirements, and error detection and correction are significantly different for voice and data transmission. Peer protocols between partners and network elements are well established in voice networks; they are a mass of confusion in data communications.

The combination of differences and similarities in voice and data transmission has interesting implications for network managers, who are confronted with creating a cost-effective, flexible, and reliable network that meets the organization's needs. Fulfillment of this mission translates to the need to share network components where feasible and to separate functions where necessary. Network elements are shared where the data and voice requirements are close; they are separated where the requirements conflict. Strategies for data network and voice network management can be examined so that appropriate philosophies and practices developed for each can be applied to the other.

Although the basic transmission medium for data and voice is the same, there are some startling differences in voice and data requirements, as can be seen in Table 1.

■ *Accuracy.* Data transmission requires high accuracy, preferably better than one part in 1 million; worse than 0.1 percent introduces significant overhead and possible errors in the ultimate data transfer.

Voice transmission is insensitive to error rates that would destroy the possibility of data transmission. One percent error is barely perceptible on a voice call; 10 percent error is acceptable.

■ *Bandwidth.* Bandwidth requirements can vary from one or two bits per second (fire and security alarms, for example) to several million (high-speed file transfer). Channel occupancy requirements vary widely and can be extremely sporadic. An alarm network has very low channel occupancy, using the channel only when an event occurs. Depending on protocol, file transfer can take up to 80 to 90 percent of the channel. A terminal session is bursty—long silences interspersed with rapid chunks of data transmission. The terminal user thinks and keys, and the computer responds.

Voice bandwidth and channel occupancy requirements are fairly constant—about 300 to 3,400 Hz and an average 40 to 45 percent occupancy in each direction.

■ *Delay.* Data transmission is insensitive to widely varying delays in the same conversation. Certain traffic, such as an

Data and voice characteristics

CHARACTERISTIC	DATA	VOICE
BANDWIDTH	WIDELY VARYING 1 BIT/S TO MBIT/S	CONSTANT 300- TO 400-Hz CHANNEL
CHANNEL OCCUPANCY	WIDELY VARYING 1 PERCENT TO 90 PERCENT BURSTY	FAIRLY CONSTANT
DELAY REQUIREMENTS	INSENSITIVE TO INCONSTANT DELAY	MUST BE CONSTANT AND LOW (0.5 SEC)
ERROR SENSITIVITY	PREFER LESS THAN ONE IN 1,000,000 BIT/S OVER 0.1 PERCENT; INTOLERABLE	INSENSITIVE TO 1 PERCENT; 10 PERCENT ACCEPTABLE
ERROR DETECTION AND CORRECTION	MUST BE PROGRAMMED	PARTICIPANTS MANAGE
PROTOCOLS	WIDELY VARYING, INCOMPATIBLE	STANDARD, ALMOST COMPLETE CONNECTIVITY

interactive terminal session, is sensitive to the amount of delay. However, this delay need not be held constant as long as it is less than a certain amount. Data can be buffered or flow-controlled to handle momentary congestion in the network or a device.

Although voice transmission is insensitive to error, it is extremely sensitive to delay: Delay must be small. Satellite feasibility tests by Bell Labs determined that delay, for example, cannot be greater than 0.25 to 0.50 seconds, after which point voice communications is nearly impossible. Constant delay is the key to intelligibility.

■ *Protocols.* Protocols for data conversations vary widely; even two devices that nominally speak the same protocol — for example, X.25 — may not be able to communicate. Protocol technology has advanced substantially since its inception; there are a number of old protocols, such as Telex and 3270 bisychronous, that need to be supported and are too expensive to modernize. Furthermore, high-level protocols, such as transport and session, are not yet standardized.

On the other hand, voice networks demonstrate full connectivity. Almost any phone can be connected to almost any phone in the world and if the partners can understand each other, voice communications can take place.

■ *Error correction.* Protocols are necessary to provide error correction in data transmission. Often, the underlying transmission media do not provide the end-to-end reliability required for data communications, and sophisticated error detection and correction techniques are required. Compared to people who are partners on voice calls, computers are ill-equipped to detect and correct errors.

Because voice calls have two intelligent beings as partners, the transmission system does not have to provide for error recovery or for sophisticated protocols. Humans can ask to have phrases repeated, if necessary.

Although the goal for network management is the same for voice and data networks, the optimal solutions differ. The solutions vary depending on the characteristics of data and voice. Nevertheless, significant cooperative planning is possible, and significant sharing of facilities is desirable.

Voice networks are inherently circuit switches — a transmission path connecting the two partners is dedicated to the call. This characteristic follows because constant delay is critical to voice calls. In expensive transmission media, such as transoceanic cables, the average 40 percent occupancy in each direction on the circuit is exploited to carry more circuits by such techniques as time-assigned speech interpolation (TASI). Usually, however, a constant 300- to 3,400-Hz path is dedicated for the duration of the call. With the emergence of cheap fiber optics, there is no compelling economic reason to abandon this practice.

Generally, circuit switches make inefficient data switches. Data switching uses various buffering schemes to make optimal use of network elements. Insensitivity to nonconstant delay means that data in a call can be queued during periods of momentary activity peaks. Because of the synergy between data computation and communications, advances in computer technology can be exploited to create better data communications switches. Lower memory costs mean that buffering can be exploited throughout the network to reduce sensitivity to overload. Lower computation costs mean that more sophisticated communications protocols that increase reliability and throughput can be put in place.

X.25 could not have been implemented 15 years ago, for example, because the packet assemblers/disassemblers on network ends require memory and buffering. Within the nodes themselves, buffering is used to reduce sensitivity to overload. High-level data link control and Advanced Data Communications Control Procedure satellites use sophisticated transmission schemes, maintaining packets, windowing, and checksums to ensure integrity of link. These newer protocols need the computing horsepower for increased reliability and more sophisticated error detection. Cheap memory is used to buffer packets to allow frames to remain outstanding. Protocol conversion and local area network drivers are other examples of communications techniques that were dependent on the evolution of cheap, powerful computation.

Some pitfalls

Mixing data and voice on the same network can be catastrophic. Data calls can cause near-fatal congestion on voice networks optimized for voice traffic. Conversational terminal traffic, which is commonly carried over telephone networks and modems, can tie up capacity so voice traffic is not sustainable. Excessive dial-tone delay was noted at a Bell Labs location when significant terminal traffic was placed over the voice Private Branch Exchange using modems. Local telephone networks have been expanded beyond standard voice engineering guidelines because of increased modem traffic. Voice calls have short holding (conversation) times, usually about five minutes. Data calls can go on for hours. Expanding the voice network to carry the additional data traffic can be cost-prohibitive. A better solution is the creation of a separate data-switching network to carry the terminal traffic.

Carrying voice over data networks is a worse idea. The usual digitizing scheme for voice takes 56 kbit/s; a modern standard is 32 kbit/s (see "Third-generation codecs pave way for future digital networks," Data Communications, September 1984, p. 173). This bandwidth is huge by data network standards. There are schemes, such as linear-predictive coding (LPC), to reduce data bandwidth for voice, but they tend to be expensive and inflexible. LPC usually breaks down when more than one person is talking on one end of a connection; the method is highly sensitive to human speech. Because voice and data are different, one switch handling both kinds of communications ends up saddled with an unnecessary complication of function, increasing possibilities for failure through unaccounted-for interactions between its two different modalities.

Additionally, acrobatics are necessary to ensure that delay is kept constant to provide intelligible voice communications. These acrobatics play havoc with schemes, such as buffering and flow control, that are used to increase network capacity. For example, packetized voice can force significant and expensive enhancements to a packet-switched network used to carry the voice call (see "Leased-line tariffs, services restructured," DATA COMMUNICATIONS, February 1985, p. 45).

Although wholesale and indiscriminate mixing of voice and data networks is not desirable, a certain amount of facility sharing is both possible and desirable. Essentially, transmission facilities can be shared, whereas switching capabilities cannot be shared. Sharing of transmission facilities can occur at several levels, from local area wiring to long-distance trunk lines. Limited sharing of switching facilities can be effectively used for timely trials of communications services, for low use, for off-peak re-use of facilities, and for backup.

The first recommendation for integrating voice and data network management is to build and maintain separate voice and data switch networks while searching for the means to share transmission facilities. Consider the use of

---

1. Five levels. *The traditional North American voice network hierarchy demonstrates an application of the gravity model of calling. High-usage trunks connect various offices.*

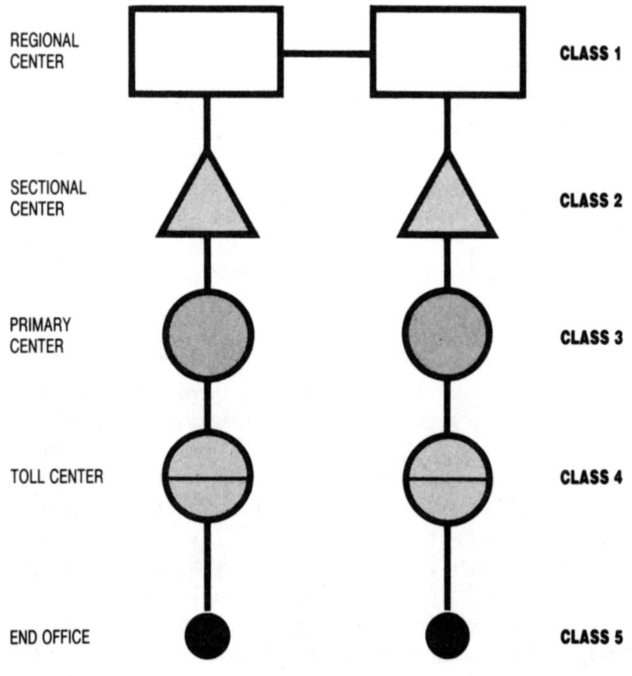

---

2. Typical voice. *This corporate voice network makes use of tandeming for interlocation switching. This design is most appropriate for large private-line networks.*

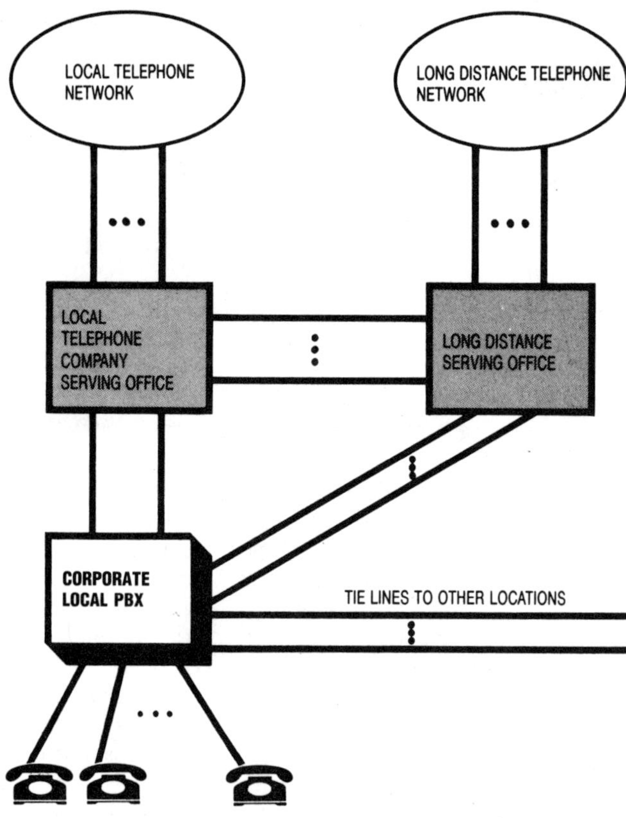

---

several data networks with interconnections between them (see "The middle ground between public and private networks," DATA COMMUNICATIONS , July 1985, p. 115). Often a particular network, say Systems Network Architecture, is optimized for specific applications. It is sometimes better to gateway separate networks than to attempt to put everybody's traffic on the same switching network. It may be better, for example, to maintain an X.25 network for Digital Equipment Corp. VAX machines with a gateway to host SNA, and not create one monster network to carry all the traffic an organization generates.

A major lesson from voice networks is the gravity model of calling: Calls are more frequent between parties that are geographically close. This observation leads to a hierarchical structure of voice switching and transmission networks—from local key equipment, PBX or Centrex, central offices, and an interoffice hierarchy in the traditional telephone network. Figure 1 shows the traditional five-level hierarchy in the North American Network; Figure 2 shows a typical corporate voice network.

In data networks, this hierarchical approach might lead to several LANs tied together with a data PBX that afforded access between the LANs and to connections outside, such as commercial data networks or circuits to other locations. The LANs are used for immediate, in-office communications. The data PBX provides for tandeming, that is, connecting LANs for local, interdepartmental communications, as well as to the outside world. The data PBX

3. Recommended data. *This corporate data network should include tie lines and local data PBXs. They can coexist with other networks.*

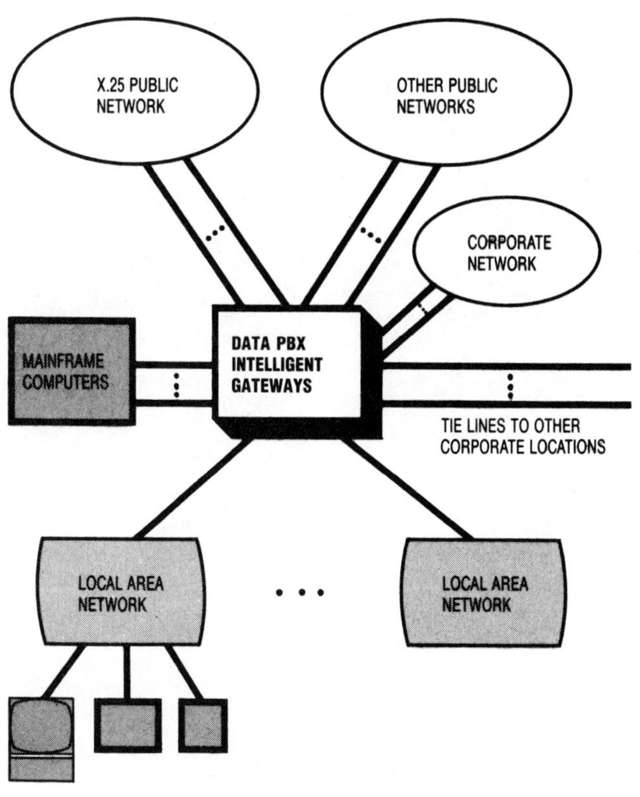

can be expanded into a collection of intelligent gateways that allow internetworking between diverse LANs and larger networks (see "Gateways link long-haul and local networks," DATA COMMUNICATIONS , July 1984, p. 111). Figure 3 shows a proposed corporate data network structure that makes use of tandeming.

Another observation is that it is cheaper to buy bandwidth in bulk. For example, a T1 channel (1.544 Mbit/s) can provide a number of voice channels and data circuits at a substantially lower cost than buying the circuits individually (see "Long overdue, T1 takes off—but where is it heading?" DATA COMMUNICATIONS , June 1985, p. 120). Furthermore, with appropriate terminating equipment, it is possible to shift the allocation of voice and data circuits as needs change over time, be it over the course of a day, a month, or a year. A large-capacity connection could be used during the day to provide circuits for inter-office communications; during the night it could be reconfigured to provide bulk file transfer for data processing at a back-office host located off-site.

Sharing of transmission facilities extends to office wiring. Short-haul wiring can usually be done by twisted pair for both voice and data networks. Telephone-like wiring makes use of twisted pair for both voice and data networks. Similar cabling uses twisted pairs for connecting RS-232-C from terminals to computers or switches. The IBM Cabling System uses twisted pair for connecting stations to the Master Access Unit. An implication for voice networks is that digitization should occur closer to the telephone set:

Channel banks could be placed where the Master Access Units are located, and T1 used to carry to the PBX or the Central Office. If digitization is brought to the wiring closet, fewer wires are needed to go to the PBX. This tactic also creates an interchangeability of wiring between the data and voice PBXs, so cabling can be adjusted as loads require; in case of outages, spares are automatically built into the network.

Figure 4 shows a proposed integrated local corporate data/voice network. Both data terminals and voice telephones are connected by twisted pair to twisted-pair punch-down blocks in wiring closets. LAN controllers or cluster controllers are wired on the other side of the block for data networking. The local data controllers and the voice twisted pair are carried over campus wiring to their respective PBXs or switches. Note that a distributed voice PBX could have channel adapters distributed throughout the campus, possibly at the same location as the LAN controllers.

The voice and data PBXs provide campus interconnections and access to the off-campus services through data- and voice-specific connections as well as through cross-connection to broadband carrier networks. The broadband carrier network, possibly T1, could connect to other locations as well as to an integrated voice and data local office. Note that other patch panels and cross-connection devices are possible and may be desirable. For example, a cross-connection might allow termination of PBX circuits on either voice-specific or broadband equipment. The idea is to build as much modularity and interchangeability into the network as possible, which will provide flexibility for backup and load balancing.

Another data network concept is being implemented in voice networks. Traditionally, a telephone has been thought of as the termination of a twisted copper pair that extends from the PBX or the central office to the set. Increasingly, however, the telephone is viewed as a voice terminal, similar to a data terminal with abilities to signal the switch to perform such functions as hold or three-way calling, which were performed electromechanically by outboard key system units.

A paramount consideration in planning networks is backup planning for failure. Network problem management consists of these phases: detection, isolation, work-around, and restoration. A network fault must first be detected, implying a need for telemetry of network performance. Both voice and data network suppliers are guilty of not providing an integrated, standard means of reporting network outages. For example, there is no standard for terminals controlling electronic telephone switches. When the fault is detected, the failing network elements must be identified and removed from service. Also, a clearly stated backup plan must be in place for a work-around while the network element is out of service. In some cases, noncritical work can be deferred. In other cases, dial backup over public networks is appropriate. Finally, restoral of service must take place.

Effective backup planning will dictate the use of interchangeable network elements as well as patch-panel or cross-connect facilities to bypass failed elements. Major advances are being made in both the voice and data arenas to provide centrally controllable cross-connection

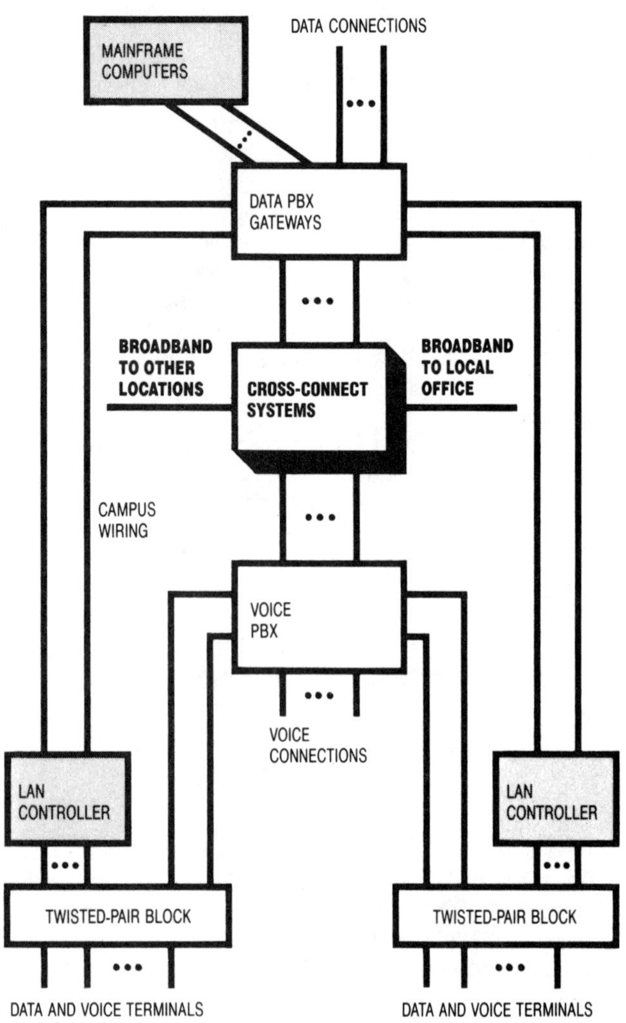

4. Integration. *This proposal for a local voice and data network uses cross-connection to form links to broadband networks. It is a design for corporations.*

devices to meet this need. Digital Access and Cross-connect System, T1 cross-connect devices mixing data and voice centrally, and remotely controlled PADs are examples are existing cross-connect devices. The manager of an integrated voice and data network should be alert to the possibility of interchanging voice and data transmission facilities.

The key to successful integration of voice and data networks is knowing when to use the same facility for voice and data and when to use different ones. Use of the same components can lead to reduced cost through load sharing, and better and cheaper backup provision. Indiscriminate mixture of voice and data on the same facilities can result in substandard performance obtained at great expense. ∎

Nicholas Papadopoulos has a bachelor's degree in engineering sciences from the University of California at San Diego and master's and doctorate degrees in engineering and economics from Harvard University. Before starting Thyrsos Consulting, Papadopoulos worked at Bell Laboratories in Murray Hill, N. J., and at Data Architects.

David W. Campt, University of California, Berkeley, Calif.

Interconnectivity: Risks may be substantial, but the benefits are great

Nowadays, with various options available, users do not have to wait for official standards to link dissimilar equipment.

As the general business environment gets more competitive, computer and communications departments feel the heat. Driven by corporate desires to simultaneously cut costs and accelerate services, communications managers are realizing that they cannot rely on the general advance of technology to allow that to happen; instead, they must consider other strategies.

Adopting a new approach can range from changing the network topology, acquiring more up-to-date technology, or breaking away from a firm's historic computer and communications suppliers. Users do this to take advantage of the many new opportunities in the more competitive computer industry. In addition to established companies encroaching on others' established turf, new entrants are constantly entering the market, trying to leapfrog over the veterans with new technologies.

When contemplating such a move, of course, a communications manager must look at networking issues. Will new processing equipment fit into the network and be accessible to all the users who eventually may want the machine? Will the new computer be able to share data with the extant devices? Will state-of-the-art communications devices offer better price-performance characteristics but perhaps limit networking flexibility?

Without question, many users are not even contemplating such issues. Even though they may be limiting their networking options and not reaping the benefits of new technology, many managers are content to stick with the computer or communications vendors their firms have historically used. This is not unreasonable. Companies that remain loyal to one vendor may find that their suppliers are more attentive to problems, and certainly will not encounter the situation of many vendors pointing at each other as the cause of the user's problems.

What follows are four stories about users who have dared to venture down the multivendor road. Even though all of the companies involved are satisfied customers, it is clear that networking between vendors does create challenges. Finding a product that can link different vendors' equipment can be a major task itself, and after the link is installed, the user may have to patiently work with the supplier to iron out the kinks.

Perhaps most importantly, a tool that flexibly links different vendors' products is likely to create work. Communications staff may have to invest substantial amounts of energy to make sure the new connectivity options are easy to use and properly controlled. The multivendor environment is, after all, more complex (a fact that makes some managers decide to return to a simpler configuration).

Still, if the new, mixed-vendor setup is properly handled, the benefits to the organization can be great. In many cases, interconnectivity products solve the problem of multiple terminals on people's desks, and can lead to a more cost-effective use of processing capability. As one user found, links between different vendors can expand a company's options in selecting equipment, because it has fewer concerns about connectivity.

Similar to widely accepted communications standards—which will eventually replace all ad hoc multivendor links—easy connections between different vendors expand the arena of competition. Thus, the benefits of interconnectivity extend to all users, whether a particular company pursues the multivendor environment or not.

Securities Industry Automation Corp.

For several years, SIAC (Securities Industry Automation Corp.) has used a Sperry (now Unisys) mainframe to support its trading and market data reporting for the New York Stock Exchange bond market.

A subsidiary jointly owned by the American and New York Stock Exchanges, SIAC provides computer services to the American Stock Exchange, the New York Stock Exchange, and the securities industry nationwide. On the mainframe resides the SIAC Automatic Bond System, a piece of software that matches available bonds to bond traders' requests. Hundreds of traders and order-room clerks access the mainframe via 3270 terminals, which historically have been connected to the Sperry host via a Collins Radio Corp. (a subsidiary of Rockwell) 8561 front-end processor. About 60 lines were connected, operating at speeds of 2.4 kbit/s or 4.8 kbit/s.

Several years ago, it became clear that the Collins machine, in the words of Steven Oliphant, a member of the SIAC development team, was "rapidly reaching the end of its useful life." Maintaining a more than 10-year-old machine was becoming increasingly difficult, the device had reached its maximum capacity, and there was no upgrade path available from Collins. SIAC then began a plan to upgrade the Collins equipment.

In addition to migrating to more current front-end processing techniques, SIAC had other goals in mind. A good percentage of terminal usage is comprised of inquiries into a database, so there was a desire to speed up terminal response time by reducing the path length to the host. One way of doing this was to use a front-end processor that could actually handle database inquiries, thus leaving database updates to be handled by the mainframe. Such a solution would not only reduce the response times, but also some of the load on the host.

As do all mainframe vendors, Sperry offered a front-end processor, the DCP product line, and SIAC considered using the company's products for its solution. SIAC eventu-ally decided to upgrade the Collins front-end processor to a machine from Tandem Computer, a company that markets a number of fault-tolerant machines that can double as front-end processors and host computers. SIAC has a number of Tandem machines in-house, and has a lot of experience with the company's equipment.

After choosing the Tandem equipment, SIAC still had to find a means of connecting the Tandem and Sperry hosts. This task was relatively unusual at the time, since SIAC was one of the first to make the attempt, and there were few alternatives.

After evaluating the alternatives that existed, the organization decided to use Network Systems Corp.'s Hyperchannel to implement the link. There were some problems, however. The initial version of the Tandem-to-Sperry link had a number of bugs, something any user of a newly developed product should expect. "One might say we did some development work for NSC," Oliphant says, "in terms of finding some of the problems with the equipment. With any new communications software, there are going to be things to shake out in the user environment that the vendor cannot find." NSC was responsive to the problems, Oliphant adds, saying its hardware was very reliable (Fig. 1).

Although the SIAC's next major network improvement is still being pondered, SIAC plans to continue upgrading and expanding its network. Future expansion toward a more distributed configuration was, in fact, part of the reason SIAC wanted an intelligent front-end processor. "There are a number of different things you can do with a Hyperchannel," says Oliphant. One possibility is using Hyperchannel

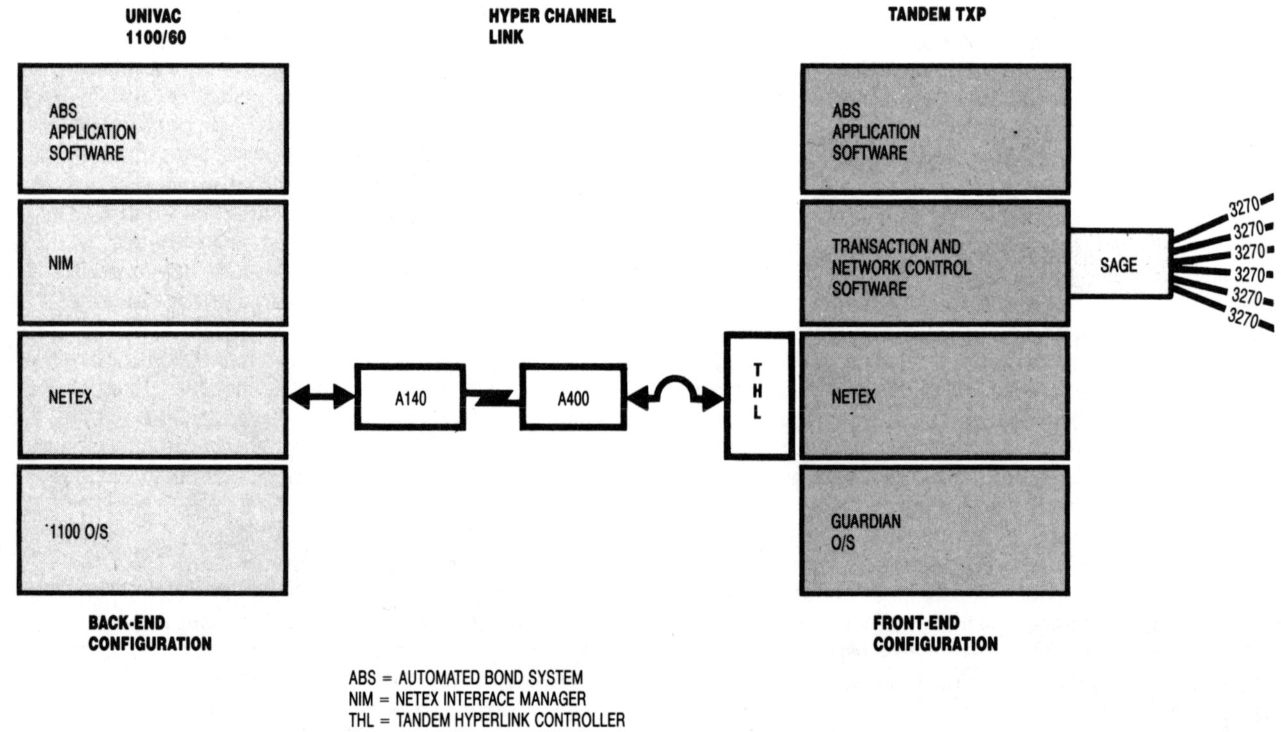

1. SIAC. *As much as possible, the SIAC network is modeled after the OSI model. The Sage 6100 communications subsystem offloads all 3270 polling from the Tandem front-end processor. NSC Hyperchannel software provides Tandem-to-Unisys connections and may be used to support network enhancements.*

to link the Sperry and Tandem machines and an in-house IBM mainframe. Currently, the only way for the machines to share data is by outputting tape to a tape drive and reading that data into the other machine.

Also, a number of SIAC employees need to connect to both the Tandem and Sperry machines. Instead of putting multiple terminals on a desk, SIAC equips those users' microcomputers with communications cards for both mainframes. This still requires that multiple lines be run from one office, however.

"Obviously, in a full networking solution you want to interconnect all of the hosts together and have one terminal that can connect to each one," says Oliphant. "I am blue-skying with this, but these are the kinds of things that are possible when you have a Hyperchannel in-house," he adds. "SIAC is also currently using the Hyperchannel hardware connecting its remote peripherals to its IBM mainframes."

Westinghouse

Given IBM's dominance of the mainframe computer market, almost every vendor in the industry has had to form some type of strategy to ensure that its equipment is compatible with Big Blue. These offerings, as well as third-party connectivity equipment, can give users the opportunity to acquire other vendors' processing equipment without forming a segregated networking topology.

In fact, many users have turned toward non-IBM communications gear not because the equipment provided more versatile connectivity, but because of better prices or performance. But little in the computer industry is permanent, including users' preferences. Some users have ventured down the alternate vendor route and, for one reason or another, later gone back to Big Blue's fold.

Several years ago, some of Westinghouse's 34 business divisions began to replace IBM 2701 and 2703 front-end processors (these products were predecessors of the 3705) with Comten front-end processors of various sizes. At the time, Comten's equipment included a few features that IBM's did not, one of the most important being the ability for both batch and interactive terminals to select the target host in realtime.

Because of these advantages, Comten became the standard front-end processor supplier for several of Westinghouse's large computer centers. This continued for a few years until about 1984, when IBM released the 3725. After that product became available, the Comten base at Westinghouse began to undergo a gradual erosion, as some computer centers let Comten leases expire and picked up new leases for 3725s.

Westinghouse Communications Systems in Pittsburgh, Pa., is charged with providing telecommunications and data services to Westinghouse business units. According to Charles Winschel, manager of Data Communications Systems, the users who switched were by no means dissatisfied customers. "Most of the users who replaced the Comten did not view the equipment as a major source of any kind of problem," he says. Winschel has the task of providing some coordination between the 34 largely autonomous computer and communications departments. One of the primary reasons for the erosion of the Comten base, says Winschel, was the additional functions provided

by the 3725 and the Network Control Program. As a result, some managers no longer saw enhanced value in the Comten gear.

Users had other motives for switching to IBM as well. Because Comten equipment must completely meet the specifications of any new release of SNA, there is usually a several month lag between the availability of new SNA capabilities on IBM's equipment and on Comten's. "I believe there has generally been a 10-to-14-month lag in the availability of new releases," says Winschel. "In some environments, this can be a problem."

Moreover, many managers did not want to face the potential hazards of the multiple-vendor environment, Winschel adds. "One manager simply said, 'With the network growth and increasing complexity, I would rather be in a single-vendor situation.'" Although Westinghouse uses multiple vendors extensively, he continues, the well-known vendor finger-pointing issue has not been a major problem.

"Any time you get finger pointing at a low level, you can always go to a higher level. Eventually, you can always bring vendors to the table. If each of the vendors claims 'It's not my problem,' you just have to say to them, 'Look, I have a problem. I am the customer, and we are are going to work together until we find my problem.'" Vendors have usually responded to Westinghouse, he says, and not deflected responsibility.

While some computer centers have switched from Comten to IBM front-end processors, others have stayed with the smaller vendor, in part to remain insulated from each new wrinkle of SNA. Some managers think being on the front lines of using a new IBM product is not desirable. "No one wants to be the pioneer," says Winschel, "because he is the one with the arrows."

Another reason for the loyalty some computer center managers pay to Comten is the effectiveness of its equipment. "The hardware has been extremely reliable," says Winschel. "Our analysis of the two hardwares says that hardware is not an issue in either company's equipment."

While Comten's support has been generally good,. Winschel points out that IBM's support is more consistent across different locations: "Local support from Comten vacillates; it is really situation- and area-dependent. At any time you might find that Pittsburgh has excellent support, while it might be less excellent in Chicago because of some recent promotion or something." This variance should not be surprising, Winschel says, given Comten's relatively small size. With a large company such as IBM, he points out, an expert can be found very quickly.

Beyond the realm of front-end processor hardware, Westinghouse has also ventured into the world of IBM alternatives. More than 50 percent of the company's mainframes are based on IBM architecture, and a number of these machines, such as NAS, are plug-compatibles. In addition, the broadcast and credit companies have historically used Burroughs (pre-Unisys) mainframes, although the credit division has, within the past 18 months, explored the use of an IBM mainframe.

This movement toward IBM does not necessarily represent a movement away from Burroughs, but rather emerges from the fact that the company wants to maximize its options for buying software packages, and more is available on IBM equipment. "For any particular need in the credit environment, you can fill books on commercially developed software for IBM, and that simply isn't true for Burroughs," says Winschel.

Since it did not have an IBM machine, the Pittsburgh-based credit company contracted with a Westinghouse subsidiary in New Jersey to use some of its excess capacity on its NAS mainframe. Until the credit company gets its own IBM machine, the credit company must make sure all of its remote offices around the country have reliable links to both the Burroughs and IBM machines. Conceivably, the design of these links should reflect the fact that a terminal user will spend more than 80 percent of terminal time accessing the Burroughs machine.

To implement the links, the credit company is relying on a nationwide T1 network that Westinghouse is building for all of its subsidiaries. To any user in the credit department, it appears that there are two separate paths to the machines. In actuality, a local multiplexer routes the user over a long-haul link, and a multiplexer in Pittsburgh routes the user either to the local Burroughs mainframe or to the IBM machine in New Jersey.

The T1 network is only one aspect of Westinghouse's strategy for consolidating its various internal networks. "On the first level of the ISO [International Organization for Standardization] model, we are building a physical network to serve the corporation's voice and data needs," says Winschel. As a result, the corporation has an active program to integrate disparate networks' transmission media under T1.

The other part of Westinghouse strategy operates at the network level. About two years ago, the corporation implemented a private packet-switched network, Wespac, that is designed to serve the general connectivity needs of the corporation's computers. "Penetration is growing very, very rapidly. The X.25 interface to these computers is a tremendous capability," says Winschel. This network is Westinghouse's principle strategy for providing more integrated communications between the corporation's computers, the ranks of which include a number of minicomputers from a variety of vendors, such as Prime, Hewlett-Packard, and Digital Equipment Corp.

The main hub for Wespac is located in Pittsburgh, with main U. S. switching nodes in Livingston, N. J., near New York, Baltimore, Atlanta, Charlotte, N. C., Orlando, Houston, Sunnyvale, Calif., and Chicago, plus Brussels and London internationally (Fig. 2). The network supports hundreds of access circuits, the majority of which are not dialed. Small minicomputers or groups of PADs (packet assemblers/disassemblers) reside at about 400 access locations, split equally between terminal PADs, used for input only, and addressable host PADs. Corporate electronic mail is run through four Prime 850 machines, and a CDC computer acts as a front-end processor to a Cray in Pittsburgh that supports Westinghouse engineering and scientific research around the world.

While this network consolidation is taking place, Westinghouse is continuing the development of its many IBM-based networks, which handle much of the corporation's current traffic. "We are moving IBM traffic to the packet-switched network, although only a very small percentage

2. Wespac 1986. *The U. S. backbone is shown with international connections. Small minicomputers and groups of packet assembler/disassemblers reside at about 400 remote locations. Terminal PADs are used for input only. Electronic mail and scientific computing are carried over the packet-switch network.*

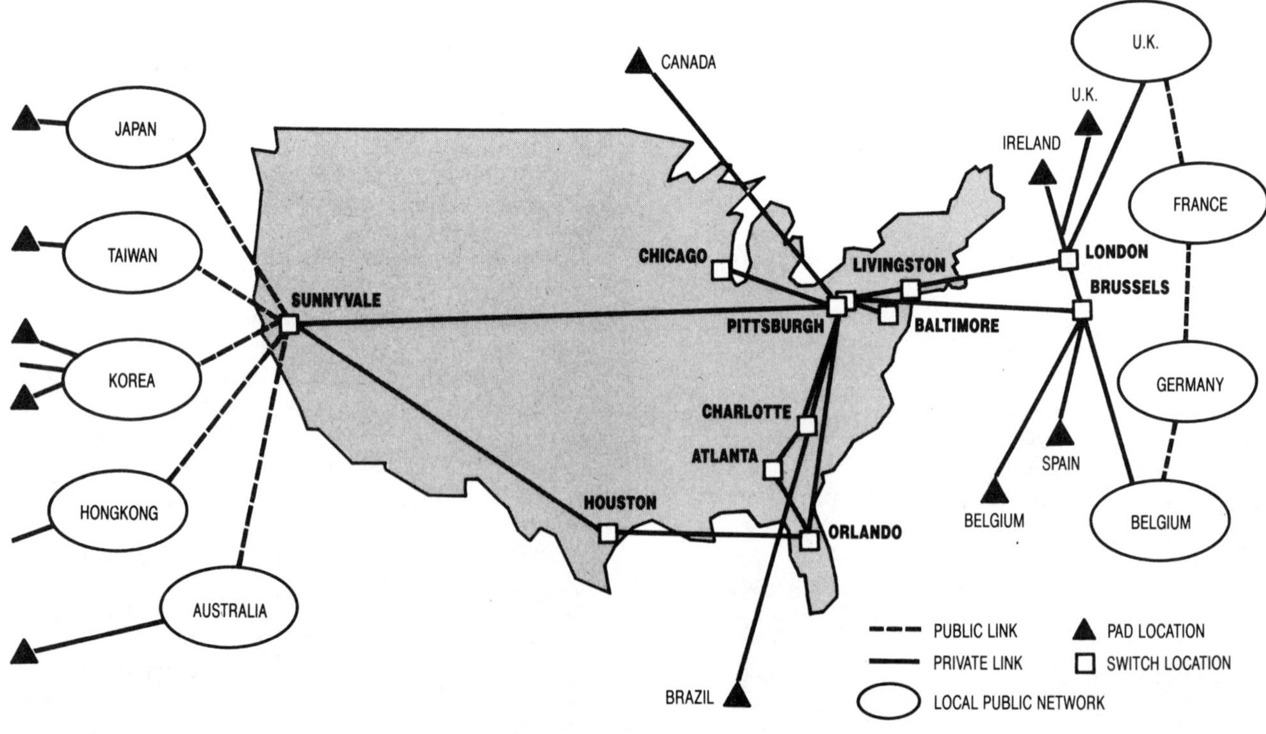

[has been migrated] at the moment," says Winschel. There is no intention to move batch traffic or large file transfers from SNA onto the packet network, although "the PC Network is a natural for X.25." The dual network strategy leans toward putting traffic as much as possible onto Wespac, for the X.25 network is easier to maintain.

Occasionally, Westinghouse will use a minicomputer vendor's SNA products for linking to IBM mainframes, although generally speaking the corporation prefers the X.25 links. "The minicomputer products typically provide one-way connectivity to IBM, meaning that they can look like an IBM PU 2 in an SNA network, for example," says Winschel. "That's great for getting them into the IBM world, but it doesn't do a darn thing to get people from the IBM world to them." Winschel looks forward to the advancement of IBM features such as LU 6.2 to help alleviate this problem.

Down in Maine

While some organizations have only recently begun to address multivendor connectivity, others have faced the challenge supporting diverse vendor's equipment for quite some time.

Prior to 1977, the government of the State of Maine used all IBM mainframes. But starting in 1972, the network used by that state government began to be based primarily around a Honeywell mainframe, the current incarnation of which is a DPS 852 triple processor configuration with about 600 terminals. A few years ago, a reorganization caused the state's data processing department in the capitol of Augusta to incorporate an IBM mainframe as well;

---

3. Maine in the early days. *Terminals were specific to an application, and some users were required to use more than one terminal to access the same machine.*

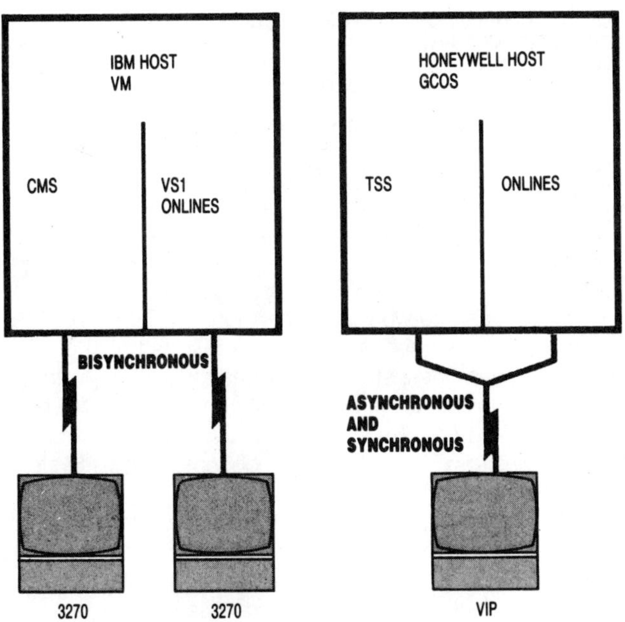

GCOS = GENERAL COMPREHENSIVE OPERATING SYSTEM
TSS = TIMESHARING SUBSYSTEM
VM = VIRTUAL MACHINE
VS1 = VIRTUAL STORAGE 1

---

the state's Department of Transportation moved and left behind its IBM model 370 135 mainframe, with the proviso that the Bureau of Data Processing continue to provide IBM support.

Initially, it seemed as though the Honeywell time-sharing services and user facilities were stronger. Eventually, though, that changed. "It seemed that during the late 1970s IBM poured a lot of money into CMS (one of the company's operating systems, the Conversational Monitor System) and its facilities, and opened up the operating system to third-party developers," says Carl Weston III, the state's deputy director of central computer services. "The pendulum swung toward IBM in terms of ease of development."

As a result, the computer services group, which supplies computing services to 70 to 80 state agencies, acquired a variety of applications for the IBM machine from a number of sources. As the range of IBM-compatible software advanced, management noticed that an increasing number of agencies kept their databases on the Honeywell host, but developed their new user tools on the IBM machine (Fig. 3).

As more and more users' desks became the residence of more than one terminal, it was clear that a terminal standard was necessary. Even though it was considered far from perfect, the 3274 terminal was chosen as a standard because of the wide support it gets in the industry. Since the state must put most of its contracts out for bidding, the computer services group did not want to greatly limit its future options by standardizing on a Honeywell terminal and the associated protocols.

Choosing the IBM terminal did not, however, resolve the standardization issue. The Honeywell mainframe supported IBM's bisynchronous 3270 protocol, but the IBM was configured to support SDLC (synchronous data link control). "It looked like we would have one terminal on each desk, but we would still have to run two lines," says Weston. "We needed a gateway that would take data from each terminal and point it to the right machine."

Finding a gateway that could accomplish this was far from easy. When the department started looking for this equipment, many vendors were marketing equipment that could perform this routing function for asynchronous protocols, but most of the gear could not handle more sophisticated protocols. The department investigated a variety of major players, including Honeywell, IBM, and Sperry. Different bids were taken from IBM, Burroughs, Univac (then selling Varian equipment), but all had problems. It was not that the hardware could not do the job; instead, the software investment required was beyond the resources of the data processing department.

One important criterion was that the equipment keep response low by minimizing "double buffering," which Weston describes as what happens when a front-end processor is line-attached to another front-end processor. "The Honeywell could do the switching, for example, but it could not channel-attach to either device," says Weston. "It would have been basically a front-end to a front-end."

Although protocol converters, such as the IBM Series/1, were also evaluated, and some equipment brought in and tested directly, response times were not adequate, in some cases twice as much. The computer services department also considered building the facility in-house, but did not want to shoulder the entire development burden. Says Weston: "We wanted a situation where the vendor was also in bed with us and had a commitment to develop this capability."

After five years of fruitless searching, the department became intrigued when Comten claimed its Model 3690 front-end processor could do the job. Following discussions with Comten's technical staff, Maine's processing professionals decided to install the company's equipment for a 90-day trial. "In our contract," says Weston, "we listed the things we wanted the product to do, specified how we would measure the performance, and agreed that Comten had 90 days to make it all work" (see "Populations in the trial period"). It took Comten engineers about four days to provide the switching capability to the initial test set of 14 lines, Weston adds, and the purchase was completed in about six weeks.

Now the Comten machine is channel-attached to the IBM 4381, and is line-attached to the Honeywell front-end processors (Fig. 4). All of the terminals that are linked directly to the Comten machine or to the IBM host (either directly or through IBM 3705 front-end processors) can go through the Comten machine and access the Honeywell DPS 852, and most recently Model 88, applications. Currently, users at Honeywell terminals cannot link to IBM applications.

Users select the environment they want through menus. They can choose the VM (Virtual Machine) or MVS (Multiple Virtual Storage) operating systems on the IBM machine, or the Honeywell machine. When servicing users who want Honeywell applications, the Comten front-end processor essentially functions as a protocol converter between the IBM SDLC protocol used by the terminals and the IBM bisynch protocol that the Honeywell host can understand.

As originally planned, the ability for users to switch between the two mainframe environments has allowed them to conveniently access the productivity tools on the IBM host and connect to the Honeywell databases. As is often the case, however, once a communications capability is in place, new uses for it seem to multiply rapidly. The department plans to incorporate an enhancement to the Comten front-end processor called the integrated protocol converter, which gives the front-end the ability to handle

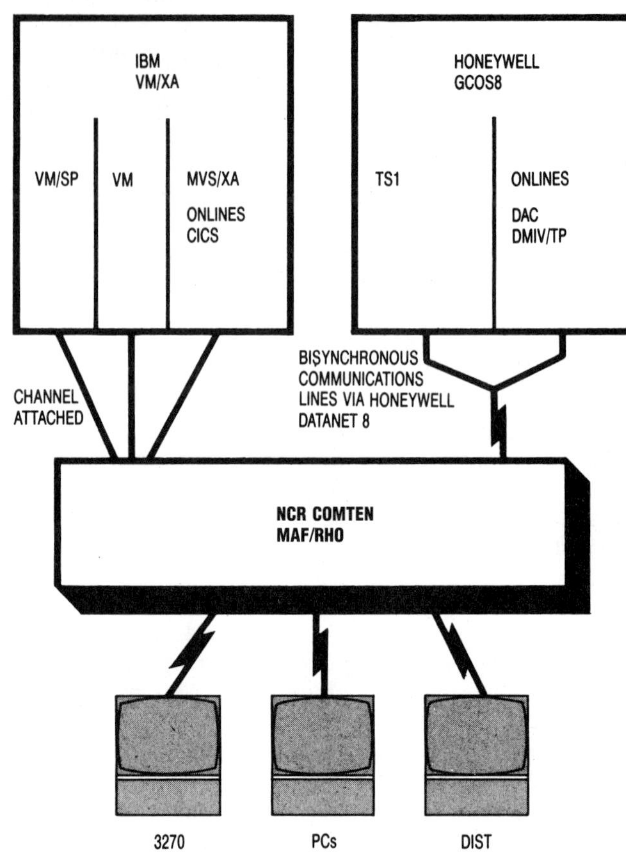

4. Progress in Maine. *The IBM 3270 and PC compatibles, plus any distributed processor capable of emulating a 3270 device (such as a Wang or IBM Series 1 or 8100) use SNA.*

asynchronous devices. With this capability, state employees will be able to work at home more easily.

Since the initial installation, Maine's Department of Administration has installed a redundant backup to the network, upgrading the Honeywell front-ends to Datanet 8/30s, and adding Wang IDS, a software product that allows transfer of Wang-formatted documents over System Network Architecture networks.

More importantly, the state can provide a whole range of new services to the general public. "We can set up some sort of network where people can get information about post-secondary educations, for example, on a dial-in basis," says Weston. "The dial-in facility is tough for us, though, because it opens up security problems."

Without a doubt, using a third vendor to implement communications between different mainframe vendors has provided Maine with capabilities it could not have had

Populations in the trial period

1) Six 3270 bisynchronous and SNA terminals on point-to-point and multipoint lines operating half-duplex.
2) One 3270 3777 SNA multipoint line operating full-duplex.
3) Two bisynchronous RJE (Remote Job Entry) point-to-point connections operating half-duplex.
4) One asynchronous start-stop line (TTY line) operating half-duplex.
5) VM (Virtual Machine) Passthrough software applications operating half-duplex, passing from an IBM machine through the Comten equipment to Honeywell.
6) Three MAF/RHO bisynchronous lines connected to the Honeywell Datanet.

otherwise. In fact, Weston envisages that the state will continue to replace its IBM 3705s with Comten equipment. His advice for users who want to venture into the multi-vendor environment: "If you are not afraid of the other [non-IBM] companies and don't regard them as unknowns, I think it is easier." Still, he adds, "I don't think anyone would do it [use multiple vendors] if they did not have to."

Chrysler

In any corporation, the task of providing disparate users with somewhat integrated access to information is formidable. But for a company that designs and manufactures complex products, the problems are even thornier: integrating office automation and data processing functions with both computer-aided design/computer-aided manufacturing (CAD/CAM) equipment and the machines running the factory floor. For such manufacturing companies, the diversity of related computerized operations makes the multiple vendor interconnection problem especially important, and quite difficult.

For several years, Chrysler Corporation has slowly nudged its computer environment—dominated by DEC minicomputers and IBM and Control Data mainframes—toward one in which users in varied parts of the company could have easy and quick access to information generated in totally separate divisions. This might allow, for example, a marketing department to have instant access to the latest work of the design department.

Although this kind of interconnectivity has long been a goal of Chrysler's information-processing professionals, a key ingredient of the connectivity was almost stumbled upon, in the sense that it was purchased for another purpose.

Chrysler's engineering center has historically relied mostly on CDC and DEC computers, while the company's less technical sectors have tended to use IBM mainframes. Several years ago, when it became clear that the company needed a means of connecting the engineering group's computers—both to each other and to the rest of the business—an elaborate strategy was adopted.

"Our basic strategy was to have a common database for product design so that we could have a single instance of product information in electronic form," says Walter Weglarz, manager of technical computer center systems and operations-engineering. Once this goal was achieved, different parts of the engineering division would be able to refer to the same automobile part in the same way. At the time, each of its vendors had its own databases which were, of course, incompatible with the other vendors. In order to pursue its goal of a common database, Chrysler had to invent its own graphics and CAD/CAM standards, a task those industries are only recently beginning to address (Fig. 5).

A similar situation was true in communications as well, for CDC, IBM, and DEC have separate communications architectures, and these were used for linking different Chrysler machines within each vendor's product line. For links between different vendors, the company established its own internal communications standard, a variant of the bisynchronous protocol.

The topology of this home-grown link between the company's engineering and business systems was not

5. Cyberman. *The CAD terminal displays a wire-frame representation of an H-body car, used in the LeBaron GTS and Dodge Lancer.*

very sophisticated. "This was done via a store-and-forward-type operation. It wasn't machine-to-machine communications," says Weglarz. "We basically had the classical node in the middle situation where dissimilar processors would connect to that machine with the same standard Chrysler-developed protocol."

Although this solution worked for five to 10 years before the implementation of LCN in 1982, increased processing and communications needs eventually began taking their toll on the link. "Eventually the capability of the store-and-forward operation—even using short-haul cables and internal dedicated lines—was not enough to handle the bandwidth necessary for high volumes of data," says Weglarz. At the time, Chrysler was limited to the 56-kbit/s services offered by AT&T and the local carrier. As a result, data transfers were often done by sending data to the middle switching node, then outputting the data to magnetic tapes. These tapes would then be hand-carried to the target machine.

In addition to these difficulties, the engineering computer center was facing the more typical problems of modern corporate computer centers. The technologies that drive computational speed (for example, the speeds of memory chips and central processing units) have been advancing faster than the technologies that govern input/output capacity (for example, disk retrieval algorithms and channel speeds). As a result, getting faster and faster processors did not necessarily have the expected payoff in increased productivity for computer users. "It was obvious we had to extend the number of computers, not simply have bigger and faster computers that would be starving for I/O," says Weglarz.

LCN to the rescue

As a result, about five years ago Chrysler began looking for a way to permit more data sharing between its more than 20 CDC machines, and the mainframe vendor's Loosely Coupled Network (LCN) provided the means. One of its primary functions is to allow multiple CDC mainframes to be linked together, making it possible for users at one terminal's machine to easily call applications and inspect data on other mainframes. For Chrysler, this would help make the common design database more

CHRYSLER ENGINEERING'S
TECHNICAL COMPUTER CENTER
HOST COMPUTER NETWORK

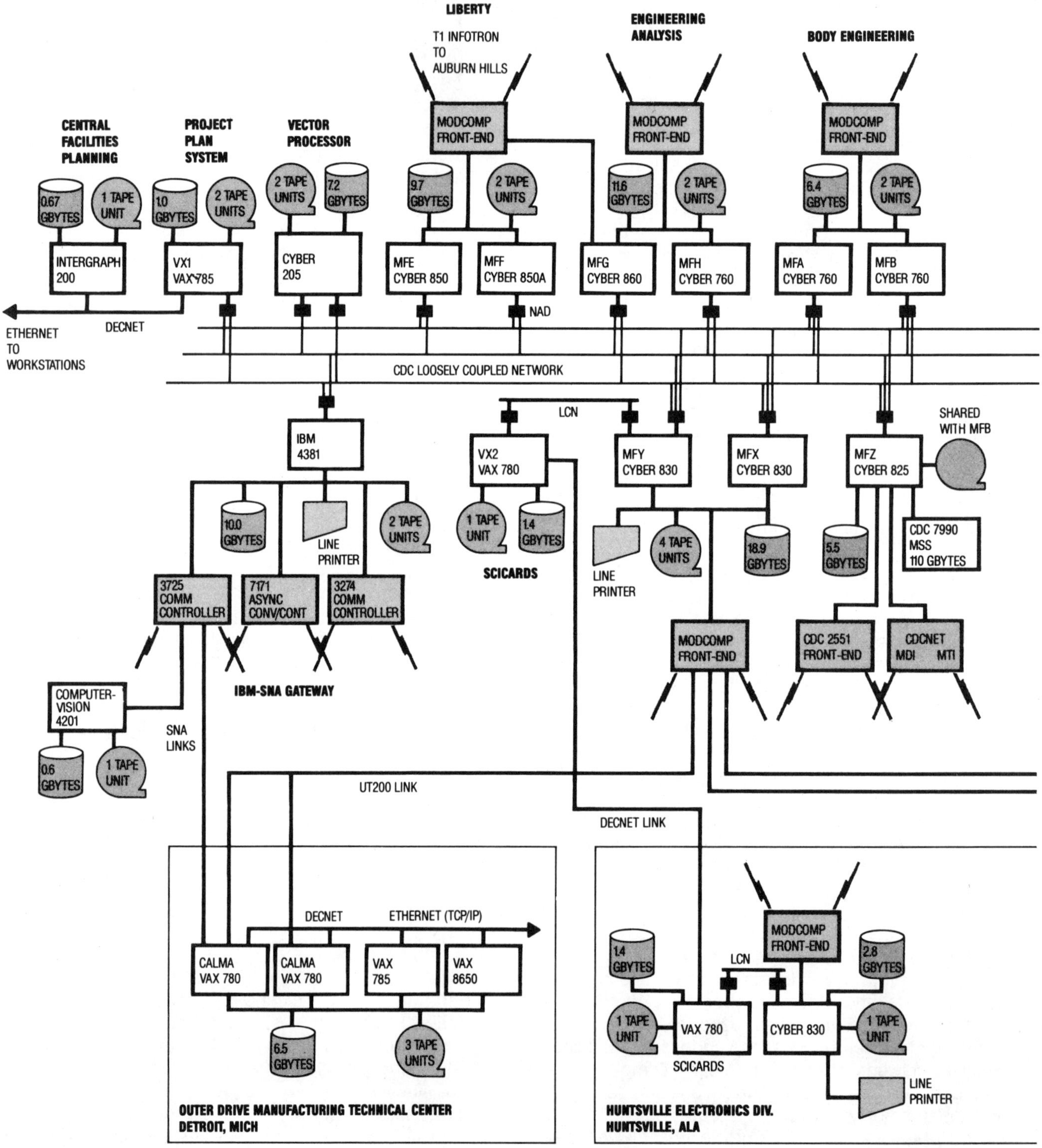

6. Chrysler. *Mainframes numbersX, Y, and Z perform electronic storage. Once data is taken from a sending machine, it is stored only in this archive, until a specified data threshold is reached, where it is sent on to a third level of electronic filing. Engineers can create panels and steering geometry, fitting out vehicles with cargo and components.* ■

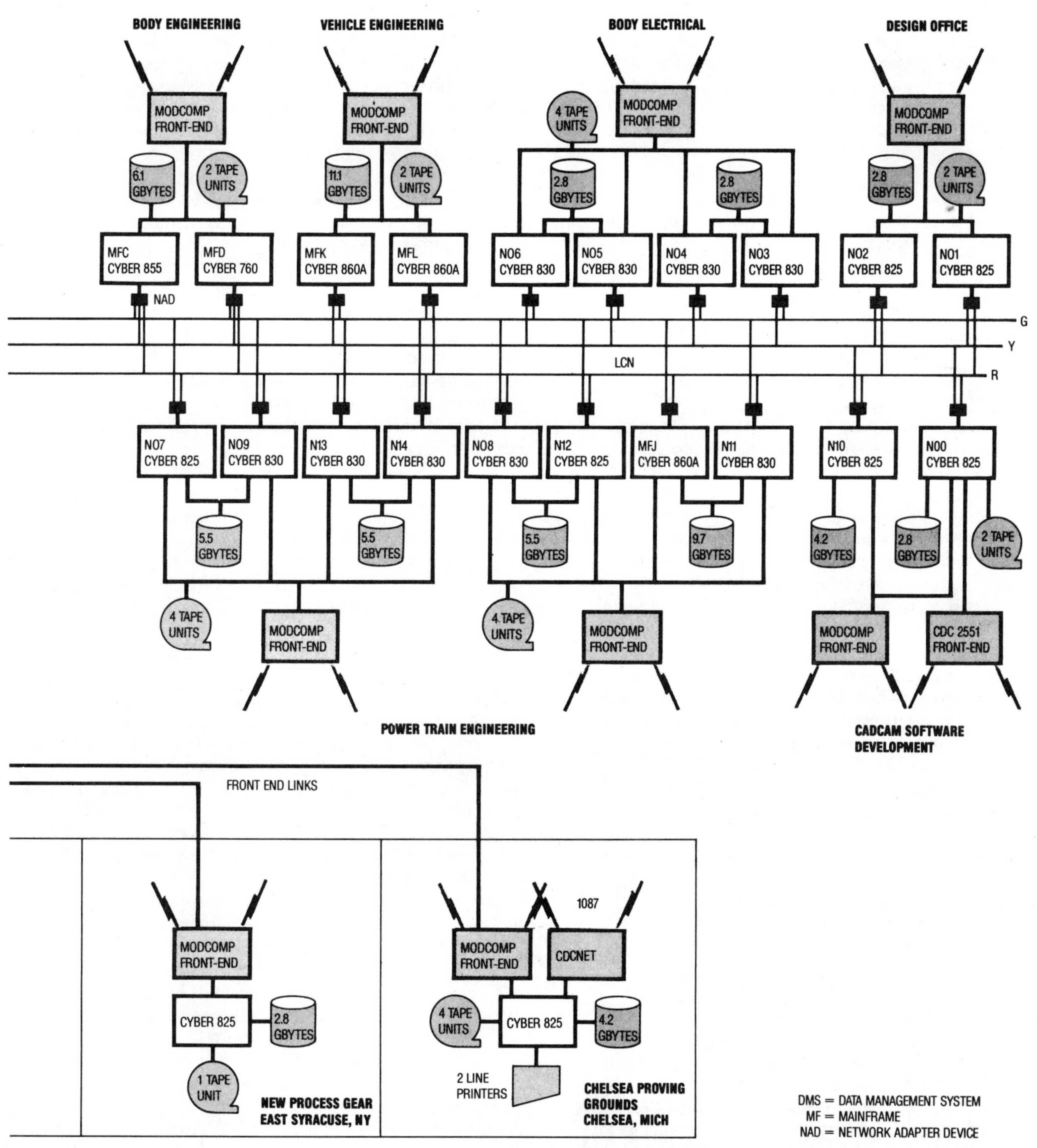

accessible. Thus, for example, an employee in the advance product development group could make a future design concept available to other areas of the company. The manufacturing division might use this information to determine the possible impact of this design on manufacturing operations.

CDC's LCN is a combination hardware-software product operating similarly to NSC's Hyperchannel. Time-driven, at Chrysler the product works over a semi-rigid coaxial network managing remote and local trunks (Fig. 6). The product is heavily weighted toward software, so that data translation functions are microcoded into network access devices strung out along the network, saving processor cycles on both sending and target machines. The RHF software supports primary and secondary data channels with Chrysler achieving actual throughput in the range of six to 10 Mbit/s on multiple trunks in parallel.

Chrysler expected LCN to help provide better management of its CDC-resident data, as well as allow better use of the various computers in the engineering center. LCN would make it easier to run a computational task on the appropriate CDC machine.

As use of LCN continued, communications management discovered that LCN could also accommodate non-CDC machines. LCN provides something akin to a high-speed mainframe channel extension, as well as software that allows a user to transfer data at very high speeds between dissimilar mainframes.

Obviously, this would give the computer center even more flexibility in assigning each task to the optimal computer. "Even though we did not originally expect it," says Weglarz, "we wound up with a multivendor network, with no concerns about data conversions being done twice on different computers. We actually could do [the conversion] in the network access device, and the data was easily transportable from any computer to any other computer." As a result, Weglarz says, it was easier to apply any vendor's advantages and output the data anywhere on the network.

For example, analysts in the automotive design group frequently need finite element analyses. For a very small job, an analyst might compose and run the job on his or her microcomputer. However, it might take a microcomputer hours, or even days, to complete a large model. With LCN in place, the analyst can compose the model locally, then send it to a computer that will accomplish the task in a length of time dictated by the analyst's needs.

Transferring the LCN's potential into reality was not a trivial issue. As with many other highly touted products in the communications field, users who purchase a communications product providing a good deal of flexibility must be willing to invest substantial amounts of effort in customizing the product for their needs.

For starters, Chrysler computer center management had to structure the network so that each work group was directly connected to a computer (or cluster of computers) appropriate for its needs. Doing this properly minimizes the need for network access and decreases response time for the most common transactions.

Perhaps more important, management had to create applications that could give engineers more computational flexibility without requiring them to navigate either the network or the vagaries of each machine. For instance, the previously mentioned automotive designer should (and does) only need to specify the resource by a mnemonic to send data. "The people who are using these machines are engineers, designers, technicians, and clerks. They do not need to be computer experts," says Weglarz.

To insulate the users from the network topology and the idiosyncracies of each computer, computer center programmers wrote the software that takes the analyst's request, builds the appropriate job control language, routes the job to the machine, retrieves the output, and presents it to the user. If desired, the user can specify that the job be run on any available machine, and Chrysler's networking software will choose the machine (Fig. 6).

Although making the LCN tool work well required significant effort, the benefit to the Chrysler Corporation was quick in coming. "We found there were limitations to how well you could effectively interconnect our complex of computers relying on manual intervention," says Weglarz. "With the advent of a single delivery mechanism," he continues, "the staff could be redirected to other activities; [they became] more productive."

Moreover, Chrysler is in a much better position to choose the best software for its needs, with less regard for compatibility considerations. Ironically, the file transfer flexibility that LCN provides gives the automaker more freedom of choice with hardware and software. It has far fewer worries about gear being unavailable to users on their existing machines. Says Weglarz: "The networking capabilities enable us to improve how we spend money on computer resources."

This extends to input/output devices as well. A supplier may have a peripheral device for its machine that is more suitable for a particular task. It might be available today on IBM and not until a future time on CDC, or vice versa. Software will not have to be rewritten for the plotter or peripheral to run on a CDC or a VAX machine.

Weglarz's vision of future improvements focuses more on other vendors than on CDC. "We emphasize the need for wider bandwidth in the 80-Mbit/s range as well as adopting the communications ISO standard. If I want to get brand X computer that has technical prowess for a certain job, I want it to connect to LCN." He adds that as a potential customer, Chrysler would rather get a prospective computer vendor and CDC together to implement that link rather than go around LCN and make a connection some other way.

Even though quite satisfied with the capabilities that LCN has provided, Weglarz is quick to point out that there is at least one other product, Network System Corporation's Hyperchannel, that provides many of the same capabilities as LCN. And while happy with LCN, he looks forward to further industry standardization, such as that which is taking place because of international standards and LU 6.2. This will allow better matching of jobs and computer resources. "Why aim a cannon at a fly on the wall when you can use a flyswatter?" he asks. ∎

David W. Campt has a B.S.E.E. from Princeton and worked for several years as software editor for DATA COMMUNICATIONS. *He is now studying at the University of California-Berkeley's School of Public Policy, focusing on issues in technology.*

Robert B. Morse, Northern Telecom Canada Ltd., Islington, Ont.

A game plan for managing the merger of mixed networks

Until the ideal network management tool exists, users should create a central in-house service bureau and rethink their design methods.

Users faced with problems in network measurement and modeling may be able to learn some lessons from Northern Telecom Canada, which recently had to define its requirements and plan its future directions in these areas.

Despite its status as a vendor of data communications equipment, Northern Telecom Canada, like any other large company, has a mixed telecommunications network along with the usual problems associated with network management. The business systems division provides all business computing needs for Northern Telecom Canada, ranging from payroll to telecommunications. Its specific responsibility is to implement and operate the internal communications networks of NT Canada, not to design or sell equipment. The mandate is to provide cost-effective, reliable service.

The business climate is the same for any other organization taking responsibility for its own telecommunications, dealing with carriers on all matters from service due dates to CRTC (the Canadian Radio and Telecommunications Commission, the equivalent of the U. S. Federal Communications Commission) implications. And Northern Telecom Canada pays the same tariffs as any other organization.

Northern Telecom Canada operates a voice network of some 40 PBXs (with the odd Centrex as well), with approximately 850 tie lines in Canada. The network is managed from Toronto with links to the United States, where there is an equivalent, slightly larger network, managed by Northern Telecom Inc., Dallas, Texas. The two operate as one through sophisticated networking software developed by Northern and operating in the various PBXs.

The fact that the composite U. S.-Canada network is managed from two separate locations is worthy of special mention. The Canadian and U. S. regulatory scenes are so different that considerable expertise, resident in the appropriate country, is essential. For example, tariffs for T1/DS1 services are so different that while it is cost-effective to move heavily into T1 in the United States, analog at Telpak rates must still prevail in Canada. Telpak is a Canadian method of buying circuits in bulk: Telpak A is a group of 12, Telpak B is a group of 24, and Telpak C is a clump of 60. The break-even point on Telpak A, for example, is about seven circuits, so that if a network manager needs fewer than seven lines it is more cost-effective to stay with existing configurations. This leads to such considerations as number of tandem legs, routing and alternate routing, billing methodology, and even numbering plans.

The trick has been to balance the cost savings of buying Telpak circuits in groups with the risk of having all circuits running along the same route. Twelve circuits coming in from different locations may not qualify for Telpak rates, yet safety and security demands for alternate routing may demand such measures. It would be very difficult to manage, negotiate, and operate north and south of the border from one location. A further difference is evident in the maintenance methodology. In the United States, Northern favors employing its own technicians to manage local service and the PBX, while in Canada this function is largely left with the carriers or interconnects.

Northern Telecom Canada also operates a private packet-switched network, NTelpac. There are some 23 nodes worldwide with more than 22 mininodes, making it one of the largest packet networks of its kind in the world (overshadowed only by those owned by Federal Express, Bell Canada, the German Bundespost, and the like). Most of the nodes are in Canada (stretching from Calgary to Montreal) and the United States (from Santa Clara, Calif., to West Palm Beach, Fla.). Overseas there are nodes in Maidenhead, England; Galway, Republic of Ireland; and Frankfurt, West Germany. NTelpac trunks run at 56 kbit/s.

Northern has various other data networks between major data centers to individual users, as well as other services, including Telex, TWX, facsimile, teleconferencing, and electronic mail. The major Northern Telecom data centers use IBM hosts, which have direct connections provided by telephone companies for communications, but Northern is trying to get these mainframe communications onto NTelpac. The manufacturing organization mainly uses Hewlett-Packard equipment and MS-DOS-based microcomputers and Apple machines (used for graphics) are also spread throughout the organization.

The major data centers have network connections between them, with nodes in Toronto, Ottawa, Ann Arbor, Mich., and Research Triangle Park, N.C. At this point, all of this equipment is partially integrated onto the packet network, with the ultimate target of 95 percent of Northern's traffic pushed onto NTelpak. Northern's business systems division is in the process of converting the IBM Synchronous Data Link Control communications onto the network.

As technology advances, the job of the telecommunications manager seems to become more complicated. There is the promise of sophisticated tools to help, but there is a great deal more information to deal with. Decisions with far-reaching ramifications have to be made in an environment that is changing faster than ever before. Long gone are the days when the management of a voice network consisted of adding a tie line when users complained about the constantly busy network.

Integrating voice and data

Data networks have also grown. A few years ago there were only point-to-point circuits, multidrop or not. Managing today's networks has proven difficult for traditional voice managers to handle (often the data center takes care of it) and a new way of thinking has to be applied to the tasks. Bits and bytes instead of Erlangs and communications call seconds, the number of seconds in a minute multiplied by the number of minutes in an hour, translate into a multiplicity of both hardware and software tools required to measure and manage data and voice. Specialized hardware, in the form of data analyzers and trapping devices for data, and analog test sets for voice, has to be examined and used.

Voice and data networks today are managed and measured differently. For data, statistics on response time, throughput, and error rate generally are required, whereas for voice, statistics on the traffic carried and the quality of transmission are more meaningful. Some network modeling tools are available, many of them microcomputer-based, but only a few organizations have the sophisticated tools necessary to give a true picture of a large tandem voice network or a combined voice and data network. Of those available, it may be difficult to justify the expense without first using the tool to demonstrate that money can be saved. Gathering the data to run these tools can be a major exercise, itself a deterrent to getting the tool.

Another realization is that Poisson and even Erlang modeling are seriously inadequate for the newer networks where queueing, alternate routing, and the extended holding times of data calls must be considered. Newer tools are needed. Networks designed using Poisson formula usually work because they are over engineered, but the network ends up with far more capacity than it needs.

Increasingly, corporations are bringing their separate voice and data network management teams together, the separation between the two becoming smaller as they move toward T1/DS1-based digital voice and data networks. This may indicate a simplification of the network manager's task.

Not so. The prospect of integrated networks, such as Integrated Services Digital Network (ISDN), brings a new area of functions, coupled with additional pressures for the manager. These networks require a shift in thinking. Users want end-to-end service, and it won't be enough for the applications manager to say "it's a line problem." Problem situations must be managed from inception to completion without delay and, it is hoped, without trouble to the user. Unfortunately, the network management and measurement tools appear to be lagging behind.

Before proceeding it may be advantageous to define what is meant here by the integrated network, because voice and data networks are already beginning to share digital facilities, and some corporations are beginning to combine voice and data management.

Integrated has three meanings:
- *Integrated Transmission Facilities*—analog voice and data, digital voice and data on the same routes. Digital voice, data, and image are multiplexed on the same trunks and ultimately everything is packetized at the switches.
- *Integrated Equipment*—digital switches and digital transmission gear together with network management equipment and user interfaces all designed and implemented as a whole.
- *Integrated Management Structures*—sophisticated, integrated tools, appropriate metrics easily generated, and the required people organization to go with them.

At all stages in these processes, telecommunications managers need a way to measure what is going on in any portion of the network at any given time. They must also have the means to process this information for modeling purposes, to predict the effects of changes, reconfigurations, and for what-if analyses. With this type of informational ability, most managers would agree that they could more effectively manage their networks.

To the user, the terminal in California must appear directly connected to the application in Ontario. The network manager must handle all the interim equipment, facilities, and connections without the user's notice.

Voice management

Figure 1A shows a voice network management structure typical in many organizations. Most of the work is done in the areas of implementation and operations together with the administration functions. Network design has for the most part consisted of an annual review of the telephone company study, at least in Canada. This is often received months after the data is collected and hence, although better than nothing, has questionable value.

Other design functions would include the addition or deletion of locations from the network and the addition of trunks to compensate for complaints of too many busy signals. Unfortunately, overcapacity is not so easily identified and dealt with, although the use of Call Detail Recording (CDR) data and a microcomputer program can help in this area.

1. Voice Management. A) shows how voice management is usually thought of; B) a less traditional presentation method, gives a truer sense of the forces and factors involved. Complexities of function are difficult to adequately describe on a typical voice network. Electronic trouble tickets would be of tremendous value.

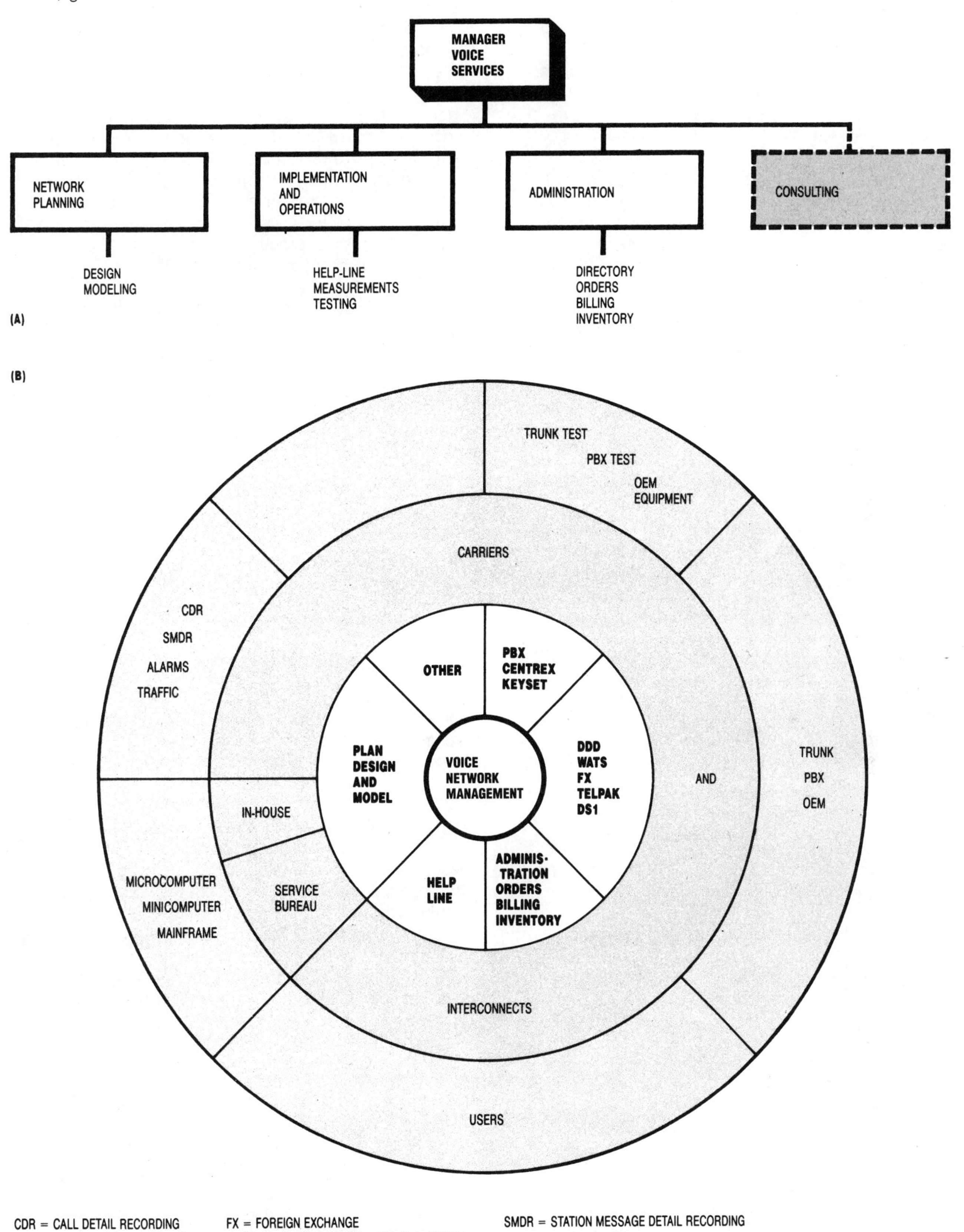

CDR = CALL DETAIL RECORDING   FX = FOREIGN EXCHANGE   SMDR = STATION MESSAGE DETAIL RECORDING
DDD = DIRECT DISTANCE DIALING   OEM = ORIGINAL EQUIPMENT MANUFACTURER

Figure 1B, while appearing very complicated is in fact a rather simplistic view of the voice manager's empire as it presently stands. It illustrates what such managers are trying to do and the forces that influence them. In the center is the network management team, with the first surrounding circle showing their areas of direct responsibility. The next layer shows the main source of influence on the functional areas, and it is clear that the carriers are far and away the major force.

Closer examination of this diagram reveals how little control the manager really has, because local telephone companies may limit operations and choices. The final layer may be the most important, showing the information sources and how they are used to generate meaningful statistics to manage networks. Surprisingly, the ability to get data is rather limited, with most of it coming from CDRs or from the carriers.

How many organizations are actually using alarm and traffic data from the PBXs? Most available switches do generate the data, but unless users draw the data from the switch it may be lost. Some switches, for example, generate copious amounts of data, but unless some provision is made to capture it, the data is dumped or overwritten hourly.

How is CDR/SMDR (Call Detail Recording/Station Message Detail Recording) processed? With a small network it can be done in-house, perhaps on a microcomputer. On larger networks, more power is needed and data collection alone is a major task. A service bureau may prove quite effective, but changes take time and money.

Traditionally it is necessary to eyeball the CDR output for network design purposes. It can reveal a great deal. For example, the amount of long distance to a particular location will help with WATS (Wide Area Telephone Service) and Foreign Exchange design. Various manipulations of call records can show tie-trunk (network) usage. This data may be fed into a microcomputer to derive meaningful information to assist in network design efforts.

The problems with collecting data on voice management illustrate the problems with network management as a whole. The information itself is collected a bit at a time, creating a fuzzy picture. No matter how the information gathering is done, all telecommunications managers long for a better way, an automated method of gathering the needed data and generating useful reports.

The outer circle also shows testing and is very limited. Without a good testing scheme, users are almost totally dependent on the outcome of local telephone companies' routine maintenance schedules. Users of large networks know from experience that some portion of the network is always out of service, suggesting that preventative maintenance is not rigorously performed. In an ideal world, maintenance should be proactive, not reactive. No one would dispute that the ability to quickly, simply, and economically test all facilities on a regular basis would create much greater reliability, far fewer trouble reports, and a happier user community.

Testing ability is severely limited, however. Many PBXs have the ability to do limited trunk testing and to take faulty trunks out of service and print a report. This function can be programmed to occur at specified times, but such tests are normally limited to the capabilities of the PBX, such as loss and noise. More sophisticated and hence more effective testing can be achieved using standalone minicomputer-based devices that can conduct a variety of tests on both digital and analog facilities as well as processing alarms. The only real drawbacks to the minicomputer-based devices are their expense and their external relation to a switch.

Add to all this the need for automatic trouble ticket generation and management reports (preferably tailor-made), and it becomes apparent that there are many deficiencies in the technology that have yet to be resolved.

But the technology is not the only issue. Once hardware and software are chosen, and data is exchanged, it is still necessary to build an infrastructure to complete the network management process.

Even small networks will benefit from the automatic generation of electronic trouble tickets. Backed by a computer's power, these tickets have already done some analysis, correlating related alarms to suggest possible trouble sources or avenues of approach. These tickets will demand attention and cannot be ignored. They can be forwarded again electronically as the escalation procedure—the contingency plan followed automatically in case of a problem—is followed and, upon final resolution, all parties involved are notified. As far as technical and non-technical management reports are concerned, templates for routine operations may suffice, but the ability to create new ones will also be provided.

Data management

Figure 2 takes into account that many organizations are not set up with a centralized communications management function. Rather than show all the variations that can be managed by a data center, a separate data communications group, or a group consisting of both kinds of experts, the basic features and functions are depicted irrespective of how an organization is structured, recognizing that in the future there will have to be some consolidation of communications and computing.

Again the network management group sits in the center of the organizational structure, surrounded by users and the equipment for which they are responsible. The administration and design functions are shown. Again the circle attempts to show the forces of influence on the network; the carriers have a major role, but the vendors also have an increasing role. Here, unlike with voice, the vendors have a much greater say in how things are done. If there is a problem with, say, some IBM communications gear, a user's impulse has been to call IBM, not the carrier involved, such as AT&T. Much communications-related software is available and used to good effect, but it is limited and places further limitations on how things are done. An intelligent modem, for example, is intrinsically an analog to a digital converter and, hence, cannot be used on purely digital facilities. Much of the software is only effective for a given protocol.

Packet-switched networks are the exception here. Of course they do not yet handle all protocols, but for those that they do, management is excellent and the tools effective. Line loading, switch load, error statistics, alarms reporting, and alternate routing are givens. Detailed operational and management reports are available and used.

This is all very well for the large user with a packet-switched network. But for non-packet-network users, the previous restrictions apply. Consider also the basic terminal user without the resources of a large mainframe, such as a user working on a dedicated processor in some vertical application. The user is effectively working blind.

Indeed any kind of monitoring or management probably means commissioning a study from a carrier or consultant or, alternatively, purchasing expensive line-monitoring equipment and the means to process the collected data. Again microcomputers are available as are minicomputers, but the data gathering process is nonetheless tedious and

---

2. Data services. Users can be associated with terminals, microcomputers, minicomputers, or mainframes. The packet networks can be public or private. Circuit-switching may *be running on the voice backbone. Other areas, such as image and facsimile, can also fit into this schematic, enabling it to extrapolate to other kinds of transmission.*

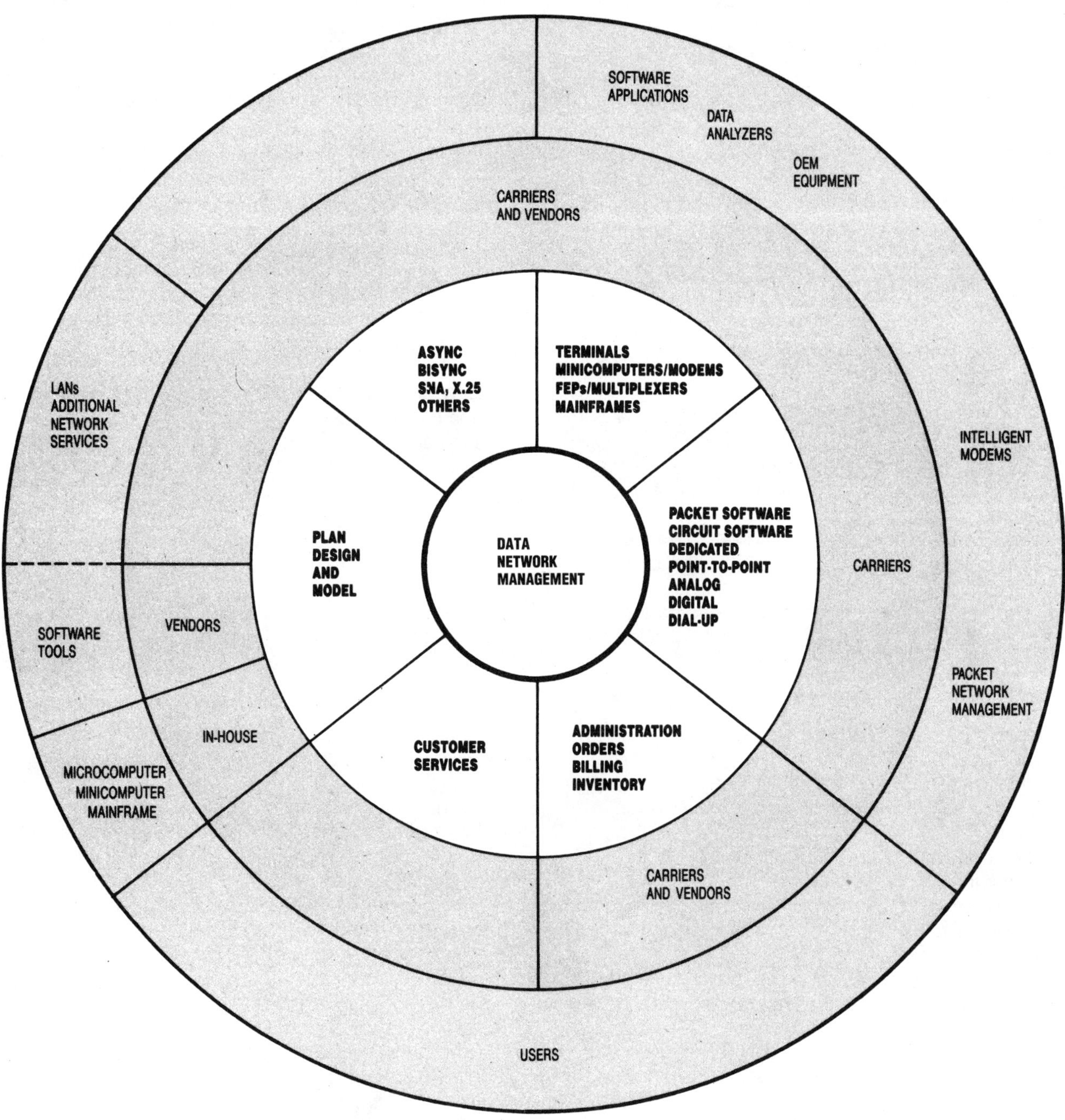

ASYNC = ASYNCHRONOUS
BISYNC = BISYNCHRONOUS
FEP = FRONT-END PROCESSOR
LAN = LOCAL AREA NETWORK
OEM = ORIGINAL EQUIPMENT MANUFACTURER
SNA = SYSTEMS NETWORK ARCHITECTURE

difficult. Here more than anywhere, the results are only as good as the data input.

Managing the complexity

What are the essentials in managing both voice and data? To know the health of any network in real time, whether voice or data, requires:

- Alarm monitoring and reporting.
- Line and trunk testing, both automatic and manual.
- Throughput and response time statistics.
- Line and switch loads.

Many additions may be made to this list. Add to these items the need for:

- Meaningful management reports and metrics.
- Automatic trouble ticket generation.
- Electronic databases of inventory, operating in real time.
- Active electronic directories.
- Billing process.

Complete the process with the requirement for a management setup that, from a single screen, will enable the user to:

- See the overall network in graphical form.
- Zoom in on a particular node or line component.
- Separate voice from data at any location.
- Look out into all networks.
- Look back into the applications.
- Collect and process data regardless of format—CDR or packets, for example.
- Analyze CDR and other data to provide what-if analysis and other statistics.

What is needed is not yet fully available. Network management, then, is often executed in a haphazard and uncoordinated fashion. Voice networks are managed with a combination of carrier-provided studies, CDR manipulations, and microcomputer programs. Some vendors claim to have standalone hardware/software devices that will allow modeling, but none have yet integrated data and voice into a single model. Usually the voice is modeled and the data added later. This is not an optimal situation.

As for testing, everyone is on his or her own. Users must choose whether to buy additional equipment, use PBX facilities, or try some other method. On the pure data side, computer networks may be in better shape than on the voice side, but there are still limitations. Does anyone really know yet how best to make use of those expensive communications facilities? Certainly not with existing tools (though packet networks are the exception). Here neither the carriers nor the vendors can be of much help. When response times start to rise, it is not easy to determine if it is the application, the front-end processor, the line, or the cluster controller that is at fault.

With preventative maintenance and testing there are no established guidelines or standard tools. Although an irate user is not required to indicate a problem (as seems to be the case with voice), this situation is only slightly better than that with voice management and measurement. The question of where network management is heading can be handled in two parts: where networks are going and how they should be managed; and the tools needed and how they will be made available.

There is hope, however. Over the next five years most major manufacturers and carriers will make available more powerful and progressively more integrated tools. The ultimate, of course, will be the all-things-to-all-people setup that can be bought off-the-shelf.

In the meantime, a combination of available tools using a modular implementation scheme can be used effectively. The intention is to trade in obsolete portions as newer technology becomes available.

A word of caution: Don't think that it's only a question of changing the tools. It will also be necessary to rethink the management philosophy. The distinction between voice and data is fast disappearing as the integrated and digital world emerges and the differences between the computing facility's communications group and the traditional data communications group becomes less and less apparent. In short, telecommunications managers are well advised to think of integration on a much broader scale than they may have in the past.

The future in both Canada and the United States is undoubtedly all digital. It will come more slowly in Canada due to the initial digital tariffs filed by the telephone companies. Today in Canada, for example, 24 interexchange tie lines are cheaper than their equivalent T1 spans. Canadians cannot help but look enviously at their neighbors in the United States.

The future holds the promise of dynamic networks offering bandwidth on demand, and networks of DS1 (the Canadian equivalent of T1) carriers. Many managers are already grappling with the problems involved in breaking up the DS1 into 24 lines of 56-kbit/s streams and the sharing arrangements between voice and data, but these problems are all solvable. Multiplexers are plentiful and feature-rich, and 56-kbit/s lines and DS1 cross-connects are already in use by the carriers; they will soon be available to the private network user.

The picture should become fairly simple, with networks evolving to combinations of DS1 links between major locations, smaller groups of digital 56-kbit/s circuits to smaller locations, and single digital circuits, perhaps multiplexed, and even analog circuits to light traffic areas.

Technology is not the problem. What is of concern is how telecommunications managers should set themselves up to manage it all. Pose two basic questions: Is it really necessary to manage a DS1 network? And who will run that network?

To answer the first question, we can draw a comparison between three interconnected digital cross-connects, each with nine facilities attached, and a Rubic's Cube. Take that another step and break each of those DS1 facilities down into the component 24 × 56 parts, and the case for sophisticated network management is made.

Possibilities for responsibility of the Transmission Facilities Management (TFM) function include the existing voice group, the data group, the computing facility, or some other group. If this question isn't answered, the liaison between the various parties will be very complex.

In the center is the new organization termed TFM group. In concept, it can be visualized as being totally responsible for *all* transmission facilities. This may not always be practical, even in a large organization, but the function is needed. If a separate group cannot be justified, it may be possible to create the initial group using staff assigned from the other major groups, such as one from voice, one from data communications, and one from MIS (Management Information Systems). They may even be maintained within their original reporting structures, but the important thing is that they have defined, first-priority responsibilities within the TFM function. Figure 3 should be considered in conjunction with Figures 1 and 2 because they are still valid.

Transmission facilities management

TFM appears to each group (voice network, data center) as a common carrier or retailer of bandwidth. If the voice service manager decides that two extra lines are required between locations, an order is placed with TFM. TFM, in turn, has established lead times, probably based on its relationship with the appropriate carriers, and it provides the service at predetermined and published rates within the company.

TFM in effect owns the digital facilities, the digital cross-connects, and the multiplexers. Costs for these items are built into the TFM rates to users. TFM may have to carry a certain amount of overhead in terms of spare capacity. But by operating on behalf of the entire corporation, this can be managed and minimized.

The next layer of the circle shows the relational links to the rest of the corporation. Other users may be included (local area networks, for example), but the principle is the same. The final layer is shown as user services and problem management. It should be noted that it is one layer removed from TFM.

With TFM in place, consider the process for a new user:
1) User requires new access to an application.
2) User contacts Application Services at Data Center.
3) Application Services verifies validity of request.

4) Application Services contacts TFM and requests connection between the points.
5) TFM inputs data into Network Modeling and assigns bandwidth, updates inventory, revises spare capacity, advises on costs, and adjusts Data Center billing.
6) Application Service issues user I.D., logon, and password; advises of user start date
7) TFM sends month-end bill to Data Center, which sends it to user.

Consider problem management with TFM, using a voice network problem as an example. The assumption here is that the problem was not spotted with centralized diagnostic tools:
1) A user at remote location identifies that there is a problem.
2) A user calls local building telecommunications contact (could be an internal operator).
3) Local contact does first-line review, determining if the problem is merely a misdial ("finger trouble") or a real problem, and so generating a trouble ticket.
4a) If the problem appears to be with the local switch, who calls local telephone company and copies trouble ticket to Voice Services for information purposes? Responsibility is still with the local contact.
4b) If the problem appears to be network-related, trouble ticket is transferred to Voice Services.
5) Voice Services uses available tools to determine if the problem is with PBX hardware or software and either deals with the problem or, if network-related, transfers trouble ticket to TFM for resolution.
6) In all cases of trouble ticket generation TFM can monitor all tickets.

With TFM, there is still a tremendous amount of operational independence and responsibility remaining in individual groups. They will still need the tools to manage their networks, so that the voice group, for example, will still have to handle PBX software and hardware, table updating, CDR for billing purposes, and may still have responsibility for network design in terms of queueing time, alternate services such as WATS, and even Grade of Service (the number of busy signals in a given hour). These all translate, however, into orders for facilities to TFM.

TFM, on the other hand, will be responsible for the performance and provisioning of the digital backbone network. As such, TFM will require sophisticated design tools, which will enable them initially to design the network based on voice parameters with a data overlay and subsequently to perform integrated voice and data design and modeling. What-if scenarios will be of particular use to establish the viabilities of alternate routing, variations in queueing times, and effects of long data calls.

Clearly, there is no single way to do it all. Consolidation into digital networks will result in a single interface point for network testing, but the type of device to be used for that testing is as yet unclear. It may be that existing network management equipment common to data communications will prove to be the answer. Specifically, the electronic matrix switch, with its abilities to monitor, test, and control the attached circuits, may be a solution. Add this capacity to the other information already available from a PBX—in the form of traffic data and network performance statistics from a data center—and there may be enough control and

---

*3. **TFM** The second ring shows the relational links between the in-house common carier, Transmission Facilities Management, and the rest of the corporation.*

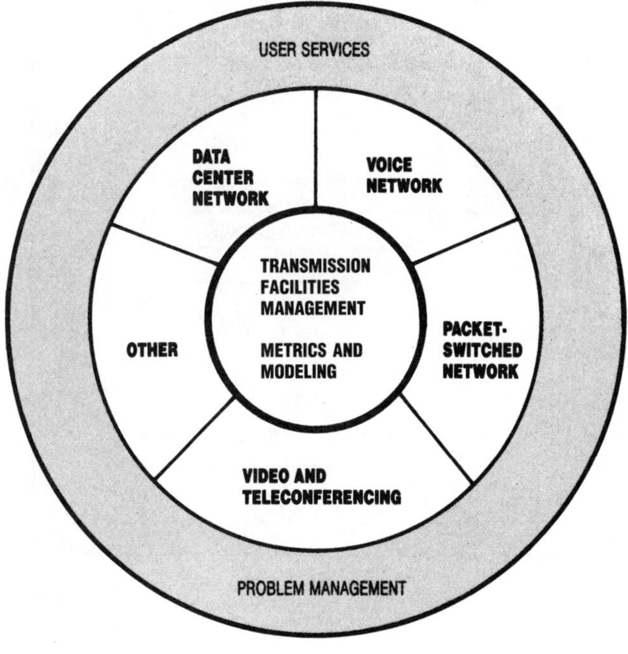

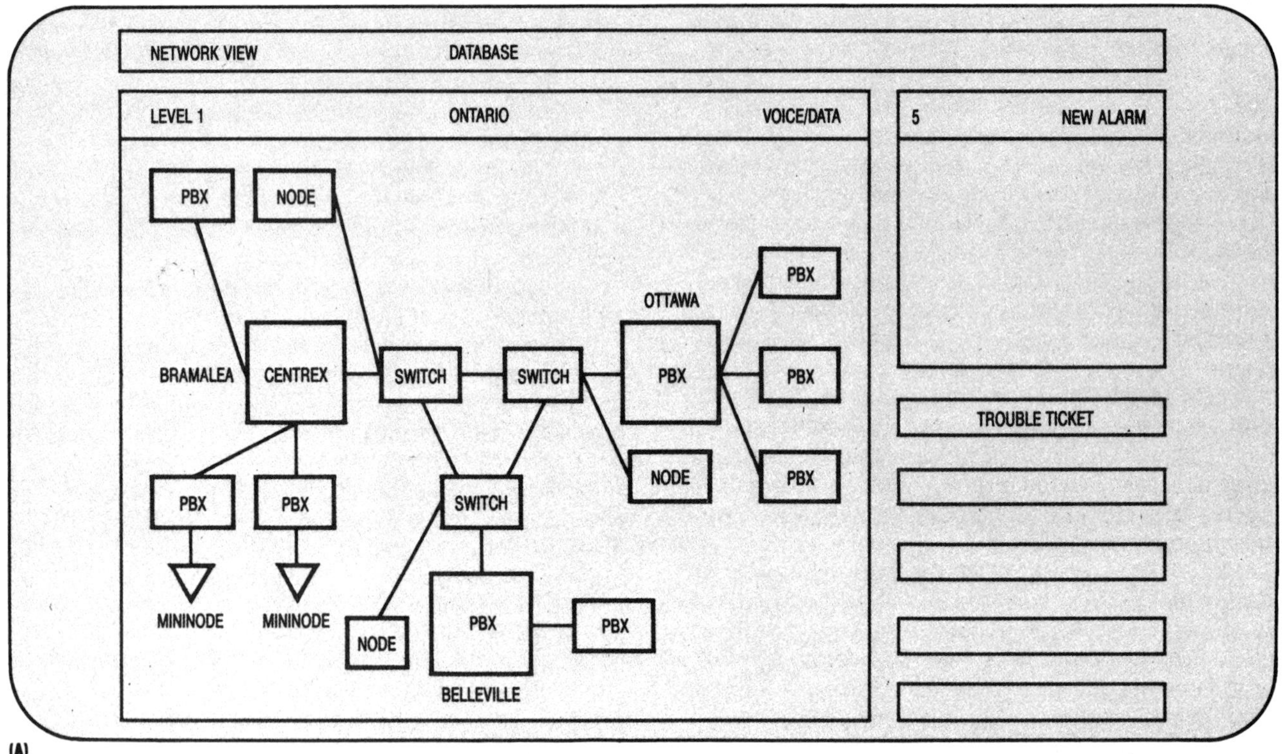

(A)

(B)

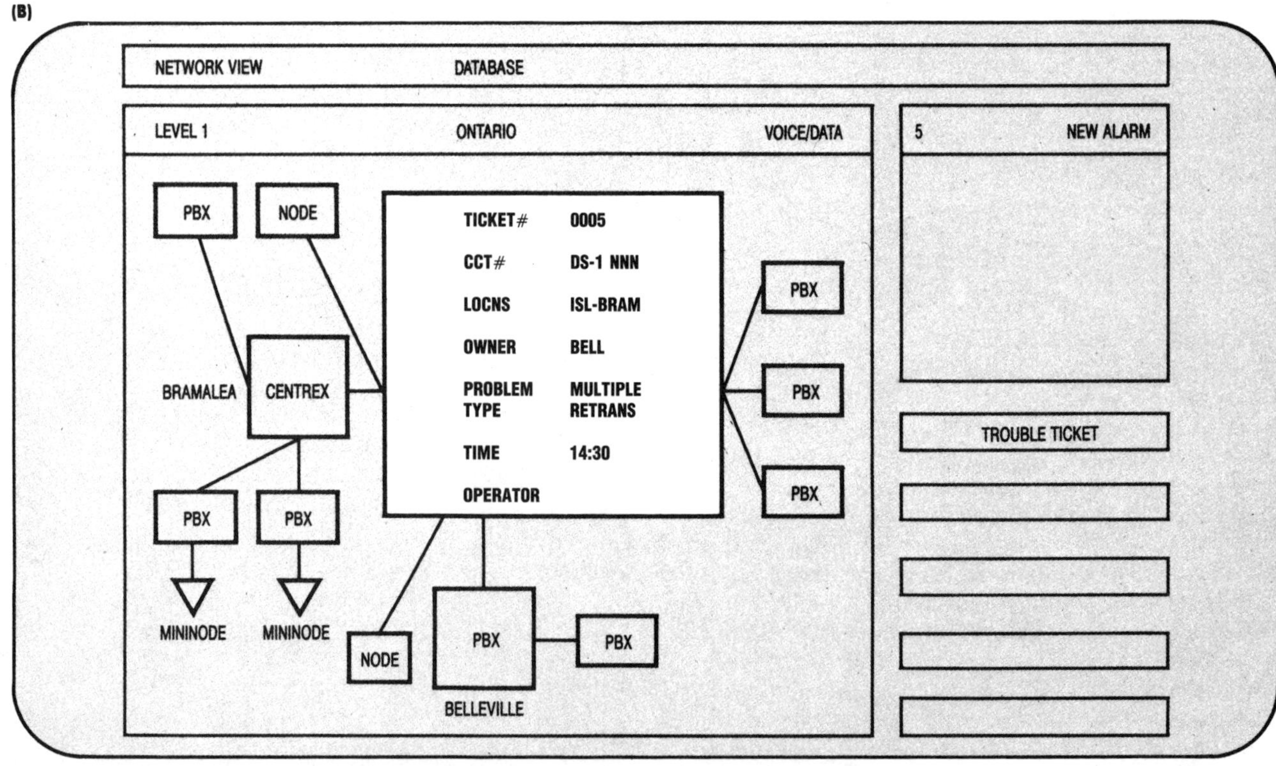

BRAM = BRAMALEA   LOCNS = LOCATIONS
CCT = CIRCUIT   RETRANS = RETRANSMISSION
ISL = ISLINGTON

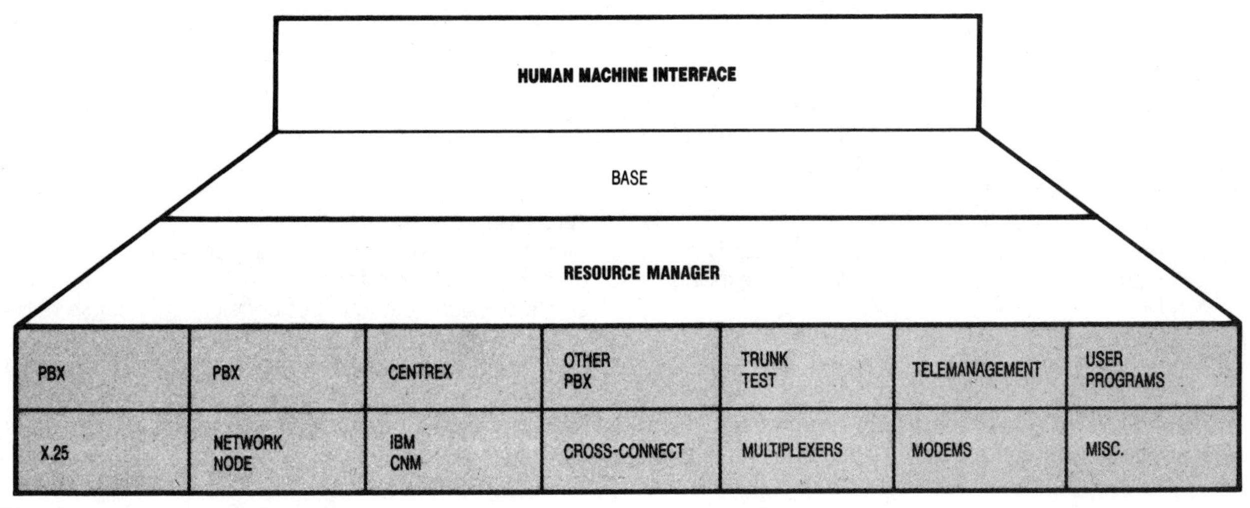

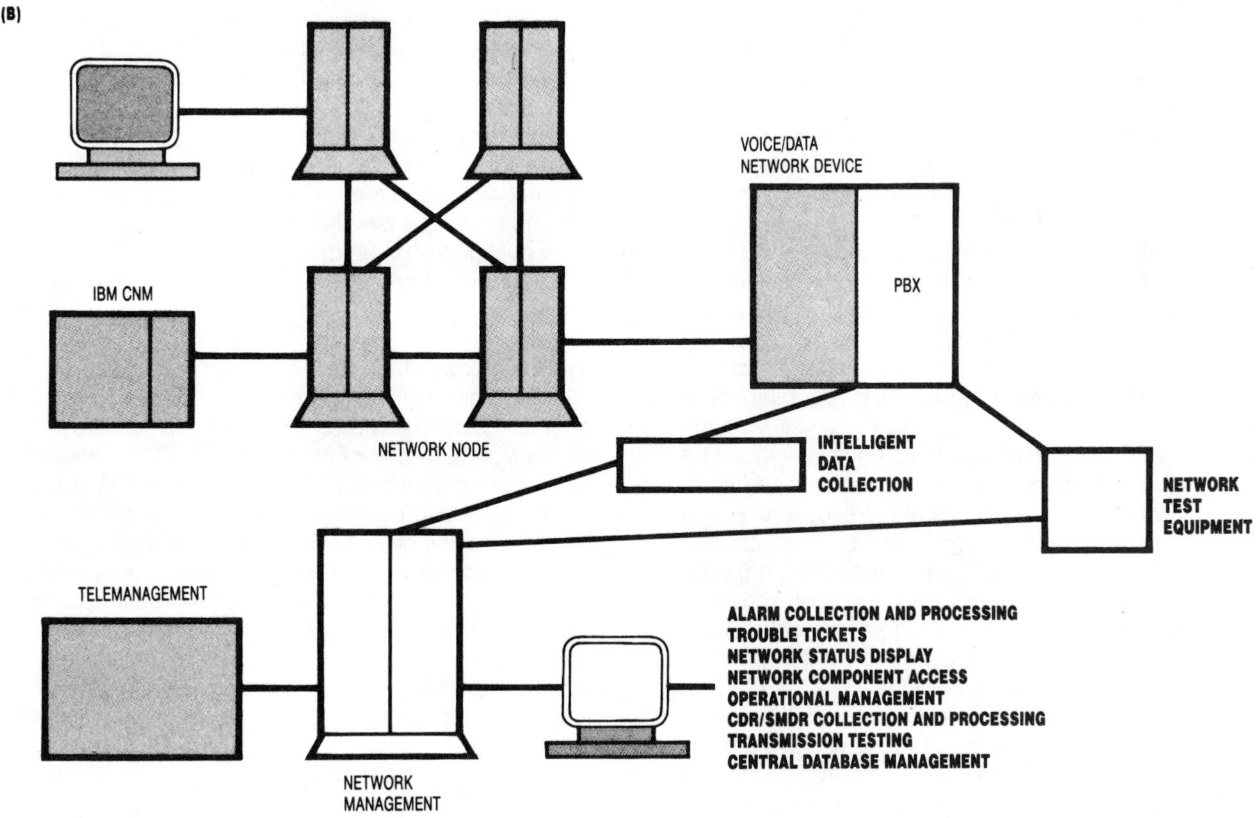

CDR = CALL DETAIL RECORDER
CNM = COMMUNICATIONS NETWORK MANAGEMENT   SMDR = STATION MESSAGE DETAIL RECORDERS

information available to form the basic structure of the ideal network tool. Automated trouble ticketing would be desirable as well.

Even though the total picture is still somewhat unclear, it is worthwhile pressuring manufacturers and carriers into providing a sophisticated answer to the question of testing.

Better models

Of more importance is the relevance of tools to model networks and their worth in giving meaningful data in terms of management reports and statistics. Many telecommunications groups are designing voice networks based on various manipulations of CDR data. Some microcomputer programs are available using Erlang B or similar formulas, but these cannot effectively model existing mixed networks.

The problem is really one of calibration. The existing formulas can give a reasonable prediction of what is happening at a given level of performance. For example, if it can be established that the grade of service is really P.02 (two busy signals out of every 100 calls) then the microcomputer program will be able to give reasonable indications of what effect one more or one less line will have. However, in most cases, that program may be indicating a base-line performance level appreciably different from fact. These programs generally do not have the sophistication to deal with certain network realities. These include, for example, tandem networks where, when reaching a busy signal, a certain number of users will hang up and not try again, a certain number will try again, a certain number may be queued, and a certain number may be rolled over to alternative services. Such exercises in modeling may prove quite futile.

Recent developments in network modeling by Bell Northern Research have led to the creation of what are termed "two-moment models." Most existing programs are only "single-moment models," which means that they only have one algorithm to model all conditions, and must therefore use approximations when conditions refer to overflow or queueing. The "two-moment model," however, has more than one algorithm and the smarts to dynamically change its algorithm when conditions indicate. These programs have the necessary complexity to accurately model a network with various levels of queueing, overflow, and alternate routing. This may be attempted iteratively with a microcomputer if desired and if a spare month is available.

The first two-moment programs are already in use with the major Canadian carriers, and they can be contracted for a network study. The results can be astonishing, with true savings of up to 30 percent on network costs stemming from the more accurate network models they generate. Also available is a single-node optimizer program, which can save a lot of expense on individual PBXs.

The cost of such a service is not small, but it can be justified, not just once but annually. This will have the advantage of keeping networks up to date, maintaining the highest possible service levels, and minimizing costs. Further, the output of the total network study may then be used to calibrate a micro- or minicomputer-based tool on a link-by-link basis. The calibrated microcomputer may then be used to adjust the network with a high degree of confidence, perhaps monthly as conditions change.

The next level of the new design programs are sophisticated data network modelers, which should be on the market this year. These should be followed by integrated voice and data modelers. A number of manufacturers are actively working in this area, so there should be some choice. Users may want to buy the entire package, but it might be more advantageous to purchase packages of more limited functions and contract for a major study annually to calibrate a less sophisticated tool. The latter method has the advantage of gaining the most up-to-date measurements at least once a year.

Wish list

All the desired network management functions should be available at a single terminal—not necessarily on one single physical terminal, but certainly on a single network, with perhaps a central minicomputer base with remote collection and with computing devices at each network node.

Such perfect network management undoubtedly will have a number of consoles, because in a large network multiple problems often exist simultaneously. Each console would have access to all functions available to the network management setup as a whole. Any one of a number of network experts on staff would be able to sit at any terminal, switch from one communications mode, such as voice or data, to another, and window between applications. Flexibility is the keyword.

Operators will be able to look at the composite network (Fig. 4a) and immediately window to trouble ticket information (Fig. 4b), selectively zero in on a node, and then separate out the voice or data connections. This network management setup (Fig. 5) will tie together all fragments previously mentioned. Because of its modularity, it will accommodate planned growth.

The carriers are offering increased services through Centrex and Megastream (a Canadian partial T1 service) offerings, giving users the ability to control and alter network configurations on demand. These facilities are being integrated into the new management techniques and practices.

Although these management technologies are not available today, there are some interim steps that can be taken. Components are available. Microcomputer-based gear—whether hardware, software, or combinations of the two—will initially collect and manipulate CDR data and monitor alarms for a small number of switches. Later versions will also be able to handle traffic data generated by PBXs. Larger devices will handle CDR data, alarms, and traffic reports for a large voice network and have similar capacities for data networks. These will be interconnectable and will provide the basis for full-scale network management. Perhaps the biggest problem, though not the most unpleasant, will be which to choose. Users want integrated network management, not components, with intelligence and flexibility. ■

Robert Morse has been a telecommunications professional for 27 years. In Canada, he has worked for Northern Telecom Canada, Toronto Dominion Bank, and the Government of Ontario. In England he worked for Cable and Wireless for 11 years. He has a bachelor's degree with first class honors from Woolwich Polytechnic and is a registered Professional Engineer with the province of Ontario.

Thomas J. Routt, Network Systems Consulting, Seattle, Wash.

SNA to OSI: IBM building upper-layer gateways

Big Blue has ventured into new terrain with products linking some of its line to X.400, MAP, and other protocol standards.

Long regarded as a leader and not a follower, IBM has received little recognition, especially in the United States, for its capability and willingness to comply with emerging worldwide standards for intervendor communications. But recent announcements confirm that Big Blue is indeed committed to interconnecting via the Open Systems Interconnection (OSI) architecture and protocols that bear the endorsement of the world's standards-setting community.

While architectures are nothing new, it has classically been the case that the architectures, protocols, and products of various manufacturers have been fundamentally incompatible with one another. These incompatibilities did not arise by chance but were built in during the design process. Indeed, they were intended to maximize a vendor's market share by locking users into proprietary solutions.

The electronic Tower of Babel that resulted, even among the various products of individual vendors, expressed itself organizationally in the following forms:
- Multiple, incoherent solution sets that duplicate human and capital resource expenditures;
- Inability to deliver critical information on a timely basis to the appropriate decision makers;
- Inability to provide users transparent access into all targeted resources due to incoherent implementations;
- Loosely defined migration strategies; and
- Absence of leadership within user organizations to properly manage information as a resource.

Obviously, few if any users have benefited from such situations. In fact, the majority of manufacturers remain unenriched by the existence of multiple, incompatible network architectures. Only IBM appears to have significantly expanded the worldwide market share of its network architecture through the successful marketing of a proprietary approach, as there are approximately 20,000 licensed Systems Network Architecture (SNA) sites of at least two mainframes and/or departmental processors each.

Objectives of open systems

In response to the increasing recognition among users and manufacturers alike of the need for an open set of communications standards, the International Organization for Standardization (ISO) formally initiated OSI standardization activities in March 1977. OSI is an ongoing effort to meet the following objectives:
- To provide an architectural reference point for defining standardized procedures that enable the interconnection and subsequent effective exchange of information between dissimilar processing environments;
- To permit internetworking among various networks of the same type so that transparent communication can be achieved as easily through an interconnected combination of networks as over a single network;
- To serve as a common framework for defining services and protocols consistent with the agreements contained in the OSI reference model, developed by ISO Technical Committee 97; and
- To accelerate the introduction of interoperable, multivendor products and services.

Even IBM could not ignore such aims. Because SNA remains its centerpiece of proprietary communications, IBM's recognition of the potential of OSI to create significant business opportunities is significant. These opportunities are especially evident in the multivendor environments of large users and in potential government procurements. Also, other manufacturers are accelerating their efforts to research, develop, and announce products that conform to the ISO International Standard (IS), Draft International Standard (DIS), and Draft Proposal (DP) protocols defined at each of the seven OSI layers. The primary catalyst for this stepped-up vendor activity derives from the elaboration

Table 1: ISO OSI and IBM SNA architecural layers and services

	INTERNATIONAL ORGANIZATION FOR STANDARDIZATION (ISO) OPEN SYSTEMS INTERCONNECTION (OSI)		IBM SYSTEMS NETWORK ARCHITECTURE (SNA)	
	LAYER	SERVICES	LAYER	SERVICES
7	APPLICATION LAYER	■ PROVIDES APPLICATION-PROCESS (FOR EXAMPLE, APPLICATION PROGRAM, DEVICE, OR TERMINAL OPERATOR) INTERFACE INTO DISTRIBUTED INFORMATION SERVICES (DOCUMENT DISTRIBUTION, ELECTRONIC MAIL, DISTRIBUTED TRANSACTION PROCESSING)	TRANSACTION SERVICES	■ PROVIDES END-USER (SAME AS OSI APPLICATION PROCESS) LOGICAL INTERFACE INTO IBM'S DISTRIBUTED TRANSACTION ARCHITECTURES (SNA DISTRIBUTION SERVICES, DOCUMENT INTERCHANGE ARCHITECTURE, DISTRIBUTED DATA MANAGEMENT)
6	PRESENTATION LAYER	■ IDENTIFIES, NEGOTIATES COMMUNICATIONS TRANSFER SYNTAX ■ FORMATS DATA (BINARY, ASCII, CCITT INTERNATIONAL ALPHABET NO. 5, EBCDIC, GRAPHICS, NUMERICS)	PRESENTATION SERVICES	■ FORMATS DATA FOR PRESENTATION (IMAGE OR HARD-COPY, 3270, 5250, SNA CHARACTER STRING, GENERAL DATA STREAM) ■ RESPONSIBLE FOR DATA REPRESENTATION BETWEEN END USERS ■ RESOLVES NETWORK ADDRESSES AND NAMES ■ SELECTS SESSION PROFILE ■ OFFERS NETWORK SERVICES (CONFIGURATION, SESSION, MANAGEMENT, MAINTENANCE, AND MEASUREMENT) ■ PERFORMS SYNC-POINT PROCESSING
5	SESSION LAYER	■ SUPPORTS APPLICATION PROCESS DIALOG ■ BINDS/UNBINDS COMMUNICATIONS ■ EXCHANGES NORMAL AND EXPEDITED DATA	DATA FLOW CONTROL	■ CORRELATES DATA EXCHANGE AND SYNCHRONIZES FLOW BETWEEN SNA HALF-SESSIONS ■ ENFORCES CHAINING AND BRACKETS PROTOCOLS ■ GENERATES CHAINING RESPONSES (HALF-DUPLEX FLIP-FLOP, HALF-DUPLEX CONTENTION, FULL DUPLEX) ■ ASSIGNS SESSION SEQUENCE NUMBERS
4	TRANSPORT LAYER	■ PROVIDES END-TO-END INFORMATION INTERCHANGE AND CONTROL ■ PROVIDES FOR ESTABLISHMENT, DATA TRANSFER, AND TERMINATION OF CONNECTIONS BETWEEN SESSION ENTITIES	TRANSMISSION CONTROL	■ REGULATES SESSION DATA FLOW ■ PACES HALF-SESSION DATA EXCHANGES ■ CORRELATES BUFFER AND PROCESSING CAPABILITIES OF DIFFERENT NODE TYPES ■ SEQUENCES SESSION MESSAGES ■ VALIDATES SESSION-MESSAGE SIZE ■ ENCRYPTS/DECRYPTS MESSAGES ■ PROVIDES BOUNDARY-FUNCTION MESSAGE CONVERSION
3	NETWORK LAYER	■ SELECTS NETWORK ROUTING SERVICE ■ SEGMENTS AND BLOCKS NETWORK MESSAGES ■ PROVIDES EXPEDITED DATA TRANSFER ■ PROVIDES ERROR DETECTION, RECOVERY, NOTIFICATION	PATH CONTROL	■ SELECTS NETWORK ROUTING ■ PROVIDES CLASS-OF-SERVICE (VIRTUAL ROUTE, TRANSMISSION PRIORITIES, EXPLICIT AND REVERSE EXPLICIT ROUTE, TRANSMISSION GROUPS) ■ SEGMENTS AND BLOCKS MESSAGES ■ PERFORMS PATH INFORMATION UNIT TRANSMISSION HEADER CONVERSION
2	DATA LINK LAYER	■ INITIALIZES DATA LINK BETWEEN ADJACENT NODES ■ TRANSFERS DATA OVER LINK ■ PERFORMS ERROR DETECTION AND CORRECTION ■ DISCONNECTS LINK	DATA LINK CONTROL	■ SAME FUNCTIONS AS OSI DATA LINK LAYER
1	PHYSICAL LAYER	■ PROVIDES PHYSICAL INTERFACE THROUGH ELECTRICAL, MECHANICAL, PROCEDURAL, AND FUNCTIONAL MEANS	PHYSICAL CONTROL	■ SAME FUNCTIONS AS OSI PHYSICAL LAYER

and implementation of user-defined OSI protocols within General Motors' (GM's) Manufacturing Automation Protocol (MAP) and Boeing Computer Services' Technical and Office Protocols (TOP).

Superficial similarities, deep differences

Table 1 presents the architectural layers and services of the ISO OSI Reference Model and of IBM SNA. Note that the service definitions in the equivalent layers of each of the seven-layer architectures are somewhat similar. However, that is where their similarity ends. SNA is a proprietary IBM communications template from which to define, design, and implement interconnection and resource sharing among IBM and IBM-compatible communications network products. By contrast, the ISO OSI reference model (the architecture) and the protocols that have been and are being defined at each of its layers (the implementations) serve as a nonproprietary, public-domain reference point from which to develop standardized procedures that allow for the interconnection and effective exchange of information among open systems. (Open systems are defined as dissimilar operating environments that reflect this common architectural reference point.)

IBM's positions on the definition and implementation of gateways from SNA to OSI have recently been formalized in the *IBM Systems Journal*. They are as follows:
Recognition of the major business case for open systems. This is especially important to large corporate and government users opposed to the use of vendor-proprietary architectures.
■ Recognition that the majority of corporate and government users may have their own internal standards organization and/or be members of the following international organizations: ISO, the International Telegraph and Telephone Consultative Committee (CCITT), European Computer Manufacturers Association (ECMA), Committee of European Communities (CEC), European Committee for Standardization and the European Committee for Electrotechnical Standardization (CEN/Cenelec), Conference of European Postal and Telecommunications Administrations (CEPT), American National Standards Institute (ANSI), National Bureau of Standards (NBS), and Institute of Electrical and Electronic Engineers (IEEE). All of these major European and U. S. standards organizations have acknowledged the OSI reference model and the resultant protocol specifications as the final international authority on connectivity and resource sharing among open systems.
■ Support for the OSI direction of developing one set of international standards as the best possible approach to the resolution of incompatibilities. A noteworthy example of this is the increasing degree of cooperation between ISO and the CCITT through the mutual publication of identical standards.
■ Support for the OSI direction of developing a single set of international protocol-test criteria and test suites.
■ Support for first-party testing and verification for OSI standards conformance. First-party testing, in this context, means that the manufacturer performs product-conformance testing with its own set of tests, which are determined to be acceptable to a user or verification body.
■ Recognition that OSI standards should not be static phenomena but rather should facilitate functional

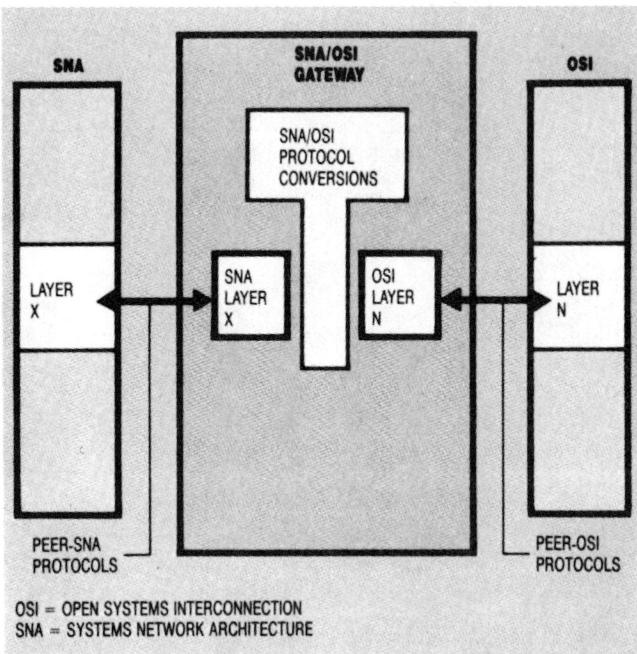

1. Gateway. *In the gateway approach, SNA and OSI protocols think they're talking to peer layers, while the gateway performs SNA-to-OSI protocol transformations.*

modularity without creating obsolescence.
■ Participation in MAP and TOP development and demonstration.
■ Participation in OSI implementation organizations whose members include key vendors and users, such as the Corporation for Open Systems (COS).
■ Commitment to the development of SNA/OSI gateway products. However, it is apparent that SNA will remain the internal, proprietary architectural centerpiece for any IBM communications product development. In other words, while OSI gateway products have been and will continue to be developed and announced, SNA appears likely to remain IBM's fundamental template for distributed communications.

The generalized approach by which IBM has elected to implement gateways between the SNA and OSI protocols is shown in Figure 1. Note that the protocol or protocols operative within SNA Layer "X" are recognized at the same SNA layer in the SNA/OSI gateway function. Peer-OSI protocols, implemented at any OSI Layer "N," are recognized between the native OSI environment and the SNA/OSI gateway. Therefore, layer entities at each end perform as if they are communicating with peer layers elsewhere in the network. SNA-to-OSI and OSI-to-SNA protocol conversions occur within the gateway, transparent to the operations in either the SNA or OSI environments.

The spread of intelligence

Interconnection products may be classified according to their degree of intelligent functioning (Table 2). The spectrum of interconnect intelligence distinguishes between the use of proprietary and OSI gateways. Note that the relative placement of other interconnect approaches is also shown.

Note in Table 2 that, in the column entitled Approach, the terms Repeater, Bridge, and Intermediate System

Table 2: Spectrum of interconnect intelligence

INTELLIGENCE	APPROACH	WHAT IT CONNECTS	DESCRIPTION	EXAMPLES	COMMENTS
HIGH	OSI GATEWAY	INTERNET MULTIPLE NETWORKS	PROTOCOL TRANSLATIONS TO LAYER 7	IBM SNA/MAP COMMUNICATIONS SERVER	NONE
	PROPRIETARY GATEWAY	INTERNET	PROTOCOL TRANSLATIONS TO LAYER 6	DECNET/SNA	NONE
	TERMINAL EMULATOR	DISSIMILAR ENVIRONMENTS	PROTOCOL TRANSLATIONS AT LAYERS 2 THROUGH 6	IBM 3710	WITHIN DATA TERMINAL EQUIPMENT
	PROTOCOL CONVERTER			INTEGRATED X25 PACKET ASSEMBLER/ DISASSEMBLER	SEPARATE DEVICE
	INTERMEDIATE SYSTEM (ROUTER)	TWO OR MORE PHYSICALLY DISTINCT NETWORKS	OSI LAYER 3 PROTOCOL (SUCH AS OSI PLP X.25)	IEEE 802.3 TO 802.4 THROUGH PLP X.25	ONE COMMON INTERNET ADDRESS ON ROUTER
	BRIDGE	TWO PHYSICALLY DISTINCT NETWORKS	LAYER 2 TRANSFORM	IEEE 802.3/802.4	NETWORKS MUST HAVE CONSISTENT ADDRESSING SCHEME AND FRAME SIZE
LOW	REPEATER	IDENTICAL ENVIRONMENTS	TRANSPARENT EXTENSION	IEEE 802.3/802.3	SAME PROTOCOLS, SPEEDS

MAP = MANUFACTURING AUTOMATION PROTOCOL
OSI = OPEN SYSTEMS INTERCONNECTION
PLP = PACKET-LEVEL PROTOCOL
SNA = SYSTEMS NETWORK ARCHITECTURE

(Router), have been formalized within the MAP and TOP architectures. Protocol converter, terminal emulator, and proprietary gateway are used by IBM and other vendors. The term OSI gateway is derived from ISO.

The use of repeaters is a technique defined low on the spectrum. Repeaters are transparent devices used to interconnect segments of an extended network (usually a local area network, or LAN) at the Physical Layer (OSI Layer 1). This Layer 1 interconnection assumes that the segments are networks of the same type, with identical protocols and speeds. For example, a repeater might interconnect two IEEE-802.3 carrier sense multiple access/ collision detection (CSMA/CD) LAN segments, each of which supports such Physical Layer characteristics as Manchester encoding, a 10-Mbit/s data rate, as well as 50-Ohm-impedance coaxial cable as a transmission medium.

The bridge approach provides for network expansion by connecting physically distinct networks at the Data Link Layer (OSI Layer 2). This approach assumes that the networks to be interconnected define a consistent addressing scheme and frame size. The bridge transform postulates a common Layer 2 protocol. For example, a bridge might link an IEEE-802.3 CSMA/CD LAN with an IEEE-802.4 token-passing bus LAN. The Layer 1 and 2A (Medium-Access Control, or MAC) protocols within each LAN are distinct. However, there exists a common Layer 2B Logical Link Control (LLC) protocol, for example the IEEE-802.2 LLC.

The Intermediate System (Router) approach allows for the interconnection of two or more physically distinct networks through implementation of an OSI Layer 3 protocol. The Intermediate System (Router) device contains one common network address that is known to all attached networks. The constituent network Physical Layer and data link layer protocols are not constrained to any of the compatibilities required by the repeater and bridge approaches. An example of the Intermediate System (Router) approach is the selection of the ISO Packet-Level Protocol (PLP), ISO International Standard 8208 (equivalent to CCITT Recommendation X.25), as a Layer 3 protocol transform common denominator to enable the interconnection of distinct IEEE-802.3 CSMA/CD and IEEE-802.4 token-passing bus LANs.

Protocol converter and terminal emulator approaches lie between intermediate system (router) and proprietary gateways on the spectrum of interconnect intelligence. These techniques share two features. They both connect dissimilar environments and they both perform protocol translations at Layers 2 through 6 (converting, for example, ASCII data into a 3270 data stream, the representation and formatting of which is defined as a Layer 6 function).

IBM offers several protocol converters (Fig. 2), including the following:

- Model 3708 Network Conversion Unit;
- Model 7426 Protocol Converter;
- Model 7171 ASCII Device Attachment Control Unit; and
- Model 3710 Network Controller.

These protocol converters all support conversion from asynchronous ASCII data streams into synchronous EBCDIC streams. The asynchronous ASCII presentations may be TWX, IBM 3101, or other equipment manufacturer (OEM) start/stop protocols.

As Table 2 indicates, a proprietary gateway is a conversion environment that "internets," that is, attaches separate networks, in addition to providing protocol converter or terminal emulator functions up through Layer 6. One such example is the Decnet-SNA gateway from Digital Equipment Corp. (DEC). It enables DEC VT-Series asynchronous ASCII display devices attached to DEC VAX processors, which are running gateway management software and are connected to a DEC PDP-11/2X, to appear as either Physical Unit Type 2 (PU T2) with Logical Unit Type 2 (LU T2) devices or as PU T1/LU T1 3777 remote job entry (RJE) devices. The gateway also permits VT devices to access a Distributed Office Support System (Disoss) running on an IBM host under Customer Information Control System/Virtual Storage (CICS/VS). In addition, it allows IBM 3270 display stations to access VAX-resident applications.

Finally, an OSI Gateway interconnects disparate networks and performs protocol translations through Layer 7 OSI protocols. In the OSI Gateway case, each constituent proprietary environment that participates retains its unique internal protocols, with common reference and transform through a suite of OSI protocols defined up through Layer 7, the Application Layer.

The preceding discussion has covered the relationship between the SNA and OSI architectures and focused on IBM's commitment to defining gateways between these two environments. Table 3 illustrates major IBM-announced products which provide service and protocol translation from SNA into OSI. As shown, IBM has announced products that provide for conversion from SNA to services and protocols defined within all seven OSI layers. The remainder of this article focuses on products that provide conversion from SNA Layers 4 through 7 to OSI Layers 4 through 7, beginning with SNA-to-X.400 Layer 7 implementation.

X.400 and SNADS compared

The CCITT published the Message Handling Systems (MHS) Recommendation X.400-Series within the 1984 Red Book as Recommendations X.400, X.401, X.408, X.409, X.410, X.411, X.420, and X.430. The purpose of MHS is to provide capability for a user-defined message of any *content* to be transparently encapsulated within a standard *envelope*, for subsequent delivery to any defined electronic mail destination. The primary MHS objectives, defined by CCITT Study Group VII, are as follows:
- To develop standard tools for interconnecting computer mailboxes (referred to as store-and-forward Computer-Based Message Systems);
- To define general-purpose, application-independent, store-and-forward message-transfer services and their associated protocols;
- To provide for a range of electronic office communi-

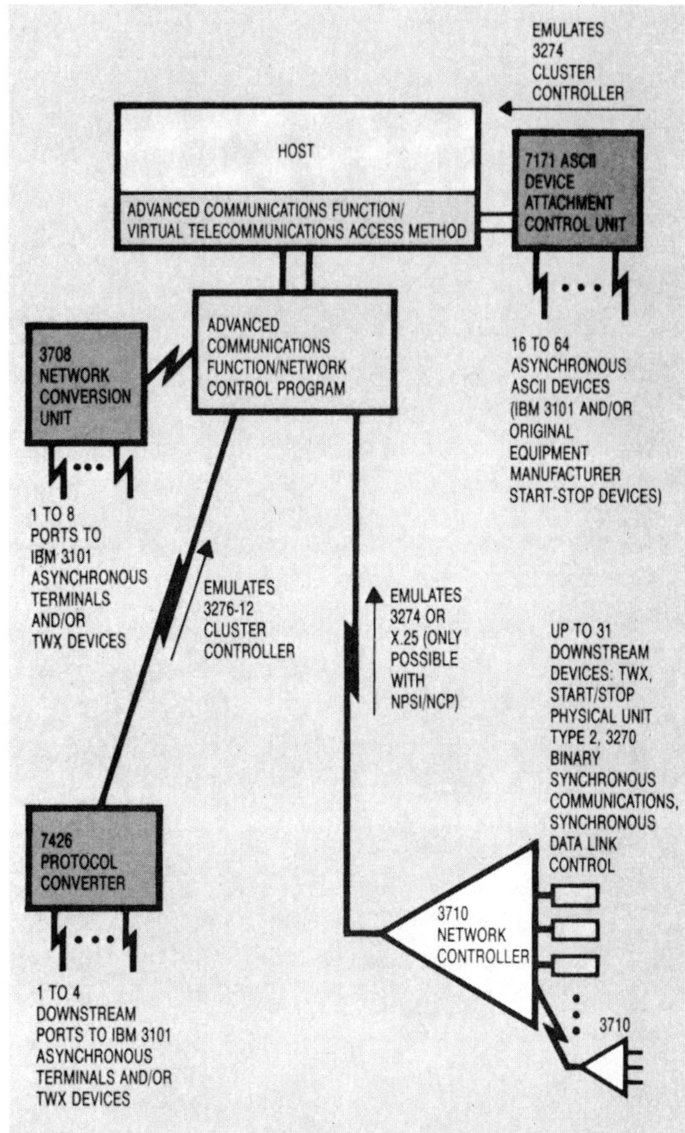

cations functions; and its final objective is
- To support access from a heterogeneous array of terminals and services.

The MHS functional model (Fig. 3a) defines a comprehensive message-handling environment that includes the following:
- Originator and recipient users;
- User Agents (UAs), which are functional elements that represent users within the MHS model and interact directly with users to prepare and submit messages for routing to proper destinations;
- The UA-to-UA relationship, within which UAs cooperate to perform message-delivery functions; and
- Message Transfer Agents (MTAs), which relay messages from submitting UAs to delivery UAs through the Message Transfer System (MTS).

MHS also defines an Interpersonal Messaging (IPM) System, which provides users with an IPM service. IPM

Table 3: Summary of SNA to OSI products

	IBM PRODUCT	FUNCTION	OSI LAYERS
1	X.400 DISOSS CONNECTION	DISOSS SNADS/DIA MESSAGE TRANSFORM/RELAY TO AND FROM X.400 MESSAGE TRANSFER FACILITY	7,6
2	X.400 MESSAGE TRANSFER FACILITY	ACF/VTAM-DEFINED X.400 MHS MESSAGE TRANSFER AGENT ENTITY (MTAE)	7,6
3	SERIES/1 REAL-TIME PROGRAMMING SYSTEM MAP COMMUNICATIONS SERVER AND THE SERIES/1 EVENT-DRIVEN EXECUTIVE MAP APPLICATION SERVER	SERIES/1-BASED SNA/MAP CONVERSIONS TO AND FROM FTAM THROUGH TOKEN-PASSING BUS	7,6,5,4,3,2,1,
4	GENERAL TELEPROCESSING MONITOR FOR OPEN SYSTEMS INTERCONNECTION (GTMOSI)	ACF/VTAM-RESIDENT TELEPROCESSING MONITOR (MVS) THAT PROVIDES COMMUNICATIONS WITH X.400, FTAM, ACF/NCP NPSI, OTSS, OSNS, VTAM API, CICS/VS, IMS/VS, TSO, AND MSNF	6,5,4
5	OPEN SYSTEMS TRANSPORT AND SESSION SUPPORT (OTSS)	MVS/SP-, VSE-, OR VM-RESIDENT CTCP APPLICATION THAT SUPPORTS ISO CLASS 0 AND 2 TRANSPORT AND ISO SESSION KERNEL	5,4
6	OPEN SYSTEMS NETWORK SUPPORT (OSNS)	MVS/SP-, VSE-, OR VM-RESIDENT CTCP APPLICATION THAT MANAGES ALL NPSI-DEFINED TYPE 4 VIRTUAL CIRCUITS OVER PACKET-SWITCHED DATA NETWORKS (PSDNs)	3
7	COMMUNICATION AND TRANSMISSION CONTROL PROGRAM (CTCP)	HOST-RESIDENT USER APPLICATION PROGRAM THAT ESTABLISHES SNA SESSIONS WITH NPSI-RESIDENT GATE/DATE	3,2,1
8	NCP PACKET-SWITCHING INTERFACE (NPSI)	ACF/NCP REGION WITHIN MODEL 3705, 3275, 3720 COMMUNICATIONS CONTROLLERS THAT PROVIDES SNA PATH INFORMATION UNIT TRANSPORT THROUGH A PSDN	3,2,1
9	GENERAL ACCESS TO X.25 TRANSPORT EXTENSION (GATE)	NPSI REGION THAT ALLOWS A HOST-RESIDENT CTCP APPLICATION PROGRAM TO MONITOR PSDN VIRTUAL CIRCUITS (VCs) AND X.25 NON-SNA DATA TERMINAL EQUIPMENT (DTEs)	3,2,1
10	DEDICATED ACCESS TO X.25 TRANSPORT EXTENSION (DATE)	NPSI REGION THAT ALLOWS CTCP TO MANAGE PSDN VCs THAT ARE DEFINED TO SNA NODES THROUGH REMOTE NETWORK INTERFACE ADAPTERS (NIAs) AS WELL AS TO REMOTE X.25 NON-SNA DTEs	3,2,1
11	PROTOCOL CONVERTER FOR NON-SNA EQUIPMENT (PCNE)	NPSI REGION THAT PROVIDES LU 1 (3767) EMULATION TO HOST FROM REMOTE NON-SNA X.25 OR NON-SNA START/STOP DTEs	3,2,1
12	INTEGRATED PACKET ASSEMBLER/DISASSEMBLER (IPAD)	NPSI REGION THAT FUNCTIONS AS AN X.29 PAD AND SUPPORTS REMOTE PSDN-ATTACHED X.28 START-STOP DTEs TO SNA HOST	3,2,1
13	TRANSPARENT PACKET ASSEMBLER/DISASSEMBLER (TPAD)	NPSI REGION THAT ALLOWS A HOST APPLICATION TO CONTROL A REMOTE X.3 PSDN PAD ASSOCIATED WITH A NON-SNA DTE	3,2,1
14	X.25 SNA INTERCONNECT (XI)	TRANSPORTS X.25 DTE TRAFFIC THROUGH SNA NETWORKS	3,2,1
15	NETWORK INTERFACE ADAPTER (NIA)	MODEL 5973 HARDWARE FEATURE THAT ATTACHES TO THE FOLLOWING: ■ 4361 HOSTS, SYSTEM/36, SYSTEM/38, 8100 DEPARTMENTAL PROCESSORS THAT CONTAIN INTEGRATED COMMUNICATIONS ADAPTERS (LOCAL NIA); AND ■ MODEL 3174, 3274, AND 5294 CLUSTER CONTROLLERS (REMOTE NIA)	3,2,1
16	ENHANCED LOGICAL LINK CONTROL (ELLC)	ASYNCHRONOUS BALANCED MODE EXTENDED (ABME) MODULO-128 LAPB SUPPORT FROM MODEL 4361, 8100, SYSTEM/38, OR SYSTEM/36 ATTACHED TO PSDN THROUGH LOCAL NIAs (NIA-TO-NIA)	2
17	QUALIFIED LOGICAL LINK CONTROL (QLLC)	ASYNCHRONOUS BALANCED MODE (ABM) MODULO-8 LAPB SUPPORT FROM ANY LOCAL/REMOTE NIA TO NPSI THAT HAS BEEN PROVIDED SINCE NPSI RELEASE 3.1. NPSI DOES NOT SUPPORT MODULO-128.	2
18	INTEGRATED X.25 ADAPTER (REMOTE)	PROVIDES X.25 EMULATION TO A PSDN FROM SERIES/1, SYSTEM/88, AND 5251 MODEL 12 CLUSTER CONTROLLER	3,2,1
19	INTEGRATED X.25 ADAPTER (LOCAL)	PROVIDES X.25 PROTOCOL BETWEEN EITHER OF THE FOLLOWING ■ SYSTEM/38 AND SYSTEM/38; OR ■ SYSTEM/38 AND SYSTEM/36 WITH NO INTERVENING PSDN	3,2,1
20	SHORT HOLD MODE/MULTIPLE PORT SHARING (SHM/MPS)	HARDWARE FEATURE FOR MODEL 4361 HOST, SYSTEM/36, AND SERIES/1 THAT PROVIDES X.21 INTERCHANGE POINT	1

ACF = ADVANCED COMMUNICATIONS FUNCTION
API = APPLICATION PROGRAMMING INTERFACE
CICS = CUSTOMER INFORMATION CONTROL SYSTEM
DISOSS = DISTRIBUTED OFFICE SUPPORT SYSTEM
FTAM = FILE TRANSFER, ACCESS, AND MANAGEMENT
ISO = INTERNATIONAL ORGANIZATION FOR STANDARDIZATION
LAPB = LINK ACCESS PROCEDURE BALANCED
LU = LOGICAL UNIT

MAP = MANUFACTURING AUTOMATION PROTOCOL
MHS = MESSAGE-HANDLING SYSTEM
MSNF = MULTISYSTEM NETWORKING FACILITY
MVS = MULTIPLE VIRTUAL STORAGE
NCP = NETWORK CONTROL PROGRAM
NPSI = NCP PACKET-SWITCHING INTERFACE
OSI = OPEN SYSTEMS INTERCONNECTION
PAD = PACKET ASSEMBLER/DISASSEMBLER

SNA = SYSTEMS NETWORK ARCHITECTURE
SNADS = SNA DISTRIBUTION SERVICES
SP = SUPPORT PROGRAM
TSO = TIME-SHARING OPTION
VM = VIRTUAL MEMORY
VS = VIRTUAL STORAGE
VSE = VIRTUAL STORAGE EXTENDED
VTAM = VIRTUAL TELECOMMUNICATIONS ACCESS METHOD

service is defined within the MTS as a specific class of cooperating UAs. It provides MTA access to CCITT Telex and telematic services.

ISO has endorsed the CCITT X.400 MHS through elaboration and publication of the Message Oriented Text Interchange Systems (MOTIS) Draft International Standards 8505, 8883, and 9065 (see "For further reading"). In the SNA world, IBM's Document Interchange Architecture (DIA) and SNA Distribution Services (SNADS) model provide functionality similar to the X.400 MHS/MOTIS model (Fig. 3b). SNADS is an asynchronous, store-and-forward, generalized object-delivery service. The DIA specification defines the following distributed transaction processing services:

- Document Distribution Services;
- Document Library Services;
- Application Processing Services;
- File Transfer Services; and
- Session Services.

DIA users are referred to as DIA Source/Recipient Nodes (SRNs). SNADS users are called, cleverly enough, SNADS Users. The DIA/SNADS object distribution approach is functionally quite similar to the X.400 Message Handling System. The DIA and SNADs components of this approach are referred to as DIA Office System Nodes (OSNs) and SNADS Distribution Service Units (DSUs), respectively.

X.400 defines several Layers 7 and 6 protocols to provide message-handling services (Fig. 4a). Message Transfer Protocol, also called the P1 Protocol, defines the relaying of messages between Message Transfer Agent Entities (MTAEs). It also defines other interactions necessary to provide message-transfer sublayer services. The P1 Protocol is specified within CCITT Recommendation X.411 (see "For further reading").

The Interpersonal Messaging Protocol (P2) is a content-specific protocol; that is, it defines a standardized message content structure. It is used as a peer protocol between cooperating User Agent Entities (UAEs). The P2 Protocol, defined within CCITT Recommendation X.420, provides the following:

- Standardized syntax and semantics used to construct User Agent Protocol Data Units, which in turn comprise the contents of messages exchanged between IPM Service UAEs;
- Operations that an IPM UA must perform to exchange protocol elements; and
- IPM UA rules for use of the Message Transfer Layer (MTL) Service in providing the IPM Service.

The Submission and Delivery Protocol (P3) governs communication between the MTAE and the Submission and Delivery Entity (SDE), to provide MTL services that have been defined by the UAE. The P3 Protocol's objective is to enable UAs that are remote from their associated MTAs to obtain access to MTL Services. The P3 Protocol, defined within CCITT Recommendation X.411, invokes the Reliable Transfer Server, articulated within CCITT Recommendation X.410.

The IBM DIA/SNADS protocols provide services and functions quite similar to those provided by the P1, P2, and P3 MHS protocols (Fig. 4b). A Document Interchange Unit (DIU) data stream provides for DIA distributed transaction processing services (described above) between SRNs and

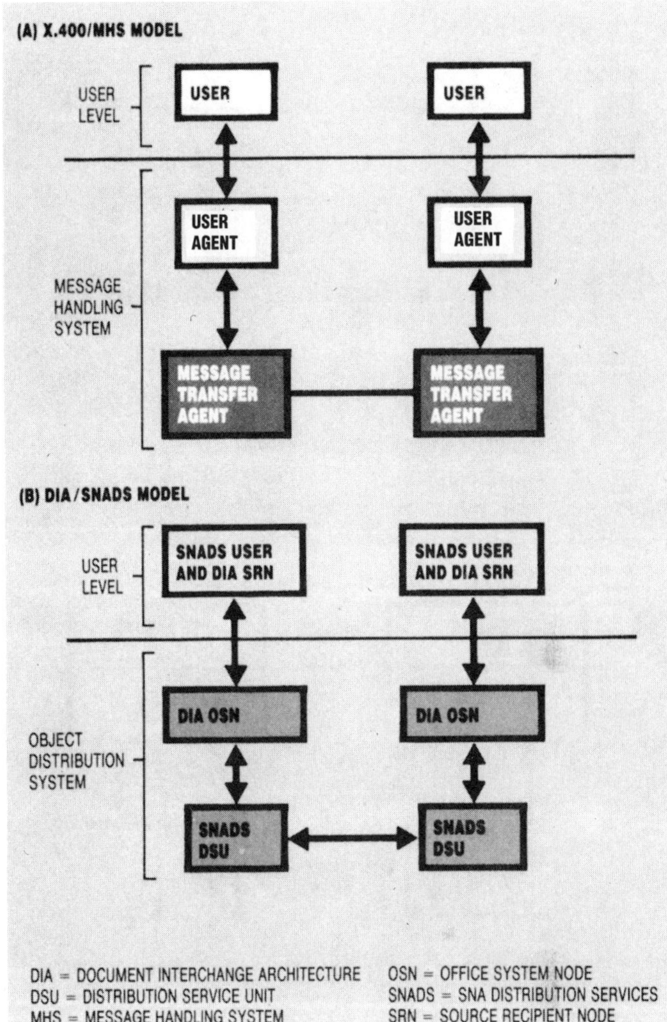

3. Functionally similar architectures. *Users of both X.400/MHS (a) and DIA/SNADS (b) invoke the services of agents that call upon a messaging substratum.*

OSNs. A SNADS Interchange Unit (IU), which can be either a SNADS Distribution Interchange Unit (which IBM also calls a DIU) or a SNADS Acknowledge Interchange Unit, defines a data stream to support remote Object Distribution services between DSUs on behalf of SNADS users. Revisable-form and final-form text document content architecture data streams define the content of the objects distributed by DIA and SNADS. These Distribution Objects, which include text files, documents, image streams, and binary data, are encapsulated within DIA Document Interchange Units and SNADS Interchange Units.

Linking the distribution architectures

Figure 4 depicts the X.400 MHS and DIA/SNADS functional models and indicates their architectural and protocol similarities. The protocol represented by each arrow in the X.400 diagram is functionally equivalent to the one represented by the corresponding arrow in the DIA/SNADS diagram.

IBM has noted the functional similarity of the X.400 and DIA/SNADS models and protocols. On March 3, 1987, in

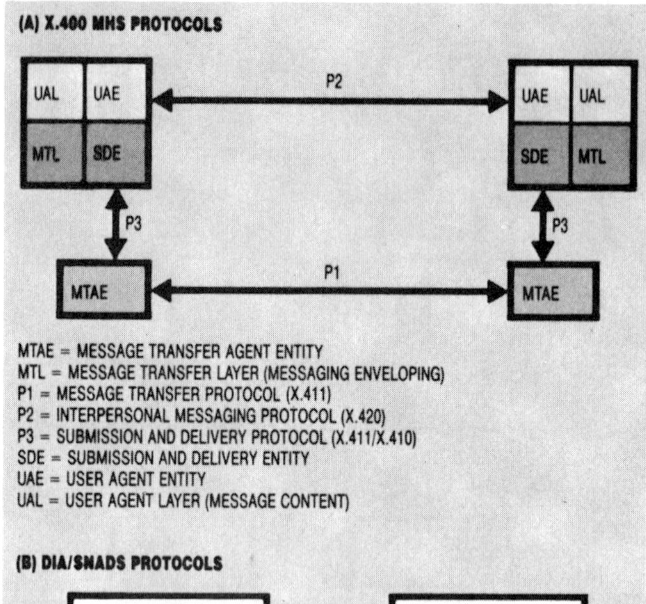

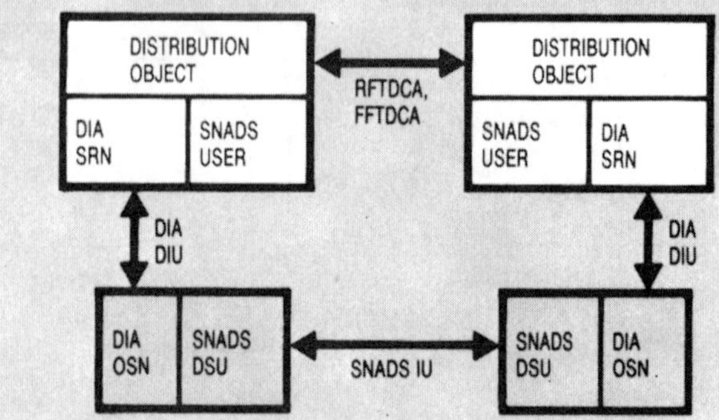

Paris, the company announced two program products that provide gateway functions between the two environments, namely, the X.400 Disoss Connection and the X.400 Message Transfer Facility. Figure 5 illustrates the relationships between these two IBM X.400 products.

■ X.400 Disoss Connection is a program product that transforms and relays messages between Disoss and the X.400 Message Transfer Facility program product. Disoss operates within a CICS/VS runtime environment; therefore, the X.400 Disoss Connection is a CICS transaction program.

■ The X.400 Message Transfer Facility program product is an Advanced Communications Function/Virtual Telecommunications Access Method (ACF/VTAM) application that generates an X.400 MTAE and utilizes the X.400 P1 and P3 protocols as envelopes to encapsulate P2 contents (see

Fig. 4 for the architectural reference).

Figure 5 also indicates that X.400 Message Transfer Facility supports the use of the P1, P2, and P3 protocols, which are OSI Layer 7 (Application Layer) and Layer 6 (Presentation Layer) protocols, over the following layers:

■ OSI Layer 5 (Session Layer) and Layer 4 (Transport Layer) protocols, through the IBM Open Systems Transport and Session Support (OSTSS) Release 2 program product, announced on March 3, 1987, and

■ OSI Layer 3 (Network Layer) protocols, through the IBM Open Systems Network Support (OSNS) Release 2 program product, announced on the same day.

This SNA/OSI communications environment is operated through the use of the IBM General Teleprocessing Monitor for Open Systems Interconnection (GTMOSI) program product, which orchestrates user application definitions into X.400 MHS through X.400 Message Transfer Facility via OSTSS and OSNS.

MAP support

During November 1980, GM formed the MAP Task Force as a vehicle to investigate and identify common communications standards for factory systems (which comprised programmable controllers, computers, networks, and other devices). GM had committed to factory automation. However, it had determined that appropriation requests for plant-floor systems allocated as much as 50 percent of total costs to networking.

These high network cost allocations were due to the fact that factories, like many user environments, employ programmable equipment from a wide range of manufacturers, each of which defines and implements its own set of proprietary and fundamentally incompatible architectures, protocols, and interfaces. The MAP Task Force was convened to address the resulting incoherence by establishing a uniform set of communications standards for use within GM and for adoption by other major users. The MAP architecture that grew from these efforts is based upon the OSI protocols.

Realizing MAP's importance to the factory market, IBM sought to offer compatibility. On November 5, 1985, it announced the Series/1 Real-time Programming System (RPS) MAP Communications Server (MCS) and the Series/1 Event Driven Executive (EDX) MAP Application Server (MAS) to provide a communications and application gateway between SNA and certain MAP applications (Fig. 6). The MCS supports connections between open systems through a network interface unit attached to an IEEE-802.4 LAN and through the RPS X.25/High-level Data Link Control (HDLC) Communications Support (XHCS) program.

The Communications Server supports MAP network user access to files and applications residing on a System/370 43XX or 30XX host through File Transfer, Access, and Management (FTAM), which is defined in a series of ISO specifications published as ISO/DIS 8571 (see "For further reading"). It also supports directory services, which provide users with network applications information. FTAM is a Series/1 RPS Programming Request for Price Quotation (PRPQ). The FTAM PRPQ supports ISO/DIS 8571/1 through 8571/4.

These ISO/DIS FTAM specifications are concerned with the manipulation of identifiable bodies of information that

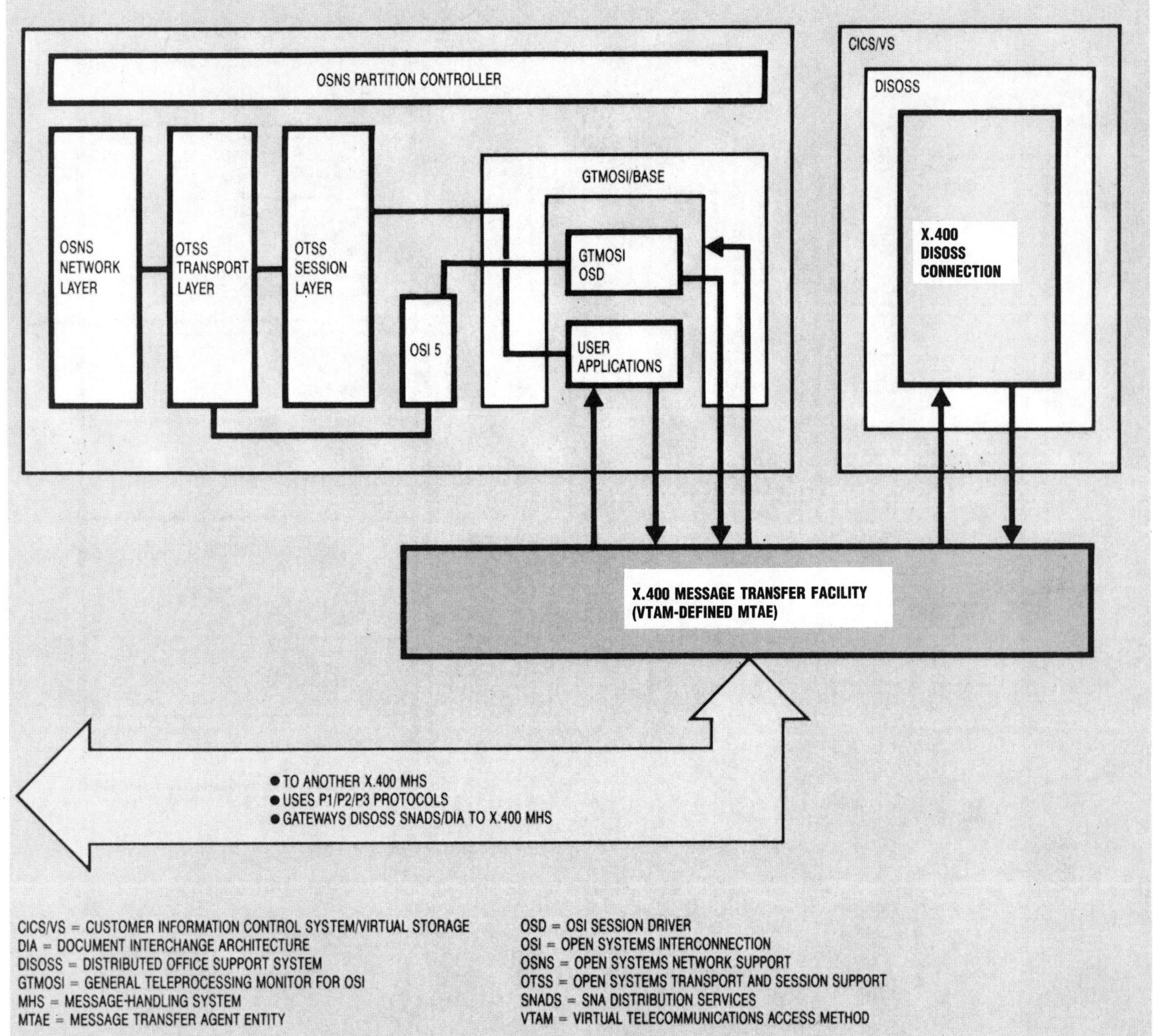

can be treated as files and stored within open systems or passed between application processes (OSI user processes). FTAM, therefore, defines a basic file service, which provides facilities for file access, transfer, and management. ISO/DIS 8571 does not, however, specify the local (intravendor) interfaces to file-access or transfer mechanisms.

The FTAM file service definitions and protocol specifications are file-expressed in the context of a virtual filestore (a file-mapping structure commonly referred to by open systems), as distinguished from any real, local filestore definitions that exist within real, heterogeneous systems. Within this context, each real end system that behaves as an open system assumes responsibility to map the virtual filestore descriptions and operations into real, local file management functions.

ISO/DIS 8571 also specifies a file access structure, which consists of an abstract syntax of hierarchical structures, including the simple cases of flat and unstructured files. The file access structure is essentially a hierarchical, ordered tree, which consists of an ordered set of File Access Data Units. These may be related in sequential, hierarchical, network, or relational fashion.

The Series/1 EDX MAP Application Server uses the RPS MCS to transmit messages between programs residing within an Application Server (Series/1) Node. Like the MCS, MAS provides connections between open systems through a network interface unit attached to an IEEE-802.4 token-passing bus LAN. The MAS uses the XHCS program to access the network interface unit.

The EDX MAP Application Server also codes and decodes Manufacturing Message Format Standard (MMFS)

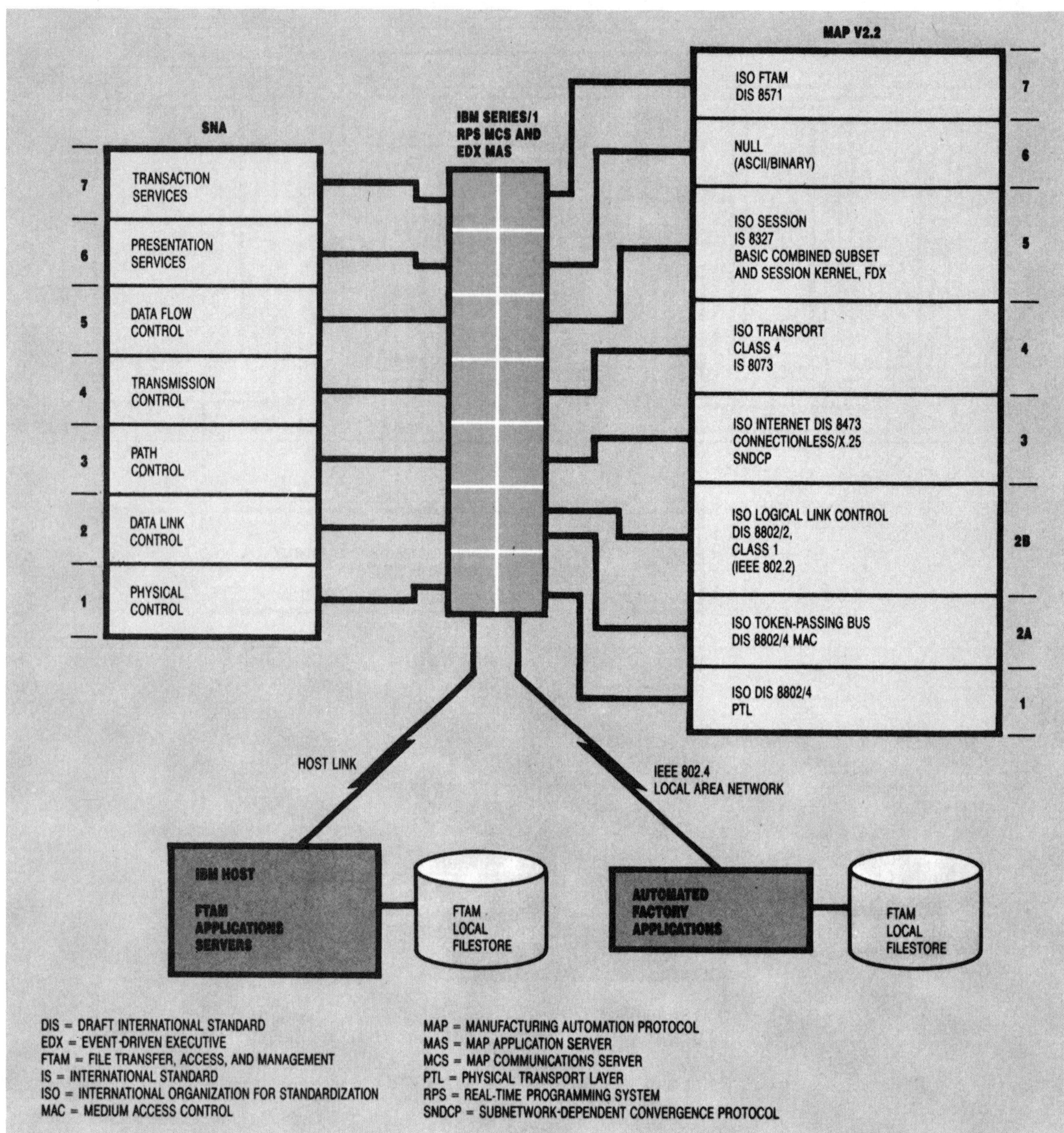

6. For factories. *The Series/1 Real-time Programming System MAP Communications Server and Event Driven Executive MAP Application Server link SNA with a subset of the map protocol suite via protocol gateway capabilities. Here, MAP's Layer 7 is File Transfer, Access, and Management; Layers 5 through 1 are OSI protocols.*

messages. These MMFS formats are used to address the bidirectional transfer of digitally encoded manufacturing information. In so doing, the MAP Application Server provides MMFS application- and presentation-layer protocols, which enable communications between the following:

■ Programmable controllers;
■ Numerical controllers;
■ Robotic controllers;
■ Specialized systems, including vision systems, probe systems, and welding controllers; and
■ Data terminal equipment, including hosts, minicomputers, and workstations.

GTMOSI

The General Teleprocessing Monitor for Open Systems Interconnection (GTMOSI) is an ACF/VTAM-resident teleprocessing monitor that runs within a Multiple Virtual Storage (MVS) address space. Its objective is to provide

7. GTMOSI. *IBM's General Teleprocessing Monitor for Open Systems Interconnection provides a communications basis for dissimilar operating environments. It can run either in isolation or in conjunction with other IBM-to-OSI products. It can also work with a variety of host packages, such as CICS, IMS, TSO, and MSNF.*

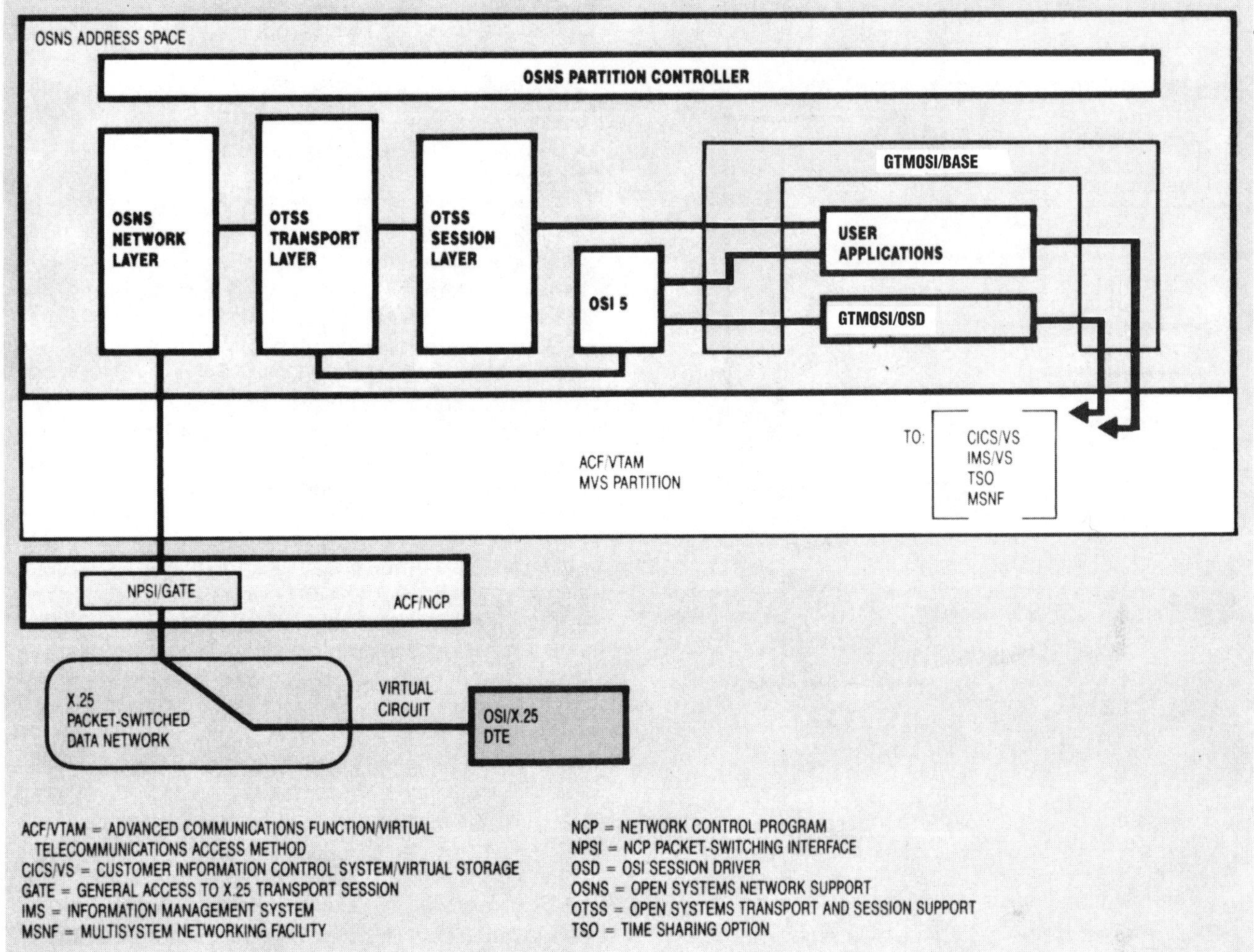

communications between dissimilar processing environments. GTMOSI heterogeneous connections are defined as connections between terminals (and/or hosts) and IBM host-resident applications. X.25-recommended physical-, frame-, and packet-level protocols are selected for Layers 1 through 3, and other non-SNA protocols are selected for Layers 4 through 7. GTMOSI interconnects terminals and applications via any of the following:

- ACF/Network Control Program (NCP) Packet Switching Interface (NPSI) and ACF/VTAM;
- Open Systems Transport And Session Support (OSTSS);
- Open Systems Network Support (OSNS);
- VTAM Application Program Interface (API);
- CICS/VS;
- Information Management System/Virtual Storage (IMS/VS);
- Time Sharing Option (TSO); and
- Cross-domain SNA through Multisystem Networking Facility (MSNF).

Figure 7 illustrates the GTMOSI operating environment. Note that the GTMOSI/Base runs within an MVS partition under ACF/VTAM, either in isolation or in conjunction with OSTSS/OSNS if OSI session-level connections are re-

quired. The OSNS Partition Controller is the OSNS address-space manager for GTMOSI/Base, OSI 5 (OSI session-level service), OSTSS, and OSNS.

GTMOSI uses the ACF/VTAM interface to connect to other environments, such as CICS/VS, IMS/VS, TSO, or MSNF. It also uses either ACF/VTAM or OSTSS to connect to the network. OSTSS, in turn, uses the OSI network level interface provided by OSNS (which itself uses the ACF/VTAM interface to NPSI).

OSTSS and OSNS
As shown, the GTMOSI OSI Session Driver (GTMOSI/OSD) component propogates OSI 5 primitives to VTAM and CICS/VS through macros that structure the GTMOSI/OSD API. There is also a GTMOSI/General Access To X.25 Transport Extension (GATE)-Fast Connect component, which provides a host operating environment for Communication and Transmission Control Program (CTCP) to support ACF/NCP-resident NPSI GATE and Fast Connect options through a packet-switched data network (PSDN) virtual circuit to non-SNA X.25 or OSI Data Terminal Equipment (DTE).

Open Systems Transport and Session Support (OSTSS)

8. OSTSS. *Open Systems Transport and Session Support provides an interface from SNA applications into OSI Class 0 and Class 2 Transport and Session Protocol functions.*

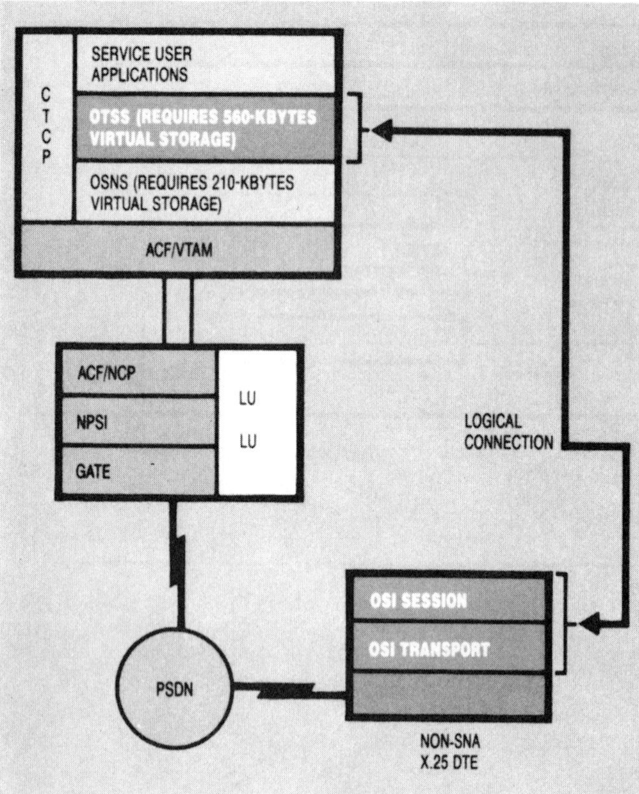

provides an interface from IBM environments into OSI Layer 4 (Transport) and Layer 5 (Session) functions. It can be used as the OSI Layers 4 and 5 basis from which to construct applications (such as those based upon X.400 and FTAM).

OSTSS is a host-resident CTCP application program that resides within the same address space as Open Systems Network Support (OSNS). Therefore, as shown (Fig. 8), application data that is passed through OSTSS is in turn sent to OSNS and on to NPSI (within ACF/NCP), which in turn communicates it to a PSDN. Also note in the figure that OSTSS communicates peer-to-peer with OSI Session and Transport Layers shown within the remotely attached non-SNA X.25 DTE.

OSTSS supports the OSI Transport Layer (Layer 4) in the following modes:
- Class 0 Transport, which provides transport connection establishment/release, normal data exchange with and without Transport Protocol Data Unit (TPDU) segmentation and reassembly, and protocol-error recognition; and
- Class 2, which provides, in addition to all Class 0 functions, such features as TPDU concatenation, separation, network-expedited data transfer, multiplexing, demultiplexing, and explicit flow control.

OSTSS also supports the following modes and features of the OSI Session Layer (Layer 5):
- Session Kernel, which provides session-connection establishment/release and normal data transfer;
- Half-duplex;
- Typed data;

- Major synchronize and resynchronize (in the absence of Transport Expedited Service);
- Minor synchronize; and
- Exceptions.

OSTSS does not, however, support the following elements of the OSI Session Layer:
- Full-duplex;
- Expedited data;
- Activity management;
- Capability data exchange; and
- Negotiated release.

On March 3, 1987, IBM Paris announced OSTSS Release 2. Like OSTSS Release 1, Release 2 supports MVS/Support Program Version 1 or 2. However, it also supports the Virtual Storage Extended (VSE) and Virtual Machine (VM) operating systems.

Open Systems Network Support operates within the host-resident CTCP and provides, in concert with NPSI, a means to connect IBM hosts to other IBM hosts or to non-IBM hosts through an X.25 PSDN. OSNS invokes the services of the NPSI GATE facility within an NPSI-resident communications controller. OSNS manages all virtual circuits (characterized as Type 4) that run through NPSI over single or multiple physical circuits through PSDNs. OSNS runs within a single address space, or partition, and is initialized and terminated through an internal host CTCP-management function called Partition Control.

In the parlance of OSI, OSNS provides Network-Layer Service Primitives to the Transport Layer (Layer 4). IBM defines an API at the interface between Layers 3 and 4, across which these primitives are delivered. On March 3, 1987, IBM announced OSNS Release 2, which, in addition to the Release 1 support of MVS and VSE, also runs within a VM operating system.

Figure 9 provides an OSNS architectural view. Note that OSNS defines SNA connections into Path Control (SNA Layer 3) and a Primary Half-Session within the host. The Secondary Half-Session is defined within the NPSI GATE facility. A non-SNA X.25 DTE, connected to NPSI through a PSDN virtual circuit managed by GATE, is defined into OSNS through DTE-to-DTE (end-to-end) addressing and the X.25 Packet-Level Protocol.

Figure 10 indicates the placement of OSNS within an MVS host, as part of CTCP. SNA LU-to-LU sessions are defined from OSNS to GATE. GATE, in turn, controls an NPSI virtual circuit through a packet-switched data network to a non-SNA X.DTE.

While OSNS implements a Layer 3 interconnection, it is by no means SNA's only link to the lower three layers of OSI, as shown in Table 3. The next article in this two-part series will cover the extensive remainder of IBM's techniques and offerings for marrying SNA with X.25 and its related protocols. ■

Thomas J. Routt is president of Network Systems Consulting, a firm that provides worldwide network architecture consulting to Fortune 1000 corporations concerned with migration to SNA and/or OSI. Previously, Routt was manager of Boeing Network Architecture for Boeing Computer Services Co. In this capacity, he managed global network planning, design, and implementation for The Boeing Company. Routt holds an M.B.A. degree in information

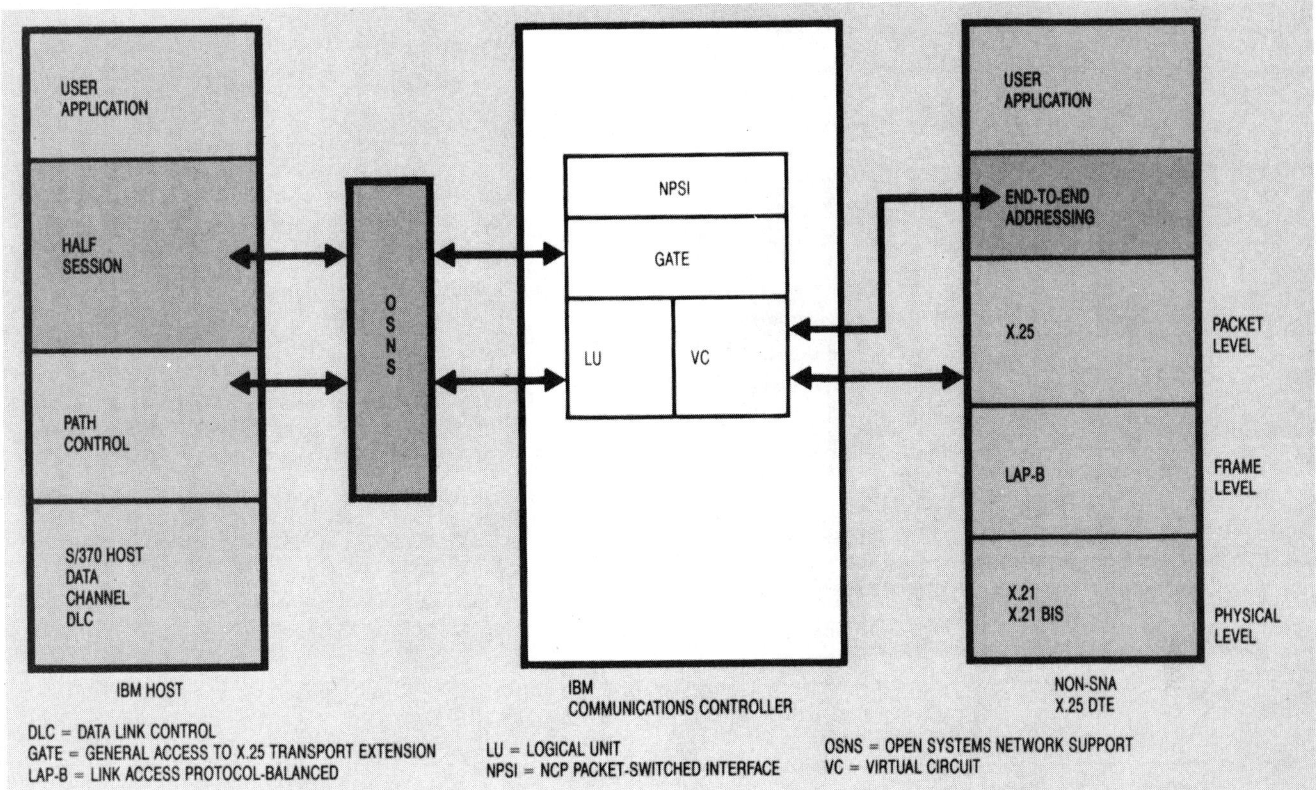

systems (Beta Gamma Sigma) from Southern Illinois University and a B.S. degree in environmental science (Honors) from Western Washington University.

For further reading

Aschenbrenner, J. R., "Open Systems Interconnection," *IBM Systems Journal,* Vol. 25, Nos. 3/4, 1986, pp. 369-379.(IBM OSI Position Paper).

CCITT Recommendations:

X.410: *Message Handling Systems: Remote Operations and Reliable Transfer Service.*

X.411: *Message Handling Systems: Message Transfer Layer.*

X.420: *Message Handling Systems: Interpersonal Messaging User Agent Layer.*

Francois, P. and A. Potocki, "Some Methods for Providing OSI Transport in SNA," *IBM Journal of Research and Development,* Vol. 27, No. 5, September 1983, pp. 452-463.

IBM Documents, Order No.:

GB11-8201-0: *General Teleprocessing Monitor for Open Systems Interconnection General Information Manual,* First Edition, September 1986.

GH12-5450-0: *Open Systems Transport and Session Support General Information,* First Edition, September 1985.

GH12-5145-2: *Open Systems Network Support General Information,* Third Edition, May 1985.

GG22-9225: *OSI and SNA: A Perspective, Installation and Migration (Paper).*

GL23-0146-0: *Introducing Real-Time Programming System Manufacturing Automation Protocol Communications Server, Event Driven Executive Manufacturing Automation Protocol Application Server,* First Edition, November 1985.

IBM Europe, "IBM and OSI: An Interconnected Future, "IBM Europe, Tour Pascal, 22 Route de la Demi Lune, 92075, Paris, France.

International Organization for Standardization/International Standards (ISO, 1 Rue de Varembe, Geneva, Switzerland):

7498: *Information Processing Systems—Open Systems Interconnection—basic reference model.*

8327: *OSI Layer 5: Session Protocol.*

8073: *OSI Layer 4: Transport Protocol Class 4. ISO/Draft International Standards:*

8473: *OSI Layer 3: Internet Subnetwork Dependent Convergence Protocol.*

8802/2: *OSI Layer 2B: Class 1 Connectionless Logical Link Control* (same as IEEE-802.2).

8802/4: *OSI Layer 2A: Token-Passing Bus Medium Access Control* (same as IEEE-802.4).

8802/4: *OSI Layer 1: Token-Passing Bus Physical Transport Layer, Broadband* (same as IEEE 802.4).

8505: *Information Processing—Text Communication— Functional Description and Service Specification for Message Oriented Text Interchange Systems (MOTIS).*

8883: *MOTIS Message Transfer Sublayer, Message Inter-*

*10. **OSNS itself.** IBM's Open Systems Network Support, a host-resident application, mediates between SNA Half-Sessions and X.25 Layers 1 through 3 environments.*

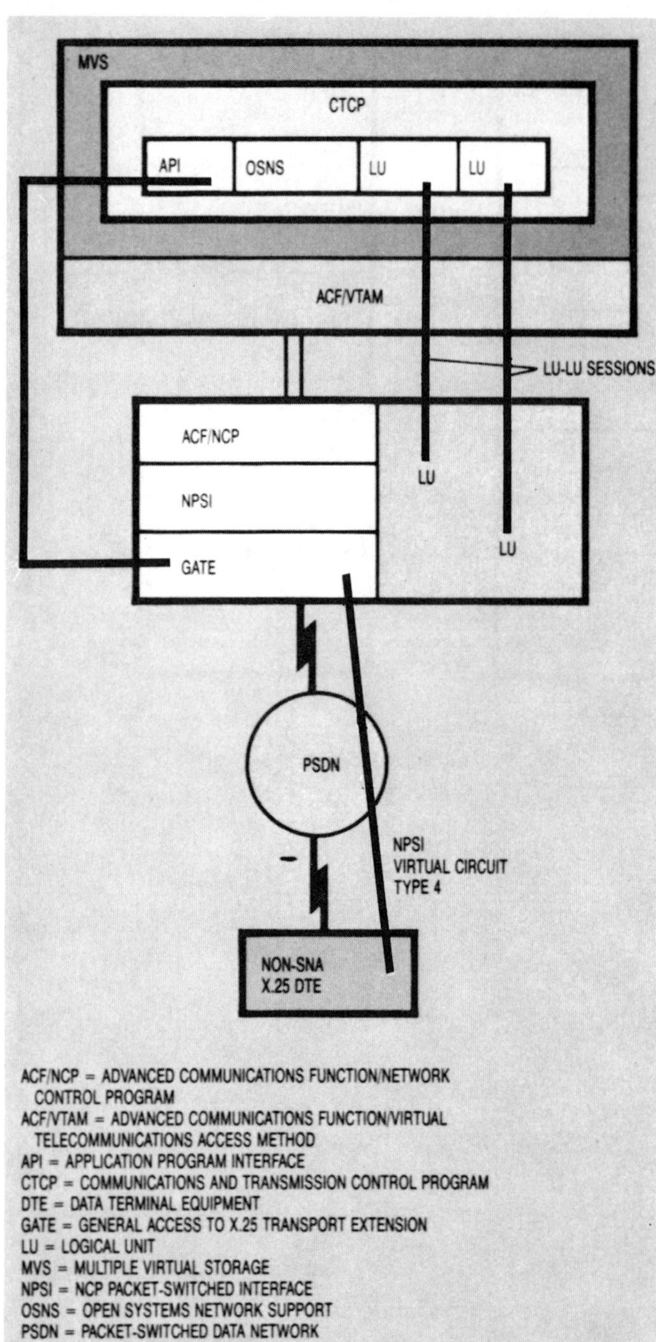

change Service And Message Transfer Protocol.
9065: MOTIS User Agent Sublayer—Interpersonal Messaging User Agent—Message Interchange Formats And Protocols.
8571/X: Information Processing Systems—Open Systems Interconnection—File Transfer, Access, and Management (FTAM), as follows:
8571/1 (Part 1): General Introduction.
8571/2 (Part 2): The Virtual Filestore Definition.
8571/3 (Part 3): The File Service Definition.
8571/3 (Part 4): The File Protocol Specification.

Network trauma: Making ends meet when two firms merge

Can network managers continue to cope with America's corporate craze? Here is how a few survived.

When Wall Street's investment bankers give the nod to a CEO to acquire or merge with another company, chances are no one calls in the network manager to approve the deal. Perhaps they should, considering the importance of communications in corporate America. Indeed, the fallout from such lofty activities as mergers and acquisitions often creates an unwanted maze of complex networking problems.

Inevitably, these high-stakes mergers often mean late nights for the network manager, who must unravel knotty network integration problems—problems that CEOs often want solved yesterday (see "I heard it through the grapevine"). Billion dollar deals are made high up in an organization, says Jack W. Fetzer, Lockheed Corp.'s director of telecommunications. "If they do decide to do it, the decision won't be based on the number of communications lines you are going to get or the color of their computers," he says.

Between 1983 and 1986 the number of corporations involved in acquisitions or mergers doubled, while the cost of these deals quadrupled. So far this year it's been more of the same: The value of such activity could climb as high as $225 billion by year's end (see "Market Activity"). And there is no respite in sight. The economic forces that spawned merger mania are expected to be as strong as ever. The new financier—the corporate raider—and new types of debt financing are entrenched on Wall Street. The Reagan Administration shows no signs of abandoning its laissez-faire philosophy or raising antitrust barriers. And the present low interest rates are keeping the cost of borrowing capital low enough to initiate takeover bids.

The chances that network consolidation will be required are great when the merging companies are in the same business. A CEO will often perceive integrating computer and communications facilities as an obvious cost-saving measure that can be quickly accomplished in these cases.

Just how that integration is achieved depends on the compatibility between the computers in the merging networks—and the ingenuity of the network manager (see "Five tips to survive the deluge").

Managers like Fetzer, who have been through the merger mill, agree that sometimes substantial network integration is inappropriate. For example, when Lockheed Corp., the aerospace giant, acquired electronics manufacturer Sanders Associates Inc. last spring for about $1.2 billion, Lockheed decided not to try to merge the Sanders computing facilities into the parent network. "We've tied Sanders into our System Network Architecture network to take advantage of PROFS, but we have not tied them too closely," says Fetzer. PROFS, the Professional Office System developed by IBM, is a software package that provides general office automation functions and is used by Sanders to transmit financial data.

No attempt is being made to integrate the core business of the two companies: the engineering function. Lockheed will keep on manufacturing aircraft and Sanders will stick to producing electronic gear.

"There is no connection to our CAD/CAM network," Fetzer says, referring to the sophisticated computer-assisted design/computer-assisted manufacturing network pioneered at Lockheed. "We can ship engineering jobs across the network using SDLC [synchronous data link control] protocols, but except in very rare occasions, we don't use common files," he says.

When merger partners share a common business, however, integrating computer and communications facilities is more problematic. If you are as lucky as Jerry Vallone, manager of telecommunications for United Jersey Bank (Hackensack, N. J.), you will find application-level compatibility and enough excess capacity on your host computers to carry the new loads. This year United Jersey has been aggressively acquiring smaller banks.

I heard it through the grapevine

The first inklings may come from the business page of the morning newspaper or through the office grapevine, but once word of a merger hits the network control center, things happen quickly.

Walter Pemberton, vice president of communications and computer services at Northwest Airlines, says he first got word that the Minneapolis-based carrier was acquiring Republic Airlines in early January 1986. By May, he and his staff had developed the plan to merge the two large, incompatible, airline reservation networks. And by October the job was done.

When forest product giant Champion International acquired its competitor, St. Regis, "we heard about it through the rumor mill, the same as everyone else," says Paul Inderhees, a network consultant at Champion's headquarters in Hamilton, Ohio.

The deal to acquire St. Regis—the target of several previous takeover bids—was cut in July 1984 during a secret weekend meeting between the companies' two CEOs and was formally approved by the boards in late August.

A network consolidation plan was offered to management the following June and the "cloning of a data center from Dallas, Texas, to Hamilton, Ohio," was completed in October, says Gary Crawford, director of systems development at Champion. Crawford insisted on a team approach to plan and document the myriad details needed to execute the three-part integration plan. The plan consisted of two test phases and an implementation phase.

"Everyone in MIS was frightened about how to merge the two data centers," Crawford says. It was perceived to be "a difficult and time-consuming chore. For five months we were totally committed to the merger and some other efforts suffered, but it was sucessful," he says proudly.

"At UJB it's been simple. All the banks we've been taking over have been IBM shops," says Vallone. The merger of recently acquired Commercial Bancshares Inc. and the Franklin Bancorp into the UJB network, for instance, was almost painless.

"At Franklin we found 3705 front-ends connected to a mid-range mainframe. Connecting their system to our mainframes was no great engineering feat," Vallone remarks. "We just moved their front-ends off their mainframe and linked them via dedicated lines to ours."

When UJB merged the resources of its two new acquisitions onto the corporate mainframe, it had an effect on the bottom line. "Their host is going away. That saves money. Just compare the lease of a computer against the lease of a 56-kbit/s line," Vallone says. The savings could be as high as tens of thousands of dollars a month.

Merge or shut down

Sometimes, though, compatible businesses and hardware may not be enough. Enter ingenuity—often the key to making a network merge work. Witness Champion International Corp., which acquired St. Regis Inc. in 1984, making Champion one of the top five forest products companies in the country.

Champion and St. Regis ostensibly had an ideal networking situation. Both companies coincidentally were built around IBM 3033 and 3081 mainframes, and both had applications that supported the forest products industry. But appearances can be deceiving.

The St. Regis data center, located in Dallas, was the nerve center of an extensive network. The network handled 300,000 transactions daily in support of accounting, order entry, payroll, and other general business functions for the company's widely distributed manufacturing plants. About 100 manufacturing operations were spread across the country, so dedicated leased lines were needed to keep approximately 1,000 terminals in touch with the Dallas host computers. By comparison, the Champion network was small. Champion had only about 50 to 75 remote terminals. Communications to the Hamilton, Ohio, data center from remote sites used dial-up facilities.

The St. Regis applications were expected to disappear eventually as Champion folded the new business into its own operations. In the meantime, the problem facing Gary Crawford, Champion's Director of Systems Development, was whether to merge or to close the St. Regis center, and how to do it. As Crawford was finding his way around the

Lines of luck. *Gary Crawford, Champion International Corp., used telecomm lines already installed at a backup site to switch operations to a new corporate home.*

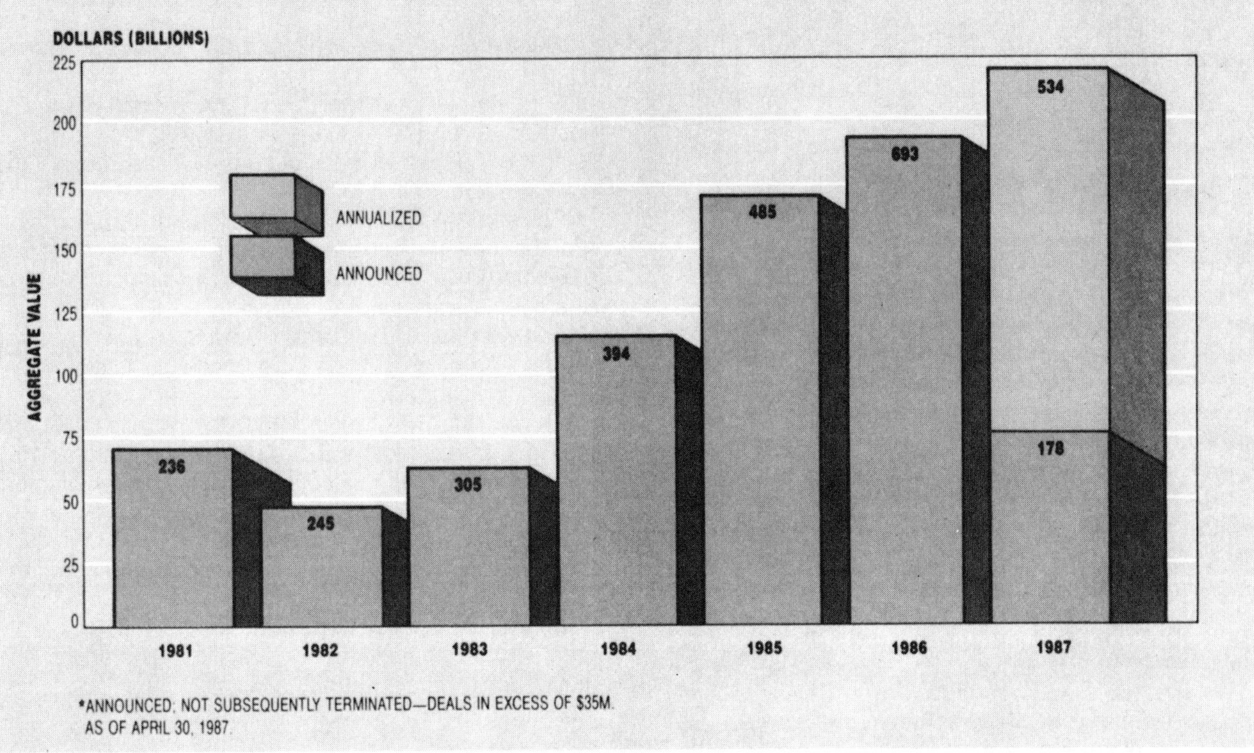

Five tips to survive the deluge

What does it take to survive the stress of merger? A big dose of adaptability can help. That was the consensus among dozens of network managers and planners interviewed for this report. Here are some tips they give that may help you survive a merger:

■ **Don't panic.** No matter how difficult the job initially seems, there is a way to whip it into shape.

■ **Start putting together a plan.** Almost all of the networking professionals interviewed agreed that it is impossible to pin down all the variables in a situation as fluid as a merger. What is important to realize is that even a sketchy plan is better than no plan whatsoever.

■ **Inventory your resources.** Even as the plan is being developed start gathering data on hosts, terminals, communications lines, and usage. The database will change, but trying to hit a moving target is better than having no target at all.

■ **Aim for perfection, but be satisfied with results.** The most elegant network integration solution may not be possible under tight time constraints. Do the best job you can with the time you have. Be satisfied with the results.

■ **Test, test, and test again.** Begin testing the merged networks as soon as possible. Don't look for reasons to wait for one or two weekends before cutover to get started.

■ **Encourage your personnel.** The long hours and the demands on key workers can lead to morale problems if they are not addressed. Keep 'em happy.

Dallas data center, corporate executives started selling off parts of St. Regis. The restructured company would have no use for two data centers.

The question Crawford finally grappled with was how to move the St. Regis applications to Hamilton. Crawford got a break when he discovered an extensive backup and emergency recovery system St. Regis had installed at a different site. St. Regis had outfitted the backup center with operating systems and applications tapes, backups, and—most importantly—valuable leased lines.

"The shell location had a duplicate set of lines," Crawford says. "From a line point of view, we simply flipped the operation from Dallas to Hamilton."

Since St. Regis and Champion had identical computers, Crawford made the decision to re-create the St. Regis environment in Ohio instead of at the recovery center. "We both had 3081s at the time. We took our backup computer and created the Dallas environment in Hamilton. We flew up the Dallas recovery tapes and mounted them as if Hamilton was the recovery site. We picked up the recovery files and installed them using the recovery plan developed by St. Regis," Crawford recounted.

On three separate weekends in the fall of 1985, Crawford re-created the Dallas applications environment in the Ohio shop. Each weekend, he says, "we had 15 to 20 users at remote sites come in on Saturdays to run the new setup." Finally, one weekend about four months after the experiment began, the Dallas operation was completely cut over to Hamilton.

"It was fortuitous we had the same hardware," Crawford says. "If we hadn't, we would have had to convert applications one at a time. It might have taken two years and cost

Airline ace. *Walter Pemberton, Northwest Airlines, merged Republic's IBM-based network with Northwest's Sperry-based network in just four months.*

$9 million a year." Crawford admits he was lucky. He found computer compatibility and his management gave him enough time to make a studied response to merging the two networks.

Will it pass the 'intelligence test?'

Walter Pemberton, vice president of communications and computer services, Northwest Airlines, Minneapolis, Minn., was hardly as fortunate as his counterpart at Champion. When Northwest announced the takeover of Republic Airlines in January 1986, Pemberton inherited two extensive, incompatible networks (see figure). What's more, Northwest's management was betting that if it could quickly consolidate its operations, it could stay competitive, so management pushed Pemberton hard to merge the networks. He had four months to get the job done.

The two network control centers were situated across the tarmac from one another at the Minneapolis-St. Paul International Airport. On the Republic side, Pemberton found an IBM shop with mainframes channel-attached to 3705 and 3725 controllers. The 3705s were linked to a mix of terminal types in reservation offices around the country, using Airline Link Control (ALC) protocols—a proprietary IBM transaction-processing facility. The 3725 controllers communicated via SNA protocols to the Republic field stations at airports.

The Northwest network is built around two Sperry 1184 computers and an 1194 computer. Communications between the Sperry mainframes is handled via a 50-Mbit/s fiber optic Hyperchannel local area network. Remote concentrators multiplex data from reservations and field stations to the 1184s. The communications protocols used throughout the network conform to the P1024 protocols sanctioned by the Societe International Telecommunication Aeronautique, a not-for-profit worldwide airline communications network.

Here is how Pemberton merged the networks in time. Under deadline pressure, Pemberton says, "it was impractical to standardize on either IBM or Sperry." He opted instead for a quick fix that essentially left two networks in place, but provided protocol translation between them at the host level.

To secure a physical connection as quickly as possible, Pemberton approved the installation of nearly three dozen 9.6-kbit/s telephone lines to link the two data centers. Later the copper lines were augmented by a fiber optic link, as the network loading increased. But the real challenge was to get the mix of IBM terminals to communicate with the Sperry mainframes.

The quickest way to link the IBM terminals to the Sperry network was to load the IBM host with the standard P1024 protocols. The protocol translation bridging requirement between the SNA and ALC communications protocols and the P1024 was handled by the IBM processor.

Once the merged networks were tested, Pemberton discovered that some of the terminal definition input on the IBM side of the network performed differently than expected when it reached the Sperry host. A transaction translation program was devised that reformatted the code coming from the IBM side into Sperry code.

Architectural arbitrator. *Bard Haerland is merging the best of the Burroughs-Sperry network and communications products into the newly created Unysis Corp. network.*

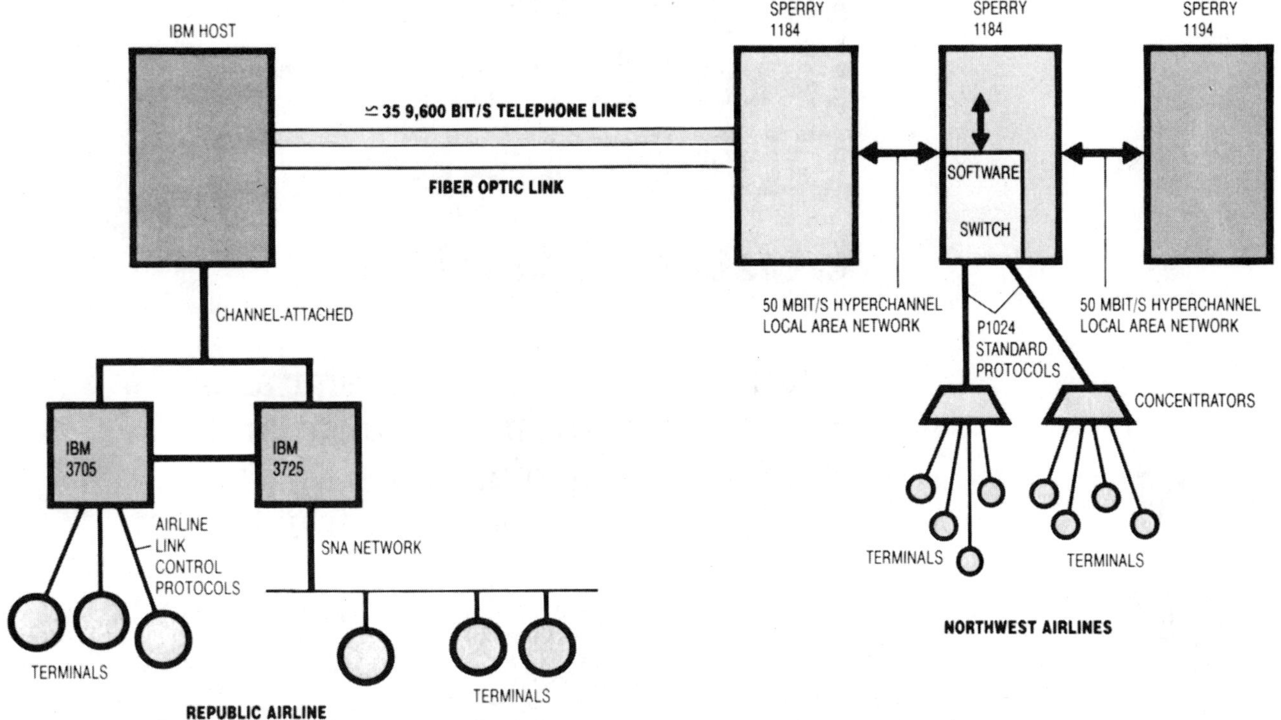

Across the tarmac. *Merging two incompatible airline networks under tough deadline pressures took nearly three dozen 9.6-kbit/s telephone lines. Once the physical link was in place, the quickest way to put the IBM terminals in communication with the Sperry network was to load the IBM host with the standardized airline communications protocols.*

"I think the situation we faced was unique. And the solution we came up with wouldn't stand the test of intelligence," says Pemberton. "But it did allow us to merge the two systems in a very short time."

Although Pemberton inherited two networks with incompatible hardware, he managed to make them interoperable by using standardized airline industry communications protocols. The computer industry is aware of the problems incompatibility creates and for years it has been paying lip service to standardization. But despite its best efforts communications transparency is still elusive.

Dissecting the product portfolio

The incompatibility gap, which is still a chronic industry problem, became a gaping abyss to two giants of the computer industry—Burroughs Corp. and Sperry Corp.—when they merged to form Unisys last year. One of the new company's biggest problems was standardizing its communications architecture.

Bluebell, Pa.-based Unisys started life with two voice networks with different internal structures. It also had a continually changing backbone environment—and, as Bard Haerland, Unisys vice president of worldwide telecommunications, puts it, "two data networks that can only communicate by looking like something else."

Almost as soon as the merger was announced, internal users, as well as the company's customers, were keeping a close watch for signs of networking direction. In truth, both the new company's internal network architecture as well as its commercial data communications philosophy were still on the drawing board. On the positive side, the two partners shared some working assumptions that made the network integration job easier. "This is not a traditional merger," Haerland says. "Usually you have a clear winner and loser. What we did at Unisys is really sit down with and decide what is best technically and in terms of personnel," he explains.

A task force, consisting of communications managers from the Unisys functional organizations such as marketing and manufacturing, dissected the Burroughs-Sperry product portfolio, searching for communications facilities that could best support network applications. The products they found mirrored the two very different approaches taken by the merger partners. Burroughs, with its mainframe bias, emphasized dedicated access.

"The Burroughs approach was that a terminal could always find an application on the mainframe," Haerland says. "Sperry always said we could get you to an application."

BUDS, the Burroughs Unified Data Network, was built around time-division and statistical multiplexing—so it was architecturally out of sync with Sperry's packet-switching approach.

The committee favored the Sperry architecture, Haerland says, because Burroughs lacked a communications processor. "They didn't have a dedicated communications processor. Without one in the the product portfolio we had some clear choices."

Unisys is now making the transition to a packet-switching network throughout the company, but merging 100,000 users into a worldwide network takes time—time that contributes to the hidden costs of acquisition. ■

Michael W. Cerruti and Maurice Voce, Intel Corp., Phoenix, Ariz.

Zap data where it really counts— Direct-to-host connections

Attaching directly to a mainframe channel, bypassing the front-end, can pay off for high-speed links to LANs, or to other mainframes.

Connectivity used to mean mainly the interconnection of terminals and host processors. Now, of course, it has evolved into a much grander issue, encompassing not only terminal applications, but also the need to connect diverse islands of automation—consisting of microcomputers, minicomputers, and mainframes, plus various network topologies and a wide range of peripherals.

For increasing numbers of users, a key component of this broad connectivity challenge is making a connection to a mainframe, such as an IBM System/370. The host connection not only opens extensive databases to authorized users, but also provides access to the programs resident in the mainframe. Host access also lets users exploit the mainframe's considerable processing power for performing data-intensive tasks.

In addition, a mainframe connection allows multiple network workstations to simultaneously run the same complex application program resident on a mainframe, and to accomplish tasks cooperatively with it.

For example, to make reservations and seat assignments for individual airline flights, travel agents can use workstations in their offices in cooperation with a remote airline mainframe. After logging onto the network, the agent identifies the customer's flight number, then sends the necessary data to the remote mainframe for processing (Fig. 1).

The mainframe in turn provides information to the agent regarding the type of craft involved and kinds of seats available. Based on that information, the agent can readily book reservations, enter and check locally maintained accounting data, and then return the selection information to the central mainframe where it can be stored and then retrieved by the airline for its use.

This type of cooperative interaction, here between an airline mainframe and processors at travel agencies, is becoming increasingly common. Among the benefits offered, one is to relieve the central mainframe of performing the entire processing task itself—and thus avoid becoming overloaded—while travel agents can be provided with locally maintained data required to run their business. Further, with this cooperative interaction, the various workstations share in accomplishing work efficiently—usually within a more reasonable time frame than is possible if the mainframe did the entire job.

Connectivity crisis

Whatever the application, the need to boost organizational productivity by pooling resources and distributing information effectively between users and the mainframe is becoming an important part of the overall connectivity picture. But at the same time that users are recognizing the potential of the mainframe connection—or perhaps because of this recognition—a phenomenon that some observers have termed a "connectivity crisis" is occurring in many networks.

Many users purchased their computers believing that they would connect easily with mainframes and other processors; others selected their equipment without giving the issue of mainframe connectivity any consideration. The crisis is felt when users realize that they were not sold "instant" connectivity when they invested in their computing devices. Further, when users realize that traditional methods for connecting diverse tools to the mainframe are not always as easy or as efficient as anticipated, the crisis deepens.

The mainframe connection has been traditionally accomplished by linking to a mainframe or I/O (input/output) channel through telecommunications solutions. (As used here, telecommunications refers to remote access.) Principally, these links have been used to connect terminals, remote peripherals, and remote mainframes to the central

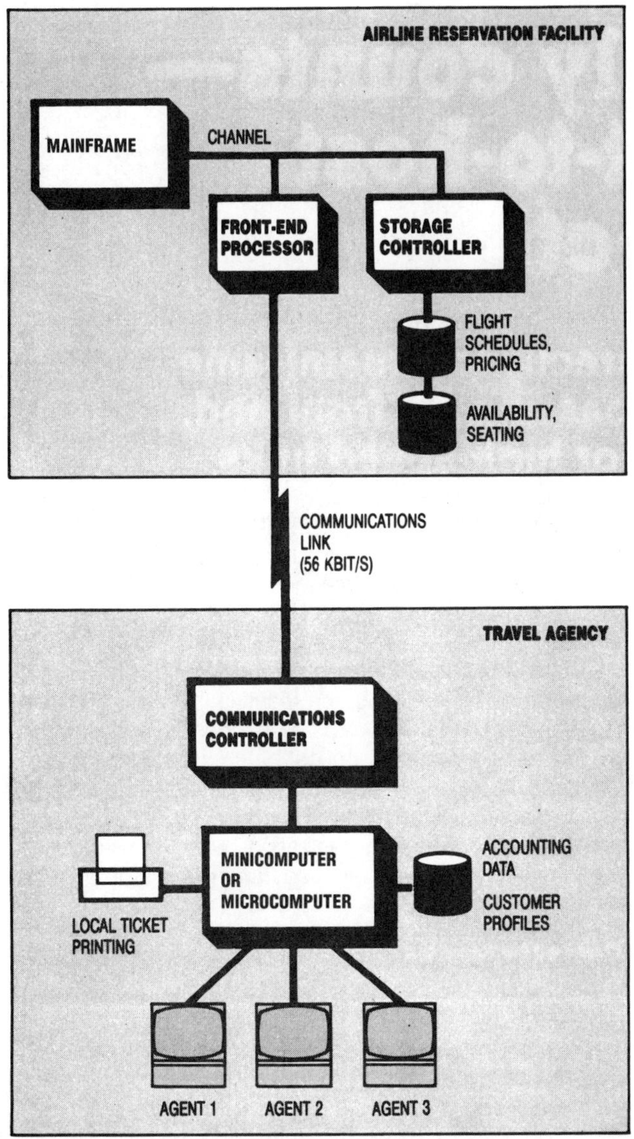

1. Cooperative processing. *A mainframe connection allows multiple network workstations to run the same complex application programs resident on the mainframe.*

mainframe. In such applications, telecommunications connections allow remote users to move screen images of data interactively. File transfers, however, are handled somewhat less efficiently. Addressing these non-time-critical data transfers with the traditional telecommunications link has nevertheless been quite successful.

Telecommunications connections are optimized for terminal-oriented messages. In today's computing environment, however, a broader orientation is needed if diverse computer networks and peripherals are to be connected in a more symmetrical peer-to-peer relationship with the user's mainframe.

The connection must also be broad enough in scope to support different sizes of data, satisfying diverse users with differing data transfer requirements. In addition, the connection should be easy enough to implement so that the mainframe becomes an accessible server for the various

devices, instead of an inflexible center around which all other tools must be configured with comparatively greater effort or difficulty.

As Figure 2 shows, telecommunications solutions use terminal emulation hardware and software and associated communications processors to connect to the mainframe. Generally, they are limited to maximum data transfer rates of 56 kbit/s. This rate is inadequate to sustain acceptable interactive response times (the goal is no more than three seconds) on networks supporting hundreds of users or applications that involve the transfer of large amounts of information in real time.

The bottleneck

The problem with telecommunications solutions is that they require 12 to 13 minutes, on average (in the case of a 56-kbit/s digital facility), to move a 1-Mbyte file between mainframe and microcomputer on a network. Although higher transmission speeds such as T1 are available, they are still limited to transferring data in terminal mode, which limits the transfer block size.

Such high data transmission speeds saturate the processing bandwidth of the front-end communications

2. Old solutions. *Telecommunications uses terminal-emulation hardware and software and associated communications processors to connect to the mainframe.*

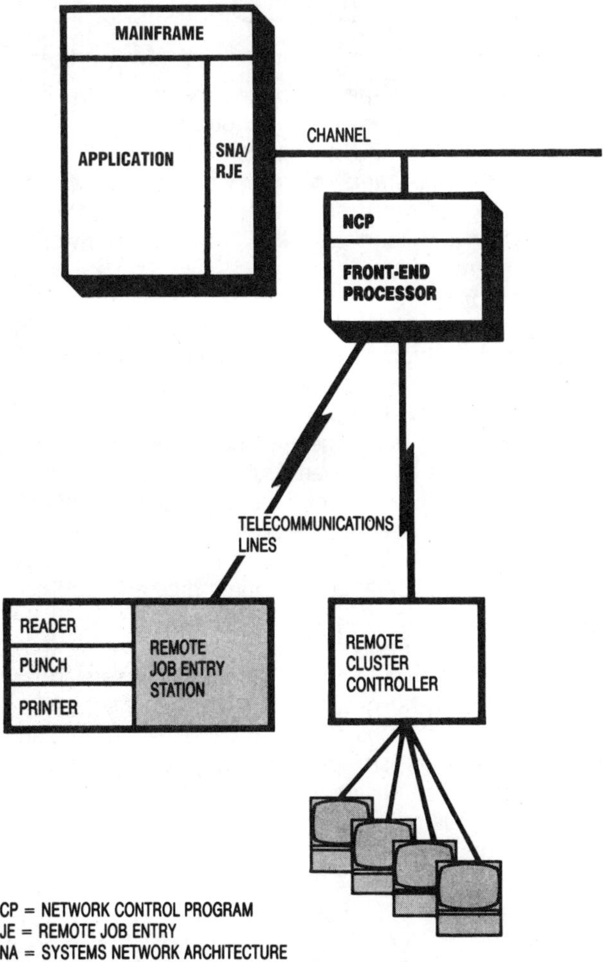

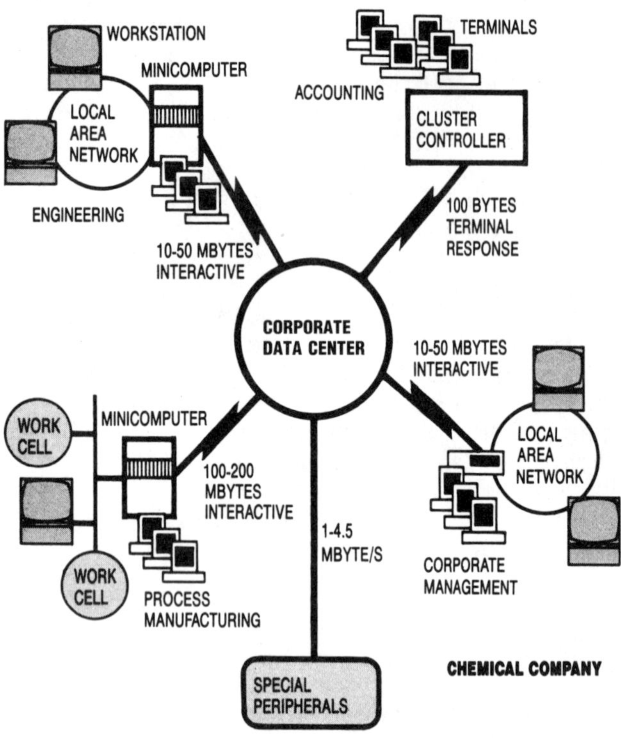

3. Connectivity needs. *A chemical company's accounting department transfers to the mainframe via a cluster controller. The processing plant connects via LANs.*

controller, thereby greatly increasing the cost of the connection. As a result, users face a bottleneck that can hamper throughput and, subsequently, productivity. Moreover, the mainframe link must be able to accommodate ever higher transmission speeds such as 100 Mbit/s supported on new fiber-based LANs (local area networks).

Chemistry lesson

To understand the demands placed upon a mainframe link by users with different types of mainframe attachments and varying data transfer requirements, consider a typical chemical company (Fig. 3).

The accounting department is one of the company's major data users. The department is in the same building as the mainframe, but beyond the maximum allowable distance for local attached devices. The department connects to the corporate mainframe primarily by terminals and remote peripherals, and it shares data and applications running on the mainframe.

Accounting, in a transaction mode, typically sends small data blocks (2 kbytes) to the mainframe. It uses standard telecommunications links, such as synchronous data link control over leased lines, for such small data transfers, and its users find this transmission method adequate. When the department has to transfer larger data blocks, however, accounting finds transmission considerably slower (the previously mentioned 12 to 13 minutes per megabyte). Such batch transmissions are typically performed during off-peak hours.

A second company group, those in the processing plant, connect to the corporate mainframe via local area net-

works, terminals, and other computing devices. In this way, the group can perform real-time processing tasks, access applications on the mainframe, and share data with other groups in the company. This user group represents medium-sized data exchanges of 100- to 200-kbyte blocks.

The company's engineering organization connects to the mainframe chiefly via other computers such as departmental minicomputers used for local data "crunching." The engineering group relies on the mainframe for the temporary or permanent storage of data that later can be extracted for further analysis. The transferred blocks of data can be as large as 50 Mbytes and require data transfers approximating local disk-transfer rates (250 kbyte to 1 Mbyte per second; for these comparisons, one byte equals 8 to 10 bits).

In our scenario, a fourth group, the corporate management team, connects via local area network attachments to the corporate mainframe so that the group can tap into its shared databases and programs. These users, like those of the engineering staff, require the equivalent of disk-transfer rates for large amounts of data: 50 or more Mbytes at a time.

Yet with a telecommunications link to the mainframe, all four groups, which represent very different sets of expectations, connections, and distances from the mainframe, must rely on the same connectivity performance characteristics.

Ultimately, because a telecommunications link favors terminal-type connections, the result is that data transmission can be slowed down to an unacceptable level when bulk file transfers or time-critical batch transmissions are required. Thus this link is likely to fail to efficiently meet the mixed demands of the different user groups in the chemical plant scenario—and in organizations with a similar dichotomy of local communications and mainframe-access configurations.

Reconsidering the problem

It is clear that connectivity is not just a matter of installing cable—it involves much more than fitting a computing tool or new user into a wiring scheme. Instead, connectivity must, by definition, also include the capability of connecting diverse applications with varying data transfer requirements to a range of mainframes. It must also provide organizations with a "comfortable," user-oriented way of interacting with the mainframe.

What has been lacking is a connectivity approach removing the mainframe from its position at the center of the network universe, making the mainframe an accessible server, and featuring direct attachment to the mainframe by varied user communities at channel speeds (3 Mbyte/s maximum).

Connecting to the mainframe means opening the machine's architecture so that the mainframe becomes a productive, integral part of the user's world, not a monolith around which everything else must be designed and configured. What is needed to realize such a connectivity scenario is a bidirectional bridge directly between the IBM mainframe and diverse users that can be incorporated into existing architectures in order to protect the user's investment in already-installed devices. Replacement costs are thus avoided.

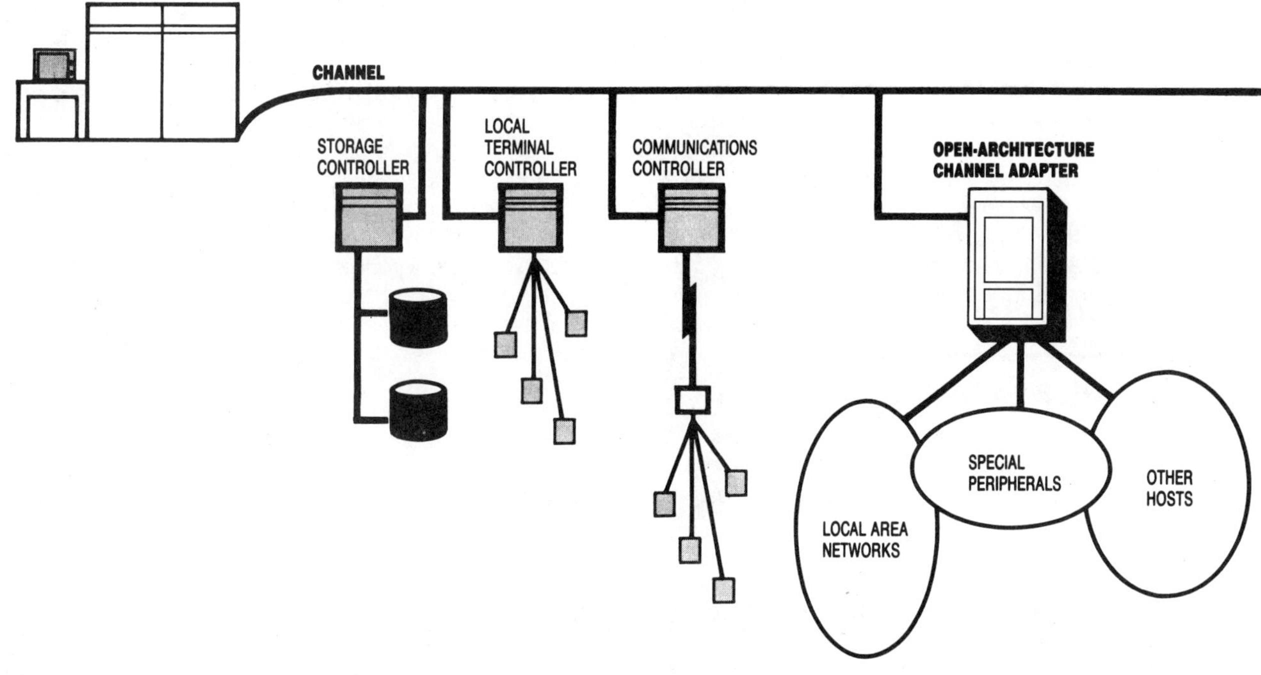

Recognizing the growing need to make the mainframe easier to access as a node on a network, IBM now offers built-in connectivity on its new 9370 computers. The 9370's integrated communications controllers enhance local area network-to-mainframe connectivity by opening the latest IBM mainframe architecture to a broad range of users. Architecturally speaking, that was accomplished by enabling the built-in controllers to interface directly to local area networks and to other computers, without having to go through front-end processors. But these built-in connectivity devices are not available for the entire family of IBM computers. Therefore, they do not meet the connectivity challenges posed by "closed" System/370-type mainframe architectures.

Another product that has attempted to address System/370-type connectivity is the multisource channel adapter, a device that provides a pathway for connecting to the mainframe various computing tools, such as local area networks and high-speed peripherals. Until recently, however, most channel adapters have been designed with proprietary interfaces. That has restricted users to connecting only those products offered by the channel-adapter vendor, thus severely limiting user choice of those computing tools. In addition, most of the adapters have been special-purpose connectivity products capable of handling only one type of connection, and have not supported general attachment for multiple devices.

A nonproprietary open-architecture channel adapter can bring less limiting solutions to users and serve as a connectivity "platform." It can go beyond the terminal orientation of telecommunications links. Shown in Figure 4 is an open-architecture channel adapter, which is an interface device that attaches directly to the mainframe channel at channel speed. It allows the user to readily connect multiple applications through standard protocols, such as IEEE 796, without changing software at the application level.

Channel-attached connectivity devices act as high-speed (3-Mbyte/s) interfaces between various types of IBM-compatible mainframes and local area networks, minicomputers, other mainframes, microcomputers, and specialized peripherals such as optical disks. Such connectivity allows original equipment manufacturers (OEMs) to customize their applications by using programmable interfaces.

Enhancing performance

Channel-attached connectivity opens an IBM mainframe to a wide array of non-IBM devices, networks, and computers. This would be similar to IBM—in a departure from its tradition—"going public" with the bus architecture of its comparatively low-cost microcomputer so that vendors could build applications for a variety of environments (such as LANs and archiving tapes) by using add-in printed-circuit boards.

An immediate benefit of the open-architecture channel adapter application is that peripheral manufacturers who wish to supply products for the mainframe are spared the expense of developing connectivity technology and can focus on product development.

The adapters can also connect mainframes to minicomputers, such as the DEC (Digital Equipment Corp.) VAX, so that VAX users can exploit the resources of both computers. The adapters also allow users to connect various LAN topologies to the mainframe.

The adapter allows multiple connections through a single

175

channel attachment, minimizing the number of channel attachments. And it handles combinations of applications concurrently, so that disparate elements—such as LANs, optical disks, and minicomputers—can share the mainframe economically. The ability to connect diverse applications concurrently lets users multiplex the bandwidth of the channel for slower devices. Adapters that provide a buffer for data flowing at channel speeds to slower applications offer an effective way to enhance channel throughput. The open-architecture channel adapter allows users to define their application priorities by user or message type—that is especially important when multiple applications coexist in a single adapter.

When evaluating potential adapter vendors, users should be on the lookout for vendor-sponsored development

---

Connectivity guidelines

Some general connectivity rules for effecting a high-speed direct-to-mainframe link apply to a number of different applications and to evolving technological changes:

1. The channel adapter should support industry standards such as those adopted by the International Organization for Standardization (ISO) and the IEEE. Examples: the Open Systems Interconnection (OSI) model and token ring and Ethernet networks.

2. Tools for network management should be provided.

3. An important feature to consider is the ability to support multiple device types so that the channel adapter looks to be whatever the mainframe deems is appropriate for the type of function being connected. This avoids the expense and performance inefficiency of multiple layers of protocol conversion software on the mainframe.

4. Look for a channel adapter that can be readily configured with a wide range of adapter boards to support standard applications. This will reduce development time in obtaining specific application solutions. It also enables a simple connectivity to support a number of different connections, such as to a Digital Equipment VAX minicomputer, an Ethernet or token ring LAN, a Manufacturing Automation Protocol application, or an ASCII terminal. These multiple mainframe-connectivity applications could also be run simultaneously.

5. Where there is a time-critical element to the data flow, such as in engineering and scientific environments, look for a high-speed interface of at least 3-Mbyte/s transmission in a data streaming mode (not limiting transmission to a predetermined amount).

6. Choose a vendor carefully, because the vendor's experience, technical knowledge, service, and support are key to the connectivity's success. Pick a vendor whose record shows long-term reliability. Look for a vendor who can help develop and test applications, perhaps by providing a development laboratory. And not least, make sure the vendor can provide training and field support for the entire connection, including the application.

---

facilities. Where such resources exist, users have access to technically knowledgeable personnel who can help with testing implementations, providing important assistance with application development.

Another vendor-evaluation criterion is vendor experience in providing mainframe-related products and support. The vendor's commitment to ongoing research and development, and its long-term viability, are more obvious points for consideration (see "Connectivity guidelines").

Besides standard connections, the open-architecture channel adapter is designed to deliver tools and methodologies for those users requiring customized applications. The tools include libraries of application routines and development environments that allow simulation of a final configuration during the implementation cycle. Methodologies include protocols that make tasks easier to perform, such as a disciplined methodology for interfacing to the adapter's control unit.

Evolving expectations

The open-architecture channel adapter enables a user to connect several applications concurrently—an efficient approach—which makes the mainframe accessible to many different users and applications. That technology is based on industry standards such as IBM's OEM interface or Federal Information Processing Standard 60.

Attaching to megabyte-per-second channels becomes even more critical as channel speeds steadily increase. Amdahl has already announced a 4.5-Mbyte/s channel. And there is speculation that IBM will move into fiber optics, which should drive channel rates even higher—to at least 12 Mbyte/s.

The speed associated with local area network technology is also on the rise. Standard LAN technology currently offers 1.25 Mbyte/s (the equivalent of 10 Mbit/s) capability. Thus the 3-Mbyte/s data-transfer rate offered by channel-attached adapters is more than adequate for most LAN applications.

However, as LAN speeds increase further, the bottleneck will be moved back to the channel. Users must assure themselves that the connectivity interface between the LAN and the mainframe is adaptable enough to accommodate improved performance on both sides in a constant evolutionary game of catch-up.

The emergence of new peripheral devices requiring connection to the mainframe will also continue. The adapter's channel-speed performance will be a boon for interfacing between the mainframe and advanced devices treated as peripherals, such as aircraft simulators, optical disks, and CAD/CAM (computer-aided design/computer-aided manufacturing) workstations. ■

Mike Cerruti is strategic marketing manager for Intel's System Interconnect Operation. He has worked with mainframe software and channel connect technology for the past 15 years. Maurice Voce is product marketing manager for Intel's System Interconnect Operation. He has had more than seven years' system engineering and marketing experience ranging from mainframes to personal computers and networks. Voce holds a B.S. in mathematics and computer science from UCLA.

Charles Morel, CXI Inc., Mountain View, Calif.

LAN gateways: New opportunities for PC-to-host connectivity

The micro-to-mainframe link is being redefined, enabling LAN workstations to exploit the power of large computers.

Until recently, only individual microcomputers with micro-to-mainframe links were able to enjoy the benefits of mainframe resources. Now, via shared gateways, mainframe resources can be made available to every microcomputer on a LAN.

Back when microcomputers first made the corporate scene, MIS (management information systems) and data communications managers looked for ways to connect desktop computers both with each other and with mainframes. To initially serve those two needs, two separate connectivity strategies were implemented: local area networks (LANs) and micro-to-mainframe links. LANs connected groups of microcomputers together; and micro-to-mainframe links connected individual microcomputers to mainframes.

The gateway concept has widened the alternatives. But not every gateway delivers the same assortment of features and benefits. To distinguish between the most functional gateways and ones that are less so, it would help to examine what gateways are and how they work.

The term gateway, as used in this article, is meant to describe a gate or opening between the distributed intelligence on a LAN and the central intelligence of a mainframe. This definition distinguishes a gateway from a bridge, which communicates between similar or dissimilar networks, such as two adjacent LANs.

To a microcomputer on a LAN, a gateway makes the mainframe available as a resource of CPU processing power, storage, information, and applications. To a mainframe, looking at the world through its traditional centralized network, a gateway is indistinguishable from the IBM-type 3270 cluster controllers and terminals that exist in a hierarchical Systems Network Architecture (SNA) or bisynchronous (BSC) network.

A gateway is best seen as precisely what it is: a device that distributes or serves the presentation of mainframe sessions (terminal interactions with a host application) among a number of nodes on a LAN. In other words, a gateway is a communications server (see "The coaxial gateway"). Although they operate in LAN environments, gateways are micro-to-mainframe products. The functionalities and benefits gateways bring to the user of a LAN are, therefore, of a micro-to-mainframe nature.

Extensive gateway product lines are available that fit into local (coaxial-cable distance), remote, and LAN environments. Although most LAN vendors offer a LAN gateway in their product lines, their gateways vary from mere terminal emulation to full micro-to-mainframe link functionality. The difference between terminal emulators and micro-to-mainframe links is enormous. To put it simply, terminal emulators merely permit a microcomputer to act like an IBM 3278 or 3279 dumb terminal—essentially a keyboard and screen. In its capacity as a dumb terminal, a microcomputer with a terminal emulator can only access interactive applications on the mainframe—applications written for access by dumb terminals.

Hundreds of programs

By contrast, a true micro-to-mainframe link allows a microcomputer to complement the mainframe, providing intelligence (processing power) and storage, in addition to the basic dumb terminal emulation. A true micro-to-mainframe link can also take advantage of the hundreds of application programs that have been developed for the micro-to-mainframe marketplace. Those advanced programs are made possible by the presence of an application program interface, or API, in the micro-to-mainframe connection.

An API may be manifested in the micro-to-mainframe control software or in the connection hardware. The API allows microcomputer applications to use the micro-to-mainframe link. However, simply having an API available does not automatically do the job. The API provided in the

The coaxial gateway

A gateway is a communications server: a node that distributes mainframe sessions to client workstation nodes. When a gateway is connected via coaxial cable to a cluster controller, it embodies Open Systems Interconnection (OSI) Level 5 (session) and distributes Levels 6 (presentation) and 7 (application) to client nodes. The served distribution may include the gateway microcomputer, although some gateways dedicate their microcomputers to the server role.

Levels 1 through 4 are handled by the cluster controller. By emulating this controller, a remote gateway communicates directly with the mainframe front-end processor and processes Levels 1 through 5, including all the link level and higher-level protocols.

In SNA (Systems Network Architecture) terms, Layers 1 through 5 correspond to PU (physical unit) functionality; Layers 6 and 7 correspond to LU (logical unit) functionality. The LU is available to client workstation nodes through the LAN medium. In these terms, a LAN is merely a method of session distribution.

Because the SNA protocol for each session is processed by software, LAN protocol layers are separate and unrelated. This means that any microcomputer on a LAN can carry out terminal emulation, through the medium of the LAN and the gateway, with no additional hardware in any of the client microcomputers. As the figure shows, the server and client can exist in the same node. Some gateway servers require dedicated microcomputer nodes—in effect sacrificing the host microcomputer to the needs of the LAN.

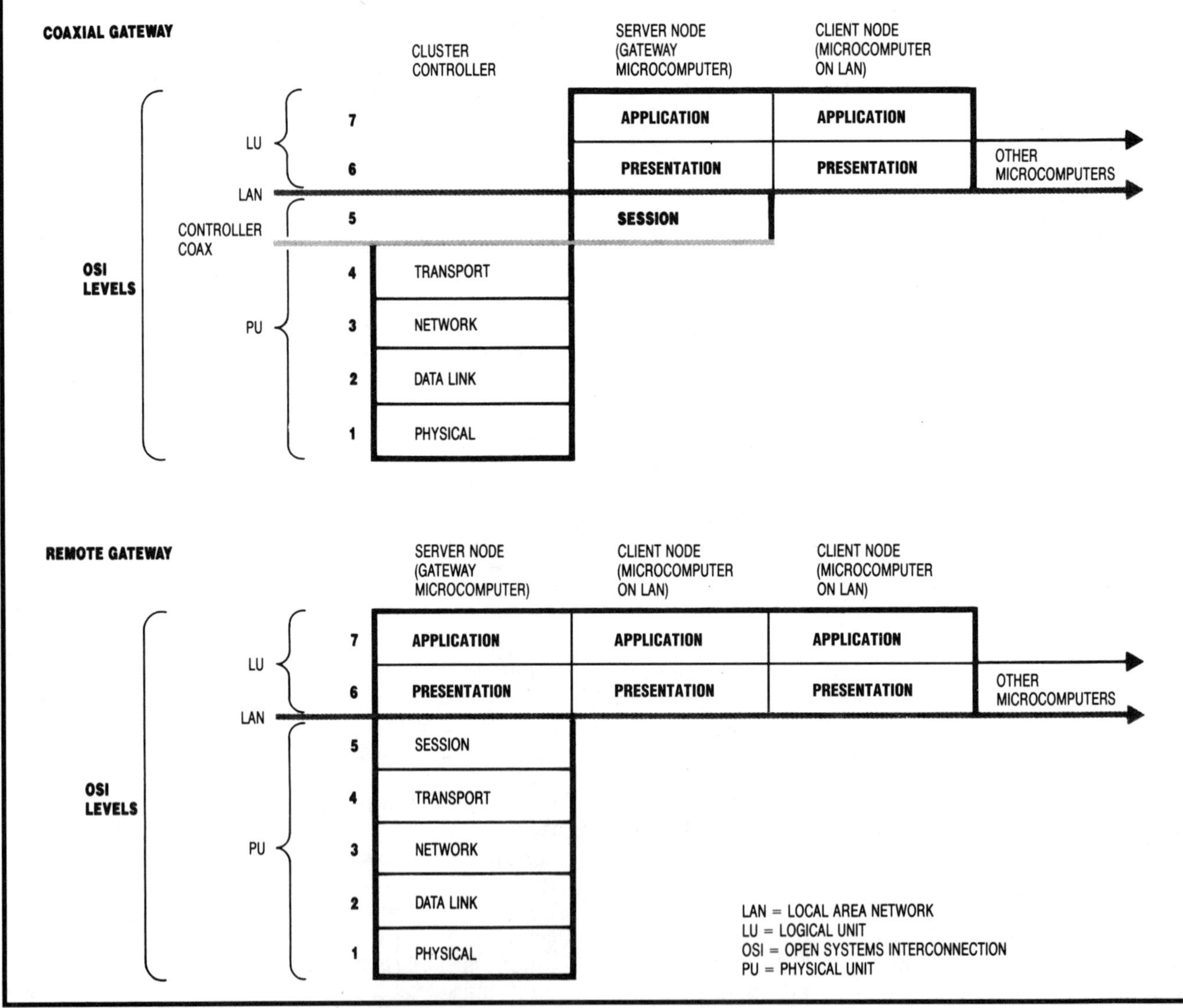

link must be supported by many micro-to-mainframe application-software packages in order for the user to gain the desired capabilities from a micro-to-mainframe link.

From a management perspective, the most desirable APIs are uniform across all types of micro-to-mainframe links (coax, remote, and LAN environments), not in just one or another. This is also desirable from an implementation standpoint, because applications written for one environment will then also work in the other two—beneficial in corporate implementations where it is likely that micro-to-mainframe links will exist in connections environments other than LANs. Since the more-advanced and more-intelligent file transfer programs are basically mainframe software packages that rely on an intelligent microcomputer counterpart, they also require a capable API at the micro end of the link.

True micro-to-mainframe capabilities might not be the only gateway feature that interests a communications manager. That person might also appreciate the manner in which some gateways can be created: through software upgrades of existing micro-to-mainframe links. A software approach enables a single micro-to-mainframe link to take on a variety of identities without replacing interface boards and even without replacing chips. In addition, upgrading an existing micro-to-mainframe link does not obsolete the application software written for that link's API.

Connectivity evolution

To understand the communications environment in which a gateway operates, we should look first at the 3270 architecture that provides the context for today's micro-to-mainframe communications. In the original 3270 Information Display System, mainframe intelligence was made available to a variety of terminals on a time-sharing basis. Information was distributed through cluster controllers (such as the 3274) to terminals connected via coaxial cable. Cluster controllers were either channel-connected directly to the mainframe or remotely connected, by means of synchronous modems and phone lines, to the mainframe's front-end processor (such as IBM's 3705/25 Communications Controller and equivalents) (Fig. 1).

The most common terminal devices were the 3278 (monochrome) and 3279 (color) display terminals, and the 3287 printer. The terminals were connected to the cluster controller by coaxial cable. These terminals required the intelligence of the cluster controller to echo each keystroke back to the terminal screen. This hardware-level mode of communications IBM calls CUT (control unit terminal) mode. All 3278/79 coaxial-connected terminal emulation boards are configured as CUT-mode devices. They allow a microcomputer to present itself to a mainframe in the guise of a 3278 or a 3279, and carry out functions limited by that relationship.

In 1983, to enlarge the functionality of this network, IBM developed a form of communications called DFT (distributed function terminal) for certain new coaxial-connected terminal-like devices, including the 3270 PC. The DFT mode is significantly different from the CUT mode in four ways:
■ It offloads high-level protocol (SNA/SDLC or BSC—SDLC is IBM's synchronous data link control) and keystroke processing from the cluster controller to the DFT device;
■ it supports multiple concurrent mainframe sessions;
■ it supports message-level APIs, permitting the applications to transmit blocks of data instead of a character at a time; and
■ it assumes a programmable microcomputer device.

On CUT-mode devices, the keyboard/display APIs have evolved to take advantage of the intelligence found in CUT-mode emulators implemented on programmable microcomputers. Originally, the only bidirectional dialogues officially supported between these CUT-mode terminal devices and host computers were through the keyboard/display. The main-frame did not distinguish between an emulator on a microcomputer and any

other CUT-mode device in the network. Therefore, to take advantage of the microcomputer intelligence, keyboard/display APIs were implemented that were transparent to the mainframe's normal network operation; that is, they were meant to simulate the keyboard/display interaction.

By liberating micro-to-mainframe communications from the need to use the keyboard/display-level API of CUT-mode communications, DFT facilitated the development of advanced applications that recognized the presence of intelligence at both ends of the communications links. The message-level API provided by the new DFT-mode devices facilitates microcomputer-to-mainframe communications by using data blocks, or messages, as dictated by the application at hand. This method contrasts with arbitrary device limitations such as display size, as in a keyboard/

---

1. The environment. *Gateways typically operate in the IBM 3270 micro-to-mainframe world. Here, mainframe intelligence is time-shared by a variety of terminals.*

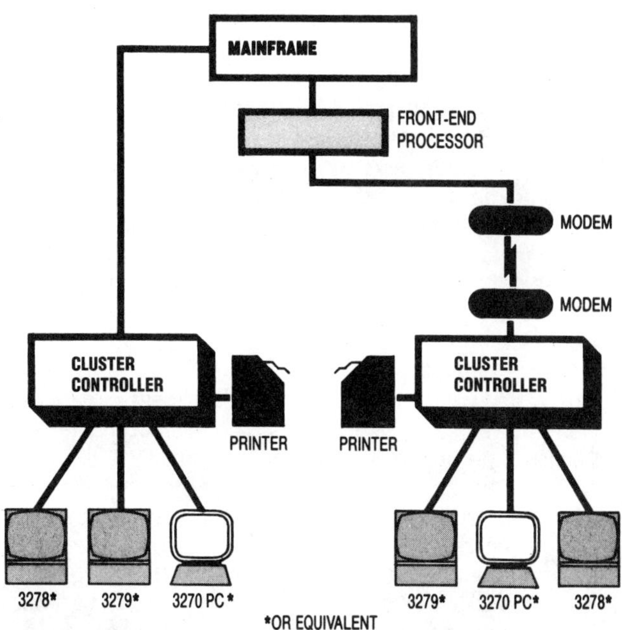

display API.

In 1984, IBM merged two of its most technologically successful creations, the 3290 Information Panel and the PC, into one device: the 3270 PC. This device had the capacity to access a number of host sessions concurrently. Together, DFT and the 3270 PC made mainframe sessions, in effect, a distributable commodity. Since DFT-mode devices permit up to five concurrent sessions on a single coaxial line, those sessions are used concurrently and independently to up to five workstations.

The gateway provides the communications path to the mainframe. It distributes the mainframe sessions to the workstation nodes throughout the LAN. The task of the workstation node is to implement the OSI (Open Systems Interconnection) presentation layer (see "The coaxial gateway"). As the name implies, this layer presents data to the user and is also responsible for the user's interaction with the device. In the LAN gateway environment, the gateway is charged with all the physical and logical communications functions normally found in single micro-to-mainframe links.

Gateway-to-workstation communications are provided by the LAN facilities, thereby binding the mainframe communications functions in the gateway with the presentation layer functions found in the workstations. In this configuration the workstations share the resource-serving capabilities of the gateway with exactly the same facilities and functions found in single micro-to-mainframe links.

Connections and sessions

In terms of micro-to-mainframe communications functionality, gateways come in the two varieties mentioned earlier: coaxial and remote. Coaxial gateways connect directly to a cluster controller. Remote gateways emulate a cluster controller and connect to a mainframe's front-end processor (communications controller) via synchronous modems and phone lines. In both cases, the gateway function is identical; only the communications connection is different.

Figure 2 graphically depicts both a coaxial and a remote gateway. Note that the coaxial-connected gateway is attached directly to an existing cluster controller as a DFT-mode device, thereby obtaining up to five concurrent sessions from the controller. The cluster controller provides physical communications services to the mainframe for all its attached devices, including the coax gateway. The controller provides physical communications services to the mainframe through a channel connection, or is remotely connected over the telephone network to the front-end processor. In contrast, the remote gateway emulates a cluster controller connected to the mainframe's front-end processor over the telephone network. Here, physical communications to the mainframe is the responsibility of the remote gateway.

There are two main component types in these configurations: gateways and workstations. The microcomputer gateway node provides a physical and logical protocol path between the mainframe and the microcomputer workstation nodes serviced by the LAN. Multiple sessions are provided by the mainframe through the gateway, and the gateway in turn serves these sessions to the workstations on the LAN. The workstation takes this session service from the gateway and presents one or more sessions to the user. Typical 3270 sessions provided through these gateways to the microcomputer workstation nodes include: host-addressable printers; and display terminals with alphanumeric keyboards, host-defined-graphics, and multiple-sessions with windowing and alphanumeric and/or host graphics.

Gateways come in a variety of "sizes," determined by the number of sessions a gateway can distribute concurrently. A basic coaxial-connected gateway can distribute the five concurrent host sessions (including printer sessions) supported by DFT-mode communications. If the gateway also emulates, for example, an IBM 3299 multiplexer (which combines up to eight coaxial channels), it can support up to forty (8 5) concurrent host sessions.

Since a remotely connected gateway emulates a cluster controller (such as the IBM 3274), the number of host sessions it can distribute concurrently is determined by the number of terminals supported by the controller device it

emulates. A 3274 can connect up to 32 devices (coaxial cable attachments). Mixes of CUT-mode (single-session devices) and DFT-mode (multiple-session devices) are supported on single 3274s. However, a maximum of 128 sessions can be accommodated (combinations of single and multiple sessions per device) on one 3274.

Creating bottlenecks

There are practical limits involved, of course. Heavy concurrent demand slows link performance. As in any other shared configuration, overuse of a finite resource causes bottlenecks. Many parameters determine when a resource goes critical, such as the performance characteristics of the gateway, the mainframe data link, the LAN environment, and the demand placed on the gateway resource by the

---

2. Connections. *The coaxial-connected gateway is attached to a cluster controller, providing communications services to the mainframe via a channel attachment.*

MICRO-TO-MAINFRAME NETWORK WITH LAN GATEWAYS

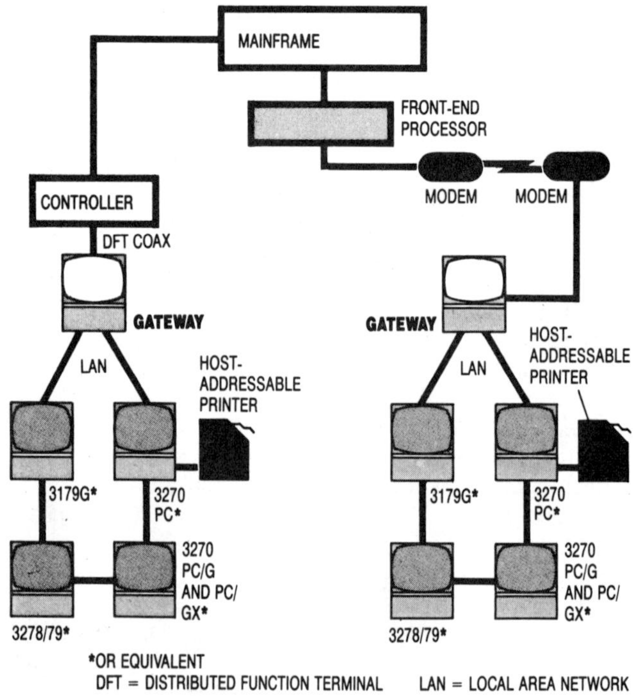

client workstations.

The performance characteristics of the gateway itself involve several factors. The chief concern in this area is the microcomputer CPU cycles (processing time) required versus those allocated to the gateway. Is the microcomputer dedicated to the gateway function, or is the gateway one of several services residing in that same microcomputer node? Secondly, does the gateway provide any special hardware to assist the microcomputer, such as a coprocessor board to offload some of the processing and memory requirement for the gateway service?

Matching the throughput on the mainframe communications link to the rest of the gateway environment is important. If the data link is too fast, the gateway will be overrun with incoming traffic. Where the data link is too slow, response time will suffer, and outbound traffic will back up in the gateway waiting for service to the mainframe.

The general performance of the LAN, such as the protocol overhead and speed, is a factor in the performance of the gateway. The LAN must provide adequate bandwidth — dependent on user response-time expectations — for gateway service, balancing the data rate on the mainframe link with the service demand and data rate across the LAN. This "well-tuned-LAN" environment can be adversely impacted by demand for other shared resource services on the LAN, such as heavy utilization of file servers.

Demands on the gateway by multiple workstations for continuous printer, interactive, or file transfer service can affect overall performance on even a well-tuned gateway. The point at which these demands degrade gateway service is determined by a combination of the above parameters.

Because there are many factors affecting the performance characteristics of the gateway-workstation configuration, it is a reasonable strategy to install more than one gateway on a LAN. This spreads the load by increasing the number of available sessions and reducing traffic on each data link to the mainframe. Optimally, however, workstation software needs to support session seeking (hunt for a needed session) by the workstation-node microcomputers. This is so that a microcomputer's session request will automatically receive a session allocation from the nearest gateway with available sessions (Fig. 3).

During the software installation at the microcomputer workstation, several gateways that are acceptable — as to session availability and security, for example — are specified in an ordered list according to the user's preference. When the user activates the workstation, it will seek service from the gateways in the order that was specified. For instance, during the workstation installation, suppose gateways A, B, and C are indicated. At program execution (run time), the workstation software attempts to connect first with gateway A. If A is busy (that is, all available sessions are already assigned to other workstations), the subject workstation tries B, and so on. In this way, the user procedures are simplified, and service is provided to the workstation on the first available gateway.

Sharing resources

Installing gateways on a LAN enables data communications managers to leverage existing investments in both micro-to-mainframe and LAN technologies. Savings are thus realized in link products, cluster controllers, and line, modem, and port costs. Gateways also put microcomputers under a kind of standardization and control, since all nodes have the same connection type and share common software.

For microcomputer users on the LAN, however, the key benefits are resource sharing. This is why most LANs are centered around file servers. These devices make files and software available to the various LAN workstations. Of course, the file server is a kind of peripheral — it looks to each microcomputer like a dedicated hard-disk drive.

Resource sharing brings with it the issue of security for mainframe resources, especially databases. Because

communications is itself a natural hazard to security, many managers have been reluctant to link remote intelligence to centrally stored data.

Micro-to-mainframe communications is largely a matter of software, however, and security can be maintained readily through implementation of three different software approaches. The first is through cooperative processing, which utilizes the intelligence at both ends of the communications line.

The second approach is password protection. Problems, however, arise when a single password can be shared by a variety of workstations. Additional security can be provided by restricted user access: by key authorization or lockout provisions.

The third software approach is implementation of the security scheme provided by the original 3270 design, in which each physical device on the network had a name that is fixed logically in the memory of the mainframe. However, with the advent of gateway technology, these physical relationships no longer exist.

With a LAN gateway, the software allocates sessions (resulting in SNA network names) to requesting workstation nodes. Security is compromised unless the gateway can accept these device names and the mainframe's perception of a fixed environment and map them into the LAN. This mapping must be done in such a way that the LAN still has the capabilities of resource sharing and the flexibilities of a LAN while maintaining requisite physical security.

Switching between sessions

A gateway provides each LAN workstation with many additional capabilities, such as text support for host-addressable keyboard displays and printers, multiple host sessions, windowing, and access to mainframe graphics. These capabilities allow users working on projects that require information from their workstations and the mainframe to switch between a workstation session and up to five host sessions. One of the latter can be a graphics session. In addition, two notepad sessions (special on-screen images usually used for assembling information copied from other session screens) are locally available. With windowing, all five host sessions, the two notepad sessions, and the microcomputer session may appear concurrently on the screen.

One of the newest and most interesting workstation capabilities is "all points addressable" (APA) or vector graphics. While traditional IBM 3279 Model S3G-type micro-to-mainframe graphics puts the processing burden on the mainframe, APA graphics allows the microcomputer to construct its own graphics images. This construction is guided by processing of display commands sent by the mainframe. APA graphics images can also be composed on one microcomputer and transmitted to the others on the LAN. (For a more in-depth discussion of IBM 3279 S3G and APA graphics, see "Graphics developments.")

An API is an important capability that resides in a workstation connected to a mainframe via a gateway — through it the user can access mainframe applications.

An application developed for a single workstation coaxial or remote micro-to-mainframe link can also run on a coaxial or remote gateway-equipped LAN, depending on the APIs provided by the vendor of the micro-to-mainframe connection and application. Because the gateway/workstation configuration emulates a standard coaxial or remote micro-to-mainframe link, the mainframe applications that require interaction with these standard devices operate with no differences when interacting with a gateway workstation.

Those mainframes that provide extensive data transfers between the mainframe and microcomputer applications do so through APIs provided by the micro-to-mainframe environments. Because only one common API is often required for many network topologies, the time required to develop and maintain micro-to-mainframe supporting programs is significantly reduced.

Cooperative processing (processing that is shared by both microcomputer and mainframe) makes the most of connected microcomputer and mainframe intelligence. Applications range from communications software that arbitrates microcomputer contention for access to mainframe data, to software that creates "virtual disks" on mainframe disks for microcomputer data storage. With cooperative processing the user gets the benefit of the combined efforts of both the microcomputer and mainframe for many important functions and capabilities, such as computing resources, databases, processing, and

---

3. Session seeking. Installing more than one gateway on a LAN spreads the load and increases the number of available sessions, reducing traffic on mainframe data links.

SESSION SEEKING

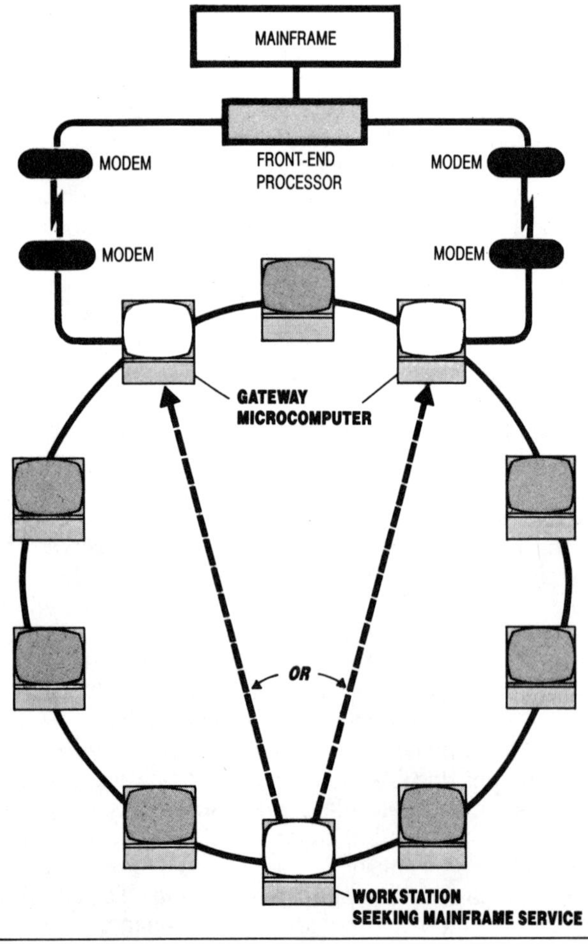

Graphics developments

The purpose of graphics is to express as many as thousands of words in a simple image. The first popular graphics terminal for the IBM 3270 product line was the 3279 Model S3G. Essentially, the S3G graphics technology displayed images using mainframe programmable symbols or character sets. This technology is available as a feature of certain micro-to-mainframe links.

The benefit of using a micro-to-mainframe link is not only to allow the generation of the graphics, but also the storing of graphics images for later presentation or to be printed off-line using the microcomputer. However, this technology has several drawbacks. It is mainframe-processing intensive, with images requiring 64 kbytes of data for transmission. Also, the microcomputer requires special hardware (such as plug-in cards) capable of displaying images based on programmable symbol sets.

Recently, further advances in graphics were realized with DFT (distributed function terminal)-mode devices. IBM provided a new graphics capability known as "all points addressable" (APA), or vector, graphics with the 3179G terminal and special versions of the 3270 PC known as the 3270 PC G and G/X. The unique capability of APA graphics is that, unlike the programmed symbol-set graphics used with S3G graphics, the mainframe processing and data transmission are both reduced. There is no need for specialized hardware based on programmable symbol sets.

With APA graphics, the image is presented to the terminal or micro-to-mainframe link as image orders — that is, commands describing how the graph should be constructed at the microcomputer. As an example, the host sends a series of orders to draw a line from coordinate A to coordinate B on the screen. The APA graphics orders facilitate further off-line editing and processing by the microcomputer.

---

transactions. Cooperative processing can even involve broadcast transactions from one node to selected multiple nodes throughout the network.

Exceptional care should be taken in the evaluation of gateway choices. The "Gateway evaluation checklist" contains a list of questions helpful in selecting the gateway best suited to a user's needs.

Future hopes vs. present realities

Communications software is going through a dramatic evolutionary stage. Much recent talk has been devoted to IBM's APPC (Advanced Program-to-Program Communications) and LU (logical unit) 6.2, the protocol used by APPC. As an architecture, LU 6.2 allows host-independent, application-to-application communications, regardless of the types of processors or language involved. The logical units communicating via APPC can co-exist on a LAN, or at different nodes on a larger network. APPC provides peer-to-peer communications among applications (see "Program-to-program communications—a growing trend,"

Gateway evaluation checklist

1. What is the network protocol (such as SNA/SDLC or BSC)?

2. Will the configuration require workstation usage to be primarily interactive or file transfer?

3. What kind of concurrent mainframe sessions (text displays, graphics displays, printers) can the gateway provide for each workstation?

4. How many workstations (nodes) will require concurrent service?

5. How many workstations (nodes) will require shared access to service?

6. Will there be priorities of service among workstations, or will they be serviced equally?

7. Does the gateway provide secure access to host resources?

8. How many mainframes are required to be accessed from the workstations?

9. What are the memory and other resource requirements of the LAN (local area network) node that comprise the gateway?

10. What are the memory and resource requirements of each LAN workstation?

11. Is the gateway API (application program interface) compatible with industry-standard micro-to-mainframe applications?

12. Is there some assurance that the gateway vendor will remain in business and continue to provide products that perform current-technology functions?

13. Can you upgrade your single terminal link to network server status with gateway software?

14. Does the gateway vendor support DFT (distributed function terminal)-coax, IBM 3299-coax, and remote connections with gateway products?

Data Communications, February 1984, p. 87).

For now, however, applications talking to applications do not take the place of humans talking to applications through devices such as terminals. For the latter, plenty of applications already exist. Also, applications that employ APPC are still largely hypothetical: They do not exist yet in any substantial quantity (only one, to the author's knowledge). Also, they do not yet address substantive requirements, such as high-volume, time-critical file transfers or virtual disk resources. Meanwhile, there is more work to do than there are programmers to do it, and there are still thousands of applications that talk to microcomputers as terminals or micro-to-mainframe links.

As a future reference, however, we can say the ideal form of micro-to-mainframe functionality would allow interactive human communications, hardcopy output, and program-to-program communications. In addition, this ideal form would support all the micro-to-mainframe programs that already exist—it would consist of a hybrid: existing micro-to-mainframe links and LU 6.2. ∎

Charles Morel was founder, CEO, and chairman of CXI. He has a B. A. in computer science from San Diego State University. Following the acquisition of CXI by Novell, Morel entered the Stanford Graduate School of Business as a Sloan Fellow.

Are users up in the air over network management?

AT&T and IBM have already announced comprehensive net management strategies. Will users land on solid ground?

Managing a network was once a simple affair. Daniel Cavanagh, a 48-year-old networking veteran and senior vice president at Metropolitan Life Insurance Company, remembers the good old days of network management. Anyone with more than five years in a corporate data center probably can, too.

"In voice communications," Cavanagh says, "someone was doing network management for you as soon as you had the dial tone. Your involvement in network management was nil. In data communications, you had to arrange for point-to-point connections. Sure, you had to define the size of the line you needed, whether it was 9.6 kbit/s or whatever. And you had to figure out what you were going to do if it broke. But that was about the extent of it."

Remember those days? Well, forget them. They are gone. Today, network management is a whole new ball game. The size and complexity of networks have increased dramatically in the past several years, fueled by the decline of processing costs as well as corporate America's rush to install personal computers. On the telephone side, new tariffs and the dismemberment of the Bell System have made the old way of doing business obsolete. Mother Bell, the ultimate network manager, disappeared without leaving a forwarding address.

Users coping with network management responsibility today are faced with an embarrassment of riches. More than two dozen vendors are pushing products into the marketplace (see "Vendor comparison: Network management" following this article). The network management features and functions being offered in these products vary as widely as the platforms available, which range from microcomputer-based systems to mainframes.

The dominant U.S. computer manufacturer, IBM, and the largest U. S. network provider, AT&T, have staked out the high ground with all-inclusive network management strategies, but both products have weaknesses. Regardless of which way users turn, however, they all are looking for the same thing: an automated system that provides status and alarm conditions, fault isolation, reconfiguration, and accounting on a network-wide basis.

The sheer size of networks has grown dramatically in the past several years. For example, in the late 1970s a typical IBM Systems Network Architecture (SNA) network was able to keep upwards of 2,000 devices up and running. By the end of 1984 that network was juggling 5,000 devices, and today the typical network can embrace upwards of 100,000 devices, all contending for network resources.

As network size was exploding, the rules governing the game were also changing. T1 offerings made it possible—and profitable—to carry both voice and data on digital backbones. In mid-1982, AT&T filed a tariff for T1 bypass technology, and in early 1984 the service became generally available as the newly restructured AT&T began offering Accunet T1.5 services. The new services had some cost benefits that were hard to ignore.

Street speak

A 1.544-Mbit/s T1 pipe can be divided into a minimum of 24 voice-grade private lines or 24 56-kbit/s Dataphone Digital Services (DDS) circuits. Maria F. Sbrilli, telecommunications analyst with Wall Street brokers Smith Barney, Harris Upham & Co., says T1 starts to make economic sense in a network with as few as 13 or 14 voice-grade private lines or three to five DDS lines.

"Considering that voice-compression techniques are able to pack as many as 88 'near-toll-quality' conversations on a single T1, there are very few situations in which T1 is not a preferable economic alternative to private lines, provided a minimum bulk traffic requirement is present," she writes in a recent report. Sbrilli says T1 circuit demand is expected to increase at a growth rate of 30 percent to 40 percent per year through 1990.

The momentum pushing private networks to become bigger is not going to slow anytime soon. The spread of T1 and the growth in size of networks share a common driver: inexpensive processing power. As the cost of processing plummeted with improvements in semiconductor production technology, inexpensive 8-bit processors propelled personal computers into the corporate network and quickened the pace of distributed processing across the computer network.

Inexpensive processing also powered the digitization of the telephone network. One of the earliest fully digital switches, AT&T's 4ESS, was brought on line in Chicago in January 1976. Today's state-of-the-art 5ESS switch was brought on line in March 1982, and T1—which has been used since the 1960s for interoffice trunking—was introduced as a commodity service called Accunet just two years later.

Have the tools needed to monitor and control large voice-data networks kept pace with the accelerating rate of change in network architecture? Big users are saying no. "Quite simply, the class of diagnostics and user information we need to manage a complex network is not available" in current network management products, says Cavanagh.

Voice-data dichotomy

Part of the blame for the slow rollout of better network control products rests with users, says Douglas W. Fagg, president of Pactel Spectrum Services, a third-party private-network service supplier based in Walnut Creek, Calif. Fagg says the dichotomy between voice and data expertise on many networking staffs may have slowed the demand for new products.

"The new technology really needs tools from both telecom and the host computer," he says. So what the users must do is develop "the ability to become masters at Open Systems Interconnection [OSI] Level 1 and Level 2," Fagg says.

The problem, though, is that very few people have a command of both the physical and logical aspects of the network. What is required is people who are fluent in both telecommunications and computers. Without such fluency, users cannot speak the right language to demand the network control tools they need.

"The days of managing a net from just the logical or OSI Level 2 layer using emulation tools are gone. The days of inferential diagnostics are gone. Ten years ago when you saw a device disappear you knew the point-to-point link went down. Now your data can pass through a dozen nodes. The telephone people, the Level 1 physical layer people, already know how to break problems apart using loopbacks. The computer people know how to analyze. The two disciplines need to come together," Fagg says.

This leaves networking professionals with few choices. If in-house staff is not getting results and vendors are unresponsive, dozens of third-party service providers, like Fagg's Pactel Spectrum, stand ready to help with network management chores. The arms-length subsidiary of Pacific Telesis, created two years ago, provides diagnostic, restoral, and configuration management services to its clients on a contract basis. Its strength is a team of data-voice experts backed up by a set of custom tools, Fagg says.

The Pactel Spectrum toolbox is loaded with remote test computers and remote loopback devices. A remote test computer is located at each client's node and there are remote loopback devices at pressure points in the network. Both types of devices are designed to be transparent to the user's network, making it possible, for example, to send data from a remote loopback device regardless of whether the client is running on X.25, HDLC (high-level data link control), or asynchronous protocols.

Telemetry from the remotes is sent to a cluster of VAXs at PacTel Spectrum's control center that are loaded with inventory information and test diagnostics. The software driving the entire test system is written so that it can be readily customized to each client's needs.

Integration options

Another option is to build network management from the ground up using in-house tools that integrate the control and status information from several vendors' products. Avant-Garde Computing Inc. (Mt. Laurel, N.J.) and Datacomm Management Sciences Inc. (East Norwalk, Conn.) are two firms that offer devices to do this, but each has taken a different tack.

Net/Alert, Avant-Garde's first product introduced in the late 1970s, won early acceptance as a performance-monitoring tool for leased-line networks because it captured status, performance, utilization, and availability from a wide variety of vendor devices. The company's follow-on product, Net/Command, consists of a network workstation and remote access units that allow the network operator to prioritize and filter the alerts and status information coming from multiple network and host monitoring, management, and diagnostic products made by different vendors. Net/Command, its developers say, gives the operations manager the ability to continually modify the alert and status thresholds of dozens of different management tools.

Here is how it works. The Net/Command system consists of two components: a workstation and access units. The workstation communicates with one or more access units via communications links. Each access unit, which can be attached to a different vendor's products, performs three functions: access and control; alert filtering; and Net/Command management.

These functions are performed by three types of boards. An access module performs access and control of the attached devices. The filter module filters the alerts received from the attached devices, and an applications controller board performs the Net/Command management functions. Each board contains a 68020 microprocessor and local memory, and they communicate across a VMEbus in the access-unit backplane.

The processed access-unit data is fed to the workstation, there the information is processed further and put into a standard screen format for display (Fig. 1). "Operators want a single workstation that tracks and monitors a hierarchy of intelligent tools," says Timothy P. Ahlstrom, Avant-Garde's president. "Each network management tool might be sending 10,000 alerts a day, but only 10 might be significant. The operator has to know what those 10 are."

Datacomm Management Sciences' Automated Network Management and Control System (ANMACS) works differ-

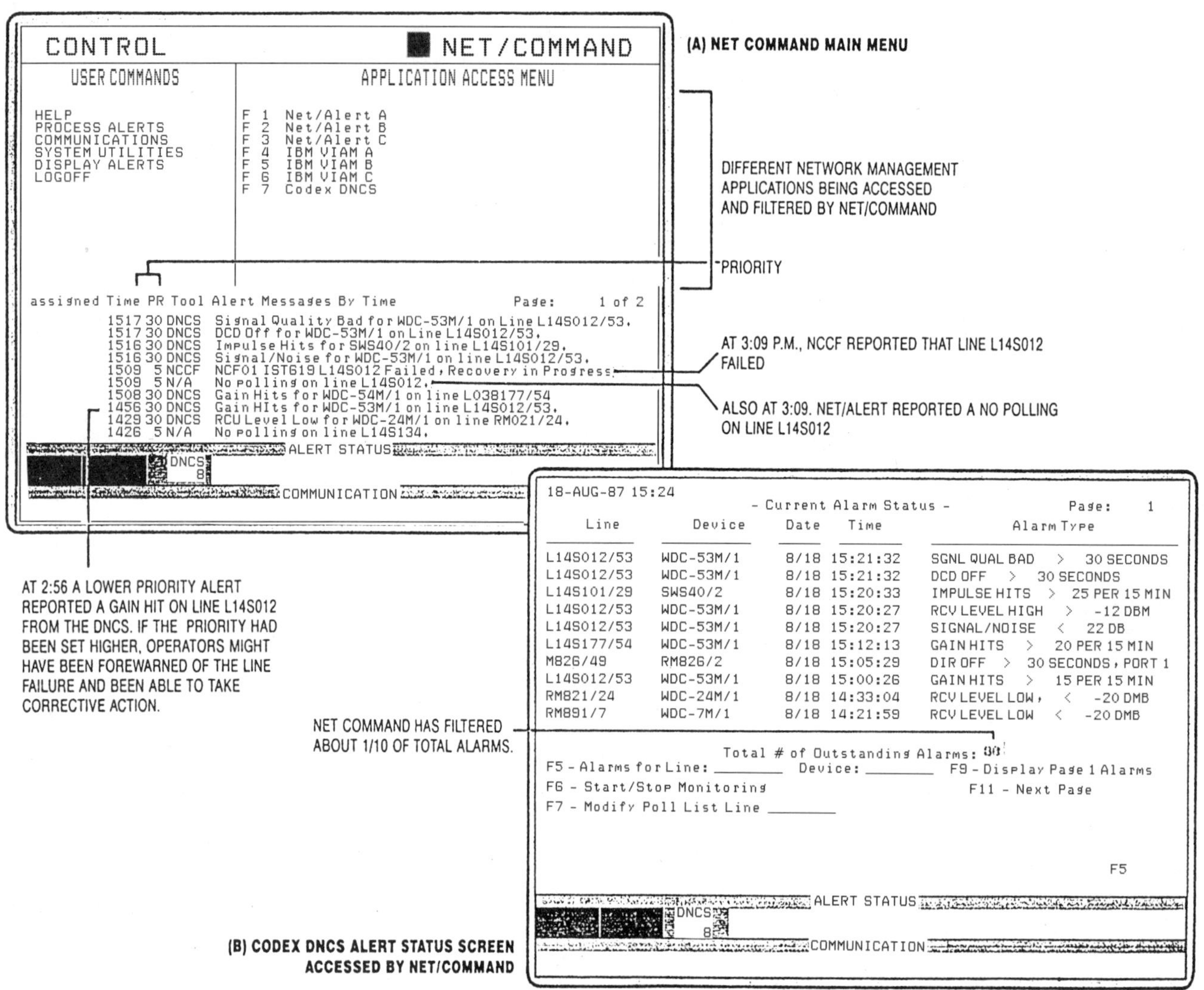

ently. It masks network management information transmitted from remote nodes and substitutes its own control information instead.

"We ignore their telemetry. We do all our own alarms because all alarms are created equal," explains Robert Geist, vice president of product technology at Datacomm Management. "For example, the number of bits used to send alarms from Racal or Codex multiplexers is not the same because the underlying hardware is not uniform."

Geist refers to ANMACS as an overlay. If an overlay is not used, Geist asks, "how do you know what data to keep and what to throw away. For example, how do you know BER [bit error rate] on the trunk is being handled the same way by two different vendors. One vendor may use a short frame count while another uses a long frame count. There are plenty of questions like this."

On the data side of the network, ANMACS typically links the front-end communications processor to a switching cabinet (Fig. 2). The cabinet, which functions as a spare switch, provides circuit access to the digital access cabinet. The matrix switch within the digital access cabinet provides the circuits that allow an operator to test the incoming line. Alarm information is sensed at the digital access cabinet based on the status of the incoming leads.

The digital access cabinet is connected via modem to the analog access cabinet. The analog access cabinet, which functions much like its digital counterpart, monitors the voice frequency portion of the network. Both data and voice access cabinets can be remotely located and transparently connected to the test bus using dedicated links.

Not every manager, though, can take the time to build a management system from the ground up or can afford third-party services. Another choice is to wait for a vendor to come along with better management products.

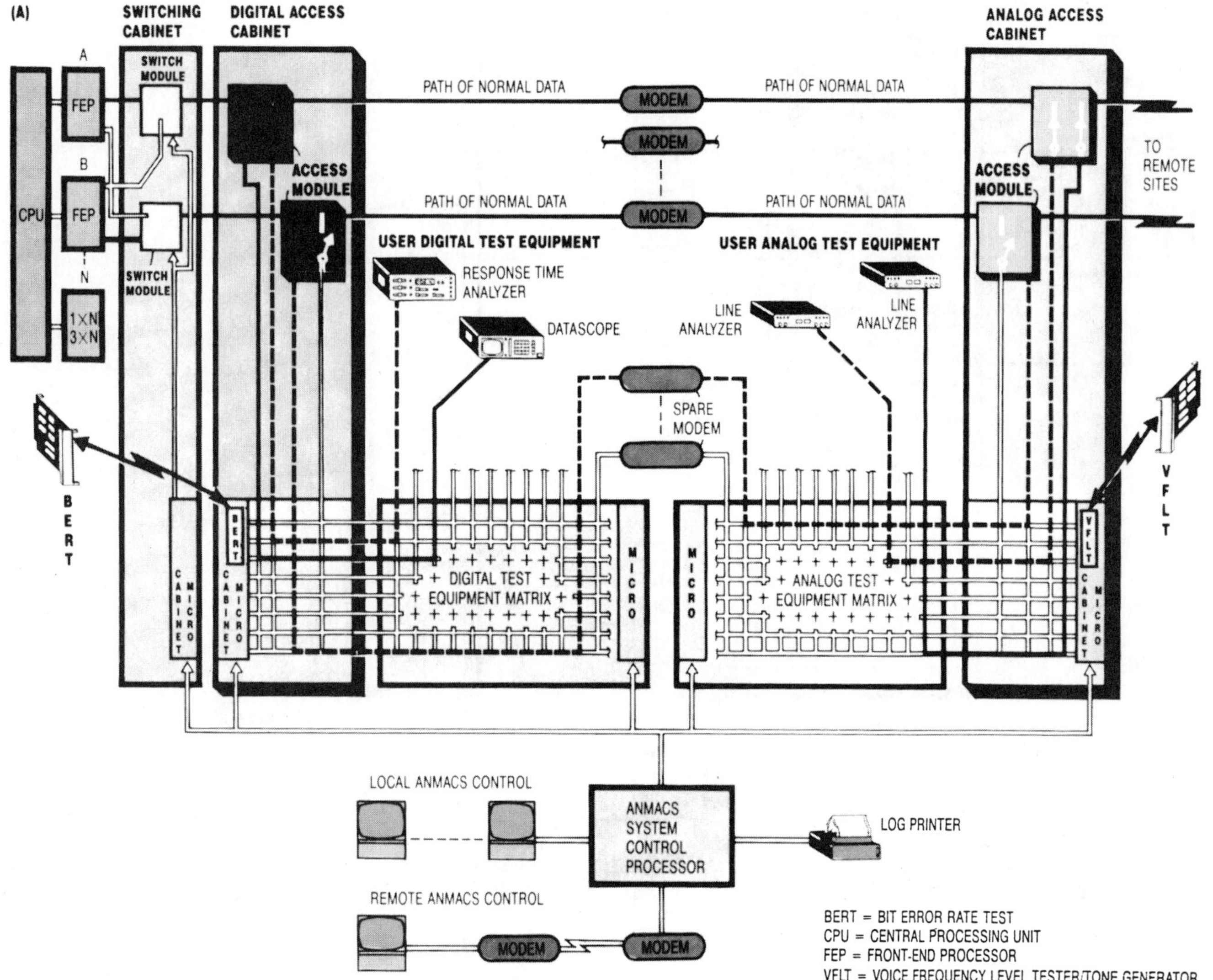

2. The way to overlay. *Datacomm Management Sciences' Automated Network Management and Control Systems (ANMACS) performs as an overlay function on existing network management gear. It ignores other vendors' telemetry and enables operators to perform tests and diagnostics directly on the effected data and voice circuits.*

This could explain why IBM's huge installed base greeted last year's announcement of a new network management product called Netview with huzzahs—despite the product's noticeable warts. At long last, it seemed, the giant was responding to the complaints of users like Gary Herron, manager of network software support for the First Union Bank (Charlotte, N.C.).

"The tools available for network management are difficult to use," says Herron, who oversees telecommunications at the bank's 800 branches. The bank's network is IBM-dominated. Herron says his network management problems became more acute as the bank evolved from strictly SNA to a more open architecture.

Netview, IBM said, would make managers' jobs less complex. "It became clear in the early 1980s that customers were having difficulty with the four or five network management products they had to learn," explains Robert B. Bailey, manager of network management products at IBM (Research Triangle Park, N.C.).

Initially, IBM set out to answer its customers' needs, Bailey says, by revamping several older IBM management products, including:

■ Network Communications Control Facility (NCCF). Introduced in the late 1970s, it provides a pipeline out of VTAM (Virtual Telecommunications Access Method) for network management information flowing from controllers and terminals to the network control terminal.

■ The Network Problem Determination Application (NPDA) provides status information about many kinds of hardware on the network.

■ The Network Logical Data Manager (NLDM) was introduced in the early 1980s. It monitors the network logically, looking for the breakdown of individual communications sessions not signaled by NPDA.

Other products that were put under the Netview umbrella include the VTAM Node Control Application, a tabular listing that gives the network operator a summary of network resources on a single screen, and the Network

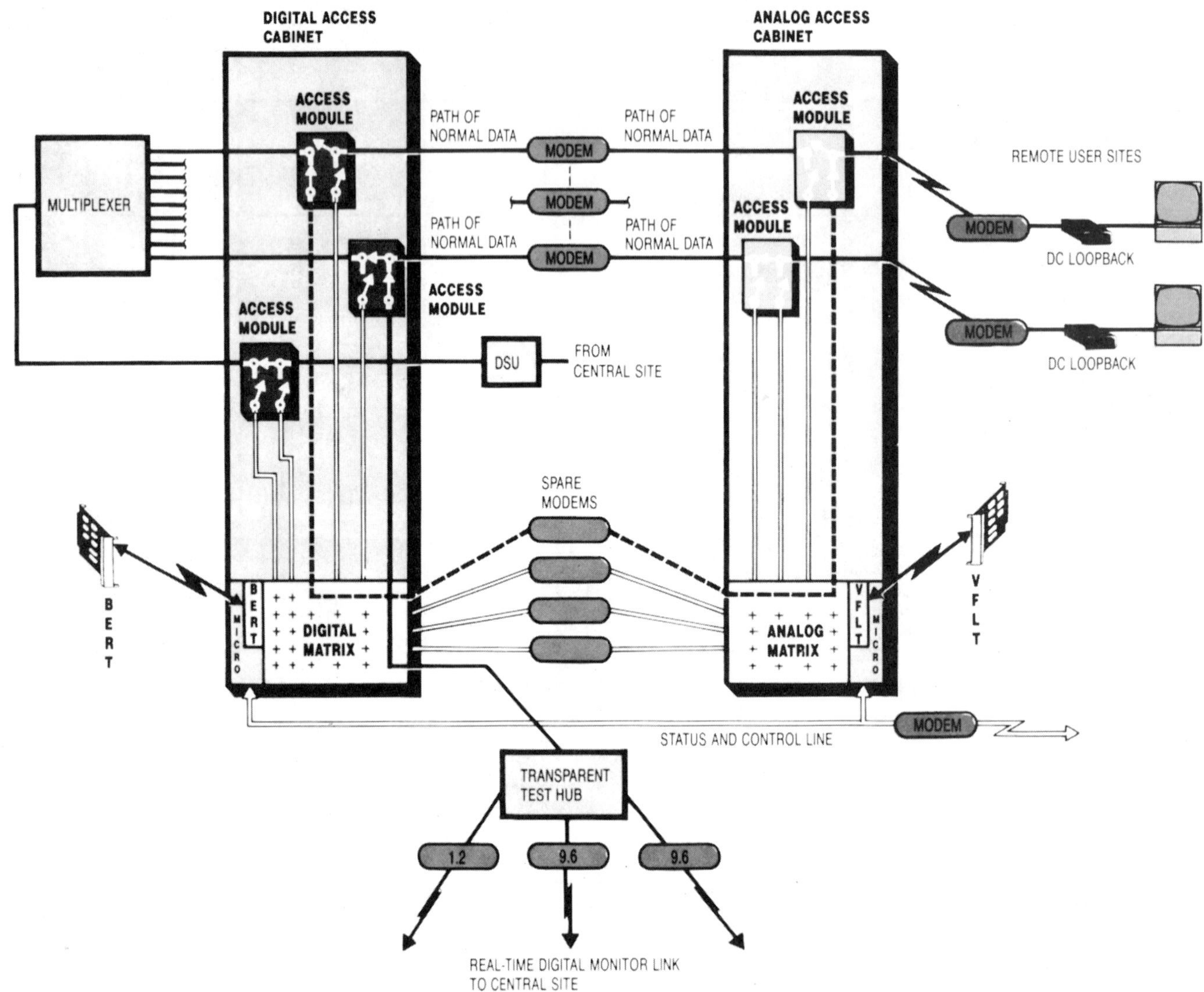

Management Productivity Facility, a program that assists the operator in selecting diagnostic routines.

According to Bailey, users were looking for "commonality between the products." What they got was a standard function key setup, the consistent use of color across tabular screen displays, and common keyword designations so that users find it easier "to navigate between the products," Bailey says. The revamping has not satisfied everyone.

Netview, its critics say, is a kludge. George Colony, president of consulting firm Forrester Research (Cambridge, Mass.), has said that Netview is so resource-intensive it can chew up 5 percent to 15 percent of any circuit during periods of normal loading. Another complaint is that the NCCF, NPDA, NLDM, and other tools that form the core of the product cannot communicate. Cincom Systems Inc., an IBM competitor in SNA management tools, says that Netview has the same database problems that flawed its earlier network management products.

"The flaws are the same as they were in the older products," says Vicki Duckworth, a senior product manager at Cincom. "The communications network management [CNM] records used to create the databases are done the same old way. You don't have common interfaces and common records between the databases underlying Netview."

Responding to such criticisms, Bailey says, "my answer is twofold. First, Netview is a first step. Database management is obviously to come. Common database access is something we continue to focus on. Second, had we taken the final step and lost all vestiges of the older products, customers would have a logical concern about where we left them. Customers are concerned about migration. They don't want to be left behind."

The product definition of Netview continued to change, however. In September 1986, four months after Netview was announced, IBM unveiled a complementary network management product. It was a bombshell. Netview/PC

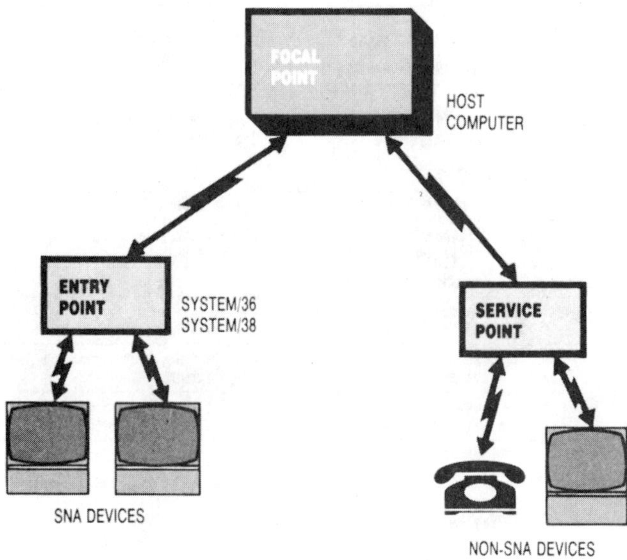

3. Opening gun. *To cement Netview/PC within Systems Network Architecture, IBM defined network management focal points, entry points, and service points.*

opened an SNA network to management information from non-IBM data and voice devices not running in an emulation mode. As part of a drive to create an Open Network Architecture, IBM was going to provide competitors with a set of protocols they could use to send their own alert information to Netview in a native mode. Now it was vendors who were lining up and shouting huzzahs.

Says Avant-Garde's Ahlstrom: "Netview is becoming a de facto standard." Rick L. Mantz, assistant vice president of engineering at Timeplex Inc. (Woodcliff Lake, N.J.), also calls Netview "a de facto standard."

"I've never looked at IBM as a product innovator," explains Robert S. Alford, vice president of circuit-switching development at BBN Communications (Cambridge, Mass.), "but anything they do has tremendous impact. When IBM does something like this, they make it easy for us and guys like Timeplex to follow."

A move of such magnitude in SNA required a new vocabulary to cement the changes (Fig. 3). The focal point, resident on a host, would provide centralized network management application support within the SNA environment. Entry points, such as the System/36 or System/38, are SNA-addressable devices that concentrate network management data from downstream SNA devices and pass it to the focal point. Service points are either IBM or non-IBM devices like personal computers that convert non-SNA network management message formats into SNA network management formats and send them to the focal point for processing.

"The service point is really a processing entity," explains Jack Drescher, product manager for Netview/PC at Research Triangle Park. "It does the processing for the focal point. Between the service point and the downstream device, an SNA connection is not needed. You can use async, X.25, or whatever protocol you require," he says.

Initially, vendors of service-point equipment were providing only a status summary of their network equipment and

alerts to the focal point. When a third round of Netview announcements was made in June 1987, a generic alert format was defined. The generic alert format standardized alert reporting and eliminated the need to maintain libraries of product-specific information on the host.

Service points and entry points introduced physical layer reporting that was previously unavailable in SNA network management. With the June announcement, physical layer reporting was taken to its logical conclusion.

As part of that announcement, IBM said it was throwing its considerable marketing presence behind the T1 network management gear developed by Network Equipment Technologies (Redwood City, Calif.). A joint marketing and development agreement with NET gives IBM access to NET's T1 switch technology—a switch with a rich set of management and diagnostic functions. It also brings dynamic bandwidth management to Netview and it gives IBM the right to use in Netview the proprietary network management protocols developed by NET.

Putting T1 management under Netview in a hierarchical network architecture turns out to be a good way to sell host computers. One analyst who declined to be identified put it this way: "T1 cannot be its own world forever. T1 data must be integrated into a database management system to be useful. IBM's strategy is to keep Netview fully compatible with T1 so that T1 management tools generate cycles in host computers. The added processing burden will draw customers to bigger computers and will also sell expensive software packages."

If buying a bigger host is a problem, users can turn to the Unified Network Management Architecture (UNMA) being developed by AT&T. UNMA has some options that hark back to the good old days when network management was in the carrier's hands. UNMA, which was announced

---

4. Reaching out. *For AT&T's UNMA hierarchy to be successful, vendors, local carriers, and other interexchange carriers must adopt the Network Management Protocol.*

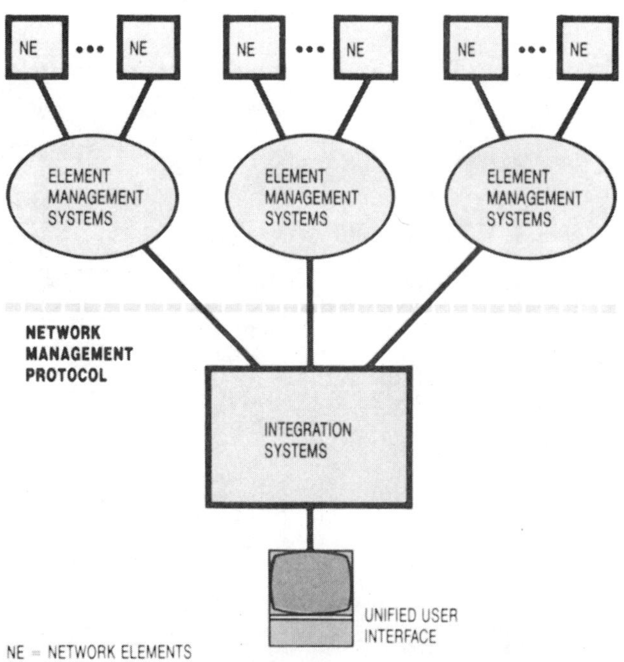

Article continues on page 198.

189

Vendor comparison: Network management

VENDOR AND MODEL	AT&T DATAPHONE II LEVEL IV SYSTEM CONTROLLER MODEL 300	AT&T DATAPHONE II LEVEL IV SYSTEM CONTROLLER MODEL 400	ATLANTIC RESEARCH NTS 3000 NETWORK RESTORATION, TEST, AND MANAGEMENT SYSTEM	ATLANTIC RESEARCH NTS 4000 DISTRIBUTED NETWORK RESTORATION, TEST, AND MANAGEMENT SYSTEM
SYSTEM CHARACTERISTICS				
Hardware configuration	Standalone	Standalone	Rackmount, PC-based	Rackmount, PC-based
Processor type	AT&T-3B2	AT&T 3B2/400	16-bit multibus or IBM PC	16-bit multibus or IBM PC
TECHNICAL CONTROL FEATURES				
Alarm conditions	Facsimile modem failure, streaming modem or DSU, no response multiplexer alarm, no answer/hold time	Streaming modem or DSU, no response multiplexer alarm, modem failure, no answer/hold time	Device failure, overload, service degradation	Device failure, overload service degradation
Number of alarm levels	User selectable –1 to 60 min.	User selectable	5, user selectable	5, user selectable
Alarm types	Console message, printer message, LED	LEDs, printer message, console message	CRT display, printer log, database log	CRT display, printer log, database log
Fallback switching	Central site operator controlled	Central site operator controlled	Automatic and manual	Automatic and manual
Switching method	Contact vendor	Contact vendor	Electromechanical, 1×N, magnetically latching A/B	Electromechanical, 1×N, magnetically latching A/B
Monitoring	Continuous local and remote	Real time	Local, continuous, and on-command	Local/remote, continuous, and on-command
Remote devices required for monitoring	Proprietary modems, DSUs, and multiplexers	Proprietary modems, DSUs, and multiplexers	Interview/Comstate test equipment (optional)	LSC-6 PC node controller provides remote control
Type of monitor signal	Sidestream and extended control channel	Sidestream and extended control channel	Direct or dial-up	Direct or dial-up
NETWORK MANAGEMENT FEATURES				
Database management system	Proprietary	Proprietary	Proprietary	Proprietary
DBMS acquisition	Included	Bundled with system	Included	Included
Data recorded	Network status-device and facility faults, alarms, system access, test results, multiplexer traffic	Network status-device and facility faults, alarms, system access, test results, multiplexer traffic	User-definable alarms, trouble ticket configuration inventory, personnel databases, etc.	User-definable alarms, trouble ticket configuration inventory, personnel databases, etc.
Reports generated	Network map, inventory profiles, trouble tickets, trending, user-defined color graphics, management reports	Trouble tickets, faults, activity summary, trending, history, color graphics, management reports	Unlimited user-defined reports on alarms, configurations, trouble tickets, inventories	Unlimited user-defined reports on alarms, configurations, trouble tickets, inventories
Other network management services supported	Remote support all network devices/facilities by AT&T, automated trouble reports	Remote support all network devices/facilities by AT&T, automated trouble reports	Other services supported via user-definable data management system	Other services supported via user-definable data management system

VENDOR AND MODEL	CINCOM SYSTEMS NET/MASTER	CODEX CORP. 4840/4850/4860 NETWORK MANAGEMENT SYSTEMS	CXR TELCOM CORPORATION SYSTEM 100 AUTOMATIC TRUNK TEST SYSTEM	DATA SWITCH INTELLINET MODEL 3205/3215/3225
SYSTEM CHARACTERISTICS				
Hardware configuration	Software only for IBM host	Standalone	Software only	Standalone
Processor type	IBM 43XX, 30XX	Data General MV Series	PC, XT, AT, or compatible	68000, 68020
TECHNICAL CONTROL FEATURES				
Alarm conditions	Any alert record fed to IBM's VTAM	Analog, digital, user definable	Inoperative trunks, trunk transmission tests outside user-definable specifications	Response time, line down, control unit I/O, line utility equipment failure, etc.
Number of alarm levels	—	Infinite	4 thresholds/test-36 total	From network to device
Alarm types	Any 3270 alarm feature	Message, audible, logging	CRT and/or printer report	Graphics display, audible alarm, printer message
Fallback switching	Not applicable	Manual, automatic	Not applicable	Full matrix
Switching method	Not applicable	Not applicable	Not applicable	Full matrix
Monitoring	Local/remote, real time, continuous or on command	Continuous, local, and remote	Not applicable	Continuous, local and remote, real time
Remote devices required for monitoring	Not applicable	Codex system modems	Not applicable	Proprietary line monitoring units
Type of monitor signal	Mainstream	Sidestream	Not applicable	Independent
NETWORK MANAGEMENT FEATURES				
Database management system	Proprietary	Proprietary	Proprietary	Proprietary, SAS, SLR
DBMS acquisition	Bundled	Proprietary	Bundled	Bundled
Data recorded	Configuration, activity, reference, inventory, hardware, alarms, modem type alerts, operator, performance	Configuration history, alarms, inventory, personnel, trouble tickets	Trunk operative faults, transmission test results, out of specification flags for tests	Activity, alarms, single transaction
Reports generated	Network schematics, audit trails, trouble tickets, inventory, account summary, current activity, history, etc.	Alarms, history, inventory, user definable	Trouble tickets, activity summary, demand test results, current activity	Alarms, audit trails, account summary, current account history, real time utilization
Other network management services supported	Failure, performance, configuration management; access control	Monitoring, fallback, configuration	—	Multiple Data Switch products

*Explanation of abbreviations and acronyms can be found at end of table.

AVANT-GARDE COMPUTING NET/ALERT PLUS	AVANT-GARDE COMPUTING NET/GUARD	AVANT-GARDE COMPUTING NET/COMMAND	CASE COMMUNICATIONS INC. CASE 5130, 5150	CASE COMMUNICATIONS INC. CASE 5200
Standalone	Standalone	Standalone	—	—
Concurrent Computer 3200	Concurrent Computer 3200	Motorola 68000 Series	Convergent Technologies	Convergent Technologies
Line down, no polls, error threshold, power failure, response time, user-defined performance	9 security alerts, 5 thresholds except on Alert, 7 functional	User-defined filtered alerts, network management tool alarms	DTE power failure, modem power failure, signal quality, line level, phase jitter	DTE power failure, modem power failure, signal quality, line level, carrier offset
—	2	User-defined maximum	2	—
Audible alarm, color graphics display	Audible console, graphic display	Audible, color graphic display	LED, console (color coded), audible	LED, console (color coded), audible
Net/Switch	Automatic disconnect	Optional automatic or manual	Automatic	Automatic
Full matrix	—	Electronic switch, manual	Not applicable	Not applicable
Local/remote, real time, continuous or on command	Continuous local and remote real-time monitoring	Local and remote, continuous	Local and remote, continuous	Local and remote, continuous
Proprietary line monitoring units	Proprietary interface control unit	Proprietary access units	Proprietary modems and multiplexers	Proprietary modems and multiplexers
Sidestream	Sidestream	Mainstream	Sidestream	Sidestream
SAS, Lotus, MICS, Symphony	—	Proprietary	Unify	Unify
Bundled with system	Bundled with system	Proprietary bundled, SAS	Bundled	Bundled
Configuration alarms, usage, performance, availability, traffic volume, characters	User activity alerts, session activation, port utilities audit trail, class profile	Network alarms, network configuration, electronic mail	Network configuration, hardware activity, line activity, alarms, histories, line troubles	Network configuration, hardware activity, line activity, alarms, histories, line troubles
Over 250 variations of standard reports and over 110 color graphic charts, unlimited number of user-defined reports	Activity summary, current activity alerts, user profiles, port utilization	Network operations event log, network alarm reporting	Network lists, trouble reports, activity summary, configuration	Network lists, trouble reports, activity summary, configuration ticket, trouble ticketing
Performance management, configuration management	Access control, terminal emulation, protocol conversion	Failure management, performance management	Diagnostics, soft strapping, central monitoring, dial backup, multiplexer support	Diagnostics, soft strapping, central monitoring, dial backup, multiplexer support

DATA SWITCH CONTROLNET 200	DATA SWITCH CONTROLNET 250	DATA SWITCH MATRIX SWITCHING VSM, WSM, TSM	DATA SWITCH MASS+ MULTIPLE ACCESS SWITCHING SYSTEM	DATA SWITCH DSM DISTRIBUTED SWITCH MATRIX
—	Standalone, mini-based	—	—	—
IBM PC/AT-339 or compatible	Multibus architecture	Data Switch designed	Data Switch designed	Not applicable
Equipment, component, line failure, pin status	Equipment failure, streaming modem or DSU, line down, power failure, network interrupt	Two (software programmable)	Carrier detect plus 1 optional	Digital state alarms, analog level alarm
Multiple, user defined	Multiple, user defined	—	—	—
LED, console, audible, audit trail	Audible, LEDs, printer message, console message	Audible, CRT, printed log	Audible, CRT, printed log	Audible, CRT, printed log
Automatic, full matrix	Automatic, full matrix	Automatic	Automatic and manual	Semi-automatic
Matrix	Full matrix	Full electronic matrix (except T-1, hard contact)	Electromechanical, A/B, 1×N	Full electronic matrix
Local, remote, on command, continuous	Local and remote	Local and remote	Local and remote	Local and remote, on command
None	None	T-Bar Data Compression Recorder	Data Compression Recorder	—
Independent	Independent	Mainstream	Mainstream	Mainstream
Proprietary Data Switch	Proprietary	80 character per connection	Proprietary	Proprietary
Bundled	Bundled with system	Priced separately	Priced separately	Priced separately
Configuration hardware, history, activity, security, and trouble-shooting	Configuration, activity, hardware, alarms, operations performed, protocol, equipment type, security	Configuration, hardware, activity	Configuration, hardware, activity	Configuration, activity, and hardware
Trouble tickets, memo, network status, audit trail, configuration status	Alarms, audit trails, account summary, current activity history	—	—	Port database, configuration activity, alarm summary
Diagnostic, performance management, remote access, configuration management	Performance management, diagnostics, configuration management, remote access	—	None	Failure management, configuration management

Compiled by: Diane P. Falten, Assistant Editor/Analyst, Datapro Research Corp.

Vendor comparison: Network management

VENDOR AND MODEL	DATACOMM MANAGEMENT SCIENCES ANMACS	DATACOMM MANAGEMENT SCIENCES NETWORK SERVICE MANAGER (NSM-1000/4000)	DATATEL DCP3800 NETWORK MANAGEMENT SYSTEM	DIGILOG NETWORK ANALYSIS AND MANAGEMENT SYSTEM (NAMS)
SYSTEM CHARACTERISTICS				
Hardware configuration	—	—	PC-based	—
Processor type	DMS SCP-III (8086)	DEC PDP 1173	IBM XT or AT	DEC MicroVax I
TECHNICAL CONTROL FEATURES				
Alarm conditions	Up to 11 EIA pins, transmit and receive voltage/frequency level, power failure, patch and break, F/B	Response time distribution, no polls, response time average, processing time average, timeout	Equipment failure, streaming modem, service degradation, line down, no polls	8–12 digital signals, analog levels, user test scan results
Number of alarm levels	—	2	1	Depends on configuration
Alarm types	Audible, console message, printed log, alarm report	Graphic display, alarm report	Audible alarm, LEDs, console or printer message	Audible alarm, console alert graphic display, log print
Fallback switching	Automatic and manual	MTRX 500/8000	None	Automatic and manual
Switching method	A/B, 1×N, manual and electro-mechanical, 3×N	MTRX 500/8000	Not applicable	A/B, relay type 1×N, full electronic matrix switch
Monitoring	Local and remote, on command	Local and remote, continuous, passive	Local/remote, real time, continuous or on command	Local and remote, continuous, scheduled
Remote devices required for monitoring	Remote access system	1 line access module per circuit	Proprietary modems, multiplexers, DSUs	Modem wraparound unit, access system, matrix switch
Type of monitor signal	Mainstream	Independent, noninterfering	Mainstream/sidestream (both automatically)	Sidestream, mainstream, dedicated low-speed channel
NETWORK MANAGEMENT FEATURES				
Database management system	Proprietary–SCP III	Proprietary	Proprietary	Proprietary
DBMS acquisition	Bundled	Bundled	Bundled with system	Bundled
Data recorded	Audit trail of all operator actions, alarms and abnormal conditions, and test result data	7-day database by hour for application, lines, and application by line; 7 days by control unit and device	Configuration, alarms, reference, inventory, hardware, modem type, activity	Configuration, inventory activity, trouble tickets
Reports generated	Audit trail, as above; alarm status	26 reports for network operation, network management, network planning	Trouble tickets, alarms, inventory, audit trails, activity summary, current activity, history	Configuraton, inventory and activity summaries, trouble tickets
Other network management services supported	Automatic BERT and voltage/frequency level testing (Autoscan), remote control tests	Real-time alarms, trend analysis, service-level agreements	Monitor, diagnostics, access control, DDS with secondary channel	Failure management, configuration management, automated scheduled testing

VENDOR AND MODEL	DYNATECH DATA SYSTEMS DYNANET 57	DYNATECH DATA SYSTEMS DYNANET 150	DYNATECH DATA SYSTEMS DYNANET 240	DYNATECH DATA SYSTEMS PRISM DYNANET 310
SYSTEM CHARACTERISTICS				
Hardware configuration	Standalone	—	—	Standalone
Processor type	Intel 8086	IBM PC/XT or compatible	Intel 80286, 8085, DDS	80186, Z80
TECHNICAL CONTROL FEATURES				
Alarm conditions	Equipment failure, system failure	Equipment failure, system failure, RS-232-C signal threshold violations	System faults/errors, user assignment criteria interface lead based alarm	Performance quality, availability
Number of alarm levels	Multiple	Multiple	Multiple, user defined	2
Alarm types	Audible, LEDs, console message, printed log	Audible, console messages, printed log	Audible, CRT display, printed log	Audible, graphic CRT display
Fallback switching	Matrix	Electromechanical switching	Automatic and manual	Automatic, manual
Switching method	1×N, M×N, manual, electro-mechanical, A/B, full matrix	Electromechanical—A/B, access and equipment substitution	Full matrix, A/B, 1×N, M×N, electromechanical	Control of switching
Monitoring	Local and remote, continuous or on command	Local and remote, continuous or on command	Local/Remote, continuous and on command	Local and remote controls
Remote devices required for monitoring	None	None	Standalone remote monitors, modem wraparounds	None
Type of monitor signal	Mainstream or sidestream	—	Mainstream, sidestream, dial-up	—
NETWORK MANAGEMENT FEATURES				
Database management system	Proprietary	Proprietary	Proprietary	Proprietary
DBMS acquisition	Bundled	Bundled	Bundled with system	Bundled
Data recorded	Configuration, hardware activity, operations performed, line trouble	Configuration, operations performed	Network configuration, hardware activity, line activity, alarms, histories, line troubles	Performance measurement data
Reports generated	Network lists, trouble reports, activity summary, configuration	Trouble tickets, configuration, activity summary	Line, network, alarm activities, network configurations, trouble reports, diagnostic operations	Performance profiles of the network
Other network management services supported	Remote switching, testing, and monitoring	Remote switching, testing, and monitoring	Remote switching, alarming, monitoring, and test diagnostic access	Real-time alarms, communication switch control

DIGILOG NETWORK DIAGNOSTIC AND TEST SYSTEM (NDTS)	DIGILOG MODEM DIAGNOSTIC AND TEST SYSTEM (MDTS)	DIGITAL COMMUNICATIONS ASSOCIATES (DCA) SERIES 9000 NMS	DIGITAL COMMUNICATIONS ASSOCIATES (DCA) NMS PC V2.0	DYNATECH DATA SYSTEMS DYNANET 52
—	—	Mini-based	PC-based	Standalone
IBM PC	IBM PC	Sun 3 workstation	PC/AT or compatible	IBM PC/XT or compatible
Fault detection	Fault detection	Equipment failure, traffic overload, service degradation, line down, power failure	Equipment failure, traffic overload, service degradation, line down, no polls	Equipment failure, system failure
Multiple operator controlled	Multiple operator controlled	4	1	Multiple
Audible alarm, console message, graphic display	Audible alarm, console message, graphic display	Audible, printer message, console message, graphics	Audible, printer message, console, screen border	Audible, console message, printed log
Automatic	None	Automatic	Automatic	Electronic, electromechanical
A/B, 1×N, N×M	None	Electronic switch	Electronic switch	1×N, M×N, manual, electromechanical, A/B, full matrix
Local, remote, continuous	Local, remote, continuous	Local and remote, real time continuous or on command	Local and remote, continuous or on command, filter, real time	Local and remote, continuous or on command
NS System II	WRB/1 wraparound box	Multiplexers	Proprietary modems, multiplexers	None
Overlay (mainstream)	Sidestream	Mainstream	Mainstream	Mainstream, sidestream, or dial-up
None	None	—	—	Proprietary
None	None	Bundled with system	Bundled with system	Bundled
Configuration, activity	Configuration, activity	Configuration, activity, reference, alarms, modem type	Configuration accounting, reference, inventory, hardware, alarms, activity history	Configuration, hardware activity, operations performed
Configuration, activity	Configuration, activity	Network schematics, bar graphs, trouble tickets, account summary, current accounting, history	Network schematics, inventory, trouble ticket, alarms, audit trail, account summary, current account, history	Network lists, activity summary, configurations
None	None	Failure, performance, configuration management; monitoring; diagnostics	Failure, performance, configuration management; monitor; diagnostics	Remote switching, testing, and monitoring

DYNATECH DATA SYSTEMS DYNANET 325	DYNATECH DATA SYSTEMS PRISM DYNANET 350	DYNATECH DATA SYSTEMS CMS—CHANNEL MANAGEMENT SYSTEM	EMCOM CORP. NCS70 SERIES	GENERAL DATACOMM INDUSTRIES NETCOM-7 NCM-70
Standalone	—	Standalone	Standalone	—
80186, Z80	80186, Z80	—	Information not available	Proprietary
Equipment failures, streaming modem or DSU, traffic overload, service degradation	Performance quality	—	Over 250 network, line, controller, and terminal-related alarms	All network interfaces, Mega Mux, GEN*NET, DDS
2	2	—	None to all	Not applicable
Audible, graphics display	Audible, CRT display	LEDs, channel activity	Console message, audible alarm, printer display	Audible, CRT, printer
Automatic, full matrix	Yes, automatic	Automatic, full matrix, manual	Not applicable	Auto/semi-automatic
Electromechanical, full matrix, A/B, 1×N, electronic matrix	Control of switching	Electromechanical, full matrix, 1×N	Not applicable	Single, gang, A/B, test and access, 1×N
Local and remote	Local and remote controls	Local and remote	Continuous, remote	Continuous or on command
Proprietary line monitoring units	None	—	None	Proprietary modems, monitor boards
Sidestream	—	—	Mainstream	Sidestream, mainstream
Proprietary	Proprietary	Proprietary	MICS & SAS-based	Proprietary
Bundled with system	Bundled	Bundled with system	Separately priced	Bundled
Configuration, activity, reference, hardware, alarms, performance measurement data	Performance measurement data	Configuration, activity, operations performed	Line utilization, line activity, response time, error and status real time/retrieval, line trace/trap	All network events configuration, inventory
Network schematics, performance profiles of network, trouble tickets, alarms, audit trail, histories	Performance profiles of the network	Activity summary, current activity	By line, controller device, application, usage availability, current activity, message accounting	Event summary, trouble tickets, inventory, configuration, graphics
Failure, performance, configuration management; monitor; diagnostic	Real-time alarms, communication switch control	Configuration management	Planning data, performance trends	Host CPU interface, NMC-to-NMC interface, satellite controller

Vendor comparison: Network management

VENDOR AND MODEL	GENERAL DATACOMM INDUSTRIES SDC-51	INFINET 90/40	INFINET 90/50	INFINET 90/70
SYSTEM CHARACTERISTICS				
Hardware configuration	—	Standalone	Standalone	Standalone
Processor type	Proprietary	DEC Microvax II, SUN	DEC Microvax II, SUN	DEC Microvax II, SUN
TECHNICAL CONTROL FEATURES				
Alarm conditions	All network interfaces	Line failure, devices failure, all network interfaces	Line failure, device failure, network interfaces	Line failure, device failure, network interfaces
Number of alarm levels	Not applicable	2	2	2
Alarm types	Not applicable	CRT display, audible, printer message	CRT display, audible, printer message	CRT display, audible, printer message
Fallback switching	Auto/semi-automatic	Automatic	Automatic	Manual
Switching method	Single, gang, A/B, test and access, 1×N	A/B, fallback, dial backup	A/B, fallback, dial backup	Manual
Monitoring	Remote continuous	Continuous, local and remote	Continuous, local and remote	Continuous, local and remote
Remote devices required for monitoring	Proprietary modems monitor BDS	Proprietary modems	Proprietary modems	Proprietary modems
Type of monitor signal	Sidestream	Sidestream	Sidestream	Sidestream
NETWORK MANAGEMENT FEATURES				
Database management system	Not applicable	Proprietary	Proprietary	Proprietary
DBMS acquisition	Not applicable	Bundled and free standing	Bundled and free standing	Bundled and free standing
Data recorded	All network events reported back to NMC-70	Configurations, hardware status, activities, alarms, call record information, channel status, alarms	Configurations, hardware status, activity, alarm, call record information, channel status, equipment I.D.	Configurations, hardware status activity, alarms, call record information, channel status, equipment I.D.
Reports generated	Not applicable	Problem reports, trouble tickets, activity reports, inventory detail, network availability	Problem reports, trouble tickets, activity reports, inventory detail, network availability	Problem reports, trouble tickets, activity reports, inventory, accounting, network availability
Other network management services supported	Not applicable	Automatic escalation of alert levels in trouble ticket system	Automatic escalation of alert levels in trouble ticket systems	Supports performance management subsystem, automated escalation of alarms

VENDOR AND MODEL	IBM NETVIEW PC	INTERNATIONAL DATA SCIENCES (IDS) SERIES 9000 NM&TCS	INTERNATIONAL DATA SCIENCES (IDS) DIGITAL MATRIX SWITCH (DMS)	NEC AMERICA NETWORK CONTROL AND MANAGEMENT SYSTEM (NCMS)
SYSTEM CHARACTERISTICS				
Hardware configuration	PC-based software	—	—	Standalone
Processor type	IBM PC/XT, PC/AT	IBM PC	IBM PC	NEC Network Processor
TECHNICAL CONTROL FEATURES				
Alarm conditions	Alerts, equipment failure, line down, no poll, power failure, error threshold	Equipment failure, CRT failure	Equipment failure, CRT failure	Line Parameters, EIA conditions (user programmable thresholds)
Number of alarm levels	—	2	5	1
Alarm types	Console message	Audible alarm, LED, console message	LED, console message	Console message, color graphics display, audible
Fallback switching	—	Manual	Operator initiated	Console command
Switching method	—	Electromechanical, A/B, ABC, 2×N	256-by-256 matrix	Not applicable
Monitoring	Local and remote	Local and remote, on command	Local and remote, on command	Continuous, local and remote
Remote devices required for monitoring	—	Inherent in module, CRT signal status	Module signal status monitor ports	NEC SPN Series modems
Type of monitor signal	—	Mainstream	Mainstream	Sidestream
NETWORK MANAGEMENT FEATURES				
Database management system	—	Dacom-NET application soft	Dacom-NET matrix software	NEC proprietary
DBMS acquisition	—	Included	Included in matrix	Bundled
Data recorded	Alarms	Configurations, activity alarm database	Configurations, activity alarm bases	Configuration, hardware, reference, alarms, inventory, trouble tickets
Reports generated	Trouble tickets, alarms	Journal, activity, and statistical reports	Journal, activity, and statistical reports	Current and historical alarm, trouble ticket, modem attributes, modem, hardware, and circuit inventory
Other network management services supported	Monitoring	Distributed intelligence	Continuous self test, distributed matrix switch	Eye pattern diagnostics, BERT/BLERT, auto test, auto poll test, line parameters

INFOTRON SYSTEMS CORP. INTEGRATED NETWORK MANAGER (INM)	INFOTRON SYSTEMS CORP. ADVANCED NETWORK MANAGER (ANM 800)	INFOTRON SYSTEMS CORP. ADVANCED NETWORK MANAGER (ANM 1500)	INFOTRON SYSTEMS CORP. ADVANCED NETWORK MANAGER (ANM INX)	IBM NETVIEW
—	—	—	—	Software only
68000	IBM PC/XT or AT	IBM PC/XT or AT	IBM PC/XT or AT	IBM mainframe
Trunk, equipment, line failures; errors; all network alarms	Line, devices, all network interfaces	Line, devices, all network interfaces	Line failure, device failure, all network interfaces	Service degradation, line problems, response time, equipment failure
2	1	1	—	—
Color graphics, audible, alarm window	Audible, console message, and event printer	Audible, console message, and event printer	Audible, console message, and event printer	—
Automatic	Manual and automatic	Manual and automatic	Manual and automatic	—
$1 \times N$	Full matrix, $1 \times N$	Full matrix, $1 \times N$	Full matrix, $1 \times N$	—
Local and remote, on command or continuous	Continuous, local and remote	Continuous, local and remote	Continuous, local, and remote	Local and remote
Proprietary	Monitor boards, remote monitor	Monitor boards, remote monitor	Monitor boards, remote monitors	—
Mainstream	Mainstream, passive	Mainstream, passive	Mainstream, passive	Mainstream
Proprietary	Proprietary	Proprietary	Proprietary	—
Bundled	Bundled	Bundled	Bundled	—
Configuration, system events, alarms, and statistics	Configuration, events, status operation message, call record information, channel status, alarms, equipment I.D.	Configuration, events, status operation message, call record information, alarms, channel status, equipment I.D.	Configuration, events, status, operations message, call record information, alarms, channel status, equipment I.D.	Alarms, hardware
Network schematic, current activity, activity summary	Configuration, alarm history, call records, channel status, current activity, trend profiles	Configuration, alarm history, call record, channel status, current activity, and trend profiles	Configuration, alarm history, call record, channel status, current activity, trend profiles	—
Failure, performance, configuration management; performance analysis	Failure management, performance management, configuration management	Failure management, performance management, configuration management	Diagnostics, primary console operation	Hardware monitoring, session monitor, status monitor, control facility

NEC AMERICA NCMS-320	NORTHERN TELECOM/ SPECTRON NMS	PARADYNE 5530	PARADYNE ANALYSIS 6510	PARADYNE ANALYSIS ENTRE
Standalone	—	Standalone	Micro-based	Software package
NEC XL/32	DEC/PDP-11	IBM Series/1-Paradyne	68010	IBM PC or PC compatible
Equipment failure, line down, streaming modem or DSU, service degradation, error threshold	Lead state, equipment failure, traffic overload/underutilization	ID line parameter, EIA	Streaming modem or DSU, line down, network interfaces, error thresholds	ID line parameter, EIA
1	4	—	10 line parameters/10 EIA lead	—
Audible, console message, graphics display	Color-coded real-time display	Console message, printed log	Printer message, console message	Console message, printed log
Manual	Console command	On-console command	Console command	On console command
Manual	Electromechanical, A/B, full matrix, $1 \times N$, $N \times M$	$1 \times N$, matrix	Console command	1×1
Local and remote, real time, continuous or on command	Local and remote, continuous or on command	Continuous, local and remote	Local and remote, continuous or on command	Continuous, local and remote
Proprietary modems	Remote datascope, store-and-forward device	Proprietary modems with monitor board	Monitor boards	Proprietary modems with monitor board
Sidestream	Dial-up	Sidestream	Sidestream	Sidestream
Proprietary	Proprietary	Proprietary relational database	Proprietary relational database	None
Bundled with system	Bundled	Bundled	Separately priced	Not applicable
Configuration, activity, alarms, reference, inventory, hardware, modem type	Alarm, performance, data, audit trail, trouble tickets	Terminal, circuit, modem, vendor, customer defined for relations	Inventory, hardware, alarms, modem type, vendor, location, equipment	Modem type, physical location
Network schematics, inventory, trouble ticket, alarms, history	Exception reports, histograms on availability, performance, trouble tickets, and status	Trouble tickets, user-defined reports	Trouble tickets, alarms, inventory, vendor performance, equipment performance, alert statistics, summary report	System configuration, alarm sort
Monitoring, diagnostics, configuration management, fallback	Control of test equipment, T1 mux, and non-NT vendor network products	Automatic escalation of alert levels in trouble ticket system	Diagnostics	None

Vendor comparison: Network management

VENDOR AND MODEL	RACAL-MILGO CMS 2001	RACAL-MILGO CMS 2050	RACAL-MILGO CMS 2060 SERIES	RACAL-MILGO CMS MATRIX SWITCH
SYSTEM CHARACTERISTICS				
Hardware configuration	Mini-based	Mini-based	Mini-based	—
Processor type	DEC Professional Series	DEC Micro PDP 11/53	DEC Micro PDP 11/73	—
TECHNICAL CONTROL FEATURES				
Alarm conditions	Equipment failure, stream modem or DSU, service degradation, line down, power failure	Equipment failure, streaming modem or DSU, service degradation, line down, power failure	Equipment failure, streaming modem or DSU, service degradation, line down, power failure	Events, definable 8 alarms/connection
Number of alarm levels	EIA alarm mask/analog	EIA alarm mask/analog	EIA mask/analog threshold	Definable
Alarm types	Audible, printer message, console message	Audible, printer message, console message	Audible, printer message, console message	LEDs, console message
Fallback switching	Automated, manual, operator	Automated, manual, operator	Automated, manual, operator	Automatic with user activity
Switching method	A/B, 1×N, manual, full matrix, electromechanical, electronic	Manual, A/B, 1×N, full matrix, electromechanical electronic	Manual, A/B, 1×N, full matrix, electromechanical, electronic	Time/space, any to any time
Monitoring	Continuous or on command, local and remote	Local and remote, real time, continuous or on command	Local and remote, real time, continuous or on command	Continuous background diagnostics, customer actuated
Remote devices required for monitoring	Proprietary modems, multiplexers, DSUs, wrap devices	—	Proprietary modems, multiplexers, DSUs, wrap devices	Utilize scopes or monitors, EIA/voltage/frequency signals
Type of monitor signal	Mainstream/sidestream	Mainstream/sidestream	Mainstream/sidestream	Mainstream, noninterruptive
NETWORK MANAGEMENT FEATURES				
Database management system	Proprietary	Proprietary	Proprietary	Console accounting
DBMS acquisition	Bundled with system	Bundled with system	Bundled with system	—
Data recorded	Configuration, inventory, activity, reference, hardware, alarms, modem type, operations performed	Configuration, activity reference inventory, hardware, alarms, modem type, operations performed	Configuration, activity, alarms, reference, inventory, hardware, modem type, operations performed	Disk (dual 40MB)
Reports generated	Network schematics, history, inventory, alarms, activity summary, current activity	Network schematics, inventory, alarms, activity summary, current activity, history, performance trends	Network schematics, inventory, alarms, activity summaries, current activity, history, performance trends	Connection status, group status, port types, pending alarms, alarm status
Other network management services supported	Monitoring, diagnostics, configuration management, access control, line quality	Performance, monitor, diagnostics, configuration, line quality analysis	Performance, monitor, diagnostics, configuration, line quality analysis	CMS diagnostics

VENDOR AND MODEL	TIMEPLEX PROPHET NETWORK MANAGEMENT SYSTEM FOR SWITCHING MICROPLEXER NETWORKS	TIMEPLEX LINK NETWORK MANAGEMENT SYSTEMS FOR LINK/1 AND LINK/2 SYSTEMS	TIMEPLEX SENTINEL 424 MANAGEMENT CONCENTRATOR	TIMEPLEX LINK/VIEW
SYSTEM CHARACTERISTICS				
Hardware configuration	PC-based	PC-based	Standalone	Software only
Processor type	IBM PC/XT	IBM PC/XT, PC/AT	—	—
TECHNICAL CONTROL FEATURES				
Alarm conditions	Real time network status and error information	Failure	—	Equipment failure, line down, no polls, power failure
Number of alarm levels	—	—	—	—
Alarm types	Audible, display, and printout	—	Audible, CRT, printers, visual	Console message
Fallback switching	—	—	—	—
Switching method	—	—	—	—
Monitoring	Local and remote	Local and remote	—	Local and remote, continuous or on command
Remote devices required for monitoring	Microplexer multiplexer, network monitoring/configuration	LINK/1 or LINK/2 Facilities Management System	—	LINK/1 or LINK/2 Facilities Management System
Type of monitor signal	—	—	—	Passes LINK/1 or LINK/2 alarms to Netview PC
NETWORK MANAGEMENT FEATURES				
Database management system	—	—	—	—
DBMS acquisition	—	—	—	—
Data recorded	Configuration, network reports, port parameters, operational status, network configuration	Configuration, network port parameters and routing, operating statistics, and report generation	Alarm conditions, any data sent or received via the command terminal	Alarms alarms
Reports generated	Network and port configuration, operating statistics	Network configuration statistics, diagrams	Date/time charges in alarm conditions, out of data sent and received by command terminal	Alarms, history
Other network management services supported	Downline loading of network configuration, management, and diagnostics	Downline or uploading of LINK/1 or LINK/2 system parameters	Monitoring of all communications with all devices attached	Failure management, monitoring

RACAL-VADIC VA9000	SYMPLEX MAESTRO NETWORK MANAGEMENT SYSTEM	TELEPROCESSING PRODUCTS MULTIDROP NETWORK MANAGER (MNM)	INFINET PERFORMANCE SYSTEMS SMART
PC-based	—	—	Standalone
IBM PC or XT	Zenith-Intel 8088/80286	Proprietary	80X86; 280
Equipment failure, traffic overload, service degradation, line down, error threshold	Compression rate, trunk utilities, host utilities, signal level, dial-back, line error	Link lost, out of service, carrier lost, failed response, streaming, terminal	Equipment failure, traffic overload, service degradation, line down, no poll, response time
2	5	2 levels, open or close	4
Audible, LEDs, printer message, console message	Audible alarm, graphic display, printed report	Audible, console message, and graphic display	Audible, graphic display, console message, log
Manual	Not applicable	No	Not applicable
Manual	Not applicable	Not applicable	Not applicable
Local and remote, real time, continuous or on command	Local and remote	Local and remote, continuous or on command	Local and remote
Monitor boards	Any Symplex product card or standalone	TP-504, -503, or -552 CSU/DSUs	Proprietary line monitoring units
—	Mainstream	Mainstream	Not applicable
Proprietary	Proprietary	Proprietary-TeleProcess	ISAM
Bundled with system	Bundled	Bundled with system	Bundled with system
Configuration, activity, inventory, hardware, modem type, alarms, history	Current status configuration	Configuration, inventory failed scans, alarm archive, line files, drop files	Configuration, response time utilities, availability, activity alarms, operations done, transaction type
Inventory, alarms, audit trail, activity summary, current activity, history	Activity summary, current activity, alarm conditions	Inventory, activity summary, current activity, line information, drop information	Alarms, activity, summaries current activity, history, exceptions available, throughput, response time, transaction type
Performance, monitor, diagnostic, configuration, access control	Failure and performance management	Performance management	Performance management, monitoring, configuration management

VERILINK CORPORATION
VERINET

VERILINK CORPORATION VERINET
PC-based (or mini)
IBM PC, DEC VAX
Equipment failure, service degradation, line down, error thresholds, power failure
User selectable
Audible, graphics display, printer message, console
Automatic, full matrix, manual
Full matrix, A/B, 1×N, electronic switch
Local and remote, real time, continuous or on command
Standalone remote monitors
Mainstream
Proprietary
Separate
Configuration, activity, inventory, hardware, operations parformed, alarms
Network schematics, trouble ticket, inventory, history, alarms, audit trails, activity summary, current activity
Failure, performance, configuration management; monitor; diagnostics

BERT = Bit Error-Rate Test

BLERT = Block Error-Rate Test

CPU = Central Processing Unit

DBMS = Database Management System

DDS = Dataphone Digital Service

DOS = Disk Operating System

DSU = Data Service Unit

DTE = Data Terminal Equipment

EIA = Electronics Industries Association

I/O = Input/Output

LED = Light Emitting Diode

MICS = Manufacturing Information and Control Systems

VTAM = Virtual Telecommunications Access Method

Vendor support

AT&T UNIFIED NETWORK MANAGEMENT ARCHITECTURE

Avanti Communications Corporation
Dyna Tech Communications Inc.
Timeplex Inc.

IBM NETVIEW/PC

Companies that have announced or are expected to announce their intention to provide products for use with Netview/PC:

Applied Systems Technologies, Inc.	Ft. Lauderdale, FL
Bytex Corporation	Southborough, MA
Communications Management Systems	McLean, VA
Digital Communications Associates	Alphretta, GA
Doelz Networks	Irvine, CA
Dynatech Communications, Inc.	East Greenwich, RI
Dynatech Data Systems	Springfield, VA
Emcon Corporation	Plano, TX
Paradyne	Largo, FL
Telenex Corporation	Mt. Laurel, NJ
TESDATA Systems Corporation	Herndon, VA

Vendors that have announced Netview/PC applications:

Avanti Communications Corporation	Newport, RI
BBN Communications Corporation	Cambridge, MA
Datatel, Inc.	Cherry Hill, NJ
DMW Group, Inc.	Ann Arbor, MI
General DataComm, Inc.	Middlebury, CT
Infotron Systems Corporation	Cherry Hill, NJ
MCI Telecommunications, Inc.	Washington, DC
Network Equipment Technologies	Redwood City, CA
Racal Milgo	Sunrise, FL
Racal-Vadic	Milpitas, CA
StrateCom, Inc.	Campbell, CA
Teleprocessing Products, Inc.	Simi Valley, CA
TelWatch, Inc.	El Dorado Hill, CA
Timeplex, Inc.	Woodcliff Lake, NJ
Ungermann-Bass, Inc.	Santa Clara, CA

in September, provides network control options for users that range from on-premises network control to contract management performed at specialized AT&T network control centers. The crucial element in the UNMA scheme is a set of communications protocols; AT&T must get these protocols adopted by other vendors for the scheme to succeed.

AT&T's way

AT&T's strategy for UNMA is to make a virtual network management system out of three network entities: customer-premises equipment, the local exchange service, and the AT&T interexchange services. Network management information from the three entities will be funneled to a network console at the customer site or to an AT&T network control center.

In the AT&T hierarchy (Fig. 4), network elements such as computers, multiplexers, and other customer-premises gear continue to carry on proprietary network management dialogues with their respective communications front-ends, which AT&T is calling element management systems. The element management systems pass their information to a central site for processing. However, before this can happen, the equipment vendor, the local carrier, and the interexchange carrier have to adopt a set of communications protocols called the Network Management Protocol.

"The NMP, it's our name," explains Richard Roca, director of AT&T's Data Architecture Center, AT&T Bell Laboratories (Holmdel, N.J.), "but it uses existing OSI standards. The NMP defines a set of OSI building blocks needed to define network management functions. In a sense, the name defines a particular group of functions that can be executed through the application layer. The NMP is a snapshot of the OSI building blocks taken at a particular time. In this sense, it is much like MAP [Manufacturing Automation Protocol] or TOP [Technical and Office Protocols]."

Given AT&T's preeminence in network control, Roca says, UNMA's biggest strength will be the logical structure it will impose on incoming network management data. "For example, you have to order the severity of the alarms coming into your network control center. To do this you have to look at where they are coming from, when they arrive, and the severity of the alarm. All this information should be subject to a logical structure. Our background as a carrier suggests we are not new to this business," Roca says.

However, in business, or more precisely, business relationships, the UNMA is vulnerable. AT&T has to enlist widespread support for the NMP to make UNMA fly. According to Roca, AT&T collected 250 inquiries at a recent trade show. But vendors familiar with UNMA are not yet jumping on the bandwagon (see "Vendor support").

"AT&T didn't make it clear they were going to make it easy to work with them," says Alford at BBN Communications. "Also, they didn't show me why I should follow them. IBM has the installed base."

Codex Corp.'s Lou Kreig, director of advanced development, says the Mansfield, Mass.-based company was asked to go public when AT&T announced UNMA. They chose not to. "The issue is one of independence. We don't want to align with any one vendor" of network management gear, says Kreig, who added, "but we do think that standards will solidify the market."

Codex went out of its way to emphasize that its 9800 Network Management System, which was announced in September, would follow evolving OSI standards. At present the 9800 supports only Codex products, but that is going to change. The architecture of the 9800 is designed to be consistent with common management information services and protocol (CMIS/P), which is under review by the International Organization for Standardization. The CMIS/P is scheduled to reach standard stature late in 1988.

Standards, like CMIS/P, offer the best hope of being able to seamlessly weave together several vendors' network management products. With standardized products, users will be able to fashion a custom network management tool tailored to the requirements of their networks. But a full suite of network management standards is still years away . . . and so are the dreams of the perfect network management tool. ∎

Frank da Cruz and Christine Gianone, Columbia University Center for Computing Activities, New York, N. Y.

Shopping for software that lets PCs chat with mainframes

Look beyond the user interface; consider file transfer, connection parameters, and terminal emulation. Get to know Kermit, XModem, et al.

Without question, people want their personal computers to communicate with other computers. The best way to accomplish this goal, however, is not always readily apparent. While communications software packages offer an increasingly popular approach to the problem, they must be chosen with care. To help readers make intelligent choices, this article presents the key features of communications packages, in particular those designed to work with the RS-232-C physical interface commonly used between personal computers and modems.

In theory, a local area network made up of personal computers (PCs—any microcomputer, not necessarily IBM PCs), a few gateways, and a mainframe doesn't need additional communications software. But this arrangement presumes that equipment is purchased according to a consistent plan designed with networking in mind. In practice, most organizations acquire their computer equipment in a fit of afterthought. They end up with a mix of PCs, minicomputers, and mainframes for which compatible networking options are neither available nor affordable.

Often, the only device that is common to all elements in this mix of machinery is the humble RS-232-C asynchronous communications port. Even when comprehensive networking solutions exist, the cost of attaching hundreds or thousands of PCs—at $500 to $1,500 per machine—to a Token Ring or Ethernet can be daunting. Moreover, those who want to dial in from home, or dial out to external services, must still be accommodated.

No wonder, then, that communications software is becoming a preferred means of connecting PCs to other computers. Hundreds of RS-232-C communications packages are available, such as Crosstalk, Blast, Relay Gold, Smartcomm, VTERM, Kermit, PC-Talk, ProComm, Red Ryder, HyperACCESS, and ASCII Pro. If selected intelligently, they provide an effective, economical way to fill the gaps in an organization's network. PC-resident data communications programs typically cost from $20 to $500 per PC (some are free, others cost more).

Evaluating RS-232-C communications packages can be a complicated process. Buyers must weigh carefully the job they require the software to perform against the product's cost. Reviews and surveys of communications packages appear frequently in the popular computer publications, and they can help. But surveys consisting mainly of charts in which, say, 100 popular software packages are compared on the basis of, say, 20 arbitrarily chosen features are unavoidably superficial. Moreover, many articles concentrate on frills and conveniences while skipping over such key issues as connection establishment and maintenance, terminal emulation, and file transfer.

What's an RS-232-C package?

A software program that runs on such PCs as the IBM PC, IBM clones, Apple II, or Macintosh, an RS-232-C communications package can communicate asynchronously with remote computers through RS-232-C serial ports—either directly or through modems. Unlike specialized products that emulate synchronous terminals in the IBM mainframe, Wang, or similar networks, the RS-232-C communications package does not require the use of special adapters (for example, an Irma board) and connections (like coax).

Communications packages for PCs must have two fundamental capabilities: terminal emulation and data transfer. The former connects the PC to a minicomputer or mainframe as though the PC were a terminal, thus making it possible for users to conduct timesharing sessions or to access an application on a central, shared system. Data transfer lets the user exchange information between a PC and a minicomputer or mainframe (or another PC).

To accomplish terminal emulation, the user needs only the PC-resident software; for error-free data transfer,

User interface

Before communications software can connect computers to each other it must communicate with a human—the user. This aspect of the program, known as the user interface, includes the prompts, commands, menus, function keys, and other features that let the user talk to the program; it also includes the displays through which the program communicates with the user.

There are many styles of user interface: command line, interactive prompt and command, menus and arrow keys, mice, and windows. The fundamental trade-off is ease of learning versus ease of use. Ease of learning is important if many people will be using the package infrequently or if there is rapid personnel turnover, so that relatively little time need be "wasted" in learning and training. A user interface designed for ease of learning presents all the choices in menus. The penalty is that menus for everything are always shown, which slows down the expert.

At the other extreme are programs that favor the expert, providing only terse and cryptic commands, sometimes with no way for a novice to get help—short of reading the manual. A compromise, "menu on demand," lets the expert issue rapid, terse commands, while still allowing the novice to see a menu at any point by entering a special help key.

There is an oft-neglected aspect of the user interface that falls into the ease-of-use category: Can the package be used by people with disabilities like motor impairment, blindness, or deafness? If you can depress only a single key at a time, how can you enter complicated Ctrl-Alt-Shift key combinations? If a PC is connected, for example, to an ASCII-oriented speaking device or a Braille terminal, how can multicolor animated graphics screens be deciphered? How will a person who cannot hear know when the package is beeping or whistling to signal an important event? Often, the fancier the user interface, the less it lends itself to use by the disabled.

Another item of minor importance, but the absence of which can be a nuisance, is the ability to access system functions without actually leaving the program. To change directories, list files, display a file, or delete a file, the user should not have to exit the communications program and then restart it afterward. This can be time-consuming, especially on floppy-disk-based systems, and even more so when settings—or the connection itself—must be reestablished.

Commercial communications packages tend to place great emphasis on the appearance and style of the user interface, primarily for marketing reasons. But for most people, the user interface should not be a key factor in evaluating a product. It only lets the user specify the real work to be done, and it should take up a relatively small proportion of the total time spent with the package. Ultimately, it is much more important to know whether, and how well, the product can perform the required tasks.

however, the receiving computer must have a companion program. The cost for commercial minicomputer- or mainframe-based communications programs—typically $1,000 to $100,000—is much higher than it is for PC versions.

Making the connection

Initially, what impresses the user most about any program is its interface (see "User interface"). But perhaps the most important aspect of any communications package is its set of mechanisms for establishing a connection—that is, matching communications parameters to the communications medium on the other end, monitoring the connection once established, and breaking the connection.

Any communications program should allow control over such communications parameters as bits per second, parity, duplex, flow control, and the number of data, start, and stop bits per character. Each of these parameters is important to a satisfactory connection between computers. In selecting a communications package, be sure that it supports all the parameters and settings required by all the computers with which it must communicate.

For example, most minicomputers and mainframes from Digital Equipment Corp. (DEC) employ X-on/X-off full-duplex flow control to prevent data overruns; if the communications package for a particular PC does not support X-on/X-off, then data transferred between the PC and the DEC system could be lost.

IBM mainframe ASCII TTY (teletypewriter) line-mode connections, however, are half-duplex, and they exercise a line-turnaround "handshake" discipline. Thus, a transmission sent to the IBM mainframe before it has sent a special handshake character, such as Control-Q, will not be accepted.

Certain popular mainframes and minicomputers, as well as public data networks like Telenet and Tymnet, use even, odd, or mark parity; they will not recognize characters unless the right parity is applied. And if a communications package cannot distinguish parity bits from data bits, the wrong characters will be displayed on the screen. Table 1 shows typical RS-232-C communications parameters for various equipment.

Some communications packages support only a limited range of transmission speeds. They may be designed to work only for dial-up connections at speeds up to 1.2 or 2.4 kbit/s. In this case, should there ever be a need to connect two computers directly, the transmission would be limited to these relatively low speeds.

Even if dial-up transmissions are the only connections foreseen, these are unattractively slow speeds. Several recently announced modems operate faster than 9.6 kbit/s on ordinary voice-grade telephone connections. Thus, any communications package should be able to operate at 9.6 kbit/s or faster. The fastest speed supported by most minicomputers, mainframes, and front-end devices today is 9.6 kbit/s, although some support 19.2 kbit/s.

Microcomputers such as the IBM PC/AT and the Macintosh can drive their RS-232-C ports to speeds of 38.4 kbit/s or faster, and two such PCs connected back to back can actually transfer data at these speeds. But the higher the speed, the more important it is to have an effective flow-control mechanism supported by the machines on each end of the connection.

Table 1: Typical communications parameters

COMPUTER	FRONT END	DUPLEX	FLOW CONTROL	PARITY	TERMINAL
Data General MV	None	Full	X-ON/X-OFF	None	Dasher
DEC PDP-11	None	Full	X-ON/X-OFF	None	VT52, VT100
DEC VAX	None	Full	X-ON/X-OFF	None	VT52, VT100
DECSYSTEM-20	PDP-11	Full	X-ON/X-OFF	Even	VT52, VT100
Honeywell DPS8	DN335	Half	X-ON Handshake	None	VIP7300, 7800
HP-1000, 3000	None	Full	ENQ/ACK	None	HP262x
IBM 370 Series	3705 TTY	Half	X-ON Handshake	Mark	TTY
IBM 370 Series	7171 P.E.	Full	X-ON/X-OFF	Even	Various*
Prime minis	None	Full	X-ON/X-OFF	Mark	TTY, PS300

P.E. = 3270 Protocol Emulator, TTY = ASCII Linemode Connection.
*Delivered with support for 13 popular terminals, configurable for more.

Unless computers are hardwired together with dedicated transmission lines, the communications connection to other computer gear is probably made with asynchronous dial-up modems. These devices communicate special control information to the PC via RS-232-C modem signals, such as Data Terminal Ready, Data Set Ready, and Carrier Detect. Most communications packages can control and monitor these signals, thereby detecting when the connection is broken or initiating the break and hanging up the phone. When a package is used interactively, modem control is largely superfluous because a broken connection is obvious. For unattended operation, however, modem control is important to avoid the excessive telephone bills that could result when the communications package fails to notice a broken connection and leaves the phone "off-hook."

Modems may be either external or internal. The external devices are controlled in a consistent way to accommodate RS-232-C; they rarely pose a problem to communications software. Although generally more expensive than internal modems, the external units are interchangeable between different computers.

Internal modems are built specifically for certain computers and sometimes require special software. A particular software package will not necessarily operate correctly with a specific internal modem, so buyers should understand a package's compatibility limitations. It is also important to check whether the networked modems will support the same modulation techniques and speeds.

Some communications packages are designed to be used only with modems. To make these devices communicate when two computers are connected directly by a cable, certain modem signals must be "faked" by cross connections or jumper wires within the cable connectors. Such a fake-out cable is called a null modem, or, modem eliminator (Fig. 1)—readily available either from a computer supply house or in the form of an adapter that can be connected to the modem cable. But different devices may require different signals connected in different ways, so users should be prepared to experiment (a breakout box will help). Such tinkering can be avoided if the communications software package can be configured to ignore modem signals when two computers are directly connected.

Dialer control. Many PCs can be connected to other computers only by telephone. So-called smart modems, like those manufactured by Hayes, are able to dial the telephone if they receive commands in the right format from the PC. This means that the communications package must understand the dialing language of the modem. Although the Hayes "AT" language has become a de facto industry standard, not all autodial modems conform to it (prominent counterexamples include DEC DF series modems and selected models from Racal-Vadic, U S Robotics, and Ventel). Be sure the communications package supports the modem's dialing language.

Dialing software simplifies connection establishment, thus concealing the details of the dialing language. The user merely tells the program what number to call. Some packages go a step further and include a telephone directory so that the user need remember only names, not phone numbers.

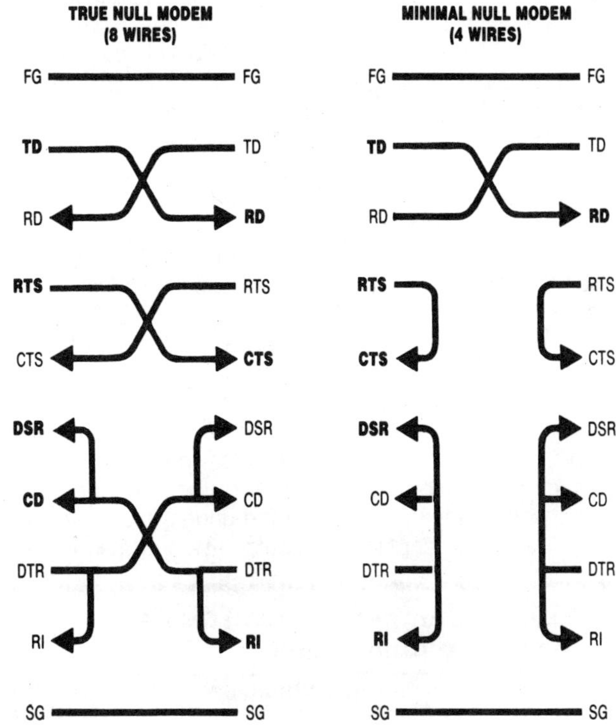

1. Null modems. *RS-232-C asynchronous modem signals must sometimes be faked by jumper wires within the cable connections—known as the null modem.*

FG = FRAME GROUND, PIN 1
TD = TRANSMITTED DATA, FROM PC TO MODEM, PIN 2
RD = RECEIVED DATA, FROM MODEM TO PC, PIN 3
RTS = REQUEST-TO-SEND, FROM PC TO MODEM, USED WITH HALF-DUPLEX MODEMS, PIN 4
CTS = CLEAR-TO-SEND, FROM MODEM TO PC, DITTO, PIN 5
DSR = DATA SET READY, INDICATES MODEM IS IN DATA TRANSMISSION MODE, PIN 6
SG = SIGNAL GROUND, PIN 7
CD = CARRIER DETECT, INDICATES THAT MODEM IS CONNECTED TO OTHER MODEM, PIN 8
DTR = DATA TERMINAL READY, TELLS MODEM THAT PC IS READY TO COMMUNICATE, PIN 20
RI = RING INDICATOR, TELLS PC THAT THE PHONE IS RINGING, PIN 22

Debugging communications parameters. Often, a user can only guess the right combination of speed, stop bits, parity bits, data bits, duplex, and flow control for a particular connection. What if the guess is wrong? What tools does the communications package offer to determine the offending parameters?

If the package allows the parameters to be set independently, they can be varied until the connection works; the number of combinations, however, might be endless. To reduce the guesswork, the communications package should include debugging tools, such as special display or logging of received characters (preferably including their eight-bit numeric values). If examination of the log reveals a byte with a numeric value of 193 (= 11000001 binary) where one would expect an ASCII "A" (= 01000001 binary), then a good guess might be seven data bits with odd or mark parity rather than eight data bits with no parity. The package should also include a troubleshooting guide (see Table 2).

Saving parameters. After discovering the proper settings for communicating with a particular machine, the next task is saving them for later use. To alleviate the tedium of setting five or 10 communications parameters for each communications session, the package should allow settings to be collected into configurations that may be saved under mnemonic names.

Some packages come with a set of configurations for popular dial-up services, such as Dow-Jones, Compuserve, MCI Mail, and The Source. These built-in configurations shield the user from having to know anything about data communications parameters. But when connecting to a service that the package doesn't recognize—for example, from a home office to a mainframe—it should be possible to manipulate the communications settings and save them. The appropriate settings, for example, for a company's DEC VAX, IBM 3090, Harris 800, plus a local Telenet PAD could be accomplished by typing just the associated configuration name.

Script language, unattended operation. Just as a communications package may store communications settings or telephone numbers, it can also allow repetitive interactive tasks, like log-in sequences, to be automated via scripts. Such short "programs" look for specific outputs from the remote computer and provide appropriate responses. When the package, or the underlying operating system, allows a script to be executed at a predetermined

Table 2: Sample entries from a troubleshooting guide

SYMPTOM	POSSIBLE CAUSE	CURE
Blank, dark screen	PC turned off	Turn on PC
Total garbage on screen	Wrong speed	Try another speed
Spurts of garbage on screen	Noise	Hang up and redial
Uniform mixture of good and bad characters on screen	Parity	Select a different parity
Typed characters appear twice	Duplex	Select full duplex
Typed characters don't appear	Duplex	Select half duplex
Random gaps in screen text	No flow control	Use flow control or a slower speed

2. Script language. *Dialing a Hayes modem to establish a connection with Unix can be done with script language, which makes a built-in dialer control unnecessary.*

set speed 1200	BITS PER SECOND
set parity none	PARITY
output AT\13	WAKE UP THE MODEM
input OK	LOOK FOR ITS 'OK'
output ATD7654321\13	GIVE MODEM'S DIALING COMMAND
input CONNECT	LOOK FOR DESIRED RESPONSE
pause 1	WAIT A SECOND
output\13	SEND A CARRIAGE RETURN
input login:	LOOK FOR LOGIN PROMPT
output chris\13	SEND USER ID, FOLLOWED BY CARRIAGE RETURN
input Password:	LOOK FOR PASSWORD PROMPT
echo Connecting to Unix System:	
echo Please type your password:	
connect	LET THE USER TAKE OVER

time, then it is possible to carry on a canned dialog with no human operator present. For instance, a PC might be programmed to "wake up" at midnight, set the proper communications parameters, dial the office minicomputer, log in, deposit the day's transactions, fetch and print the day's mail, log out, and hang up. Script languages vary from the primitive and cryptic to full-blown programming languages complete with variables and conditional branching. Figure 2 shows a simple script for dialing a Hayes modem to establish a connection to a Unix and then log in. It illustrates how a script can be used in place of built-in dialer control.

The "output" commands send the indicated text strings to the Unix machine ("\13" is a code for carriage return), and the "input" commands search the incoming data for the indicated strings. If any of the input commands fail, the script is automatically terminated. This is an important feature of a script language. Suppose, for instance, a nightly script sends the day's work to a mainframe and then deletes it from the PC's hard disk. If the data cannot be successfully transmitted, then the script should not forge ahead stubbornly and destroy all the day's work.

Scripts are essential for unattended operation; they are also useful in setting up procedures for relatively unskilled operators, such as data entry clerks. For the typical interactive user, however, scripts are a minor convenience rather than a necessity.

Terminal emulation

The PC has increasingly replaced the terminal in many organizations. In addition to its other capabilities, a properly programmed PC can act like, or emulate, a terminal. Thus, it can be used to conduct a dialog with a remote computer. Keystrokes are transmitted via the communications port, and characters that arrive at the port are displayed on the screen. On half-duplex connections, the sender's keystrokes are also echoed locally by the PC on the screen. On full-duplex connections, terminal emulation can be a tricky business because characters may arrive at the port at the same time as the user is typing; communications programs vary in their ability to handle both events at once, especially at higher speeds.

It should be stressed that terminal emulation does not provide any automatic error control—anymore than a real terminal would. Bare characters are sent back and forth with absolutely no error-recovery mechanism. If a package claims to supply error-checking data transfer, the buyer should understand that this claim applies to the package's file transfer functions and not to its terminal emulator. A noisy telephone line would probably leave garbage on the screen during terminal emulation even though files could be transferred successfully.

In addition to sending and displaying characters, a terminal emulator attempts to imitate the repertoire of special effects of particular ASCII video display terminals, such as the DEC VT100 series, the IBM 3101, the Televideo 920, or the ADM3A. This means that the program responds to screen control sequences sent by the host just as the real terminal would. For example, the ASCII sequence "ESC [5 ; 7 H " sent to a DEC VT100 positions the cursor at row 5, column 7; "ESC [0 J" clears the screen; so a PC programmed to emulate a VT100 would understand the same sequences and perform the same actions. When emulating a terminal, the package should also provide mapping between the function keys of the terminal and those of the PC, so that they transmit the same sequences. If the VT100 PF1 key sends "ESC 0 P," the IBM PC's F1 key might be programmed to send that sequence.

Today's video display terminals possess a formidable array of features for tabbing, highlighting, partitioning the screen, erasing and inserting text, positioning the cursor, drawing figures, changing colors, switching character sets, activating printers, and so forth—all controlled by host-transmitted escape sequences. A package may emulate such a terminal completely, or it may emulate a subset of its functions. Some terminals have features that cannot be emulated by certain PCs. For example, the DEC VT100 allows switching between 80- and 132-column modes, but an IBM PC can only display 80 columns. To get 132 columns on the IBM machine, a special board may be needed. Another example is the VT100's "smooth scrolling" feature, which allows a file to glide slowly up the screen. The DEC Rainbow can do this; the IBM PC cannot.

The emulation provided by a communications package should be complete enough to allow access to any host-resident software that is designed to control the appearance of the terminal's screen; full-screen text editors like EDT on VAX/VMS or GNU EMACS on a Unix machine are good tests. Another is IBM 3270 protocol emulation as performed by the IBM 7171 or other protocol converter. If emulation is incomplete, the screens may appear fragmented and jumbled, characters or lines may overwrite each other, or gaps and transpositions may occur.

Terminal emulation is a key function for users who engage in a lot of interactive dialog with a remote computer, especially when screen control is involved. In this case, it is essential that the communications package be capable of emulating a terminal that the remote computer supports, such as a DEC VT100 or -200 series with DEC VAX/VMS or a Data General Dasher with DG minicomputers. Terminal emulation is less important for brief or noninteractive encounters, such as occasional sessions primarily for file transfer.

Redefining and translating. Since a PC keyboard may have a different layout than that of the emulated terminal, it may be helpful to "move" the misplaced keys to their familiar locations (no, not with pliers). For instance, the Escape (ESC) key (important to much host-resident software) is notoriously mobile, appearing in many different locations even on PCs from the same maker (the IBM and DEC keyboards spring to mind). If one is accustomed to finding ESC immediately to the left of the "1," but the PC has "`" (accent grave) in that position, the "`" could be redefined to transmit ESC (and vice versa). Similarly for function keys; the VT100 PF keys are on the right, whereas the IBM PC's F keys are on the left; some VT100 users may find it more convenient to assign the PF keys to the PC's numeric pad.

A package might also make it possible to assign any arbitrary character string to a key, so that the user could transmit commonly typed items (name or log-in sequence, for example) with a single keystroke. Such many-to-one assignments are called keyboard macros, and there are limits to the number of characters that may be represented by a single key.

Key redefinition is important if a user's application requires frequent switching among terminals and PCs having different keyboard layouts. It is also helpful when switching the same PC between different hosts. If the user is accustomed to typing the Backspace key to erase a character but one host uses ASCII Rubout for this function while another uses Control-H, the suitable character can be assigned to the Backspace key.

Character sets. The ability to handle European and non-Roman character sets (keyboard input as well as screen output) is important for those who deal in languages other than English. It is common practice in Germany and Scandinavia, for instance, to assign umlaut, slashed, or circled vowels to the ASCII bracket positions. PCs and host computers must agree on these conventions in order for characters to be displayed as intended rather than in Anglo-American ASCII. Translation of outbound and arriving characters is, therefore, an important function of the communications package. To satisfy the needs of multi-national companies, or users with international business dealings, the package should not be restricted to seven-bit ASCII but should allow for eight-bit international character sets in line with such International Organization for Standardization (ISO) Recommendations as 2022 ("ISO 7-Bit and 8-Bit Coded Character Sets—Code Extension Techniques") and 6937 ("Coded Character Sets for Text Communication").

Text screen memory. A special advantage of emulating a terminal on a PC is that the PC may surpass the capabilities of the terminal. The PC's memory may be used to hold hundreds of lines that have scrolled off the top for later recall. Current or previous screens may be dumped to a disk file or printer at the touch of a button.

Graphics. For PCs that have a color monitor, the commu-

Kermit vs. XModem

Two of the most commonly used public-domain error-checking communications protocols, XModem and Kermit, differ in several ways.

■ XModem uses eight-bit binary bytes in its packet fields and, therefore, requires an eight-bit transparent communications link. It cannot function, even for text files, when parity is in use. Similarly, when any device in the communications path is sensitive to control characters, such as Control-Z or Control-S (which occur in the XModem packet control fields), XModem packets are subject to interference. For this reason, XModem cannot operate in conjunction with X-on/X-off or other in-band flow control. Kermit, on the other hand, encodes its packets as though they were lines of text and, therefore, does not have these restrictions.

■ XModem packets are sent in only one direction. The responses are bare, unchecked control characters such as Control-F for acknowledgment, Control-U for negative acknowledgment, or Control-X for cancel. Corruption of XModem responses into other valid responses is possible, and it can cause a file transfer to terminate prematurely or, worse, corruption of the file. Kermit uses fully error-checked packets in both directions and is more robust in the face of transmission errors.

■ XModem uses fixed-length packets. There is no length field. If a file's length is not an exact multiple of 128 bytes, then extra bytes will be transmitted. Furthermore, if a computer, multiplexer, or other device cannot handle bursts of 132 characters, XModem packets will not get through. Kermit packets include a length field. Packets can be adjusted to accommodate small buffers, and a short packet can be sent at the end, so there is no confusion about the exact end of file. XModem includes no mechanism for transmitting the file name, so it has no way of sending multiple files in a single session. Kermit does this routinely.

■ XModem makes no distinction between text and binary files. But since the conventions for representing text files on different computers can vary, the results of an XModem text-file transfer between unlike file systems can be surprising. Kermit specifies a common intermediate representation for text files during transmission so that incoming text files can always be stored in a useful form. However, this places the burden on the user to select text or binary transfer mode.

■ Both the XModem and Kermit protocols have seen a number of extensions over the years. XModem has no formal or consistent way to negotiate the presence or absence of given features, whereas feature negotiation is built into the basic Kermit protocol. A pair of variant XModem programs will not necessarily be able to communicate, whereas any pair of Kermit programs will automatically fall back to the greatest common set of options. XModem and Kermit protocol extensions include the following features:

Multiple files. Modem7 and YModem can transfer multiple files in a single batch, XModem cannot. The ability to perform multiple file transmission is built into the basic Kermit protocol.

Eight-bit data through seven-bit channel. XModem does not have the ability to pass eight-bit data through a seven-bit channel. Kermit supplies this as a negotiated feature (commonly available).

Alternate checksums. XModem-CRC uses a 16-bit cyclic redundancy check to achieve greater reliability and tries to adapt itself to eight-bit checksum only. XModem programs automatically. Kermit supplies an optional 12-bit checksum as well as a 16-bit CRC, which is negotiated with automatic fallback to the single-character checksum.

File transfer interruption. Both XModem and Kermit allow file transfer to be interrupted with no ill effects. Kermit also includes the ability to cancel the current file in a group and proceed to the next one.

Compression. Kermit programs may negotiate compression of repeated bytes. XModem lacks a compression option.

Long packets. YModem allows 1-kbyte fixed-length packets for greater efficiency. Kermit extensions permit variable-length packets up to about 9 kbytes; they are negotiated with automatic fallback to regular-length packets.

Sliding windows. Kermit programs may negotiate simultaneous and continuous transmission of packets and their acknowledgments on full-duplex links, with a window of up to 31 unacknowledged packets and selective retransmission of lost or damaged packets. (This option is not yet widespread among Kermit implementations.) Sliding windows are not possible in XModem because its responses carry no sequence number (an XModem variant called WModem simulates sliding windows but this version will only work if there are no errors).

File attributes. YModem transmits a file's name, size, and creation date. XModem does not. Kermit always transmits the name, and the ability to communicate a wide range of other file attributes may be negotiated (but, like sliding windows, this is not yet a widely implemented Kermit feature).

Checkpoint/restart. Neither XModem nor Kermit has the ability to restart a file transfer after the connection is broken. ZModem, however, does.

Kermit also differs from XModem by including a file-server mode of operation, in which the remote Kermit program receives all of its instructions from the PC Kermit in packet form. Kermit servers can transfer files and perform a variety of file management functions, such as deletion, directory listing, and changing directories.

Implementations of Kermit can be had for most PCs, minicomputers, and mainframes. XModem implementations are found mostly on PCs, rarely on minicomputers or mainframes. Basic XModem is somewhat more efficient than basic Kermit, because the packets are slightly longer and there is less encoding overhead. The situation is reversed when the Kermit package is given the ability to perform compression, long packets, or sliding windows.

nications program should be able to set the fore- and background text screen colors. A well-chosen color scheme can reduce operator fatigue or even wake up the user during the less exciting hours of the day.

In order to access graphics-oriented applications on the mainframe or minicomputer, such as SAS Graph, SPSS Graphics, Plot 10, Tella-Graf, or various computer-aided design packages (not to mention certain dial-up shopping services), the communications package must emulate a graphics terminal or a standard known to the application, such as Tektronix 4010, 4014, or other model; DEC ReGIS, HPGL, GKS, GDDM, or NAPLPS. Graphics-terminal emulation is found in only a few communications packages (usually for an additional cost); and certain PCs (like the IBM) need a special monitor and graphics board.

In recent years, graphics have tended to be done directly on the PC by such packages as Lotus, MacPaint, and others. It is not usually possible to connect one PC to another in order to access the remote PC's graphics applications, though certain highly specialized packages do allow this type of connection. Merely running Crosstalk from PC A to PC B will not result in Lotus on PC B putting a color pie chart on PC A's screen. More commonly, the graphics package exists on both PCs, and their data files are moved from one computer to another using a file transfer protocol built into the communications package.

File transfer

". . . transfers your data over phone lines at the speed of light!" was a claim that once appeared in an advertisement for a communications package. While it's true that electricity travels through wires at near light speed, it is not (yet) true that one electron is equivalent to one bit of data. In fact, at the most common speed used for dial-up data communications, 1.2 kbit/s, a single bit is pretty big—about 150 miles long! A character (generally represented in transmission by 10 bits) is 1,500 miles long; two characters, like OK, would span the North American continent.

Spurious advertising claims notwithstanding, transmission speed is a technological issue; data transfer is a software issue that includes such questions as how to make effective use of the transmission medium and how to smooth over the differences between computers. Specific areas to watch out for include the following:
■ Can binary files be transferred?
■ Can text file formats be converted to useful form between unlike elements in a network?
■ Can a group of files be sent in a single operation?
■ Can file-name collisions be avoided?
■ Can a file transfer be cleanly interrupted?

ASCII vs. error-checked protocols. Communications packages offer two basic types of data transfer: raw and error-checked. Transmitting raw data, the most common form of transmission, is usually referred to as using the ASCII protocol. This means that the data is sent as is—as ASCII characters—from one computer's communications port to the other. The advantage to this method is its simplicity. No special software need be resident on the remote computer, beyond its text editor or a Type or Copy command. The disadvantages, however, explain why error-checked protocols have evolved. They are as follows:
■ The data sent using the ASCII protocol will be corrupted if there is noise on the communications line.
■ Data will be lost if the receiving computer cannot keep up with the sender.
■ Binary (nontextual) files generally cannot be transferred this way, since many computers will either ignore the parity bit or act on control characters rather than accept them as data: Control-C, Control-S, and Control-Z are frequent culprits.
■ This method works for only one file at a time.

A refinement of ASCII protocol incorporates X-on/X-off or some other method of flow control to reduce the chances of data loss. In this case, both computers must support the same method of flow control, but corruption of the data (including the flow control signals themselves) remains a problem—as does file delimitation and the restriction on binary files.

To achieve reliable, correct, and complete transmission of files between computers, neither the ASCII nor the X-on/X-off protocol are sufficiently trustworthy. The communications package must include a true error-correcting file transfer protocol. Error-checked data transfer requires cooperating programs on each end of the connection to exchange messages, which are called packets, according to agreed-upon formats and rules (similar to those used on the telephone: One person dials; another person, hearing the phone ring, picks up and says hello; the caller is identified. The two parties take turns talking. If one doesn't understand what the other says, a repetition is requested. Good-byes are exchanged, and the phones are hung up). Key to the success of this interaction, of course, is that the conversation is conducted in the same language. A file transfer protocol operates similarly: The two processes "connect," identify the files that are being transferred,

---

3. Comparing packets. *Kermit and XModem both transfer files between computers in blocks of data, or packets. The packets are error-checked via calculated checksums.*

(A) XMODEM

(ALL FIELDS ARE 8-BIT BINARY)

SOH = ASCII CONTROL-A (SOH, START OF HEADER)
BLOCK = 8-BIT BINARY 'BLOCK' (PACKET) NUMBER, 1-127 (RECYCLES)
−BLOCK = 255 MINUS THE BLOCK NUMBER (1's COMPLEMENT OF BLOCK NUMBER)
DATA = EXACTLY 128 BYTES OF UNENCODED 8-BIT DATA (A CP/M DISK BLOCK)
CHECK = AN 8-BIT BINARY CHECKSUM

(B) KERMIT

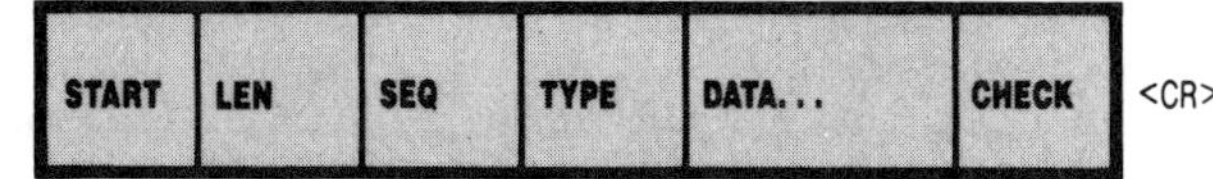

EACH KERMIT PACKET FIELD EXCEPT DATA IS A SINGLE CHARACTER.
EACH FIELD EXCEPT START IS COMPOSED ONLY OF PRINTABLE ASCII
CHARACTERS. THE PACKET IS NORMALLY TERMINATED BY A CARRIAGE RETURN.

START = CONTROL-A (SOH), BUT IT CAN BE REDEFINED
LEN = PACKET LENGTH, 0-94, ENCODED AS A PRINTABLE ASCII CHARACTER
SEQ = PACKET SEQUENCE NUMBER, 0-63 (RECYCLES), PRINTABLE
TYPE = PACKET TYPE, S F D Z B Y N, ETC.
DATA = FILE NAME, FILE DATA, ETC., DEPENDING ON TYPE, PRINTABLE ASCII
CHECK = 8-BIT CHECKSUM, FOLDED INTO 6 BITS AS A PRINTABLE CHARACTER

Software worksheet: Know your options

CONFIGURATION

Make and model of your computer:____

Operating system and version:____

Memory:_____________________ (K) Floppy drives:___________________ Hard-Disk Capacity:___________________ (M)

Communications interfaces:____

Modem make and model:____ [   ] Internal [   ] External

Name of communications package:____

Communications package vendor:________________________________ Phone:__________________________

Package memory size:____________________________ (K) Package disk occupancy:___________________________ (K)

Before proceeding, be sure that the communications package is compatible with your computer's configuration!

COST

(a) What is the unit cost of the package? $_________

(b) Is source code included, so that you can make changes and fix bugs? Is there is an additional charge for source code? Cost of source code, if you want it: $_________

(c) Is copying allowed? If so, go directly to (f).

(d) How many PCs will you need it for? _____________ Is there a volume discount? If so, enter discounted cost: $_________

(e) If a site license is available, what does it cost? $_________

(f) Enter best total price for PC versions $_________

(g) Do you also need minicomputer or mainframe versions? If so, enter total cost for mini or mainframe versions $_________

(h) Total cost to your organization $_________

DOCUMENTATION, TRAINING, AND SUPPORT

Is the manual ...

[   ] thick and unmanageable?

[   ] thin and cryptic?

[   ] just right?

How important is the manual?

[   ] Must be consulted frequently

[   ] Occasional lookups required

[   ] Does the manual have a good index and table of contents?

[   ] Is training available?

[   ] Is training necessary?

[   ] Is telephone support available and included in the package price?

WHAT IS YOUR PRIMARY USE FOR THE PACKAGE?

[   ] Long interactive remote sessions. Communications parameter settings, terminal emulation, and key definition are the most important features.

[   ] Infrequent remote sessions mainly for the purpose of data transfer. Concentrate on the user interface, script language, and file transfer protocol.

USER INTERFACE

[   ] Is help available at all times?

[   ] Does the user interface favor the novice user? (Menus at all times)

[   ] Does it favor the expert user? (No menus)

[   ] Is the package equally convenient for both novice and expert? (Menu on demand)

[   ] Can canned procedures be set up for unskilled users? (Scripts, command files)

[   ] Can local operating system functions be accessed without leaving the package?

[   ] Can the package be used by the disabled?

COMMUNICATIONS PARAMETER SETTINGS (always important)

Bits/Second: 0,110,300,1200,2400,4800,9600,19200,etc.

Maximum: ___________

DUPLEX

[   ] Full (e.g. for DEC minis)

[   ] Half (e.g. for IBM mainframes)

ECHO

[   ] Remote (e.g. for DEC minis)

[   ] Local (e.g. for IBM mainframe linemode connections)

DATA BITS

[   ] 5 (Baudot)

[   ] 7 (ASCII)

[   ] 8 (national characters)

STOP BITS

[   ] 1 (for most connections)

[   ] 1.5 (rarely used)

[   ] 2 (used only for 110 bits per second or less)

PARITY SELECTION

[   ] None (all bits used for data)

[   ] Even (required by some mainframes, front ends, public networks, etc.)

[   ] Odd (ditto)

[   ] Mark (ditto)

[   ] Space (rarely used, but sometimes handy)

CHARACTER SET SELECTION

[   ] 5-bit Baudot (used in Telecommunication Devices for the Deaf)

[   ] 7-bit US ASCII (most common in English-speaking countries)

[   ] 7-bit "national ASCII" (Norwegian, German, etc.)

[   ] 8-bit "extended ASCII" (e.g. use of IBM PC 8-bit character set)

[   ] Support for international standard non-Roman character sets

[   ] User-definable or downloadable character sets

FLOW CONTROL SELECTION

[   ] X-on/X-off (e.g. with DEC computers)

[   ] ENQ/ACK (e.g. with Hewlett-Packard computers)

[   ] RTS/CTS (for half-duplex modems)

[   ] Half-duplex line turnaround handshake (e.g. with IBM mainframes)

[   ] Other: ____

[   ] None (can flow control be turned off?)

DEBUGGING

[   ] Special display of all received and transmitted characters

[   ] Logging of all received and transmitted characters

[   ] Can you collect communications settings into recallable configurations?

CONNECTION ESTABLISHMENT

Support for RS-232-C asynchronous modem signals (RTS, CTS, DSR, CD, DTR, RI):

[   ] Does the package monitor Carrier Detect (CD) and Data Set Ready (DSR) from the modem?

[   ] Does the package assert Data Terminal Ready (DTR)?

[   ] Can the package drop DTR to hang up the phone?

[   ] Does the package respond to Ring Indicator (RI) so that it can be called from outside?

[   ] If you have a half-duplex modem, does the package support RTS/CTS?

[   ] Does your PC have an internal modem?

[   ] Does the package support this internal modem?

DIALER CONTROL:

[   ] Does your modem provide automatic dialing?

[   ] What dialing language is used by your modem?

____

[   ] Does the package support automatic dialing?

[   ] Does the package support your modem's dialing language?

[   ] Does the package provide a phone directory?

[   ] Can the package operate over direct connections, without modems? That is, can it be told to ignore CD and DSR? (If not, you will need the "fakeout" (minimal) null-modem cable from Figure 1).

Script language for automatic login, unattended operation:

[   ] Access to all necessary package commands from script language.

[   ] Conditional execution/termination of script commands.

[   ] Fancy script programming features (variables, labels, goto's, etc.)

[   ] Unattended operation (e.g. late at night, when phone rates are low).

[   ] Can the program be suspended and resumed without dropping the connection?

TERMINAL EMULATION:

What terminal(s) does the package emulate? _______________________

[   ] Is the maximum speed for full-duplex terminal emulation sufficient for your needs?

[   ] Does the package emulate a terminal that is supported by the computers you wish to communicate with?

[   ] Is the terminal emulated fully enough for use with all desired software applications on these computers?

[   ] Is any special hardware (like a 132-column board) required in the PC?

[   ] Does the package support fore- and background colors? (Do you need them?)

[   ] If a graphics terminal is emulated, does your application support it?

[   ] Screen rollback (view screens that have scrolled away)

[   ] Screen dump (save current or previous screens in PC files)

[   ] Printer control (copy displayed characters to printer, print whole screen)

[   ] Print or save text screens in alternate character sets

[   ] Print or save graphics screens

[   ] Function keys

[   ] Key redefinition

[   ] Keystroke macros

[   ] Translation of displayed characters, alternate character sets

FILE TRANSFER PROTOCOLS

[   ] ASCII (this is not an error-correcting protocol)

[   ] X-on/X-off (this is not an error-correcting protocol)

[   ] Xmodem

[   ] Kermit

[   ] Proprietary (Blast, MNP, etc): ___________________________

[   ] Other: ____

[   ] Do the systems you're communicating with support the same protocol(s)?

[   ] Does the package transfer both text and binary files?

[   ] Do text files arrive on the target computer in useful form?

XMODEM OPTIONAL FEATURES

[   ] Modem7-style transfer of multiple files

[   ] XModem-CRC for more reliable error checking

[   ] Ymodem 1K packets for increased efficiency (half duplex)

[   ] Ymodem filename transmission

[   ] Checkpoint/restart (Zmodem)

[   ] Wmodem continuous transmission (full duplex)

[   ] Do the computers you wish to communicate with support the same XModem options?

KERMIT OPTIONAL FEATURES

[   ] 8-bit data through 7-bit links (e.g. links with parity)

[   ] Repeated character compression for improved efficency

[   ] 12-bit checksum, 16-bit CRC, for more reliable error checking

[   ] File transfer interruption

[   ] Long packets (up to 9K) for improved efficiency (half duplex)

[   ] Sliding windows for improved efficiency (full duplex)

[   ] Transmission of file attributes

[   ] Server operation

[   ] Remote host commands and file management

request retransmission of lost or damaged information, identify the end of the file, and then disengage.

A special caveat: The fact that many newer modems provide error correction does not eliminate the need for file transfer software. An error-free data stream from modem to modem does not guarantee correct data from computer to computer. Issues of end-to-end flow control and error correction, file delimitation, and format conversion must still be addressed within the computers themselves.

Error-checking protocols. Two well-known error-checking file transfer protocols are XModem and Kermit. Many commercial packages include one or both of these protocols (sometimes alongside, proprietary protocols), but there are also hundreds of public-domain or freely sharable Kermit or XModem programs. The major advantage of XModem and Kermit is that they are ubiquitous. The protocol specifications are open and public, and large bodies of Kermit and XModem software are available. The cost to a large organization for these programs is minimal, compared with the per-CPU licensing fees required for commercial packages. Furthermore, chances are greater that a Kermit or XModem program will exist for any given computer.

In the case of Kermit programs, source code is included, which encourages their adaptation to a wide range of computers. Noncommercial versions of Kermit can be had for more than 250 different machines and operating systems, ranging in size from the smallest microcomputer to the largest supercomputer, and Kermit is included (at no extra charge) in about 100 different commercial software packages. According to a recent announcement from Telebit Corp. (Cupertino, Calif.), Kermit protocol is even beginning to find its way into silicon. XModem is also available for a wide variety of computers, but it was designed primarily for microcomputer-to-microcomputer links. It is most widely known by its commercial implementations, and it is a fixture in programs like Crosstalk.

Kermit, XModem, and other error-checking protocols do not all offer the same features (see "Kermit vs. XModem"). Kermit won't talk to XModem and vice versa. Each must be evaluated according to several criteria: Is there a version of the protocol available for all the computers that must communicate? Can the protocol accommodate all the necessary communications parameters? Is the performance acceptable? Is the software affordable?

XModem is more properly called the Christensen protocol after its designer, Ward Christensen, who originally intended it only for communications between CP/M microcomputers. Christensen put his original 1977 Modem program into the public domain, and it was modified by others over the years; some protocol features were added, resulting in protocol variants with names like Modem2, Modem7, XModem, YModem, ZModem, and so forth.

The Kermit file transfer protocol was originally developed in 1981 at the Columbia University Center for Computing Activities for CP/M, MS-DOS, the DECSystem-20, and IBM mainframes with VM/CMS; that is, for use in microcomputer-to-mainframe applications. It was shared freely with other institutions, with sources and documentation included. Everyone was, and is, permitted and encouraged to copy and share, to make improvements, and to contribute new versions.

Kermit and XModem both transfer files between computers in blocks of data, or packets (see Fig.3). They require a program running on each computer to compose, send, read, decipher, and act on the packets. Each packet is error-checked via calculated checksums, and retransmission is requested when packets have incorrect checksums. Deadlocks are broken by timeouts and retransmission. Missing or duplicate packets are caught using packet sequence numbers. Both protocols are half-duplex stop-and-wait, which means that the next packet is not sent until the current packet is acknowledged.

Most commercial RS-232-C communications packages claim to include XModem, Kermit, or both. In general, the commercial XModem implementations include none of the Modem7, YModem, or ZModem options but often do include support for cyclic redundancy checks. Thus, they can transfer only a single file at a time and only through transparent eight-bit communications channels. Commercial Kermit implementations vary from the bare-bones to the very advanced, but all versions can transfer text files through seven-bit links, and they can handle multiple files in a single operation. It is not always apparent from vendor literature exactly which options are supported. Buyers who are interested in these features should call the company and confirm whether the package includes them. After all, one of the advantages of commercial offerings is telephone support from the vendor.

More asynchronous protocols

XModem and Kermit are not the only asynchronous communications protocols available. Others include UUCP, Blast, MNP, X.PC, Poly-Xfr, DX, Compuserve, FAST, and DART. Most of these protocols are proprietary, and they are found primarily in commercial packages. They often include advanced capabilities, such as checkpoint/restart, bidirectional file transfer, and sliding windows.

But all proprietary protocols have these drawbacks: They must be purchased in conjunction with commercial packages, and if no package is available for a certain computer, then another protocol and set of packages must be found. Of the commercial packages, Blast probably comes closest to Kermit in covering a wide variety of hardware, and it exceeds Kermit in many design and performance areas. The drawback is the cost: $250 for the PC version; $450 for a PDP-11 version; and more for larger minicomputers or mainframes. Since the Blast protocol is inherently full duplex, a special "Blast box" front end must be purchased for half-duplex machines. Kermit, however, may be used either full or half duplex.

Shopping for communications software can be a full-time job. The accompanying checklist may help during the evaluation process (see "Software worksheet: Know your options"). The first step is deciding what communications features are needed; then go out and find them by checking the vendor literature or calling the company. ∎

Frank da Cruz is senior network planning officer at Columbia University's Center for Computing Activities (CUCCA) and author of Kermit: A File Transfer Protocol. *Christine Gianone is CUCCA's Kermit administrator. Frank da Cruz and Chris Gianone are co-authors of a forthcoming book on data communications software and protocols. Both hold masters degrees from Columbia.*

Gilbert Held, 4-Degree Consulting, Macon, Ga.

Making the most of the versatile breakout box

Handy and economical tools for troubleshooting all kinds of data communications problems, active and passive breakout boxes can prevent finger pointing when networks fail.

A portable, hand-held tester used primarily to examine the condition of the conductors at the physical-interface level, the simple breakout box, in the right hands, can be one of the most powerful tools available for testing and troubleshooting communications.

There are many types of breakout boxes, ranging from simple monitoring devices to units that permit the operator to readily change the state of leads, patching one conductor to another. Most breakout boxes are designed for use on RS-232-C interfaces, while some work with wideband V.35 interfaces or Centronics parallel printer interfaces. The discussion here focuses on devices designed for use on the ubiquitous RS-232-C interface, although general descriptions contained in this article, without reference to specific RS-232-C conductors, are also appropriate to breakout boxes designed for use on other types of physical interfaces.

The breakout box was originally designed to provide a visual indication of the state of the conductors at the physical interface. This examination can be between data terminal equipment (DTE) and data communications equipment (DCE), between two DTEs, or between two DCEs. The simplest type of breakout box is passive, providing a number of light-emitting diodes (LEDs), which are lit or not, depending on the voltage level on a particular conductor.

One end of a breakout box normally contains a "male" plug DB 25-P connector, while the opposite end of the breakout box contains a "female" socket DB 25-S connector. In the RS-232-C standard, DTEs and DCEs are supposed to have female DB 25-S connectors, while the cable connecting DTE to DCE has male DB 25-P connectors on each end.

In most situations, the breakout box can be easily inserted into either end of the cable connection between DTE and DCE (Fig. 1). The top portion of the figure shows the standard cabling of a DTE to a DCE; the bottom shows how the breakout box can be inserted between one of the devices and the cable. In actuality, the breakout box can be inserted between the DTE and a cable connector, between the DCE and a cable connector, or right between DTE and DCE. To allow insertion directly between devices, many breakout box manufacturers have incorporated two ribbon cables to tie the separate device connectors to each end of the test unit.

Some of the more expensive breakout boxes have dual-gender connectors attached to each end of the ribbon cable connected to the device. These ensure that the technician using the breakout box will always be able to insert it into a network segment, regardless of the type of cable end or device connectors encountered.

Passive breakouts

Basically, passive breakout boxes (Fig. 2) provide the user with the ability to monitor either all or a subset of the conductors at the physical interface. Some lower-cost units allow the user to monitor only pins 2, 3, 4, 5, 6, 8, and 20—the key data and control leads used with most asynchronous transmission applications. Others include two rows of interface-circuit probe points and an additional LED display labeled TEST, with a patch point wired to the TEST LED. This creates a spare LED.

A typical passive breakout box will monitor eight interface leads at one time; the TEST LED is used to provide the operator with the ability to monitor any other lead. This is an economical design, since LEDs normally cost more than probe points. Also, by reducing the number of LEDs, both the size and the complexity of the breakout box are reduced. Typical retail cost for such devices ranges between $75 and $100.

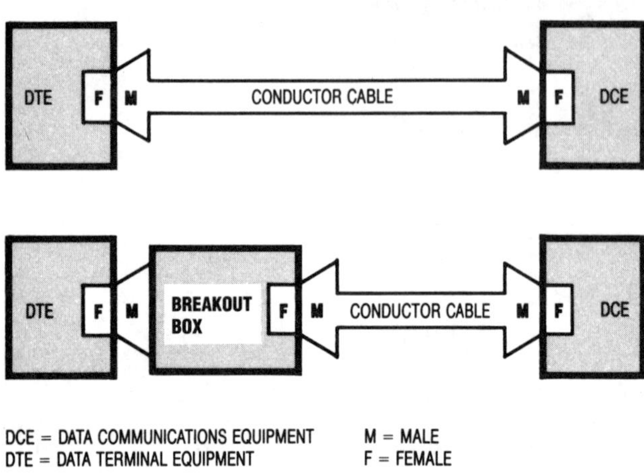

1. Using the box. *Breakout boxes can be installed between a DTE and a DCE, between two DCEs, or between a cable and either a DCE or DTE.*

When a single row of unicolor LEDs are included in the breakout box, the device is considered a "single-state monitor," a definition that is derived from the RS-232-C standard for data and control signals. In the RS-232-C specification, a positive voltage at or greater than +3, and less than or equal to +15, is defined as a "logic 0" or "space." A negative voltage at or less than -3, but not less than -15, is defined as a "logic 1" or "mark." Here, voltages between the logic 0 and logic 1 delimiters are considered a transitory state.

When only one set of LEDs is used in a breakout box, the LEDs normally light up in response to a positive voltage, denoting a logic 0 or signal space. The absence of illumination on the LED can indicate either a negative voltage or a transitory voltage. Thus, only when the LED is illuminated can the breakout box user be assured of the state of the conductor's signal.

In comparison to single-state breakout boxes, the use of a second row of LEDs changes the device into a "tri-state" unit. This type of breakout box normally uses red and green rows of LEDs, with a pair of LEDs assigned to each conductor to be monitored. Generally, breakout boxes are designed to illuminate red LEDs when a positive voltage is present and green LEDs when a negative voltage level occurs. Thus, if neither LED is lit, the monitored conductor is in a transitory (no-voltage) condition.

As an alternative to the use of dual rows of green and red LEDs, some breakout boxes employ a single row of LEDs that can be illuminated in either color. While this type of device is functionally equivalent to a breakout box that uses two separate rows of LEDs, it does permit color-blind people to use the device.

Still other breakout boxes are constructed with dual pairs of red and green LEDs. One pair of LEDs is used on the DCE side of the interface; the second pair is used to represent leads on the DTE side of the interface.

Since a passive breakout box can only monitor the condition or state of interface conductors, its role is limited to the examination and verification of control signal conditions. As an example of a possible use of this device, consider a dial-in modem connected to a computer port.

Suppose users complained that the only response to dialing the switched telephone network number of the line connected to the modem was constant ringing—the classic "ring no answer" (RNA) communications problem. By inserting a passive breakout box between the modem and the computer port, the operator of the breakout box can usually determine the culprit initiating the RNA.

Port diagnosis

Prior to receiving a call, the computer port will normally have pin 20 (Data Terminal Ready, or DTR) "raised," or in the ON condition. If this condition is not observed, the chances are very high that the computer port is the RNA culprit. Potential solutions to the problem range from removing and reinserting the board on which the computer port is located (known as reseeding), replacing the board with a spare, or checking the computer's communications software.

The next step in this observation process is to determine if the modem has conductor 6 (Data Set Ready, or DSR) in the ON condition. If not, the modem will not pass the RI (Ring Indicator) signal to the computer port when an incoming call arrives, thus causing the RNA predicament.

The breakout box user may then arrange for an associate to dial the modem while the tester observes the control signals. The absence of pin 6 or pin 22 (RI) being ON means that the modem is probably causing the RNA condition. Possible solutions to this problem can range again from the reseeding of a board in the modem, refas-

2. Passive box. *With a mini patch cord, the status of any conductor can be displayed on the TEST LED. Here, the Ring Indicator (pin 21) lead status will be displayed.*

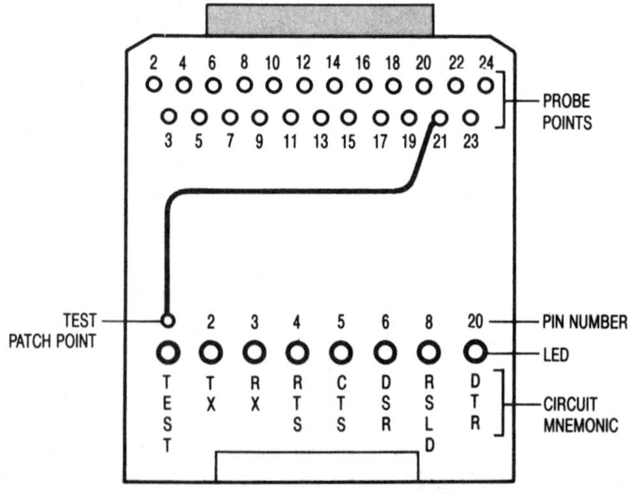

tening connectors, or replacing either a modem board or the whole modem.

If both the DSR and RI signals are high (register a positive voltage), then the computer port is not correctly responding to the modem. This indicates that the computer port, and possibly also the communications software, need to be examined. In many instances, the deactivation of one or a group of lines by the computer console operator, through either a standard operating procedure or testing, may not have been followed by an appropriate command to place the line back into service. In such situations, a request to the computer operators to reactivate line "XXX" should cause the DTR signal to reappear and return the connection to normal.

Active breakouts

In comparison to a passive breakout box, an active breakout box contains patch and cross-connect probe points for both DTE and DCE sides of devices undergoing tests. In addition, an active breakout box contains a set of switches that can be used to break open the data and control lines of the physical interface. These devices are also commonly called breakout switches.

Some active breakout boxes are battery-powered, while other devices are powered from the line they are monitoring. At the high end of this product category, several breakout boxes include positive- and negative-voltage sources that can be used with jumpers or mini patch cords to simulate control signals. These normally sell for between $275 and $350.

In a typical high-end, active breakout box, the positive- and negative-voltage sources are included so an operator can simulate any of the RS-232-C conductor signals he or she may require. This control-signal simulation is accomplished by the operator first patching one end of a jumper wire (supplied with the breakout box) to the appropriate voltage source.

The operator can then connect the opposite end of the jumper wire to one of the 50 probe points on the device, each of which is associated with a simulated conductor signal on the DTE or DCE side of the breakout box.

As an example of the use of the voltage sources and probe points, consider an operator who wants to observe the reaction of a device to the presence of a RI signal but does not have a dial-network circuit available in which to place an actual test call. By connecting the active breakout box to the RS-232-C port on the device and then patching a jumper wire from the positive voltage source to the probe point associated with pin 22 (RI), the operator can simulate the occurrence of that signal. Then, by observing the other LEDs, the operator can note the response of the device to an RI signal.

Probe points

The two rows of 25 probe points on a typical active breakout box can be used for patching and simulating RS-232-C data and control signals at either side of the device. This all-inclusive patching capability permits the operator to use a jumper wire to connect any signal or data conductor on one side of the device to any other signal or data conductor on the same side or the opposite side of the device. To understand the value of using probe points, consider an operator that is working with a ring-start communications device, such as a port on a port selector.

If the operator desires to connect a terminal directly to the port selector, no RI signal will occur (since the connection bypasses the switched telephone network). In this situation, the technician would examine other control signals activated by the terminal and determine the effect of jumping one of the terminal control signals to the RI signal.

By using the probe points, the technician could, for example, first cable the active breakout box to a port on the port selector. One jumper wire could be used to patch a positive voltage to the DTR probe point, thus simulating that control signal without actually cabling the terminal to the port selector port. Next, the technician could jumper the DTR probe point to the RI probe point, in effect forcing the RI signal to become active whenever a DTR signal is present.

If the operator then notices the flashing of an LED on either pin 2 or pin 3, this would indicate that the port selector is activated by forcing the RI signal high. It would then begin to transmit a sign-on message to a nonexistant terminal simulated by the use of the active breakout box. The LED may flash either on pin 2 or pin 3 because the port on the port selector may be configured as either a DTE or a DCE. If it is configured as a DTE, data will be transmitted on pin 2, whereas if the port is configured as a DCE, data will be transmitted on pin 3.

Once the required jumpering is noted, the operator can use the information to fabricate an appropriate cable. For the previous example, pin 20 (DTR) would be jumpered to pin 22 (RI) in a cable to ensure that each time a directly connected terminal was turned on, the port selected would receive the required RI signal.

Connectors and switches

The dual-gender connectors that come with the cables attached to an active breakout box ensure that the device can be connected to any standard RS-232-C connector, without requiring the operator to search for an adapter. To understand the utility of dual-gender connectors, consider the RS-232-C cabling standard. In this standard, DTEs and DCEs are supposed to be built with female socket connectors, while cables connecting the devices are supposed to have male connectors on each end, allowing such cables to be fastened to both devices.

However, in reality, DTEs and DCEs may not conform to the connector standard, and the resulting cable used to connect the two devices (a DTE to a DTE or DCE) will likewise deviate from the standard. With the inclusion of dual-gender connectors, breakout box operators do not need cable adapters or "gender-mender" devices.

The 25 breakout switches on an active breakout box can be used to break open data and control lines when the left side of each switch is pushed down. When examining the operations of two devices, the breakout switches are useful for enabling and disabling data and control signals. By using these switches, a technician can easily examine the effect of changes in control signals of one device on another, without requiring that the devices be operating.

Consider the previous example where a terminal is directly connected to the port of a port selector. To find out if the port selector interprets a drop of the DTR signal as a disconnect request, the operator could simply flip the DTR breakout switch to drop that control signal. Then, by either examining the port selector console or the port interface on the port selector, the operator will be able to determine if the absence of DTR causes the port selector to disconnect the terminal.

On the port interface, a technician will first note some activity on either pin 2 or pin 3 (again, depending on whether the port is configured as a DTE or DCE). This is evident because the green LED associated with that pin will light up. This occurs because, according to the RS-232-C standard, a transmitter will always be at a negative voltage when not transmitting.

The pin-reversal switch enables the operator to easily reverse pins 2 and 3 in an RS-232-C test application, such as when connecting two DTEs or two DCEs together. Some breakout boxes, however, require an operator to use two jumper wires to patch the probe points of pin 2 to pin 3 and pin 3 to pin 2.

Active vs. passive

The patching and control-signal simulations of active breakout boxes enable them to be used in a variety of situations where a passive device may be of little or no use. Consider the versatility of the active breakout box in several typical communications scenarios.

■ Suppose a communications port on a microcomputer is directly cabled, through a conduit, to a port on a protocol converter located in a computer room. After the microcomputer loads its communications program and enters its terminal emulation mode, it turns out that data entered from the keyboard fails to be displayed on the microcomputer's monitor. Since there is a possibility that (1) the communications cable was crimped when snaked through the conduit, (2) the software was configured incorrectly, or (3) the protocol converter was not operating correctly, problem elimination should be used to isolate the impairment. By using an active breakout box, in this case as a loopback plug (taking a signal received and looping it back), the technician obtains a mechanism for physically checking the cable.

Figure 3 illustrates the use of an active breakout box as a loopback plug. By inserting the device between the cable and the protocol converter port, it can be used to check the continuity of conductors in the cable by using breakout switches with jumpers or mini patch cords.

In the example, Transmit Data (TD) is patched to Receive Data (RD), Request to Send (RTS) is patched to Clear to Send (CTS) and DTR is patched to both DSR and Data Carrier Detect (DCD). The switches on the breakout box for each of the circuits are placed in the open position, thereby disabling any signals emanating from the port on the protocol converter.

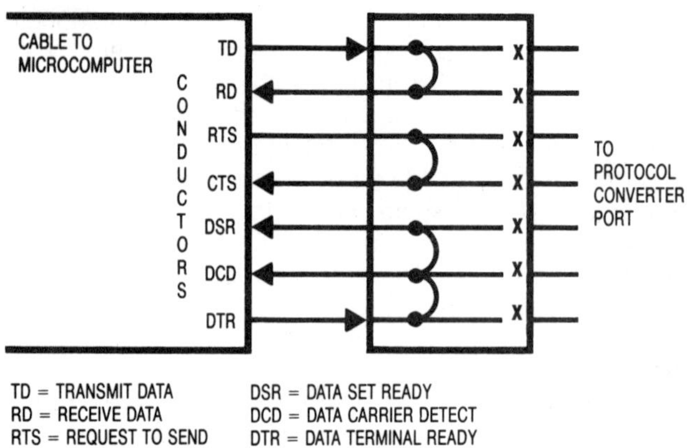

3. Loopback plug. *Looping back signals can be accomplished through an active breakout box. This allows testing of both transmitting devices and cables*

Although the breakout box will only confirm whether or not the microcomputer is functioning as a terminal, the breakout box could also be connected directly to the computer's communications port. If characters are echoed back to the computer's display when the breakout box is connected to the computer's communications port, while no characters are echoed back when the device is inserted between the cable and the protocol converter port, then the technician can safely assume that the cable is defective.

■ With interface modification, an active breakout box probably finds its primary use. By using its patching capability, technical control center personnel can determine special cabling requirements that may be necessary to make devices with incompatible control signals compatible.

Consider the direct connection of a terminal device to a port selector that operates as a ring-start device. This means that the port selector must receive a signal on pin 22 (RI) in order to be placed in operation. Since a directly cabled terminal does not provide an RI signal, the technician could insert an active breakout box between the cable and the port selector port connector, then, through the use of jumpers or mini patch cords, attempt to derive the required signals prior to fabricating a cable. In this situation, one possible solution might be to jumper or patch DTR to RI. Then, when the terminal is turned on and DTR becomes high, it forces RI high, activating the port selector.

■ Another common data communications problem is determining whether an interface device operates as DTE or DCE. While the original RS-232-C standard was developed to govern the serial data interchange between DTE and DCE equipment, it is now quite common to have DTEs connected to DTEs and DCEs connected to DCEs. In such situations, technicians must first determine the "personality" of each device to be connected (whether DTE or DCE) and the conductor flow requirements, and then fabricate the appropriate cable to permit the incompatible devices to communicate.

4. Null modem. *By using the breakout box, users can easily determine what kind of conductor cabling will be required to make a null modem.*

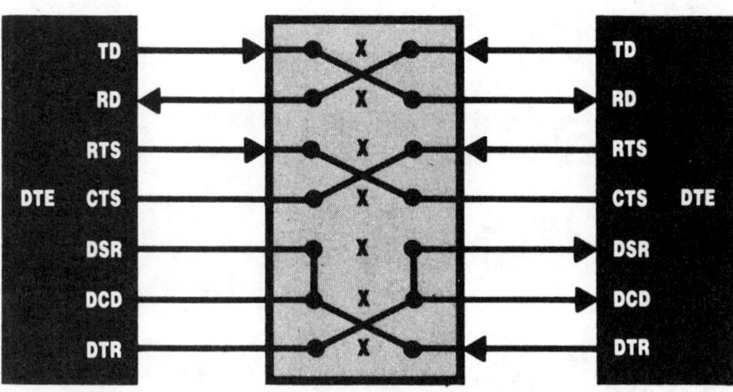

TD = TRANSMIT DATA
RD = RECEIVE DATA
RTS = REQUEST TO SEND
CTS = CLEAR TO SEND
DSR = DATA SET READY

DCD = DATA CARRIER DETECT
DTR = DATA TERMINAL READY
DTE = DATA TERMINAL EQUIPMENT

X = INDICATES A BREAKOUT SWITCH IN OPEN POSITION

In the example where a microcomputer is cabled to a protocol converter, another incompatibility problem can arise if the protocol converter port is configured as a DTE device. To verify this, the technician can connect a breakout box to the port of the protocol converter. Since the RS-232-C standard specifies that a transmitter will always be at a logic 1 (negative voltage) when not transmitting, the green LED associated with pin 3 on a three-state breakout box will light up if the protocol converter port is configured as a DCE. If the protocol converter port is configured as a DTE, then the green LED on pin 2 will be illuminated.

Since some protocol converters can be programmed through a configuration port, it might be possible to simply change the port to a DCE port in order to achieve compatibility with the microcomputer operating as a DTE. If this is not possible, then the technician must determine the appropriate control signals and data path connections required to develop a null modem cable to connect one DTE to another. This can be accomplished by either examining the manuals of the protocol converter and the microcomputer's asynchronous communications adapter to determine their control signal requirements or by using a breakout box to determine the required control signals.

The technician can connect the breakout box to the protocol converter port to observe its control signal outputs. This is accomplished by noting which red LEDs are lit. (At rest, they generate a positive voltage.) Next, the technician can verify the control signal inputs to the protocol converter port by first patching pins 2 to 3 and 3 to 2, which connects the transmit-data and receive-data conductors of the microcomputer to the appropriate transmit and receive conductors on the protocol converter port. This procedure is called for because it was previously determined that the protocol converter port is configured as a DTE and because conductors 2 and 3 must be reversed for two DTEs to operate.

Once pins 2 and 3 are reversed, the technician can apply a negative voltage (control-off) to each potential input and note the results. This is accomplished by placing one end of a mini patch cord into the negative voltage source on the breakout box and the opposite end of the patch cord to each potential input source.

If the protocol converter port stops operating when a negative voltage is applied on a conductor, a working control input has been located. The control inputs on the microcomputer's asynchronous communications adapter can be similarly determined to develop a DTE-to-DCE wiring chart. This can then be used by the technician to verify null modem conductor assignments. Figure 4 illustrates the use of an active breakout box, configured as a modem eliminator cable, to verify the conductor arrangement prior to fabricating the required cable.

Cable verification

Pin connections of a cable can also be examined by using an active breakout box. If cable has not been installed, each end of new cable can be connected to the breakout box, and the operator can apply either a positive or negative voltage to each of the conductor probe points on one side of the breakout box and examine the LEDs on the other side. Open conditions (broken connections) and continuity of conductors (where voltages flow evenly end-to-end) can then be noted.

To illustrate the use of an active breakout box to perform cable testing, assume one end of a mini patch cord is connected to a voltage-source probe point. If the operator patches the other end of the cord to pin 2 and the LED associated with pin 3 on the other side of the device lights up, this indicates that pins 2 and 3 are reversed. Similarly, if the operator patches the other end of the cord to pin 20 and pins 6 and 8 light up on the other side of the breakout box, this indicates that DTR is tied to DSR and DCD.

If a cable is already in place, it is usually too difficult to remove for testing. In such situations, an active breakout box can be placed at one end of the cable and a passive breakout box placed at the other end. A positive or negative voltage can be patched to each conductor probe, with results noted at the end of each cable.

As indicated, the breakout box is a very useful and practical piece of network diagnostic hardware. Because of its low cost and high usefulness in testing and troubleshooting, it is quite common for technicians to carry one around in the way that engineers used to wear slide rules. And since other types of communications test equipment — line monitors and protocol analyzers — are now being manufactured with built-in breakout boxes, this added functionality can be viewed as a testament to the versatility of the handy, standalone breakout box. ∎

Gilbert Held, director of 4-Degree Consulting, is an internationally recognized author and lecturer on data communications subjects. Twice a recipient of the Interface Karp Award and a winner of the American Association of Publishers Award, Held is the author of 15 books and more than 60 technical articles. He also conducts seminars on data communications testing, troubleshooting, and capacity planning.

Malcolm Hamer and Jim Heilmann, Citicorp, New York, N. Y.

How one firm created its own global electronic mail network

A pre-X.400 solution overcame vendor incompatibilities while integrating five different software packages.

How does a company provide 19,000 users with intercommunications when it has a network of 47 processors, each running one of five different electronic mail software packages? The answer, in Citicorp's case: Give all users access to a single common directory. The Citicorp configuration is the result of a three-year plan to interoperate different vendors' electronic mail software packages. The company used a set of internal Citicorp standards, known as the Citidex Electronic Mail Standards.

The evolution of Citicorp's intracompany electronic mail service started in 1981 with a pilot installation in London. The main ingredients were a DEC (Digital Equipment Corp.) PDP-11/70 computer plus the popular off-the-shelf electronic mailbox software package, Comet. The pilot was initially limited to Citicorp's London staff, but it became so talked about that personnel at other European branches started to ask for mailboxes on Comet. The computer was connected to Citicorp's global telecommunications data network, and soon staff throughout Europe were intercommunicating via electronic mail—named Citimail.

Use of Citimail then spread to other regions, and by mid-1983 Citimail was accepted as the primary means of international person-to-person nontransactional communications within the corporation. (All communications regarding financial transactions continue to be conducted via a totally separate message-switching network, which has a high level of security and the necessary audit trails to guard against misplaced messages.)

Comet (supplied by Maxcom, based in Waltham, Mass.) is designed for the DEC PDP-11 series of machines. A PDP-11/70 or -11/84 processor, running Comet, can support about 64 concurrent sessions. This is the typical session demand created by 1,600 users in one time zone, or as many as 4,800 users spread around the globe (so

that advantage can be taken of nonoverlapping working hours).

Comet's efficiency results from a conservative database structure. But the database is not continuously self-reorganizing, so the application has to be "taken down" (preventing users from gaining access) for a few hours on weekends to run database reorganization routines. Also, Comet has only a primitive line editor, rather than the kind of full-screen editor available on more recent packages such as DEC's All-in-One. (An example of the Comet line-editor's crudeness: The operator cannot back up the cursor beyond the line on which it is.)

Easy to manage

Nevertheless, Comet seems to gain rapid acceptance by new users, possibly because of its very simple command structure: There is only one command level, no menus, and only a handful of command verbs to remember.

In 1983 another PDP-11/70 had to be added in London. (By this time a backup machine had already been added to the original configuration to guarantee continuity of service in the event of a hardware failure.) Demand for Citimail grew so rapidly that this second node was full within a few months, so that a third node was needed. This third node was placed in New York to serve Citicorp staff in North and South America. It consisted of a PDP-11/70 plus a backup. The multiple-machine environment, with nodes in London and New York, was handled using the standard multinode Comet software. This software makes node intercommunications transparent to the user.

In parallel with the growing popularity of Citimail, several areas of the corporation had started to look for integrated office automation (OA) and electronic mail solutions to their internal day-to-day business requirements. Three organizational areas implemented such packages. One area de-

Message types and type codes

CODE	TYPE
01	ORDINARY TEXT MESSAGE
02	USER-REQUESTED ACKNOWLEDGMENT
03	SYSTEM-REQUESTED ACKNOWLEDGMENT
05	NEGATIVE ACKNOWLEDGMENT (MESSAGE UNDELIVERABLE)

DIRECTORY UPDATE MESSAGES	
50	ADD A NEW LOCATION CODE TO THE DATABASE
51	MODIFY AN OLD LOCATION CODE IN THE DATABASE
60	ADD A NEW USER
61	DELETE AN OLD USER
70	ADD A NEW DISTRIBUTION LIST
71	DELETE AN OLD DISTRIBUTION LIST
80	ADD MEMBER(S) TO A DISTRIBUTION LIST
81	DELETE MEMBER(S) FROM A DISTRIBUTION LIST
90	CHANGE A USER'S NAME OR A DISTRIBUTION LIST NAME
91	CHANGE A USER'S NODE NUMBER

ployed a network from San Antonio, Tex.-based Datapoint, whose electronic mail feature is called E-Mail. This feature offered close integration of electronic mail with word processing, plus full-screen editing of electronic mail messages. Two other areas chose DEC's All-in-One package, which has similar characteristics.

By late 1983 it became clear that a problem was arising. Users on the local OA-based packages wanted to exchange messages with Citimail users, who numbered about 6,000. The only way they could do this was to be enrolled on both services, using the OA-based service for within-division communications and Citimail for communications with other areas, particularly overseas branches. To try to solve this problem, a committee was set up to investigate how the various packages could be made to communicate with each other.

While less ambitious than the CCITT X.400 standards, the internal Citicorp standards are dominated by a concern with directory and addressing issues. These issues have a very different scope with an intracompany network than with public electronic mail networks.

Arguing the philosophy

The investigating committee had one major advantage over the CCITT X.400 committees: The eventual population that would be using the consolidated network was limited to a well-defined set of human beings: Citicorp employees, who currently number about 100,000. This makes the addressing problem many orders of magnitude simpler than the public electronic mail problem of potentially addressing any human being on the planet. Even so, some members of the committee argued that it would be impossible to continue with the basic Comet scheme of addressing people by their names. They proposed, instead, the use of personnel numbers.

After some lively debates, the personnel-number approach was rejected because it was awkward and redundant. In any case, users must supply enough information about a desired addressee to uniquely identify that addressee in the directory. So why not use that information directly? In the end it was agreed to construct a unique identifier for every employee by adding a suffix to each name. The suffix took the form of *Location:Group*, where Location identifies the geographical location, and Group identifies the person's functional working area. In the case of common last names, middle initials would be pressed into service to provide a unique key if first name, location, and group all coincided.

It was also agreed that the location code would be based on IATA (International Air Transport Association) airport codes, to minimize the number of characters appearing in message headers. (For example, Los Angeles would be identified as LAX.) Because some of the airport codes are somewhat obscure, it was decided to prefix them by a two-letter region code, to guide users to where the city might be. So the location code for Los Angeles becomes USLAX. Brussels takes the region code EU for Europe, so the location code for Brussels is EUBRU. Hong Kong is APHKG, where AP stands for Asia/Pacific.

The group codes were based on abbreviations already widely used in the Citicorp telephone directory, such as INV for Investment Banking Sector, IND for Individual Banking Sector, IB for Institutional Banking Sector, and AUD for Audit Division. So, three similar entries in the directory might be: John A. Smith (USLAX:INV); John B. Smith (EUBRU:IND); John B. Smith (APHKG:IB).

Another point to which the committee members agreed: Users would not, generally, key in these location/group suffixes, such as "(USLAX:INV)"; in most cases the suffix would be appended by the electronic mail software package. If, in the *To:* line of a message, the user keys "John A. Smith," or even just "J. A. Smith" where there are no other J. A. Smiths, then this will be accepted immediately and confirmed by the electronic mail software.

'Will the real John Smith . . .'

The addressee confirmation takes the form of a repetition of the *To:* or *CC:* line after the one entered by the user. It may differ from what the user enters: Names are shown as they appear in the directory ("John A. Smith" where the user typed just "J. A. Smith"). Also, the suffix is appended. The confirmation reassures the user that the correct John A. Smith has been identified. However, if the user types an ambiguous name, the electronic mail package will offer a choice of possible names, giving the suffix for each.

For example, the dialogue might go as follows: (The regular text is that typed by the user; the italics represents that generated by the electronic mail software package.)
To: John B. Smith
Ambiguous name.

Do you wish to see 2 similar names (Y/N)? Y
1 John B. Smith (EUBRU:IND)
2 John B. Smith (APHKG:IB)
Corrected name or number: 2
To: John B. Smith (APHKG:IB)
In this example, the final line of text is the addressee
confirmation for the *To:* line.

Users who are aware of the ambiguity (from a previous
attempt to send a message to one of the John B. Smiths)
can key the name and suffix themselves, to avoid being
taken through the above process. Or they may type just
the name and answer the resulting prompts. Experience
has shown that only a low percentage of names is ambiguous without the suffix, so that it is rare for users to have to
go through a dialogue like the one above.

What turns out to be much more common is that the user
is unsure of how the first name or initials appear in the
directory and will therefore type just the last name. This
results in the electronic mail software package offering a
number of possible names, from which the user makes a
choice. Users in these circumstances have reported (in
various surveys and interviews) that they have found the
suffix extremely useful in identifying the user they are
seeking. They are more likely to know the city and the part
of the company in which the user works than the first name
and initials. Users also report that the suffix has been useful
in identifying where people are located. (On some messages with many addressees, it was previously difficult to
sort out who one's fellow addressees were.)

Other important philosophical points that the committee
soon accepted were:

■ Every electronic mail node in the corporation, once linked
with the other nodes, must hold a directory of all users on
all nodes. Users then have the perception of all being on
the same node, since they can then send messages to
anyone on any node without first identifying the addressee's node.

■ The complete directories held in each node must be kept
fully synchronized (identical) using minimal manual operations. Human intervention for the directory-update function
should be performed only by the System Administrator of
the node that has the mailbox of a user whose directory
entry is being created or changed.

■ No node is allowed to send a message to another node
without every addressee being positively identified from the
complete directory. So, barring directory synchronization
failures, internodal messages should always be accepted
at the receiving node, and manual intervention to deal with
undeliverable messages should be a very rare occurrence.
This is in contrast to many distributed public networks,
where "wild" messages (those with unvalidated addresses)
can be sent to another node.

Seamless and hands-off

The investigating committee's next assignment was to
define a set of internodal message types. These message
types would be needed to achieve the committee's dual
objectives: a "seamless" integration of the different vendors' packages and a minimal human intervention in the
maintenance of directory synchronization.

Two general classes of messages were specified: user
and directory update. User types were subdivided into
ordinary text and acknowledgments.

The vast majority of messages passing between nodes
during normal operation are ordinary text. A small proportion are acknowledgments. The latter generally occur only
when the sender specifically requests that receipt of the
sent message be acknowledged.

To allow for the possibility of a node operating in a
positive-acknowledgment mode for all messages, two
types of acknowledgments were defined: sender-requested and network-requested. Sender-requested
causes the destination node to issue an alert that receipt
of the message will be acknowledged if it is read.

Network-requested, on the other hand, is generated
automatically by the receiving node when the associated
message is placed in the user's in-box. It is thus proof that
it got to the destination node but does not mean that it has
been seen by the addressee. If necessary, a message may
be flagged for both types of acknowledgment.

The other type of message—directory update—represents a very small proportion of traffic. It is mixed in with
the user messages on the same physical internodal links.
At most, there are a few hundred updates a week across
the whole network, which represents less than one percent
of the total internodal traffic.

Before looking at the various types of directory update
messages that the committee defined, it is necessary to
understand the directory-database structure being considered. This structure represents the minimum requirements
for an electronic mail package that is to meet the Citidex
standards. (Individual electronic mail packages may have
additional elements in their directories.)

The model database structure consists of three parts: an
individual user part, a distribution list part, and a location-
code table. A distribution list is thought of by its name, such
as Electronic Mail Committee, plus a set of "pointers" that
point to the directory entries of individual users who are
members of that list. This means that the directory entry for
users may be changed without having to make any
changes to the distribution lists on which they are.

Character count

The model for the individual-user part of the directory
database consists of:
■ Name (32 characters maximum)
■ Location code (8 characters maximum)
■ Function code (8 characters maximum)
■ Node number of user's mailbox (4 digits)
■ Last update sequence number (2 digits)

The committee allowed for eight characters in the location code, even though the initial scheme used only five.
The use of four digits for the node numbers was meant to
reduce to nil the possibility of running out of node numbers.
In practice, it is unlikely that the number of nodes would
exceed 50.

The model for the distribution list part of the directory
database consists of:

- List name (32 characters maximum)
- Location code (8 characters maximum)
- Function code (8 characters maximum)
- Last update sequence number (2 digits)
- Pointers to individual directory entries of list members

All location codes must be explicitly defined in the database's location-code table. All new entries or changed entries in the individual-user part of the database must be checked against this table—to make sure that the location code is a recognized one—before the directory update is allowed. A consequence of this procedure is that, before a node can advise the other nodes of the first user in a new location, the location code for that location must be broadcast to the other nodes. Only then can users with that location code be added. This structure was defined in order to eliminate the possibility of "lost" users (without a recognized location) being entered in the directory due to keying errors by System Administrators.

To keep directories synchronized, 10 types of directory update messages were defined (see table). These types were needed to cover all the possible update actions relating to individual users' directory entries, to distribution lists, and to the location-code table.

The assumed creation method for distribution lists is to first create an "empty" list (message type 70) and then add members to it (message type 80). This was thought to be a cleaner method of handling list creation than to include the initial members in the list-creation message.

Primitive is better

The next step was to define the exact format of the messages that would be passed between the electronic mail nodes. While the idea of a layered protocol like X.400's had intellectual appeal, it was agreed that a more primitive arrangement would be easier to implement in the short term. The approach selected was to use the traditional message switching approach of a message header with well-defined fields and field labels, plus a unique message-termination character.

Figure 1A is the format of the message as it passes between two nodes. At the destination node, the message is presented to the recipient in whatever format that user's package employs. An example of such a format is shown in Figure 1B.

In the internodal message (Fig. 1A), the message header consists of a number of fields, each labeled with a three-digit field label preceded and followed by a colon (for example, :801:). Each field is terminated by a "carriage return."

Only the second and third digits of the field labels are significant. The extra digit, which is always 8, was added so that, in the future, nonmail message types—identified by a different initial digit—could be intermixed with mail messages on the same network.

The message terminator is a single hyphen on a new line, followed immediately by a carriage return. The internodal message-handling software prevents—by "space stuffing"—a hyphen in the message text from causing a premature termination of a message. Space stuffing inserts

(A) EXAMPLE OF AN INTERNODAL TEXT MESSAGE

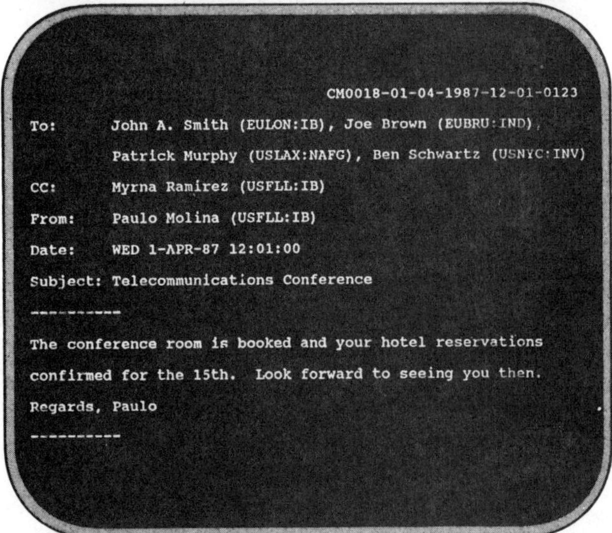

(B) HOW THE ABOVE MESSAGE WOULD APPEAR TO ONE OF THE ADDRESSEES

a space after a text-resident hyphen. A hyphen is only a terminator if it is in the left-most column and has no character or space between it and the carriage return.

Easier debugging

This method of message termination was chosen over a nonprintable reserved character because the committee had a strong preference for using recognizable printable characters wherever possible. It was felt that such a method would make software debugging easier: sample messages could be readily analyzed from a printout, instead of an operator having to interpret strange characters displayed on a network-analyzer screen.

The committee defined 26 field labels. An ordinary text message may use up to 10 of these. Directory update messages tend to use somewhat fewer field types. In the example (Fig. 1A), field :810: contains the message type code, which determines what header fields must be present and what optional fields may be present. Field label :839: appears only in an ordinary text message and is the start-of-text indicator.

The :800: field contains the number of the node to which this particular copy of the message is being sent (node 0011). In this example, the source node will send similar copies to nodes 0002 and 0013, because the message is addressed to users on these nodes. The :801: fields contain *To:* addressees; the :802:, *CC:* addressees. The *From:* line appears in field :803:. Note that the message comes from a user on node 0018. Field :820: contains the message ID; :821:, the date/time stamp; and :830:, the subject.

The fifth digit on the end of the node number in the :801: and :802: fields is an acknowledgment-request code. 0 is for no acknowledgment; 1, sender-requested acknowledgment; 2, network-requested acknowledgment; and 3, both types of acknowledgment.

Although not illustrated in this example, fields :801: and :802: may contain distribution-list names. In this case, the node number that precedes the distribution list name is set to a "wild card" number of 0000, because distribution lists may contain members on more than one node. The receiving node must disassemble each list to determine if any of the list's members are on that node.

If the distribution-list name is the only addressee of the message, the software sends copies of the message only to nodes with addressed members. (This approach prevents the sending node from aimlessly sending copies of user messages to all nodes, regardless of whether the messages contain addressees for those nodes or not.) However, if the message is also addressed to other individual users or distribution lists, disassembly of a distribution list at the receiving node may result in no users being found belonging to that node. (Disassembly of the list refers to an electronic mail software operation to place copies of the message in their proper mailboxes.) In the *To:* and *CC:* lines, as displayed on the screen of the message recipients, only the distribution-list names appear, not the names of the list's members.

Change administration

Although user messages are intended only for the nodes of their addressees, directory-update messages are broadcast to all nodes. A directory update occurs when a node's System Administrator adds, changes, or deletes a directory entry. The update is immediately implemented on the node in question, which then automatically sends update messages to all the other nodes. A node receiving an update message automatically carries out the update, normally without human intervention. However, if a problem arises (such as an update sequence-number gap or a failure to find the original directory entry), incoming update mes-

2. Modification message. *This directory update illustrates a change in the user's organizational group (from IB to INV) and location (from London to Tokyo).*

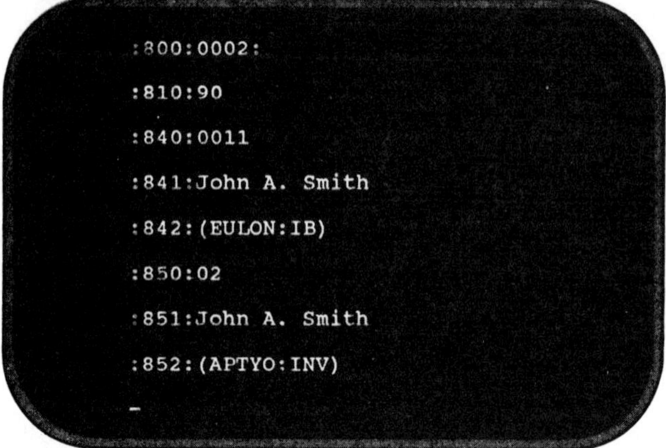

sages will be "spilled" to the receiving node's System Administrator.

Figure 2 illustrates a modify-name and/or -suffix update. In this example, the user's name is unchanged, but he has moved to a different organizational group (from IB to INV) and to a different location (from London to Tokyo). Field :840: contains the sending-node number. This is the node on which the sending user has his mailbox. Field :850: contains an update sequence number. The directory entry at each node should have an update level of 01 prior to processing this update, and an update level of 02 after. The :851: and :852: fields contain the new directory entry.

The committee defined the formats of each message type: which fields were required and which optional; also, which could appear only once (like the *From:* field), and which could appear one or more times (like a *To:* or *CC:* field). Thus, there are four classifications for a header field: RS (required, single), RM (required, multiple), OS (optional, single), and OM (optional, multiple).

Operational restrictions

In defining how the network would actually work, the committee established a number of rules. Some are:

■ Each node or group of nodes must have a System Administrator to establish new mailboxes, to change directory entries for the node's users and for distribution lists, and to remove users who leave the company.

■ No "proxy" additions would be allowed. That is, one node's administrator cannot force another node to create a new mailbox for a user on that other node. The rationale: 1. None of the software packages was capable of opening a new mailbox on the basis of an incoming update message; 2. There are other pieces of information required to open a new mailbox, such as the new user's initial sign-on password. Mailbox-creation is thus under the sole control of the System Administrator of the node in question.

■ In principle, a distribution list can be created by any System Administrator; also, any System Administrator can add members to an existing list. However, the committee initially adopted a conservative operational approach to have each list "owned" by a specific administrator, who would make all the additions to and deletions from the list. This avoided having two add-member updates generated at the same time from different nodes—with the same update-level number in field :850: (Fig. 2)—which would result in the second one being rejected.

The distributed-management approach—with no single overall administrator—is particularly suited to operations in a global organization, where time differences make central control almost impossible. The major ingredients of this approach are a System Administrator for each node, and a "democratic" database-updating scheme in which each node broadcasts its updates to all the others.

Getting to the nitty-gritty

The implementation of the standards was carried out by different project teams for each electronic mail software package. For Comet and All-in-One, joint projects were set up with the vendors. The latter provided programmers to write add-on software modules to implement the standards.

In the case of the Datapoint E-Mail subnetwork, a team of Citicorp programmers wrote a gateway program to run on a Tandem Non-Stop processor. The gateway provided an interface between the entire Datapoint subnetwork and all the other nodes in the network. Datapoint provided no support for this project. Tandem hardware was used because the part of Citicorp that uses E-Mail had a number of other Tandem-based applications under development. The plan was to run the gateway on a machine shared with some of these applications.

The phasing of the implementation was arranged to minimize programmer time spent on testing for logical flaws. First, the standards were installed on the Comet nodes, taking over from the vendor's own multinode Comet arrangement. However, the nodes could be rolled back to multinode Comet operation if things went wrong.

The use of the *Location:Group* suffix was then introduced into the directories. This caused some initial performance problems because of the way the directory look-up algorithms worked. However, after some "fine-tuning" of the search algorithm, the average look-up time (the time that elapses from the user typing the *To:* line, followed by carriage return, to the *To:* line being confirmed back to the user) was restored to about one second per name.

Exchange of user messages between the nodes under the standards was relatively trouble-free from day one. Only the directory update messages caused any significant trouble. Initial reject rates on incoming update messages (requiring intervention by the administrator) were somewhat higher than expected. However, after further software debugging, they were brought down to a level—a few per week—that could be easily handled by administrators as a standard operating procedure.

All the Comet nodes were DEC machines, and the lower protocol layers were well taken care of by Decnet. There-fore, at the link level, the exchange of messages between

Comet nodes was accomplished relatively easily.

In the second phase of implementation, work was com-pleted on the Datapoint E-Mail gateway, and tests were started between it and the Comet subnetwork. This was somewhat more complex than the first phase because software for the lower protocol layers had to be debugged at the same time as the electronic mail data-exchange software. Initially, a proprietary Citicorp protocol was used to provide Layer 2 (Data Link) and Layer 4 (Transport) services. However, this was replaced at a later stage by X.25, combined with a proprietary Layer 4 protocol for message-delivery assurance.

Tough task

The most rigorous standards-testing period occurred with the message exchanges between the Comet nodes and the E-Mail gateway. The two teams had made different assumptions about what was meant in the standards. For example, clarification was needed of which fields were optional and which mandatory. In the end, the "right" answer to each difference of interpretation was decided by negotiation between the teams. As a result of this testing period, the standards were updated to make them more explicit on the points where problems had arisen.

In the third phase of implementation, work was com-pleted on adapting the All-in-One software to the stan-dards. By this stage, the standards were well-defined and substantially free of logical flaws and omissions. As a result, the testing evinced fewer surprises than in the E-Mail/ Comet tests. All-in-One was ready for interconnection after several weeks of pilot operation.

At about this time the physical interlinking of the nodes was starting to become a problem. Provision had been made in the standards for any node to act as a tandem switching point for messages between other nodes. How-ever, this feature had not been applied in practice because too many of the nodes were already stretched to the performance limits of their hardware.

Each node was therefore connected to each other node. This was relatively easy in the case of the DEC-based nodes because of the use of Decnet. However, the connec-tion of the E-Mail gateway to all the Comet nodes was a nightmare, since there were at that time seven separate channels (two of them international ones) to be continu-ously monitored. To simplify the network, an Electronic Mail Message Tandem (EMMT) was developed to allow the network to be changed from a fully connected mesh to a quasi-star configuration.

The EMMT is a DEC PDP-11/70-based application that communicates with DEC-based nodes via Decnet and with non-DEC nodes using one of several protocols that it supports. To determine the routing for a particular mes-sage—if Decnet addressing does not take the message to its final destination—the EMMT looks at the first line of the message header (the :800: field). For example, the Comet node in Singapore can deliver a message to the E-Mail gateway by using Decnet to get the message as far as the EMMT. The EMMT then accepts the entire message from Decnet, stores it on disk in case of problems, looks at the

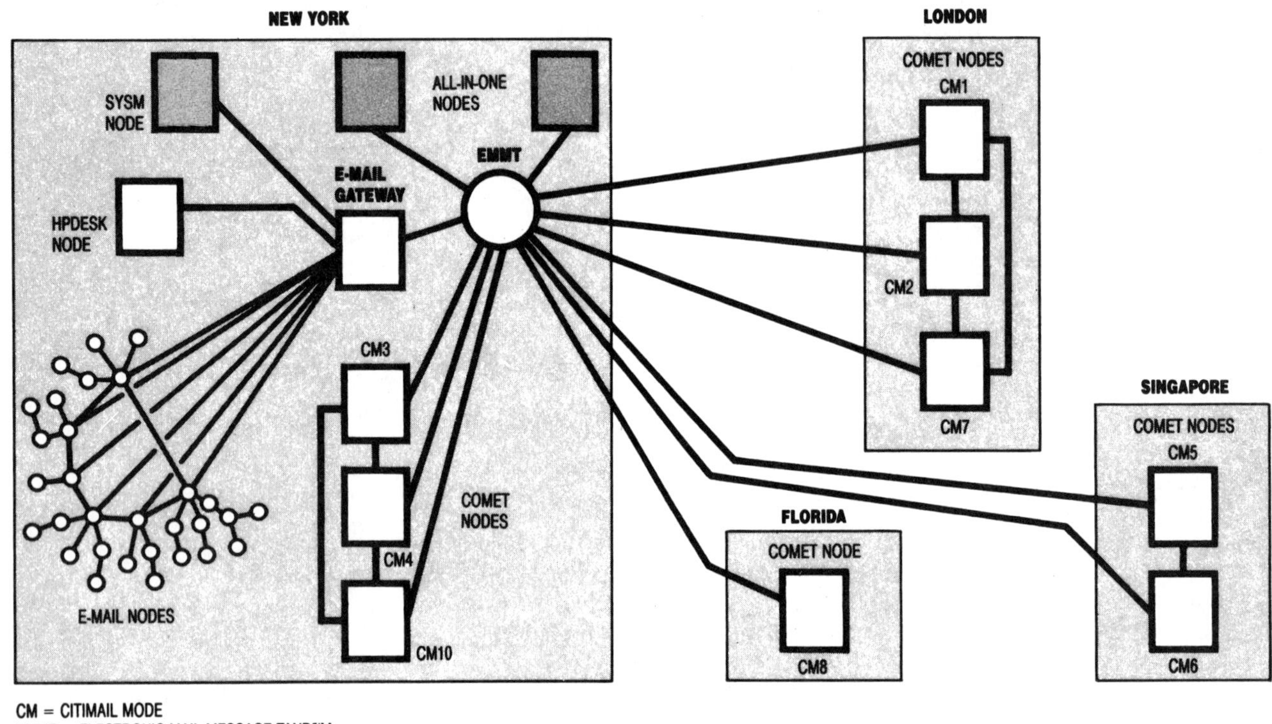

first line of the message header to identify the destination node, and selects the appropriate outgoing route. Then the EMMT sends the message to the E-Mail gateway, using the protocol chosen for that route.

Continuous operation

Each non-DEC node need only be connected to the EMMT in order to achieve full intercommunication with all the DEC-based nodes on the network. In effect, the EMMT acts as the hub of the global Decnet. In addition, having no electronic mail package to support, the EMMT is a reliable Decnet node. That is, there is no risk of having its operation as a tandem point on the Decnet being disrupted by housekeeping routines that are common on the actual electronic mail nodes.

Once the EMMT was operational, the final cutover of the first All-in-One node was completed. At this point, there were three different vendors' electronic mail software packages providing a seamless, global service to about 16,000 users.

Subsequent to the initial three implementations, the Citidex standards were implemented on the Hewlett-Packard HPDesk package, which runs on an HP3000, and the SYSM package (from Boise, Idaho-based H & W Computer Systems), which runs on an IBM mainframe. Because the numbers of users on these nodes were relatively small, and because organizationally they came under the same area that uses the E-Mail subnetwork,

they were connected into the E-Mail Gateway, rather than directly to the EMMT. (In principle, they could have been connected to the EMMT.)

For the System Administrators, the only significant difference between the original environment of separate subnetworks and the new integrated network is the need to handle a number of spilled messages each day. As mentioned earlier, some of these are update messages that, for one reason or another, could not be processed at the receiving node. Administrators would typically telephone each other to expedite handling a spilled update message.

The rest of the spilled messages are user types that cannot be delivered because of database conflicts. The most common cause of an incoming user message being spilled to the administrator is the user message overtaking an update message that affects a user message's address-ee. The administrator finds out why the message was not processed automatically, tries to fix it, then either sends it on its way or rejects it back to the originator.

Each electronic mail package handles the generation of outgoing update messages in a different way, and it is possible for updates to lag behind user messages in some of the packages. The same result can occur when incoming update messages are placed in a queue for processing that is longer than the queue for incoming user messages.

For the user—apart from the implementation of the new addressing scheme using the location/group suffix—the operation of each node has hardly changed.

In defining the various internodal message formats, the investigating committee had to arrive at a definition of a standard set of user services. These services—in X.400 terms, user-agent services—would be available to the entire population of users in the corporate network. This was necessary because of the desire to limit the complexity of the Citidex standards, bearing in mind that they would be implemented by add-on modules for off-the-shelf electronic mail software packages.

Software clout

Comet, being the simplest of the three original packages (Comet, E-Mail, and All-in-One)—and the one with the most users—strongly influenced the selection of the standard set of services. Some examples of services that were and were not included:

Included

■ *Forwarding of messages.* Messages can be forwarded, by either the sender or recipient, to one or more other users. The original message, complete with header as it appears on the workstation screen, becomes the new message text. As an internodal Citidex message, the forwarded message has only one header with field labels such as :801:. The consequence of this rule is that users on, say, Comet, who receive a forwarded message from a user on E-Mail, will see the original message with the *To:*, *CC:*, *From:*, and *Subject* arranged in the E-Mail format—not the Comet format. This did not lead to any complaints or misunderstandings.

■ *Answering received messages.* The provision of this capability in a given software package has minimal impact on the standards, and its omission on any node does not affect other nodes. However, allowance was made for answering of messages by way of a header field, :831:, which is an undefined extra-header line. Its principal use is to enable the inclusion of the *Subject* line from the original message to which the answer is being given. Where :831: is used in this way, the committee recommended that *Re:* be inserted before the contents of the original subject line. To preserve the generality of field :831:, this *Re:* is inserted as textual content by the sending node.

■ *Distribution lists.* Distribution-list names appear in the :801: and :802: header fields. The disassembly of a distribution list into its members takes place within the software of the node receiving the message and is invisible to the user. In other words, disassembly is aimed only at deciding into which mailboxes to place the message. The distribution-list name is what users see in the *To:* or *CC:* line. Of course, a node may hold additional local distribution lists that the other nodes do not know about, provided that messages leaving the node have the actual users' names substituted for the local distribution-list name in the message header.

■ *Nesting of distribution lists.* The committee agreed that, since all software packages would be able to cope with nesting, this would be allowed under the standards. In other words, some or all of the members of one distribution

list could be the names of other distribution lists. Interestingly, at one committee meeting, someone raised the question, "Do we have to check for recursive distribution-list definitions?" For instance, should the software identify and reject an attempt to add List A as a member of List C if List C is a member of List B and List B is a member of List A? This could cause the message-delivery software to get stuck in a loop when it tries to disassemble List A. It was finally agreed that recursive-nesting protection was required but that it was sufficient to search through four layers to detect nesting if unlimited searching was impracticable.

Not included

■ *Blind carbon copy (BCC).* There is no header field in the standards for BCC. Comet's designers believed that an electronic mail service should be conducive to good manners. Accordingly they dismissed the idea of supporting BCC. They argued that if you want a third party to see a copy of a message that you have sent to someone else, you should use the forwarding facility for getting the message to that party after you have sent it in the normal way. At least on Comet, you cannot forward a message that has been edited since it was sent, nor can you forward a message that you have composed but not yet sent. This is another example of Comet's good-manners philosophy: You cannot pretend to a third party that you sent a message that you did not really send.

■ *Silent acknowledgment of message receipt.* The issue of acknowledgments was mentioned earlier. Comet warns: "Reading this message will send an acknowledgment. Do you wish to continue?" Comet's designers considered it bad manners to let the sender know that the recipient has read the message without the recipient being aware of what is going on. Although some software packages allow the sender to have a "silent" acknowledgment, the committee specified the Comet treatment.

The inclusion of a network-requested acknowledgment was a concession to software packages with full tracking of messages. It allowed the display of "Message placed in in-box at destination node" by the sending node. The committee left it to the network implementers to decide whether they would design their software to send out all messages tagged for network-requested and sender-requested acknowledgments. In the end, nobody opted for creation of acknowledgments by default. It was generally recognized that users are annoyed by nonvital acknowledgment-requested messages.

■ *Non-text attachments to messages.* Although some electronic mail packages support the attachment to messages of nontext files (such as spreadsheets and graphics), the committee decided not to support this under the standards. Message text was defined as strings of ASCII printables plus carriage return or carriage return/line feed. This "lowest common denominator" of electronic mail service could be supported by all the software packages. The software modules written to implement the standards had to remove any attachments from messages sent outside the node (they are acceptable within the node) and

The global story

The accompanying figure illustrates how the Citicorp Global Telecommunications Network (GTN) provides both user access and host-to-host Decnet links. The former is for workstations that are connected to the GTN and then GTN-switched to the DEC (Digital Equipment Corp.)-based nodes (Comet and All-in-One — see Figure 3). The host-to-host, internodal traffic is via permanent point-to-point channels operating at 4.8 or 9.6 kbit/s. The user-workstation access — provided on demand — is to one of (typically) 64 asynchronous, switched ports on each node.

The user gains access to the GTN by inputting an ID and password (mainly for accounting purposes), then a service-selection code to establish a session with the desired electronic mail node — such as "CM4." The GTN establishes a switched connection to electronic mail, selecting the first available port in the group of 64. The node makes a security check, affirms permissible access, and completes the connection. At the end of the session, the connection is cleared.

If users are at locations where workstations are not directly connected to the GTN, they can access the GTN by making a dial-up connection through the local telephone network.

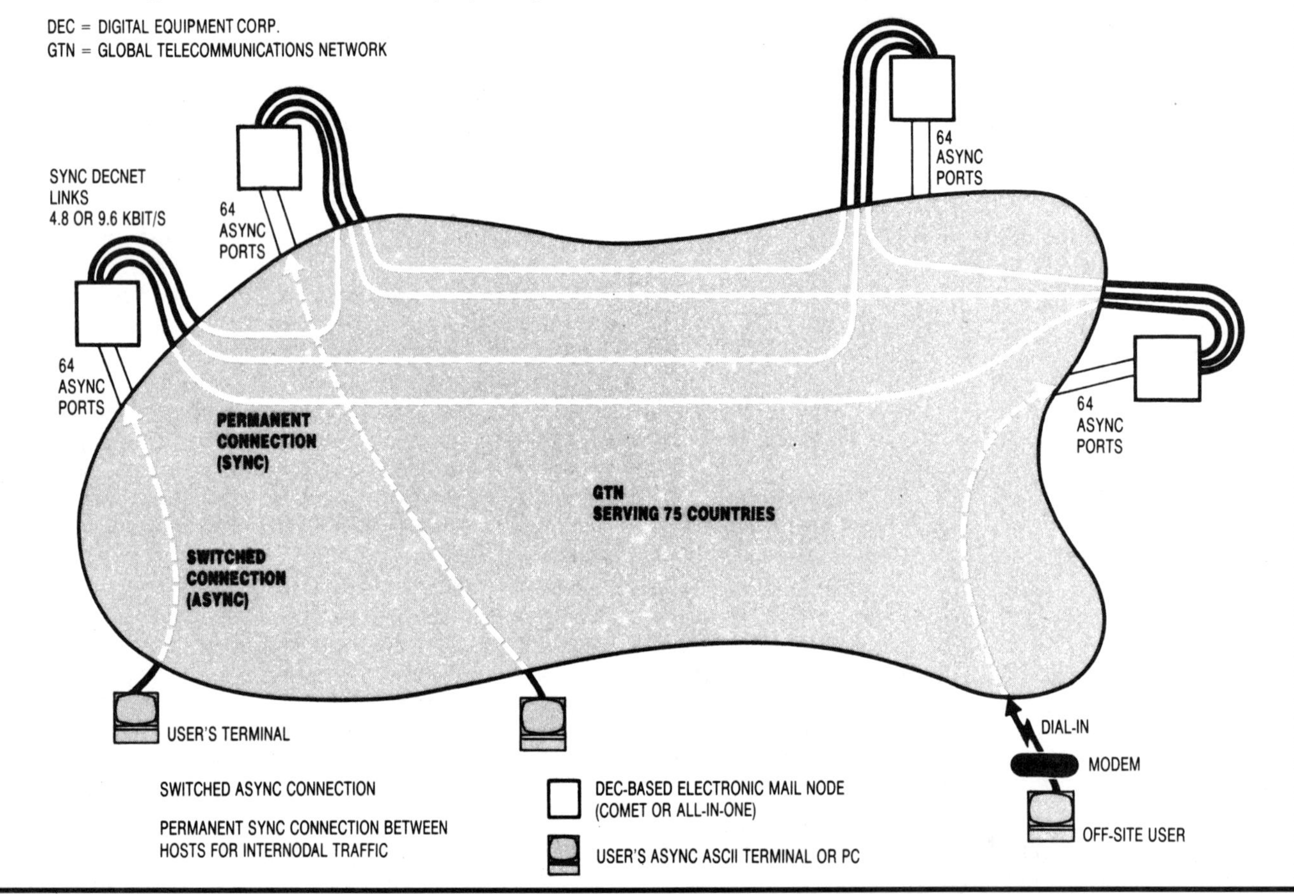

warn senders that their attachments were not being sent to certain addressees. (While in principle only ASCII printables were allowed in the message text, this was broadened slightly by the committee to include Ctrl-G [bell], which some users like to include in their messages to get the recipient's attention.)

Current configuration

Figure 3 shows the complete network as it looks today. The second All-in-One node has been connected into the network. There are now nine Comet nodes: three in New York (serving the United States and Canada), three in London (serving Europe, the Middle East, and Africa), two in Singapore (serving the Asia/Pacific region), and one in Pompano Beach, Florida (serving South America, Central America, and the Caribbean). Except for London, the Comet sites now use the newer PDP-11/84 machines, which are functionally similar to the PDP-11/70 but use more modern components and are therefore physically smaller and cheaper to maintain. CM9 (Citimail node 9) — not shown — is allocated to South America, but is not yet implemented.

With the HPDesk and SYSM implementations, the total number of different software packages that are interworking under the Citidex standards is now five (DEC's All-in-One, Comet, Datapoint's E-Mail, HPDesk, and H & W's SYSM). Current volume is about 200,000 messages a day (counting a message with, say, three addressees as three separate messages). Of these, about 10,000 messages pass between nodes in different locations using the Citidex standards, and about 40,000 additional pass between collocated nodes. Wherever possible, members of the same organization have been given mailboxes on the same node, to minimize internodal traffic.

While most nodes are linked via Decnet for host-to-host communications, user-workstation access is asynchronous ASCII at 300 bit/s, 1.2 kbit/s, or 2.4 kbit/s (depending on what is supported at the user's location). This access is achieved via Citicorp's Global Telecommunications Network (GTN), which has nodes (mainly CASE Communications DCX switching statistical multiplexers) in 75 countries (see "The global story"). Workstation access is always to the node on which users have their mailboxes, regardless of the location from which they are calling.

In accessing a Comet node, users operate in teletype mode and employ the simple line editor mentioned earlier. All-in-One offers full-screen editing, provided that the user has a DEC terminal—or has a PC communications package that emulates a DEC terminal. (All-in-One defaults to teletype mode—with its simple line editor—if the workstation does not respond to the DEC handshake.)

At any one time, there may be as many as 64 users accessing each Comet node. The Comet subnetwork has a theoretical capacity of close to 600 concurrent sessions.

However, this level of activity does not actually occur, because of time differences.

While somewhat less elegant than the X.400 series of standards, the Citidex Electronic Mail Standards represent a significant practical step toward linking different vendors' electronic mail software packages. What is perhaps most important about these standards is that they take care of not only the exchange of user messages and acknowledgments but also the much more complex directory issue.

The committee members believe that solving the directory problem is crucial to the success of electronic mail. They doubt that Citicorp's electronic mail network would have achieved its popularity if users had been burdened with complex addressing schemes. Even something as apparently harmless as having to prefix a person's name with a node number (such as *73:John A. Smith*) would probably have been a deterrent. The way the different software packages interwork under Citidex is genuinely seamless: All users appear to be on one large node. ∎

Malcolm Hamer and Jim Heilmann are vice presidents of Citicorp. Hamer is responsible for corporate-level standards-setting in data communications. A physics graduate of Oxford University, England, he has worked in telecommunications for 17 years. He holds an M. B. A. from New York University and has co-authored three books on telecommunications. Heilmann is responsible for global Citimail development and operational standards. A Business Administration graduate of Marist College, New York, he entered the field of telecommunications 13 years ago.

Jay R. Jaeger, Wisconsin Department of Transportation, Madison, Wis.

A state builds a roadway between DEC and IBM

Workers in Wisconsin's Department of Transportation found an easy way to connect its IBM mainframe complex to CAD/CAM setups based on DEC VAX minicomputers.

How can designers and mechanical artists working on VAXes efficiently access large IBM-based resources? The Badger State of Wisconsin's Department of Transportation (DOT) was faced with this sticky problem but managed to overcome it, a task that was probably more daunting than designing roadways and solving transportation hassles.

Data transfer of large files, often up to 10 Mbytes, required that tapes be carried by hand between computers. Users and programmers wanted to be able to merge Intergraph drafting functions with IBM's text editor in order to facilitate the production of highway-design plans. VAX users also wanted to be able to access faster, enhanced, IBM-based laser printers.

As are most state agencies, the DOT is continually asked to do more work with fewer resources. Although the state budget has been growing by about 9 percent each year, the DOT has not shared in the growth: In fact, the department's staff of 3,900 employees has decreased slightly over the past 10 years. Only a shrewd use of networking technology has enabled the department to keep up.

The challenge to Wisconsin's DOT has been even more acute than that facing similar agencies in other states. In terms of available dollars per mile of road, Wisconsin ranks below the national average, and the DOT is responsible for the maintenance and improvement of some 12,000 miles of Wisconsin state highways. Declining transportation revenues during the past decade have caused more reliance on advanced technology to support the department's data processing and design responsibilities. The Hill Farms Regional Computing Center in Madison, run by the state's Bureau of Systems and Data Processing, is responsible for supporting the DOT's enormous load of engineering design, mapping, and administrative functions.

The center's computing facilities use IBM 3090-200 and Amdahl 5890-200 mainframe computers operating under MVS/XA (Multiple Virtual Storage/Extended Architecture) and two DEC VAX machines operating under VMS Release 4.5 (Fig. 1). Each of eight transportation-district design and project management offices in the network handles about nine counties, supporting its region's roadway design and maintenance requirements.

The district design centers use IBM 327X terminals and remote job entry (RJE) printers attached to the hosts through Systems Network Architecture (SNA) and Intergraph drafting workstations (Fig. 2). These are linked to the VAX machines by synchronous data link control point-to-point communications lines. Note that Figure 1 shows the computer networking hardware resources while Figure 2 depicts the extensive range of services offered by those resources as well as the software modules that make the network possible.

Until 1986, the department used an SNA RJE connection to provide the link between its DEC- and IBM-based resources. The connection was slow and cumbersome to use, especially for binary file transfer, which was the preferred format for the graphics files.

With the RJE operating at only 9.6 kbit/s, file migration for archival use was impractical and backups were technically impossible. The data rate was too slow and the RJE function did not support the DEC backup command. DOT draftsmen and programmers often complained that they had to work around, not with, the setup.

DOT computer operators used to spend four to five hours per week mounting disks and tapes for VAX backup and off-line file storage. The DOT staff recognized that an efficient data transfer network could, however, automatically schedule backups and file migration for non-peak hours on the department's IBM mainframe. With the need

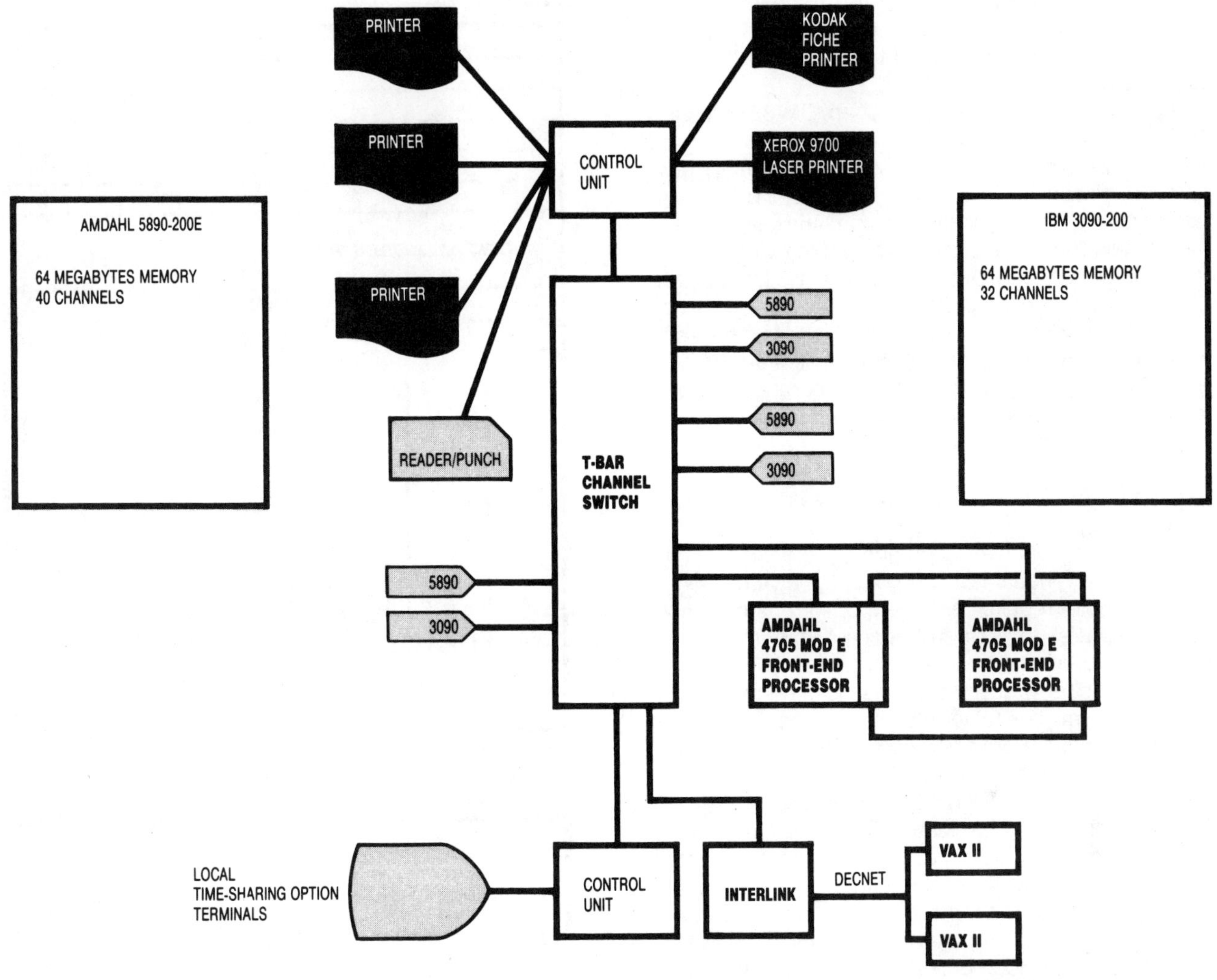

to increase service and efficiency, the DOT team began to study the possibility of obtaining a better DEC-to-IBM link that would meet current and future needs without breaking the budget.

Wish list

Program-to-program communications and file transfer were the two primary functional requirements for the sought-after link. Terminal emulation, security-setup compatibility, and ease of implementation were also important considerations. Bidirectional file transfer was one of the most important parts of the request, necessary to provide for the transfer of complete files from IBM to VAX, VAX to IBM, and from VAX to VAX.

Because of the large volume of information processed by DOT—1.8 Gbytes on the two VAXes and 4.2 (out of a total of 150) Gbytes on the host—the link required high speeds to save operating time and costs. Allowing for

long-term file-migration needs, and with the knowledge that the DOT had to be able to back up and restore 300-Mbyte disk packs in less than two hours and 675-Mbyte disk packs in less than four hours (if the process took longer, backup/recovery would not be practical), programmers were able to calculate the required data-transfer rate (Fig. 3). Based upon an estimate of 2,900 sessions that were being conducted each month by graphics users (which factored growth into the existing accounting records), the DOT originally calculated a need for 180-kbit/s transfers. When the files were found to average 2,000 blocks each instead of 1,000, the requirement was set at 360 kbit/s. The 33 percent utilization figure is a DOT standard for channel or communications-line use; if the figure runs higher, it usually means someone will be waiting at least part of the time, and a second pipe needs to be added on.

Using the host for archival storage was the most cost-effective solution. Continued use of the VAX disks to support the Intergraph workstations was twice as expensive as disk space on the IBM mainframe. To use the hosts as backup, however, the hardware-software combination that would support DEC-to-IBM transfers had to have a sustained disk-to-disk data-transfer rate of at least 400 kbit/s. Use of the IBM CPU (central processing unit) had to be less than 5 percent and that of the VAX CPU less than 20 percent.

Terminal emulation in the form of an IBM 3278-to-DEC VAX bridge was necessary for administrative uses and to free high-use graphic workstations for their primary purpose. Terminal emulation for file housekeeping also eliminated the need for asynchronous communications lines. The solution had to be compatible with the VAX VMS operating system as well as with DOT's security software on the mainframe (Cambridge System's Access Control Facility Security Software). Access control was required to be active at all times, especially during file transfers.

The DOT's VAXes support up to 30 simultaneous users, so the DEC-to-IBM link needed to support numerous simultaneous communications sessions. As many as 16 sessions would have to be available bidirectionally at the same time. Restrictions on supported session types were not acceptable.

The requirements mentioned above were the minimal conditions for vendors invited to bid on the DOT effort. Other functional requirements were optional, that is, not required for a vendor to be the successful bidder. However, since each function was necessary for the DOT to accomplish its goal, a cost factor was included by a DOT evaluation team. This factor represented the cost that the state would incur in providing support for these functions if the vendor did not.

By the end of 1985, DOT had composed the link's requirements. The request for bid (RFB) was structured so that the lowest-cost bidder meeting the mandatory requirements would then get the job (see "Functional and technical requirements"). The formula used to determine lowest total cost was the sum of total product costs, installation costs, costs to provide optional functions, maintenance costs, and education costs.

Compare and contrast

Two companies responded to the DOT's RFB. Network Systems' Hyperchannel and Interlink Computer Sciences' 3711 Gateway (MVS) products were reviewed. Product specifications and five-year, life-cycle costs were both considered before making the final decision.

The Hyperchannel solution involved a high-speed channel connection capable of up to 3.4-Mbyte/s operation and supporting software used in network operations. It provided task-to-task communications and file transfer but did not have record access, character translation, job submission, terminal support, file deletion, or proxy functions. Since it was largely a hardware solution, applications would have had to be written to accomplish backup, VSAM (Virtual Storage Access Method) file access, terminal emulation, and transparent file access.

Interlink's 3711 Gateway included a channel-attached

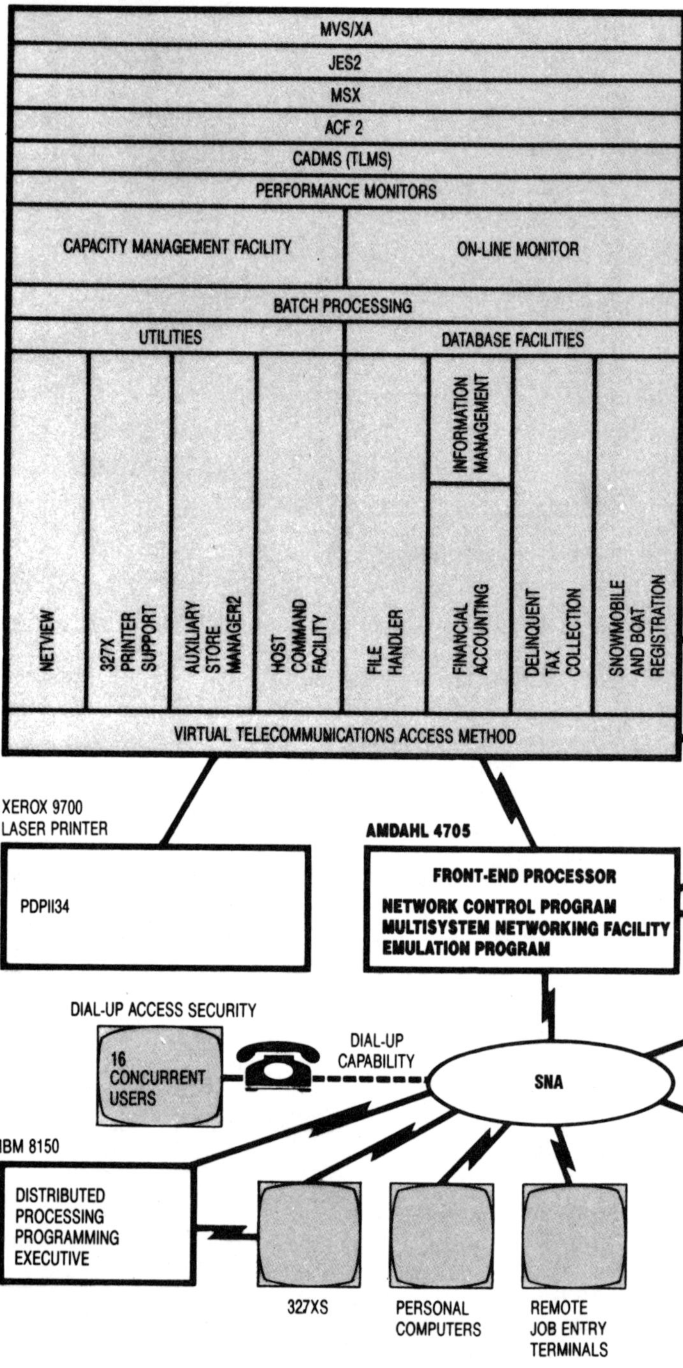

2. Computing services. *Traditional data processing for the Department of Motor Vehicles and Tax Records is supplied, as are ad hoc information-center requests. CAD/CAM*

applications are supported through the SNA links to district offices in Superior, Rhinelander, Green Bay, Waukesha, Wisconsin Rapids, La Crosse, and Eau Claire.

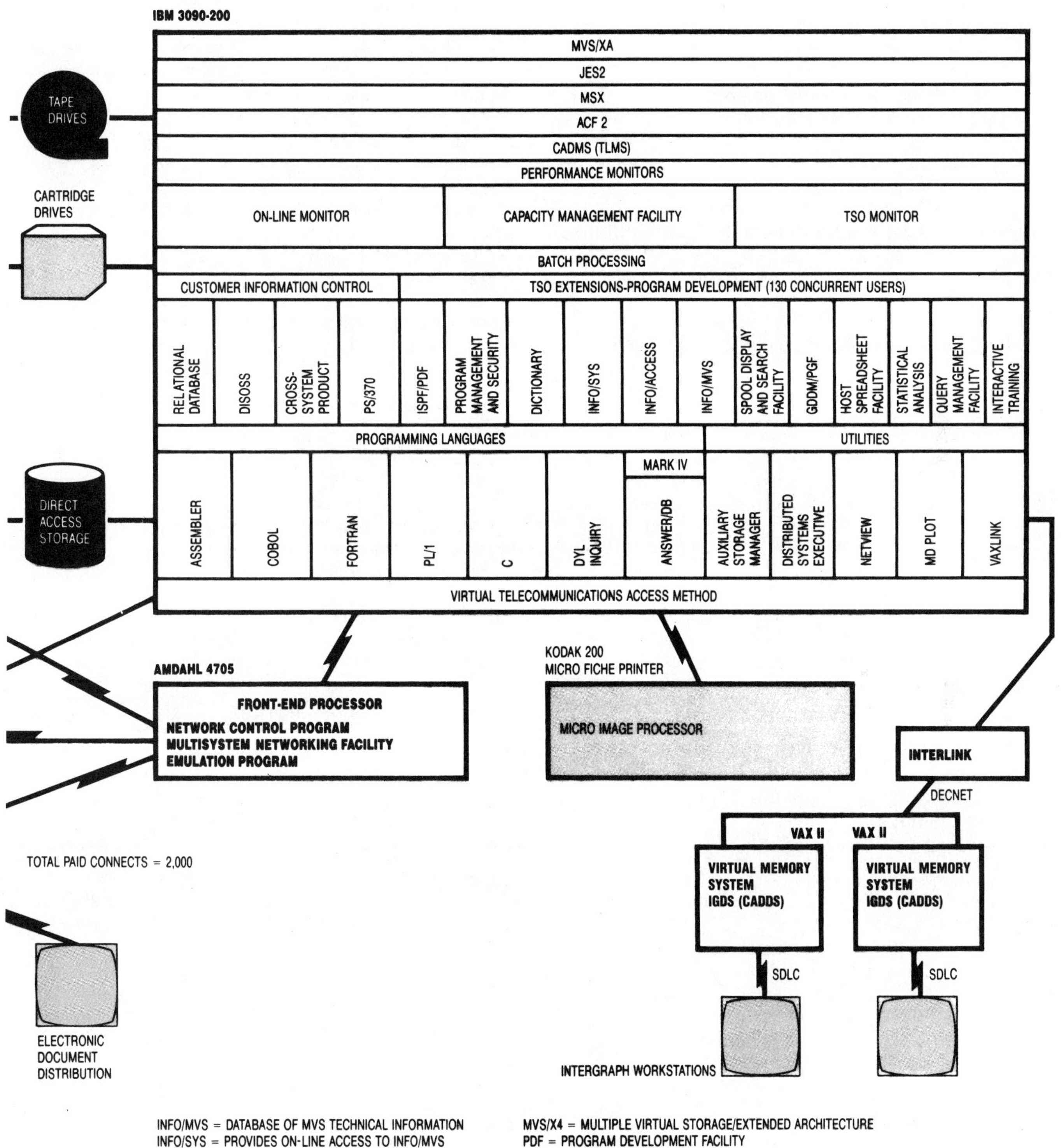

INFO/MVS = DATABASE OF MVS TECHNICAL INFORMATION
INFO/SYS = PROVIDES ON-LINE ACCESS TO INFO/MVS
INTERLINK = DECNET CHANNEL INTERFACE TO MVS
ISPF = INTERACTIVE SYSTEM PRODUCTIVITY FACILITY
JES = JOB ENTRY SUBSYSTEM
MD PLOT = PROVIDES GDDM OUTPUT TO PEN PLOTTERS
MSX = MULTIPLE SYSTEMS DRIVER/MULTIPLEXER

MVS/X4 = MULTIPLE VIRTUAL STORAGE/EXTENDED ARCHITECTURE
PDF = PROGRAM DEVELOPMENT FACILITY
PGF = PRESENTATION GRAPHICS FACILITY
PS/370 = PERSONAL SERVICES
TSO = TIMESHARING OPTION
VAXLINK = MVS-DECNET SUPPORT

Functional and technical requirements

The Wisconsin Department of Transportation's evaluation team determined that the following would be required of any vendor providing a DEC-to-IBM file-transfer mechanism.

Mandatory functional requirements

- IBM/VAX and VAX/VAX program-to-program communications:
—must be bidirectional.
—must be at the record level.
—if not transparent, describe the sequence of subroutine calls that will be written to modify the VAX or IBM programs.
- IBM-to-VAX and VAX-to-IBM file transfer:
—must transfer complete files from the IBM to either the VAX 11/780 or the VAX 11/785 and back.
—must allow for no translation between ASCII and EBCDIC files.
—must allow for transferring files with no character-set translation.
- Continous data transfer rate:
—must be able to transfer information between memory on the IBM machine and memory on either VAX at a bidirectional, continuous, sustained rate of 1 Mbit/s.
—must be able to transfer information on a file on the IBM and a file on either VAX at a bidirectional, continuous, sustained rate of 400 kbit/s.
- CPU use:
—for the continuous 400-kbit/s disk-to-disk transfer rate, CPU use must be less than 5 percent on the IBM and less than 20 percent on the VAX.
- IBM ACF2 security:
—must work with existing ACF2 installation but may require specially written code.
—must use the first eight characters of the DEC User Authorization File user-name field or provide a translation table from a DEC user name to an assigned eight-character host name.
—must be active for file transfer.
—must be active during transparent record access.
- Restricted access to VAX machines:
—must prevent unauthorized IBM users from accessing DEC machines using the installed ACF2 security; this may require specially written code.
—must use the ACF2 Logon ID.
—must be active for file transfer.
—must be active during transparent record access.
- Multiple sessions:
—must support at least 16 simultaneous communications sessions.
—must not place restrictions on either type or direction of sessions.

Mandatory hardware and software requirements

- IBM channel interface:
—must be made to the IBM 3081K Block Multiplexer Channel.
—must conform to IBM channel standards defined in "IBM System/360 and System/370 I/O Interface Channel to Control Unit OEM's Information," order number GA22-6974-7 or later revision.
- DEC VAX Unibus interface:
—must be a standard Unibus interface and conform to the DEC VAX Hardware Handbook.
—must allow use on either the first or second VAX Unibus Adapter.
- DEC VAX interface power requirements:
—must consume no more than 15 amperes of power from the Unibus backplan 5-volt power supply.
DEC VAX interface backplane space requirements:
—must not require more than three hex slots on the Unibus backplane.
- No modifications to DEC or Intergraph:
—description should be given of any DEC directories that will need to be modified.
- No modification to IBM host software:

---

network controller that attaches to the Decnet network through Ethernet. Synchronous and asynchronous interfaces were also available.

Operating at 450 kbit/s, the gateway used software residing on an IBM mainframe to provide bidirectional file transfer, record-level access to data from the DEC side, data translation through a data-field translation dictionary, job submission, printout movement, data-set-protection attribute manipulation, file deletion, and full proxy support. The proxy feature meant that users who were logged on to one Decnet node could transparently access the mainframe as another Decnet node without being required to send passwords over the network. Interlink also provides a task-to-task interface that allows a program on the IBM host to communicate as a peer with programs in the Decnet.

The center chose the Interlink gateway for installation on a 30-day acceptance test in January 1986. Before the DOT officially accepted the product, though, department protocol required that the product meet development standards.

First, the hardware and software had to stay up and running. DOT requirements stated that all equipment must meet a standard of performance by operating at an availability level of 98 percent or better. Calculation of the availability level was computed by dividing the Productive Operational Use Time, or the maximum number of hours that the equipment is intended to be available for use by the state, by the sum of that time plus the net downtime. The availability level turned out to better the 98 percent operating floor. The gateway was able to come back on line automatically even when the DEC or IBM machines went down.

Second, to verify the specified data-transfer rate, the DOT's programmers made copies and backups of files with

—description should be given of any IBM libraries that will need to be modified.

—description should be given of any EXITS used and their purpose.

—amount of shared memory should be specified.

■ Floor space:

—must not require more than 25 square feet.

Optional functional requirements

While not required for a bidder to be successful, each function is necessary for the processing center to accomplish its goals. For each requirement that the bidder does not meet, a cost factor will be included by the evaluation team.

■ Record translation during file transfer:

—software must allow the center to tailor ASCII-to-EBCDIC and EBCDIC-to-ASCII translation tables.

—software must support translation of a record on a field-by-field basis with these four formats: ASCII-to-EBCDIC or EBCDIC-to-ASCII; binary byte reversal for 2, 4, or 8 bytes; floating point for all formats; and "as-is" fields that are not translated.

■ VAX VMS backup support:

—must support IMAGE backups, with and without RECORD and VERIFY options.

—must support INCREMENTAL backups, with and without RECORD and VERIFY options.

—must support writing DEC backup information to IBM tape without placing the entire SAVESET on either the IBM or DEC disks.

—must support a transfer rate of SAVESET information of 2 Mbit/s.

■ Transparent ACF2 use:

—must not require any modifications of existing ACF2 data structures.

—The center must not be required to write any code.

■ Transparent access to IBM files:

—must support read and write access to the following:

IBM sequential data sets; IBM partitioned data set members; IBM VSAM RRDS (Relative Record Data Set) data sets, including read, write, add, and erase; IBM VSAM ESDS (Entry Sequenced Data Set) data sets; and IBM VSAM KSDS (Key Sequenced Data Set) data sets, including read, write, add, and delete of records.

—In addition, must be able to accomplish all read and write functions from any high-level VAX language using the standard RMS support subroutines for that language.

■ Access to DEC RMS files:

—must support read and write access to the following: RMS sequential files in record mode, as well as RMS indexed files in record mode, including read, write, add, and delete of records.

—Must also be able to accomplish all read and write functions using a vendor-supplied set of subroutines for the IBM host that use standard linkage conventions and that may be called from assembler, Cobol, VS Fortran, and PL/1 programs.

■ Print access to IBM from DEC:

—must connect to IBM JES2 (Job Entry Subsystem).

—must allow routing output to be sent to any local or remote site.

—must allow specification of a form number.

—must allow specification of number of copies.

■ Terminal access to IBM from VAX:

—must allow VT100 users to log on to IBM.

—must translate all 3270-family commands to VT100 commands, including intensity, protect, and extended highlighting.

—must translate all VT100 keystrokes and cursor positioning to 3270 inbound data streams.

—must function with IBM Interactive System Productivity Facility text-editor software.

■ Terminal access between VAXes:

—must allow users on one VAX to log on to a second VAX. Once connection is established, the terminal must behave as if directly attached to the remote VAX.

random data using the standard DEC copy and backup commands. They further confirmed, through benchmark testing with actual user data, a transfer rate in excess of 400 kbit/s.

Troubleshooting

A problem arose with the DOT's IBM mainframe, the first 3090 installation for the gateway. First, the faster channel speeds of the 3090 exposed an error in the Auscom microcode, a set of third-party IBM channel boards for non-IBM devices installed in the Interlink 3711 network controller. Timing problems with the software, created because the 3090 is a dyadic machine (has two CPUs), initially caused the task-to-task and file-transfer functions to fail during testing.

Three Auscom boards were used for input/output and one for the driver/receiver module, the connection between the applications program and the device. It was in this module that the error was exposed. Under certain circumstances, the Auscom never notified the driver of the failed status presentation because of the faster 3090 channel speeds. The boards would not properly deliver a status message requested by the mainframe and, furthermore, would not notify the driver of the presentation of the failed-status message. To remedy this, the gateway device driver was modified to monitor the Auscom boards, detect a missing status presentation, and report it to the host.

The interaddress-space communication code was initially patched and later replaced altogether. The original code was written by someone who was not familiar with multiprocessor technology; once the old code was ripped out and completely rewritten, DOT users had no further recurrence of the problem.

The DOT also discovered there was no method to

3. Transfer rates. The original estimate of 1,000 blocks per file turned out to be 100 percent too small; DOT user files are actually closer to 2,000 blocks

ORIGINAL CALCULATION		REVISED CALCULATION
2,900	SESSIONS/MONTH	2,900
× 2	MACHINES	× 2
× 2	FILES/SESSION	× 2
11,600	FILES	11,600
× **1,000**	**BLOCKS/FILE**	× **2,000**
× 512	BYTES/BLOCK	× 512
× 8	BITS/BYTE	× 5
47,513,600,000	BITS/MONTH	**95,027,200,000**
÷ 22	DAYS	÷ 22
÷ 10	HOURS	÷ 10
÷ 3,600	SECONDS/HOUR	÷ 3,600
60,000	BITS/SECOND	120,000
× 3	(33 PERCENT UTILIZATION)	× 3
BITS/SECOND 180,000		**BITS/SECOND 360,000**

specify space allocation when running backups. The department needed a way to specify space allocation because the VMS backup utility cannot precalculate the size of the backup save-set file, a special file with a distinct format to which DEC's backup utility sends its output. Programmers installed a command option that allowed users to control file size allocated on the mainframe.

The DOT used the gateway solution in file transfer and task-to-task modes only during the first six months following the installation; line-mode terminal emulation was added later. When DEC VT-terminal emulation was developed, the Hill Farms center began to take advantage of full-screen emulation.

In the near future, the DOT plans to migrate to TCP/IP (Transmission Control Protocol/Internet Protocol), using the Department of Defense protocol to replace Decnet. As the DOT moves heavily into Unix-based workstations, it will run TCP/IP alongside the Intergraph Xerox Network System, using synchronous data link control less and less. The first part of the project, the installation of Media Access Control (MAC)-level protocol-independent Ethernet bridges, has been bid. The second part of the migration will consist of the installation of a channel-attached TCP/IP box that makes it possible for the workstations to talk directly to the Wisconsin MVS hosts. ■

Jay R. Jaeger earned a B. S. in electrical engineering and an M. S. in computer science from the University of Wisconsin, Madison. Project leader for the Graphics Technical Support section, he has worked for the Wisconsin Department of Transportation since 1975. He is currently with the Computer Science Systems Engineering Unit in the DOT's Bureau of Systems and Data Processing.

Weiming Hu, Digital Equipment Corp., Littleton, Mass.

Making ends meet: Interconnecting electronic mail networks

Gateways and translation strategies are proposed for backbone networks to interchange incompatible electronic documents on multivendor networks.

The typical corporation today employs multiple electronic mail networks, invariably supplied by multiple vendors. And companies attempting to implement a corporation-wide electronic mail network find out quickly that they need to interconnect diverse machines and mail services. This is no simple chore, but there are some logical approaches that make sense—and work.

One such interconnect strategy based on gateways uses an enhanced backbone network to provide common mail service. This backbone supports its own independent mail protocol, plus a series of gateways into each constituent mail component, mapping between foreign mail services and the backbone network.

The backbone network exists as a subnetwork within a company's overall networking structure. Nodes comprising the backbone support a common set of services, which include electronic mail, translation services, and gateways. Within the backbone network, all mail items use a standard "envelope." In this way, the contents of these envelopes (the message bodies) are kept in their original (native) form while they are in the network. Foreign machines and networks—those which are not part of the backbone network—are connected to the backbone by gateways implemented on backbone nodes. The translation services supported by the backbone nodes are used to perform the required gateway functions.

In offices, this backbone network can be implemented by minicomputer-based departmental servers connected via electronic mail. Each server provides a local mail service for work group users, whether they use microcomputers, standalone word processors, or terminals. Through gateways, departmental servers also allow access to other machines and networks, such as enterprise-wide mainframes and outside mail services.

Gateways allow users of different mail services to exchange mail by bridging the differences between mail protocols. To do this, both the mail envelope and the message body need to be translated.

The envelope needs to be translated when a mail item goes into a different hardware/software configuration because it contains protocol-specific routing and handling information. Since recipient names and addresses are needed to properly route and process the mail item, they must be changed into the format expected by the destination mail service. Address translations are frequently performed as part of envelope translation. Backbone gateways translate envelopes into the standard form used by the network when the mail item is first relayed into the network, which is then translated into the proper target form when the mail item leaves the backbone for the target mail service.

Message bodies, like envelopes, also require translation if the originating and target services are different. At a minimum, the destination mail service needs to know how to display the message body. To be useful to the recipient, the message body must also be received in a form that can be modified and processed. In most offices, message bodies are frequently word processing documents.

There are two types of word processing documents: revisable or final form. A revisable-form document contains imbedded format codes and structural information, such as indentation marks and tab settings, which describe the layout of the document as well as the textual information itself. This imbedded information is used by the word processing program when a user edits (revises) the document. The additional formatting and structural information make the revisable word processing document a more complex object than the traditional plain-text messages.

A revisable-form document must be converted into a final-form document before it can be printed. The final-form

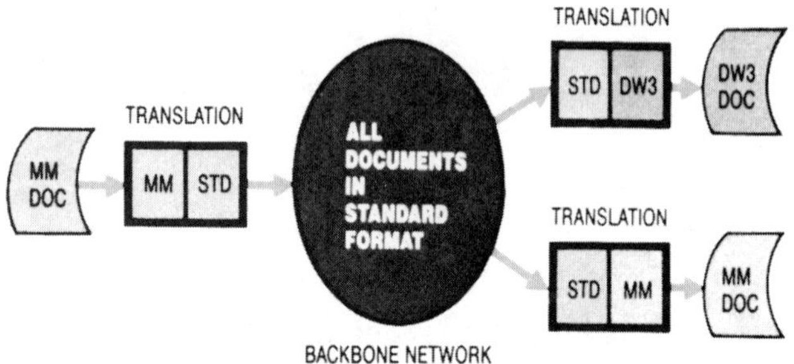

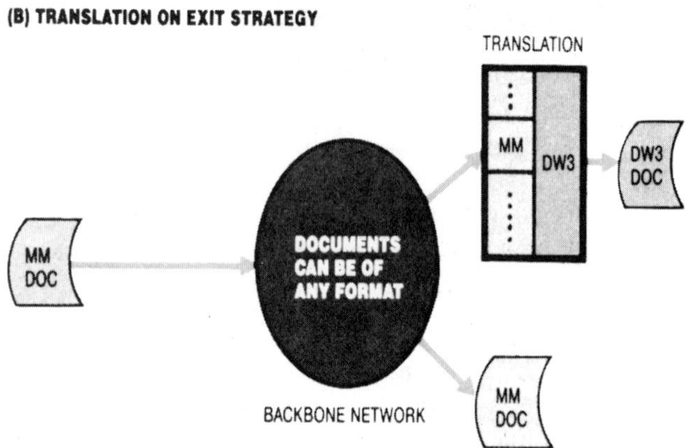

1. Translation strategies. *In A, a Multimate document is translated twice. In B, the document is translated only if necessary when it leaves the network.*

document contains those character sequences that cause the printer to produce the desired effect (such as spacing, character font selection, and carriage control). The conversion step applies all the specified formatting operations to produce the result, so that, for example, the correct number of spaces may be inserted to justify the text properly. Thus, the final-form document is an image of the revisable-form document after the formatting operations have been performed.

Because the formatting information is stripped when a revisable-form document is converted into a final-form document, the final-form document is not suitable for further revisions. Therefore, if a document is to be modified in the future, it must be retained in revisable format. Because of this usefulness, documents should be maintained in their revisable form when they are to be interchanged. Their existence is especially critical in multivendor networks where the sender and recipients may all be using different word processing software.

The interchange of revisable-form word processing documents as message bodies is difficult to achieve because the revisable document formats used by different word processing vendors are incompatible. A Wang Office user, for example, would not be able to read, let alone modify, an IBM DisplayWrite3 revisable-form document created on an IBM PC. The translation of revisable-form documents is therefore needed to achieve the desired information transfer between heterogeneous work groups.

Document translation strategies

Two possible strategies are available for translating message bodies consisting of revisable-form documents: auto-translation on entry and translation on exit.

In Figure 1A, auto-translation on entry is based on the definition of a standard revisable-document format to which all documents are translated when they enter the backbone network. Since all documents in the network are constrained to this standard format, they can be processed by any node within the network. Mail items are translated as required when they exit the network via gateways.

When a Multimate document, for example, is relayed into the backbone network, it is automatically translated into the standard revisable format. The document is relayed in this form while it remains within the network. And if, for example, the recipient requires DisplayWrite3 format, the document will be translated from the standard revisable format when it exits the backbone network.

This alternative has the advantage of simplicity. The implementation of gateways is simplified by the adoption of a network-wide standard document format. Since all documents in the network are guaranteed to be in this form, each gateway only needs to be capable of translating between this standard format and the destination document format. Having a single message-body type also simplifies the logic of the backbone mail service itself.

This simplification comes at a cost. The weakness of this approach is that needless translations are frequently required. In the example just given, the document is translated twice even if the recipient is also a Multimate user. These extra translations incur processing overhead and also increase the likelihood of loss of fidelity.

Translations can destroy document fidelity because of the "lowest common denominator" effect. This occurs because all word processing programs do not have identical capabilities. Features that are unique to a given word processor cannot be preserved during translation. Only those features that are supported by both document types are preserved, and other information is lost. For example, the underline attribute would be lost when a document is converted into a format that does not support underlining. This degradation is also cumulative. So, as the translated document is translated yet again, more information may be lost until the amount of information reaches that subset of features supported by all word processors.

To eliminate needless translations, backbone networks can use a translation-on-exit strategy for message bodies. Rather than automatically translating everything into a standard revisable format, this approach translates documents only when required. Furthermore, such translations are delayed until the very last moment. The last moment is defined as the moment the mail item exits the backbone network—hence the term "translation on exit."

Under this approach, the backbone network is augmented to handle foreign document types. Documents are submitted to the backbone network in their original revisable format and remain in that form while they are in the network. Translations take place only when required. They are carried out only when a mail item leaves the backbone for an environment that cannot use the original format.

Mail items leave the network when they go through a gateway to enter a different mail service or when they are retrieved from a mailbox by recipients. In the first case, mail items must be translated so that the foreign mail setup can process it. In the latter case, mail items must be translated so that recipients can work with them.

Re-examining the earlier example from the translation-on-exit perspective, the user sends the same Multimate document into the backbone network (Fig. 1B). This time the document is not translated when it enters the network but remains in its native format while it is relayed within the network. When it reaches the gateway node to the DisplayWrite3 user, it is translated into the destination format. When it reaches the gateway node for another Multimate user, however, the document exits untranslated.

The translation-on-exit strategy better preserves document fidelity by avoiding translations wherever possible and reducing information loss. This strategy, however, requires software that can perform the necessary translations between all document types that are supported. For example, the gateway node to the DisplayWrite3 user must be capable of translating from all supported document types to the destination document type. This capability is provided by a translation function located on each backbone node.

The translation function is simply a collection of translator programs residing on each gateway node that performs document translations upon demand. A standard document format (such as IBM Document Content Architecture Revisable Format) usually operates in these translations.

Within the translation programs themselves, all translations are carried out in two steps. First, the document is translated into a standard intermediate format. Then it is translated from the standard intermediate format into the appropriate destination format. All supported document types have a translator that translates to the standard intermediate format and also an inverse program that translates the intermediate format into its own format.

Given this structure, only two translators need to be written for each document type. Because the standard intermediate document format itself may not be a perfect match for all supported document types, the translations to and from the standard intermediate format may diminish document fidelity. Thus, the document format chosen to be the standard intermediate format should ideally be a superset of all the supported document types.

The strategy of going through a standard intermediate format can be selectively bypassed where the preservation of fidelity is critical. In particular, the set of translators can be augmented by including direct translators that go from one document type to another without going through the intermediate format. This approach can be very effective where the two document types have similar features that are not supported by the intermediate format. The drawback of this approach is, of course, that more translators need to be written.

The gateways

Gateway software modules connect diverse electronic mail programs. They perform the transformations required to allow two different mail services to exchange mail. To support the translation-on-exit strategy, gateways must:

■ Perform protocol conversion by translating incoming and outgoing mail envelopes. This is necessary so that the mail item can be relayed properly. (Envelopes always need to be translated; translation on exit refers to the contents of these envelopes, that is, the documents.)

■ Identify and tag incoming mail objects so that the destination gateway node knows the proper translator to invoke. In general, the mail items can contain arbitrary application-specific objects such as spreadsheets or database transactions.

■ Translate outbound mail objects into the format expected by the destination on the other side of the gateway. For example, all documents should be translated into a Wang revisable format when a mail item is forwarded through a gateway to a Wang machine.

Note that there are two types of translators: one for protocol (mail envelope) conversion, which is invoked on both entry and exit to the network, and one for message body conversion, which is only invoked upon exit. The first type of translation is specific to the protocols of the originating and target systems and is implemented by each gateway individually. The latter type of translation is common to all gateways and is provided by the backbone's translation functions.

Within the framework of the X.400 Message Handling Systems reference model (see "Electronic mail standards to get rubber-stamped and go worldwide," DATA COMMUNICATIONS, May 1984, p. 159), mail functions can be divided into the User Agent and the Message Transfer Agent sublayers. The Message Transfer Sublayer contains programs called Message Transfer Agent Entities (MTAEs), which perform the mail-relaying functions. The User Agent Entity (UAE) allows the user to prepare, submit, and receive mail. The UAE interacts on the user's behalf with the MTAE. Mail services must have compatible User Agent and Message Transfer sublayers to exchange mail. It is the task of gateways to achieve this commonality between two dissimilar mail services.

Each of the three generic gateway types can be characterized by the protocols that are used to interface with backbone nodes. Essentially, the choices are:

■ Interface at the Message Transfer Sublayer using a relay protocol. The software within this sublayer, the MTAEs, perform the store-and-forward delivery functions.

■ Ballot box Interface at the Message Transfer Sublayer using a submission and delivery protocol.

■ Interface at the User Agent Sublayer. The gateway software interacts with the backbone UAE, which in turn interacts with the Message Transfer Sublayer on its behalf in sending and receiving mail.

The type of gateway to implement depends upon the needs and capabilities of the destination machine and network.

■ *Interface via relay protocol.* This type of gateway makes connections at the Message Transfer Sublayer by implementing an MTAE to perform mail relay functions. The protocol used between two MTAEs is called a relay protocol.

The relay protocol implies that both MTAEs can perform routing and relay functions within their respective domains. This approach is usually used when making a connection to another networked mail service. Using this approach, a mail item destined for a node in the foreign network is first relayed to an attached backbone node. The gateway on that node translates the mail item and then relays the result to an MTAE of the foreign network. From that point on, the foreign network takes care of delivering the mail item to the intended recipient. The gateway also performs the reverse operation of accepting mail from the foreign MTAE destined for recipients reachable by the backbone network.

Figure 2A illustrates a possible interface to IBM Systems Network Architecture Delivery System (SNADS) using this approach. The gateway resides on a backbone node. When relaying a mail item to an IBM host, the gateway node would translate the message bodies and exchange SNADS

---

2. Backbone and SNADS. *In A, the document is translated on the backbone node and then relayed to the recipient. In B, the document is relayed as is to the recipient.*

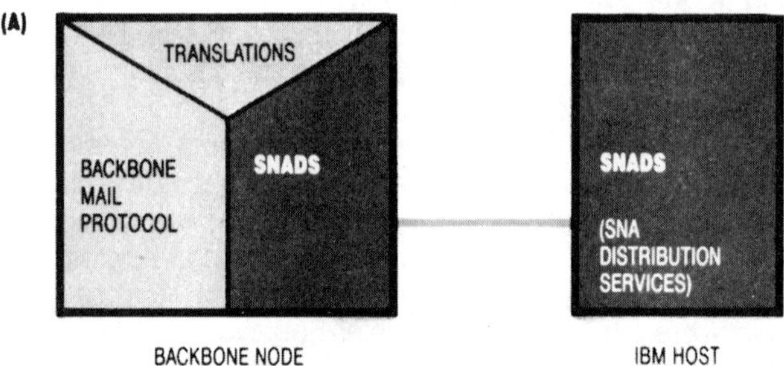

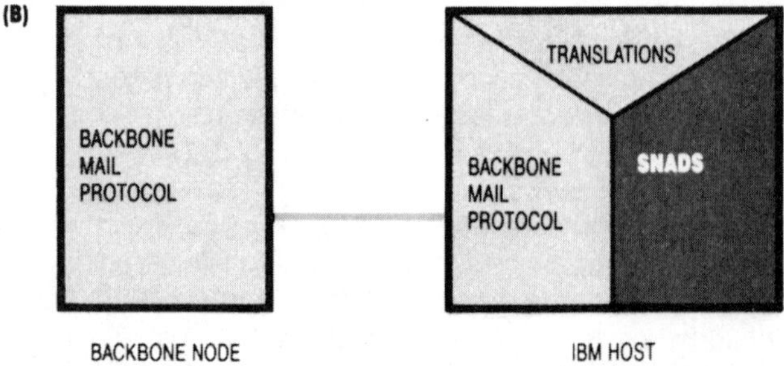

SNADS = SYSTEMS NETWORK ARCHITECTURE DISTRIBUTION SERVICES

Distribution Interchange Units (DIUs) using SNA/LU 6.2 (Logical Unit) with the IBM host. The host then takes care of relaying the DIUs within its own domain.

Figure 2B outlines a different variation. Here, the gateway software is implemented on the host, where the host performs all the required translations and can also exchange backbone network protocol elements directly with backbone nodes. In this approach, the host would appear to be just another backbone node.

The configuration shown in Figure 2A is easier to implement than that shown in Figure 2B because placing the gateway software on a backbone node allows it to use translation functions. A gateway implementation on a non-backbone node will need to re-implement these programs if it is to provide the same services.

■ *Interface via submission and delivery protocol.* This type of gateway also makes connections at the Message Transfer Sublayer. Instead of an MTAE, a Submission and Delivery Entity (SDE) is implemented. The SDE talks to the backbone MTAE through what is called a submission and delivery protocol. All routing and relaying functions are done by the MTAEs of the backbone network. The SDE on the foreign processor is responsible only for submitting outbound mail to a backbone node and for end-point distribution of received mail items to its own users.

Figure 3 illustrates how this approach can be applied to a multi-user word processing machine. First, the word processor is augmented with an X.400 Reliable Transfer Server to achieve the physical transfer of mail items (see "What is X.400"). This function can be implemented by a file transfer program. A set of user interface programs supplying the User Agent (UA) functions and the SDE are then added to complete the required software.

A user wishing to send mail would interact with the UA on the workstation. After the mail item has been created, the SDE uses a submission protocol to pass the mail item to the MTAE on the backbone node. The backbone network will then relay the mail item to the intended recipients. Note that the SDE does not perform any routing functions. All processing, including any required translations, are deferred to the backbone node.

In the reverse direction, if a received mail item is destined for a recipient on the word processor, the backbone network would relay it to the nearest backbone node. If the mail item is not in the format expected by the destination, the contents would be translated. The MTAE of the backbone node then establishes a session and delivers the mail item to the proper destination SDE.

The single-node orientation of the submission and delivery protocol makes it more appropriate for linking up to standalone machines than for networked mail services. The offloading of processing to the backbone nodes and the absence of the relaying functions make this protocol easy to implement. This is, therefore, the protocol of choice for making connections to machines that do not already have native mail services.

■ *Interfacing with the User Agent.* The two previously described approaches work with the MTAE of the backbone network. They use either a relay or a submission and

3. Reliable transfer. *The sender uses a submission and delivery protocol to relay mail to the backbone. This transfer is carried over a reliable transfer service.*

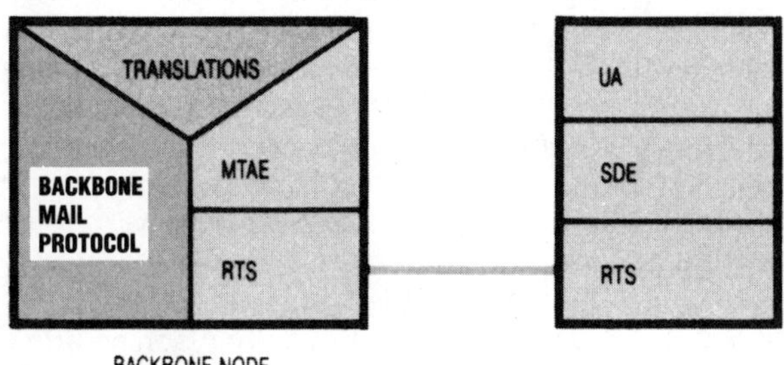

delivery protocol. This third approach does not directly implement any mail protocols. Instead, the target machine acts as a user, appearing to the backbone as a directly connected user and not as a peer machine (Fig. 4A).

The user works with an interface program on his or her own machine. This program buffers the user from the network, sending and receiving mail. This interface program then makes the appropriate requests to the actual UAE on the backbone node. These requests are typically issued over the usual user terminal protocols such as TTY or 3270. As far as the backbone network is concerned, the user logically resides on the backbone node itself.

In the simplest case, the interface program is a terminal emulator. Using this program, the user appears to the backbone node as a normal user of the backbone mail service. This user would see and use the standard backbone mail user interface. The backbone node directly supplies all the mail functions.

A more sophisticated variation is illustrated in Figure 4B. Here, the interface program presents an independent set of user interfaces. This interface executes on the user's machine and is separate from the normal interfaces as seen by the users of the backbone network. The user would interact with the local interface program, which is usually tailored to the particular machine. This interface then makes asynchronous requests to the UAE on the backbone node.

The distinguishing feature of these approaches is that communications takes place with the UAE rather than the MTAE of the backbone node. The chief advantage of this approach is that minimal software is required. Specifically, mail protocols do not need to be implemented. Protocol conversion is also not required since the user uses backbone mail services directly. If document translations do need to be performed, they can still be done by the translation functions of the backbone network.

This approach does impose extra overhead on the backbone node by shifting more of the processing to it. For example, the backbone node has to be involved whenever a microcomputer user sends or receives mail.

Interfacing at the User Agent Sublayer also imposes its own overhead. Going through the User Agent and the

---

What is X.400?

The X.400 series of CCITT/ISO (International Consultative Committee for Telephone and Telegraph/International Organization for Standardization) recommendations define a set of electronic mail standards. Mail services implemented in conformance to these standards are expected to be able to interchange mail much as the ISO protocols allow multiple vendors' networks to be easily interconnected.

A collection of standards are embodied within the X.400 series recommendations. X.400 itself presents a reference model for mail interchange. It defines objects such as the mail envelope and active agents such as the Message Transfer Agent Entities. As a reference model, this is independent of the specific mail protocols, which implement these objects and agents, and can be used to describe existing mail services.

The X.400 series also specifies a particular set of protocols and message formats. For example, X.411 specifies a particular Message Transfer Sublayer protocol. Full X.400 compliance means that one also implements the actual mail protocols and message formats specified by the standards.

The universal adoption of the X.400 protocols would simplify interconnecting mail services. If all mail services use the same mail protocol and document format, for example, then they can directly exchange mail. This by itself does not, however, eliminate the requirement for heterogeneous interconnects.

First, the convergence to a single set of mail protocols is unlikely to occur overnight; standards take time to be universally adopted. During the period between now and when the standards are universally implemented, there will likely be a wide variety of mail networks that use different mail protocols. Those mail services that are X.400 compliant will initially be yet another foreign mail service to the one with which the user must interconnect. Furthermore, there will still be the installed base of users who cannot readily switch over to new mail services.

What's more, using a common mail protocol also does not solve the general problem of exchanging application-specific objects. Even if the sender and receiver are using the identical mail protocol, for example, neither will be able to exchange documents created by different word processors unless translations are performed. Therefore, the X.400 standards help in narrowing the scope of the problem but do not eliminate it altogether.

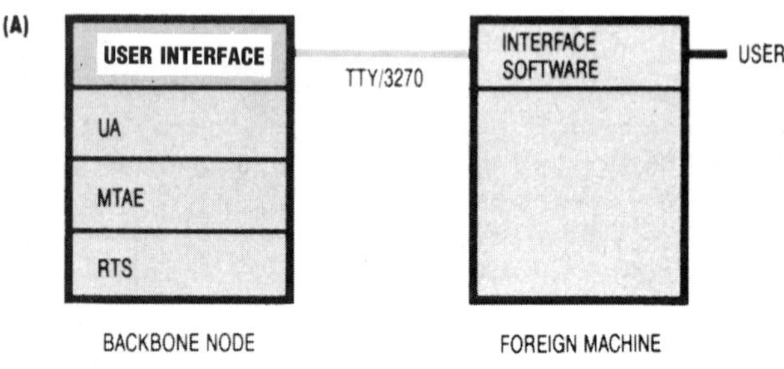

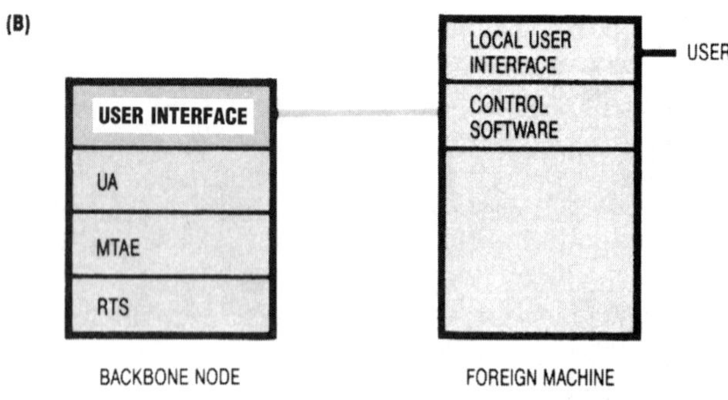

MTAE = MESSAGE TRANSFER AGENT ENTITY
RTS = RELIABLE TRANSFER SERVER
UA = USER AGENT

4. Agents and entities. *In A, the user software makes it appear that the user is directly connected to the backbone. In B, the local software interacts with the backbone.*

associated user interfaces is more costly in terms of host cycles and connect time than the alternative of connecting directly with the MTAE because of the need to go through these extra software layers.

Integration example

Figure 5 illustrates how a company-wide electronic mail network can be assembled using these components. The core of the enterprise-wide mail service is the backbone network of departmental servers. The departmental computers would provide the normal office automation and data processing functions as well as the backbone node capabilities. In particular, these departmental computers would be easily networked, able to transport different foreign document types, support multiple gateways, and make translations. Attached to each departmental processor are the various machines of the local users. These processors may include traditional terminals, microcomputers, and shared-logic word processors. In addition, some backbone nodes would contain links to the corporation-wide mainframes and public mail networks.

Different gateways would be used to tie the various machines to the backbone network. For example, mainframes would interface via relay protocols, word processors would use submission and delivery protocols (because they generally don't have enough intelligence to use relay protocols), and the terminals and microcomputers would use the backbone mail service directly.

To begin with, a user on a Wang word processor creates the original document in revisable format and sends it to recipients on each type of machine and network. The SDE on the word processor submits the document and an envelope to the attached departmental computer, which serves as a backbone node. The departmental processor translates the envelope into the standard backbone format and encapsulates within it the original document. It also identifies it as a Wang revisable-format document.

The backbone network then routes the mail item. Eventually, copies are routed to the gateways connected to each of the destinations.

At the gateway to the IBM mainframe, the envelope and the document are both translated. The gateway node uses SNADS to relay the result to the IBM host. SNADS takes over relaying within the SNA network.

The recipient, using a conventional terminal, would receive the mail in a mailbox on the attached departmental processor. Before the document is examined, it would be translated into the word processing format used by the office automation software running on a departmental computer. Once the document is in this format, the recipient can view the item or modify it further.

The microcomputer recipient is treated as a normal user of backbone node mail. When the mail item has been routed to the local node, it is deposited in the user's mailbox on the backbone node. If the user desires, the document can be translated into a favored word processing format and downloaded to a microcomputer. The document can then be locally examined and modified independent of the departmental computer.

When the mail item is routed to a recipient who is also using a Wang word processor, the gateway node translates the mail envelope from the standard backbone format into the format expected by the SDE on the word processor. Since the document is already in the required format, it is not translated. It is delivered as is to the SDE on the word processor, which then distributes the mail to the appropriate user on the machine.

The mail service achieves this integration not by imposing a single standard but by allowing existing de facto standards to work together. Therefore, individual users and work groups can retain the tools and procedures that have evolved to suit their specific needs.

To summarize, a successful network of heterogeneous machines and networks:

■ Uses backbone distribution to form a core.

■ Uses a family of compatible gateways supported by

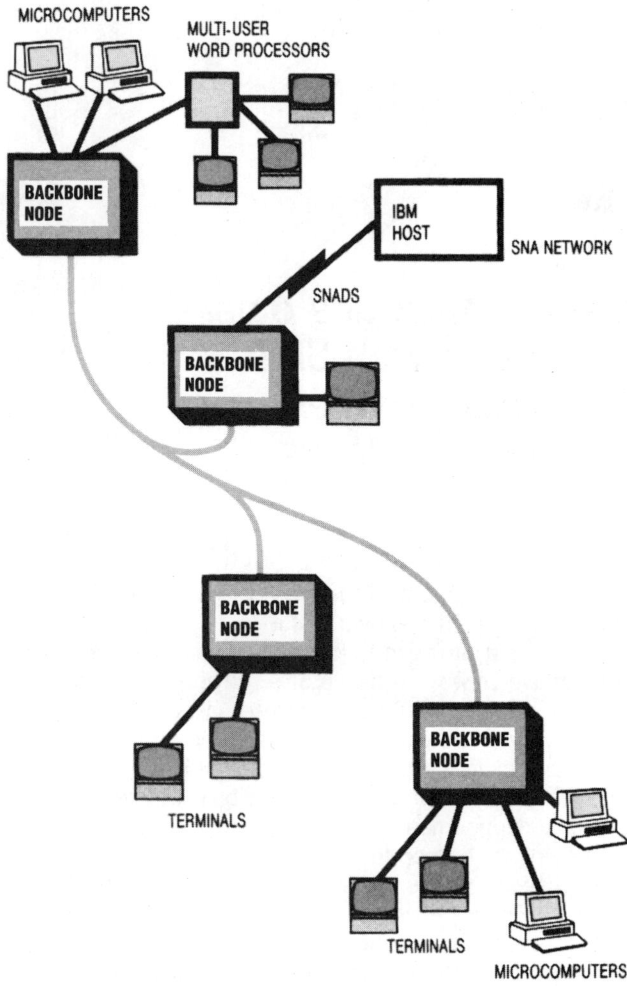

5. Multiple pathways. *This backbone network of four computers connects equipment from a variety of vendors. The machines have differing capabilities and limitations.*

translation services that tie together a variety of machines and mail services to this backbone network.

■ Supports a variety of gateways to suit the requirements and capabilities of different machines.

■ Obeys the invariant that all objects circulate in their native format while they are in the backbone network and are translated appropriately when they exit.

The result of this effort is a mail service that can be used to integrate the diverse machines and networks present in today's multivendor environments. ■

Weiming Hu received his B. S. (1982) and M. S. (1983) in electrical engineering and computer science from M.I.T. He is currently a principal software engineer with the Secure Systems Group at Digital Equipment Corp. in Littleton, Mass. Previously, he was the designer and project leader for a number of gateways to the Honeywell Bull mail product at the Office Communications Software Group of Honeywell Information Systems in Billerica, Mass.

Jill Ann Huntington, Datapro Research Corp., Delran, N. J.

OSI-based net management: Is it too early, or too late?

AT&T's latest salvo manages data plus voice; interworks with SNA applications, network devices, and public switched networks.

An old battle is heating up again in the data communications arena. The players: IBM and AT&T. The playing field: the network management market. Not exactly an even match, considering IBM's commanding lead. But this time it's not just one network management scheme versus another: It's OSI-based network management, which most agree holds out to users the last best hope of achieving true end-to-end control over multivendor networks.

AT&T last month announced several new products, including the key component of its OSI-based network management strategy—Accumaster Integrator. The Accumaster Integrator uses SNA Management Application, developed by Cincom Systems Inc. (Cincinnati, Ohio), to obtain logical network management data on SNA networks from either IBM's NetView or Cincom's Net/Master. The Accumaster Integrator is in beta test and will be generally available in the fourth quarter of this year.

AT&T concurrently announced Accumaster Management Services, a network management service (typically off-site) administered by AT&T staff. Each AT&T staff team will be dedicated solely to one customer. Also announced is Release 2 of the Accumaster Consolidated Workstation, featuring an X Window-based display.

The distinguishing feature of the Accumaster network management product family is its OSI-based implementation, built on AT&T's Unified Network Management Architecture (UNMA). Up to this point, UNMA's OSI-based approach has appeared to be more of an idea than a solution. Indeed, some users have viewed OSI as an esoteric subject—until last September, when IBM announced that its NetView would support OSI by mid-1990.

OSI is definitely moving into the mainstream. In the short term, however, due to IBM's massive installed base of SNA networks, NetView's market presence will continue to dwarf OSI-based management systems. SNA will never go away, and AT&T does not expect that it will.

AT&T is not aiming to dislodge SNA, nor does it want to replace NetView with its own SNA network management system. Rather, AT&T's goal is to set the standard in the industry for OSI-based network management—by providing a graphics-based integrating package that will send and receive commands and information to and from hosts, network management subsystems, and various devices in a multivendor network environment.

To make the Accumaster Integrator viable in the SNA market, AT&T is providing a mechanism for capturing SNA management data from NetView (or Net/Master) and correlating that to alerts from various physical devices monitored on the network. The Integrator's Alarm Correlation feature isolates the most likely source of multiple alarm faults—including those cases where the fault may be a logical error (such as a modem malfunction). The Integrator draws on a network device profile stored in a comprehensive configuration database to provide the Alarm Correlation feature. AT&T is clearly targeting multivendor network management, and the Accumaster Integrator presents the first tangible step toward supplying a product that is capable of addressing the growing OSI market.

Both NetView and the Accumaster Integrator provide integrated network management, but their approaches, designs, strengths, and limitations are different (Table 1). The Accumaster Integrator provides several advantages over NetView: immediate OSI support, superior physical network management capability, and comprehensive management for voice networks.

On the other hand, NetView provides superior logical network management—particularly of SNA networks. Most of all, NetView has a three-year lead over the Accumaster Integrator and has evolved to become a de

Table 1: Comparing network management

FEATURE	ACCUMASTER INTEGRATOR	NETVIEW
HARDWARE	AT&T 3B2 (SUPERMICRO-BASED)	SYSTEM/370 (HOST-BASED)
OPERATING SYSTEM	UNIX	MVS
UNDERLYING PROTOCOLS	NMP (AN IMPLEMENTATION OF OSI MANAGEMENT PROTOCOLS)	LU6.2 (PROPRIETARY)
VENDOR SUPPORT	17 VENDORS HAVE PLEDGED TO DEVELOP NMP INTERFACES TO THEIR PRODUCTS. MORE THAN 40 VENDORS HAVE JOINED THE OSI/NM FORUM IN LESS THAN SIX MONTHS.	MORE THAN 40 HAVE PLEDGED TO DEVELOP NETVIEW/PC INTERFACES OVER THE PAST TWO YEARS. NUMBERS HAVE NOT INCREASED SIGNIFICANTLY IN RECENT MONTHS. FEW VENDORS HAVE ACTUALLY RELEASED NETVIEW/PC PRODUCTS.
USER CUSTOMIZATION	USING C LANGUAGE.	USING CLISTS AND REXX (A STRING-PROCESSING LANGUAGE).
CONSOLE DISPLAY	GRAPHICS-BASED WITH WINDOWING CAPABILITY, RUNNING ON A SUN WORKSTATION.	TEXT-BASED, RUNNING ON AN IBM PC OR PS/2.
TERMINAL EMULATION ACCESS TO OTHER PHYSICAL DEVICE MANAGEMENT SYSTEMS	YES	NO
SAA COMPLIANT	NO	YES
OSI COMPLIANT	YES	WILL SUPPORT OSI BY MID-1990.
PRIMARY SOURCES OF REVENUE FOR VENDOR	AT&T EXPECTS SUBSTANTIAL REVENUE FROM ITS ACCUMASTER MANAGEMENT SERVICES AND FROM PROVIDING DATA TO LECs ON THE CUSTOMER-ALLOCATED PORTION OF THE PUBLIC NETWORK.	IBM DERIVES SUBSTANTIAL REVENUE FROM BOTH SOFTWARE LICENSES AND SELLING ADDITIONAL MAINFRAMES IN THE LONG RUN.
PRICE	$300,000*	MONTHLY LICENSE FEE $705-$1,255. (NETVIEW/PC HAS ONE-TIME COST OF ABOUT $2,000)

*TYPICAL CONFIGURATION INCLUDES INTEGRATOR SOFTWARE, ONE 3B2-600, TWO INTEGRATOR WORKSTATIONS AND CABLE, PLUS ACCESS TO THREE ELEMENT MANAGEMENT SYSTEMS ONE OF WHICH IS THE SNA MANAGEMENT APPLICATION. THE UNMA APPLICATION, A NET/MASTER OPTION, IS MARKETED BY CINCOM AND PRICED SEPARATELY.

facto standard. Users know that NetView will be around for a long time.

One of NetView's weak spots is its method for linking with non-IBM devices and network management systems—namely, NetView/PC. When the product was first introduced in 1986, IBM boasted that NetView/PC would become a de facto standard for consolidating network management information from devices on a multivendor network.

"The approach we used for NetView/PC could be accepted by the standards people," said Jack Drescher, then IBM's product manager for NetView/PC in Research Triangle Park, N. C. (see "An analysis of IBM's NetView/PC: Potential, potential, potential," DATA COMMUNICATIONS, November 1986, p. 81). Now, more than two years later, NetView/PC's drawbacks have dispelled that hopeful prediction and hindered IBM's efforts to win support from an overwhelming majority of vendors.

Chief among these drawbacks is that NetView/PC is awkward and expensive to implement. Another major limitation has been the inability of NetView to respond to NetView/PC alerts. Version 1.2 of NetView/PC, with a scheduled availability date of May 1989, is designed to provide this support.

IBM also hoped that NetView/PC would extend NetView's reach into managing voice networks. Concurrent with NetView/PC's introduction, IBM announced two Rolm products that used NetView/PC to pass call detail information and alerts from PBXs to NetView. However, with IBM's December 1988 sale of Rolm comes doubt about Big Blue's ability to comprehend the voice market and deal with voice management effectively.

These two gaps in the NetView scheme—capturing data from other vendors' devices and managing voice communications—are weaknesses that AT&T hopes to exploit with the Accumaster Integrator. Both multivendor network management and voice management were primary considerations when AT&T designed UNMA and the Accumaster Integrator.

The new Accumaster Integrator, described in the context of AT&T's Unified Network Management Architecture, lends itself to several comparisons with NetView. Although the comparisons that follow here are not intended to be exhaustive, they should furnish a starting point for evaluating the Accumaster product announcements (see "Glossary" for an explanation of terms).

Three-tiered architecture

AT&T's Unified Network Management Architecture aims to provide end-to-end management of voice and data networks in multivendor environments. It is a three-tiered architecture that follows the ISO/CCITT Open Systems Interconnection (OSI) standards and management framework—to the extent they are defined (Fig. 1).

This standards-based approach contrasts sharply with the direction IBM took several years ago in developing NetView. IBM instead chose to create a de facto standard, designing NetView (and its predecessors, Network Communication Control Facility, or NCCF, and Network Problem Determination Application, or NPDA) to manage networks conforming to SNA's proprietary architecture developed primarily to connect IBM equipment.

NetView and UNMA each provide some network management integration by allowing the user to monitor both logical and physical aspects of the network from one central interface. (Network management products that provide a "logical network view" measure the network as represented by actual traffic passing over it. Products controlling the physical network monitor and control the actual circuits and network nodes.)

UNMA starts with the Accumaster product line on the physical side and (in its initial implementation) enables the user to view actual displays from components on the logical side, such as IBM's NetView or Cincom's Net/Master. This feature is sometimes referred to as a cut-through capability.

To provide the cut-through capability, AT&T has included a 3279 emulation package as part of its Accumaster Integrator. Thus, the Accumaster Integrator console will have the capability of displaying information just as it appears on the NetView console. The Accumaster console (a Sun workstation) will be a terminal defined in SNA and, as such, will have the capability of accessing SNA applications, such as Cincom's Net/Master or IBM's NetView. At present, AT&T has no plans to develop its own logical management package for SNA networks.

In contrast, IBM begins with NetView on the logical side and integrates physical network management through its Link Problem Determination Aid (LPDA) and NetView/PC. Similarly, Enterprise Management Architecture (EMA), from Digital Equipment Corp. (DEC, Concord, Mass.), starts with the Executive control program on the logical side and provides Access Modules that communicate with remote hardware using OSI-based protocols.

Both data networks and voice networks can be managed via UNMA. More important, however, UNMA supports the customer-allocated portion of the public network. It lets users tie together three network management domains: the customer premises, the local exchange network, and the interexchange network.

AT&T can provide UNMA customers with the means to integrate information from public networks with data from their private network management systems. IBM's NetView and DEC's EMA stop short of the public network and offer instead much more sophisticated logical network management capabilities, particularly at the applications level.

Since OSI management standards have not yet solidified, how soon can an integrated solution for managing multivendor networks appear? IBM has decided to wait until mid-1990, when most OSI management standards will have reached International Standard status (Table 2).

AT&T is not waiting—the Accumaster Integrator uses Network Management Protocol (NMP), AT&T's implementation of OSI standards as they exist today. AT&T pledges to modify NMP and its products to conform to any changes that the OSI committees may dictate. In the interim, AT&T is proactively seeking support for NMP and is heavily involved in the OSI Network Management/Forum.

A Unified User Interface is the focus of UNMA's three-

Glossary

The following terms are useful in understanding the new AT&T network management product. They are not presented in alphabetical order because, in part, each term builds upon an understanding of its predecessor in the list.

OSI (Open Systems Interconnection): an architectural model designed to enable computerized systems in multivendor environments to share information. The OSI model defines an open system as one that obeys OSI standards in its communications with other systems. This contrasts with proprietary architectures, such as IBM's Systems Network Architecture (SNA), which are designed primarily to support one vendor's equipment.

DIS (Draft International Standard): the last stage in the OSI standardization process before final approval. Draft International Standards are usually stable enough to allow vendors to commence implementation, although they are still subject to minor modifications before becoming International Standards (ISs).

DP (Draft Proposal): the stage in the OSI standardization process before DIS. Draft Proposals define the scope of the standard and, while subject to modification, are usually stable enough to guide vendors in developing product architectures.

UNMA (Unified Network Management Architecture): a three-tiered architecture that serves as AT&T's blueprint for future network management products and services. UNMA is an open architecture that employs interfaces based on OSI standards.

Network elements: network equipment and services that comprise an organization's network. These include physical devices on the network, such as modems, multiplexers, PBXs, LANs, and hosts. Also included are local exchange carrier (LEC) networks, interexchange services, Postal, Telephone, and Telegraph agencies (PTTs), and international network services. Network elements form the first tier of AT&T's UNMA.

EMS (Element Management System): a system that manage network elements. The term encompasses the plethora of devices on the market that provide network management for certain pieces of the network. Large networks typically employ many separate EMSs to control different vendors' products and services. Examples of EMSs include systems that manage modems, multiplexers, and DSUs (such as the Codex 9800 INMS, Racal-Milgo's CMS 2000, and AT&T's Dataphone II Level IV).

AT&T also uses the term *element management system* to describe certain operations embedded in the phone company's networks that analyze traffic over telco switches, support trouble ticket facilities, and provide related services. EMSs form the second tier of AT&T's UNMA.

NMP (Network Management Protocol): the protocol used in UNMA to communicate information from various vendors' element management systems to the Accumaster Integrating System. NMP is fully compliant with the OSI seven-layer model and the currect definitions of OSI management framework and management information services. NMP performs the same function as do LU 6.2 and SSCP-LU for IBM's NetView/PC.

Accumaster Integrator: AT&T's Unix-based system capable of automatically uploading information from other EMSs via the NMP interface. AT&T announced this product on January 31. According to AT&T, the product will eventually provide overall, end-to-end network management of all network elements in an organization's network.

ACW (Accumaster Consolidated Workstation): an MS-DOS based system that displays a consolidated network view by providing separate windowing sessions to various AT&T EMSs. Release 2 of ACW, announced in January, will allow users to communicate with IBM host applications (using NetView or Cincom's Net/Master) while maintaining active sessions with other EMSs.

NCCF (Network Communication Control Facility): IBM's host-based network management software that provides the operator interface and network logging facilities. NCCF operates as an application program under ACF/VTAM. IBM enhanced NCCF (renamed "The Command Facility") and incorporated it into NetView in 1986.

NPDA (Network Problem Determination Application): IBM's network management product that uses a series of panels to provide operations with information needed to perform problem determination and resolution. An enhanced version NPDA (renamed "The Hardware Monitor") was incorporated into NetView in 1986.

EMA (Enterprise Management Architecture): Digital Equipment Corp.'s OSI-based network management strategy. Like UNMA, EMA provides for multivendor network management using an interface based on OSI standards. Seven vendors have pledged to support EMA. Digital has yet to publish its interface implementation.

---

tiered architecture. Machine-to-machine interaction occurs between the three tiers; human-to-machine interaction occurs at the Unified User Interface.

Tier 1 is made up of network elements, which may include customer premises equipment (CPE), such as modems, multiplexers, LANs, hosts, and PBXs. Local exchange carrier (LEC) networks, interexchange services, Postal, Telephone, and Telegraph agencies (PTTs), and other international network services are also considered network elements.

Tier 2 consists of Element Management Systems (EMSs), which manage network elements. An EMS provides what may be called "local" management capabilities—operations, administration, maintenance, and provisioning functions of managing a particular network element group. Today, most large networks include multiple EMSs, since vendors have traditionally supplied multiple network management products for different devices and services. It is not unusual to find different EMSs for computer hosts, matrix switches, T1 resource managers, and Ethernet

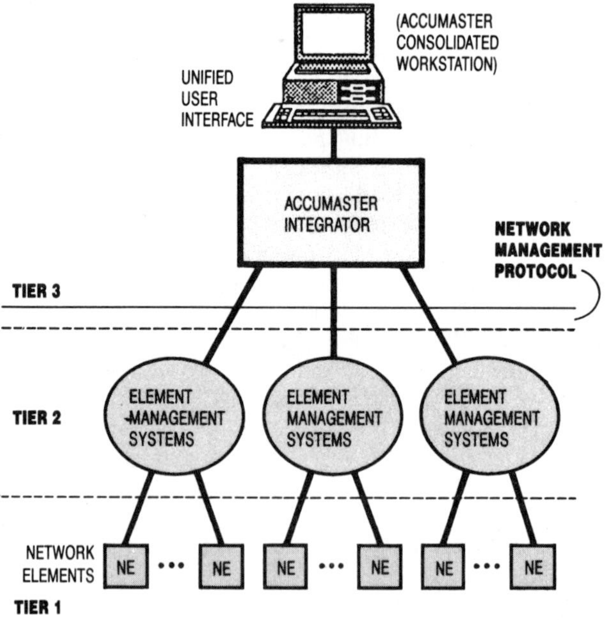

1. Three tiers. UNMA's Tier 1 consists of Network Elements; Tier 2 has Element Management Systems; and Tier 3 is the Accumaster Integrator.

LANs—all in the same corporate network. Each EMS is, all too often, an island unto itself. The inability of disparate EMSs to share information prevents the user from obtaining an end-to-end view of the network.

Customers have access to about 20 AT&T EMSs. An additional 100 network-based EMSs deployed by AT&T are not currently customer-accessible. Over the next decade, AT&T plans to make more of these systems accessible, providing customers with additional trouble ticketing information as well as alarm and performance information on AT&T facilities.

Tier 3 aims to provide the end-to-end view by supporting communications between EMSs and the Integrating Network Management System. This integrating mechanism, the Accumaster Integrator, is the heart of the UNMA strategy. The Accumaster integrating system will communicate with individual EMSs through a common protocol stack. This stack (Network Management Protocol), is AT&T's implementation of OSI management specifications as they exist today. Under UNMA, management integrating packages (such as the Accumaster Integrator) also communicate among themselves via the standard protocol stack (Tier 2-to-Tier 3). UNMA allows communications based on native (proprietary) protocols between the Network Elements and their respective EMSs (Tier 1-to-Tier 2). Communications based on standard protocols between Tiers 1 and 2, however, may evolve in the future.

The Accumaster Integrator provides cut-through capabilities to the EMSs, allowing users to exercise full capabilities of each EMS. This feature gives AT&T's product an edge over IBM's NetView.

As part of the Accumaster product announcements,

AT&T unveiled a special application it developed under joint agreement with Cincom Systems. This application, called the SNA Management Application, provides logical information about SNA networks to the Accumaster Integrator.

Also at Tier 3, the Unified User Interface creates the image of a virtual network, so to speak. The Accumaster Consolidated Workstation's enhancements found in Release 2 support this concept by bringing screens from 10 element management systems into one central screen (up to six at any one time, using windowing capabilities). These element management systems include NetView, Net/Master, several AT&T voice management systems, and any element management systems that support VT100 terminal emulation.

Implementing OSI net management

As of January 1989, AT&T had published four Network Management Protocol documents (TR 54004 through 007) to guide other vendors in implementing the interface between their proprietary Element Management System products and the Accumaster Integrator. AT&T's work on NMP, as described in these documents, provides the best insight available to date regarding the practical mechanics of implementing OSI network management.

Based on the OSI seven-layer reference model, NMP is also consistent with the OSI Management Framework and Management Information Services to the extent to which these are defined. NMP is implemented in Layers 4 through 7 of the OSI model and is independent of specific implementations of Layers 1, 2, and 3. NMP is subject to some modification because it depends on some OSI standards that are not yet finalized (see "NMP Status").

AT&T divides its application layer services into two categories: transaction services and file transfer services. Transaction services depend on Common Management Information Service (CMIS), Remote Operations Service Elements (ROSE), and Association Control Service Elements (ACSE). Enhanced transaction services, which provide for two-phase commitment and chaining plus similar sophisticated facilities, require Commitment, Concurrency, and Recovery (CCR) in addition to CMIS, ROSE, and ACSE. File transfer services require ACSE and FTAM. AT&T's implementation of these for NMP, are outlined in document TR54004.

In addition to NMP's implementation across Layers 4 through 7, AT&T has also published NMP application message sets for configuration management and fault management. OSI specifications covering these two functions, as well as for security management, are closer to final approval than are those for performance and accounting management. AT&T is currently working on message sets for the latter as well as for the other remaining UNMA network management functions, although progress to some extent depends on OSI committee progress.

AT&T, however, sees no reason to wait for these functions to attain Draft International Standard (DIS) status before embarking on implementation. The company is developing products that conform to OSI Draft Proposals (DPs), even though DPs are subject to modification. AT&T

Table 2: OSI management status

	OSI MANAGEMENT STANDARDS			EXPECTED REGISTRATION DATES		
TITLE	**REFERENCE DOCUMENT**	**WORKING DOCUMENT**	**DRAFT PROPOSAL**	**DRAFT INTERNATIONAL STANDARD**	**INTERNATIONAL STANDARD**
OSI MANAGEMENT FRAMEWORK	DP 7498-4	COMPLETE	COMPLETE	COMPLETE	OCTOBER '88
OSI MANAGEMENT INFORMATION SERVICE OVERVIEW	N 2683	COMPLETE	COMPLETE	JULY '89	JULY '90
STRUCTURE OF MANAGEMENT INFORMATION	N 2684	COMPLETE	COMPLETE	MAY '89	JULY '90
COMMON MANAGEMENT INFORMATION SERVICE (CMIS)	DP 9595	COMPLETE	COMPLETE	COMPLETE	SEPTEMBER '89
COMMON MANAGEMENT INFORMATION PROTOCOL (CMIP)	DP 9596	COMPLETE	COMPLETE	COMPLETE	SEPTEMBER '89
CONFIGURATION MANAGEMENT	N 2686	COMPLETE	COMPLETE	JULY '89	JULY '90
FAULT MANAGEMENT	N 2687	COMPLETE	COMPLETE	JULY '89	JULY '90
SECURITY MANAGEMENT	N 2688	COMPLETE	SEPTEMBER '89	JULY '89	JULY '90
ACCOUNTING MANAGEMENT	N 2689	COMPLETE	SEPTEMBER '89	APRIL '90	APRIL '91
PERFORMANCE MANAGEMENT	N 2673	COMPLETE	SEPTEMBER '89	APRIL '90	APRIL '91

pledges to modify its products to comply with any OSI changes, but it expects those changes to be minor. Despite this aggressive approach to product development, it will take a number of years for AT&T to develop full functionality in all its targeted functional areas.

Although AT&T has pledged that it will modify NMP to conform to final OSI specifications, users must realize that the OSI guidelines leave room for differences in vendor implementations—differences that can tarnish the lure of interoperability. Within each OSI layer are not only mandatory services but also optional ones that a vendor may or may not choose to implement. Vendors may opt to extend protocol definitions. For example, AT&T adds a parameter constraint in the ACSE Protocol for NMP that is not required in the ISO standard. Thus, users must be aware that while OSI-based implementations are *open,* this does not mean that they are identical.

Developing interfaces

Since multivendor connectivity under UNMA depends on vendor acceptance of NMP, AT&T proposes that other vendors use the published NMP specification and message sets to develop UNMA interfaces to their products. DEC, Hewlett-Packard, and a few other pioneers, however, are also developing different OSI implementations. Equipment vendors do not have unlimited resources, and many will be forced to choose between AT&T's NMP and other alternatives.

Industry analysts have viewed the lack of vendor support for NMP as a major hindrance to user acceptance of UNMA. AT&T has recently pledged to take a more proactive role in promoting NMP among equipment vendors for LECs and PTTs. AT&T lists 17 equipment vendors supporting NMP (Table 3). This list will undoubtedly grow before early 1990, when the OSI/Network Management (NM) Forum plans to stage an interoperability demonstration.

Before this demonstration becomes a reality, however, the Forum must select a protocol-stack and message-set implementation. This will probably amount to choosing a slightly modified version of AT&T's NMP. While Forum membership does not indicate full-fledged support of AT&T's NMP, each vendor in the Forum has made a substantial commitment to an OSI-based approach to network management—an approach that is much more amenable to AT&T's scheme than IBM's or even DEC's.

It is interesting to note that at the April 1988 IBM Telecommunications Consultants Conference, IBM was proudly pointing out that "maybe two or three vendors" had pledged support for AT&T's UNMA, compared with about 40 vendors supporting NetView/PC. While support for NMP and membership in the OSI/NM Forum has increased substantially over the intervening months, the momentum behind NetView/PC support has remained stationary, at best.

Consensus setting

AT&T played an instrumental part in the July 1988 formation of the OSI/NM Forum. The founding members included Amdahl, British Telecom, Hewlett-Packard, Northern Telecom, Telecom Canada, STC PLC (UK), and Unisys. Forum membership has increased to more than 40, including five new voting members. New voting members include Digital

NMP status

The following section briefly describes the OSI layers and protocols in which Network Management Protocol is implemented. The status of each OSI component is listed to provide a general picture of the degree to which NMP is subject to change.

OSI Layer 4—International Standard Status (finalized). The transport layer establishes (node-to-node) network connections, provides end-to-end data acknowledgment, terminates network connections, and performs related tasks.

OSI Layer 5—International Standard Status (finalized). The session layer establishes endpoint-to-endpoint sessions, specifies duplex or half-duplex service between session users, and coordinates session termination.

OSI Layer 6—International Standard Status (finalized). The presentation layer ensures compatibility between incoming file, record, and data formats, as well as the format requirements of the receiving systems.

OSI Layer 7—Portions have attained International Standard Status (partially finalized). Within the application layer are several sublayers used for network management, including:

- ASCE (Association Control Service Elements): International Standard (finalized)
- FTAM (File Transfer, Access, and Management): International Standard (finalized)
- ROSE (Remote Operations Service Elements): Draft International Standard (relatively stable)
- CCR (Commitment, Concurrency, and Recovery): Draft International Standard (relatively stable)
- CMIS (Common Management Information Service): Draft International Standard (relatively stable)
- CMIP (Common Management Information Protocol): Draft International Standard (relatively stable)

Communications Associates Inc., MCI Communications Corp., and Microtel Ltd. New vendors pledging associate membership include Avant-Garde, Contel Technology Center, Fujitsu America, Hekimian Laboratories, Infotron, NCR Corp., Network Equipment Technologies, Prime Computer, Racal-Milgo, Siemens A.G., and Telwatch.

The OSI/NM Forum's main goal is to accelerate delivery of OSI management-based products by forming a consensus on protocol options, message sets, and management object definitions. Forum members anticipate that such a consensus will not only promote product implementation development but also influence international bodies to adopt standards supporting (or, at least not conflicting with) those implementations. Forum members have pledged to promote Forum-adopted platforms within the international standards bodies.

The Forum plans to stage an interoperability demonstration in mid-1990 and is in the process of defining the messages that will allow that demonstration to take place. These messages address *event management,* which includes fault management and configuration manage-

ment. The closure date for a Forum consensus on messages is planned for mid- to late 1989. At the same time, the Forum will be working toward a consensus on management architecture, including object definitions that name and define management data.

In January, the Forum achieved its first major milestone when it defined a seven-layer protocol stack for conveying management information. The protocol stack includes X.25 and IEEE 802.3 for the transport layers and is fairly close to AT&T's published definition of NMP.

AT&T has indicated that it will modify NMP to comply with whatever the OSI/NM Forum adopts and, ultimately, with whatever OSI committees adopt. Clearly, each vendor represented in the OSI/NM Forum has individual reasons for joining and will vote for an implementation that promotes those goals. Thus, there is no guarantee that OSI/NM Forum members will automatically adopt NMP without modifications.

On the other hand, regarding anticipated OSI/NM Forum decisions, AT&T has stated that the technical work done on NMP will not change. Furthermore, AT&T's John Miller, director of network management, has stated that "the Forum's goals are totally aligned with AT&T's goals."

DEC is moving full steam ahead in garnering support for its own OSI-based approach—Enterprise Management Architecture (EMA). Announced in Cannes, France, in September 1988, EMA employs a director-entity approach that allows multiple "directors" (digital network management systems) to manage "entities" (analogous to AT&T's Network Elements) on multiple domains.

Directors can exchange management information with, and even take over management duties of, other directors in different domains (in the event of a malfunction). This exchange is possible since EMA specifies a standard OSI-based format for information exchange. At this time, however, DEC has not announced peer-to-peer exchange with its directors and NetView or the Accumaster Integrator. According to DEC, EMA was two and a half years in development.

DEC's EMA has support from seven vendors, including Codex, DCA, Stratacom, Timeplex, and other equipment and software providers. Several of them have pledged support for both EMA and NMP. While the momentum behind the OSI/NM Forum is undoubtedly pushing DEC to reconsider its declination, the company has not announced intentions of joining to date.

DEC has stated that it will deliver OSI-based management products by the end of 1989. It could thus damage AT&T's bid to wield primary influence over the direction of OSI-based implementations. If AT&T's supporters continue to increase in number and if DEC announces no viable strategy for linking to NetView, that damage will probably be minimal.

Adding logical data

Last summer, AT&T and Cincom Systems Inc. announced an agreement to jointly develop an application that will provide logical data to the UNMA integrating system. Cincom currently produces Net/Master, widely accredited as the only real competition to IBM's NetView.

Table 3: Vendor support for NMP

AVANTE-GARDE COMPUTING INC.

AVANTI COMMUNICATIONS CORP.

COASTCOM T1 NETWORKING PRODUCTS

DIGITAL COMMUNICATIONS SYSTEMS INC.

DYNATECH COMMUNICATIONS INC.

EMCOM CORP.

GENERAL DATACOMM INC.

HEKIMIAN LABORATORIES INC.

INFOTRON SYSTEMS CORP.

INTEGRATED TELECOM CORP.

KAPTRONIX INC.

NEWBRIDGE NETWORKS

PARADYNE CORP.

RACAL-MILGO

SYNC RESEARCH INC.

TELINQ SYSTEMS

TRIDOM CORP.

Benefiting from Cincom's expertise in SNA, the resulting application, called the SNA Management Application (SMA), resides in the IBM host and allows the Accumaster Integrator to interface with either IBM's NetView or Cincom's Net/Master. The application will support SNA customers by extracting logical information (messages and screens) from IBM systems and displaying them on the Accumaster Integrator Console (Fig. 2). Using this approach, the Accumaster Integrator could include peer-to-peer interfaces with other logical network management systems, such as DEC's EMA.

The SMA builds on the functionality that Net/Master currently provides, according to Cincom, but will not preclude UNMA customers from using IBM's NetView. Furthermore, the SMA does not depend on IBM's Network Performance Monitor (NPM), adds Cincom. The current Net/Master product requires access to the NPM, which IBM could bundle with NetView at a future date. (There have been no indications so far that IBM intends to do that, however, and Datapro believes that this is unlikely.)

The UNMA roll call

1. The Accumaster Integrator. Featuring an X Window-based interface, the product takes logical network management information from the SNA Management Application (an optional feature) and correlates it with physical device data transmitted (via an NMP interface) from various vendors' EMSs. One of the Integrator's most striking aspects is its Alarm Correlation feature. While not infallible, this feature provides a distinct advantage over NetView's implementation of capturing physical device alerts through

NetView/PC—particularly when the network administrator must resolve multiple simultaneous alarms.

The Alarm Correlation feature compares alarms as they are received, determines the most likely cause of the alarm, and suppresses secondary alarms linked to the original problem. To accomplish this, the Integrator uses internal logic in combination with network device profiles stored in a configuration database. The feature can help operators determine what to do first and whether the alarms are related by isolating the most likely source of the alarm.

As impressive as this feature is, it is obviously not perfect, since the Accumaster Integrator chooses the *most likely* cause. In the future, says AT&T's Miller, the company will expand this area and will continue to enhance the algorithms that drive the feature. Also, at present, the Alarm Correlation is not user-programmable in the sense that it includes user exits for extensive customization.

The marketability of the Accumaster Integrator hinges on UNMA's open NMP interface, which allows the user to integrate data from other vendors' element management systems. Codex, Racal-Milgo, and other vendors offer modem and multiplexer management products that far outsell AT&T's Dataphone II, for example. Of course, the Accumaster Integrator can only provide information from other EMSs if the manufacturers develop the requisite NMP interface. Seventeen major vendors have already pledged to develop NMP interfaces. Four of those vendors, including Racal-Milgo and Infotron, have already implemented NMP interfaces on their products. The number of vendors supporting NetView/PC is about twice AT&T's figure; however, the momentum behind NetView/PC is surprisingly low, given IBM's installed base of SNA networks. If NetView/PC supporters numbered in the hundreds, AT&T would not have poured so much into the UNMA/NMP development effort.

The *new* Accumaster Integrator not only consolidates but also integrates by processing information. Initially, the product provides control in two clearly related areas: fault management (alarm integration) and configuration management. The Integrator includes a configuration database of all network components. Device profiles include device types, names, locations, and how these devices are interconnected. The product draws on this information to produce real-time graphic displays of network configurations. The Integrator's graphics capabilities also support fault management—including the use of icons to represent network devices and color codes to indicate fault severity and importance. More important, the product allows the user to track down logical or physical faults from one console.

For example, if an alarm comes in from the SMA, the operator can view data from the NPDA Hardware Monitor and query to get a picture of the route from the host through each of the SNA service nodes. The operator can then examine the status of each to see whether or not there is a physical problem correlating to the logical alarm. Also, the Integrator enables an operator to claim "ownership" of

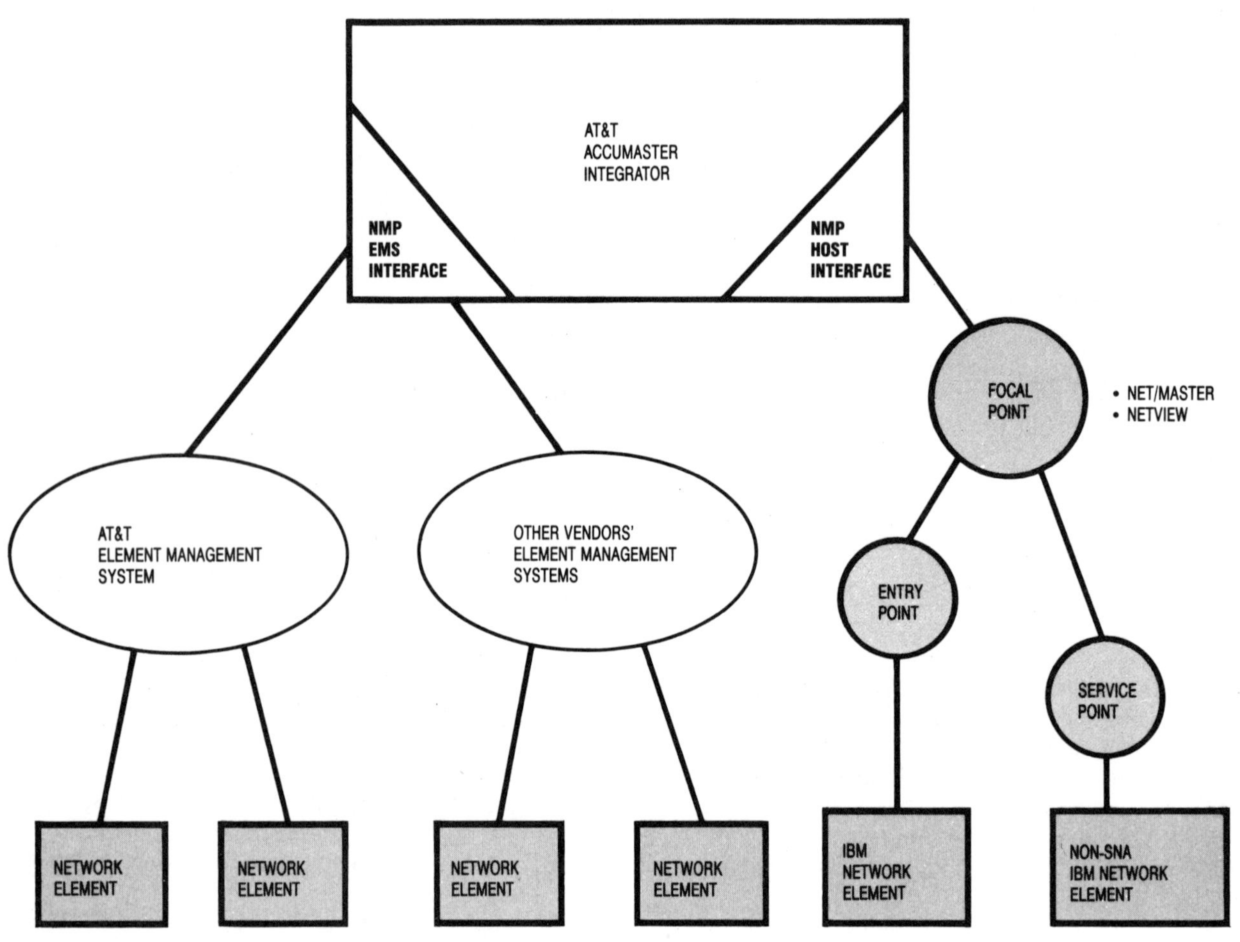

an alarm by setting a flag to indicate to other network operators that the alarm is being handled. An electronic mail feature enables network operators and administrators to communicate information about faults and problem resolution on line.

Besides processing management data through the NMP interface, the Accumaster Integrator includes terminal emulation capabilities to enable the user to cut-through to the individual EMSs. That important feature gives the user the full effect of operating at the EMS console—such as a StarKeeper console. This provides an advantage over the NetView/PC implementation, which presents generic alerts or character strings (extracted from the other physical network devices using code points) rather than the actual EMS console display.

To facilitate an end-to-end view of the network, the Accumaster Integrator creates a unified, "virtual network" composed of both private and public network elements. It does so by combining information from customer premises EMSs with information from EMSs controlling those portions of the public network partially allocated to the customer. Under UNMA, this integrating system may reside either on the customer premises *or* in the public network, or in both simultaneously.

2. Accumaster Management Services. Besides the Accumaster Integrator, AT&T now offers an integrating service called Accumaster Management Services. This service will be administered from various Network Operations Centers (NOCs) that physically reside either in AT&T's network or on the customer's premises. NOCs will be staffed by AT&T personnel teams dedicated solely to a specific customer. When under contract for NOC services, the customer will receive three categories of services: provisioning, fault management, and analysis. Provisioning includes procurement and follow-through on all equipment and service orders, including station moves, changes, and relocations. Fault management includes call receipt, trouble tracking, repair verification, restoration planning, and implementation services. Analysis includes regular, detailed reports on numerous aspects, including response time and meantime to restore.

There are roughly 10 NOCs already in service. About half of these are on the customer's premises. Pricing is on a contract basis and depends on options chosen. Contracts can be designated as five days per week (normal, or expanded business hours) or seven days per week, up to 24 hours per day. This service is available immediately.

3. *Accumaster Consolidated Workstation, Release 2.*The first release of the ACW was announced in September 1987 and became available in mid-1988. Release 2 of the ACW runs on an AT&T 6312 Work Group System (WGS) and uses multitasking applications software to monitor multiple Element Management Systems simultaneously. The 6312 WGS supports the MS-DOS operating system.

The ACW's 3270 terminal emulation facility provides IBM host access from NetView or Cincom's Net/Master. Users can communicate with host applications while maintaining active sessions with other EMSs. ACW Release 2 now supports up to 10 EMSs, displaying the status of six of these simultaneously using the windowing feature. In this release, AT&T has also added VT100 terminal emulation and 513 emulation. The 513 emulation feature gives users the capability to access the AT&T System 75/85's (PBX) Centralized System Management and other vendors' EMSs. The VT100 capability enables users to access network management systems that support VT100 terminal emulation. This includes AT&T network-based information, such as the Management Information Systems Report. MISR is a network administration report system designed to support Software Defined Networks.

ACW operators can observe network changes in real time and interact with the appropriate system to perform testing, problem diagnosis, troubleshooting, and reconfiguration.

4. *Accunet T1.5 Information Manager (AIM).* This is the first AT&T product adapted to UNMA standards. AIM works either as a standalone EMS or as an EMS under the Integrator. AIM features audible signals and graphics displays, and it focuses on configuration management, alarms, and error performance. The product does not display real-time utilization of T1 lines. AIM keeps various records on failed circuits for 31 days.

The AIM software package costs about $3,000 and will be available to Accunet T1.5 customers in April. There will also be a onetime fee of approximately $1,000 per circuit accessed to initiate service. To implement AIM as a stand-alone system, the customer must provide a PC and a 9.6-kbit/s private line link to the AIM system.

5. *NetPartner Network Management System.* AT&T's integrating system for LECs is the NetPartner Network Management System (NMS). AT&T introduced NetPartner NMS in 1988, although there are no figures available on how many units have been sold. This product is a hardware/software combination that gives Centrex customers restricted access to the phone company operations embedded in the phone company's network. Specifically, NetPartner translates information that is currently within the phone company's operations into a form that is easier for customers to understand, manipulate, track, and alter. The phone company maintains control over what the customer can access.

NetPartner NMS features a three part architecture, comprised of host equipment at the phone company, customer premises equipment, and operations at various phone company sites.

NetPartner also provides a 3270 terminal emulation capability that provides access to IBM's NetView or NCCF/NPDA or Cincom's Net/Master. In this configuration, NetPartner appears like a cluster controller to the IBM host computer. NetPartner has a menu-driven, graphics-based user interface. The phone company customizes each menu to show only those functions that the customer's company has purchased. Currently, one NetPartner NMS can support five to 10 customers—up to 20 users simultaneously. The phone company defines the number of users per customer. Future NetPartner enhancements are planned, including an ISO-based interface to specific customer premises-based and interexchange carrier products. Some artificial intelligence-based capability is also planned.

AT&T is directing its NetPartner marketing efforts at both phone companies and end-users. AT&T is seeking to convince LECs that end-users are willing to pay extra for the control facilities that a NetPartner-equipped LEC can offer. AT&T is trying to persuade end-users to demand NetPartner capability from their local telcos. AT&T is particularly pursuing those users interested in ISDN capabilities. Pricing information on NetPartner is not yet available.

Nine ways to support users

Network management systems are used to help obtain real-time information on network performance and traffic characteristics, diagnose problems, and reconfigure to meet changing needs. In the past, network management was characterized by separate management systems devoted to providing these services for a particular vendor's product or group of products.

AT&T, however, proposes with UNMA to integrate data from disparate management systems and collectively provide critical network management functions. Specifically, UNMA defines nine functions to support users in managing their networks. The first five of these functions are included in the OSI functional model of management.

■ *Fault management.* The goal of fault management is to maintain network availability at an acceptable level. On a day-to-day basis, this means quick and accurate problem detection and problem determination.

The UNMA management integrator correlates alarm information from various devices to pinpoint the event or fault that may have caused multiple alarms. UNMA calls for complete audit trail of the fault management process, supported by trouble tracking.

In April 1988, AT&T published the Network Management Protocol Fault Management Message Set Specification. This document outlines how NMP enables users to control alarm reporting, manipulate alarm information, and set alarm reporting parameters.

■ *Configuration management.* The goal of configuration management is to manipulate network configurations to adapt to changing needs and traffic patterns or to isolate problems. To support this, the network management product must collect information on the current state of the network, noting changes; modify network attributes; and change configuration.

The UNMA definition of this function has four basic aspects: network inventory management, change management and provisioning, name management, and actual connections (relating inventory items to their physical layout). Network inventory management involves tracking all devices and services on the network. Change management and provisioning supports both scheduled and unscheduled movement of telephones, modems, terminals, circuits, and other network components. Name management governs the network directory. In April 1988, AT&T published the NMP Configuration Management Message Set Specification.

■ *Performance management.* The goal of performance management is to identify and correct potential problems before they cause a fault. To accomplish this, the management system must collect data on current network and resource performance levels and maintain performance logs.

UNMA provides the capability to correlate information from multiple EMSs to assist the users in identifying network performance trends. UNMA users will have the capability to monitor selected network components via user-definable measures and thresholds. UNMA will provide both recent history and current performance data, which the user can analyze in order to identify network performance trends.

■ *Accounting management.* This function informs users of costs incurred and enables users to set accounting limits.

Under UNMA, users can compare usage and billing information across related voice networks and subnetworks and potentially obtain more complete billing, verification, and chargeback information. Chargebacks may include charges for fixed-cost items such as telephones or terminals as well as usage; UNMA supports comparison of vendor bill verification and comparison of vendor bills with inventory and internal measures.

■ *Security management.* Security management encompasses access control, authorization facilities, and partitioning the network. The OSI definition of security management also includes support for encryption and key management and the maintenance and manipulation of security logs.

UNMA supports tracking log-on attempts and violations to prevent unauthorized network access. UNMA also supports multiple network management permission levels. Under UNMA, network administrators can manage the network from either one or several different network management operation centers by partitioning the network.

■ *Planning.* While not defined as an OSI management function, planning is widely accepted as a major network

No OSI-based product supports all nine functional areas defined by UNMA.

management subsystem. The goal of planning is to design and optimize models that describe potential changes to the network. Consolidating usage trends and performance data supports this. Planning typically involves collecting performance data, consolidating usage trends, and analyzing future requirements.

UNMA outlines three common types of planning: capacity planning (day-to-day fine-tuning, such as adding or rearranging trunks); contingency planning (backup and disaster recovery, including estimated costs); and strategic planning (new applications, growth plans, acquisitions, reorganizations).

■ *Operations support* This encompasses managing the staffing and operation of a network management center.

UNMA defines four aspects of operations support: creating network management center procedures (for trouble logs, maintenance fixes, shift changes, etc.); analyzing work and information flow at the center; analyzing network management center staff requirements; and preparing user training and development plans.

■ *Programmability.* The goal of programmability is to customize the network management package to meet corporate needs. There are no "off-the-shelf" solutions in network management. Programmability is critical because each network is different and networks are characteristically in a state of flux.

UNMA provides parameterization of key characteristics and provides flexible report capabilities, customizable scripts, and custom programming options. It supports programmability in C language.

■ *Integrated control.* The goal of integrated control is to create the image of a single virtual network, even though it may actually comprise diverse, separate management systems. UNMA currently provides consolidation of multiple network control screens into a single, windowing workstation—the Accumaster Consolidated Workstation.

These nine generic function descriptions provide a useful framework for evaluating integrated network management products. Currently, there is no single OSI-based product or service that provides comprehensive, integrated support in all of these functional areas. Over the next decade, AT&T plans to evolve UNMA and the Accumaster product line to fill this gap. ■

Portions of this article were adapted from the January 1989 issue of "Datapro Reports on Communications Software."

Jill Huntington is an associate editor/analyst with Datapro. She holds a B. S. in business and English from Wake Forest University, Winston-Salem, N. C., and a master's degree in Computer Science from the University of Virginia in Charlottesville. Within the computer industry, she has held positions in programming, teaching, and technical writing. Prior to joining Datapro, Huntington was employed as a programmer/analyst with NCR Corp. (Dayton, Ohio).

Alan J. Weissberger, Data Communications Technology, Santa Clara, Calif.

The evolving versions of ISDN's terminal adapter

Several 'TAs'—protocol converters for plugging your existing data devices into ISDN—are already available. But beware of their many differences.

Existing data communications equipment and interfaces are not compatible with the Integrated Services Digital Network (ISDN): Some type of adaptation is required. The device that will do this, the terminal adapter, or TA, will be an essential ingredient in the acceptance and growth of ISDN. While only a handful of TAs has been introduced to date, these ISDN "protocol converters" will probably proliferate exponentially in the 1990s with the spread of ISDN.

A terminal adapter maps a non-ISDN terminal, PC, or modem into an ISDN basic-rate interface (2 B + D, with two B channels at 64 kbit/s and a D channel at 16 kbit/s). Analog telephones and facsimile machines may also be attached to some TAs via an RJ-11 phone connector.

The functions of a TA include providing: rate-adaption and data-format conversion for a B channel, X.25 packet-switching interfaces for both B and D channels, digitization of analog instruments for a B channel, out-of-band signaling (as per CCITT Q.931 and Q.921 standards) on the D channel, and the four-wire ISDN S/T physical layer interface (as per the CCITT I.430 standard).

The TA, which is commonly implemented as a standalone unit or as a PC circuit card, may support both circuit-switched and packet-switched services (Table 1). Significantly, all circuit-mode ISDN terminals (those that operate over either circuit-switched connections or dedicated lines) will need to support TA procedures on the B channels in order to communicate with existing non-ISDN terminals that gain access to ISDN circuit-mode services via a TA.

In the case of ISDN packet switching (non-circuit-mode service), the TA can also convert X.25- or asynchronous-terminal data streams to the ISDN packet format. The TA would then communicate over a virtual circuit with another such TA, or directly with an ISDN packet-mode terminal.

To understand the functions of ISDN terminal adapters, it is necessary to understand ISDN's reference points and functional groupings (Fig. 1). For a more detailed discussion of these two ISDN topics, refer to "Standards makers cementing ISDN subnetwork layers," Data Communications, October 1987, p. 237.

The functional groupings are collections of ISDN functions, which may be physically realized in a "box" (standalone unit) or on a plug-in circuit card. The reference points are conceptual boundaries that separate the various functional groupings. All reference points need not be physically present in every ISDN interface; functional groupings may be combined, or one function may be null.

There are two ISDN terminal equipment types: TE1 and TE2. TE1 is an ISDN terminal, whereas TE2 is a terminal incompatible with ISDN recommendations. TE2 requires a TA for conversion, located at the R reference point. All existing terminals, facsimile machines, and computers would be classified as TE2s. However, if a PC has an integral ISDN card, it could be considered a TE1, since it has full access to the D channel.

Terminal equipment refers to either a TE1 or a TA. Both provide the ISDN user-to-network interface.

Primary-rate access

The NT2 (network termination 2) could be a PBX, LAN (local area network), communications processor, or multiplexer that concentrates two or more TE1s or TAs at the S reference point. It is used in primary-rate access (23 B + D) and is generally not present in basic-rate applications where the TE1 or TA is directly connected to the NT1 (sometimes called NT) at the T reference point. In this case, the S and T reference points are coincident.

In addition to the point-to-point service shown in Figure 1, there is a basic-rate, point-to-multipoint (or passive bus) configuration. This permits as many as eight TEs to share

Table 1: Summary of TA procedures

ISDN SERVICE	TA PROCEDURES	R INTERFACE(S)	ISDN CHANNEL(S)
CIRCUIT SWITCHED	V.120 (U.S.)	V.24, V.35	B,H
	V.110 (EUROPE, JAPAN)	V.24, V.35	B
	DMI-1* (AT&T, U.S.)	V.35	B
	DMI-2 (AT&T, U.S.)	V.24	B
	T-LINK (NTI, CANADA, U.S.)	V.24, V.35	B
	X.30 (WEST GERMANY, SCANDINAVIA, JAPAN, U.K.)	X.21	B
PACKET SWITCHED	X.31 CIRCUIT MODE	X.25**	B
	X.31 PACKET MODE	X.25**	B,D,H

* EQUIVALENT TO V.110 AT 56KBIT/S.

** ASYNC OR SYNC TERMINALS MAY BE SUPPORTED BY CUSTOMER PREMISES PADs OR A TA WITH INTEGRAL PAD. X.25 INCLUDES PACKET, DATA LINK, AND PHYSICAL LAYERS.

DMI = DIGITAL MULTIPLEXED INTERFACE
ISDN = INTEGRATED SERVICES DIGITAL NETWORK
NTI = NORTHERN TELECOM INC.
PAD = PACKET ASSEMBLER/DISASSEMBLER
TA = TERMINAL ADAPTER

a single 2 B + D interface to the NT1 or NT2. TEs can communicate only with the NT, however, and not with each other, unless the optional NT2 does local switching.

The standards in effect at the various reference points specify how signals flow across the physical interfaces separating the functional blocks. The S and T physical interface (Fig. 1) characteristics are electrically identical: CCITT Standard I.430 for basic-rate access or I.431 for primary-rate access.

(The ANSI T1E1 committee is working on a standard for the primary-rate interface, applicable at reference points S, T, and U, and compatible with existing channel service units [CSUs]. This specification will likely be electrically equivalent to the DS-1 [T1] specification, rather than to the I.431 electrical characteristics.)

Most terminal adapters to date provide the S/T basic-rate access, physical layer interface (I.430). The R interfaces are physical layer interfaces for existing terminals operating under the following standards: V.24/V.28 (RS-232-C/D), V.35, X.21, and X.25 (X.21*bis*).

The U interface, for the basic-rate physical layer on the network side of NT1, facilitates full-duplex transmission over the two-wire digital subscriber loop. A 2B1Q line code (two bits represented by one quaternary symbol) with echo cancellation (EC) has been standardized for use in North America. It is an appendix to CCITT G.961 (I.AB), "Digital System Transmission." 2B1Q EC is also now being considered by Japan and several European countries.

Some TEs and TAs intended for point-to-point operation will incorporate the U interface, so that the single unit will permit direct access to the digital subscriber loop. In that case, the S and T reference points are null and the I.430 interface doesn't exist.

The general terminal adapter configuration is shown in Figure 2. A typical operation would have one TE2 on the left communicate with the TE2 on the right, while a second TE2 on the left communicates with the TE1 on the right. Note that the TE1 and TA must use the same B-channel procedure—such as V.110 or V.120—in order to communicate. Also, the TE1 and TA both support D-channel signaling (Q.931, Q.921) and the S/T interface (I.430). Finally, future TAs may incorporate NT1 functions (U interface), depending on the availability and performance of 2B1Q LSI (large-scale integrated) chips.

TA requirements

The distinguishing functions of ISDN terminal adapters depend on the bearer service—the actual communications capability. Circuit and packet modes require different B-channel protocols, both requiring:
1. adaption from the R-interface rate to a 64-kbit/s B channel or 16-kbit/s D channel (the latter for ISDN packet switching)
2. data format conversion

1. ISDN basics. The reference points are conceptual boundaries that separate the various functional groupings. All reference points need not be physically present.

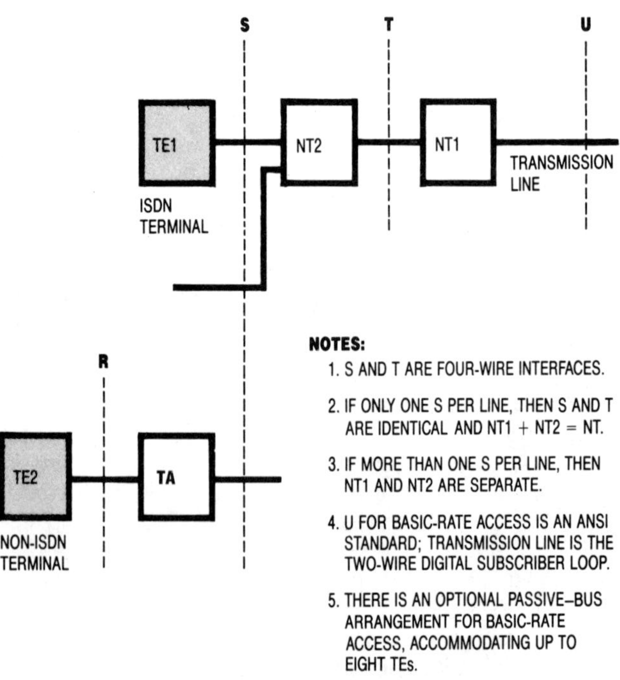

3. D-channel data link and network layer procedures (CCITT Q.921 LAPD [Link Access Procedure D] and Q.931 call control), and

4. control of, and response to, R-interface-lead (V.24) state changes by regulating end-to-end data flows.

There may be one or more R-interface ports per terminal adapter box, with three being typical. An important TA function is to map R-interface in-band signaling (such as the Hayes AT—Attention-Code—command set [Hayes Microcomputer Products, Atlanta, Ga.] or CCITT V.25*bis* autodial) into ISDN D-channel signaling (Q.931 procedures). Alternatively, manual dialing, through a keypad on the TA, is possible.

For circuit-mode ISDN access, a transparent 64-kbit/s (either restricted or unrestricted for ones density) path is available between the two end points, and a compatible rate-adaption procedure must be chosen (transparent means that the switch does not look at the B channels' information content). In Europe, that procedure is likely to be CCITT V.110; in Canada, T-Link; and in the United States, V.120, T-Link, and DMI-2. Each of these procedures (discussed later) has its own frame format, protocol modes, techniques to include R-interface status (such as V.24 leads), error detection, and flow control.

TAs may also support analog phones, facsimile machines, and modems, all via the 3.1-kHz audio bearer service. Some ISDN phones provide a TA function for a V.24 or V.35 port, enabling the connection of a non-ISDN terminal (TE2).

For packet-mode ISDN access, either B- or D-channel packets are available on most ISDNs provided by the local exchange carriers. The TA converts X.25 DTE (data terminal equipment) or asynchronous-terminal transmissions at the R interface to Q.931 messages and X.25 packets at the S/T interface.

There are official (CCITT) and unofficial (DMI and T-Link) TA standards. The three CCITT TA standards are summarized in Table 2 and discussed later.

The three categories of CCITT ISDN TA standards are for:

■ *Circuit-switched service for X.21 DTE:* X.30 (I.461). Only countries with X.21 DTEs (especially West Germany) will support X.30. There are no operational units in the United States, and none are planned. (X.21 is currently supported by West Germany, Japan, and the Scandinavian countries.)

■ *Circuit-switched service for V.24 (asynchronous/synchronous) and V.35 (synchronous) DTE:* V.110 (I.463) and V.120. V.110, based on X.30, will be used in Europe and possibly Japan; V.120, in the United States and Canada.

■ *Packet-switched service:* X.31 case A (circuit mode, B channel), X.31 case B (packet mode, B or D channel). Many European countries will support case A; X.31 case B will be supported in the United States, Canada, and Japan.

De facto standards

The official TA standards, V.110, V.120, and X.31, will be discussed later in this article. The two types of unofficial TA standards, DMI and T-Link, are used extensively by present TAs and therefore deserve consideration.

DMI, the Digital Multiplexed Interface, is AT&T's computer-to-PBX interface. It uses a four-wire, 1.544-Mbit/s (T1) link that contains 23 DS-0s (64 kbit/s each) for data and one DS-0 for signaling. Several computer and PBX manufacturers are using AT&T's DMI over in-house wire or over a T1 link. AT&T's Digital Station sets (attached to the System/75 and System/85 PBXs) and ISDN basic-rate terminals and TAs (75XX) use DMI rate adaption for circuit-switched B channels. Vendors wishing to communicate with those products must also use DMI rate adaption, either on digital station sets attached to their PBXs or in basic-rate terminals and TAs.

DMI-1 is for 56-kbit/s data terminal equipment (DTE). It is compatible with V.110 at that rate. DMI-2 is for V.24 DTE (less than 20 kbit/s). The DMI-2 is based on HDLC (high-level data link control) framing but not HDLC elements of procedure (there is a DMI header instead of the HDLC address and control fields). Since most existing terminals support V.24 (RS-232), DMI-2 is used extensively. DMI-3 is based on LAPD framing and procedures. It will probably

2. Adapting terminals. *The general terminal adapter configuration is shown here. In a typical operation, one TE2 on the left communicates with the TE2 on the right, while a second TE2 on the left communicates with the TE1 on the right. The TE1 and TA must use the same B-channel procedure—such as V.110 or V.120—in order to communicate.*

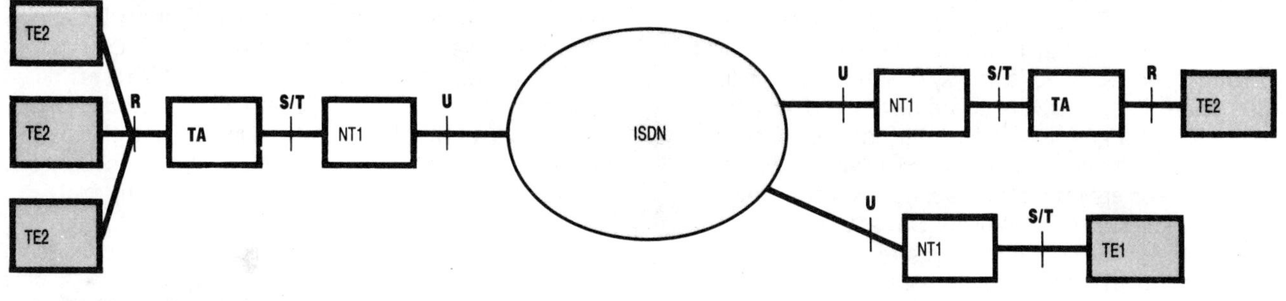

Table 2: Comparison of TA standards

	V.110	V.120	X.31
ISDN BEARER SERVICE	CIRCUIT	CIRCUIT	CIRCUIT/PACKET
RATE ADAPTION	1-3 STEPS	FLAG STUFFING[1]	FLAG STUFFING
MULTIPLE DESTINATIONS	NO	NO	YES
HDLC BASED	NO	YES	YES
B CHANNEL MULTIPLEXING	DEPENDS ON Q.931[2]	YES—LLI	YES—LCN
D CHANNEL OPERATION	NO	NO	YES (CASE B)
ERROR DETECTION	NONE	CRC—V.41	CRC—V.41
ERROR CORRECTION	NONE	RETRANSMISSION	RETRANSMISSION
FLOW CONTROL	LIMITED (X BIT)[3]	YES—WINDOW	YES—WINDOW
CONNECTIONLESS DATA LINK OPERATION	YES	YES (UI FRAME)	NO
TYPE OF DTE/DCEs AT R	ASYNC/SYNC (BIT TRANSPARENT)[4]	ASYNC/HDLC/BIT TRANSPARENT	X.25 SYNC[5]
R STATUS TRANSPORT	S,[6] X BITS	HEADER IN I FIELD (1 OR 2 OCTETS)	PAD FUNCTIONS (LIMITED)
USE OF UARTs, HDLC LSIs	NOT POSSIBLE	YES	YES

1. THE ADDITION OF FLAG CHARACTERS.
2. NOT CURRENTLY SUPPORTED: NEED TERMINAL-TO-SUBRATE CONFIGURATION, MAP, ADDRESSES.
3. UNIDIRECTIONAL: FROM TA TO TE2 BASED ON TA BUFFER THRESHOLDS.
4. ALL INFORMATION AT THE R INTERFACE IS IN THE TA FRAME THAT APPEARS AT THE S/T INTERFACE.
5. TE2 TO TA FLOW CONTROL NOT SPECIFIED.
6. THE S BIT REPRESENTS V.24 LEAD STATUS.

BEARER = INFORMATION-CARRYING
CRC = CYCLIC REDUNDANCY CHECK
DCE = DATA CIRCUIT-TERMINATING EQUIPMENT
DTE = DATA TERMINAL EQUIPMENT
I FIELD = INFORMATION FIELD
LCN = LOGICAL CHANNEL NUMBER
LLI = LOGICAL LINK ID
LSI = LARGE-SCALE INTEGRATION (CHIPS)
PAD = PACKET ASSEMBLER/DISASSEMBLER
TA = TERMINAL ADAPTER
UART = UNIVERSAL ASYNCHRONOUS RECEIVER/TRANSMITTER
UI = UNNUMBERED INFORMATION

migrate to V.120 and frame relay (see "Streamlined packet scheme gathers growing support for future networks," DATA COMMUNICATIONS, July 1988, p. 62).

T-Link is the circuit-mode TA protocol used in Northern Telecom's (NTI's) Datapath (circuit-switched digital network), CPI (Computer-to-PBX Interface), and ISDN terminal products. With Datapath and ISDN devices, T-Link rate-adapts user data onto individual 56- or 64-kbit/s channels for transmission through NTI's digital circuit-switching products (such as the DMS-100 central office switch and the SL-100 PBX). For CPI implementations, T-Link runs on each of the 24 DS-0 channels in a four-wire T1 link.

Datapath and T-Link are currently offered publicly in the United States in the RBOC's public switched digital networks (PSDNs) and digital Centrex services (such as BellSouth's AccuPulse and Nynex's Switchway 56). Also, private-T-Link users include: McDonnell Douglas, Trans-America, University of California at Davis, University of Michigan, Merrill Lynch, and Anheuser-Busch.

According to NTI, there are more than 1,500 DMS-100s installed in the United States; Datapath software has been ordered for more than 800 of them. T-Link coverage can be extended beyond these DMS offices through the use of Datapath channel units installed on D4 channel banks in other central offices or on DMS remotes. (A D4 channel bank converts analog signals to T1 via a channel unit.)

Several TA vendors, including Harris Dracon and Racal-Milgo, are supporting T-Link (Fig. 3) for ISDN applications on Pacific Northwest Bell, Southern Bell, and Bell Canada networks, as well as for interworking with existing Datapath Switched 56 services.

NTI's strategy is based on the premise that multiple rate-adaption protocols already exist and will continue to do so for several years. In order to facilitate interworking between ISDN and existing services (such as Datapath), NTI is encouraging TA vendors to support T-Link as well as CCITT Recommendations V.110 or V.120. If NTI is successful, multiprotocol TAs and IWUs will become available. (An IWU is an interworking unit—a device that carries circuit-mode data and converts between ISDN and non-ISDN, such as Datapath and the PSTN [public switched telephone network].)

NTI has publicly disclosed T-Link through Bellcore document TR-EOP-000277, entitled "Datapath Network Access Interface Specification." In addition, NTI has recently established a Datapath/T-Link licensing program for CPE (customer premises equipment) vendors and has jointly developed a T-Link chip with Intel (see "The TA marketplace").

3. Vendor version. *Northern Telecom's T-Link, in this ISDN configuration, is the circuit-mode TA protocol in the company's Datapath (circuit-switched digital network), CPI (Computer-to-PBX Interface), and ISDN terminal products. With Datapath and ISDN devices, T-Link rate-adapts user data onto individual 56- or 64-kbit/s channels.*

DATAPATH/ISDN INTERWORKING (SINGLE SWITCH) USING T-LINK

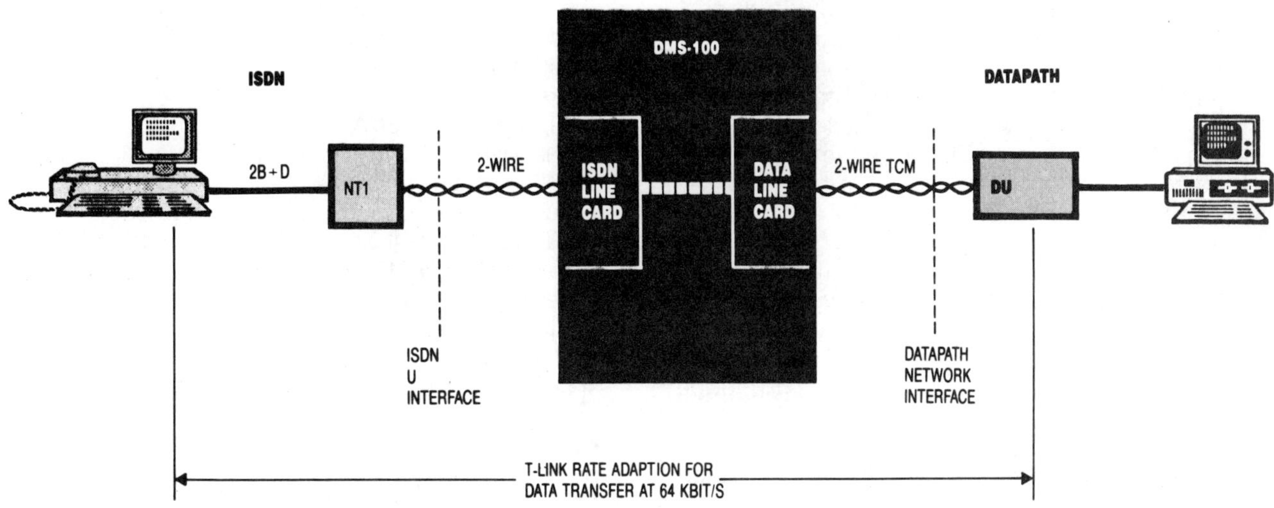

V.110 was created primarily in Europe and is well accepted there. IBM has developed a V.110 TA (its 7820) for West Germany, France, and the United Kingdom. Recently, IBM added call-control support in the 7820 for AT&T's 5ESS and NTI's DMS-100.

European circuit switching

The 1984 CCITT version of V.110 was only for synchronous V.24 or V.35 terminals and did not provide for ISDN-to-PSTN internetworking. The 1988 V.110 adds capabilities to support the following: asynchronous V.24 terminals, a network-independent clock (to interwork with synchronous PSTN modems or with other synchronous networks where the DCE [data circuit-terminating equipment] must be the timing master), and an optional in-band parameter-exchange procedure (when out-of-band call control is not available end-to-end). These additional capabilities came from ECMA 102, the European Computer Manufacturers Association standard for rate adaption.

The V.110 rate-adaption (RA) technique is based on X.30 (I.461) and I.460. Those standards involve subrate multiplexing of a B channel via intermediate rates of 8, 16, and 32 kbit/s. There are one to three V.110 RA steps, depending on the terminal's speed and whether it is synchronous or asynchronous.

■ Synchronous 48- and 56-kbit/s terminals are directly adapted to 64 kbit/s, using 32- and 64-bit frames, respectively. The overhead bits in those frames create a 64-kbit/s bit stream.

Synchronous rates of 600 bit/s, 2.4, 4.8, 9.6, 14.4, and 19.2 kbit/s use two-stage rate adaption (Fig. 4):

■ RA1: Bit repetition to create an 80-bit frame at an intermediate rate of 8, 16, or 32 kbit/s. There is a 17-bit frame-alignment pattern required for synchronization of the 80-bit frame. RA1 is based on I.461 (X.30).
■ RA2: Bit positioning of one, two, or four bits for every eight bits at 64 kbit/s corresponding to intermediate rates of 8, 16, or 32 kbit/s, respectively. This is specified in I.460.

Async rates to 14.4 kbit/s use three-step rate adaption (Fig. 4):

■ RA "zero" (first step) is based on V.22 asynchronous/synchronous conversion. It produces a bit stream defined by $2^n \times 600$ (where n = 0 to 5). Specifically, stop-bit padding is employed for rates of: 50, 75, 110, 150, 200, 300 to 600 bit/s, and 3.6 to 4.8, 7.2 to 9.6, 12, and 14.4 to 19.2 kbit/s (these are the standard rates that are input to RA1). Start, stop, and parity (if any) bits are included with each data character in the bit stream.
■ RA1: (same as previous RA1) for rates of 600 bit/s, 2.4, 4.8, 9.6, and 19.2 kbit/s.
■ RA2: (same as previous RA2)

There is also underspeed/overspeed detection (as per V.22), which requires manipulation of stop bit(s) in the V.110 frame. This is for asynchronous clocking irregularities.

The 80-bit V.110 frame contains a 17-bit frame-alignment pattern, user data (with bit repetition due to rate differences), three bits identifying the terminal's data rate, three bits for clock synchronization adjustment, four "snapshots" of V.24 leads DTR/DSR (data terminal ready/data set ready), two snapshots of RTS/RLSD (request to send/received line signal [or carrier] detector), and two snap-

The TA marketplace

For the next two or three years, the majority of North American terminal adapters and TE1s will need to include DMI and/or T-Link rate adaption. When IBM announces V.120 products, or Bellcore provides specifications for a V.120 internetworking unit between ISDN and PSTN, implementation of the V.120 standard will also be necessary in customer premises equipment.

The ISDN terminal adapter market will prosper at least until the mid-1990s, when ISDN interfaces and interoperability should begin to be built into more and more data and telecommunications devices. In the interim, TAs will be essential to fill the transition-to-ISDN void. Specifically:

■ The existing population of terminals, workstations, and PCs need access to an ISDN for data services; they certainly will not be readily discarded and quickly replaced by ISDN terminals.

■ Network-supplied interworking units (IWUs) will provide circuit-switched TA connections between a PSTN (public switched telephone network) and an ISDN. This will enable synchronous and asynchronous PSTN-attached terminals and PCs to access ISDN hosts and PCs through TA plug-in cards.

■ The same companies as are making ISDN voice/data terminals (NTI, AT&T, Siemens, NEC, Fujitsu) are also making TAs in order to offer their customers a complete ISDN solution. A TA with a digital phone is compatible with an ISDN centrex service.

■ Computer manufacturers are not in a hurry to build ISDN interfaces for their products. Instead, they are concentrating on the older standards—OSI, SNA, and TCP/IP applications—for wide area and local area networks. As a result, ISDN "server" TAs will be needed for computers to access an ISDN.

■ Traditional modem-and-multiplexer companies (such as Codex, Hayes, Milgo, General DataComm, Microcom, and Timeplex) will offer TAs to protect their installed customer base. Meanwhile, ISDN will begin to erode the modem and multiplexer markets in the 1990-92 time frame.

Functional types. TA products are likely to be divided into low, medium, and high functionality. A representative sample follows:

■ A TA circuit card for an IBM PC with B-channel circuit-switched voice/data, B-channel packet data, and D-channel packet data. Optionally, this product could also digitize voice (pulse-code modulation) for one B channel.

■ A TA standalone "box" for asynchronous terminals, PCs, and hosts. ISDN circuit- and packet-switching services will be supported for data at rates up to 19.2 kbit/s. An important feature: Several terminals can share an ISDN B channel, depending on the TA procedure. A packet assembly/disassembly (X.3, X.28, X.29) function will be required for packet-mode attachment of asynchronous ASCII terminals.

■ A TA box for X.25 DTE. This requires support of X.31 for B- and D-channel packet data. An important feature: virtual-circuit concentration, where several X.25 DTE devices share a B channel.

■ A TA box for X.21 DTEs. This requires support of X.30 and ISDN circuit switching. West Germany, Japan, the Scandinavian countries, and the United Kingdom are the only ones known to have X.21 DTE attached to public networks.

■ A TA box for IBM SNA terminals and cluster controllers. This is a family of products. V.120 will be used for circuit-switched (B-channel) rate adaption; X.31 for packet switching in controller-to-host communications. A 3270-to-ISDN coaxial multiplexer will connect remote 327X terminals to a 3274/3174 controller via circuit-mode ISDN access. (AT&T's 3270 Data Modules do this now.)

■ A TA circuit card or box within a PSTN-ISDN IWU, which includes a modem pool. Bellcore plans to specify IWU standards for the RBOCs, which will include V.120 terminal adaption.

■ A TA circuit card or box for a PBX, computer, front-end processor, or T1 multiplexer using the ISDN primary rate. DMI-2 or T-Link is likely to be used for DMI and CPI, respectively. V.120 will be used for rate-adapting IBM products. R-interface ports will include V.24, V.28, V.35, X.21, and X.25.

TA products are already available from AT&T (the dominant vendor today—see table), Harris, Fujitsu, NEC, Infotron, and Hayes, among others.

AT&T ISDN terminal adapters

TERMINAL ADAPTER	R INTERFACE	BRI CHANNEL AND PROTOCOL CAPABILITIES
7505, 7506, AND 7507 TELEPHONES WITH DATA OPTION	EIA-232-D DCE 0.3-19.2 KBIT/S 1 PORT, ASYNCH	D CHANNEL, X.25 B CHANNEL, DMI MODE 2 B CHANNEL, DMI MODE 3
7500 DATA MODULE (BASIC)	EIA-232-D DCE OR DTE 0.3-19.2 KBIT/S 1 PORT, ASYNCH	D CHANNEL, X.25 B CHANNEL, DMI MODE 2 B CHANNEL, DMI MODE 3
7500 DATA MODULE (DUAL PORT)	EIA-232-D DCE 0.3-19.2 KBIT/S 2 PORTS, ASYNCH	D CHANNEL, X.25 B CHANNEL, DMI MODE 2 B CHANNEL, DMI MODE 3
7500 DATA MODULE (SYNCH RS232)	EIA-232-D DCE 0.3-64 KBIT/S 1 PORT, SYNCHRONOUS	B CHANNEL, DMI MODE 2 B CHANNEL, DMI MODE 1 B CHANNEL, DMI MODE 0
7500 DATA MODULE (SYNCH V.35)	CCITT V.35 DCE 48-64 KBIT/S 1 PORT, SYNCHRONOUS	B CHANNEL, V.110 B CHANNEL, DMI MODE 1 B CHANNEL, DMI MODE 0
3270 DATA MODULE (MODELS T AND C)	CATEGORY A COAX 2.358 MBIT/S, 1 PORT (T); UP TO 8 PORTS (C)	B CHANNEL, PROPRIETARY

DMI MODE 0: 64 KBIT/S
      1: 56 KBIT/S
      2: HDLC FRAMED
      3: LAPD-BASED

BRI = BASIC-RATE INTERFACE
DCI = DATA CIRCUIT-TERMINATING EQUIPMENT
DMI = DIGITAL MULTIPLEXED INTERFACE
DTE = DATA TERMINAL EQUIPMENT

4. Adapting rates. *There are one to three ISDN V.110 (I.463) rate-adaption steps, depending on the terminal's speed and whether it is synchronous or asynchronous.*

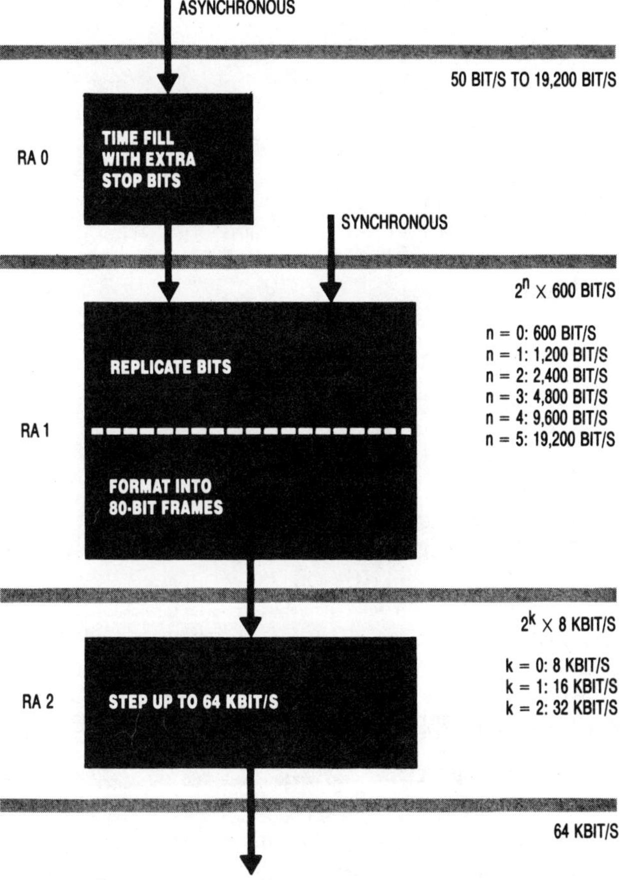

shots of a shared-function X bit: clear-to-send/asynchronous flow control/loss of frame synchronization. (A snapshot is the status at a moment in time. It occurs four times in a frame as a result of the interrogation of a modem pin.)

The clock-adjustment bits are for a network-independent clock, which is needed to work with synchronous PSTN modems or other synchronous DCE that must be timing masters. In the case of a network-independent clock, the ISDN S/T interface timing cannot be used by the TA and therefore must be adjusted to that of the external DCE timing source.

V.110 is a physical layer procedure that lends itself to "bit-engine" (bit level rather than byte level) processing. Its disadvantages include:

■ the lack of error detection on the V.110 frame;
■ a complex frame-alignment procedure when the intermediate rate is not known;

■ difficulty in detecting a change in data rates that alters the intermediate rate (such as when a PSTN modem's data rate "falls" back/"falls" forward);
■ no procedure in companion standards (Q.931 or I.515) for subrate multiplexing of a B channel; and
■ an incomplete specification for flow control (the TA is not required to look in-band for an X-off or X-on character).

Finally, commercially available UARTs (universal asynchronous receiver/transmitters) for the R interface and USRTs (universal synchronous receiver/transmitters) for the S/T interface cannot be used because of the rigid bit-alignment requirements for V.24 leads with data leads at the R interface and the complex frame-alignment pattern at the S/T interface. Siemens, Mitel, and SGS-Thomson (an Italian-French joint venture) plan to produce V.110 LSI devices.

Domestic circuit switching

V.120 was originated in the United States by the Exchange Carriers Standards Association (ECSA) T1D1 committee (now T1S1 and T1E1). It is based on the use of LAPD framing and procedures, with flag-stuffing rate adaption for 64-kbit/s B channels. Unlike V.110, V.120 may also be used on H0 (384 kbit/s), H11 (1.536 Mbit/s), and H12 (1.920 Mbit/s) channels. (The H channels are formed out of multiple B channels for a primary-rate interface.)

Using a LAPD-based protocol preserves the equipment vendor's investment in hardware and software and offers additional features for terminal adaption. These features include: error detection, error correction (via retransmission), flow control, and statistical multiplexing of terminal data streams onto one B channel.

The statistical multiplexing capability makes efficient use of the 64-kbit/s B-channel bandwidth when multiple terminals or PCs with "windows" (partitioned screen) desire access to the same host computer. It is ideal in a multiplexer or cluster-controller environment, such as 3270. The multiplexer ports can be identified by a subaddress in the Setup message (to be discussed).

Figure 5 shows three different types of V.120 TEs connected to an ISDN. TE1 is in native mode (directly supports ISDN) and is typically a terminal or computer accommodating multiple sessions. The single TE2 is a non-ISDN device, accessing the ISDN through a TA. This TE2 could be a terminal or a PC with windows. If the latter, it would generate multiple data streams, typically two to four.

Each of the paired TE2s is either an ISDN multiplexer or an ISDN cluster controller. Each TE communicates with each of the other TEs through the ISDN switch.

The V.120 frame is consistent with HDLC and LAPD and consists of flag, address (two octets), control (one or two octets), information (zero to n octets), frame-check sequence or FCS (two octets), and flag. (The unnumbered frames have a one-octet control field. The information field's first two octets optionally contain a V.120 header carrying the R-interface status.)

V.120 does require protocol-processing software. But existing HDLC formatter LSIs can be used for the hardware implementation.

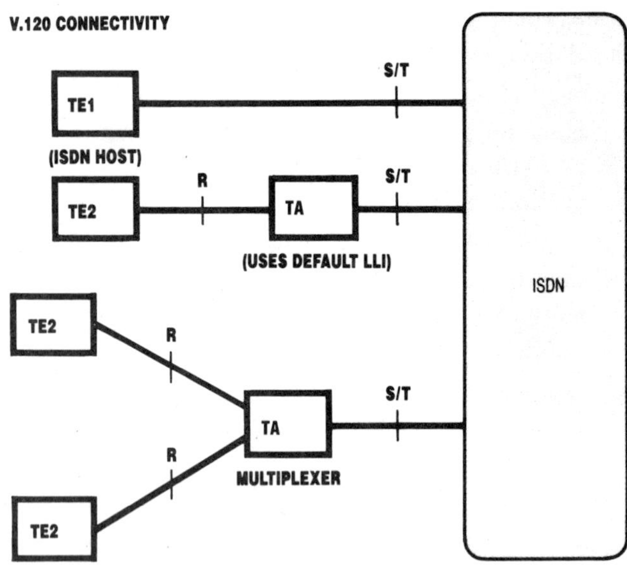

5. Terminal equipment. *Shown are three types of V.120 TE connections. Each TE communicates with each of the other TEs through an ISDN circuit-mode connection.*

There are three R-interface terminal types possible in V.120:

1. asynchronous protocol sensitive
2. HDLC protocol sensitive, and
3. bit transparent.

The TA monitors the status of the R-interface data stream and, for the first two terminal types, passes it along in the V.120 header.

With the bit transparent, the status is just encapsulated. An example of the latter is in automated teller machines. The bit-transparent mode can also be used to encapsulate synchronous character-oriented data streams, such as bisync. Each supported terminal requires a logical link, identified by a 13-bit, logical-link ID (LLI) address value (256 to 2,047) in the V.120 address field.

LLI management is a network layer procedure, which includes creation, setup, collision resolution, and clearing of logical links sharing the circuit-mode connection. The procedure is by a TA-to-TA exchange of four Q.931-like messages: Setup, Connect, Release, Release Complete.

These messages are carried in a B channel (V.120 Information frame with LLI = 0) or in a D channel (Q.931 User-to-User Information message, if provided by the network).

There is also a default LLI = 256, which eliminates the LLI management procedure and thereby simplifies V.120 implementation for rate adapting a single non-ISDN terminal. In that case, R-interface parameters may be exchanged by the Q.931 lower-layer compatibility-element XID frame, or they could be known in advance. (The

XID—or exchange station ID—is an HDLC frame.)

V.120 is strongly supported by IBM, Bellcore, the RBOCs, and AT&T. IBM believes V.120 is the most advantageous way of carrying SNA-SDLC (Systems Network Architecture-Synchronous Data Link Control) terminal data streams on an ISDN circuit-mode connection. 3270 SNA cluster controllers and PCs with windows are ideal for the V.120 environment. Bellcore plans to specify a V.120-based IWU for ISDN-PSTN circuit-switched data calls.

AT&T, Bellcore, and the RBOCs want to standardize TAs and IWUs in public networks, basing them on LAPD for consistent implementations. Since both V.120 and frame relay are based on LAPD with virtual-circuit multiplexing, AT&T, IBM, and NTI view V.120 as a stepping stone to a frame-relay packet service. CCITT Study Group (SG) XVIII, T1S1, and T1E1 have expressed support for the enhancement of V.120 for frame-relay applications. This topic will be taken up by SGXVII in the next study period—1989 to 1992.

Computer companies such as IBM, NCR Comten, Harris, ICL North America (Stamford, Conn.), Teleos (Eatontown, N. J.), and Wang have shown interest in implementing V.120. AT&T and Bellcore have been very active in the standards effort. We can safely assume that V.120 will be extremely popular in the United States.

Switching packets

CCITT X.31 is the standard governing ISDN packet switching for TE1 and X.25 DTE (see "How packet-mode transmission services will evolve in ISDN," DATA COMMUNICATIONS, April 1988, p. 201). X.31 functions include rate adaption to an ISDN channel (B, D, or H) and coordination between X.25 and Q.931 call-control procedures. Service descriptions for ISDN packet switching are also included in X.31.

There are two versions of X.31: case A, or circuit mode (formerly, minimum integration scenario); and case B, or packet mode (formerly, maximum integration scenario). Both versions use X.25 packet layer protocol (PLP) on the bearer channels and include extensions to Q.931 for packet data calls.

In X.31 case A, the packet switching is done by a packet handler in an external packet network. The ISDN provides only a circuit-switching service and only B-channel packet switching is available. A circuit-switched call to an external access unit (the packet handler) is set up using Q.931 procedures. X.25 PLP is then used on top of X.25 LAPB (Link Access Procedure-Balanced) on the B channel. Rate adaption to 64 kbit/s is via flag stuffing or, optionally, via X.30 (I.461). The latter would only be useful when interworking with digital transmission networks utilizing subrate trunks (8, 16, 32 kbit/s)—a capability that has not yet been implemented.

In X.31 case B, the ISDN offers integral packet switching; there is a packet handler in the ISDN. The ISDN service provided is packet mode, and both B-channel and D-channel packet switching are available from the ISDN packet handler. X.25 PLP is used on top of LAPB (B channel) or LAPD (D channel). Rate adaption to 64 kbit/s (B) or 16 kbit/s (D) is via flag stuffing. D-channel packet switching is particularly attractive for ISDN basic-rate access (see "The D-channel packet TA"), since it provides the user with a data transport service in addition to call control. Packet switching on the D channel may be used concurrently with circuit-switched B-channel calls, thereby increasing the throughput of the basic-rate interface.

There is no recommendation governing PAD (packet assembler/disassembler) service on an ISDN. The support of asynchronous access by or through an ISDN is not within the scope of X.31.

However, packet-network PADs can be accessed by an X.31 TE1/TA via X.25 PLP procedures and the appropriate PAD protocol (X.29). X.31 TAs with async terminals attached will provide the PAD function. Alternatively, a self-contained PAD could connect to an X.31 TA at reference point R, appearing as an X.25 DTE. This would be required to interface many asynchronous terminals (eight or more) to an ISDN packet service. Finally, SNA-SDLC cluster controllers could be connected to an X.31 TA with integral SNA PAD for ISDN packet access.

At the host site, an X.31 TA could interface to an IBM 37X5 front-end processor that has a Network Packet-Switching Interface installed. The 37X5 appears as an X.25 DTE to the TA.

Telling the difference

Given the multiplicity of TA procedures, how does a TA/TE1 distinguish between them for a circuit-switched call?

The Q.931 "Lower Layer Compatibility" element in the Setup or Connect message can be used when out-of-band signaling is available end-to-end (single ISDN or ISDN-to-ISDN). Code points have already been reserved for the X.31, V.110, and V.120 terminal-adaption standards.

Otherwise, when the ISDN call is to or from a PSTN, or Circuit-Switched Digital Network (such as switched 56/64 kbit/s), and out-of-band signaling is not available end to end, there are three alternatives:

1. Always know the rate-adaption procedure prior to call setup. Hang up when the TA/TE1 does not recognize the framing pattern.

2. Use "self-identification" in a multiprotocol TA to determine the rate-adaption procedure based on the framing pattern or initialization sequence. This method consists of multiple single-protocol rate-adaption devices bridged together on a B channel, with a logical summing of the "can't identify" indications of the individual components (based on uniquely identifying the framing pattern). If no device can identify the framing pattern, the call is cleared (the TE/TAs are incompatible with each other). Otherwise, the device that has identified the framing pattern is connected to the B channel. This implementation would typically be used by a multiprotocol-host TA, accepting calls from a variety of remote TEs and TAs.

One problem with this method is when a multiprotocol TA calls a single-protocol TA. If an incompatible rate-adaption protocol is chosen initially, several time-outs and, possibly, several call attempts might be required before a

The D-channel packet TA

In the United States, RBOC-provided ISDNs will emphasize D-channel packet switching, for several reasons:

- It enables RBOCs (regional Bell operating companies) to include their packet networks (available, but for the most part not tariffed) in an ISDN (Integrated Services Digital Network). They would then get revenue from a packet-switching service, besides offering a more comprehensive network.

- It makes ISDN centrex (local RBOC-provided voice/data networking) much more versatile—instead of handling only circuit-switched calls, the ISDN centrex can simultaneously handle packet-switched calls. In many cases, this added functionality will forestall PBX purchases or private-network bypass. For example, a local host computer can be accessed by terminals/TAs through D-channel packet procedures. This configuration could substitute for a local area network or a data PBX.

- In passive-bus (multipoint) installations, the B channels will be in great demand for voice and file transfer applications, leaving only the D channel available for lower-speed (up to 19.2-kbit/s) data.

- Packet access at 16 kbit/s can be adequately handled by most ISDN packet switches and terminal equipment. Northern Telecom's DMS-100 supports up to six D-channel packet TEs along with two B-channel TEs. Alternatively, up to eight D-channel TEs can be accommodated if the B channels are not used.

- D-channel packet switching is easier to implement in TE (terminal equipment) than is B-channel packet switching, resulting in lower-cost equipment.

Because of the RBOCs' ISDN-inspired, D-channel packet-switching emphasis, most TA vendors plan to provide D-channel packet switching for products sold in the United States. Some TAs may also provide B-channel packet access. X.31 TAs generally interface to one X.25 data terminal equipment or to one or two asynchronous terminals. In the latter case, they also provide a packet assembly/disassembly (X.3, X.28, X.29) function. It is envisioned that future TAs will accommodate up to 8, 16, or 32 asynchronous terminals with integral PAD and X.31 capability. This would provide the equivalent connectivity of today's PADs.

match occurs. Another potential difficulty is when two multiprotocol TAs are connected and each attempts a different sequence of rate-adaption procedures.

The TAs could oscillate between procedures, even though one or more procedures could be common to both. The call would eventually be cleared due to repeated time-outs, without any information having been exchanged. For these reasons, it is recommended to start with V.120 and proceed through a prioritized sequence of rate-adaption procedures.

3. Use the in-band Protocol Identifier (PID) sequence,

6. Internetworking. *When an ISDN interfaces with the public switched telephone network, the interworking unit (IWU) handles all call control with the terminal adapter. An in-band rate-adaption technique may be necessary, depending on the ability of the IWU's internetworking functions to handle out-of-band signaling.*

ISDN-PSTN DATA INTERNETWORKING (V.120)

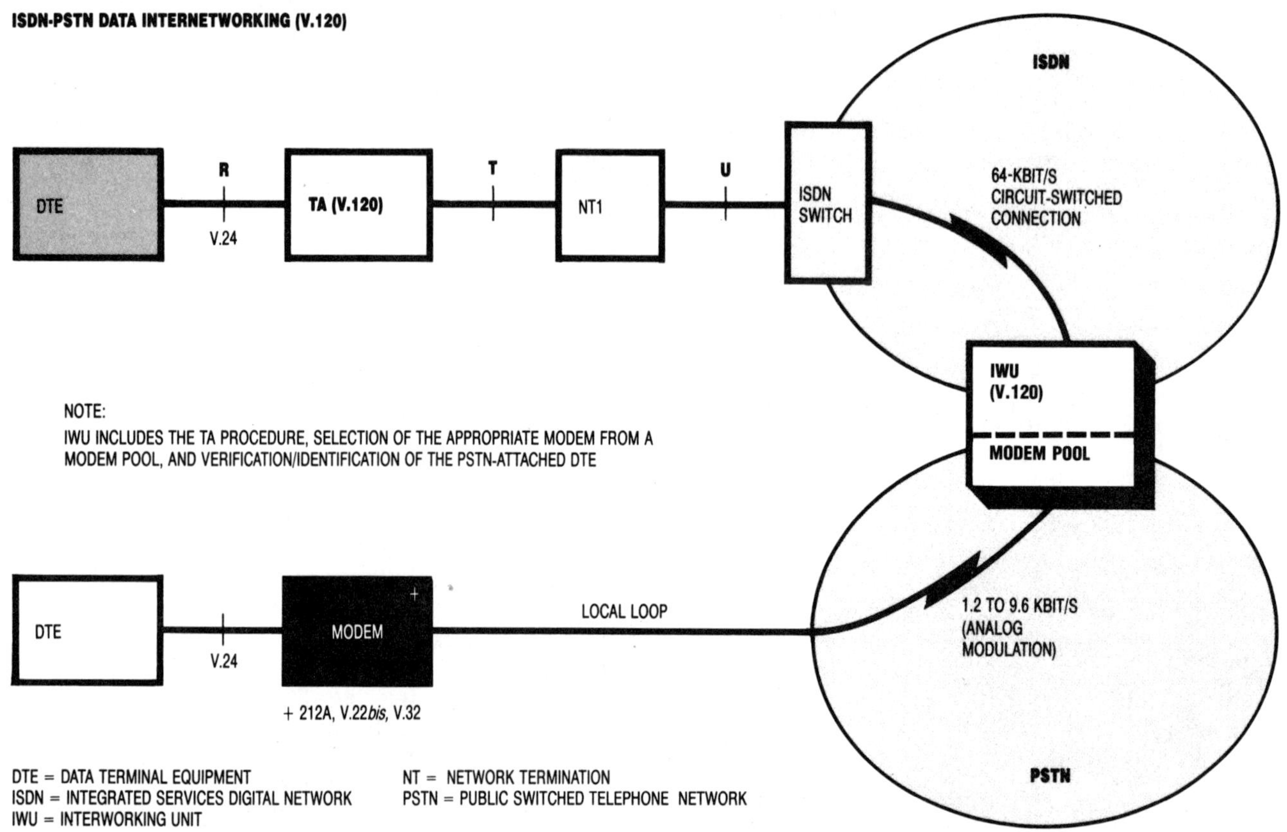

which precedes the rate-adaption frame-alignment pattern. The PID involves the successful exchange of two different synchronization bytes (transmitted and detected 32 times), followed by a PID byte pair (transmitted three times and detected at least twice). Eight bits of the PID byte pair identify which rate-adaption protocol(s) can be supported by the calling TA. The called TA sets only the bit position, corresponding to the rate-adaption protocol to be used, in the returned PID byte pair (also transmitted three times).

If none of the indicated rate-adaption protocols can be supported, a null byte pair is returned, and the call may be cleared. If the PID is not supported (such as by existing single-protocol TAs), a timer will expire and one or more default rate-adaption protocols may be tried before clearing the call.

While the PID requires additional software, and a transparent "escape" mode (escape from the framing-pattern search) on LSI rate-adaption devices, it does explicitly identify which rate-adaption procedure is to be used for each circuit-switched call. An added benefit is the identification of nonstandard rate-adaption procedures (T-Link and DMI-2).

Methods 2 and 3 are appendices to CCITT I.515— Parameters for ISDN Interworking. AT&T prefers the former,

while NTI advocates the latter method for rate-adaption identification. The choice between them must be made by the implementer, based on the functionality desired in the TA products.

Figure 6 illustrates ISDN-PSTN internetworking, where an in-band rate-adaption technique may be necessary, depending on the ability of the IWU's internetworking functions to handle out-of-band signaling. When the capability is in the PSTN, the identification of rate-adaption method must be done in-band.

In ISDN-PSTN internetworking, the IWU handles all call control with the TA. Currently, there is no standard that maps R-interface autocalling with Q.931, V.110, or V.120 procedures. This mapping is presently left up to the implementer. ∎

Alan J. Weissberger is an independent consultant specializing in the implementation of telecommunications standards, technology assessment, and technical market research. He is a participating member of the ECSA T1S1, T1E1, and T1M1 ISDN standards committees and a senior member of the IEEE. He holds an Sc.D. from MIT and an M.S.E.E. from Northeastern University. Weissberger wishes to thank Larry Smith of AT&T and Ed Juskevicius of Bell Northern Research for their valuable contributions to this article.

Lee Mantelman, DATA COMMUNICATIONS INTERNATIONAL

OSI on PCs: Bringing the world to the desktop

As European researchers bring full open standards to microcomputers, vendors in several countries come to market with the first products.

You can call anyone who has a telephone, anywhere in the world, and exchange any kind of audible information. Wouldn't it be great to be able to do the same with the microcomputer?

Corporate network managers have long heard how Open Systems Interconnection (OSI), the suite of protocols put forth by the International Organization for Standardization (ISO), was supposed to allow computers to interwork as easily as telephones. But evidence of this promise has been conspicuously absent—until very recently.

The promise of OSI generated much of its following while network managers were puzzling over how to link their large computers. Since then, however, lots and lots of little ones began sprouting up all over—and users started linking them in all sorts of ways.

Tower of Babel, part 2

Now, OSI is also seen as a way out of the micro mess. While products to put the lower OSI layers (such as X.25, which encompasses the bottom three OSI layers) onto personal computers have been available for years (see "PAD power at the PC: Adding zip to the packet-switching network," DATA COMMUNICATIONS, October 1988, p. 64), only recently have upper-layer protocols matured enough to begin applying them on the PC level.

Most would agree that it makes sense to combine universal computing with universal communications. And this is not just a utopian ideal: Even IBM implicitly endorsed the concept by building OSI into its Systems Application Architecture, for which a key platform is the Personal System/2.

Users, in fact, may soon be demanding full-suite OSI on PCs—this the result of the spreading popularity of the X.400 electronic messaging protocol. Consultants at London-based Ovum Ltd. forecast that, in the United States,

the United Kingdom, France, and Germany, over a half-million personal computers and 150,000 larger machines will be using X.400 to communicate with each other by 1994 (as opposed to a mere 500 computers at the end of 1988).

Though these are still early days for OSI-on-a-PC (or OSI PC, for short), several parallel efforts are under way around the world to fatten the modest micros with software based on ISO's rich seven-layer cake. These include:
- Three European Community   backed research projects;
- U. S.-based vendors Retix and Touch Communications Inc.;
- British Telecom (BT), both on its own and in collaboration with Provo, Utah-based Novell Inc.;
- A France Telecom subsidiary, in collaboration with 3Com Corp. of Santa Clara, Calif.;
- One vendor in Australia, and another in London, who are teamed with Banyan Systems Inc. (Westborough, Mass.);
- Wheathampstead, England-based NET-TEL Computer Systems Ltd.;
- The Canadian vendor Sydney Development Corp.; and
- Japan's Oki Electronic Industry Co. Ltd.

Early prototypes

Compared to the stagnation of only a few years ago, the OSI PC scene is now bursting with activity. The first highly visible effort to marry OSI software with microcomputer hardware was the Carlos (Communication Architecture for Layered Open Systems) project.

Carlos, an Esprit (European Strategic Program for R&D in Information Technology) program, was designed to result in "precompetitive" working prototypes, which European vendors could then take to the product stage. The program was carried out by a consortium consisting of a number of Danish companies, including main contractor RC Computer A/S, project manager Fischer & Lorenz A/S (an OSI consulting firm), software house Sysware ApS, and the U. K.'s Case Communications Ltd.

According to David Brown, director of research at Case, "It was decided to implement OSI on two different sets of hardware, a PC and a plug-in card on a packet switch." These different configurations reflected a pair of attitudes about the distribution of OSI code. Some researchers felt that "it seemed very heavy-handed to have the full seven-layer stack in a PC, with every stack repeated over and over in every PC," says Brown. "We thought some economies and performance could be gained by pulling portions out and centralizing them."

To that end, the researchers developed three types of network nodes: an OSI PAD with Layers 6 and 7; an OSI Box with Layers 1 through 5; and an extended (but non-switching) PAD with all the layers. The OSI PAD was to be aimed at users, while the OSI Box would have been geared toward public network carriers.

"Back in the early 1980s, we thought of Layer 5 as a potential public service, like X.25 is today," explains Poul Mølgaard, department manager for RC Computer, "but there's not been any trend toward bringing in such a service."

More germane, another set of Carlos researchers set out to build an OSI PC. In fact, three types of OSI PC were envisioned: one with all the OSI layers, which would be able to talk directly to an X.25 network; one containing Layers 6 and 7, to talk to the OSI Box; and a middle-layer version acting as a LAN server for the upper-layer versions.

Since the Carlos project was completed last year, the participants have begun to develop products based on it. One, an RC product called the OSI-Board (not yet available), will provide user and application interfaces to the same OSI protocols as Carlos, namely File Transfer, Access, and Management (FTAM) and Virtual Terminal (VT). RC cut the OSI stack somewhere in the middle of the seventh layer, so 6 1/2 layers are on the board and the rest of the application layer runs in PC/AT software.

Of course, OSI on a PC is only useful if there is OSI on the destination computer — unlikely in the case of VT (see "Is VT sputtering?").

Iberian nap

The OSI PC was implemented on an RC-manufactured personal computer. Because it had to be multi-tasking, the OSI software ran under Digital Research's Concurrent DOS. The trouble was that running all seven layers on the PC itself left too little memory and processor capacity to run any applications.

There were two alternatives to the Carlos OSI PC scheme, each pursued in a separate follow-on project. In Cactus (Carlos Addition for Clustered Terminal User Agents), the bulk of the OSI code would run on a Unix workstation separate from the PC. For Sesta (Standard Esprit System Transfer Adaptor), "we're basically dumping Carlos onto a board," says Mølgaard. In both projects, however, VT would be eclipsed by the X.400 messaging standard.

The Sesta team, comprising Fischer & Lorenz, RC Computer, and a Portuguese company called INESC (set up by several Portuguese universities and the Portuguese PTT), set out to migrate the Carlos OSI software onto a PC/AT (or compatible) board. (Sesta means "siesta" in Portuguese.)

While Sesta was intended to free up the PC's processor and memory for applications, it was also seen as a way to quicken the OSI software. The researchers have no exact performance figures yet but plan to test the board later. Still, they're aiming more for versatility than for speed.

"Following standards is not always the most efficient way to do things," says Mølgaard. "You could always implement a more efficient system if you know who you're going to talk to. OSI is not better or quicker in that sense. Openness — the multivendor aspect — is the real advantage," he says.

One key development in Sesta is the implementation of an X.400 User Agent, or UA (Fig. 1). Layers 1 through 5 on

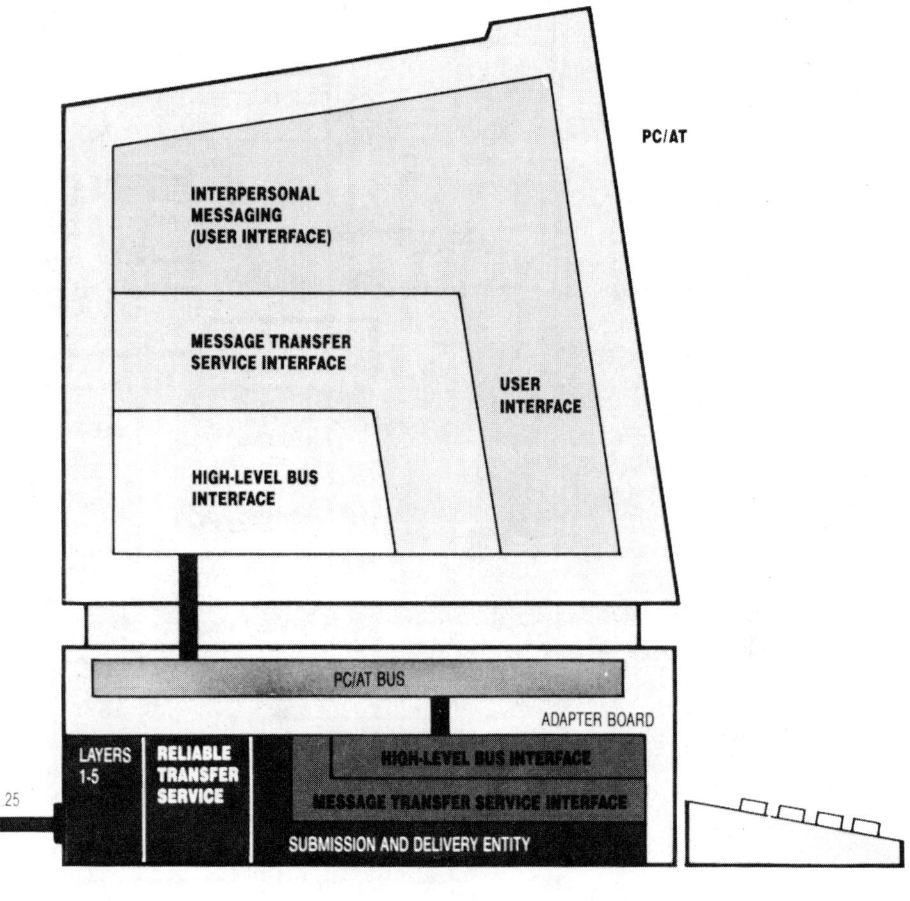

1. Sesta la vie. *The Sesta project puts all seven layers (except for the X.400 user interface module) on a board in the PC. The high-level bus and the message transfer service interfaces link the board with the PC-resident software by running in both locations.*

the adapter board make the OSI session-layer service available for the Reliable Transfer Service (RTS), which provides checkpointing, session recovery, and the reliable transport of Application Protocol Data Units. The Submission and Delivery Entity handles the X.400 P3 (Submission and Delivery) and Remote Operation Service protocols, as well as the encoding and decoding of the P2 (Interpersonal Messaging) protocol.

All these modules, like the Interpersonal Messaging (IPM) module (which handles the menu-driven user interface), are standard X.400 and OSI components. Specific to Sesta are the Message Transfer Service Interface and the High-Level Bus Interface, which join the IPM with the rest of the OSI stack.

Several vendors (including Retix and BT) have beaten the Sesta team to the market with OSI boards. Others are doubtless on the horizon or perhaps already available. But the point of Sesta was not to corner the market, or even to be the first one there. According to Mølgaard, it was to "be out early enough to get a reasonable market share. It is important to release just in time—neither too early nor too late. The Sesta project is expected to be completed in June, while the UA development is planned to finish by the end of the year.

Desert bloom

The other extension of Carlos, called Cactus, involves the development of a clustered UA to give PCs easier access to X.400. The project involves two additional partners, the Universidad Politecnica de Madrid and the Universidad Politecnica de Catalunia, in Barcelona.

While Sesta aims to devise precompetitive prototypes, "the Cactus team will say, 'here's the software, if you want to come and have an almost-free license, you're welcome to it,'" says Erik Lorenz Petersen, director of Fischer & Lorenz.

Cactus's claim to fame is that it is an implementation of the 1988 version of X.400. In the version completed in 1984, the UA had to be on line to receive messages. This "hanging around waiting for the phone to ring" would tie up a single-tasking operating system such as MS-DOS, meaning that any PC running an X.400 UA could do nothing else.

There are two ways around this problem. One, chosen by Cactus, is to implement the P7 protocol. An X.400 feature introduced in the 1988 version, P7 allows the PC to perform word processing, spreadsheet, or other functions while a Message Store receives incoming messages on its behalf.

The other solution, favored by vendors who want to start selling product, is to stick with the old version and use a dedicated PC to run the UA and to act as an X.400 LAN mail server.

One drawback in using 1984 X.400 is that the server and client PCs must communicate using either a nonstandard protocol or the P3 Submission and Delivery Protocol. The former means that the LAN workstations must be running a single vendor's software, not true OSI. The latter, according to Cactus literature, leads to "inflexible message control flow, excessive storage demands, inadequate message redirection capability, and cumbersome BAS [Basic Activity Subset] session requirements."

However, Ovum predicts that P7-based products and services will not begin to appear in force until 1991. In fact, because Cactus was conceived in 1986, before the latest draft of X.400, the researchers decided to "intercept" the protocol and use a version being promoted at the time by the European Computer Manufacturer's Association (ECMA).

For the lower five OSI layers, Cactus uses software developed in Carlos. All these modules reside in a Cactus

Box (Fig. 2), which may be connected to a public or private X.25 network. The Cactus box is implemented on a Sun workstation running Unix.

With the Cactus Box acting as OSI server, Cactus PCs need only run part of the UA (called the Mailbox Client or MBC) and a simplified RTS. This RTS, which also appears in the Cactus Box's LAN processor board, ensures that messages are delivered intact from the PC to the Box. (Note that PCs can attach via dial-up or multiplexer links as well as over a LAN.) The full RTS handling the Cactus Box's wide area network (WAN) board ensures delivery from the Box to the other end.

The Message Transfer Agent (MTA) and its submodules are standard 1984 X.400, but the Mailbox Server (MBS) module is new to the 1988 version. The MBS and the MBC constitute the User Agent.

For administration, Cactus implements Manager Functions that communicate with the PCs using the Global Task Mailbox. Another specialized module, the Directory Mailbox, provides access to the Cactus directory.

The European Commission was expected to give Cactus a final review this month.

While a long-range project such as Cactus can focus on the latest and greatest X.400 protocol set, commercial implementers have to base their kit on the more established version.

"Today's products stop at 1984," says Joan May, project leader at Case for Carlos and Cactus. "I would think the 1988 X.400 would be more useful in Electronic Data Interchange [EDI] than the 1984, because it has the presentation services," she says.

Peter Westwood, chief operating officer of North Ameri-

can operations for Sydney Development Corp. in Vancouver, B. C., agrees with her. "I think the 1988 standards are more suitable to PC and LAN use than the 1984 standards," he says, "and as those standards have just been approved, it will take some time before they stabilize."

Although Sydney offers X.400 on a PC under MS-DOS, running on a Novell LAN, the firm is not selling the package to users but only through OEMs, value-added networks, "and to the occasional large corporate user," says Westwood. "We're not sure there's a shrink-wrap market. I think the technology is still evolving too much. Everyone's implementing a slightly different version of X.400, and they're all a pain in the neck to interoperate," he says.

In contrast to Sydney, "Retix seems to be trying to move into the limelight," says Westwood. "In my perception, they've made a dramatic change in their focus. They're going after the mass user market," he says. Sydney and Retix compete in supplying OSI software to OEMs.

Retix has announced a Cactus-like X.400 (1984) LAN service that uses a Sesta-like OSI PC card. The two are part of an offering called Retixmail, which was launched at CeBIT in English, French, and German versions. (Retixmail was announced in the United States in November 1988.)

The OSI PC card, called PC-320, handles the transport layer and below (Fig. 3). An unusual feature is that the card provides two stacks; a connection-oriented stack, which can provide multiple channels over X.25 WANs; and a connectionless one for use over LANs. A 1.5-Mbyte memory helps the board handle both stacks and will enable Retix to migrate other

3. Retixmail. *The Retix X.400 package consists of a dual-stack wide are network card with Layers 1 through 4, Message Server software with Layers 5 and 7, and User Agent code in each PC.*

layers down to the board.

At present, though, the BAS form of the session layer, the RTS, the MTA, and the Interpersonal Messaging protocols are part of a module called the Message Server. This module runs under standard single-tasking DOS on a dedicated PC or compatible called the OpenServer 400.

A copy of the network operating system must be running on the OpenServer as well. To appeal to a vast array of users, Retix has enabled its package to run over any network operating system compatible with DOS 3.1, including Novell NetWare, Microsoft Networks (MS-Net), 3Com's 3+, the IBM PC Network or PC LAN Programs, or Olivetti's Olinet-LAN.

The client DOS PCs run their own copies along with Retix UAs. Users access Retixmail by running it as an application under Microsoft Windows, logging onto the server, submitting and retrieving messages, and logging off. An option will alert users of new messages, even during a different windows application.

Instead of a 1988 X.400-style Message Store, Retix divided the messaging function into store (handled by the file server) and forward (handled by the OpenServer). A message to be sent (or one that is received) passes over the LAN or the WAN to the file server, whence it is relayed to one or more users on the LAN or in the outside world, or both.

The advantage of avoiding a Message Store is that the file server need not be modified. "It's kind of a neat way of doing it," says Cactus project leader May.

Retix is not worried about competing with Cactus-derived or other 1988 X.400-based products. "The older version of X.400 will be around for a long time, just as people are still buying 1984 X.25," says Tom Kernan, Retix manager of European marketing in Cranford, England.

As with other LAN hardware/software combinations, the larger the LAN, the lower the per-user cost. A hundred-user package costs between $7,000 and $7,500, while a ten-user network would run just under $5,000.

Though Retix may have been the first vendor on the OSI

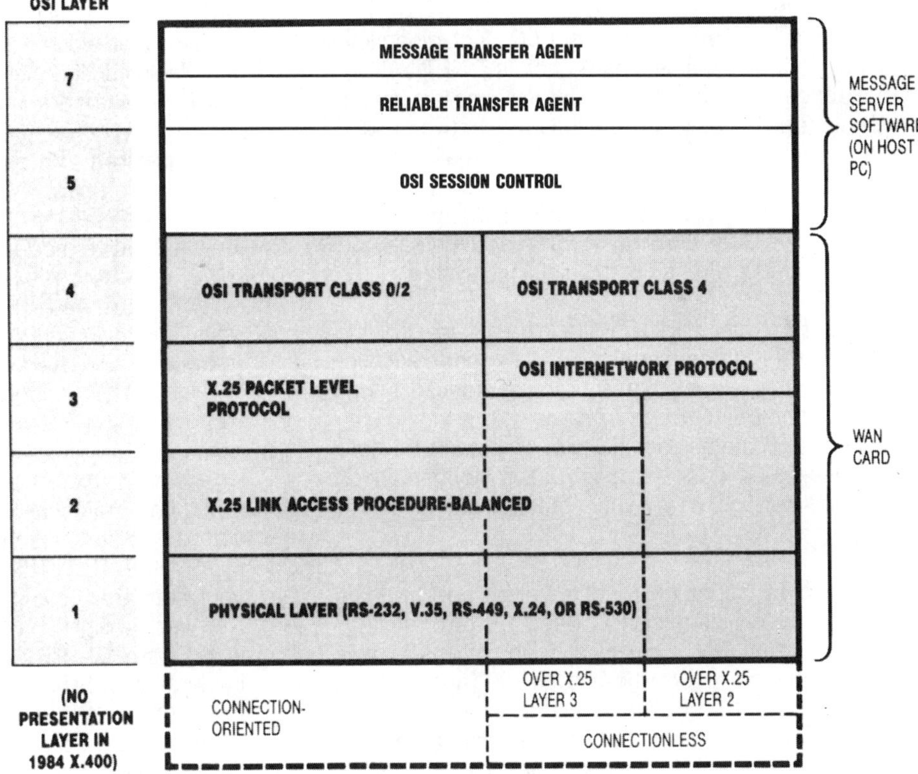

PC scene, it won't be for long. This summer, BT plans to release PC400, a LAN mail package based on 1984 X.400. For £9,500 (about $16,400) users will get a PC/AT with an OSI communications card, UA and MTA software, and documentation. A typical 256-user network would cost £18,000 (about $31,000).

One unique feature of PC400 is on-screen fax, with which users can send and receive facsimile images in the X.400 envelope. They can also view, magnify, shrink, and otherwise manipulate the images on the screen of a standard PC.

Several departments in the British government have put the BT product to a commercial trial. Although BT has not announced the availability of PC400 internationally, "we're interested in doing that," says Martin Cassidy, BT's LAN business manager in London. "We'll be announcing other OSI protocols running on PCs," he adds.

BT's architecture is roughly the same as Retix's, but there are a few differences. For example, the session and RTS protocols reside on the BT board instead of in PC memory. And the BT package also tweaks DOS to perform some multitasking.

PC400 will run over a number of LANs including Novell NetWare, which BT markets as part of its T-NET LAN product range. BT, one of Novell's largest resellers internationally, is codeveloping a link with Novell between MHS (Message Handling Service), the NetWare mail package, and PC400. "The MHS/X.400 mapping will be Novell's product, and they haven't announced when it will be available," says Gary Muchmore, sales and marketing manager of X.400 in BT's communications systems division.

Novell's approach is that OSI is for external use only. That is, X.400 and its brethren may be fine for communicating with the outside world, but are far from ideal for use among workgroup members. "There's no one who wants to use X.400 to communicate from a PC to a PC. It would be like killing a flea with a sledgehammer," says Stephen Hochschild, manager of product marketing at Novell.

Touch

Touch Communications Inc. (Scotts Valley, Calif.) begs to differ. The company is pushing OSI as a LAN operating system, using true OSI to link PCs. Touch claims to have about 50 customers among the *Fortune* 1000 and the U. S. government as well as European users.

Touch has recently shipped its first production user OSI package based on a TOP 3.0-compliant stack. The software, in versions for the MS-DOS, VAX VMS, and Macintosh operating systems, includes an upper-layer module for FTAM and a lower-layer module to handle ISO Transport Class 4 and the IEEE 802.3 protocols. The DOS software costs $395 (or $1,340 with hardware); the Mac version costs the same but is $940 with hardware. Code for the VMS runs from $3,000 to $11,000.

Because it uses 750 kbytes of memory, the Touch OSI code requires an intelligent Ethernet card with 512 kbytes of on-board memory for the MS-DOS computer. The protocol stack runs on the card, while two other modules run with the applications in the PC.

Currently available applications and future OSI-based applications from Touch access the OSI network via a network services module. Third-party OSI applications can be written to use the programmatic interface module, which gives developers access to services atop the OSI seven-layer stack or directly to any of the underlying layers. The OSI code now offers FTAM, though Touch expects its first mail product using X.400 by year's end.

To illustrate how the FTAM software works, Andrew Lauta, manager of product marketing at Touch, cites the MS-Net-like FTAM redirector that Touch has implemented under DOS.

"A file request from Lotus 1-2-3 or dBase would generate an interrupt 21, which generally signals a disk or local file access," says Lauta. "Software in the network services module intercepts the disk request and decides whether the request is local or should go out over the OSI LAN and do an FTAM file transfer," he says. In effect, the FTAM redirector extends the interrupt 21 to the remote OSI server.

In the Mac world, the Touch software now supports only the Macintosh II, which can practically handle an Ethernet card and a larger memory.

Poor performer?

OSI has long been lambasted on performance grounds. "No one can say that the performance of 7-layer stacks can match a native-mode implementation of a network protocol," says Novell's Hochschild. But Lauta comes back: "We measure performance from the user interface," he says. "We sat users down and tested the time it took to perform certain remote tasks, compared with the times for TCP/IP [Transmission Control Protocol/Internet Protocol] running MS-Net," says Lauta. "They were roughly the same."

One anomaly: According to Lauta, Touch sees OSI's role in the corporate world as the link between workgroups based on different technologies, such as DECnet, Network File System, TCP/IP, and so on. "We're not saying give up your NetWare," says Lauta, "we're saying, if you want your NetWare workgroup to talk to IBM or DEC or Apple networks, use OSI." But the workgroup vendors are moving to implement OSI links on their own, undermining the need for an OSI-based workgroup. "Our product doesn't do everything we want it to do, but it's the first step in the vision," says Lauta.

In answer to the BT/Novell partnership, 3Com, Novell's archrival in PC network operating systems, has also teamed with a European vendor for an X.400 tie-in. Telesystemes Reseaux, the Paris-based subsidiary of France Telecom, will devise two products for 3Com: an X.25 router and an X.400 gateway for LANs, both based on PC hardware platforms.

Télésystemes, Retix's X.400 center of competence in France, will base 3Com's X.400 package on the Retix OSI protocols. The trick will be to make the software run under 3+Open, 3Com's LAN answer to IBM's Operating System/ 2. The products are due, in both French and English, this summer.

Another leading LAN operating system vendor, Banyan Systems Inc. (Westborough, Mass.), is working with two companies to build X.400 gateways: Xionics Ltd. in London and Datacraft Data Communication Pty Ltd., Croydon, Victoria, Australia. While Xionics links the Banyan network to a Unix box running X.400 and X.25, Datacraft is porting its X.400 code to the Banyan server and using the native X.25 gateway. Datacraft plans to ship early in the second quarter 1989, but the Xionics product is still in beta test.

In late August, NET-TEL, a small firm outside London, began offering an X.400 mail product for networked PCs called Route 400. Though similar to Retixmail in design, Route 400 does not require windows. It can work with any LAN software that supports a shared file server, since it uses the file service-level interface provided by the LAN software rather than Netbios. Other features include remote asynchronous and X.25 dial access.

The product's strength is in its MTA, which offers a number of management features. It lets the administrator monitor messages moving through the OSI stack and set levels of log-in information for all layers, to increase diagnostic detail. Route 400 costs £5,000 (about $8,600) for the MTA plus £100 (about $175) for each UA (less with volume discount).

Meanwhile, in Tokyo, Oki Electronic Industry Co. Ltd. of Warabishi, Japan, demonstrated OSI software for FTAM running on its 80286-based microcomputer at the Interoperable Networking Event last November (see "Flexibility or heresy? The struggle to redraw MAP," DATA COMMUNICATIONS, November 1988, p. 49). All seven layers ran on the PC.

"Almost all the memory was used for the OSI software," says Ito Noburo, section manager in Oki's computer systems division, "but in the future, with larger memory on the PC, I think OSI will be able to run along with other software."

Though Oki already offers the presentation and application layers as products for its minicomputer, the PC code it showed for those layers was only a prototype.

Thus, although the technology is just beginning to evolve, vendors around the world are discovering the possible marriage of universal computing and global communications by means of the OSI PC. ∎

Joseph Fernandez, Software Developments Pty. Ltd., Chatswood, New South Wales, Australia

SNA and OSI: Which manages multivendor networks best?

SNA is here to stay, but OSI is coming on strong. How do the two compare? Can they peacefully coexist?

In the past, Open Systems Interconnection (OSI) and Systems Network Architecture (SNA) development efforts have concentrated on improving network connections. Now the focus has shifted to management of the heterogeneous networks that these improved connection options are making possible. Network management architectures have been promulgated by IBM and by the International Organization for Standardization (ISO) committee responsible for OSI standards. IBM has titled its network management architecture Open Network Management. The OSI equivalent is known simply as OSI Management.

IBM's Open Network Management (ONM) architecture divides network management into four categories of SNA Management Services: Problem Management, Performance and Accounting Management, Configuration Management, and Change Management.

■ Problem Management is the handling of an error condition in the network, from initial detection to resolution. In ONM, it is defined to consist of Problem Determination, Problem Diagnosis, Problem Bypass and Recovery, Problem Tracking and Control, and Problem Resolution.

■ Performance and Accounting Management is the determination and reporting of statistical measures of network performance in such areas as responsiveness, availability, and network-resource usage. It consists of Response-Time Monitoring, Availability Monitoring, Utilization Monitoring, Component Delay Monitoring, Performance Tuning, Performance Tracking and Control, and Accounting.

■ Configuration Management is the control of information that identifies network resources and their interrelationships (no services specifications yet).

■ Change Management is the planning, control, and application of changes to the network components. (Again, no services specifications yet.)

The Configuration Management service is meant to provide up-to-date information on network device names, locations, support and service contacts, and the like. It is meant to help an organization systematically implement and track hardware, software, and microcode changes.

To date, only the SNA Management Services subcategories of Problem Determination, Problem Diagnosis, and Response Time Monitoring have been specified.

OSI equivalency?

The OSI Network Management architecture is divided into five categories of management services: Fault Management, Accounting Management, Configuration and Name Management, Performance Management, and Security Management. These categories are known as Specific Management Functional Areas (SMFAs).

■ Fault Management is the detection, isolation, and correction of abnormal operation. It includes fault notification, logging, tracing, diagnostic testing, and corrective action.

■ Accounting Management is defined as the determination of costs for usage of resources and the assignment of corresponding charges.

■ Configuration management consists of facilities to initialize and shutdown managed objects, to set or change their configuration parameters, to collect status information, and to associate names with managed objects.

■ Performance Management is defined as the evaluation of the behavior of the managed objects. It includes facilities for gathering and logging statistical data.

■ Security Management supports the management of authentication, access control, and data encryption.

Draft specifications of these SMFAs have been produced in the form of OSI working papers.

As shown in Figure 1, there is considerable correlation between the IBM and OSI definitions of network manage-

1. Management services. *Both SNA and OSI architectures categorize network management operations at a high level: SNAMS for IBM and SMFA for OSI.*

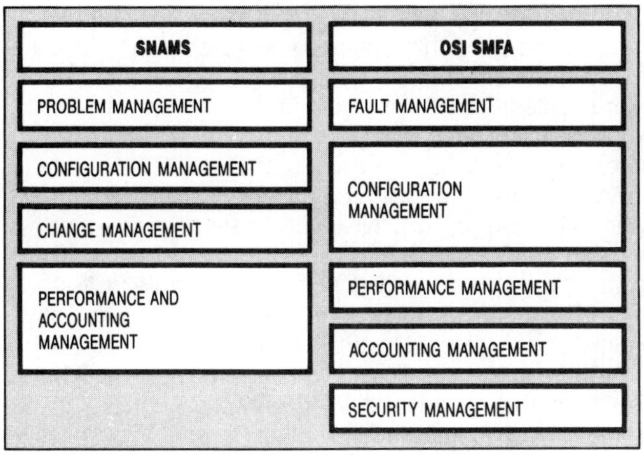

SNAMS = SNA MANAGEMENT SERVICES
SMFA = SPECIFIC MANAGEMENT FUNCTIONAL AREAS

ment services. OSI Configuration management, for example, includes IBM's Change Management. Similarly, IBM specifications state that each network management category in the architecture provides for Security Management.

Network management models

Each of the two architectures bases its model of network management on a set of management entities. In both cases, the management entities represent logical units that implement specified sets of management functions.

IBM's Open Network Management architecture uses a model based on three entities—a Focal Point, an Entry Point, and a Service Point.

■ An Entry Point—where network management data is inserted into an SNA network—is an SNA node. It usually has a number of attached devices for which it provides network connections. Its management role is to transmit data for itself and the attached devices to the Focal Point and receive management data from the latter. It obeys network management commands from the Focal Point.

■ A Service Point, like an Entry Point, transmits and receives management data to and from a Focal Point but does not provide SNA connections for attached devices. It converts management data from non-SNA devices to SNA format and inserts the data into a focal point of an SNA network.

■ A Focal Point performs centralized network management. It communicates with attached Entry and Service Points and controls all network components through them. The Focal Point transmits management commands to Entry Points and Service Points, and receives their responses; it receives management data in SNA format from Entry Points and Service Points and performs processing of this data and its display for network operations purposes.

Known as OSI Systems Management, the OSI network management architecture is based on the concept of monitoring, controlling, and coordinating network resources, with reference to all seven OSI layers. Provision is also made for management to occur wholly within the individual layers.

OSI Systems Management has developed the model for management activities. These are carried out by management processes that operate on managed objects. A managed object is an abstraction of a resource to be managed; that is, it represents the management view of an OSI resource. The managed object can send notifications, such as reports or events, to a management process.

There are two kinds of management processes: managing processes and agent processes. The agent processes operate directly on the managed objects, affecting management operations at the request of the managing process and relaying notification back to the managing process. A computer in an OSI network can implement one or more agent or management processes in any combination (Fig. 2).

The OSI management model

OSI network management involves communicating and processing data on managed resources. The data can, for example, be the resource as named through a specific convention, together with information on its configuration, past problems with its operation, or current interactions with other resources.

The OSI management standardization activities have recognized that complex manipulation of a range of data is necessary, so considerable attention has been devoted to modeling network management data. IBM's network management architecture has yet to address this area.

The OSI Management Information Model is based on the theory of object-oriented design developed in the study of programming languages. Managed objects can be physical entities, such as modems, or logical entities, such as programs, which implement communications protocols.

The managed object usually has a number of attributes that characterize it. Attributes have values, which are typically the items of information that OSI Systems Management needs to manipulate.

For example, an error counter is defined as an attribute, the value of which is a quantity that a management process would wish to read. Five management operations applicable to attributes have been defined: get attribute value, set attribute value, derive attribute value, add attribute value, and remove attribute value.

An attribute value can consist of more than a single value; it can have a structure encompassing a set of values. Here, the Add-and-Remove operations may add or remove members of such a set.

The five operations that manipulate attribute values must be directed at the managed object to which the attributes belong. The managed object is responsible for performing the appropriate operations.

There are two other operations, Create and Delete, which are defined to act directly on managed objects.

The OSI model defines two hierarchical relationships in which objects participate: inheritance and containment.

A managed object is considered to belong to a managed-object class consisting of all objects that possess the same attributes, support the same operations, and issue the same notifications.

Classes are arranged in a hierarchy; inheritance is a relationship between classes. Each class inherits the distinguishing characteristics (attributes, operations, and notifications) of the class above it in the hierarchy and adds some new ones.

For example, if "network" were to be defined as one class, "packet-switching network" could be defined as another class below it in the inheritance hierarchy.

The second hierarchical relationship, that of containment, applies to individual managed objects. A managed object can contain other managed objects, each of which in turn contains further managed objects. This relationship is used to create a naming scheme.

At any given level in the containment hierarchy, a managed object at that level has what is called a Relative Distinguished Name (RDN), which distinguishes it from other objects at the same level. The full name of a managed object is obtained by "walking" down the containment hierarchy from the highest level to the managed object itself, concatenating the RDNs of each managed object along the path.

OSI's network management architecture defines the concept of a Management Information Base (MIB)—a repository of all management information. The management model will develop the structure of information for network management and storage in the MIB.

However, the OSI architecture quite properly does not define specific database techniques, so that there are no unnecessary constraints on the implementation of the MIB. While it is a single logical repository, it may be implemented in either a centralized or distributed fashion.

Comparing the SNA and OSI models
While the IBM and OSI definitions of Management Services are very similar, their models for network management are quite different.

IBM's model is a hierarchical one, closely aligned with the traditional structure of SNA. Just as SNA has a Systems Services Control Point (SSCP) as the heart of the network, the management architecture has a Focal Point at the center of management communications and functions.

Entry Points and Service Points are slaves of the Focal Point, reflecting the relationship between SNA node type 2 (PU—Physical Unit—2) and the SSCP node type 5 (PU 5).

The OSI model, on the other hand, is built on the concept of distributed management processes that interact with each other. Again, the management architecture reflects the communications architecture, which in this case was developed over the last decade to address peer communications between computers from different vendors.

In the case of IBM architectures, the close mapping between its management architecture and its communications architecture makes it easy to implement the management structure within a traditional SNA network. The practi-cal result has been that a user organization can build an SNA network using products from a number of different vendors, all of which implement the management architecture, and which can therefore all be effectively managed under that architecture. Many implementations can be made compliant with the management architecture (and in many cases already are) by the addition of the documented Entry Point functions. Similarly, a vendor can implement a Focal Point that conforms fully to the architecture, and this has also already been done.

Mix and match of SNA-compatible products works well when it is done wholly within an SNA network. For example, a user organization can install: cluster controllers and communications controllers from IBM and from PCMs (Plug-Compatible Manufacturers), all functioning as Entry Points; one or more IBM or PCM S/370 host machines; and an IBM or third-party Focal Point implementation on the S/370 host to manage the whole network. And all of this can be in strict compliance with SNA Network Management architecture.

User organizations benefit from the compatibility between different implementations of Focal Points and Entry Points, since they can freely take advantage of individual product strengths such as user-friendliness, performance, and reliability.

The OSI model of distributed management processes lends itself more readily than the IBM architecture to implementation in a heterogeneous network, where equipment from different vendors is connected together. In such a network, the emphasis is usually on peer connectivity, with the freedom to access applications and data anywhere on a network, without reliance on a large centralized mainframe. This access is, of course, subject to security measures, but the point is that the networking architecture makes peer communications possible. The OSI model extends to detailed modeling of management information, providing a basis for consistent and comprehensive implementation of network management functions.

Network management protocols
SNA uses a layered set of protocols for end-to-end data transmission. Following the adoption by ISO of a seven-layer model for OSI, a seven-layer model has been defined by IBM for SNA.

The highest layer—the application layer in the OSI model—is known in SNA as the transaction services layer, and it handles message units known formally as Request/Response Units, or RUs. It is at this level that network management information is exchanged between Entry Points and Service Points on the one hand and the Focal Point on the other hand. The network management information, sometimes known as Communications Network Management (CNM) messages, is carried by the lower protocol layers in the same way that data is carried between user terminals and host programs.

Before IBM's adoption of a formal network management architecture, a variety of different RU formats was used to convey network management information. Perhaps the major contribution of the formal architecture has been its

2. OSI Management. *Distributed management processes are the basis of OSI Management. An individual OSI open system can implement agent processes, as well as manag-ing processes in any combination. A computer in an Open Systems Interconnection network can invoke any or all of these processes.*

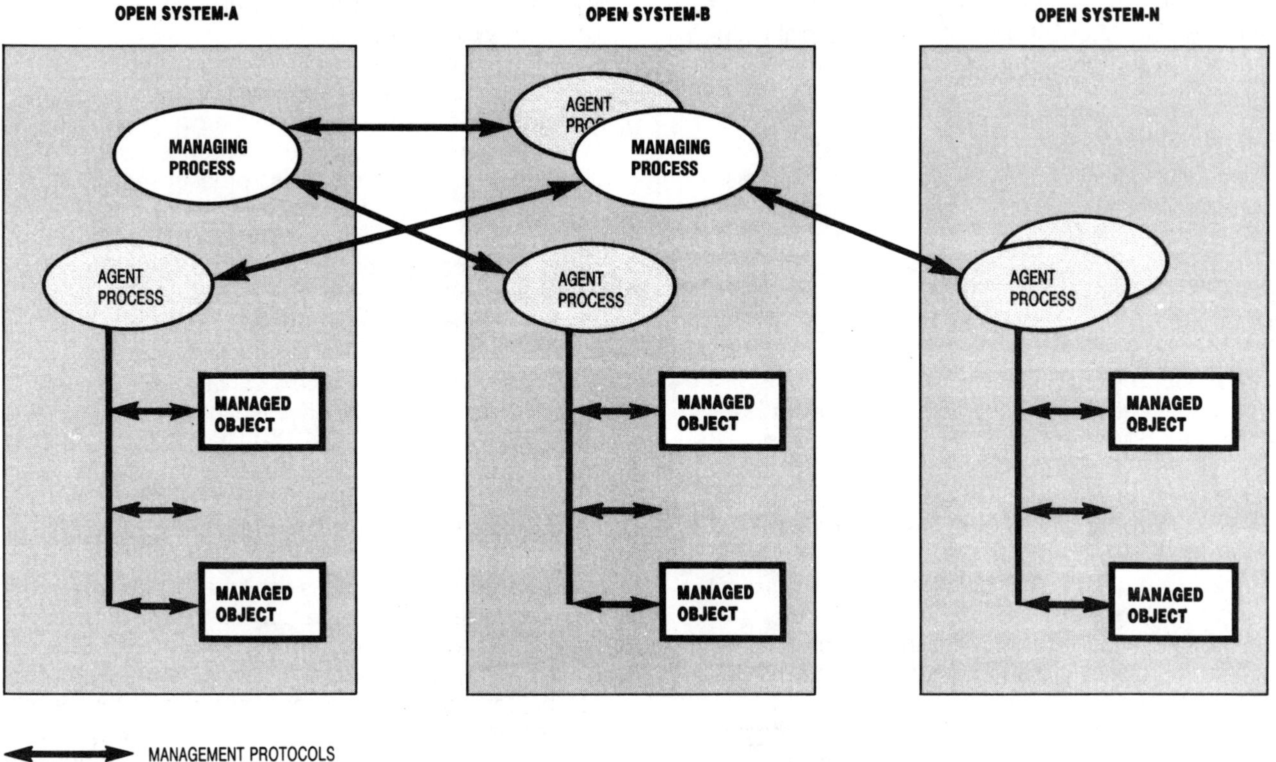

standardization on a single RU format, the Network Management Vector Transport (NMVT), for all management functions.

The NMVT format is shown in Figure 3. There are several key points to note here:

■ The three-byte header of this RU is a code that distinguishes the network management NMVT records from all the other RUs carried by an SNA network. This provides an easy way for an implementer of an Entry Point, Service Point, or Focal Point to recognize relevant records and, conversely, to create management records in the correct format.

■ The body of the NMVT consists of management data in a format that the SNA management architecture calls a vector. The data is defined by two quantities, a length and a key; length is the number of bytes in the vector and a key is a code that uniquely specifies the management function to which the data applies.

■ In an NMVT, the vectored data is hierarchically structured. The NMVT is defined to hold a single major vector. This merely acts as an envelope for a number of subvectors. Each subvector can act as an envelope for a number of subfields, each of which has the vector format of a length field followed by a key field followed by the data.

The NVMT format provides a structured way to communicate management data, with the chosen structure lending itself to modular processing by receivers and creating by transmitters.

The architecture currently defines only three major vectors that can be exchanged between a Focal Point and an Entry Point or Service Point. These three major vectors are built of subvectors, some of which are common to multiple major vectors, and others are specific to a major vector. The common subvectors typically carry such information as device identification, date, and time.

Finding and diagnosing problems

SNA Management architecture has to date only specified management services for Problem Determination, Problem Diagnosis, and Response-Time Monitoring.

The central concept, in the architecture's Problem Determination and Diagnosis services, is that of an Alert, sent by an Entry Point or Service Point to a Focal Point, to notify the Focal Point of a detected network problem. The problem information is communicated in an NMVT containing an Alert major vector.

IBM originally took the approach of providing most of the problem information through a Basic Alert subvector, carried in the Alert major vector. The Basic Alert subvector contained information that categorized the type of error to some degree, and most important, a set of three device-specific code points.

Each code point was a two-byte index that selected

an appropriate message screen on the Focal Point; this message screen contained device-specific information on the problem. It was assumed that the developers of any new network device would generate a set of problem information screen displays for that device type, and that this set would be installed at the Focal Point host before the new device type was introduced into a network.

The approach required considerable work to support each new SNA device type on the part of IBM, other product developers, and the user organizations. It also meant that, over a period of time, the Basic Alert subvector would be dependent on a very large number of device-specific screens. This made maintenance and growth a problem for IBM, for other SNA product implementers, and for user organizations.

From basic to generic alerts

As part of its definition of a network management architecture, IBM specified a new Alert structure, the Generic Alert. This consists of a set of subvectors defined in a way to allow the exchange of common management data for a variety of device types. Associated with Generic Alert are:

■ An alert type, a code that specifies one of five severity levels for the problem.

■ A description code that provides information on the category of problem, distinguishing, for example, hardware problems from software problems.

■ A "probable causes" subvector that provides more detailed categorization of the type of problem.

■ An optional "user causes" subvector that conveys diagnostic information for problems that can be resolved by an operator.

■ An optional "install causes" subvector that conveys diagnostic information regarding problems caused by incorrect installations.

■ An optional "failure causes" subvector that conveys more detailed information on the failing equipment type.

■ A "cause undetermined" subvector, included if none of the previous three subvectors can be generated.

■ A "recommended actions" subfield suggesting how the problem could be rectified.

■ A "detailed data" subfield carrying parameter values, typically those that are product-specific.

The Generic Alert is based on the concept of the Focal Point maintaining tables of text messages relating to problem conditions that are less product-specific than those formerly maintained for Basic Alerts. The subvectors and subfield carry indices into these message tables, allowing the Focal Point to select appropriate messages and combine them into meaningful displays. The message strings act as building blocks of a complete screen display.

The subvectors and subfield contain code points. A code point is a two-byte code that provides two indices into the Focal Point tables of text strings. The first index selects a default text string, providing the most general information relating to the problem. The second selects a replacement text string, supplying more specific information.

The Focal Point text strings can be encoded with embedded parameters that can be substituted with values from the data contained in the received subvectors. For example, detailed identification of a device having a problem can be carried in a subvector; a code point can be used to select an appropriate generic problem message; and the device identification can be inserted at the appropriate point in the message before being displayed to an operator at the Focal Point.

The Generic Alert is seen by IBM as the major facility for problem management in a mixed-vendor network. The associated subvectors and subfields have code points reserved for non-IBM use. IBM's network-management-ar-

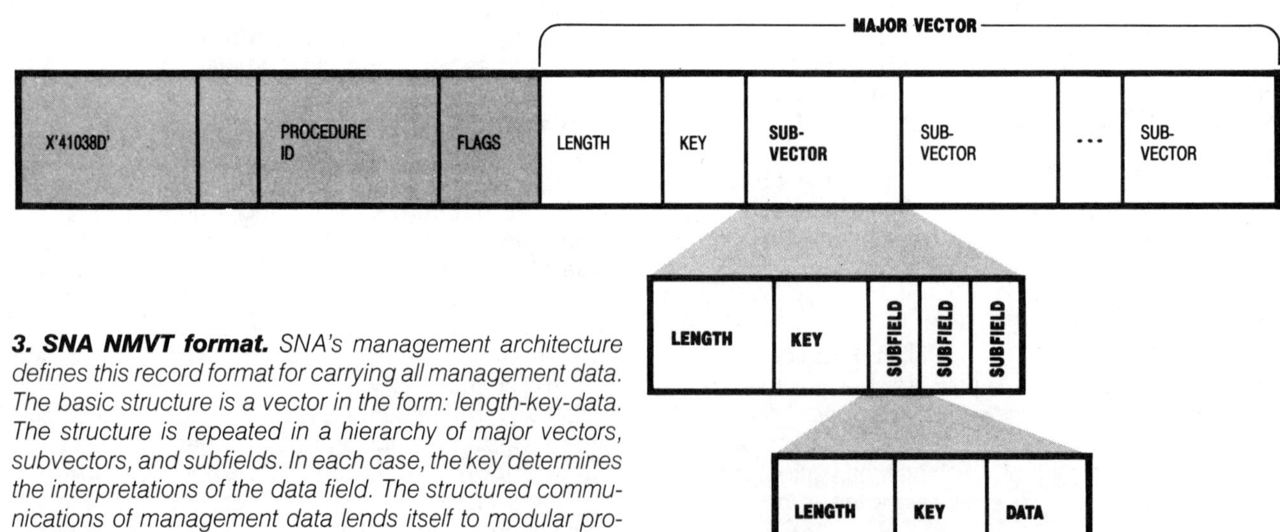

3. SNA NMVT format. *SNA's management architecture defines this record format for carrying all management data. The basic structure is a vector in the form: length-key-data. The structure is repeated in a hierarchy of major vectors, subvectors, and subfields. In each case, the key determines the interpretations of the data field. The structured communications of management data lends itself to modular processing.*

chitecture manuals state that these code points will never be allocated to IBM products but will be reserved for third-party suppliers and customers to use.

Response-Time Monitoring

Response-Time Monitoring is the capability of the Focal Point to determine the delays between input and corresponding output at network elements, such as terminals. The delay times are usually measured at the Entry Point or its non-SNA counterpart attached to a Service Point.

The Focal Point can send the Entry Point or Service Point an NMVT requesting that this information be gathered and returned—either immediately or when triggered by events such as session terminations. The Entry Point or Service Point returns an NMVT containing its response and may subsequently send NMVTs with response time data.

The OSI network management architecture's SMFAs (see Fig. 4) constitute a somewhat informal definition of management services. (Management functions constitute the formal definitions of these services.)

A set of management primitives has been defined that will be useful for many management operations. Known as Common Management Information Services (CMIS), these are implemented by OSI machines in OSI networks communicating through an application layer protocol, the Common Management Information Protocol (CMIP).

The management functions use CMIS, and can use other application layer services to effect their operations. In actuality, they implement a high-level protocol, the Specific Management Information Protocol (SMIP). However, SMIP has a less tangible existence as a protocol in its own right, consisting of particular parameters within CMIP along with the use of other protocols, such as the OSI File Transfer, Access and Management (FTAM) protocol.

CMIS defines services for sending and retrieving management information, commands, and responses. Because OSI networking resources are modeled for management purposes as managed objects, CMIS includes services for creating and removing these representations of resources, along with the commands and information that reference these managed objects.

CMIS operates over an end-to-end logical connection at the application level, and specifies how the association should be established and cleared. It is specified as a number of primitives, each with a set of mandatory and optional parameters.

The CMIP specification defines the format of the messages exchanged in order to implement the CMIS primitives and the sequences in which they are exchanged. CMIP is based on a Request/Response dialogue, just as SNA network management and other protocols are.

CMIP message formats are defined in the ISO language ASN.1 (see "ASN.1, an OSI language"). This language requires the use of strictly defined data types to express the syntax of message elements.

CMIP is intended to provide a common framework for the transmission of a variety of management information on the large range of managed objects that occur in practice in networks. These object types and their attribute types are also being defined in ASN.1 in the standards documents related to the OSI Management Information Model.

The individual management functions that collectively specify operations for Fault Management, Configuration Management, Performance Management, Accounting Management, and Security Management will define their parameters using ASN.1.

The CMIP specification uses English text to describe the procedures used to implement the protocol's logical sequences. However, ISO is considering the possibility of using a formal language for this as well. If adopted, this is likely to be one of two languages, Lotos or Estelle, each currently in use for other ISO and CCITT standards definitions.

The OSI SMFAs for Fault Management, Configuration Management, Accounting Management, Performance Management, and Security Management have begun defining the actual functions that will provide these services. Of these, only Fault Management and Configuration Management have firm definitions at this stage.

Fault Management has defined two functions: Error Reporting and Information Retrieval; and Confidence and Diagnostic Testing.

Configuration Management has defined three functions: Object Management, Relationship Management, and State Management.

Performance Management is expected to make use of the Confidence and Diagnostic Testing function defined for Fault Management. There are also proposals for: Workload Monitoring, Response Time Monitoring, and Statistical Analysis.

Accounting Management has proposals for: Communications Instance Accounting and Accessing Accounting logs.

Security Management has proposals for: Audit Trail, Security Alarm Reporting, Auditing and Alarm Reporting Management, and Security Object and Attribute Management.

OSI Management also has a Common Management Functional Area that will identify functions of general use. In its current form it defines two functions: Management Service Control and Log Control.

A total of five of these functions have reached the ISO Draft Proposal stage: Error Reporting and Information Retrieval, Object Management, Relationship Management, State Management, and Management Service Control. Considerable work remains to be done on the others.

Optional parameters

In OSI, the Error Report is the equivalent of the SNA Alert. An Error Report contains one mandatory and 11 optional parameters. The mandatory parameter is the error type, which categorizes the error into one of the following types: Communications, Quality of Service, Processing, Equipment, or Environmental.

The optional parameters are:

■ Probable cause code.

■ Severity, which can have a value of critical, major, warning, or indeterminate.

■ Trend indication, showing recent changes in severity.

4. CMIS, CMIP. *CMIS implementations on two OSI systems communicate using an application-layer protocol, CMIP, which itself runs over a complete set of OSI lower-level protocols. OSI is now defining a set of management functions that will use CMIF and other protocols, constituting an SMIP protocol.*

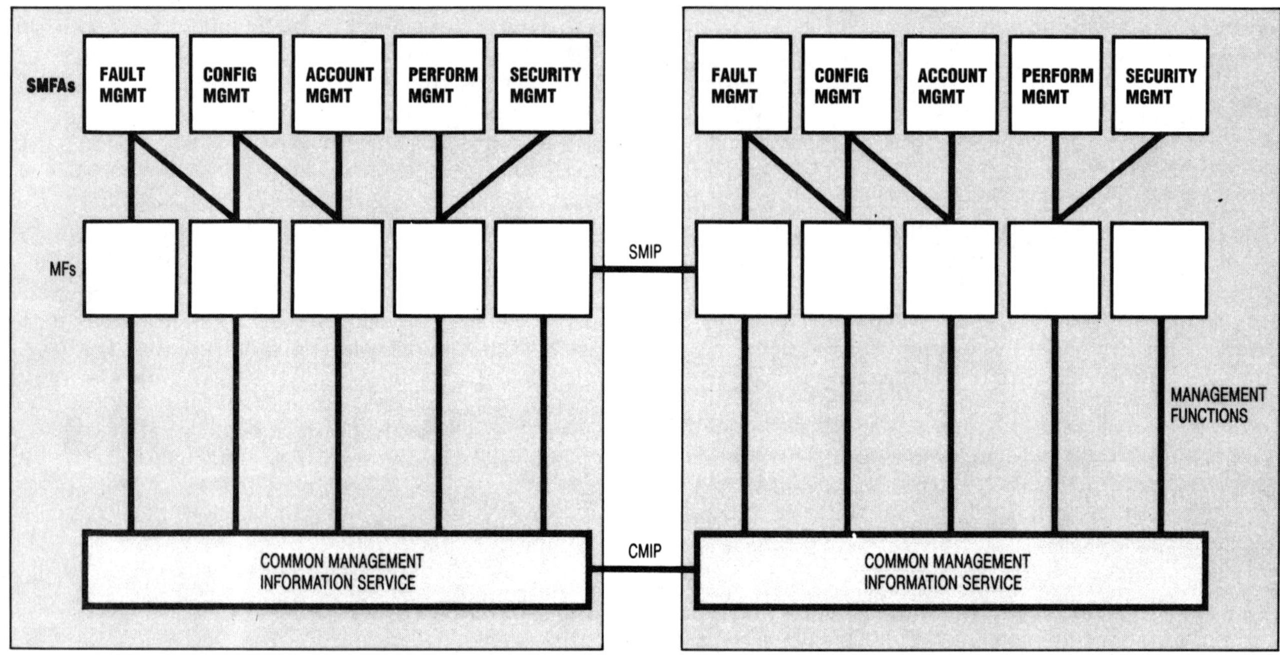

CMIP = COMMON MANAGEMENT INFORMATION PROTOCOL
CMIS = COMMON MANAGEMENT INFORMATION SERVICE
MF = MANAGEMENT FUNCTION

SMFA = SPECIFIC MANAGEMENT FUNCTIONAL AREA
SMIP = SPECIFIC MANAGEMENT INFORMATION PROTOCOL

(NOTE· THIS IS A SIMPLIFICATION. THE FUNCTIONS MAY ALSO USE OTHER SERVICES, SUCH AS FTAM)

Back-up status, showing whether the resource having the problem has been backed up.
■ Diagnostic information, which can include relevant counter values.
■ Proposed repair action.
■ Threshold information, information on error thresholds that have been reached.
■ State change, showing past and present configuration states of the managed object.

The error type, probable cause code, severity, and repair action parameters all have counterparts in the SNA Alert. The SNA architectural specifications already include extensive lists of codes to categorize error types and probable causes and to specify actions. ISO is just beginning to consider this issue.

The other parameters do not have counterparts in the SNA Alert. The alert structure instead provides for sending additional product-specific data in a detailed data subvector.

The Object Management function, developed for OSI Configuration management, uses the object-oriented model to perform operations in OSI networks. It consists of operations to create, rename, and delete managed objects; to read and change attribute values; to report any of these events to another open system; to read attribute values; and to list the managed objects in another open system.

State Management defines managed objects as possessing two kinds of states: operational and administrative. The operational state of a managed object can be "disabled," "enabled," "active," or "busy." The administrative state can be "locked," "shutting down," or "unlocked."

Under the Management Information Model, the administrative state and operational state each constitute an attribute of the managed object. The possible states then become allowable attribute values.

The background to this model is the theory of "finite state" machines. This increasingly well known programming technique represents a process as a machine with a well-defined number of states and well-defined input events, where each input may cause a transition between states.

The State Management functions define inputs of "enable," "disable," "new user," "user quit," "capacity increase," and "capacity decrease" for the operational state. It defines inputs of "unlock," "lock," and "shut down" for the administrative state.

These states and inputs lead to state-transition diagrams that specify the administrative and operational behavior of the managed open system.

OSI relationships

Relationships between managed objects of particular significance for Configuration Management are formally defined as a type of attribute of the managed objects. This function defines the following types of relationships between pairs of managed objects:

- Service, where one is the provider and one is the user.
- Peer, communications between two similar objects.
- Backup, where a secondary object can provide the functions of a known primary object.
- Group, where one is the member and one is the owner.

Operations are defined to create, change, and delete relationships; to report these changes; and to list relationships and related objects. Since properties are attributes of managed objects, these operations are actually a part of the Object Management Function, with parameters carrying the attribute information.

A major practical problem with large-scale network management is that managing processes can get flooded with event reports, and in turn, subject network operators to a flood of messages. There is, therefore, a requirement for filtering. It is also necessary to be able to choose the operations to be permitted on individual managed objects.

Management Service Control provides both. Its tool is the "discriminator," one of a special class of managed objects known as management support objects, described in the Management Information Model.

Discriminators allow the selective forwarding of event reports to managing processes. Through discriminators, the managing processes can also specify criteria to determine whether an incoming operation request is to be performed by an agent process.

The operations defined are:
- Intitiate/terminate management service control.
- Suspend/resume management service control.
- Retrieve/modify discriminator attributes.

The parameters can carry discriminator criteria that can, for example, only generate OSI Error Reports if the Error Report severity parameter value is marked "critical" or "major."

For implementation purposes, IBM's architecture groups functions into sets of closely related functions. Each function has a base subset, which defines the functions that must be implemented if any of the functions in that set are to be implemented.

Optional subsets

In addition, each function set can include one or more optional subsets. There may be dependencies between some of the optional subsets, so that the implementation of a particular optional subset may require the implementation of another optional subset. The subsets can thus be represented as consisting of a mandatory base and optional towers.

This definition of base and optional subsets is a practical way of providing a large measure of implementation flexibility, while still retaining compatibility between independent implementations of the architecture. Some implementations may be on lower-powered processors, so that implementers have to be selective in the number of functions they implement. The base subset defines the mandatory functions that will ensure compatible operation with other, more powerful implementations.

The seven-layer OSI model has services and protocols defined with a large number of options included. As a result, there is a danger that two different implementations may choose different options—and, therefore, not work together.

Much of the practical work in the OSI arena in the last two years has been to address this problem, taking the form of definitions of "functional standards." These are standard profile sets that pick specific options in each layer.

The Corporation for Open Standards in the United States and its counterparts in other parts of the world have been active in this area, and so have the MAP (Manufacturing Automation Protocol) and TOP (Technical and Office Protocols) groups. In addition, national governments are now publishing Government OSI Profiles (GOSIPs), which define in each case the OSI option set to be operated by all government agencies in their respective countries. This has been done in the United States and United Kingdom, and a number of European governments and the Australian government are working on GOSIPs of their own.

SNA and OSI

Each architecture is a complex specification with many implementation options. In each case, there is the potential for independent implementations to be incompatible.

IBM's approach to solving this incompatibility problem is the grouping of features into base and optional subsets, with rules for their selection. OSI has begun to follow IBM's approach and define functional units consisting of clearly specified sets. But the OSI effort goes beyond this to address conformance specification and testing, where different vendor implementations can be independently verified.

There is clearly a strong need for independent conformance certification to support the IBM architecture as well. For example, at least one product on the market that claims to conform to the SNA Management Architecture inserts multiple major vectors into an SNA NMVT record, although the architectural specifications clearly forbid this.

While the overall categorization of management services by IBM and ISO is very similar, their approaches to management protocols are very different.

SNA Management Services, for example, uses a vectored packing of all data into a single record type. Data can consist of binary values or text strings, and the interpretation is determined by the definition of the subvectors and subfields that contain the data.

OSI Management's protocol specifications are based on the fundamental concept of separating the presentation syntax from the transfer syntax. The presentation syntax, ASN.1, is a language that defines relevant data structures in the style of strongly typed programming languages, and management protocols can be formally expressed in this language. The transfer syntax is a set of encoding rules that define the bit patterns to be transmitted.

Some recently released IBM products use SNA LU session protocols, rather than NMVTs, for some management functions. The formal specifications for SNA Management Services do not allow the use of these protocols, so that these implementations currently exist outside the SNA

ASN.1, an OSI language

A formal language developed expressly for OSI application-layer standards, Abstract Syntax Notation One, or ASN.1, is defined in a pair of ISO standards.

The OSI committee has taken the apoproach of separating the protocol data structures from their representation for transmission. The protocol data structures represent an abstract set of definitions that can be used to specify protocols.

When two open systems are to communicate, they first agree on a common representation for each of the defined data structures — so that the bit patterns they exchange are interpreted the same way by each party.

This is similar to high-level programming languages that have a formally defined syntax. A programmer expresses instructions in terms of this syntax. When these instructions are to be executed, a representation has to be developed that can be understood by the computer that will execute them. This representation is the machine code produced by the language compiler.

ISO's separation of the protocol data structures from their transmission representation has two major advantages. First, a formal protocol specification need only define the syntax of the protocol and is therefore a much easier document to comprehend than one that defines both the protocol structures and the bit representations. Second, the protocol representation can, if necessary, be changed independently of the protocol syntax by using different encoding rules. All that is necessary in this case is for both ends in a particular communication to agree on the new set of encoding rules.

The ASN.1 protocol data structures are defined in ISO standard 8824. A basic set of encoding rules for the representation of the ASN.1 protocol data structures is defined in ISO standard 8825.

The fundamental ASN.1 concept is the datatype, that is, a defined set of possible values with an associated name. Any variable quantity is defined to be a variable of a particular datatype, which limits the legal values it can assume.

For example, there could be a datatype DayOfWeek, defined to consist of the set of values (Monday through Sunday). If a variable is defined to be of datatype DayOfWeek, it is then restricted to having one of these seven values. In practice, these values will be represented by codes, but the representation is separated from the abstract definition, and can be considered separately.

This concept of datatyping is what the so-called "strongly typed" programming languages, such as Pascal and Modula-2, are based on. A programmer with experience in one of these languages will find ASN.1's concepts and notation familiar.

The formal term "datatype" is usually abbreviated to "type." The example, DayOfWeek, is of a simple type, with the legal values directly specified. More complex types can be created by defining structured types consisting of combinations of other types.

Each type has an associated tag value used in the implementation to distinguish different types. ASN.1 defines four classes of tags, allowing the same tag value to be re-used in different contexts. These four classes are:

- universal, the class of tag values assigned by ISO 8824 itself to the general types it defines;
- application, a class defined by an application-layer standard;
- private, where tag values can be assigned by one or more implementors for their own purposes;
- context-specific, where the meaning depends on the particular context in which the tags are used.

ISO 8824 also allows a user to construct ASN macros, which, as in programming languages, are user-defined notations for combinations of language structures. An ASN macro definition specifies the syntax for a type definition and a value definition.

ASN.1 is a language for specifying protocol message formats — not the procedures used to exchange them in valid sequences. In order to specify the procedures, the implementation of the protocol is usually modeled as machine with well-defined states, a protocol "finite-state machine." Describing these state changes: "State transition tables." Together with the descriptions of the actions performed by the protocol finite-state machine, these constitute a formal specification of the procedures.

An ISO specification language may be used at a later date to define procedures in this way. Errors in interpretation are much less likely to occur when formal languages such as ASN.1 are used to create specifications. They also raise the possibility of formal proof of the correctness of an implementation.

Network Management architecture. It might be expected that IBM will extend the architectural specifications of their Open Network Management in the near future to include these protocols, or alternatively, replace current SNA LU-based implementations with ones that do conform to the architecture.

The OSI network management architecture is based on a Management Information Model, which is used to describe the diverse elements that make up a network, and the actions necessary to manage them. The model naturally leads to the OSI MIB, a conceptual repository of all management information.

IBM's architecture has not yet defined a model for network management data. There is an urgent need for this in order to provide a consistent basis for the protocol and service definitions.

For example, the NMVT structure specifies two levels of nesting (that of major vector into subvectors, and subvectors into subfields). Yet one of the most commonly used subvectors, the Product Set ID subvector, is defined itself by other subvectors, in violation of this rule. Apparently, a third level of nesting was deemed necessary, but this has not been added to the NMVT definition.

Another very evident concern is that subfields and subvectors have grown very rapidly in number and complexity, and consistency is becoming a major problem. A data model that structured all managed objects would make protocol requirements clear from the outset, and would allow a much cleaner definition of protocols. Presumably, IBM has recognized the need for such a model and its definition is imminent.

Multivendor environment

The major trend in networking today is the interconnection of equipment from a variety of computer and communications vendors. Networks have become heterogeneous and will become increasingly so. A network management scheme must therefore cope with equipment from multiple computer and communications vendors.

IBM has devoted a large amount of its resources to its SNA communications architecture and its corresponding network management architecture. It can be expected to continue to do so.

However, IBM has also provided support for internatioal standards such as X.25, and can be expected to continue to provide products that support ISO standards as well. In 1988, it announced that an implementation of CMIP would be available in March 1990.

All the other major computer vendors have announced a strong commitment to OSI, and this implies a commitment to the OSI Management Framework. Most of these vendors do not have the same kind of major investment in a proprietary networking architecture that IBM has. They can be expected increasingly to devote their product development efforts and energies to the OSI architecture.

Digital Equipment Corp. is the only vendor with a proprietary networking architecture that can be considered a rival to IBM's SNA, both in terms of market share and range of function. However, DEC has announced that it will migrate its Digital Network Architecture to OSI, and has declared as an objective being the premier supplier of OSI networks. DEC's network management can therefore be expected, in the medium to long term, to be based on the OSI Management Framework.

Merger?

One view expressed in the industry is that SNA and OSI networking architectures will merge. It seems very unlikely that this will happen within 15 years. IBM does have its major investment in and commitment to SNA, suggesting the company is not likely to replace SNA with OSI. We can look at the pattern of IBM's support of X.25 as an illustration.

X.25 was first issued as a CCITT standard in 1976. Twelve years later, it is offered as an option to IBM's own SDLC (Synchronous Data Link Control) in virtually all the relevant IBM communications products; it can be used in place of SDLC on appropriate links, and, for example, is used extensively in this way in Europe.

X.25 has not, therefore, replaced an IBM standard but rather coexists with it. ISO is equally unlikely to move the OSI standards in the direction of SNA. The OSI standardization effort achieved a critical mass about two years ago; it has been the subject of successful demonstrations.

Over the last 10 years, the OSI committee has acquired extensive experience in developing standards within its operational framework. This is now showing up in the accelerated pace of standards development. A management scheme for the multivendor networks that are becoming common must therefore support both SNA and OSI management architectures.

Heterogeneous networking has brought with it another trend — that of peer networking. Users are finding that they need to be able to access data located on a variety of different machines. This cannot be supported effectively if access needs the involvement of a centralized host.

IBM has itself recognized this trend and, during the last few years, has refocused its SNA architectural efforts on retrofitting peer communications features into SNA. In a multivendor network, the pattern of peer communications becomes even more evident.

User organizations will tend to choose networks that satisfy applications requirements. An organization's network will actually consist of a number of subnetworks, each one possibly supplied by a different vendor. The subnetworks will be linked in a peer fashion, allowing connections between networks and access (where authorized) to data located on any network.

These peer connections cannot effectively be achieved under a hierarchical network management architecture. For example, if Change Management has to be carried out at a centralized mainframe, this can delay or even preclude the dynamic addition or removal of nodes at different points in a network. Users must be free to alter each one of the subnetworks independently, dynamically, and flexibly.

Each of the subnetworks is likely to have installed network management products that manage that subnetwork efficiently. This suggests that the most effective management scheme for the entire network is one that relies on communications and cooperation between the individual network management schemes on a peer basis.

This hypothetical network actually consists of SNA and OSI networks, each managed in accordance with its corresponding architecture. Communications and cooperation between the two architectures can be effected by mapping between these two management architectures in a way that is not visible to users of management services.

This interfacing occurs at the application level and requires a mapping between different data representations — in one case, the OSI Management Information Model, and in the other, the equivalent IBM management data representation, which still has to be defined. ■

Joseph Fernandez works in the research group of Software Developments Pty Ltd. He holds a B.Sc. degree from Makerere College in Uganda and a Ph.D. in Physics from Washington University in St. Louis, Mo. Pamela Bray, graphic artist at Software Developments, generated the artwork for the illustrations used in this article.

Roger L. Koenig, Koenig Communications Consulting, San Jose, Calif.

How to make the PBX-to-ISDN connection

Here are your options for making the big move — from your current, proprietary digital network design to one based on the ISDN standards.

Growth produces change. Your company's sales organization has to move from its current suburban headquarters site to a new office building in the city. In the kickoff planning meeting, your CEO expresses grave concerns about the possible negative impact on revenues that might result from a lapse in communications between the sales organization and its customers. The sales VP makes it clear that he wants no degradation in voice or data services.

The new sales office will need a high level of connectivity with headquarters. From the standpoint of continuity and economy, incoming Direct Inward Dialing (DID) numbers, voice mailboxes, and attendant (private-operator) services should be provided centrally from the headquarters facility. Each salesperson's desktop PC must continue to have 19.2-kbit/s access from the new location to the mainframe's inventory database, price-quoting program, and electronic data interchange and electronic-mail applications.

A tough scenario to implement? Are leased lines to the new facility the only answer? And are they going to add significantly to your telecommunications expenses? What options do you have in equipment selection? Will you need to add another T1-multiplexer node at the new site? How is your maintenance staffing going to be affected?

In today's world of private digital networking, your options are rather limited. Figure 1 shows a current solution for networking the new sales office to headquarters.

To achieve integration of voice-calling features between the two facilities, you would invariably need to buy a new PBX from the same vendor as the one at headquarters. With luck, the PBX vendor's proprietary common-channel networking scheme should, over T1 lines, support the required centralized attendant service, DID integration, and voice-feature transparency (sharing the same features between headquarters and the remote site).

Providing voice-mail service to the sales office from the headquarters' voice processor could be tougher, however. The voice processor needs to receive forwarding-number identification and called-extension status (busy, unavailable, answer supervision) information from the sales office's PBX, through the network. The processor also needs to be able to activate message-waiting displays at the remote-site extensions.

Success in providing voice mail service from the headquarters location will depend on how well the PBX and voice processor share information over their proprietary data link. If a new voice processor is needed at the sales office, the two processors will exchange messages by dialing-up connections through the private network.

Switching and sharing

Asynchronous 19.2-kbit/s data connections from PCs to the headquarters mainframe may be supported economically with an X.25 packet assembler/disassembler (PAD), serving as a statistical multiplexer. The new sales-office PBX, with its proprietary digital telephones, switches data from each PC to the multiplexer channels.

The PBX's data-switching feature also provides for a sharing of local printers and file servers, in addition to concentrating data channels to the mainframe. Providing voice and data to each desktop over a single twisted-pair cable is inexpensive and easy to maintain compared to an overlay of local area networks.

A new T1 multiplexer is needed at the sales office to

1. Proprietary solution. *Here is a current digital solution for networking a new sales office to headquarters. Both PBXs should be from the same vendor. With luck, the PBX vendor's proprietary networking scheme, over T1 lines, will support the integration of the required voice features between the two sites.*

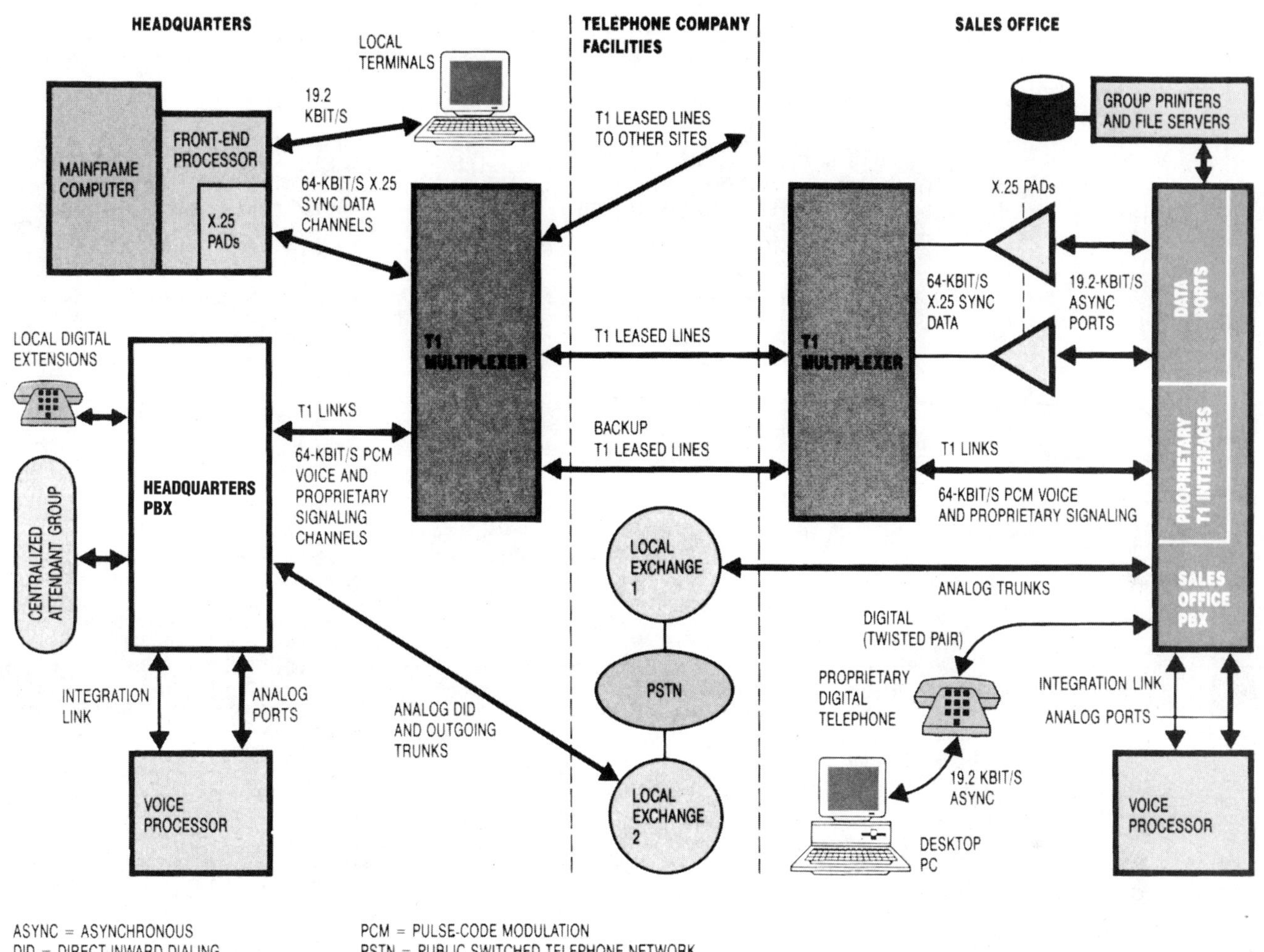

manage the leased T1 lines back to headquarters. Its functions are:

■ To allocate DS-0 (64-kbit/s) channels for synchronous data connections between the PADs and the mainframe;
■ To combine the PBX's voice and common-channel messaging channels with the data connections; and
■ To provide alternative routing in case of T1-link failures.

Redundant leased T1 lines, with separate routing, are needed to ensure continued operation of the sales office in the event of a backhoe disaster.

Will the Integrated Services Digital Network (ISDN) standards make any difference in solving the aforesaid networking problem? Would standardized ISDN networking save money—either in equipment purchases, transmission costs, or in maintenance?

The answer to both questions is yes. ISDN networking promises multivendor-feature integrations, more networking options, and lower costs to users. To understand why, it is helpful to look at how private networks implemented with ISDN standards are different from the proprietary digital networks that are widely implemented now.

During the 1980s, a number of proprietary digital networking techniques were developed by PBX vendors. Most vendors with PBXs that support 500 lines or more now also offer what can be called a "digital networking option." This option uses T1 lines to carry voice, data, and signaling between the PBX nodes in a network.

The first generation of T1 connections to PBXs simply performed the functions of a D3 channel bank—essentially providing tie-line connections with 24 digital PCM (pulse-code modulation) channels. Emulating the analog tie lines that preceded them, these T1 interfaces used "on-hook, off-hook" signaling bits and in-band tones in each channel to establish connections and pass numbering information between networked PBXs.

Subsequently, however, the desire to implement a uniform set of PBX features across networks exceeded the capabilities of in-band signaling to carry this more complex

PBX common-channel T1 networking comparison

PBX	T1-BASED COMMON-CHANNEL NETWORKING	SIGNALING CHANNEL AND LINK ACCESS USED	T1 BEARER CHANNELS	MESSAGE SET AND PROTOCOL USED FOR PRIVATE DIGITAL NETWORKS
AT&T Definity System 75/85	Distributed Communications System (DCS)	A separate, proprietary, data link carries signaling between nodes. An HDLC link access protocol is used.	24 channels per T1 link.	AT&T's DCS uses a proprietary message set between System 75/85 nodes. Messages are transported with an implementation of the X.25 protocol.
Ericsson MD110	T1 links can connect distributed nodes (Line Interface Modules) in a star configuration.	One 64-kbit/s D channel per T1 link is used for signaling. The link access is proprietary.	22 channels per T1 link.	The MD110's distributed architecture uses a proprietary message set and protocol over the D channel established on each T1 or 2.048 Mbit/s connection link.
Fujitsu F9600	'ISDN Network Transparency' available in the first quarter of 1990.	One 64-kbit/s D channel per T1 link is used for signaling. ISDN LAPD access is implemented.	23 channels per T1 link.	Fujitsu's new ISDN networking will use CCITT Q.931 basic call-establishment messages and protocols. 'Supplementary services' messages are based on the Australian PTT extensions, which are similar to evolving ECMA recommendations.
Intecom IBX	InterExchange Link (IXL)	One 64-kbit/s signaling channel is used per T1 link. The link access protocol is proprietary.	InterExchange Links support 21 bearer channels per T1 link.	Intecom's IBX distributed architecture uses a proprietary message set and protocol between IBX nodes.
Mitel SX-2000	Mitel SuperSwitch Digital Network (MSDN)	One 64-kbit/s D channel per T1 link is used for signaling. HDLC link access is implemented.	23 channels per T1 link.	Mitel's MSDN is an implementation of the United Kingdom's Digital Private Network Signalling System (DPNSS). It conforms to British Telecom-recommended specifications. Mitel-specific transparent messages have been added.
NEC NEAX 2400	Common Channel Interoffice Signaling #7 (CCIS #7)	One 64-kbit/s signaling channel is used per T1 link. The link access protocol is proprietary.	23 channels per T1 link.	NEC's CCIS #7 uses a proprietary message set based on a subset of the CCITT recommendation for Signaling System Number 7.
Northern Telecom SL-1 SL-100	Electronic Switched Network (ESN)	One 64-kbit/s signaling channel is used per T1 link. The link access protocol used is LAPD.	23 or 24 channels per T1 link.	Northern's ESN uses a proprietary message set and protocol to network SL-1 and SL-100 nodes. The ESN message set may be carried over primary-rate interfaces, which conform to CCITT standards at Layers 1 and 2.
Rolm 9750	Rolm 9750 Business Communications System (multinode distributed architecture)	The proprietary Control Packet Network (CPN) can use T1 channels dynamically for signaling between nodes.	'Extended Digital Interties' carry up to 24 channels per T1 link.	Rolm's 9750 distributed architecture uses a proprietary message set and protocol for communications between nodes. Signaling messages share bandwidth with bearer channels over T1 or fiber optic links that connect nodes.
Siemens Saturn	Corporate Network (CorNet)	One 64-kbit/s D channel per T1 link is used for signaling. ISDN LAPD.	23 channels per T1 link.	CorNet uses CCITT Q.931-basic call-establishment messages and protocols. 'Supplementary services' messages are defined by Siemens, closely following evolving ECMA recommendations.

ECMA = European Computer Manufacturers Association
HDLC = High-Level Data Link Control
ISDN = Integrated Services Digital Network
LAPD = Link Access Procedure-D

PRI = Primary-Rate Interface
PTT = Postal, Telegraph, and Telephone
SS7 = Signaling System 7

information between network nodes.

Most current T1-networking options use some type of common-channel signaling implementation to carry digital messages between PBX nodes—either over a dedicated separate data connection or one that is shared with voice and data channels. Messages regarding the call-processing and management of a group of connected channels are generated by the software of each networked PBX.

For example, Mary Allen, in the new sales office, has an urgent matter to discuss with the payroll manager at headquarters. She calls, finds the manager's extension busy, and uses the PBX's camp-on (call back when free) feature. The following dialogue of messages might be exchanged over a common signaling channel between the two PBXs:

Sales Office PBX: Request call to extension 2254; extension 6120 is calling with class of service (calling privileges) level 11, text string: "Mary Allen."

Headquarters PBX: Extension 2254 is busy.

ISDN PBX NETWORKING DIRECTIONS	STATUS OF PBX-TO-EXCHANGE ISDN PRIMARY-RATE INTERFACE
AT&T is designing implementations of open ISDN PBX networking based on CCITT Q.931 and evolving ECMA recommendations for supplementary messages. DCS networking capabilities will be migrated to ISDN primary-rate. SS7 support on PBXs will depend on user demand.	Available since 12/87 on System 85. Current features supported are Automatic Number Identification (ANI) and Call-By-Call Selection. New features now in certification.
Ericsson's current implementation of the Digital Private Network Signalling System (DPNSS) in the U.K. will become part of an ISDN networking option in the U.S. during 1990. DPNSS features will be added to Q.931 primary-rate connection capabilities, available at the same time.	PRI-to-exchange connections demonstrated in Australia, Norway, and at AT&T trials. Primary-rate Interface availability in the U.S. is first quarter of 1990.
ISDN primary-rate networking, providing feature transparency between Fujitsu PBXs, will be available within the year on the F9600 and selected Omni products. Fujitsu will respond on an individual basis to requests for an open specification of their ISDN networking implementation.	A primary-rate exchange interface for the F9600 will be available in the third quarter of 1989. Availability for selected Omni PBXs is the first quarter of 1990.
Intecom will adopt ISDN networking standards as they become available. Networking standards based on CCITT Q.931 and Q.932 recommendations are preferred since these would provide a uniform interface for PBX-to-PBX and PBX-to-exchange applications.	A primary-rate exchange interface for the IBX is currently in development and will be available in mid-1990.
Mitel's MSDN currently offers common channel networking functionality equivalent to, and in many cases beyond, CCITT Q.931 and the extensions coming from the ECMA committee. Mitel is also developing Q.931-based SX-2000 networking for future compatibility.	Primary-rate exchange interface available in the U.K., implementing the British Digital Access Signalling System 2 (DASS2). Mitel has not announced an availability date for the U.S.
NEC will migrate its CCIS #7 proprietary networking to an international ISDN standard. This migration will be driven by 'cost-effective user benefits and public exchange capabilities.' The desire is to implement only one international networking standard based on CCITT recommendations.	A primary-rate exchange interface for the NEAX 2400 will be available in the U.S. between the fourth quarter of 1989 and the first quarter of 1990.
Northern Telecom has been a proponent of PBX networking based on a subset of the public exchange Signaling System 7, called the Remote Operation Service Element (ROSE). Northern's exchange-to-PBX ISDN networking and PBX-to-PBX networking are to be based on a common implementation.	Available since 11/88 for the SL-1. Supported features are ANI, Call-By-Call Selection, and NB+D. NB+D supports signaling for up to 16 primary-rate lines (383 B channels) on one D channel.
Rolm declined to comment for this survey. IBM's recent agreement to sell Rolm Systems to Siemens Corporation is expected to influence Rolm's directions in ISDN networking.	Rolm has not announced an availability date for a 9750 primary-rate exchange interface.
CorNet will be available on Saturn PBXs in the third quarter of 1989, and is currently shipping with the Siemens HiCom PBX in Europe. CorNet will continue to be upgraded to ECMA recommendations, leading to CCITT Q.932 and Q.933.	A primary-rate exchange interface for Saturn PBXs will become available at the same time as the CorNet interface: third quarter of 1989.

(Mary Allen hears busy tone from the local PBX and activates the camp-on feature.)

Sales Office PBX: Extension 6120 requests a camp-on to extension 2254.

Headquarters PBX: Camp-on confirmed.

(Mary Allen hears a confirmation tone and hangs up, waiting to be rung back when the payroll manager's line becomes free. The payroll manager receives a message on her displayphone: "Camp-on from Mary Allen, Ext. 6120.")

These messages are usually assembled into packets, along with other messages, and sent over a common data channel between the PBXs. A voice connection between the two locations is never needed during this signaling dialogue.

The table, "PBX common-channel T1 networking comparison," summarizes the common-channel networking implementations using T1-carrier facilities that are being provided by several leading PBX vendors. (The table is not all-inclusive.) Marketing managers from each of the PBX companies were interviewed to assemble the information shown.

Keeping it the same

Today's common-channel networking options offer a high degree of feature transparency between networked PBX nodes. Feature transparency refers to the ability of PBX users to have the same calling and data features across a network of PBXs as they have available at their local PBX. Mary Allen's ability to camp-on to a headquarters extension is an example of feature transparency.

Call-processing information, such as an extension's class of service, is sent across networks to allow remote-site users to share trunking facilities and other calling privileges. A centralized attendant service option is provided over common-channel networks by most PBX vendors. An exception is Northern Telecom's (NTI) SL-1, which currently provides the centralized-attendant feature only over conventional tie lines.

Most common-channel T1 networking in use today is in proprietary, closed implementations. Closed means that no published specification for interworking is available to users, network integrators, or other third-party vendors. PBXs in proprietary networks share most features only with PBXs from the same vendor.

The most widely implemented examples of proprietary T1 networking in the United States are AT&T's Distributed Communications System (DCS), NTI's Electronic Switched Network (ESN), and NEC's Common-Channel Interoffice Signaling Number 7 (CCIS #7).

Despite NEC's choice of names, its CCIS #7 uses a proprietary message set, which is based on a subset of the CCITT recommendation for Signaling System Number 7.

Richard Minthorne, director of product management for NEC America, says that there are no plans to publish an open specification for NEC's CCIS #7.

"This might change in the future if other vendors implemented SS #7 for networking," says Minthorne. NEC's long-term direction, he explains, is to migrate its CCIS #7 networking to the international ISDN standard. This migration will be driven primarily by central office ISDN capabilities. Minthorne stressed that "there need to be cost-effective user benefits to migrate private networks to ISDN."

NTI's ESN is now being offered over the company's SL-1 and SL-100 primary-rate ISDN interfaces. Using the first layer of CCITT ISDN standards, these interfaces structure the T1 bit stream into 24 DS-0 clear (full 64-kbit/s) channels.

In addition to standard ISDN 23 B+D channel use, an implementation option is to provide common-channel signaling for managing up to 16 primary-rate lines (383 B channels — 24 × 16, minus the one D channel) over a single D channel. This N × B + D arrangement provides further bandwidth conservation by using the one D channel for all the channels' signaling.

Proprietary protocol

Consistent with ISDN standards for the data link (Layer 2) of the OSI (Open Systems Interconnection) reference model, Link Access Procedure-D is used to convey messages over common D channels. Still, the actual protocol and structure of messages (corresponding to the upper levels of the OSI reference model) for NTI's ESN remain proprietary to NTI, however. This currently precludes the possibility of interworking through a direct primary-rate connection with an ESN network by any other vendor or service provider.

On the question of networking openness, Bob Hoffman, Product Manager for ISDN Network Services at NTI, responded that the company has already published its first specifications for exchange-to-PBX ISDN primary-rate connections.

"Northern's is a full-product family across public and private networks. I see exchange-to-PBX and PBX-to-PBX ISDN networking as being the same. We need to accommodate customer needs and will continue to talk with other vendors to arrive at common standards," Hoffman says.

AT&T's DCS has been implemented in networks across the United States for roughly six years now. DCS messages are exchanged among System 75, System 85, and Definity nodes over a virtual data circuit using implementations of high-level data link control and X.25 protocols. With a separate common-channel data circuit, all 24 channels of connected T1 links may be used as bearers for voice or data traffic.

Dick Davis, Supervisor of Systems Planning For Definity Generic 2 at Bell Laboratories, says that DCS networking will remain proprietary to AT&T.

"The direction is to create an open [networking] specification with ISDN standards. DCS will retain its current networking features, with new features to be introduced as needed. We intend this to be a smooth transition [to ISDN networks], compatible with the DCS installed base," says Davis.

AT&T development efforts are focused squarely on

networking its PBXs with an implementation of the CCITT ISDN recommendations Q.931 and Q.932 (see "When will ISDN networking come together?"). A vendor executive who is participating in AT&T's ISDN trials speculated that we may see a product announcement for ISDN networking of Definity in six to 12 months.

"Networking features such as calling- and connected-party identification are available now [on Definity primary-rate connections]," says Bell Labs' Dick Davis. "It may take two to three years before all of the DCS-enhanced networking features are available on ISDN. In the interim period, we will see hybrid DCS and ISDN networks, with interworking of basic features."

AT&T's recent Definity PBX announcement included primary-rate features for AT&T virtual private network support and load sharing in automatic call distribution applications. N × B + D capabilities were also announced, providing signaling control for up to 20 primary-rate interfaces (479 B channels — 20 × 24, minus one D channel) over a single D channel.

Ericsson's MD110, Intecom's IBX, and IBM/Rolm's 9750 PBXs are designed with what are loosely defined as distributed architectures.

Distributed PBX architectures received a lot of attention in the early 1980s. It was during that period that so-called fourth-generation PBXs were introduced, typified by the CXC Rose, Ztel's PNX, Intecom's IBX, and Rolm's 9000 CBX. Distributed architectures offer the following advantages for network implementers:
- Absolute feature transparency between nodes;
- The ability to share large amounts of bandwidth (connection channels) between nodes; and
- Centralized management and programming.

Similarities predominate

Differences between the capabilities of distributed and networked architectures have blurred in recent years. Both, in fact, use similar principles to exchange call-processing messages between nodes over a common data channel. Distributed software architectures communicate information on network activity to each node on a continual basis, increasing — compared with the networked case — message content and frequency. On the other hand, networked architectures pass information between nodes as the result of an event or query, sending messages to only those nodes involved in a particular transaction.

Comparing feature transparency of networked and distributed architectures, however, is becoming a nonissue. One has to look very hard to find usable features that a networking approach cannot implement.

The main advantage that remains with distributed architectures is their ability to efficiently share large amounts of connection bandwidth over coax or optical-fiber links. High-capacity links are only really useful where "dark fiber" (unmultiplexed optical-fiber cables) can be economically installed, such as within building complexes, in campus environments, or along utility company rights-of-way.

Mark Housley, product marketing manager at Rolm, explains that interconnecting distributed 9750 nodes with

T1 links is an option for customers who are not able to install optical fiber.

"The preferred method of connection is to install internode links, which support 365 channels each via optical fiber, versus 24 channels provided over Extended Digital Interties." Extended Digital Intertie is the name given to Rolm's proprietary T1 interconnection product.

Nodes in a Rolm 9750 installation communicate signaling and management messages over a virtual data circuit, called the Control Packet Network (CPN). CPN uses available connection channels of either internode links or Extended Digital Interties to transport message packets between nodes. The implementation—similar to that of other vendors—is entirely proprietary to Rolm.

Marketing managers at Rolm declined to comment on the anticipated directions for ISDN networking of the 9750. Sources close to the company indicate that after the effects of IBM's sale of Rolm's development and manufacturing facilities to Siemens are more fully assimilated, Rolm is expected to begin development of ISDN networking soft-

---

When will ISDN networking come together?

When asked about networking with ISDN Centrex, a research manager at one regional Bell operating company (RBOC) comments: "We're still trying to determine the direction internally."

ISDN Centrex (containing PBX-like features), with the ability to integrate with private PBX networks, may still take several years to evolve. A significant problem is that there is currently a lack of ISDN networking standards in ISDN protocol Layers 3 and above. And, unfortunately, arriving at a common standard is hampered by political and commercial interests.

ISDN standards are constructed using the Open Systems Interconnection seven-layer reference model:
- Layer 1 (physical) specifications for primary-rate (DS-1) connections are in CCITT recommendation I.431.
- Layer 2 (data link) protocols for the D channel (called Link Access Procedure-D) are contained in Q.920 and Q.921, which was ratified at the November 1988 CCITT plenary session.

These first two layers are considered stable and have been widely implemented in primary-rate interface chip sets and controller firmware. The trouble begins at Layer 3, the network layer.

CCITT recommendation Q.931 ("ISDN User-Network Interface Layer 3 Specification") covers messages and protocols for basic call set-up and supervision over primary-rate ISDN interfaces. This is the Layer 3 specification that has been implemented to make exchange-to-PBX primary-rate connections in the United States.

Q.931 does not cover the voice and data features that are expected of modern PBX networks, however. Even rudimentary features, such as call transfer, forwarding, and call waiting, are not covered by Q.931.

These so-called supplementary services are the specification's void that both standards committees and manufacturers are attempting to fill. The definition of these supplementary services will eventually be incorporated into CCITT recommendation Q.932, called "Generic Procedures for the Control of ISDN Supplementary Services." Q.932 will be submitted for ratification at the 1992 CCITT plenary session.
- **ECMA and ANSI.** There are two main standards committees at work on the upper layers of ISDN primary-rate networking. The European Computer Manufacturers Association (ECMA) has become the focal point of ISDN networking-standards creation in Europe.

ECMA committee TC32/TG6, which is working on a definition of supplementary services, represents a variety of interests. These interests include those of AT&T, IBM, Northern Telecom (NTI), and Siemens.

The American National Standards Institute's (ANSI) T1S1 is a subcommittee that has grown out of the original T1 committee. The latter was formed five years ago by the Exchange Carriers Standards Association. T1S1 is the U. S. focal point of ISDN networking standards.

A member of the ANSI T1S1 committee explains: "T1S1 is composed of four major groups: regional operating companies, interexchange carriers, manufacturers, and users. Most of the user representation is from government organizations."

Doug Spenser, Data Interfaces Supervisor at Bell Labs, has been a member of ANSI T1S1, ECMA TC32/TG6, and CCITT study groups relating to ISDN networking standards. He describes how the ANSI and ECMA committees go through three stages in the development of a recommendation.

"Stage 1 is the determination of architectures and topologies," he says, "Stage 2 is 'What do you want the protocol to do?' At Stage 3, you actually decide on the message set and protocol. The ANSI and ECMA committees are only at Stage 1."

Another member of T1S1 comments: "The committee is driven in two directions. One direction is with the RBOCs and NTI, who support networking based on Signaling System Number 7 [SS7]. The other direction is set by a group of manufacturers who support networking with extensions to Q.931, the same as the ECMA [TC32/TG6] committee. Bellcore's [Bell Communications Research's] technical recommendations [based on SS7] are in conflict with ECMA recommendations.

"T1S1 is mostly dominated by the interests of the RBOCs. They want an ISDN networking standard that will facilitate their implementation of virtual private networks."
- **Who's ahead?** The consensus of the committee members interviewed was that ECMA TC32/TG6 is farther along in the definition of ISDN networking standards than is T1S1. There is a faction in the ANSI committee (composed of several companies also represented in ECMA) that inputs TC32/TG6 recommendations to T1S1. IBM is one of the supporters of ECMA recommendations

ware based on Siemens's set of CorNet standards. Rolm has already demonstrated ISDN primary-rate interfaces in Europe on the now-withdrawn 8750 PBX.

Ericsson's MD110 is also promoted as a distributed-architecture PBX. Since the MD110's internal switching is built on a European 30 B+D (2.048 Mbit/s, instead of 1.544 Mbit/s) framing structure, the preferred method of connecting MD110 nodes in North America is through media that support 2.048-Mbit/s transmissions.

Optical-fiber, microwave, or copper links are frequently installed to establish groups of 2.048-Mbit/s connections between MD110 nodes. When standard T1 lines (at 1.544 Mbit/s) are used, eight channels per link are restricted by converters, yielding 22 B+D connections (one B channel is used for synchronization). And, again, the protocol for signaling and messages sent on the D channel is proprietary to Ericsson.

Ericsson has been an active participant in international ISDN development. Primary rate exchange-to-PBX connections on the MD110 have been demonstrated in Australia,

---

in the United States. The ECMA committee recommendations are widely expected to become CCITT recommendations in 1992.

Simon Wilders, ISDN product manager at StrataCom (Campbell, Calif.), was a representative to the ECMA TC32/TG6 committee through 1988. He estimates that the networking features of Q.932 will be fairly well defined by the committee by the end of this year.

When asked about the direction of standards activities, Bob Hoffman, product manager for ISDN Network Services at NTI, comments: "It's going to take quite a while for a standard to shake out of the ANSI committee." Hoffman explains that a subset of TCAP [see below], called the Remote Operation Service Element (ROSE), has been defined to implement call-associated messaging for ISDN networking to customer premises.

TCAP stands for Transaction Capabilities Application Part. It is an applications protocol that forms part of the North American public network implementation of CCITT SS7. Current public-network TCAP applications involve database inquiries for credit card calling and 800-number translations (see "Knocking on users' doors: Signaling System 7," DATA COMMUNICATIONS, February, p. 147).

Building on the existing TCAP protocol, applications may be created with SS7 to encompass ISDN networking features, such as:

- Call-forwarding management
- Camp-on to extensions
- Virtual private network management
- Centralized attendant services.

A message set and protocol based on TCAP provides an alternative to ECMA's definition of the supplementary services currently lacking in ISDN-user networking standards. This is the definition desired by many of the RBOCs. Implementation of ISDN features on the public network would be easier if customer premises equipment was able to communicate with public exchanges. This implementation could be facilitated via a subset of the language that the public network is already growing to understand: TCAP.

Bellcore and NTI have been working on ROSE (a TCAP subset), which would satisfy the needs for supplementary services in both PBX-to-PBX and PBX-to-exchange networking applications.

With ROSE as an upper-layer standard to network PBXs, the RBOCs could offer users a smooth migration from PBX-based private networks to virtual private networks and ISDN Centrex. SS7-based supplementary-service definitions bring to the RBOCs less time and a lower cost to implement ISDN networking services.

Development of ROSE-based networking software appears to be well under way. "The Northern SL-1 and DMS-100 have been linked with a ROSE network. Networking based on ROSE is now being discussed with the RBOCs," says NTI's Hoffman.

Bell Labs' Spenser comments: "The RBOCs could offer virtual private networks with either Signaling System 7 or Q.931-based [ECMA] protocols. Q.931 would take more work, but Q.931 and SS7 can be made to interwork. The part of the Q.931 message which can't be handled locally can be sent over SS7."

■ **'Management and maintenance.'** Jim Neigh, head of the Systems Interworking Department at Bell Labs, believes that the ANSI T1S1 committee will recommend two standards based on Q.931 and on SS7.

"Signaling System 7 was designed for the public network. It contains a lot of management and maintenance overhead that customer premises equipment can't make use of," says Neigh, "People are saying that a skinny SS7 could be done, but you need Q.931 for [primary-rate] connections to the exchange anyway. Q.931-based [ECMA] standards have more advantages for private and virtual private networking. AT&T will only support SS7 [PBX networking] if the demand materializes."

Neigh says that AT&T is working on its own implementations of Q.932, staying close to the ECMA standards. "AT&T will publish an open specification for its implementation and evolve its products to be compatible with future standards," he notes, adding: "If you wait for the ANSI standards committee [T1S1], it will be 1992 or '93 before we see products. Vendors can't afford to wait."

Indeed, most PBX vendors are not waiting. First implementations of Q.931-based networks, with vendor-specific extensions, are becoming available this year and in 1990. Neigh says that the implementation of open multivendor ISDN PBX networks in the United States will depend on customer demand. "If a sufficiently large RFP [request for proposal] requiring ISDN interworking comes forward, then we could see a multivendor network in a couple of years. If not, it may be several years."

Norway, and in AT&T Communications trials. The British Telecom pre-ISDN networking standard, Digital Private Network Signalling System (DPNSS), is currently available on the MD110 in the United Kingdom (see "The British DPNSS experience").

Larry Minzey, Ericsson product manager, says that DPNSS will become a T1 networking option on the MD110 in the United States during the first quarter of 1990.

"Basically, the top 10 DPNSS features will be supported, including centralized attendant service," says Minzey. "DPNSS network features will complement Q.931-based MD110-to-exchange and MD110-to-MD110 primary-rate ISDN capabilities, which will be available at the same time."

Only one primary-rate networking technique has so far been used to implement multivendor PBX networks: British Telecom's DPNSS. As a subsidiary of British Telecom, and an active vendor in the U. K. marketplace, Mitel of course offers DPNSS on its SX-2000 PBX. Mitel also offers DPNSS networking in the United States over T1 links between SX-2000 PBXs; it is called the Mitel SuperSwitch Digital Network (MSDN). MSDN is reported to have more than 60 network installations in the United States and Canada.

The British DPNSS experience

In the early 1980s, British Telecom (BT) organized a committee of PBX manufacturers (Plessey, GEC, and Mitel) to work on a common channel   signaling standard for PBX digital networking. The committee developed a PBX interconnection standard designed to provide a set of networking features for both voice and data calls. It named its handiwork the Digital Private Network Signaling System, or DPNSS.

Having no accepted ISDN networking standards at the time, the committee built on telecommunications standards that did exist. With the International Organization for Standardization's (ISO) seven-layer Open Systems Interconnection model in hand, the DPNSS was constructed as follows:

■ Layer 1: 2.048-Mbit/s digital links with the same channel and framing structure as that used for 30-channel pulse-code modulation. This is defined under CCITT specifications G.703 and G.732.

■ Layer 2: High-level data link control, the link access protocol defined under ISO specification 4335.

■ Layers 3 through 7: The DPNSS signaling set and compelled protocol (acknowledgment required for each message transmitted) was defined (contained in BT Network Requirements 188) to perform network routing, end-to-end transport, presentation of features, and the exchange of network management information.

The committee's intention was to provide an extensive set of PBX features with DPNSS, but still leave manufacturers with the ability to develop and implement unique networking capabilities. Although DPNSS defines supplementary services for relatively sophisticated applications (such as centralized attendant service and text messaging), manufacturers are still able to implement networking features of their own through "nonspecified information" strings.

DPNSS private networks were first implemented in early 1986. Acceptance since then has been swift. Of 11 U. K. private network managers interviewed in 1988, eight were using DPNSS in their digital networks. Frequently cited reasons for choosing DPNSS were multivendor-PBX feature integration and the ability to use future ISDN offerings from British Telecom to incorporate off-network locations into virtual private networks.

Virtually all RFPs (requests for proposals) for networked PBXs in the United Kingdom now require DPNSS capabilities. DPNSS network users include major government, financial, manufacturing, and transportation networks. For example, the Central Computer and Telecommunications Agency (CCTA) runs the largest DPNSS network in the country for Her Majesty's government. It links 60 PBXs serving over 35,000 extensions in the Westminster area of London.

DPNSS is also being deployed in the broader CCTA network of 170,000 government extensions. CCTA has been the proving ground for DPNSS feature integration between vendors. PBXs from Ericsson, GEC, Plessey, and Mitel are all now a part of the government's DPNSS network.

Plessey, the U. K. market leader, has also been a leader in the implementation of DPNSS on its ISDX PBXs, providing "the feature of the month," as a former Plessey engineer described it. Mitel and GEC are not far behind. Ericsson has only recently entered the DPNSS networking market.

British Telecom's promotion of the DPNSS standard is not totally altruistic. They intend to gain by wooing users from private networks and onto virtual private networks and ISDN Centrex, providing value-added revenue to BT.

To accomplish this, the Digital Access Signaling System 2 (DASS2) specification was created (in 1983) to be a compatible subset of DPNSS. British Telecom began installing DASS2 primary-rate (2.048 Mbit/s) connections between customer PBXs and public exchanges last year.

DPNSS and DASS2 are often termed "pre-ISDN" or "U. K. ISDN" standards. They diverge from CCITT Q.921- and Q.931-specified ISDN primary-rate networking standards at Layer 2 and higher. But with the large installed base of DPNSS networks in the United Kingdom, and BT's current roll-out of DASS2 connections to the public network, it is likely that the island nation will also remain an ISDN island for some time to come.

Indeed, this was found to be a major concern among multinational network managers interviewed in the United Kingdom. With the European continent building ISDN private networks based on Q.931, gateway functions will be needed to connect U. K. sites with those on the continent. Gateways will surely lead to extra complications, feature limitations, and expense for users.

Leo Lax, assistant vice president for ISDN marketing at Mitel, explains that MSDN uses the "transparent capabilities" of DPNSS to exchange Mitel-specific messages (such as text strings for Mitel's on-line telephone directory).

"MSDN is well featured. Users are not satisfied with fewer features [over a network] than they have at a local node," says Lax.

Based on Q.931

Mitel has produced a feature chart that favorably compares MSDN telephony features with those specified by CCITT standards Q.931 (with extensions) and Signaling System #7. Lax adds that Mitel is developing networking capabilities based on Q.931, "since you need to do Q.931 for public exchange connections anyway." He anticipates that the CCITT will adopt "supplementary service" features, similar to those currently used in DPNSS, when the Q.932 specification is fully developed.

Migrating from DPNSS networking to CCITT-standard networking is not seen as particularly difficult. "In addition to differences in the actual format of the messages, DPNSS is a compelled protocol [requiring an acknowledgment for each message transmitted], while Q.931 is not. This will need to be accommodated [by software changes]," Lax notes.

Fujitsu's flagship PBX, the F9600, is billed as "a ground-up ISDN switch." Mike Albers, director of product planning for Fujitsu Business Communications Systems, says general availability of primary-rate interface capabilities is anticipated for late 1989 and early 1990.

Currently dubbed simply ISDN Network Transparency, Fujitsu's PBX-to-PBX networking feature is based on CCITT Q.931. The supplementary service messages (which are needed to implement the majority of PBX features) are designed from Australian PTT (Postal, Telegraph, and Telephone agency) specifications, according to Albers.

Although similar to evolving European Computer Manufacturers Association recommendations for Q.932, the Australian extensions "won't work with other U. S. [networking] implementations," Albers says, explaining that Fujitsu anticipates evolving its ISDN networking implementations as further standards become available.

Will Fujitsu publish an open specification of its ISDN networking implementations? "Fujitsu would respond on an individual basis to requests for a primary-rate networking spec. There are no plans to publish an open specification [as Siemens has done for its CorNet], however," Albers says.

Siemens has taken a bold lead in promulgating a worldwide ISDN PBX networking standard called CorNet (for Corporate Network). Originally created from the German PTT specification, TR6, CorNet has been installed on over 150 Siemens Hicom PBX nodes in Europe. The 700-page CorNet specification was first introduced in February 1988 and is available from Siemens for a small fee.

Scott Augerson, director of product management at Siemens Information Systems, says "CorNet will be available on the Saturn product line in the U. S. during the third quarter of 1989. Primary rate exchange-to-PBX interfacing [Automatic Number Identification and Call-By-Call Selec-

tion] will also become available at the same time. Ninety voice and data features will be supported over CorNet in the first release."

Augerson explains that CorNet is a "living" specification. "CorNet implements CCITT Q.931 now, and will be upgraded as Q.932 and Q.933 become available. Siemens has taken its best guess at the Q.932 supplementary service messages. If the messages turn out to be different, we will change CorNet when Q.932 is released," he says.

Augerson is not aware of any multivendor demonstrations being planned for CorNet. He says that the National ISDN Users Group will be soliciting vendor participation for an ISDN demonstration event in the fall of 1990, however.

To date, the majority of PBX vendors have requested copies of CorNet, according to Augerson. None of the vendors in this survey, however, said that they were considering incorporating CorNet compatibility into their products. The most likely U. S. implementer, among large PBX suppliers, is the Rolm Systems division.

What is being gained?

Why are so many PBX vendors putting so much development effort into networking with ISDN standards? What will ISDN networking do that the proprietary implementations don't do now? Consider again the earlier networking problem—connecting the new sales office to headquarters. Figure 2 shows a networking solution that implements ISDN standards.

T1 leased lines still provide the most economical traffic medium between headquarters and the sales office (you pay fixed monthly lease charges rather than measured rates per call). Back-up lines have been replaced by primary-rate interfaces to the local exchange. If connections on the leased lines are lost, all voice and data traffic can be immediately routed over primary-rate connections back to headquarters.

Providing back-up does not mean that the public exchange must understand PBX-feature messages. The sales office PBX (or headquarters T1 multiplexer) simply requests 64-kbit/s clear-channel connections, as needed, from the public network.

This is done with the local D-channel connection to the exchange. Supplementary service messages, which are used to activate PBX features, may be carried as user data over the public network D-channel. This type of network back-up is a near-term solution. Only rudimentary ("pipeline") ISDN transport capabilities are required of the public exchange network. You don't need to wait for your local operating company to offer ISDN features that are on a par with those provided by your PBXs.

In addition to providing back-up, the primary-rate interfaces have consolidated the local exchange connections, replacing a bank of analog trunks. This should make fault isolation and maintenance easier. Having the primary-rate interfaces in place also provides an inexpensive way to handle peak traffic periods—simultaneous with existing T1 lines—between headquarters and the sales office without adding T1 lines. Over all, the transmission economies have been improved.

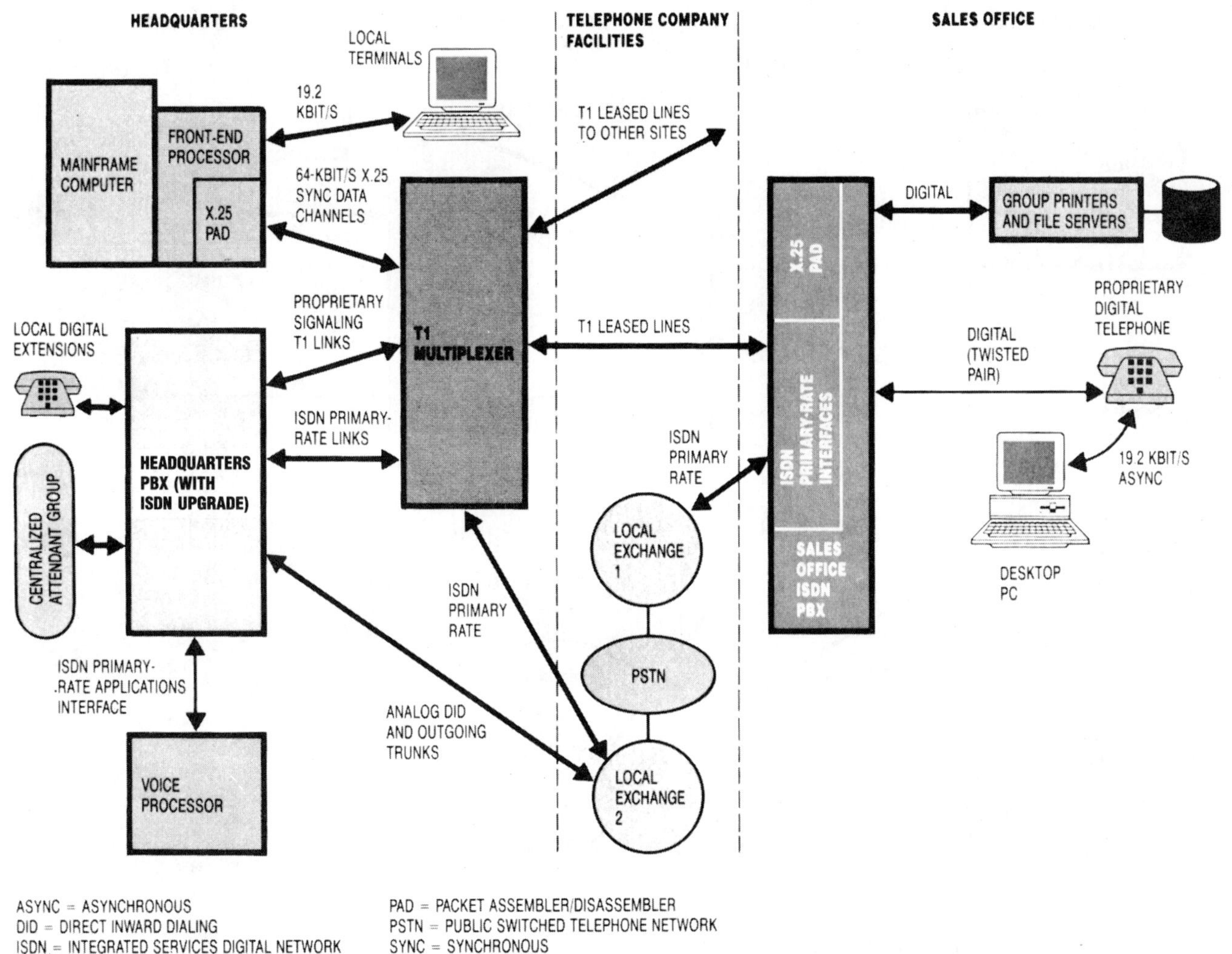

2. Private ISDN solution. In this networking solution, which implements ISDN standards, T1 leased lines still provide the most economical traffic medium between headquarters and the sales office. If connections on the leased lines are lost, all voice and data traffic can now be routed over primary-rate connections back to headquarters.

The most dramatic difference between the proprietary and ISDN networking solutions is the reduction in equipment needed at the new sales office. For example, you don't need to buy an extra voice processor. With forwarding-number identification, message waiting, and called-extension status messages available in a standard ISDN protocol, the headquarters voice processor can provide a full set of voice-mail features across the network. To accomplish this, the voice processor will need to be upgraded to enable the connection of a primary-rate applications interface to the headquarters PBX.

And there is also no longer a need for an end-node T1 multiplexer at the sales office. Using standard D-channel messages, both the T1 multiplexer at headquarters and the ISDN PBX in the sales office can monitor link performance, enabling connection rerouting from either site.

Now that the PBX can manage the entire data connection back to headquarters, the next logical step is to provide the X.25 PAD function internally. This eliminates the bank of PBX data ports (Fig. 1) that were needed to route data through an external (X.25) multiplexer.

Statistically multiplexing the 19.2-kbit/s channels into 64-kbit/s X.25 packet data provides a much more efficient use of the primary rate and T1 DS-0 channels than subrate speed adaption (padding each 19.2 kbit/s up to 64 kbit/s). Statistical multiplexing is even more efficient than subrate multiplexing (putting three 19.2-kbit/s connections into one 64-kbit/s channel).

With ISDN networking, the PBX has assumed many of a T1 multiplexer's roles at a network end. For the management of private network backbone traffic, the functions of the T1 multiplexer are still very much needed, however.

Using open ISDN networking standards, you will also have a choice of vendors from which to purchase the sales office PBX. You can pick the most cost-effective product without worrying about being locked into a vendor's proprietary networking scheme.

Yet another networking solution is looming on the ISDN

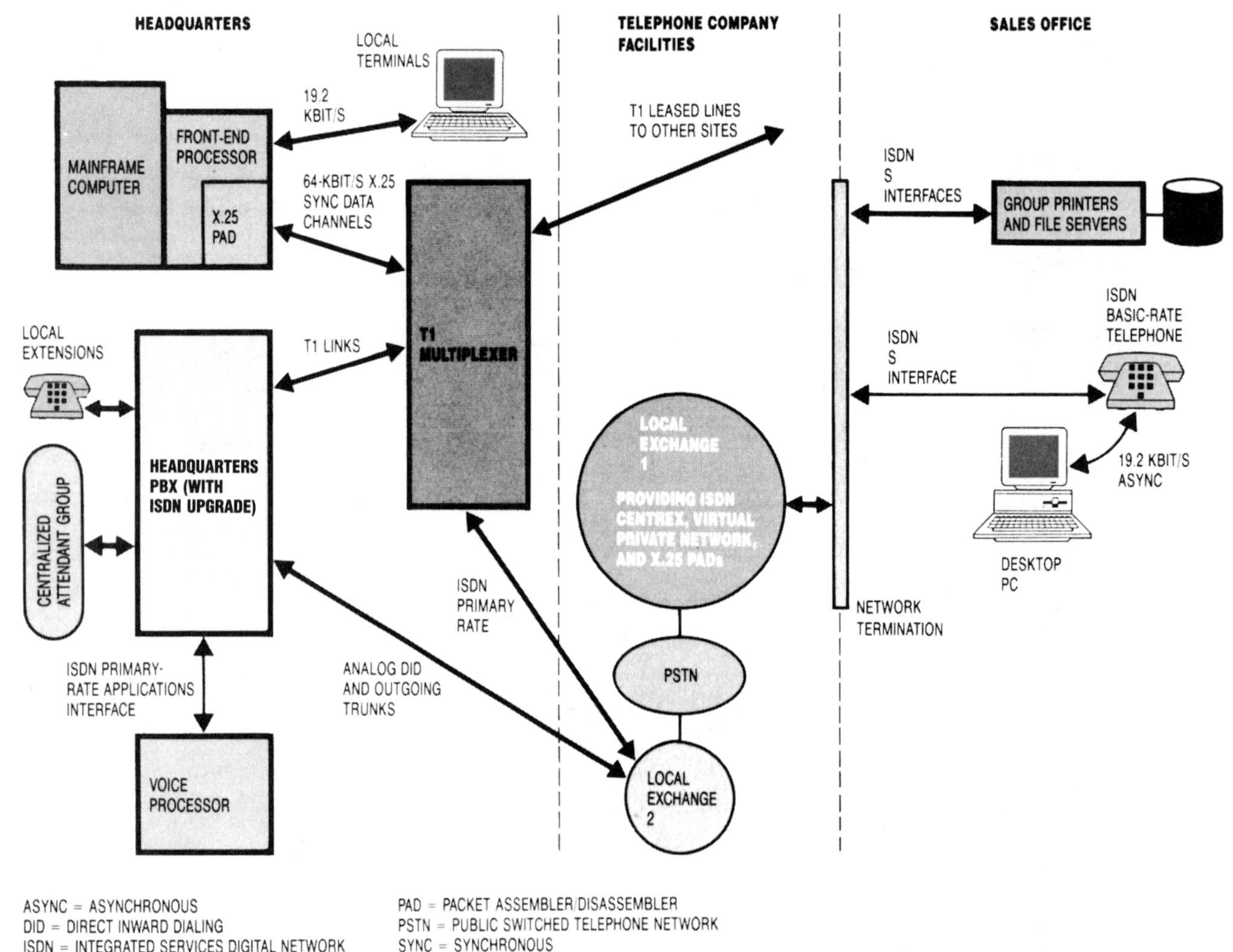

horizon, however. Figure 3 shows a network connecting the sales office to headquarters using an ISDN Centrex service. In this implementation, the only telecommunications equipment needed for the sales office are ISDN basic-rate telephones.

The ISDN Centrex alternative

Data connections from the desktop PCs are plugged directly into the back of the telephones. The local exchange provides an X.25 PAD facility for an efficient concentration of data into primary-rate channels. And a numbering plan can be established that gives the sales office a virtual private network to headquarters. There are no leased lines to the new location.

Unlike the ISDN PBX solution, private network integration with ISDN Centrex requires that the local exchange be able to understand, and generate, a full set of PBX feature messages. For your company to achieve the feature transparency and centralization of resources desired, the local exchange's operating company must offer ISDN capabilities equivalent to your PBXs. This will obviously take longer to evolve than the simple ISDN transport and call establishment abilities required of the operating company in Figure 2.

Providing a full set of ISDN features and solutions is definitely a top-agenda item for the Bell operating companies, just as it is with foreign PTTs. ISDN Centrex also provides new opportunities to private network implementers. For example, by using ISDN standards internally, private networks will be able to make use of ISDN Centrex and virtual private networking as a cost-effective means of serving off-network locations. ∎

Roger Koenig is an independent consultant providing market-research, technical-specification, and international development   planning services to manufacturers of telecommunications products. He previously spent nine years with Rolm, involved with PBX design and development. He holds an M.S. in Engineering Management from Stanford and a B.S.E.E. from Michigan State.

U.S. Companies Involved In ISDN Trials And Service Rollouts

Company	Switch	Access	Carrier	Status	Note
Aetna, Hartford, Conn.	AT&T 5ESS	Basic	Southern New England Telephone	Installation underway	
Alverno College, Milwaukee	Siemens EWSD	Basic	Wisconsin Bell	Started March 1988, ends 1989	Trial.
American Express, Phoenix, Ariz.	AT&T System 85 PBX/4ESS	Primary	AT&T	Started July 1988	First customer of AT&T's Primary Rate.
American Transtech, Jacksonville, Fla.	AT&T System 85 PBX/4ESS	Primary	AT&T	Started Dec. 1987	Beta test site for AT&T's Primary Rate.
Arizona, State of, Phoenix	Northern Telecom DMS-100	Basic	US West Communications	Started Nov. 1986, officially ended	
Boeing Co., Seattle	AT&T 5ESS	Basic	US West Communications	Scheduled start Nov. 1988	
Carnegie Mellon University, Pittsburgh	AT&T 5ESS	Basic		Contract pending	
Chevron Corp., San Francisco	Northern Telecom SL-100/DMS-100	Primary/Basic	Pacific Bell	Installation underway	
Contel Corp., Atlanta	AT&T 5ESS	Basic	Southern Bell	Started April 1988	Paying customer.
Control Data Corp., Minneapolis	NEC NEAX 61E	Basic	US West Communications	Started Nov. 1987, ends Nov. 1988	Trial.
Duke University, Durham, N.C.	AT&T 5ESS	Basic	Southern Bell		
Eastman Kodak Co., Rochester, N.Y.	Northern Telecom SL-100 PBXs	Primary		Started Aug. 1988	First Primary Rate using two SL-100s.
Federal National Mortgage Assoc., Washington	AT&T 5ESS	Basic	C&P Telephone	Started June 1988	
First Data Resources Inc. (American Express subsidiary), Omaha, Neb.	Northern Telecom SL-1 PBX and AT&T 4ESS	Primary	AT&T	Unannounced	
Glaxo Inc., Research Triangle Park, N.C.	SL-1 PBX and DMS-100	Primary/Basic	GTE South	Started June 1988	First Primary Rate/Basic Rate in one trial.
Hardees, Rocky Mount, N.C.	Northern Telecom DMS-100	Basic	Carolina Telephone	Scheduled start Jan. 1989	
Hayes Microcomputer Products Inc., Norcross, Ga.	AT&T 5ESS AT&T 5ESS	Basic Basic	Southern Bell Pacific Bell	Started April 1988 Sept. 1987 to Sept. 1988	Using ISDN to develop ISDN products.
Hershey Foods Corp., Hershey, Pa.	AT&T 5ESS	Basic	Contel of Pennsylvania	Scheduled start Oct. 1988	Will include ISDN satellite transmission.
Honeywell Information Systems (Honeywell Bull), Minneapolis	Northern Telecom DMS-100	Basic	US West Communications	Started Jan. 87, officially ended	Applications included data/voice transmission between office and employees at home.
Intel Corp., Chandler, Ariz.	AT&T 5ESS	Basic	US West Communications	Started Feb. 1987, ended Aug. 1987	Trial.
Johns Hopkins Medical Center, Baltimore	AT&T 5ESS	Basic	C&P of Maryland	Contract pending	
Lawrence Livermore Laboratory (University of California), Livermore, Calif.	AT&T 5ESS	Basic	AT&T Federal Systems		
Lockheed Missiles and Space Co. Inc., Sunnyvale, Calif.	AT&T 5ESS	Basic	Pacific Bell	Started Sept. 1987, ended Sept. 1988	Trial.
Mass. Institute of Tech., Cambridge	AT&T 5ESS	Basic		Scheduled cutover Oct. 1988	Using AT&T 5ESS as PBX for private network.
Mather Air Force Base, Sacramento, Ca.	AT&T 5ESS	Basic	AT&T Federal Systems	Started Aug. 1988	Model for ISDN deployment at 50 bases.
McDonald's Corp., Oakbrook, Ill.	AT&T 5ESS	Basic	Illinois Bell	Started Dec. 1986	
McDonnell Douglas Corp., St. Louis		Primary	AT&T	Unannounced	
Microcom Inc., Norwood, Mass.		Basic	New England Telephone	Installation underway	Part of centrex contract.
Motorola Inc., Schaumburg, Ill.	Northern Telecom DMS-100	Basic	Illinois Bell	Planning stage	
NASA, Washington	AT&T 5ESS	Basic	AT&T Federal Systems		
Nice Corp., Ogden, Utah.	Northern Telecom SL-1s	Primary			Telemarketing company using private ISDN.
North Carolina State Univ., Raleigh	Northern Telecom DMS-100	Basic	Southern Bell		
Northeast Utilities, Hartford, Ct.	Northern Telecom SL-1s	Primary			PBXs in Rocky Hill Ct. and Meriden, Ct.
Pennsylvania, State of, Harrisburg	Northern Telecom DMS-100	Basic	Bell of Pennsylvania	Contract pending	Statewide network with ISDN in Harrisburg.
Pratt & Whitney, East Hartford, Conn.	AT&T 5ESS	Basic	SNET		
Prime Computer Inc., Natick, Mass.	AT&T 5ESS	Basic	Southern Bell	Started April 1988	Paying customer.
Rockwell Communication Systems, Richardson, Texas.	AT&T 5ESS with two remotes.	Basic	Southwestern Bell	Scheduled start Dec. 1988	40 buildings in a campus environment will be linked via ISDN.
Shearson Lehman Hutton Inc., New York	AT&T 5ESS	Basic	New York Telephone	Started June 1988	Part of 8,000 line centrex contract.
Shell Oil Co., Houston	AT&T 5ESS	Basic	Southwestern Bell	Start Sept. 1988	Plan to use 5,000 ISDN lines.
Southern Methodist University, Dallas	Siemens EWSD	Basic	Southwestern Bell	Started Feb. 1988	
SunTrust Service Corp., Atlanta	AT&T 5ESS	Basic	Southern Bell	Started April 1988	Paying customer.
3M Corp., St. Paul, Minn.	AT&T 5ESS	Basic	Southwestern Bell	Started Aug. 1988	Plan to use 3,165 ISDN lines.
Tenneco Inc., Houston	AT&T 5ESS	Basic	Southwestern Bell	Started June 1988	Plan to use 3,900 ISDN lines.
Texas A&M University, College Station	GTE GTD-5 EAX	Basic	GTE Southwest		
University of Arizona, Tucson	AT&T 5ESS	Basic	US West Information Systems Inc.	Planning stage	Using AT&T 5ESS as PBX in private network.
University of Connecticut, Storrs	AT&T 5ESS	Basic	SNET		
University of Indiana, Bloomington	Northern Telecom DMS-100	Basic	Indiana Bell		
University of Maryland, College Park				Unannounced	
University of South Florida, Tampa	AT&T 5ESS		GTE South	Started Oct. 1987	
U.S. Dept. of Treasury, Wash.				Contract pending	
U.S. Bank of Oregon, Portland	Northern Telecom DMS-100	Basic	US West Communications	Started March 1987	Trial.
Virginia, State of, Richmond	AT&T 5ESS	Basic	C&P of Virginia	Started April 1988	
West Virginia University, Morgantown	AT&T 5ESS	Basic	C&P of West Virginia	Scheduled start Dec. 1988	Plan to use 660 ISDN lines.

Note: This chart was compiled by *CommunicationsWeek* with information provided by Teleos Communications Inc., Eatontown, N.J., as well as from news releases and published reports. Carriers, switch manufacturers and their affiliated laboratories are not listed.

Edwin E. Mier, editor at large, DATA COMMUNICATIONS

LAN gateways: Paths to corporate connectivity

Until OSI arrives, integrating LANs into corporate networks or creating a backbone binding different protocol stacks hinges on unlocking the mysteries of LAN operating systems.

Maintaining domestic tranquility within a typical departmental LAN is not that hard—as long as the servers all run the same network operating system (NOS) *and* LAN-attached users limit their networking scope to accessing local LAN resources. But corporate communications managers are increasingly tasked with integrating isolated "isLANs" into their backbone network infrastructure. And many are finding that, on entering into these multimegabit local domains, they truly are strangers in a strange LAN.

The big difference, of course, between managing a departmental LAN and managing a LAN in the corporate environment is that the latter involves the efficient design and deployment of gateways, as well as ensuring that users on both sides of those gateways are able to effectively communicate and move data on an end-to-end basis.

Part of the problem relates to the fundamental differences between classic wide area networking and LANs. Corporate backbones have traditionally been typified by leased-line data rates, point-to-point logical connections, and a finite set of well-established (and usually usertunable) protocols, such as X.25 and SNA. Folding LANs into this environment, however, means understanding and accommodating a burgeoning assortment of new and different protocol stacks, high-level software interfaces, and a confusing array of two-sided software-based functions (client-server, requester, redirector, and so on), which may or may not map well to your backbone technology.

Establishing end-to-end connectivity between a single LAN station across a wide area network (WAN) to a remote destination can be difficult enough. Many, though, are now facing the prospect of traversing multiple LANs, perhaps a mix of different IEEE 802 adaptations (or even standardized *and* proprietary topologies) to allow a source in one domain (borrowing from the vernacular of both IBM and the TCP/IP community) to communicate with a resource in another.

Yet, unfortunately, the situation promises to get worse before it gets better; to wit:

■ *Quickly changing software landscape.* The leading LAN operating software suppliers are all in the process of supplanting their existing first-generation software designs with new versions. Major enhancements to NOS architectures will affect more than just performance and user interfaces. For instance, previously standalone (separate software, and usually separate node) router, bridge, and gateway functions are being integrated into server-based or operating system based megapackages. And while this all-in-one approach may enhance the individual LAN NOS's ability to work over a variety of WAN and LAN environments, it will also likely complicate the internetworking of LANs running different suppliers' LAN NOSs.

■ *Planned obsolescence?* With greatly enhanced gateway and communications-server software has come proportionately larger resident-memory requirements to run it. And as memory-intensive functionality goes up, performance tends to decline. In some cases, new releases have even required abandoning the hardware base they had been running on and migrating to totally different, higher-horsepower microprocessors.

IBM's LAN operating software, which two years ago ran on PCs and hard-disk PC/XTs, now only runs on 286-based hardware (ATs and most PS/2s). Indeed, the larger resident-memory requirements have effectively shut MS-DOS-based machines out of certain LAN communications roles and, where already running, have necessitated the transfer of these communications software functions to new, more expensive OS/2-based platforms.

■ *Stacking one on top of the other.* A proliferation of protocol stacks is in some cases being addressed by carrying

Coming to terms with gateways

There is a good analogy between today's network industry and the early days of the railroad industry. At first, independent railroad companies built their own rail systems, in some cases with different track gauges. Forming a foundation for the industrial age, these separate railroads grew to meet the expanding transportation needs of their regions. But inevitably there came a time when customers wanted to ship freight across the boundry of two incompatible rail lines.

Because of the different track gauges, interregional excursions were impossible, necessitating the laborous and time-consuming manual transfer of freight from the cars of one rail company to the cars of another. Eventually, of course, standard rail gauges were adopted and rail cars made by all the manufacturers could travel anywhere in the country. Unfortunately, an enormous amount of track and equipment was made obsolete in the process.

Unlike railroads, successful standardization of transportation lanes for the information age—networks—has not been realized. Until this happens, the gateway is a primary means of converting between the different protocols used in our diverse network architectures. In spite of the gateway's current importance to free movement of data, the definition of a gateway is a bit foggy because of its many applications. In fact, it's not just gateways that are underdefined these days, it's also the network operating systems (NOS) that create the environment in which gateways operate.

■ **A nose for NOSs.** First a definition. A sensible set of criteria for a NOS is that it must provide a minimum of file, print, and communications services to clients running one of the following workstation operating systems: Unix, DOS, OS/2, or Macintosh O/S.

But what about DECnet, IBM's SNA, and other architectures that primarily support terminals—or terminal emulation—but not client-server relations. These architectures deploy gateways as well, but for purposes of this discussion they are considered special cases. The gateways on the terminal-supporting networks allow minicomputer or mainframe hosts to convey information, to dissimilar systems, as agents for dumb terminals.

Bridges for host-based networks differ substantially from bridges on true NOS-based, client-server networks such as 3Com, Novell, IBM token ring, and Banyan, among others. LANs in which both the user station and the shared resource servers (file server, print server, modem server) have an operating system are said to have a client-server architecture. Unlike host bridges that do everything for the terminal, NOS bridges divide the protocol-conversion chores equitably between the user's station and the gateway node (see figure). When a user on a client-server LAN sends data to a dissimilar system, say, a host that supports 3270 terminals, the user's workstation runs an emulation program that converts user data into a format appropriate for the target system. In the case of the 3270 gateway, the user's workstation converts its PC data stream into the 3270 data stream. "Data stream" in this context means a mix of data and native control characters that is specific to the formatting and outputting needs of a given station or printer.

Once the user data—for example, a request for a specific record—has been formatted by the emulation program on the user's node, it gets passed to the gateway node using the LAN's native communication protocols (for instance, XNS running on Ethernet). When the

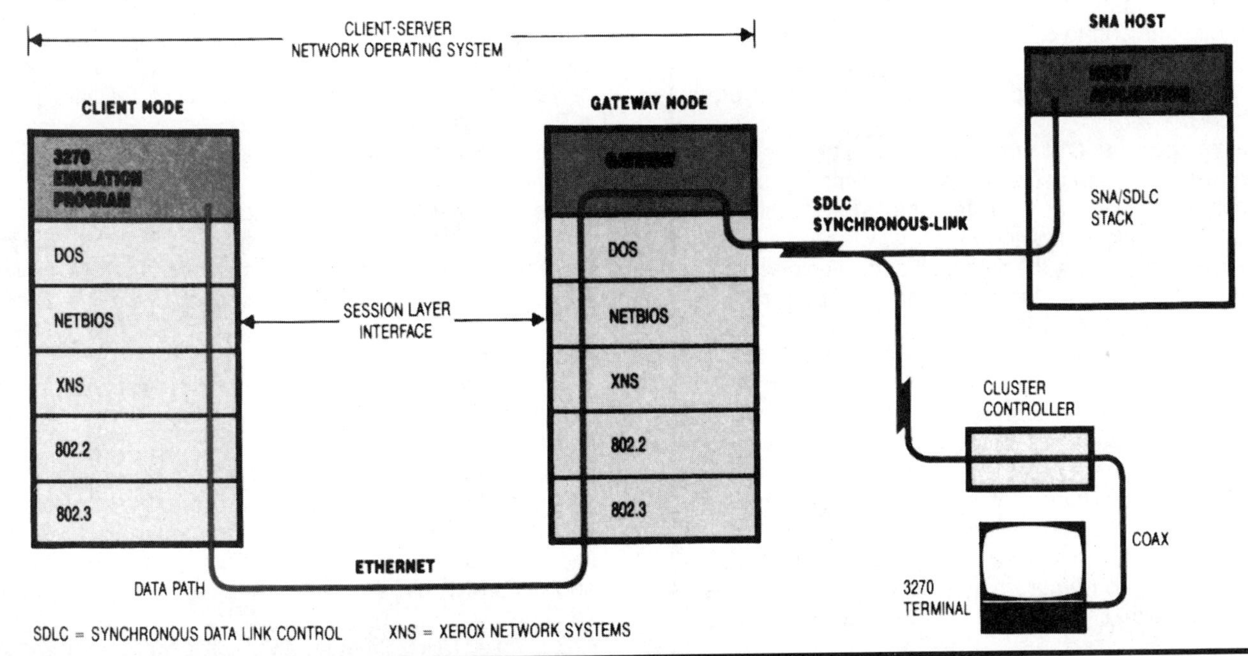

gateway node receives the data from the emulation application, it packages it up in the communications protocol required by the target system, in this case, SNA/SDLC, and then ships it through a local or remote link to the host computer.

■ **Gateway vs. bridge.** If someone tells you that he has a gateway between two similar networks, he probably means a remote bridge. It is easy, for instance, to confuse X.25 remote bridges with X.25 gateways. The bridge just ships a LAN's upper-layer protocols and user data over a wide-area packet network to a LAN that uses the same protocols and data stream — transparent to the user stations. An X.25 gateway, on the other hand, requires the user station to run an emulation program that converts data to the format used on a dissimilar system — often an asynchronous host, in the case of X.25. The gateway then takes the converted data from the user's node and ships it over a packet network to the target network using X.25 protocols. This is very different from an X.25 bridge.

Here's another way to think of this: When a user's station communicates through a bridge (or router), it maintains its identity; it is still a PC or Mac or Sun or other client. But when a user's station communicates through a gateway, it functionally becomes something else: a 3270 terminal, a 5250 terminal, a VT 220 terminal, whatever.

Of all the devices in the network segmentation spectrum (repeaters, bridges, routers, etc.), gateways are the most likely to have low throughput. Gateways often suffer from the impediment of low-speed links supported by modems, although, by definition, a gateway does not necessarily communicate through a telephone line. In IBM's architecture, for instance, 3270 gateways can tranfer PC requests to mainframes through an end-to-end token ring link. But even in the case of a high-speed link, gateways still have the innate disadvantage of time-consuming multilayer protocol conversion.

■ **Waiting for OSI stacks.** When will the computer industry be freed of the burden of making its stations imitate other stations just to talk across heterogeneous networks? When, like the railroads, will our networks support a diversity of data-exchange vehicles from any vendor, all traveling on the same protocol tracks? The answer is likely the same as the answer to the question: When will OSI become widespread?

Gateways may always be with us in some form or another, but a better technique for clients from dissimilar NOSs to interact is through OSI standard protocol stacks. When different operating systems use the same stack, a world of efficient and dependable cross-architecture communications is possible. WAN/LAN bridges and routers running standard protocols are the key to barrier-free data transportation in this futuristic world. *—Steven S. King*

an entire LAN protocol stack, or its most important layers, within another stack (layered above it, as it were) to achieve end-to-end connectivity (such as, say, AppleTalk layered above DECnet, or 3270 LU2 protocols on top of Netbios). This inevitably involves additional and duplicated communications processing, with the resultant performance loss accepted as the price for simultaneous support of both protocols.

■ *Data "whiplash."* Unlike a typical WAN connection, LAN-WAN integration entails sending data across a combination of links, which may range from a 1.2-kbit/s asynchronous phone line to a 16-Mbit/s synchronous token ring. This hurry-up-and-wait syndrome carries with it two big problems: an increasing likelihood of buffer overflows, especially at critical junctions such as terminal servers; and a mismatch of link flow-control mechanisms, which invariably are determined based on the characteristics of the particular transmission segment. The result in both cases can be lost user data.

■ *You say tomato.* Tending to confuse users even more, there is no standard industry use of LAN communications software terminology. To one vendor, "supporting" a particular protocol may mean implementing that particular protocol stack. To another it can mean something entirely different, such as supporting just the programming interface for that protocol. There is a big difference (see "Coming to terms with gateways").

Aside from different interpretations for the same term, vendors also employ different terms to describe what amounts to the same software function. Take, for example, the Berkeley BSD "Sockets" interface — a Unix de facto standard mechanism for accessing TCP/IP, analogous to Sun Microsystems' Network File System (NFS). Sockets is referred to as a "client-server function" by one vendor, a "remote procedure call" by another, and yet another calls it an "interprocess communications" facility.

These semantic differences are in some cases subtle, but they can nevertheless confound a user's ability to effect connections. Take, for example, Novell's and Apple's differing aspects of "Netbios compatibility."

Netbios is actually two distinct types of software:

■ The set of layered protocols (read stack) that is loaded into IBM PCs and compatibles so they can communicate on a LAN.

■ The session-level programming interface, similar in function to IBM's Advanced Program-to-Program Communications (APPC), that makes it easy for PC-DOS application software to set up sessions with applications on other nodes, allowing many types of data access, data transfer, and messaging functions.

The Netbios session-layer interface is widely supported on LANs from diverse vendors, the Netbios stack, on the other hand, is not robust and is used by IBM, but not on most of the LANs from 3Com, Novell, and Banyan.

Apple's Netbios services consist of a board and software for the Mac II (called TokenTalk and promised for release later this year) that allows it to connect to an IBM token ring and perform as a client (or requester, if you prefer) to IBM servers.

But TokenTalk will not mean that the Mac can run

appllications software or programs that access LAN services via the Netbios session-layer interface. Further, a Mac II running TokenTalk cannot act as a gateway for other nodes on an AppleTalk LAN.

Novell's NetWare 286, on the other hand, does support the Netbios session-layer application interface, allowing any Netbios-aware software applications to run on top of it. But NetWare 286 does not support or implement the Netbios protocol stack, and subsequently cannot access or communicate with IBM servers on an IBM LAN (IBM's current token ring LAN and PC Network LANs all support the Netbios stack and the Netbios applications interface).

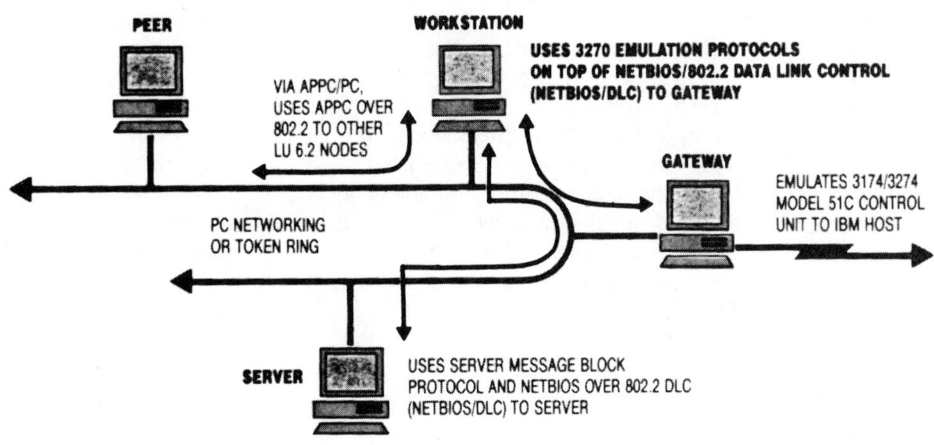

1. IBM connectivity. *In addition to a basic server attachment, an IBM PC or PS/2 station can converse across a token ring to a 3270 gateway and a LU6.2 peer. If necessary, all three interfaces are loaded at once, leaving little memory for applications.*

Communications managers can be better prepared to deal with these disturbing trends and developments by understanding how the leading LAN vendors differ in their software-design approach, especially as it pertains to their current products' protocol and gateway support—and their plans for the future regarding these functions.

LAN NOSs—in transition

To understand the new realities of linking LANs and their operating systems, a little history is in order.

In the past 18 months, an accelerated evolution has been under way throughout the LAN industry—from what might be called first-generation, PC-DOS- and MS-DOS-oriented networking packages, to more advanced versions that take advantage of the multitasking, queue-driven operating environment of full 32-bit desktops. For the most part, this equates to OS/2-powered PS/2s, but not exclusively. Apple Computer's mid-June flurry of gateway and connectivity enhancements, for example, clearly favors the Motorola 68020-based Mac II, the only model now sporting the 32-bit Nubus, as Apple's new gateway/server node of choice.

Last November's delivery by IBM of its new OS/2 LAN Server software, coupled with Version 1.1 of its OS/2 Extended Edition operating system, played a major role in sparking this new LAN NOS genre.

Among the first to follow suit was 3Com with early availability of its 3+Open operating system, which has as its base IBM's OS/2 kernel (the relatively "unadorned" Standard Edition). The OS/2 kernel is coupled with 3Com's own version of server software (the LAN Manager), and its own repertoire of built-in software programming interfaces and supported protocol stacks.

3Com archrival Novell counterattacked with the announcement of its NetWare 386. The first version (3.0) is slated for delivery in the fall, but it is in a later release (Version 3.1, due out early next year) that Novell is promising to incorporate its full array of different protocol stacks and software interfaces.

And as mentioned, Apple recently unveiled a bevy of AppleTalk connectivity products (most due out this fall) including Phase II of AppleTalk. While not a drastic overhaul of the original AppleTalk, Phase II enables Apple-Talkers to traverse multiple segments of Ethernets and token rings, as well as other AppleTalks. The keystone of Phase II is substantially enhanced internet router software, which Apple says will be capable of keeping straight the locations of thousands of local and remote AppleTalk nodes (which, notably, can include DOS-based PCs and VAX/VMS minicomputers) over multisegment, multitopology LANs.

Big Blue's gateway blues

In spite of all this apparent movement toward mature LAN technologies, the industry's ability to move data freely between its vastly differing architectures is barely out of the Stone Age. Nowhere is this more evident than with IBM, where gateway communications from LANs into wide-area SNA networks and to IBM hosts are not easily facilitated with Netbios.

In April 1987, IBM brought out the LAN Support Program, which offered either Netbios on top of the IEEE 802.2 protocols or just 802.2 (the latter for a couple of particular applications—3270 terminal emulation across the LAN and for PCs running APPC/PC [APPC for the PC], offering a session-layer interface directly to low-level transport services, see Figure 1).

This new combination "Netbios/DLC" protocol stack is now the mainstay of IBM LANs; the "DLC" refers to the data link control layer, of which logical link control (LLC) is a sublayer. As discussed later, it seems that now, with soon-to-be-delivered OS/2 enhancements, IBM may finally be able to segregate Netbios LAN operations from its future ideal: to run APPC throughout both IBM SNA wide area networks and SNA local area networks—efficiently swapping out 802.2 LLC (to be used over LANs) with Synchronous Data Link Control (SDLC) and/or X.25 over the long haul.

IBM has a lot to gain, of course, if it can compel its users to buy PS/2s by the bushel. If it can get them to also abandon their PCs, so much the better. Big Blue has a strategy to do this, largely via OS/2, and as long as it doesn't push users too hard, it may well succeed.

The strategy seems to hinge on future communications capabilities, particularly as they pertain to the interworking of PCs and PS/2s on the same LAN.

Users of IBM's PCs have long lamented the fact that the MS-DOS operating system only allows access to 640 Kbytes of usable memory on PCs. This is problem enough for standalone PCs, but on networked PCs the accelerating growth of memory requirements for communications protocols and LAN software interfaces has made the 640-Kbyte workspace impossibly inadequate for many applications.

For example, to access a token ring based OS/2 LAN Server as a workstation "requester" (including redirector, messenger, and receiver components), a PC needs assorted LAN software loads that require over 400 Kbytes of memory—leaving less memory than what is required for most applications, not to mention their data.

The same is true today for any PC that is configured to perform as a server—even on a LAN consisting only of other PCs. Performing as a file server requires the PC LAN Program in the server PC, and also in any requester PCs on the same LAN (it's the same program, just configured differently). But the latest PC LAN Program version (1.3, issued last year) now requires at least a 286-based AT (and ideally a PS/2) to be the server. The previous release allowed a hard-disk XT to be a server.

Even to run through IBM's 3270 LAN gateway, memory requirements both for the gateway and for PC workstations that access it are sizable—and growing (see table). Including the DOS 3.2 operating system, a 3270 LAN gateway needs about 260 Kbytes of memory for communications system software (plus about 30 Kbytes more if users elect to add the Server-Requester Programming Interface, or SRPI, which IBM now encourages as the standard for LAN applications that use LU2.0 communications for 3270-emulation applications). Even an MS-DOS workstation on a LAN that communicates off-LAN to a 3270 host through the gateway needs system software requiring on the order of 160 Kbytes (not counting the MS-DOS operating system). The left-hand column of the table shows memory requirements for a DOS-based PC with APPC, 3270 emulation, and the network interfaces all loaded—an extreme case, for power users only.

For the memory-requirement reasons already discussed, it is increasingly undesirable to run an MS-DOS PC as both a LAN server and as a gateway. There is also the reason that PC gateways have a greater proclivity to "lock up" than do PCs engaged in other activities.

The reason, says Dick Kamerer, senior product planner with IBM Entry Systems Division, is all the interrupts that a gateway receives. As the PC is interrupt-driven (unlike the multitasking, queue-driven PS/2) when two interrupts are received at exactly the same time, a lock-up results. This may not be catastrophic in some PCs, but the only real remedy is to shut down the gateway PC and reboot it (any data in transit when this happens is lost). Naturally, the more gateway traffic the gateway PC gets, the greater the chances of this happening.

"The worst combination to put into a gateway," says Kamerer, "is large files and an AT bus." His recommendation, echoed by nearly everyone at IBM these days: Get a PS/2.

Duplication of effort?

Besides the Netbios/DLC stack currently in use on IBM LANs, the way LAN workstations get to, and through, gateways appears somewhat less than elegant.

Ed Hurry, technical planner with IBM's Entry Systems Division in Austin, Tex., acknowledges that a Netbios/DLC session establishment is first conducted between the workstation and the gateway. (In the case of a

PC (MS-DOS) memory requirements (bytes)

REQUIRED OPERATING SOFTWARE	WORKSTATION PC, XT, XT-286, AT, OR PS/2	GATEWAY PC, XT, AT, OR PS/2	SERVER PC/AT OR PS/2
MS-DOS 3.3 (OR 4.0)	48K (75K FOR 4.0)	48K (75K FOR 4.0)	48K (75K FOR 4.0)
PC LAN PROGRAM (v1.3)	46K (REDIRECTOR ONLY)	46K (REDIRECTOR ONLY)	350K (SERVER CONFIGURATION)
LAN SUPPORT PROGRAM (v1.1) OVER TOKEN RING	35K (60K IF PC NETWORK)	35K (60K IF PC NETWORK)	35K (60K IF PC NETWORK)
PC 3270 EMULATION PROGRAM (v3)[2]	160K (MINIMUM FOR WORKSTATION)	200K (MINIMUM FOR LAN GATEWAY)	—
APPC/PC (v1.11)	203K	—	—
PC MEMORY REQUIRED FOR LAN OPERATING SOFTWARE	500K TO 540K	340K TO 380K	440K TO 500K
MAXIMUM MEMORY AVAILABLE IN 640-KBYTE PC FOR ALL OTHER APPLICATIONS	100K TO 140K	260K TO 300K	140K TO 200K

1. PCS NEED A PREVIOUS, SINCE-WITHDRAWN VERSION OF LAN SUPPORT PROGRAM (v1.0). THE LATEST VERSION IS NOT SUPPORTED ON PCS AND REQUIRES HARD-DISK XT, AT, OR PS/2.

2. THE NEW IBM PERSONAL COMMUNICATIONS/3270 PROGRAM, SCHEDULED TO BE AVAILABLE IN JULY, RUNS THE 3270 EMULATION PROTOCOLS ABOVE 802.2 DLC, EFFECTIVELY BYPASSING NETBIOS. MEMORY REQUIREMENTS FOR WORKSTATIONS COULD BE SLIGHTLY LESS THAN SHOWN; MEMORY REQUIREMENTS FOR THE GATEWAY ARE GREATER, HOWEVER.

3270-emulation gateway, the gateway must then establish a logical 3270 session with the host.) The LAN workstation then communicates to the gateway in the appropriate format (3270 or asynchronously, for example), but each message is encapsulated within Netbios/DLC frames for LAN transport to the gateway. The gateway then strips off the Netbios layers and passes on what's left.

This procedure is regarded as inefficient since Netbios incurs a lot of protocol-processing overhead, especially when it is just an envelope carrying asynchronous-message traffic from a workstation to a gateway's modem line.

Experts agree that two other protocols—XNS (Xerox Network Systems) and DEC's Local Area Transport (LAT) protocol—handle this much more efficiently and with much less LAN overhead. IBM declined to comment on the relative efficiency, or lack thereof, of Netbios/DLC in this environment.

It appears that this Netbios/DLC process will be streamlined somewhat in the OS/2 world of the future by running SNA protocols—and not Netbios/DLC—right on top of 802.2 LLC, thus eliminating the requirement to convert LAN workstation requests and frame formats to their most appropriate wide-area-SNA equivalent, along with all the overhead and processing that entails.

While OS/2 offers greater communications capacity, capability, and flexibility, not all of the necessary pieces are available from IBM yet. Indeed, the current version of the OS/2 Extended Edition (1.1) contains no inherent gateway capabilities. (The abilities of an OS/2 Extended Edition to communicate as a standalone node are present, and they are impressive, but the added functionality to manage these communications links for other stations over a LAN simply haven't been included yet.)

AppleTalking

Apple Computer Inc., with a long-held and well-deserved reputation for marching to the beat of a different drummer, is apparently getting in step with the rest of the LAN world.

Apple makes it abundantly clear that it has no intention of departing from its existing AppleTalk design or protocols, and that it has, with the June introduction of AppleTalk Phase II, just refined, expanded, and added to it. A key element of Phase II is a new Internet Router software package, which tracks and routes AppleTalk sessions between thousands of AppleTalk-speaking nodes scattered over interconnected LANs (Ethernets and token rings, as well as AppleTalk, see Fig. 2). AppleTalk Phase I had a maximum limitation of 254 network nodes.

In addition, AppleTalk Phase II adopts use of IEEE 802.2 packet framing, which allows it to also incorporate the framing/address of the particular underlying 802 LAN that the AppleTalk frame is traversing (802.3 for Ethernets, 802.5 for token rings, and so on). Phase I AppleTalk used only the 48-bit addressing and framing structure of Ethernet/802.3, not the full protocol. This change also now allows AppleTalk routers to do selective "multicasting" and zone broadcasting of messages to select groups of machines, instead of

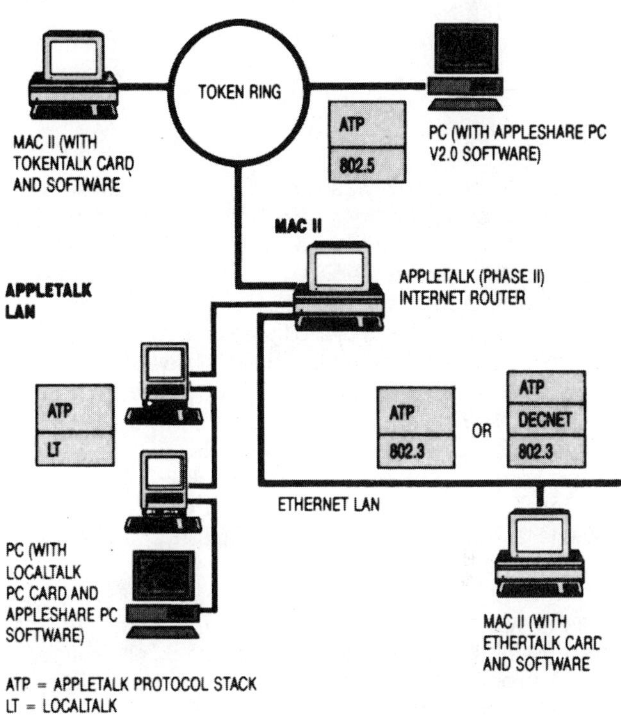

2. Apple LAN togetherness. *With the upcoming Apple Mac II router, AppleTalk clients on token ring, Local Talk and Ethernet LANs can access common resources.*

its earlier Phase I "general broadcast" to all machines.

Apple has shown itself to be very selective about how it plays along with others—especially IBM LANs and its development partner, DEC. For example, the new June product (to be available this fall) enables a Mac II user to plug in an 802.5 board, attach to an IBM token ring (just 4-Mbit/s rings for now), and communicate with IBM's PC LAN servers (and reportedly also OS/2 LAN servers) as a workstation requester (client).

The Mac II board includes all the necessary software components included in the IBM PC LAN Program and the IBM LAN Support Program, and handles full token ring compatibility, including source routing. (Apple says this is assured because it uses the same token ring chips from Texas Instruments that the numerous third-party token ring products use; IBM has developed proprietary VLSI [very large-scale integration] chips for its own token ring cards.) The Apple code also reportedly provides full Netbios/DLC compatibility.

But here's the rub. The Mac II token ring product does not allow the Mac to assume a server role on the token ring, just a client-requester role (unlike IBM nodes running the PC LAN Program, which can be either). And neither is the Mac equipped with the token ring/Netbios connection able to serve as a gateway to an AppleTalk, which would theoretically enable other Macs to patch through to also access the IBM servers on the token ring.

Neither does Apple support the popular Netbios applica-

293

tion programming interface (API). "We don't support it, in part, because it's written for Intel microprocessor-based MS-DOS machines," says Robert Wohnoutka, Apple's manager of product marketing for AppleTalk network systems. "The Netbios API tells you, for example, to write things to a particular Intel register. We're Motorola microprocessor-based, not Intel."

MacRouting

"AppleTalk isn't 802-anything," says Wohnoutka, almost proudly. But he winces when asked why Apple doesn't do a gateway, based on the Mac II-Netbios product, for AppleTalk-to-Netbios translations. He says this is due to the wide disparity between AppleTalk protocols and Netbios. As a result, mapping between the two is extremely difficult, if not impossible. One major difference is routing.

"In Netbios, there's no routing definition, which is why it'll never be adopted as a standard," Wohnoutka says, adding: "All Netbios has is source routing, if you call that routing." He notes that the Internet routing scheme Apple employs is more akin to the routing of TCP/IP, where routers dynamically track which nodes are where, what the best route to take is, and then modify the DLC layer addressing to reflect the best route.

Unlike the robust, Layer 3 and 4 protocols of a TCP/IP router, IBM's source routing is based on an "enhancement" made to the the 802.5 frame specification. This feature allows an optional routing field within each frame, which is used by end stations and bridges, not routers, to specify the path through a complex of bridged rings. This low-level approach to routing differs considerably from the philosophy of TCP/IP, XNS, and other popular stacks, which do not route at the data link level (Layer 2).

"With source routing," Wohnoutka says, "you can't, for example, figure a 'best route' on a real-time basis."

It should be noted that AppleTalk's new routers, which Apple recommends be dedicated Mac nodes, are not gateways, and don't provide translation to other platforms. Whether they physically connect an AppleTalk to an Ethernet, or an Ethernet to a token ring, "Our routers only route AppleTalk protocols," notes Wohnoutka.

This means that, while Apple LAN communications products enable communications across multiple, different-LAN segments, the destination of any AppleTalk-generated message "has to be an AppleTalk/AppleShare service," says Wohnoutka. He adds that this need not necessarily be a Mac: It could be a PC loaded with "AppleShare for PC" software, which makes the PC an AppleTalk Filing Protocol (AFP) "client" in the AppleTalk world, or a VAX loaded with "AppleTalk for VMS" software.

Novell novelty

Novell is hanging its hopes for a continuation of past glories on its next-generation LAN NOS: NetWare 386. Novell's product emphasis has long been on server software, with cooperative workstation "shell" programs that load into the other LAN PC workstations.

And Novell makes clear that it doesn't intend to abandon that approach. Jabbing at IBM's bloated and memory-intensive OS/2 operating system, Novell states in its preliminary NetWare 386 technical documentation that: "Like the other dedicated NetWare server products that have preceded it, NetWare 386 is designed specifically as a network server operating system. It does not attempt to graft network functionality onto a workstation operating system."

However, when it comes to gateways that enable off-LAN egress, and onto-the-LAN access, Novell has responded with software products that all run as MS-DOS applications, and which Novell admits may not—and perhaps even should not—run on the server.

"With NetWare 286 (Version 2.15 is the latest), all our gateways now run on a DOS machine," says Richard King, vice president of software development with Novell's network products division. He adds that this arrangement has proved effective, and efficient, since communications from any LAN workstation to a gateway "don't need to go through the server's core operating system, except for bridged connections."

A long-touted and impressive feature of Novell's server communications software has been its bridging capability. Up to four different LAN segments, of different LAN types (token ring, Ethernet, and Arcnet, for example) can be connected through the server. This has been possible because Novell's and LAN board vendors' substantial efforts to write drivers that convert the format of the particular underlying LAN to NetWare's internal routing format.

"We have a third-party LAN certification program for doing this," says King, adding that "we've certified over 100 adapters." Novell still writes and maintains drivers for 3Com's cards, IBM's, and its own.

Novell has made its server-based routing particularly efficient. When the router determines that a message is to go from one LAN segment to another (as opposed to into the server for, say, a file access or print session) the message forwarding is done in less than 200 machine instructions, according to King. Depending on the speed of the server's processor (say, 10 MHz), this means that message forwarding between disparate LANs involves only a few milliseconds of delay.

To date, Novell has not developed any particular gateway products optimized for its LAN network-server operating system: Instead, it has acquired gateway experience and products through acquisition (Novell's archrival 3Com largely did the same thing).

Novell's acquisitions included Santa Clara Systems in 1986, CXI (offering its PCOX line of micro-to-mainframe links) in 1987, and this year added Excelan (with extensive TCP/IP experience as well as VAX expertise).

The major planned NetWare 386 enhancement that will affect on- and off-LAN gateway communications is Novell's concept of Network Loadable Modules, each of which would contain a different set of protocol stacks and/or program interfaces. Novell says it plans modules for Netbios, Named Pipes (considered by many an enhanced successor to Netbios for interprocess communications), AT&T's Transport Level Interface (TLI, for Unix), as well as

Gateway advice for the LANlorn

Here are a few general design considerations and recommendations, culled from the collective advice of vendor product managers and experienced users:

■ Consider the right protocol stack for the right job. Experienced users have found that certain LAN protocols are better for different types of LAN traffic. DECnet/LAT and XNS, for example, reportedly are better suited to short-message and bursty asynchronous-terminal traffic than, say, Netbios/DLC. Similarly, TCP/IP is lauded for its suitability for very large files.

■ Be wary of back-to-back, high-speed LAN segment mismatches. Try to avoid, if possible, gateway or router connections of relatively low-speed LAN segments (say, 1-Mbit/s Starlans or 2.5-Mbit/s Arcnets) to much higher-speed ones (10-Mbit/s Ethernet or 16-Mbit/s token ring, for example). Bridges, which do minimal processing, still need to be able to handle large buffered queues. With routers and gateways, where processing is much greater, buffer overflows are increasingly likely.

■ Examine flow control on a link-by-link basis. Where data routinely passes over a combination of local and long-haul links from source to destination, be sure each end of each link can throttle the other. A half-duplex phone-line link from a computer port directly into an asynchronous communications server, for example, can spell disaster if the host begins dumping voluminous files into the server, which cannot then intermittently interrupt the host.

■ Get the whole story from gateway vendors. Be sure you understand what the product does, what it supports—and what it doesn't. Also, get estimates of throughput based on your particular environment (type of messages, message length, number of messages expected per unit of time, and protocol or protocols used).

■ Keep gateways on LAN segments where they're most used. It may even be a good idea to add another duplicate gateway on another LAN segment, rather than run inordinate amounts of traffic through a router or bridge from stations seeking a gateway to the LAN segment where the gateway resides. It not only adds traffic to two LAN segments unnecessarily, but it increases the likelihood of congestion problems at the crossover point.

■ Do a risk assessment before packing too many key functions on the same LAN node. It may appear to be cheaper at first glance to also house a gateway (even more than one gateway) on the same node as, say, a file server. But weigh the prospects of data lost because of lock-ups or buffer overflows resulting from high gateway volumes. A traffic analysis to determine the optimal "probability of blocking," and then engineering so that load generally doesn't exceed capacity, is the goal.

■ Nesting, or layering LAN protocols on top of each other, can in some cases yield simultaneous compatibility. But the duplicated protocol processing can overwhelm nodes. Memory and processing requirements where a mix of protocols are employed often exceeds the sum of the parts if they were to operate individually.　　—*E.E.M.*

Sun Microsystems' Network File System (NFS, also a Unix-oriented client-server protocol), and AFP and the AppleTalk protocol stack.

While much attention and detail in this article has focused on the widely diverse protocol stacks that the leading LAN operating system suppliers now support, likely to be just as important to corporate network planners in the 1990s is the growing array of divergent APIs, client-server protocols, interprocess communications facilities and other new high-level software services.

While it is beyond the scope of this article to delineate each, suffice it to say for now that these areas, too, are likely compatibility trouble spots that will be encountered in coming years. As with all facets of data processing and data communications, thorough planning is essential in this complex, evolving environment (see "Gateway advice for the LANlorn").

The existence of many different permutations of TCP/IP running over today's massive Ethernets is an example of this syndrome, at a lower level. Due to Unix's popularity and its widespread adaptation by so many different computer makers, different protocol implementations were bound to evolve (as much, it seems, to distinguish all the different offerings as to provide bona fide functions or points of reference).

Still, there is progress. For instance, Unix experts say that, as long as support for the same TCP/IP protocol functions is available within an extended network, support for Sun's NFS, Berkeley's Sockets, AT&T's TLI, and others can be adjusted and tweaked to accommodate differences. Coexistence is possible.

IBM similarly has embarked on a campaign of issuing different APIs for virtually every different communications-protocol variation (SRPI for programs using LU2.0/3270 communications, Common Programming Interface—C language (CPI-C) for LU6.2 applications, ACDI for modem-oriented asynchronous applications, and so on). An IBM insider, however, advises communications managers that adherence to these APIs, or lack of adherence to them, may make only minor differences to compatibility. The difference between the CPI-C interface for LU6.2, and the existing APPC interface, for example, may involve only a few added commands—from perhaps a hundred or more that they have in common.

These new features, interfaces, and functions bear watching, to be sure, but it may be years before certain ones establish themselves as de facto standards. And buyers' preferences for those that enjoy the most widespread support will be a key factor. ■

Edwin E. Mier, editor at large for DATA COMMUNICATIONS, *is also president of Mier Communications Inc., a communications and networking consultancy in Princeton Junction, N.J. Mier, who holds a BA degree from Lehigh University, specializes in connectivity issues and problems.*

Dean Wolf, Fujitsu Inc., and Steven S. King, DATA COMMUNICATIONS

Making the most of ISDN now

Although reports coming in from ISDN trials praise the high speeds and low error rates, it's apparent that new application planning criteria are needed.

Over the past few years, the noise level from discussions about ISDN theory and internals has grown to an acronym-laden roar—CCITT I.430, SS7, Q.931, 2B1Q, V.120, TE2, and so on. Unfortunately for readers of technical publications, much of this flood of verbiage refers to elements of digital networks that lie outside of a user's domain.

But in the realm of customer data terminal equipment (DTE) and workplace ISDN applications, things are a lot more familiar than the ISDN theory articles would have it. In the course of a user's daily interaction with ISDN, for instance, computers converse with ISDN terminal adapters (the modem-like device that connects non-ISDN computers to ISDN networks) using familiar Hayes AT and X.25-PAD command sets. Q.931 signaling procedures running on the ISDN D channel's Link Access Procedure-D (LAPD) protocol are there too, just as the articles predicted, but they exist well below the level of user operations.

Introductory articles have also given us some very large expectations about what ISDN will deliver. With all that's been said, it is easy to assume that local ISDN services and high-speed terminal adapters (TA) will arrive just in time to meet upcoming demands for increased communications bandwidth, allowing computers to exchange data briskly, at 19.2 kbit/s or even 64 kbit/s. And if that's not fast enough, according to the ISDN gurus, we will be able to order up a couple of ISDN B channels, add some compression, and go for 200 kbit/s, desktop to desktop.

Of course, it's not that simple. Many of the ISDN pilot sites aren't running at 64 kbit/s yet, let alone 200 kbit/s. In fact, most are running at 19.2 kbit/s or less. Given the constraints of existing hardware and software, some initial ISDN applications have been limited to the snail's pace of channels that were designed at the height of the analog era. Let's face it, even today, few communications pro-

grammers are coding applications with error-free 64-kbit/s digital lines in mind.

For insight on the implications of ISDN for existing communications setups, consider what happened when the industry first added high-speed analog modems to its arsenal of communications gear. These modems talked to each other at dazzling speeds across voice-grade lines. Unfortunately, the process of goosing throughput exposed previously unconsidered weaknesses in computer-to-modem links, in data rates available on installed ports, and particularly, in production communication software.

In addition to throughput bottlenecks in the non-ISDN elements of their networks, early ISDN users are finding that their application software is not always well suited to a near-error-free environment. These pioneers have discovered that communications software doesn't stop giving time-consuming acknowledgments for every packet just because it's on an ISDN line. In most cases, communications software such as Kermit, Crosstalk, or ProComm doesn't know that it's not talking to an analog modem. This is because the TAs do such a good job of emulating a modem on the DTE side of their interfaces.

Eventually, ISDN ports will be built into every computer, as RS-232 and similar ports are today. But until then, computers will need a TA between them and the switching nodes on a digital network. Consequently, it is the features and limitations of both the TA and the central office switch that determine what services are available to today's ISDN users.

Basic-rate services

Although not available in all possible combinations, the fundamental set of ISDN basic-rate data services consists of:
■ B-channel circuit-switched (BCS) service for one or two B channels on an as-needed basis, with data rates up to 64 kbit/s. BCS can be asynchronous or synchronous, and is

protocol-independent, in that it does not assume X.25 or other protocols. Some, but not all, central office switches can provide a permanent B channel circuit as a provisioned service.

■ B-channel packet-switched (BPS), an X.25 service on the B channels on a permanent or switched basis, to 64 kbit/s. Some switches allow BPS on one B channel only and may require BPS to be permanent in initial offerings.

■ D-channel packet-switched (DPS), an X.25 service on the D channel at sub-16-kbit/s data rates. Circuit switching is not available for current ISDN D-channel implementations.

In spite of all the attention given ISDN's 64-kbit/s data rates and advanced interfaces such as synchronous V.35, much of the initial application work is being conducted with asynchronous equipment at speeds of 19.2 kbit/s or less. This makes sense, considering that currently there are few computers or front-end processors (FEPs) with asynchronous RS-232 ports running at 64 kbit/s. Generally, TAs support the 64-kbit/s rates with synchronous protocols.

Because of the lack of widespread support for 64 kbit/s, TAs use a rate-adaption technique that lets them provide user equipment with speeds of 56 kbit/s, 48 kbit/s, or less on the B channels. TAs come with one or two RS-232 or V.35 ports that can be used to access the BCS services concurrently. At sub-19.2-kbit/s speeds there are typically a variety of TA rate options: 300 bit/s, 1.2 kbit/s, 2.4 kbit/s, 4.8 kbit/s, 9.6 kbit/s, and 19.2 kbit/s.

In the case of X.25 packet switching for the B channels, it is important to distinguish the nominal 64-kbit/s rate from the throughput class of the X.25 virtual circuits, generally 9.6 or 19.2 kbit/s. Multiple virtual circuits can run on a single ISDN channel; their throughput class is independent of the channel speed. If the connecting computer has an X.25 FEP, the TA's internal X.25 PAD can be turned off. When the TA's PAD is on, it can be configured with familiar syntax, such as the Hayes AT or CCITT X.28 commands (see Table 1).

Manufacturers of ISDN-capable central office switches generally provide a B-channel packet-data facility as a provisioned (preassigned) service. This means that the function is set up specifically via a service order, in a

Table 1: Typical ISDN Terminal Adapter Commands

X.28 commands

(All commands are followed by <CR> except <CTRL>P)

PAD command	Function
CLR	Clears a virtual call
INT	Transmits an interrupt request packet
MENU	Switches to off-line command mode
PROFn	Selects a profile
PROF?[n]	Reads a profile (the currently active one if number is omitted)
PAR?n	Reads a parameter value
R	Requests reestablishment of a virtual call
RESET	Transmits a reset request packet
STAT	Requests status of a virtual call connected to the DTE
n…n	Sets up a virtual call
SETmin	Changes or establishes a parameter value
SET?min	Changes or establishes a parameter value and then reads it
<CTRL> P	Escape character

X.28 result codes

Code	Description
COM	Call connected
ERR INC	Error
RESET	Reset
FREE	Call status
ENGAGED	Call status
PAR (list)	Parameter value
CLR CONF	Clear confirmation
CLR ERR	Local procedure error
CLR RPE	Remote procedure error
CLR PAD	Call cleared by PAD
CLR DTE	Call cleared by terminal
CLR OCC	Called number busy
CLR INV	Invalid call
CLR DER	Called number out of order
CLR NC	Network blocked
CLR NA	Access denied
CLR NP	Called number not assigned

AT commands

Command	Parameter	Function
AT		Attention code; precedes all commands except A/ command
A/	None	Repeats last command (Don't use prefix AT)
Dn	n = up to 30 digits	Dials a call (tone dialing only)
En	n = 0	Do not echo commands
	n = 1	Echo commands
H	None	Disconnect a call
O	None	Returns to on-line state
Qn	n = 0	Sends result codes
	n = 1	Suppresses result codes (quiet mode)
Sr=n	r = 0-16	Register number
	n = 0-255	Sets register 'r' to value 'n'
Sr?	r = 0-16	Reads contents of register 'r'
Vn	n = 0	Numeric output of result codes
	n = 1	Verbal output of result codes
Xn	n = 0	Result codes 0-8 and 30-33 (See Result Codes table)
	n = 5	Preceding result codes and 21-23
%I	None	Request to send INTERRUPT packet (for PAD)
%Pn	n = 0-3	Selects specified profile (for PAD)
%P?n	n = 0-3	Reads specified profile (for PAD)
%R	None	Requests to send RESET packet (for PAD)
%S	None	Requests call status (for PAD)
MENU	None	Switches to off-line command mode

AT result codes

Numeric	Verbal (DPS/BPS)	Verbal (BCS)
0	OK	
1	CONNECT	
3	NO CARRIER	
4	ERROR	
7	BUSY	
8		NO ANSWER
21	ENGAGED*	
22	FREE*	
23	TRANSFER*	
30		CALL REJECTED
31		B-CH BUSY
32		INCOMPATIBLE
33		L1 DEACT

*Expanded result codes

manner similar to that of placing a subscription order with a value-added network for X.25 service. Current AT&T 5ESS switch software allows provisioning of a single permanent BPS channel per basic-rate interface (BRI). Switched BPS service will become available with the next 5ESS software release for nondedicated applications. The Northern Telecom DMS-100 switch allows both B channels to be configured as packet-switched, permanent service.

On many ISDN installations, the most attention has been given to the basic rate's packet-switching D channel (DPS), which supports X.25 as the B channel does, only at lower speeds. Part of the reason for this attention is economic, in that the D channel is quite inexpensive compared to the high (but descending) costs for the B channels.

The D channel runs at 16 kbit/s between the TA and the ISDN switch. But because this channel is also used for call set-up and network management signaling, the full 16 kbit/s is not available to the user.

Whenever possible, user equipment is configured to interface with a TA at 19.2 kbit/s, while the TA transfers through the network as fast as current loading conditions allow. The D channel can be shared by multiple devices—on the same BRI—in which case throughput can bog down to unacceptable levels. Trials on a single D-channel attached device on lightly loaded networks have clocked end-to-end throughputs of up to 14 kbit/s. It must be stressed that only ISDN-optimized software can attain these speeds.

Packet heaven

Because of the multiple-virtual-circuit facility of X.25, calls can be set up between multiple DPS- or BPS-connected computers in terminal-to-host configurations (see Fig. 1).

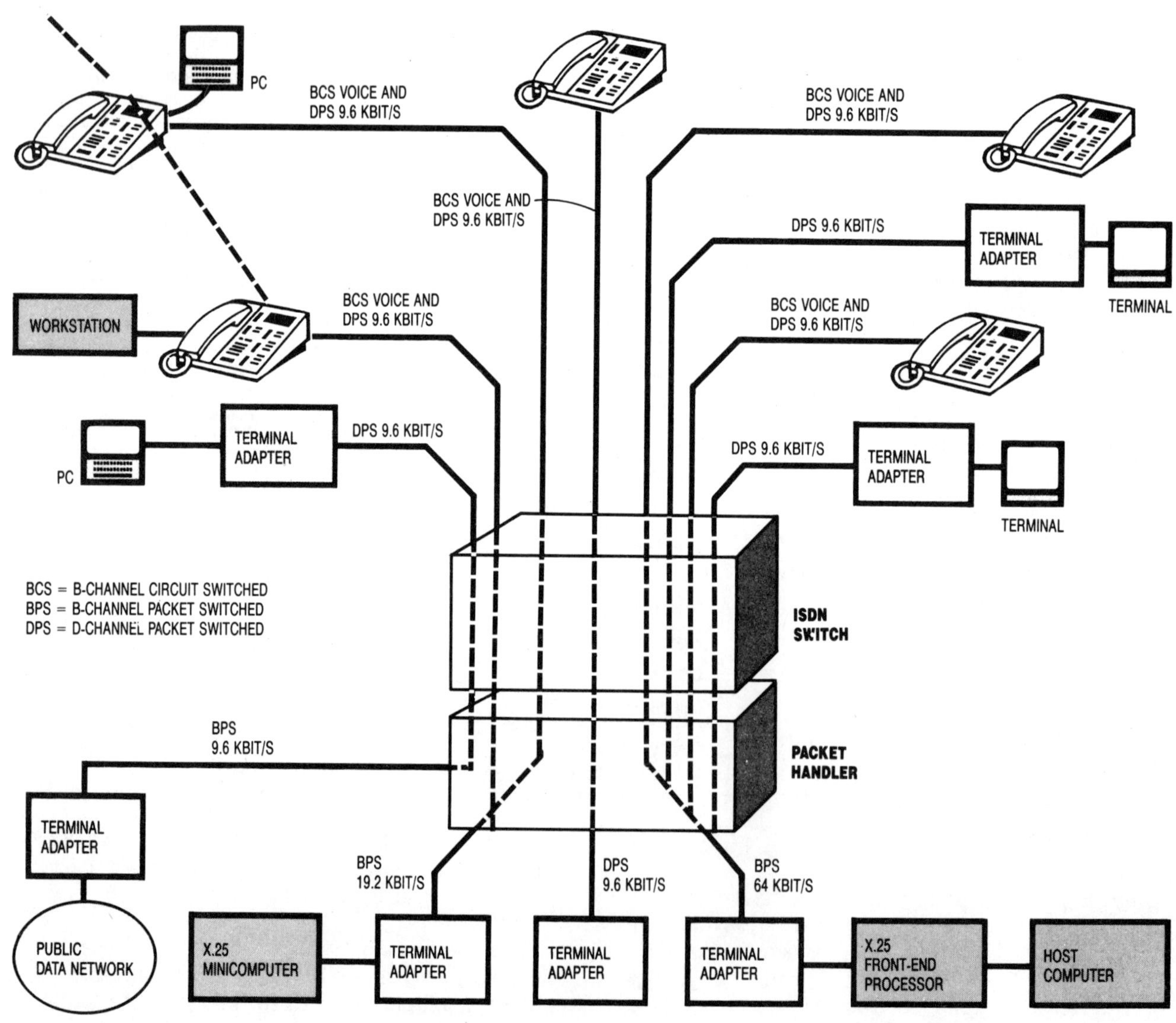

1. Packet-switched. The ISDN central office switch freely mixes circuit-switched and packet-switched channels. The advantage of packet switching is that channel bandwidth is allocated to a call only upon the appearance of data from a terminal device. This data is typically divided into packets of 128 or 256 bytes.

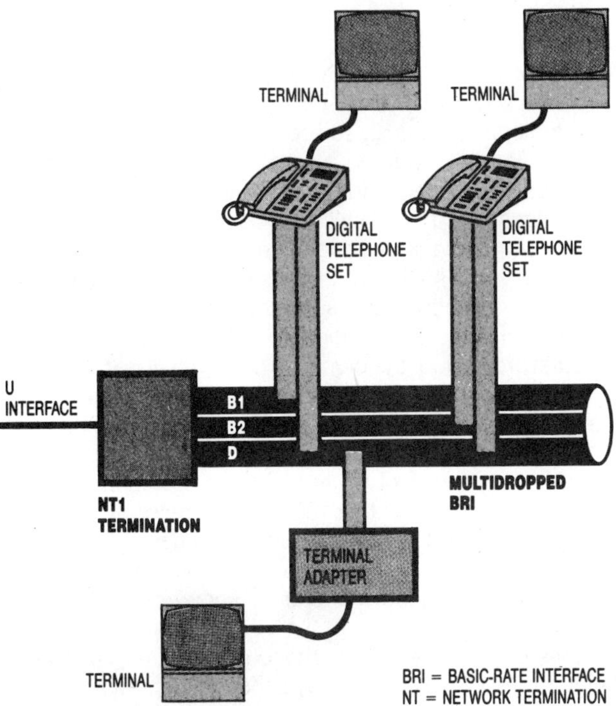

For example, several DPS TAs can create logical channel connections through a central office packet handler to a single BPS-connected computer. BPS service can provide greater throughput than DPS service because of the higher speed of the channel and the ability to request a higher throughput class (an X.25 feature that defines the maximum data rate of a virtual circuit — for instance, 19.2 kbit/s).

Packet switching on the B and D channels brings a number of advantages to X.25, such as the ability to multiplex multiple logical links on the 2B+D channels. The end effect of X.25 on an ISDN is error-free communications from TA to TA. For circuit-switched ISDN, without X.25 error correction, bit-error rates are related to the quality of the local loop, something on the order of one in 10^{-6} bits.

The 5ESS allows abbreviated dialing for X.25 packet-switched calls via a feature called 4-Digit Intercom. Northern Telecom has an automated dial feature called Direct Call, which allows prestoring of the destination address at subscription time.

There will increasingly be alternatives to ISDN's classic one-BRI-per-TA configuration. The availability of these alternatives varies greatly from vendor to vendor, but it usually involves multiple TAs sharing a single basic-rate line. For instance, the ISDN specifications allow up to eight terminals to be multidropped per line.

The advantage of multidropping is greater utilization of the 2B+D line (see Fig. 2). In this configuration, two digital telephones with integrated TAs share the line with a stand-alone DPS TA. The two B channels are fully occupied by the telephone users and the D channel carries the traffic for three terminals. ISDN trials have shown that response times for DPS users can become noticeably slower if more than three or four terminal users simultaneously share the D channel for a typical interactive application such as on-line text editing.

Note that the ability to utilize a BRI in the manner described is dependent on the bandwidth requirements of a given application. For example, if PCs are given D-channel access and the application calls for continuous PC-to-PC or PC-to-host file transfers, it is recommended that the BRI be configured to allow only a single PC to have D-channel access. A BRI configured in this manner could support two voice-only telephones and a PC via a stand-alone DPS TA.

Trials and errors

Given that the majority of in-place software and hardware has been designed to transfer data on the lower-speed, error-prone channels that typify the analog age, a choice that faces users is: either down-size expectations for ISDN, or, upgrade existing components, often at considerable expense and effort. Judging from the trials, there will be a lot of both going on, as ISDN becomes widely available.

To fully comprehend the effects of high-grade digital links, it is necessary to examine the entire end-to-end application, including FEP-to-host communications, packetizing software, port-to-bus interfaces, and file transfer methods. All these components are potential bottleneck areas.

Overengineering the ISDN interface to support a full 64 kbit/s for an application that is throughput-limited to 9.6 kbit/s (such as 3270 protocol conversion) obviously results in excessive cost and wasted bandwidth. This is due to the underutilization of the high-cost TA and FEP with, for example, 64-kbit/s V.35 interfaces.

Suppose you have an application running at 19.2 kbit/s. You feel the application could benefit from a speed upgrade to 64 kbit/s with ISDN BCS service. Before upgrading your network components — such as communications controllers for a host computer — talk to your equipment supplier. Ask for references of users with network environments similar to yours who have installed the application on currently available 56-kbit/s Dataphone Digital Service (DDS) links. Were there any bottlenecks? Was the application able to completely utilize the 56-kbit/s line?

Generally speaking, if an application can fully utilize a 56-kbit/s DDS circuit to obtain a response time or throughput improvement, it is a candidate for ISDN's full 64-kbit/s B channels. If your equipment suppliers have participated in ISDN compatibility tests, you may benefit from their experience and insight about the applications that work best in such an environment. Available ISDN features can vary somewhat, depending on the manufacturer.

The experience of early ISDN users has shown that the penalty for ignoring the basic layered approach of OSI becomes a greater factor with the higher speeds of ISDN. The penalty is failure to achieve full utilization of the 64-kbit/s B channel. Some users were unable to take advantage of the higher speeds because of unnecessary overhead and duplication—both avoidable with the OSI layered approach.

These inefficiencies have been particularly evident at sites where users ran their own software on top of the D channel's X.25, resulting in redundant packetization, flow control, and error checking. Consequently, even if the ISDN is well-tuned, application software duplicates communications functions, with adverse effects on throughput.

IBM network protocols that support X.25 tend to have a different type of bottleneck (see "IBM supports X.25, doesn't it? Clearly, it depends," DATA COMMUNICATIONS, March 1987). IBM's Network Packet Switching Interface (NPSI) contains a great deal of internal overhead, because it is constrained to convert X.25 on the network side to SNA on the host side in both directions.

BCS represents a real opportunity for upgrading SNA links, but for many users of IBM mainframe networks that require X.25 connectivity NPSI must be considered for its effects on throughput. In cases such as these, where the bottleneck is the FEP's communications method, it may be more cost-effective to utilize lower-cost/lower-speed ISDN components to provide connectivity. For example, choose TAs with RS-232 interfaces that support 9.6-kbit/s DPS and 19.2-kbit/s BPS, rather than V.35 interfaces and 64-kbit/s BPS.

Another user experience involved a site that was previously using short-haul modems and an ancient file transfer program with its own custom blocking, error checking, and flow control. This was definitely not a well-layered, OSI-compliant protocol stack. When the short-haul modems were replaced with 64-kbit/s ISDN, with the original communications software was retained, no performance improvement was detected.

With all the problems stemming from running old software on new network links, the question arises: Why not just use a non-error-checking approach that relies on the near-error-free ISDN environment for data integrity?

There have been and will continue to be cases where users move data with non-error-checking procedures on an ISDN. But, keep in mind that, even with the B and D channel X.25 packet services, error correction is only between the TA's—it is not end-to-end.

This means that errors will not be corrected when introduced by the cables and connectors between the TA and DTE, the DTE ports, or the DTE software itself. For instance, if there is a local source of noise interference that is causing bit errors in the DTE's RS-232 port, the most perfect D-channel session in the world can't stop this corruption of data.

That brings us to today's popular error-checking software products. In fairness to existing communication software, it must be said that not all non-ISDN optimized software products are worthless at the new speeds and error rates. End-to-end error correction and flow control is so critical to many applications, existing packages using Kermit, Xmodem, or proprietary transfer protocols will be used widely on ISDN.

Considering that ISDNs will often be employed to connect dissimilar systems, the fact that mature communications products such as Kermit run on so many different platforms is in their favor. And if these mature products have advanced features such as sliding windows, variable packet sizes, and X.25 line-turnaround control, it is likely that they will perform adequately (but not superlatively) on an ISDN.

Packet sizes on ISDNs are generally 128 kbit/s or 256 kbit/s, as specified by the user at provisioning time. On error-free lines such as an ISDN, it is normally recommended that communication software block size be set as high as possible, to reduce protocol overhead. With such good channels, the performance hits from retransmitting one of these long blocks should be few and far between.

Further, the block boundaries of the user software may not relate well to ISDN packet boundaries. This is likely the case when asynchronous software blocks its data in 128-byte increments—not uncommon. After several bytes of protocol are added, the block will no longer fit in the ISDN 128-byte packet. In some cases, two 128-byte packets will be sent for a single 128-byte block of user data.

Very long packets, 2 kbytes or more, are one method used by the makers of ISDN optimized software to maximize throughput. But other ISDN developers will say that long packets are just a Band-Aid, and what is really best for ISDN lines is an error-correcting technique that doesn't use conventional send-a-packet, acknowledge-a-packet algorithms.

Some of the fastest asynchronous software available today for ISDNs does not use standard stop-and-go acknowledging, but instead sends a constant stream of data, with unacknowledged cyclic redunancy checks (CRCs) included every 2 kbit/s, and minimal handshaking at one-minute intervals. With this streamlined approach, an acknowledgment is sent at the end of a file or group of files. In the rare event of a CRC-detected error, subsequent blocks are discarded and retransmission is started at the point of the error.

Besides higher speeds and greater efficiency, ISDN optimized communications software has other advantages over conventional software. (ISDN optimized software includes: HyperAccess, from Hilgraeve Inc., Monroe, Mich.; Excellnet, from ExcellTech Inc., Yankton, S.D.; IS NET, from Newbridge Networks, Herndon, Va.; and Manylink, from Netline Inc., Provo, Utah.) Just as pre-ISDN software has been optimized for the dominant analog modem technologies, ISDN software has been optimized for the emerging terminal adapters. This often involves collaboration between hardware and software makers to develop software drivers, configuration scripts, and user interfaces that are particularly well-suited for TAs.

The down side of this new software is its proprietary nature. Unlike the mature protocols (such as Kermit and Xmodem) that run on hundreds of different hosts and modems, new ISDN software supports a very limited repertoire of platforms. Consequently, to reap the rewards of ISDN-optimized software, it will in most cases be necessary to buy new software for every system in the application.

The correct method of planning for ISDN, while not particularly obvious, is quite similar to traditional network planning methods. The worst thing is to rush out and provision BRI lines without a good idea of communications requirements. Before even thinking about TAs and BRI lines, consider the capabilities and limitations of your application, end-to-end, all layers, hardware, and software. Next, look at TAs.

Do the right thing

Says AT&T senior engineer Harris Barbier: "You really need to know the capabilities of your TA before provisioning." He adds that the user manuals for TAs are a good place to go for specifications and tips on how to set up BRI lines so they will match the features of the TA. Some of the parameters are: packet size, variable sliding window size, number of virtual circuits, and throughput class for packet circuits.

With Centrex service, it is the telephone company's responsibility to enter in the switch the parameters for the ISDN line, but the telco cannot do this without accurate information from the user. Therefore, the user must carefully plan the network—not only how each BRI will be used but also down to specific parameter settings for DPS and BPS. A configuration profile that is established for each digital subscriber line (DSL, same as a BRI) is called a translation. The translation tells the central office how the line is to be used—such as voice only or voice and data—as well as specific voice and data characteristics of the telephone or terminal adapter at the other end. Table 2A gives typical translation options for the AT&T 5ESS D channel. This is a sampling of default values and their interpretations. In some cases, these defaults can be modified from the TA.

■ *Packet size.* The 5ESS allows a packet size of 128 or 256 bytes. Users with heavy terminal-character traffic would

select 128, while those with file transfer requirements might choose 256 when their TA supports this value.

■ *Window size.* The switch's D channel window size is two or three packets. For a clean loop set the window to three, for a dirty loop set it to two.

■ *Reverse charging acceptance.* The reverse-charging option tells the switch whether an incoming caller may reverse the charges for the call. This value defaults to no.

■ *Flow-control negotiation.* If the flow-control parameter is set to "yes," TAs may negotiate the window size, packet size, and throughput class for both directions (independently) of the D channel. If this parameter is set to no, the default settings for these parameters will apply.

■ *Fast select acceptance.* This is an X.25 feature for quick calls in applications such as automated credit card approval. It allows data (a credit card number, for instance) to travel with the initial call-request packet. The default for this parameter is "no"—meaning fast select calls are not accepted.

■ *Intercom address indicator.* A four-digit number may be entered for fast dialing inside an AT&T exchange. This is for users of this AT&T service.

X.25 B-channel default settings (see Table 2B) control the parameters that support packet data on the B channel. With the current software on the 5ESS and DMS-100, BPS is a permanent-connection-only service. The X.25 B channel translation functions are similar to those for the D channel, but the values a user chooses for window and packet sizes may differ.

■ *N2 retransmissions.* This is an integer from two to 16 that controls the number of retransmissions for LAPB, level-two frame retransmissions. A value of two is typical for applications on a good loop; a higher value is necessary for a dirty loop.

■ *T1 retransmission time-out.* For this parameter, measured in tenths of a second, a setting of 20 would allow 2 seconds for a LAPB-level retransmission time-out.

■ *Window size.* Unlike X.25 parameters for the D channel, the B channel may have a window size of two to seven packets. Users in areas with problematic loops should keep this number low (two); otherwise, better performance may be gained by increasing it. But high window-size values require more memory in the TA and switch.

■ *Packet size.* The packet size of the ISDN B channel is independent of the D channel. Depending on the capabilities of the TA, this may be set to 256 to lower protocol overhead.

The proper translation settings are a function of application requirements and the capabilities of the terminal adapters and central office switches. TA manufacturers and switch providers are gathering a wealth of implementation experience in this emerging technology area, so the new ISDN user should never be alone when it's time to make things work. ■

Dean Wolf is Manager of Product Marketing with Fujitsu's ISDN Systems Group. He has 13 years experience in the field of data and voice communications. He holds a bachelor's degree from Southern Illinois University, Carbondale. Wolf acknowledges the technical and editorial support of Jim Weldon.

Stephen Fleming, Licom Inc., Herndon, Va.

Get ready for T3 networking

DS-3 will be as commonplace as today's T1 because of coming availability and cost-effectiveness. Here's what to expect and how to implement the new technology.

Many corporate managers are administering T1 networks that are growing at a rate that puts crabgrass to shame, and new users are clamoring for more and more bandwidth. Increasingly, data communications managers are eyeing T3 equipment as a solution to the problems raised by this expansion. Carriers and vendors, aware of the growing interest, are offering equipment and services at the T3 rate (44.736 Mbit/s—commonly called 45 Mbit/s).

As an indication of increasing T3 acceptability, a recent study by Ken Bosomworth of International Resource Development showed the T3 equipment market climbing from $20 million in 1988 to a predicted $330 million in 1994. Similarly, he says, the T3 services market should go from $20 million in 1988 to $900 million in 1994.

To better understand many of the issues related to T1 and T3 networking, one should be familiar with North American regulations (see "The digital hierarchy"). They dictate how digitally multiplexed signals may be transmitted over the public network in the U.S. and Canada. Different hierarchies of signals are used abroad, making direct interchange of voice or data signals with North American networks impossible.

Before it can be justified, a T3 backbone must prove itself economically. In late 1988, AT&T amended its Tariff No. 9 to significantly improve the economics of T3 circuits. The previous tariff involved a complicated scheme of mileage bands. There is now a fixed charge of $6,000 per month and a simple mileage charge based on airline miles between cities. The charge varies from $180 per month for one-year contracts to $150 per month for three years to $130 per month for five years. Carriers other than AT&T offer similar arrangements, often for even lower prices.

A comparison of these charges versus standard T1 charges is shown in the figure. (The T1 calculations assume typical AT&T monthly rates of $2,600 fixed and $14.85 per mile with a 15 percent volume discount; the T3 calculations assume a three-year rate.) As can be seen, a T3 circuit can be cost-justified by as few as four T1s on links of less than 50 miles. (Recall that a T3 represents the equivalent of 28 T1 circuits.) At the other extreme, 10 T1 circuits will always cost more than a T3, regardless of distance. With non-AT&T carriers, the principle remains unchanged, although the break-even points may vary.

Flexibility and control

Implementing a T3 corporate backbone provides users with a measure of flexibility and control over the network. At the low-speed end, circuits may be either 56 kbit/s or 64 kbit/s. These may be used for voice or data services. Clear-channel circuits at 64 kbit/s may also be used for the bearer (B) channels of ISDN.

Intermediate circuits are often referred to as fractional T1 or FT1. These consist of some subset of a full T1 in multiple-DS-0 bundles. For example, one-half of a T1 (768 kbit/s) or even one-quarter of a T1 (384 kbit/s) may be adequate for many videoconferencing applications, without dedicating an entire T1 circuit. Many carriers have begun offering fractional T1 service to capture users who have outgrown 56-kbit/s services but who cannot yet justify a full T1. With the proper switching functions, these may be consolidated within a T3 networking multiplexer.

Full T1 circuits may be switched between sites on demand. The bit rates of these circuits may be 1.544 Mbit/s (the standard T1, including the framing bit), 1.536 Mbit/s (a T1 payload, without the 193rd framing bit), or 1.344 Mbit/s (24 channels of 56 kbit/s each).

The capability to switch this variety of circuits allows the user to put up and take down circuits of differing rates on the T3 backbone as requirements change, without having to work through an external network provider. This can take the form of reducing lead time for a circuit order, time-of-

The digital hierarchy

Digital transmission techniques were introduced in the former Bell System in the early 1960s for efficient transport of voice signals. At that time, data formed an increasingly smaller percentage of network traffic. Therefore, the basic digital transmission structure is centered around human voice communication.

A plot of amplitude versus time for a speech sample would show significant high-frequency components. Luckily, a successful conversation (involving both understandable speech and a recognizable speaker) requires less than 4 kHz of audio bandwidth. After being processed by a low-pass filter, a speech sample loses its high-frequency components and is ready to be digitized.

The maximum analog frequency to be reproduced is 4 kHz. Therefore, according to the Nyquist theorem (the rate at which data can be transmitted without incurring intersymbol interference cannot be more than twice the bandwidth in Hertz), an 8-kbit/s sampling rate was adopted. By sampling the voice signal every 125 microseconds, its essential information is extracted in analog format and readied for digital encoding (see Fig. A). This pulse-amplitude modulated (PAM) signal contains all the information in the original signal up to approximately 4 kHz. (Because of operational considerations, the actual cutoff in digital telephony is lower than 4 kHz, but the principle remains the same.)

■ **Pulse-code modulation.** The modulation scheme chosen for early digital transmission standards is the easiest to implement: pulse-code modulation. The PAM signal is quantized (see Fig. B) by mapping into discrete amplitude levels, each with a unique binary code. (The example in the figure uses four-bit coding.) Naturally, additional discrete mappings reduce the quantization error and improve the fidelity of the coded signal. The example shows four-bit coding, for a total of 2^4 — or 16 — possible coding levels. Actual devices were designed to implement eight-bit coding, providing 2^8 — 256 — quantization levels. This is sufficient for satisfactory reproduction of the human voice.

Note that by creating eight-bit codes 8,000 times per second (8 kbit/s), the bit rate of a digitized voice signal is eight multiplied by 8,000, or 64,000 bits per second. This is the basic 64-kbit/s channel that is the foundation of much of the digital network. Such a digital channel is often referred to as a DS-0 (digital signal, level 0).

■ **Time-division multiplexing.** The original deployment of digital transmission was driven by a desire to conserve copper pairs outside telephone offices. Each analog voice signal in the existing telephone network consumed a physical pair of copper wires from a subscriber location to a telephone central office. Once the basic building block was digital, it became feasible to multiplex the digital signals together into a higher-order digital signal. The interleaving method used, time-division multiplexing, led to defining the next level of the digital hierarchy as being equivalent to 24 DS-0 signals. This level is referred to as DS-1 or T1.

The multiplexing function to create a DS-1 signal was originally handled by a network element known as a digital channel bank or D-bank. Now, of course, numerous devices offer T1 interfaces.

■ **T1 format.** DS-1 is formed by byte-interleaving 24 DS-0 channels. The per-frame aggregate capacity, deduced from 24 channels of eight bits each, is 192 bits. Repeating the frame 8,000 times per second would result in an aggregate bit rate of $192 \times 8,000 = 1,536,000$ bits/second, or 1.536 Mbit/s.

This, however, is not the DS-1 rate, since a 193rd bit is added to each frame for timing and alignment purposes. This 193rd bit is called the framing bit and brings the aggregate bit rate to the T1 rate of 1.544 Mbit/s.

The framing bit is used to repeat a specific pattern throughout a "superframe" consisting of 12 frames. This pattern is used by receiving terminal equipment to identify and align the incoming bit pattern. The most common framing pattern used defines a D4 framing structure (named after the AT&T D4 channel bank). A newer standard, called extended superframe format (ESF), uses a 24-frame pattern (see "The hidden treasures of ESF," DATA COMMUNICATIONS, September 1986). The extended size of the superframe allows for the transmission of a six-bit cyclical redundancy check and for a 4-kbit/s embedded operations channel.

Note: Each voice circuit in a T1 appears to consist of a 64-kbit/s channel. In actuality, telephone switching re-

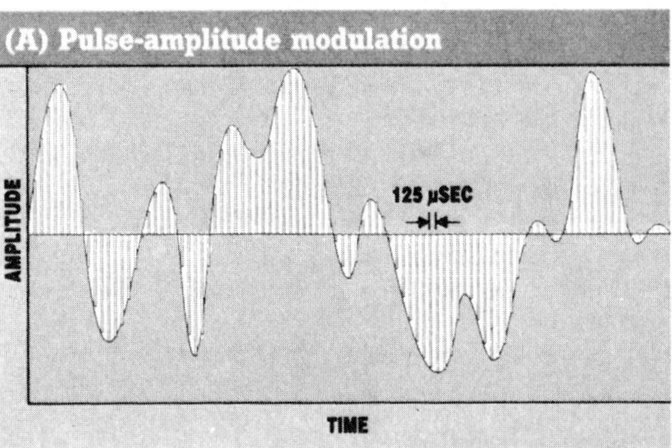

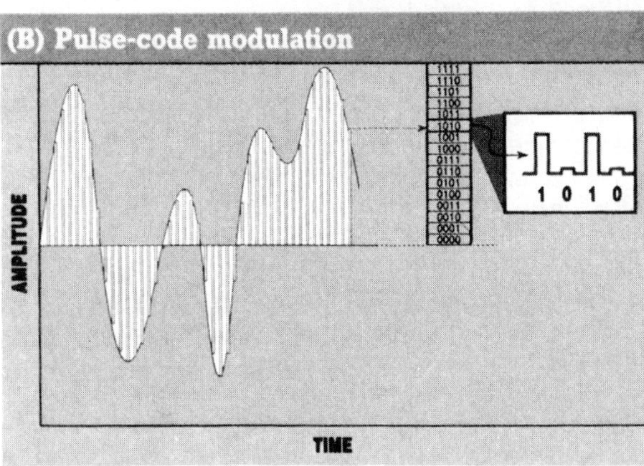

quired a fraction of this bandwidth to handle call-processing functions. In North America, this was handled through robbed-bit signaling: Every sixth frame, the least significant bit is removed from each eight-bit sample and used for signaling. This results in imperceptible degradation for voice traffic. Data traffic, however, can only rely on the untouched seven bits. Instead of a 64-kbit/s clear channel, therefore, DS-0 data circuits have an effective bit rate of only seven bits multiplied by 8,000 per second, or 56 kbit/s.

■ **T3 format.** At a rate of 1.544 Mbit/s, the T1 rate was sufficient for many needs, but not for all. On dense, high-volume routes, higher bit rates were required. The first step in this direction was made with the DS-2 rate, consisting of four DS-1s. (An intermediate rate, DS-1C [3.152 Mbit/s] is sometimes used, but is of no concern to this discussion.) The individual bits from each tributary are bit-interleaved.

DS-2 would appear to have a bit rate four times that of a DS-1, or 6.176 Mbit/s. In actuality, another layer of framing is added at the DS-2 rate. This framing ensures correct byte alignment as before, but also allows for variances in clock rates among tributary DS-1s (asynchronous operation). Special stuffing bits are included, as required, to ensure identical bit rates before bit interleaving. "Fast" signals receive less stuffing; "slow" signals receive more stuffing; adjustments are made continually to achieve a common reference level. These stuffing bits are removed at the far end of the transmission span. A total of 17 framing and stuffing bits are added to each DS-2 frame, leading to an aggregate DS-2 bit rate of 6.312 Mbit/s (8,000 × 17 added to 6.176 Mbit/s).

At this speed, the DS-2 signal can still be carried over copper pair, but the limitations inherent in copper transmission become more restrictive. Specially shielded cable is required to reduce crosstalk and susceptibility to electromagnetic interference. This cable requirement limited the acceptance of DS-2 installations, and it has never reached the wide deployment seen by DS-1 equipment.

By the end of the 1970s, however, a way around the limitations of copper pair was on the horizon. Transmission technologies based on the nearly limitless bandwidth of optical fiber were emerging from the laboratory, and a new layer of the digital hierarchy seemed appropriate. Based on technology available at the time, an asynchronous DS-3 rate was defined as the combination of seven DS-2 signals (equivalent to 28 DS-1s or 672 DS-0s). Framing and stuffing bits, as well as rudimentary error checking and internal communications, were added to the DS-2 tributaries to generate an aggregate bit rate of 44.736 Mbit/s.

Notice that the information content, or payload, of a DS-3 is equal to 672 64 kbit/s = 43.008 Mbit/s. The additional 1.728 Mbit/s of overhead represents the sum of the DS-1 framing bit, the DS-2 framing and stuffing bits, and the variety of DS-3 overhead bits. In terms of network efficiency, the DS-3 format devotes 96 percent of the transmission bandwidth to payload, with approximately 4 percent overhead.

Although the DS-3 was designed to be created from multiple DS-2 signals, there was an obvious inefficiency in using two separate devices for the DS-1-to-DS-2 and DS-2-to-DS-3 multiplexing functions. (The generic names of these devices are M12 and M23, pronounced em-one-two and em-two-three.) A new type of device was created, dubbed the M13 (one-three), which accepted DS-1 inputs and produced DS-3 output (and the reverse).

Note that the DS-3 (or T3) is often referred to as consisting of 28 DS-1s. This is correct, but it is more accurate to describe it as consisting of seven DS-2s. The DS-2 rate has not been eliminated, but simply shifted to an internal rate within the M13. None of the limitations of the DS-1 and DS-2 frame formats are removed by asynchronous DS-3 devices.

■ **North American digital hierarchy.** Coincidentally, as fiber optic technology exploded out of the laboratory, a far-reaching shift took place in the U.S. network. The divestiture of AT&T meant that no single entity would be capable of setting universal standards for the North American network. The technological advances did not slow, however, and higher and higher bit rates became economically feasible. After an abortive attempt at a DS-4 (274.176-Mbit/s) standard, major manufacturers basically went their individual ways with optical fiber equipment operating at a variety of bit rates. Overhead channels, multiplexing schemes, and the number and type of tributary were all decided on a per-manufacturer basis. Optical links between equipment from different vendors became impossible. DS-3, however, was retained as a common denominator and became the standard interconnect for all high-speed fiber gear designed for use in the public network.

Since all high-speed links were asynchronous, bit-stuffing penalties continued to mount. Multiple levels of bit-stuffing (DS-1 to DS-2, DS-2 to DS-3, DS-3 to proprietary) continued to require additional bandwidth for synchronization control. At the same time, the high bandwidth of optical fiber encouraged manufacturers to implement additional overhead functions. Payload efficiency dropped dramatically, but this was acceptable, given the vast capacity of these new transport elements. Hub offices began terminating dozens or, in some cases, hundreds of DS-3 signals.

By the late 1980s, the North American digital hierarchy looked like what is shown in the table.

North American digital hierarchy						
LEVEL	BIT RATE	DS-3	DS-2	DS-1	DS-0	EFFI-CIENCY
DS-0	64 KBIT/S	–	–	–	1	100%
DS-1	1.544 MBIT/S	–	–	1	24	99%
DS-2	6.312 MBIT/S	–	1	4	96	97%
DS-3	44.736 MBIT/S	1	7	28	672	96%
3 x DS-3	≈ 139 MBIT/S	3	21	84	2,016	93%
12 x DS-3	≈ 565 MBIT/S	12	84	332	8,064	91%
24 x DS-3	≈ 1.2 GBIT/S	24	176	664	16,128	86%

day circuit changes, or quick response to a temporary overload condition in some part of the network.

Realistically, T3 networks are not for everyone. Who can justify the investment required to operate a 45-Mbit/s circuit? One group that can is *Fortune* 500 corporations that have already installed nationwide T1 backbones. Smaller organizations with unusually high communications requirements (typically, service companies) also have T1 networks in place today. In any network where multiple T1 circuits have been placed or planned between locations, it may be appropriate to consider T3 service.

Another segment consists of organizations with rights-of-way, such as public utilities, railroads, pipelines, and state and local governments. One of the most cost-effective ways to implement a T3 network is to own the optical fibers required for transmission. Right-of-way organizations have an advantage, since they do not have to go through the negotiations necessary to lay a cable across private property and public thoroughfares. Although the up-front costs of a fiber installation can be significant, they are often offset by eliminating the recurring monthly charges associated with leased T1 or T3 circuits.

T3 technology issues

Once the decision to go to T3 has been made, a number of questions about technology need to be answered.

One of the choices to be made early in the process is whether to lease or purchase T3 circuits. The options involved in each choice are summarized in Table 1.

The first solution is the traditional way of managing communications: leasing the circuit from a service provider. This provider may be the local telephone company, an interexchange carrier (IXC), an urban-bypass organization, or a friendly right-of-way company. In each case, the service provider takes care of bringing a T3 pipe to the customer premises and keeping it working. The fees for such a service are often justifiable if the user organization is not set up for network monitoring, troubleshooting, and repair.

Alternatively, the T3 circuit may be leased only between carrier points-of-presence. Since T1 circuits to the premises are readily available, this combination avoids the problem of providing a dedicated fiber pair to the premises to complete a broadband connection: the "last-mile" problem. This option can be attractive when terminating an entire T3 at a private user's location is not feasible, either because of prohibitive placement cost or traffic patterns.

The alternative to leasing is to own the T3 transmission equipment outright. This implies that the user must have access to one of two facilities: an optical fiber cable or a digital microwave transmission path.

Optical fiber has a much higher transmission capacity than digital microwave. By installing a private cable, a user establishes ownership of transmission resources and, for a one-time cost, avoids the recurring expenses associated with a leasing arrangement. However, it is often impossible to install cable without owning a right-of-way. Placing private fiber cable is normally only practical for short-haul networks within a campus or urban area.

In addition, locating and repairing cable breaks (caused by construction, accident, or malice) can be time-consuming. To get around such difficulties, some users have resorted to leasing "dark fiber" from a telephone company, bypass operation, or IXC. Dark fiber means that the monthly charge pays only for dedicated access to the optical fiber and for cable maintenance; the user is responsible for providing optical multiplexing equipment, network monitoring, and terminal maintenance. This can be especially practical in an urban setting where a private right-of-way would be prohibitively expensive.

Because of the right-of-way and maintenance problems inherent in optical fiber cable, users have turned to digital microwave radio as a T3 transmission medium. Operating basically over line-of-sight paths, these networks provide reliable error-free transmission of a T3 signal across an urban area. Newer units can even be mounted indoors, transmitting through a window, so that tower installation and maintenance is eliminated.

Digital microwave radio has three problems. First, the electromagnetic spectrum is strictly licensed by the Federal Communications Commission. Overcrowding of the airwaves has closed off certain portions of the spectrum in densely populated urban areas. Second, strict spectrum allocations imply that digital microwave cannot be readily upgraded in bandwidth. While a 45-Mbit/s optical fiber can be readily converted to 565 Mbit/s, a 45-Mbit/s digital microwave setup is probably destined to remain at 45 Mbit/s.

Finally, digital microwave devices are inherently limited to line-of-sight distances—sometimes even shorter,

T1 and T3. Using standard AT&T rates, a tariff comparison shows that leased T3 lines carrying the equivalent of 28 T1s are more economical than multiple T1 lines. For distances of less than 50 miles, only four T1s are required to break even.

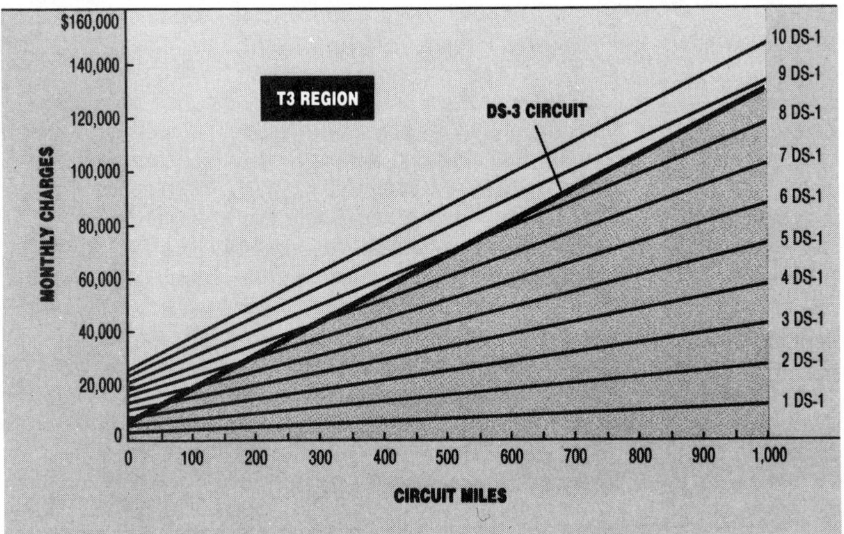

T3 Networking

owing to weather conditions or other hindrances. This is manageable in urban-distance settings, but can cause problems for interstate or national networks.

Many private networks mix optical fiber and digital microwave. The fiber can be used in high-density areas, with microwave hops to lower-density remote locations. Alternatively, the main network can be placed entirely on fiber, with T3 microwave used for emergency restoration in the event of a cable cut. Dual-media transmission is especially attractive to service-critical networks such as banks, airlines, and other on-line transaction-processing companies.

After choosing between leased and owned facilities, the data communications manager must decide what equipment to use to terminate these facilities. With leasing, the terms of the lease may dictate use of a particular vendor's equipment. When using private fiber cable or microwave, the terminal choices are entirely the responsibility of the data communications manager.

Equipment choices

All private optical networks share the advantages of near-limitless upgradability. The data rate of modern single-mode fiber reaches many tens of Gbit/s. Whether the fiber cable is owned or leased, users have abundant options when shopping for optical fiber terminals. The 1980s boom in optical installations for the public network has led to dozens of available products from numerous vendors; capacities currently range from a single T3 (45-Mbit/s) to 36 T3 circuits (1.7-Gbit/s). Future installations are expected to operate at even higher speeds. Although these Gbit/s devices are only of interest to telephone operating companies and IXCs, they will certainly be available to private-network users when the need arises.

Once transmission issues have been solved, the user must decide what T3 multiplexing equipment is required for the application. There are three major choices:

- Asynchronous M13s.
- DS-3 cross-connects.
- T3 add/drop multiplexers.

The traditional method of obtaining T3 circuits is via an M13 multiplexer. This device collects up to 28 T1 signals and uses two steps of time-division multiplexing to produce a T3. There are tens of thousands of M13s in service in the public network today; 10 years of manufacturing experience and economies of scale have brought them down to surprisingly low prices ($4,000 to $10,000). The rate and format of the M13 signal are defined in Bellcore document TR-TSY-000009.

These devices have been optimized for bundling T1 circuits for point-to-point transmission in the BOC and IXC markets. They are the T3 equivalent of the "dumb" channel bank—adequate for basic transport, but often inadequate for complex corporate networks. They are usually appropriate only in point-to-point networks that do not require much in the way of flexibility or performance monitoring.

A modification of the T3 standard, known as C-bit parity, was published by AT&T in document PUB 54014, which describes the Accunet T45 service offering. While not adding any flexibility or control to the M13 standard, C-bit parity does provide rudimentary far-end performance monitoring over T3 lines. This standard has not gained the widespread deployment of the traditional M13s.

At the other extreme is the new entry of 3/1 and 3/1/0 digital cross-connect systems (DCS). These are sometimes referred to as DACS (Digital Access and Cross-connect System) products, after the AT&T product line of the same name—or as wideband cross-connects. The types differ in that the 3/1 DCS demultiplexes DS-3 signals to the DS-1 rate, while 3/1/0 machines demultiplex through the DS-1 rate to DS-0, or 64-kbit/s, rate. DCS 3/1 or 3/1/0 devices incorporate an internal switching matrix, providing circuit-switched flexibility and significant network management features. The DCS excels in "hub-and-spoke" networks where T1 circuits from a variety of T3 sources must be interconnected. These products tend to be optimized for dozens or hundreds of T3 ports; although their features may appeal to corporate-network users, their capacity (and price tags) can be overwhelming.

A third multiplexing alternative exists in the form of the T3 add/drop multiplexer (ADM). As the name implies, these units allow the individual T1 circuits to be added and dropped at a particular site. When deployed along a T3 route, these devices can provide the T1 switching functions of large 3/1 cross-connects for a single T3 circuit. Some vendors also provide DS-0-level switching for some or all of the 64-kbit/s circuits within a T3. This provides the user with electronic control of the T3 bandwidth, network surveillance, capital-cost reductions at intermediate sites in a T3 route, and compatibility with the huge installed base of T3-based fiber and radio networks.

Synchronous ADMs can be especially valuable in overcoming the limitations of a T3 microwave network. By

Table 1: Facility choices

	LEASED T3 CIRCUITS	OWNED OPTICAL FIBER	OWNED DIGITAL MICROWAVE
ADVANTAGES	SIMPLICITY MINIMUM STAFFING REQUIREMENTS PERFECT FOR LONG-HAUL T3 NETWORKING	ONE-TIME COST 'UNLIMITED' CAPACITY VARIED EQUIPMENT OPTIONS EASY UPGRADES COMPATIBILITY WITH NEW SERVICES PERFECT FOR CAMPUS ENVIRONMENT	ONE-TIME COST RAPID SET-UP PORTABILITY NO RIGHT-OF-WAY ISSUES PERFECT FOR METROPOLITAN AREA NETWORK
DISADVANTAGES	RECURRING MONTHLY COST LIMITED NETWORK CONTROL LIMITED FLEXIBILITY	REQUIRES RIGHT-OF-WAY VULNERABLE TO CABLE CUTS REQUIRES ON-CALL MAINTENANCE	WEATHER DEGRADATION FCC LICENSING RESTRICTIONS LIMITED BANDWIDTH

providing efficient bandwidth allocation, a synchronous T3 ADM can maximize the utilization of a single T3 pipe. With digital microwave, the difference between a single highly filled T3 and two poorly utilized T3s can determine whether a network is economically or technically feasible.

It is worth noting here that a fourth class of multiplexing equipment will be entering the market within the next few years. These devices, based on the Sonet hierarchy (see "Sonet calms choppy waters"), promise to offer a level of flexibility and performance well beyond the traditional M13. Because of their synchronous nature, Sonet networks will provide many of the benefits of the DS-3 cross-connects and T3 add/drop multiplexers for multi-DS-3-rate fiber. Since Sonet networks are incompatible with the installed base of fiber transmission, however, DCS machines or T3 ADMs will still be required to connect Sonet networks with the existing North American network.

T3 ADMs may be directly integrated into intelligent T1 multiplexer networks, acting as a higher-level circuit switch

---

Sonet calms choppy waters

No description of high-speed networking would be complete without a discussion of Sonet. This new standard, an acronym for Synchronous Optical Network, is supported by dozens of vendors and public network providers in North America, Europe, and Japan. It operates at multiples of T3 bandwidth. Initially, products will be offered at the following bit rates (OC stands for optical carrier): OC-1, 51.84 Mbit/s; OC-3, 155.52 Mbit/s; OC-12, 622.08 Mbit/s; OC-48, 2.49 Gbit/s.

Sonet brings order to the current chaos of high-speed fiber optics, where each vendor has established independent proprietary bit rates and protocols. In the United States, the first phase of the Sonet standard has been published as ANSI T1.105-1988 and T1.106-1988.

As a synchronous standard, Sonet is well-suited for switching tributary signals within a higher-bandwidth pipe. Initially, switching will be limited to T1 and DS-0 signals, but other service offerings will be defined as time goes on. One future example: a publicly switched Ethernet interface that would allow you to dial a 10-Mbit/s channel cross-country or around the world. Sonet networks operating at OC-3 and higher rates will also be used as the basis for interconnection of broadband services such as Distributed Queue Dual Bus metropolitan area networks and high-definition television.

Sonet is fully backward-compatible with the ANSI synchronous T3 format; it is partially backward-compatible with older asynchronous T3 equipment such as M13s. It does not affect users of digital microwave radio, since there is little need for a synchronous standard higher than T3 for these applications. It will be deployed by the BOCs in the early 1990s. Depending on its success in that arena, other network providers and corporate-network users will follow suit.

---

for a broad mixture of T1 tributaries. The same can be said for asynchronous M13 networks.

Although the DS-1 and DS-3 external interfaces are identical, the internal architectures are quite different. The asynchronous M13 bit-interleaves and bit-stuffs DS-1 signals to the DS-2 rate, repeating the process from DS-2 to DS-3. The T3 ADM, on the other hand, synchronously aligns each incoming DS-1, allowing identification of each DS-0 circuit. Therefore, the T3 ADM first demultiplexes the DS-1 tributaries into the component DS-0 signals. After passing through a time slot interchanger (TSI), the signals plus overhead channels are remultiplexed in a single stage from DS-0 to DS-3.

A DS-3 interface may be provided on one or both sides of the TSI. When equipped on a single side, the device acts as a DS-1-to-DS-3 multiplexer, with internal DCS. When equipped on both sides, the device can add and drop individual DS-0 or DS-1 signals to a DS-3 path. Unlike asynchronous designs, there is no limitation on how many DS-0 or DS-1 signals may be added or dropped.

By implementing the DS-0 internal switching matrix, the ADM provides far greater flexibility in circuit arrangement than the hard-wired multiplexing of an M13. The ADM can also switch proprietary or unframed T1 signals at the full 1.544-Mbit/s rate (rather than the 1.536-Mbit/s or 1.344-Mbit/s rates common to other devices). This is accomplished by arbitrarily splitting the signal into 24 bytes of eight bits each, carrying the 193rd bit separately in the T3 overhead, and reuniting the elements in the correct sequence at the receiving terminal. Unframed T1 video signals or non-D4-compatible T1 signals can be carried transparently within such a device.

In addition, the synchronous T3 transmission format (ANSI standard T1.103-87) — also known as Syntran — used in a DS-0 ADM integrates performance monitoring and an embedded control channel into the T3 bit stream. A nine-bit cyclical redundancy check (CRC9) is performed at the DS-3 rate for remote performance monitoring. Also, a 64-kbit/s embedded operations channel permits communications both between individual nodes and between the network and network management devices. For T3 users, the synchronous T3 format provides the same benefits that the extended superframe format (ESF) provides for T1 users.

Compatibility issues

Most data communications managers have learned the importance of compatibility with the public network the hard way. Proprietary interfaces, unless in a pure single-vendor network, often turn out to be more troublesome than useful. When choosing T3 network equipment, there are new network compatibility issues involved.

First, the equipment must be compatible with the existing T3 standards. Luckily, the T3 world consists of well-defined interfaces, so compatibility is not usually a problem here.

One area of concern with T3 is facility compatibility. A number of AT&T and Bellcore publications specify the interface required for a DS-3 signal to be carried over T3 equipment. These specifications make up the Digital Signal Cross-connect, Level 3 (DSX3) standard. The standard includes specifications for line coding, signal pulse shape, clock rates, frame format, and other parameters of interest to equipment vendors. Any device meeting this DSX3 specification can transport over any T3 equipment, whether optical or microwave, from any vendor.

A second area of concern is terminal compatibility. Once the signal has been successfully transported, issues of terminal compatibility arise. Two major camps of terminal standards exist and have been formalized by Bellcore: the synchronous T3 and the asynchronous T3. These two signals are not directly end-to-end compatible, but must be translated by a third device.

The synchronous standard, being newer, is more fully documented and does not allow much vendor freedom in implementing the specifications. This ensures that any device built to this standard will work successfully with any other, regardless of vendor.

The asynchronous standard is older and has been interpreted differently by vendors. Many of them have added proprietary extensions to provide value-added features or to make up for deficiencies in the format (such as the C-bit parity variation, noted earlier). Their unique implementations of the asynchronous T3 interface can cause compatibility problems ranging from disabling minor features to major network inconsistencies. These solutions dictate that a user employ a single-vendor network.

Since installing T3 equipment in a private network almost always implies connection with new or existing T1 equipment, the issue of T1 compatibility must also be addressed. As with DS-3, AT&T and Bellcore have published details of the T1 interface, collectively referred to as the DSX1 specification. Again, the standards have left room for vendor interpretation, leading to possible inconsistencies.

The most common T1 interface consists of a 1.544-Mbit/s signal channelized according to D4 format. This allows network equipment to identify and switch individual DS-0 (64-kbit/s) signals. This standard was established by AT&T and is nearly universal within the public network. It is normally referred to as D4-channelized or DACS-compatible. The payload data rate of a channelized T1 is 1.536 Mbit/s.

The lockstep limitations of the D4 format led some T1 equipment vendors to ignore the 64-kbit/s boundaries and use a proprietary organization of data within the DS-1 frame. An unchannelized signal requires access to the entire 1.544-Mbit/s T1 format. This allowed more flexibility in transporting varied rates of voice and data, but created incompatibility with the DACS networks installed throughout the public network. Many vendors now offer both options: channelized for public compatibility and unchannelized for maximum bandwidth efficiency. Installations using both types of signals must ensure that their T3 equipment can transport both efficiently.

Yet a third variation exists with unframed T1 signals. These normally represent the output of certain T1 video codecs or encryption equipment. Unlike the unchannelized signals, these do not even meet the DSX1 framing standard, but only the clock rate and associated requirements. Again, in a network that must transport unframed T1 signals, it is important to verify that the T3 equipment will be compatible.

Future compatibility

Finally, it is important to note that the DS-3 formats do not represent the final step in network evolution. As higher bit-rate standards evolve, T3 equipment purchased today must be integratable into new networks that will be installed throughout the 1990s.

The user making the leap to T3 will find that all the network management capabilities of T1 products are still available. Indeed, by offering single-point monitoring of all T1 circuits in a network, the addition of intelligent T3 devices can actually make the network operator's life simpler, not more complicated.

Early in the T3 equipment decision-making process, a communications manager will realize that most T3 equipment is optimized for traditional BOC and IXC applications. This can be adequate in some circumstances, but these devices do not lend themselves to the sophisticated management and control requirements of private networks.

A new generation of T3 devices is appearing on the market from a number of sources—from traditional telephone company transmission-equipment suppliers to T1

Table 2: Performance monitoring parameters

PARAMETER	ASYNCHRONOUS T3	SYNCHRONOUS T3
DS1		
BIT ERROR RATE		✓
BIPOLAR VIOLATIONS	✓	✓
SLIPS		✓
CRC6 VIOLATIONS	ESF ONLY	ESF ONLY
AIS DETECT		✓
FRAME LOSSES		✓
ERRORED SECONDS		✓
SEVERE ERRORED SECONDS		✓
DS3		
BIT ERROR RATE	PARITY-BASED	CRC-BASED
PARITY ERRORS	✓	✓
BIPOLAR VIOLATIONS	✓	✓
CRC9 VIOLATIONS		✓
AIS DETECT	✓	✓
FRAME LOSSES	✓	✓
ERRORED SECONDS	✓	✓
SEVERE ERRORED SECONDS	✓	✓

AIS = ALARM INDICATION SIGNAL
CRC6 = 6-BIT CYCLIC REDUNDANCY CHECK

multiplexer manufacturers to small start-up companies. All, however, have a common goal: to create intelligent T3 devices for the emerging private marketplace. These devices are a distinct departure from the "dumb" ones used in huge quantities by telephone companies and IXCs.

Communications managers will also have to analyze the T1 circuits currently used in their networks. For seamless operation, the T3 equipment should support all types of T1 circuits likely to be used. Managing different types of T1s on different types of T3 equipment ensures confusion.

Networks with an emphasis on data will tend to use unchannelized T1s in order to pack the maximum number of data circuits into the available bandwidth. This is especially common in networks where one vendor supplies all the T1 multiplexing equipment. These circuits will also be used for T1 video codecs, where channelization is meaningless.

Voice networks will tend to use D4-channelized circuits. Thesecircuits are generated by standard channel banks; they are alsoavailable on most modern T1 multiplexers. Naturally, D4-channelized T1s can also be used for transport of data at any number of bit rates, depending on the capabilities of the T1 equipment.

A possible complication arises with the availability of adaptive differential pulse-code modulation (ADPCM) equipment in private-network multiplexers. ADPCM transmits high-quality voice at 32 kbit/s, 21.3 kbit/s, or even 16 kbit/s, instead of 64 kbit/s. DS-0 switching implies that pairs, triads, or quads of ADPCM signals will be switched as units, which slightly reduces the efficiency of the switching matrix. The problem may be alleviated with the realization that T3 bandwidths bring an end to many of the original arguments for ADPCM. With 28 T1 circuits available, maximum utilization of a single T1 may not be an issue.

Finally, many vendors are considering the use of ESF circuits for enhanced fault isolation and troubleshooting. Although it may not be economical to convert all existing circuits to ESF, it is important to allow new circuits to take advantage of this improved range of functions.

Network surveillance consists of alarm reporting and performance monitoring to continually verify the health of the network. Alarms can consist of equipment failures, carrier failures, or entire node failures. Performance monitoring provides diagnostic information for individual circuits, either before or after a failure. Statistics can be reported for both T1 and T3 levels, as shown in Table 2. Effective use of performance thresholds can encourage preemptive equipment maintenance and minimize network downtime.

Surveillance in the public network is typically handled by multimillion-dollar surveillance centers operating on dedicated mainframes. In the private-network world, a dedicated microcomputer or technical workstation is often a more realistic alternative. The user's workstation is only half the issue. Comprehensive network surveillance requires both intelligent network management devices and intelligent network elements capable of measuring performance statistics such as slips, frame errors, CRC errors, and bipolar violations (see "How to detect frame slips in voice-band PCM channels," Data Communications, October 1988). Therefore, even sophisticated network surveillance can obtain and display only elementary alarm information from less sophisticated T3 devices such as M13s.

Many network management products really provide only network surveillance. Reaching into the network to rearrange circuits, either in response to a service request or to a service problem, often requires a technician moving cables on a patch panel.

Newer T3 devices solve these problems by giving the operator direct control over DS-0 and DS-1 connections within the network, resulting in such benefits as time-of-day switching of T1 or T3 or the reserving of bandwidth for an anticipated videoconference. Again, this requires comparable levels of sophistication both for the T3 network elements and for the centralized management software.

Survival

Network disaster recovery is critical at the T3 rate — not many networks can survive the simultaneous loss of 672 circuits. Disasters take many forms. Fiber optic cable cuts are not uncommon; with modern high-bit-rate fiber, a single cable cut can affect a quarter of a million circuits. Both long-haul and local-access circuits are at risk. Central office fires, such as the one at Hinsdale in Chicago, are rare but devastating. Even operator errors, such as disconnecting the wrong cable at the wrong time, can constitute a network disaster.

The first line of defense is battery backup and internal redundancy; T3 equipment built to BOC standards typically has multiple layers of protection switching built in, so that no single module failure can cause loss of service. The BOCs typically specify protection-switching times of 60 milliseconds or better to restore full service over backup modules.

The next defense is network redundancy: By routing redundant T3 circuits over separate physical links, users can protect against even catastrophic carrier-node failures. With excess bandwidth available on unaffected routes, manual or automatic disaster plans may be implemented to restore some or all circuits affected by the disaster. This can take several minutes — longer than the 60 milliseconds specified for equipment protection, but still greatly superior to the hours or days required for manual restoration.

The best defense is autonomous network recovery. For example, survivable T3 ring architectures provide rapid restoration of all circuits in a fraction of a second, without the lag time required to consult central human or computerized network management mechanisms. Such arrangements are now being implemented in the public network. Private users, with their sensitivity to even brief periods of downtime, will almost certainly follow suit. ∎

Stephen Fleming has a BS summa cum laude in physics from Georgia Institute of Technology (Atlanta). He has worked at Bell Laboratories, where he specialized in optical fibers, and at Northern Telecom, where he specialized in multiplexers and cross-connects. He wrote this article when he was Licom's director of marketing for T3 and Sonet products. He has since returned to Northern Telecom.

John M. McQuillan, McQuillan Consulting, Cambridge, Mass.

Routers as building blocks for robust internetworks

Linking LANs with smart segmentation devices — particularly routers — will provide users with a foundation for the next generation of wide-area networking.

In the past, traffic aggregation and multiplexing were performed primarily by packet switches, multiplexers, and concentrators. Increasingly, however, local area networks serve as the lowest-cost, highest-speed, and most popular traffic multiplexers. As a consequence, many organizations have concluded that their wide-area data network may evolve to become an internetwork of LANs.

Hierarchical networks such as IBM's SNA are built around a multitier structure with micros, minis, and mainframes and extensive distribution of processing services throughout the network. Such networks have been the mainstay of many computing facilities throughout the 1980s (see Fig. 1A).

In the 1990s, a new kind of network architecture will grow rapidly to assume importance at least equal to that of the previous two structures (see Fig. 1B). In a LAN-interconnection network, all the user devices appear to be on a uniform network architecture with equal access to all other clients and servers. Peer-to-peer communication is possible at high speeds through such a network without hierarchical data communications or data processing.

Interconnected LANs replace WANs

The two major computer vendors, IBM and Digital Equipment Corp., have both begun to develop and sell LAN interconnection solutions based on peer network architectures. DEC has been selling Ethernet-based networks to engineering departments for years. DEC's new generation of routers and SNA gateways is intended to provide LAN interconnection solutions for the entire corporation.

IBM has been the leading proponent of hierarchical networks sold to the central processing group. Recently, however, IBM has introduced a broad range of new products based on standards, including TCP/IP and FTAM (File Transfer, Access, and Management) on both MVS and VM. IBM also offers interconnection with Ethernet and 802.4

LANs in addition to its own token ring. The challenge for DEC is to sell LAN-interconnection technology to the MIS manager. The challenge for IBM is to build a new generation of networks. While neither vendor is likely to abandon its traditional market, both will be competing for the emerging market of centrally purchased internetworks.

Thus, the stage is set: Organizations are interconnecting their LANs driven by the decentralization and distribution of processing. Other contributing factors include the widespread availability of low-cost, high-bandwidth fiber optic transmission for local, metropolitan, and wide-area communications. Furthermore, the industry has responded by developing several generations of attractively priced bridges and routers for interconnecting LANs.

For the last 10 years, most corporations have standardized on a small number of wide area network (WAN) architectures. Traditionally, these have been dominated by the major computer suppliers (IBM, DEC, and others) and the X.25 packet-switching standard. We are now recognizing the emergence of a new WAN standard — the extended LAN. Sales of X.25 WANs may reach a peak and begin to decline by the early 1990s. Even IBM and DEC may begin to see their WAN sales slow as a result of competition from their LAN products.

Fast and simple LAN extension

The two main technologies for LAN interconnection are bridges and routers. Bridges are fairly simple devices. They work at Layer 2 in the OSI protocol hierarchy. When segmenting an extended LAN, bridges use the low-level node addresses, seeing only a "flat" address space with no hierarchical grouping represented with logical addresses. That means that they are independent of any higher-level protocols, though these may run in conjunction with a router.

Bridges need to process only the Media Access Control

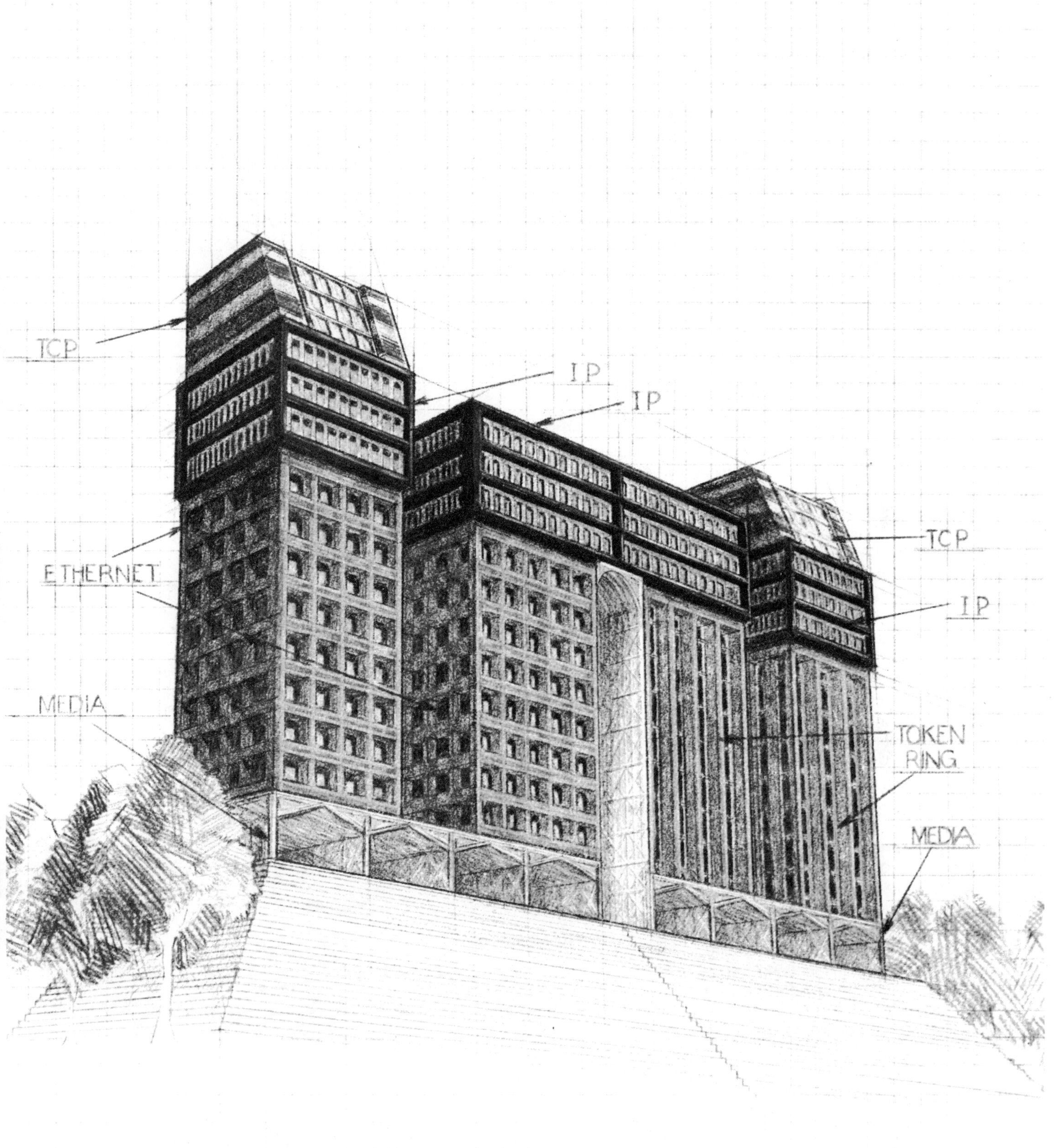

TCP
ETHERNET
MEDIA
IP
IP
TCP
IP
TOKEN
RING
MEDIA

(MAC)-level header on the LAN, a function that can be carried out partly or entirely in hardware. Bridges are, therefore, very fast. They only need to do two things. First, they must filter all the packets on the local area network, detecting which ones can remain local and which ones must be sent to another LAN. The second task is called forwarding, which is transmitting any of these remote packets to one or more other LANs.

These functions may be fixed or adaptive and some bridges can be programmed to carry them out on a selective basis. In general, bridges are used to interconnect similar LANs, but this is not essential. It is possible to bridge between very different LANs as long as both are running a compatible protocol suite at Layer 3 or above (see Fig. 2).

Bridges have a variety of applications, such as connection of coax LANs and twisted-pair LANs or extending local area networks to larger distances and greater numbers of ports. One of the more important applications is to improve the throughput and reduce the congestion on a LAN by dividing it into two pieces and isolating the traffic of each LAN from that of the others. Thus, it is quite common as local area networks grow for bridges to be introduced and for the networks to divide and multiply in a process resembling cell mitosis.

Bridges are very attractive to network managers because they can be inserted in a manner that is completely transparent to the computers and workstations at the source and destination. A customer can operate DEC, Hewlett-Packard, Sun, Apollo, and other computers over the same extended LAN. In contrast, the customer of a WAN technology such as SNA, DECnet, or X.25 has to select a single standard for a wide-area protocol and implement a network of compatible processors.

With bridges, there is no need to re-number any of the computers on the network, or to change the protocols or message headers after the bridges have been introduced. Further, bridges are capable of forwarding many different protocols concurrently so that the network manager does not need to know in advance which protocols are used. Finally, it is possible to bridge LANs at almost any speed and distance. Most organizations start slowly at first, linking a few local networks together.

Begin building bridges

It may be appropriate in the early stages of a network's evolution to install a low-end bridge on a PC platform by adding a couple of LAN inter-face cards. These imbedded bridges offer a way to get started without much investment or commitment.

As time goes on, most organizations conclude that it is necessary to have special-purpose bridges where traffic levels exceed a few hundred packets per second. Extremely high-speed bridges are available between LANs in the same building. These bridges come with two local area network ports and act as a node on each LAN. Other bridges operate over wide-area distances. These units come with a LAN interface and an interface to a transmission circuit such as a DS-0 or DS-1 line. For intermediate distances, it is possible to link bridges by fiber or other transmission equipment.

There has been some controversy about how bridges should operate. The IEEE 802 group has been working since 1984 on MAC bridging. Two proposals for bridge management protocols have been analyzed in detail: source routing (originally proposed for token ring) and spanning tree (originally proposed for Ethernet).

Spanning tree bridges are designed to be used by any Ethernet-style product, even those developed before 802.3. Source routing bridges add a routing information field to the basic frame format, requiring some participation by the

1. Evolving network models. *Traditional networks are hierarchical and vendor-specific, giving users little chance for desk-to-desk interaction. Peer networks, however, allow direct interaction of all intelligent nodes.*

end stations. This makes it harder to apply to products already installed in LANs today.

The advocates of source routing claim that it will be applicable to much higher-speed LANs (as much as 100 Mbit/s for the Fiber Distributed Data Interface [FDDI] standard) by avoiding table look-ups in the bridges. Some of the debate concerns whether it is more important to be backward compatible to existing LANs or to plan for future LANs. IEEE 802.1 decided that transparent spanning tree bridges offer the best solution in terms of robustness, compatibility with existing 802 standards, and stability.

The spanning tree protocol has broadened the scope of bridges. Originally, bridges were capable of forwarding on one path only, without any intelligence regarding the network topology. This meant that bridges could not be linked to form a network that contained loops. The spanning tree protocol algorithm manages these loops, keeping certain links inactive to prevent packets from circulating forever. Some bridges are even capable of sending traffic on multiple paths simultaneously.

Another very attractive feature of bridges is that most of these products are intelligent and are capable of learning which nodes are local to each LAN automatically. There is no need to configure a bridge network. It is enough simply to turn the equipment on and let it discover the LAN's configuration and establish its own address table.

State-of-the-art bridges today are capable of filtering 20,000 packets per second and forwarding more than 10,000 packets per second for prices ranging from $2,000 to $20,000. At $20,000 there are advanced WAN bridges capable of alternate routing and good network management. For $2,000 the bridge is local only, with lower packet-processing rates and rudimentary network management. This price performance is an order of magnitude better than conventional packet switches and multiplexers, and two orders of magnitude better than earlier front-end processors in mainframe-oriented network architectures.

All in all, bridges remain the technology of choice for interconnecting small numbers of local networks or those that are in proximity to each other, as well as connecting LANs in applications where extremely high performance is essential.

Enterprise-wide internets

Routers are a complementary technology to bridges. Routers operate at Layer 3 in the OSI hierarchy, which means they are specific to a particular protocol such as TCP/IP, XNS (Xerox Network Systems), DECnet, or OSI. Routers exchange information with each other via a management protocol, in order to establish routes through the networks that interconnect them. In this way, routers form an internet or a "network of LANs." Routers offer improved

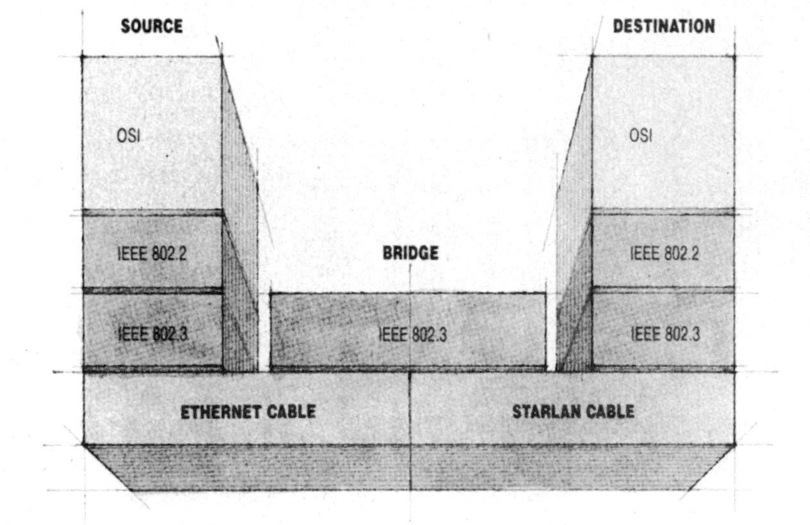

2. Basic bridge architecture. *Bridges are low-level network management devices that can be implemented completely or mostly in hardware. Though they don't offer sophisticated network management, they are fast and cheap.*

reliability because they have adaptive routing algorithms, extensive traffic-filtering capabilities, and some security measures (see Fig. 3).

One of the prerequisites to using a router is to standardize on one or more protocols and addressing structures in the network. In order to use routers in a large LAN interconnect environment it is essential to have a protocol that is based on a hierarchical, not flat, address structure.

Usually, router management schemes determine routes based on the top-level address structure (analogous to an area code in the telephone network), then when the packet arrives at the destination router and it is sent into the destination network, that network must take responsibility for delivery to the address within that "area code." Routers are designed to interconnect highly diverse media. The original routers for the Arpanet (called gateways) were TCP/IP devices that could link Ethernet, X.25, radio, and satellite networks.

Along with the advantages of greater reliability, security, and network management information come some drawbacks. Introducing routers in a network means that the end points must all adhere to a uniform address numbering plan. Breaking a LAN into two pieces with a router is not as simple as splitting a LAN with a bridge. In general, bringing in an additional router means renumbering some of the computer systems.

But there are compensations. It is not possible to bridge one LAN segment onto another without limits. After bridging several segments in a row, fundamental network timing limits prevent further bridging. With routers, this problem goes away. Customers can build networks with hundreds of routers using today's technology. Advocates of routers point out that they can serve to protect one network from problems or disturbances on another.

It is quite common for large bridged networks to suffer from "broadcast storms" because some LAN protocols that are broadcast in nature are passed through each bridge,

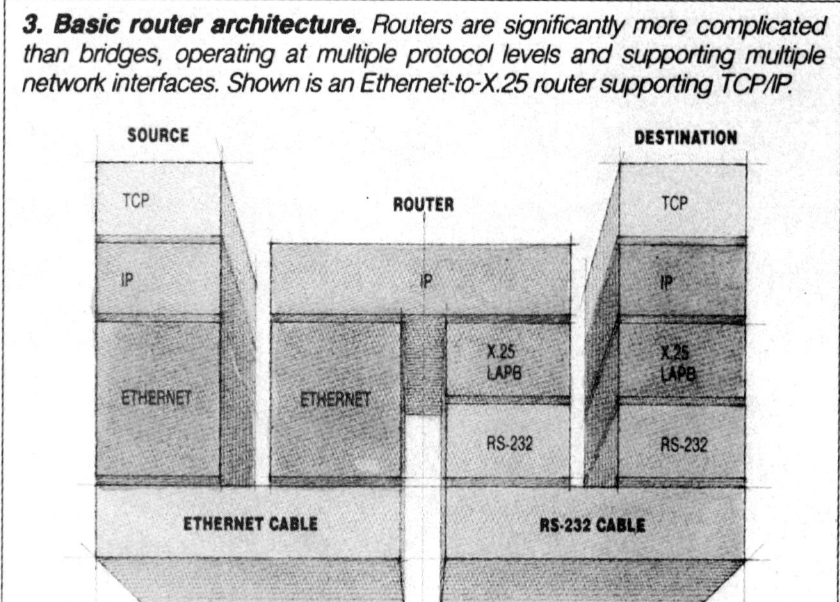

3. Basic router architecture. *Routers are significantly more complicated than bridges, operating at multiple protocol levels and supporting multiple network interfaces. Shown is an Ethernet-to-X.25 router supporting TCP/IP.*

multiplying the traffic level on the extended network enormously. In the case of malfunctions or improperly set parameters, some extended LANs have been rendered unusable because of such broadcast storms. Routers, on the other hand, forward only traffic that is explicitly addressed to them, blocking uncontrolled broadcast traffic.

One of the most important innovations in recent years is the development of multiprotocol routers. Initially, most routers were specialized to a particular protocol suite. Recently, several companies have developed routers that can concurrently route several different protocols such as TCP/IP, DECnet, XNS, and OSI. This is tremendously important for organizations that have not yet been able to standardize on a single protocol. However, there are other protocols (DEC's Local Area Transport and some SNA protocols) which cannot be routed, and so must be bridged. Many routers can also bridge.

In comparison with bridges, routers are somewhat more expensive and often slower. State-of-the-art routers are usually limited to a few thousand packets per second and cost about $10,000 to $20,000. Although a fast router will out-perform a slow bridge, routers are generally slower than bridges because their job requires a fairly significant amount of processing in software.

But speed is relative. A router that is capable of handling 2,000 packets per second is fast enough to connect an Ethernet to a T1 line at full bandwidth. In fact, such a router could interconnect two LANs and two T1s at full efficiency if the packet lengths are sufficiently long. And there are routers available today that are capable of speeds of up to 10,000 packets per second in certain circumstances.

Making the choice

So, which is best—bridges or routers? While many vendors enjoy debating the question, it is often not really relevant for users. Why? Because most customers find that the question has an easy answer for them. If they value an open architecture with standard interfaces and want to preserve flexibility to use any protocol they desire, then the choice is clear—they must use bridges.

On the other hand, some organizations have been able to develop a strongly defined, unified architecture around one or a small number of standard protocols. In this case, where the emphasis is on a clear vision of the future, routers can help to make this vision a reality.

Some people have observed that two-port bridges can, as many LAN segments are interconnected, lead to inefficiencies because traffic from the source segment may have to flow through many intermediate segments on its way to the destination. This reduces some of the traffic isolation advantages that may have motivated the use of bridges in the first place. Multiport bridges that can connect four or more LAN segments are a potential solution to this problem. On the other hand, multiprotocol, multiport routers can fill this product requirement as well.

Whenever there is a difficult choice, such as bridges versus routers, the customer may want to have his cake and eat it too. Now that is possible with the arrival of hybrid bridge/routers, which are available from such companies as Cisco, Halley Systems, and others. In fact, both bridges and routers continue to improve over time, as shown in Figure 4, with a trend toward product consolidation.

Most large customers with many LANs to interconnect are likely to use some bridges locally and some routers remotely and for backbones, favoring hybrids. At the same time, there will still be a market for low-cost bridge-only products and for single-protocol routers.

As networks grow larger and more numerous and as communications processors get faster, customers are tending to use routers for WAN communication. They provide better management and more complete isolation of local communications. On the other hand, as LANs get faster—FDDI and 802.6, for example—bridges may be favored for the highest-speed communication (over 100,000 packets per second) because it is difficult to carry out such high-speed processing in software.

As FDDI technology is used in the local area and T3 circuits become prevalent in wide-area networking, both bridges and routers will be built to interconnect low-speed LANs with FDDI and FDDI with T1 and T3 circuits.

View from above

The movement to a LAN-interconnect architecture has profound consequences throughout any organization in several areas: technical architecture, organizational structure, and network strategy.

A LAN-interconnection network makes it possible to

unbundle data processing from data communications. Traditionally, minicomputers carried out many different functions, including terminal support, database access, WAN communication, electronic mail, and others. Once a LAN-interconnection architecture is installed, these functions can be split among a number of specialized processors.

Terminal servers are used to interconnect terminals with multiple hosts, not just one. File servers and database servers offload the data-handling function. Specialized electronic-mail servers can run on 386-based processors and specialized servers such as bridges and routers carry out the WAN communications. The minicomputer or other specialized CPU is relegated to the role of a MIPS server.

This is an important transition from the era in which terminals had to be purchased from the same vendor as the host computer. Now PCs serve as universal workstations and are purchased as commodities. In fact, workstations, servers, bridges, and routers are all quickly entering the commodity phase. They are purchased based on price and performance rather than on brand name.

Unfortunately, a LAN-interconnect architecture gives the network management staff a much more difficult job than in the past. Instead of a centralized network with tight configuration control over all workstations, the future lies with extremely flexible and open systems with thousands of users supported by their local departments. Local area network interconnection is a centrifugal force that is leading to a dispersed architecture of microservers instead of more centralized minis and mainframes. It is also leading to an era of local control and management of highly distributed networks.

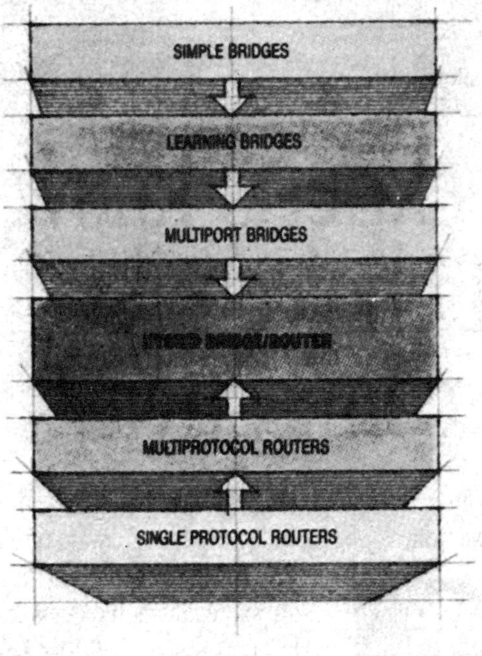

The second major consequence of LAN-interconnection architectures is a shift in organizational structure in many companies. Traditional organizations are structured hierarchically. This leads in turn to a hierarchical information flow with batched information sent upward in the organization at periodic intervals.

This organization and information flow causes long delays in the decision-making cycle that are familiar and frustrating to everyone. Many companies are trying to flatten their organizational pyramid in an effort to become more responsive to the demands in the marketplace and to shorten their decision cycles. LAN-interconnection networks are a way to assist in this effort.

Decentralization and downsizing

As a company evolves its business practices and flattens its organizational pyramid, it can use nonhierarchical computer networks to send information on a peer-to-peer basis throughout the organization. The information can be streamed from one desk to another instead of being batched from one department to another.

The best early example of such an application is electronic mail. In time, interconnected LANs will make this kind of communication possible for all sorts of business processing. The revolution of network structure will cause — and it must reflect — profound changes in organizational structure.

The third consequence of LAN-interconnection networking is a shift in strategic thinking. The traditional model for competition in business is based on value. In this theory, the relevant equation is: Value = Quality ÷ Price.

The new theory is that there is a third dimension to competition. Companies can not only compete by improving their quality or by dropping their price but also in a third way: by competing in time. The new equation is: Value = Quality ÷ (Price × Delay).

An important new competitive edge is improving the delay the customer sees in working with the supplier. This delay might be in ordering the part, getting satisfactory customer service, upgrading to a new capability, or some other aspect.

Local area network = interconnection technology makes an organization more nimble. Since rapid response is key to future competitiveness, LAN interconnection can play a vital role in improving a company's position in its marketplace.

The interconnection of LANs to form a new kind of WAN is a critical step in the establishment of enterprise networks. Even when the fundamental technologies of bridges and routers become well established, there will still be a number of problems remaining in network management, operations, and security. Installing these network segmentation devices is the first step in a new era of internetworking. ∎

John M. McQuillan is a well known authority on computer networks with 20 years of experience, including the development of the SPF routing algorithm for the Arpanet, which serves as the basis for many LAN routers today, IP and DECnet Phase V among them.

4. A separation that won't last. *Though they started out as unrelated devices from different vendors, bridges and routers are in the process of converging.*

Jim Carlo and John Hughes, Texas Instruments, Dallas, Tex.

Token ring compatibility: It's time to plug and play

IBM and TI once promised to cooperate for the sake of token ring interoperability, but nothing is that simple. TI's token ring experts detail the compatibility issues still facing vendors and users alike.

Back in 1985, when IBM announced its first token ring LAN products and Texas Instruments introduced its first token ring chip, both companies promised a program of compatibility testing to ensure interoperability of future LAN products.

Since then, separate implementations by IBM and by third parties using TI's token ring chip sets have contained vastly differing hardware interfaces and protocol software. Many of the early interoperability issues have been resolved, allowing networking successes on sites that vary from small law firms to research facilities to huge corporations. The result of these successes, however, is new and more complex demands for token ring product interoperability.

When taking stock of token ring, it is important to remember that the network landscape has changed drastically since the standard's introduction. Today, dozens of manufacturers are supplying token ring functions in myriad forms, from off-the-shelf PC cards to interfaces embedded in routers, servers, and mainframe communications controllers.

But not just the devices that use token ring have evolved. The complexity and interconnection of the LANs supporting token ring have radically changed since the initial work by IBM, TI, and the IEEE.

In response, the 802.5 token ring standard has changed and indeed is still changing, as problems of internetworking and higher data rates on unshielded twisted pair replace the earlier issues of waveforms, timing, and frame structure. But even with the ongoing efforts, and in spite of all the innovation in devices and topologies, it is possible today to say that product interoperability is highly achievable.

Birth of a standard
Token ring development by IBM and TI was under way as early as 1982; the IEEE was involved in creating the 802.5 standard at this point as well. By 1985 the fundamental characteristics of access were solidified and codified by the IEEE 802.5 committee in a Blue Book. This document contained a description of Media Access Control (MAC) frames for establishing the ring, but not necessarily for controlling and managing the ring. Since 1985, the IEEE has issued several addenda to the standard. These have been combined in a draft form into a Common Reference Document, which is expected to be formally published by the end of the year (see Table 1 for a list of the document's contents).

Fortunately, very few problems have resulted from various vendors' interpretations of the IEEE 802.5 standard. This is due in part to the other two major references on token ring—one from IBM (Token Ring Architecture Reference Manual) and one from Texas Instruments (TMS380 User's Guide)—that have served to lead the standards.

Currently the standard covers both 4 Mbit/s and 16 Mbit/s token rings, but the form of the standard is necessarily an abstraction that does not define actual hardware and software. Consequently, variation in vendor implementation is still very much an issue. The bit order of token ring addresses at various interfaces, for instance, still remains a design concern, as does Ethernet compatibility.

Acknowledging that product interoperability largely depends on standards interpretation, in 1988 the industry formed a vendor-neutral foundation to facilitate the spread of technical information on token ring. This group, the Open Token Foundation (OTF), will not directly define standards such as 802.5. What it will do is provide a forum for vendor technical discussions, disseminate information, and be a united voice for communicating common vendor needs to the standards bodies.

The combination of a strong vendor coalition under OTF and continuing work in 802.5 and related IEEE committees should ensure that token ring technology meets and exceeds high expectations held by the end-user community.

Token Ring

To understand all the ramifications of multivendor token ring networks it is helpful to understand the two major ways that token ring devices can interact: communications and coexistence.

Communications between two token ring nodes means that a meaningful (to an application) transfer of data takes place. It is the process by which nodes send and receive packets between their respective applications. Both nodes must run the same suite of protocol software (for example, TCP/IP or XNS), but these nodes can differ in the details of their hardware and software implementation.

Coexistence, in contrast, is the process by which nodes pass only management data without interfering with each other's operation. For nodes to coexist, they can run different upper-layer software but must contain the same MAC layer capabilities described in IEEE 802.5. This allows initial ring establishment and MAC network management processes and basic ring functionality.

For coexistence, each node must recognize which frames on the ring are to be processed and which frames are to be discarded. Device-addressing standards are most important for coexistence. When a node that can't coexist is added to a ring, quite simply, the ring crashes or will not initialize correctly.

The TI chip sets and documentation have been conceived to ensure that token products of all types will

The Open Token Foundation

The Open Token Foundation (OTF) is a private nonprofit organization composed of users and vendors of token ring products who are dedicated to expanding the interoperability of multivendor token ring products and broadening their use.

Founded in December 1988 with 40 affiliated members representing 23 companies, the OTF was formed to establish an open, vendor-neutral standard that allows all vendors' token ring products to work together in the same network. Its founding members include: 3Com Corp. (Santa Clara, Calif.); Madge Networks Ltd. (London); Memorex Telex Inc. (Tulsa, Okla.); National Semiconductor (Santa Clara, Calif.); NCR (Dayton, Ohio); Proteon Corp. (Westborough, Mass.); Racore Computer Products (Los Gatos, Calif.); Standard Microsystems Corp. (Hauppauge, N.Y.); Texas Instruments (Dallas); and Vance Instruments (Chantilly, Va.).

■ **OTF's objectives.** OTF's three main objectives are:
1) To make itself the major forum for facilitating communication between network vendors, network resellers, and users of token ring products;
2) To increase and broaden the membership to represent the full range of organizations concerned with token ring: vendors, resellers, and end users;
3) To publicize and promote uniform technical standards for networking and communications.

OTF's goal is to openly provide specific information to any vendor in order to achieve industrywide plug-compatible token ring network products. That information includes specifications and other guidance necessary to make implementing token ring standards easy and cost-efficient.

OTF also publicizes and popularizes other groups' formal standards. Foremost among these is the IEEE 802.5 standard, which is familiar to all vendors who are creating token ring products.

Simply establishing standards does not guarantee interoperability. Standards organizations, such as IEEE, the International Organization for Standards (ISO) and ANSI only provide overall guidelines for product design and are not specific enough to make sure all products conforming to a standard will work together. In other words, vendors can conform to standards without making their equipment interoperable with competitors' products.

Consequently, OTF's role is to encourage vendors to design products that comply with standards and work with other token ring systems without modification.

For example, OTF seeks to convince IEEE to add extensions to the 802.5 standard that will minimize the risk that any vendor will introduce products that can't operate with third-party token ring products.

Such interoperability problems occurred when IBM introduced Version 3 of its 3270 Terminal Emulation Program. IBM wrote key startup commands directly to its Token Ring Adapter card, bypassing software interfaces previously used—maintaining conformance with the IEEE standards, but compromising compatibility with third-party products. As a result, several third-party vendors were forced to redesign existing products.

IBM is not the only company to introduce new products that negated existing interoperability, nor do its actions represent an unusual event. OTF serves to remind IBM and other vendors who might take this course: If they want interoperability, then they must go beyond the letter of standards compliance and plan designs with interoperability in mind.

■ **OTF activities.** Among OTF's more important duties is coordinating the standards implementation activities of different token ring members. OTF saves these companies from having to research competitors' products on their own and then make design adjustments.

In addition, to prove multivendor interoperability among token ring products, the organization has begun coordinating public demonstrations using interconnected member products. The foundation held the first such demonstration at Networld in Dallas in September 1989, with more than 20 companies participating, including Apple and IBM.

When OTF establishes its interoperability test lab, manufacturers will no longer have to duplicate efforts throughout the industry to determine which products are capable of functioning properly together. Instead, OTF will assume responsibility for testing and certifying compliance of member's products with interoperability standards. The lab will also handle benchmarking the actual performance of interoperable token ring products.

Token Ring

Table 1: IEEE 802.5 reference documents

ANSI/IEEE Standard 802.5–1988

Common Reference Document, November 1988, containing:

A. Station Management Review	Defines 16 network management MAC frames
E. Management Entity Spec	Aligns network management with 802.1
F. 4/16-Mbit/s Operation	Defines physical layer for 16 Mbit/s
H. Support for LLC III	Procedures for LLC Type III use
I. Early Token Release	Defines early token release at 16 Mbit/s

Other IEEE Drafts

B. Voice Grade Media Attachment	Telephone cable recommended practice
C. Reconfiguration	Two counter-rotating rings
D. Multiple Ring Networks	Source routing definition
G. Conformance Testing	Definition of conformance tests
J. Fiber Optic	Fiber cable attachment
K. Token Ring Media	Unshielded/shielded cable

MAC = MEDIA ACCESS CONTROL
LLC = LOGICAL LINK CONTROL

Table 2: Coexistence and communication

These token ring elements:	Need to be the same between nodes for:	
	Coexistence	Communication
Physical Layer Signaling	Yes	Yes
MAC layer and frames	Yes	Yes
Address and network management	Yes	Yes
Source routing header filtering	Yes	Yes
LLC layer SAP address filtering	Yes	Yes
LLC type (I, II, or III)	No	Yes
Upper layer protocol (TCP/IP, Netbios)	No	Yes
Card/PC hardware interface	No	No
System processor (80XXX, 68XXX)	No	No
PC machine type	No	No

coexist. It is up to the vendors and higher-level protocols to enable communications between nodes for the purpose of transferring applications data. It has been TI's experience over the last four years that the majority of token ring interoperability problems have been in communications (protocols, applications) or connections (cabling, connectors) not in coexistence. See Table 2 for a summary of coexistence and communications requirements.

Applying these concepts to the industry groups, IEEE is primarily involved in coexistence issues, while OTF is involved in both coexistence and communications issues.

Much work is under way to address the problems of robust communications on token ring networks. As indicated by recent announcements from such vendors as Microsoft (Redmond, Wash.), 3Com Corp. (Santa Clara, Calif.), and Novell Inc. (Provo, Utah), the use of one vendor's software over another vendor's hardware is being resolved by using open interfaces.

All corners of the industry are directing energy toward bridging, one of the major outstanding issues. Particular attention is being paid to compatibility between source-routing and transparent spanning-tree bridges on the same token ring. The IEEE 802.5 and IEEE 802.1 committees are continuing to work toward a resolution in this area, and many vendors are tailoring their own approach to that standards work.

Source routing, as the name implies, means that the source device determines the packet's route. With transparent spanning-tree routing the routing decisions are made by the intermediate devices (bridges) in a manner that is transparent to the end devices.

A bit of order, please

In general, interoperability difficulties can be divided into four major areas: frame formats, protocol stacks and interfaces, physical connections, and bridging.

Figure 1 illustrates the token ring frame format and its relationship to the OSI protocol model. The start of the frame, typically called the MAC header, contains the MAC destination and source addresses. Unlike Ethernet, 802.5 token ring defines a routing information field to support directed transmission of frames across source-routing bridges. The logical link control (LLC) header, which is described by IEEE 802.2 standards, comes next in the frame.

Other protocols, such as Netbios and TCP/IP may have their own headers following the LLC field. The information field that conveys the applications data is next, followed by the MAC trailing fields. For coexistence, the MAC, routing, and LLC fields must be decoded by all nodes on the ring. For communication between nodes, the same complete protocol stacks are required.

Because of its position in the history of LAN access techniques, Ethernet has had a pervasive influence on the culture of network engineering. Unfortunately, address-bit ordering for token ring is very different than it is for Ethernet. This difference caused several conceptual and many real problems with using addresses to achieve compatibility between token ring and Ethernet.

Key to the address-bit ordering issue is the 48-bit MAC address that is obtained by network vendors from the IEEE. Issued in blocks, these registered device addresses are called Organizationally Unique Identifiers (OUI) and are handed out with no knowledge on the IEEE's part of the type of network on which they will be deployed.

When a vendor obtains a block of MAC addresses from the IEEE, it is understood that no other vendor will be assigned the same addresses, with the goal that every token ring or Ethernet device will have a unique address.

This would be straightforward except that the order in which the 802.5 token ring standard requires that the address be presented to the MAC layer is the reverse of that required by Ethernet. Consequently, if a vendor uses the same MAC-layer algorithms for its token ring and Ethernet products, the addresses will go out on the wire backwards for 802.5—hence, no guarantee of unique address.

Because of the huge number of IEEE addresses, identical addresses resulting from reversed bit order can be expected to only occur rarely. But with the possibility of different vendors using different bit orders for the MAC address, communications between vendor stacks and

Token Ring

1. Token ring frame internals. The 802.5-defined frame is designed for robust internetwork environments with multiple protocols, routing options, and network management needs. Much of token ring's robustness comes from its logical link control fields, which feature service access points for multiprotocol stacks.

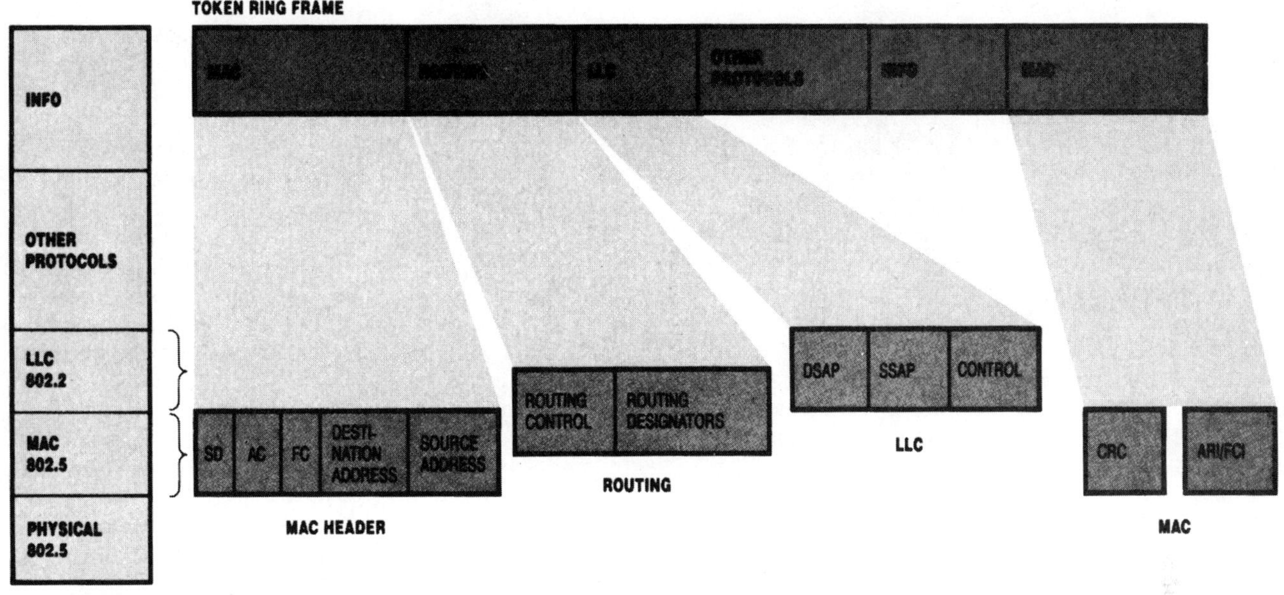

applications is not assured unless the correct bit order is used.

It is important to note that on the token ring, the MAC address and the protocol identifier are differently ordered within the frame. This can create confusion, and only time will determine whether token ring frames abide by this IEEE convention. Bridging between nodes on different network types is complicated by this bit-order swapping, requiring extra development effort and software overhead in devices.

Additionally, cyclic redundancy check protection between stations is lost. When to swap bits and what to swap are ongoing issues. One solution might be for the IEEE to grant all vendors a second block of OUIs with opposite bit order. Then uniqueness between nodes will be preserved.

LLC for posterity

With the addition of token ring to its stable of access methods, IBM also chose to use IEEE 802.2 LLC Type 2 (see Fig. 2). The LLC standard is a subdivision of the data link control layer that can supply nonguaranteed delivery (LLC Type 1) or guaranteed delivery with sliding windows and acknowledgments (LLC Type 2).

LLC Type 2 uses a connection-oriented protocol with sequencing and packet acknowledgment services that are often associated with OSI transport layer or synchronous protocols such as SDLC (synchronous data link control) and HDLC (high-level data link control). With LLC Type 2, a sequence number for each packet is added to the frame so that correct frame sequencing and acknowledgment are possible. Automatic retries for disrupted frame transmission are also supported.

TI provides LLC Type 1 and Type 2, which may be deployed either in RAM (loaded from floppy into memory) or in a programmable read-only memory (PROM) chip on the token ring network interface card. A third variety of LLC, Type 3, has been specified for industrial and other applications that need a fast acknowledgment without the necessary overhead of the Type 2 connection services.

When announced with the original token ring products in 1985, LLC was not in use on commercially available LANs. As of this writing, however, LLC has been widely accepted and is supported in the drivers of practically all token ring card offerings.

Figure 2 illustrates how the key protocol stacks on token ring use the different LLC types. LLC Type 2 is shown on top of LLC Type 1. This is because LLC Type 2 actually requires LLC Type 1 to establish the connection. APPC (advanced program-to-program communications, IBM's peer-to-peer protocol) and IBM's PC LAN program use the LLC Type 2 process. XNS (Xerox Network Systems), TCP/IP, and OSI (MAP/TOP) stacks generally use the LLC Type 1 and provide sequenced protocol at the transport level.

Finally, token ring LAN management software interfaces directly with the MAC layer to provide connection-management services.

A major advantage of LLC is that it defines an additional address-selection field in the token ring frame. This field can be used to allow different protocols to coexist on the same transmission line. This address-selection field is called a service access point (SAP).

When nodes running different protocols coexist on a LAN, each node looks inside the LLC destination SAP (DSAP) field of each passing packet to determine whether it contains a familiar protocol type. If a node doesn't recognize the protocol type indicated, it ignores the packet.

Figure 3 illustrates how the SAP supports the use of different protocols on the ring. The MAC protocol layers filter frames by address. The frame is then passed to the LLC protocol layer, where additional address filtering can occur based on protocols.

Table 3 illustrates key SAPs used by token ring vendors. In Figure 3, when SAP = FE the frame is routed to the OSI protocol stack, when SAP = F0 the frame is routed to the Netbios protocol. This feature allows multiple protocol stacks to exist in the same machine or in different machines on the same LAN.

Because only 6 bits are allowed for SAP differentiation, only 128 different SAPs are permitted. With today's multiplicity of vendors and protocols and internetworking, 128 SAPs are inadequate. To make things worse, SAPs have been self-assigned in the past, with vendors choosing their own values in an unorchestrated way.

This a key area where OTF is assisting vendors by publishing SAPs for all popular protocols. IEEE has also helped by defining an additional 40-bit protocol designation. This can be used by vendors to supplement the SAP values in the information portion of the frame.

Hardware/software issues

Hardware and software compatibility has long been a thorny issue for token ring users. Most users want to have the option of purchasing hardware from one source and software from a second source. But for this to work, all cards must work in all makes of PCs, and all the possible PC-card combinations must work with all types of network operating software. This is not the case today, in part because of great variation in the implementation of buses, interrupts, timing, and other I/O functions of PCs.

One of the first compatibility stumbling blocks dates back to 1985 when IBM chose to implement token ring on a shared RAM card while TI introduced a direct memory access (DMA) chip set. The card from IBM mapped a portion of its internal RAM—that containing the frames received or transmitted—into the PC memory map. Thus, the PC's CPU provided the data transfer support from the card to the system.

__2. LLC and typical SAPs.__ Depending on the needs of the higher-level protocols, vendors build their stacks on top of either LLC Type 1 or LLC Type 2. Because IBM's PC LAN Program has no formal transport level, it gets guaranteed delivery by running on LLC Type 2, allowing sliding windows and retry functionality.

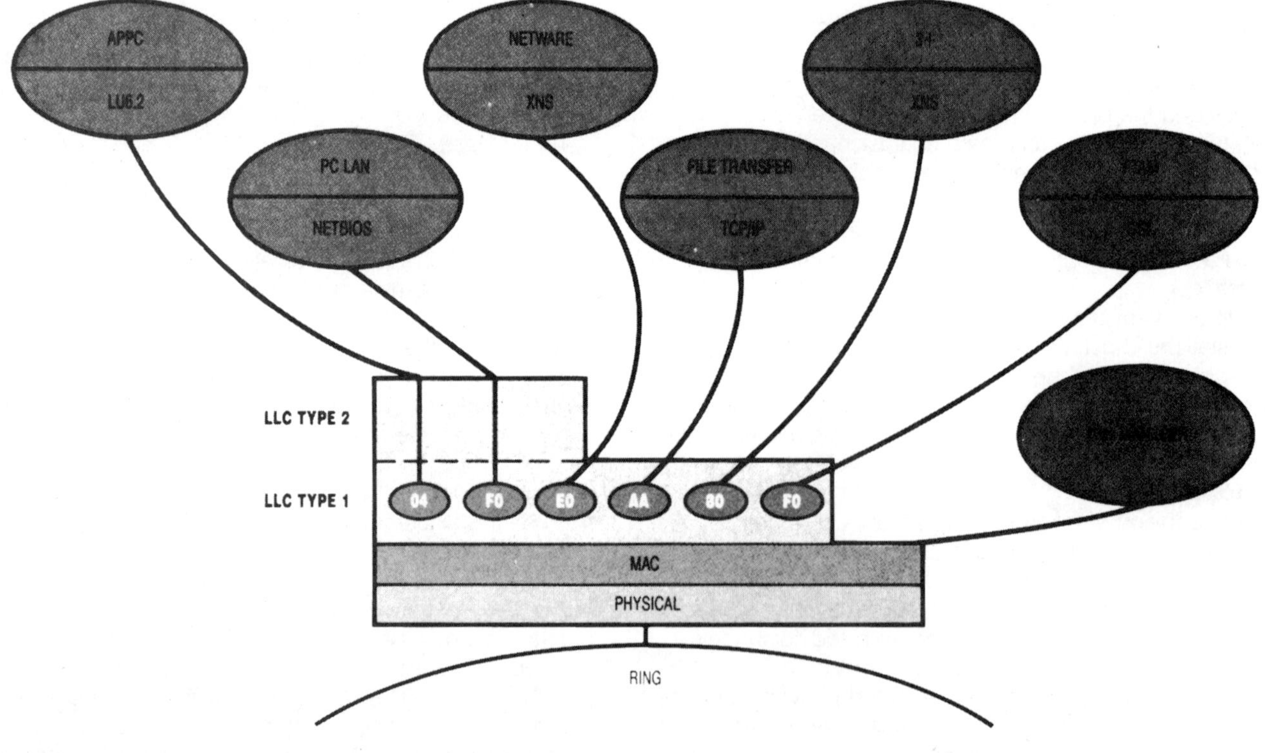

Token Ring

The chip set from TI implemented a complete DMA controller. Thus, the chip set could control both the address and data buses, avoiding bottlenecks inherent in transfers controlled from the PC side.

The shared RAM interface provided good performance for small packets, while the DMA interface provided high speeds for larger packets. This is the effect of a somewhat time-consuming chip setup process that takes place before each DMA transfer. Shared memory does not have this setup requirement, but neither does it have the transfer efficiencies for large packets of DMA.

DMA has been at a disadvantage for some machines, in particular the IBM PC/XT, where a DMA card could not be used. For the PC, implementations using DMA chip sets created internal buses to operate in the pseudo-DMA mode. For such advanced machines as the 80286, 80386, and the IBM RT, DMA is efficient and increasingly popular.

There are advantages to both methods, depending on the application and the architecture of the computer supporting the token ring hardware. Both methods will undoubtedly persist, and extolling the virtues of one technique over the other does not aid vendors' communication compatibility. However, the conclusion is that both communication and coexistence between the two card types is possible.

Figure 4 illustrates how the shared memory and DMA access methods can be matched at the same place in the protocol stacks. Approach A in the figure is similar to IBM's method. It uses LLC Type 2 on-card and a shared RAM access method. The implementation in B is used by many of TI's OEMs and also interfaces with a DMA access method at LLC Type 2 (or Type 1).

Both implementations can be accessed at the same 802.2 interface, using the interface specified in the IBM Token Ring Network Adapter Technical Reference Manual. Alternatively, the vendor interface could be at the 802.5 layer, as shown at C in the figure. This is also specified in the IBM document. Microsoft LAN Manager has its own LLC and Netbios, and consequently interfaces with TI's chips at the 802.5 level.

Some vendors are now specifying other MAC-layer software interfaces. 3Com, for example, is offering its LAN Manager interface and Novell has its adapter interface (see "Vendors plot ways to give LAN users access to multiple protocol stacks," DATA COMMUNICATIONS, Newsfront, September 1988). In the near future interfaces defined by such vendors will provide the needed compatibility to achieve communication between vendor products.

Occasional problems with the above layered architecture stem from the lack of conformance of specific software packages, written to a high-layer interface but using a lower-layer hardware function.

As an example, IBM's 3270 program is written to the IEEE 802.2 interface shown in Figure 4 except that during initialization it uses a card-specific hardware register to determine the interrupt level setting. This single violation of the interface requires that any hardware needing to run the high-level program also have this specific hardware register. That is not the case when layers are properly adhered

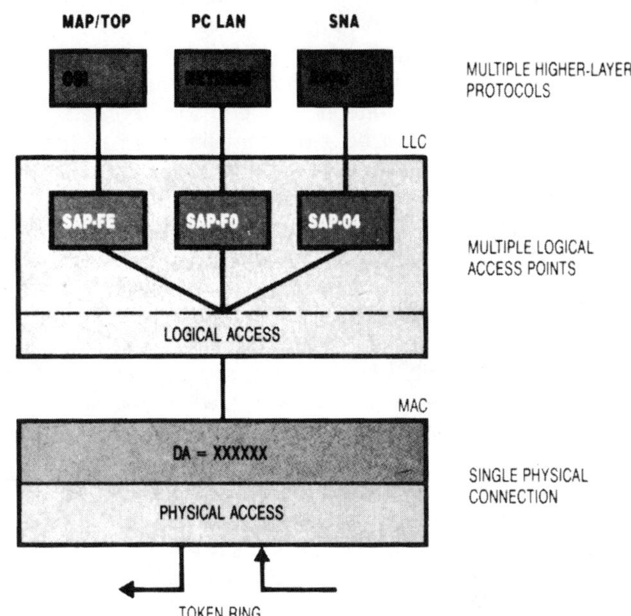

3. One node, many protocols. *LLC's service access points will demultiplex packets coming from the MAC level to multiple protocol stacks in the same node.*

APPC = ADVANCED PROGRAM-TO-PROGRAM COMMUNICATIONS
LLC = LOGICAL LINK CONTROL
MAC = MEDIA ACCESS CONTROL
MAP/TOP = MANUFACTURING AUTOMATION PROTOCOL/TECHNICAL AND OFFICE PROTOCOLS
SAP = SERVICE ACCESS POINT

Table 3: Sample service access points

Service access point	Usage
00	Null SAP
FF	Global SAP
02	Individual LLC sublayer management function
03	Group LLC sublayer management
FE	OSI network layer protocol
80	3Com protocol (XNS)
04	SNA protocol
05	SNA path control group SAP
E0	Novell NetWare
F0	IBM Netbios protocol
F8/FC	IBM remote initial program load (IPL)
AA	TCP/IP SNAP protocol
4E	EIA-RS 511 manufacturing message service
06	Arpanet's internet protocol
18	Texas Instruments' test software protocol

LLC = LOGICAL LINK CONTROL
SNAP = SUBNETWORK ACCESS PROTOCOL

to. The future solution to this problem is that higher-level software scrupulously avoid dependence on any hardware-specific features.

The physical layer of a token ring consists of cable and wiring concentrator components. It is noteworthy that many so-called interoperability problems with token ring have actually been found to stem from cable and concentrator misconfiguration.

The wires of the shielded cable are color-coded to match colors on the token ring connectors. These connectors come in small bags with 12 components, and connection is clearly described and color coded.

For a token ring using unshielded twisted pair, an RJ-11 connector is used. Unfortunately, the unshielded cabling colors are not standardized and is sometimes old and has already been wired. This is the source of many problems with token rings running over unshielded pair.

The relationship of wiring distances and the number of nodes often confuses users and vendors alike. Different vendors claim different allowable distances between nodes based on a well-defined trade-off between number of nodes and wiring type and wiring distance.

The article "How to design and build a token ring LAN" (DATA COMMUNICATIONS, May 1987) gives a detailed procedure to determine cable distances versus node count and cable type. The tables in that story are calculated from the IEEE 802.5 receive specification, where a specific receive signal level (and thus cable loss with distance) is required. The allowable loss from transmitter to receiver is a combination of two parameters. First is cable attenuation, both to the node and between separate wiring concentrators. Second is the loss in each wiring concentrator relay, even though the node is bypassed.

Much progress has been made in this area through vendor training and documentation, but care must be taken to design products that facilitate proper cabling and connection.

Although not widely known, in a token ring LAN, either source-routing or transparent bridging can be used. A full discussion of the differences between bridges is contained in the IEEE *Network Magazine,* January 1988.

Building bridges

To understand communication and coexistence between bridges, there are three items to consider:
- The properties of the end node wishing to transmit frames across a source-routing bridge.
- The properties of the source-routing bridge.
- The properties of the transparent bridge.

Because a transparent bridge places no requirements on the network's end nodes, it is not necessary to consider the properties of those nodes when using such a bridge.

A key difference between Ethernet and token ring protocols is that token ring has added an address recognized indicator/frame copied indicator (ARI/FCI) bit sequence set by the receiving station. These ARI/FCI bits, located at the end of the frame (see Fig. 1), are very important for correct bridge operation. The ARI or A bit is set by a station if it recognizes the source address in a frame and should copy the frame. The FCI or C bit is set if the copy operation is successful.

These bits were not intended to be used in normal ring transmission. However, some vendors' higher-level proto-

---

__4. Options at the hardware-software juncture.__ Token ring card vendors have many ways to transfer data, implement LLC, and interface their drivers to the TI chip set. For example, drivers in use today access LLC on the card with shared RAM or DMA. Vendors also have the option of interfacing drivers directly to the 802.5 layer.

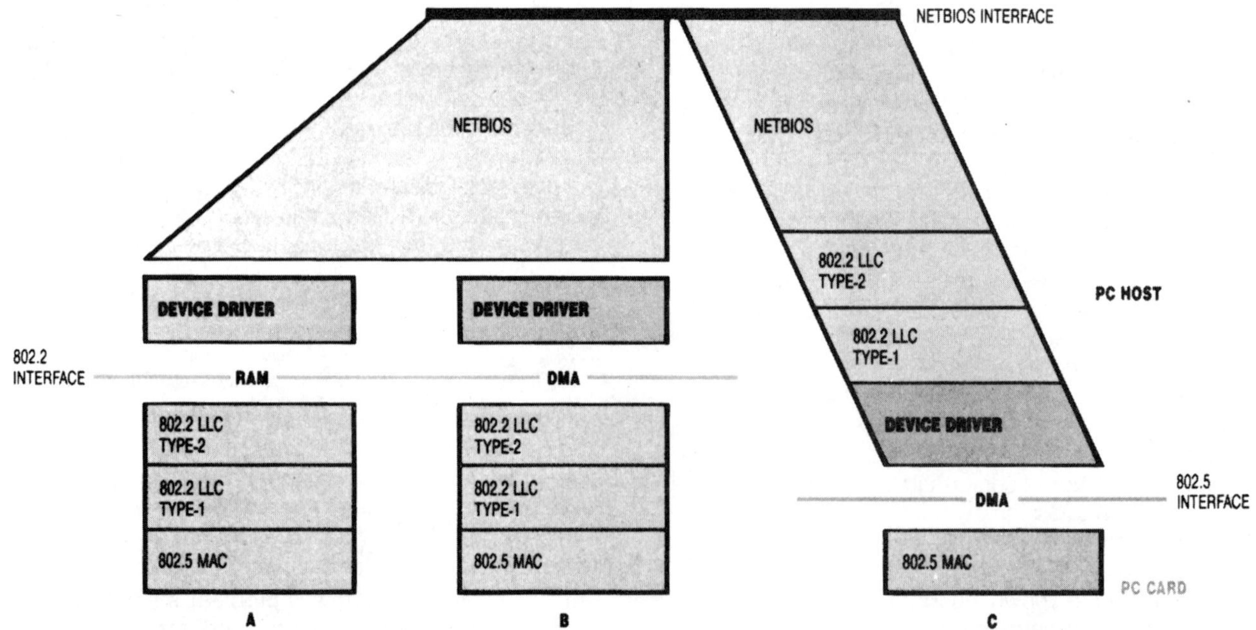

cols and application software use these bits to determine if the frame was transmitted and received correctly. Thus, a bridge must handle these bits correctly because the setting of the ARI/FCI bits is part of the MAC processes that aid ring management and prevent duplicate addresses on the same ring.

Following are nine rules that token ring bridges must honor to ensure interoperability.

1 Bridges should set ARI/FCI for all copied frames intended for forwarding.

2 Do not set ARI/FCI for those frames that are not to be forwarded. For source-routing bridges, this copy-and-forward decision can be done rapidly by scanning the routing information field of the incoming frame for the correct bridge sequence numbers.

3 Always decode the first bit of source address to determine if a routing field is present. Many systems have failed coexistence because this first bit went unchecked, and the system decoded the frame incorrectly. The presence of this field is denoted by a one in the first bit of the source address.

In source routing, the originating station designates a frame's route by embedding a route description in a field of the transmitted frame. For token rings, this routing-information field is located after the MAC header and before the LLC header.

4 Each station must have a way to determine the routing path for a station on another ring. To do so, the node must send out exploratory route frames. These frames pass over all source-routing bridges, looking for the destination address. Once the destination is found, the frame, along with the correct route information, is returned by the destination station. The frame originator then stores this information.

Once a partnership between end nodes is established, each node stores information about the other in a parameter table. If LLC Type 2 is used, then route determination occurs together with setting up the logical link.

5 Each station must store a routing information field along with the destination address to direct frames through the source-routing bridge.

The copying and forwarding algorithms for a source-routing bridge are specified by IEEE 802.5D. The bridge must forward exploratory route frames and be able to recognize, in the correct order in the routing information field, both its own bridge number and its partner's.

6 Each bridge must have a unique 16-bit number—consisting of a 12-bit ring number and a 4-bit bridge number—that is obtained during initialization or by receiving specific bridge management frames (LLC frames).

7 In a transparent bridge, address tables should be established by examining the source addresses of frames on the bridge's own ring. Frames with a destination address not found in these tables are assumed to be from another ring and are forwarded.

8 A spanning-tree bridge must not copy or forward MAC frames which have a destination address equal to the source address. If it does so, the duplicate address test will fail.

During token ring station initialization, a duplicate address test frame is transmitted by the station being added to the ring. This frame must not be copied and forwarded, thereby setting ARI/FCI.

9 Each spanning-tree bridge must be cognizant of the frames it transmits (even those with a different source address) so that it does not update its spanning-tree tables with off-ring frames.

All frames that are transmitted by a token ring node can also be received. A node must be able to distinguish frames originating on its own ring from those coming from another ring. The latter should not be used to update a node's address tables.

Future efforts

The preceding rules should allow compatible operation between bridges and end nodes on a token ring. However, effort is still required to determine how both spanning-tree and source-routing bridges can coexist on the same ring.

The IEEE 802.5 committee once defined a bridge that was transparent to source routing. In that definition, one side of the bridge followed source-routing prototcols and the other followed transparent spanning-tree protocols. Though this definition has been removed from the latest draft revision of the standard, IBM recently announced a product using a similar algorithm. For both bridge types on the same ring, several problems remain. Among them are determining which routing method should take precedence and handling parallel bridges with spanning-tree algorithms.

Eventually, the authors believe, token ring bridges will be predominantly of the source-routing type. Because both source-routing and transparent bridge are available today, though, end-node products tend to use protocol software that offer the user a choice of bridge.

Once end nodes have the algorithms to control source routing through networks—and they eventually will—the source-routing bridge, which is simpler to implement, will be the bridge of choice. Until that happens, however, both bridge types will be used.

This article has provided guidelines for achieving compatible coexistence and communication between token ring products. Guidelines notwithstanding, it is up to implementers and testing organizations to produce and validate the error-free hardware and protocols that will make interoperation a reality. ∎

Jim Carlo, a senior member of the technical staff in Texas Instruments' semiconductor open systems department, has been active in TI's token ring development program since 1982. He was responsible for establishing the original verification program to ensure that TI's silicon chip set met IEEE and IBM specifications. Currently responsible for high-speed fiber network development, he holds a PhD in electrical engineering from MIT.

John Hughes, manager of TI's semiconductor open systems department, has managed TI's token ring program since 1982. Hughes has also served as the Corporation for Open Systems lower-layer subcommittee manager and is currently a member of the board of directors of both the Open Token Foundation and Sparc International. He holds both a BA and an MA in electrical engineering from the University of Texas at Austin.

David Greenfield, special to DATA COMMUNICATIONS

Multivendor token ring networks come of age

In the past it may have been incautious to consider alternatives to IBM-made token ring products; in the future it will be incautious not to.

During the past year, a series of developments in the token ring industry have made front-page news. Early in the year came IBM's introduction of 16-Mbit/s token ring over shielded twisted pair. Later, the introduction of a new generation of adapter cards employing bus mastering was followed by a flurry of vendor announcements promising to support 16-Mbit/s token ring over unshielded twisted pair.

As the year progressed, Apple Computer Inc. brought out its new TokenTalk product line, including a token ring adapter for the Macintosh II. And finally, this fall delays for Texas Instuments' 16-Mbit/s token ring chip set caused much concern and commotion.

Since its introduction in 1985 by IBM, token ring has had to share the LAN limelight with 10-Mbit/s Ethernet. Today, however, with its 16-Mbit/s speeds, efficient access technique (token passing), and structured cable plant, token ring is gaining dominance on many fronts. Indeed, current projections expect token ring installations to surpass Ethernet installations by 1991.

Considering its evolving capabilities, the full impact of token ring technology has not been felt yet. With plans by Ungermann-Bass and Proteon, among others, to move 16-Mbit/s onto unshielded twisted pair, all that remains is for TI to release its 16-Mbit/s chip, which was originally scheduled for release this past September. TI is currently shipping samples; full production is expected by the end of the first quarter of next year.

The new TI chip set will support both 16 Mbit/s and 4 Mbit/s. Whether it actually ships in January as currently planned is anybody's guess. When TI is successful in bringing the product to market, the proliferation of token ring cards will be accelerated, driving down costs and encroaching on what has traditionally been Ethernet's prime real estate: high-speed backbones and graphics-intensive environments.

By adopting token ring as the means for interconnecting its mainframe, minicomputer, and PC product lines, IBM has all but assured token ring of a predominant position in the LAN marketplace. But beyond Big Blue's cheerleading, consumers will continue to purchase token ring LANs for several reasons. One is the protocol's robustness. Unlike Ethernet, its main competitor, the token ring protocol includes the tools for network management in its specification.

A second advantage to token ring is its topology. The natural fault-tolerant qualities of the dual-wired ring become increasingly desirable as network downtime becomes increasingly unacceptable.

Third-party paradise
Much as the IBM PC brought about a whole universe of compatible products, token ring's success has been driven by its open standard (IEEE 802.5) and ongoing efforts by vendors to make hardware interfaces and network software work together. Today's token ring is a veritable third-party paradise, and will remain so until the inevitable market consolidation comes and players are either swallowed up or driven out.

In spite of the high level of third-party activity, in many circles IBM is synonymous with token ring. According to Brad Baldwin of Dataquest, a San Jose, Calif.-based market research firm, IBM's dominance among U.S. vendors in worldwide shipments of token ring network interface cards (NICs) hovers at 77 percent. By the time third-party 16-Mbit/s adapters hit the market, that percentage could be even higher, considering IBM is already shipping its 16-Mbit/s product.

Even with its lead, IBM's dominance will undoubtedly erode; to date there are at least 15 third-party vendors manufacturing their own token ring adapters for PCs. To compete with IBM's unyielding presence, manufacturers have tried to keep their prices low, while offering higher functionality than the counterpart IBM products. Prices for third-party boards range between $395 and $500 for 8-bit boards and $499 and $750 for 16-bit boards.

The average price for the 8-bit card reviewed later in this article is about $520, nearly $130 lower than its IBM equivalent. There is less price spread in the Micro Channel architecture product arena; IBM's card lists for $750. Racore differentiates itself in a crowded marketplace with the lowest-priced line of network cards—all under $500.

The third-party adapters often include a number of fancy features for their short buck. For example, 3Com and Tiara have designed their cards to handle both 8- and 16-bit buses, allowing the same adapter to run in both AT and PC machines. The classic PC/XT uses an 8-bit bus to move data between the CPU and memory. In contrast, the AT employs a 16-bit bus. Adapters that can use the wider bus to transfer data in 16-bit chunks (all other factors being equal) will have higher performance than cards with 8-bit buses; see Table 1 for bus size and other evaluation criteria for available token ring cards.

The feature that may have generated the most hoopla is bus-mastered direct memory access (DMA). This is the ability of a network interface card to take control of the bus and transfer data directly into PC memory without the help of the PC processor. With traditional data transfer methods access to the bus was centralized at the (PC) host processor. Bus mastering allows multiple adapters to vie for direct control of the bus and PC memory. Performance is increased by allowing the adapter, not the host, to perform the brunt of the transfer operations.

A major user concern, interoperability of token ring products from different vendors, has been largely solved. At NetWorld in Dallas this fall, the Open Token Foundation (OTF), a consortium of vendors advocating token ring compatibility, demonstrated the products of over a dozen vendors functioning on four internetworked LANs—without failures of basic ring operation.

"Our work at NetWorld proves to users and vendors alike that off-the-shelf products from multiple manufacturers can indeed function properly when put to the test," claims Colin Mick, OTF's executive director.

Indeed, Mick's claim was confirmed by every vendor, installer, and end user contacted—at least when speaking about simple configurations of a few rings with similar protocol software. Some speculated that interoperability may be an issue when bridging between many LANs, particularly when they include both token ring and Ethernet access methods.

Chips ahoy!
For those ready to buy lots of token ring cards now, perhaps the biggest drawback of the third-party offerings is lack of support for 16-Mbit/s speeds. All third-party vendors with the exception of Ungermann-Bass (UB) use TI's TMS380 chip set, which was codeveloped by TI and IBM. Many have promised high-speed adapters, but all are constrained by vaporous chip sets.

TI promised delivery of its 16-Mbit/s chip set last September. To date, TI is still in testing. Full shipments are not expected out until the first quarter of next year. UB, which currently is the only other source of 4-Mbit/s chip sets, is still in the process of developing a strategic plan for its 16-Mbit/s token ring.

TI's TMS380 chip set consists of five main components: the system interface chip, communications processor chip, protocol handler chip, and the ring interface chip pair. The system interface chip transfers the data between the host PC and the adapter using DMA techniques.

The communications processor is the controlling chip, containing a 16-bit CPU with 2,750 bytes of RAM. The communications processor executes the 16 Kbytes of adapter control program located in the protocol handler's ROM. This firmware provides management services, reliable ring operation, and diagnostics. The communication processor also buffers transmitted and received frames in its RAM.

Adapter criteria
Selecting the right NIC for your LAN is important, and performance no doubt will be a critical issue. But perspective is needed. According to a study released in January 1988 by the National Software Testing Laboratories, even an extremely fast network adapter can only increase system performance by around 20 percent. In contrast, a fast multi-user database system can increase network performance by 300 percent over a slower database system.

The PC hardware, operating system, protocol stack, and application software all affect network performance substantially. And no matter how fast the card runs, the network will always run only as fast as its slowest component. Adding memory to a network card, increasing the card's bus width, or optimizing the card driver software are for naught if another component's performance is sluggish. Concern for network performance extends beyond the NIC to every facet of the network. And while performance is important, compatibility, reliability, and other qualities are as essential.

The performance factor considered most important by the manufacturers contacted was the card's driver software. See Table 2 for a list of cards and driver support for common network operating systems (NOS). The driver is generally one or two files loaded into the PC and the adapter's memory. The driver provides a standard interface with which the NOS interacts. Ariel Gomez-Ortigoza, president of Lantana (San Diego, Calif.), one of the few manufacturers of bus-mastered DMA cards for the Micro Channel, claims that a 100 percent difference can be seen between well written and poorly written drivers. Unfortunately, the driver's quality is also the most difficult of the NIC criteria to determine.

Generally speaking, a quality driver will at least have the critical portions of its code written in assembler. Some manufacturers have chosen to write their drivers completely in assembler. Other manufacturers write the code at least partially in a higher language like C. Determining the quality of the driver simply by asking the vendor is virtually impossible. One easy way to weed out poor drivers is to purchase a card whose driver has been certified

Multivendor networks

by the manufacturer of the NOS, Novell for example, which has a vested interest in good performance and dependability.

Aside from the driver, adding memory to the token ring card is probably the most obvious way for a vendor to improve its adapter's performance. IBM's Network Adapter II and Network Adapter/A both contain 16 Kbytes of memory on board. Third-party vendors have exceeded this considerably. Table 1 enumerates RAM size for token ring cards covered by this article. The 16 Kbytes or more additional memory augments the 2,750-byte packet buffer allotted by TI, allowing a greater number of packets to be stored on the card simultaneously.

Says Leon Adams, open systems manager at TI: "It's pretty evident that the larger the packet buffer, the greater the network performance. However, the impact would

Table 1: Network interface card characteristics

CARD VENDOR	PRODUCT	DATA TRANSFER METHOD	SHARED MEMORY WINDOW (KBYTES)	CHIP SET MANUFACTURER
3COM	TOKENLINK	DMA, I/O PORT, BUSMASTER DMA	N/A	TI
	TOKENLINK PLUS	DMA, I/O PORT	N/A	TI
GATEWAY COMMUNICATIONS	G/TR AT ADAPTER	BUSMASTER DMA	N/A	TI
	G/TR PC ADAPTER	I/O PORT	N/A	TI
IBM	NETWORK ADAPTER II	SHARED MEMORY	16	IBM
	NETWORK ADAPTER/A	SHARED MEMORY	16	IBM
	NETWORK 16/4 ADAPTER	SHARED MEMORY	16–64	IBM
	NETWORK 16/4 ADAPTER/A	SHARED MEMORY	16–64	IBM
LANTANA TECHNOLOGY	CYPRESS II	BUSMASTER DMA	N/A	TI
MADGE NETWORKS	MADGE PC RING NODE	I/O PORT	N/A	TI
	SMART AT RING NODE	BUSMASTER DMA	N/A	TI
	MC RING NODE	BUSMASTER DMA	N/A	TI
	SMART MC RING NODE	BUSMASTER DMA	N/A	TI
NCR	NCR PC TOKEN RING-16	SHARED MEMORY	8	TI
	NCR PC TOKEN RING-8	SHARED MEMORY	8	TI
PROTEON	P1346	BUSMASTER DMA	N/A	TI
	P1347	BUSMASTER DMA	N/A	TI
	P1342	SHARED MEMORY	8	TI
	P1840	BUSMASTER DMA	N/A	TI
PURE DATA	PDI8025	BUSMASTER DMA	N/A	TI
	PDUC8025	BUSMASTER DMA	N/A	TI
RACORE COMPUTER PRODUCTS	M8112	SHARED MEMORY	8	TI
	M8110	BUSMASTER DMA	N/A	TI
	M8111	SHARED MEMORY	8	TI
TIARA	LANCARD/T*PC	SHARED MEMORY	16	TI
	LANCARD/T*AT	SHARED MEMORY	16	TI
UNGERMANN-BASS	NIUPS/TR	SHARED MEMORY	16–32	UB
	PC-NIU/TR	SHARED MEMORY	32	UB
WESTERN DIGITAL	TOKENCARD WS	SHARED MEMORY	8	TI
	TOKENCARD	SHARED MEMORY	8	TI

LLC = LOGICAL LINK CONTROL   DMA = DIRECT MEMORY ACCESS

Multivendor networks

depend on [network] loads. You may only notice the difference under heavy traffic conditions."

Just how much RAM should be allocated for buffering packets? It depends on the environment and the particular device. Servers, for example, generally have more packets addressed to them than clients and thus require larger buffers. Some environments are more likely to generate higher amounts of traffic. Some manufacturers will include an additional 128 Kbytes, using a majority of the RAM for on-board protocol processing that IBM conducts in the PC's memory.

Ungermann-Bass includes the most on-board RAM of any token ring adapter. However, while the TI chip set implements token ring's media access control (MAC) and logical link control (LLC) protocols in firmware (see this issue's cover story for explanations of LLC and MAC), UB

DATA RATE (MBIT/S)	BUS SIZE (IN BITS)	LIST PRICE	REMOTE BOOT PRICE	REMOTE BOOT STANDARD	HOST ARCHI-TECTURE	MAXIMUM INTERRUPT LEVEL	INTELLIGENT/ DUMB	AMOUNT OF RAM ON CARD (KBYTES)
4	8/16	$595	$49	N	AT	9	D	16
4	8/16	$945	N/A	N	AT	12	I	256
4	16	$695	N/A	N	AT	8	D	128
4	8	$595	N/A	N	PC	4	D	2
4	8	$650	$65	N	AT	4	D	16
4	16	$750	$65	N	MCA	4	D	16
16/4	8	$895	$65	N	AT	4	D	64
16/4	16	$895	N/A	N	MCA	4	D	64
4	16	$750	N/A	N	MCA	4	D	48
4	8	$499	$80	N	PC	4	D	16
4	16	$749	$80	N	AT	8	I	128
4	16	$599	$80	N	MCA	3	D	16
4	16	$799	$80	N	MCA	3	I	128
4	8/16	$650	N/A	Y	AT	6	D	16
4	8	$399	N/A	Y	PC	6	D	16
4	16	$550	$50	N	AT	9	D	2.8
4	16	$650	$50	N	AT	9	D	18
4	8	$495	$50	N	XT	6	D	2.8
4	16	$750	N/A	N	MCA	6	D	18
4	16	$650	$70	N	AT	9	D	16
4	16	$725	$80	N	MCA	10	D	64
4	8	$399	$70	N	XT	2	D	18
4	16	$499	$70	N	AT	4	D	18
4	16	$499	$70	N	MCA	4	D	18
4	8	$595	N/A	N	PC	6	D	64
4	8/16	$795	N/A	N	AT	6	D	64
4	16	$1095	N/A	Y	MCA	2	D	512
4	16	$695	N/A	N	AT	4	D	256
4	8	$499	$39	Y	XT	6	D	2.8
4	8	$599	$39	Y	XT	6	D	128

Table 2: A selection of token ring cards and drivers

CARD VENDOR	CARD	IBM PC LAN PROGRAM	OS/2 LAN MANAGER	NETWARE 2.1	BANYAN VINES	DCA 10NET	3COM 3+	3COM 3+ OPEN
3COM	TOKENLINK	x		x	x		x	x
	TOKENLINK PLUS	x		x			x	x
GATEWAY	PC ADAPTER	x		x				
	AT ADAPTER	x		x				
IBM	ALL	x	x	x				
LANTANA	ALL	x		x				
MADGE	ALL	x	x	x	x	x		x
NCR	ALL	x		x				
PROTEON	P1346	x		1Q, '90	x			
	P1347	x		1Q, '90	x			
	P1342	x		1Q, '90				
	P1840	x		1Q, '90				
PURE DATA	PDI8025	x		x				
	PDUC8025	x		x				
RACORE	ALL	x		x				
TIARA	ALL		x	x				
UNGERMANN BASS	ALL	x	x	x				
WESTERN DIGITAL	ALL	x	x	x	x			

uses its 512 Kbytes of RAM for the same purpose. The reason, explains Jeff Ellerbruch, UB's token ring product manager, was to ease programming changes, in case IBM had altered the token ring protocol.

Pick a transfer method

Token ring vendors move data between their adapters and PC memory with one of three methods: shared memory, DMA, or I/O ports; and there are variations to each of these (see Table 1). IBM and UB chose shared memory, also termed memory-mapped I/O. This method maps a portion of the PC's memory to the adapter's memory creating what is called a shared-memory window. Incoming data from the LAN is processed and moved into the adapter's memory. The PC is then notified and reads the data directly from the card as if it were its own memory.

The advantage of shared memory is its compatibility with the range of PC platforms. Vendors like shared-memory transfer because it works with virtually all types of PC buses and processors.

The problem with shared memory is its window size. The memory used for the shared-memory window is unavailable for other PC applications. With a large window, more data can be moved, but the chance for memory conflicts with other I/O cards is increased.

With shared memory, if the window is too small, the amount of data handled in each operation is limited and transfers are inefficient, particularly for larger packets. Consequently, most shared-memory cards, including IBM's, have a 16-Kbyte window, which represents a bal-

ance between robbing too much memory from the PC and allowing too small a window size for the needs of the network card.

Avoiding the shared-memory approach, the TI chip set uses DMA to move the data between the PC host and the

Using an intelligent card isn't always the right choice.

adapter. With DMA, a peripheral has direct access to the host's memory and no memory window is required.

One issue with DMA is that the processor is not ready, by default, for DMA operations. To set up each DMA transfer various parameters need to be established with the processor. The time overhead incurred in this setup is costly. Small increments of transfer (8 or 16 bits) is another inefficiency of conventional PC DMA, sometimes called slave DMA.

Some token ring vendors have improved DMA with cards containing a bus controller chip that can gain control of the bus without all the overhead of standard, PC-based DMA. This is called the busmaster approach.

We have covered the DMA and shared-memory methods of transfer, the third method uses the PC processor's I/O ports. Most cards use the PC's I/O ports to transfer control information from the PC to its I/O cards and back. Some network cards even employ this technique to transfer data coming off the LAN into the PC's address space. Although still in use, the I/O port method has been discarded in favor of shared-memory transfer or DMA transfer variants on newer cards.

It takes smarts
Intelligence is another prime card-evaluation factor, and vendors provide all sorts of intelligence levels for their cards. TI's token ring chip set includes a protocol manager that processes the token ring protocols on board. As far as MAC-layer processing is concerned, every token ring adapter is intelligent. Most manufacturers use this processor only for the MAC layer. Consequently, in the area of higher-layer protocol processing these cards may be considered dumb.

A few vendors, however, have gone beyond the requisite MAC-layer processing to process higher-layer protocols on the card itself. These intelligent cards are of two different types. The first is typified by the TokenLink product line from 3Com, which incorporates on the adapter an Intel 80186 that can load higher-level protocols such as 3Com's transport software onto the adapter for processing.

The second approach to card intelligence is shown by the Smart card line from Madge Networks (London, England). The Smart card uses TI's communication processor to process higher-layer protocols in addition to the MAC layer. According to Mark Richer, Madge's director of development, the Smart card downloads NOS protocol software (such as NetWare's) onto the card, saving the PC from the protocol processing duties. With NetWare, protocols include LLC, IPX (internetwork packet exchange), and SPX (sequenced packet exchange).

Adding another chip, such as 3Com's 80186, uses precious adapter space and increases the cost of the board. However, by staying within the same chip-set family as the PC, 3Com does not have to rewrite the function calls used in its driver software. In contrast, Madge's most difficult step, said Richer, was developing in the TI programming environment. Every protocol that gets loaded onto the adapter was rewritten to function on the TI chip. While this presents a bit of a Herculean task at first, the development of the TI programming environment will make later ports significantly easier.

Using an intelligent card may not always be the right choice. Its big advantage comes in freeing up some memory and faster processing if the PC host is slow. But Richer says that memory saving only amounts to about 14 Kbytes under NetWare.

Moreover, in a 80386-based system, processing the protocols at the host, even when heavily loaded, may still be faster than processing the protocols on a much slower Intel or TI chip on the network card. This latter concept has prompted some vendors to claim that their dumb cards are faster than the typical smart card. This obviously depends on many variables, such as drivers, host PC speed, transfer type, and packet size. A number of parties, including DATA COMMUNICATIONS are in the process of testing the performance of token ring cards. Results are expected to be available by early next year.

Alas, with the current enormous population of PC/AT compatibles, add-on cards, and memory-starved software, conflicts are bound to arise. Some of these demons can be avoided, others may prove unsolvable for certain equipment mixes.

DMA channel number conflicts between NICs and other cards, for example, are largely solved by offering a range of DMA channel selections. Other problems, such as those related to bus timing on the host PC, are unsolvable at the user level. Following are some of the pitfalls to watch for when venturing into the land of third-party PCs and token ring products.

IRQ and I/O settings
Most token ring adapters include a wide range of IRQ (interrupt request) and I/O address settings from which to choose. So in a machine loaded with devices, there is a greater chance for the boards to function. Tom Carson, an administrator of a 275-station LAN at McData Corp. (Broomfield, Colo.), found that even cards with a range of interrupts may still have their share of problems.

The Proteon P1344 card, for example, supplies various interrupts (3 to 12). However, when the card is configured with a Novell driver only a few choices remain. The first token ring card installed in a machine may not conflict, but additional cards in the same machine (particularly for servers) will conflict either with LPT 1 and 2 or COMM 1 and 2. If that happens you must disable the printer interrupts. But on some machines the interrupts cannot be disabled easily or at all.

Carson reported a similar problem with Western Digital's WD8005TR card. The card provided an ample number of interrupts but was limited to only two I/O addresses. Consequently, only two WD805TR cards could be placed in one file server.

Not even IBM is free from card configuration problems. Mark Rader, a senior field engineer at Network Services (Fairfax, Va.), comments that the IBM token ring board, supports IRQ settings for 2, 3, 6, and 7. In many machines, IRQs 2 and 6 are used for the other controllers leaving IRQ's 3 and 7. However, the parallel one port uses IRQ 7 and the second serial port uses IRQ 3.

Normally on IBM machines, disabling the serial and parallel ports is a routine task — just remove the adapter. However, some compatibles integrate the two ports onto the motherboard, making it especially difficult to disable them. In a server with serial and parallel printers and a mouse it may be that no interrupts are left for the NIC.

Similarly, says Rader, IBM's token ring board only supplies two I/O address options, A20 and A24. Thus only two IBM cards can be placed in a single machine. Some operating systems, such as NetWare and Vines, enable a server with four NICs, interconnecting four different networks. With IBM cards this configuration is problematic.

Bus timing
Some glitches cannot be avoided with any type of card. These often occur on rogue AT clones that don't conform to the IBM bus specification.

Explains Ben Wilson, senior engineer at Racore Computer Products: "Some ATs have problems passing status information between the card and the host PC. The problem is their bus timing. Specifically, the time required to drop the channel-ready line. The TI chip set uses the channel-ready line to insert the wait states necessary for buses on the adapter and motherboard to synchronize. Without bus synchronization host-adapter data transfer cannot occur."

The channel-ready line should be activated when the adapter reads or writes from I/O, according to the AT specification. However, some compatibles maintain control of the line for too long, not allowing it to be activated by the adapter. Thus, the card cannot function with the host.

One machine in which Wilson has seen the problem is the PS/2 Model 30 286. Although the PS/2 Model 30 has an AT bus, it does not recognize the channel-ready signal activated by the card. Instead, manufacturers must modify their 16-bit cards to pass the status information in 8-bit transfers.

In closing, don't let all these potential snags dissuade you from the many benefits of multivendor token rings. Except for the conflicts with PCs and card settings outlined above, interchanging 802.5 adapters from different vendors on the same network should not cause faults.

Choosing token ring cards is somewhat of an involved process these days because of the wide range of available card architectures and driver software. This is the result of an assortment of capable vendors jockeying for position in what is expected to be an enormous market in the next decade.

As a result, the varying claims of battling vendors can make understanding the underlying technology difficult. The forces behind the diversity are not purely engineering ones, either. So it is helpful to remember that, as with many key technologies, IBM exerts an influence on product development that is both obvious and subtle.

Early on, for instance, shared memory was an ideal way for token ring cards to transfer data into PCs and XTs. Though bus mastering is now considered more efficient for 16-bit cards, IBM has persisted in its shared-memory technique, even in the Micro Channel environment where bus mastering is highly supported. And of course, what IBM does affects what some of the third-party card makers do, hence the large array of busmaster, shared-memory, and other transfer methods.

But none of the transfer-method considerations affect basic interoperability. At this point in the industry's development the question is not whether all these cards will work together, but whether all the various parts and pieces—including cables, connectors, card settings, card drivers, network operating software, and application software—can be made to work together.

In the future, the performance gains and memory conservation that vendors are touting today will need to be augmented by ease of integration. Fast cards and low memory requirements will do users little good if the integration of cards into working systems remains a black art. ∎

Jerry Yochelson, Systems Strategies Inc., New York, N.Y.

HLLAPI: The bridge from DOS and Unix to mainframes

This emerging 3270 interface standard can put a new face on aging host applications without touching them.

Empires have risen and fallen over 3270 terminal emulation. There are three reasons for this. The first is the enormous value of the data stored in IBM (and compatible) mainframes, which are generally accessible only through 3270 (and compatible) terminals. The second is the value of the application software that accesses and manipulates this data. And finally, users and upper management are pressing for new and better means of meeting their interactive processing requirements.

In response to the latter, MIS and data processing managers may have to modify existing software or migrate some applications to a distributed processing environment. But while doing so, they must not interrupt their own controls or user access to the central site.

There is a relatively simple and cost-effective solution to these conflicting demands: the high-level language application program interface. HLLAPI is an emerging host-connectivity software standard that specifies the programmatic interface to IBM 3270 terminal-emulator software (see "HLLAPI standards"). It typically operates on PCs under DOS, and on microcomputers and minicomputers under Unix.

HLLAPI enables MIS, data processing, and data communications managers to extend the capabilities and lifetimes of the existing IBM 3270 applications on their mainframes without altering a line of source code in their mainframes to accomplish this. With HLLAPI, managers can postpone, perhaps indefinitely, that day of reckoning when they have to modify or convert a decade-old application program whose authors, documentation, and even source code may be long gone.

Further, managers can use HLLAPI to improve terminal-operator productivity (in certain cases even eliminating manual data entry). They can also simplify user interface to mainframe applications, improve response time at terminals, and reduce loading on communication lines.

Perhaps the most important benefit of HLLAPI is that it simplifies the development of new, distributed applications on PCs and Unix computer systems. For example, HLLAPI applications running on a networked PC or minicomputer can concurrently access data from multiple sources (different remote mainframe computers, different databases on the same mainframe, or local databases). Then the application can combine that data with operator input and then update one or more remote and local databases.

The history of HLLAPI

HLLAPI had its genesis in 3270 terminal emulation. Originally, emulation was performed in the firmware of special-purpose hardware to implement IBM plug-compatible terminals. As the use of minicomputers grew, this emulation began a migration to software. The advent of the PC was soon followed by add-on 3270 communication boards and emulator software. In one survey there were almost 300 companies offering a 3270-emulation product (see "Ensuring that your emulator really acts like an IBM," DATA COMMUNICATIONS, January 1986).

The first PC emulators performed only 3278 (or predecessor) display and keyboard emulation and some 3287 printer emulation. The emulator's communication board typically connected the PC via coaxial cable to a local 3274 (or compatible) cluster controller. There were no user programming capabilities except for an escape key (hot key) that allowed the user to enter a local DOS command (which generally had no direct relation to the emulated session).

HLLAPI evolution under Unix was influenced by the operating environment. Unix typically operates on microcomputers, minicomputers, or larger computers that have the processing and the I/O power to handle multiple terminals and host connections. (Microcomputer, in this context, typically means a computer based on an 80386

331

HLLAPI

processor.) Unlike lower-powered PCs, these computers can support multiple bisync/SNA communication boards so that links can be maintained to geographically separated hosts.

On Unix systems, this capability, along with the capability to serve multiple users, promoted the development of 3274 controller emulators and communication boards. The terminals on a Unix system with 3274 emulation access one or more remote mainframes in the same manner as a 3278 hard-wired to a cluster controller and connected to a single host.

Since Unix systems are configured with multiple ASCII terminals of different types (for example, a VT100 or HP2621), the emulation software has to map the keys and display features of the particular terminal into the native 3270 terminal keys and 3270 display characteristics. This is also the case for PC displays and keyboards.

To support this, emulator developers saw the need to organize their software into components that separated the characteristics of the local terminal from the functions of the line (communication) side of the 3270 emulation. This evolved into the concept of presentation space, an area in computer memory that contains the data that represents the 3270 display.

As data is received from the host (line side), the emulation software places it into the presentation space. The terminal side of the emulator maps the presentation space data into its most equivalent representation on the terminal display.

When an operator enters data, function keys, or defined key sequences at the keyboard, the emulator transforms these (as needed) into 3270 representation, performs any local 3270 processing (such as preventing writing into protected fields) and places the data into the presentation space (and on the display). When the operator hits the enter key or any other host-attention key, the emulator causes previously entered data to be sent to the host.

Since the set of 3270 functions is fixed (at least until IBM's next release), emulator developers encode these functions into subroutines in order to more readily accommodate their development of terminal-specific mapping routines. These subroutines access and manipulate the presentation space and perform the 3270 functions. From this point, it is a minor evolution for emulator developers to extend these subroutines into a 3270 application program interface (API).

With an API, users can develop applications that go far beyond simple terminal mapping. These applications can intercept and manipulate terminal input, add information to the locally displayed data, and process the data received from the host and the data entered locally into a presentation space. The general relationship of 3270 terminal emulation software to HLLAPI is shown in Figure 1.

This type of API is often provided with various kinds of communication software packages including SNA, bisync, and X.25. As might be expected, different emulator vendors have had their own set of API functions for the same protocol. Moreover, the functions are most likely to be provided for only one programming language, such as C.

Note that C is a high-level language, and that there are

3270 APIs for other HLLs, but there was no industry standard for 3270 APIs until IBM entered this arena in 1983 with its 3270 PC, a PC/XT bundled with special software and hardware. The hardware includes a 3278 terminal interface board that supports IBM's Distributed Function Terminal (DFT) mode. With DFT, a 3270 terminal or 3270 emulator can have multiple host sessions concurrently.

The software—the IBM 3270 PC Control Program—supported DFT with the addition of windows that allowed a user to view either a full screen or multiple partial screens containing a fraction of the display from different sessions. In a subsequent release of the program, IBM added low-level API software, which made emulator functions available through special DOS software interrupts (similar to system calls in other operating systems).

Applications using DOS system calls are typically programmed in assembler code. Most of the HLLs that run on a PC (such as Microsoft C and Borland Turbo Pascal) are able to make these calls, but the result is nonportable software.

In 1986, IBM introduced HLLAPI to provide an interface from compilers to the emulator, which is less dependent on the PC and DOS. There are two IBM DOS versions of the interface: HLLAPI 3.1, for use with the 3270 Workstation Program, and EEHLLAPI 1.2, included with the PC 3270 Emulation Program, Entry Level 1.2.

What can HLLAPI do for you?

HLLAPI capabilities are usually grouped into the following categories:

Unattended operation or programmed operator. Any combination of keystrokes routinely entered by a terminal user can be stored in a HLLAPI program, which enters the

HLLAPI standards

Although IBM HLLAPI is the de facto standard, work has begun on formal HLLAPI standards. In March 1989, Bell Communications Research (Bellcore) issued Technical Advisory TA-STS-00780, "Generic Requirements for a Bellcore 3270 High Level Language Application Interface." The stated purpose of this advisory is to document generic requirements for a Bellcore 3270 HLLAPI for connected workstations or processors. These workstations or processors can be based on any architecture and run any operating system (DOS, OS/2, or Unix). The advisory further states that "One of Bellcore's objectives is to design software that is hardware-independent, thus removing application dependencies for a specific vendor."

The advisory contains an attachment that states Bellcore's anticipated generic requirements for 3270 HLLAPI. This includes support for asynchronous ASCII communications in which both the host and the terminal can be asynchronous. VT100, VT52, and Teletype 33 type terminals are specified for support.

Although this advisory is not the work of an industry users' organization, it does indicate the increasing use of HLLAPI and the movement to standardization.—*J.Y.*

HLLAPI

1. Applied HLLAPI. *With HLLAPI, users can develop applications that go beyond simple 3270 terminal mapping. Such applications can intercept and manipulate terminal input.*

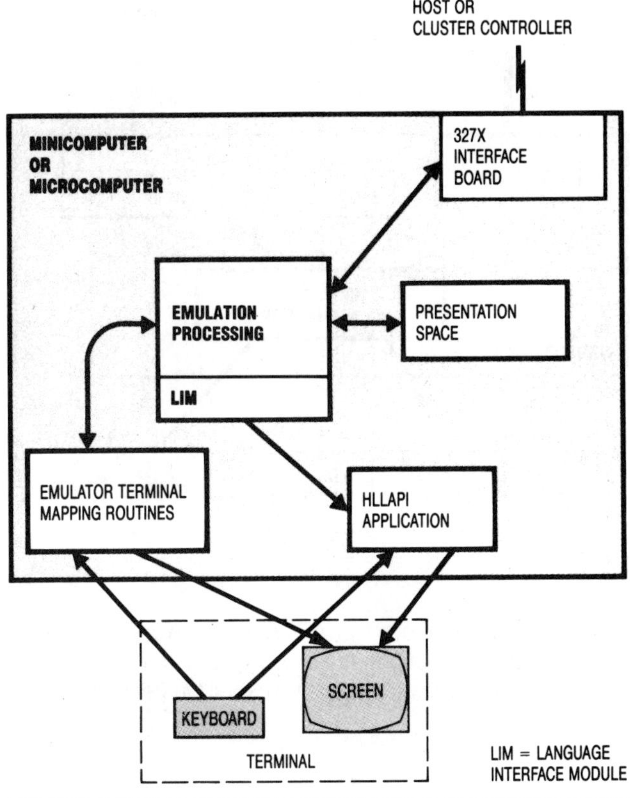

keystrokes at later, predefined times. The programmed operator concept includes automated host log-on/log-off, automated invocation of HLLAPI application programs, and automated data entry into a series of host screens based upon minimal operator input and interaction.

Keystroke filtering. HLLAPI can intercept operator keystrokes and substitute other, more complex, strings for them (keyboard macros), delete them, and perform local validation on certain fields.

Creation of a single input screen or view of multiple host sessions. A HLLAPI application can be programmed to provide a user with a single composite interface to multiple host applications and then populate the data fields of these applications from a single set of information entered by the user. This is valuable when a terminal user has to enter similar or identical information into multiple screens for different host applications.

Data extraction. HLLAPI can transfer data between different applications residing on the same or different hosts.

Improvement of the host user interface. Host interfaces typically are terse and uninformative, often having rigid data formats and cryptic messages. This is partially based upon limitations on the amount of data it is desirable to communicate, because of utilization of the mainframe and communication facilities. With HLLAPI, the intelligence and help data is distributed to the PC, microcomputer, or minicomputer. This allows custom, user-friendly data-entry screens to be implemented that replace existing screens without modifying the host application or increasing communications overhead.

The first applications end users generally create with HLLAPI are automated log-ons or scripts for their most commonly used or repetitive host applications. An example is a HLLAPI menu interface to IBM's Disoss electronic mail program. With a few keystrokes, a user can sign on, read messages, prepare new messages and log off. Other examples are translation programs, which extract and format data from mainframes for use on PC spreadsheet or database programs.

HLLAPI programs can hide the IBM host environment from a novice terminal operator. Such programs handle all mainframe interactions, such as log-ons and error code processing. This allows a user to create a program that emulates an expert mainframe user while not requiring much expertise or much effort from the PC operator.

Menus and help screens can be incorporated in HLLAPI programs to create a highly interactive, easy-to-use, and easy-to-learn front-end to a host application. This preserves the investment in mainframe hardware and software while eliminating the need for the PC operator to be knowledgeable of, or trained in, the use of an operating system or the details of 3270 data entry.

Beyond these almost intuitive uses are a broad range of more powerful implementations. Consider the following, based on actual cases.

■ *Case 1, the problem:* You are the communications manager of a large retail chain that has its own private credit card. Authorization checking is done on terminals connected to an SNA network communicating with the host.

For competitive reasons, management wants to add two major national credit cards. Each card has its own authorization network and each network uses a slightly different variant of bisync. You are required to authorize all credit purchases. However, you cannot have sales personnel make telephone calls for each transaction, and you do not want to rework the host software or to add parallel networks.

The solution: Replace the operations center 3270 terminals with a microcomputer or minicomputer operating under Unix. With Unix, the computer can support multiple ASCII terminals (six in this case) operating as 3270s, as well as three 3274 emulation cards that connect to the mainframe and to the other credit authorization networks. Two of the cards have modified firmware that handles the bisync variants. The configuration is shown in Figure 2.

Then, implement a HLLAPI application in the computer that intercepts all reject transactions from the host and can also enter authorization requests on the two other networks. Each credit card carries a unique first digit to identify itself (for example, 3 = American Express, 4 = VISA, 5 = MasterCard). When the application receives a rejected authorization request from the host, it examines the credit card number. If it begins with a recognized digit, the application creates a new authorization request and sends it to the appropriate network. If it is returned from the network as authorized, the application sends it back to the host as an operator override accept.

In all other cases, an operator receives the reject message as before. Nothing has to be changed in the host to support this. There are additional cost benefits from replacing the 3270s with ASCII terminals.

■ *Case 2, the problem:* You are the data processing manager at a large manufacturing firm with a dozen warehouses and many locations across the country. You have implemented a CICS (Customer Information Control System) to gather on-line inventory-control information and manage distribution of centrally purchased materials.

The system uses data entry from 3270 terminals at various locations, with processing at several corporate data centers. Despite its advantages, this method of data collection requires a certain amount of manual data preparation and a significant amount of manual data entry. Because of this, there has been an ongoing rate of data-entry errors, which has resulted in delayed shipments and misplaced orders. In addition, the volume of data has been increasing, so that terminal response time has begun to slow down.

You have been investigating the possibility of imprinting all inventory containers with bar code (along with human-readable) information and capturing this information at each location with hand-held bar-code readers. This would greatly reduce errors, speed the information flow and probably reduce data-entry staffing requirements. However, you want to avoid any modification of the CICS program, which is part of a large, complex host system running at multiple centers.

The solution: Replace the 3270 terminals used for entering this data with a PC containing a coaxial adapter card (connected to a 3274) and a bar-code reader input port. Create a HLLAPI application that interfaces with the host and also reads the bar-code input. Now, when items are received at the loading dock, warehouse personnel read the affixed label, verify that the part number and quantity in the container are as described, and capture the corresponding bar-code data from the label with the scanner.

An operator at the PC terminal enters the scanned data and keys in any additional information. The HLLAPI application combines scanned data and keyed information and formats the host data entry screens. In addition to practically eliminating errors, the application is able to reduce the number of host interactions because it maintains it own local database in the PC. This improves on-line response time as well as achieving the other goals.

Both of the above cases are instances of using HLLAPI for value-added data entry. Here, we start with data-entry operators at a 3270 terminal and end with operators at a 3270-like terminal. However, the terminals are smarter, can acquire the data from other than the operator, and process transactions faster. This is in contrast to using HLLAPI to hide the 3270 interface, typically for those users who are doing most of their computing locally and need only occasional access to the mainframe.

HLLAPI runs in the presence of a 3270 software-based

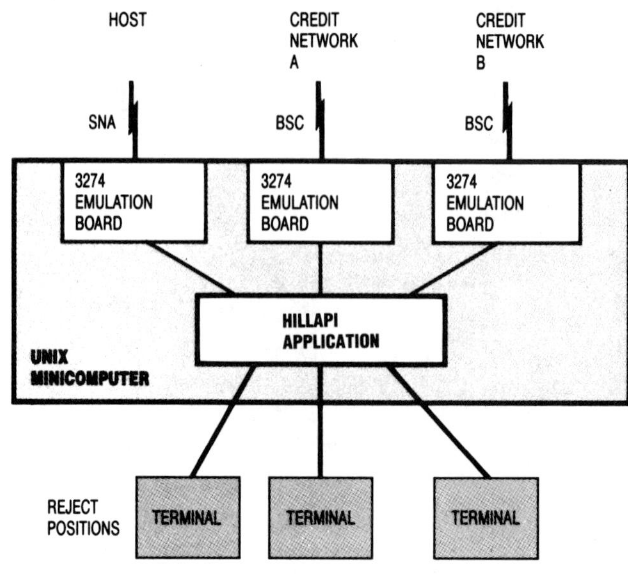

2. Making connections. *In this scenario, the HLLAPI application is being used to connect credit card networks that support either SNA or bisynchronous communications.*

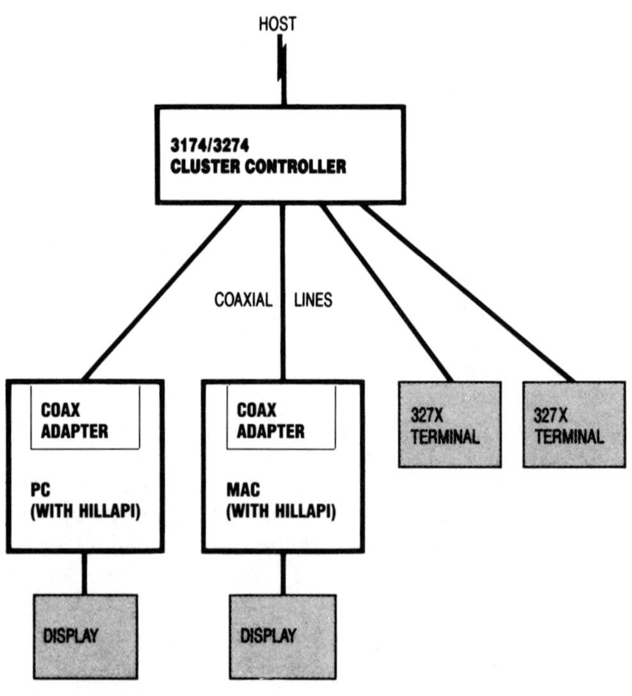

3. Cards. *Here's how HLLAPI typically works with PCs running 3270 emulation. A PC, PS/2, or Apple Macintosh with a coaxial adapter connects to a 3274 cluster controller.*

emulator, which generally operates in one of three configurations:

1. In a PC, PS/2, or Apple Macintosh with a 3278/3279 terminal coaxial adapter card connected to a 3274 cluster controller on a Type A coaxial line, as shown in Figure 3. These cards are available from Attachmate (Bellevue,

4. Adapters. *In a LAN, a PC, PS/2, or Macintosh has a LAN adapter rather than a coaxial card and uses the LAN to access gateway servers.*

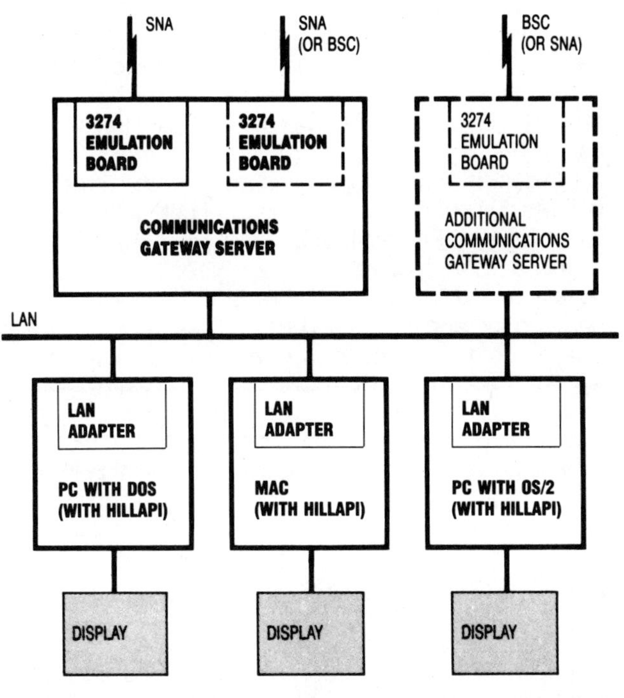

5. Unix HLLAPI. *HLLAPI configured on a Unix system contains one or more 3274 controller emulation boards for concurrently accessing multiple hosts.*

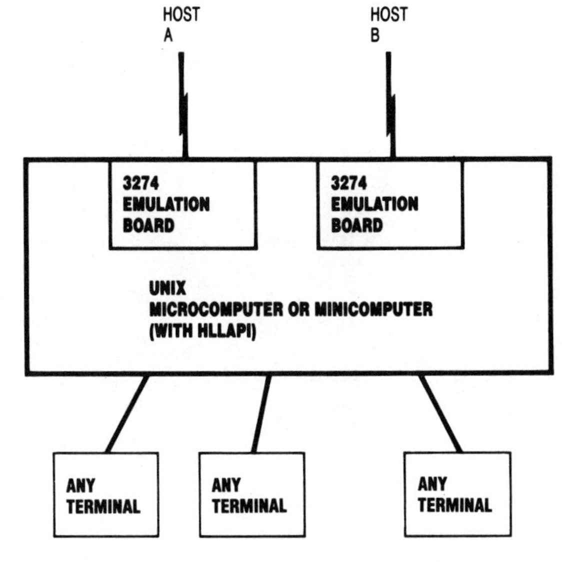

Wash.), Digital Communications Associates (Alpharetta, Ga.), and IBM, among others. It is also possible to connect to a 3274 on an IBM token ring. In this configuration, the PC can concurrently access only one host (however, if the host front-end is connected to other host front-ends, there can be alternate sessions to the hosts).

2. In a PC, PS/2, or Macintosh connected via a LAN to a gateway computer. Here, the gateway, which may be a micro- or minicomputer running Unix (or Xenix), contains a 3274-type controller emulation board and operates as a communication server for PC client workstations. As shown in Figure 4, the PCs are connected by a LAN adapter, rather than a coaxial card.

As also shown, a PC can have concurrent access to multiple hosts either through additional controller boards in the gateway or through access to multiple servers. In addition, the host protocols can be different. Such gateway hardware and software is available from Attachmate, Banyan (Westboro, Mass.), Digital Communications Associates, Harris (Dallas, Tex.), IBM, and Novell (Pravo, Utah), among others.

3. In a Unix computer system containing one or more 3274 controller emulation boards for concurrently accessing multiple hosts (see Fig. 5).

This configuration is logically equivalent to the previous gateway configuration, but all the hardware and software reside in one computer. As described above, Unix allows essentially any kind of terminal to act as a 327x. Such Unix hardware and software is available from AT&T (Bridge-water, N.J.), Pyramid Technology (Mountain View, Calif.), and NCR (St. Paul, Minn.), among others.

3270 emulation and HLLAPI software is available from several vendors including AT&T, Digital Equipment Corp. (Maynard, Mass.), Pyramid Technology, Rabbit (Malvern, Pa.), and Systems Strategies (New York, N.Y.). DEC and Sun offer 3270 emulation but do not currently offer HLLAPI. The number of HLLAPI vendors for Unix is appreciably smaller than for DOS. In general, the software will run on a unique emulator board, but there are packages that will run on different (or compatible) boards.

DOS, Unix, and OS/2

HLLAPI is available under DOS, Unix, and OS/2. OS/2 Communications Manager 1.1 provides EHLLAPI, which is compatible with entry emulator HLLAPI (EEHLLAPI), used in the PC 3270 Emulator Program, Entry Level, Version 1.2.

Which operating system and, for DOS, which configuration (standalone or LAN) is best for your requirements? The answer depends on the nature of your application, the requirements of your users, and your existing PC, LAN, and micro-/minicomputer configuration. Other factors may have to be considered such as the need to access concurrently more than one mainframe and the number of users who require concurrent host connectivity.

A DOS standalone configuration (as the term implies) would be the choice when you have a standalone requirement (one or a few users) or need to merge the mainframe data or functions with existing PC programs (such as a spreadsheet or a slide-preparation program). You would also have PCs or a 3274 controller with available ports to connect the emulation cards. OS/2 is more powerful than DOS because of such features as multitasking and support for larger memory addressing than DOS allows, and like DOS could be used in standalone HLLAPI or LAN configurations.

HLLAPI

If you need access to a mainframe from multiple PCs or you already have a PC LAN network, you should consider a LAN configuration. If you already have a PC LAN network, you may be able to add the 3274 emulation board to a nondedicated gateway, or install a dedicated communications gateway PC and then install HLLAPI software on the appropriate PCs. It may not always be cost-effective to implement a LAN network for the sole purpose of a providing multiple users with access to mainframes, particularly if your application is primarily value-added data entry as described in the previous examples.

If your application is this type of data entry, you should consider HLLAPI under Unix. This may also prove to be the most cost-effective alternative if you require concurrent access to multiple hosts or will have multiple terminals requiring HLLAPI service (as in the credit-network example). Additional cost benefits may derive from the use of low-cost terminals in place of PCs and the elimination of the need to implement a network, as in the LAN configuration. A Unix microcomputer dedicated to HLLAPI can support up to 32 terminals; a minicomputer can support 100 or more.

HLLAPI applications that require larger memory benefit from implementation under OS/2 or Unix, which do not have the memory addressing limitations of DOS. LAN server and Unix HLLAPI configurations typically use 3274 boards, rather than a 3270 board. This allows greater flexibility when associating 3270 device addresses with any user's terminal. In a DOS standalone configuration, the PC can have only the addresses associated with the controller port to which it is connected. In a LAN gateway or Unix implementation, the definition of each host session can specify a set or range of device identifications, rather than a single emulated device.

Unix and certain DOS or OS/2 HLLAPI applications may operate in foreground (under direct operator control) or background (free-running once they are initiated). Applications that are entirely automatic and do not require operator interaction can operate in the background. This allows a user to initiate multiple HLLAPI applications to run concurrently and independently.

It should be noted that no matter what configuration you initially implement, with a small amount of software planning, you can migrate your application to other configurations (even if this involves porting to another vendor's HLLAPI) with relative ease. As described in the next section, HLLAPI is rapidly becoming standardized.

A proper Unix HLLAPI implementation will support the same functions and overall HLLAPI application structure as DOS HLLAPI. This is particularly significant for complex HLLAPI applications that must be cast in the form of a sequence of processes, accessing the host sessions and passing control and presentation spaces from one process to the next.

HLLAPI programming

The communications between a HLLAPI application program and a host computer are referred to as host sessions. A host session is the logical connection between a presentation space in the local computer and an inter-active application running under CICS, CMS, TSO, or VM in a host. The current connected presentation space is the active session to which a HLLAPI application is connected.

HLLAPI applications are programmed using function calls. Each HLLAPI function has a number associated with it. There are over 40 HLLAPI function codes, which can be divided into the categories shown in "HLLAPI function code categories."

In addition, HLLAPI programs must be concerned with session parameters, which are set both with Function 9 (Set Session Parameters) and with function return codes. Session parameters allow an application to specify and control certain aspects of the interface between the application and HLLAPI, such as specifying what HLLAPI will recognize or generate as an end of text indicator (defaults to binary zero). Return codes typically indicate errors.

When a HLLAPI application calls a HLLAPI function, it will generally be making a call to a language interface module (LIM), a software bridge between the HLL compiler in which the HLLAPI application was written and the common (to all HLLs), lower-level 3270 API routines. Each HLL compiler (Basic, C, Cobol, Pascal, and the like) used to program a HLLAPI application must have a unique interface into HLLAPI, often in the form of an LIM.

The need for a software bridge to translate function calls from different HLLs to common subroutines is not unique to HLLAPI. Each compiler has its own unique method of storing data and of calling subroutines, even those that appear to be similar in form and function. For example, y = sin(×); /* C, sine of x*/ and y := Sin(×); {Pascal, sine of x} will generally transfer information in and out of their sine subroutine in different manners. Different implementations of the same language — for example Lattice C and Microsoft C — must generally have their own LIMs.

A LIM has no HLLAPI functionality. It is a software library that manipulates the parameters used in the calling application into the form and format expected by the API. Then it calls the API function. When the API returns to the LIM, the LIM manipulates the results into the form and format understood by the HLL program and then returns to the application.

A LIM is not the only way to implement a software bridge. In fact, it is a comparatively high-overhead alternative. A lower-overhead approach would be to "hard code" the language interfaces into the emulator. However, this would prevent other compiler interfaces from being developed without access to the HLLAPI vendor's source code. With the LIM approach, an interface can be constructed for any language by following the LIM design guidelines set down by IBM. Unix HLLAPI implementations tend to avoid the LIM approach to save overhead, and because most Unix applications are written in C.

Application design

As mentioned above, you generally do not need the source code or even the documentation to design a HLLAPI application that will interface with an existing mainframe application. The approach to take when designing any HLLAPI application is to consider that you are writing a detailed instruction manual for a terminal operator of the host application who has limited experience.

When operators first sit in front of a screen, they must generally look at the screen (is it on?) and then specify where they are by taking some action that sets them to a known state in regard to their host application. This may be a simple procedure such as entering CLEAR or it may require a complex series of actions such as routing through a VTAM (Virtual Telecommunications Access Method) network to the desired host application.

Once the initial state is established, the operator must enter data and control keys, determine the response by looking at certain parts of the screen (both the data and operator information area), interpret the response, and go on to the next step. Each step must be analyzed:

logging on, selecting an application from a menu, processing each transaction, and handling all possible host, operating system, and network responses, including error conditions.

The HLLAPI program must function as an expert operator and avoid calling upon the human operator for assistance.

Above and below HLLAPI

A number of vendors offer 3270 scripting languages that allow a user to implement programmed operator applications without having to write real programs. A user first writes the script using a word processor and saves it as an ASCII file. The vendors typically include prewritten subroutines for performing common tasks such as connecting with the mainframe, drawing lines and boxes on the screen, and looking for specific data in the 3270 session. At run-time, the user loads the scripting oftware that will interpret the file and execute the sequence of interactions with the mainframe.

These languages are not standardized, and many use proprietary interfaces into their vendors' emulator software. However, because of the growing use of HLLAPI, some vendors have developed scripting languages that generate HLLAPI functions so that the scripts can be run over other vendors' emulators.

There is a price for all this high-level portability: run-time overhead. This overhead starts with the emulator formatting the data and placing it into the presentation space, and the application then retrieving it. To this is added the LIM processing, another cost for prtability. If a scripting language is also being used, your microcomputer or PC has quite a bit of processing to do before it actually sends and receives data to and from the mainframe.

As noted above, certain HLLAPI packages avoid the LIM overhead by only implementing a C language interface or by not supporting the implementation of user LIMs. In addition, when HLLAPI runs with a 3274 board, the underlying emulator that directly accesses the SNA data stream, unaltered and unprocessed.

This has been referred to as raw-mode data format (as opposed to the cooked-screen format). When this feature is provided, it typically requires that applications be written in the vendor's 3270 API. This is not a standard interface, but will markedly improve processing speed and allows the implementation of new mainframe-to-API applications that have some of the capabilities of LU6.2, without requiring LU6.2 support in the mainframe, micro-, or minicomputer.

HLLAPI is a powerful tool for extending the life and capabilities of current mainframe 3270 applications and for implementing new ones. It is easy to learn and use, is available from many vendors, and is on its way to becoming a standard for host connectivity. It can bridge DOS, OS/2, and Unix, offering almost limitless opportunities for the creation of responsive, distributed applications with centralized control. ■

Jerry Yochelson is the director of research at Systems Strategies. He has been involved in the design of software products for more than 10 years.

Section 3
Protocols

John Reynolds and George Wilson, Software Research Corp., Natick, Mass.

Ensuring that your emulator really acts like an IBM

Beware! Many 3270 emulation packages are only minimally tested before being released. Users must begin to insist that the products be fully tested.

Ever since computers became important to corporations, data processing and communications managers have struggled with the problem of providing timely access of information to anyone who needs it. Part of the challenge has been to provide communications links between many different computers throughout an organization. In the past few years, this task has been made more difficult by the proliferation of mini- and microcomputers.

Today, and for at least the next decade, the communications manager's goal is to provide an information network in which microcomputers, minicomputers, and mainframes are all able to access and distribute information among themselves—mere standalone processing is no longer enough.

For most large companies, IBM equipment lies at the heart of the network and, therefore, must be given significant attention. Consequently, one of the most important steps in putting together a flexible network is to implement products that allow mini- or microcomputers to communicate with IBM mainframes. These products are often in the form of emulators that allow the processor to emulate some variety of an IBM 3270 terminal.

The need to provide 3270 emulation has produced a significant cottage industry. In order to compete, minicomputer manufacturers are forced to provide 3270 emulation capability. Third-party manufacturers are providing less expensive 3270 workalike terminals as an alternative to IBM. However, the greatest explosion has occurred in the market for emulation boards that allow an IBM PC or compatible microcomputer to behave like a 3270 terminal, thereby facilitating access to an IBM mainframe. Currently, there are approximately 250 to 300 companies manufacturing or marketing some sort of 3270 emulation product. Approximately 30 percent of

these manufacture add-on boards for microcomputers, while the remainder are minicomputer and terminal manufacturers.

Most companies that are manufacturing 3270 emulation boards are small, fledgling start-up firms, typically with fewer than 100 employees. These companies often lack sophisticated product design practices, product development methods, and product testing procedures. Furthermore, most of these firms provide only a minimum level of documentation that is often very incomplete and difficult to read and understand.

Due to the lack of resources, most of these companies lack sufficient post-sale technical support for their boards. A common problem for many manufacturers of small emulation boards and minicomputers is the lack of sufficient IBM expertise necessary to develop perfect 3270 emulation products. Because of this scarcity of IBM expertise, users should be very careful about buying a 3270 emulator.

Plainly stated, although a product may claim to emulate a real 3270, many times it will not operate as such. In fact, the product may not work at all.

A defective 3270 emulator could conceivably cause a disaster for a company, especially for one buying a large quantity of emulators. To illustrate, the average emulation board costs approximately $1,000. If a company purchases 10,000 boards before discovering that they are defective, it could theoretically incur a loss of millions of dollars. In addition to the out-of-pocket expense, a defective board could also harm personal productivity, since it could cause the destruction and misrepresentation of data.

The major reason defective 3270 emulation products are slipping out of manufacturers' doorways and into the hands of unsuspecting users is that the manufacturers are not testing their products adequately. Many of the manufacturers are very short on capital and are thus forced to distribute a small amount of resources among many areas (for example, marketing, development, and manufacturing). As these companies struggle to slash expenses, the first area neglected is often product testing and quality control. The problem is compounded because many of the firms only produce one product and must bring it to market as quickly as possible in order to survive. Consequently, the emulation board may be introduced to the market without ever being tested.

But defective emulators are not a problem limited to undercapitalized start-up companies. Many larger mini-computer manufacturers also fail to test the 3270 emulation feature on their minicomputers and terminals. Such companies usually lack both adequate testing methods and personnel with sufficient IBM expertise. Sometimes, they simply fail to make the commitment to provide a quality product.

Test before you buy

Because of the volatility and embryonic state of the 3270 emulation industry, no standards for product testing and product quality have been established. Therefore, manufacturers can claim 3270 compatibility without having to prove it. This is in contrast to more established industries (such as electronics) where product standards exist. For example, the electronics industry established the Underwriter's Laboratory (UL) safety standard as a method to ensure that all products of similar categories are safe. Every product is tested for safety using the same predetermined industry standard. Since no 3270 emulation standard exists, users themselves must place pressure on manufacturers to establish quality standards for testing and to validate emulators before releasing the product to market.

In the meantime, how can an MIS manager comfortably choose a 3270 emulation product (microcomputer board, minicomputer, or terminal) with the assurance that the product is truly 3270 compatible before making a major purchasing decision?

One option a communications manager has is to trust the manufacturer's claims and to assume that the product has been subject to thorough and comprehensive testing. Of course, this approach is risky and could prove disastrous.

Another way to ensure that the company invests in a quality 3270 emulation product is to do the testing internally. However, this would require a major commitment of company resources, and the company itself may not have much expertise about the innards of the 3270 protocol.

In the meantime, a 3270 product can be validated both by testing the functionality of the product and by investigating the stability and the support provided by the product's manufacturer. Pure functionality testing determines if the product works. Investigating the manufacturer's stability helps a buyer determine if the company can provide adequate support and if it will have the longevity to continue that support. Stronger companies will be more likely to test a 3270 emulator before releasing it to the market.

As will be discussed, the user also has a few options for testing emulators. No matter which option is chosen, an emulator should be tested thoroughly, because it can fail in a multltude of ways.

Problems with emulators

There are three primary types of 3270 emulators:
- Coaxial, 3278 terminal emulators.
- Remote, 3274 cluster controller/3278 terminal emulators.
- Local, 3274 cluster controller/3278 terminal emulators.

Coaxial emulators (Fig. 1) are connected to a real 3274 cluster controller via a coaxial cable, and they only emulate a 3278 terminal. The cluster controller, in turn, is connected to a 37X5 communications controller via an RS-232-C connection and modems or modem eliminators; the 37X5 is linked to the mainframe through a direct channel connection.

Remote emulators (Fig. 2) replace a combination of the 3274 cluster controller and the 3278 terminal. These emulators are also connected to a 37X5 communications controller via an RS-232-C connection and modems or modem eliminators. Remote emulators can be used with both SNA (Systems Network Architecture) and BSC (Binary Synchronous Communications) protocols.

Local emulators emulate the 3274 cluster controller and the 3278 terminal that are directly connected to the mainframe via a channel connection.

(Despite these general rules, remote emulation is becoming increasingly popular and cost-effective, even when the host is located at the same facility. Using remote emulation reduces connect time with the mainframe because the microcomputer processes all the information in MS-DOS, then uses communications facilities only when the user wishes to transmit or receive data.)

The problems usually begin only after the 3270 emulator has been purchased and installed. Shortly after the user logs on to the first 3270 session with the emulator, it may be discovered that many of the functions of a 3278 terminal cannot be performed, or that attempting some functions even crashes the line. For example, it is common to find a BSC 3276 emulator that has an extra byte of erroneous data between the end of transmission and the padding characters. This causes the host mainframe to retry the device continually until the host concludes that the cluster controller is inoperative. The session is then terminated.

Often the unsuspecting buyer purchases an emulator based solely on its ability to log on. Unfortunately, the chosen product often cannot adequately perform specific 3270 functions. For example, such commands as READ BUFFER or READ MODIFY might be located in fragile areas of the application. If an emulator cannot process these fragile commands, the entire application will not operate, rendering the emulator and the application useless.

Interestingly, there tend to be different problems with coaxial emulators, depending on how they are connected to the mainframe. A coaxial emulator is more

1. Coaxial linked emulator. *All emulators linked by coaxial cable—emulating only a 3278 terminal—are attached to 3274-type cluster controller units. In some cases, the 3274 is locally attached to the mainframe; in others, the 3274 controller is linked to the mainframe via long-haul lines and intervening modems.*

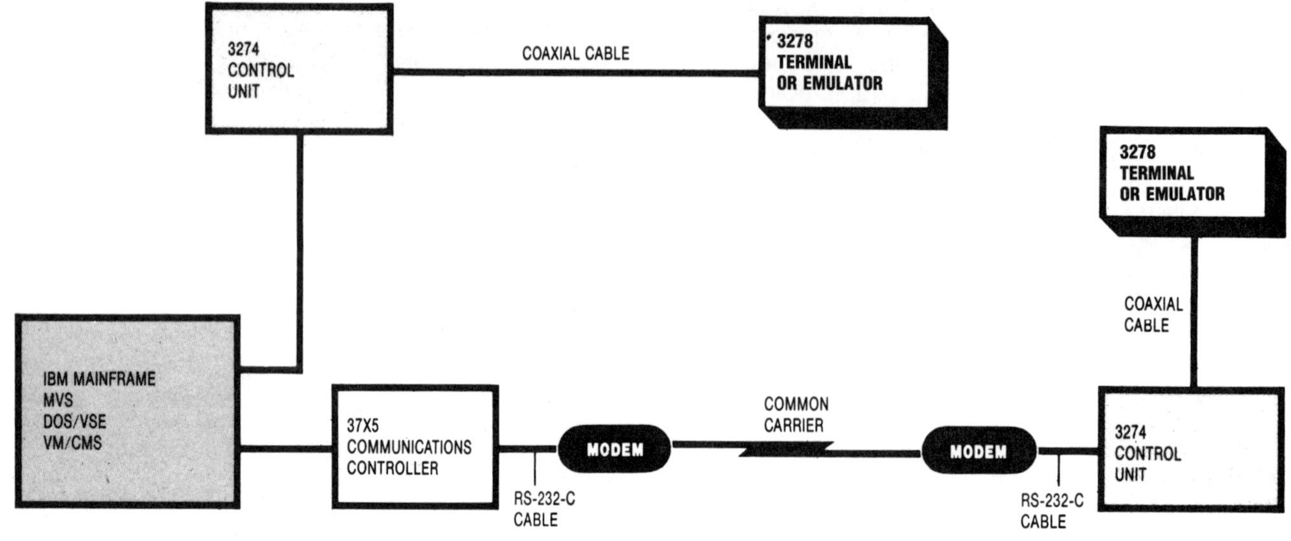

likely to have problems with speed, possibly resulting in the loss of a session. For instance, the remote emulator can fail when the communications line speed is changed from 2.4 kbit/s to 4.8 or 9.6 kbit/s. Conversely, when a problem occurs with a coaxial emulator attached to a channel-connected 3274 cluster controller, the consequences tend to be more severe. In this situation, an inadequate emulator has a much greater chance of crashing the operating system due to faulty channel command words (CCWs).

One of the most common problems that occurs with coaxial emulators, especially microcomputer boards, is that they often fail load testing. In such a test, large amounts of data are transmitted from the mainframe to the emulator. A real 3278 terminal is a high-performance machine, capable of receiving buffers with large amounts of data. A microcomputer emulator board is not as sophisticated and, because of the overhead processing of the emulator, cannot receive data as fast as an IBM 3278. The emulator buffer on the emulator cannot necessarily receive, process, and display data as fast as it is being sent by the mainframe. However, a good emulator will guarantee the integrity of data, thereby preventing data loss and/or data corruption.

In addition, a defective emulator can bring down an entire line, disrupting many terminals or resulting in the partial display and corruption of data. Corruption of data can even be more dangerous than a line crash because the user may still assume the data is correct. Some emulators react by losing program control, in which case the user cannot execute any commands and must restart the emulator.

Many inadequate emulators lose complete program control and, in the worst case, crash the operating system. This loss of program control usually occurs when a vendor designs and develops a coaxial 3278 emulator on a remote connection and then installs it on a channel-attached 3274 cluster controller.

A very common problem is inoperative keyboard functionality. This problem occurs when an emulator's keyboard is incorrectly mapped and does not precisely match an actual 3278 keyboard. For example, on some emulators, in order to perform a PF10 function, the user may have to press the keys ALT and E simultaneously. As this example suggests, some of these illogical keyboard mappings are extremely difficult to remember and use.

In addition to having 3278 keys mapped non-intuitively, some emulators simply do not have correct (or any) provisions for all the functions of each 3278 function and character key. The product may incorrectly process a PF13 key, for instance. Again, problems like this can make emulators and applications useless.

Keyboard mapping problems usually occur because the emulator has not been tested against the host. These problems manifest themselves in many ways. For instance, the SYSTEMS REQUEST key may not work, or the cursor may not stop blinking. Inadequate keyboard mappings could also result in the mishandled processing of certain operations, such as PROGRAM READ BUFFER, SET BUFFER ADDRESS, and REPEAT TO ADDRESS. These problems are generally warning signs that more serious quality problems—such as a loss of program control and shifting data—are on the horizon.

A significant percentage of emulators tested will not properly execute a complete set of application commands. This very common problem is extremely hard to predict because of the almost infinite number of variables possible with each application's command structure, and because each sequence of commands and orders is unique.

All too often, 3270 emulator users are victims of broken promises. Several emulation boards advertise that they have file transfer capabilities. But of all the products making those claims, almost none of them can transfer a file without serious constraints. For example, a few of the emulators can transfer a file if the data is limited to an 80-byte record under a single application, such as TSO (Time Sharing Option) or CMS (Conversational Monitor System). Unfortunately, most data fails to meet such strict prerequisites. Since these emulators do not provide a general file transfer capability that allows a user to transfer different size files between different applications, many "file transfer facilities" are highly limited.

These emulators also promise to correctly process 3270 field attributes, but in a number of these products this promise is unfulfilled. IBM's 3270 protocol defines 32 basic field attributes that are controlled by the host application program. A good application may implement field attributes to optimize the terminal operator's interactive session. A poor emulator might incorrectly process the attributes sent by the host, such as AUTO-SKIP, NUMERIC PROTECTED, or HIGHLIGHTED. If these attributes are not recognized, the user may not be able to enter data, since the application will not accept invalid field attributes.

(IBM frequently enhances 3270 features, adding to the difficulty of keeping an emulator current. For example, recent additions to actual 3270 terminal features include seven-color display, reverse video, and blinking fields. Of course, if the emulator does not provide support for new features, certain types of applications may not be usable.)

Emulators often fall down when confronted with a throughput test. As the name implies, this type of test measures the speed at which data streams can be sent or received by the emulator to or from the communications line. Because an emulator is a software program that imitates the 3278 and/or 3274 circuitry, it cannot process data streams with the speed of the actual devices.

For example, in one such throughput test, a particular 3278 coaxial emulator was discovered to be over 80 percent slower than a real 3278 terminal. This through-put discrepancy occurred during a test that measured the terminal and emulator's ability to process a particular 605-byte data stream for a duration of three minutes. Within that time, the IBM 3278 processed 373 iterations of the data stream, while the emulator was only capable of processing 69. This type of discrepancy is common with all emulators but varies greatly from one product to another.

Essentially, most emulators are very slow. If speed is very important—such as for file transfers—there is not much a user can do other than to choose the fastest one with the greatest capability.

Avoid a lemon

Due to the number of 3270 problems, it seems evident that a wise company should take action to protect itself from unknowingly purchasing a defective emulator. Because the 3270 emulation industry is in an embryonic state, users must not assume that an emulator has been tested by a manufacturer. Even if testing is performed, there are currently no quality standards accepted by the entire industry. Therefore, the only way a user can avoid purchasing a lemon is to test an emulator before purchasing it.

Once an organization has determined which type of device (e.g., microcomputer, minicomputer, or terminal) it wishes to use to emulate a 3270 workstation, and once it has determined whether to have a remote or coaxial connection, the organization is ready to do some test driving. This should include:

1. Developing a test plan that includes the 3270 emulation objectives. The most important reasons for purchasing the 3270 emulator (for example, single file transfer, uploading/downloading of files, or electronic mail) should be prioritized.

2. Developing a plan to consider such criteria as quality of customer service, the quality of product documentation, and the stability of the company. Any user will discover the importance of these last criteria after the emulator freezes several times, support from the manufacturer is unattainable, and it becomes evident that the relevant section of the documentation reads like hieroglyphics.

3. Selecting several products that claim to meet the desired feature/function criteria necessary for the 3270 emulator. By reading product brochures and advertise-

---

2. Remote emulator. *Some units take the place of both the 3274 cluster controller unit and the 3278 terminal. In this example, a communications controller and modems link the emulator to the host. A local emulator (not shown) takes the place of a terminal and a directly attached control unit.*

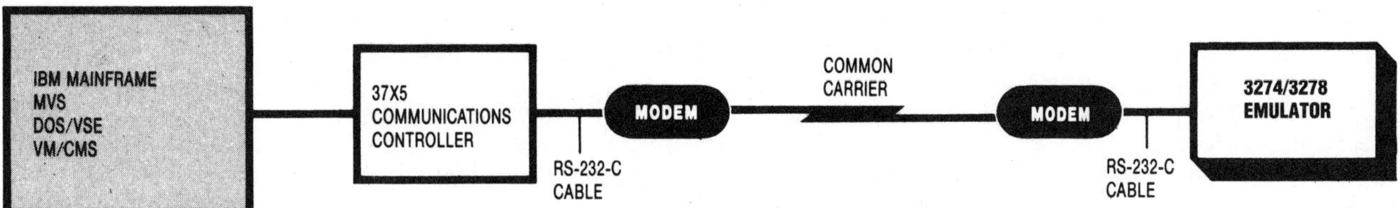

MVS = MULTIPLE VIRTUAL STORAGE
DOS/VSE = DISK OPERATING SYSTEM/VIRTUAL STORAGE EXTENSION   VM/CMS = VIRTUAL MACHINE/CONVERSATIONAL MONITOR SYSTEM

ments, a user can select a number of emulators to test, based on claimed features and functions. Usually, a company can afford to purchase several microcomputer boards to test, but it is not feasible for a company to purchase a minicomputer or terminal strictly for testing purposes. A minicomputer or terminal can be leased or possibly loaned to a company if the manufacturer is made aware of the possibility of a future purchase.

While developing the testing plan, the user must determine the most effective 3270 testing method. Several options are available.

One method used by many 3270 emulator manufacturers (and that could conceivably be employed by users) is to develop a microprocessor to test the emulator. The microprocessor tests the emulator by attempting to duplicate the 3270 data streams sent to a 3278 by an IBM mainframe in a real 3270 session. This method has its limits, however, because it means that an emulator is testing an emulator.

Alternatively, the company could test the product by subjecting the emulator to a sample of the application that it is expected to support, such as a payroll or general ledger application under CICS (Customer Information Control System) or IMS (Information Management System). However, this approach can only disqualify an emulator that fails. If an emulator correctly processes the test functions, it may create an illusion that the emulator is fully 3270 compatible.

Certifying an emulator against one or two applications only confirms that the emulator can execute a subset of 3270 functions that reside in the specific application. Since any one application usually uses no more than 30 to 40 percent of the most predictable 3270 functions, 60 percent of the product's 3270 functionality would be entirely untested. Trouble could ensue when an additional 3270 function, such as READ BUFFER, is added to the application. The result could be as serious as a loss of program control.

In addition, it is difficult to measure one emulator against another using a subjective method because it is almost impossible to manually replicate a complete test for each individual emulator.

Another method for testing in-house is to develop a software application that tests the 3270 emulator's ability to perform all the 3270 orders, commands, and screen-formatting options, and does so in every operating environment. This method is the most effective since it provides a consistent test that replicates all the operating conditions of a real 3270.

The problem with developing any test in-house is the drain on the resources of an already burdened computer/communications department. Usually, it is not feasible to divert attention away from applications programming in order to develop a subjective test or to write a testing program.

There is an alternative approach that a user can call upon to test a 3270 emulation product. An MIS manager can purchase or rent (via time-sharing) a standard 3270 quality assurance program produced by a third-party software vendor. If properly designed, the 3270 testing program would ensure that a user's purchase decision is correct and would detect any emulator deficiencies before purchase.

Such a program could be used by a company even after an emulator has been purchased. The test can be used to validate every emulator before installation. In addition, the computer/communications department could use a 3270 emulation test to detect communications problems that occur after installation. For instance, many times when a problem arises, a manager does not know whether the problem resides in the network, the emulator, or the application. A good 3270 emulation test program can quickly determine whether the problem resides in the emulator. It thereby saves many hours of troubleshooting.

Attributes needed

Regardless of the method chosen, there are fundamental standards that any 3270 test must enforce. The test procedure must exercise all functions of a real 3270 terminal, however rarely used a particular function might be. All field attributes and processes must be investigated as well. There are 32 basic field attributes (for example, BASIC NUMERIC FIELD and AUTOSKIP) and well over 1,000 combinations of advanced attributes (for example, REVERSE VIDEO and TARGET FIELD) that an application might need.

The test must be able to determine whether an emulator can operate and perform all 3270 functions while operating under any combination of IBM software applications. For example, 3278 data sequences operate differently in TSO than in CICS, and an emulator should be tested for every application environment where it might be used.

The savvy data processing/communications manager will evaluate more than just the compatibility of an emulator. An evaluation of the documentation that accompanies a product will help a user determine whether the product can be operated easily. Usually, documentation that is poorly organized, confusing, and shabbily produced is a sign that the emulator is difficult to use and that the manufacturer probably rushed the product in order to market it more quickly.

Before making a final decision, the buyer should evaluate the company as a business. Certain factors, such as size, maturity in the marketplace, diversity of product line, and product support of a company, will help a buyer determine the stability of a manufacturer.

Of course, purchasing an inadequate emulator will neither be the end of the world nor subject the company to total communications chaos. Still, a defective emulator would simply cause a great deal of unexpected aggravation and expense for the information systems department. ■

John Reynolds is Software Research Corp.'s director of advanced systems and is responsible for all the consulting and testing services for the company. George Wilson is SRC's manager of consulting services and has worked with many developers of 3270 emulation products. Software Research markets a 3270 quality assurance package to hardware vendors and user corporations.

David L. Anderson, Temple, Barker, and Sloane Inc., Lexington, Mass.

LDI: Why data communications managers should be more interested

Logistics data interchange
is beginning to catch the eye
of corporate management. How
will it affect your network?

Logistics data interchange (LDI) — the use of a computer network to transmit logistics information electronically within a company or to external suppliers, transportation carriers, or customers — is becoming one of the fastest-growing applications of data communications technology.

Logistics information consists of real-time data on company operations — such as the flow of inbound materials, production status, product inventories, customer shipments, and incoming orders. LDI is a subset of the more general communications concept of electronic data interchange (EDI) within and among companies. EDI includes the movement of financial, marketing, and messaging data in addition to the flow of logistics information. Such information could be considered the lifeblood of a company, encompassing all aspects of external and internal data interchange needed to run a successful and efficient business.

From an external perspective, companies need to communicate with various parties — for example, suppliers, financial institutions, transportation carriers, and customers — about order shipments and billing. Internal operations departments exchange information about production scheduling, material and product inventories, shipments among company facilities, and matters relating to planning and control. These separate groups must also perform such tasks over long distances, especially if production facilities are overseas while consumer markets and administrative services are in the United States.

Faced with the high capital costs and increased competition, many companies are attempting to enhance customer service and to reduce costs by developing closer internal ties between such operations as material handling, production, and distribution. External sharing of logistics information with suppliers, carriers, and financial institutions is helping these companies create new opportunities to reduce material and product handling costs.

A January 1985 survey conducted by the National Mass Retailing Institute looked at current practices and future trends in physical distribution. The results showed that 38 major retailing companies (representing $25 billion in annual sales) have already given LDI facilities substantial attention and have singled out these capabilities for primary focus in the future. For example, of companies with over $1 billion in sales, 55 percent now have electronic store ordering, 27 percent have electronic supplier data exchange, and 36 percent have electronic carrier data exchange. The survey respondents expect that by 1987 these percentages will grow to 73 percent, 54 percent, and 81 percent, respectively. Similar surveys in other industries have recently shown comparable results.

The implications of this information are clear: Communications management must prepare for a substantial increase in LDI among a variety of internal and external organizations over the next few years. All indicators suggest that LDI will soon be essential to many companies' physical distribution processes because it will improve control over goods moving from suppliers, through production, to customers. In this way it will increase product competitiveness and enhance sales. In some cases, the impact on in-place networks will be minimal, perhaps requiring only a new dial-out modem and minimally increased communications costs. In other cases, an LDI undertaking may require the installation of new networking hardware and software that will connect the company to its suppliers or to third-party networks.

Pinpointing the exact origin of LDI is difficult, but development began with discussions held in the late

1960s among executives involved with traffic and distribution. While many then agreed that LDI was theoretically possible and even necessary, implementations were initially stymied by inconsistencies in the transaction data format and in the processing equipment across separate companies. The first standards (covering, for example, data formats, network protocols, and interchange capabilities) for cross-company transmission of logistics information emerged in 1975. But direct use of these standards did not begin until the late 1970s and was confined to the exchange of waybill data among carriers in the railroad industry and to limited data-sharing experiments among a few industrial firms.

In the 1980s, however, many sectors of the business community have taken more interest in LDI. Three major factors have contributed to this development.

The most important factor may be the financial restructuring of the U. S. economy in the early 1980s. High interest rates (currently two times historical levels) mean high inventory financing costs. And the high cost of holding inventories — often 30 to 50 percent of a firm's short-term debt — has forced many companies to significantly alter their strategies for material and product handling. In the past, rules about physical distribution have been designed only to control inventory levels; now, decisions are aimed at increasing the frequency of inventory turnovers. Companies are attempting to increase the flow of product inventory information among suppliers, carriers, and customers in order to help reduce overall costs.

A second major factor behind the new interest in LDI has been the rapidly rising operating costs, exacerbated by continued growth in the volume of manual paper processing. In response to these problems, many companies have computerized logistics data for their material-handling and distribution operations. Once management procedures for internal transactions were automated, these firms looked for ways to link central facilities electronically with remote locations and even with outside suppliers and carriers in order to speed the exchange of logistics information and to reduce the cost of such communications.

The third major cause of increased interest in LDI has been the advancement of data communications and computer technologies themselves. Operating dedicated lines for domestic or international communications within and between companies has been a very expensive proposition until very recently. Because of communications technologies that permit multiple access to dedicated lines and the wide availability of satellite networks, the cost and complexity of distributing information worldwide has been dramatically reduced. In addition, the growth of internetworking communications software, which allows unlike processing equipment to interact, may soon permit the transfer of logistics data without costly conversion programs.

For example, Lykes Bros. Steamship Company Inc., a major U. S. shipping line based in New Orleans, needed to extend the reach of its in-house equipment control procedure to manage its worldwide inventory of shipping containers. Although its IBM mainframe tracked and managed information on containers at sea, in ports, and in transit between inland locations, Lykes needed to tie overseas locations into its network. Rather than develop a totally new scheme, Lykes uses General Electric Information Services' Intelligent Network to collect data on its container status worldwide and to update its master equipment database on the in-house computer. The expansion was accomplished without expensive conversion programming, since interface technology (IBM 2780/3780 emulator software) was readily available in the GE network. The network allows Lykes to better serve its customers both by providing up-to-date information on its container location and status worldwide and by helping shippers replace physical inventory holdings with information flows.

Associations as catalysts

Despite the willingness of individual companies, or groups of them, to engage in LDI, widespread progress would remain impossible without the coordination of standards. One source of this leadership has been industry trade associations. The Transportation Data Coordinating Committee (TDCC) has been involved with the development of LDI standards since the early 1970s. In addition to developing standards, the TDCC has been one of the major forces behind cross-company information exchange experiments.

Originally founded to help transportation carriers better coordinate the flow of information on interline shipments, the TDCC has expanded its scope to include all forms of LDI. The TDCC has ongoing committees that work on designing specifications for new hardware and software equipment to facilitate information interchange. In addition, the organization is sponsoring the Warehouse Information Network System (WINS) experiment, which involves the use of LDI formats for data transactions between a group of public warehouses, their customers, and carriers. Finally, TDCC has developed an interface software program to promote EDI, the more general form of LDI that includes both logistics and nonlogistics data transmissions among companies.

TDCC's program, called EDI Software, provides the interface between the sender's and the receiver's internal programs, which may be operating on different makes or models of computers and may use different internal data structures. EDI Software includes a routine that takes data from a user's fixed-format record, edits it according to the EDI standards, and constructs transaction sets for the transmission; a similar routine performs the opposite function for receiving data.

Although not currently as active in developing LDI facilities as the TDCC, the nation's banks could become a major force in this area. Deregulation of the U. S. banking industry has allowed financial institutions to expand the range of services offered to customers. In particular, the National Association of Freight Payments Banks (NAFPB), in operation over 25 years, has discussed the expansion of operations to enable a broader flow of logistics-related information through the banks and among their customers. This would allow

1. Basic link. When a vendor provides the logistics EDI, the customers need only be concerned with basic connectivity, not with developing software standards.

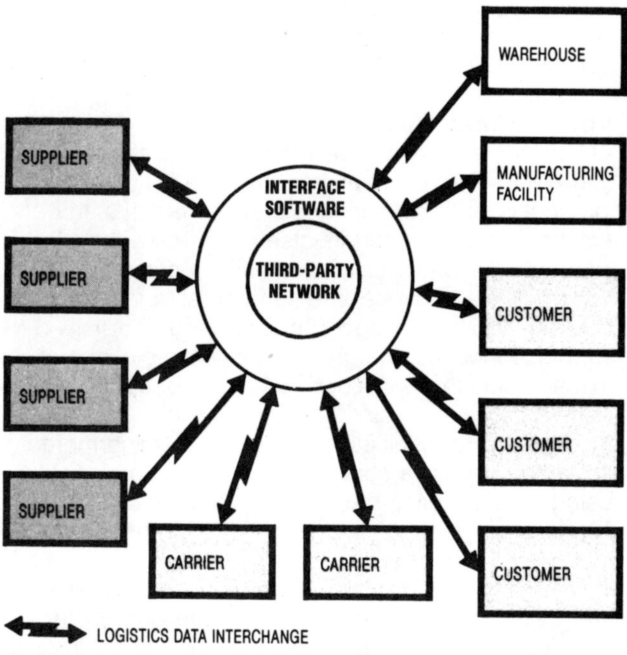

banks belonging to NAFPB to capture more company transactions in their payment services.

The Bank of Boston, for example, as part of its Freight Management Services, offers clients LDI services for freight bills. The freight bills are transmitted electronically to the bank, which then processes the data for payment and retransmits the audited bills back to the client's computer.

However, as in any transactions interchange mechanism, significant processing volumes must be realized quickly to bring costs down to levels competitive with current procedures. This means that "third-party" vendors are likely to be the cornerstone of any full-scale logistics information exchange scheme.

Vendors as LDI providers

In addition to industry organizations, such as the TDCC and freight payment banks, a number of major communications and computer companies are trying to foster growth in LDI schemes. Such industry giants as AT&T Information Systems, IBM, and General Electric Information Services are all actively marketing third-party services for LDI. Not limited to logistics information exchange, these networks and their associated hardware and software allow users to experiment with a wide range of cross-company communications (Fig. 1).

Already in existence are third-party networks that facilitate such interchange yet do not require users to make substantial hardware and software investments. AT&T's Accunet Digital Services and Tymshare's EDI-Net are just two examples.

AT&T's Electronic Order Exchange (EOE) operates through the AT&T Communications Network and provides a facility for intercompany transaction process-

ing. It can be used to transmit purchase orders as well as provide information on price and product listings, item availability, order and shipment status, invoices, and payment terms. EOE is particularly effective for repetitive reorder situations, standard product lines, high-volume established customers, or interfaces with a select number of critical suppliers. Although some customization is required to permit external EOE linkages, EOE does not require extensive revamping of existing in-house order-entry procedures. All such third-party data exchange facilities are basically in the start-up phase, and actual logistics information sharing is only a small percentage of their total transactions. However, the participation of the industry leaders in electronic LDI suggests fast growth for such services over the next few years, particularly as companies realize the relatively low cost of implementing LDI through third-party networks.

Internal LDI: Already under way

Most arrangements for the sharing of logistics information that occurs within a company were installed in the 1970s. At that time both mainframe logistics software and the introduction of minicomputers brought electronic transfer costs below those of voice- and paper-oriented communications. These networks were usually set up for separate management of manufacturing process phases that are discrete: for example, the handling of materials, inventory control, or outbound distribution (Fig. 2). As a result, logistics decision making within companies rarely considered issues of corporatewide materials or product handling.

As mentioned earlier, pressures to reduce costs during the early 1980s pushed many companies to

2. Internal. An LDI network will make interactions between separate units faster and more efficient. Voice and paper communications will still be desirable.

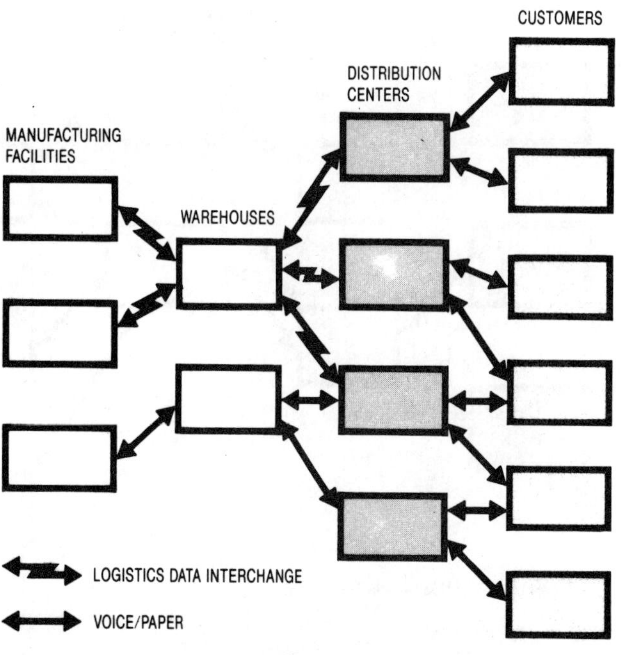

improve the exchange of logistics information within and across their operating divisions. In many cases, this consisted of tying additional locations into existing networks, as in the case of Lykes Bros. Steamship Co. The addition of terminals in distribution centers, for example, allowed more direct communications with central production and warehouse facilities and often made the flow of products more efficient. Rarely, however, did a company install entirely new facilities designed to manage the flow of materials and products (from supplier to customer) throughout its entire manufacturing and distribution process. Enhancements to the network achieved marginal efficiency improvements in existing operations. But prospects for additional gains were limited because logistics management mechanisms, which were designed and run separately, lacked communications capabilities.

For example, Ralph M. Parsons Co., a U. S.-based engineering and construction firm, implemented a worldwide procurement tracking procedure by combining the General Electric Information Services Shared Application service with in-house computer resources. While Parsons had internally developed procurement tracking software on its in-house hardware, it had no way to share information with joint-venture partners, perform real-time input, receive output and inquiries, and audit all transaction information. In conjunction with General Electric, Parsons developed communications software so that partner firms could link to the computers of both companies and have worldwide access to the central Parsons database. The network allows direct local-number dial-up from points as diverse as Yokohama, Paris, and Abu Dhabi.

The absence of two major requirements has slowed the increased use of internal LDI linkages: coordinated logistics control mechanisms and the economic justification for connecting internal logistics facilities. Many companies, however, have designed and successfully operated partially coordinated logistics control activities, such as those for the distribution or material resource planning (DRP and MRP) processes.

Not fully interested
Although many firms have seen the advantages of DRP and MRP schemes, relatively few have fully installed integrated logistics management mechanisms. In general, the state of the art in internal company logistics information-sharing facilities remains a cross-division communications process rather than an analysis or decision support linkage. (Sophisticated-decision-support connections might allow, for example, operations management to monitor and react to logistics information transmissions.)

Still, the opportunities for LDI are becoming more apparent, and data communications managers are being increasingly called on to implement LDI facilities. For instance, point-of-sale or point-of-use (POS and POU) mechanisms — designed to record transactions immediately and enter them into a control database — are major new developments in information transfer facilities that could form the basis for improved internal or external information sharing. Stop & Shop Inc., a major food retailer, uses POS data to help control inventory costs and improve profit margins; the company also sells POS (cash-register) transaction data to suppliers to assist their competitive analyses. These procedures allow the faster update of data concerning the flow of materials and products within the com-

---

3. External connections. *Most companies are very hesitant to explore communications links to outside vendors. Today, connections between the companies are often primitive. Still, very significant savings can be achieved if computer links are implemented between the companies up and down the logistics chain.*

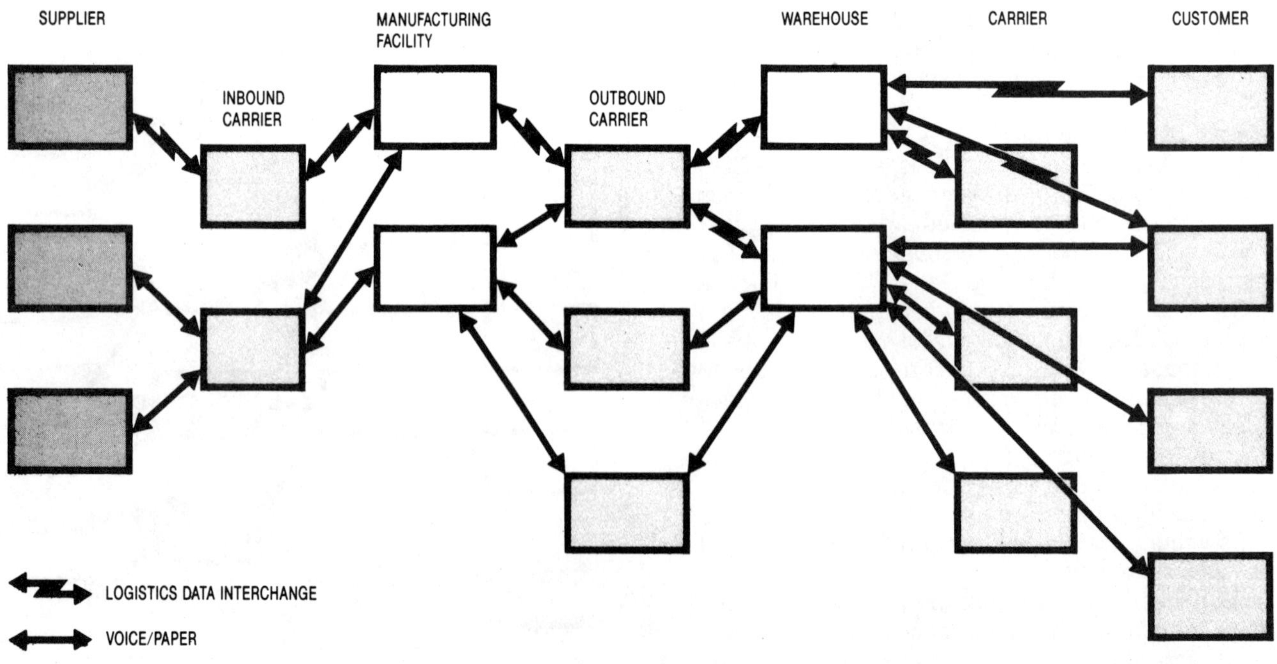

pany's and supplier's manufacturing and distribution operations, thereby allowing better monitoring of overall logistics events as well as the ability to influence in-process activities.

While internal logistics information transfer is currently being upgraded in many companies, external communications is still quite limited. A growing number of firms are implementing new facilities that allow customers direct electronic access to supplier or carrier shipment information (Fig. 3). Today, however, the services provided (including some downloading) are often somewhat primitive. For example, a dial-up information exchange service that allows only visual inspection of current in-transit movements may be of little use to major customers who need extensive input data for their own planning processes.

As noted above, the development of standards for electronic data interchange presents a continuing problem for cross-company logistics information exchange. At present, various communications standards are available for use:

- ANSI (American National Standards Institute) ASCX.12 covers general business transactions involving purchase orders and invoices.
- Automotive Industry Action Group's Electronic Data Interchange (EDI) conventions are designed for transactions with the auto industry.
- Uniform Communications Standard (UCS) is primarily used in the retail food business.
- Warehouse Information Network Standards (WINS) facilitates communications in the warehouse industry.
- Automated Carrier Interface (designed for ocean carriers), Rail Waybill Interchange (RWI), and Motor Carrier Waybill Interchange (MCWI) are all used primarily by transportation carriers.

An example of a third-party vendor that offers clients a variety of EDI communications software standards is TranSettlements Inc., which supports a full range of transportation-related EDI services for carriers, shippers, and shipper-service organizations. The TranSettlements' computer and communications facilities provide each participant with a single interface through which they can achieve full EDI with all participants. In-bound Wide-Area Telecommunications Service (WATS) facilities are available for dial-in access to TranSettlements' central computer at 4.8 kbit/s using IBM's 2780/3780 bisynchronous protocol.

TranSettlements' services include an electronic billing system, an electronic bill of lading, and an electronic remittance notice. These allow participants to receive, acknowledge, analyze, store, reformat, and forward information on the network. TranSettlements also supports several EDI standards. Logistics transactions options include purchase orders, order acknowledgments, material releases, advance shipment notices, commercial invoices, and payment/remittance advices. Transportation transaction options include bills of lading, shipment information and tracing, freight invoicing, and payment/remittance advice.

Although carriers, shippers, and intermediaries have worked together over the last 15 years to develop LDI standards acceptable to all parties, progress has been slow. Outside the transportation industry, cross-company logistics information sharing among other industrial firms has been limited to the ongoing experiments of small groups of participants.

In an effort to reduce some of the mystery associated with electronic information interchange, a number of industry groups are sponsoring shared network approaches to EDI. The Transnet direct ordering procedure, developed by the Motor and Equipment Manufacturers Association (MEMA), uses General Electric Network Services to allow wholesale distributors direct access to the supplying manufacturer's computer for ordering purposes. Original sponsors include some major U. S. manufacturers, such as Champion Spark Plug, Federal-Mogul Corp., and Wagner Electric Corp. Originally tested in 1974 and 1975, Transnet has expanded rapidly and now encompasses most major suppliers and distributors. Currently, companies using Transnet need not dedicate elaborate hardware or highly trained technicians. The communications requirement is that in-house computers be able to emulate an IBM 2780 or 3780 remote-job-entry terminal at 2.4 kbit/s or 4.8 kbit/s. For low-speed operations, a modified TWX (teletypewriter exchange) terminal or Touch-Tone telephone is all that is required. The Transnet data center establishes identity with the requisite security code and transmits orders in accordance with standard industry formats. The Transnet computer checks each order for invalid part numbers, advises the customer of discrepancies, and responds with a printed acknowledgment of the order.

Although current computer and communications equipment can handle such information sharing, little software has been developed that allows easy interfaces among incompatible company transaction procedures. In addition, many companies have yet to accept the underlying economic rationale of logistics information exchange; upper management is sometimes put off by the investment in new manufacturing and distribution control procedures required to integrate the flow of data on materials and products with planning or decision-support processes. However, as competitive pressures grow and automation becomes less costly, LDI schemes will be seen as more feasible options.

Getting ready

Moving a company toward increased LDI use can be a way for data processing or data communications managers to leverage existing network capabilities into a new cost-cutting tool for their corporations. In evaluating LDI's appropriateness for a company, the precise objectives for using LDI should be clarified; the cost and benefits of various approaches must then be examined. Next, representative suppliers and carriers should be polled to determine their interest in exchanging logistics data. If some investment in LDI is still a viable option, an internal study of how such a network would operate (given the logistics management procedures currently in place) should be undertaken. The results of this study should give a company enough information to evaluate the two essential alternative strategies for implementing a logistics EDI network:

4. No strangers allowed. *When the environments are small or the company has a very high security concern, a small private LDI might be appropriate.*

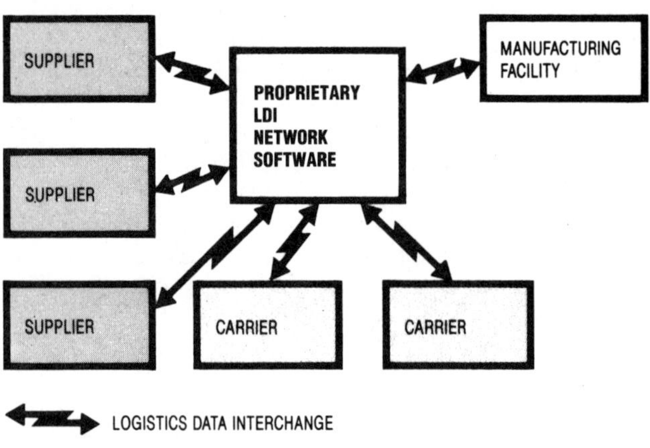

■ *Strategy 1:* Develop a "closed network" scheme. This approach is most useful when only a small number of participants are involved (for example, a company and a limited group of suppliers, distributors, and carriers). If some of the participants already have communications capabilities, all can share in the hardware and software upgrading costs necessary to implement the network. Such an arrangement is also useful if security issues are critical or if other factors require highly specialized information exchange (Fig. 4).

■ *Strategy 2:* Operate on a "third-party" network. When a larger number of participants is involved, or when investment costs for participants may be prohibitive, relying on an outside network is often optimal. Public networks, involving low access charges and generally minimal interface requirements—sometimes only a terminal and a modem—are an economical alternative if all participants are willing to conform to network requirements. Future software developments by these and other suppliers will automatically convert company data to exchange compatible information and should boost the use of such public networks.

Before a company seriously considers setting up an innovative scheme for controlling shipping activity, an "LDI audit" of available in-house and carrier arrangements should be undertaken. First, the company should investigate the flexibility of extant communications facilities to handle logistics data. Second, the corporation should examine what shipment tracing and control information may be available (by either computer or voice access) from carriers. Finally, initial shipment control network designs should be developed and reviewed with vendors. ■

This is Part One of a two-part article. Part Two will examine the experiences of various companies as they implemented LDI schemes. It will also discuss basic procedures involved in an LDI audit.

David L. Anderson, a vice president of the management consulting firm Temple, Barker, and Sloane Inc., has been with the company for two years.

Jon Dhuse and George R. Hayek, Intel Corp., Chandler, Ariz.

Standard protocols are needed for distributed microcontrollers

A nine-bit protocol is proposed as a standard. The supposed benefit: Increased product functionality and reduced costs.

With the recent advancement of micro-computers and other tools that ease user access to processing power, an important application of communications technology is often overlooked. Small, dedicated applications—perhaps resident on distributed microprocessors—have particular communications needs that are not addressed by the heavily touted industry standards. Because the sales volume of these products is often much higher than that for self-contained computers, the incremental cost of a communications facility has a significant impact on overall product costs and is therefore a major concern.

For instance, the home entertainment area is undergoing the rapid emergence of serial bus schemes for interconnecting stereo, television, and video cassette recording equipment. However, the products are in such a competitive market that cost, not standards, drives the serial interface implementation. The least expensive solutions are typically not the best in terms of performance and quality, so, unfortunately for consumers, these criteria are often considered design trade-offs.

In these types of applications, very large-scale integration (VLSI) microcontroller products are frequently used to perform dedicated tasks requiring intelligence. Several popular microcontroller products contain universal asynchronous receivers/transmitters (UARTs) on the same chip. This existing serial interface hardware can be used advantageously to fulfill the communications requirements. It is important that the industry be aware of specific asynchronous interprocessor communications protocols based on these serial interfaces.

The protocol provides a serial interconnection scheme that adapts itself to many multiprocessor and distributed control applications. Applications requiring remote con-trollers, data acquisition, and sensing are likely candidates for such a protocol.

A primary design goal for this asynchronous nine-bit interprocessor protocol (NBIP) is to allow for flexible system configurations; accordingly, NBIP allows for both low-performance (dumb) devices and intelligent stations. Low-performance devices, capable of little or no error checking and status reporting, have minimal firmware devoted to the serial protocol. The home entertainment bus is an example application for this type of device. A television connected to the bus would have no status to report back to the user, and an occasional transmission error is significant.

At the same time, NBIP provides for intelligent stations with error checking, acknowledgment capabilities, and polling schemes. In the modern copier, distributed microcontrollers handle specific functions, such as feeder or display control. Here, data integrity between microcontrollers is important. For example, most users would find it unacceptable to receive 100 copies when they only requested one.

The NBIP architecture also accommodates either fixed or adaptive system designs. In a fixed system, the "master" station would have implicit knowledge of the number and types of peripherals that existed in the system. A terminal concentrator designed to handle up to 10 terminals on a multidrop line is one such case. The master station knows that it is only talking to terminals, that there can be at most 10 terminals, and that each communicates in the same message format.

In an adaptive system, there can be variable numbers and types of devices. Upon initialization, the "master" determines the current system configuration. In the copier, the users have various options. They may want the basic unit, which only copies single originals, or they may desire the deluxe model, which includes a feeder, collator, and stapler. The serial protocol is designed to allow one master station to determine which options are present and to operate accordingly. This means that one software program can be used in all models, reducing the overall product cost.

Data link, addressing, command features

The access control protocol for NBIP requires a single active master on the link with one or more slave devices. Data can be transmitted by both the master and the slaves, but all transfers are initiated by the master. The protocol allows for a master/slave pair to change roles, forcing an additional constraint on the interconnection when more than one possible master resides on the link. (A device that starts out as a slave and can become a master is called a slave master.) The constraint is that all communications take place on a single line, so any potential master can talk with all of the slaves. This requires half-duplex communications, for there is no provision for collision detection or access priority resolution.

Figure 1a illustrates a full-duplex connection. Notice that the active master can transmit to and receive from both slaves on the link. However, if the slave master later becomes the active master on the link, it will be unable to communicate with the other slave unit. The half-duplex connection, shown in Figure 1b, solves this problem and allows any station to transmit and receive data to and from all other stations on the network.

The primary unit of information in this protocol is the "word." A word consists of nine data bits, which are preceded by a start bit and followed by a stop bit when transmitted. There are two types of words—data and address—and each word's type is indicated by the

---

1. More flexible. *In (a), if the slave master assumes master status, it cannot communicate with the slave. In (b), both possible masters can talk to the slave.*

(A) FULL-DUPLEX CONNECTION

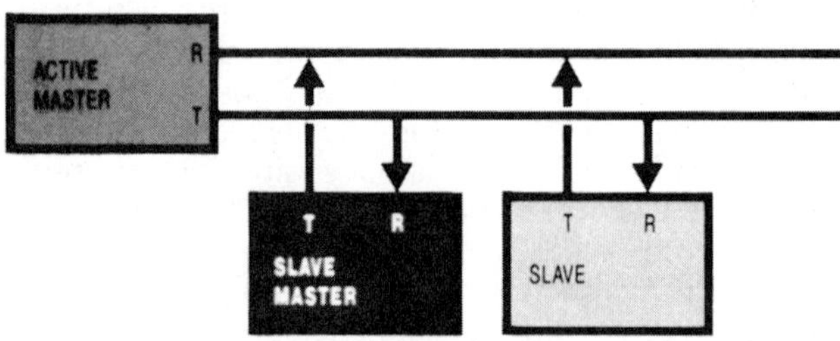

(B) HALF-DUPLEX CONNECTION

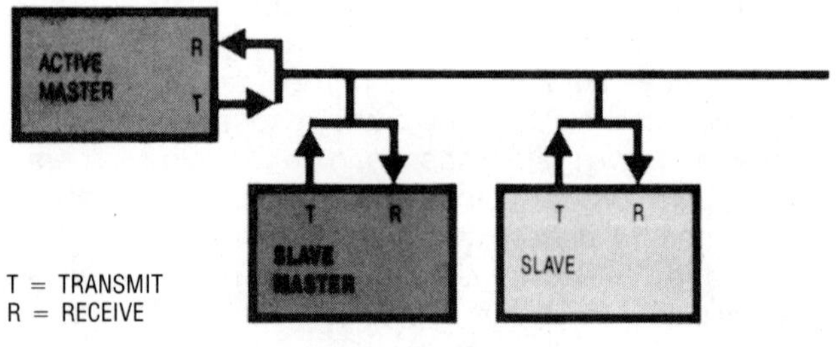

---

2. Small difference. *Frame formats 1 and 2 are almost identical, except that frame format 2 includes a checksum field to allow more complete error checking.*

FRAME FORMAT 1

FRAME FORMAT 2

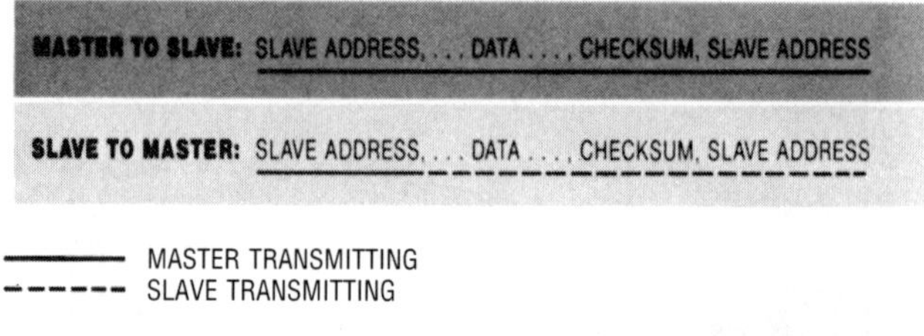

---

value of the ninth bit. A group of words is called a frame, and communications take place in one of two frame formats.

The design goal of a flexible communications network creates the need for different levels of data integrity. This is achieved by the existence of two frame formats, referred to as frame format 1 and frame format 2 (Fig. 2.)

In both formats, a frame begins when a master transmits a slave's address. Encoded into this address word is a control bit that indicates the direction of data flow, either master to slave (defined as a write) or slave to master (defined as a read). The transmission of the slave address is followed by data flowing one way or the other. The master closes the frame it is transmitting either by sending a new slave address or by resending the same slave's address.

A slave can respond with data after being selected by the master. In this case (Fig. 2), the slave closes the frame by sending its own address. This has the effect of telling the master that the transmission is complete, as well as indicating to the master the origin of the data for error-control purposes.

The difference between the two formats is that in frame format 2, a word of checksum information is inserted between the last data word transmitted and the closing address. The checksum is calculated by summing the opening address and data bytes in the message, truncating to the least significant eight bits, and taking the complementary negation of the sum. When a device communicating in frame format 2 receives the closing address, the device checks to see if the sum of checksum and the previously received data words within that frame is zero; a nonzero result indicates an error. Frame format 2 is recommended for applications where the data integrity is a more stringent requirement and a simple parity check is insufficient.

Data in frame format 1 consists of either eight or seven bits and a parity bit for error checking. Parity, when included, covers all nine bits of the word and is defined to be even parity. Data in frame format 2 can only be eight bits; no parity is allowed because the eight-bit checksum value may not meet the requirements of having even parity and being the checksum. For example, the checksum for the hexadecimal bytes "04" and "16" is "E6," which has odd parity.

The address structure is the key to the NBIP protocol. Address words serve one of two functions. They either indicate the particular slave with which the next communications will take place or they serve as data link control. As will be discussed later, eight addresses are reserved by the protocol for data link commands.

An address consists of a six-bit address field, a write/read bit that indicates the direction of data flow, a parity bit, and an address/data bit that distinguishes between an address word and a data word. This basic structure is shown below:

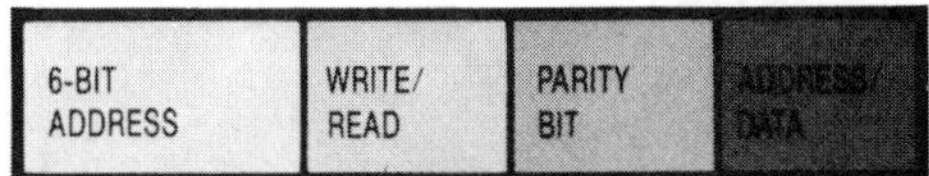

The address field supports 64 unique addresses, but eight of these are reserved for special functions. The remaining 56 addresses are available as slave addresses using one-word addressing. An additional 448 slave addresses can be employed through the use of a two-word (extended) address. The eight reserved addresses are delineated below. Seven of them are used for address extension, and the other serves as a broadcast address that all slaves will recognize.

Reserved addresses

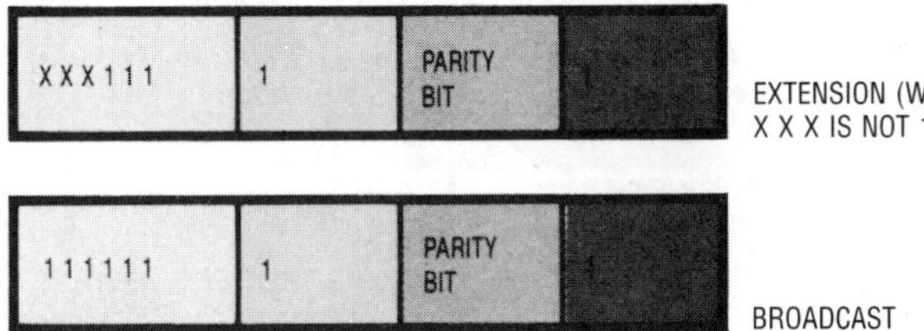

Extended addressing is accomplished by combining one of seven extension addresses with a normal address word. The address word following an extension is always treated as a slave address, even if it is identical to one of the reserved addresses. Extended addressing therefore yields 7 × 64 = 448 addresses. The total addressability of the protocol is 56 + 448 = 504 unique slave addresses. Figure 3 shows a network with three slave stations, two with base addresses and one with an extended address. Note that although the second byte of the extended address looks like a reserved address, it is not interpreted in that manner.

The command structure provides the ability to determine and control the state of the serial link network. The command repertoire includes commands to reset slaves, poll slaves for status information, query slaves about their serial link capabilities, and configure them to different modes. Other commands provide for an acknowledge request and response and for transferring

3. Larger networks. *Although not really required in the small network here, extended addresses allow one master to address up to 504 unique slave addresses.*

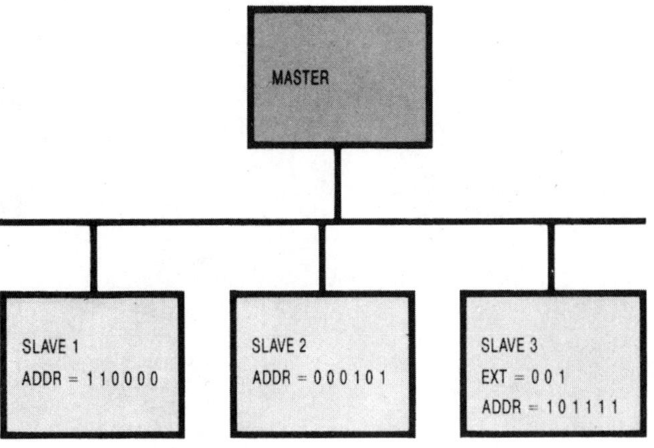

SLAVE ADDRESS FRAME(S)

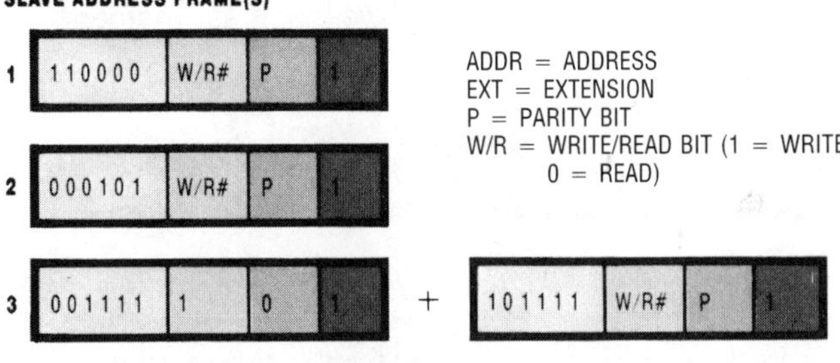

link master status between potential masters. The command formats are as follows:

The RESET command tells the addressed slave to reset itself. The RESET causes that microcontroller to execute a software initialization sequence that puts the device into a known state.

The POLL command requests that the addressed slave return a byte of status information. The status byte includes such information as device not ready for data, data available, and parity/checksum or framing error on the previously received message.

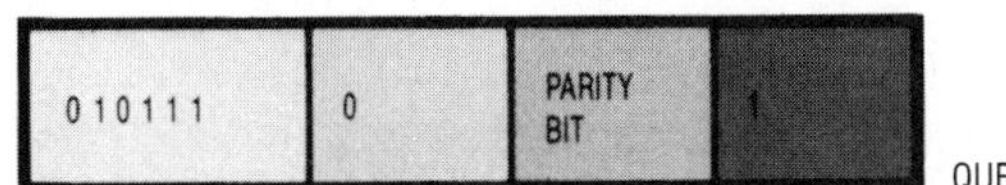

The QUERY command lets the master determine the type of slaves on the network. After receiving a query, a slave returns two bytes. The first byte specifies the capabilities of that slave, such as type of error checks, frame format,

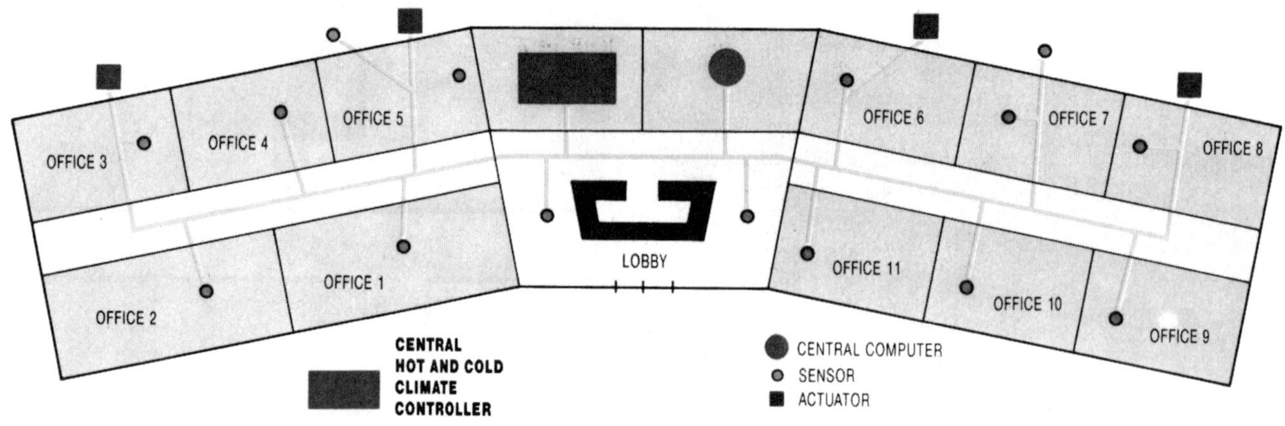

4. Weather report. *The nine-bit protocol could be used in a single-story building that is divided into separate offices spaces. A program in the central computer would allow it to govern each climate device in the building. A multidrop serial link can connect the sensors and the actuators to the computer.*

or acknowledgments. The second byte specifies the current configuration of the slave, such as whether the acknowledge feature is enabled.

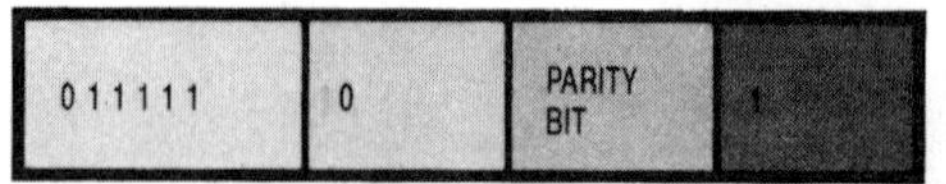

CONFIGURE

The CONFIGURE command is used to program a slave's serial port into nondefault modes. On reset, each serial port defaults to frame format 1 with acknowledge disabled. These can be changed using CONFIGURE, and then confirmed using the QUERY command.

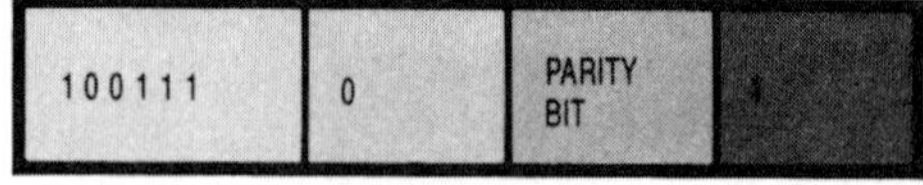

REQUEST ACKNOWLEDGE

This command indicates that the master requests an acknowledgment from the addressed slave. The slave then transmits its own address to indicate an acknowledgment if no parity, checksum, or framing errors were encountered on the prior frame.

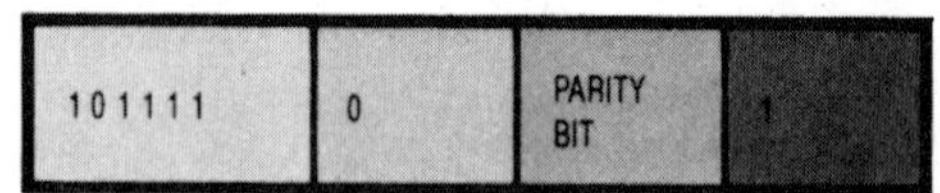

TRANSFER MASTERSHIP

This command is used to transfer master status of the network from the current master to a slave master that wants to be master. Upon receiving this command, the slave sends an acknowledgment to the previous master and then takes over the bus master status. The old master reverts to a slave mode upon receiving the acknowledgment.

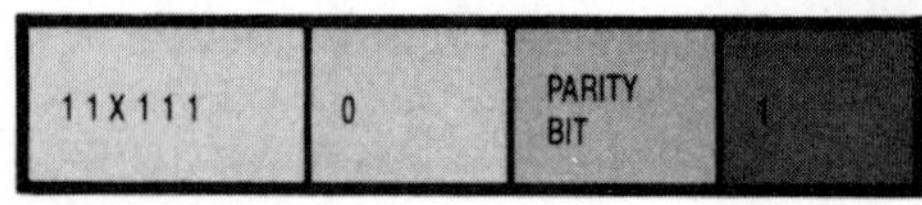

RESERVED

This command is reserved for future commands that have not yet been specified. (The designation "x" means that the bit has not yet been defined.)

An example application for NBIP might be a climate controller for an office building. Suppose that the building is a single-story structure divided into many individual spaces that are used as offices. Since the occupants have different climate requirements, each is billed separately for heating and cooling.

A climate-control system that uses some central intelligence to organize its operation should reduce the cost of heating and cooling the structure. A flexible controller should be able to perform such actions as adjusting the temperature of different spaces in the building to suit the time of day and season. It should be able to exploit alternative sources of heat and cold when appropriate, and it should control the turning on of large, power-consuming devices in order to minimize their operating cost.

Low-speed network

The architecture and physical layout of the system is shown in Figure 4. A central computer has the responsibility for overseeing the building climate. This may be one of many tasks, such as security and lighting control, that it must perform. The computer follows a program that has been designed to accommodate the building's structure and the weather patterns of the environment, as well as the needs of the individual tenants. This interconnection scheme is a multidrop serial link, and the exchange of information between the central computer and the various nodes is accomplished by using the nine-bit serial protocol. Transmission rates over 100 kbit/s are not required, so inexpensive cabling and line drivers/receivers can be used. For example, a simple twisted-pair cable and RS-485 differential transceivers can be used to build a network up to 4,000 feet long with a data rate of 100 kbit/s, a speed that would be suitable for this application.

The remote nodes fall into two categories, sensors and actuators. The group of sensors contains devices that measure and report temperature, humidity, and the presence of sunlight, while the actuators are such machines as heat pumps, humidifiers, sun shades, and vent fans. The central computer uses a polling method to determine the conditions at each of the sensor locations, then drives the actuators to ensure that climatic conditions meet requirements.

Suppose a sensor reports that a certain area is colder than it should be. The main computer may choose to turn on a heat pump, vent air from a warmer space, or open the sun shades to admit heat-giving sunlight. It may be programmed to do whichever would be most effective in terms of cost, speed, and energy efficiency. Manual overrides also exist, so that a person could control the computer, if necessary.

The messages between the computer and the remote nodes use frame format 2 of the NBIP, which adds a checksum to ensure the correctness of the transmitted data. The messages to the sensors are initiated by the central computer and start by the transmission of the sensor's address. The addressed sensor responds by transmitting a frame of data followed by a checksum and the closing address. Messages to the actuators also start by the transmission of the actuator's address and continue with the central computer sending data that is interpreted by the actuator as commands. The message is closed by the transmission of the checksum and closing address.

Why use a network?

The alternative to an integrated climate controller is a group of individual thermostats, one or more placed in each individual office space. These units typically open or close vents to admit warm or cool air as needed from a central air conditioner. One drawback of such an approach is that there is no communications between the thermostats, so no coordinated effort can be achieved to reduce the total operating cost.

A network with centralized control that performs such coordination has a major disadvantage. When the central computer fails, the entire climate system breaks down. A trade-off study would indicate the risk involved if the system failed versus the cost for backup systems. Such failures might be serious if, for instance, some offices contained expensive computer hardware that must remain cool.

In addition, an integrated approach allows the modification of the entire building climate from a single location; no one need visit and adjust individual thermostats scattered throughout the entire building. An arrangement such as this provides for more customization of individual climates within the building and allows the cost of climate control to be fairly divided. Although the initial cost of an intelligent climate controller runs about 35 percent higher than a nonintelligent one, vendors of intelligent climate controllers generally contend that the additional cost can often be recovered within three years. ∎

Both Jon Dhuse and George R. Hayek are with Intel's microcontroller operations, developing single-chip microcomputers. Dhuse holds a B. S. in computer engineering from the University of Illinois. Hayek received a B. S. in electrical engineering from Georgia Institute of Technology.

Dave Anderson, Temple, Barker, and Sloane, Lexington, Mass.

LDI: A bright future, despite a few obstacles

Several industry trends are helping logistics data interchange overcome its previous impediments to growth. This is the third and final article in a series.

Logistics data interchange (LDI) — the use of any computer network to transmit logistics information within a company or to external vendors, transportation carriers, or customers — has accelerated the trend away from paper documentation and toward electronic communications. Despite the advantages of installing very sophisticated LDI networks, the progress of LDI has been somewhat slower than expected. Fortunately, some of the new computer and communications technologies will naturally push companies into more sophisticated LDI structures. If data communications managers and strategists are aware of these new technologies and the key forces behind LDI's overall progress, they can play the crucial role in helping companies use communications networks to cut operating costs.

During the last 10 years, dramatic advances have been made in the physical mechanisms companies use to produce, store, and move their goods. The growth in automated factories and robotic warehousing devices and the improved service quality of transportation procedures have allowed companies to speed up the flow of products from plants to customers. However, the information transmitted on the status of these movements has not always kept pace with the movements themselves. It is not uncommon for the product to arrive at the customer before the paperwork, often leading to customer service problems, such as unwanted inventories or payment delays.

To fully realize the cost savings of the new just-in-time manufacturing and distribution schemes, companies are beginning to demand that communications networks "catch up" with the physical channels. As a result, many data communications managers will be required either to upgrade the information and analysis capabilities of existing logistics communications networks or to install new LDI procedures that will increase information flow efficiency and productivity.

To do this, data communications managers will have to address a variety of difficult issues over the next few years — escalating numbers of standards and protocols, new and exotic internal and external networks, and increased network complexity.

Protocol standardization, although widely acknowledged to be a key factor behind the long-term success of LDI, continues to make only slow progress. One of the major problems is the large number of organizations involved in establishing LDI standards: ANSI (American National Standards Institute), EIA (Electronic Industries Association), IEEE (Institute of Electrical and Electronic Engineers), ISO (International Organization for Standardization), NBS (National Bureau of Standards), and the TDCC (Transportation Data Coordinating Committee), among others.

Is there a way out of the LDI standards morass? As discussed in the second article, industry groups, such as the Automotive Industry Action Group (AIAG), have been established to develop standard communications and document guidelines for LDI between suppliers and original equipment manufacturers (OEMs) within the U. S. automobile manufacturing industry. Similarly, General Motors Corp. has pursued development of the Manufacturing Automation Protocol (MAP) — a standard set of protocols that sets the stage for intra- and interplant communications among all types of in-plant manufacturing operations (material flows, work stations, and product inventories). Boeing's similar push of TOP (Technical and Office Protocols) is a related set of standard protocols that can also foster the increased use of LDI.

In this manner, standardization will continue to occur on an individual industry basis or an industry/supplier

The best way for data communications managers to be kept informed on LDI standards is to monitor, join, or initiate an industry-specific LDI standards committee.

basis. For example, working groups within the electrical, chemical, office products, and aluminum industries have already adopted the ANSI X.12 transactions standards for intercompany LDI. The role of associations, such as AIAG, will also become more important but only for groups associated with particular industries. The more general associations, such as TDCC, may become less important as industry-specific LDI groups become dominant, although such groups as TDCC may increasingly deal with interindustry communications rather than intra-industry (supplier/OEM) issues.

The best way for data communications managers to be kept informed on LDI standards is to monitor, join, or initiate an industry-specific LDI standards committee. However, managers should make sure that their LDI group represents mainstream thinking, not radical or untried approaches to LDI, because conflicting views on both standards and LDI network architecture will continue to exist in the future.

As companies have increasingly automated plant operations, some have run across problems in integrating computerized operations across manufacturing and distribution functions. Companies may, for example, have an MRP (manufacturing resource planning) scheme that controls material flows throughout the production process. At the same time, a separate, unlinked automation facility may coordinate machine tool, robotic, and assembly operations. Similarly, the integration of workstation and material information flows with the overall (supervisory) computer network has often been unattainable, dampening the cost savings and productivity gains achieved with automation.

An emerging solution to integrating disparate computers within and among automated factories is the local area network (LAN). Unlike prior factory communications schemes that required separate wiring, LANs operate through a single trunkline with plug-in connections. Such flexibility allows easier adaptation of manufacturing processes to changing customer requirements and reduces production costs by allowing work flow to be altered on a real-time basis.

Often, multiple LANs may exist in the same plant. A plant control scheme is generally organized on a hierarchical basis, ranging from controls at and across individual workstations, through controls over material flows among workstations, and up to overall supervisory work flow controls.

At the lowest level of the hierarchy, such operations as machine stations and material sources are linked, allowing communications to and from manufacturing locations on supply requirements. Such LANs are generally proprietary, designed for specific and simple communications that control and report on work flow.

At the next highest level, plantwide LANs control overall material and product flow within a facility. For example, a midwestern manufacturer of batteries uses a LAN to coordinate delivery of parts to nearly 20 different machine locations and a storage area. Scanning devices keep track of parts flow, allocating products to the correct location. The LAN coordinates six separate flow control operations which is safer than a central computer control scheme that would make the entire plant vulnerable to one machine malfunctioning. These networks may be commercially available, but customized interfaces are often needed between proprietary and commercial LANs.

Finally, at the highest level, LANs can be used to redistribute work loads across manufacturing stations, alter existing "orders" (as to number, manufacturing speed, or features in some cases), and work around problem areas. Such "intelligent" LANs are still in prototype, since they generally require a standardized communications protocol (such as MAP) across a variety of general purpose and proprietary systems operating within a factory.

Perhaps the most ambitious and sophisticated LAN effort to date is being undertaken by Electronic Data Systems Corp. (EDS) for its parent company, General Motors Corp. Although billed as the nation's largest private telephone network, the $350 million arrangement will connect much more than just telephones. The current objective is to standardize communications and tie together GMC's computers with those of its suppliers, factories, dealers, and offices. Once the network is established, GMC can improve its parts delivery to assembly plants and increase assembly line automation. In addition, GMC intends to sell space on the network to suppliers and other companies for LDI operations.

GMC expects the network to be a major weapon in its battle for global motor vehicle markets. For example, by the early 1990s, the following scenario will be able to take place: A car dealer enters a customer's order into a computer. The order is directly transmitted to a central computer, aggregated on the basis of multiple dealer messages, then sent to assembly facilities and parts suppliers. The order specifies when to have parts available and when to begin vehicle assembly, and it also instructs internal factory manufacturing and assembly stations about how to build the car, what color to paint it, and what accessories to install.

How should the typical data communications manager evaluate the role of LANs in his or her company's LDI automation? As mentioned in the previous article, a manager should first conduct a complete audit of existing LDI mechanisms. Next, the manager should investigate commercially available LANs and the capabilities of proprietary products. Finally, the manager should develop a long-term (minimum five-year) LDI communications plan that describes both architecture and implementation plans.

This long-term plan should also include one or more "pilot projects" for testing alternative LAN/LDI schemes. Since full implementation for even a single-plant LAN using MAP-type standards may take two or three years, choosing the wrong product can be costly. Another advantage of pilot projects is the opportunity they afford a manager to decide between what could be called a "telephone network" and a "bulletin board" LDI configuration. The telephone network configuration allows a large number of two-way information flows and is used in most current LAN implementations of LDI. The bulletin board configuration makes relevant information centrally available to all users and helps avoid message collision. This configuration may also simplify software development and allow high-level controllers easier access to broad-based data on plant operations, improving efficiency, and reducing production costs.

Moving toward ACHs

As discussed in the previous articles, some of the nation's leading companies (including AT&T, IBM, and General Electric) continue to make major investments in networks and software designed for third-party LDI arrangements. These networks focus on providing both intra- and intercompany information exchange.

Perhaps the best example of these new networks and how they will work is provided by automated clearinghouses (ACHs). Established and operated by the U. S. Federal Reserve System, ACHs provide a mechanism for banks and other financial institutions to clear both debit and credit transactions using either an electronic network or a magnetic tape exchange. At present, over 30 ACHs are operating in the United States, with a monthly volume of nearly 35 million electronic transactions — still a small share of the country's total financial transactions.

The most interesting aspect of ACH operations lies in their inherent economies of scale. Federal Reserve System studies have shown that for each 10 percent increase in transaction volumes, total ACH operations costs rise only 6 to 7 percent. This implies that as volume increases, costs per transaction decline. Since ACHs are already less expensive than most paper transactions, such networks can make exceptional cost savings possible.

Adoption of an ACH arrangement for LDI operations seems to be natural and even necessary for companies seriously interested in electronic data transfer. Although third-party operations provide the *ability* to engage in LDI, the formation of an electronic transactions clearinghouse of major shippers, vendors, and carriers is probably required to *implement* the process. By themselves, the networks are insufficient to launch widespread LDI acceptance.

One of the most advanced third-party LDI arrangements that could be used as a basis for an ACH operation for logistics data has been developed by the McDonnell-Douglas Electronic Data Interchange Co. As with most third-party vendors, the McDonnell-Douglas network consists of a nationwide intelligent communications network (EDI*Net) and software (EDI*Translator) capable of translating internal company data and documents into standard EDI document formats.

EDI*Net allows direct computer-to-computer transfer of business documents between companies with different computers, data, and document formats. Operating over the Tymnet network, EDI*Net communicates with nearly any intelligent device that supports asynchronous, bisynchronous, or X.25 communications protocols at speeds ranging from 300 bit/s to 9.6 kbit/s. Messages can be sent or received 24 hours per day, while complying with industry standards such as ANSI X.12 and the Uniform Communications Standard.

EDI*Translator accepts internal company LDI data in anymachine-readable format and converts it into standard EDI document formats for transmission on EDI*Net. The translation facility has two operational subsystems: a sending subsystem that creates standard document formats from internal company data for transmission to other companies, and a receiving subsystem that edits an inbound message to the LDI network for conformity to industry communications standards and notifies senders of message errors. (EDI*Translator was developed by Metro-Mark Integrated Systems Inc., although McDonnell-Douglas has exclusive worldwide marketing rights to it.)

The McDonnell-Douglas facilities reflect the state of the art in third-party vendor schemes, requiring few internal changes in company operations to take advantage of LDI. However, the ease with which company data is translatedand sent to other companies is only a small part of the process involved in implementing better data communications within an organization.

As mentioned, the automation of manufacturing and distribution systems has rapidly increased the speed of product movements between vendor, plant, and customer. Sometimes, products even arrive before their documentation. While third-party vendors can speed up document flow outside of companies, the major barriers to improved communications are usually within company facilities. As a result, a company may be able to rapidly transmit full order documentation electronically via a third-party network, but the receiving company may not have integrated the inbound information into internal communications facilities. This defeats some or all of the benefits of LDI. Data communications managers, therefore, should not look at third-party LDI arrangements as a complete solution to their problems, but only as one piece of a very complex cross-company and interfacility communications puzzle.

Although questions remain about the integration of company and third-party LDI schemes, the role of these facilities as the primary intercompany LDI networks of the future is becoming more clear. A major issue that has yet to be addressed, though, is the ownership of LDI networks. Current third-party LDI networks are privately owned. However, the banking industry's experience with electronic data interchange has shown significant economies of scale in the operation of industry-owned ACHs. It is likely that industry groups, such as AIAG, may join together in developing an ACH-like network for logistics data over the next 10 years.

For the data communications manager, the choice of an external LDI network should involve an evaluation of several characteristics, including communications standards supported, access to the network, conformance to message requirements, difficulty of linkage to internal information facilities, and necessary investments. The primary benefits of third-party LDI networks — minimal capital investment and ease of use — are certainly more preferable to the costs and time required to develop a private LDI network for intercompany communications. However, the third-party networks only facilitate external messages transmission, often the simplest and least disruptive aspect of integrated LDI networks within a company. Before signing up with a third-party vendor, a data communications manager should establish a long-term LDI communications plan for the company so that the role of the external LDI networks is well known to all potential users.

Major trends
Three major trends in telecommunications and computers — deregulation of global communications networks, the rapid growth in fiber optics as a transmission medium, and the development of "intelligent" computers — will further reduce LDI costs and improve service diversity and quality over the next 10 years. The net result will be even more incentives (from a cost and customer service perspective) for companies to introduce electronic LDI systems rapidly.

Influenced by the deregulation of the communications industry, rapid changes are occurring worldwide in the procedures and technology of both intra- and intercountry communications. The advent of multiple service suppliers in the same market is leading to rapid declines in service costs, and the rapid growth of the computer as the primary user/generator of information has created the need for advanced communications.

Typically, telecommunications companies and those seeking to engage in LDI face many of the same problems in developing interfaces among diverse computers. Telecommunications companies will also be working to break down cross-company communications problems, thus speeding up the development of translation facilities and unified message standards and protocols. Overall, communications managers should expect continued declines in information interchange costs as well as an improved ability to operate LDI on a global and country-specific basis.

Besides telecommunications deregulation, the rapid trend toward substituting fiber optics for copper wire will not only reduce communications costs, but it will also make it possible for the next generation of communications networks to handle the growing traffic among computers, such as LDI. Fiber optics can be used for both internal LANs within factories and cross-ocean communications cables. In addition to allowing far greater capacity, fiber optic lines reduce costs by requiring fewer signal repeaters. This technology promises to dramatically reduce the costs and increase the capacity of communications networks and, by extension, external and internal LDI systems.

Finally, advances in artificial intelligence (AI) — the ability to make machines mimic certain human decision techniques — promise to both make LDI systems more user-friendly and automate a variety of basic LDI functions. Subfields of AI relevant to LDI include automated problem-solving, expert systems, and natural-language processing. Automated problem-solving will, for example, allow a company's computer to query vendors on order status, access a variety of data banks sequentially to determine current conditions, and even alter a delivery date if necessary. Expert systems will eventually allow computers to do a certain degree of cognitive thinking, although such products are decades away. Natural-language processing will enable the computer to understand languages, simplifying communications between companies. In all, AI will help make LDI systems easier to use and reduce the need for communications standards.

Where do we go from here?
From all indications, prospects are exceptionally bright for a rapid increase in LDI among companies over the next decade. New facilities are being developed, telecommunications costs will continue to decline, and technology will be easier to use and will fully automate many mundane functions (such as order inquiry/status). The next generation of technology (LANs, ACHs, AI) will lead LDI toward future products that are even more revolutionary. Data communications strategists should be aware of some of the more general long-term trends.

However, the banking industry's long-term experience with electronic data interchange has shown significant economies of scale in the operation of industry-owned ACHs.

From LANs to interplant integration. LANs will revolutionize collocated and intrafactory communications over the next five years, setting the stage for interplant arrangements that will integrate an entire company's operation, from vendor procurement through customer delivery. The interplant LDI facilities will almost certainly operate over any third-party communications equipment, linked with proprietary/commercial LANs within plants or office buildings.

From ACHs to LICHs. Assuming that domestic ACHs develop among companies during the coming decade, the next step will be the development of a worldwide ACH (dubbed LICH for logistics information clearinghouse). LICHs will function both within a region (such as Europe and the Far East) and between regions.

From communications to smart networks. The next generation of LDI facilities will clearly allow improved communications of basic logistics data among companies. However, the real promise of future LDI facilities is their ability to replace many of the basic company procurement, production planning, inventory control, and customer service staff functions with automated facilities. If computers will be able to use artificial intelligence to replace some of the more basic control and monitoring functions now performed by company staff, significant cost reductions and job upgrading will be possible. ∎

Dave Anderson has been employed by Temple, Barker, and Sloane Inc., Lexington, Mass., for two years. He holds a Ph. D. in transportation and economics from Boston University.

Gilbert Held, 4-Degree Consulting, Macon, Ga.

Using flexible software to access many hosts from a microcomputer

Want to clear those terminals from your desk and still be able to get around? Try a microcomputer with a helping of emulation software.

Rather than sit before multiple sets of screen and keyboard, many users who must communicate with more than one host have traded in their terminals for microcomputers. This revolt has been made possible by emulation programs that enable the small machines to mimic the necessary terminal protocols. Each terminal has a specific set of commands and codes that the attached computer uses to tell it how to present data to the user, and special-purpose software allows microcomputers to speak the various dialects of "terminaleze." While other software allows a microcomputer to operate like asynchronous terminals or to do more sophisticated file transfer procedures ("Evaluating microcomputer communications software," March, p. 209), emulation packages turn the microcomputer into a terminal polyglot.

The simplest emulation programs transmit and receive information on an asynchronous, line-by-line basis. These programs emulate the teletype, or TTY, terminals that were among the first used in data communications. The TTY protocol became a standard because of the straightforward nature of line-by-line operations and because it was based on ASCII (American National Standard Code for Information Interchange). With advances in the technology, full-screen display terminals gave application designers the ability to address any point on the screen. Such flexibility, however, had a price. No longer would there be a simple, uniform way for any host computer to address any terminal.

Various data processing companies took different tacks on how to manage terminal screens, so the terminals that they produced were largely incompatible. Thus, users of host-based applications that were written to display information on a full-screen basis had to have the proper terminal available. Also, access to different kinds of hosts called for multiple terminals, often on the same desk. Now, to alleviate some of these problems, sophisticated emulation programs for microcomputers have begun to reach the market.

An appropriate terminal emulator will mimic the terminal's display attributes, such as inverse video, blinking, and underlining, on the microcomputer's screen. In such cases, the communications program must convert the microcomputer's character set to the character set of the terminal being emulated and vice versa. This includes a conversion of the control-character sequences sent to the terminal to manipulate its display attributes as well as printer control character sequences (for printing in boldface, compressed mode, and so on).

Keyboard and command code differences

The keyboard of a microcomputer is very similar to those of most asynchronous terminals. However, full-screen terminals are built to operate with specific protocols and usually have several unique keys. Thus important differences may exist between the keyboard of the terminal being emulated and the microcomputer's keyboard. When no direct one-to-one mapping of the keys is possible, most communications programs require that the user enter a two- or three-key sequence or combination on the microcomputer in order to simulate the desired keystroke.

Table 1 shows a portion of the command codes recognized by several popular asynchronous, ASCII-coded terminals. Note that an application program developed on a host computer to use the functions of any of the three terminals listed in Table 1 could not be used with either of the others. The incompatibility between the command codes recognized by a microcomputer and those recognized by such terminals

Table 1: Terminal command-codes

	TERMINAL		
FUNCTION	HAZELTINE EXECUTIVE 80	IBM 3101/20	TELEVIDEO 950
CURSOR UP	ESC,FF	ESC,A	VT
CURSOR DOWN	ESC,VT	ESC,B	LF
CURSOR RIGHT	DLE	ESC,C	FF
CURSOR LEFT	BS	ESC,D	BS
CURSOR HOME	ESC,DC2	ESC,H	RS
ERASE SCREEN	ESC,FS	ESC,L	ESC,*
ERASE TO END-OF-LINE	ESC,SI	ESC,I	ESC,T
ERASE TO END-OF-PAGE	ESC,CAN	ESC,J	ESC,Y

BS = BACKSPACE ESC = ESCAPE RS = RECORD SEPARATOR
CAN = CANCEL FF = FORM FEED SI = SHIFT IN
DC2 = DEVICE CONTROL 2 FS = FILE SEPARATOR VT = VERTICAL TABULATION
DLE = DATA LINK ESCAPE LF = LINE FEED

normally precludes using a microcomputer for anything other than line-by-line transmission (TTY terminal emulation).

To enable a microcomputer to emulate a specific vendor's terminal, the communications software must convert the ASCII control codes that perform screen functions on the microcomputer into their equivalents on the terminal being emulated. Thus, for example, to emulate a Hazeltine Executive 80 terminal, a program would transmit the characters "ESC, FF" to the host when the "cursor-up" key on the microcomputer keyboard is pressed. A program that emulates a Televideo 950 terminal would transmit the "VT" character, a 3101 emulator would send "ESC, A," and so on.

Conversely, the command codes generated by the host computer must be converted into control codes recognized by the microcomputer. Upon receipt from the host of characters representing a certain function, an emulation program would thus generate the equivalent code on the microcomputer. A program operating on, say, an IBM Personal Computer (PC) would translate a "cursor-up" character from the host into an "RS" character (ASCII 30), the PC's "cursor-up" function code.

Emulation categories

Every asynchronous microcomputer communications program enables the computer to operate as a TTY by transmitting and receiving data on a line-by-line basis. Therefore, all such programs can be classified as terminal emulators. Once TTY emulation is eliminated from consideration, asynchronous emulation programs can be classified into three general categories:

■ Specific terminal emulation.
■ Multiple terminal emulation.
■ User-definable terminal emulation.

It should be noted that while some programs fall into only one of these categories, the scope of certain others brings them under two or three headings.

Examples of specific terminal emulation programs include SmarTerm 100, SmarTerm 125, and SmarTerm 400 from Persoft Inc. (As in the article referred to previously, the programs reviewed here were selected for illustrative purposes only. The review should not be construed as an endorsement by either the author or the magazine. In addition, readers are cautioned that it is the policy of many vendors to update their programs on a periodic basis. Therefore, a feature currently missing or inadequate on the version of software examined in this article may be added or revised in a later release.)

SmarTerm 100 permits an IBM PC to function as a Digital Equipment Corp. (DEC) VT100-series terminal, such as the VT100, VT101, VT102, or VT52. The program implements most of the features of VT100 terminals on the IBM PC, including character attributes, line and character insertion and deletion, and full local-printer support. All VT100 keys are mapped to corresponding keys on the microcomputer keyboard. This permits a microcomputer operator to use popular DEC full-screen editors.

The program allows both ASCII and binary programs or data files to be transferred to and from the host computer. In addition, SmarTerm 100 supports two different 132-column video boards available for use on the IBM PC. On microcomputers without direct 132-column display capability, the program uses horizontal scrolling of the conventional 80-column display to permit users to view any portion of the internally maintained 132-column display area.

Persoft's SmarTerm 125 extends the DEC VT100-series terminal emulation provided by SmarTerm 100 to include emulation of the VT125. It also adds support of DEC's Remote Graphics Instruction Set (ReGIS), a set of graphics-function description commands. Subject to certain hardware limitations, SmarTerm 125 emulates all functions of the VT125 ReGIS language on an IBM PC, including position, curve, vector, text, down-loadable character sets, shading, multiple writing planes, and custom writing patterns as well as DEC macrograph facilities, which are macros used to describe screen graphics. With the graphics emulation capability of SmarTerm 125, microcomputer operators can use a variety of popular host-based graphics products.

Another product in the Persoft SmarTerm series that warrrants attention is SmarTerm 400. This program allows an IBM PC to function as a D100, D200, or D400 terminal from Data General Corp. It also transfers ASCII or binary programs and data files between IBM PCs and hosts that talk to Data General terminals. Like other members of the SmarTerm series, SmarTerm 400 implements virtually all features of the aforementioned Data General terminals on the microcomputer.

Multiple-product, user-defined terminal emulation

Besides the Persoft series of specific terminal emulators, many communications software vendors incorporate VT100 emulation capability into their microcomputer programs. The popular DEC emulator may also be offered as an option. Users of BLAST (Blocked Asynchronous Transmission, from the Communications Research Group in Baton Rouge, La.) can opt for DEC VT100- or Data General D200-series emulation.

Table 2: Softerm PC's terminal emulations

ADDS REGENT 20	HONEYWELL VIP 7205
ADDS REGENT 25	HONEYWELL VIP 7801
ADDS REGENT 40	HONEYWELL VIP 7803
ADDS REGENT 60	IBM 3101 MODEL 10
ADDS VIEWPOINT	IBM 3101 MODEL 20
DATA GENERAL D200	LEAR SIEGLER ADM-3A
DATAPOINT 3601	LEAR SIEGLER ADM-5
DEC VT52	TELEVIDEO 910
DEC VT102	TELEVIDEO 925
HAZELTINE 1400/1410	TELEVIDEO 950
HAZELTINE 1500	TTY COMPATIBLE
HAZELTINE 1520	USER DEFINED
HEWLETT-PACKARD 2622A	

TTY = TELETYPEWRITER

Table 3: Softerm PC's user-definable terminal functions

ANSWERBACK	
HOME CURSOR	
CLEAR SCREEN	
ERASE TO END-OF-LINE	
ERASE TO END-OF-SCREEN	
INSERT LINE	
DELETE LINE	
PRINTER	ON OFF
INVERSE VIDEO	ON OFF
LOW INTENSITY	ON OFF
UNDERLINE	ON OFF
BLINK	ON OFF
CURSOR UP	
CURSOR DOWN	
CURSOR RIGHT	
CURSOR LEFT	

One of the most comprehensive multiple-product terminal emulation programs marketed as of this article's writing is Softerm PC, from Softronics of Memphis, Tenn. In addition to basic TTY emulation, Softerm PC includes exact emulations of 24 popular terminals, providing all keyboard and display functions. It also supports both conversational-mode (line-by-line) and block-mode (screen-at-a-time) data transfer. The specific terminals emulated by Softerm PC are listed in Table 2.

Besides the listed terminals, Softerm PC includes a general-purpose, user-defined terminal emulator. This portion of the package lets the user specify parameters required for the emulation of a terminal not specifically included with the program.

The program's user-defined terminal emulation capability provides TTY-standard (ASCII) carriage return, line feed, and backspace processing while permitting user definitions for most of the common terminal functions. Functions that are user definable with Softerm PC are listed in Table 3.

Besides providing a comprehensive set of terminal-emulation modules, Softerm is a program rich in communications features. The program provides an exceptionally explicit method of defining the user's hardware environment, more detailed than many communications and noncommunications packages. In addition, Softerm contains many features that other programs lack. These include the ability to modify the appearance of the user interface and to log screen images to disk.

A comprehensive printer-control definition capability lets the user select the page length and width and set the way the printer handles lines longer than the page width. A cursor-definition feature permits the user to have the screen cursor displayed as an underline, partial block, half block, or full block. If a color monitor is used, the user can select from a set of eight colors the specific foreground and background colors to be displayed. Between the cursor and color definitions, users can explicitly configure their displays to meet their personal visual preferences.

Another valuable feature included in Softerm is a Fortran-77 source-code program that can be used to obtain micro-to-mainframe protocol compatibility. When transferred to a user's mainframe, this program lets developers construct micro-to-mainframe applications on top of Softrans, a proprietary Softerm protocol. Softrans incorporates a CRC-16 (cyclic redundancy check) polynomial algorithm for error-free block transfer of data as well as a data compression algorithm to enhance line efficiency.

Operation

In addition to the Softrans protocol, users of Softerm can also specify the use of an XModem protocol contained in the program for file transfer operations. Since Softerm's user manual exceeds 350 pages, the major problem faced by many users of this program will probably involve becoming familiar with the wealth of features included in the program and how to use them.

The program's "communications agent," a configuration module, is loaded the first time Softerm is

1. Initial setup. Softerm automatically seeks the standard input/output communications and printer ports (COM and LPT) and adjusts its settings accordingly.

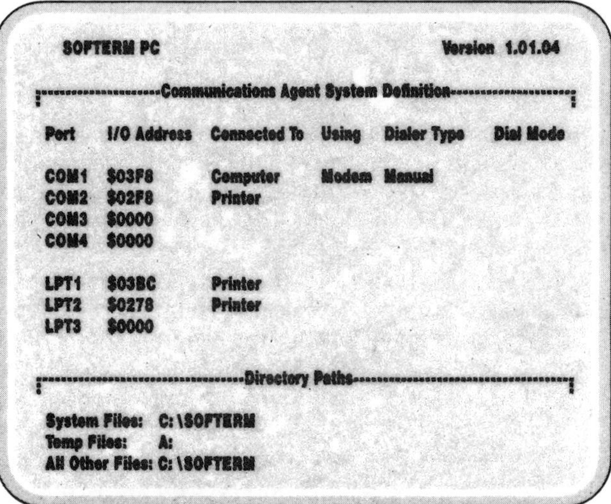

executed as well as upon user command thereafter. This module automatically tests the microcomputer for the presence of standard communications COM1 through COM4 and line printer ports LPT1 through LPT3, setting default values for all ports encountered. The IBM PC operating the program in the example contains two communications ports and two printer ports (Fig. 1).

If the default settings of the communications agent do not accurately reflect the attached devices, the user can easily toggle the field values to select the most appropriate entry from a series of predefined settings. This is accomplished by using the Tab key to position an inverse-video field over the display choice that the user wishes to change. Then, with either the space bar or the cursor keys, the user can toggle through the available choices, pressing the Enter key to accept the displayed entry.

Since in the example no device was connected to the COM2 and LPT2 ports, "nothing" was selected for these field values (Fig. 2). Similarly, since a Hayes Smartmodem was to be used with a tone-dialing line, the appropriate field entries were selected. Softerm version 1.01.04 (the version used for this article) supports 18 different types of modems. The user can thus select the appropriate modem by simply pressing the space bar or cursor key once the inverse-video field is positioned under "dialer type."

Once the appropriate information is defined to the communications agent, the user must press the Alt and Enter keys simultaneously for the program to accept the current screen format. For persons accustomed to simply pressing the Enter key to conclude an operation, the program's reliance on numerous combinations of the Alt key with other keys may require a period of adjustment. Fortunately, simply pressing the Alt and "?" keys together displays an appropriate help screen matching the user's point of progress in the program.

This assistance is usually sufficient to permit the user to move rapidly through the program.

After the initial configuration is completed, a "default port definitions" screen is displayed (Fig. 3). This screen consists of a column of fields corresponding to the options available for each port that was defined to the communications agent. Since the options for some ports are not applicable to other ports, a significant number of blank entries appear in the table. For example, only six options are applicable to the IBM PC's serial communications port COM1.

As with all definition menus in the program, the user can easily change a port definition by moving an inverse-video bar over the item to be changed and then pressing the space bar or cursor key until the desired parameter is displayed. The "bits/character" option toggles between the values of seven and eight, while the choices available for "parity" are none, odd, even, mark, and space. The "stop-bits" field toggles between one and two, while the serial-port option "speed" can be set to a value from 50 bit/s to 9.6 kbit/s (in bit/s).

The "rcv pacing" option defines the type of pacing control the program will use when receiving data. This option is obviously only applicable to a COM port connected to a computer. It can be toggled between X-on/X-off, data terminal ready (DTR), and none, with a DTR selection allowing the DTR signal to be used for pacing control. For data transmissions, the "xmit pacing" option indicates whether or not the program should respond to a pacing signal when transmitting data.

When a printer is attached to a COM port, the "fill character" option permits the user to have the program generate a pad character or a user-specified character to provide pacing control for nonintelligent printers that do not respond to X-on/X-off. In addition, the user can specify the number of these characters to be sent to the printer after the transmission of a carriage return (Fill after CR), after a line feed (Fill after LF), or after a form feed (Fill after FF). The user can also decide whether or not the program should automatically generate a line feed after each carriage return (LF after CR) in the data being transmitted.

While the preceding options are more comprehensive than those encountered in most communications programs, Softerm also includes six additional printer-port options to enable the user to configure hard-copy output in almost every way imaginable. These options permit the user to specify the length (in lines) of the forms used in the printer ("page length"), the number of lines to be skipped over when printing a page, equivalent to the top margin ("page skip"), and whether or not the printer has the capability to execute a form feed when it is sent an ASCII form-feed character ("hardware FF").

The "page width" option defines the number of columns available on the printer, while the "fold long lines" option indicates whether print lines exceeding the number of printer columns are to be folded or truncated. The last printer port option, "graphic char set," permits the user to indicate whether or not the printer has the capability to print graphics characters. If not, the program will automatically translate such characters into spaces for all printing operations.

Video and printer definition
The third and final screen in the communications agent permits the user to define video characteristics and printer macros. These macros can be extremely useful. In fact, they are a unique attribute of Softerm that should be incorporated into all programs that work with a printer.

Figure 4 illustrates the "video and printer definitions" menu. The "printer macro strings" permit the user to predefine up to 10 command strings that can be used to initialize a printer to a desired printing format. Thereafter, whenever a Softerm print function or utility requests a printer command string, the user can simply press a function key to initiate one of the predefined character sequences. Thus pressing function keys could be used to place the printer in an emphasized print mode, compressed print mode, and so on.

After the communications agent definition is completed, the Softerm "setup options" screen is displayed (Fig. 5a). From this menu users can select a specific terminal emulation activity ("load emulation"), change the communications parameters ("terminal options"), and perform other basic functions, including initiating a session ("online operation") or exiting to DOS (Disk Operating System).

When the load emulation option is selected, initially the selection "TTY compatible" will be displayed under "emulating" on the screen illustrated in Figure 5a. By using the space bar or cursor keys, the user can toggle through the 24 available emulations.

Once the appropriate emulator is selected, it can be used with the previously configured communications, display, and printer parameters. Alternately, the user may select the terminal options menu to change one or

more parameters. Different configurations can be saved to disk using the "save configuration" option and recalled by using the load configuration option.

The "disk utilities" option illustrated in Figure 5b permits the user to display the current directory as well as to rename and delete files and to set a default path through a hierarchical file structure without having to exit the program.

Once online operation is selected from the Softerm menu, the only deficiency in this otherwise extremely powerful program becomes noticeable. When this option is selected, the screen clears and the cursor is positioned at the top left-hand corner of the screen, with no notification of what the user is to do next. Only from trial-and-error or from reading the (350-page) manual can a user determine that the proper step is to press the Alt and "2" keys followed by "F2" in order to obtain a pop-up menu of the program's "dial utilities options" (Fig. 5c). Selections from this menu permit the user to enter and list information in a dialing directory (which Softerm calls the "phone book"), to dial the number associated with a name in the directory, to terminate a call ("hangup"), and to print the directory.

This procedure may be frustrating to a novice initially. However, a short time working with the program reveals the power of the dial utilities. Users can build a virtually unlimited dialing directory, since additions to the phone book are logged to the disk file named Softerm.Fon. Once the names and numbers are entered, the user simply specifies the name of the entry to be dialed. The program automatically searches the phone book and retrieves and displays the telephone number and communications parameters of the matching name in the phone book. Next, the user can change any entry or, if the selection is satisfactory, have the number dialed by pressing the Alt and Enter keys.

While SmarTerm is a power-packed communications program with a comprehensive set of terminal emulators, its many options and the extensive use of microcomputer and communications terminology in its

---

4. Display, output. *Besides setting preferred display colors, this menu lets the user control the printer by associating command strings with function keys.*

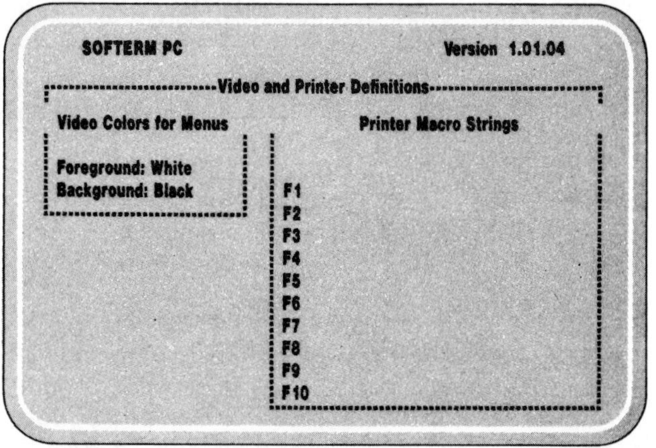

(A) SETUP OPTIONS

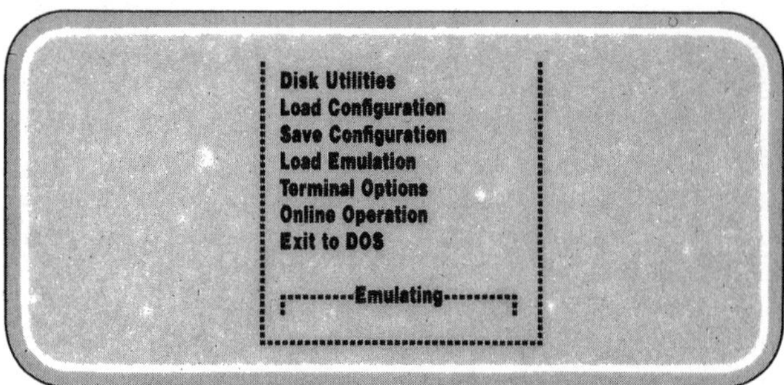

(B) DISK UTILITIES

(C) DIAL UTILITIES OPTIONS

documentation makes it a difficult program to master. Users with minimal communications requirements are best advised to look elsewhere for simple TTY terminal emulation. Those who need access to only a single host or type of host may be satisfied with single-terminal emulators like the Softerm series. However, those who want to configure their hardware environments and wish the flexibility of many terminal emulation capabilities in one package should consider a program like SmarTerm. ∎

Gilbert Held, director of 4-Degree Consulting, is the recipient of the 1984 Karp Award. He received the 1983 American Association of Publishers award for writing "the most outstanding microcomputer software program in the science/humanities category." Held is the author of 12 books and over 50 technical articles.

Lloyd Wanveer and Patrick Driscoll, Tymnet Inc., Cupertino, Calif.

Merger issue: Integrating SNA with a packet network

Software lets users replace dedicated leased lines between IBM terminals and hosts to relieve reconfiguration troubles.

Corporate buyouts, multinational corporations, and the lure of new technology have created a hodgepodge of networking schemes within many large corporations. A single corporation, for example, might have an IBM Binary Synchronous Communication (BSC) network for remote job entry (RJE) workstations and terminal clusters; a Systems Network Architecture (SNA) network of RJE, 3270, and 37X5 nodes; and an asynchronous network supporting a variety of computers and terminal equipment. What's more, large networks have been known to consist of as many as 25 independently operated subnetworks — each requiring its own bandwidth, maintenance, and management.

The possibility, though seldom realized, of network data sharing can sometimes result in as much as a 70 percent savings in operating expenses. Consolidation may also relieve staffing problems by simplifying network operation, and by reducing the need to involve highly skilled staff in routine maintenance tasks.

Packet-switching technology offers a way to create integrated multivendor private networks. In a packet network, leased lines are deployed between network nodes, and routing is designed to optimize bandwidth in a multiprotocol environment. Communicating equipment supporting a variety of protocols may share bandwidth (leased lines or satellite) by using a common intranetwork protocol for transmitting user data.

The approach to SNA packet-switching integration described here results in significantly reduced telecommunications costs, flexible multivendor interconnectivity, dynamic network reconfiguration, increased network uptime, and a reduction in the time and staff required for maintaining asynchronous, BSC, and SNA networks.

SNA is a highly protocol-dependent network architecture. As such, it represents a great challenge to multivendor network integration. SNA logic is distributed among the host, the 37X5 communications controller, and a terminal cluster controller or RJE device. SNA protocols mediate successful communications between these devices up a hierarchy from a terminal to an owner host. Thus, for communications between hierarchical SNA components, there must be a compatible software interface. Packet-switching technology can provide several levels of SNA support, as well as support for BSC, X.25, and asynchronous networks. IBM equipment may use the transmission services of a packet-switched network configured with the following software:

- SNA/SDLC interface, providing complete SNA compatibility for Physical Unit Type 2 (PU T2) and PU T4 control units.
- SDLC interface, compatible with SNA at the data link control layer.
- 3270 protocol conversion utility, providing 3270 translation for asynchronous character and block-mode terminals.

SNA support logic is distributed throughout the network as required by downloading software to packet nodes from a supervisory node. A single packet node may be configured with any number or types of interfaces. One node may connect SNA 3270 control units, serve as any host interface, provide 3270 protocol conversion, and connect a cluster of asynchronous terminals. Dedicated hardware is not required.

The basic objective of SNA integration is to allow the packet network to be used in place of dedicated leased lines between IBM terminals and hosts. Interfaces to the packet network for BSC, SDLC, and SNA/SDLC equipment permit IBM terminals and hosts to share network bandwidth with other equipment (Fig. 1). Leased lines may be deployed to optimize bandwidth for the aggregate needs of the organization. The result is a simplified network topology and significantly lower leased-line costs.

The SDLC interface — compatible with SNA at the data

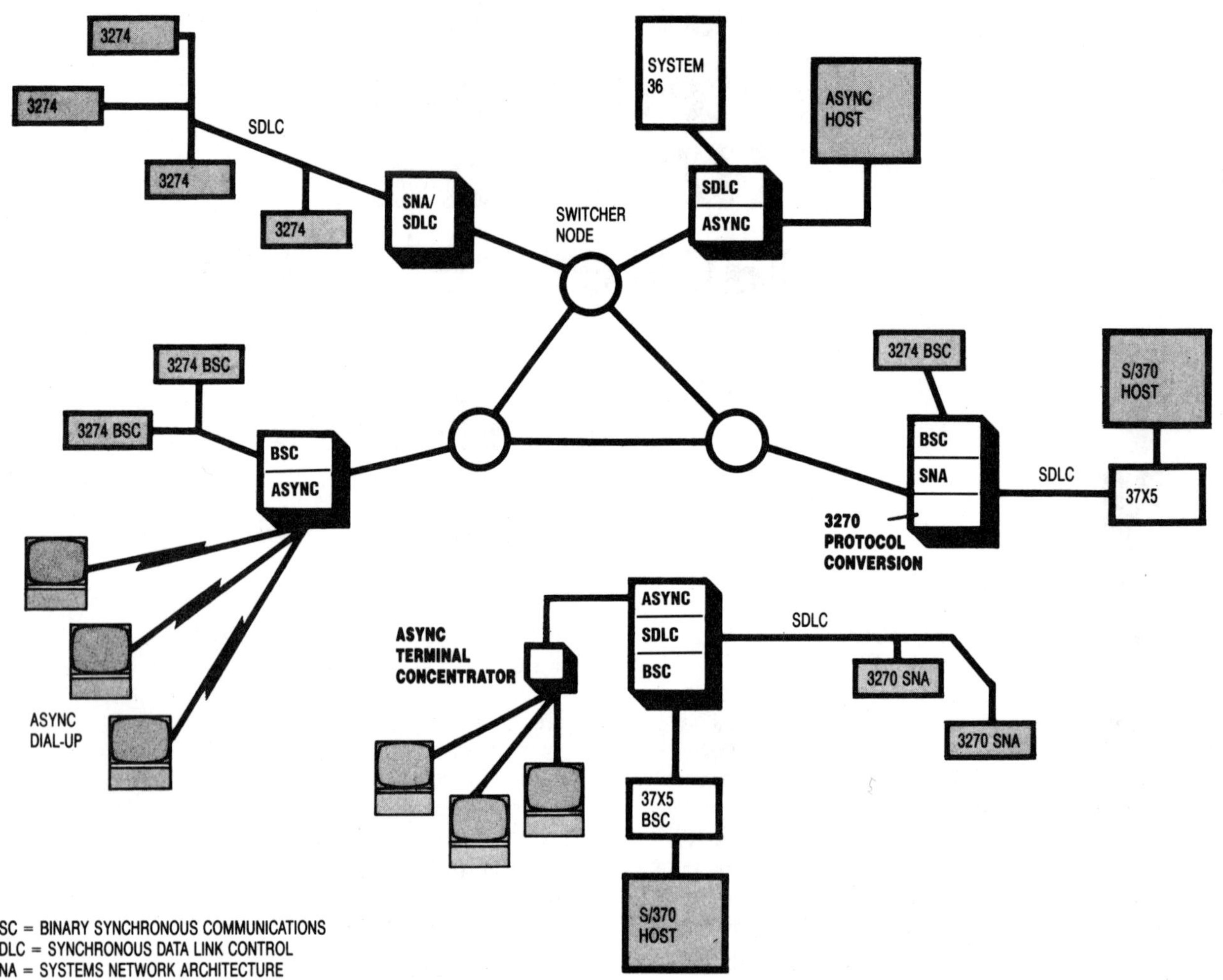

link control layer—achieves this objective. It supports PU T1 (pre-SNA devices), PU T2 (IBM 3270, 8100, System 3X, for example), and PU T4 (37X5), and is transparent to all logical unit types. Higher-level SNA protocols are transparent to the packet-switching interfaces and are transmitted, end-to-end, through the network (Fig. 2A).

The SNA/SDLC service consists of separate terminal and host interfaces, each of which is compatible with the interconnected device at all SNA layers. Capabilities beyond those provided by SNA may be introduced between interfaces, as long as the output is compatible with the interconnected device (Fig. 2B). Where SNA is a protocol-dependent proprietary architecture, the packet network, acting as a distributed gateway, can offer access to SNA services for non-SNA terminals and hosts (Fig. 2C).

Dynamic reconfiguration

In SNA the physical, or explicit, route is the same for each session between a pair of users until the routing table of an network control program (NCP) is changed. Each time a logical unit (terminal, host, or application program) is added or moved to a different location, the NCP routing

tables in each intervening 37X5 must be updated. The same is true when a new cross-domain routing path (a path over or through an area controlled by a host processor or a specific partition within a host) is authorized, when a logical unit (LU) must be deleted, or when the explicit routes are redefined to rebalance the distribution of traffic in the network.

Redefining NCP routing tables requires that all 37X5s between two users, and all subordinated 37X5s and PU T2s, be brought down and regenerated once NCP tables have been updated. This results in frequent network downtime, and the need for a standing army of highly skilled systems programmers to do routine maintenance tasks.

The SNA/SDLC host interface in a packet-switching node alleviates this problem by providing a screen behind which the physical configuration of the SNA network may be changed without modifying the NCP routing tables (Fig. 3). The network can expand and change without frequent network downtime or the involvement of SNA systems programmers.

Essentially, the packet network serves as a boundary

368

2. Three flavors. *(A) The SDLC interface adds value by allowing network bandwidth to be shared by SDLC, asynchronous, and other synchronous protocols; (B) the SNA/SDLC interface allows easy reconfiguration and improves fault tolerance; (C) the application level provides 3270 protocol conversion.*

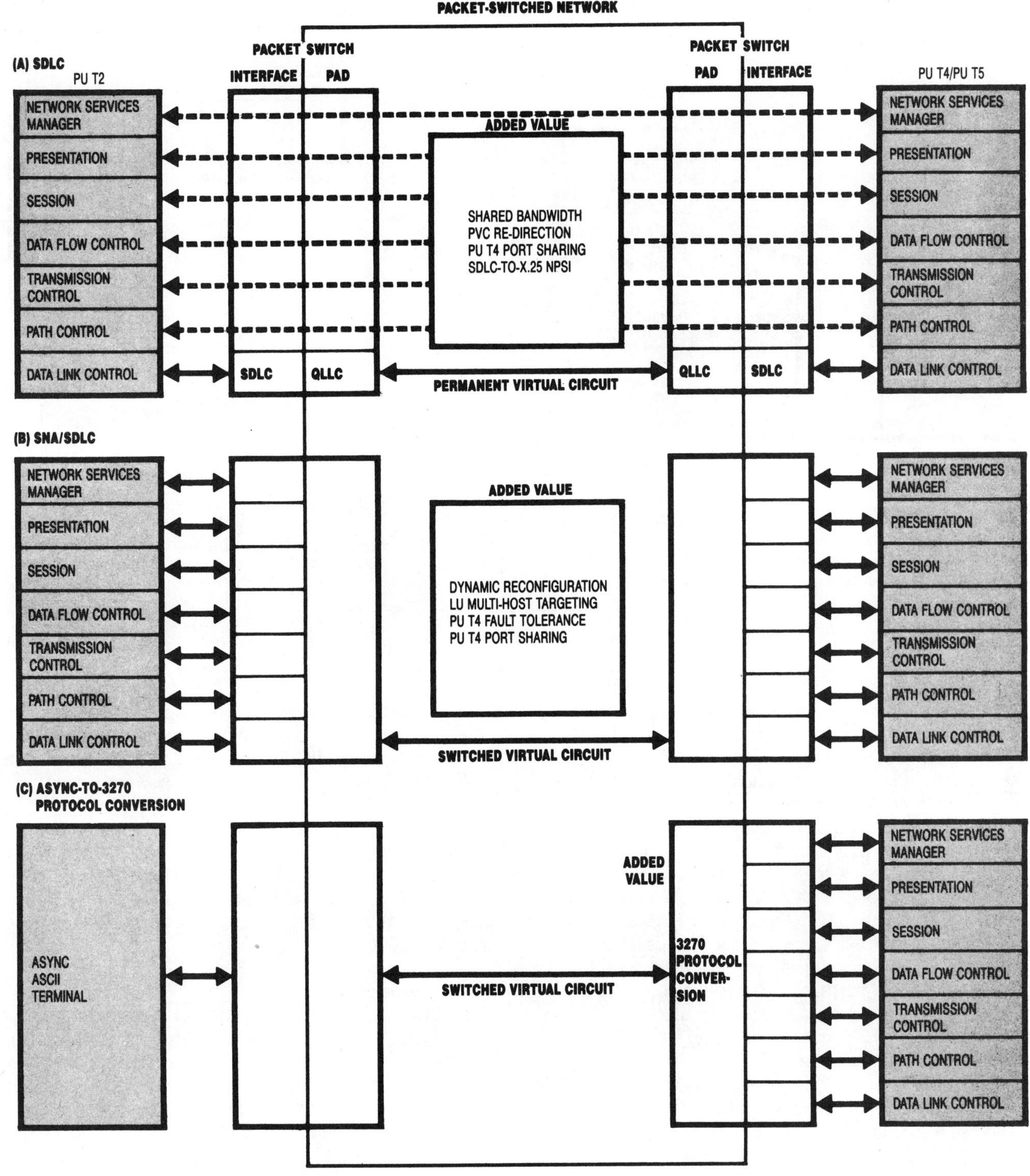

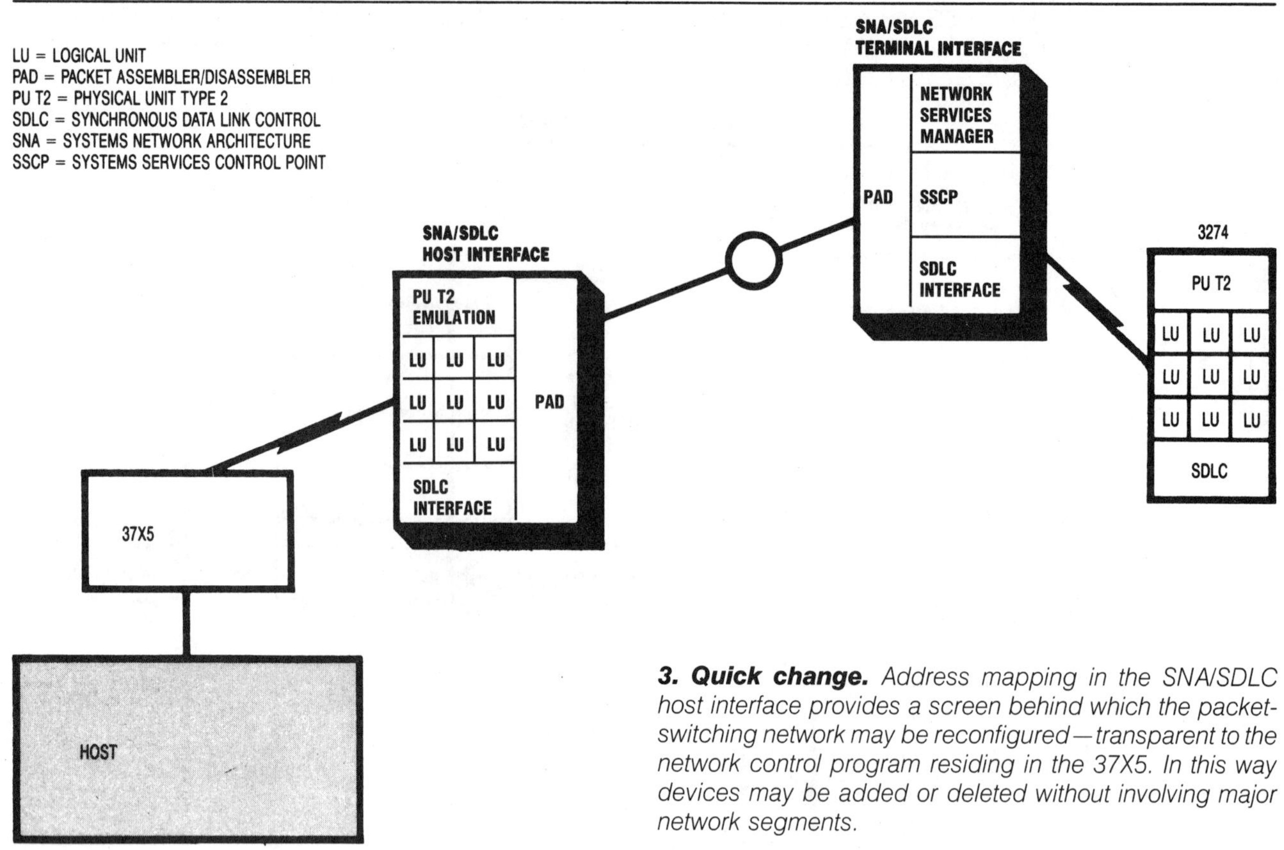

*3. **Quick change.** Address mapping in the SNA/SDLC host interface provides a screen behind which the packet-switching network may be reconfigured—transparent to the network control program residing in the 37X5. In this way devices may be added or deleted without involving major network segments.*

between SNA PU T2 and PU T4 units. SNA/SDLC host and terminal interfaces act as partners to the local SNA nodes, providing a local protocol interface as a proxy for the expected partner. The SNA LU address of each terminal in a 3270 cluster is mapped onto a pool of dummy LUs in the SNA/SDLC host interface. The dummy LUs are defined to a local 37X5 NCP and remain stable regardless of actual changes to the network configuration. The location of terminals and their selected destinations are dynamically redefined to the packet network supervisor as required. Reconfiguration does not disrupt the network.

The SNA design requires that each LU in the network be owned by a specific host. The owner host is responsible for confirming that an LU is authorized to access a particular application. As a consequence of this requirement, all devices sharing a link must have the same owner host. This means that each terminal in a 3270 cluster or a multidropped network of 3270 controllers must have the same owner. Even though many users may be working primarily with applications in other hosts, the sessions must be established through the owner host, and all messages must be transmitted through that host's local 37X5 NCP. Routing to the target host is handled by Multi-Network Systems Facility (MNSF), an SNA host software program.

The LU mapping in the SNA/SDLC packet network interface enables any host in the network to be selected on a logical unit basis, that is, by each device. Host access is not restricted to LUs owned by the host. Each terminal in a terminal cluster or in a multidropped network is able to select a host destination individually. The destination may be different each time the user logs on the network. Packet network switched virtual circuits are used in place of MSNF cross-domain communications.

In the SDLC implementation, a separate permanent virtual circuit is established for each physical unit (rather than each LU) in a multidropped network. Each physical unit may target a different host directly. In contrast to the SNA/SDLC interface implementation, however, each targeted host must own the physical unit.

The packet network provides password protection, validating that a user is authorized to access the targeted host. IBM host subsystems (CICS and IMS) provide another level of password protection to ensure that the user is authorized to access a particular application. There is no loss of security.

Enhancements

The obvious advantage of multihost targeting for the SNA/SDLC service is configuration flexibility since applications and terminals may be configured and reconfigured without regard for ownership. In addition, 37X5 throughput is improved for the following reasons:

■ Intermediate routing nodes (IRNs)—including the owner's local 37X5 in a cross-domain session—are not required.
■ If necessary, traffic from the multidropped network may be distributed among several 37X5 ports. To the user, improved throughput means faster response time than is usually expected from a multidropped network.
■ Bandwidth use is optimized using packet network adaptive routing algorithms designed specifically for that purpose.

Reducing port count. An alternative to a multidropped

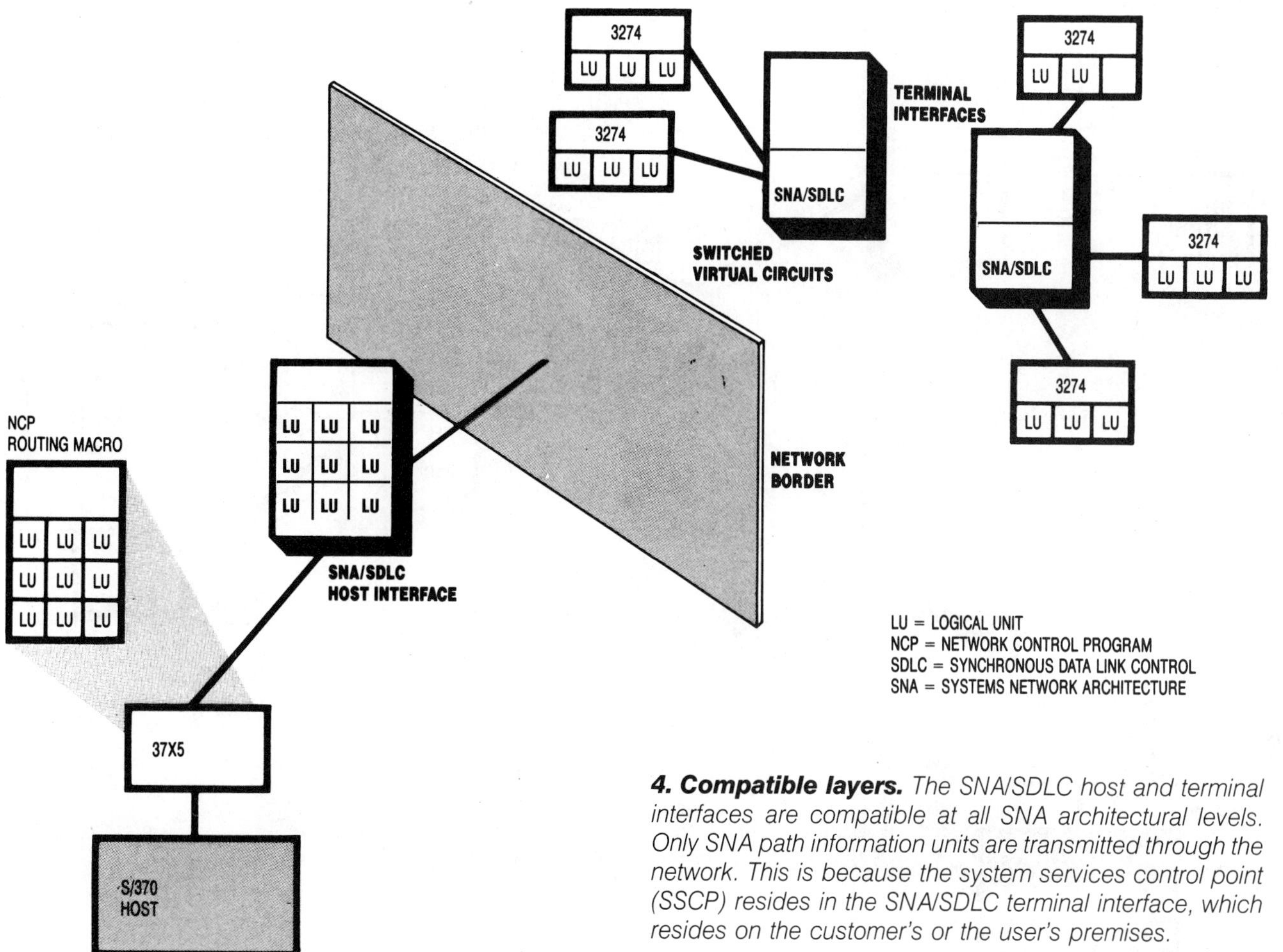

4. Compatible layers. *The SNA/SDLC host and terminal interfaces are compatible at all SNA architectural levels. Only SNA path information units are transmitted through the network. This is because the system services control point (SSCP) resides in the SNA/SDLC terminal interface, which resides on the customer's or the user's premises.*

SNA network is one in which each 3270 cluster is connected to a 37X5 by a point-to-point link. When the available ports on the front-end are exhausted, the network must either be reconfigured as a multidropped network or another 37X5 front-end must be added.

An SNA/SDLC host interface can be used to reduce the 37X5 port count without reconfiguring the network or adding 37X5s. A single host interface may serve numerous SNA/SDLC terminal interfaces to which PU T2 nodes are connected by point-to-point or multipoint links.

PU T4 fault tolerance. SNA restricts PU T2 nodes to a single link connecting the node to an upstream PU T4. If that PU T4 or any upstream PU T4 goes down, all connected PU T2 nodes are disabled until the failed unit is regenerated. If the PU T2 link or an upstream single-link transmission group goes down, the node is disabled until the link is recovered. Using the packet network switched virtual circuit capability, PU T2 nodes may be re-routed— with minimal service disruption—to an alternate PU T4 node if an upstream component fails.

Inside the interface

The SNA/SDLC service involves interaction between two interfaces: a terminal interface for downstream PU T2 nodes; and a host interface connecting to a PU T4 (Fig. 4). Any two terminal and host interfaces in the network may interact, a capability which is supported by switched virtual circuits.

The terminal interface appears to a downstream PU T2 as a host SNA Systems Services Control Point (SSCP). The PU T2 establishes a session with the packet-switching carrier's SSCP and is temporarily bound to it as if it were the owner host SSCP. When the SNA/SDLC terminal interface starts running, it immediately activates sessions with the PUs and LUs of all attached control units. The first thing that a user sees when he switches on a 3270 terminal is a menu. This menu prompts the user for identification, password, and destination selection.

The switched virtual-circuit connection between the terminal and host interface is established by the packet-network supervisor using tables that translate the SNA symbolic name provided by the user to a destination packet-node number. This is entirely transparent to the user. The local session that was used to send the menu to the controller is then unbound. The terminal is ready to transmit when the host interface is bound to the host SSCP.

The host interface acts as a gateway in a similar manner to that provided by IBM in NCP for BSC devices as well as to the gateways that are provided by many non-IBM computers. The interface appears to an upstream 37X5 as a link-attached PU T2 control unit. It emulates a PU T2

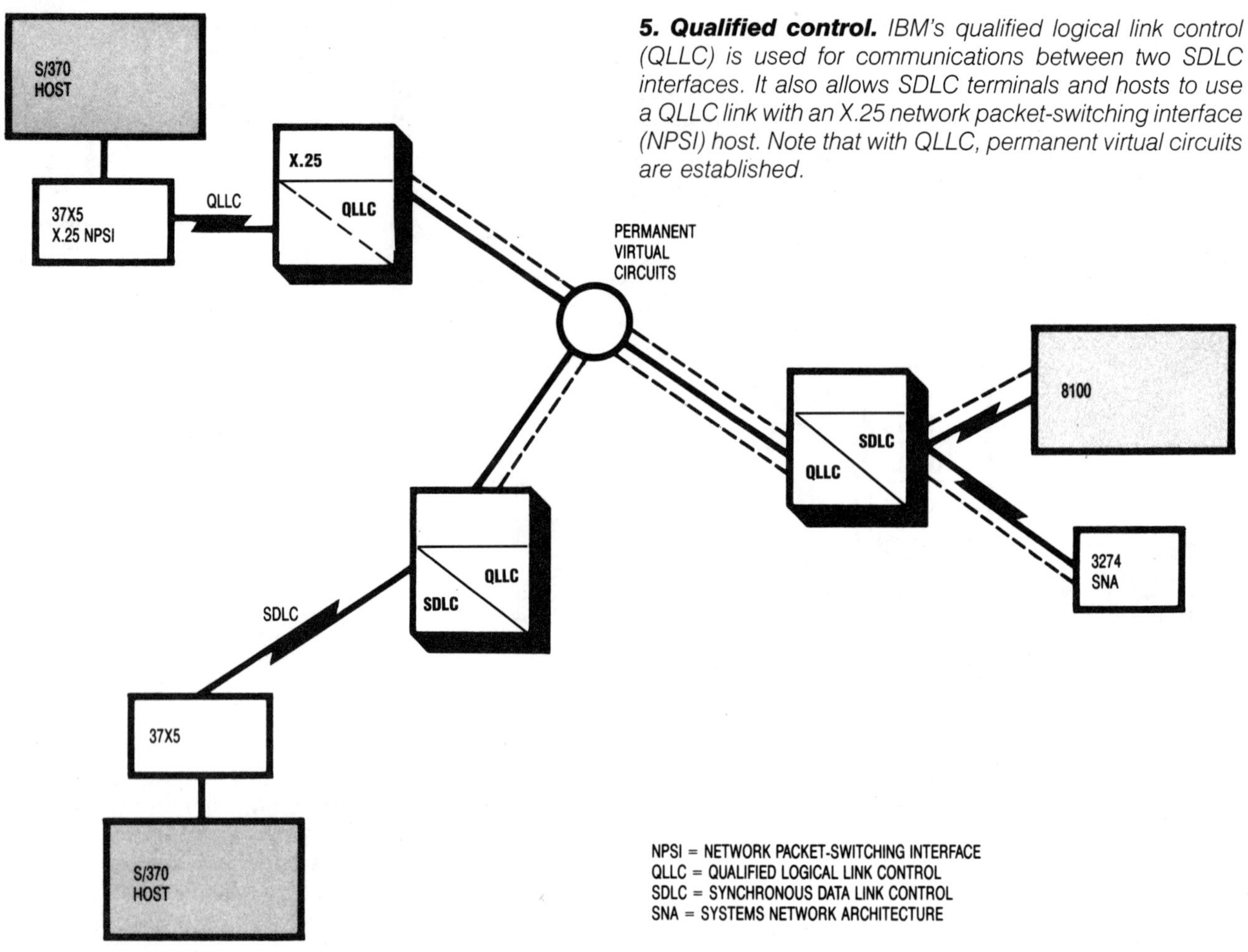

5. Qualified control. *IBM's qualified logical link control (QLLC) is used for communications between two SDLC interfaces. It also allows SDLC terminals and hosts to use a QLLC link with an X.25 network packet-switching interface (NPSI) host. Note that with QLLC, permanent virtual circuits are established.*

network services manager (NSM), which controls a pool of dummy LUs. LU addresses of downstream devices are mapped onto these dummies. The NSM is used by the host SSCP to bind the PUs and LUs in the interface to a host application.

The SDLC supervisory frames are handled locally by the SNA/SDLC terminal and host interfaces. They are not passed through the network. These messages are command frames used to control interaction between a secondary and primary station (for example, polling, poll acknowledgment, and flow control). When the SDLC control field is formatted for information transfer, a packet assembler/disassembler (PAD) in the interface converts the SDLC FID4 (format identifier for the full network address) to the intranetwork protocol. Only SNA path information units (PIUs) are passed through the network.

Just SDLC
The SDLC-only interface is compatible with SNA at the data link control layer. Higher-level protocols and codes are transmitted through the packet network transparently. Unlike the SNA/SDLC interface, the SDLC interface maintains the SNA-defined relationship between the owner host and downstream LU using permanent virtual circuits. As a result, the benefits of transparent reconfiguration, multi-host targeting, and PU T4 fault tolerance do not accrue. How-

ever, since the SDLC service is compatible with SNA only at the data link control layer, it is the more flexible in terms of the types of SNA devices it can interconnect.

All equipment using the SDLC discipline may be connected, including 37X5 controllers, all pre-SNA and SNA/SDLC cluster controllers, processors emulating PU T2, and many protocol converters. Future SNA protocols and products that use the SDLC link protocol can be supported without modification to the interface.

SDLC support can be provided by the interaction of two SDLC interfaces. The interface acts as a primary station to a PU T2 (an IBM 3270 control unit, for example), which is always a secondary station. On the other side of the connection, the interface acts as a secondary station to the upstream PU T4, always a primary station. The interface appears to the host as a point-to-point or multipoint secondary station.

A single SDLC interface can support both primary and secondary ports so that terminals and hosts may be interconnected through the same interface. Each SDLC interface may provide up to 16 ports, each of which supports a maximum of 32 stations. Additional interface slots may be added to the node as required.

The SNA/SDLC interface handles all SDLC procedures locally. The SDLC interface handles some procedures locally, and others between interfaces on either side of the

SNA and X.25

IBM support for X.25 is a welcome indicator that IBM backs the efforts of international standards-making organizations toward open systems interconnection. IBM supports X.25 with the X.25 Network Packet-Switching Interface (X.25 NPSI), a software product that runs under ACF/NCP in a 37X5 front-end processor, and with microcoded X.25 configuration support for 3270 cluster controllers.

The X.25 NPSI product allows 3270 terminals configured with X.25 support to share a public or private packet-switched network with devices supporting a wide range of non-SNA protocols. In addition, the X.25 NPSI Protocol Conversion Network Entry (PCNE) subsystem permits asynchronous TTY terminals to use IBM host subsystems to gain access to asynchronous host applications. PCNE does not provide ASCII-to-EBCDIC 3270 protocol conversion.

As a practical matter, however, IBM X.25 support is limited and carries a high cost/performance penalty. For one thing, X.25 microcoded support for 3270 control units requires approximately 72 kbytes of control storage. The ability to use X.25 support without sacrificing other SNA configuration support features is restricted to the newer 3270 terminal models. Configured with a hardware expansion unit, these control units have sufficient memory (320 kbytes) to support the interface without sacrificing features or degrading performance.

Microcoded X.25 support for older 3270 SNA models (31C and 51C) entails some sacrifice of capability. By increasing memory to 256 kbytes, the full complement of SNA features, including X.25, may be run. But no more than eight terminals may be supported in a cluster without seriously degrading response time. IBM provides X.25 support for these models without a memory expansion unit, in which case, only the basic keyboard functions are supported for up to eight terminals.

IBM does not support interconnection to X.25 NPSI for 3270-21C models, pre-SNA 3270 SDLC, or 3270 BSC equipment. An X.25 PAD/multiplexer must be obtained from a third party in order to connect these units to an X.25 network interface.

The limitations of IBM 3270 X.25 support cost users money for the following reasons:
- Hardware expansion units must be purchased.
- For the large installed base of older 3270 SNA/SDLC equipment, up to four times the number of 3270 control units may be required to support a native 3270 network.
- X.25 PAD/multiplexers must be acquired to support 3270 SNA/SDLC, SDLC, and BSC equipment for which IBM X.25 support is unavailable.

Performance will be also degraded by the large additional burden on the front-end processor. The degree of performance degradation is difficult to estimate since the performance level will vary, depending on a user's particular hardware/software configuration.

Although the X.25 NPSI interface supports switched virtual circuits, as a practical matter this capability can be used only by asynchronous terminals using the NPSI PCNE subsystem. Native 3270 equipment are bound by the SNA conventions which require that all sessions, local and cross-domain, be established through a single owner host supporting Multi-Network Systems Facility (MNSF).

Rather than attempting to force SNA to conform to a standard interface, such as X.25, another approach to the integration of SNA, BSC, and packet-switching networks is to make the network interface conform to IBM equipment protocols. There is then no need to modify or augment the SNA host, front-end, or 3270 configuration support software or degrade performance. This approach acknowledges the fact that SNA is a de facto standard which, at least in the United States, must be considered on a par with X.25.

---

circuit. No SDLC procedures are handled end-to-end, that is, between end-users. All procedures used to control interaction between a secondary and primary station — for example, polling and flow control, and unnumbered frames — are handled by the local SDLC interface. They are not passed through the network.

SDLC unnumbered SNRM (set normal response mode) frames and information frames are passed through the network and handled locally by the interfaces. Internal handling of these procedures allows any number of point-to-point secondary stations to share a multidrop host link. Remote control unit addresses are mapped one-to-one to addresses in the host interface. This capability may be used to reduce the 37X5 port count for point-to-point networks as was described for the SNA/SDLC service.

When the SDLC control field is formatted for information transfer, a PAD in the interface converts SDLC to the Qualified Logical Link Control (QLLC) protocol for transmission through the network. The QLLC protocol, serves as the data link control discipline which allows two SDLC interfaces to communicate.

The QLLC protocol serves a dual purpose: In addition to

linking network interfaces, it is compatible with IBM's X.25 Network Packet Switching Interface (X.25 NPSI). Those 3270 SDLC control units with insufficient memory to support IBM's microcoded X.25 support may access an X.25 NPSI host using an SDLC interface on the terminal side and an X.25 interface on the host side (Fig. 5). (See "SNA and X.25.")

The primary and secondary ports on a pair of packet nodes are connected with a permanent virtual circuit. An operations monitor is provided which, among other functions, allows a permanent virtual circuit to be redirected. This allows the SNA network to be reconfigured without changing the physical network.

Higher service

Here 3270 protocol conversion results from the interaction of a slot in a packet-switching node that acts as a 3270 translator, and an SNA/SDLC, BSC, or X.25 host interface. Asynchronous character and block-mode terminals are interconnected to the packet network through a standard asynchronous interface using dial-up (up to 2.4 kbit/s) or leased-line facilities (up to 9.6 kbit/s). Asynchronous ASCII

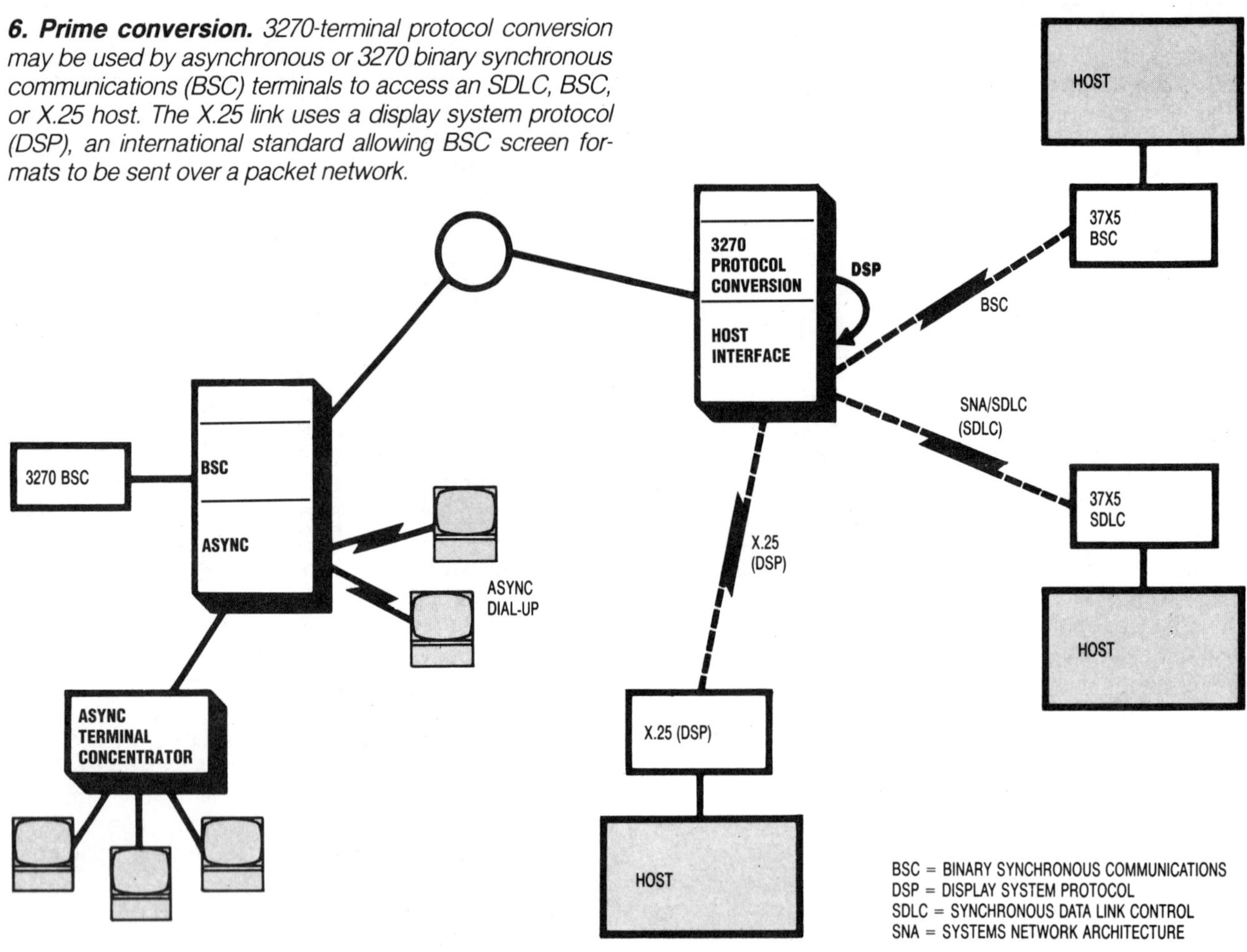

6. Prime conversion. *3270-terminal protocol conversion may be used by asynchronous or 3270 binary synchronous communications (BSC) terminals to access an SDLC, BSC, or X.25 host. The X.25 link uses a display system protocol (DSP), an international standard allowing BSC screen formats to be sent over a packet network.*

messages are transmitted to the translator using the intranetwork protocol.

All protocol conversion takes place at the host side of a circuit. Because the translator slot may reside in the same packet node as a number of other terminal and host interfaces, it can rightly be described as a service — a utility of the network that may be used as required. Unlike most protocol converter/cluster controllers, asynchronous terminals may alternate between native mode operation for communications with an asynchronous host, and 3270 mode operation for interaction with any of the major IBM host subsystems (for example, CICS, TSO, IMS, CMS).

Protocol conversion

The translator slot on the network interface converts ASCII to EBCDIC, and translates native screen handling codes to 3270 control characters. On the input side, character mode data is blocked for presentation to 3270 applications. The translator negotiates field attributes with a number of screen handlers on the output side. Most 3270 screen attributes are supported, subject to the inherent limitations of the asynchronous terminal.

Local screen copy and host-initiated printing is supported via a port attached printer or a printer connected through a separate circuit. The printer appears to the host as an IBM 3287 printer. Display System Protocol (DSP) is

used as the interface between the translator and an SNA/SDLC, BSC, or X.25 host interface slot (Fig. 6). DSP is a protocol for transmitting BSC through a packet network standardized through joint agreement of Transpac, Telenet, and Tymnet. The SNA/SDLC and BSC interfaces convert between DSP and SNA/SDLC or BSC for transmission over the host link. If the host is connected through an X.25 interface, the DSP format is retained for transmission to a front-end communications processor supporting DSP.

The use of DSP as an intermediate protocol between the translator and host interfaces provides a bonus for BSC networks. Native 3270 BSC terminals are connected to the network through an interface that converts BSC to DSP. Since host interfaces are designed to accept DSP-formatted data in conjunction with the 3270 translator, 3270 DSP formatted data originating at a 3270 BSC station may be converted to SNA/SDLC or X.25 format at the host interface without a special translator slot.

The BSC-to-SNA/SDLC translation is a valuable aid to organizations in the process of migrating from BSC to SNA networks. It may also be used to extend the life cycle of 3270 BSC equipment. ■

Lloyd Wanveer, systems planner at Tymnet Inc., received her B. A. from Washington University in St. Louis. Patrick Driscoll is Tymnet's manager for network interface development in Cupertino.

Donald H. Czubek, Communications Solutions Inc., San Jose, Calif.

Understanding IBM's electronic mail architectures

DIA and SNADS both perform application-level electronic mail functions. This guide for the perplexed differentiates between the two methodologies.

IBM markets a wide range of office automation products capable of supporting electronic mail users. These products are implemented on three different levels (Fig. 1). On the mainframe is the software cornerstone of IBM's office strategy, the Distributed Office Support System (DISOSS). At the departmental processor level are the Personal Services products for System/36 and System/38, as well as the older 5520 Administrative System and the 8100's DOSF (Distributed Office Support Facility) software. At the single-user workstation level are the Personal Services/PC package for the IBM PC, the 6580 Displaywriter, and the 8815 Scanmaster.

In an effort to ensure that all of its office electronic mail products are compatible, IBM has defined standard architectures at both the data transport and application levels. The structured data transport protocols are delineated by Systems Network Architecture (SNA). Most of IBM's office products support SNA's new Advanced Program-to-Program Communications, but some use the older Logical Unit Type 2 support defined for 3270s and asynchronous ASCII communications.

At the applications level, all IBM office products support Document Interchange Architecture (DIA) or SNA Distribution Services (SNADS), or both. There is considerable confusion about why two different application-level architectures are used to perform a single function and about which network components use SNADS and which use DIA. This article will attempt to show how these architectures work together to perform electronic mail functions.

The role of Document Interchange Architecture

The IBM office network is made up of products that are either requesters or providers of services. These services include document distribution (electronic mail), document libraries, application processing, and file transfers. Some products, particularly departmental processors, are hybrid devices that act as both requesters and servers. The requesters act on behalf of network users to request such services as electronic mail. The requested functions are performed by the service providers (see table).

DIA defines the interaction between a user of an office network and the components of the network that actually supply the network services. In DIA terms, the user makes requests for office services such as electronic mail and library access through a workstation called a Source/Recipient Node (SRN).

The components of a DIA network that actually perform the requested office functions are called Office System Nodes (OSNs). The most important example of an OSN is IBM's mainframe-based DISOSS package. Departmental processors, such as System/36, System/38, 5520, and 8100, have OSN capability either available or announced by IBM. The role of DIA is to standardize the way SRNs interact with OSNs to request office services.

While Figure 1 shows the architecture of document distribution, Figure 2 provides a simple example of document distribution showing the actual products in an office network. User A wants to distribute a document from a Displaywriter to User B, who is also a Displaywriter user. Both Displaywriters are connected to the same DISOSS.

User A will first initiate a DIA SIGN-ON REQUEST, which will cause a DIA session, or logical connection, to be established between the Displaywriter (a DIA SRN) and DISOSS (a DIA OSN). Note that the DIA session is just between User A's Displaywriter and DISOSS, and is not an end-to-end connection between the two Displaywriters.

At this point, User A has made a request for distribution, and the document to be distributed resides in DISOSS. DISOSS will respond to the request for distribution by putting the document into an output queue that is associated with User B.

User B will issue a DIA SIGN-ON REQUEST to begin a

1. Office architectures. *Architectural relationships of IBM electronic mail products, including mainframes, minicomputers, and microcomputers, are shown.*

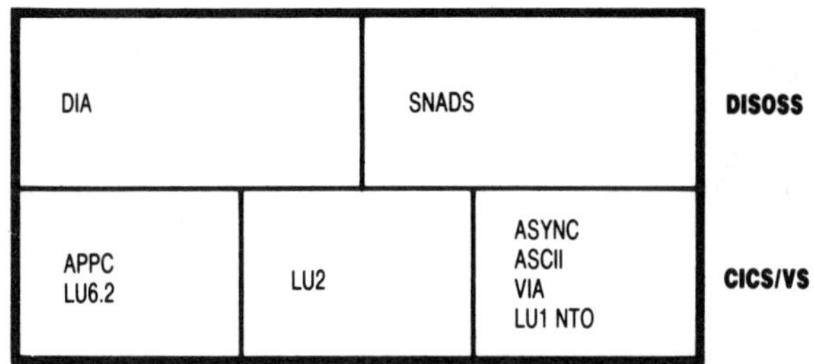

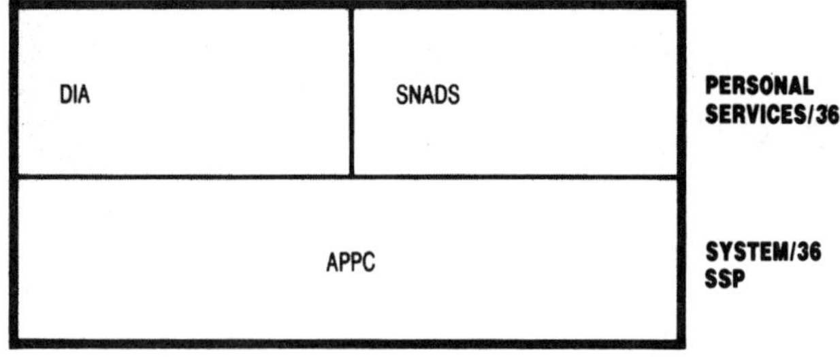

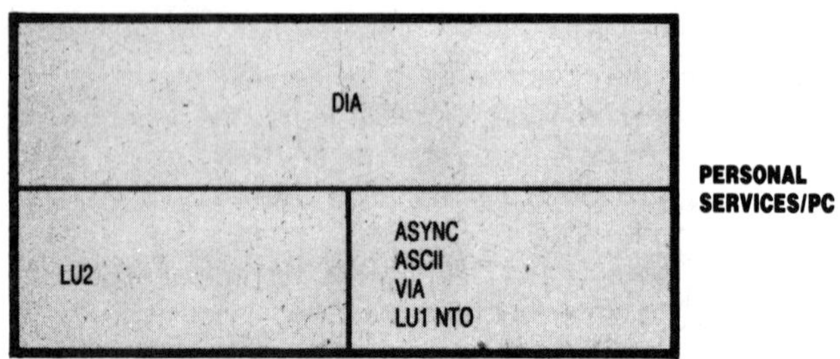

APPC = ADVANCED PROGRAM-TO-PROGRAM COMMUNICATIONS
CICS/VS = CUSTOMER INFORMATION CONTROL SYSTEM/VIRTUAL STORAGE
DIA = DOCUMENT INTERCHANGE ARCHITECTURE
DISOSS = DISTRIBUTED OFFICE SUPPORT SYSTEM
LU = LOGICAL UNIT
NTO = NETWORK TERMINAL OPTION
SNADS = SYSTEM NETWORK ARCHITECTURE DISTRIBUTION SERVICES
SSP = SYSTEM SUPPORT PROGRAM

2. Office network. *When only one Office System Node is used, DIA is used to handle document transactions. When two or more are involved, SNADS must come into play.*

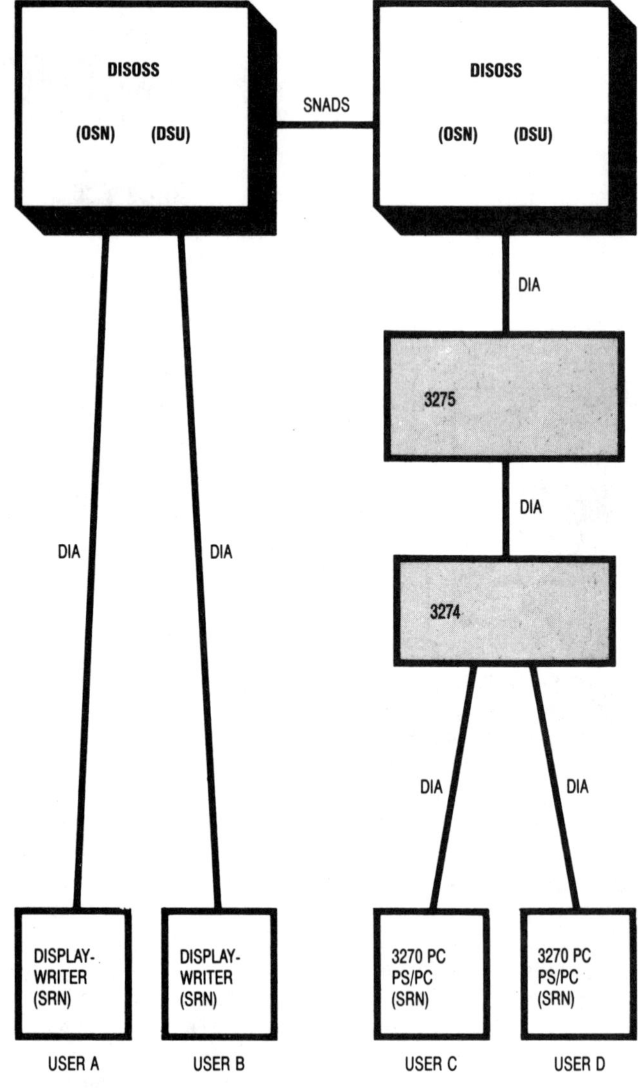

DIA = DOCUMENT INTERCHANGE ARCHITECTURE
DISOSS = DISTRIBUTED OFFICE SUPPORT SYSTEM
DSU = DISTRIBUTION SERVICE UNITS
OSN = OFFICE SYSTEM NODES
PS/PC = PERSONAL SERVICES/PERSONAL COMPUTER
SNADS = SYSTEM NETWORK ARCHITECTURE DISTRIBUTION SERVICES
SRN = SOURCE/RECIPIENT NODE

DIA session with DISOSS. User B can request a list of documents in the DISOSS output queue, which is, in effect, B's mail box. User B can then retrieve the document that was previously distributed by User A.

DIA, by itself, is capable only of performing document distributions that involve only a single OSN and the SRNs directly attached to it. To perform document distributions in more complex office networks with more than one OSN, SNADS must also be used.

SNADS provides generalized delayed delivery. It defines a store-and-forward network made up of components called Distribution Service Units (DSUs). As the data to be delivered moves through the SNADS network, it may be

Requests and products

REQUESTORS	REQUESTOR/SERVERS	SERVERS
PERSONAL SERVICES/PC	PERSONAL SERVICES/36	DISOSS
DISPLAYWRITER	PERSONAL SERVICES/38	
SCANMASTER	5520	
DISOSS = DISTRIBUTED OFFICE SUPPORT SYSTEM		

Glossary of terms

APPC Advanced Program-to-Program Communications. A subset of SNA (Systems Network Architecture) functions and protocols used specifically to allow programs on one site to communicate with programs at another using LU 6.2. APPC is designed to make SNA more usable in a distributed application.

Conversation Verb Interface (CIV) IBM's structured application program interface for distributed LU 6.2 application programs.

DIA Document Interchange Architecture. An application-level architecture that defines protocols and data structures for the consistent exchange of documents and files amoung distributed office applications, such as DISOSS and Personal Services products. DIA supports such functions as distribution, application services, and document library.

DISOSS Distributed Office Support System. An application subsystem that provides a variety of office automation functions, including document distribution services and library services. Allows users to send, receive, distribute, and file documents. Utilizes various IBM protocols, such as DIA and SNADS.

DIU Document Interchange Unit. The data structures used to carry out operatons in SNADS and DIA networks.

DOSF Distributed Office Support Facility. DOSF manages text and data used on IBM 8100 equipment.

DSL Distribution Service Level. Used to select a route in a SNADS network based on priority, capacity, and safe delivery of messages.

DSU Distribution Service Unit. The components of a SNADS network that are responsible for data delivery, routing, and queuing.

EDD Electronic Document Distribution. EDD is a set of software services for the Displaywriter allowing documents to be filed and distributed to other Displaywriters and hosts running DISOSS.

LU 6.2 Logical Unit 6.2. Part of IBM's Advanced Program-to-Program Communications that provides a standard communications protocol for distributed application programs.

OSU Office System Node. The OSN performs document distribution, library services, application services, and file transfers on behalf of network users.

Personal Services A series of IBM software products (PS/PC, PS/36, and PS/370) that run on the PC, System/36, and 370-type mainframes, respectively, and provide a connection to DISOSS. The Personal Services products allow users to request distribution and library services.

SNADS SNA Distribution Services. An application-level architecture that provides asynchronous (delayed delivery) distribution of documents and files between users. SNADS implements a store-and-forward mechanism that allows information to be stored until the path to the receiver is available.

SRN Source/Recipient Node. The SRN requests through DIA that the OSN perform certain functions on behalf of network users. These functions include document distribution, library services, application services, and file transfers.

queued indefinitely in intermediate DSUs. It is important to remember that SNADS is separate from DIA and is a broadly applicable architecture not limited to document delivery functions.

The role of SNA Distribution Services

The delayed delivery capability of SNADS means users do not need a complete end-to-end connection across a SNADS network before they can begin to send data. Each of the nodes that makes up a SNADS network contains queues that can hold data indefinitely. DSUs are the SNADS network nodes, and as data moves through the SNADS network it is forwarded from one DSU to the next. If a communications path between two DSUs is not currently active or available, the sending DSU will queue the data until the communications path becomes available. The data may be queued several times for indefinite periods as it moves through a SNADS network. This is why SNADS is said to provide delayed delivery.

Looking at Figure 2 from the SNADS point of view, the DISOSS units in our sample network are SNADS DSUs, while the Displaywriters are simply users of the SNADS network. The Displaywriters and their users are beyond the scope of the SNADS networks; they are simply the sources and destinations of documents being distributed.

SNADS comes into play when document distributions are performed across multiple DIA OSNs that are also SNADS DSUs. This is the case when we distribute a document from User A to User C in Figure 2. The distribution operation starts the same way as in the first example — User A initiates a DIA session with the adjacent DISOSS setup and used DIA protocols to request that DISOSS perform the distribution. The document to be distributed now resides in a DISOSS queue and User A ends the DIA session. Note that DIA is still used to request that the distribution be initiated.

When DISOSS begins the process of distributing the document, it finds that the intended recipient is on the other DISOSS. The document must first be sent to the other DISOSS before User C can gain access to it. SNADS is used to send documents between DISOSS units.

If the communications facilities connecting the two

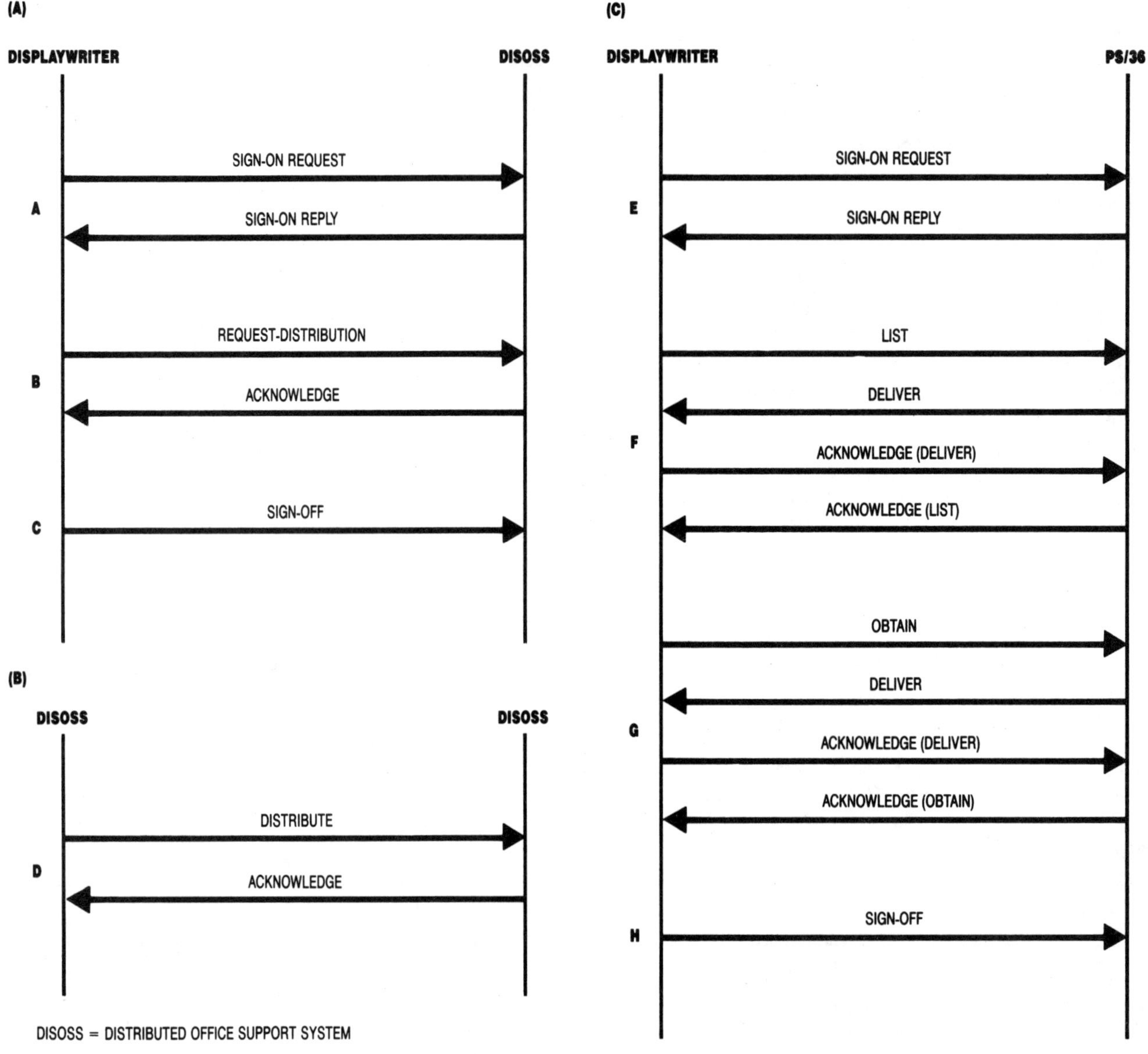

3. SNADS point of view. *The same office network that appears in Figure 2, expanded to show how SNADS operates with DIA. (A) and (B) show the sign-on and sign-off mechanisms operating in DISOSS; (C) shows the operating structures in Personal Services. Receiving and sending Distribution Service Units orchestrate the process.*

DISOSS facilities are not available, the DISOSS on the right will queue the document for transmission and it will be sent whenever a communications path becomes available. The document may remain queued for milliseconds or days. If there were multiple DISOSS DSUs between the sender of the document and the recipient, delays could be introduced at each intermediate DSU.

In Figure 2, DISOSS is an implementation of the SNADS architecture. SNADS is already widely implemented, not only in DISOSS, but in IBM's departmental processors, including System/36, System/38, 5520 Administrative System, and 8100 Information System. All of these products have, or will have, SNADS support.

Let's look at how all these technologies work together. User A at the Displaywriter on the left will be sending a document to User D, who is using an IBM Personal Computer running the Personal Services/PC software. This distribution operation will involve the use of SNA's LU 6.2 (Advanced Program-to-Program Communications, or APPC) and LU 2 at the data transport level, and DIA and SNADS at the application level.

A typical electronic mail operation

DIA initiates the distribution. The first protocol exchange is between User A's Displaywriter and its adjacent DISOSS. The purpose of this interchange is to request initiation of distribution to User D. The Displaywriter, since it is a Source/Recipient, can request that distribution be initiated, but *it* is performed by the OSN, DISOSS.

The data transport protocol used by the Displaywriter's Electronic Document Distribution (EDD) software is LU 6.2. Each of the DIA protocol exchanges between the Display-

4. APPC/DIA Interaction. *APPC, SNADS, and DIA work together to implement an electronic mail network. Both DIA and SNADS use APPC as the transport mechanism.*

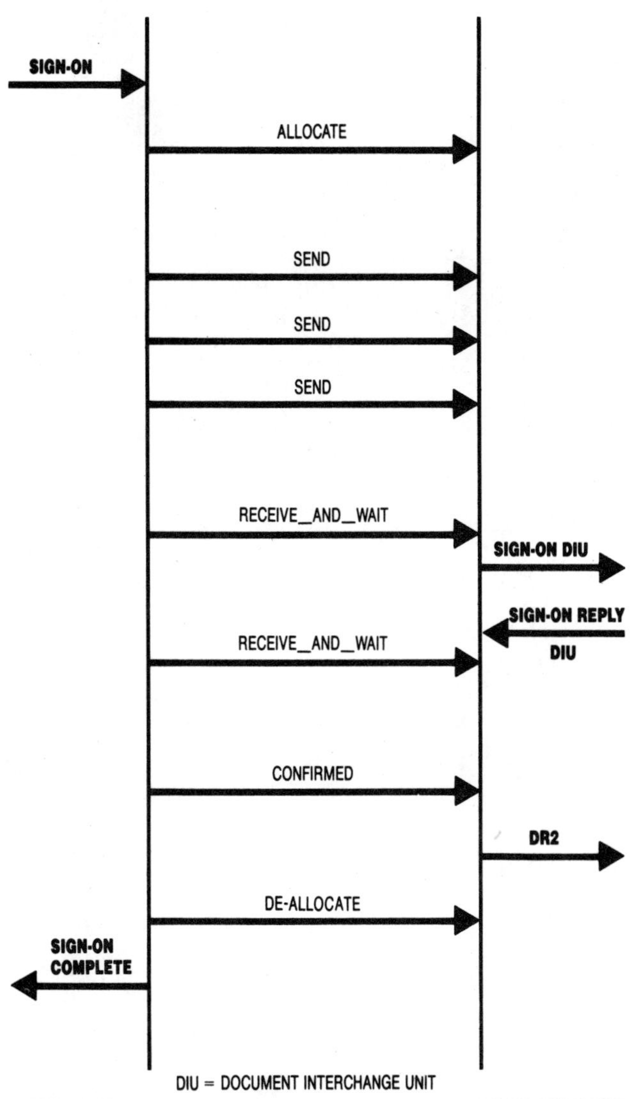

writer and DISOSS will be carried on a separate LU 6.2 conversation. LU 6.2 uses conversations to manage and control access to SNA sessions.

First, a logical connection must be established between User A and DISOSS. This connection, called a DIA session, is initiated by a DIA SIGN-ON REQUEST (Fig. 3). The SIGN-ON REQUEST contains the user's I. D. and password as well as a list of the DIA function sets to be used on the DIA session. The SIGN-ON REPLY indicates whether the sign-on operation was successfully completed or an error condition occurred. The document distribution operation is initiated by a REQUEST-DISTRIBUTION command. This DIA command carries the list of recipients as well as indicators that request confirmation of delivery and priority. The REQUEST-DISTRIBUTION command also carries the document to be distributed. The ACKNOWLEDGE command indicates whether the distribution operation was successfully initiated. It is important to understand that this is not an acknowledgment of delivery, but that the distribution was initiated by DISOSS. Confirmation of delivery will, optionally, occur later, when the document is actually received by the recipient. The DIA session is terminated by a SIGN-OFF.

At this point the document distribution process, requested by the Displaywriter, is ready to begin. The request for distribution was made using DIA protocols; the distribution process itself will involve the use of SNADS. DISOSS and SNADS actually perform the distribution.

The actual document distribution process now begins in DISOSS. DISOSS checks the destination address to see whether the recipient is local (attached to the same DISOSS equipment) or remote (attached to another DISOSS node or some other OSN/DSU). If the distribution is local, the document is simply put into the output queue that is associated with the local user.

If the recipient is attached to another OSN/DSU, SNADS will be used to deliver the document to the target OSN. To determine the target OSN/DSU, DISOSS performs the SNADS directing function, determining the destination DSU name, based on a user I. D. In our example, the destination DSU will be DISOSS User B. After the directing function is completed, the DSU will perform the SNADS routing function. This involves looking up the destination DSU name in a routing table to find the path to the destination. Multiple routes may be defined between DSUs. The most appropriate route is determined by matching the requested Distribution Service Level (DSL). The DSL specifies the priority, level of data protection, and the required queuing capacity of intermediate DSUs.

In Figure 3, DISOSS uses the SNADS DISTRIBUTE command to send the document to its destination DSU. In this example, the document is sent directly to the destination DSU. The DISTRIBUTE command may, in some networks, travel through several intermediate nodes before arriving at the destination DSU. The DISTRIBUTE command is used to move the document through these intermediate store-and-forward nodes. When the document is successfully delivered to a DSU, it replies to the sending DSU with an ACKNOWLEDGE command.

In solicited delivery of mail, the document will remain in the destination DSU until the user solicits delivery to the workstation. The remainder of this example shows how a user at a DIA SRN can check the output queue (mailbox) and retrieve selected documents from the OSN/DSU.

In Figure 3, User B must first logically connect with the adjacent DISOSS. This is again accomplished by sending the DIA SIGN-ON command and waiting for its reply. Next the user will check the contents of the output queue in the adjacent OSN. This is the user's mailbox. The DIA LIST command solicits a list of documents that have arrived for this user. This list is built by the OSN/DSU and sent to the user's SRN in a DELIVER command. Receipt of the list is acknowledged by the SRN; then the OSN/DSU acknowledges completion of the entire LIST operation. The user uses this list to select mail to be retrieved from the OSN/DSU.

The documents the user wants to read are retrieved by sending an OBTAIN command from PS/PC to DISOSS. The document is sent to the SRN in a DELIVER command. Receipt of the document is acknowledged by the SRN, then the OSN/DSU acknowledges completion of the entire obtain operation. Multiple documents can be retrieved in a

APPC, DIA, and SNADS

Most of IBM's mainstream office products use Systems Network Architecture's (SNA's) Advanced Program-to-Program Communications (APPC) to support DIA and SNADS operations. APPC is the underlying communications protocol used by DISOSS, System/36-Personal Services/36, System/38-Personal Services/38, Displaywriter, Scanmaster, 5520 Administrative System, and 8100.

When a DIA SRN that supports APPC signs on to its adjacent OSN, the DIA command processor uses the APPC Conversational Verb Interface. The application software in the SRN creates a SIGN-ON Document Interchange Unit (DIU) and issues an APPC ALLOCATE verb which will allocate an LU 6.2 conversation on an existing SNA session. The ALLOCATE verb also carries the name of the transaction software program to be started by the remote logical unit. This transaction software program will be run inside the mainframe Customer Information Control System (CICS) program that DISOSS will use to parse and execute the SIGN-ON command that follows.

The transaction program name is carried in a Type 5 Function Management Header, a data structure sent to initiate a remote program. This header is built by the logical unit and placed in the LU 6.2 output buffer. Note that it is not actually sent until either the output buffer is full or a verb is issued that forces transmission of the output buffer.

The SIGN-ON DIU itself is written by issuing one or more APPC SEND verbs. Again, the data is not actually transmitted until either the output buffer is full or a verb that forces transmission is issued. After the SIGN-ON DIU is written to DISOSS, receipt of a SIGN-ON reply is anticipated, so an APPC RECEIVE-AND-WAIT verb is issued.

The reply is read by issuing an appropriate number of RECEIVE-AND-WAIT verbs. The last RECEIVE-AND-WAIT verb will also receive an indicator that requests an APPC confirmation. The CONFIRMED verb satisfies this request by sending an SNA DR2, a definite response indicator, which serves as an acknowledgment to DISOSS. The APPC conversation is then de-allocated, and the DISOSS sign-on operation is complete for the network user.

single operation. Each document is sent in a separate DELIVER command. The DIA session is then terminated by a SIGN-OFF command from the SRN (Fig. 4).

It is expected that most vendors who compete with IBM in the workstation marketplace will provide similar support within two years. Two vendors, Digital Equipment Corp. and Data General, are already supplying Source/Recipient Node capability through their implementations of APPC and DIA. Wang and Honeywell have also announced products supporting these architectures. ■

Donald H. Czubek is a founder and vice president of Communications Solutions Inc. Czubek has 15 years of data communications product design experience, most recently with Four-Phase Systems.

David G. Matusow, Computer Task Group Inc., Phoenix, Ariz.

BTAM, VTAM, X.25: Uneasy alliance

Linking different machines over an X.25 network requires patience and hard work. And though problems may never disappear completely, the results can be worth the hassles.

Be careful in interconnecting machines with different access methods, whether from the same or different vendors. A lot can go wrong. In particular, it is important to be knowledgeable about both environments. Even so, however, linking such machines, especially with a sophisticated network protocol, can be an arduous process.

One recent example of such a struggle occurred when a worldwide financial services company (call it "company A") had to draw on data owned by a Compuserve-like information provider ("company B"). The need to access the data regularly and readily pointed to a direct connection between the company's respective mainframes. However, although both utilized IBM mainframes, operating systems, and access methods, the connection was anything but straightforward.

Company A's host ran Systems Network Architecture (SNA) under the Virtual Telecommunications Access Method (VTAM), while company B's host used the Basic Telecommunications Access Method (BTAM), which is an older, non-SNA environment (Fig. 1). Since both of these machines already had X.25 interfaces to a public packet network for various other purposes, it was decided that the links (the existing leased lines from both company A and company B to the packet network) could be used to save both time and money in creating a new way of joining the two companies.

The X.25 link from A's host was IBM's NCP Packet Switching Interface (NPSI) running under the Network Control Program (NCP). It would be used to dial out to company B's host, which ran X.25 software from Comm-Pro Associates Inc. in Redondo Beach, Calif.

IBM has had little experience doing dial-out from NPSI. Thus, the support and documentation it provided were far from optimal. In fact, very little hands-on experience with such environments was to be found anywhere. This was compounded by the fact that NCP Packet Switching Interface is not widely used and has many operating problems.

Even after these problems were resolved, however, the connection was not totally stable, nor is it to this day. For example, if the host processor is loaded more heavily than usual, thereby causing a change in the operating speed of the teleprocessing monitor, the connection does not always work. Almost all of the problems occur during the initial handshaking that is required to start the connection. Once the connection gets beyond this point, problems usually disappear.

Plan ahead

Early investigation showed that data could be passed from SNA to non-SNA environments using one of the following three methods:

■ *Full SNA emulation.* Emulations of full SNA subarea nodes were the most flexible but also the most complex and hard to implement of the methods. Few off-the-shelf products were available.

■ *Passthrough applications.* These programs, software emulations of cluster controllers, were simpler and more readily available. Each half of the software communicated with one environment, such as ASCII and 3270. However, only single sessions or groups of sessions could be set up between machines. Increasing throughput between the machines would require meshing data from multiple sessions. The delicate balance between the two halves of the implementation would become increasingly difficult to support.

■ *Hardware emulations.* Protocol converters are effective for low-speed (less than 9.6-kbit/s) data transfer and simple interactive traffic but offer limited speed and throughput for heavy traffic between computers.

An easier solution to the requirements for both data

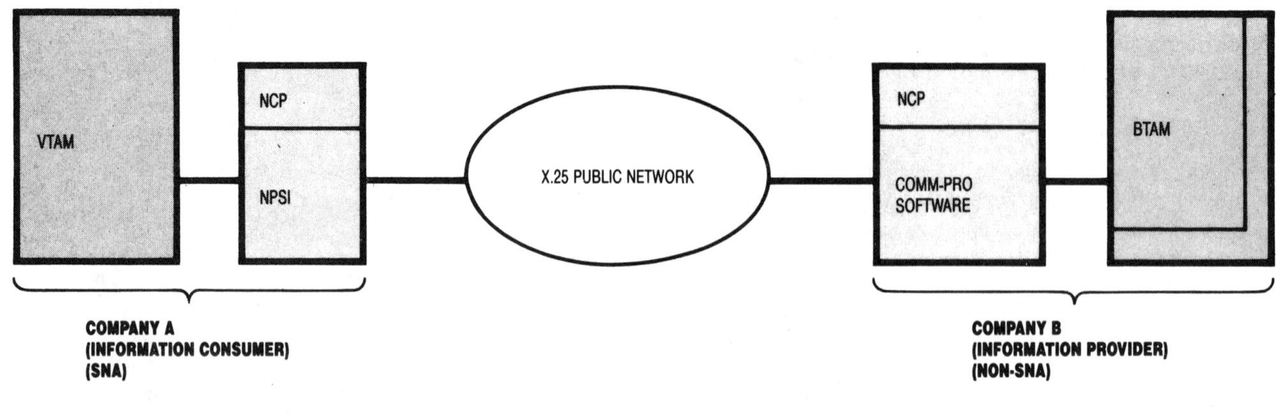

transfer and interactive traffic was needed. The answer was sought in the X.25 communications standard. It was felt that an X.25-based solution could avoid many low-level "bits-and-bytes" implementation details.

As with all intercomputer connections, even between machines in a single company, a great deal of detailed preplanning was necessary. The companies held many discussions to ensure that link- and packet-level parameters, such as packet-size and logical-channel numbers, were consistent between the parties. Even such careful planning might not have covered every parameter that could have caused a glitch, though luckily no problems were encountered at this stage.

In configuring the X.25 parameters for the connection, each company was constrained in some way by the software components it used. For example, company B's range of logical channel numbers was limited by the Comm-Pro software. Only a certain packet size offered by the network vendor could be used. Moreover, the equipment owned by each company used a different character code. The ASCII data favored by B's environment had to be translated into EBCDIC (Extended Binary Coded Decimal Interchange Code) for company A's SNA gear.

It was decided that the link would utilize switched virtual circuits (SVCs). This method of connection allows the creation of multiple, nonpermanent, virtual point-to-point links from fewer permanent physical circuits. Using SVCs allows multiple logical sessions to be multiplexed between the two endpoints, which reduces connection cost.

Life's hard for NPSI

Company A's NPSI software, residing in the 37X5 front-end processor, performs protocol conversion between SNA and the X.25 network. This conversion consists of two basic parts:
- NPSI takes outbound messages, strips off the SNA headers, packetizes the remaining (raw) data, adds X.25 headers, and sends the packets into the X.25 network. The opposite is done for arriving data.

- The software also simulates an SNA device for the host-based SNA software products. This includes implementing such SNA logical unit (LU) functions as session setup and problem notification.

The most difficult task facing NPSI is to keep each network pleased with the requests and responses it provides. For example, it must satisfy pacing requirements on both the SNA and X.25 sides. With X.25, the software must keep track of the number of outstanding packets, both on the link as a whole and on each virtual circuit.

The physical link is paced to a maximum of seven unacknowledged packets. Upon reaching this threshold, acknowledgment must be made before any more packets can be passed. In addition, two outstanding packets are permitted on each SVC. The need to satisfy both the physical and virtual links results in a very complex acknowledgment scheme.

On the SNA side, NPSI is simpler, but also more constrained. It appears to the host as an unsophisticated 3767 SNA printer, a physical unit (PU) type-1 device. PU 1 is the simplest physical-unit type in SNA, supporting few of the higher SNA enhancements. One of its limitations is that it allows only single request units (RUs) to be sent and received. (By contrast, a device of PU and LU types 2 can handle multiple outstanding RUs.) Thus, NPSI cannot keep track of the sequence numbers used to count outstanding packets. This restriction reduces the throughput of the session by requiring constant acknowledgments.

A buggy ride

With very few companies running NPSI, the amount of support from IBM for both procedural questions and technical difficulties varies from little to nonexistent. As a result, there are several bugs in the software. Some of these are easy to find and resolve, while others can be quite elusive. One major difficulty involved a departure of the "call out" methodology from the documented procedures.

One of the most troublesome tasks was to call out from

2. Startup. *One task calling another allows company A to establish a call request, via a logically defined terminal (A), through a packet network (B). Events that follow the generation of the requested task include a link to the access method, from there to the front-end processor, and then an X.25 call-request sequence.*

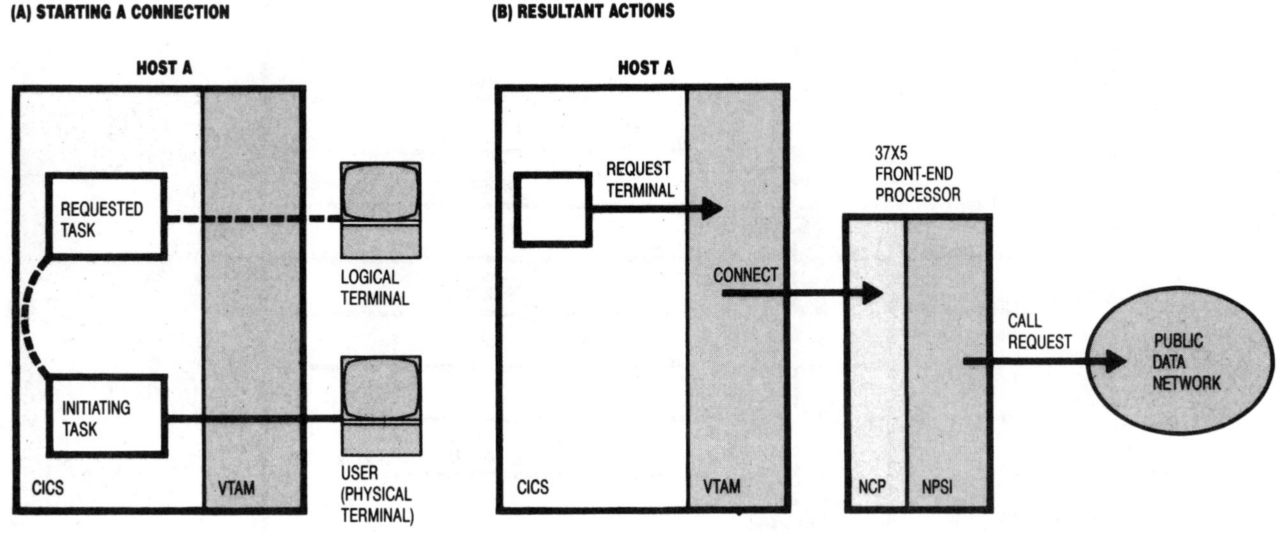

NPSI through the packet network to company B. Trying to implement this function led to many confusing problems that still defy resolution. A problem in the parameter definitions between NPSI/NCP and VTAM meant that the session would not complete, even when the documentation was followed explicitly.

The parameters in question were the DIALNUM parameter in the VTAM switch major node (VBUILD = TYPESWNET) and certain parameters in the NPSI generation. The NPSI manual was extremely confusing, making conflicting statements in different places. Here, it stated that the two numbers should be the same. There, it stated that VTAM would respond to NPSI by taking the IDNUM from NPSI and subtracting one from it.

By experimentation, it was discovered that VTAM did subtract the incoming IDNUM by one. However, the IDNUM had to be specified properly in the NPSI generation. The solution was to specify what was actually an improper IDNUM in the VTAM definition. Circumventing this problem was an exercise in illogic that allowed the session to be set up and completed.

Later, a method was found of specifying the same number in the NPSI generation and in VTAM. Though this took care of the original problem, it created another one: Half the SVCs that NPSI generated could not be used because the IDNUM would result in a hexidecimal number, something that NPSI would not tolerate.

The network connection between the two computers was

3. Trouble. *After a successful X.25 connection, company B's software sent two problematic messages, a log-on request and a command that should have stayed internal to company B's gear (the WRITE INITIAL command, meant for supporting terminals, was supposed to be intercepted by B's front-end processor).*

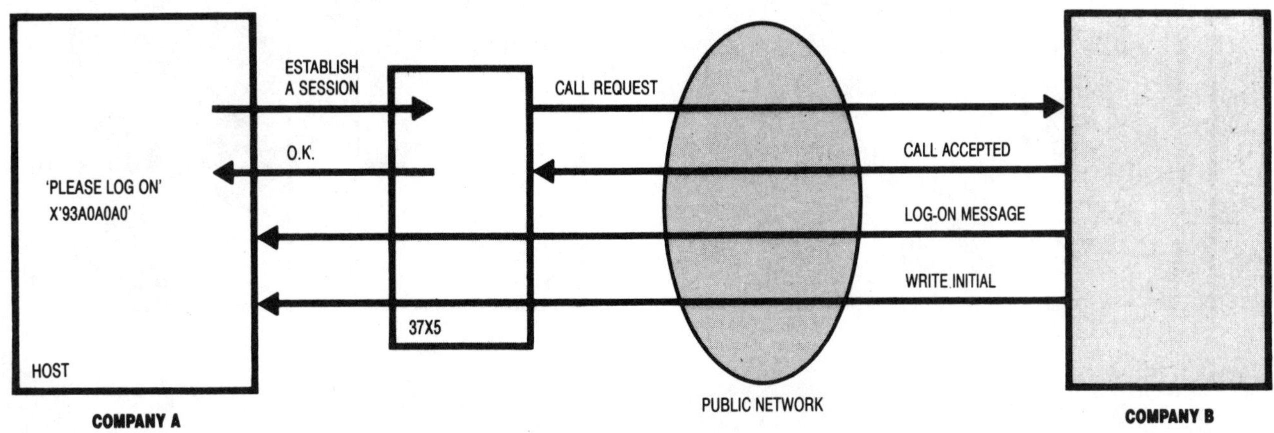

4. Mixup. *The hosts think of each other as terminals, so Host A believes Host B's message includes a log-on destination, but it does not. What's worse, A can't figure out B's ASCII message. And all of this is happening while A's software is trying to set up an internal session. This problem was resolved by keeping A quiet for a while.*

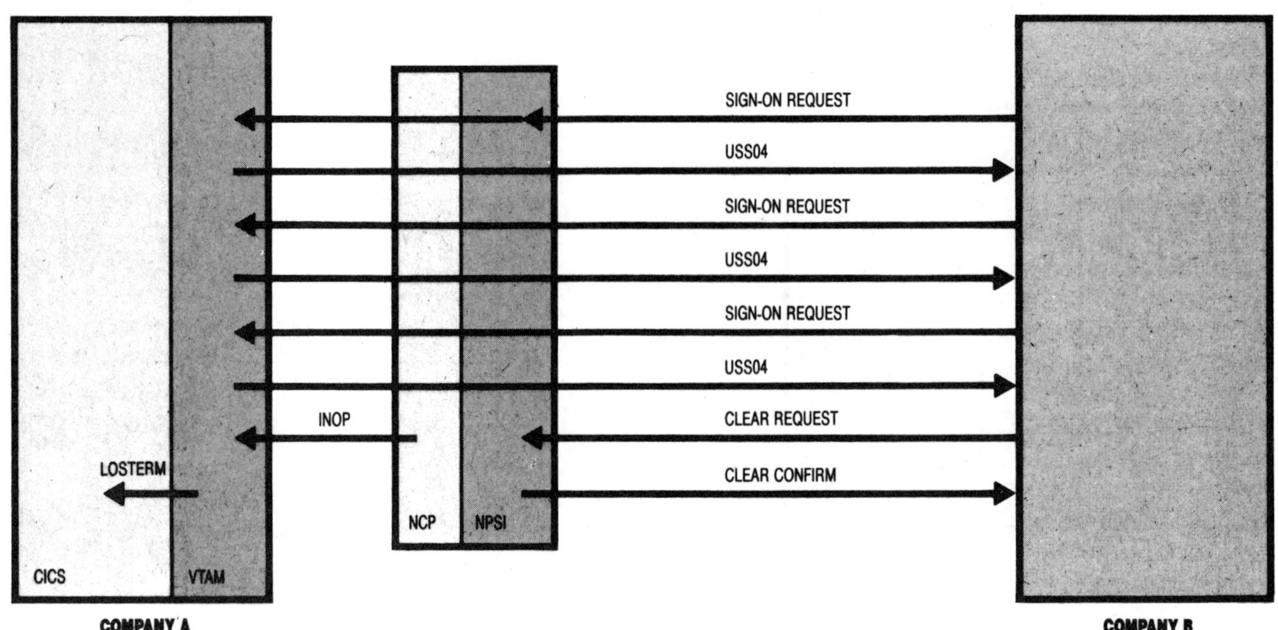

CICS = CUSTOMER INFORMATION CONTROL SYSTEM
INOP = INOPERABLE (MEANS B HAS DISCONNECTED)
LOSTERM = LOST TERMINAL
NCP = NETWORK CONTROL PROGRAM

NPSI = NCP PACKET-SWITCHING INTERFACE
USS = UNFORMATTED SYSTEM SERVICES
VTAM = VIRTUAL TELECOMMUNICATIONS ACCESS METHOD

5. Bottom line. *If the hex message arrived when the application was ready, the connection could be made (A). Otherwise, the session ended in error (B). Even after all the network and access-method problems were solved, this millisecond timing problem remains, causing failure on about 1 percent of log-on attempts.*

(A) CODE ARRIVES AFTER APPLICATION ATTACHED

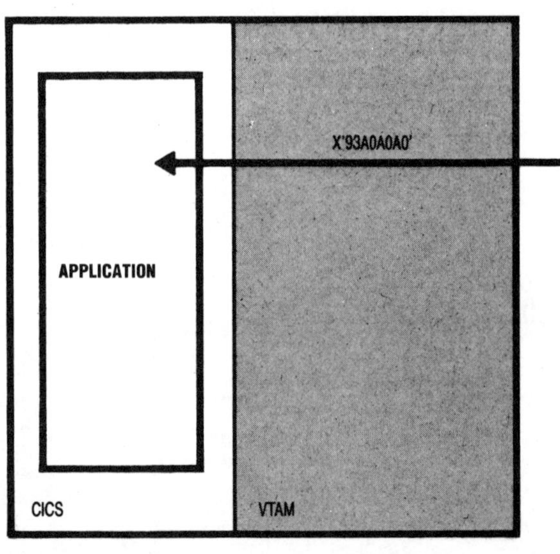

(B) CODE ARRIVES BEFORE APPLICATION ATTACHED

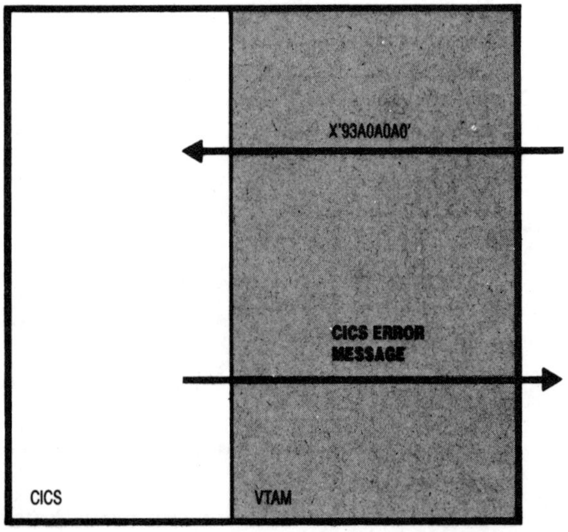

CICS = CUSTOMER INFORMATION CONTROL SYSTEM
VTAM = VIRTUAL TELECOMMUNICATIONS ACCESS METHOD
X'93A0A0A0' = THE ODD-PARITY ASCII EQUIVALENT OF WRITE INITIAL

complete at last. Unfortunately, the difficulties thus far encountered were only the first of a tortuous set of problems caused by the time-independent or unsynchronized operation of the large software components. Two such major headaches arose: one in establishing an SNA session between VTAM and NPSI, and another caused by an errant message packet sent from company B to company A.

■ Session setup. The first major synchronization problem, getting a connection through VTAM, was due to the fact that data activity on the X.25 link (which provides the logical connection between A and B) is not synchronized with the session setup between VTAM and NPSI, although the SNA session relies on the intermainframe link.

The configuration involved an X.25 call initiated from company A to company B. To accomplish this, the following sequence was to be carried out:

■ A Customer Information Control System (CICS) task requested the attachment of another, new task to one of a set of terminals logically defined for connecting to company B (Fig. 2A).

■ CICS recognized that it does not have an active session with the requested terminal and asked VTAM to make the connection.

■ VTAM, in turn, asked NPSI to send an X.25 CALL REQUEST command, which included the address of the destination computer, to the public network (Fig. 2B).

■ Company B responded with a CALL ACCEPTED packet (Fig. 3) and the X.25 switched virtual circuit was completed.

■ At this point, any data that the 37X5 receives from company B is held until NPSI responds ("O.K.") to VTAM's initial request for session establishment.

■ Once the SVC is active to VTAM, the buffered data continues through to CICS. VTAM normally expects this data to be log-on data.

Unfortunately, this is not the way it happened.

Company B's host was sending out a log-on request message as it normally would to terminals. It then expected log-on data to be sent back. Also, BTAM is idiosyncratic in that it must issue and process a WRITE INITIAL command to turn the line around before it can read incoming data. This command is supposed to be handled by B's NCP and not go any farther, but instead it was packetized and sent to company A. Thus, as Figure 3 shows, company A received an X.25 packet containing company B's log-on request and a second packet immediately thereafter containing the hexidecimal code X'93A0A0A0' (the odd-parity ASCII equivalent of WRITE INITIAL).

The first packet (the log-on request) was sent into VTAM. VTAM, expecting this data to be an SNA log-on request, tried to find the specified destination. However, VTAM had trouble with the incoming ASCII data. When it searched its tables to find the specified destination, VTAM was not able to match the input request. VTAM would then send back a message ("USS04") that the destination was unknown (Fig. 4). This would happen three times in a row, since B was set up to request a log-on three times. There was no synchronization between these exchanges and the rest of the session setup to CICS.

At the same time, company B would receive the response, a CICS message, from VTAM. Company B's computer was expecting a response to the log-on request of a user I.D. and password. Since this did not occur, company B's computer would break the session.

Many attempts were made to circumvent this sequence. The first effort was trying to get VTAM to set up the session more quickly. If it could be done before the three messages went out through VTAM, the messages could be isolated in CICS. This was unsuccessful.

However, a solution was finally found: to eliminate the error message VTAM was issuing. This was done by specifying in the unformatted system services (USS) table that no error message be issued. Since VTAM would not signal that it did not accept the data coming in, company B's host had no knowledge of a problem. This allowed enough time for the session to CICS to be completed.

■ *Hex message.* Now the CICS session was in place, but the second major synchronization problem appeared in trying to support the X'93A0A0A0' message, which CICS did not know how to interpret. It was at this point that very difficult timing problems started appearing. These problems, caused by related events occurring at unpredictable times with respect to each other, were highly sensitive to loading conditions of the processors, which affected timing. For example, sometimes CICS would receive the hexidecimal X'93A0A0A0' after the transaction program was attached to the terminal (Fig. 5A). In this case, the application program would request a log-on I.D. and password and the connection would proceed as planned.

At other times, however, CICS would receive the hexadecimal message before the application was attached (Fig. 5B). CICS, in this instance, would think the data included a transaction code in the first four bytes (CICS's default location for the transaction code). When this happened, CICS would transmit an error message, which company B's host would misinterpret as a command meaning "disconnect." To handle these cases, a dummy program (a sort of "null subroutine") was written and associated with a new CICS transaction code of X'93A0A0A0'. The dummy program would simply discard the hexidecimal message and return control back to CICS.

There was one other problem at an even higher level. Since the access method runs in a way uncoordinated with the application processes, the applications would have to interrogate the condition of the CICS application program interface (API) to know whether it should be receiving data from the line or was free to send data. However, between checking the API and actually issuing the appropriate command, the interface condition would sometimes change. This brought on a form of deadlock when the application would try to send but VTAM would not allow it to because new data had arrived on the line for processing.

To work around the uncertainty in the API, the application had to be modified to carefully interrogate some of the operating information kept by CICS in its internal control blocks. Normally, a user program would never have to look at these structures. However, this was the only way that the application would work at all with any regularity. ■

David G. Matusow, senior telecommunications consultant, works in the Phoenix, Ariz., office of the Computer Task Group Inc. in Buffalo, N. Y. Matusow holds a B. A. in political science and a B. S. in computer science, both from Purdue University in Lafayette, Ind.

William Stallings, Comp/Comm Consulting, Great Falls, Va.

Interfacing to a LAN: Where's the protocol?

Users must be assured that their network devices are compatible. To accomplish this requires the use of a host-to-front-end protocol—but there is no standard.

The IEEE-802 standards and the FDDI optical-fiber local area network standard, soon to be adopted, solve many of the problems caused by the use of different protocols and interfaces for LANs. The acceptance of these standards by both vendors and customers means that customers have a wide variety of standardized LAN equipment to choose from. However, one significant area in need of standardization has been overlooked, and it has to do with the way in which customer equipment is connected to the LAN.

In IEEE-802 jargon, the following protocols are needed to connect to a LAN: physical, medium access control (MAC), and logical link control (LLC). These protocols specify the logic needed for end-to-end functionality. The next-higher layer (usually the network layer) must be able to invoke the services of the LLC in order for user applications to employ a LAN.

In considering the implementation of a network-LLC interface, two possibilities arise: (1) network and LLC both execute in the host processor; or (2) LLC and below are offloaded onto a front-end processor (FEP).

The FEP approach is attractive for several reasons: It relieves the host of the network processing burden and thus enhances efficiency. Also, the FEP can be procured from a different vendor than the supplier of the attached devices, so that the user has more flexibility in selecting equipment to attach to the network: It is not necessary that the attached equipment support the particular type of local network that the user has implemented; it is only necessary that the FEP and the attached devices share a common, standardized interface. The potential drawback of the FEP approach is that a new protocol is needed, known as a host-to-front-end protocol (HFP).

Before exploring the implementation of an HFP and the standards-related issues it raises, we need to look at the protocol architecture requirements of a local network.

As Figure 1 shows, a LAN communication architecture involves the three layers mentioned earlier—physical, MAC, and LLC. The physical layer provides for attachment to the medium. The MAC enables multiple devices to share the medium's capacity in an orderly fashion. And the LLC provides for data link control across the network.

The figure also indicates that higher layers of software will make use of the LLC. Put another way, the LLC provides the service of transmitting frames of data across the LAN, and that service is invoked by a higher layer of software. The IEEE-802 standards and the optical-fiber ring standard from ANSI 3T9.5—the Fiber Distributed Data Interface (FDDI)—use this three-layer architecture.

The three LAN layers correspond to the lowest two layers (physical and data link) of the ISO's Open Systems Interconnection (OSI) model (see "Of local networks, protocols, and the OSI reference model," DATA COMMUNICATIONS, November 1984, p. 129). The next layer, then, would be the network layer. In the context of a LAN, most functions traditionally associated with the network layer are not needed. For example, the LLC layer provides for the routing and addressing needed to transmit protocol data units from source to destination. Also, if the connection-oriented LLC service is used, the LLC layer provides for logical connections, flow control, and error control. Above that, the recently approved ISO connectionless network-layer standard, which provides an internetworking protocol, is needed so that the hosts on the LAN can be connected, via a gateway, to hosts on other subnetworks (see "Internetworking in an OSI environment," DATA COMMUNICATIONS, May 1986, p. 118).

Figure 2a shows this architecture. The LLC layer moves frames of data from one station on the LAN to another. The network layer provides internetworking capability. The transport layer provides end-to-end reliability. Thus, the user of the transport layer is guaranteed that its data will

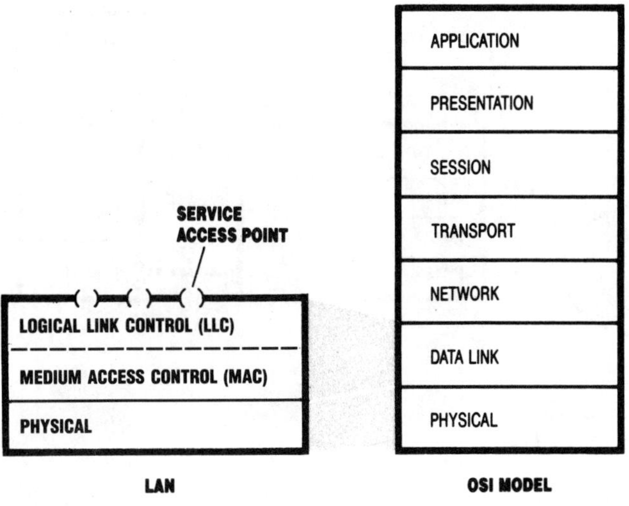

1. Three layers. *The logical-link-control layer provides for data link control across the network. Higher layers of software will make use of the LLC.*

be delivered with no losses and no misorderings. Above the transport layer are user-oriented layers (session, presentation, application) that handle communication functions beyond reliable data transfer.

We can trace the operation of this architecture on a single unit of user data in Figure 2b, which is keyed to event times marked on Figure 2a. At some time t0, the session entity presents a block of data to the transport entity. The transport entity encapsulates this data with a transport header and passes the resulting unit to the network-layer entity (t1), which adds its own header and passes the resulting unit to the LLC (t2). The LLC in turn adds its own header and passes the resulting unit to the MAC (t3). MAC produces a frame that includes both a MAC header and a MAC trailer, and this frame is transmitted across the LAN (t4). The MAC frame includes a destination station address, and the frame will be copied by the station with that address (t5). The user's block of data then moves up through the layers, with the appropriate headers and trailers stripped off at each layer (t6, t7, t8, and t9).

The FEP

The preceding discussion and Figure 2 assume that all layers of the architecture are implemented in the same processor. That is not always the case. Often, some of the lower layers are offloaded onto a front-end processor.

Consider a local network as consisting of not only a transmission medium, but also a set of intelligent devices that implement the network protocols and provide an interface for attaching subscriber devices (terminals or computers). We will refer to these intelligent devices as FEPs. The FEPs collectively control access to and communications across the local network. Subscriber devices attach to the FEP through some standard communications or Input/Output interface. The details of the local network operation are hidden from the devices.

---

2. Internetworking architecture. *To interconnect hosts via a gateway (a), an internetworking protocol is needed. Its operation can be traced on a single unit of user data (b).*

The user's data moves up through the layers, with the appropriate headers and trailers stripped off at each layer (t6, t7, t8, t9). The transport layer provides end-to-end reliability.

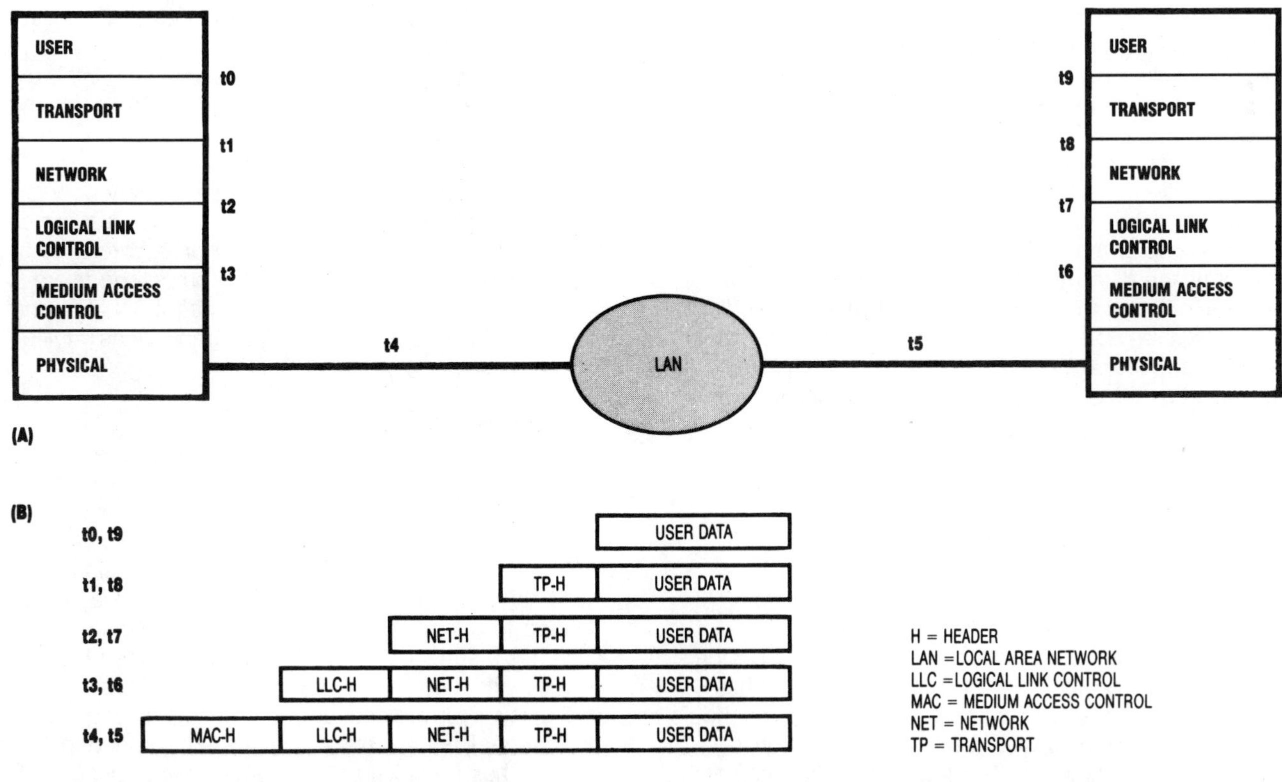

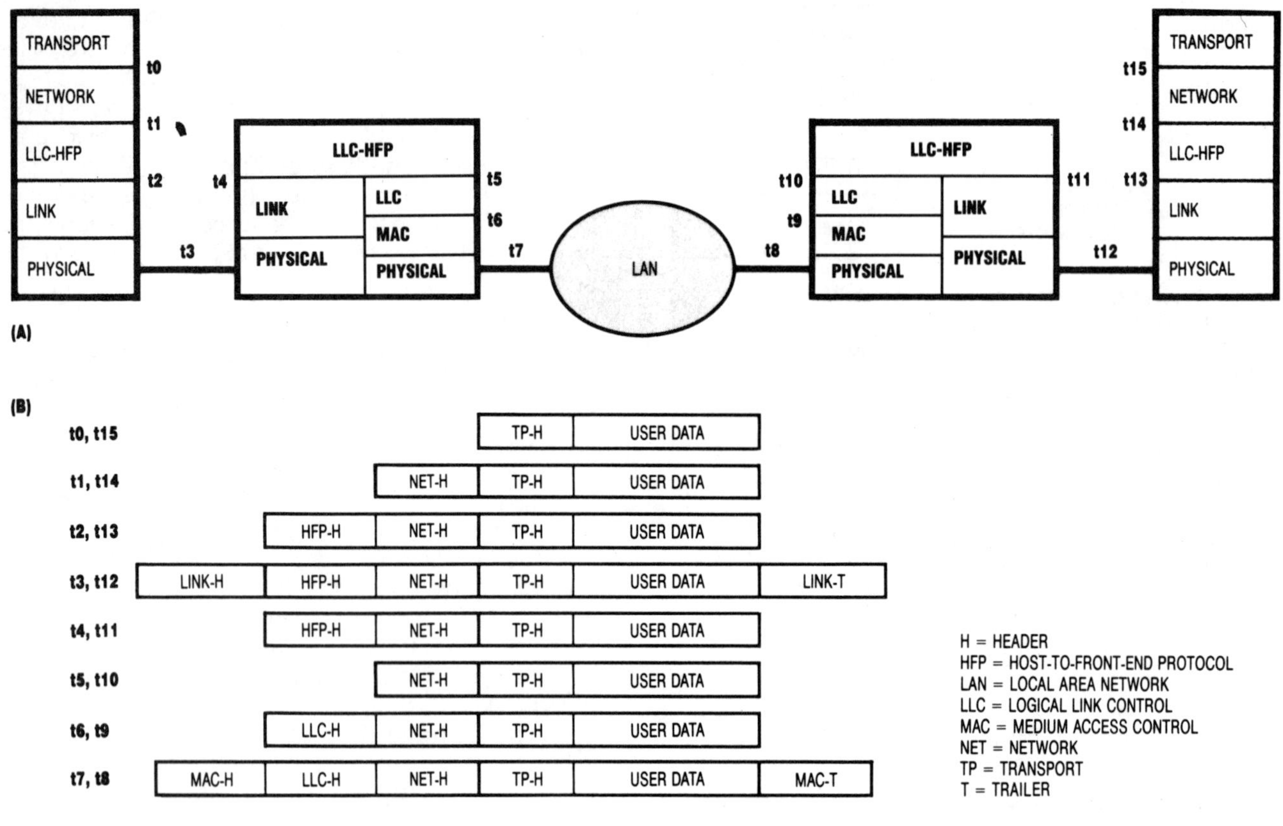

The FEP architecture is commonly used by independent local network vendors (those who sell only networks, not the data processing equipment that uses the LAN). Thus, as noted, in many cases the FEPs in a local network configuration are supplied by a different vendor than the supplier of the terminal and computer equipment.

The FEP is a microprocessor-based device that acts as a communications controller to provide data transmission service to one or more attached subscriber devices. It transforms the data rate and protocol of the subscriber device into that of the local network transmission medium and vice versa. Data on the medium is available to all attached devices—each FEP screens the data for reception based on the attached address or addresses.

In general terms, the FEP performs the following functions:
- Accepts data from attached device.
- Buffers the data until medium access is achieved.
- Transmits data in addressed packets.
- Scans each packet on medium for own address.
- Reads packet into buffer.
- Transmits data to attached device.

The FEP can either be an outboard or an inboard device. As an outboard device, it is a standalone unit. The hardware interface between the outboard FEP and the attached device is typically a standard serial communications interface, most commonly RS-232-C. Almost all computers and terminals support this interface. As an inboard device, the FEP is integrated into the chassis of the data processing device—for example, a minicomputer or terminal. An inboard FEP generally consists of one or more printed-circuit boards attached to the device's bus. Communication is typically by means of direct memory access (DMA) across the bus.

The FEP approach is becoming increasingly popular, since a customer can mix a variety of vendor equipment on a LAN but use a single-vendor FEP product to simplify network management. In the highly competitive microcomputer area, a variety of vendors offer LAN FEPs that connect to the popular system bus organizations (Multibus, for example).

The device-FEP interface

Remember that the discussion centering on the scenario of Figure 2 assumes that all of the protocol layers are integrated and executed on a single processor. Now assume instead that the LLC and below reside on an FEP.

The architecture of this approach is not as straightforward as you might have expected. Additional layers are needed to link an FEP and its attached station. Figure 3 assumes a serial communications link between the FEP and the attached device. Thus, a physical-layer protocol and a link-layer protocol are needed to exchange data across that link. One more protocol is also needed. This protocol has no universally accepted name, but it is often referred to as HFP. To identify this protocol as referring to

Table 1: Logical link control service primitives

UNACKNOWLEDGED CONNECTIONLESS SERVICE

```
L-DATA.request (local-address,remote-address,l-sdu,service-class)
L-DATA.indication (local-address,remote-address,l-sdu,service-class)
```

CONNECTION-ORIENTED SERVICE

```
L-DATA-CONNECT.request (local-address,remote-address,l-sdu)
L-DATA-CONNECT.indication (local-address,remote-address,l-sdu)
L-DATA-CONNECT.confirm (local-address,remote-address,status)

L-CONNECT.request (local-address,remote-address,service-class)
L-CONNECT.indication (local-address,remote-address,status,service-class)
L-CONNECT.confirm (local-address,remote-address,status,service-class)

L-DISCONNECT.request (local-address,remote-address)
L-DISCONNECT.indication (local-address,remote-address,reason)
L-DISCONNECT.confirm (local-address,remote-address,status)

L-RESET.request (local-address,remote-address)
L-RESET.indication (local-address,remote-address,reason)
L-RESET.confirm (local-address,remote-address,status)

L-CONNECTION-FLOWCONTROL.request (local-address,remote-address,amount)
L-CONNECTION-FLOWCONTROL.indication (local-address,remote-address,amount)
```

ACKNOWLEDGED CONNECTIONLESS SERVICE

```
L-DATA-ACK.request (local-address,remote-address,l-sdu,service-class)
L-DATA-ACK.indication (local-address,remote-address,l-sdu,service-class)
L-DATA-ACK-STATUS.indication (local-address,remote-address,service-class,status)

L-REPLY.request (local-address,remote-address,l-sdu,service-class)
L-REPLY.indication (local-address,remote-address,l-sdu,service-class)
L-REPLY-STATUS.indication (local-address,remote-address,l-sdu,service-class,status)

L-REPLY-UPDATE.request (local-address,l-sdu)
L-REPLY-UPDATE-STATUS.indication (local-address,status)
```

a front-end whose highest layer is LLC, it shall be called an LLC-HFP.

To understand the need for an HFP, consider again the case of an integrated architecture (Fig. 2). At t2, the network entity passes a block of data to the LLC for transmission. How does the LLC know what to do with this data block? That information is contained in the link control primitive (command) used by the network layer to invoke the LLC. The link control primitives are listed in Table 1. For example, if the unacknowledged connectionless service is used, the network entity would use the following primitive and associated parameters to invoke the LLC:

L-DATA.request (local-address,remote address, 1-sdu, service-class) where:

local address	= local LLC service access point
remote address	= destination station (MAC) address and destination LLC service access point
1-sdu	= block of data being passed to LLC for transmission

service class = desired priority

Exactly how this information is passed to an LLC entity will depend on the implementation. For example, if the LLC is invoked by a subroutine call, the L-DATA.request call is compiled into a machine-language subroutine branch, and the parameters of the call are placed somewhere in registers or memory, to be picked up by the called routine. The details are not, and should not be, part of the LLC standard. The internal implementation of this interface depends on the machine language and operating system and upon optimized design choices.

The subroutine-call approach works fine if the network and LLC entities execute in the same processor. But in the case of the example in Figure 3, they run on separate processors. A way is needed for the network and LLC entities to exchange primitives and parameters, and that function of the LLC-HFP-LLC-HFP provides a way for the network and LLC entities to communicate. In the host, the LLC-HFP entity presents an interface with the network entity that mimics the LLC. This setup allows the network entity to use calls such as L-DATA.request as if the LLC and network were running on the same processor. In the FEP, the LLC-HFP behaves like any other LLC user.

Table 2: LLC-HFP header and primitives

HEADER

FIELDS	FUNCTION
SERVICE ACCESS POINT	SPECIFIES USER OF LLC SERVICES
PRIMITIVE CODE	SPECIFIES WHICH LLC PRIMITIVE IS BEING INVOKED
PARAMETER COUNT	SPECIFIES NUMBER OF PARAMETERS
PARAMETER	THIS FIELD OCCURS ONCE FOR EACH PARAMETER AND CONSISTS OF TWO SUBFIELDS
LENGTH	SPECIFIES THE LENGTH IN OCTETS OF THE VALUE SUBFIELD
VALUE	SPECIFIES THE VALUE OF THE PARAMETER

PRIMITIVE CODES

```
 1  L-DATA.request
 2  L-DATA.indication
 3  L-DATA-CONNECT.request
 4  L-DATA-CONNECT.indication
 5  L-DATA-CONNECT.confirm
 6  L-CONNECT.request
 7  L-CONNECT.indication
 8  L-CONNECT.confirm
 9  L-DISCONNECT.request
10  L-DISCONNECT.indication
11  L-DISCONNECT.confirm
12  L-RESET.request
13  L-RESET.indication
14  L-RESET.confirm
15  L-CONNECTION-FLOWCONTROL.request
16  L-CONNECTION-FLOWCONTROL.indication
17  L-DATA-ACK.request
18  L-DATA-ACK.indication
19  L-DATA-ACK-STATUS.indication
20  L-REPLY.request
21  L-REPLY.indication
22  L-REPLY-STATUS.indication
23  L-REPLY-UPDATE.request
24  L-REPLY-UPDATE-STATUS.indication
```

Table 3: LLC-HFP system control block format

WORD	NAME	DESCRIPTION
1	STATUS	NETWORK INTERFACE UNIT (NIU) OR HOST STATUS INFORMATION, SUCH AS WHETHER OR NOT READY TO RECEIVE DATA
2	DIRECTIVE	MANAGEMENT-RELATED COMMANDS AND ACKNOWLEDGMENTS
3	COMMAND POINTER	POINTS TO AN AREA OF MEMORY THAT CONTAINS ONE OR MORE COMMANDS. EACH COMMAND CONSISTS OF A COMMAND CODE AND A LIST OF PARAMETERS.
4	FRAME POINTER	POINTS TO A BUFFER CONTAINING A BLOCK OF DATA BEING PASSED BETWEEN THE LLC AND THE LLC USER
5-8	ERROR COUNTERS	ERROR-RELATED STATISTICS

The operation of Figure 3's architecture can now be traced. At t1, the network entity passes the user's data plus a network header to LLC-HFP, using the L-DATA.-request call. LLC-HFP appends a header and passes the result to the link layer (t2). In this case, the link layer is an ordinary point-to-point data link control protocol, such as the High-level Data Link Control (HDLC). Table 2 suggests a format for the header. Note that the header identifies which user is invoking the services of the LLC, the primitive being invoked, and the parameters associated with that primitive.

Again, this scenario assumes an outboard FEP and the use of a data link protocol, such as HDLC, across the host-FEP interface. If the FEP is a communications board, then there will be no link and physical layer protocols as such between the FEP and the host. In most cases, the FEP and host processor will connect to the same backplane bus and exchange information through a common main memory, with the FEP typically using DMA, as stated earlier. In this case, a specific area of memory is shared and is used to construct a system control block for communication. The system control block fulfills the same function as the header mentioned above. As an example, Table 3 gives the system control block format used in an Intel product.

One issue remains to be examined. Whether the host-FEP exchange is achieved by a header or by a system control block, a specification of that exchange is needed. The specification would include not only the formats discussed above, but also such protocol functions as initialization, flow control, management functions, and recovery. If both the FEP and the host are provided by the same vendor, that specification can be proprietary. If, however, the FEP and the host are from different vendors, then a standard specification would be preferable. As stated, it is likely that FEPs will be from a different vendor than the vendor for the attached devices. Indeed, there may be attached devices from a number of different vendors. Thus, the case for a standard for the host-FEP exchange is a strong one. Unfortunately, no such standard exists or, as far as is known, is even contemplated by IEEE 802, ANSI X3T9.5, or the ISO.

A transport-level FEP

With today's microprocessors, it makes sense to offload even more of the processing burden from the host. An increasingly popular approach is to house all layers up through transport in the FEP. This relieves the host of all processing associated with establishing and maintaining a reliable end-to-end connection.

Figure 4 depicts this architecture. Note the similarity to Figure 3—the same reasoning applies here. In this case, the user of the transport layer executes on a different processor than does the transport entity. Hence, a transport-level host-to-front-end protocol (TP-HFP) is needed to allow the transport user to exchange primitives and parameters with the transport entity. The TP-HFP header will contain a code specifying which primitive is being invoked and a list of parameter lengths and values. In the case of an inboard FEP, the primitives and parameters can be exchanged by means of a system control block.

Table 4 lists the primitives for the ISO transport protocol standard. The ISO transport protocol standard, like the LLC, has the concept of a service access point (SAP), so

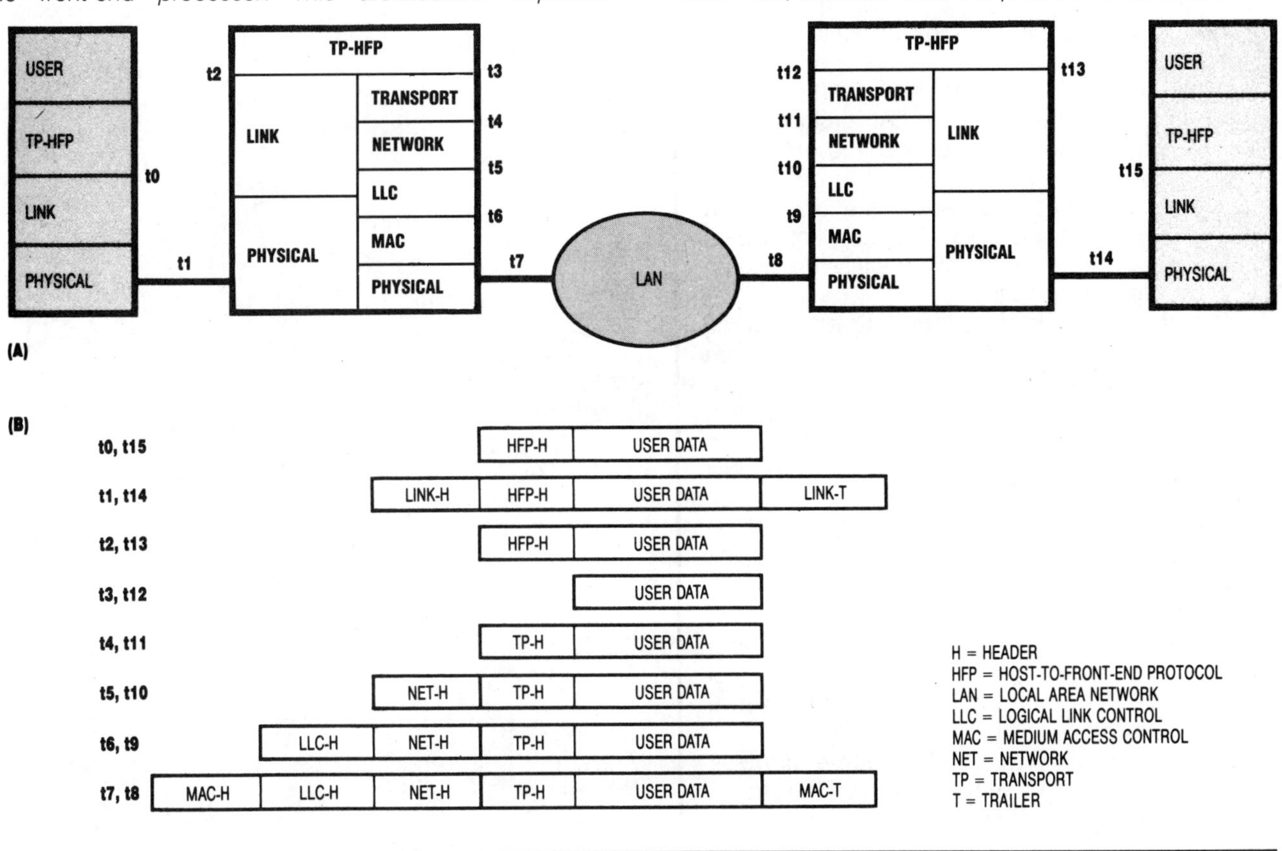

Table 4: ISO transport service primitives

```
T-CONNECT.request (Called Address,Calling Address,Expedited Data Option,Quality of Service,Data)
T-CONNECT.indication (Called Address,Calling Address,Expedited Data Option,Quality of Service,Data)
T-CONNECT.response (Quality of Service,Responding Address,Expedited Data Option,Data)
T-CONNECT.confirm (Quality of Service,Responding Address,Expedited Data Option,Data)

T-DISCONNECT.request (Data)
T-DISCONNECT.indication (Disconnect Reason,Data)

T-DATA.request (Data)
T-DATA.indication (Data)

T-EXPEDITED-DATA.request (Data)
T-EXPEDITED-DATA.indication (Data)
```

that a transport entity can have multiple users. The first six primitives listed in the table are used to establish and subsequently tear down a logical connection between transport SAPs. Most of the parameters are self-explanatory. The quality-of-service parameter allows the transport user to request specific transmission services, such as priority and security levels. The remaining primitives are concerned with data transfer. The expedited version requests that the transport entity attempt to deliver the associated data as rapidly as possible. Note the similarity of these primitives to those for the LLC.

Although placement of the transport layer and those below in the FEP is becoming popular, making desirable a standard specification for TP-HFP and a transport-level system control block is not in sight. (For current and projected LAN standards activity, see "LAN standards.")

The exact functions performed by the HFP will depend on the architecture employed. For example, an LLC-HFP will need to pass different primitives and parameters than a TP-HFP. In any case, some format, such as that indicated in Table 2 or 3, is needed. Other characteristics of an HFP are relatively independent of the protocol layer involved. Specifically, the HFP must be:

■ Reliable, to ensure no loss of messages.

LAN standards

The key to the development of the local area network market is the availability of a low-cost interface. The cost to connect equipment to a LAN must be much less than the cost of the equipment alone. This requirement, plus the complexity of the LAN protocols, dictates a very large scale integration solution. However, chip manufacturers will be reluctant to commit the necessary resources unless there is a high-volume market. A LAN standard would ensure that volume and also enable equipment from a variety of manufacturers to intercommunicate.

That is the rationale of the IEEE 802. Its standards are being processed by the International Organization for Standardization (ISO).The standards are in the form of a three-layer communications architecture, which is matched against the ISO's better-known Open Systems Interconnection (OSI) reference model in Figure 1.

The logical link control (LLC) layer provides for the exchange of data between service access points (SAPs), which are multiplexed over a single physical connection to the LAN. The LLC provides for both a connectionless, datagram-like and a connection-oriented, virtual-circuit-like service. Both the protocol and the frame format resemble those of the High-level Data Link Control (HDLC).

The medium access control (MAC) layer provides for the regulation of access to the shared LAN transmission medium. For each MAC specification (carrier-sense multiple access with collision detection, and token ring), a physical layer specification tailored to the topology and MAC algorithm of the corresponding MAC protocol is provided.

The IEEE-802 standards are designed for low-to medium-speed LANs, up to 20 Mbit/s. Work on high-speed LANs has been performed within the ANSI X3T9 technical committee on I/0 interface standards. A subcommittee, called X3T9.5, has developed a proposed standard called the Fiber Distributed Data Interface (FDDI), which will soon be adopted as an ANSI standard. FDDI specifies the MAC and physical layers and assumes the use of the IEEE-802 LLC layer. The MAC layer is a token-ring specification, similar to that of IEEE 802. The physical layer specifies a 100-Mbit/s optical-fiber ring.

- Connection-oriented, to maintain the state of a dialogue with each user of the HFP.
- Multiplexed, to allow multiple higher-level users.
- Individually flow-controlled by the user.

Overall, the HFP must examine each command that it receives, verify the parameters associated with the command, and reformat as necessary for communication. ∎

William Stallings is president of Comp/Comm Consulting. He has a B. S. E. E. from Notre Dame and a computer science Ph. D. from M. I. T. This article is based on material in the second edition of his book, Local Networks, *recently published by Macmillan. He is also author of* Data and Computer Communications *(Macmillan, 1985).*

Roy Evans, NCR Corporation, Cambridge, Ohio

Programmable net simulators make protocol tests easier

Simulators test multiple-layer mixed-protocol products at development sites without host connections.

Running full-function communications protocol tests using dedicated connections to host computers can be costly and difficult. For example, a typical test scenario involves installing a host or network node connection and then developing a test application program to control the host from a remote site. Thus, two communications sessions are required—one session to control and one to perform the test. The net result is that network response time suffers.

Yet test verification is crucial when applications must work in conjunction with a feature-rich product, such as the IBM Systems Network Architecture (SNA). Exercising the entire range of communications protocol functionality for SNA end-user products is difficult through a fixed network. Users may spend dozens of days trying to test a product's response when SNA negative responses are received from the host computer. Or weeks may go by trying to verify a product's capability to reassemble segmented data messages from the host or the SNA network.

Readily creating such test situations requires a flexible, operator-responsive communications test capability. NCR Corp. recently used a simulator to perform quality assurance acceptance tests on a communications processor using an X.25/SNA communications protocol channel.

The unit tested was a programmable communications processor designed for installation in a bank's branch offices. It will provide a communications interface between automated teller machines (ATM) at the branch and IBM SNA host computers at remote data centers by means of an X.25 packet-switching network.

The communications processor is connected to several data entry terminals and gateways by means of a local area network (LAN). Each gateway unit on the processor LAN has four RS-232-C ports for connecting ATMs. One gateway unit on the LAN is soft configured to provide the X.25/SNA channel to an IBM SNA host.

A typical installation for this bank processor is shown in Figure 1 . The X.25/SNA channel is created by loading communications gateway 1 with X.25 networking protocols. Gateways 2 and 3 are loaded with SDLC protocols to provide the links to the automatic teller machines at the bank. Other gateways may be added to the LAN. The SNA protocol software is resident in the bank processor. Pascal applications also reside in the processor, controlling communications between the ATM and the IBM SNA host.

The physical X.25/SNA channel is designed to handle high-speed synchronous modem connections to a packet-switching network accessing SNA host computers. To allow different SNA host computers independent access to any single bank processor at a branch office, two separate SNA Physical Units (PUs) reside in each processor unit. Three secondary Logical Unit (LU) session ports are available with each PU. When a PU is activated, it communicates over its own X.25 virtual circuit established by a separate X.25 call-request sequence. Thus, each network host—linked to one of the two physical units in the bank processor—has its own virtual circuit connection through the packet network. Likewise two data centers can maintain communications with one branch processor.

For example, a processor's RS-232-C port on its X.25/SNA gateway can be connected directly to a full-duplex modem at a branch. A four-wire telephone line connects the branch modem to the network modem at the network entry node as shown in Figure 2. One SNA host computer on this network could then establish a call to one of the PUs in the bank processor while another central computer makes a link to the second PU in the same processor. With three LUs on each PU, as many as six SNA data transfer LU-to-LU sessions could be active, three sessions with each central computer.

The simulator chosen to test this network product was the Chameleon II Protocol Simulator/Analyzer by Tekelec,

Calabasas, Calif. Several other communications simulators were considered during an evaluation period. A total of four companies demonstrated their simulator product at our development site. Table 1 shows a breakdown of the criteria used to choose the test simulator.

Full protocol analysis and simulation capabilities were available on all of the simulators for roughly the same price, approximately $18,000 (Fig. 1). Test programs for Synchronous Data-link Control/SNA (SDLC/SNA), higher-level data link control (HDLC)/X.25, and Binary Synchronous Control (BSC) were important criteria in the selection process as were X.25 certification procedures and tests. It was discovered that some test libraries were in development and not available. The Tekelec Chameleon had fully developed test libraries, and its X.25 test library included a series of HDLC, Link Access Procedure Version B (LAP B) and Level 3 test scenarios.

The ATM SDLC links and the host X.25/SNA channel on

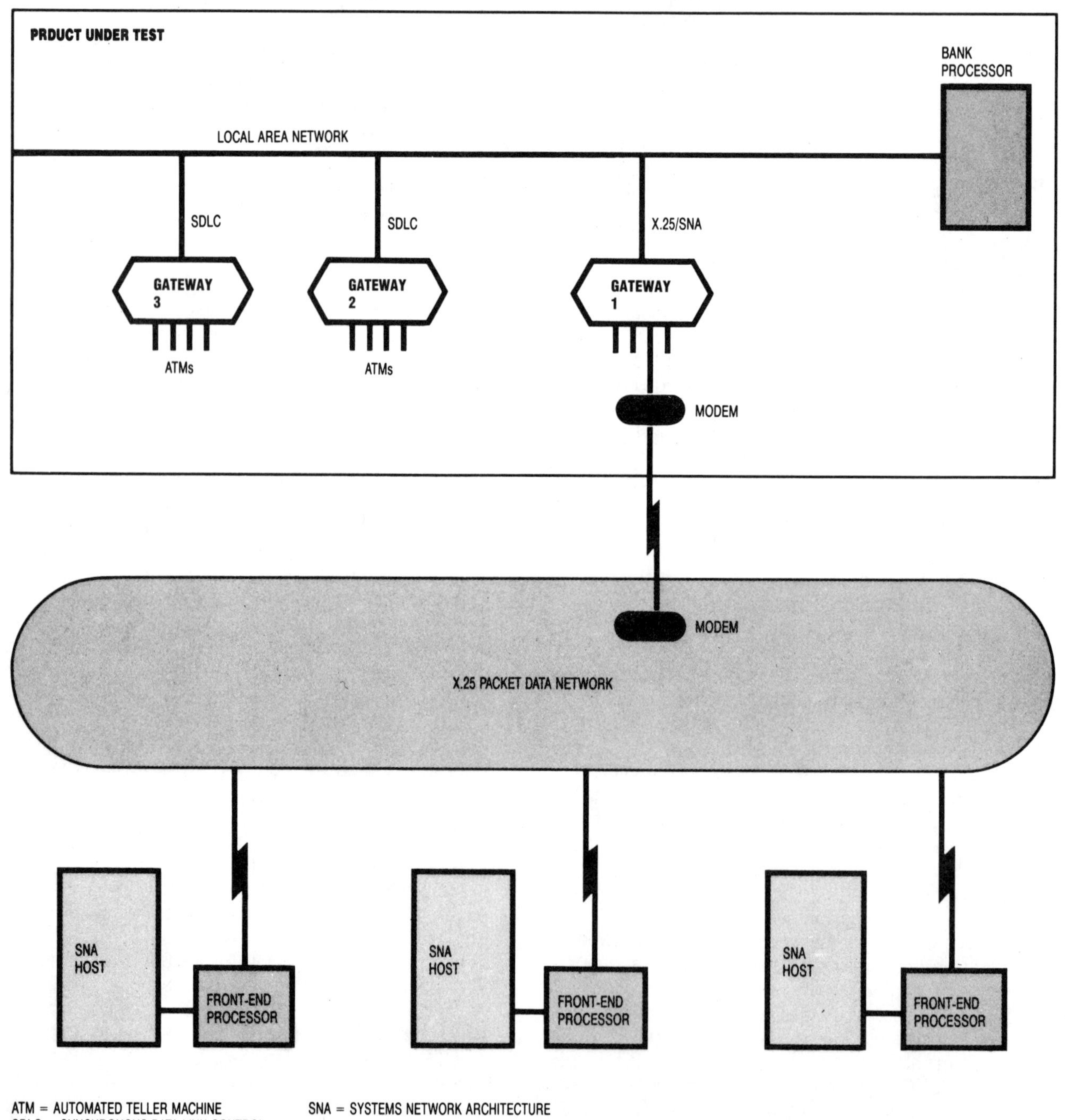

*1. **Network configuration.** Automated tellers, using SDLC links, communicate with the local bank processor. The processor communicates with remote hosts via an X.25/ SNA channel. This is created by loading gateway with X.25 networking protocols Gateways 2 and 3 are loaded with SDLC protocols to provide links to the bank's ATMs.*

the bank processor were tested using the Chameleon simulators as shown in Figure 3. Two Chameleons simulated a total of eight ATMs on secondary SDLC links. The ATM SDLC link testing was eventually supplemented with IBM-compatible personal computers.

Another Chameleon was used to drive the X.25/SNA connection by simulating the X.25 network entry node and SNA's Path, Transmission, and Data Flow protocol functions. Gateway I is configured and loaded with X.25 communications software. Two NEC America Inc. DSP 9600 RIII modems were linked via a 4-wire full-duplex circuit connected to the bank processor and the Chameleon network simulator. The modems were chosen for their high-speed capability and easy switching between 4.8, 7.2, and 9.6 kbit/s transmission rates. A three-way toggle switch on the modem's front panel provides speed selections.

The data scope monitor connected passively to the modem cable is a Digilog Inc. (Montgomeryville, Pa.) DLM IV. The data scope captures and records accurate time relations on data messages. The scope provides a protocol layer decode for the HDLC link level or X.25 packet level. When the Chameleon is running in automatic HDLC link handling mode, link headers and trailers are transparent to it. On these occasions, the data scope provides the HDLC link monitoring.

Before the bank processors were actually delivered, an X.25 packet assembler/disassembler (PAD) proved to be a handy testbed. The PAD, with one asynchronous terminal, appeared to the Chameleon much as the bank processor, except for absence of SNA protocols. When the bank processor with its X.25/SNA gateway became available, it simply replaced the PAD. The asynchronous terminal was used to facilitate sending and receiving screen data in packet form to the Chameleon. Being able to practice protocol programming on the Chameleon and initially

experimenting in developing an X.25 packet-level handler on it improved the overall test schedule.

Simulator testing the channel

Final customer acceptance required full functional exercise of all the protocol layers. This necessitated testing all SNA layers riding on top of the two X.25 layers.

The X.25 interface was tested first. The Chameleon's library of X.25 HDLC/LAPB and packet-level tests was used extensively during software integration tests. Locally programmed tests were also developed on the Chameleon and run against the HDLC and packet level.

The SNA test required full functional exercise of the product's SNA transmission service (TS), profile 4 and function management (PM), profile 4 session rules and data flow protocol functions. The test consisted of such items as running SNA full duplex, running SNA half duplex flip-flop (signal, change direction indicators, etc.), initialize and terminate protocols, quiesce, shutdown, segmenting, chaining, and so forth.

Two types of software quality assurance tests were performed on the bank processor to verify the X.25/SNA connections. One series of tests exercised the communication line protocols. It simulated the IBM SNA host and its protocol activities. The other tests were targeted to the banking processor, which contains the application interface to the multisession X.25/SNA host communications port. The application interface defines the way user-produced applications talk to SNA host computers over LU-to-LU sessions. The processor is programmable in Pascal. The communications interface to Pascal applications programs was extensively used and tested while running simulated X.25/SNA data transfer exercises.

Various X.25 and SNA protocol tests with data transfer exercises were developed and run over a three-month

2. Multiple sessions. *Several SNA host computers gain independent access to a single bank processor since each processor accommodates two SNA Physical Units and three Logical Units. When a PU is activated, it communicates over its own X.25 virtual circuit. As many as six SNA data transfer LU-to-LU sessions could be active.*

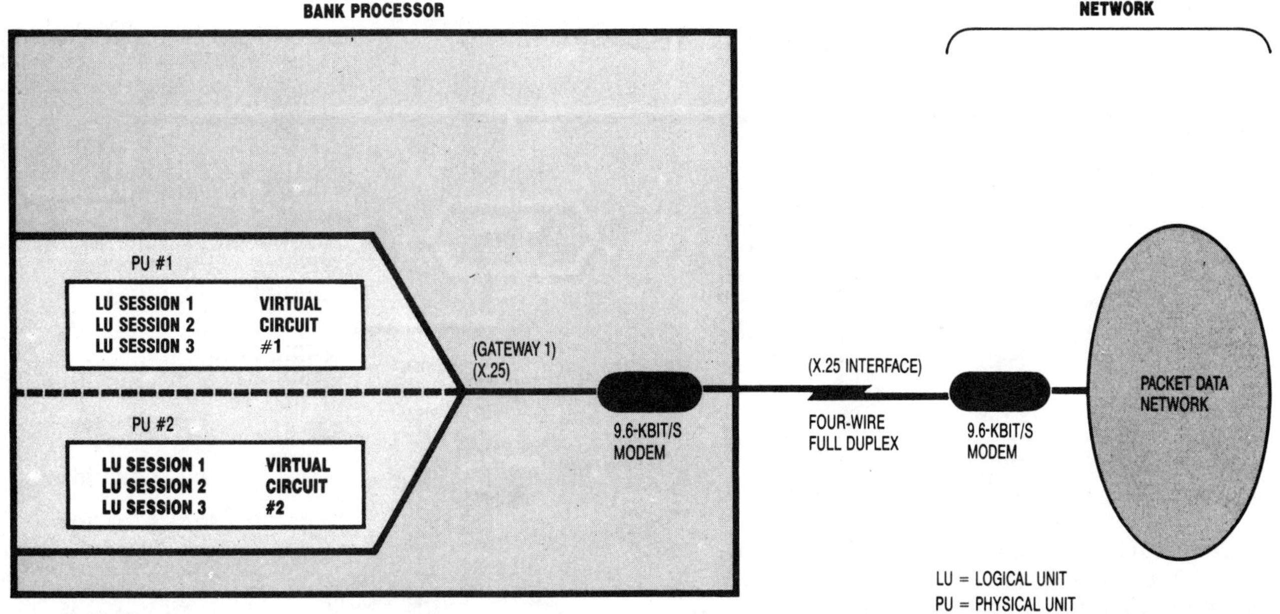

period. The job required one communications test engineer writing the Chameleon programs and another programmer producing Pascal application programs on the bank processor. All the SNA rules and appropriate X.25 functions were touched on at least once during the tests. Combinations of possible situations and some boundary conditions were also addressed. The X.25/SNA qualified logical link control (QLLC) layer was tested for basic functionality. This is a minimal, SDLC-like protocol layer. QLLC uses the Q bit in the X.25 packet header to flag a QLLC command.

Tests run on the Chameleon simulator were written in the SIMP/H programming mode to test the various SNA functions. In this mode, the HDLC link in X.25 runs automatically and transparently to the programmer. Only HDLC information frames are visible and used by the programmer. These information frames become the X.25 packet header and SNA headers once the programming is complete. The Chameleon maintains a trace buffer of HDLC information frames sent and received. This trace is printable and was used extensively in trouble-shooting design problems.

Figure 4 shows a sample program and test results. The Chameleon test scenario activates both PUs in the processor, then it activates and binds three LU sessions on each PU. The test cycles and repeats, exchanging SNA exception response data messages back and forth over each of the six LU data transfer sessions. During these test cycles, the Chameleon SNA host simulator sends an exception response data message and waits for a data message from the processor. When the Chameleon receives a response, it sends a data message on the next LU-to-LU session which, in turn, loops through all six sessions over and over. Figure 4 shows the X.25 and SNA header-built subroutines. These routines, used with others, effectively become communications handlers for the protocol layers. This test was run overnight and over weekends for stability verification.

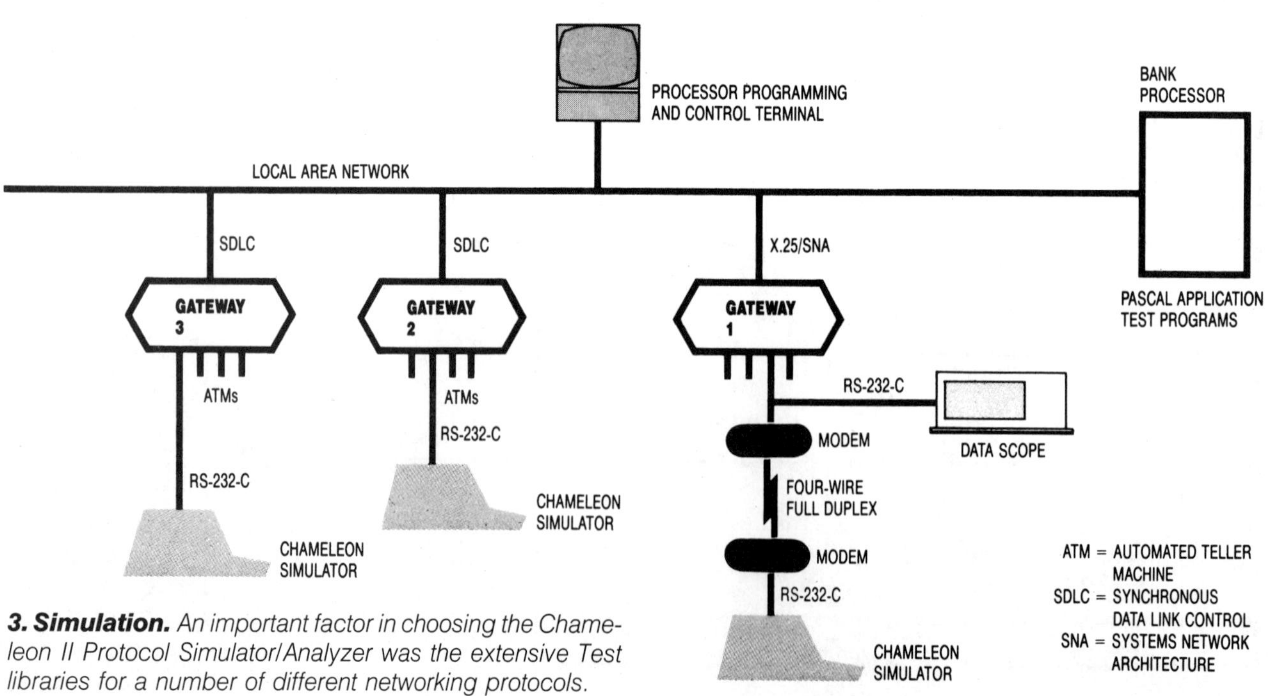

3. Simulation. *An important factor in choosing the Chameleon II Protocol Simulator/Analyzer was the extensive Test libraries for a number of different networking protocols.*

The program consisted of 355 lines of Chameleon Basic program statements. Approximately 250 lines in the program were used to establish the two X.25 virtual circuit calls, perform QLLC functions, handle X.25 packet-level acknowledge protocol, and build SNA headers. Once the lines of code were debugged, they remained the same and became the basis for the entire series of SNA tests.

Figure 5, the trace printout of SNA data transfer exercise, shows portions of the Chameleon's trace buffer printout, which includes a communications sequence from X.25 call establishment to SNA data transfer. Annotations are added to mark the different communications phases.

The trace display is given in hexadecimal eight bit byte representations. In the format of the trace display an R or T represent received or transmitted messages. The messages tagged R come from the bank processor. The messages tagged T are sent from the Chameleon, which is simulating an SNA host through an X.25 network.

There is a time stamp indicating when the message occurred. The next column contains the total number of bytes in the message in terms of HDLC I-frames. HDLC header, field check character, and flags are not seen in this Chameleon mode. The HDLC link level is handled automatically and transparently to the program. The final entry is the message bytes sent or received. The first three message bytes throughout the panel are X.25 headers. The byte fields relate directly to the description in the CCITT standard for X.25.

For example, the hex FB and FF of the first two messages are the packet identifiers for a DTE Restart Request from the bank processor and a DCE Restart Confirm from the network (or, in this case, the Chameleon). The next two sets of processor-network exchanges are call requests from the processor's two physical units establishing two virtual circuits on logical channels 06 and 05. All the remaining traffic is over one or the other of these two X.25 circuits.

To sample decode an SNA header in the above trace, consider the request header in the first activate physical unit (PU #1). The hexadecimal bit field is 6B 80 00. Using the current IBM SNA reference summary, hex 6B decodes to an RU category of session control (SC), format one with only one message in a chain. Hex 80 decodes to definite response requested.

The last two large message transactions in the panel show the SNA data transfer between simulator and bank processor. The first message is from the host-network simulator to the bank processor. Since the message is sent in SNA exception response mode, only a packet-level acknowledgment is returned. The second data message is from the bank processor. That message is also sent in exception response mode.

Good measure

The tests conducted under simulation proved to be a good measure of how the network performed under actual conditions. In fact, an examination of the effectiveness of the test technique was conducted simultaneously on an actual product at a customer site. The customer location was far enough removed so that both efforts ran more or less independently. A large portion of the software bugs discovered at both sites tended to be common network problems. There were, however, many software and hardware problems that proved to be unique to each effort. One advantage of simulator testing was the ability to recreate and debug problems discovered at the product development site.

The customer EFT testing was constrained when working with the actual banking terminals and communications network equipment. With simulation equipment, much larger configurations running faster and higher overall transfer rates were possible.

Eventually, the test equipment was augmented with IBM-compatible personal computers with communications hardware and software. The PCs were used to drive the SDLC banking machine gateway units, which permitted larger configurations operating at maximum speed.

The PC communications boards with software were purchased for $1,195 each. The software, however, is not nearly as extensive as that available on the Chameleon simulator. But the overall data transfer rate of the PCs

---

4. Sample test. *Tests run on the Chameleon simulator were written in SIMP/H to test the various SNA functions. Here are the X.25 and SNA header building routines.*

```
2870 REM /////////////////////////////////////////////////////////////
2880 REM //  SUBROUTINE TO SEND $0 AS DATA PACKET //
2890 D = 0
2900 M = 0
2910 I = 0
2920 MOD = 01
2930 LCN = @(40*PU+1)
2940 P(R) = @(40*PU+2)
2950 P(S) = @(40*PU+3)
2960 BUILD Q,D,MOD,LCGN,LCN,P(R),M,P(S),I,$0
2970 REM //  ALSO, ENTRY POINT FOR SNA BUILD SUBROUTINE  //
2980 TRAN
2990 UND
3000 TDISPF
3010 NRM
3020 @(40*PU+3) = @(40*PU+3) + 1
3030 if @(40*PU+3) < 8 GOTO 3050
3040 @(40*PU+3) = 0
3050 RETURN
3060 REM
3070 REM
3080 REM //  SUBROUTINE TO SEND SNA HEADER WITH PACKET HEADER.  //
3090 LCN = @(40*PU+1)
3100 P(R) = @(40*PU+2)
3110 P(S) = @(40*PU+3)
3120 BUILD Q,D,MOD,LCGN,LCN,P(R),M,P(S),I,FID,MPF,RES1,EFI,RES8,DAF,OAF,
        SNF,REQP,RUC,RES1,FI,SDI,BCI,ECI,DR1I,RES1,DR2I,ERI,RES2,QRI,
        PI,BBI,EBI,CDI,RES1,CSI,EDI,PDI,CEBI,$0
3130 GOSUB 2980
```

5. Trace Printout. *The Chameleon's trace buffer printout includes a communications sequence from X.25 call establishment to SNA data transfer. Annotations are added to mark the different communications phases. The trace display is given in hexadecimal eight bit byte representation. R and T represent received or transmitted messages.*

```
        (X.25 virtual circuit establishment)                    (SNA Exception Response data exchange with first LU-LU session on PU #1)

R 04:24:45:39:80   5  10 00 FB 00 00   (DTE restart request/confirm)     T 04:26:25:09:70  198  10 06 CC 2C 00 02 01 00 01 03 90 00 48 45 4C 4C 4F 20
                                                                                                54 48 45 52 45 20 37 30 30 30 20 53 59 53 54
T 04:24:45:64:60   3  10 00 FF                                                                  45 4D 20 5F 20 31 31 31 31 31 31 31 31 31 31
                                                                                                31 31 31 31 31 31 31 31 31 31 31 31 31 31 31
R 04:24:50:79:50  16  10 06 0B 0E 05 16 00 00 00 00 00 00 C3 01 00 00                           31 31 31 31 31 31 31 31 31 31 31 31 31 31 31
                                                                                                31 31 31 31 31 31 31 31 31 31 31 31 31 31 31
T 04:24:51:11:40   3  10 06 0F   (Call request/accept for PU #1)                                31 31 31 31 31 31 31 31 31 31 31 31 31 31 31
                                                                         (SNA data sent to      31 31 31 31 31 31 31 31 31 31 31 31 31 31 31
R 04:25:11:22:20  16  10 05 0B 0E 06 16 00 00 00 00 00 00 C3 01 00 00     the processor)  ==>   31 31 31 31 31 31 31 31 31 31 31 31 31 31 31
                                                                                                31 31 31 31 31 31 31 31 31 31 31 31 31 31 31
T 04:25:11:54:10   3  10 05 0F   (Call request/accept for PU #2)                                31 31 31 31 31 31 31 31 31 31 31 31 31 31 31
      .            .           .                                                                31 31 31 31 31 31 31 31 31 31 31 31 31 31 31
                                                                                                31 31 31 31 31 31 31 31 31 31 31 31 31 31 31
      .            .           .                                                                31 31 31 31 31 31 31 31 31 31 31 31 31 31 31
   (SNA activate PU and LU, session bind for first LU-LU session)                               31 31 31 31 31 31 31 31 31 31 31 31 31 31 31
                   | X.25 |    SNA TH     | SNA RH |
T 04:25:15:03:30  21 |10 06 22|2D 00 00 00 00 00|6B 80 00|11 01 01 05 02 00   R 04:26:25:59:00   3  10 06 E1  (X.25 packet level acknowledge)
                      02 01 40   (activate PU #1)                         R 04:26:26:23:20  212  10 06 EC 2C 00 02 03 00 01 03 90 00 48 69 20 74 68 65
                                                                                                72 65 20 43 68 61 6D 65 6C 65 6F 6E 20 20 48
R 04:25:15:37:50   3  10 06 41                                                                  69 20 74 68 65 72 65 20 43 68 61 6D 65 6C 65
R 04:25:15:82:40  32  10 06 42 2D 00 00 00 00 00 EB 80 00 11 11 40 40 40 40                     6F 6E 20 48 69 20 74 68 65 72 65 20 43 68 61
                      40 40 40 40 00 00 07 01 00 00 00 00 00 00                                 6D 65 6C 65 6F 6E 20 20 20 20 20 20 20 20 20
T 04:25:16:44:10   3  10 06 41                                                                  20 20 20 20 20 20 20 20 20 20 20 20 20 20 20
T 04:25:17:65:60  21  10 06 44 2D 00 02 00 00 00 6B 80 00 0D 01 01 05 02 00   (SNA data received 20 20 20 20 20 20 20 20 20 20 20 20 20 20 20
                      02 01 01   (activate LU #1)                          from the processor) ==> 20 20 20 20 20 20 20 20 20 20 20 20 20 20 20
R 04:25:17:99:80   3  10 06 61                                                                  20 20 20 20 20 20 20 20 20 20 20 20 20 20 20
R 04:25:18:44:20  14  10 06 64 2D 00 00 02 00 00 EB 80 00 0D 01                                 20 20 20 20 20 20 20 20 20 20 20 20 20 20 20
T 04:25:19:04:60   3  10 06 61                                                                  20 20 20 20 20 20 20 20 20 20 20 20 20 20 20
      .            .           .                                                                20 20 20 20 20 20 20 20 20 20 20 20 20 20 20
                                                                                                20 20 20 20 20 20 20 20 20 20 20 20 20 20 20
T 04:25:23:46:80  48  10 06 88 2D 00 02 01 00 00 6B 80 00 31 01 04 04 B0 30                     20 20 20 20 20 20 20 20 20 20 20 20 20 20
                      40 00 00 00 85 85 00 00 00 00 00 00 00 00 00
                      00 00 00 00 00 00 00 00 00 00 00 00 00 00 00    T 04:26:27:00:10   3  10 06 E1  (X.25 packet level acknowledge)
R 04:25:23:83:00   3  10 06 A1        (bind LU session #1)                      .
R 04:25:24:27:30  13  10 06 AB 2D 00 01 02 00 00 EB 80 00 31
T 04:25:24:87:70   3  10 06 A1
      .            .           .
      .            .           .
```

LU = LOGICAL UNIT   SNA = SYSTEMS NETWORK ARCHITECTURE
PU = PHYSICAL UNIT

outperformed the Chameleon by a factor of 3 to 1. Because the Chameleon was easier to program, it was used in most of the testing.

The maximum-configuration, maximum-speed performance tests revealed several communication gateway hardware timing errors. These errors would manifest themselves after several hours of continuous data exchange. When a bug finally affected a customer, the problem was already solved, the fix tested, and the product was ready for installation.

The Chameleon's ability to handle large programs is constrained. At approximately 360 lines of Basic code the program memory is full. The simulator is capable of calling subprograms from a diskette. However, the time needed to exchange the resident program with a diskette program and then restore the main program in memory is a problem.

Therefore, all test scenarios were single, memory-resident programs. Only one or two SNA functions could be tested at a time. Also, running interpretive Basic on the Chameleon made it difficult to perform any maximum throughput rate performance testing.

Overall tests showed that the simulator was a very capable tool for communications testing. It fulfilled our expectations, and the growing base of communications test software proved to be a big plus in meeting tight test schedules. ∎

Roy Evans, a Project Leader of Communications Quality Assurance at NCR Corp., Cambridge, Ohio, holds an M.S. from West Virginia University in Electrical Engineering. He has also studied advanced mathematics at California State University and is a part-time instructor in Electrical Engineering at Kent State University.

Po Chen, Motorola Inc., Phoenix, Ariz.

How to make the most of ISDN's new LAPD protocol

Doing LAPD in software appears to be more costly and less efficient than the hardware-based alternative.

The most visible part of the Integrated Services Digital Network (ISDN), at least to most users, will be the S/T interface, over which subscriber voice or data terminal equipment will connect with, say, a serving PBX. But what most ISDN users will not see is the sophisticated new protocol that makes ISDN access possible—even where multiple customer devices share a single ISDN access, in classic point-to-multipoint fashion.

The link access procedure "D" (LAPD) and affiliated higher-layer protocols handle the handshaking (commands and responses), signaling, and control for all of the voice and data calls that are set up through the ISDN D channel (see "Some ISDN background and elementals").

LAPD evolved from LAPB of the CCITT X.25 protocol. And, perhaps ironically, either LAPB or LAPD can be used to process data that is transmitted in "packet mode" within an ISDN B channel.

The LAPD protocol provides framing, sequence control, error detection, and recovery for multiple logical data links on the same D channel. There has been some discussion at the T1D1 ISDN committee to also adopt the LAPD protocol for data transmission on the B channel. Data transmitted in the packet mode, therefore, would be processed and framed according to the LAPD protocol. Using LAPD in this way, multiple logical data links can be supported on a B channel using statistical multiplexing.

The LAPD protocol encompasses two major functions: 1. the bit-level protocol that deals with such operations as framing and cyclic redundancy [error] checking (CRC); and 2. the element of procedure that deals with the handshaking between peer entities at both source and destination terminal equipments.

Two types of operation are supported by the LAPD protocol: acknowledged and unacknowledged operations. Unacknowledged operation uses unnumbered information frames. Information transfer in the acknowledged operation can be done with either a single- or multiple-frame transmission. In the single-frame operation, no more than one unacknowledged frame can be outstanding at any time. On the other hand, the multiple-frame acknowledged operation allows several sequence-numbered unacknowledged information frames to be outstanding at any time—dependent on the implementation's buffer space.

Each ISDN basic access at the S/T interface can support multiple terminal devices. In order to have each device support multiple logical data links, the data link address has a format that consists both of a service access point identifier (SAPI) and a terminal equipment identifier (TEI). Together they specify a data link connection identifier (DLCI). (These identifier terms are specified by the CCITT.)

The SAPI allows 64 service access points to be specified. For instance, a SAPI value of 0, representing messages sent in the packet, is related to the call control procedures. The SAPI identifies a point at which OSI (Open Systems Interconnection) Data Link layer services are provided to a Network layer entity by a Data Link layer entity. The TEI for a point-to-point data link connection may be associated with a single terminal. A terminal may contain one or more TEIs. The TEI for a broadcast data link is associated with all user Data Link layer entities containing the same SAPI.

The LAPD address field is constructed as follows (octet 1 is a flag):

	BIT						
8	7	6	5	4	3	2	1

SAPI		C/R	EA0	OCTET 2
TEI			EA1	OCTET 3

Some ISDN background and elementals

The Integrated Services Digital Network (ISDN) has been pursued for years by switching-equipment manufacturers and telephone operating companies. The major purpose of this effort is to provide enhanced data-and-voice switching services to both business and residential subscribers over existing telephone wires.

Most of the U. S. telephone switching equipment today is analog and is due for upgrading. ISDN provides a migration path for those analog central office and PBX switches, while extending to users digital end-to-end services such as voice, data, telex, security management, and energy management.

Most new commercial and residential buildings contain four-wire twisted pairs. However, the majority of existing buildings still have two-wire cabling. To provide the integrated voice/data services to both four-wire and two-wire cabling plants, two different interfaces are recommended by the CCITT, labeled S/T and U (see figure for the positioning of these interfaces).

ISDN access

The S/T interface is intended for use on the four-wire twisted pairs between the subscriber terminal equipment and the remote PBX termination. On the other hand, the U interface is for a two-wire twisted pair between the subscriber terminal equipment and the central office switch, or between a network termination 1 (ISDN designation NT1) and the central office switch. The ISDN will provide each subscriber with simultaneous access to two B channels (64 kbit/s each) for voice and data and to one D channel (16 kbit/s) for data, control, and signaling for both voice and data call-connection establishment and disconnect.

The interfaces

NT1 includes functions equivalent to the OSI's Physical layer. These functions include line termination, Layer 1 line maintenance and performance monitoring, timing, and Layer 1 multiplexing.

NT2 includes functions equivalent to Layer 1 and higher layers of CCITT X.200 (OSI). PBXs and terminal controllers are examples of NT2. NT2 functions include Layers 2 and 3 protocol handling and multiplexing, switching, and concentration. Note that NT1 and NT2 can be combined and their functions provided by a PBX.

TE (terminal equipment) includes functions equivalent to Layer 1 and higher. Examples of TE are digital telephones, data terminal equipment, and integrated workstations. TE functions include protocol handling, maintenance, and interfacing. TE1's interface complies with the ISDN user-network interface; TE2's does not.

TA (terminal adapter) includes functions equivalent to Layer 1 and higher. It enables a TE2 to be served by an ISDN user-network interface.

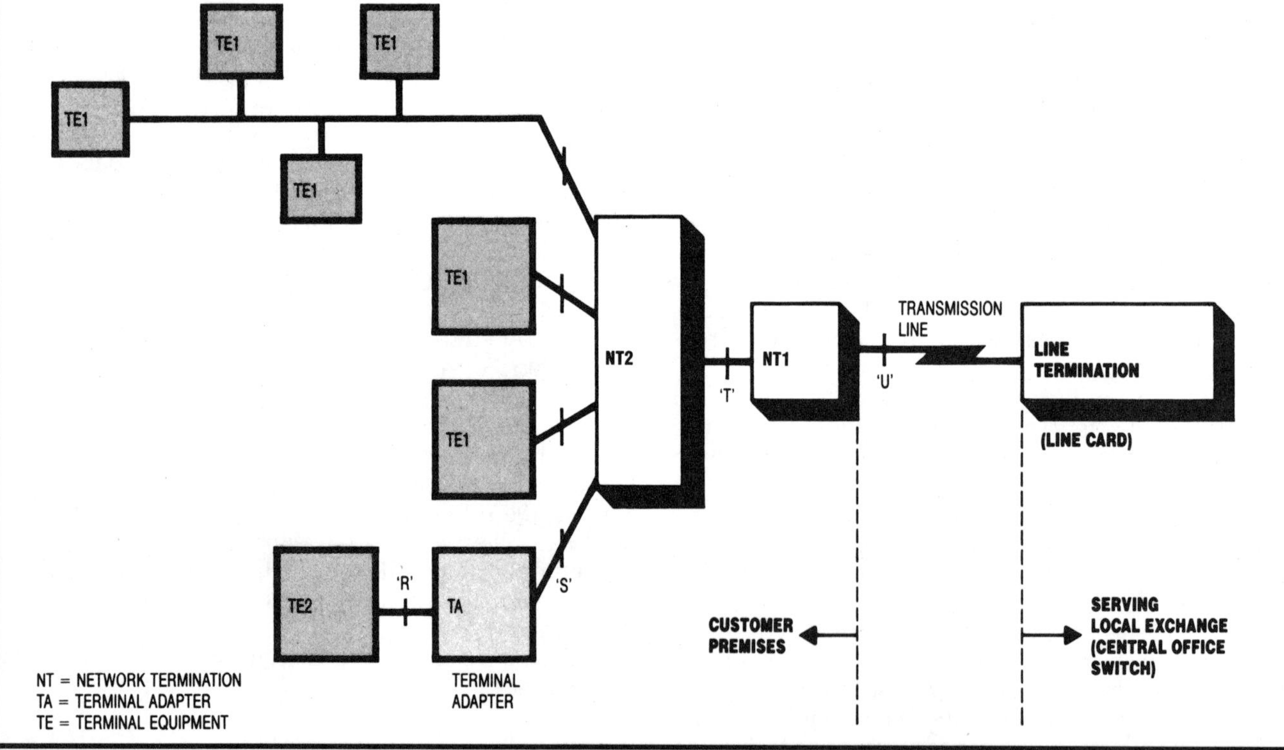

where C/R = command or response and EA = effective address to indicate the length of the address field is one or two octets.

For the LAPD frames, the address field should have two octets. Bit 1 in octet 2 set to 0 (EA0) means that another address is to be transmitted; bit 1 in octet 3 set to 1 (EA1) indicates that the associated address is the last one in the transmission.

The TEI assignment procedure can be carried out by the terminal equipment after being initiated by the user. The terminal equipment identifier is obtained by exchanging messages (such as identity checks or identity requests) with peer equipment at the exchange termination—a private branch exchange or telephone company central office.

Two procedures

The LAPD protocol's evolution from LAPB came about in order to serve multiple terminals on a single subscriber loop. The major differences between LAPD and LAPB:

■ Timers. There are four timers associated with LAPD; two with LAPB. The four are T200, T201, T202, and T203 (CCITT nomenclature). T200—equivalent to LAPB's T1—is started after the frame has been transmitted. The default value is set to 1 second. T201 keeps track of the time between retransmissions of the TEI identify-check messages. T202 keeps track of the time between retransmissions of the TEI identify-request messages. T203—equivalent to LAPB's second timer—keeps track of the time between activations of link-supervision sequences. This can help detect a faulty data link connection condition—no activity in time T203 indicates a fault.

■ The link address field is extended from one octet in LAPB to the two shown earlier in LAPD, to accommodate SAPI and TEI fields.

■ Statistical multiplexing is needed to provide several data links on a single D or B channel. LAPB is strictly point to point.

■ The unnumbered information (UI) command is added in LAPD. When an OSI Layer 3 (Network) or management entity requests an unacknowledged information transfer, the UI command shall be used to send information to its peer at the destination. (Each layer has a management entity; the concept is still evolving.) UI command frames do have sequence numbers; therefore UI frames may be lost without notification to the management entity. (After a time-out period, the Layer 3 or management entity assumes that the UI frame is lost, and requests a retransmission.)

The requirements

The LAPD protocol handler is needed at both the subscriber and the exchange terminations to handle the bit level protocol for data and telephony signaling on the D and, possibly, B channels. Many data terminal manufacturers emphasize the necessity to transmit packetized data over the B channel in order to take full advantage of its 64 kbit/s capacity.

The effective data rate for combining the B and D channels (64 and 16 kbit/s, respectively) is 80 kbit/s, full duplex. At the subscriber site, the software-intensive approach to process the LAPD protocol without a DMA (direct memory access) controller will have difficulty in meeting the prescribed speed requirement and still maintain the quality (error frequency) of the data link. Software is inherently slower; DMA, which defines the hardware-intensive approach, enables operation three to four times faster. This will be explained further.

At the exchange equipment, it is common to have eight subscriber lines terminated on a single line card of a private branch exchange or of a central-office switch. However, some manufacturers choose to terminate only one line on a line card in order to prevent any disruption in service to

1. ISDN terminal. Here, data link controllers (DLCs) handle the LAPD (link access procedure D) protocol in the B and D channels. The incoming data is processed by the DLCs for such functions as address recognition of the terminal equipment identifier field, zero-bit deletion, flag detection and removal, and cyclic redundancy check.

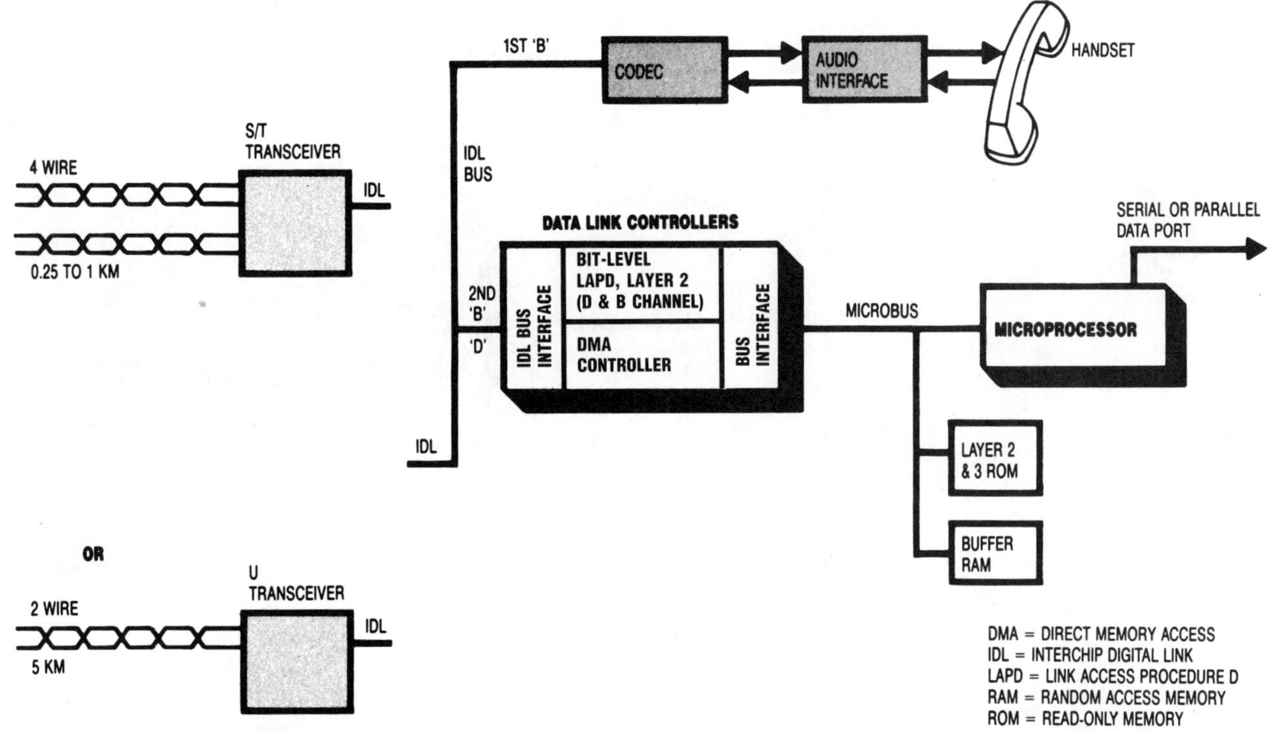

other subscribers when replacing a line card.

Therefore, two options are available to execute the LAPD protocol at the exchange equipment: Either execute LAPD on each line card (eight D channels), or execute LAPD for several line cards at the level above the line card. This latter level is at the network processor, which handles multiple line cards.

Not-so-low overhead

If the LAPD protocol is processed at the line card, the effective data rate for eight D channels is 8 × 16 or 128 kbit/s full duplex. Since LAPD can only be executed on a per-line basis, a certain amount of overhead—caused by task switching—is incurred to perform the LAPD protocol on multiple data links. This is complicated by the fact that a software-intensive solution that does not have a DMA controller to execute the movement of a block of data will interrupt the microprocessor once every character. This is a significant burden to the microprocessor and will degrade its performance.

For the second option, where LAPD is executed at the level above the line card, a multiplexer is needed. This is to multiplex several (multiples of eight) D channels into a higher-speed (Mbit/s), packetized data stream. The result: more efficient execution (less task-switching) of LAPD.

The alternatives

To implement the LAPD protocol, processing is required for the following: bit-level protocol, which deals with the framing, CRC, and zero insertion/deletion (to ensure that there are no more than five consecutive 1 bits in the data field, to prevent them from being mistaken for the starting and ending frame delimiters); element of procedure, which deals with the handshaking related to the establishment and breaking of link connections. Bit-level protocol can be handled by the data link controller (DLC) chip (available from several sources) with additional circuitry to handle differences between LAPB and LAPD. The element of procedure can be performed by either software or micro-coded hardware.

There are many highly integrated (VLSI or very large-scale integration) X.25 protocol controllers available today. They can handle both the Data Link layer (LAPB) and the Physical layer functions on a single chip at a Mbit/s speed. When enough demand develops for a LAPD controller, expect to see a single-chip embodiment of such a device for ISDN applications.

Advantages and disadvantages

What follows are implementation experiences of the software- and hardware-intensive approaches, with a comparison of the two. The software-intensive approach requires a DLC, circuitry to handle address-field recognition, and a microprocessor. The DLC takes care of the bit-level protocol. LAPD's element of procedure is done in software, which requires about a 12- to 16-kbyte program.

When the DLC controller receives data, it performs the address field recognition, checks the CRC bits, strips off the header, then interrupts the microprocessor on a character-by-character basis if the address of the received data is matched. The microprocessor must read the interrupt register, error or status register, then move the

---

__2. Adapting to ISDN.__ The case where the LAPD (link access procedure D) protocol is executed only within the D channel, to establish and disconnect the voice and data calls, is depicted here. ISDN operates synchronously. So data that is transmitted over the second B channel to an asynchronous DTE is processed by a rate adapter.

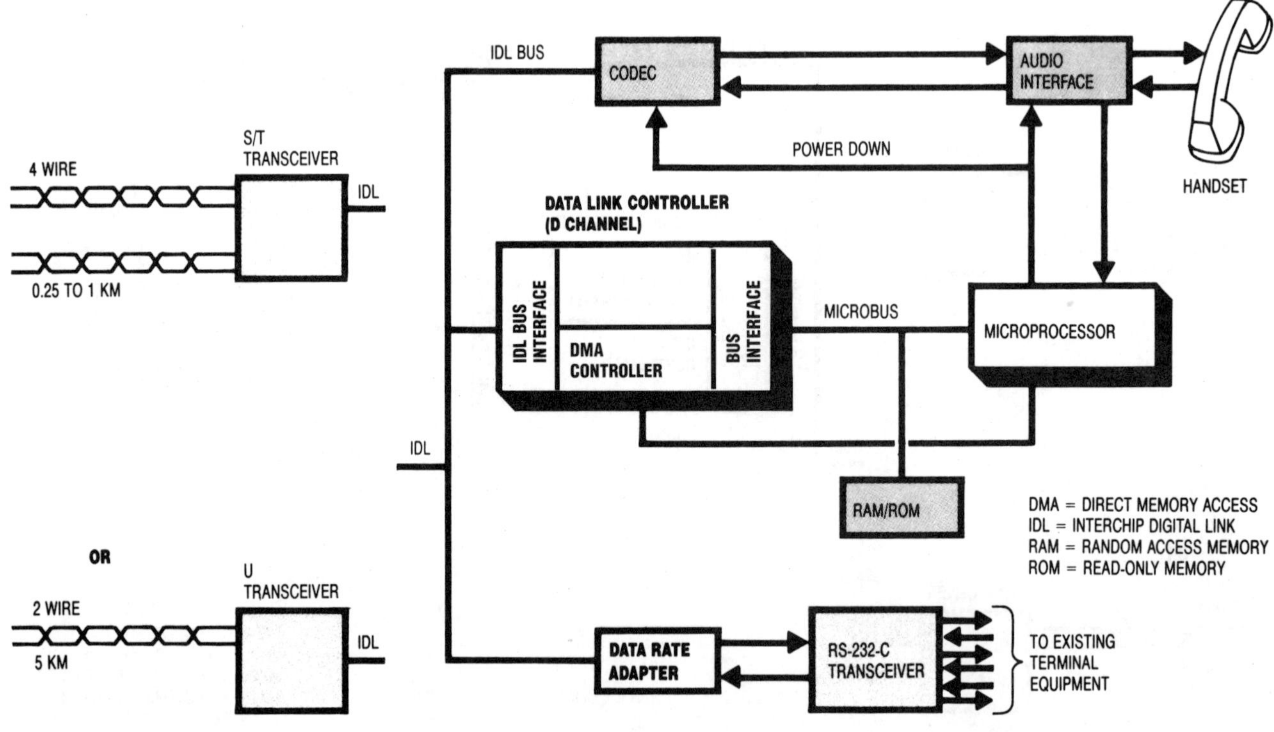

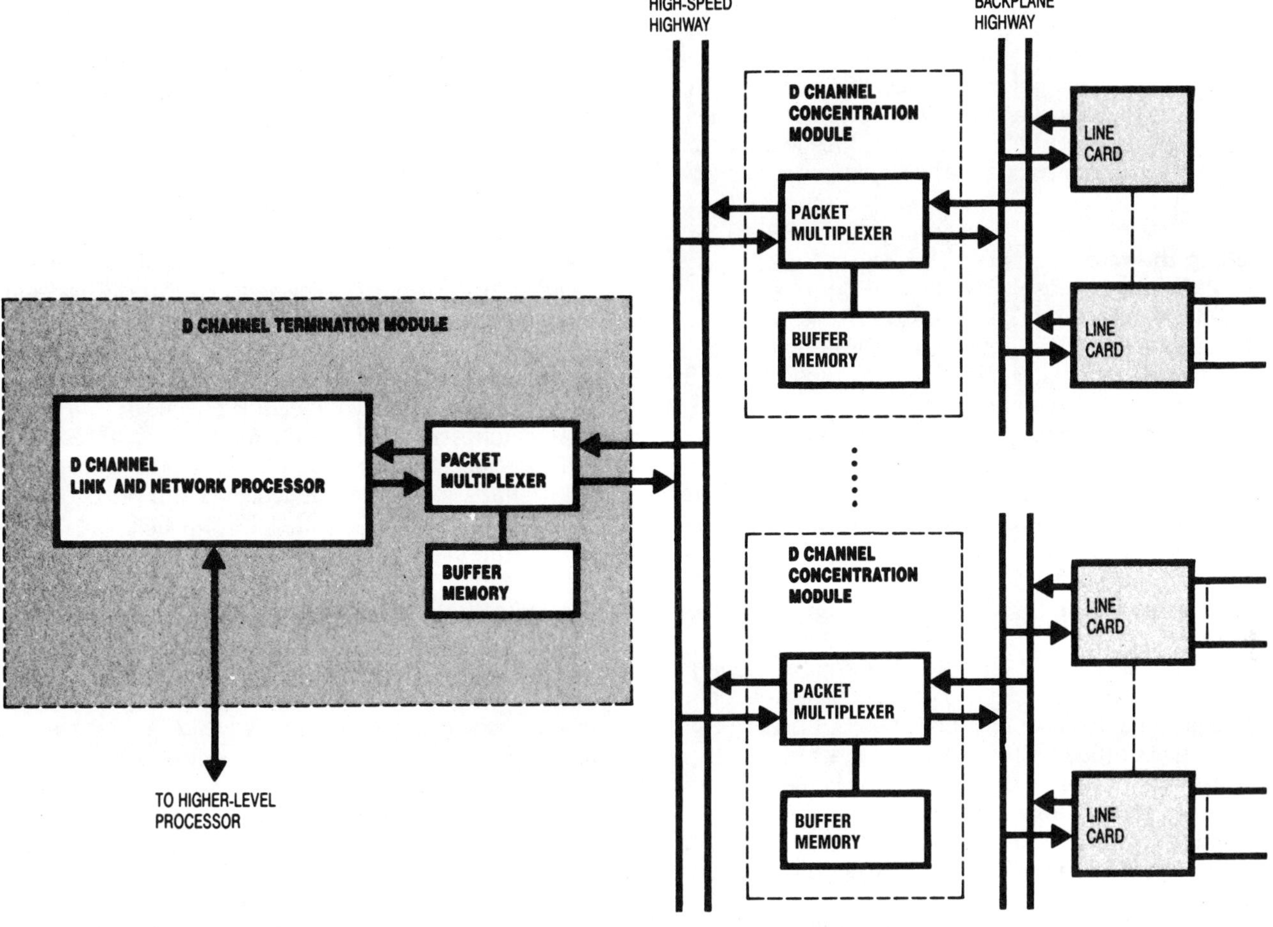

3. Muxing the LAPD protocol. *It is not optimally efficient to process the LAPD (link access procedure D) protocol at a line card for all D channels. A more efficient approach—requiring fewer LAPD-protocol chips—is shown. Many D channels from several line cards are multiplexed into a data stream carried by the backplane highway.*

character from the buffer to the memory, which takes about 12 microseconds for a microprocessor. For the data rate of 64 kbit/s, full duplex, the microprocessor has to move a character within 62.5 microseconds [$(1 \div 2 \times 64$ kbit/s$) \times 8$ bits/byte] after the interrupt is issued by the data link controller. Otherwise, the data link will become unreliable. For a microprocessor, this interrupt-handling overhead represents 20 percent of the total available processing time—a substantial burden.

Experience indicates that the maximum achievable data rate is 64 kbit/s, full duplex, using this software-intensive approach. Any higher rate will make the data link unreliable due to data overrun.

On the other hand . . .

In the hardware-intensive approach, the LAPD bit-level protocol is processed with dedicated hardware, such as two DLCs. The built-in DMA controller and other necessary circuitry perform address recognition. The controller relieves the burden caused by interrupts to the microprocessor on a character-by-character basis. Therefore, the microprocessor can dedicate more processing time to handle both the element of procedure of the LAPD protocol and the Network layer protocol for call processing.

Assume that the first B channel is used to carry digitized voice, the second B channel is for data, and the D channel carries signaling and control messages for voice and data call connection and teardown. A block diagram is shown in Figure 1 in which DLCs are used to handle the LAPD protocol in the B and D channels. As shown, the incoming data received from the S/T or U transceiver is processed by the DLCs for such functions as address recognition of the TEI field, zero-bit deletion, flag detection and removal, and CRC. The data, stripped of flags and CRC, is stored in the buffer memory and later fed to the microprocessor for further processing, when necessary. This processing is in accord with the element of procedure of the LAPD protocol and the Network layer protocol. Furthermore, data received for the second B channel is processed by the microprocessor and moved to a workstation, through the buffers, for further processing.

The digitized voice destined for the first B channel is demultiplexed from the received serial data stream and fed to a PCM (pulse code modulation) coder/decoder (codec). The codec's output is then fed into an audio interface and the handset.

Similarly, outgoing data transferred from the workstation via the read/write buffers is first processed at the micropro-

403

cessor according to the LAPD's element of procedure and the Network layer protocol. The Network layer protocol may be performed by the microprocessor of the workstation. Then data is sent to the two DLCs for framing, CRC calculation and insertion, and zero-bit insertion. Outgoing voice signals are sampled and digitized by the PCM codec, then fed to the S/T or U transceiver. The S/T or U transceiver multiplexes data coming from the second B channel with data from the D channel and digitized voice from the first B channel into a single data stream, encodes them, and transmits the data stream over the two- or four-wire twisted pairs.

Matching the rate

Figure 2 depicts the case where the LAPD protocol is executed only within the D channel, to establish and disconnect the voice and data calls. ISDN operates synchronously. So data that is transmitted over the second B channel to an asynchronous DTE is processed by a rate adapter, to convert the synchronous transmission to asynchronous (the reverse procedure occurs in the other direction). The rate adapter also changes the data rate from a higher speed (64 kbit/s) to a lower one (up to 19.2 kbit/s) and vice versa. The slower data is handled by an RS-232-C transceiver, which transmits and receives data between the rate adapter and the DTE.

The rate adaption is obtained through a multistage process. User data at 19.2 kbit/s or below is first converted from asynchronous to synchronous by bit-stuffing — adding "stop" bits. Thus, the user data becomes 600 bit/s times an even number ($600 \text{ bit/s} \times 2^n$, where n is a positive integer greater than zero). Bit repetition and frame addition are done to convert the user data into 64 kbit/s. The microprocessor and the data link controller can be further integrated into a single chip to reduce the chip count and cost.

Optimizing efficiency

It is a common cost-beneficial practice to have eight subscriber loops terminated on one line card. But, it is still not optimally efficient to process the LAPD protocol for all D channels right at the line card. A more efficient approach — requiring less LAPD-protocol chips — is shown in Figure 3. Many D channels from several line cards are multiplexed into a data stream carried by the backplane highway — which interconnects the packet multiplexers and the line cards. A LAPD organizer (packet multiplexer) in the D channel termination module, which includes the built-in DMA, detects the frame boundary, conducts a CRC, and then reorganizes the input data stream.

This reorganization results in very high speed (Mbit/s) back-to-back (no gaps between frames) data packet frames that are transmitted over an even higher-speed (multi-Mbit/s) multiplexed highway. The frames are then processed by the D channel link-and-network processor, which handles LAPD and the Network layer data on a packet-by-packet basis. The major advantage of this approach: It eliminates the overhead caused by the many task switchings when the LAPD protocol is performed on each frame segment of the 16-kbit/s D channel.

So far, we have focused mainly on the basic access rate of the ISDN interfaces. The LAPD frame organizer and the architecture shown in Figure 3 also apply to the primary rate of access. The primary rate at the ISDN S/T interface reference points (not shown in Figure 3) is 1.544 Mbit/s (United States) or 2.048 Mbit/s (Europe). The differences between the basic and primary access rates include their data rates: The basic rate provides the 2B + D ($2 \times 64 + 16$ kbit/s) user-network interface, while the primary rate provides the 23 B + D ($23 \times 64 + 64$ kbit/s) interface. Other differences: Basic access provides both point-to-point and point-to-multipoint configurations, but the primary rate supports only point-to-point. This implies that for each direction of transmission, only one source and one destination are connected to the primary interface.

The applications of the primary rate ISDN interface include: linking two PBXs, linking a PBX to an ISDN central-office switch, and extending the primary rate to data communications users. LAPD will be used to process the signaling and control messages in the D channel for those data frames carried over the 23 B channels.

The architecture of Figure 3 can be used to handle the LAPD protocol for those primary rates that terminate at the S/T interface. With this approach, the LAPD protocol is not processed in the D channel at the termination of each primary rate of access. Instead, many of those D channels are demultiplexed from their primary rates and preprocessed by the LAPD organizer into back-to-back packets. Then the packets are transmitted over a higher speed (Mbit/s) data highway into a dedicated processor, where the LAPD element of procedure is processed. Three orders of magnitude higher throughput of the LAPD processing is achieved with this architecture.

Comparing approaches

A strictly software-intensive solution cannot handle the LAPD protocol at data rates higher than 64 kbit/s, full duplex. The data rates at the subscriber and at the exchange equipment are 80 kbit/s (BD channels) and 128 kbit/s (eight D channels), full duplex, respectively. It appears that the best alternative at the subscriber site to reduce the excessive host overhead caused by interrupts is to use a DMA technique to move the received data without the host processor's attention. In that way, the processor receives the interrupt signals only at the end of each data frame. This allows it to dedicate more processing time to the higher-layer protocols.

At the line cards of the switching equipment, it is more efficient to process data frames from many D channels with a frame organizer, which reorganizes and multiplexes the incoming low-speed signals into higher-speed back-to-back frames. Then, a dedicated processor (any high-performance microprocessor, such as a 32-bit one) can better handle the LAPD and even the Network layer protocols. This approach reduces processing requirements, thereby providing a cost-effective ISDN upgrade. The approach also minimizes changes to the line cards of existing digital central office switches. ∎

Po Chen conducts strategic product planning and market development of data communications, including networking of ISDN and LAN products, at Motorola. He received his B.E.E. from the National Taiwan University, M.E.E. from the University of Hawaii, and Ph.D. from the School of Electrical Engineering, Purdue University.

James I. Falek and Mary A. Johnston, BBN Communications Corp., Cambridge, Mass.

Standards makers cementing ISDN subnetwork layers

ISDN standards will radically alter the way users access networks. By 1996, T1 will be out and a much leaner X.25 will be in, thanks to the lower three layers of ISDN.

Integrated Services Digital Network (ISDN) standards are an attempt to bring the sophistication of data communications protocols to the world of circuit switching. Initially, the aim of the international and American standards activities was to replicate existing circuit-switched voice and data services. Recently, however, the physical, logical link, and network layers of ISDN have begun to solidify. These three layers, collectively called the subnetwork layers, may form the basis of most future networking technology.

ISDN standards cover both circuit and packet switching. In the past few years, many of the circuit-switched recommendations have been discussed and finalized. Most of these are expected to pass in the 1988 plenary session of the International Telegraph and Telephone Consultative Committee (CCITT). Because the work on packet-mode standards had a much later start, these standards are in much rougher form. Standards for Layer 1, the physical layer, are essentially complete, as are those for Layer 2 (that is, Link Access Procedure-D, or LAPD). These maintained much of their initial form of 1984. The Layer 3 (network layer) protocol is much less solid. However, a version is expected to be approved in 1988. The period from 1988 to the next plenary session in 1992 will see an effort to expand the capabilities of packet-mode services as well as to develop more user-oriented applications and services.

In the short term, this means that X.25 packet-switching networks will undergo little change from the way they operate today. Although gateways to ISDN will be necessary, the ISDN packet-mode protocols will not require major changes to the way X.25 operates. However, after 1992, significant changes to the X.25 protocol are envisioned that will take advantage of wideband ISDN and the expected widespread availability of fiber optics. Consequently, tracking the status of the standards is important to both product developers, who must immediately seize hold of recommendations to support their next-generation equipment designs, and to users. Users can gauge the status of standards as mile markers, anticipating that commercially acceptable, debugged products based on those standards will hit the market two or three years after CCITT approves them.

ISDN is a layered protocol that follows the general guidelines set forth in the Open Systems Interconnection (OSI) seven-layer model. This fact alone differentiates ISDN from telephony standards in that it is being defined in terms of data communications guidelines, rather than circuit-switched analog signaling specifications. ISDN is bringing the worlds of data communications and telephony closer.

This article will serve as an overview and primer for those who want to understand ISDN in the context of the ISO (International Organization for Standardization) layers. It is expected that three methods for packet switching across an ISDN will be approved in 1988, with significant work being completed on a fourth mode. As noted above, these standards do not change existing packet-mode protocols such as X.25, but will fundamentally affect their future implementation.

Circuit-switched and packet-mode services use the same channel types and protocols. However, the protocol requirements for packet support are much more extensive because they must work with existing standards, most importantly, X.25.

Interfaces and channel types

To a large degree, the issues of interfaces and channel types have been agreed upon since the 1984 CCITT plenary session and are not expected to change extensively in 1988. An understanding of their format is critical to any analysis of ISDN because they provide the framework through which the protocols and applications flow.

1. Unifier. *The ISDN user-network interface separates the network (or networks) from the user. The user sees a single ubiquitous interface to a single network.*

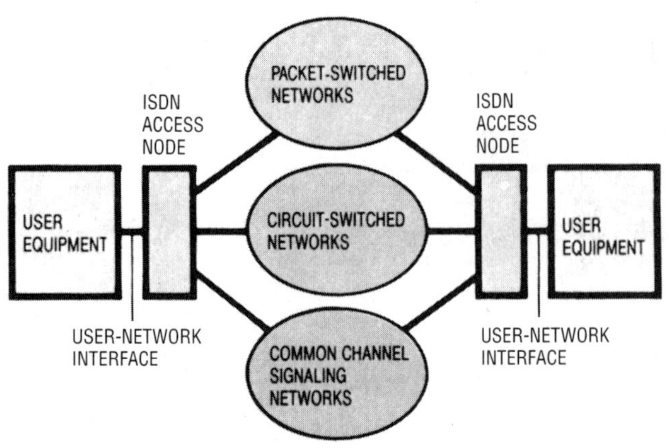

ISDN defines a full network architecture (Fig. 1). This architecture separates access functions (how to get into the network) from actual network functions (those internal to the network). Of key importance to ISDN is how access nodes interact with the user rather than how elements within the network interact with each other.

The user-network interface is comprised of all the equipment between a user's customer-premises equipment (for example, a private branch exchange, or PBX) and the network (Fig. 2). Each device in the user-network interface has a particular function or set of functions and is called a functional grouping. The interfaces between functional groupings are known as reference points. Functional groupings are considered to be an extension of either the network's or the user's equipment. Network termination (NT) equipment handles the communications from the network while the terminal equipment (TE) is responsible for the communications from the user.

Network Termination 1 (NT1) devices define the boundary of an ISDN and are responsible for the basic OSI Layer 1 functions. These devices handle the physical and electrical termination of the network and perform signal conversion, timing, and maintenance of the physical line. They also protect the user from changes in the transmission technology of the local subscriber loop by providing a fixed, standardized physical interface.

In contrast, Network Termination 2 (NT2) devices are usually more intelligent than NT1 devices. NT2 devices perform the link layer functions and usually network layer functions as well. When the NT2 does not have the network layer protocol capability (for example, if the host has an X.25 front-end), the NT2 passes along to the terminal equipment the original Layers 2 and 3 frame that was received from the NT1. An NT2 device may be a switch, multiplexer, local area network (LAN), PBX, or a terminal controller.

A Network Termination 1,2 (NT12) is a single device that has the functionality of an NT1 device combined with the functionality of an NT2 device. The NT12 will handle the

---

2. Various points of demarcation. *The user-network interface is divided between network equipment and terminal (user) equipment. In the United States, the terminal equipment includes everything from the NT1 to the TE devices, whereas in Europe, ISDN users will control all devices from the NT12 to the TEs.*

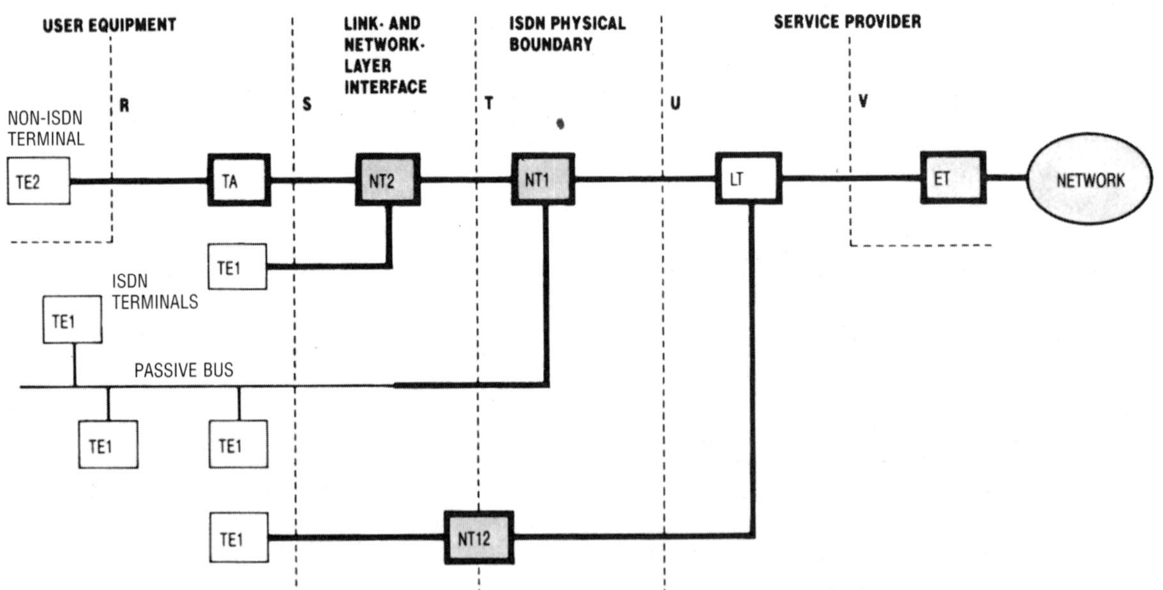

physical, link, and network layer protocols.

Besides the three NT functional groupings, there are three other functional groupings (TE1, TE2, and TA) that describe terminal access to an ISDN. Terminal equipment (such as telephone handsets or computer terminals) is considered to be either ISDN-compatible or pre-ISDN. ISDN terminal equipment is referred to as Terminal Equipment 1 (TE1). TE1s can just plug into an NT2 or NT1 and begin to communicate in the ISDN environment. Pre-ISDN terminals, known as Terminal Equipment 2 (TE2), will use their pre-ISDN connectors (such as RS-232-C) to connect to an ISDN Terminal Adaptor (TA). The TA will, in turn, connect to an NT2. A TA can be a separate device hanging off an NT2 or can be part of an NT2 device. Most NT2s are expected to have multiple dedicated TA ports.

Reference points are the logical connectors between the functional groupings in the user-network interface. The reference points refer to the separation of the functions between any two functional groupings. The S reference point separates an NT2 device from terminal equipment. The T separates an NT2 or TE1s on a passive bus from an NT1. The U separates an NT1 from the line-termination equipment while the V divides line-termination from exchange-termination equipment.

Each of the reference points has somewhat different characteristics. The S and T physically consist of two twisted-wire pairs—one to transmit and one to receive—allowing full-duplex communication. The range of S and T reference points is 3,300 feet (1,000 meters) in a point-to-point configuration or up to 500 feet (150 meters) in a multidrop passive-bus configuration. The U interface will have a maximum length of 2,500 to 6,500 meters. The V interface will be a nonstandard interface between the LT and ET and will be found in the central office.

The U reference point is a full-duplex interface running over a single pair of twisted wires. The conversion from four to two wires (NT1 to LT), needed to maintain consistency with current telephone networks, is done by an echo-canceling algorithm. This algorithm won out recently over the competing "Ping-Pong" method, ending a controversy that had brewed for some time.

The echo-canceling protocol that will be codified in the 1986 CCITT Gray Book uses a connected equalizing network to electrically balance the communications network. When transmitting, half of the transmitted power is absorbed by the cable and the other half is absorbed by the equalizing network. Due to the inexact splitting of the power, echoes of the transmitted data are reflected back to the sender. An attached filter cancels the echoes by testing all incoming transmissions and comparing them with the previously transmitted data. If there is an exact match (including particular physical and electrical characteristics), the information is deemed to be an echo and is removed from the transmission line.

In the United States, both the NT1 and NT2 functions are considered to be part of customer premises equipment, requiring the use of a nationally standardized U interface to permit competition among the manufacturers of premises equipment. In Europe, however, the NT1 function has been delegated to the public common carrier, eliminating the need for a standard U interface.

At this time, it is unknown whether Europe will eventually adopt a U standard to promote terminal portability on a global basis. For international companies and the U. S. government, which hope to gain economies of scale by purchasing equipment from a single source, this lack of international acceptance of the U interface could have significant consequences.

Data is transferred between NT and TE, either packet-switched or circuit-switched networks, through channels. ISDN has only a few types of channels, documented in the 1984 Red Book. Two of these, the B and D channels, will be the most widely used between now and 1992. The channels are as follows:

- The A channel is the 56-kbit/s analog channel used in the telephone network today.
- The B, or bearer, channel is a 64-kbit/s bidirectional digital voice-grade (high-quality) channel that does not carry any signaling information. B channels will be the backbone of the ISDN user-network interface. They will carry voice and data using either circuit switching or packet switching.
- The C channel is a digital channel that will be used with the A channel during the transition to ISDN. The C channel will operate at 8 or 16 kbit/s and carry signaling information, interactive data transfer, and teleaction information (tele action refers to a low-speed communications service for short messages).
- The D channel handles both the transfer of user data and signaling information. "Signaling" refers to the passing of information for the establishment, maintenance, and clearing of ISDN channels. Currently, signaling information in the network—such as ring, busy, and caller number—is passed along in-stream with the call (in-band signaling). The ISDN user-network interface uses out-of-band signaling over the D channel for more efficient transfer of data and overall use of the bearer channels. Since signaling occurs in bursts and is not time-consuming, the D channel will be idle for part or most of the time. Therefore, the D channel can be used more efficiently by passing low-speed packet data and telemetry information when not in use by the bearer channel. This gives a user the choice of transmitting packet-switched data over either the B channel or the slower D channel. The transmission of signaling information will have a higher priority on the D channel than that of packet-switched data.
- H channels are formed out of multiple B channels. These wideband channels are beginning to attract a great deal of attention among standards bodies. They will generally rely on fiber optics to support multimegabit data rates. The H channels will be used for fast facsimile, video, high-speed data, high-quality audio, and packet switching. Some H channel types mentioned in the CCITT 1984 Red Book include the following:
- The H0 channel (384 kbit/s);
- The H11 channel (1.536 Mbit/s); and
- The H12 channel (1.920 Mbit/s).
- The H4 channel (approximately 135 Mbit/s) will have enough capacity to connect to high-performance LANs. Higher bandwidths will be created as needed from some combination of the H and B channels.

Channel access is defined as the configuration of channels used to transfer user data and signaling information to and from an ISDN. The two types of channel access currently defined are as follows:

■ The basic-rate interface (BRI) channel is intended for a single terminal point-to-point connection, access to multiple terminals using a star or bus topology, or access to a small PBX. Basic-rate interfaces consist of two B channels at 64 kbit/s and one D channel at 16 kbit/s (commonly called 2B + D). Thus, the effective basic access rate bandwidth totals 144 kbit/s (64 + 64 + 16).

■ Primary-rate interface (PRI) channels are intended for connection to a large PBX or LAN. The primary access rate is intended for use in place of T1 lines. Currently, there are two T1 rate standards, one for North America and Japan (1.544 Mbit/s) and another for Europe (2.048 Mbit/s). The 1.544-Mbit/s PRI uses 23 B channels at 64 kbit/s and a single 64-kbit/s D channel for signaling. The 2.048-Mbit/s PRI uses 30 B channels and a single 64-kbit/s D channel.

Beyond the arena of physical interfaces and channel types lie the protocols of ISDN. Packet-mode standards are much more fluid and incomplete than the interfaces and channel types. As with most current standards activities, ISDN protocols attempt to follow the OSI seven-layer model as much as possible. Most ISDN work has concentrated on the three lower layers, physical, data link, and network, as described below.

Physicallayer protocols

The basic-rate interface allows for both point-to-point and multidrop passive-bus connections. The frames transmitted by the network to the terminal equipment have a different format than the frames transmitted in the other direction. Frames are transmitted by the network and the terminal equipment every 250 microseconds (millionths of a second). Four thousand frames a second carrying 48 bits per frame yield an actual data-transfer rate of 192 kbit/s. Yet the frame actually carries only 36 bits of B and D channel data. One-quarter of each frame, or 12 bits, is overhead, making the nominal data-transfer rate 144 kbit/s.

NT frames are the frames transmitted by the network to the terminal equipment. TE frames are the frames transmitted by the terminal equipment to the network. The first two bits of both the NT and TE frame are used for framing

alignment (synchronization) (Fig. 3). The NT and TE frames contain two octets of bits to transmit B1 channel information (B1 bits), two octets of bits to transmit B2 channel information (B2 bits), and four bits to transmit D channel information.

In the NT frame, the L bits are used to electrically balance the entire frame, whereas in the NT frame, the L bits balance each octet of B channel information and each individual D channel bit. This is done to avoid line-code violations as well as to limit the content of the signal received by the NT in the passive-bus configuration.

The A bit in the NT frame is used to activate or deactivate a TE, allowing the device to come on line or, when there is no activity, to be placed in low-power-consumption mode. The S bits currently have not been assigned and are reserved for future standardization. The E bits in the NT frame are the echoes of the previously transmitted TE frame's D channel bits.

When the NT receives a D channel bit from a TE, the NT will echo that bit in the next immediate E bit position. The TE expects that the next incoming E bit is the echo of the last transmitted D bit.

The TEs using a passive-bus configuration need to arbitrate to transmit D channel information (arbitration of B channel information is handled at Layers 2 and 3). When a TE has D channel information to transmit, it will watch the bits arriving on the line from the NT. A specified number of continuous E bits with the binary value of one will indicate that the D channel is currently not in use. When that number is reached, the TE will transmit its D channel information.

After receiving a D channel bit, the NT will echo that bit in its current frame's next E bit position. The TE will evaluate the next incoming E bit from the NT. The TE will continue to transmit only if the incoming E bit has the same value as its last transmitted D channel information bit. If the bits' values are different, the TE will assume that a D channel collision has occurred, stop transmitting on the D channel, and begin the D channel arbitration process again.

---

3. Frame variances. *Although the basic-rate interface frames are the same size (48 bits), the NT frames (frames transmitted from the NT) have a different format than the TE frames (sent from the TE). This is due to the different responsibilities of the NT and the TE, especially when using the passive bus architecture.*

BASIC-RATE TE FRAME

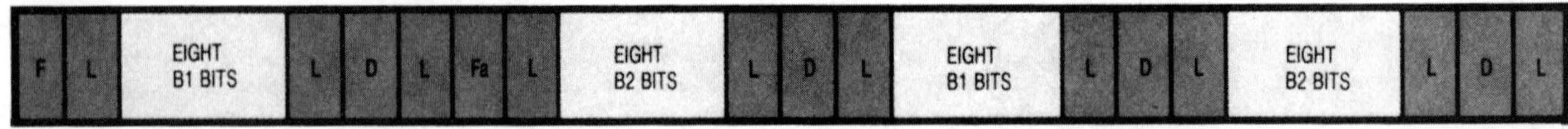

BASIC-RATE NT FRAME

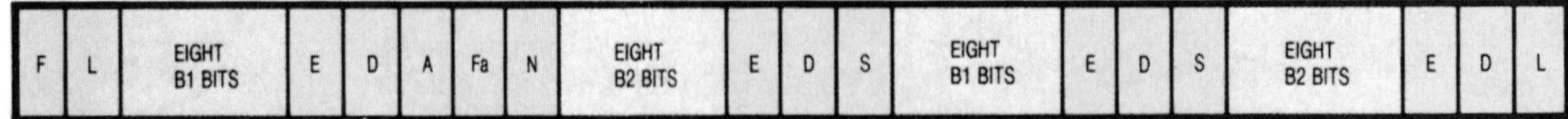

A = ACTIVATE/DEACTIVATE BIT
B1 = B1 CHANNEL BITS
B2 = B2 CHANNEL BITS
D = D CHANNEL BIT
E = D CHANNEL ECHO BIT
F = FRAMING BIT
Fa = AUXILIARY FRAMING BIT
L = DC BALANCING BIT
NT = NETWORK TERMINATION
TE = TERMINAL EQUIPMENT

The number of continuous E bits of value one that must be received by the TE prior to sending D channel data is contingent upon the type of information that the TE needs to transmit. Signaling information is given a higher priority than nonsignaling information. As such, the number of continuous E bits of value one that is needed to transmit signaling information is less than with nonsignaling information. Currently, eight E bits of value one must be "seen" by the TE to send signaling information and 10 E bits of value one to send nonsignaling information.

Following the successful transmission of a LAPD (Layer 2) frame, the number of continuous E bits of value one needed by a TE is incremented by one (for that type of information). This allows the other TEs on the multipoint passive bus the opportunity to access the D channel. After all the TEs have accessed the D channel, the number of E bits needed by the TE is decremented down to its previous level. When a TE does not have any D channel information to send, the TE will transmit binary ones on the D channel, allowing the previously described process to transpire.

The primary-rate interface will be used to replace the current T1 communications. Whereas the basic-rate interface is complicated by the multipoint passive bus, the primary rate is complicated by having two frame formats, the 1.544-Mbit/s frame and the 2.048-Mbit/s frame (Fig. 4). Each primary access frame contains an initial framing bit followed by multiple eight-bit slots. Each slot is for a particular D or B channel. The smaller primary B channel frame, the 1.544-Mbit/s frame, has 24 slots, numbered 1 through 24, with the D channel, if present, in the last slot. The 2.048-Mbit/s frame has 32 slots, numbered 0 through 31, with the D channel, if present, in slot 16. Frames are required to be transmitted every 125 microseconds (8,000 frames per second).

Over a primary-rate interface, signaling is usually done by the single D channel contained in that interface. Thus, when there are multiple primary-rate interfaces across the user-network interface, there will exist groups of B channels, each controlled by a single D channel within the individual PRI. This could be an inefficient use of bandwidth. To improve the situation, ISDN allows for the substitution of a single D channel by a single B channel. In this case, the D channel would be relieved of its signaling responsibilities and allowed to behave as a standard B

---

4. Primary frames. *The 1.544-Mbit/s primary-rate interface frame will be used in North America and Japan, while the 2.048-Mbit/s frame is for Europe.*

1.544-MBIT/S B-CHANNEL PRIMARY ACCESS FRAME

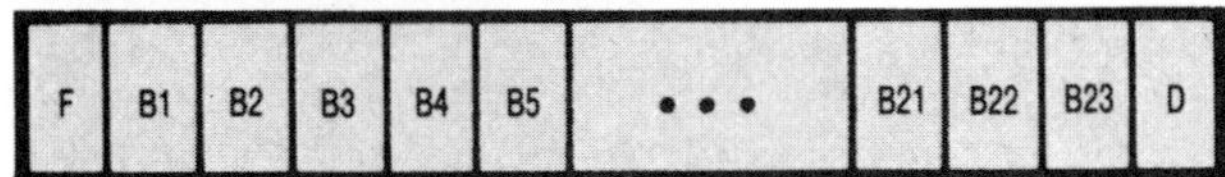

2.048-MBIT/S B-CHANNEL PRIMARY ACCESS FRAME

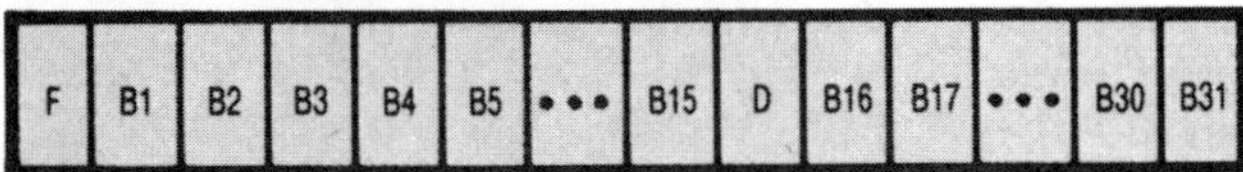

F = FRAMING BIT
D = EIGHT D-CHANNEL BITS
Bn = EIGHT B-CHANNEL n BITS

---

5. LAPD. *The LAPD frame contains a control field, command/response bit (its progenitor, LAPB, uses a byte), an information field, and a frame checksum.*

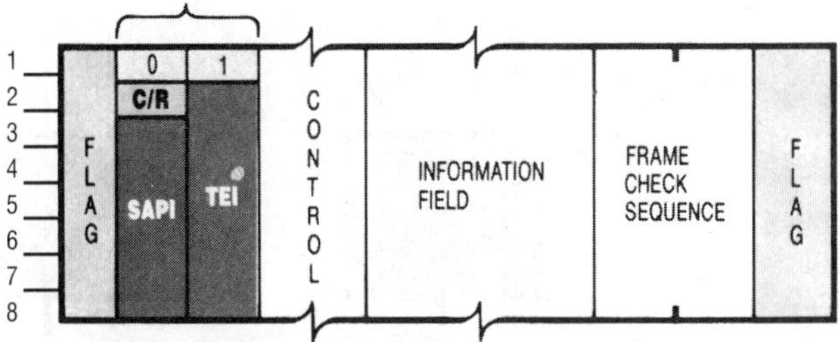

SAPI = SERVICE ACCESS POINT IDENTIFIER
TEI = TERMINAL END-POINT IDENTIFIER
C/R = COMMAND/RESPONSE BIT

---

channel. It could then be used for circuit- or packet-switched connections. One of the other D channels in the user network interface would be given the signaling responsibility first held by the original D channel as well as responsibility for this new B channel. Hence, multiple PRIs could be used with only a single operating D channel.

Link layer protocols

Layer 2, the data link layer, is responsible for the reliable transfer of information across the physical links. Its functions include synchronization, error control, and flow control. The datalinklevel protocol for the signaling channel in ISDN is a bit-oriented protocol similar to HDLC (high-level data link control) called LAPD, also known as CCITT Recommendation Q.921. The information transferred may be user-packet information or signaling information. Circuit-mode connections will not necessarily use LAPD for communications, except for signaling.

There are two different types of LAPD information-transfer service, unacknowledged and acknowledged. In unacknowledged information-transfer service, information from the network layer is transferred in frames that are not acknowledged by the receiving station. This allows for fast data transfer but provides for neither flow control nor error recovery.

By contrast, acknowledged information-transfer service is used only with point-to-point communications. Upper-layer information (such as packet data or ISDN network layer messages) is transferred in numbered frames that are acknowledged by the receiving entity. This service uses a windowing protocol (not permitted in the unacknowledged service) that allows multiple frames to be sent to an entity before requiring acknowledgment providing an effective flow-control mechanism. Unlike the unacknowledged information-transfer service, the acknowledged variety provides full error-recovery mechanisms for both transmission errors and frame-format errors.

The LAPD frame consists of several components (Fig. 5). The 2-byte address of each frame, called the Data Link Control Identifier (DLCI), is divided into the Service Access Point Identifier (SAPI) and the Terminal End-point Identifier (TEI). These provide a form of multiplexing, since the SAPI tells the LAPD entity which Layer 3 entity the transmission is intended for and the TEI similarly identifies the logical

6. Layer structure. *The design of the LAPD frame allows the selection of multiple Layer 3 entities, by means of the SAPI, and a further differentiation of multiple higher-layer entities, by means of the TEI. This brings a much richer addressing and multiplexing mechanism to the link layer than it ordinarily has.*

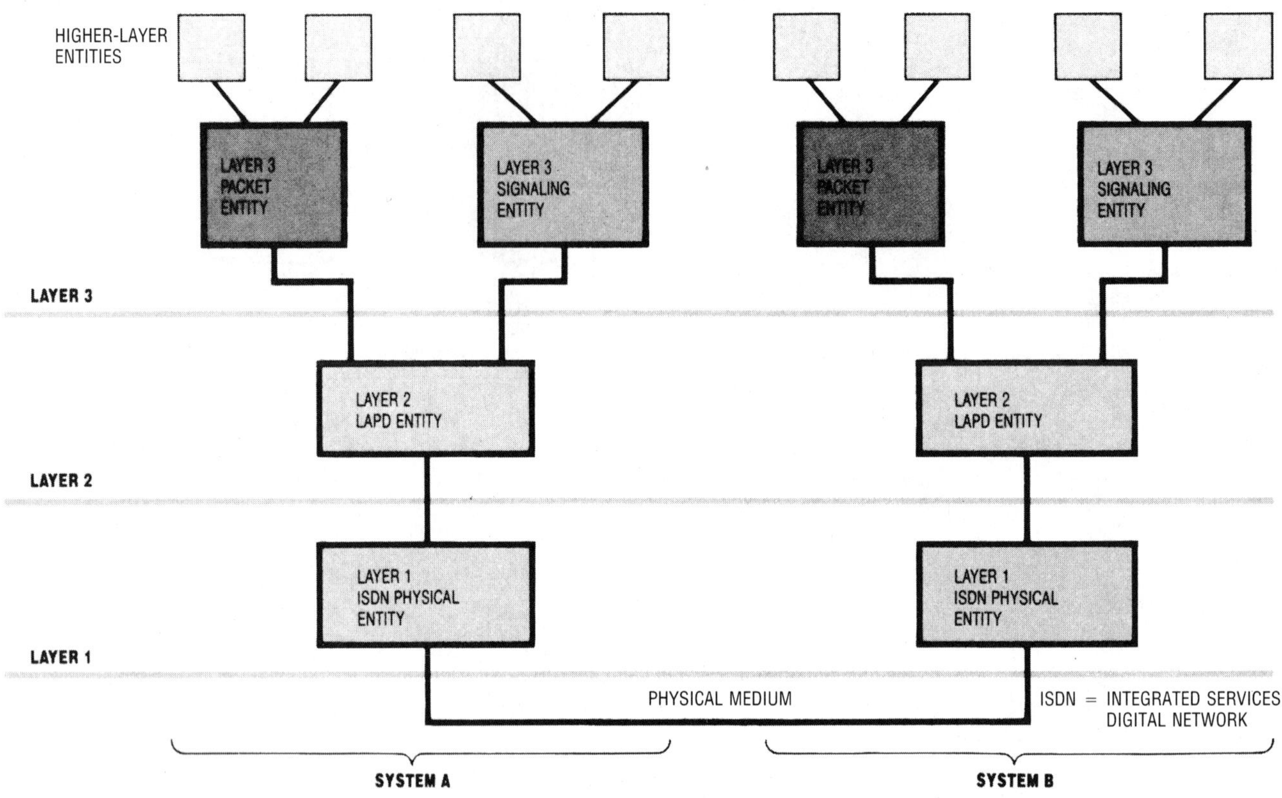

terminal within that Layer 3 entity.

The control field determines the type of LAPD frame being transmitted as well as containing the sequence numbers for the acknowledged information transfer service. The information field carries higher-layer data and is currently restricted to a 256-octet maximum. This maximum data-length value is expected to be increased in the future to more efficiently handle packet voice, LAN data, and satellite-link data. The Frame Check Sequence is the standard 2-byte CCITT-16 cyclic-redundancy checksum. Finally, the frame is enveloped by one or more HDLC flags.

The Command/Response (C/R) bit is similar to the address field used in HDLC (LAP and LAPB) to differentiate commands from responses. The TE will set the C/R bit to one for responses and reset it to zero for commands. The network side does the opposite, setting the bit for commands and resetting it for responses.

The SAPI identifies the network entity for which the information in the LAPD frame is intended. A LAPD entity will usually have more than a single Layer 3 entity above it and therefore will have more than one SAPI in use (Fig. 6). There are currently three SAPIs defined in ISDN. A LAPD frame with a SAPI equal to zero would tell the link that the frame is transporting signaling information. A frame with a SAPI equal to 16 would indicate that the frame was carrying data for the X.25 packet-mode data. A SAPI equal to 63 in a LAPD frame is used for management purposes. This process affords the user-network interface a layer of multiplexing, as well as giving the receiving link layer entity

information to determine if it supports the type of network connection being requested.

The TEI identifies the logical terminal or final destination for the Layer 3 information. One or more TEIs can be used for point-to-point data transfer besides that offered by the SAPI at Layer 2, providing another layer of multiplexing. The TEI for broadcast connection occurs when a message is transmitted with the TEI set to all ones. Broadcast TEI frames will be transmitted to all the logical terminals on the Layer 3 entity.

The control field indicates the type of frame being transmitted. There are three different formats for the control field: numbered information transfer (I format), supervisory functions (S format), and unnumbered information transfers and control functions (U format). These are shown in Figure 7. The I-format frames are used to transfer information between network layer entities. Each I frame has a send-sequence number, a receive-sequence number, and a poll/final bit, which are all independent. The S-frame format is for supervisory-control functions. The U format provides additional functionality and is used for information transfer during unacknowledged information transfer. The modifier function bits and the supervisory function bits differentiate the frame types (listed in Table 1) from one another.

ISDN's Layer 3, the network layer, has not been completed to the degree of the physical and data link layers. The network protocol, known by its CCITT Recommendation title, Q.931, must be able to both handle data transport and signaling. Although the protocol was originally to be used solely for the signaling channel, it is now intended to be used on both signaling and bearer (data) channels.

The network layer protocol uses messages to convey information between two Layer 3 entities (similar to X.25 packet layer). The components of the message are called information elements. Depending upon the type of message, some of the information elements are mandatory while others, such as those listed in Table 2, are optional. The mandatory information elements are as follows: the protocol discriminator, the call reference, and the message type (Fig. 8).

■ The protocol discriminator is used to distinguish an ISDN network message from other OSI network layer messages. Additionally, it distinguishes between other network layer messages (including X.25) and user-specific protocols. The protocol discriminator is always the first octet of a message.

■ The call reference is the second information element in the ISDN network layer message. It is used to identify the message with a connection request. The call reference is made up of call-reference length, a call-reference flag, and a call-reference value.

The call-reference value is assigned by the source of the access connection at the beginning of a call and remains fixed for the duration of the call. This value has only local significance (between TE and NT). The call-reference value will be used for identification purposes in both registration/cancellation of TEs to the NT and activation/deactivation requests from the NT to the TE. A global call-reference value may be used for broadcast messages that will affect every connection on a logical link.

The call-reference flag is a Boolean value that identifies which side initiated the connection. The destination side always sets the flag to "1," while the originator sets the flag to "0." Therefore, all call-reference values can be used simultaneously by two connections on a logical link, assigned once by the user equipment and once by the network.

■ The message type identifies the function of the message

---

7. LAPD frame control fields. *I frames help transfer higher-layer information, S frames handle flow control, and U frames help maintain the data link connection.*

INFORMATION FORMAT (2 OCTETS)	N(S)						0
	N(R)						P/F

SUPERVISORY FORMAT (2 OCTETS)	0	0	0	0	S	S	0	1
	N(R)							P/F

UNNUMBERED FORMAT	M	M	M	P/F	M	M	1	1

M = MODIFIER FUNCTION BITS
N(S) = SEND SEQUENCE NUMBER
N(R) = RECEIVE SEQUENCE NUMBER
P/F = POLL OR FINAL BIT
S = SUPERVISORY FUNCTION BITS

Table 1: LAPD control field type

FORMAT	FRAME TYPE	NAME	RESPONSIBILITY
I	I	INFORMATION	TRANSFER SEQUENTIALLY NUMBERED FRAMES CARRYING LAYER 3 INFORMATION FOR ACKNOWLEDGED INFORMATION TRANSFER SERVICE
S	RR	RECEIVER READY	INDICATES THAT THE LAYER 2 ENTITY IS READY TO RECEIVE A FRAME, ACKNOWLEDGES A PREVIOUSLY SENT FRAME, AND CLEARS THE BUSY CONDITION ESTABLISHED BY AN RNR FRAME
	RNR	RECEIVER NOT READY	INDICATES A LINK LAYER BUSY CONDITION (A TEMPORARY INABILITY TO ACCEPT INCOMING I FRAMES)
	REJ	REJECT	REQUEST RETRANSMISSION OF I FRAMES STARTING AT THE N(R) FRAME
U	SABME	SET ASYNCHRONOUS BALANCED MODE EXTENDED	BEGIN LINK CONNECTION FOR ACKNOWLEDGED INFORMATION TRANSFER SERVICE USING MODULO 128-FRAME WINDOWING
	DM	DISCONNECT MODE	INFORMS RECEIVING ENTITY THAT THE CONNECTION IS IN AN ERROR STATE AND THAT UNACKNOWLEDGED INFORMATION TRANSFER SERVICE CANNOT BE PERFORMED
	UI	UNNUMBERED INFORMATION	UNNUMBERED FRAMES CARRYING LAYER 3 INFORMATION FOR UNACKNOWLEDGED INFORMATION TRANSFER SERVICE
	DISC	DISCONNECT	USED TO TERMINATE ACKNOWLEDGED INFORMATION TRANSFER SERVICE
	UA	UNNUMBERED ACKNOWLEDGMENT	ACKNOWLEDGE SABME OR DISC
	FRMR	FRAME REJECT	REPORT OF AN ERROR CONDITION THAT CAN NOT BE RECOVERED BY THE RETRANSMISSION OF AN IDENTICAL FRAME
	XID	TRANSFER ID	USED TO TRANSFER CONNECTION MANAGEMENT INFORMATION BETWEEN PEER ENTITIES

being transmitted. It is the third information element in a message and is currently a single octet in length (currently, the extension bit is set to zero). Message types are divided into one of three categories: call-establishment, call-disestablishment, and miscellaneous messages (Table 3).

Optional information elements are at least one octet in length and are located at the end of a message. The single-octet information element has a three-bit identifier, whereas the multi-octet information element has a seven-bit identifier (Fig. 9). Many of the services that ISDN will provide will use the information elements.

There are currently three mutually exclusive scenarios for using the ISDN network layer protocol: packet-mode connections over the signaling D channel, packet-mode connections over the user-data B channels, and circuit-mode connections to packet networks via the B channel. These options are expected to be approved by the CCITT in the 1988 plenary session. Each scenario leaves the operations of existing X.25 packet networks unchanged.

However, a fourth option, known as frame-relay connection, is in the works. This option could ultimately entail extensive revisions to the existing X.25 protocol. Although it is not expected to be approved by the 1988 CCITT plenary session, frame-relay will certainly be a high priority by 1992.

The following is a description of these four options, which are depicted in Figure 10. Each option depends upon the D channel signaling connection being established between the NT and the TE. This connection can be initiated by the terminal equipment or by the network. To illustrate these sequences, let TS refer to a signaling connection initiated by the terminal and NS refer to one initiated by the network. (These are the authors' own abbreviations, not standard terminology.)

In a TS sequence, the TE sends a SETUP message with

Table 2: Selected ISDN network-layer information elements

SINGLE-OCTET INFORMATION ELEMENT

NAME	FUNCTION
LOCKING SHIFT	INDICATES THAT THE FOLLOWING IS DIFFERENT TYPE OF INFORMATION ELEMENT (GIVES THE ABILITY TO SHIFT BETWEEN INTERNATIONAL, NATIONAL, NETWORK-SPECIFIC, AND USER-SPECIFIC INFORMATION ELEMENTS)

VARIABLE-LENGTH INFORMATION ELEMENTS

NAME	FUNCTION
BEARER CAPABILITY	INDICATES THAT THE NETWORK CAN PROVIDE SPECIFIC BEARER CAPABILITIES (DATA TRANSFER RATE, DATA TRANSFER CAPABILITY)
CALL STATE	DEFINES CURRENT STATE OF CONNECTION (SUCH AS ACTIVE, DETACHED, AND DISCONNECT REQUEST)
CHANNEL IDENTIFICATION	IDENTIFY CHANNEL/SUBCHANNEL WITHIN THE INTERFACE
PROGRESS INDICATOR	DESCRIBES AN EVENT THAT OCCURRED DURING A CALL
KEYPAD	MECHANISM TO TRANSPORT IA5 (INTERNATIONAL ALPHABET 5, ALSO KNOWN AS ASCII) CHARACTERS - ENTERED BY MEANS OF A TERMINAL KEYPAD
CALLING PARTY NUMBER	IDENTIFIES SOURCE OF A CALL
CALLED PARTY NUMBER	IDENTIFIES DESTINATION OF A CALL
TRANSIT NETWORK SELECTOR	IDENTITY OF A NETWORK THAT CONNECTION SHOULD USE TO GET TO FINAL DESTINATION
LOW-LAYER COMPATIBILITY	USED FOR COMPATIBILITY CHECKING, IN CONJUNCTION WITH BEARER CAPABILITY
USER-USER INFORMATION	USED TO TRANSFER INFORMATION BETWEEN ISDN USERS THAT SHOULD NOT BE INTERPRETED BY THE NETWORK(S). EQUIVALENT TO FAST SELECT IN X.25

8. Q.931. Network layer message format includes the protocol discriminator, call-reference flag and value, message type, and optional information elements.

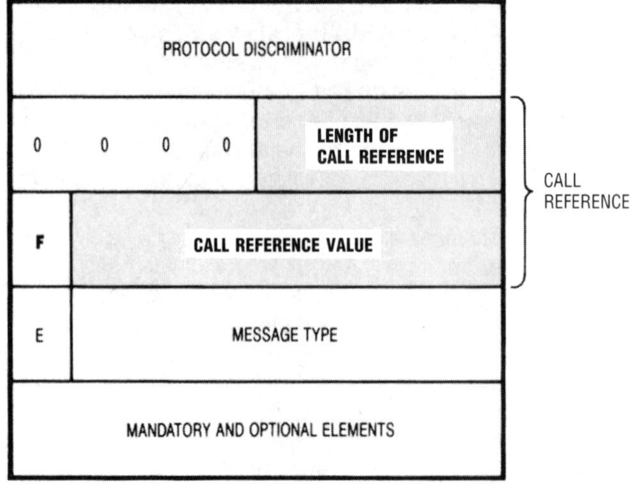

E = EXPANSION BIT
F = CALL REFERENCE FLAG

a SAPI of 0 over the D channel to the NT. The NT responds with one of four possible message sequences: a Release Complete (REL COM); a Connect (CONN); or a Call Proceeding (CALL PROC) followed by either a REL COM or a CONN message. A CALL PROC message indicates that the network will need more time to determine whether the signaling connection can be established. A REL COM or a CONN message will follow the CALL PROC message within a specified time-out. A REL COM message indicates that the connection cannot be set up at the current time. However, if a CONN message arrives, the LAPD logical link for signaling is established and other types of signaling can take place between the NT and the TE.

NS connections use the same sequence of messages to establish a signaling connection, except that the messages in the NS flow opposite to those in the TS (in the TS, the SETUP message is transmitted by the TE, whereas in the NS it is transmitted by the NT). Also, in establishing an NS connection, the NT must send a Connect Acknowledge (CONN ACK) message in response to a CONN message from the TE. This message is optional in the TS case.

■ Packet-mode over the D channel. If a signaling connection has not already been established, the TE performs a sequence similar to the TS to establish a link layer (LAPD) terminal-initiated packet connection (TP). The SETUP message used in a TP has a SAPI of 16 and a Channel Identifier information element, which tells the NT that the connection is to be established over the D channel. Upon receiving the CONN message (assuming that the network can handle packet data), the user may transmit an X.25 Call Request packet.

On the other side of the link, when the incoming Call Request is presented from the network, the NT determines if the call can be delivered based on part on the Called User Profile (CUP). This profile, stored in the NT, maintains such information as whether packet mode is allowed on the

D (signaling) channel, called party number, closed user group information, and throughput class. If the NT decides that the call cannot be processed, the call is cleared back to the network with an X.25 Clear Indication packet.

If, however, the call can be processed, the NT performs an NS (see above), if needed. After the signaling connection is established, the NT establishes a link layer packet connection between the NT and the TE. This network-initiated packet connection (NP) sequence is analogous to the NS sequence, except that the NT sends a SETUP message with a SAPI of 16 to establish a packet-mode connection. Once in packet mode, the NT relays the X.25 Call Request to the remote TE using LAPD frames whose SAPI is 16. X.25 packet layer procedures are used for virtual-circuit communications. All link layer frames use a SAPI of 16.

■ Packet-mode B channel access. Virtual circuits are

Table 3: Selected ISDN network-layer message types

NAME	DEFINITION
CALL ESTABLISHMENT MESSAGES	
ALERTING	RECEPTION OF A SETUP MESSAGE
CALL PROCEEDING (CALL PROC)	CALL ESTABLISHMENT HAS BEGUN AND NO MORE INFORMATION IS NEEDED
CONNECT (CONN)	CALL ACCEPTANCE BY CALLED USER
CONNECT ACKNOWLEDGE (CONN ACK)	RECEIPT OF CONNECT MESSAGE
SETUP	BEGIN CALL ESTABLISHMENT
SETUP ACKNOWLEDGE (SETUP ACK)	CALL ESTABLISHMENT HAS BEGUN AND MORE INFORMATION IS NEEDED BEFORE PROCEEDING
CALL DISESTABLISHMENT MESSAGES	
DISCONNECT (DISC)	INVITATION TO RELEASE A CHANNEL AND ALL ASSOCIATED CALL-REFERENCE VALUES
RELEASE (REL)	SENDING SIDE HAS RELEASED A CHANNEL AND ALL ASSOCIATED CALL REFERENCE VALUES; SENDING SIDE SHOULD DO THE SAME IF IT HAS NOT ALREADY DONE SO
RELEASE COMPLETE (REL COM)	SENDING SIDE HAS RELEASED A CHANNEL AND CONSIDERS THAT CHANNEL TO BE READY FOR REUSE
RESTART (REST)	REQUEST THAT A CHANNEL BECOME IDLE
RESTART ACKNOWLEDGE (REST ACK)	INDICATES REQUESTED RESTART IS COMPLETE
MISCELLANEOUS MESSAGES	
INFORMATION (INFO)	PROVIDE ADDITIONAL INFORMATION FOR CALL ESTABLISHMENT
STATUS (STAT)	RESPONSE TO UNEXPECTED MESSAGE OR IN RESPONSE TO A STATUS ENQUIRY
STATUS ENQUIRY (STAT ENQ)	SOLICIT INFORMATION ABOUT THE STATE OF THE CONNECTION

9. Elemental. *The optional ISDN network layer information elements transport the facilities and maintenance information about a network layer call.*

SINGLE-OCTET INFORMATION ELEMENT

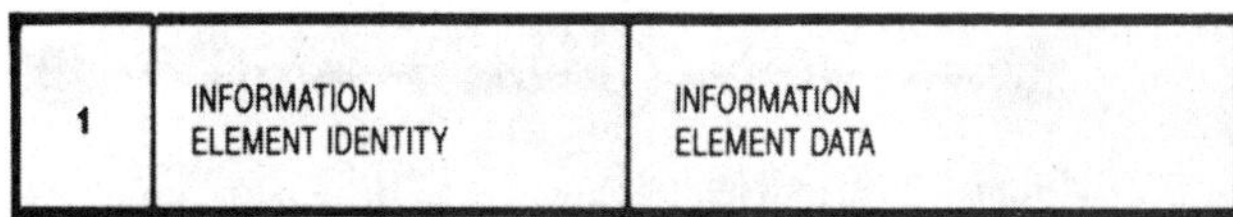

VARIABLE-LENGTH INFORMATION ELEMENT

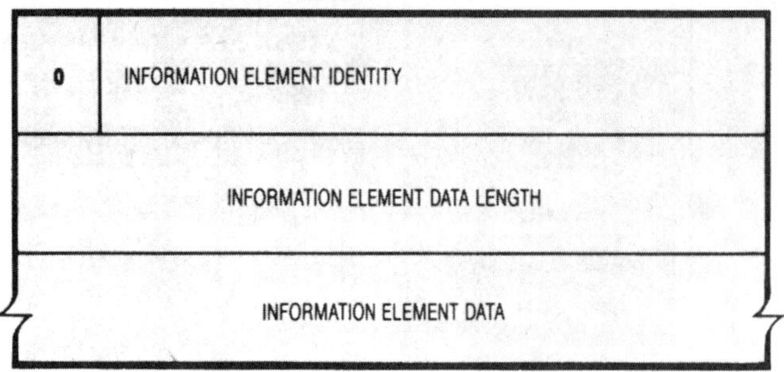

established over the B channel using X.25 Layers 2 and 3. As in the packet-mode-over-D-channel sequence, a LAPD signaling connection can be established by a TS sequence if it does not already exist. Assuming a TS connection is already established, the TE performs a similar sequence to set up a B channel as a packet-mode channel. The SETUP message goes across the D channel with a Channel Identifier information element as in packet mode. The information element indicates whether the connection can only be established on an exclusive B channel, a preferred B channel, an alternative to the preferred B channel (which could be a D channel), or any B channel. If the channel requirements cannot be met or if the NT determines that channel establishment can be met currently for other reasons, the NT will respond with a REL COM message. Otherwise the NT will respond with a CONN message or with a CALL PROC followed by a CONN or REL COM message. The CONN message carries information to the TE indicating which channel has been chosen for B channel packet mode by the NT. At this point, the TE starts sending HDLC flags on the indicated B channel. After X.25 Layers 2 and 3 come up between the TE and the NT, the TE sends an X.25 Call Request packet to the network.

When the Call Request is presented to the remote NT from the network, the NT checks the CUP. Assuming the restrictions can be met, the NT brings up a signaling connection (NS), if necessary, followed by an NP sequence. The SETUP message again goes over the D channel but the information elements indicate the desire to establish a packet-mode connection over the B channel. Then, assuming the connection can be established, the TE begins sending HDLC flags over the chosen B channel following the CONN ACK from the NT. X.25 Layers 2 and 3 are brought up and the Call Request is transmitted from the NT to the TE. Standard X.25 link and packet layer procedures are followed for communication.

10. How to. *Different procedures bring up D channel packet-mode (A), B channel packet-mode (B), B channel packet over circuit (C), and B channel frame relay (D). All the procedures are composed of similar sequences, which have been abbreviated here, for clarity, as signaling, packet, circuit, and frame relay setup.*

(A) PACKET MODE OVER D CHANNEL

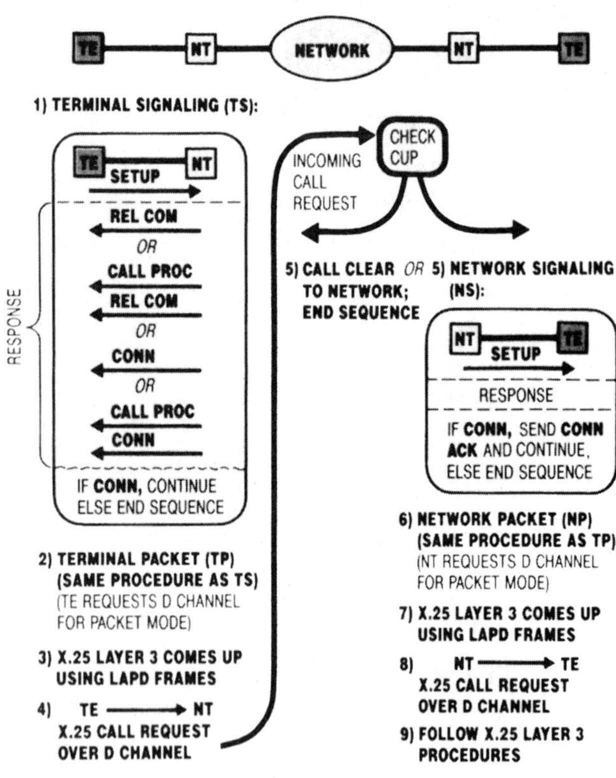

(B) PACKET MODE OVER B CHANNEL

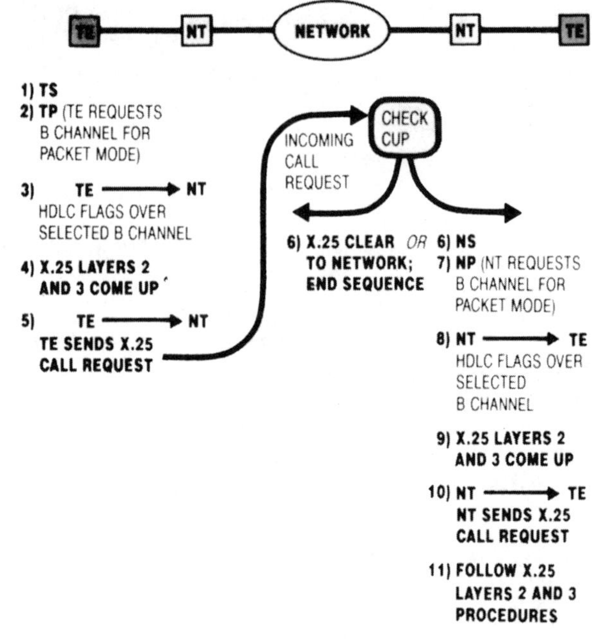

(C) CIRCUIT-SWITCHED B CHANNEL FOR PACKET ACCESS

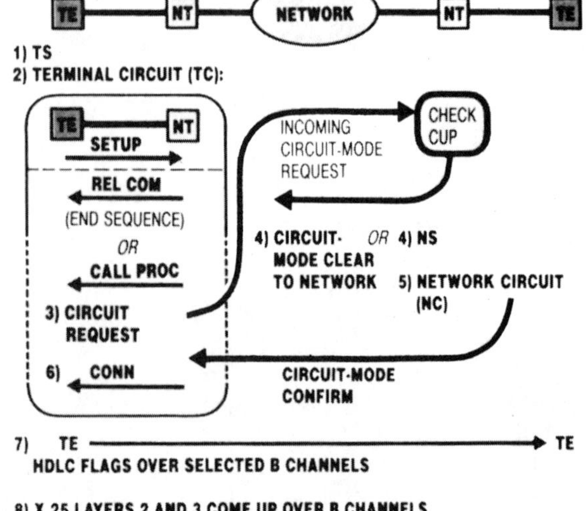

(D) FRAME RELAY

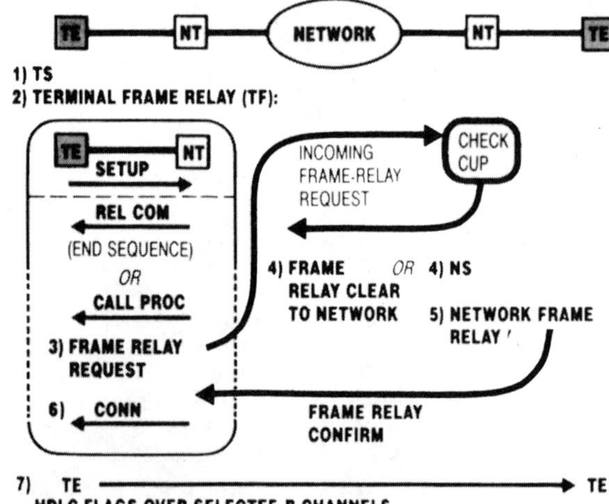

HDLC = HIGH-LEVEL DATA LINK CONTROL
LAPD = LINK ACCESS PROCEDURE-D
NT = NETWORK TERMINATION
TE = TERMINAL EQUIPMENT

■ Circuit-switched packet over the B channel. The procedures to establish a circuit-switched connection over a B channel are similar to those for packet-switched links. The TE sending the SETUP uses a Channel Information element, but the D channel is not an option as an alternative or primary channel. If the channel restrictions cannot be met, the NT sends a REL COM back to the TE. Otherwise, the NT returns a CALL PROC and a request from the attached network to establish a circuit connection.

The remote side follows procedures analogous to the packet-switched case, again with the D channel restriction for the Channel Information element. The remote NT signals the connection failure or establishment back to the local NT. If the connection failed, the local NT transmits a REL COM message to the TE. If, however, the connection can be established, the NT sends a CONN message to the TE. At this point, there is a circuit-mode connection between the local and remote TEs. To bring up packet mode, the local TE transmits HDLC flags across the network to the remote TE. X.25 Layers 2 and 3 are used from this point. This is analogous to using X.25 over leased lines.

■ **Frame-relay service.** Frame relay is a new type of packet-mode service that is expected to be commercially available in the next five years. It uses LAPD frames with the DLCI (SAPI and TEI) as a single logical-connection identifier, similar to the logical channel number of the X.25 network layer. The DLCI is comprised of 13 bits, giving over 8,000 possible virtual connections. Frame relay essentially combines the functionality of Layers 2 and 3 into a single layer.

A switch performing frame-relay switching will only need to look at the first N bits to route a frame, instead of waiting to receive the entire frame. This works similar to an Ethernet and token-ring switching mechanism. Moreover, a full network layer would not be needed. A user could choose to employ only the data-transfer phase of the X.25 packet layer protocol to transport the data in the LAPD frame.

The establishment of frame-relay connections uses procedures similar to those of circuit-mode connections. Assuming that a signaling connection has been set up over the D channel, the TE can bring up a frame-relay connection (TF). After receiving a SETUP and accepting channel restrictions, the NT responds with a CALL PROC message to the TE. Simultaneously, the NT attempts to make a frame-relay connection with the destination requested in the SETUP message.

If the remote side cannot establish the connection, the NT responds to the TE with a REL COM message. However, if a frame-relay connection can be established, the NT responds with a CONN message to the TE. The TE at this point can begin sending HDLC flags and bring up LAPD (frame relay) going from the local TE to the remote TE (end-to-end) across the specified B channel. The TE may additionally use X.25 packet layer data-transfer phase prodedures for virtual call service.

When the destination NT receives the request to establish a frame-relay connection, it first checks the CUP. If the channel restraints can be met and the signaling connection has been established over the D channel, the remote NT can begin to bring up a frame-relay connection (NF) across the remote user-network interface. If the user does respond to the SETUP message with the CONN message, the NT transmits a CONN ACK message to the TE. Additionally, the NT signals the network that the frame-relay connection has been established at the rem end. The rem TE must then wait for the local TE to initiate higher-layer communications using the selected B channel.

What to expect

ISDN standards for packet-mode support will have minimal impact on existing packet data networks during the early years of ISDN introduction. Users of ISDN circuit networks will be able to access packet networks via gateways but the underlying X.25 (or proprietary packet protocols) will remain unchanged.

However, by the mid-1990s, frame relay will begin to challenge every existing planning metric for packet networks. As Layer 3 functions are pushed into Layer 2, the underlying X.25 protocols will begin to mutate. The performance and throughput demands that users place on packet data networks will increase dramatically, demanding packet switches that can accommodate much higher throughput and capacity than is available today. This will in turn spawn a new generation of real ISDN packet switches by the mid-1990s, with wideband interfaces and much more sophisticated processing capabilities.

Today's X.25 users will have an easier time migrating than users of proprietary arrangements, such as SNA, because the ISDN standards bodies have pledged to support X.25 in an evolutionary manner. Nonetheless, the X.25 of 1996 or 2000 will look very different than today's X.25, with much less overhead for error-checking and recovery procedures.

Manufacturers of both packet and circuit switches will need to stay on top of standards, participating in their definition more than before. Users can go ahead and procure packet networks based on today's technology, but should realize that the long-term trend is for change. By the mid-1990s, some users are likely to rely on hybrid private packet network backbones combined with local packet services from the public BOCs—similar to the hybrid software-defined network/T1 solutions being introduced to support today's circuit-switched voice/leased-line data requirements. Other users will have migrated to integrated circuit/packet switches supporting primarily private networks. And still others will opt for complete reliance on public ISDN data networks to meet their requirements.

As the capabilities of packet-mode services mature and the infrastructure of ISDN increases, user data networking strategies will be due for serious reevaluations and overhauls. However, that day will not arrive until the mid-1990s.

■ *James I. Falek is a telecommunications engineer at BBN Communications Corp. He develops new packet assembler/disassemblers and is a participant in the T1D1 ISDN standards process. He holds a bachelor's degree in mathematics and computer science from Emory University (Atlanta).*

Mary A. Johnston is a senior consultant in the Telecommunications Consulting Group at BBN Communications. She holds a Masters of Public Policy from the John F. Kennedy School of Government at Harvard University and a bachelor's degree from Drew University in Madison, N. J.

Charlie Bass, Ungermann-Bass, Santa Clara, Calif.

Data networks' endangered and protected species

The world of data communications will converge on SNA and OSI, as the two protocols converge on each other. And proprietary protocols' days are definitely numbered.

Alternative data communications architectures have proliferated in recent years, but only two — IBM's Systems Network Architecture (SNA) and the International Standards Organization's (ISO's) Open Systems Interconnection (OSI) reference model — are destined to survive. All others, including popular vendor-specific architectures such as Digital Equipment Corp.'s Decnet, and open architectures such as TCP/IP (Transmission Control Protocol/Internet Protocol) and XNS (Xerox Network Systems), are an endangered species. For despite the large followings these alternatives have gathered, the world is lining up behind SNA, OSI, or both.

SNA's survival is assured through the enormous presence of IBM in the worldwide marketplace, and IBM's continued commitment to this architecture. More importantly, IBM's customers invariably contribute to SNA's survival through their confidence and investment in SNA, making it the most widely deployed data communications architecture in the industry.

Until recently, critics scoffed at the notion that the OSI reference model would evolve beyond a concept into a concrete, practical protocol suite for multivendor networking. Even fewer took seriously the idea that OSI would rise to such prominence in the networking world that it could stand shoulder to shoulder with IBM's SNA. But that is precisely what is happening.

The rise of OSI

The OSI movement has been steadily picking up momentum and followers since its founding in Europe in the 1970s. Originally, users and vendors banded together under the auspices of ISO to devise an open architectural model for heterogeneous networks. Over the past 10 years, OSI advocacy has evolved from an architectural framework to a set of specific protocols. In the process, it has grown into an international movement with a U. S. following that encompasses large private-sector users as well as government computer users who have come to recognize the importance and potential benefits of an industrywide international standard. Early endorsement contributing to OSI's momentum in the United States came from two of the nation's largest commercial users of computers and communications equipment — General Motors Corp. (GM) and the Boeing Co.

GM became the chief corporate sponsor of the Manufacturing Automation Protocol (MAP), an OSI-based networking standard aimed initially at accelerating GM's internal industrial automation program. Boeing has promoted MAP's twin, the OSI-based Technical and Office Protocol (TOP), a closely related standard for supporting office automation, scientific, and engineering applications.

Both companies have specified MAP/TOP compatibility as a requirement in future computer and communications procurement, and both have invested significant resources in promoting the virtues of OSI. In particular, GM and Boeing were instrumental in founding the MAP/TOP Users' Group (see Table 1).

With prodding from this united and committed user community, computer and communications vendors have come to realize the significance of OSI. Consequently, an impressive and somewhat unlikely collection of such vendors came together in late 1985 to form the Corporation for Open Systems, or COS (see Table 2). COS was chartered to promote the adoption of OSI standards and, in particular, to verify that individual implementations of MAP/TOP products conform to common specifications. COS can also be viewed as a move by vendors to offset the power wielded by the MAP/TOP user community and regain some degree of control in implementation strategies. While COS members recognize the potential benefits of OSI, a consolidated implementation strategy assures vendors that their investment is synchronized with their

Table 1: Major MAP/TOP corporate affiliates

Table 1: Major MAP/TOP corporate affiliates

3COM CORP.	INTEL CORP.
AEG	KAISER ALUMINUM AND CHEMICAL CORP.
ALUMINUM COMPANY OF AMERICA	LITTON INDUSTRIES AUTOMATION SYSTEMS
ARTHUR ANDERSON & CO.	M.W. KELLOGG
AT&T TECHNOLOGIES	MICHIGAN BELL TELEPHONE CO.
BOEING COMPUTER SERVICES	MINNESOTA MINING & MANUFACTURING CO.
BRIDGE COMMUNICATIONS	MONSANTO CO.
CHRYSLER CORP.	MORTON THIOKOL
CINCINNATI MILACRON	MOTOROLA INC.
DEERE & CO.	NAVISTAR INTERNATIONAL CORP.
EASTMAN KODAK CO.	NORTHERN TELECOM
E.I. DuPONT	NORTHROP CORP.
ELECTRONIC DATA SYSTEMS	ORACLE CORP.
ERICSSON INC.	PHILLIP MORRIS USA
EXXON CHEMICAL CO.	POLAROID CORP.
GENERAL DYNAMICS	PRIME COMPUTER
GENERAL INSTRUMENT CORP.	PROCTOR & GAMBLE CO.
GENERAL MOTORS CORP.	REYNOLDS METALS CO.
GOULD INC.	ROCKWELL INTERNATIONAL
HONEYWELL INC.	SHELL COMPANY OF AUSTRALIA LTD.
HUGHES AIRCRAFT	SQUARE D CO.
INDUSTRIAL NETWORKING INC.	WEYERHAEUSER INFORMATION SYSTEMS
INGERSOLL-RAND CO.	

competitors and partners and that they will not be behind or ahead of one another in the market. While it can be argued that this synchronicity reinforces OSI interoperability objectives, it also allows individual vendors to pace their investment and transition to OSI with minimal risk.

Of the various U. S. government agencies that have contributed to the OSI movement, the most notable are the Department of Defense (DOD) and the Department of Commerce (DOC). As a result of a 1985 internal study, the DOD decided that it would move its vast collection of networks from TCP/IP to OSI. This decision was made based on the conclusion that, over time, off-the-shelf OSI-compatible products would be more readily available than those based on TCP/IP despite TCP/IP's widespread acceptance in the scientific and engineering communities. The DOD is presently determining how it will make the transition from TCP/IP to OSI while maintaining the operational integrity of its networks.

In 1986, under the leadership of the late Department of Commerce Secretary Malcolm Baldridge, 15 federal agencies formed a task force to develop communications specifications for their own internal networking needs (see Table 3). The result was GOSIP (Government OSI Profile), first released in January 1987. GOSIP is essentially a restatement of TOP. Fundamental to a consistent position on OSI is the common reference to U. S. National Bureau of Standards (NBS) Implementors' Agreements as the detailed protocol specification for MAP, TOP, COS, and GOSIP. These agreements, reached in NBS-sponsored workshops, are the underpinnings that loosely hold to-

gether an otherwise disparate collection of special interest groups. The prospects for a single industrywide OSI standard would be reduced if the NBS forum did not function as a U. S. network high court. The NBS process was somewhat unstable during 1986 because of federal budget cuts and the uncertainty of the role of the NBS testing versus COS. While there was talk of privatization of the NBS network laboratory, it was generally agreed that testing and certification were the domain of COS, while NBS would play a critical role in bringing the industry together to evaluate and resolve technical issues.

The GOSIPspecification should have a galvanizing effect on the OSI movement in the United States. Traditionally, critics have complained that OSI is nothing more than a paper standard, lacking practical implementation and, more importantly, customers. This opinion is likely to change as the DOD, DOC, and affiliated agencies move to have GOSIP adopted as a Federal Information Processing (FIP) standard. Once GOSIP achieves such status, OSI will become an approved and, in some cases, a required specification for federal computer and communications equipment procurement.

To further reinforce the practical applicability of OSI, COS and the MAP/TOP committee recently announced an event to be held in June 1988 to demonstrate factory, office, and engineering applications executing over MAP-, TOP-, and possibly GOSIP-compatible networks. This event was originally distinguished from previous demonstrations of OSI interoperability by the sponsors' insistence that only readily available products and not prototypes be employed. This

ADC TELECOMMUNICATIONS
AETNA LIFE & CASUALTY
AMDAHL CORP.
APOLLO COMPUTER INC.
APPLE COMPUTER INC.
AMERICAN TELEPHONE & TELEGRAPH CO.
BECHTEL POWER CORP.
BELL COMMUNICATIONS RESEARCH
BOEING COMPUTER SERVICES
BRIDGE COMMUNICATIONS INC.
BURROUGHS CORP.
CCTA, HER MAJESTY'S TREASURY, BRITISH GOVERNMENT
CITICORP
3COM CORP.
CONCURRENT COMPUTER CORP.
CONTROL DATA CORP.
CONVERGENT TECHNOLOGIES
DART & KRAFT INC.
DATA GENERAL CORP.
DIALCOM INC.
DIGITAL EQUIPMENT CORP.
DOW CHEMICAL CO.
E.I. DU PONT DE NEMOURS & COMPANY INC.
EASTMAN KODAK CO.
THE EQUITABLE
EXCELAN
GENERAL ELECTRIC CO.
GENERAL MOTORS CORP.
GOULD INC.
GTE SERVICE CORP./TELEPHONE OPERATIONS
HARRIS CORP.

HEWLETT-PACKARD INC.
HONEYWELL INC.
HUGHES AIRCRAFT CO.
INTERNATIONAL BUSINESS MACHINES CORP.
INTERNATIONAL COMPUTERS LTD.
INTEL CORP.
ITT CORP.
MOTOROLA INC.
NCR CORP.
NATIONAL SEMICONDUCTOR CO.
NETWORK SYSTEMS CORP.
NORTHERN TELECOM INC.
ONTARIO MINISTRY OF GOVERNMENT SERVICES
    COMPUTER AND TELECOMMUNICATIONS DIVISION
PACIFIC BELL
PRIME COMPUTER
PROCTER & GAMBLE CO.
RETIX
ROCKWELL INTERNATIONAL
SPERRY CORP.
SUN MICROSYSTEMS INC.
SYTEK INC.
TANDEM COMPUTERS INC.
TELEX COMPUTER PRODUCTS INC.
TELENET COMMUNICATIONS CORP.
TEXAS INSTRUMENTS INC.
TOUCH COMMUNICATIONS
VISA INTERNATIONAL
WANG LABORATORIES
XEROX CORP.

---

objective has been compromised by the reluctance of several large vendors to participate under such conditions. In keeping with its charter, COS will provide testing tools and services to event participants. (It is notable that COS has committed only to a subset of the full MAP/TOP.)

As further evidence of the momentum of OSI, Digital Equipment Corp. (DEC), arguably the most advanced network supplier among the major vendors, has openly embraced OSI, despite recent criticism of MAP by Chairman Ken Olsen, and it has begun to migrate its proprietary Decnet architecture toward conformance with OSI standards. It should be remembered that Olsen is primarily criticizing MAP's lower two layers, which are based on broadband token-bus technology, not OSI as a whole. His remarks need to be weighed in light of DEC's limited broadband capabilities. The company has not developed broadband technology on its own and has instead relied on outside vendors. DEC has also made an enormous investment in baseband Ethernet and is understandably reluctant to make a similar investment in broadband token-bus.

Finally, DEC now is the market leader in supplying processors for factory automation, and the ascendancy of MAP will create a more level playing field. Conversely, MAP works in IBM's favor since the company has not been a

DEPARTMENT OF AGRICULTURE
DEPARTMENT OF COMMERCE
DEPARTMENT OF DEFENSE
DEPARTMENT OF ENERGY
ENVIRONMENTAL PROTECTION AGENCY
GENERAL SERVICES ADMINISTRATION
DEPARTMENT OF HEALTH AND HUMAN SERVICES
DEPARTMENT OF HOUSING AND URBAN DEVELOPMENT
DEPARTMENT OF THE INTERIOR
DEPARTMENT OF JUSTICE
DEPARTMENT OF LABOR
NATIONAL AERONAUTICS AND SPACE ADMINISTRATION
NATIONAL SCIENCE FOUNDATION
OFFICE OF MANAGEMENT AND BUDGET
DEPARTMENT OF TRANSPORTATION
DEPARTMENT OF THE TREASURY
NATIONAL COMMUNICATIONS SYSTEM

strong player in the factory. MAP provides an opportunity to increase its factory presence. An obvious consequence of Olsen's comments is that DEC's commitment to MAP is being questioned, putting its sales representatives who deal with GM in an unenviable position.

Regardless, DEC's strategy for OSI involves retaining the external characteristics (such as the user interface) and network-management features of Decnet, while internal layers are brought into OSI conformance. Even though this evolutionary approach to OSI is not consistent with MAP/TOP guidelines, it retains a valuable familiarity and comfort level for Decnet users while leveraging DEC's investment and differentiation in network management. Full MAP/TOP conformance is measured by top-to-bottom adherence to OSI specifications; DEC addresses conformance on a layer-by-layer basis and retains the overall proprietary nature of its architecture. The success of this evolutionary approach will certainly be studied by IBM vis-a-vis its own SNA strategy.

As it becomes clear that SNA and OSI are destined to be the surviving architectures of choice, other vendors will evolve their proprietary offerings to the OSI standard. MAP/TOP purists may frown on this approach, but it allows customer and vendor alike to simultaneously hold on to the past and move into the future.

SNA is an assumption

The long-term survival—and even the preeminence—of SNA is an assumption that most MIS (management information systems) directors and data communications managers have already made because of IBM's position as the world's premiere computer supplier. This, in turn, adds to the momentum of SNA as both IBM and its customers continue their commitment to and investment in SNA and, possibly more important, SNA-based applications.

But it is simplistic to assert that SNA's success relies wholly on the strength of IBM or the blind faith of its users. Remember the PCjr and PC Network? SNA will, in fact, survive for a more important reason: It is a well-conceived, flexible, and robust data communications architecture.

Why is it then that SNA is often criticized for being inefficient, unfriendly, and out of date? Much of that criticism was valid while it strictly reflected SNA's roots in an earlier generation of computing. Introduced in 1974, the architecture supported a hierarchical approach to networking, in which an all-powerful central host lorded over dumb terminals and other attached devices that wished to employ the host in a computing task on their behalf. Though valid, this model of computing became restrictive as ubiquitous intelligent workstations, especially IBM's own PC, created a peer-to-peer, server model of computing and the concomitant local network industry. SNA designers could not have foreseen the microcomputer-to-mainframe phenomenon, but it is a testament to the architecture's excellence that SNA has been extended to embrace today's full spectrum of networking needs, encompassing clusters of PCs, departmental minicomputers, and corporate hosts.

As a result of SNA extensions announced and partially delivered over the past two years, peer-to-peer communications is widely supported; mainframe hosts are not required for routing; dynamic reconfiguration is possible; the location of files is transparent; and network management is open to other vendors. The cumulative effect of these features has been the revitalization of an architecture that was near the brink of becoming obsolete. SNA is now positioned to support current and foreseen network requirements as well as any competitive communications architecture.

SNA and OSI: Comingling and coexistence

SNA's current and expected popularity should not obscure the temptation to meld the richness of SNA with the vendor independence and design economy of OSI. Primarily, IBM is in the business of selling MIPS (million instructions per second) and file storage, which the overhead problems of SNA promoted. To their credit, realistic OSI advocates do not relish being isolated from a ubiquitous SNA infrastructure and its wealth of applications.

Despite its obvious reluctance to embrace a standard it does not control, IBM is pragmatic and often opportunistic. Consequently, while the corporation continues to champion SNA and would prefer to ignore OSI, it has realized that to sell today to MAP factories and to buyers in Europe—and tomorrow to TOP offices and to the U. S. government—it must find ways to counter and accommodate the OSI challenge.

In fact, IBM has participated broadly in the OSI phenomenon. In the United States it has announced and delivered MAP-based products and is an active participant in OSInet, a community of vendors who test the interoperability of their protocol suites across an X.25-based internet. In Europe, IBM has set up centers for research, development, and testing of OSI in Heidelberg, West Germany; La Gaude, France; and Rome, Italy; and has released a special version of SNA called OTSS (Open Transport and Session Support) that is OSI-compatible at the Transport and Session layers.

It is unlikely that DEC's strategy of migrating to OSI while retaining the external characteristics of Decnet has gone unnoticed by IBM. SNA and OSI are not simply destined to compete with one another, but also, as IBM's introduction of OTSS indicates, to coexist and comingle. They may even meld to the point of being indistinguishable.

Many similarities in structure and capabilities already exist between the two architectures, including the fact that each one consists of seven layers (Fig. 1). Starting with the bottom layer, SNA consists of (1) Physical Control, (2) Data Link Control, (3) Path Control, (4) Transmission Control, (5) Data Flow Control, (6) Presentation Services, and (7) Transaction Services. By comparison, the OSI reference model's layers are: (1) Physical, (2) Data Link, (3) Network, (4) Transport, (5) Session, (6) Presentation, and (7) Application.

While specific features differ between the two models, the first two layers of each architecture provide physical connections and data transfer; Layer 3 provides routing functions, Layers 4 and 5 establish and maintain end-to-end connections; Layer 6 enables the proper interpretation of information; and Layer 7 provides the user with application-oriented services. These structural similarities increase the feasibility and probability that they will coexist and comingle over time.

Conceptually, the most straightforward way for SNA and

1. SNA vs. OSI architectures. *Similarities of structure smooth the way for the merger of the two architectures. While details differ, their objectives are similar.*

	SNA		OSI
7	TRANSACTION SERVICES	**USER SERVICES**	APPLICATIONS
6	PRESENTATION SERVICES	**INTERPRETATION**	PRESENTATION
5	DATA FLOW CONTROL	**ESTABLISH AND MAINTAIN END-TO-END CONNECTIONS**	SESSION
4	TRANSMISSION CONTROL		TRANSPORT
3	PATH CONTROL	**ROUTING**	NETWORK
2	DATA LINK CONTROL	**PHYSICAL CONNECTIVITY AND DATA TRANSFER**	DATA LINK
1	PHYSICAL CONTROL		PHYSICAL

OSI = OPEN SYSTEMS INTERCONNECTION
SNA = SYSTEMS NETWORK ARCHITECTURE

OSI to coexist is through the application of gateway processors. Rather than merge SNA and OSI, such gateways would provide a functional bridge between the two either by receiving protocol transactions on a layer-by-layer basis from one domain and transforming them into comparable functions of the other or an application process residing concurrently on both protocol stacks (Fig. 2). A layer-by-

2. Alternate gateways. *The choices are a flow between networks with a layer-by-layer transformation, or an intermediate node able to talk with both architectures.*

(A) LAYER-BY-LAYER TRANSFORMATION

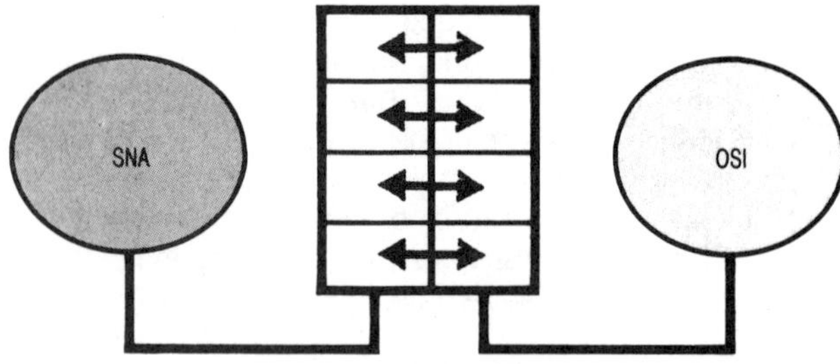

(B) DUAL-STACK APPLICATION

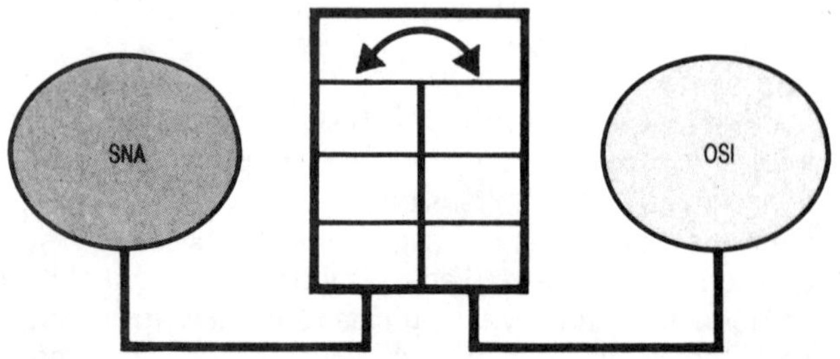

OSI = OPEN SYSTEMS INTERCONNECTION
SNA = SYSTEMS NETWORK ARCHITECTURE

layer transformation allows end-to-end connections and transparency of the gateway function, but it is far more computationally intensive and limited by the compatibility of features at each layer. Both gateway approaches can localize transformation to a server and provide common network management and access control. However, this approach requires a readily accessible, if not dedicated, resource and implies a disjointed view of the network domain. Implied in this method is that the two architectures remain separate, with crossover limited to application services. Consequently, a gateway server may be impractical or less desirable than a distributed approach that intentionally blurs the distinctions and boundaries between the two domains.

Device emulation

A simple and commonly used approach for allowing devices native to one network to communicate with devices on a foreign network is device emulation. In particular, IBM 327X terminals and controllers are being emulated on virtually all non-SNA networks in order to access IBM host-based applications. In fact microcomputer-to-mainframe communications are dominated by PCs emulating 327X terminal devices linked to an IBM host application. Originally, SNA assumed that this link was a leased line; the connection can now be leased, switched, or, in some cases, an X.25 network.

For microcomputers resident on non-SNA networks, the device emulation protocol is encapsulated and delivered to a gateway server that transmits it to a host through an SNA link protocol such as SDLC (synchronous data link control). Device emulation is limited, however, because the networks are not truly interoperable: Files can be transferred and remote users connected to hosts, but some communications, such as host-to-host, are restricted. Obviously, this device emulation technique can and will be used across OSI networks, providing the same level of SNA-to-OSI communications as alternative protocol suites (Fig. 3).

This particular mingling of OSI and SNA functions may be incidental to the more pressing objective confronting OSI providers: accommodating Netbios, today's dominant network application interface. In principal, Netbios is a Session Layer interface that is not tied to a particular underlying protocol suite. Indeed, a number of vendors support a Netbios interface on top of XNS and TCP. Consequently, it is highly probable that an enterprising vendor will soon incorporate the Netbios interface in an OSI stack, allowing OSI to support a growing number of applications including 327X/SDLC emulation packages.

Netbios is not officially part of either the SNA or OSI protocol suites and, consequently, its continuance is disquieting to much of the IBM organization. Netbios is considered a tactical, not strategic, offering, introduced by Entry Systems Division to support clusters of PCs in the absence of a viable SNA-based solution. As SNA's features are enhanced and strategic application interfaces are identified through SAA (Systems Application Architecture), Netbios is noticeably excluded. Indeed, it is anathema to the MAP/TOP organization because it is not consistent with its strategic direction. However, it has a large and growing base of support that can alleviate the near-term scarcity of OSI-based applications.

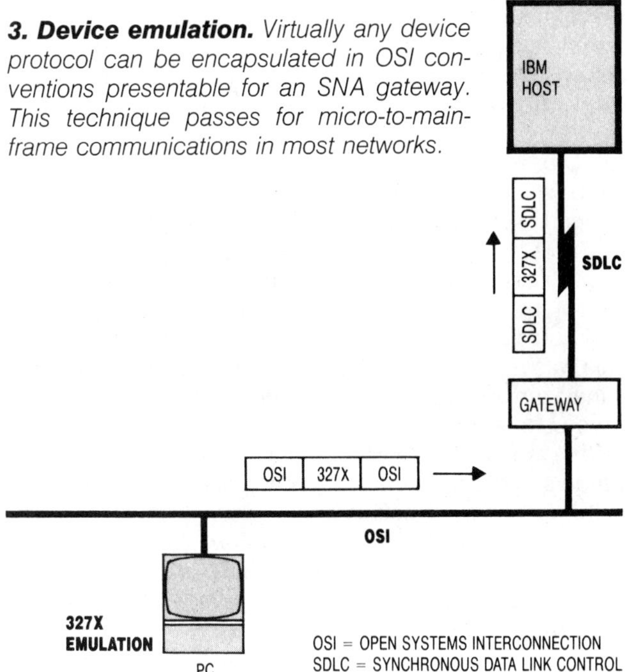

3. Device emulation. *Virtually any device protocol can be encapsulated in OSI conventions presentable for an SNA gateway. This technique passes for micro-to-mainframe communications in most networks.*

Complementing the myriad sources of 327X emulation products, IBM now supports the connection of non-SNA devices, namely ASCII terminals, to SNA hosts through protocol conversion options in its 7171 communications controllers. It is easy to imagine a new generation of SNA terminals that can switch between native and ASCII modes of operation. At this point, both SNA and ASCII (OSI) devices can easily connect to both SNA and OSI networks.

Work is under way on a Virtual Terminal Protocol (VTP) for the OSI suite. VTP will establish a uniform and generic set of terminal operations for communicating across an OSI network. Once VTP has been widely adopted, it is realistic to assume that IBM will incorporate VTP protocol conversion in its front-end processors, assuring continued SNA-to-OSI cross-connections.

Internet and interstation transmission

Another straightforward and somewhat mundane instance of SNA and OSI blending is when one acts as a transmission service (layers 1 and 2) for the other. A common example of this approach is when SNA sessions operate across X.25 packet-switched networks. While IBM was comparatively late and limited in its support of X.25, SNA now offers a number of options for taking advantage of X.25 links. This is an instance where SNA and OSI have come together with little fanfare, but with significant benefit in circumstances where long-distance dedicated lines (SNA's original transmission model) are impractical. While the X.25 interface can be functionally viewed as providing Layer 3 functions, generally, SNA treats X.25 as a simple transmission link and retains full control for routing between subarea nodes. A more provocative question is whether or not there will be examples of OSI sessions operating across SNA links? The answer is, yes.

Due to the vast array of SDLC-compatible hardware and software, it is unavoidable that this standard will be used for internet transmission between OSI networks. As before, routing (Layer 3) will remain in the client network and the SNA-to-OSI crossover will occur at the interface between layers 2 and 3.

Comparable to internet transmission services between networks is interstation transmission on a local area network (LAN). In this environment IBM has facilitated an SNA-to-OSI crossover by adhering, in its own Token-Ring PC adapter product, to the Layer 2 interface standard known as Logical Link Control (LLC) or 802.2 adopted by the IEEE-802 committee. By adhering to this LLC interface (Fig.4), a common Layer 3 client can reside on any of the IEEE-802 data link standards: 803.2 CSMA/CD (carrier-sense multiple access with collision detection) or Ethernet; 802.4 token bus; and 802.5 token-ring. The implications of this standard interface and IBM's adherence to it are remarkable. Not only can OSI layers 3 through 7 be easily wedded to IBM's Token-Ring technology, but SNA protocols can reside on token bus (MAP) and Ethernet (TOP). This will undoubtedly result in SNA and OSI protocols residing on common local networks, which will provide additional motivation to provide interoperability between the two. Gateway servers, as discussed earlier, can then be applied to achieve a dialogue between stations that reside on the same LAN but speak different protocols.

4. LLC interface. *The Logical Link Control is a single interface between Layers 2 and 3 that allows mixing and matching of SNA and OSI upper layers with all 802 standards.*

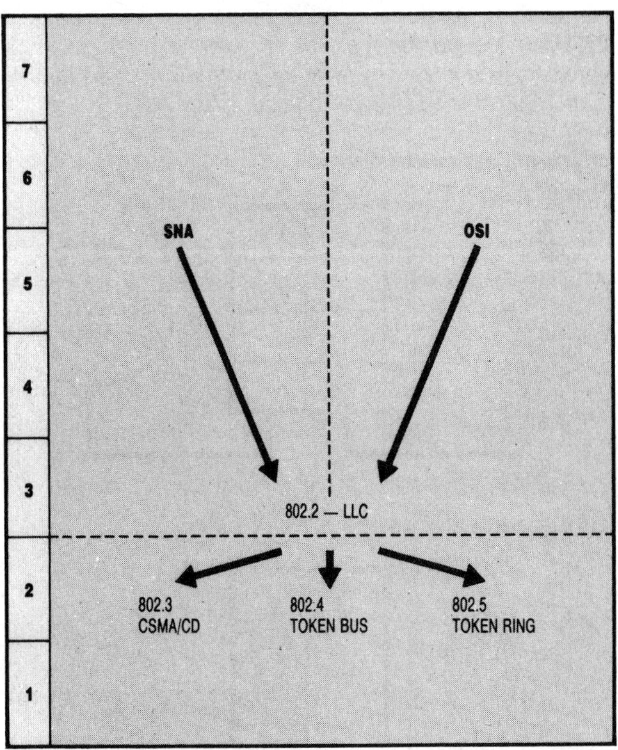

CSMA/CD = CARRIER-SENSE MULTIPLE ACCESS WITH COLLISION DETECTION
OSI = OPEN SYSTEMS INTERCONNECTION
SNA = SYSTEMS NETWORK ARCHITECTURE

Advanced Program-to-Program Communications (APPC) protocol is a recent landmark extension to SNA that supports program-to-program or peer-to-peer conversations between a broad spectrum of computing devices ranging from PCs to large hosts. The significance of APPC is its uniform treatment of any two devices on the micro-computer-to-mainframe spectrum at each end of a conversation. Prior to APPC, a 370-class host was required to manage any conversation and it was the dominant party. APPC conversations consist of a set of commands or verbs defined by an Application Program Interface (API), which are enacted by Logical Unit (LU) 6.2 operations. Consequently, for two programs to engage in a peer-to-peer conversation they must adhere to the APPC API and reside on devices supported by LU 6.2.

APPC/LU 6.2

With the introduction of APPC/LU 6.2, IBM not only set the strategic direction for distributed processing with SNA, it moved ahead of other architectures, including OSI, with provisions for interprocess communications. While Netbios was excluded, APPC was included in the list of SAA interfaces to be supported on all strategic processors.

Subsequent to its introduction, the European Computer Manufacturers Association (ECMA) in 1985 considered recommending that APPC/LU 6.2 be incorporated into the OSI standard roughly at Layer 6 by ISO. Since APPC was built outside the context of OSI, there has been some argument about whether it should be installed at layer 5 or 6. In addition to enhancing its basic functions, the inclusion of APPC/LU 6.2 would make it easier to make a port of APPC-based applications to OSI networks. As IBM migrates strategic offerings such as Disoss (Distributed Office Support System) to APPC, a wealth of applications become available through conformance with APPC. This was, undoubtedly, what ECMA had in mind. However, the other side of this proposition was the inherent advantage that IBM would gain in time and expertise in the context of OSI. This was a political fireball that ECMA preferred to drop rather than defend based on its win-win attributes. It could have been argued that the ECMA community, IBM, and ISO all would have profited from its adoption. ECMA vendors and customers would have gained easy access to IBM applications software, IBM would have made an easy entry into the OSI world, and ISO would have gained a well-defined and critical protocol. But because IBM was on the winning side of the equation, the other players were wary and the opportunity slipped away.

In January, the prospect of incorporating APPC into OSI was raised again by ECMA to a more receptive interna-

---

5. APPC API. *Like the Logical Link Control interface, this verb set is becoming the interface specification for first joining, then merging, SNA and OSI.*

API = APPLICATION PROGRAM INTERFACE
APPC = ADVANCED PROGRAM-TO-PROGRAM COMMUNICATIONS
DISOSS = DISTRIBUTED OFFICE SUPPORT SYSTEM
LU = LOGICAL UNIT
OSI = OPEN SYSTEMS INTERCONNECTION

---

6. SNA-OSI merger. *As data crosses the SNA-OSI threshold created by interfaces associated with the ISO model, the identity of each architecture is lost and is irrelevant.*

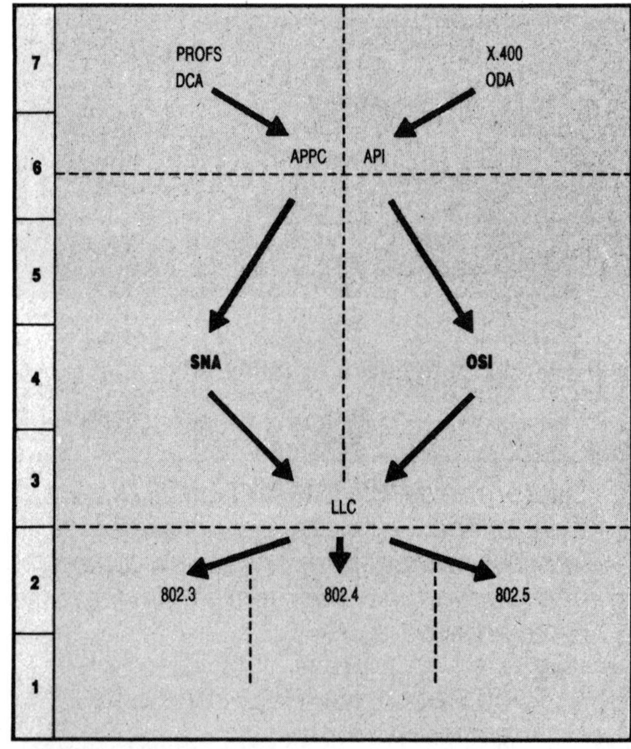

DCA = DOCUMENT CONTENT ARCHITECTURE
ODA = OFFICE DOCUMENT ARCHITECTURE
OSI = OPEN SYSTEMS INTERCONNECTION
PROFS = PROFESSIONAL OFFICE SYSTEM
SNA = SYSTEMS NETWORK ARCHITECTURE

tional audience. In the intervening year, IBM introduced APPC/VM (Virtual Machine) as part of its 9370 announcements operating on Ethernet and bisynchronous links. With its announcement came the realization that, as an interface specification, APPC API could be decoupled from the details of LU 6.2, reducing IBM's advantage (Fig. 5). Consistent with ISO's tradition of massaging a proposal and leaving its imprint, APPC is likely to emerge different than it entered. This may be timely, since IBM is massaging APPC API to resolve minor differences introduced in its different operating systems—APPC/VM is not identical to APPC/PC. By stating that, through SAA, APPC/PC and APPC/VM will converge, users can infer what they were not aware of before: that the two are different.

Applications

The upper reaches of SNA and OSI are where the application protocols most relevent to users are located and where IBM has the advantage of momentum. For document definition and interchange, IBM has defined Document Content Architecture (DCA) and Document Interchange Architecture (DIA), which its electronic messaging service PROFS (Professional Office System) is built upon. In OSI, document definition is provided by Office Document Architecture (ODA) and electronic messaging primitives are contained in the X.400 specification. Will there be a cross-fertilization of these specifications? Certainly. Many vendors have supplied transformation utilities between non-IBM-generated documents and DCA. Such utilities will exist for ODA-to-DCA transformation.

X.400 is one of the most anxiously awaited OSI protocols because it can be the basis for corporatewide messaging between disparate vendors' equipment (the Holy Grail of OSI). Given the existing support of SNA connections by these same vendors, it is likely that X.400-based messaging will occur over SNA circuits. In fact, IBM has announced two such products, the X.400 Disoss Connections and the X.400 Message Transfer Facility.

Indeed, SNA and OSI are destined to intertwine and potentially to merge to the point of being indistinguishable. Consider a distributed electronic mail service that operates between a personal computer and a VAX, based on X.400, that conforms to an APPC interface joined to OSI layers 3 through 5 with the PC residing on an Ethernet and the VAX sitting on a Token-Ring (Fig. 6). Which is SNA and which is OSI? Who cares?

OSI purists may be put off by such scenarios, but between the temptation to access SNA-based applications and IBM's posture vis-a-vis OSI, they cannot, and should not, be avoided. The real issue is the interoperability that comes with open architectures. As IBM defensively opens SNA, the identification of this amalgamation of standards is less important than what they accomplish. ∎

Charlie Bass is cofounder and director of Ungermann-Bass Inc., chairman of Touch Communications, director of Sierra Semiconductor, consulting professor of electrical engineering at Stanford University, limited partner of Sequoia Technology Ventures, and editor of Computer Networks *and* IEEE Networks. *Prior to founding Ungermann-Bass, he held a variety of positions at Zilog Inc. from 1975 to 1979, ending up as general manager of its systems division.*

William Stallings, Comp-Comm Consulting Inc., London, England

Is there an OSI session protocol in your future?

The many features of session layer standards will soon be available to users. This tutorial sorts through what they are and how they work.

The lowest four layers of the seven-layer Open Systems Interconnection (OSI) model, put forth by the International Organization for Standardization (ISO), are designed to provide users with a basic, reliable communications service. These layers (physical, data link, network, and transport) contain the protocols necessary for moving data from one host to another over a single link, a network, or an interconnected set of networks with no losses, mis-orderings, or duplications.

But not even this wealth of "basic" services is enough for most applications. For example, a remote terminal-access application might require a half-duplex dialogue. A transaction-processing application might require checkpoints in the data-transfer stream to permit backup and recovery. A message-processing application might require the ability to interrupt a dialogue in order to prepare a new portion of a message, and later to resume the dialogue where it was left off.

All these capabilities could be embedded in specific applications at Layer 7 of the OSI model (the application layer). However, since these types of dialogue-structuring tools have widespread applicability, it makes sense to organize them into a separate layer: the session layer (Layer 5). The session layer sits immediately on top of the transport layer. To support a dialogue, the session layer creates a logical connection, called a session connection (SC), that maps one-to-one onto a transport connection. The SC provides numerous services that impose structure on the dialogue between applications that takes place over a reliable transport link.

Both application developers and users would be well-advised to learn about the session layer. Developers need to know what dialogue-structuring services the session layer has to offer. Even prewritten applications may provide users with access to these services. Since these users will be able to set various session parameters, it is helpful to know what parameters are available to them.

ISO and the International Telegraph and Telephone Consultative Committee (CCITT) have jointly promulgated a standard for session services (known by ISO as the Draft International Standard, or DIS, 8326 and by CCITT as X.215). The session layer provides the means for cooperating application entities to organize and synchronize their dialogue and to manage the data exchange.

Session services

According to ISO's DIS 8326, the session layer provides the following types of services to its users:

■ Establish a connection with another session-service user, exchange data with that user, and release the connection in an orderly manner.

■ Establish synchronization (sync) points within the dialogue and, in the event of errors, resume the dialogue from an agreed sync point.

■ Interrupt a dialogue and resume it later from a prearranged sync point.

■ Negotiate for the use of tokens to exchange data, synchronize and release the connection, and arrange for data exchange to be half-duplex or full-duplex.

In addition to providing for the establishment, maintenance, and termination of session connections, the ISO session service provides a variety of ways of structuring the dialogue that takes place over those connections. The simplest of these facilities is the ability to choose two-way simultaneous (full-duplex) or two-way alternate (half-duplex) operation.

The session service also provides an optional facility for labeling the data stream with synchronization points, which serve two purposes. Synchronization points can be used to clearly isolate portions of the dialogue, and in error recovery.

Two types of sync points are defined: major and minor.

1. Session interaction structure. Dialogue units are demarcated by major sync points and may include minor ones (A). Activities are sets of dialogue units (B).

(A) EXAMPLE OF A STRUCTURED DIALOGUE UNIT

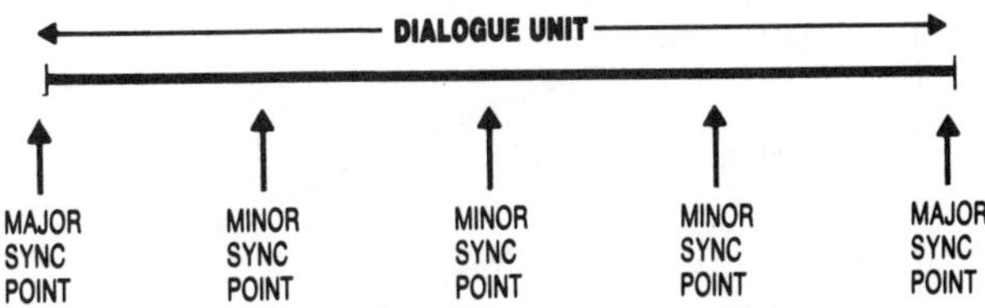

(B) EXAMPLE OF A STRUCTURED ACTIVITY

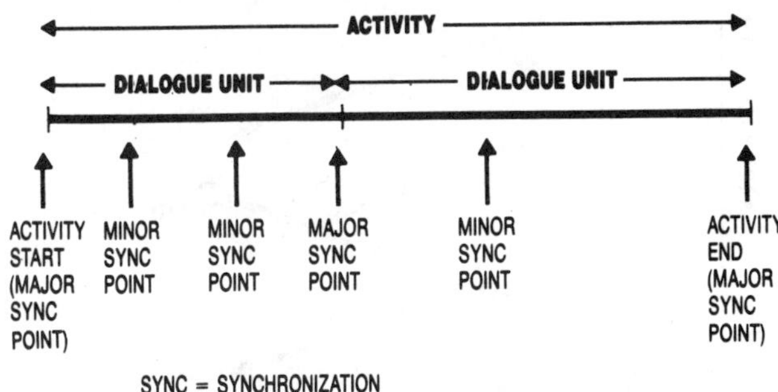

The relationship between these two is illustrated in Figure 1a. Major sync points are used to structure the exchange of data into dialogue units. The characteristic of a dialogue unit is that all data within it is completely separated from all data before and after it. After defining a major sync point, the user may not send more data until that sync point is acknowledged by the destination user. For recovery purposes, it is not possible to back up beyond the last major sync point.

Thus, the two purposes mentioned above are achieved:
■ Since the completion of one dialogue unit must be acknowledged before the next begins, the dialogue unit can be used by the session user to define application-oriented functions. For example, if a sequence of files is to be transferred, each file could be segregated into a separate dialogue unit. The sender could then be assured that a particular file had been received and accepted before attempting to send another file.
■ The dialogue units define the limit of recovery. For example, in a transaction-processing application, each transaction could be equated with a dialogue unit. When a transaction is complete and acknowledged, each side can purge any recovery information that had been saved for the purpose of permitting backup to the beginning of that transaction.

Minor sync points are used to structure the exchange of data within a dialogue. They provide more flexibility for recovery. A session user may define one or more minor sync points within a dialogue unit and need not wait for acknowledgment before proceeding. At any point, it is possible to resynchronize the dialogue to any previous minor sync point within the current dialogue unit or, of course, to resynchronize to the beginning of the dialogue unit (the most-recent major sync point). This permits the session user to make a trade-off: With frequent sync points, backup and recovery can be speeded up at the expense of saving frequent checkpoints.

In the session standard, it is not the responsibility of the session layer to save any data that has already been transmitted. The session service will simply mark the data stream as requested with a serial number; numbers are assigned sequentially. When resynchronization occurs, the session layer decrements the sequence number back to the point of resynchronization. To retransmit data that had been previously transmitted, the session user must have saved that data and must present it to the session service again.

Activities

One additional level of structuring is available as an option that may be selected when setting up the session: the activity option. An activity is defined as a logical unit of work, consisting of one or more dialogue units (Fig. 1b). The key feature of the activity is that it can be interrupted and later resumed. For example, if an activity (such as a very long database transfer) is taking place and one machine or the other needs to interrupt this process (to go down for maintenance or to handle a higher-priority task), then the session service stops the activity. The session service remembers the last serial number used, so that the activity may be resumed later with the same sync-point

2. Activities and sessions. Sessions may map one-to-one to activities (A) or may consist of several activities (B). Or, activities can also span several sessions (C).

(A) ONE-TO-ONE

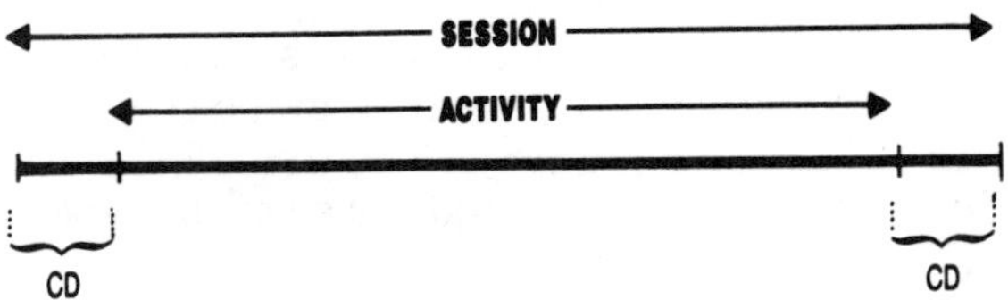

(B) MANY-TO-ONE

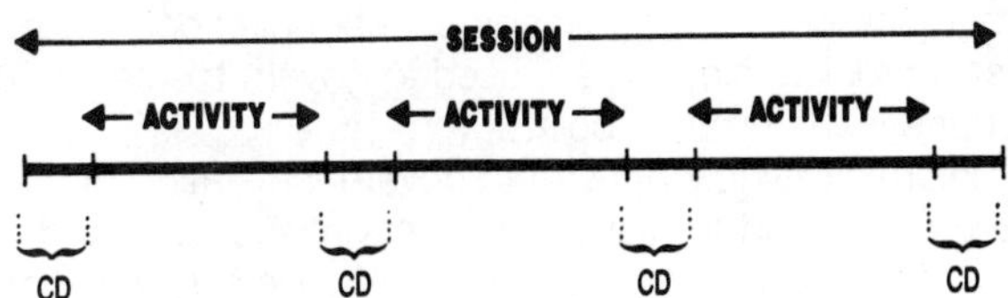

(C) ONE-TO-MANY

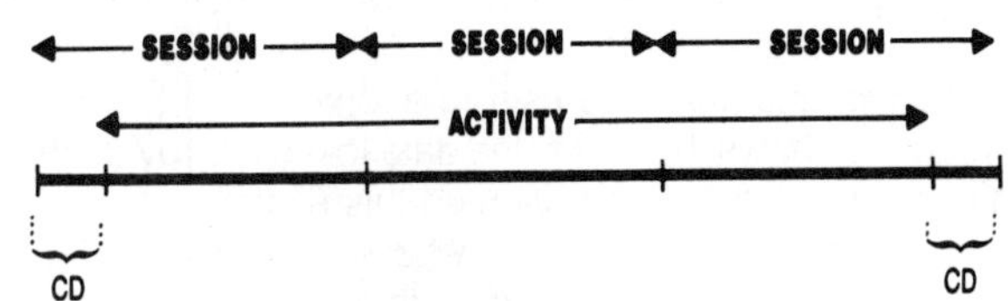

CD = CAPABILITY DATA MAY BE SENT

structure. Again, it is the responsibility of the session user to save any other context information that will be needed for resumption.

The relationship between an activity and a session connection is not fixed. As indicated in Figure 2a, it is possible to have a one-to-one correspondence. In this case, a new activity begins a new session connection, and when the activity is completed, the session connection is terminated. It is also possible to perform multiple activities in sequence over a single session connection (Fig. 2b). This approach may be desirable if session establishment is time- or resource-consuming. If two session users know they will engage in a series of activities, it makes sense to maintain the session connection. Finally, a single activity can span multiple session connections (Fig. 2c). If an activity is interrupted and is not expected to be resumed immediately, it makes sense to break the connection, freeing up resources, and begin a new connection at some point in the future when the users are prepared to resume their activity.

A final feature illustrated in Figure 2 is the use of capability data. If two users select the activity option, then, normally, data may be exchanged only when an activity is in progress. Capability data is a mechanism whereby such users can exchange a small amount of data over a session connection when no activity is in progress. For example, this feature could be used to transmit control information without going through the overhead of setting up an activity.

Token gestures

A token, in the context of the session standard, is an attribute of a session connection that is dynamically assigned to one user at a time and that grants the user exclusive rights to invoke certain services. Put another way, certain services can only be invoked by the current token holder.

The token mechanism is used in the session service to structure the dialogue. The session service provides mechanisms by which a token can initially be assigned to one of the two users engaged in a session and subsequently passed from one user to another. Four tokens are defined, as follows:
■ data token, used to manage a half-duplex connection;
■ synchronize-minor token, used to govern the setting of minor synchronization points;
■ major/activity token, used to govern the setting of major sync points and to manage the activity structure; and
■ release token, used to govern the release of connections.

Three services are associated with the token mechanism: The give-token service allows a user to pass a token to the other user of a session connection. The please-token service allows a user who does not possess a token to request it. The give-control service is used to pass all tokens from one user to another.

Figure 3 shows the use of the data token to provide the half-duplex mode of operation. In this example, the token is initially possessed by user A, who is free to transmit data. User B may not transmit normal data, but may transmit a small amount of what is referred to as typed data. An example of typed data would be the transmission of a break character from a terminal to halt the flow of data

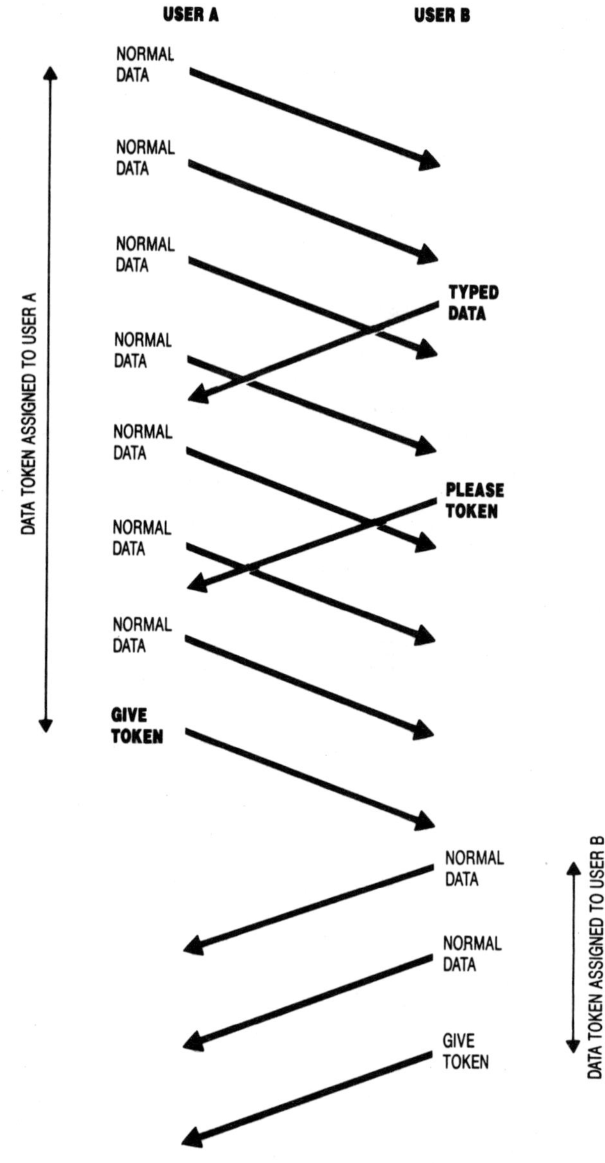

3. Two-way alternate service. *In half-duplex operation, user A sends until receiving a please token. User B can only send normal data after receiving a give token.*

from an application. User B may request the data token at any time, but the token is relinquished only at user A's discretion.

Each of the tokens is always in one of the following two states:
■ Not available. All four tokens are optional, so their use must be negotiated during connection establishment. In the case of the data and release tokens, their unavailability means that the corresponding services (data transfer, release) are always available to both users. In the case of the synchronize-minor and major/activity tokens, their unavailability means that the corresponding services (synchronization, activities) are unavailable to both users.
■ Available. An available token is assigned to one of the two users, who then has the exclusive right to use the associated service.

Table 1: The use of ISO session tokens

FUNCTION	TOKENS REQUIRED			
	DATA	MINOR SYNC	MAJOR SYNC	RELEASE
TRANSFER DATA IN HALF-DUPLEX MODE	M	-	-	-
TRANSFER CAPABILITY DATA	I	I	M	-
SET MINOR SYNC POINT	I	M	-	-
SET MAJOR SYNC POINT	I	I	M	-
START ACTIVITY	I	I	M	-
RESUME ACTIVITY	I	I	M	-
INTERRUPT ACTIVITY	-	-	M	-
DISCARD ACTIVITY	-	-	M	-
END ACTIVITY	I	I	M	-
RELEASE CONNECTION	I	I	I	I

M = MANDATORY (TOKEN MUST BE AVAILABLE AND ASSIGNED TO USER TO PERFORM FUNCTION)
I = IF AVAILABLE (IF TOKEN IS AVAILABLE, IT MUST BE ASSIGNED TO USER TO PERFORM FUNCTION)
- = WHICH SIDE OWNS TOKEN WHEN FUNCTION PERFORMED IS IRRELEVANT

Table 1 shows which tokens a user must possess to perform which functions. Note that, with the exception of the release service, each service listed in the table requires the use of a particular token and may require the use of additional tokens if they are available. These restrictions appear reasonable. For example, in the case of half-duplex operation, only the holder of the data token can set sync points.

Quality of service

Associated with each session connection is a quality of service (QOS), defined by the values of a list of parameters (Table 2). These parameters specify certain characteristics of the session as observed by the end users.

Most of these parameters (the first nine) have to do with the performance (that is, with the speed or the accuracy and reliability characteristics) of the session connection. These parameters are passed down to the transport layer to request that the appropriate quality of service be provided on a transport connection to support the session connection. The next two parameters, protection and priority, are also passed down to transport. Use of the control and transfer parameters, however, is confined to the session layer.

The quality-of-service parameters fall into two categories: prearranged and negotiated. The value of each prearranged parameter is selected and known prior to connection establishment and is not negotiated. The standard does not specify how such agreements are to be reached; the matter is left to local implementation. Note, however, that all the parameters in this category are directly supported by the transport service. Thus, their use must be agreed to by the transport service. The transport-service standard itself indicates that each of the transport QOS parameters can be either negotiated or prearranged.

If the session users in a single computer use a variety of QOS parameter values, then each time the session layer sets up a transport connection, it will have to tell the transport layer what values it wants. These would then have to be negotiated at the transport level. If, however, all the session users use the same prearranged values, then it is more efficient to also prearrange those values at the transport level.

As the session-service standard is defined, when two users set up a logical connection, some of the quality-of-service parameters will already be defined. Such parameters are givens; they are not negotiable. The standard specifies neither the method by which this prearrangement is to be made, the parameters that are to be prearranged in each computer, nor the values that these parameters are to have. In fact, one computer may have a mixture of parameter-value sets. Then all these parameters are directly supported by the transport service, which is the layer that really provides a particular quality of service. Thus, the session layer sets up a transport connection when it wants a particular set of QOS parameters, each of which may be negotiated or prearranged at the transport level.

In the case of a session service that has a different set of prearranged parameter values with different session users, then these parameters could be requested on a per-transport-connection basis and negotiated at the transport level. If the session service is providing the same set of prearranged parameter values to all session users, it would seem to be appropriate to prearrange these values with the transport service. However, the session service standard does not provide explicit guidance on these points.

The remainder of the QOS parameters are negotiated during the session connection establishment phase, as described below. Once the SC is established, the selected parameters are not renegotiated during the lifetime of the SC. If changes occur in the quality of service, these are not signaled to the session users.

The session layer standard defines the services provided by that layer in terms of a set of primitives and parameters. However, this form of definition is not intended to imply an implementation approach but to specify the service in functional terms. Thus, the primitives are not important in themselves. What is important is the way in which the user makes use of the session services.

How to use the session service

During the connection establishment phase, one user requests a session with another user on a remote host. This phase involves negotiating the characteristics of the session connection to be employed. The negotiation results either in the failure to establish a session connection or in a three-party agreement on those characteristics. (The three parties referred to in the standards documentation are the two session users plus the session service provider, which generally consists of a session layer module in each of the two computers and their connection.)

The QOS parameters are negotiated in four stages. First, the calling user (user requesting a session connection) can specify the following:
- for residual error rate and for throughput and transit delay

Table 2: Quality-of-service parameters for the session service

PARAMETER	DESCRIPTION	PERFORMANCE-RELATED OR OTHER	PASSED TO TRANSPORT?	NEGOTIATED/ PREARRANGED
SESSION CONNECTION (SC) ESTABLISHMENT DELAY	MAXIMUM ACCEPTABLE DELAY BETWEEN A CONNECTION REQUEST BY A USER AND THE CORRESPONDING CONFIRMATION BY THE SESSION SERVICE.	P	YES	P
SC ESTABLISHMENT FAILURE PROBABILITY	PROPORTION OF CONNECTION ESTABLISHMENT ATTEMPTS THAT FAIL AS A RESULT OF PROVIDER BEHAVIOR, SUCH AS MISCONNECTION, REFUSAL, OR EXCESSIVE DELAY. CONNECTION FAILURE, DUE TO USER BEHAVIOR ARE EXCLUDED FROM THE CALCULATION.	P	YES	P
THROUGHPUT	RATE OF DATA TRANSFER THAT CAN BE SUSTAINED BY THE SERVICE PROVIDER.	P	YES	N
TRANSIT DELAY	AVERAGE ELAPSED TIME BETWEEN A REQUEST TO TRANSFER DATA BY A SESSION USER AND THE DELIVERY OF THAT DATA TO THE DESTINATION SESSION USER, USING A NOMINAL DATA UNIT SIZE OF 128 OCTETS.	P	YES	N
RESIDUAL ERROR RATE	THE FRACTION OF TRANSFERRED UNITS OF DATA THAT ARE LOST, ALTERED, OR DUPLICATED BY THE SESSION SERVICE.	P	YES	N
TRANSFER FAILURE PROBABILITY	APPLIES TO THROUGHPUT, TRANSIT DELAY, AND RESIDUAL ERROR RATE. FOR EACH OF THESE PARAMETERS, THE TRANSFER FAILURE PROBABILITY IS THE OBSERVED PROPORTION OF TIME THAT THE SESSION SERVICE PROVIDER FAILS TO PROVIDE THE MINIMUM ACCEPTABLE SERVICE.	P	YES	P
SC RELEASE DELAY	MAXIMUM ACCEPTABLE DELAY BETWEEN A USER-INVOKED CONNECTION RELEASE REQUEST AND THE SUCCESSFUL RELEASE OF THE SC AT THE PEER SESSION USER.	P	YES	P
SC RELEASE FAILURE PROBABILITY	PROPORTION OF RELEASE REQUESTS THAT ARE NOT SATISFIED WITHIN THE MAXIMUM ACCEPTABLE DELAY.	P	YES	P
SC RESILIENCE	PROBABILITY THAT THE SESSION SERVICE PROVIDER WILL ABORT THE LOGICAL SESSION CONNECTION.	P	YES	P
SC PROTECTION	A FEATURE THAT SPECIFIED ONE OF OUR OPTIONS: • NO PROTECTION FEATURES; • PROTECTION AGAINST PASSIVE MONITORING; • PROTECTION AGAINST MODIFICATION, DELETION, REPLAY, OR INSERTION OF DATA; AND • BOTH PROTECTION FEATURES.	0	YES	N
SC PRIORITY	SPECIFIES THE PRIORITY OF SCs RELATIVE TO: • THE ORDER IN WHICH CONNECTIONS HAVE THEIR QUALITY OF SERVICE DOWNGRADED, IF NECESSARY; AND • THE ORDER IN WHICH SCs ARE BROKEN TO RECOVER RESOURCES, IF NECESSARY.	0	YES	N
EXTENDED CONTROL	ALLOWS A USER TO MAKE USE OF THE RESYNCHRONIZE, ABORT, ACTIVITY INTERRUPT, AND ACTIVITY DISCARD SERVICES WHEN NORMAL FLOW IS CONGESTED.	0	NO	N
OPTIMIZED DIALOGUE TRANSFER	PERMITS THE SESSION PROTOCOL TO CONCATENATE MULTIPLE SESSION SERVICE REQUESTS AND SEND THEM AS A UNIT.	0	NO	N

in each direction (which may differ), two values, namely the "desired" and the "lowest-acceptable" QOS;

■ for SC protection and SC priority, a single parameter value indicating the desired QOS; and

■ for extended control and optimized dialogue transfer, one of the two values "desired" or "not desired."

In the next stage, the session-service provider will either reject the connection request or convey the connection request to the called user. If it conveys the request, it may (or may not) downgrade the requested quality of service based on its own limitations. Then, for each of the negotiated parameters, an "available" value, specified as follows, is conveyed to the called user:

■ For SC protection, if the service provider agrees to provide the desired value, then that value is used. If the service provider does not agree, it informs the calling user that the connection is rejected.

■ For SC priority, a value equal to or better than the requested value is used.

■ For residual error rate, and for each direction of throughput and transit delay, if the service provider agrees to offer a value that is at least equal to the "lowest acceptable"

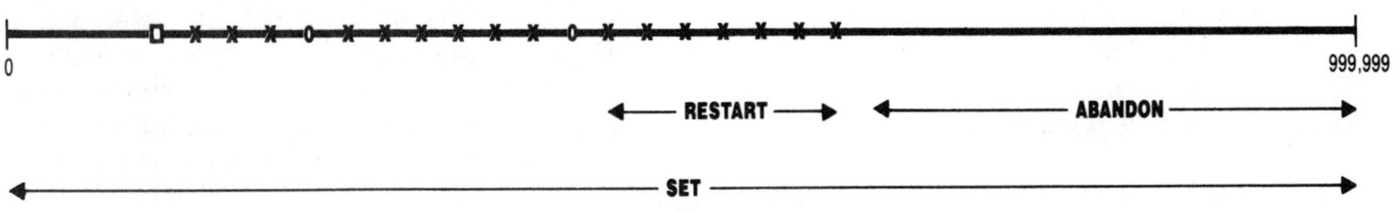

4. Synchronization serial-number assignment. *This figure illustrates the range of synchronization-point serial numbers that can be employed by a user in order to abandon, restart, or simply reset an OSI session connection, as related to the initial serial number and the serial numbers of the synchronization points.*

requested value, then the provider's value is used. If the service provider does not agree, it rejects the connection.

■ For extended control and optimized data transfer, if the "desired" value is requested and the provider does not agree, it sets the value to "not desired," and the facility is not used. Otherwise, the provider conveys the same value as the one requested.

The third stage takes place after the called user receives the connection request. The user responds by specifying each of the negotiated parameters as follows:

■ For optimized data transfer, if the called user agrees to the requested value, it specifies that value. If the requested value is "desired" and the user does not agree, it specifies "not desired." If the requested value is "not desired" and the user does not agree, it may reject the connection.

■ For each of the other parameters, if the called user agrees to the requested value, it specifies that value; otherwise, it may reject the connection.

Finally, the last stage takes place. The response from the called user is conveyed to the calling user.

Besides determining the QOS parameters during the connection establishment phase, the two session-service users also determine the availability of tokens. The calling user can request the availability of one or more of the types of tokens. For each requested token, the calling user proposes who initially owns the token: requester side ("I have it."), accepter side ("You have it."), or accepter chooses ("You decide who has it.").

During the data transfer phase, the users pass data to the session provider in blocks called session service data units and observe the discipline imposed by the tokens. For example, if there is a data token, the connection is half-duplex and the users must take turns sending data. If synchronization and resynchronization are allowed, then the holder of the appropriate tokens can set major and minor sync points.

Each point has an associated serial number that is unique within a given session connection. Major sync points are consecutively numbered in step with the minor sync points, facilitating resynchronization by the service provider. They are always acknowledged. By contrast, the user must explicitly request acknowledgment of minor sync points if tighter synchronization is desired.

When requesting resynchronization, the user indicates the value to be assigned to the serial number by selecting one of the following options (Fig. 4):

■ Abandon: any unused value greater than the current serial number.

■ Restart: any previously used value greater than the sync-point serial number that identifies the last acknowledged major sync point.

■ Set: any value.

Table 3: ISO session service subsets

SERVICE	KERNEL	BCS	BSS	BAS
SESSION CONNECTION	X	X	X	X
NORMAL DATA TRANSFER	X	X	X	a
EXPEDITED DATA TRANSFER	-	-	-	-
TYPED DATA TRANSFER	-	-	X	X
CAPABILITY DATA TRANSFER	-	-	-	X
GIVE TOKEN	-	X	X	X
PLEASE TOKEN	-	X	X	X
GIVE CONTROL	-	-	-	X
MINOR SYNCHRONIZATION POINT	-	-	X	X
MAJOR SYNCHRONIZATION POINT	-	-	X	-
RESYNCHRONIZE	-	-	X	-
PROVIDER-INITIATED EXCEPTION REPORTING	-	-	-	X
USER-INITIATED EXCEPTION REPORTING	-	-	-	X
ACTIVITY START	-	-	-	X
ACTIVITY RESUME	-	-	-	X
ACTIVITY INTERRUPT	-	-	-	X
ACTIVITY DISCARD	-	-	-	X
ACTIVITY END	-	-	-	X
ORDERLY RELEASE	X	X	b	X
USER-INITIATED ABORT	X	X	X	X
PROVIDER-INITIATED ABORT	X	X	X	X

BCS = BASIC COMBINED SUBSET
BSS = BASIC SYNCHRONIZED SUBSET
BAS = BASIC ACTIVITY SUBSET
a = HALF-DUPLEX ONLY
b = NEGOTIATED RELEASE OPTION AVAILABLE

The restart option is used for recovery to a previous point in the dialogue. However, it is up to the session user to perform any data retransmission or other recovery function; the session service merely changes the value of the serial number. The set and abandon options are used where recovery is not desired but the current dialogue is to be aborted without dropping the connection. Again, the semantics of these options is up to the individual session user.

The connection release phase is orderly. That is, release is performed cooperatively between the two session users of the connection so that all in-transit data is delivered and accepted prior to the release. If the negotiated release option was selected, then the user receiving a release request may refuse the release and continue the session connection without loss of data.

Session layer subsets

As the numerous options suggest, the session layer tries to be all things to all people. The result is that a full-blown implementation of the layer is not only complex but unnecessary for virtually all applications. Thus, it is likely that only subsets of the session service will be provided by particular implementations. The standard anticipates this and tries to impose some order by defining four subsets of the session layer. Table 3 lists the services supported by each of these subsets.

The minimum subset is the kernel, which must be provided in any implementation. In essence, it provides for the transparent use of transport connections, with none of the special features associated with the session layer. The kernel alone would be useful for very small machines such as microcomputers. The basic combined subset (BCS) adds support for half-duplex operation. This subset is useful if the principal additional operation is terminal-to-host interaction. The basic synchronized subset (BSS) provides dialogue synchronization and negotiated release (release only when both sides agree). BSS is intended for applications such as reliable file transfer and transaction processing. It is likely that most companies will implement at least BCS and that many will implement BSS.

The most highly structured set is the basic activity subset (BAS), which has most of the services defined in the standard, including those relating to activity management. However, it lacks full-duplex operation during normal data transfer (half-duplex suffices for document exchange and facsimile), minor synchronization, resynchronization, and negotiated release. The BAS is used in CCITT applications to separate documents and message text from control information. The specification of the BAS is compatible with a similar description in CCITT recommendation T.62 (Teletex and Group 4 Facsimile). Outside of this specialized application area, there may be few uses for the basic activity subset. ∎

William Stallings, who earned his Ph.D. from MIT, is president of Comp-Comm Consulting Inc. of London, England. As an independent consultant his clients include IBM, the government of India, and the National Security Agency. Stallings is the author of the three-volume series, Handbook of Computer-Communications Standards, *just published by Macmillan. This article is based on material in Volume I, which covers OSI and OSI-related standards.*

Upper layers: From bizarre to bazaar

Standards atop the OSI stack, once merely strange abstractions, are now showing up in carnival-like trade-show demonstrations. Can a thriving marketplace be far behind?

Thanks to progress at the upper reaches of the International Organization for Standardization's (ISO) Open Systems Interconnection (OSI) model, users will soon see dramatic growth in OSI-compatible products and services. Once understood only by blue-sky thinkers in standards-making groups, these protocols are becoming clear and standardized enough for implementers to actually do something with them. When, in the not-too-distant future, users can build functioning networks out of interoperable, OSI-based products, the standards will have finally arrived on earth.

Products based on standards have long benefited both the computing and the communications worlds, being more interoperable and less expensive and troublesome than their nonstandard counterparts. Communications standards made low-level networking easier, from plugging in connectors to setting up routes through packet networks and exchanging data reliably. Software standards, such as the Structured Query Language (SQL), have brought equivalent benefits to the computing world.

Until recently, however, standards have done little to hasten the convergence of these two worlds. Applications programmers have had no standard way of accessing sophisticated networking tools. They could write applications within proprietary architectures, but this locked their programs into a single environment. Unfolding upper-layer standards provide the missing link.

These layers are the farthest removed from the network hardware, or even its topology, and must in fact remain independent of such details. They support the networking requirements of application programs, which makes them software-intensive. Unlike these programs, however, they must also be independent of the processing environment.

Rooted in the specifics of neither computing nor communications, upper-layer standards can bridge these two domains. For the same reason, though, they are fated to be highly abstract, almost mystical. As the outcome of consensus, these standards offer great potential but have been slow to develop. This paradox leads to the conflict between those who hold that standards will eventually dominate networking and those who maintain that they will always lag behind proprietary technology.

Terra firmer

Protocols at the lower layers—physical (Layer 1) through transport (Layer 4)—had reached international standard (IS) status by 1984. There were also international standards at the session layer (5). But presentation (6) and application (7) were still relatively crude. X.400, put forth by the International Telegraph and Telephone Consultative Committee (CCITT), was the major application layer protocol. Another, ISO's File Transfer, Access, and Management (FTAM), was also being promulgated.

Since then, the presentation layer has attained IS standing, although it is still generating some confusion (see "Those mysterious inner uppers"). The view of the application layer has matured as well. In 1984, standards makers were trying to break the application layer into sublayers, but this approach lead to such absurdities as "function A is above function B which is above function A" and was abandoned. Now, the application layer is set forth in well-defined, though still abstract, terms (see "OSI's final frontier: The application layer," in this issue).

For example, application service elements (ASEs) are defined at the application layer. Mechanisms are described to bind ASEs together into application entities (AEs). In turn, the AEs provide a particular functionality to an application user, such as the ability to exchange revisable documents by electronic mail.

This article will consider X.400 issues and implementations as highlighted at October's Telecom '87; the status and nature of other upper-layer protocols likely to have a

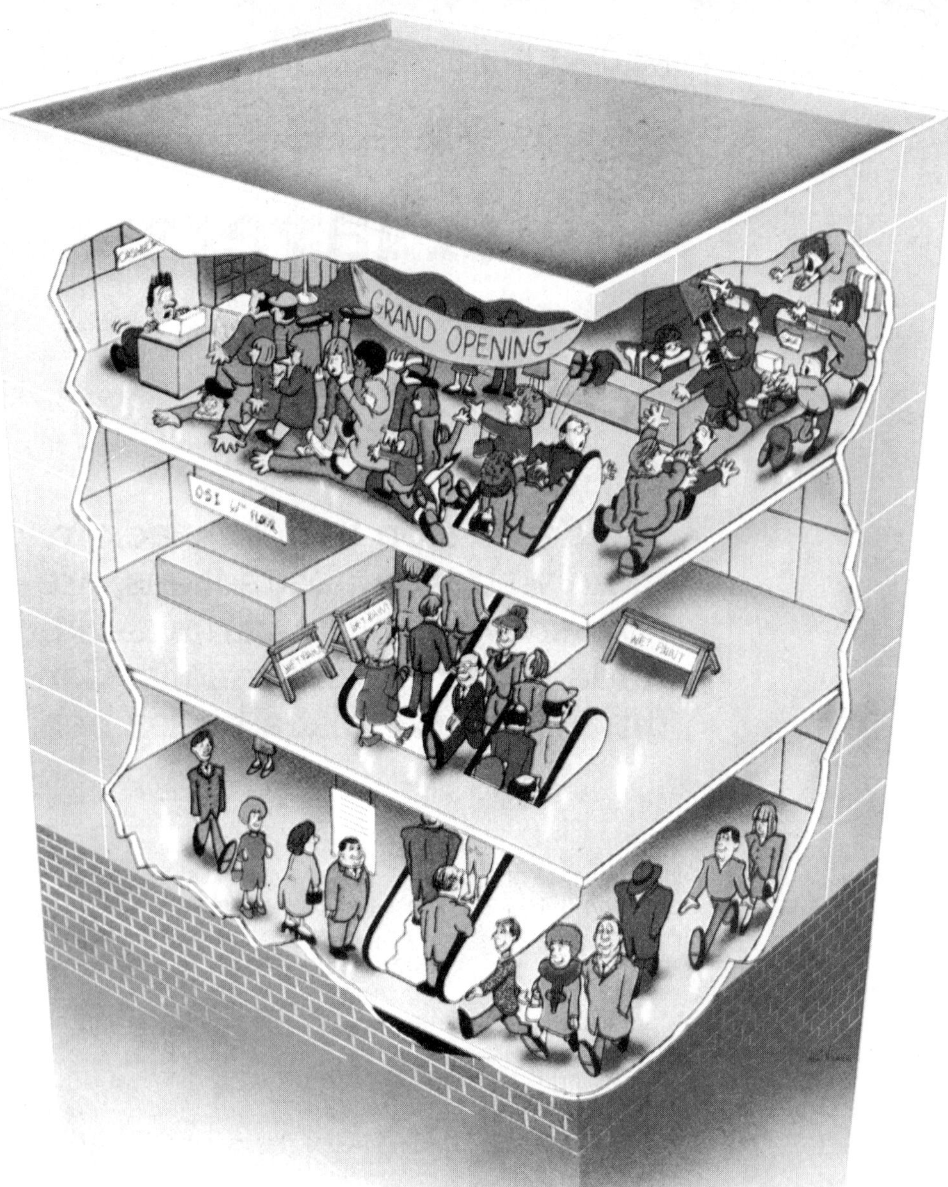

significant impact on information networking in the near future; and finally, the upcoming Enterprise Networking Event (ENE), with its display of MAP/TOP, FTAM, and other related protocols.

From Geneva and back

Interconnection extravaganzas have become almost as much a fixture of standards activity as subcommittee meetings. In the United States, the 1984 National Computer Conference and Autofact '85 shows brought attention to the Manufacturing Automation Protocol (MAP) initiated by General Motors. The CCITT X.400 message-handling protocol has been a drawing card at European shows. In 1985, three companies showed interoperating X.400 prototypes at the SICOB office equipment show in Paris. Eight organizations joined their prototypes together at the 1986 Hannover Fair in West Germany. By March 1987, 14 firms were coupled at the Hannover show. All had made commitments to bring their X.400 products to market by the end of the year.

And last October saw the largest such demonstration to date. Twenty-one vendors—from France, Germany, Japan, Switzerland, the United Kingdom, and the United States— exhibited interworking X.400 implementations at Telecom

'87 in Geneva. To participate, a firm had to be ready to announce an X.400 product within six months of the demonstration.

According to Ian Valentine, technical director of Level-7 Ltd. in Wokingham, England, the consulting firm that coordinated the Telecom effort, the show signaled the coming of age of X.400. "It shows that the technical problems of interconnection have been resolved," he says.

Two types of X.400 nodes were networked: Administrative Management Domains (ADMD), operated by national carriers, Postal, Telegraph, and Telephone (PTT) agencies, or recognized private service providers; and Private Management Domains (PRMD), run by software and equipment suppliers. While ADMDs could act as passthroughs or relays, PRMDs could not.

Each PRMD had to connect to one or more ADMD. The ADMDs, in turn, had to interconnect with each other so that there would not be more than one intermediate relay between any two PRMDs. The participants decided not to reveal to the public exactly who was connected to whom, as some carriers were negotiating permanent X.400 gateways. The network topology could be deduced, however, from the known paths between the PRMDs (Fig. 1). For example, Hewlett-Packard (HP) connected to the Japa-

Those mysterious inner uppers

The application layer protocols are likely to draw the most user attention, and for good reason: They bear the names of useful services. As the outer surface of the Open Systems Interconnection (OSI) stack, these protocols are also the most visible. The application layer is expected to grow dramatically in both number of protocols and utility. However, this growth would not be possible without a solid foundation.

Until recently, the enabling upper-layer protocols—namely session, presentation, and the common application services—were both incomplete and hard to understand. These OSI "innards" are no longer incomplete, and the veil of mystery is slowly being lifted. However, a great deal of work is still going on at each layer:

■ **Session.** The purpose of the session layer is to transfer the application's data by means of data-transfer primitives. It uses other primitives to connect, release, abort, and resynchronize sessions. (For a complete account, see "Is there an OSI session protocol in your future?" DATA COMMUNICATIONS, November 1987, p. 147.)

Initially, the session layer's designers had assumed that data transfer would be used for the majority of user data. It therefore made perfect sense to limit the primitives, except for data transfer, to being no greater than 512 bytes long. Likewise, on an abort, no more than nine bytes of user data could be carried.

In practice, however, the application-protocol writers decided that it would be more convenient to piggyback their protocol data units (PDUs) atop the session's PDUs. For example, it made sense for FTAM to do its connection negotiation at the same time as the session layer was negiotiating its own connection (especially over long-haul networks, where negotiation can be expensive).

A new version of the session protocol, due to be approved as an addendum next month, will handle such exchanges by allowing unlimited data transfer on all primitives. Implementations should be available this year. However, there may be compatibility problems.

Early implementations of File Transfer, Access, and Management (FTAM) were designed to work well with the session's version 1, but later FTAM versions can transfer more than 512 bytes of user data on a connection. Products written to the newer FTAM specification would likely have problems with session version 1. For instance, when it sent out a long-winded connection request, such a product would not know if the other side could accommodate it. Work is under way at the National Bureau of Standards (NBS) to devise implementers' agreements that overcome this mismatch.

■ **Presentation.** Just beneath the application layer, which is concerned with the meaning (or semantics) of transmitted data, is the presentation layer, which governs the way meaning is represented (the syntax). Like the transport layer, which ensures reliable delivery, presentation ensures reliable data content.

The presentation layer has two main functions. It changes the local abstract syntax (the representation native to the end node) into the commonly known transfer syntax. And it negotiates presentation syntaxes. In this negotiation, the local application gives the presentation layer a list of abstract syntaxes it wants to use. Presentation then determines which transfer syntaxes it needs to support those abstract syntaxes and attempts to agree with its peer on a set of abstract syntaxes that the two can use to communicate.

According to Mike Ellis, who chairs the Upper-Layer Special Interest Group of the NBS OSI Implementers' Workshop, "the presentation layer is difficult to understand and implement. You can't just have a programmer write to the specification and expect it to play."

Charlie Bass, cofounder of Ungermann-Bass and chairman of Touch Communications, suggests that this may have helped slow development. "The presentation layer has moved along modestly, but it is far from interpreting complex structures," he says. Others, however, are sanguine about the layer's potential.

"I expect to see growth in the presentation layer," says Gary Workman, coordinator of the Manufacturing Automation Protocol development team at General Motors. "The number of transfer syntaxes will grow, and so will the capabilities of the presentation protocol."

■ **ASN.1.** Right now, however, there is only one standard transfer syntax, called the basic encoding rule for Abstract Syntax Notation 1. ASN.1 is used to define protocols. It is analogous to the Backus-Naur Form, an abstract way of specifying programming constructs.

ASN.1 has been in use for some time. The original X.400 and FTAM protocols both used it. However, ASN.1 "is a tool that has to be used in conjunction with something else to make it useful," says Ellis.

Although it provides a standard way to define protocols, its drawback is complexity. "Conformance to ASN.1 can be complicated," says Ellis, "so you may see a more restricted subset of ASN.1." Moreover, it does not provide all the functions that a designer might want. Ellis speculates that "you may see encrypting and/or compacting algorithms for transfer syntaxes, although no such support is in the works at this time."

■ **ACSE.** The Association Control Service Element was intended to be the single repository for all common functionality among application layer protocols.

One such function is authentication. Since many application service elements might need an authentication mechanism, it makes sense to consolidate authentication in ACSE. Another such function is the application context, a shared understanding of what functions the applications may provide.

ACSE does not have a lot of meat to it right now. One reason is ongoing disagreements about what constitutes common functionality. It is easier to identify such functionality than to make it usable.

By way of analogy, Ellis points to the desirability of a single wheel size for vehicles, which would allow all tires to fit onto a common-size hub. However, truck designers prefer big tires while sports-car designers prefer small ones. "Only time will tell whether ACSE will gain enough common functionality to pay its way in the protocol stack," says Ellis.

nese PTT via the Swiss PTT and then AT&T. Telesystemes, a French firm, linked to the outside world via Transpac.

Some observers wondered if the X.400 demonstration was more smoke than fire. "These interoperability shows are minimal subsets of functionality," said Andy DeMari, president of Retix, the Santa Monica, Calif., supplier of OSI software. Retix passed on the Telecom group scene in favor of its own X.400 demonstration. Telenet, which took part in the multivendor booth, called the interoperability testing required for Telecom participation extensive. However, it "was not as rigorous as we would want for a commercial service," said Stuart Mathison, Telenet vice president for special projects, messaging.

Laurie Bride, program manager of the Technical and Office Protocols (TOP) within Boeing Computer Services in Seattle, Wash., felt that the demonstration did not go far enough.

"I told the Geneva people that when they could handle electronic data interchange, including such business forms as purchase orders and private, in-house electronic mail systems, I'd be impressed," Bride says. However, she finds the effort laudable, calling herself "a firm believer in data communications standards. It's the only way to go."

Messaging products
Clearly, vendors agree with her. Countless firms have endorsed X.400 or proclaimed their intention to implement it. Table 1 lists many of the vendors with announced products and services. Although shown in dollars, some prices were converted from other currencies and will thus fluctuate with the exchange rate. ICL's offerings are priced in pounds sterling, IBM's in French francs. Some, like IBM's and HP's, are only available outside the United States.

Many of the firms sell their code to original equipment manufacturers as well as to users. Sydney Data Products Inc. claims that its X.400 product has garnered more than

---

Worldwide X.400. *At the Telecom '87 show in Geneva last October, 12 vendors had X.400 links via nine carriers. Most of the actual links were not divulged. Though the Nixdorf and Alcatel STR machines were off site, all the firms, including the carriers, could send each other mail messages via terminals at the show.*

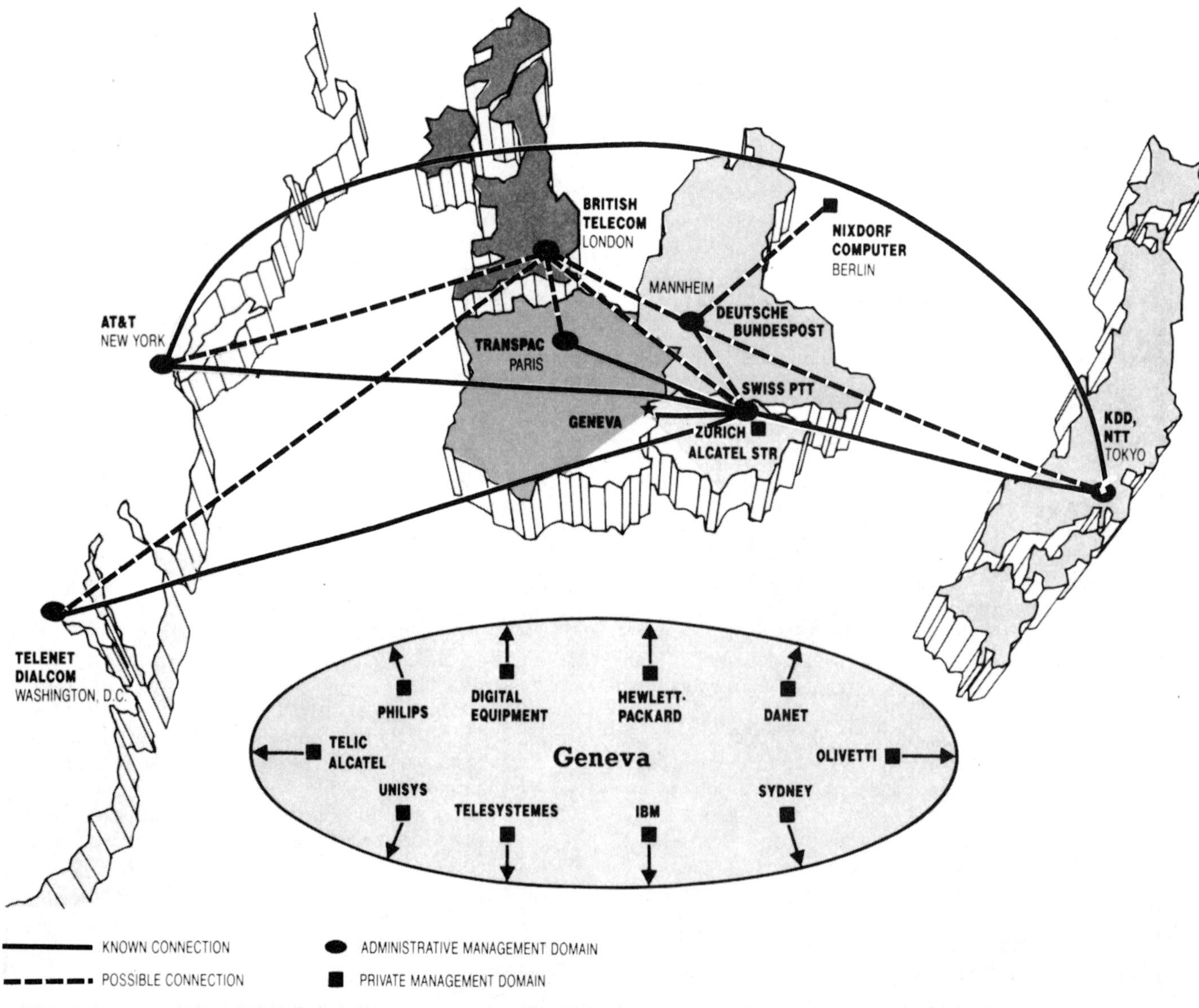

Table 1: Sampling of X.400 products

VENDOR	PRODUCT/DESCRIPTION	AVAILABILITY	PRICE	FUNCTIONAL STANDARD
AT&T PISCATAWAY, N.J. 800-624-5672	GATEWAY 400 (X.400 CAPABILITY OF AT&T MAIL SERVICE)	NOW	SURCHARGE OVER USUAL TRANSACTION CHARGE	NBS
DATA GENERAL WESTBORO, MASS. 617-366-8911	DG X.400 (X.400 GATEWAY)	NOW	$1,375 to $10,450	CEPT
DIALCOM ROCKVILLE, MD. 301-881-9020	PATHFINDER (FAMILY OF INTERCONNECT PRODUCTS)	NOW (PROFS AND TRANSIT); EARLY 1988 (WANG AND USER AGENT)	$1,000/MONTH (DOMESTIC ACCESS); $5,000/MONTH (INTERNATIONAL)	CEPT
DIGITAL EQUIPMENT CORP. MERRIMAC, N.H. 603-884-2412	MESSAGE ROUTER X.400 GATEWAY (SOFTWARE-BASED GATEWAY BETWEEN DEC'S MAILBUS AND X.400)	NOW	$3,500 to $14,000	CEN/CENELEC, CEPT, AND NBS
GENERAL ELECTRIC INFORMATION SERVICES ROCKVILLE, MD. 301-340-4000	EDI*EXPRESS, QUIK/COMM (EXISTING SERVICES WITH X.400 CONNECTIVITY)	FIRST QUARTER 1988 (QUIK/COMM); LATER IN 1988 (EDI*EXPRESS)	VARIABLE (BASED ON USAGE)	CEN/CENELEC, NBS
HEWLETT-PACKARD GRENOBLE, FRANCE 76-625-535 OR LOCAL U.S. FIELD OFFICE	OSI/X.400 (X.400 GATEWAY FOR HP9000/300 MINICOMPUTERS)	NOW (IN EUROPE ONLY)	$22,000 (INCLUDES HARDWARE; SESSION, TRANSPORT, AND X.400 SOFTWARE	CEN/CENELEC, CEPT, AND NBS
IBM EUROPE PARIS, FRANCE 47-676-754 (PRODUCTS ONLY AVAILABLE IN EUROPE)	X.400 MESSAGE TRANSFER FACILITY (MTF) FOR VM	SEPTEMBER 1988	$6,625 TO $26,500	CEN/CENELEC, CEPT
	X.400 MTF FOR VSE	DECEMBER 1988	$7,540 TO $30,150	CEN/CENELEC, CEPT
	X.400 PROFS CONNECTION	SEPTEMBER 1988	$5,480 TO $21,925	CEN/CENELEC, CEPT
	X.400 MTF FOR MVS	THIRD QUARTER 1988	$21,000	CEN/CENELEC, CEPT
	X.400 DISOSS CONNECTION	THIRD QUARTER 1988	$16,430	CEN/CENELEC, CEPT
ICL BRACKNELL, U.K. 344-424-842	OFFICE POWER/ICL MAIL (USER PRODUCT; ALSO SELL CODE TO WORKSTATION VENDORS AND ELECTRONIC MAIL NETWORKS)	NOW (LOWER-PRICED VERSION); SECOND QUARTER 1988 (DOS AND HIGHER-PRICED VERSIONS)	$2,700 TO $450,000	CEN/CENELEC
OMNICOM INC. VIENNA, VA. 703-281-1135	OSILOGIE (X.400 SOURCE CODE FOR OEMs AND LARGE USERS)	FEBRUARY 1988	$45,000 PLUS ROYALTIES	CEN/CENELEC
RETIX SANTA MONICA, CALIF. 213-399-2200	RETIX X.400 (X.400 SOURCE CODE FOR OEMs AND LARGE USERS)	NOW	$40,000 TO $140,000	NBS AND CEN/CENELEC VERSIONS
SYDNEY DATA PRODUCTS INC. LOS ANGELES, CALIF. 213-444-3000	MESSENGER 400 (SOFTWARE FOR MOST COMPUTER OPERATING SYSTEMS)	NOW	$100 TO $250,000 (DEPENDING ON LICENSING AND MACHINE)	CEN/CENELEC, CEPT, NBS
TELECOM CANADA OTTAWA, ONTARIO 613-567-5127 (OUTSIDE CANADA CALL COLLECT)	ENVOY 100 (EXISTING SERVICE WITH X.400 CAPABILITY)	JANUARY 1988 (IF APPROVED)	$.50 SURCHARGE PER MESSAGE	NBS
TELENET RESTON, VA. 703-689-6000	TELEMAIL 400 (MAIL SERVICE OFFERING; ALSO LICENSE CODE)	NOW (WITH DATA GENERAL CEO); EARLY 1988 (DEC ALL-IN-ONE, IBM PROFS)	SURCHARGE OVER USUAL TRANSACTION CHARGE	CEPT, NBS
WESTERN UNION UPPER SADDLE RIVER, N.J. 201-825-5000	EASYLINK X.400 (INTERCONNECT CAPABILITY)	JANUARY 1988	NOT DETERMINED	SUPPORTS ALL FUNCTIONAL STANDARDS

CEN/CENELEC = EUROPEAN COMMITTEE FOR STANDARDIZATION/EUROPEAN
COMMITTEE FOR ELECTROTECHNICAL STANDARDIZATION
CEPT = COMMITTEE ON EUROPEAN POST AND TELEGRAPH
MVS = MULTIPLE VIRTUAL STORAGE

NBS = NATIONAL BUREAU OF STANDARDS
OEM = ORIGINAL EQUIPMENT MANUFACTURER
VM = VIRTUAL MACHINE
VSE = VIRTUAL STORAGE EXTENDED

60 licensees. "These include more than half of the top 30 computer and communications vendors in North America and Europe," says Peter Westwood, Sydney's chief operating officer.

Some of the carriers have already set up links with other nations. For example, Telenet licenses its Telemail X.400 software to nine PTTs in various countries and has interconnection agreements with them, including UK Telemail, Italmail in Italy, Telemimo in Australia, and Ace Telemail in Japan. AT&T has announced an X.400 connection between Envoy 100, the Telecom Canada X.400 service, and AT&T Mail's Gateway 400.

For IBM users abroad, five announced products will offer gateways to X.400. The X.400 Disoss Connection and MVS (Multiple Virtual Storage) Message Transfer Facility were announced in March 1987 (see "SNA to OSI: IBM building upper-layer gateways," DATA COMMUNICATIONS, May 1987, p. 133). Corresponding products for Profs under VM (Virtual Memory) and for VSE (Virtual Storage Extended) were announced in October 1987.

IBM is not supporting X.400 domestically because "demand for it in the United States is very slow," says Donald A. Gladstone, program manager at IBM's OSI project office in Research Triangle Park, N. C. "Demand in Europe seems to be a few years ahead of that in the United States. In general, demand for both X.400 and MAP is not overwhelming; there seems to be a lot more interest than actual usage. Nonetheless, this year, we will see more X.400 and FTAM products announced and most of the announced ones shipping," he says.

Roy Cadwallader, ICL's manager of network technology in Kidsgrove, England, has been watching IBM in European standards meetings. "IBM seems to have changed their whole OSI tune in the standards arena over the last six months. My impression is that, whereas they were previously against standards, they're now behind them," he says.

In a bid for American IBM users, Telenet plans to introduce a Profs/X.400 software interface that runs on users' private IBM gear. "IBM will not be providing X.400 software in the United States for about a year, so we've taken it upon ourselves to develop a package," says Mathison.

The last column in Table 1 lists the "functional standards" that each product follows. When the 1984 CCITT X.400 recommendations were published, it became apparent that the standard was not complete in all respects. It would be possible for two vendors to build implementations that did not actually interoperate, because the lengths of fields and protocol elements were not defined (for example, the maximum length of a name), and because nothing specified what subset of the total specification could be built and still interoperate.

To overcome this quandary, groups of implementers in Europe, North America, and Japan formed to establish functional standards, as they are known in Europe (or implementation profiles in the United States). The groups have been negotiating and sharing documents to get the functional standards as close together as possible.

For instance, two of the functional standards interworked at the Hannover Fair, although "the vendors had to break the rules somewhat to make that work," says John M. Stidd

of Xerox Corp. in Sunnyvale, Calif., who chairs the X.400 Special Interest Group (SIG) at the NBS OSI Implementers' Workshop. These rules modifications are being adopted by the implementers' groups.

What's ahead for X.400
At this point, X.400 is a mature protocol. Products that implement it have proven interoperable and are being deployed throughout the world.

However, for the X.400 protocol to be truly universal, it will have to offer a directory service. Like an electronic version of the white and yellow pages, the directory service would list all subscribers. Directory work is proceeding under ISO and also under CCITT's Study Group VII.

One possible snag is getting a cohesive agreement for a convergent document, so that both ISO and CCITT use the same protocols and services. For example, in the area of security, the CCITT, representing the PTTs (which control telephone and mail directories), took the stance that authentication (granting or denying access privileges) should be handled by the directory provider. ISO, representing equipment and software vendors, thought it should be done by the Association Control Service Element (ACSE), the common locus of functionality, so that directory service would be a generic service accessible by any application.

In Solomonic fashion, the groups decided that either the directory or the application may perform authentication. However, hard problems and political/technical differences, such as how the distributed directory should work and how to get information from one domain to another, persist.

"Electronic messaging can't and won't explode until these issues are resolved. Other groups within CCITT will be hovering like vultures around Study Group VII," says Valentine. He also points beyond the directory problem to commercial issues, such as tariffing. Since messages may bounce from node to node and network to network, who pays how much for what becomes unclear.

Another twist in the road lies just around the bend in the form of a substantial revision that will come out as a joint ISO/CCITT standard in 1988. "Caveat emptor," says John Stidd. "It is uncertain how upward-compatible the current X.400 products will be, but there are enough differences to make the transition fairly expensive to go from the 1984 to the 1988 version," he says. Among the major differences are the following:

■ Security. Security provisions are now limited to password protection. The 1988 version will provide a protocol for the secure exchange of encrypted messages. It will also offer better authentication mechanisms.

■ Hard copy. Addressing will be extended in the 1988 version to allow the electronic mail service to interwork with physical postal delivery services (that is, the address will include towns, streets, and so on).

■ Mailboxes. One of the most glaring flaws in the 1984 version, at least from the U. S. perspective, concerns the user agent (UA), the software component interacting with the user, and the message transfer agent (MTA), which relays messages to other MTAs and thus supports UA-to-UA communication. MTA-to-MTA interaction uses a protocol called P1, UA-to-UA uses P2, and UA-to-MTA uses P3.

The problem with the 1984 design is that the UA had to

Table 2: State of the protocols

PROTOCOL	STATUS	PRODUCT TIME FRAME	DESCRIPTION
ABSTRACT SYNTAX NOTATION 1 (ASN.1)	IS	NOW	AN ABSTRACT WAY OF DEFINING PROTOCOL SPECIFICATIONS, CURRENTLY SUPPORTED BY ONE SET OF BASIC ENCODING RULES, WHICH CONSTITUTES A TRANSFER SYNTAX USED BY THE PRESENTATION LAYER.
ASSOCIATION CONTROL SERVICE ELEMENT (ACSE)	BECOMING AN IS	1988	PROVIDES BASIC FACILITIES FOR THE CONTROL OF AN ASSOCIATION BETWEEN TWO APPLICATION ENTITIES.
DIRECTORY SYSTEM (ISO); ALSO CALLED X.500 (CCITT)	DIS	1988-90	PROVIDES INFORMATION ON NAMES, ADDRESSES, ROUTING, AND OTHER OBJECTS NEEDED FOR GLOBAL NETWORKING.
FILE TRANSFER, ACCESS, AND MANAGEMENT (FTAM)	BECOMING AN IS	NOW	DESCRIBES HOW TO CREATE, DELETE, READ, AND CHANGE FILE ATTRIBUTES AS WELL AS TRANSFER AND ACCESS (AT FILE AND RECORD LEVEL) FILES STORED AT A REMOTE SITE.
JOB TRANSFER AND MANIPULATION (JTM)	DIS	1988 (U.K., GERMANY, JAPAN)	SUPPORTS DISTRIBUTED JOB PROCESSING, INCLUDING JOB SUBMISSION, FILE AND RESOURCE ACCESS, AND OUTPUT REDIRECTION.
MANUFACTURING MESSAGE SERVICE (MMS)	DIS	MID-1988	A COMMAND AND CONTROL LANGUAGE USED TO COMMUNICATE WITH MANUFACTURING DEVICES SUCH AS PROGRAMMABLE AND NUMERIC CONTROLLERS AND ROBOTS.
MESSAGE HANDLING SYSTEMS (MHS)—CCITT X.400:			
• 1984 VERSION	R	NOW	STANDARD FOR THE INTERCHANGE OF ELECTRONIC MAIL AMONG RECIPIENTS SERVED BY DIVERSE COMMON CARRIERS AND COMPUTER VENDORS.
• 1988 VERSION	DR	1989-90	A REVISION OF X.400 TO INCLUDE CHANGES IN PROTOCOLS AND SERVICE ELEMENTS, PROVIDING SECURITY, MAILBOXES, AND PHYSICAL DELIVERY.
NETWORK MANAGEMENT:			
• OSI MANAGEMENT FRAMEWORK	DIS	1988 (MAP AND TOP); EARLY 1990s (ISO STANDARD-BASED)	FRAMEWORK, SERVICE, AND APPLICATION LAYER PROTOCOL FOR PASSING INFORMATION BETWEEN MANAGERS AND THE RESOURCES THEY MANAGE.
• COMMON MANAGEMENT INFORMATION SERVICE	DP		
• COMMON MANAGEMENT INFORMATION PROTOCOL	DP		
OFFICE DOCUMENT ARCHITECTURE (ODA)	DIS	1989-90	SPECIFIES STRUCTURES FOR THE EXCHANGE OF PROCESSIBLE DOCUMENTS.
OFFICE DOCUMENT INTERCHANGE FORMAT (ODIF)	DIS	1989-90	AN ASN.1 ENCODING THAT CONSTITUTES A PARTICULAR REPRESENTATION FOR THE OFFICE DOCUMENT ARCHITECTURE.
PRESENTATION	IS	NOW	PROVIDES FOR TRANSFORMATION OF DATA BETWEEN LOCAL AND COMMON SYNTAXES AND FOR NEGOTIATION OF PRESENTATION SYNTAXES.
REMOTE DATABASE ACCESS	DP	1989	FACILITATES ACCESS TO DATABASES FROM INTELLIGENT WORKSTATIONS AND FROM OTHER DATABASE ENVIRONMENTS VIA A CLIENT/SERVER RELATIONSHIP.
SECURITY	SECOND DIS	EARLY 1990s	SECURITY ARCHITECTURE AND MECHANISMS THAT ADD APPLICATION AUTHENTICATION AND TRANSPORT ENCRYPTION TO BASIC OSI REFERENCE MODEL.
SESSION:			
• VERSION 1	IS	NOW	LETS USERS ESTABLISH AND RELEASE CONNECTIONS FOR DATA EXCHANGE AS WELL AS SYNCHRONIZE, INTERRUPT, AND RESUME SESSIONS.
• VERSION 2	DA	1988	ALLOWS USER DATA LONGER THAN NINE BYTES ON ABORT AND PRIMITIVES LONGER THAN 512 BYTES.
TRANSACTION PROCESSING	BECOMING A DIS	1989-90	PROVIDES SERVICES TO PROCESS ATOMIC UNITS OF WORK, A GROUP OF UPDATES THAT MUST BE DONE EITHER IN THEIR ENTIRETY OR NOT AT ALL.
VIRTUAL TERMINAL (VT)	SECOND DIS	1988-89	ALLOWS FOR THE TRANSMISSION ACROSS THE NETWORK OF TERMINAL-ORIENTED MESSAGES, INCLUDING KEYBOARD INPUT, SCREEN UPDATES, AND VARIOUS TYPES OF TERMINAL CONTROL INFORMATION.

CCITT = INTERNATIONAL TELEGRAPH AND TELEPHONE CONSULTATIVE COMMITTEE
DA = DRAFT ADDENDUM
DIS = DRAFT INTERNATIONAL STANDARD
DP = DRAFT PROPOSAL
DR = DRAFT RECOMMENDATION

IS = INTERNATIONAL STANDARD
ISO = INTERNATIONAL ORGANIZATION FOR STANDARDIZATION
MAP = MANUFACTURING AUTOMATION PROTOCOL
OSI = OPEN SYSTEMS INTERCONNECTION
R = RECOMMENDATION
TOP = TECHNICAL AND OFFICE PROTOCOLS

Will LU 6.2 weather the storm?

Controversy has surrounded transaction processing since IBM first submitted its Logical Unit (LU) 6.2 for consideration as a basis for the International Organization for Standarization (ISO) standard. After an initial rejection, IBM submitted LU 6.2 again. Persistence may have paid off. Joe Twomey, a member of Bellcore's technical staff and ISO editor for Transaction Processing (TP) protocols, says that "although ISO would never endorse a vendor's implementation, the service primitives that are produced look very compatible with LU 6.2."

The conflict, according to Laurie Bride of Boeing Computer Services, is not whether the protocols themselves are different but whether the functional services that the ISO TP protocol delivers are the same as those offered by LU 6.2. IBM's Systems Network Architecture (SNA) users wonder if they will be able to use Open Systems Interconnection (OSI) networks with full functionality or whether only a nominal subset of the LU 6.2 services will be available. Of the non-IBM vendors, says Bride, "some want to see, they won't say less functionality but better performance." A proposed compromise provides subsets that meet each criterion.

Richard DesJardins, of Computer Technology Associates, agrees that "the politics is there, but there's a strong motivation for vendors to come to terms." He gives several reasons why LU 6.2 is not exactly what ISO is looking for:

■ LU 6.2 includes a lot of the functionality currently found in OSI's session layer, so there is no need to duplicate it in the application layer. It also includes redundant or SNA-specific management capabilities, such as association control (which is how an application can be sure of the identity of its partner).

■ Rather than endorse the LU 6.2 verbs, which OSI manufacturers complain would make IBM's applications easier to support or to port than anyone else's, the standards groups will adopt an abstract service interface into which IBM will map its verbs.

■ ISO TP offers more functionality than LU 6.2.

Donald A. Gladstone, IBM's OSI program manager, agrees that the ISO standard can do things that LU 6.2 cannot. "Functional areas, valid from OSI's point of view, are being added," he says. "For example, they want full duplex, which LU 6.2 does not provide." Gladstone is confident that the TP standards will look "very similar to LU 6.2. They will be reasonably close but almost assuredly not identical," he says.

be colocated (in the same box) with the MTA to use the P3 protocol. The protocol assumes that the UA will always be attached and active. It makes no provision for the storage of messages in a central mail server. Where the UA is a minicomputer with simple terminals attached, or where the service is accessed via Telex or Teletex, as in Europe, the design makes sense. However, it does not work for people who want to use their personal computers for mail. The 1988 CCITT draft recommendation extends the P3 protocol to accommodate mailboxes (the new mailbox protocol is being called, variously, P7 or P3+).

Strategic protocols

Deployment of X.400 is half of the first phase of what may be considered OSI's grand scheme. "The number one goal of the OSI community (standardizers, product builders, and testers) must be to get the basic OSI platform, namely X.400 and FTAM, out there in working products," says Richard desJardins, a standards pioneer and associate with Computer Technology Associates Inc., a McLean, Va., systems engineering firm. Such products will be on display at ENE '88 later this year.

DesJardins, who is one of three drafters of the original OSI reference model, believes that phases two and three are also on track.

"Look, you can make all the standards in the world, but if you don't give people something they can use, they won't accept you," he says. "Our strategy for getting OSI accepted is to provide platforms for electronic mail and file transfer, then virtual terminal capability, and finally transaction processing." A number of other standards, covering remote database access, network management, security, and other functions, will also sweeten the OSI pie (see Table 2).

■ Virtual terminal. Many network users face the problem of having to access applications from a terminal quite different from the type that the application was developed to support. Microcomputer users can bridge this gulf on a case-by-case basis with terminal emulation, but others may have to have two or more types of terminal devices on their desks.

The OSI Virtual Terminal (VT) protocol is designed to provide remote, networkwide access to applications. This should allow vendors to write applications that run on a particular computer but that can also be accessed from any other processor vendor's attached terminals. For example, if an IBM 370 mainframe had an OSI VT link to a VAX, 3270 terminal users would be able to use the VAX's VT100-oriented applications.

VT Basic Class represents the terminal screen in terms of a matrix of character cells, which precludes the support of bit-mapped or vector graphics. However, says desJardins, "people will add forms, graphics, windows; these things will evolve on us." They will clearly have to, given the graphic, interactive nature of modern microcomputers.

One of these changes is already under way: Addenda to the standards documents covering the VT service and protocol specify how to handle forms-oriented VT applications. These addenda would support applications that, for example, download the characteristics of a form to a terminal system, allow a data-entry terminal operator to fill out the form, and send the completed form back to the

438

application. ("Terminal system" here refers to the OSI device that the terminal is attached to, such as the 370 mainframe in the example above.)

The VT protocol could predate and perhaps even substitute for as yet unimplemented functions of other protocols. For instance, users could perform third-party file transfers, logging onto node A from node B and transferring one of node A's files to node C. Thus, VT eliminates the need for more complex file-transfer protocols, such as an addition to FTAM that has been discussed in the standards community.

One vendor has already announced a VT-based product. Bridge Communications Inc. of Mountain View, Calif., has unveiled an OSI communications server, called CS/1-OSI, for availability in early 1988. The $9,900-to-$16,000 servers, built around multiple Motorola 68020 processors, can be joined into packet-switching networks that serve as distributed data switches providing port contention and resource sharing.

The CS/1-OSI boxes will run VT among themselves, supporting data streams of terminal-oriented interactive traffic. In the future, as hosts implement the OSI protocols, users will not need the Bridge devices to front-end for the hosts but merely to support the terminals. Of course, as terminals are replaced by personal computers that can run VT, the CS/1-OSIs will not be needed there either. However, Judy Estrin, Bridge's general manager, pointed to the "huge installed base of terminals and low-end PCs. And this product is not a replacement for PC connectivity. It's just the first in our OSI product line."

VT is not yet even an international standard. It is a second Draft International Standard, the first DIS having been put through extensive changes upon balloting (see "ISO standards route").

Implementing a VT-based product in such circumstances "was not easy," says Estrin. "We were implementing it as it was being defined. Our engineers spent a lot of time at the NBS implementers meetings," she says.

■ Transaction processing. ISO's Transaction Processing (TP) standard lets applications process "atomic" units of work. In an atomic update, either a group of updates (such as to the same, replicated file in several different locations) is done in its entirety or no update is done at all. There are no partial updates, which would lead to inconsistency in distributed databases.

Atomic updates involve vendor verbs or primitives such as commit (which completes the transaction by telling everyone to proceed) and rollback (which aborts the transaction by telling everyone to undo). These primitives are akin to a distributed version of using semaphores for file-locking, which is a centralized means of maintaining consistency.

The ISO transaction processing standard is entering its DIS phase. The standard seems to be progressing rapidly, unencumbered by earlier questions about the role that IBM-engendered protocols would play in its development (see "Will LU 6.2 weather the storm?"). Says Joe Twomey, ISO TP protocol editor: "We're on an accelerated schedule, and, astoundingly, we're meeting it." He expects TP to reach the IS stage in December 1989. However, he says, vendors will probably start implementing TP sooner.

■ Remote database access. This ISO standard will appeal to micro-to-mainframe fans. Its purpose is to allow access to small portions of files. Today, users can only download large chunks, unless they buy idiosyncratic micro-to-mainframe link products or develop their own. ISO's RDA specification has a specialization that targets the ISO SQL standard, but it could also support other access languages. In principle, such support could facilitate the use of RDA in micro-to-micro applications.

"Remote database access and transaction processing comprise the next big platform," says desJardins. "It captures 90 percent of the business." There is some question, however, about when that platform will be in place. Some standards people want RDA to hinge upon and be consistent with TP work, while others want to push forward with it to avoid the waiting period. "The position of the United States and, I believe, France is that it should use TP. We may have to wait a little while until TP is finished, but then RDA will be ready," says desJardins.

The idea of distributing pieces of a database, accessing those pieces in a uniform way, and creating secure, transparent links between them is not unique to OSI. It forms a key component of IBM's Systems Application Architecture (SAA) and Operating System/2's Database Manager. "IBM will do the same thing within SNA, but that's not heterogeneous networking," says desJardins. "IBM has good stuff, SAA is not to be criticized, but many users will also want to keep segments of the database on DEC [Digital Equipment Corp.] and HP [Hewlett-Packard] machines," he says.

■ Network management. Vendors can often sell the maturity of their proprietary network management schemes relative to that of standards. While the vendors' schemes are fairly well along, they are generally limited to their own environments. For example, to build large networks and sell a lot of modems, network modem vendors such as Codex will need network management setups that can talk to computers from many vendors. Because most such modem makers do not sell computers themselves, they will need standards. IBM's umbrella Netview product, like SAA, will not cover all multivendor situations.

However, users may not wait for standards. "It's one of the big questions about OSI," admits Paul J. Brusil, principal scientist of Mitre Corp. in Bedford, Mass., and chair of the NBS Network Management SIG. "We won't see management at the upper layers for four years at least. This could be a problem, since it gives proprietary network management schemes a long lead to get entrenched."

An ISO application layer protocol for passing information between managers and their resources, called Common Management Information Protocol (CMIP), is now a Draft Proposal (DP). Common Management Information Services (CMIS), which defines primitives that provide services to network management applications (either a manager or a manager's agent in a node being managed), is also at the DP stage. The OSI Management Framework, an addendum to the basic OSI reference model, is now a DIS.

Other documents cover a variety of specific management information services, including configuration, fault, security, performance, and account management. All are still at the Working Draft stage.

Configuration and fault management could be up for DP status in 1988, followed by security management. Brusil says that, beyond the basic structure of network management, the specifics have to be generated at each layer. "We'll start to see management from the bottom up. The farther up the layers you go, the less progress there's been," he says.

One silver lining: The Defense Advanced Research Projects Agency's Internet Engineering Task Force, maker of the Transmission Control Protocol/Internet Protocol (TCP/IP), "is seriously considering the use of CMIS and CMIP," says Brusil. Some users are now attempting to standardize on TCP/IP as an interim to OSI. This would give such users a leg up on the transition in the area of network management. Both TCP/IP and OSI components can co-reside in the same network and be managed by the same manager.

■ Security. Another area likely to be of interest to corporations is security. "We're not going to have open systems until we have secure systems," says desJardins. There are two basic building blocks of security: application authentication, which allows applications to be sure they are in contact with each other and not with an impostor; and encryption of the transport pipe, which ensures applications that the data passing between them is neither tampered with nor read.

The basic OSI reference model is not secure. A Security Architecture, which specifies where security may be added to the reference model, is nearly complete (its status is second DIS). The actual protocols must then be added to the architecture. Those are not expected until the 1990s.

ENE '88

This year's major U. S. OSI networking event is shaping up to be Enterprise Networking Event 1988 International, which will be held June 6 through 8 in Baltimore, Md. There will be nine sponsored booths in the event: General Motors, Boeing, TRW, John Deere, the Aerospace Coalition, and Process Industries will each sponsor a booth, as will the Corporation for Open Systems (COS) and Britain's Communication Networking for Manufacturing Applications and its Department of Trade and Industry. Another booth, in the United Kingdom, will be linked to the COS booth via OSI protocols.

Each of the booths will host from three to 12 vendors demonstrating implementations of the MAP or TOP specification version 3.0, except for those at the COS booth. According to Elizabeth Methiasin, technical coordinator for the COS booth, "such MAP/TOP protocols as Network Management, Directory Service, and Manufacturing Message Service are not international standards, so COS does not feel they are mature enough to adopt yet." Therefore, the vendors at the COS booth will be demonstrating what Methiasin calls COS's "platform protocols," which are FTAM and X.400. Major U. S. computer vendors, such as DEC, Data General, Honeywell, Wang, Unisys, Hewlett-Packard, and at least a half dozen others, will be demonstrating X.400.

ENE is "a demonstration of the technology but also a way of accelerating and validating it," says Andy McMillan, director of the communications and distributed systems lab at the Industrial Technology Institute (ITI). "Conformance tests will be used on equipment before it goes to the event, all the equipment will be interoperability tested as it is linked to other vendors' gear at the event, and the whole activity will be monitored and controlled," he says. Beyond the linking of actual products, McMillan states that the event is significant in that "showing interoperability will speed the products to market. It is also an opportunity to test the conformance tests themselves."

COS is overseeing the development of testing setups for implementations of its protocol set. In line with ENE, ITI, in Ann Arbor, Mich., is coordinating the development, in various locations throughout the world, of testing arrangements for all the upper-layer protocols that are not included in the COS protocol set but that are part of MAP/TOP 3.0.

MAP and TOP

Many users are excited about the latest version, 3.0, of MAP and TOP. These architectures, born of user needs, have been based on international standards wherever possible. Where the standards were premature, MAP and TOP based their versions of the required functions on a snapshot of the skeletal standard. For example, MAP version 2.1 implements network management and directory services, though the ISO standards in these areas are incomplete. Also, it was released when there was no presentation layer standard, which version 3.0 uses.

The two versions are therefore incompatible. Much more attention is now being paid to upgradability and migration strategies than a few years ago, according to McMillan. "Migration from MAP/TOP to ISO network management and directory services, when they exist, has been thought about and is an issue being worked on," he says.

McMillan cites a key factor in this new awareness: the U. S. MAP/TOP Users Group steering committee issued a statement that all releases of MAP for six years following the final 3.0 release will include mechanisms for interoperating with 3.0.

Numerous products based on MAP 2.1 have been available for some time; one based on version 3.0 (Concurrent Computer Corp.'s MAP Sub-system) has also been announced. Table 3 is derived from the MAP/TOP Product Directory, issued twice a year by ITI and the Society for Manufacturing Engineers. The directory breaks down its 221 products into six categories. (Note that references by vendors to version 3.0 conformance are not recognized by ITI or the MAP/TOP Users Group.)

Table 3 was culled from the categories of "end systems" (that is, full, seven-layer robot, cell, and programmable controllers and communications servers), "gateways," and "network products." The other categories were not included since they either had no upper-layer protocols ("network components"), were not products at all but rather services ("services"), or were original equipment manufacturer products ("OEM products"). Since far fewer TOP products than MAP products had been announced, Table 4 includes OEM offerings as well.

As can be seen from the tables, MAP and TOP specify several upper-layer protocols that either have no equivalent to, or are based on early versions of, ISO standards. The standards are as follows:

■ CASE. Common Application Service Elements, in early standards thinking, was considered a sublayer-like presentation. It was to have had four parts, including the Commitment, Concurrency, and Recovery function (see "OSI's final

Table 3: Sampling of announced MAP products

VENDOR	PRODUCT	SESSION	CASE	DIRECTORY	NM	FTAM	MMFS	MMS	PRICE	AVAILABILITY
AEG FRANKFURT, WEST GERMANY 49-69-6673-584	MAP GATEWAY	✓	✓	✓	✓	✓			N/A	N/A
CANBERRA INDUSTRIES INC. MERIDEN, CONN. 203-238-2351	CELL LEVEL CONTROLLERS:									
	MODEL 280	✓	✓			✓	✓		$10,000-$20,000	NOW
	IMACS 90 DP	✓	✓						$20,000-$80,000	NOW
CHARLES RIVER DATA SYSTEMS FRAMINGHAM, MASS. 617-626-1032	UNIVERSENET	✓	✓	✓	✓	✓			$2,000	NOW
CIMCORP INC. AURORA, ILL. 312-851-2220	CIMCELL CELL CONTROLLER	✓	✓		✓		✓	✓	N/A	N/A
	CIMROC ROBOT CONTROLLER	✓	✓			✓	✓	✓	N/A	N/A
CINCINNATI MILACRON CINCINNATI, OHIO 513-841-6200	MAP HARDWARE AND SOFTWARE FOR MILACRON ROBOTS	✓	✓				✓		N/A	NOW
CONCORD COMMUNICATIONS INC. MARLBORO, MASS. 617-460-4646	MAP HEADSTART/PC	✓	✓						$8,800-$16,000	NOW
	MAPWARE SERIES 1200/PC	✓	✓						$2,695	NOW
	MULTIBUS CONTROLLER	✓	✓						$3,500-$4,000	NOW
CONCURRENT COMPUTER CORP. TINTON FALLS, N.J. 201-758-7570	MAP SUB-SYSTEM	✓	✓	✓	✓			✓	N/A	NOW
DATA GENERAL WESTBORO, MASS. 617-870-6781	DG/MAP	✓	✓	✓	✓	✓		✓	N/A	NOW
DIGITAL EQUIPMENT CORP. MARLBORO, MASS. 617-480-4355	VAX DEC/MAP:									
	MICROVAX	✓	✓	✓	✓	✓	✓	✓	N/A	N/A
	UNIBUS AND BI	✓	✓	✓	✓	✓	✓	✓	$12,000-$16,000	N/A
GE FANUC AUTOMATION CHARLOTTESVILLE, VA. 804-978-5776	GENET FACTORY LAN NETWORK MANAGEMENT SOFTWARE				✓				$10,000	NOW
GEC AUTOMATION PROJECTS INC. SOUTHFIELD, MICH. 313-353-4800	GEM 80 PROGRAMMABLE CONTROLLER	✓	✓		✓		✓		$32,000	NOW
GOULD INC. FORT LAUDERDALE, FLA. 305-587-2900	POWERCOMM MAP	✓	✓		✓	✓	✓		$6,000	NOW
GOULD INC. ANDOVER, MASS. 617-475-4700	GOULD CELL CONTROLLER	✓	✓		✓		✓		N/A	NOW
	MAP GATEWAY	✓	✓		✓		✓		$25,000	NOW

CASE = COMMON APPLICATION SERVICE ENTITY
FTAM = FILE TRANSFER, ACCESS, AND MANAGEMENT
MAP = MANUFACTURING AUTOMATION PROTOCOL
MMFS = MANUFACTURING MESSAGING FORMAT STANDARD
MMS = MANUFACTURING MESSAGING SERVICE
N/A = INFORMATION NOT AVAILABLE

Table 3: Sampling of announced MAP products (continued)

VENDOR	PRODUCT	SESSION	CASE	DIRECTORY	NM	FTAM	MMFS	MMS	PRICE	AVAILABILITY
HEWLETT-PACKARD CUPERTINO, CALIF. 800-367-4772	HP MAP 2.1 FOR:									
	HP 1000 RTE-A	✓	✓						$18,000	NOW
	HP 9000 SERIES HP-UX	✓	✓						$16,000	N/A
HONEYWELL IASD PHOENIX, ARIZ. 602-863-5533	DPS6/MAP 2.1	✓	✓			✓			N/A	N/A
IBM CORP. BOCA RATON, FLA. 305-998-7204	MAP APPLICATION SERVER	✓	✓	✓	✓	✓	✓		$4,500	NOW
	MAP COMMUNICATIONS SERVER	✓	✓	✓	✓	✓	✓		$9,500; $1,500 FOR FTAM	NOW
INDUSTRIAL NETWORKING INC. SANTA CLARA, CALIF. 408-496-0969 X5576	NETWORK MANAGEMENT CONSOLE	✓	✓		✓				N/A	N/A
INTEL CORP. HILLSBORO, ORE. 503-640-7079	MAP 7 LAYER SOLUTION	✓	✓	✓	✓	✓			$4,490	NOW
MAXITRON CORP. CORTE MADERA, CALIF. 415-924-8060	AC107 CELL CONTROLLER	✓	✓	✓	✓		✓		N/A	NOW
	DATA PC	✓	✓	✓	✓		✓		N/A	NOW
	OASIS-COM MODULES	✓	✓	✓	✓		✓		N/A	NOW
MOTOROLA MICROSYSTEMS TEMPE, ARIZ. 602-438-3511	MAP 2.1 COMPLETE SYSTEM	✓	✓	✓	✓	✓	✓		$11,000-$22,000	NOW
STRATUS COMPUTER MARLBORO, MASS. 617-460-2000	MAP COMMUNICATIONS SUPPORT	✓	✓	✓	✓				$7,000-$10,000	NOW
SUN MICROSYSTEMS MOUNTAIN VIEW, CALIF. 415-960-1300	SUNLINK OSI	✓	✓	✓	✓	✓			$3,000 (WITH MAPKIT); $7,900-$35,000 (FOR WORKSTATION OR SERVER)	NOW
TOKEN AUTOMATION BEDFORD, MASS. 617-275-3875	MAP/X.25	✓	✓	✓	✓	✓	✓	✓	$21,000	NOW
THERMO AUTOMATION INC. LOUISVILLE, COLO. 303-665-9000	MAP-BOX	✓	✓	✓		✓		✓	$12,500-$14,800	NOW
VANCE SYSTEMS INC. CHANTILLY, VA. 703-471-9402	MAP ANALYSIS AND TEST SYSTEM				✓				$20,000	4/1/88

NM = NETWORK MANAGEMENT

Source: Fall 1987 MAP/TOP Product Directory

Table 4: Sampling of announced TOP products

VENDOR	PRODUCT	UPPER-LAYER PROTOCOL				VERSION	OEM?	PRICE	AVAILABILITY
		NM	FTAM	CASE	SESSION				
CHARLES RIVER DATA SYSTEMS FRAMINGHAM, MASS. 617-626-1032	UNIVERSENET	✓	✓	✓	✓	1.0		$2,000	NOW
COMMUNICATIONS MACHINERY CORP. SANTA BARBARA, CALIF. 805-963-9471	FTAM		✓			1.0	✓	$12,000	N/A
	CASE			✓		1.0	✓	$3,500	NOW
	SESSION				✓	1.0	✓	$9,000	NOW
OMNICOM INC. VIENNA, VA. 703-281-1135	OSILOGIE SOFTWARE		✓	✓	✓	3.0	BOTH	N/A	NOW
	OSILOGIE/PC		✓	✓	✓	1.0	BOTH	$1,995 (INCLUDES CONTROLLER BOARD)	NOW
RETIX SANTA MONICA, CALIF. 213-399-2200	PORTABLE OSI MAP/TOP SOFTWARE	✓	✓	✓	✓	1.0	✓	N/A	NOW
SUN MICROSYSTEMS MOUNTAIN VIEW, CALIF. 415-960-1300	SUNLINK OSI FOR TOP	✓	✓	✓	✓	1.0		$2,500	NOW
SYDNEY DATA PRODUCTS LOS ANGELES, CALIF. 213-444-3000	ISONET				✓	3.0		N/A	NOW
TOUCH COMMUNICATIONS INC. SCOTTS VALLEY, CALIF. 408-438-4800	FASTPORT 3.0	✓	✓		✓	3.0	✓	N/A	2/1/88

CASE = COMMON APPLICATION SERVICE ENTITY
FTAM = FILE TRANSFER, ACCESS, AND MANAGEMENT
N/A = INFORMATION NOT AVAILABLE

NM = NETWORK MANAGEMENT
OEM = ORIGINAL EQUIPMENT MANUFACTURER
TOP = TECHNICAL AND OFFICE PROTOCOLS

Source: Fall 1987 MAP/TOP Product Directory

frontier: The application layer," in this issue). Later, it was decided that CASE was just one of many ASEs, so its name was changed to Association Control Service Element (ACSE). The transition from MAP 2.1 CASE to MAP 3.0 ACSE should be painless.

■ Directory Service. MAP 3.0's directory service will be more closely based on the ISO standard than 2.1's. It adds a capability that permits remote updating of the directory database across the network. This upgrade should likewise entail no major user hassles.

■ MMFS and MMS. These manufacturing protocols are used by MAP, not TOP, since office devices presumably will not need to talk directly with robots or factory-floor controllers. MMFS, the Manufacturing Messaging Format Standard, is a highly specialized command and control language for communication between programmable machines and manufacturing devices. The Manufacturing Messaging Service (also called EIA RS-511 by the Electronic Industries Association) is derived from the MAP 2.1-specific MMFS, which makes MMFS the so-called father of MMS. However, MMS has changed so dramatically since its inception that, unlike CASE and Directory Service, upgrading from MMFS to MMS is likely to give users a considerable headache.

■ Network Management. This function is key to operating any network, and the delay in standardization is creating some real worries. "I believe the ISO effort is lagging because of the sheer magnitude of the task," says Gary Workman, coordinator of GM's MAP development team. "There's a sense of urgency," adds Bride, "but also a sense that it may not be possible. A worldwide effort is under way to strategize how to speed up the development of the network management standard."

Unable to wait for international standards, the MAP/TOP community has created an application layer network manager. Statistical counters are maintained at each layer and fed to the network manager. These counters are specifically tailored to the interests of MAP and TOP.

"Workman's counters are usable within a subnetwork type of environment, but when you start to talk about an interconnected, wide-area environment, with global as well as local concerns, we still don't have management capability," says Bride.

Yet the MAP efforts may even spur the standards work.

"The MAP network management approach is not incompatible with OSI; it's just advanced," says desJardins. "They're trying to do it first, coming up with parameters they see are needed. The MAP people are participating in OSI, so their experiences will get into the picture," he says.

FTAM

The File Transfer, Access, and Management protocol may be doing as much to spur standards implementation in the United States as X.400 is in the rest of the world. "The most critical Layer 7 protocol to the industry right now is FTAM. Most of what we're doing is file transfer," says Charlie Bass, cofounder of Ungermann-Bass and chairman of Touch Communications Inc. in Scotts Valley, Calif. "FTAM is the pillar of MAP activity in the United States," says Level-7 Ltd.'s Valentine.

FTAM has traveled a bumpy road on its way to becoming an IS, a road that illustrates the intricacy of standards development and deployment. MAP, TOP, and the Government OSI Procurement specification, or GOSIP, have gone through three stages: base standards put forth by ISO and the American National Standards Institute; a process of implementers' agreements, which narrow the standards down into practical, real-world specifications that can be implemented; and finally, further refinement into profiles, where the protocols are strung together vertically into stacks suited to the office (TOP), the factory (MAP), or government use (GOSIP).

Typically, by the time a standard has reached DIS status, the technical work on it can be considered stable. Minor editorial changes may occur, but the specifics of technical implementation stay the same. FTAM did not follow that premise.

FTAM Phase 1 was a fully functional FTAM arising from agreements in the NBS workshop that were based on the DP. Both MAP 2.1 and TOP 1.0 pointed to Phase 1 of FTAM. Later, work was begun to include other features, like record-level access, and a set of agreements called Phase 2 FTAM was developed, based on the DIS. However, at the eleventh hour, major changes were made in moving from the DIS to the IS, so the implementers, who were caught unprepared, had to work feverishly to realign Phase 2 to be compatible with the IS.

The secret of file access

The key difference between the FTAM in MAP version 2.1 and in version 3.0 is the ability to remotely access a single record from a file as opposed to having to retrieve the whole file. This capability could give the standards-based vendors a competitive edge on the proprietary ones.

"The standard upper-layer protocols tend to be less functional than those in the homogeneous environment," says Eric Spiewak, director of hardware and communications with Charles River Data Systems Inc. in Framingham, Mass. "For example, we wouldn't use FTAM to transfer data between two of our systems. The same is true of most networking vendors, if they have a mature product.

"But that could change with advanced FTAM," he continues. "MAP 3.0 provides record-level access, so you might be able to have a distributed file system that uses FTAM." Touch Communications does just that. The firm has built an OSI-based file server that it hopes will compete with the leading local area network operating systems (see "Look, up in the sky, is it OS/2? LAN Manager? No, it's Vaporwar," DATA COMMUNICATIONS, September 1987, p. 77).

Touch OSI is sold to users in PC-DOS and Vax VMS versions. The product includes a full TOP 1.0 stack running on top of Ethernet (IEEE 802.3). Above FTAM Phase 1, Touch has built something it calls Touch Streams, analogous to Sun's Network File System (NFS). An applications interface lets the user run standard DOS applications transparently over the network.

Since it is built using FTAM Phase 1, Touch OSI will be incompatible with Phase 2. However, Touch is developing a Phase 2 implementation to which it will upgrade its installed base (of more than ten) when the new version is available early this year.

"The kind of OSI networking we're creating will make it tough for the Novells and the 3Coms, so they'll have to be concerned with OSI," says Andy Lauta, Touch's product marketing manager. "Touch is not hoping to satisfy everyone or change the world, but we have a good chance in companies where OSI is required, such as those bidding for GOSIP contracts."

Lauta points to several other factors that will help the FTAM-based product compete. Touch plans to:
■ Expand its product line to include more platforms besides DOS machines and VAXs (such as Apple and Unix machines, although no such products have yet been announced).
■ Support additional networking technologies (such as IEEE 802.5 or token ring, as well as X.25).
■ Continually add to overall network services available as the OSI protocols mature, such as virtual terminal (protocol emulation), mail (X.400), and of course, network management.
■ Continue to push the server's performance to the limits of what OSI can provide. Lauta expects such performance to be better than that of TCP or NFS. "Implementations of OSI today tend be slower than Novell's Netware; we feel that they're now about the same as or a little better than IBM's PC Network," he says. "According to the Department of Defense, which developed TCP/IP, OSI should architecturally provide higher performance than TCP/IP," he adds.

Interchange, RJE

Two other upper-layer standards deserve mention, one for being broadly useful, the other for being on a dead-end track.

In the first standard, information gets packaged in a universal or common format and then moved across a network so that it can be further processed and revised in the remote setting. This standard, known as the Office Document Architecture/Office Document Interchange Format (ODA/ODIF), has reached DIS status.

The need for a document interchange standard is clear. Users who try to interchange documents between Wordstar, Wordperfect, and Macwrite formats face the problem of how to send the files and have them still look the same.

Most commercially available solutions use point-to-point, case-by-case translators. The problem is that, for n products, it is necessary to build n-squared translators. Each time a format is added, a translator must be written for every other existing format. With a standard such as ODIF, each new product only needs a translator to the common format.

Of course, the standard would have a hard time anticipating the structures that will arise as new formats reach the market. How would ODIF keep up?

"I don't believe standards ever do keep up," says Lawrence A. Welsch, manager of the office systems engineering group at NBS, the government group responsible for ODA/ODIF standards activity, "although innovation creates room for other standards. Also, a standard now will allow for many more innovations than would be possible without the standard, stimulated by the increased use of document interchange. In the same way," continues Welsch, "the IBM PC, once a standard (in this case, de facto), lead to such innovations as Lotus 1-2-3, Wordperfect, and so on." Related standards for information interchange, such as graphics and product data exchange standards, are as readily justified for similar reasons.

The other standard, known as Job Transfer and Manipulation (JTM), is less easy to justify. JTM, sometimes called "son of Remote Job Entry," is principally used by the U. K. University Network. Students create jobs, send them to computers, and get back the results. Peter T. Barry, who chairs the upper-layer standards committee in the British Standards Institute, admits that the United States has not shown much interest in JTM, principally because the same job can be done with file transfer and the job-control language of the particular machine.

"JTM does not have a long and healthy future in the microcomputer age," says desJardins. Barry agrees that other standards vying to do the same job, such as remote database access, transaction processing, and something called open distributed processing, "will, regrettably, probably overtake it, I suspect."

End of the beginning

All told, the industry may look back on this period as the end of the beginning for upper-layer protocols. After some grief caused by instability in MAP between versions 2.1 and 3.0, in such areas as MMFS, which was not downward-compatible, the upper layers are looking more and more stable.

"As soon as one of these protocols has reached an international standard status, it is appropriate for building products on, but we can't assume that we're done," says Bass.

The application layer is the one that the user—and the user's programs—sees, so standards makers and implementers have to be more responsible about how it unfolds. Stability is needed for the programming interface to the upper layers; later generations of the protocols can then be viewed as extensions.

"At the inner layers, we can accommodate some volatility in the specifications, but the top of the stack has to be more solid so people will not be afraid to build on it," says Bass. ■

For further reading:

Jones, Vincent C. *MAP/TOP Networking.* New York: McGraw-Hill, 1988.
MAP/TOP Product Directory. Ann Arbor, Mich.: Industrial Technology Institute, Fall 1987.

Evelyne Roux, Hewlett-Packard, Grenoble, France

OSI's final frontier: The application layer

Possibly the most beneficial layer of the standard reference model is the one closest to the user. This insider's report reveals structures few users have seen before.

The application layer, the topmost in the seven-layer Open Systems Interconnection (OSI) model put forth by the International Organization for Standardization (ISO), is the hottest topic in the world of OSI. The reason is clear: This layer will allow full communications between users of OSI networks. Thus, it is where the user payoffs and opportunities are to be found.

Application layer protocols are likely to proliferate. Two are already represented in current products, and more will soon follow. Understanding the concepts that underlie all these protocols can help users keep up with application layer-based products and services as they are announced.

Completely transparent multivendor networking has been, for many users, an ideal dream but a practical nightmare. Transferring an electronic mail message, for example, from an IBM computer to one from Digital Equipment Corp. (DEC) to one from Hewlett-Packard was impossible without the use of expensive, customized adaptations, such as an implementation of IBM protocols on the DEC or HP machine. But since 1977, when the ISO took up the cause, that dream has been moving closer to reality. Today, leading vendors agree that the OSI model is the key to interconnections among their heterogeneous offerings. For this reason, OSI implementations are appearing on many computers.

The OSI standards constitute a framework for defining the communications process between systems (computers and their users). The reference model, adopted by the ISO in 1984, includes seven layers that define the functions involved in communication between two systems, the services required to perform these functions, and the protocols associated with these services.

The implementation of these functions is achieved by software written to bridge the gap between the application process, which starts the communication—for instance, a program in an automated teller machine that responds to a customer's balance inquiry—and the physical medium over which the communication travels, in this case the bank's private telephone lines.

The lowest five layers in a network that conforms to the OSI model ensure that the network provides a reliable connection, if it can. The sixth, the presentation layer, ensures that information is delivered in a form that the receiving system can understand and use. The top layer of the model, the application layer, reflects the behavior of an application process that is observable in its communication with other application processes.

For each architectural layer in the OSI model, standards are being or have been defined that offer widely accepted means of meeting the layer's requirements. The standards for the four lowest layers (physical, data link, network, and transport) specify mechanisms for the transfer of information. Standards for the session and presentation layers specify, respectively, the mechanisms for checkpointing the data (for resynchronization purposes) and the syntactic representation of the semantics (that is, the encoding).

Of all the layers, the application layer contains the most functionality. Here, the decision is made whether to treat the communication as a file transfer, a virtual terminal session, or a computer-aided design session. After this choice, the complete stack of adequate protocols in the six lower layers is automatically selected.

For this reason, the widest variety of work is presently going on at the application layer. The protocols being studied in this layer include: File Transfer, Access, and Management (FTAM); Virtual Terminal Protocol (VTP); Message Handling System (MHS); Transaction Processing (TP); Job Transfer and Manipulation (JTM); Remote Database Access (RDA); and others. These protocols are at different levels of development.

The application layer is the only one that interfaces with the application process. But the application process itself is outside the scope of the OSI model; its form and function is the responsibility of the system user. (Here, "system user" refers to anything that will access the application layer. It can be a human being, a program, or a combination of the two.)

Structure

The structure of the application layer is currently being defined by ISO. This work will lead to international standards. A conceptual model of the application layer is being developed to interrelate all the standards at the layer.

The lower layers merely convey data. By contrast, OSI standards for the application layer are primarily concerned with communicating the semantics (the meaning) of information. Consider, for example, an important database that is split into several parts, each on a different computer. The computers are interconnected by a network. An application process might be responsible for some distributed information processing task, such as updating the database and keeping the components consistent. Using application layer services, the process could perform or request actions related to the objectives of the update. That is, it might write data to or delete data from a server or it might ask process to take these actions.

In ISO terminology, an open system is a system that can interoperate with (run with) other computers, perhaps of a different manufacturer, through a network. In the ISO reference model, the interoperation of real (that is, actual hardware and software, as opposed to conceptual) open systems is modeled in terms of the interactions between applications processes in these systems.

An application process is an element within a real open system that takes part in the execution of one or more distributed information processing tasks. It can be either a user's program or a person deciding, for example, to answer a letter. The application process, which is part of the local operating environment, interfaces, via the user element (UE), with the application entity (AE), a program in the system that deals with the lower-level OSI protocols (Fig. 1).

For application processes to cooperate, they must share sufficient information to enable them to interact. The shared information is called the information base. The processes must also have a common understanding of what this shared information means. For example, all the

computers involved in a flight reservation must know that "NY" means New York if they are to meaningfully use that abbreviation.

Typically, application layer standards define conceptual schemes that enable application processes to communicate successfully. Such schemes define the rules governing the transfer of data, the associated semantics, and the abstract syntax (or encoding conventions) to be used in data transfers.

To meet the communications requirements of peer application processes, the upper layers of the OSI model provide services that:
- Support the negotiation of semantics for the information being exchanged (for instance, whether to run file transfer with or without error recovery).
- Support the negotiation of commonly understood representations (a common encoding or set of encodings) for the information being exchanged.
- Enable the application processes to insert signals, uniquely distinguishable from each other, into the information stream that allow the application processes to synchronize and resynchronize their activities.
- Enable the application processes to negotiate and manage the dialogue control needed to support their information-flow requirements (specifying, for example, whether they talk both at once or one at a time).

The first of these requirements is met by services of the application layer, the second by the presentation service (that is, the services provided by the presentation layer), and the third and fourth by the session service.

Application layer model

Within the OSI environment, an application process is represented by one or more application entities. That is, each application entity represents a different aspect of the communication behavior of the application process. Figure 2 illustrates these elements. It shows a system with two application entities. Such a system can manage two OSI communications (that is, two conversations or channels of interaction) at the same time. An AE is accessed via the presentation address.

In each AE, the application process has to choose an application service element (ASE) to perform its task. A service element is a primitive defined at the interface between two adjacent layers. An ASE is a set of functionalities that supports a typical application. It represents different kinds of work that the user wishes performed, such as file transfer, mail service, or transaction processing, along with all the elements necessary to perform that kind of work. Each of the ASEs shown in the figure (ASE1, ASE2, and so on) stands for a particular ASE implemented in the computer. For example, ASE1 could stand for the X.400 standard for electronic mail and ASE2 for FTAM.

Structure of an application entity

At any given time, the application process works either with ASE1 or ASE2. The single association controlling function routes the application process to the appropriate ASE. In case of several OSI communications, the multiple association controlling function manages the coordination of the application entities. (Here, as throughout, an association

---

1. User element. *The user's application process can access the lower-layer protocols only via the application entity, which it interacts with through the user entity.*

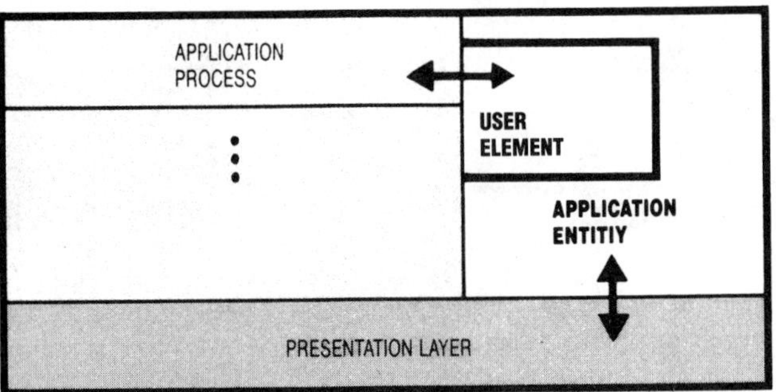

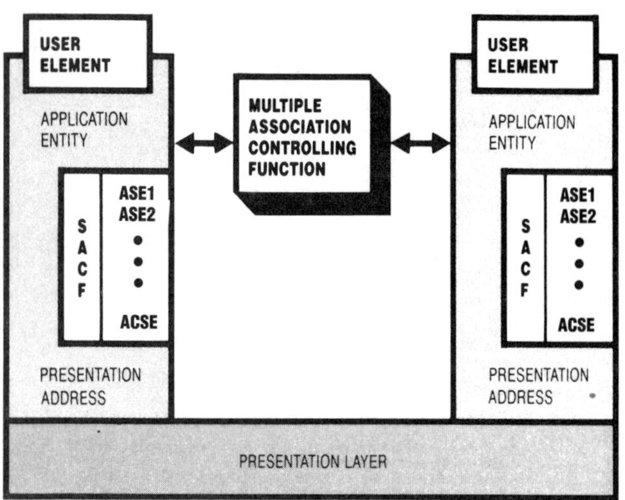

2. Layer model. *Applications use application service entities (ASEs) to do their work. Routing to ASEs is done by single and multiple association controlling functions.*

ACSE = APPLICATION CONTROL SERVICE ELEMENT
ASE = APPLICATION SERVICE ELEMENT
SACF = SINGLE ASSOCIATION CONTROLLING FUNCTION

refers to a connection at the level of the application layer.)

An application entity contains one user element and a set of application service elements. The specific combination of these different elements determines the type of application entity.

The user element represents, or acts on behalf of, the application processes. It allows the ASEs to communicate with other application entities. In sum, the user element represents the ultimate source and destination of information transfer.

An ASE is a coherent set of integrated functions that allows application entities to interoperate for a specific purpose. ASEs may be used independently or in combination to meet specific information processing goals. As mentioned earlier, the X.400 and FTAM ASEs are already defined.

Another type of ASE, the association control service element (ACSE) facilitates other ASEs working together. For example, FTAM can be used alone or in combination with another ASE, Commitment, Concurrency and Recovery (CCR), for error-recovery purposes. (CCR will be described below.) The ACSE is also used to open and release the association.

Today, only the term ASE is used. Although they had received some usage, the terms CASE and SASE are no longer in currency. A CASE, or Common ASE, represented the common functions needed for different jobs or ASEs between computers. For example, to run FTAM or VTP, it would be necessary to open a communication between the two machines. Opening a communication is thus a function common to several protocols. SASE, or Specific ASE, was used to differentiate FTAM from MHS from other kinds of application protocols. To date, however, no objective criteria have been established for distinguishing a CASE from a SASE.

Entities in an OSI environment must be addressable. Moreover, an application entity may be able to support one or more application associations. To accomplish this, each AE is attached to a presentation address, which points to one or more presentation service access points (PSAPs). An AE has at least one name by which it is identified: an application title. At any time, the application title is bound to the presentation address of the PSAP to which the AE is attached.

Application layer directory

The question arose of how to handle inquiries of the form, "What is a presentation address through which the application entity with the title 'X' can be accessed?" To this end, an application layer directory function was established. An open system should be able to perform this directory function for any application entity title, either locally or by interacting with a remote directory service.

To get the address of a remote application entity with which it wants to establish an association, an application gives the application title of the remote system to the local AE (Fig. 3). Then the application entity, through the directory service ASE, establishes a communication with a directory server to get the presentation address of the desired system. It uses this address to issue a connection request to the presentation layer. It is thus possible to establish a communication with any remote application process via an association with its AE.

Application layer components

The standardization of some specific applications, such as X.400 or FTAM, has led to the definition of modules (formerly called CASEs) containing functions that are common to all the applications. These modules cooperate with the specific ASEs to provide the service required by the application process.

The terminology around these common functions is, unfortunately, a bit murky. The problem is that several working groups have studied these functions independently, and each has defined its own model, a situation far

3. Addressing. *To address a remote system, an application sends a title (1) to an ASE, which passes it to a server (2). The address (3) goes to the presentation layer (4).*

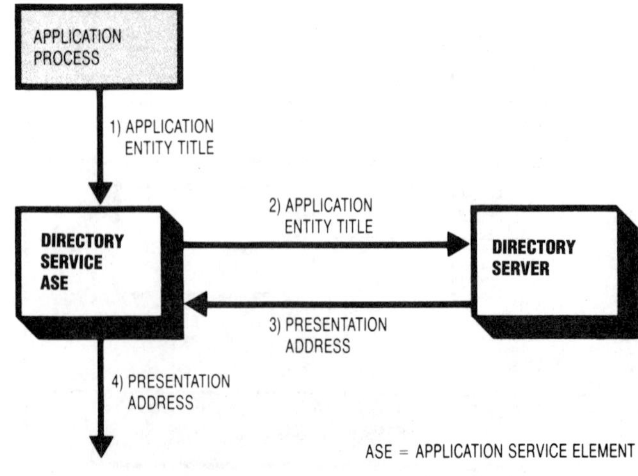

from the ideal of a single model of the application layer. To date, several modules have been defined: Reliable Transfer Service (RTS), Remote Operation Service (ROS), and Common Application Service Elements (CASE), which here denotes a specific set of functions rather than a general category of ASEs.

CASE was defined by ISO to group the common functionalities of the application layer. At present, the services provided by CASE relate mainly to association control or, more specifically, the association control service element (ACSE). (This could change, however. It is one of many application layer issues yet to be resolved.) ACSE provides basic facilities for the control of an application association between two application entities that communicate by means of a presentation connection. CASE consists of ACSE plus CCR.

The control of a single association is achieved by the following service elements:
■ Associate: Starts the use of an association by the ASE identified by a parameter transmitted to the remote system.
■ Release: Terminates the use of an association when the application has finished its communication. The request may be accepted or rejected by the remote system, but in any case, no data is lost.
■ Abort: Causes the abnormal release of an association by the underlying presentation service, with possible loss of information in transit.
■ P-Abort: Indicates the abnormal release of the association by the underlying presentation service, with the possible loss of information in transit.

For the part of the model that concerns the opening and release of the association via the ACSE, a one-to-one mapping exists between an application association and a presentation connection. This distinguishes it from ASEs. The ACSE is used to open and release an association, but after it is open, it can be used by several ASEs consecutively without being released and reopened. Different applications could run on the same association and then on the same presentation connection.

The ACSEs require access to the P-Connect, P-Release and P-U-Abort service elements. P-Connect, or presentation connect, permits the opening of a presentation-level connection. P-U-Abort stands for presentation user abort. Note that the ACSEs neither use nor constrain the use of other presentation services.

The association control protocol machine (ACPM) within the ACSE defines all the states and protocol elements necessary to properly run the protocol. It communicates with its service user (that is, with the layer above it) by means of the primitives defined in ISO documentation. Each invocation of the ACPM controls a single association.

There are plans for CASE to provide other services under the rubric of Commitment, Concurrency, and Recovery (CCR). Concurrency refers to, for example, managing several accesses to a database; commitment, to one system's assuring another that work has been done; and recovery, to a means whereby a system can correct data after an error or failure. Such services ensure the maintenance of data consistency in a distributed environment. They are especially useful in transaction processing. Typically demanded by banking applications, these services guarantee that a transaction is either completely and correctly finished or is not done at all.

Consistency is maintained by use of a master/slave relationship, which ensures that only one system has the right to ask another to commit. The master system either commits all the slaves or rolls them all back to their original states, from which the series of transactions may be reconstructed.

CCR has the following primitives:
■ Begin: Identifies the start of an atomic action (one that cannot be split).
■ Prepare: Indicates the end of transmissions by the master. (The rationale for using the term "prepare" is lost in antiquity.)
■ Ready: Indicates the readiness of a slave to commit the action.
■ Refuse: Indicates refusal by the slave.
■ Commit: Used by the master to order commitment (with confirmation).
■ Rollback: Used by the master to order rollback (with confirmation).
■ Restart: Used to restart properly after a crash.

All these primitives map directly onto the session primitives. CCR is presently defined but not yet integrated into the application layer; further work is needed.

RTS

Reliable Transfer Server was defined by the International Telegraph and Telephone Consultative Committee as part of the application layer. Its function is to interface electronic mail applications with the session layer through a presentation layer entity. It does this by grouping several common primitives used by both the MHS electronic mail application and one or more other applications.

The RTS, part of the application layer for MHS applications, provides common services and is built on top of the presentation layer (Fig. 4). RTS has minimal requirements from the presentation layer but requires many of the functionalities of the session layer. Through RTS, the message transfer layer (MTL) passes messages from the user agent layer to the network. The user agent layer prepares messages from the application layer user to be sent.

The interface between the MTL and the RTS consists of the following primitives:
■ Open: Establishment of an association.
■ Close: Release of an association.
■ Turn-please: Request for the turn (the right to send data).
■ Turn-give: Give the turn.
■ Transfer: Reliable transfer of data.
■ Exception: Indication of a transfer failure.

Work is going on within ISO to help RTS evolve by developing interfaces to the presentation layer and not only the session layer. RTS will be reviewed and probably modified in 1988.

ROS

The Remote Operation Service was originally defined as a protocol that would permit easy interconnection of a workstation or a microcomputer with its mail server. It uses a client-server model to represent cooperation between application entities. This model splits a distributed application into modules (or agents). Some of these, the server mod-

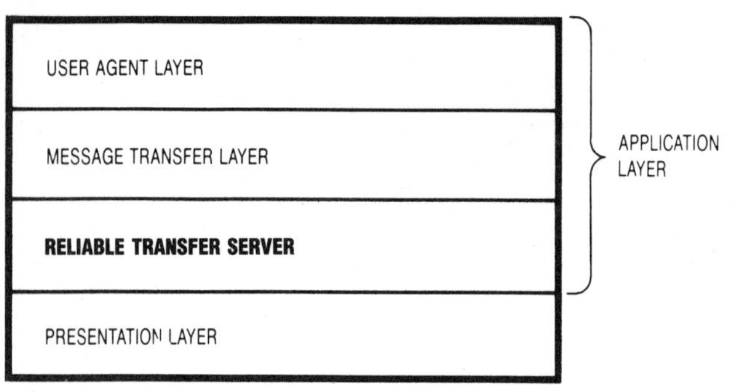

ules, provide services requested by the client modules.

The client-server model has several components (Fig. 5). The server system is a functional entity that performs a set of specific application services by means of server agents. The server agent makes its services available to the client through an access protocol. This protocol is inherently asymmetric. That is, the rights of each side are not the same. For instance, only the client has the right to initiate dialogue. Also, the two sides do not have the same sets of protocol elements.

Sometimes, several server agents will have to cooperate to provide the service. If they are remote and connected through a network, they will cooperate through an inter-server agent protocol. A client system is a set of clients accessing one or more servers. A client communicates with a server agent using an access protocol.

The way the user requests a service from a server agent is called an operation (Fig. 6). The x-access protocol (where x designates the type of application, such as filing or mailing) links two entities that are functionally complementary (in essence, the machine has been cut in two). This is in contrast to the peer entities of the OSI model, where both sides have the same number of levels. The service sublayer defines the parameters of an operation and the ROS sublayer defines how these parameters are transmitted.

In the client-server model, the generic structure of an operation is an elementary request/reply interaction. The

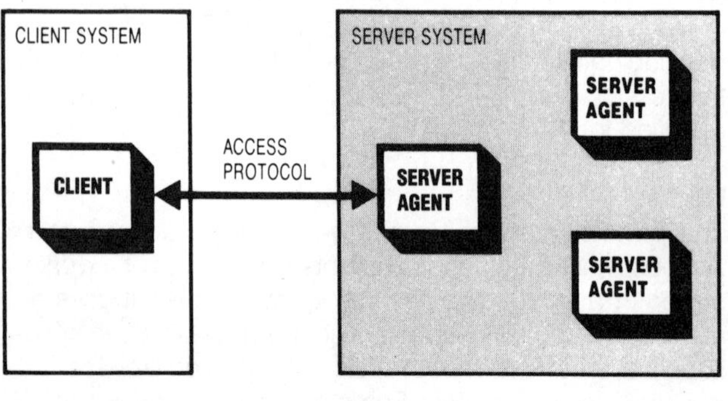

request is the invocation of the operation; the reply is the result or error. The invocation of an operation incorporates the operation type and the arguments (parameters).

If a client wants to interact with a service agent, it has to invoke a bind operation. If the bind operation yields a result, an association between the client and the service is established. At this point, an operation (other than the bind operation) may be invoked. If a client invokes an unbind operation, the association is released and no more operations, except a bind operation, may be invoked.

The Remote Operation Service is provided by a sublayer of the application layer. The ROS users, which are ASEs, are located in the application layer. They use ROS in the same manner, independent of the type of ASE and regardless of what the application is, provided it is built on top of ROS.

As is true in the client-server case, the initiating ROS user establishes an ROS association by a bind operation. If the ROS association is established, operations may be invoked. When the initiating ROS user wishes to release an ROS association, an unbind operation is issued.

It is important to understand that ROS is only a tool for ASEs to transmit information. ROS conveys some protocol information but does not know what type of information is conveyed. It does not know whether it is being used to

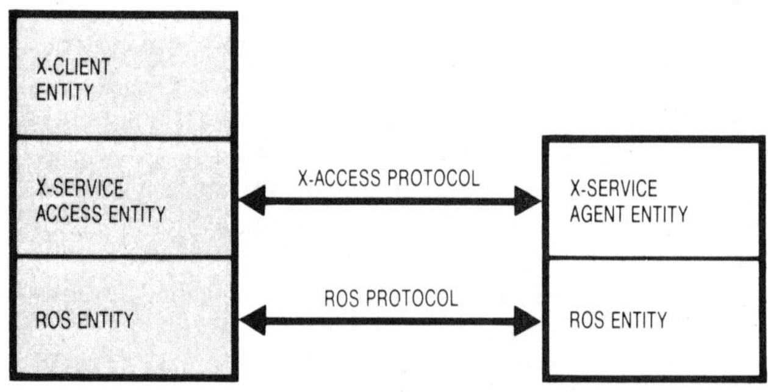

carry an order for flowers or an interoffice memo.

Today, the application layer is of key importance in the standards community. Many working groups are concerned with its structure and specification. One group within ISO is defining a model for the layer based on the needs of application processes and on the theoretical evolution of those needs. Another working group has defined a set of services and protocols that do not map with this structure of the application layer and are trying to influence the development of the application layer in a way compatible with FTAM. This is but one example of the difficulties and challenges, still ongoing, encountered in defining this last layer of the OSI reference model. ■

Evelyne Roux is Hewlett-Packard's representative on European standards committees such as the European Computer Manufacturers Association and the French division of ISO. Prior to joining Hewlett-Packard in 1985, she worked with France's Architel project on the development and promotion of OSI standards. Roux is based in Grenoble, France.

Thomas J. Routt, contributing editor, DATA COMMUNICATIONS

Under the Big TOP at Enterprise '88: TOP 3.0's debut

Even in nontechnical, administrative offices, the Technical and Office Protocols stands a good chance of eclipsing Manufacturing Automation Protocol and proprietary offerings.

TOP has gotten a bad rap. Many users think of the Technical and Office Protocols as the weaker sibling of the more acclaimed Manufacturing Automation Protocol (MAP); both are adaptations of the International Organization for Standardization's Open Systems Interconnection (OSI) model.

Moreover, most users know TOP only in its Version 1.0 form. The problem is that the only application-layer service provided by TOP 1.0 was File Transfer, Access, and Management (FTAM)—necessary, but far from sufficient, for building sophisticated network applications.

For this reason, TOP was overshadowed by MAP, which provided other required but nonstandard protocols, such as Manufacturing Messaging Format Standard. While TOP Version 1.0 provided connectivity, it lacked a rounded set of application-layer services. It could not handle graphics, remote terminal access, or network management, all features highly desirable to users.

Even electronic mail, a capability basic to most users' network checklists, especially for office applications, was not provided by TOP 1.0. This despite the fact that an international specification for electronic mail, Recommendation X.400 of the International Telegraph and Telephone Consultative Committee (CCITT), has been implemented in products for some time (see "Upper layers: From bizarre to bazaar," DATA COMMUNICATIONS, January, p. 110). TOP, therefore, was also outdistanced in the office by the more robust proprietary offerings of the major vendors.

With Version 3.0, however, the tables may be turned. TOP has a strong chance of outdistancing MAP as well as many single-vendor offerings. TOP 3.0 offers such standardized, vendor-independent application services as:
- Graphical data interchange.
- Electronic mail.
- Distributed transaction processing.

- The ability to create and interchange compound electronic documents.
- Remote file access.
- Remote terminal access.
- Network directories.
- Network management.

All these capabilities, until now, have only been offered within specific, vendor-unique, networked environments. They have generated much industry interest in TOP and will doubtless help TOP steal the show at the upcoming Enterprise Networking Event (ENE) '88 International at the Baltimore Convention Center, June 6 to 8, 1988. Moreover, a hearty number of vendors have thrown their weight behind Version 3.0, joining those that already offer TOP 1.0-based products.

This article outlines the need for TOP in businesses, describes the planned ENE configurations and tests, considers specific vendor implementations of TOP, and examines issues that can help users migrate from proprietary protocol suites to TOP/OSI or, in fact, to any standard architecture. A more detailed architectural discussion, to appear next month, will elaborate TOP 3.0's application program interfaces, examine the TOP 3.0 upper- and lower-layer specifications and protocols, and conclude with a set of TOP directions.

The business case for TOP 3.0

The fundamental reason for having a networking resource is to provide an enterprise-wide infrastructure that can deliver, format, present, and interchange appropriate data on a high-availability, timely, and cost-effective basis to decision makers, regardless of their organizational position, geographic or temporal proximities, or computational interface.

User networks characteristically combine multiplevendor

architectures, protocols, and communications products that are fundamentally incompatible. These incompatibilities have generally been vendor-engineered to lock users into manufacturer-unique solutions so that these vendors can maximize their market share. The direct results of implementing incompatible, multiplevendor architectures are as follows:

- Proliferation of various and incoherent architectures.
- Frequent duplication of human and capital resources within various departments.
- Provision of overly complex, nontransparent user interfaces into networking resources.
- Unacceptably low mean times between failures and outages and unacceptably high mean times to repair.
- Unacceptably low network resource availability.
- Unacceptably low throughput and, consequently, unacceptably high response-time profiles.
- Loosely defined network resource migration and phasing strategies.
- A general absence of user ability to effectively and economically manage the distributed information resource.

These drawbacks of incoherent vendor architectures are made worse by exponential improvements in technology. These are spurring users to implement desktop, desk-side, and departmental office workstations and processors; however, interdepartmental coordination of these efforts is decreasing.

The MAP/TOP Users Group was begun in 1985 as a specific user response to this incompatibility issue. The MAP Program at General Motors was established to devise a uniform set of communications standards for factory automation. The TOP Program at Boeing Computer Services addresses requirements for the engineering and general office environment.

More than manufacturing

TOP's potential reaches far beyond the manufacturing front office into such areas as medicine and meteorology and, with planned improvements, even into the traditional single-computer-vendor financial-service industries. Enhancements to the TOP 3.0 specification, anticipated in September, will likely incorporate International Organization for Standardization (ISO) Transaction Processing (TP) service and protocol agreements, which hold great promise for such industries as banking and insurance. Even without TP, TOP has much to offer.

The combined goal of the TOP/MAP 3.0 architectures (the MAP Specification is also currently at Version 3.0) is to provide a standardized mechanism for computer-integrated manufacturing (CIM), which integrates computer-aided design (CAD) and computer-aided manufacturing (CAM) application portability in a vendor-independent communications environment. *The user business case that propels CIM is the requirement to provide purchasers of manufactured goods with on-time, quality-assured, personalized designs at the low marginal costs classically associated with mass-produced items.*

In essence, the economies of scale engendered through the mass production associated with conventional manufacturing, at the high-volume/low-variety end of the manufacturing spectrum, need to be cost-efficiently translated into economies of choice associated with the low-volume/high-variety end. A cost-efficient translation would engender a flexible design and manufacturing process that offers timely product customization at the low unit costs classically achievable only in dedicated, line-production environments.

Factory-floor contributors to end-customer economies of choice are rendered primarily through clustering computerized numerical control (CNC) machine tools into compact "cells." In these cells, machine tools are provided just in time with work in process (that is, as few raw materials and partially completed goods are kept in inventory as possible). The immediate result is that in-factory work in process is held to a minimum, thereby dramatically reducing inventory costs and enabling on-schedule customer deliveries. Factory cells that communicate with MAP-specified protocols eliminate the "islands of automation" otherwise characteristic of these units and bring about flexible manufacturing setups.

The range of potential nonfactory applications of CIM technology is substantial as well. For example, one emerging specialty in medicine is interventional radiology. Specialized catheters with optical-fiber probes wended into the heart provide not only optical examination but also digital geometric pictures that assist in the remote use of laser cutters and sutures attached to the end of the catheter. Another example comes from meteorology. Weather prediction, modeling, and observation often employ supercomputers and other vector (as opposed to scalar) processors, which manipulate several complex geometric objects and need to communicate those objects to other, dissimilar vector processors.

Indeed, the potentials for technical office (CAD) and nontechnical office (administrative) application portability eclipse those of manufacturing. TOP 3.0 provides the fundamental basis for synthesis of dissimilar native-form knowledge bases, information models, and representation conventions through provision of common data translation and transmission standards and conventions.

ENE extravaganza

There have been several demonstrations of the TOP and MAP OSI implementations in recent years, but the most significant one to date will occur at the Enterprise Networking Event. An elaborate demonstration will show, in microcosm, an organization of the near future, complete with technical-office, administrative-office, and manufacturing functions. It will also spotlight TOP/MAP 3.0 as an important key to getting there.

The event's theme will be "An OSI Solution to Enterprise-wide Communications." ENE will emphasize the relationships between the various information creators, manipulators, and communicators within a total enterprise (a corporation, governmental agency, or university), and will demonstrate how TOP and MAP can integrate these. Specifically, the goal is to demonstrate the reality, validity, and quality of OSI and TOP/MAP 3.0-based products in

Who's doing what

ORGANIZATION	ENTERPRISE AREA OF RESPONSIBILITY	EVENT DESCRIPTION
BOEING CO. SEATTLE, WASH.	ORDER PROCESSING/SUPPLIER CONNECTION	■ SIMULATE A PURCHASER-TO-SUPPLIER CONNECTION APPLICATION GENERATE AND ISSUE A COMPUTER-BASED REQUEST FOR PROPOSAL AND OBTAIN AN ELECTRONIC RESPONSE FROM A REMOTE SUPPLIER
TRW CLEVELAND, OHIO	MANUFACTURING RESOURCE PLANNING	■ DEMONSTRATE A 'PAPERLESS' ENTERPRISE THROUGH USE OF COMPUTER-AIDED DESIGN, MANUFACTURING REQUIREMENTS PLANNING, AND COMPUTER-AIDED PROCESS PLANNING APPLICATIONS ■ RESULTING DESIGN, BILL OF MATERIALS, AND NUMERICAL CONTROL INFORMATION WILL BE SENT TO AN AUTOMATED PROFILER, WHERE A PART WILL BE MANUFACTURED
DEERE & CO. MOLINE, ILL.	JUST-IN-TIME MANUFACTURING	■ SIMULATE A SHEET-METAL MANUFACTURING CELL AND DEMONSTRATE BENEFITS OF COMPUTER-INTEGRATED MANUFACTURING ■ MAKE USE OF GROUP TECHNOLOGY (WHICH LOCATES SIMILAR EXISTING PARTS) AND DESIGN-BY-FEATURE (WHICH MODIFIES A SIMILAR PART TO A NEW APPLICATION)—ENABLES APPLICATION SCHEDULING AND NESTING TO DEMONSTRATE SMOOTH FLOW OF INFORMATION THROUGH A MAP/TOP NETWORK ■ MANUFACTURE ENGINE-SUPPORT MOUNT PLATES FOR U.S. AIR FORCE BOOTH
PROCESS INDUSTRIES, MANAGED BY ALCOA CORP., PITTSBURGH, PA.	POWER MANAGEMENT AND MATERIAL PROCESSING	■ DEMONSTRATE HOW MAP ALLOWS A PROCESS SUPERVISOR TO MONITOR AND ANALYZE SUCH DATA AS POWER CONSUMPTION, PLASTIC PRODUCTION, AND COST TRENDS ■ SIMULATE PRODUCTION OF DIFFERENT-COLORED PLASTICS USING A BLENDING MODEL ■ POWER-MANAGEMENT AREA OF THIS BOOTH WILL SIMULATE ENTERPRISE POWER PRODUCTION USING SENSORS, CONTROL SYSTEMS, AND ALARM-DETECTION SYSTEMS TYPICALLY FOUND IN CONTINUOUS, MATERIAL-FLOW PROCESS INDUSTRIES
COMMUNICATION NETWORKS FOR MANUFACTURING APPLICATIONS (CNMA), MANAGED BY BRITISH AEROSPACE PRESTON, ENGLAND	SUPPLIER/SUBCONTRACTOR TO DEERE BOOTH	■ BOOTH LOCATED AT BRITISH AEROSPACE UNIT IN NORTHERN ENGLAND AND LINKED VIA X.25 ■ COLLABORATE WITH DEERE BOOTH ■ DEMONSTRATE A DISTRIBUTED APPLICATION WHERE PARTS ORDERED IN AMERICA CAN BE DIRECTLY MANUFACTURED IN EUROPE
DEPARTMENT OF TRADE AND INDUSTRY (DTI) LONDON, ENGLAND	SAME AS CNMA	■ SIMULATE A SUBCONTRACTOR JOB SHOP FOR DEERE BOOTH BY PROVIDING MANUFACTURING RESOURCES TO PRODUCE ENTERPRISE PRODUCT ■ PROVIDE HEAVY EQUIPMENT SUCH AS LASER CUTTERS AND FULLY INTEGRATED COMPONENTS THAT CAN CARRY OUT ALL OPERATIONS IN THE PRODUCTION CYCLE (RANGING FROM REQUISITIONING THROUGH WORK SCHEDULING TO ACTUAL MANUFACTURE)
U.S. AIR FORCE/INDUSTRY COALITION WRIGHT-PATTERSON A.F. BASE DAYTON, OHIO	MANUFACTURING DESIGN	■ DESIGN ENTERPRISE PRODUCT ■ ENABLE BOOTH VISITORS TO MODIFY THEIR ENTERPRISE PRODUCT CONFIGURATION PRIOR TO ITS MANUFACTURE PROCESS AN ENGINEERING CHANGE TO AN AEROSPACE PART DRAWING, MANUFACTURE THE PART OFF-SITE, AND SHIP IT TO SHOW FOR INSPECTION THE FOLLOWING DAY
CORPORATION FOR OPEN SYSTEMS McLEAN, VA.	INVOICE	■ GENERATE INVOICES FOR THE ENTERPRISE PRODUCT USING INFORMATION FROM CENTRAL ENTERPRISE SERVER ■ DEMONSTRATE USE OF ELECTRONIC MESSAGING IN THE OPERATION OF AN ENTERPRISE
GENERAL MOTORS DETROIT, MICH.	FINAL ASSEMBLY	■ PROVIDE TWO ROBOTIC ENTITIES WORKING IN UNISON TO ASSEMBLE THE ENTERPRISE PRODUCT ACCORDING TO VISITORS' SPECIFICATIONS ■ ACCESS POSTAL DELIVERY APPLICATIONS ■ HIGHLIGHT USE OF MAP/TOP NETWORK MANAGER AND DIRECTORY SERVER FUNCTIONS

providing solutions across an entire enterprise.

ENE is aimed at the following four objectives:

■ Exhibiting interoperating systems (autonomous computation- and communications-capable processing environments) engaged in a series of related activities.

■ Demonstrating the availability to the marketplace of interoperable, multivendor systems in the context of enterprise-wide networks and application solutions.

■ Demonstrating the applicability of the systems exhibited to a broad spectrum of enterprises, including manufacturing, financial services, engineering, and others.

■ Exhibiting actual, working systems that vendors have made available to customers or intend to make available within a reasonable time after the event.

The Enterprise Networking Event is a joint TOP/MAP and Corporation for Open Systems (COS) event. The Event Steering Committee is comprised of key representatives from Apple, Boeing, COS, GM, Honeywell, Hewlett-Packard, ITI, Jaguar, Kodak, and Wang.

The event architecture will be based upon booths, each of which represents a different functional aspect of a total, integrated enterprise. These booths and their responsibilities are listed in the table (see "Who's doing what").

When visitors to the event register at the Society of Manufacturing Engineers (SME) booth, bar codes will be generated for their name tags. Once completed, the SME information file will be passed to the order-entry system maintained at the Boeing booth. Files will be available for read access by any participating FTAM node in the event.

Three event-wide applications, event information, postal messaging, and enterprise global communications, will be demonstrated simultaneously throughout the show.

The *event information application* will allow the transmittal and retrieval of files from selected FTAM-supporting nodes. These files will contain information regarding event statistics (such as booths visited and visitor-progress tracking) and booth profiles (the types of services provided at the event).

The *postal messaging application* will demonstrate the distributed use of messaging protocols between certain nodes that implement MHS. All sponsor booths will have at least one node that will exchange messages with other nodes utilizing a CCITT X.400 service. Booth visitors will be able to create text messages from X.400 user agent (UA) terminals and send these messages to other UAs in the event. UAs will be both collocated with, and remote from message transfer agents (MTAs), or message switches. UAs will access remote MTAs using privately defined protocols.

The *enterprise global application* will use TOP and MAP to demonstrate the communications required to accomplish the distributed ordering, design, manufacturing, and assembly of event giveaways (complementary materials, such as manufactured booklets). These giveaways will confirm the viability of customized mass production.

While the first application highlights file transfer, using FTAM, and the second focuses on electronic mail, using X.400, the third demonstrates the interoperation of several TOP/MAP 3.0 network functions. These include FTAM,

X.400, Virtual Terminal (VT), and Manufacturing Messaging System (a MAP protocol). VT provides interactive terminal access to remote applications, as opposed to the other services, which are primarily batch-oriented.

The event's main network topology will consist of two LANs, based on IEEE 802.3 CSMA/CD (carrier-sense multiple access with collision detection) and IEEE 802.4 Token-Passing Bus. All systems exhibited in user-sponsored booths will implement a consistent subset of the TOP/MAP 3.0 specifications. These specifications will include the COS platform, which consists of three functional protocol stacks: FTAM, CCITT X.400/MHS, and at least one of four lower-layer stacks (802.3, 802.4, 802.5, and connectionless or connection-oriented X.25).

Figure 1 depicts a high-level architectural overview of the TOP/MAP COS Enterprise Network topology. The figure indicates that IEEE 802.3 and 802.4 LANs make up the event's main network. It also shows that X.25 wide area network (WAN) interfaces will be provided, both within the main event area and to Europe.

Each booth will handle a different function, as follows:

■ *Boeing.* About a dozen vendors will take part in the Boeing booth. (Likewise, the other booths will host one or more independent vendors. Those at the Boeing booth are identified for the sake of illustration.)

This booth will be responsible for order-entry activities and will therefore maintain two file-serving activities, one for visitor tracking and another for visitors' personal data. The order-entry activity includes the reading of visitors' bar codes and the initiation of a giveaway order. Upon entry to the booth, the bar code will be read and compared against the visitor's personal files for verification of registration. The Boeing booth's topology is shown in Figure 2. The network supports MHS, FTAM, and VT application services.

The objective of the Boeing application is to demonstrate that the open systems approach to enterprise communications is beneficial to the procurement process. By selecting multiple vendors' equipment, the Boeing booth will highlight the following functions:

■ Develop a new product/part design and specification.

■ Create a request to be sent to suppliers.

■ Select suppliers that will receive the request.

■ Prepare the request to be electronically delivered to prospective suppliers.

■ Receive/evaluate supplier responses and select supplier(s).

■ Send the order to the selected supplier(s).

■ Receive order acknowledgment from the supplier(s).

The Boeing booth will use FTAM and MHS as transfer methods and Office Document Architecture and Initial Graphics Exchange Specification as data interchange formats. (These will all be discussed in depth in next month's follow-up article.)

■ *TRW.* TRW's booth will be responsible for manufacturing resource planning (MRP). The TRW staging area will maintain three file servers for storing configuration files, modification information, and order-closeout (completion) information. Each of these file servers may reside on any of the FTAM nodes (Fig. 3).

1. ENE topology. *The main network at Enterprise Networking Event will consist of two local area network backbones running TOP/MAP 3.0 protocols, linking private and user-sponsored booths, a nework management center, the Corporation for Open Systems booth, and, via X.25, a participating site in Europe.*

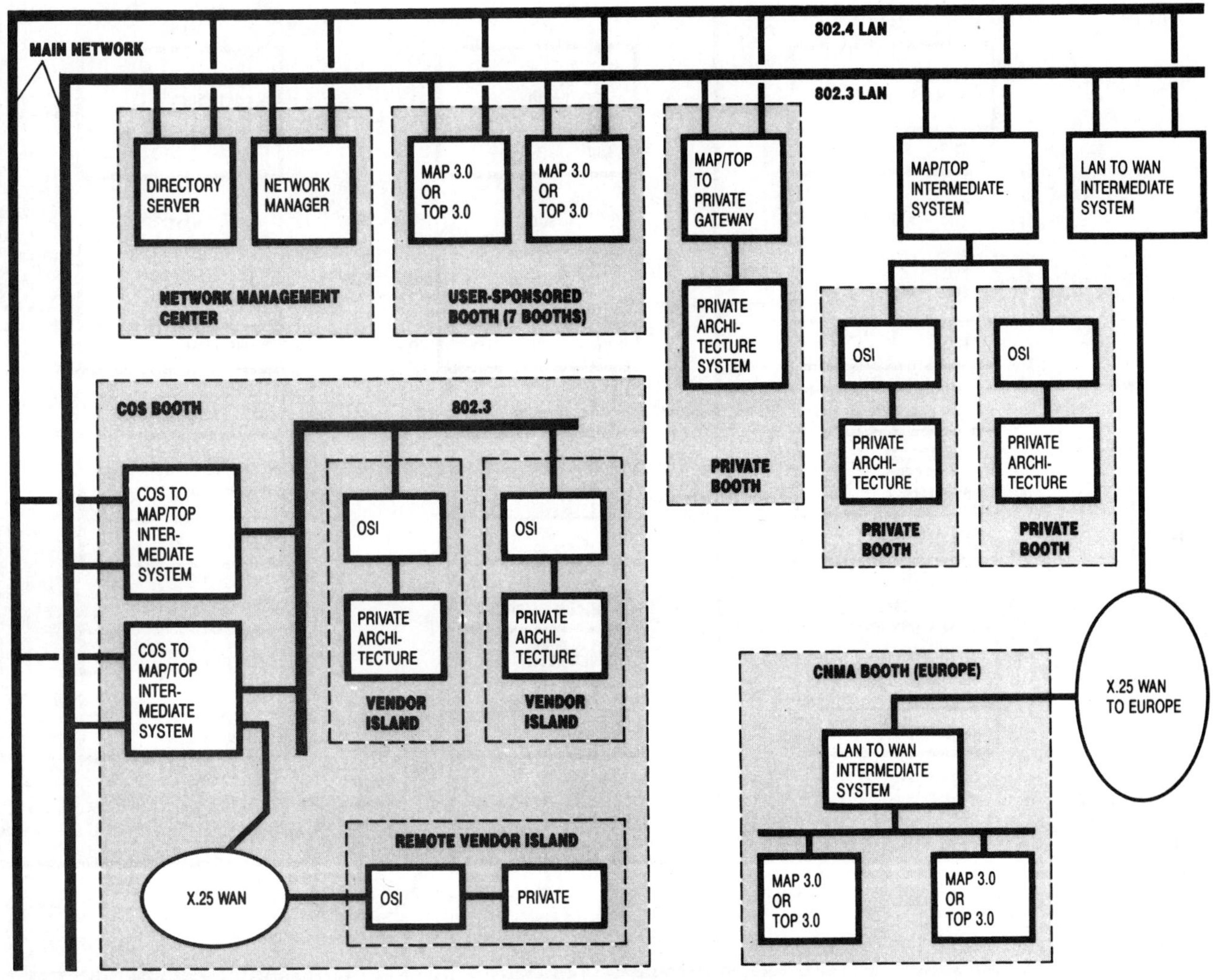

The TRW processing environment will verify orders and update them if customization takes place for an event attendee's giveaway. The TRW MRP system will also contain an actual resource-planning database that must be updated in conjunction with (though not necessarily at the same time as) the files on all connected event file servers. An 802.4/X.25 router supports MHS and FTAM.

■ *Deere & Co.* The Deere booth will be the one responsible for just-in-time manufacturing and, as such, will maintain a file server to store temporary parts lists and requests for parts lists from the assembly booth. It will request parts lists from the MRP system, arrange supplemental capacity from subcontractors, create the bill of material for each giveaway to be assembled, and deliver required parts.

■ *Process Industries.* This booth will be responsible for power management and material processing (process control) activities. In this capacity, the booth will maintain two file servers for storing power-consumption and material-request data. These file servers will collect electrical-power-demand data, simulate generation of that power, and report associated costs to other enterprise systems as part of the event information application.

■ *CNMA and DTI.* These booths will be responsible for subcontract manufacturing and will participate as single-source subcontractors for specific parts in the just-in-time manufacturing activity. The CNMA and DTI booths will maintain two file servers for the storing of part-request files.

■ *U. S. Air Force/Industry Coalition.* This booth, responsible

455

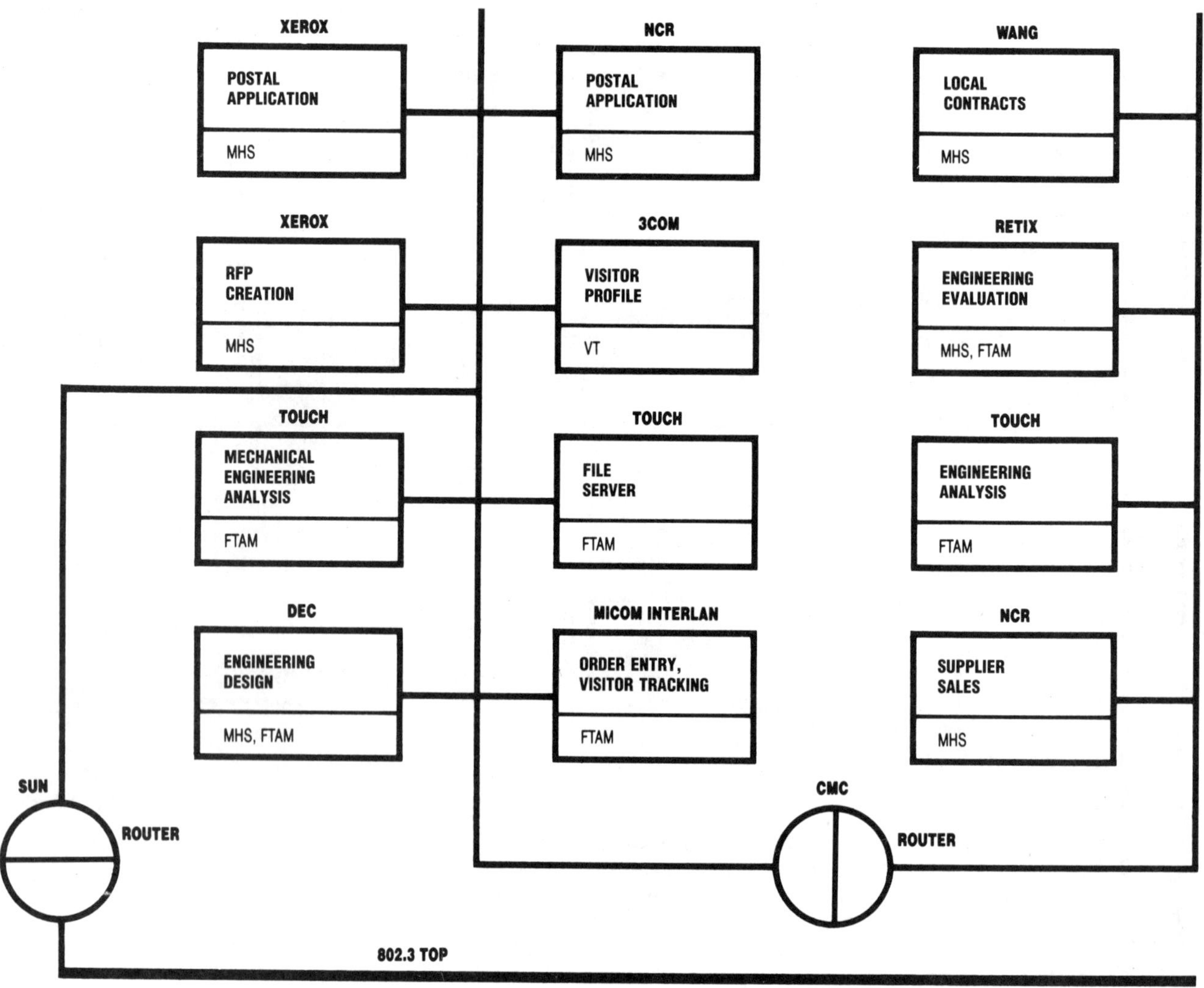

2. Boeing booth. *Boeing is playing host to 11 vendors at its ENE booth. Each vendor is responsible for a different application; all are linked via routers. The backbone runs* TOP *protocols over an IEEE 802.3 carrier-sense multiple access with collision-detection network and provides messaging, file transfer, and virtual terminal.*

for manufacturing design, will maintain a file server containing copies of event attendees' configuration files and available event-giveaway options. Upon entry to the design booth, the visitor bar code will be scanned and the design system will search for a corresponding visitor-tracking file on the Boeing, booth-resident visitor-tracking file server. The Air Force file server will verify that the customer has placed an order, modify that order, and then provide update information for the TRW MRP database.

■ *Corporation for Open Systems.* The COS booth will be responsible for invoicing activities. To do this, it will maintain a file server for temporary storage of invoice data. File-server activities will include the reading of order-closeout data and the generation of an event invoice, based on

energy costs of manufacturing and assembly.

The COS booth topology is illustrated in Figure 4, which shows 802.3/X.25 and 802.3/802.4 routers and an 802.3/ 802.3 bridge supporting MHS and FTAM application services. The COS test system will confirm that ENE participants conform to the COS platform (TOP/MAP 3.0 protocols).

■ *General Motors.* The GM booth will be responsible for the assembly activity and maintain a file server to store parts-list files prior to assembly. This activity will consist of actual assembly of the giveaway and delivery to the customer. The GM file server will initiate an order closeout following delivery, monitor physical inventory of the giveaway parts, maintain counts of various giveaway configurations pro-

456

duced, and monitor the power consumed by the booth.

The ranks of vendors committing to TOP-conformant products is swelling because of the interest and endorsement of major users. User disenchantment with vendors' communications and data-interchange incompatibilities has developed sufficient momentum to propel the TOP and MAP OSI efforts through the MAP/TOP Users Group. This significant consortium represents the major network-resource purchaser and implementer market segment. It provides critical, coordinated requirements for data connectivity and interchange to the TOP and MAP specification process as well as to the growing number of vendors developing such products.

Indeed, there is now a vendor's equivalent to the TOP users' group. The Washington, D. C.-based Computer and Business Equipment Manufacturers Association (CBEMA) has recently formed a TOP Vendors Group. The CBEMA/TOP Vendors Group membership includes AMP, Apple, AT&T, Communications Machinery Corporation, CDC, Eastman-Kodak, Hewlett-Packard, Honeywell-Bull, IBM, ICL, Intel, NCR, Texas Instruments, Ungermann-Bass, Wang Laboratories, and Xerox.

Product sampling: Retix . .

Presented below are descriptions of the TOP products available from Retix (a Santa Monica, Calif.-based software firm), Sun Microsystems (Mountain View, Calif.), and Touch Communications Inc. (Scotts Valley, Calif.), all of which have stated TOP support and/or announced products. While other vendors, including all those listed above as members of the CBEMA/TOP Vendors Group, have announced TOP direction and/or products, the three examined below provide a high degree of TOP 1.0 capability and plan to support TOP 3.0.

Retix provides several software products that implement TOP/OSI protocols. Generally, each Retix product is a portable software package that implements a single OSI communications protocol. These packages may be used independently or may be linked together to provide a full seven-layer implementation. The protocols are implemented in standard C language and are designed to be independent of the operating system to which they may be ported. Retix OSI products include several cases of non-TOP products, but only TOP products are considered here.

The majority of TOP products available today conform to version 1.0. However, it is highly likely that a number of vendors will announce TOP 3.0 products during or around the Enterprise Networking Event.

Retix TOP products include the following:

■ OSI FTAM (Phase II, for TOP 3.0 FTAM). This product consists of six major modules. TOP 3.0 specifies both initiators and responders in FTAM (as will be elaborated in next month's architectural overview). There are two protocol implementations, one each for the initiator and responder sides of an association. An Application Interface Module provides the TOP Application Interface on the initiator side. A File System Interface Module may be linked with the Responder Protocol Module to make a file server.

■ MAP 2.1/TOP 1.0 FTAM. This product conforms with Phase I FTAM requirements and supports TOP 1.0. Two FTAM packages are provided, which support the basic User Correctable service (in which the user is responsible for recovery after failure) and the Reliable service (which supports recovery after loss of a transport connection and restart of the file transfer).

■ X.400 Message Handling System. Retix has three X.400 MHS-compliant packages. Interpersonal Messaging (IPM) User Agent implements the CCITT P2 IPM protocol and

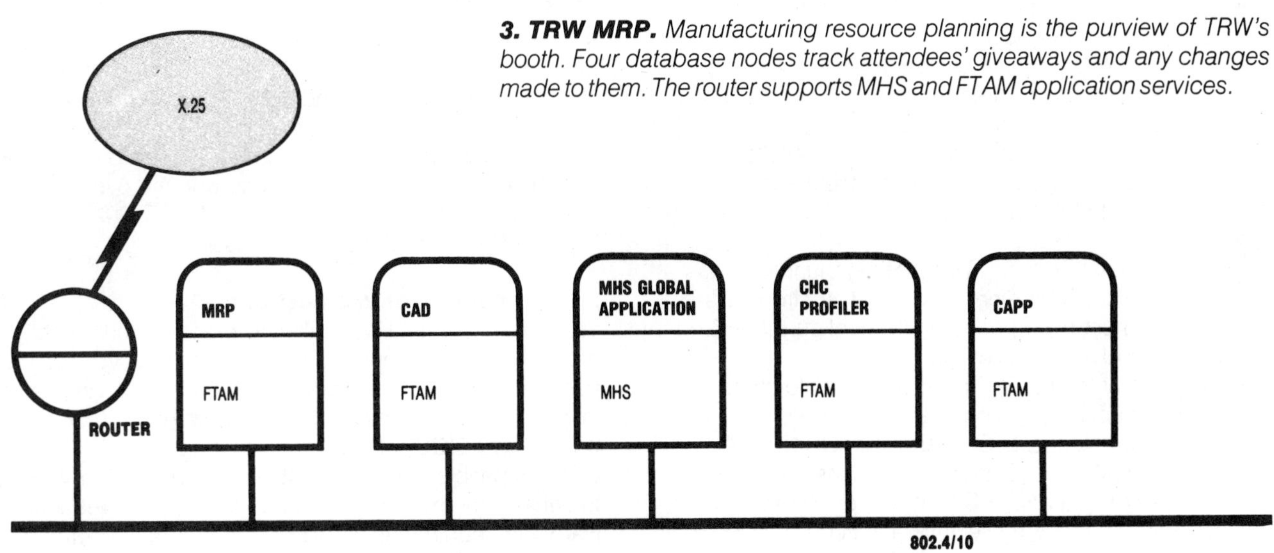
3. TRW MRP. Manufacturing resource planning is the purview of TRW's booth. Four database nodes track attendees' giveaways and any changes made to them. The router supports MHS and FTAM application services.

CAD = COMPUTER-AIDED DESIGN
CAPP = COMPUTER-AIDED PROCESS PLANNING
CNC = COMPUTERIZED NUMERICAL CONTROL
FTAM = FILE TRANSFER, ACCESS, AND MANAGEMENT
MHS = MESSAGE HANDLING SYSTEM
MRP = MANUFACTURING RESOURCE PLANNING
802.4/10 = 802.4 TOKEN-PASSING BUS LOCAL AREA NETWORK

allows a human user to send and receive messages within and among computing environments. Message Transfer Service implements the CCITT P1 Message Transfer Protocol, enabling a computer to function as a message switch (called a Message Transfer Agent). Reliable Transfer Service operates over both the full or basic activity subsets of the OSI session protocol.

■ OSI Presentation Protocol. This package implements the kernel functional unit and allows multiple presentation-service access points to be activated or deactivated at run time. The software permits registration of an abstract syntax for each presentation context and provides the ASN.1 Basic Encoding Rules. ASN.1 and other possible transfer syntaxes and corresponding user-provided encoder/decoders are registered at run time.

■ ASN.1 Compiler. This product provides a development tool for OSI application and presentation layer protocols. The compiler accepts a definition of the abstract syntax of Protocol Data Units (PDUs) in the form of ASN.1 and allows specification of the target-system word length, maximum octet and bit-string lengths, and additional implementation-specific parameters. C-language programs are produced that parse incoming PDUs and format outgoing ones.

■ OSI Session Protocol. Four packages are provided that implement Basic Combined Subsets, Basic Synchronized Subsets, Basic Activity Subsets, or all function units. Any of these is negotiable at connection establishment.

■ OSI Transport Protocol. Packages include OSI Transport Protocol Class 0/2, Class 0/2/4, and Class 4. The Class 4 package is designed for TOP 3.0 conformance and operates over a connectionless network service that implements protocols such as the ISO internetwork protocol.

■ OSI Internet Protocol. This product provides relaying and routing of data through intermediate systems, which are accessed by multiple subnetworks (LANs or WANs). Enables Retix implementation of the ISO end-system to intermediate-system protocol (see below).

■ End-System to Intermediate-System Routing Exchange Protocol. This consists of an end-system (ES) part and intermediate-system (IS) part. The ES aspect generates requests for routing information and paces the results in a cache on nonrouting systems. The IS aspect resides on routers that contain full routing tables and respond to routing requests.

■ X.25 Packet Level Protocol. This package functions as either data terminal equipment (DTE) or data circuit-terminating equipment (DCE) and can be configured as a relay between LANs and/or WANs.

■ Logical Link Control (LLC). This product conforms to ISO's 8802/2 specification, equivalent to IEEE 802.2 LLC. It includes four packages: LLC Class 1, for TOP 1.0, MAP 2.1/3.0, and GOSIP; LLC Class 2, for X.25 as a network layer protocol over a LAN; LLC Class 3, for MiniMAP and Enhanced Performance Architecture; and LLC Class 4, for combined uses of Classes 1, 2, and 3.

■ X.25 Link Access Procedure B (as DTE or DCE).

Through its Sunlink OSI products, Sun Microsystems provides OSI implementations that allow Sun workstations to communicate with the systems of other vendors. Sun Microsystems OSI products include several cases of non-TOP products, but only TOP products are considered here. Note that the Sun OSI/TOP products as well as other Sun software are built upon the foundation of an enhanced Unix operating environment.

...Sun...

Sun Microsystems TOP products include:

■ Sunlink OSI FTAM. This product supports the asymmetrical OSI FTAM protocol relationship between initiator and responder peer entities. Sunlink OSI FTAM Interface Libraries support the range of FTAM transaction- and non-transaction-oriented service primitives. The product is offered as both a "high-level" and a "low-level" interface library. The high-level interface library is intended for writing FTAM initiators, while the low-level interface library allows definition of FTAM responders as well as initiators. Sunlink OSI FTAM is written in the C programming language and supports interfaces into the Sun ASN.1 product.

■ Sunlink MHS (Message Handling System). This product, based on the CCITT X.400 Recommendations, links Sun users to public mail services based in heterogeneous computing environments. Users of standard Sun mail programs, such as the window-based Mailtool, can transparently exchange electronic messages with users of private and public mail services that conform to X.400 protocols. Sunlink MHS provides both gateway and, through the CCITT X.400-defined MTA, message-relay functions. The gateway translates standard Sun messages, which conform to the Department of Defense's (DOD's) Simple Mail Transfer Protocol specifications, to and from X.400 MHS formats. Sunlink MHS supports X.400-based exchanges from the following: private management domain (PRMD) to administrative management domain (ADMD); PRMD to PRMD over X.25; and PRMD to PRMD over IEEE 802.3 or IEEE 802.4 LANs.

■ Other TOP products in the Sunlink family include: ANS.1; Session Protocol; Transport Protocol; Connectionless Network Protocol; X.25; and IEEE 802.2 (Logical Link Control). Sunlink X.25 conforms to the X.25 Packet Level Protocol and supports the TOP/OSI Subnetwork Point of Attachment. This means that it can operate over such subnetworks as X.25, IEEE 802.3 CSMA/CD, 802.4 Token-Passing Bus, and 802.5 Token-Passing Ring.

...and Touch Communications

Touch OSI is a family of software products that enable multiple-vendor computing environments to communicate transparently over a network. Two major product implementation groups are Touch OSI DOS and Touch OSI VMS.

■ Touch OSI DOS software implements a MAP 2.1/TOP 1.0 OSI-compatible stack on an IBM PC, enabling an IBM PC to behave, for example, as an OSI print-service requester. Hardware requirements are a PC, PC/XT, PC/AT, or equivalent, with a hard disk and recommended 640K of memory. TOP-based protocols that are implemented include: FTAM, ASN.1, Connection Oriented Presentation, Session, and Transport Services, Connectionless Mode Network Service, and Local Area Network Service (ISO 8802/2—LLC 1).

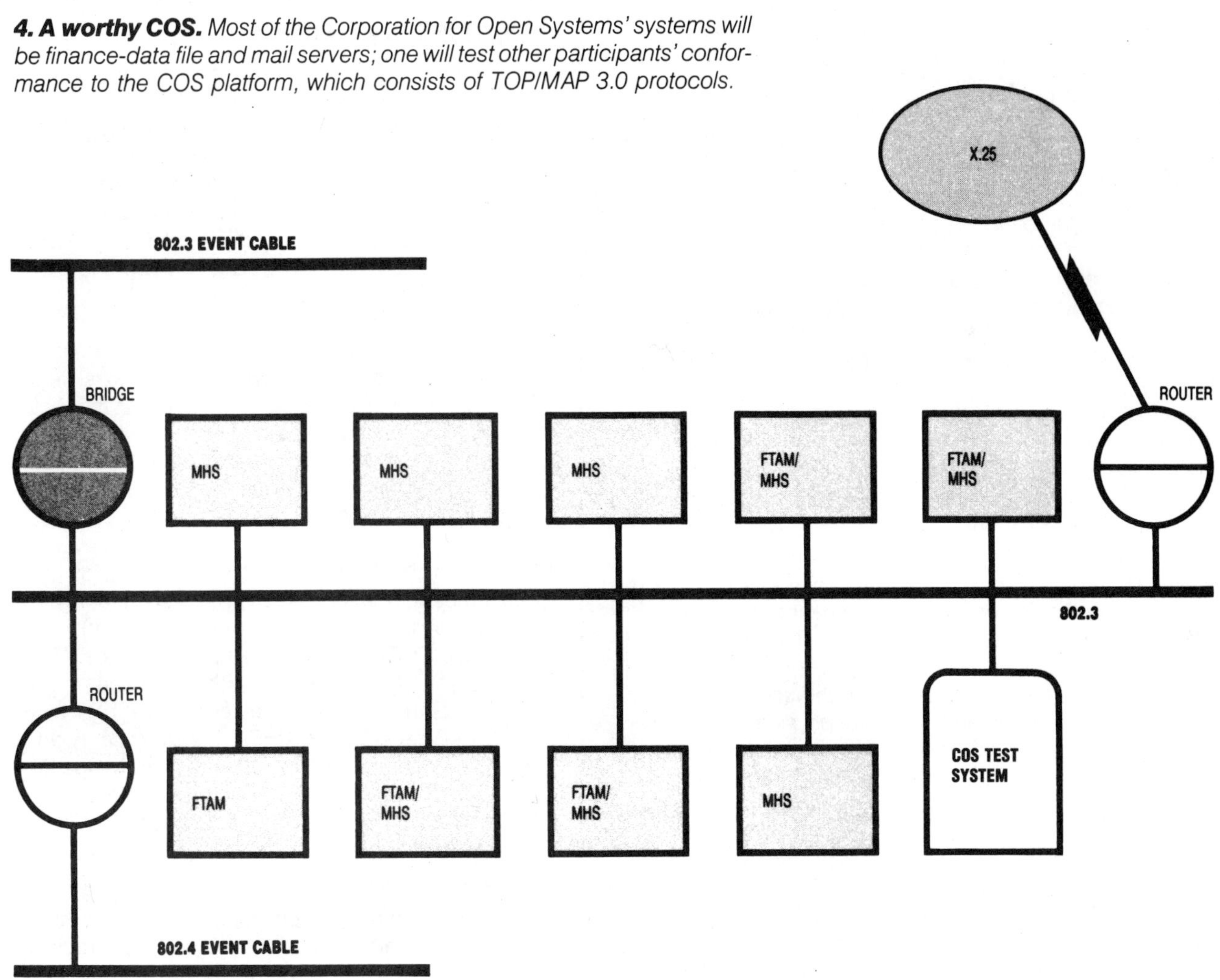

■ Touch OSI VMS software implements a MAP 2.1/TOP 1.0 OSI-compatible stack on the Digital Equipment Corp. VAX series of computers. This enables VAX and MicroVAX II computers running VMS to behave as OSI file and print servers. The TOP-compliant Touch OSI VMS protocol stack is identical to the TOP-compliant Touch OSI DOS stack. Hardware requirements are for a minimum of 3 Mbytes of main memory in either the VAX 8000, VAX 11/700, Micro-VAX II, or VAXstation series of computers.

How to migrate to standards

The TOP 3.0 architecture and protocols are designed to provide an integrated, vendor-independent set of user application services over a variety of standard LAN and WAN media. Because of the enriched set of standardized services that TOP 3.0 offers and because of the energetic push being given the protocol stack by vendors, more and more users are beginning to install TOP networks. Users who want to migrate from vendor-unique to vendor-independent approaches should follow a few simple principles.

First, plan a phased migration to either convert or replace existing proprietary equipment and services. A phased migration provides a graceful substitution of non-TOP protocols with TOP protocols (for example, replace proprietary upper-layer protocols with TOP protocols over a previously installed TOP subnetwork). One example of this is the recommendation of the TOP Technical Review Committee to discontinue installing the DOD Advanced Research Projects Agency protocol suite over TOP subnetworks (see "TOP/OSI vs. TCP/IP").

Clearly, the existing vendor-specific installed base of equipment, facilities, and applications represents a major resource base that probably must be amortized well beyond this year. However, a well-engineered, net-present-value analysis would recognize that the perpetuation of proprietary networking approaches, as opposed to the adoption of TOP, contributes major costs to the enterprise in terms of lost opportunity. Such a study would quickly indicate that the disadvantages of these approaches outweigh the costs of transition.

Users should recognize that most major vendors have committed themselves to providing TOP protocols. However, the extent to which they are provided may vary from vendor to vendor. When installing a TOP network, users should confirm that, based upon user-application requirements, the TOP architecture and protocols will provide network application functionality (in such areas as graphical application interchange, electronic mail, remote file access, remote terminal access, network directory, and network management services) greater than or equal to what it is replacing.

Any implementation of a TOP network should minimize user application impact by disassociating user applications from networking protocols. This can be accomplished by mapping user-requested network services to the interface library routines specified in TOP 3.0. In essence, the recommendation is to map an application program to the TOP/MAP 3.0 Application Program Interface Library (a standard library that includes data interchange formats). The library then interfaces with Layer 7, enabling application-program and device portability.

Potential TOP users should determine the scope of connectivity requirements and construct physical and logical topologies accordingly. In essence, adopt a network-development life-cycle approach, which recognizes that proper designs are expressions of user application requirements. Ultimately, the network must be "tuned" to the applications that most heavily utilize network buffer and line resources. On that basis, determine the following:

- Message types by application (interactive, batch).
- Message priorities.
- Existing and planned physical/logical configurations.
- Traffic volume by location and by message.
- Traffic profiles and expected worst-case profile scenarios (for example, time of day, day of week, day of month, week of year).
- Which enterprise areas exhibit the most urgent business requirements (these can achieve the highest net returns in the migration priority).

Before setting up a TOP network, establish and quantify user operational requirements, which include: throughput; expected response time; mean time between failures; mean time between outages; mean time to repair; reliability; and availability.

TOP 3.0 recommends the use of the ISO internet protocol as a baseline because a variety of LAN and WAN approaches can interface with each other through this common reference.

Maintaining consistent subnetwork types and minimizing the number of different types in a TOP network is important. One of the guiding tenets of TOP and OSI is to minimize networking and protocol options to the lowest number to achieve information interchange, and this tenet extends to the lowest two layers of the architecture.

It is essential that TOP users track resources and prac-

TOP/OSI vs. TCP/IP

A number of users have implemented Transmission Control Protocol/Internet Protocol (TCP/IP), which was engendered by the Department of Defense (DOD), over various local area network physical and link layer protocols, including TOP subnetwork protocols. In turn, TCP/IP often supports a DOD upper-layer suite, such as File Transfer Protocol (FTP) and Telnet. However, these users may find a transition from the DOD protocols to their OSI equivalents inevitable.

It is highly significant that DOD has, since late 1987, formally stated its intention to adopt the OSI protocols as its sole mandatory interoperable protocol suite. It has further stated that it will interoperate with the DOD protocols only for the expected life of systems supporting those protocols. Furthermore, the Government OSI Profile (GOSIP) and Computer-Aided Acquisition Logistics Support (CALS) have been adopted by DOD to accomplish this objective. GOSIP covers Layers 1 through 7, while CALS addresses the application program interface (that is, the set of services that reside between applications and the application layer).

Because DOD has stated alignment to the TOP/MAP/COS efforts, GOSIP is functionally comparable to the TOP common network services, including FTAM for remote file access and MHS for electronic mail, and CALS is comparable to the TOP data interchange formats, which include Office Document Interchange Format, Computer Graphics Metafile, and Initial Graphics Exchange Specification.

tice configuration management. Constant awareness of existing and planned physical and logical resources is critical in any networking environment.

For ease of maintenance, divide and conquer. Modularize and isolate components to the extent that reliance of multiple services on a particular network component should be avoided, since the removal and/or replacement of that component could involve a major effort to re-initialize services. ■

Thomas J. Routt is president of Network Systems Consulting, a firm that provides worldwide network architecture consulting to Fortune 1000 corporations concerned with migration to OSI and SNA. Previously, he was manager of Boeing Network Architecture for Boeing Computer Services Company. In this capacity, he managed global network planning, design, and implementation for the Boeing Company. Routt holds an M. B. A. in information systems from Southern Illinois University and a B. S. in environmental science from Western Washington University.

The author wishes to acknowledge the input of Laurie Bride, Boeing's manager of network architecture and program manager of the Boeing TOP Program, as well as the efforts of her staff. Their organizational assistance, interface coordination to TOP users and vendors, and review of the manuscript have proven invaluable.

Thomas J. Routt, contributing editor, DATA COMMUNICATIONS

From TOP (3.0) to bottom: Architectural close-up

Presented here is a detailed look at the way international standards are shaping up as they continue to make inroads into U. S. user firms.

The business mission of computer networks is to serve as an enterprise-wide infrastructure that can deliver, format, present, and interchange appropriate data on a highly available, timely, and cost-effective basis to distributed decision makers in a sufficiently detailed or abstracted level, at whatever organizational, geographic, or temporal distance from one another and regardless of which computer interface is currently available.

Enabling networks to meet this challenge within a multi-vendor setting has been the goal of international standards, specifically the International Organization for Standardization's (ISO's) Open Systems Interconnection (OSI) efforts. In the United States, these efforts have been embodied principally in the work of the Technical and Office Protocols (TOP) and Manufacturing Automation Protocol (MAP).

However, the TOP specification Version 1.0, published by Boeing Computer Services in November 1985 to be compatible with the then-current MAP Versions 2.1 and 2.2, provided only a narrow range of services. While several vendors implemented TOP 1.0 and users began to employ TOP in limited settings, more widespread acceptance of TOP would await Version 3.0, which appeared in April 1987 (see "Where TOP comes from").

The major distinction between the two versions is that TOP 3.0 provides a relatively complete set of application services. This set includes standard graphics application interfaces, electronic mail, and remote file and terminal access as well as network directory and management services. Such services are considered essential to many user environments.

This article, the second in a series (see "Under the Big TOP at Enterprise '88: TOP 3.0's debut," DATA COMMUNICATIONS, April, p. 155), examines the TOP 3.0 architecture at all its levels and focuses on the application-level protocols and interfaces that will bring these much-called-for services to users' multivendor networks.

Rationale

Technical and administrative offices represent perhaps the most significant settings for distributed computing. These settings have witnessed a dramatic growth in productivity tools in recent years. The proliferation of distributed office tools has matched exponential technology and attendant price-performance improvements and has led to increased user dependence upon proprietary computer network architectures, protocols, and products.

Unfortunately, user networks often contain components from multiple vendors, which may have been engineered to be fundamentally incompatible at the application-interface and communications levels. Such incompatibility engenders technical, economic, and organizational inefficiencies that make it impossible for computer networks to fulfill their business mission.

The primary goal of TOP is to accelerate the availability of cost-effective, off-the-shelf, interoperable, computer-based products. These products should satisfy the requirements of technical and administrative office users of multivendor networks. The resulting TOP specification represents the collective requirements of the MAP/TOP Users Group, which in turn is understood by vendors to represent a significant market segment. This group includes the following:

■ Hughes Aircraft, Alcoa, Jaguar Cars, General Electric, Kaiser Aluminum, Rockwell International, Ford Motor Co., General Dynamics, Chrysler Motors, Lockheed, Kraft, Grumman, Scott Paper Co., Monsanto Co., Boeing, General Motors, Du Pont, Weyerhaeuser, McDonnell Douglas, U. S. Air Force, Deere & Co., Frito-Lay, Mobil, Eastman-

Kodak, Northrop, Shell Oil, Nabisco, TRW, Proctor and Gamble, Martin Marietta, and Union Carbide.

The current TOP specification, Version 3.0, defines a suite of protocols for the seven OSI layers and for the interfaces between applications and Layer 7.

Newer and richer

The major architectural concern of TOP 1.0 was to provide error-free file transfers between cooperating end systems (Layer-4-and-above protocol environment). TOP 1.0 certainly provided connectivity within multiple-vendor environments. Noticeably absent, however, was the extended interōperation that cooperating applications could achieve with common data formats. Furthermore, there was little agreement on application-layer functions during discussions of TOP 1.0 at the NBS Implementers' Workshops.

Figure 1 illustrates TOP Version 1.0, which essentially provides for file transfer services at Layer 7 over an Ethernet-like, 10-Mbit/s local area network (LAN) using an ISO carrier sense multiple access with collision detection (CSMA/CD) at Layers 1 and 2. Note that TOP 1.0 defines a single OSI Layer 7 protocol, File Transfer, Access, and Management (FTAM), and does not specify an OSI Layer 6 protocol.

Due to these limitations, several proprietary vendor architectures at the time provided a richer set of application services than TOP 1.0. It was widely recognized that a robust suite of application-layer protocols was necessary. That recognition, and resulting upper-layer protocol agreements, led to the endorsement and publication of TOP Version 3.0. With TOP 3.0, networks can come close to fulfilling their business mission.

APIs

Increased flexibility in meeting users' networking needs is made possible by application program interfaces (APIs), standard routines that provide network-based services to application programs. Technical office applications, such as computer-aided design (CAD) packages, simulation, and scientific data analysis, frequently use graphical services. Many business office applications are also increasingly dependent on graphics. These include desktop publishing, illustration, and drafting programs, as well as integrated spreadsheets that create business graphs for presentation.

TOP 3.0 regards computer graphics application programs as those that produce or manipulate computer graphics pictures and requiring computer graphics services. This includes graphics output or display, input from an operator, interactive graphics-based applications, storage and retrieval of items in graphics databases, and graphics metafiles, the generation, interchange, and interpretation of picture descriptions.

Figure 2 illustrates TOP 3.0. The Standard TOP Application Program Interface Library provides the data-interchange formats that allow heterogeneous graphics applications to interconnect and share resources in an application-independent and device-independent manner.

Note in the figure that both the Computer Graphics

Acronyms

ACSE Association Control Service Element
ADMD Administrative Management Domain
AE Application Entity
APDU Application Protocol Data Unit
ANS American National Standard
AP Application Process, Application Profile
API Application Program Interface
ASN.1 Abstract Syntax Notation One
CASE Common Application Service Element
CCR Commitment, Concurrency, and Recovery
CGI Computer Graphics Interface
CGM Computer Graphics Metafile
CLNP Connectionless-Mode Network Protocol
CLNS Connectionless-Mode Network Service
CMIP Common Management Information Protocol
CMIS Common Management Information Services
CONS Connection-Mode Network Service
DDGL Device-Dependent Graphics Layer
DIB Directory Information Base
DIGL Device-Independent Graphics Layer
DIGS Device-Independent Graphics Services
DIS Draft International Standard
DP Draft Proposal
DSA Directory Service Agent
DUA Directory User Agent
EDIF Electronic Design Interchange Format
FDDI Fiber Distributed Data Interface
FTAM File Transfer, Access, and Management
GKS Graphical Kernel System
IDU Interface Data Unit
IGES Initial Graphics Exchange Specification
IS International Standard
MHS Message Handling System
MOTIS Message Oriented Text Interchange System
MTA Message Transfer Agent
MTAE Message Transfer Agent Entity
NPDU Network Protocol Data Unit
NSAP Network Service Access Point
ODA Office Document Architecture
ODIF Office Document Interchange Format
PDES Product Data Exchange Standard
PDU Protocol Data Unit
PPDU Presentation Protocol Data Unit
PRMD Private Management Domain
ROS Remote Operation Service
RTS Reliable Transfer Service
SMAE System Management Application Entity
SPDU Session Protocol Data Unit
STEP Standard for the Exchange of Product Model Data
TPDU Transport Protocol Data Unit
TSAP Transport Service Access Point
UA User Agent
UAE User Agent Entity
VDI Virtual Device Interface
VT Virtual Terminal

1. TOP 1.0. *The initial TOP specification provided file transfer services at Layer 7 and little else over an Ethernet-like LAN using a contention scheme at Layers 1 and 2.*

OSI LAYER	TOP 1.0 PROTOCOLS
7 APPLICATION	ISO FTAM 8571
6 PRESENTATION	NULL (ASCII AND BINARY ENCODING)
5 SESSION	ISO SESSION 8327 BASIC COMBINED SUBSET AND SESSION KERNEL, FULL DUPLEX
4 TRANSPORT	ISO TRANSPORT 8073 CLASS 4
3 NETWORK	ISO INTERNET 8473 CONNECTIONLESS AND FOR X.25 SUBNETWORK DEPENDENT CONVERGENCE PROTOCOL
2 DATA LINK	ISO LOGICAL LINK CONTROL 8802/2 (IEEE 802.2) TYPE 1, CLASS 1
1 PHYSICAL	ISO CARRIER SENSE MULTIPLE ACCESS/COLLISION DETECTION MEDIUM ACCESS CONTROL (IEEE 802.3 MAC) 8802/3 10 BASE5 (10 MBIT/S, BASEBAND, 5 MHz)

Meta-file (CGM) and Graphics Kernel System (GKS) constitute TOP 3.0 APIs, which, in turn, provide the functional interface between graphics applications and OSI Layer 7.

CGM and GKS are part of the TOP 3.0 computer graphics standards that were selected from those developed by ISO Technical Committee 97/Subcommittee 21/Working Group 2 (the formal document references are listed at the end of this article). CGM provides an Application Profile (AP, a TOP 3.0-specific OSI protocol stack) and a set of Device-Independent Graphics Services (DIGS, which provide graphics-device transparencies) for 2-D graphics (3-D ISO DIGS standards are currently under development). GKS defines a language-independent API to provide interoperability between graphic applications and hardware.

The TOP 3.0 architecture internally structures an API as the interface between the graphics application process and computer graphics services. Figure 3 shows the TOP Graphics Reference Model. APIs are implemented to provide the services of the Device-Independent Graphics Layer (DIGL, part of the API, not part of Layer 7).

The DIGL provides services that are common to all graphics architectures and hardware, and its use makes device dependencies transparent to the user. GKS specifies the DIGL component of the TOP 3.0 API.

TOP 3.0 achieves this graphics-device independence within the API by segregating all of the device-dependent graphics functionality into a separate API component, architecturally subordinate to the DIGL, called the Device-Dependent Graphics Layer (DDGL). The service provided by DDGL enables the DIGS to support specific graphics devices and workstations. The DIGL-DDGL interface is called the device interface and is specified as CGM Interchange Format within TOP 3.0.

CGM provides a picture-description metafile that contains, in device- and installation-independent form, the pictorial description of information represented by the graphics functions invoked through the API. In essence, the CGM stores output primitives and attributes. These compose the picture and can be used for archiving and transferring picture-description information. CGM is graphics-device independent and is created by a CGM generator residing at the device-driver level.

Note in Figure 3 that GKS is interfaced to CGM-related device drivers. A CGM generator residing at the device-driver level is invoked by the application-callable layer (that is, the DIGL). Correspondingly, CGM may be invoked by an application-callable, device-independent graphics system, such as GKS.

TOP 3.0 selects the Initial Graphics Exchange Specification (IGES) Version 3.0 (as shown in Figure 2) to enable exchanges of product-definition data (a subset of engineering-drawing applications that align with the U. S. Government's Computer-Aided Acquisition Logistics Support program). In essence, IGES exchanges human-interpretable product data. This data is defined by IGES as entities such as point, line, circular arc, and so on.

Product Data Exchange Specification/Standard for the Exchange of Product Model Data (PDES/STEP) is a follow-on activity to the NBS IGES effort. The PDES/STEP effort is intended to develop a richer set of data descriptions than those provided by IGES for a range of application areas. These areas include mechanical, electrical, and electronic products, finite-element modeling, piping and plant design, architecture, engineering, and construction, as well as in the preparation of technical publications.

PDES/STEP Version 1.0 is anticipated to become an ISO standard. The current direction is to incorporate PDES/STEP into the TOP specification when it is sufficiently mature but also to retain IGES.

TOP 3.0 defines Office Document Architecture/Office Document Interchange Format (ODA/ODIF) for formatting and interchanging compound electronic documents. These documents may be composed of multiple content types, such as character-, geometric-, and raster-graphics data. TOP 3.0's selection and recommendation of ODA/ODIF is formally characterized as the TOP Document Architecture (DA) Application Profile (AP). Specifically, the TOP DA AP defines an implementation of ODA/ODIF that supports the interchange of revisable- or formatted-form compound documents. The graphics objects within these documents are specified according to the TOP Computer

2. TOP 3.0. *The successor to TOP 1.0 provides a rich set of application services, including electronic mail, remote file access, remote terminal access, network directory, and net-work management. These application services are provided to assist in graphical application data interchange. TOP 3.0 also defines a standard application program interface.*

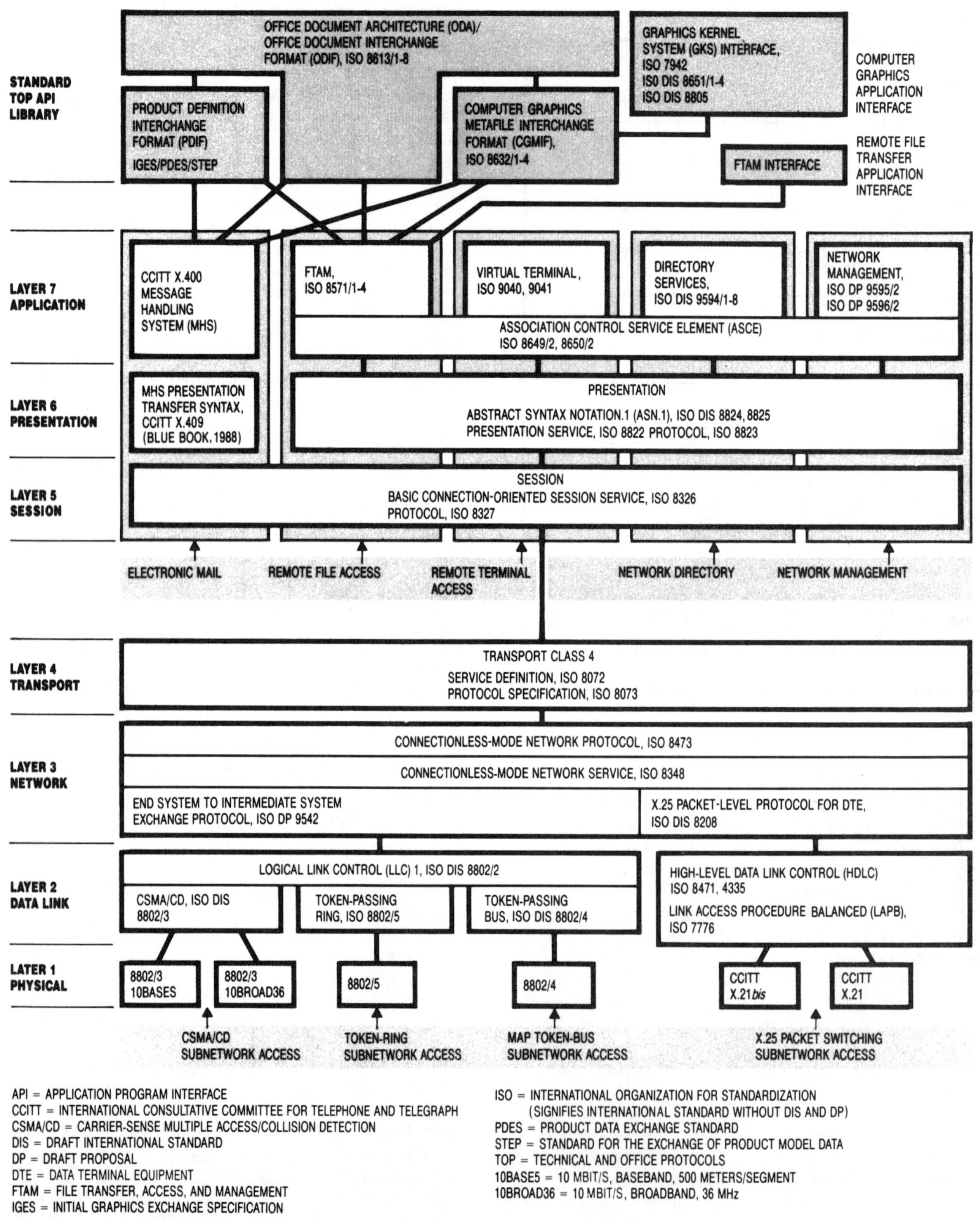

API = APPLICATION PROGRAM INTERFACE
CCITT = INTERNATIONAL CONSULTATIVE COMMITTEE FOR TELEPHONE AND TELEGRAPH
CSMA/CD = CARRIER-SENSE MULTIPLE ACCESS/COLLISION DETECTION
DIS = DRAFT INTERNATIONAL STANDARD
DP = DRAFT PROPOSAL
DTE = DATA TERMINAL EQUIPMENT
FTAM = FILE TRANSFER, ACCESS, AND MANAGEMENT
IGES = INITIAL GRAPHICS EXCHANGE SPECIFICATION

ISO = INTERNATIONAL ORGANIZATION FOR STANDARDIZATION (SIGNIFIES INTERNATIONAL STANDARD WITHOUT DIS AND DP)
PDES = PRODUCT DATA EXCHANGE STANDARD
STEP = STANDARD FOR THE EXCHANGE OF PRODUCT MODEL DATA
TOP = TECHNICAL AND OFFICE PROTOCOLS
10BASE5 = 10 MBIT/S, BASEBAND, 500 METERS/SEGMENT
10BROAD36 = 10 MBIT/S, BROADBAND, 36 MHz

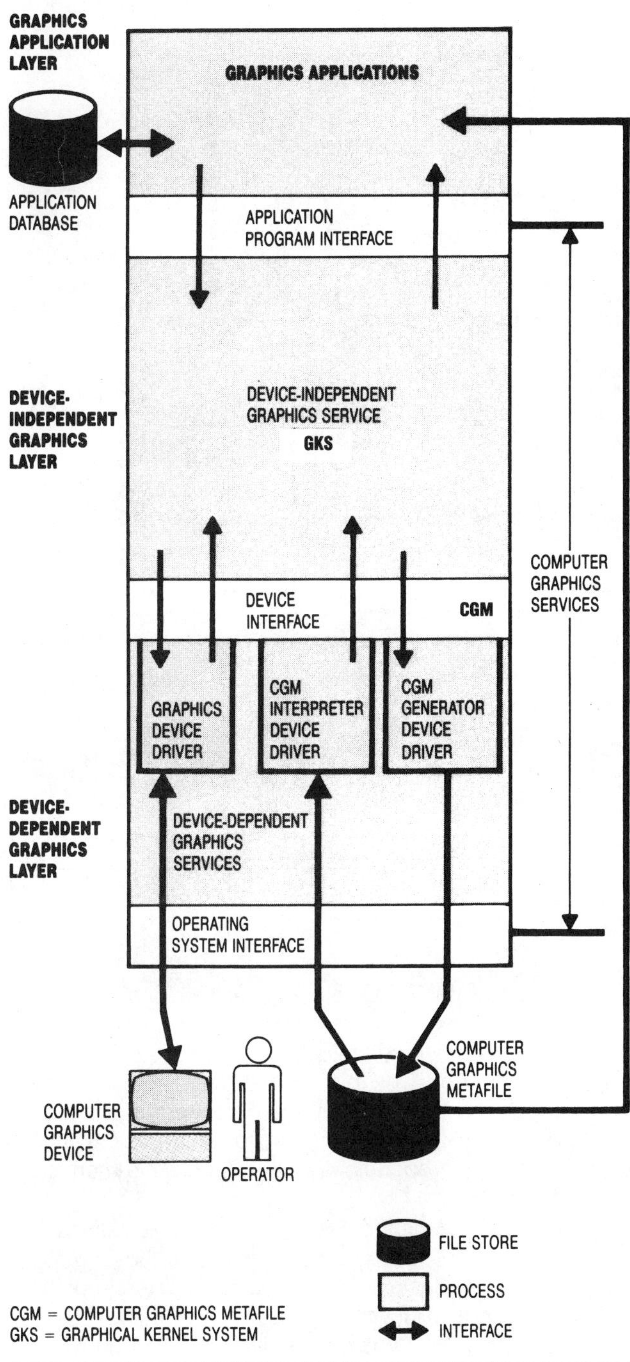

Graphics Metaphile Application Profile (TOP CGM AP).

The TOP 3.0 architecture specifies a TOP Document
Processing Reference Model (Fig. 4). In this model, a
document progresses through three processing phases:
editing, which includes both content and logical structure
editing; layout, which defines a page-oriented, physical-
layout organization; and imaging, which displays a specific
layout structure with associated formatted content and

presentation styles. The TOP DA AP specifies a combination of conformance levels for document architecture,
document profile, and interchange format.

Application layer

Note in Figure 2 that all members of the Standard TOP API
Library (such as CGM, GKS, IGES, and ODA/ODIF) are
architecturally independent of the particular electronic
delivery service invoked. Therefore, within the TOP 3.0
architecture, files created by the API Library members can
be transferred through Data Transfer Services (a TOP term
for application-layer specifications). These services include
Message Handling System (MHS), FTAM, Virtual Terminal,
Directory Services, Network Management, and Association
Control Service Element, as described below.

■ MHS. The TOP 3.0 MHS AP is based upon CCITT Recommendation X.400 (Red Book, 1984), the X.400 Implementers' Guide, and the NBS Implementation Agreements for OSI Protocols, which came out of the NBS
Implementers' Workshops. The primary objectives of
X.400-series MHS is to enable messages of any content to
be transparently encapsulated within a standard envelope
for subsequent delivery to an electronic mail destination.
These messages, which can include text, graphics, facsimile, voice, and other data types, may be transferred
within and among public and private networks.

TOP 3.0 endorses simple lines of ASCII text as the MHS
envelope contents, in conformance with the NBS Implementation Agreements. TOP will likely accommodate
future editions of the NBS implementation agreements,
including binary, facsimile, and other document types.
Also, TOP working groups have determined that there is a
requirement to carry other data interchange formats, such
as ODA, CGM, and IGES.

The TOP 3.0 MHS AP specifies the use of Private Management Domain (PRMD)-to-PRMD communications to
connect proprietary mail systems. PRMDs are defined as
privately owned and operated Message Handling Systems
grouped together for purposes of common administration.
Figure 5 shows that a given Message Transfer Agent (MTA)
may support one or more User Agents (UAs) on behalf of
users. Moreover, MTAs can communicate directly within
the same PRMD and between different PRMDs.

Vendor implementations that support PRMD-to-PRMD
services accessed by the TOP profile provide two X.400-
defined protocols: P1 Message Transfer Protocol (X.411)
for exchanges between MTA entities, and P2 Interpersonal
Messaging Protocol (X.420) for exchanges between UA
entities. While direct PRMD-to-PRMD connections support
the exchange of messages without the need for an Administrative Management Domain (ADMD, a registered
public provider of X.400-based Message Handling Services), the TOP MHS AP also specifies support for message interfaces from PRMD to ADMD and from ADMD
to ADMD.

In general, a product that supports the TOP MHS AP can
connect in an MHS messaging environment to any other
vendor's product as long as they both define gateways
conforming to the TOP MHS Application Profile. Although

4. Document processing. *The TOP Document Architecture Application Profile supports the interchange of revisable- or formatted-form compound documents using the model shown. In this model, a document progresses through editing, layout, and imaging stages on its way to final printout or display.*

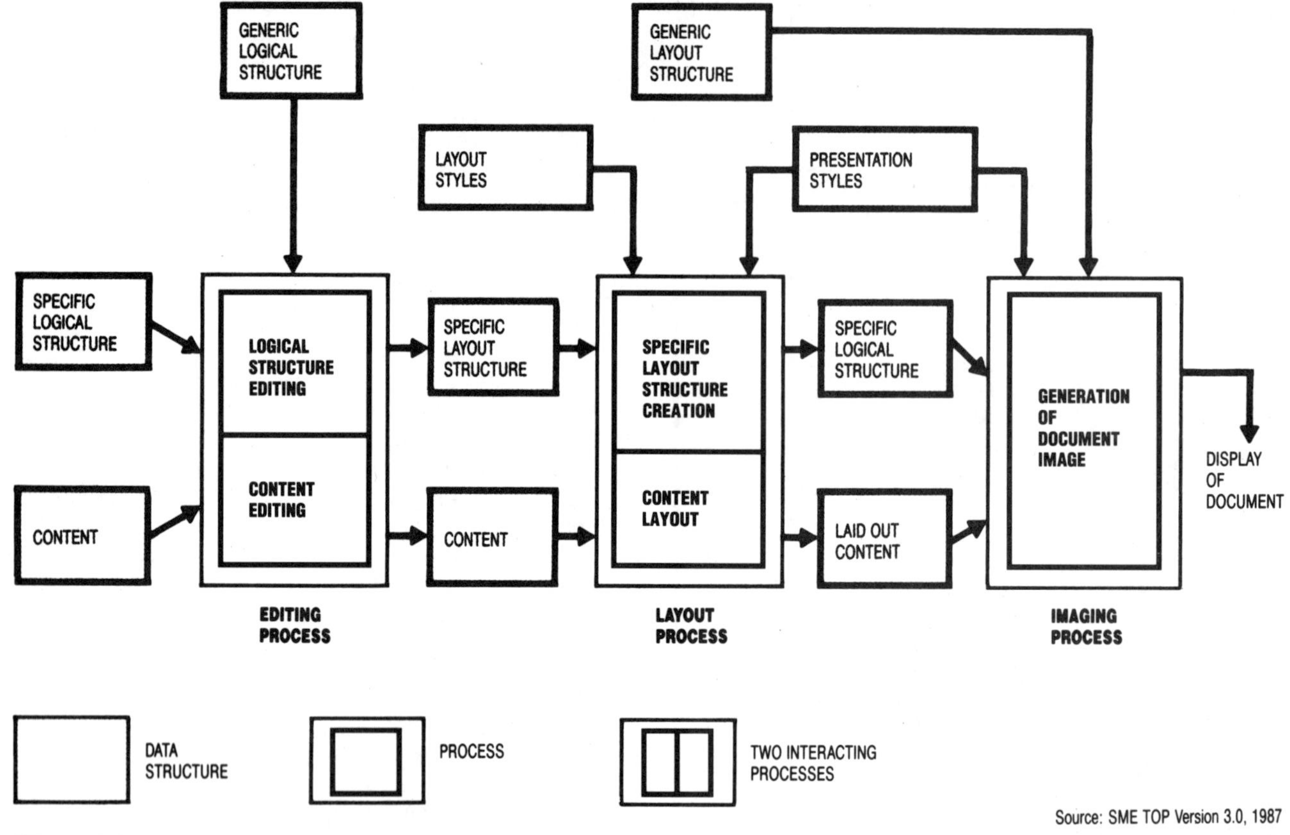

the AP conforms to CCITT X.400-1984, that CCITT recommendation uses different presentation and session protocols than does the ISO endorsement, Message-Oriented Text Interchange Standard. X.400 1988 Blue Book will align with Abstract Syntax Notation One (ASN.1) and Session Protocol.

At present, TOP 3.0 has no choice but to follow the CCITT's 1984 agreements. Note that PRMD was not specified in the CCITT 1984 recommendations and, furthermore, that X.400 1984 specifies Transport Class 0. By contrast, Class 4 was selected by NBS and Government OSI Profile for PRMD to provide a highly reliable transport service over a connectionless internet protocol.

■ FTAM. The TOP FTAM AP specifies a set of services to transfer information between application processes and filestores (which consist of file-storage and file-service mechanisms). It also supports the ability to create, delete, and transfer entire binary or text files. Moreover, it enables a process to read or change file attributes, erase file contents, locate specific records, and read or write file records.

The ISO FTAM specifications are concerned with the manipulation of identifiable bodies of information that can be treated as files and stored within open systems or passed between OSI application processes. The FTAM File

Service definitions and protocol specifications are expressed in the context of a virtual filestore (a file-mapping structure commonly referred to by open systems), as distinguished from any real, local filestore definitions that exist within real end systems. Each real end system that behaves as an open system must map the virtual filestore descriptions and operations into real, local file-management functions.

The ISO FTAM protocol is asymmetrical. It defines two types of peer entities: an initiator, which requests most activities as the master of an interaction, and a responder, which responds to initiator requests as slave. The protocol is connection- and transaction-oriented in that an initiator must establish a connection with a responder prior to request/response flows. Figure 6 illustrates the FTAM initiator/responder relationship between two TOP end systems.

The TOP FTAM AP includes nine document types. These identify file characteristics such as structure, syntax, content semantics, and permissible operations.

Whereas FTAM defines a virtual filestore used to describe the FTAM services and the mapping of these services onto the local filestore, neither the FTAM standard nor the NBS implementation agreements specify an interface to FTAM services. Note in Figure 2 that a TOP 3.0

FTAM interface is specified, shown above Layer 7. This programming interface is intended to provide application program portability.

■ The TOP Virtual Terminal (VT) Application Profile, based on the ISO VT-Basic Class, maps a specific device into a canonical form called a virtual terminal and then back into the device format expected by the application. It supports the interactive transfer and manipulation of graphic elements. TOP VT AP provides an object-based, remote, interactive, connection-based terminal service between heterogeneous TOP end systems. These are shown in Figure 7 as local terminal and remote host environments.

The TOP VT service uses an object-based model. In it, the virtual terminal is represented by an object that has a structure characterized as a 1-, 2-, or 3-dimensional array residing in the Application Entity (AE, such as instances of FTAM, VT, Network Management, or Directory Services).

Each array element may contain a single character. Attributes are defined for each element, such as color of screen foreground/background, emphasis, character repertoire, and font. The TOP VT service is interactive, and users can read or update the VT object by simulating the capabilities of a character-mode terminal.

■ TOP Directory Services support high-level references to network objects and provide information to users about the systems and services that can be invoked on a network. The relationship between directory references and directory objects is based on directory entries, which consist of sets of attributes.

The directory environment includes a collection of directory entry information in the form of a directory information base (DIB). The DIB can be accessed remotely through a directory service AP known as a Directory Service Agent (DSA). Each user application interacts with a DSA through

---

5. Message handling. *The TOP MHS Application Profile enables interconnection of proprietary mail systems that are privately owned and operated for purposes of common* *administration under private management domains. These domains support the exchange of messages without the need for an administrative management domain.*

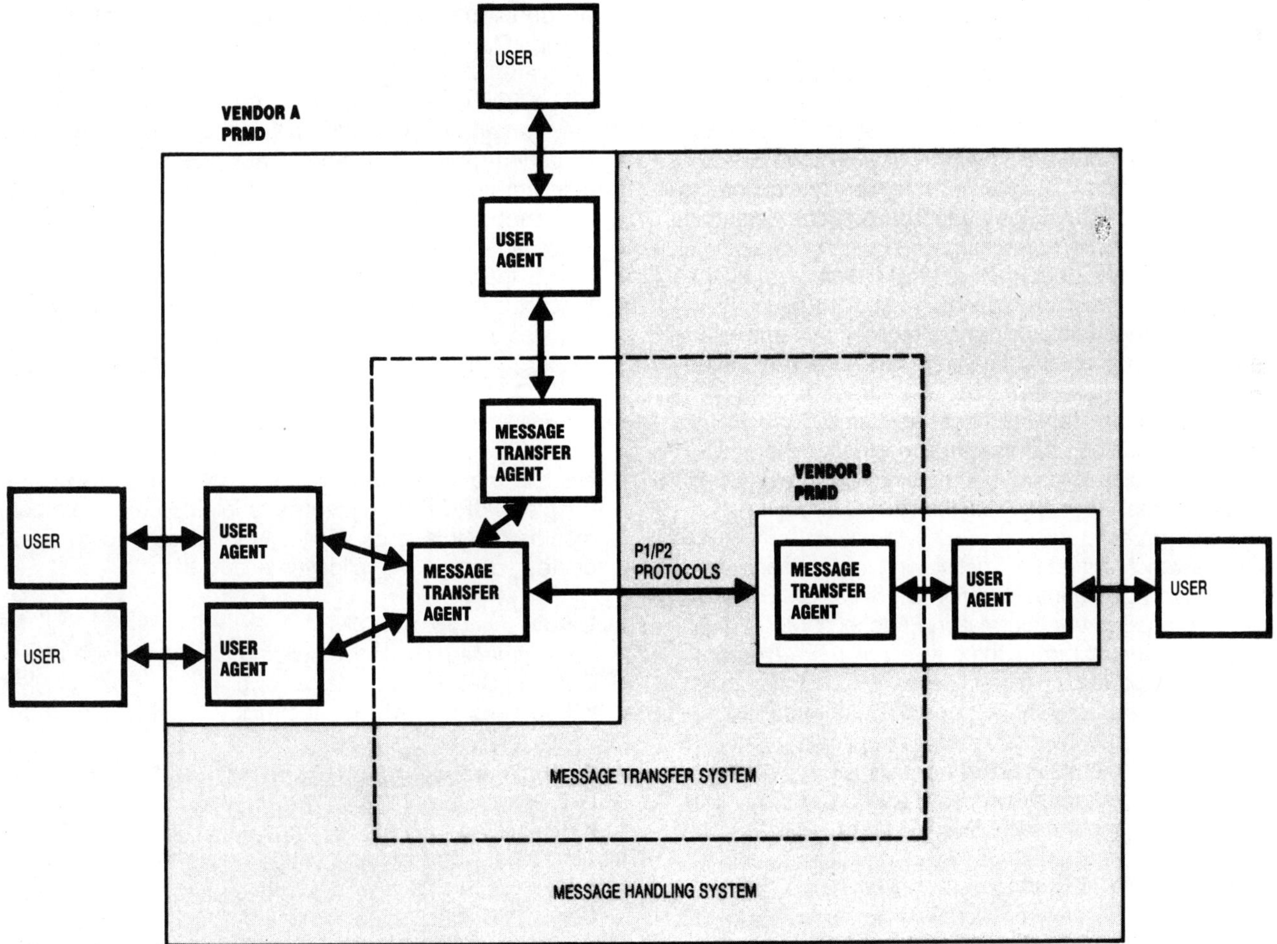

P1 = MESSAGE TRANSFER PROTOCOL (X.411)
P2 = INTERPERSONAL MESSAGING PROTOCOL (X.420)
PRMD = PRIVATE MANAGEMENT DOMAIN

Source: SME TOP Version 3.0, 1987

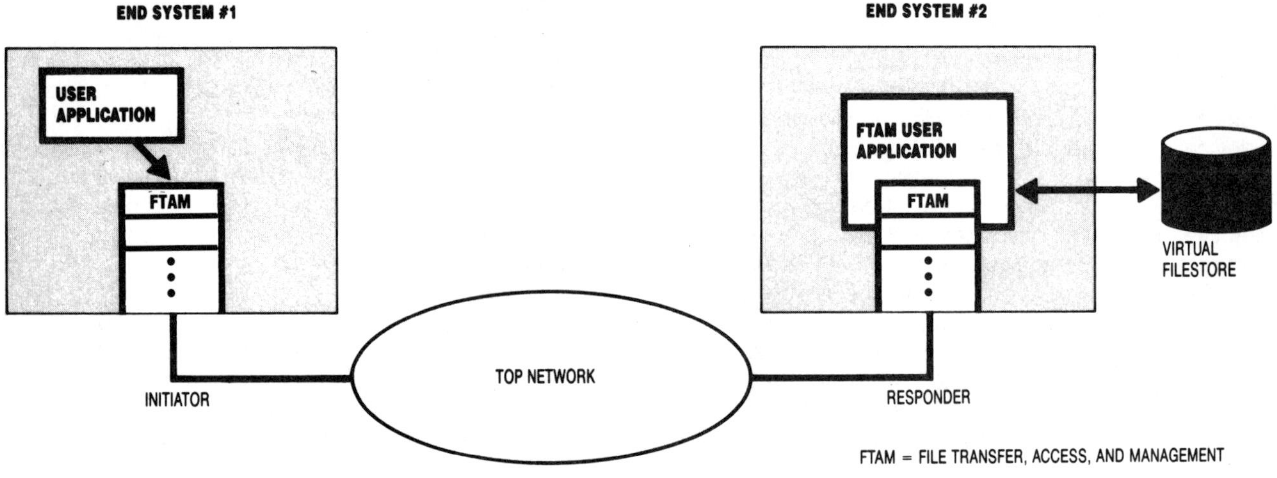

6. Initiator/responder. *TOP's File Transfer, Access, and Management Application Profile uses an asymmetrical protocol, which defines two types of peer entities. The FTAM initiator requests transactions and the responder reacts to these requests. This protocol is connection- and transaction-oriented.*

a Directory User Agent (DUA) local to the application.

The ISO directory standards specify two principal directory protocols. Directory Access Protocol defines the exchange of requests and responses between a DUA and a DSA. Directory Systems Protocol defines the exchange of requests and responses directly between two DSAs.

The DIB internally classifies directory objects according to a Directory Information Tree that exploits the hierarchical relationship commonly found among objects (for example, a person works for a department that is part of an enterprise that is headquartered in a specific country).

There are three basic directory services. A name-to-attribute binding, analogous to a "white pages" directory, binds a name to a related piece of information. A name-to-list-of-names binding, analogous to a distribution list, is used in applications such as electronic mail and routing tables. Finally, an attribute-to-set-of-names binding, analogous to a "yellow pages" directory, lists the names of objects having a given attribute.

■ TOP Network Management defines information services, Common Management Information Services (CMIS), and Common Management Information Protocol (CMIP). The overall framework supports three levels of TOP resource management: protocol management, which manages all resources associated within a specific TOP protocol layer; layer management, which provides insight into layer conditions (for example, such states as waiting or transmitting); and system management, which is supported by System Management Application Entities (SMAEs).

TOP CMIS services enable SMAEs to intercommunicate and provide TOP/OSI protocol-stack state status and management, including configuration, performance, and fault management. Configuration management involves addition, deletion, and modification of network resources. Performance management includes network measurement, analysis and adjustment procedures to determine congestion, message delay, service reliability, routing throughput, bridge throughput, and link utilization. Fault management includes fault detection, notification, isolation, and recovery.

The TOP CMIP provides the request/response service between an initiator SMAE in one TOP end system and a responder SMAE in another, which is executing management activities on behalf of the initiator SMAE. The protocol also supports an unsolicited event-reporting service between an event-intiator SMAE and a collector (responder) SMAE, the one responsible for event logging.

■ Association Control Service Element (ACSE) provides services to such application contexts as ISO FTAM and Virtual Terminal Services, TOP Network Management, ISO/CCITT Directory Services, and PRIVATE (a default value). Note in Figure 2 that ACSE is not required for MHS.

The TOP ACSE protocol provides standard services for establishing and terminating application associations. It enables TOP/OSI applications to intercommunicate common parameters, such as titles, addresses, and application context, during an application association.

Below the top of TOP

To summarize, the major building blocks provided by TOP's upper layers are as follows:

■ Electronic mail, which uses MHS services from GKS, CGM, IGES, or ODA/ODIF APIs.

■ Remote file access, which uses FTAM services from GKS, CGM, IGES, or ODA/ODIF APIs.

■ Remote terminal access, which makes use of the Virtual Terminal ACSE-ASN.1-Session Protocol stack.

■ Network directory, which makes use of the Directory Services ACSE-ASN.1-Session Protocol stack.

■ Network management, which is enabled through the Network Management ACSE-ASN.1-Session Protocol stack.

At the layers beneath the application layer, TOP 3.0 specifies OSI protocols, just as it does at the application

468

layer. Generally, Layer 1 through Layer 6 specifications are at the International Standards stage, with the exception of some network and data-link protocols, which are still draft international standards. The layers are as follows:

■ Presentation layer. The TOP ACSE protocol makes use of the Kernel functional unit (defined below) of the Presentation Service to pass information, in the form of ACSE Application Protocol Data Units (APDUs), between peer AEs. Note in Figure 2 that the TOP 3.0 architecture uses Abstract Syntax Notation One (ASN.1) as the presentation-layer facility to specify a notation for abstract syntax definition.

TOP 3.0 selects ASN.1 because the nature of user-data parameters within the presentation layer can change. That is, the application layer may require that the presentation layer carry the value of complex data types, including character strings from a variety of character sets. These values reside within multiple character sets.

ASN.1 is a generic character notation that negotiates which transfer syntaxes are to be used. Data types referenced with ASN.1 include, for example, Boolean, integer, bit string, octet string, null, sequence, tagged, any, and character string. Note also, in Figure 2, that the set of ASN.1 documents is technically aligned with the relevant parts of CCITT Recommendation X.409 (Blue Book, 1988), shown as the MHS Presentation Transfer Syntax for Layer 7 MHS.

■ Session layer. The purpose of the session layer is to provide dialogue-management services to the presentation and application layers and, in so doing, to provide peer-session users with the means to exchange data in an organized and synchronized way. The TOP 3.0 session agreements support the use of the ISO Basic Connection Oriented Session Service and Session Protocol. These agreements define the session layer into three phases, the session-connection-establishment, data-transfer, and session-connection-release phases.

TOP Session Services for FTAM are enabled through the use of two types of functional units. Kernel functional units support the basic session services required to establish a session connection, transfer normal data, and release the connection. The other type, the duplex functional unit, supports two-way session transfer services. In addition, VT and MHS use the Basic Activity Subset and the Basic Synchronized Subset of the ISO Session Protocol.

■ Transport layer. TOP 3.0 requires ISO Transport Class 4 to support the connection-oriented transport service, which provides flow control and the ability to multiplex user transmissions to the network. The ISO Transport Class 4 connection-oriented transport service is required within the TOP architecture because Connectionless Network Service is selected at Layer 3.

■ Network layer. The network layer, in essence, makes transparent to the transport layer the way in which supporting communications resources are utilized to accomplish data transfer. A primary TOP 3.0 network-layer requirement is to specify protocols that support TOP end systems attached to LANs. The TOP 3.0 LANs, specified in Layers 1 and 2, are carrier-sense multiple access/collision detection (CSMA/CD), token-passing ring, and MAP token-passing bus. It is recognized, however, that not all TOP end systems that in an open technical and administrative office environment will be LAN-attached but rather may interface through wide area networks (WANs). To this end, TOP 3.0 additionally provides for the X.25 packet-level protocol at the network layer where TOP end or intermediate systems are connected to packet-switching networks.

TOP 3.0 specifies three network-routing levels: the enterprise portion, which uniquely identifies the highest level group or organization (for example, corporation, governmental agency, or university); the intermediate system (IS)-to-IS portion; and the end system (ES)-to-IS portion. When ES-to-IS routing is provided on LAN subnetworks, TOP 3.0 dictates the use of the ISO ES-IS Exchange Protocol.

■ Data link layer. The OSI data link layer (Layer 2) performs frame formatting, error checking, addressing, and link management to ensure accurate data transmission over links between nodes. The TOP data link layer distinguishes between LAN access, which provides Logical Link Control (LLC) over CSMA/CD, token-passing ring, and token-passing bus LANs, and WAN access, which provides for High-Level Data Link Control (HDLC) and Link Access Procedure-Balanced (LAPB) if the network layer is defined by the X.25 Packet Level Protocol.

The data link layer for LAN use is subdivided into Link Layer Control and Media Access Control. Figure 8 presents the TOP 3.0 model for the data link and physical layers and indicates the Link Layer Control and Media Access Control (MAC) divisions of the data link layer for LANs. The figure also indicates that the LAN Link Layer Control sublayer is specified by IEEE 802.2.

The primary TOP 3.0 LAN is specified by IEEE 802.3 as

Where TOP comes from

TOP 3.0 consists of numerous technical specifications and agreements that derive from the collective work of various TOP Users Group technical subcommittees. Although these subcommittees have specialized in various functional areas, each of them collects, elaborates, and studies technical and administrative office requirements and specifies protocol solutions that satisfy those requirements. In addition, each committee works closely with standards organizations, such as ISO, CCITT, IEEE, and the National Bureau of Standards OSI Implementers' Workshops. All solutions proposed by TOP technical subcommittees are subject to public review and approval before being incorporated into the TOP specification.

One major positive result of that specification is to promote the design and testing of TOP products needed by the significant market segment represented by the TOP Users Group. TOP 3.0 also functions as a procurement template through which users can effectively measure vendors' responses to requests for proposals, quotations, and information. Not least, TOP serves to educate users.

7. *Virtual Terminal.* *The VT Application Profile maps a specific device into a virtual terminal and then back into the format expected by the application.*

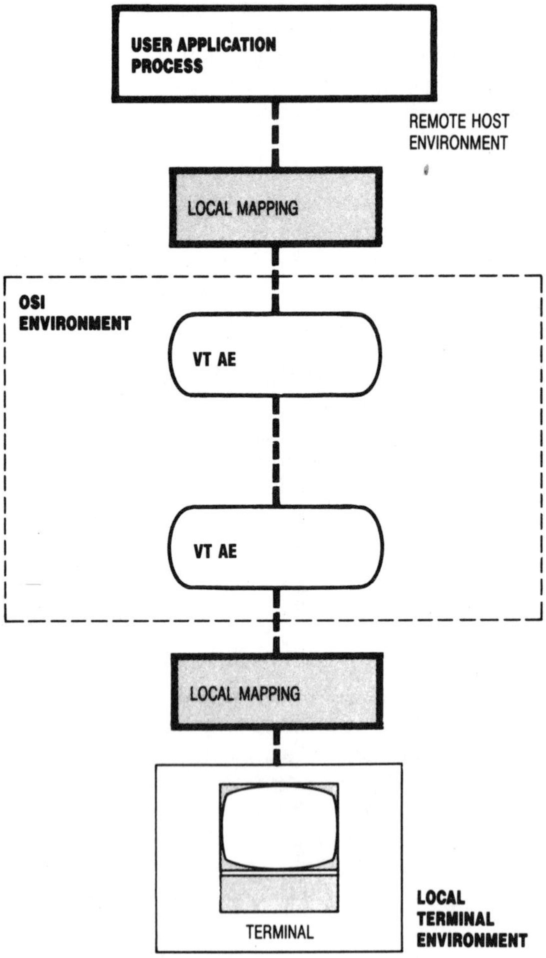

AE = APPLICATION ENTITY
OSI = OPEN SYSTEMS INTERCONNECTION
VT = VIRTUAL TERMINAL

CSMA/CD, which uses a LAN contention access method. CCITT X.25 LAPB (1984 Red Book) specifies access to public switched data networks (PSDNs). However, the IEEE 802.5 ring and IEEE 802.4 bus LANs, both of which use token passing as a deterministic access method, are also named as alternate TOP 3.0 LANs.

The reasoning behind TOP's selection of 802.3 CSMA/CD as the initial MAC sublayer protocol is the ease of migration from Ethernet Version 2.0 LANs to IEEE 802.3 LANs and the fact that a wide base of components already exists for Ethernet LANs. Additionally, CSMA/CD has been shown to be quite effective in handling a broad variety of distributed office applications, including document and graphics interchange. TOP 3.0 also supports the token-passing IEEE 802.5 and 802.4 protocols because the token-passing subnetwork access method provides a reasonably predictable, collision-free allocation of network capacity with stable throughput and response times under varying network loads and utilizations.

■ Physical layer. The primary TOP 3.0 physical-layer protocol is 802.3 baseband CSMA/CD, called 10Base5 (for 10 Mbit/s, baseband, 500 meters per segment), which utilizes the CSMA/CD media access protocol over a shielded coaxial cable. TOP 3.0 selected 10Base5 as its primary physical layer because of the large installed base of 10Base5 cabling from widespread use of Ethernet LANs, because of the graceful migration possible from Ethernet Version 2.0 to 802.3 CSMA/CD (to the extent that the two can coexist on the same cable), and because 10Base5 cable is a proven technology that provides reliable, high-speed data transfer.

One alternate TOP 3.0 physical-layer selection (refer to Figure 8) is 802.3 broadband CSMA/CD (10Broad36), which can link back to 10Base5 and provide multiple-vendor-attachment support within a broadband cable technology using CSMA/CD as the MAC protocol. Another is 802.5 token-passing ring on shielded twisted-pair cable, which links to 10Base5 subnetworks and supports multiple-vendor attachments with a performance-oriented office automation protocol under high sustained network loading conditions. A third is MAP 802.4 token-passing bus on coaxial cable (not recommended as a TOP subnetwork), which links to 10Base5 subnetworks and supports multiple-vendor attachments over both carrier band and broadband options under the MAP Version 3.0 specification. Yet another option is the PSDN permanent-circuit interface specified by CCITT X.21*bis*, which incorporates EIA-232-D, CCITT Recommendation V.35, and EIA-449.

Directions

Graphical Kernel System and Computer Graphics Metafile were the two graphics data interchange standards selected for TOP 3.0. Several graphics standards are under consideration for incorporation into TOP, as follows:

■ Computer Graphics Interface defines an interactive virtual-device interface between the DIGL and the DDGL. Recall that TOP 3.0 specifies the use of the CGM standard to provide 2-D picture interchange between end systems and the use of the GKS standard to provide an API and DIGS for 2-D graphics. The elaboration of CGI within the TOP specification will serve to standardize the API mechanism that enables end-to-end resource and data sharing between heterogeneous graphics applications.

■ Three-dimensional graphical functionality will be addressed by GKS-3D.

■ Whereas IGES 3.0, as described earlier, provides a subset of a full product data-exchange capability, future versions of TOP will likely incorporate the capabilities of PDES/STEP, to be used in conjunction with IGES 3.0. Since not all CAD/CAM setups will generate complete data, and since received product model data will continue to be interpreted by a person either as a display or as a generated plot, it is likely that IGES files will continue to be transferred to maintain data-exchange compatibility between current and anticipated environments.

■ Initial Graphics Exchange Specification 3.0 will eventually

include binary and compressed ASCII file formats.
■ Electronic Design Interchange Format (EDIF) will likely be included to provide for transfer of integrated circuit information.

Another major TOP data interchange direction is referred to as Transaction Processing. The TOP Distributed Transaction Processing Subcommittee is defining a transaction-processing model service and protocol consistent with the efforts of ISO and ANSI. TOP requirements for future incorporation of a transaction-processing protocol are that the protocol must be consistent with the ISO OSI application-layer architecture, must support the processing of subtransactions (transactions that are initiated by other transactions), must use the services of ACSE and Commitment, Concurrency, and Recovery (CCR) primitives in communicating with lower layers, and must support the multiple use and reuse of an application association.

At the data link layer, high-speed protocol standards that use optical fiber backbones, such as the ANSI Fiber Distributed Data Interface (FDDI) and IEEE 802.6 metropolitan area networks, may find their way into the TOP specification. While the FDDI and 802.6 fiber protocols are competing efforts, it is likely either that they will converge or that TOP will select one.

Future physical-layer standards under consideration for incorporation into TOP include IEEE 802.3 1Base5 (1 Mbit/s, baseband, 500 meters per segment), support for token-passing ring (IEEE 802.5) on unshielded twisted-pair wire, protocols that may result from the efforts of the CCITT on Integrated Services Digital Networks, and ANSI FDDI fiber physical interface protocols.

In all these cases, as is true of the existing TOP 3.0 physical-layer protocols such as 802.3, 802.5, and 802.4, IEEE 802.3 CSMA/CD 10Base5 remains the primary TOP subnetwork access protocol. Therefore, all other physical-layer protocols are required to provide internetworking connections back to IEEE 802.3 10Base5.

A near-future release of TOP is expected to consolidate the Transaction Processing service and protocol agreements and to incorporate stabilized text on Directory Services and Network Management. To summarize, the TOP Version 3.0 architecture provides a comprehensive set of application services to enable standardized data interchange and communications over a wide range of LAN and WAN subnetwork environments. It thereby provides a funtionally cost-effective alternative to the proliferation of proprietary networking environments. For these reasons, TOP 3.0 represents a significant step toward fulfilling the accomplishment of the user technical and administrative distributed office user business case. ■

Thomas J. Routt was recently named a contributing editor to Data Communications *and is president of Network Systems Consulting, a firm that provides worldwide network architecture consulting to* Fortune *1,000 corporations concerned with migration to OSI and SNA. Previously, he was manager of Boeing Network Architecture for Boeing Computer Services Company. In this capacity, he managed global network planning, design, and implementation for the Boeing Company. Routt holds an M. B. A.*

in information systems from Southern Illinois University and a B. S. in environmental science from Western Washington University.

The author wishes to acknowledge the input of Laurie Bride, Boeing's manager of network architecture and program manager of the Boeing TOP program, and of her staff. Their organizational assistance, interface coordination to TOP users and vendors, and review of the manuscript proved invaluable to this effort.

Selected documents that form the basis of and are related to TOP 3.0:

General

TOP: Technical and Office Protocols Specification Version 3.0, Society of Manufacturing Engineers, July 1987.

MAP: Manufacturing Automation Protocol Specification 3.0, Society of Manufacturing Engineers, July 1987.

OSI: ISO 7498, CCITT X.200, Information Processing Systems-Open Systems Interconnection-Basic Reference Model.

Application Program Interfaces

GKS: ISO 7942, Information Processing Systems-Computer Graphics-Graphical Kernel System Functional Description.
—ISO DIS 8651, Information Processing Systems-Computer Graphics-GKS Language Bindings-Part 1: FORTRAN, Part 2: Pascal, Part 3: Ada, Part 4: C.
—ISO DIS 8805, Information Processing Systems-Computer Graphics-GKS for Three Dimensions (GKS-3D) Functional Description.

CGM: ISO 8632, Information Processing Systems-Computer Graphics-Metafile for the Storage and Transfer of Picture Description Information-Part 1: Functional Specification, Part 2: Character Encoding, Part 3: Binary Encoding, Part 4: Clear Text Encoding.

ODA/ODIF: ISO 8613, Information Processing-Text and Office Systems-Office Document Architecture and Interchange Format-Part 1: General Information, Part 2: Document Structures, Part 3: Document Processing Reference Model, Part 4: Document Profile, Part 5: Office Document Interchange Format, Part 6: Computer Graphics Content Architectures, Part 7: Raster Graphics Content Architectures, Part 8: Geometric Graphics Content Architectures.

IGES: ANS Y14.26 M-1987 (Identical to NBSIR 86-3359, April 1986), Digital Representation for the Communication of Product Definition Data (V3.0).

Application-layer specifications

MHS (Message Handling Systems, Red Book, 1984): CCITT X.400 : System Model-Service Elements.
—CCITT X.401: Basic Service Elements and Optional User Facilities.
—CCITT X.408: Encoded Information Type Conversion Rules.
—CCITT X.409: Presentation Transfer Syntax

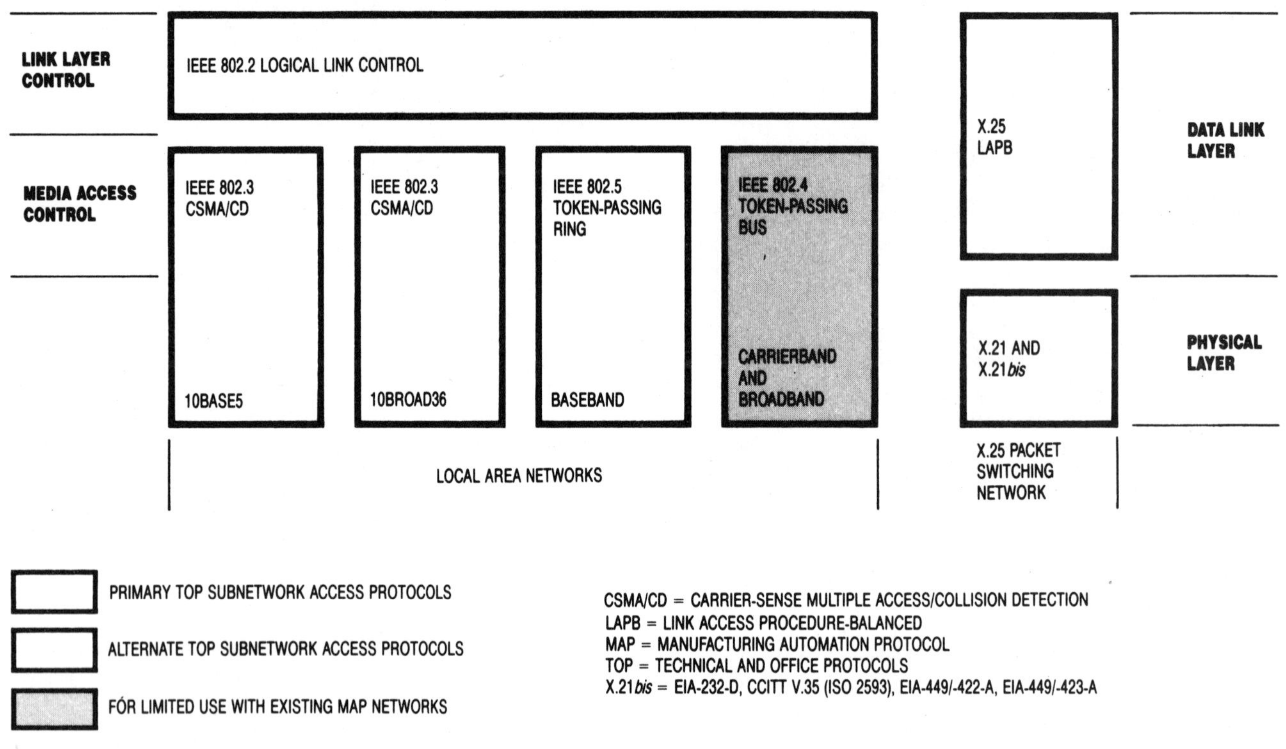

Notation.

—CCITT X.410: Remote Operations and Reliable Transfer Server.

—CCITT X.411: Message Transfer Layer.

—CCITT X.420: Interpersonal Messaging User Agent Layer.

FTAM: ISO 8571, FTAM-Part 1: General Introduction, Part 2: The Virtual Filestore, Part 3: The File Service Definition, Part 4: The File Protocol Specification.

VT: ISO 9040, Information Processing Systems-Open Systems Interconnection-Virtual Terminal Service-Basic Class.

—ISO 9041, Information Processing Systems-Open Systems Interconnection-Virtual Terminal Protocol-Basic Class.

Directory: ISO DIS 9594, Information Processing Systems-Open Systems Interconnection-The Directory, Parts 1-8; the eight ISO Directory Services sections include: (1) Concepts and services, (2) Information framework, (3) Access and system services definition, (4) Procedures for distributed operation, (5) Access and system protocols, (6) Selected attribute types, (7) Selected object classes, and (8) Authentication framework (related to security).

Network Management: ISO DP 9595, Management Information Service Definition, Part 1: Overview, Part 2: Common Management Information Service (CMIS) Definition.

—ISO DP 9596, Management Information Protocol Specification, Part 1: Overview, Part 2: Common Management Information Protocol (CMIP).

ASCE: ISO 8649/2, Information Processing Systems-Open Systems Interconnection-Service Definition for Common Application Service Elements-Part 2: Association Control.

—ISO 8650/2, Information Processing Systems-Open Systems Interconnection-Protocol Specification for Common Application Service Elements-Part 2: Association Control.

Sub-application layers

ASN.1: ISO DIS 8824, Information Processing Systems-Open Systems Interconnection-Specification of Abstract Syntax Notation One.

—ISO DIS 8825, Information Processing Systems-Open Systems Interconnection-Specification of Basic Encoding Rules for Abstract Syntax Notation One.

Presentation: ISO 8822, Information Processing Systems-Open Systems Interconnection-Connection Oriented Presentation Service Definition.

—ISO 8823, Information Processing Systems-Open Systems Interconnection-Connection Oriented Presentation Protocol Definition.

Session: ISO 8326, Information Processing Systems-Open Systems Interconnection-Basic Connection Oriented Session Service Definition.

—ISO 8327, Information Processing Systems-Open Systems Interconnection-Basic Connection Oriented Session Protocol Definition.

Transport: ISO 8072, Information Processing Systems-Open Systems Interconnection-Transport Service Definition.

—ISO 8073, Information Processing Systems-Open Systems Interconnection-Connection Oriented Transport Protocol Specification.

Network: ISO 8473 (Final Text), Information Processing Systems-Data Communications-Protocol for Providing the Connectionless-Mode Network Service.

—ISO DP 9542, Information Processing Systems-Data Communications-End System to Intermediate System Exchange Protocol for Use in Conjunction with ISO 8473.

—ISO 8348 DAD2, Information Processing Systems-Data Communications-Network Service Definition Addendum 2-Covering Network Layer Addressing.

—ISO DIS 8208, Information Processing Systems-X.25 Packet Level Protocol for Data Terminal Equipment.

—CCITT Recommendation X.25 (Red Book, 1984), Interface between Data Terminal Equipment and Data Circuit-Terminating Equipment for Terminals Operating in the Packet Mode and Connected to Public Data Networks by Dedicated Circuit.

Data Link: ISO 8802/2, IEEE 802.2, Local Area Networks-Logical Link Control.

—ISO 8802/3, IEEE 802.3, Local Area Networks-Carrier Sense Multiple Access with Collision Detection (CSMA/CD) Access Method and Physical Layer Specifications.

—ISO 8802/4, IEEE 802.4, Local Area Networks-Token-Passing Bus Access Method and Physical Layer Specification. Options and parameters as per MAP V3.0 Specification, 1987.

—ISO 8802/5, IEEE 802.5, Local Area Networks-Token-Passing Ring Access Method and Physical Layer Specification.

Physical: CCITT Recommendation X.21 (Red Book, 1984), Interface between Data Terminal Equipment and Data Circuit-Terminating Equipment for Synchronous Operation on Public Data Networks.

—CCITT Recommendation X.21*bis* (Red Book, 1984), Use on Public Data Network of Data Terminal Equipment that is Designed for Interfacing to Synchronous V-Series Modems.

—CCITT Recommendation V.35 (Red Book, 1984), Data Transmission at 48 kbit/s Using 60-108 KHz Group Band Circuits.

—EIA-449 (1977), General Purpose 37-Position and 9-Position Interface for Data Terminal Equipment and Data Circuit-Terminating Equipment Employing Serial Binary Data Interchange.

—EIA-232-D (1986), Interface between Data Terminal Equipment and Data Communication Equipment Employing Serial Binary Data Interchange (Supercedes EIA-232-C, 1969).

John McConnell, Infonetics Inc., Santa Clara, Calif.

Stepping off the OSI standards bandwagon

The international standards effort has been too slow in developing security and management services. And certain applications are flawed.

Users have been demanding better standards for some time, and vendors, having finally gotten the message, are now falling over themselves in the rush to embrace the Open Systems Interconnection (OSI) model. OSI is attractive as a framework for discussion, but the model also has some warts. Its costs, operation, and the quality of OSI-based services are rarely discussed.

Responsibility for the development of the OSI model rests with the International Organization for Standardization, or ISO (see "OSI: What is it?"). The model, which is defined in seven layers, sets out a method for developing the interfaces and protocols to make incompatible computers communicate.

The three lowest layers of the model define several fundamental network standards as well as a common, or internetworking, sublayer (see "Making computers communicate"). This sublayer makes it possible for incompatible networks to share data.

At the middle of the model is the transport layer, which is a boundary between the physical and the service environments. It frees the upper layers from concern with communications matters and provides a network-independent level of computer-to-computer communications.

The three highest layers of the model define a set of functions that computers provide to create an interworking environment. Interworking is what enables services, and the processes that support them, to communicate on a peer-to-peer basis (see "Interworking: The next wave in compatibility").

OSI, as a framework for discussion, has taken center stage. It has received the endorsements of many standards bodies, large users, and government agencies. Most major vendors have also come to grips with OSI: Digital Equipment Corp., for example, is migrating its current products toward the standard, while others, such as IBM, are attempting to coexist with it and simultaneously maintain their proprietary products (see "SNA to OSI: IBM building upper-layer gateways," DATA COMMUNICATIONS, p. 120, May 1987).

Although OSI has the limelight, developing an OSI specification takes far too long. The time needed to win approval for a specification and then to develop a product that conforms to it is often measured in years. And OSI specifications are still far from complete. Only the bottom five layers have been formally adopted as ISO standards. The remaining layers are still entwined in a time-consuming approval process.

A lot of work remains to be done in the specification of OSI-based services. Areas such as security and network management have received belated attention from standards committees, and they lag far behind the seven-layer protocols developed for computer communications. These lacks will hamper the creation of truly effective OSI operation. No architecture can claim to be complete without addressing the full range of issues and problems that arise in an open environment of different computers.

The long delays in creating standards engender problems that come back to haunt users in the future. When manufacturers are without standards, they create their own solutions.

Security

Creating a secure open environment assumes that communications can be protected from several threats, including: interception or alteration of traffic; bogus traffic; obtaining the identities of the communicating partners; and interruption of legitimate activities. To protect communications from this class of problem, security functions must be distributed among many computers and in several different layers. The problem is that in an internetworking and interworking environment the large number of subnetworks and computers involved can make security solutions difficult to implement or manage.

For example, at the internetworking level, consideration must be given to the choice of subnetworks with different security provisions for intermediate routing. Internetworking gateways must also be secured so that their behavior cannot be altered by unauthorized parties. Information concerning the security capabilities of all attached subnetworks must be distributed to the gateways so that they can incorporate security in routing decisions. Finally, traffic presented to a gateway must specify the level of security treatment it requires as it is moved across different subnetworks.

The interworking environment must also protect individual computers from attack by remote processes. Individual operating systems must be constructed to supply the necessary security mechanisms and then be integrated into the interworking environment. Protocols and services must be defined so that computers can interact and exchange the necessary information among themselves as well as with special security-management computers.

Other aspects of security involve the protection of the actual security data, such as passwords, encryption keys, and access codes, and the means for altering or distributing that information. If security features are not addressed in a timely manner, many network administrators may adopt solutions that will be incompatible with future OSI standards.

Management

Network management in an OSI environment also has many aspects that cannot be neglected indefinitely. Each network administrator must have a set of basic management options to achieve orderly growth, cost-effective operation, and reliable levels of service.

These options can only be generated with a large complement of tools, distributed to every participating computer. The tools gather and distribute different types of management information. Some tools can be active, changing local operation under remote direction, while others simply report conditions. With these tools, the network administrator can build such network management options as:

■ Performance specifications for components within the OSI environment. Operational information must be collected, processed, and delivered to managers. At this time, performance is such an unknown that even the government group charged with developing OSI procurement policies such as the Government Open System Interconnection Profile (GOSIP) has not defined any criteria for evaluation.

■ A method of determining the costs of various services within an environment. Cost factors include those for communications (attachment, transmission charges, relays, time, and volume) and computer usage (application fees, storage charges, and CPU utilization). This information should be available to applications as they request remote services. Means for distributing this information to all involved parties must also be defined.

■ Directory services that support applications by providing a range of information necessary to the OSI environment. Distributed directory services must also be constructed for interworking environments. Many OSI-based applications assume directory service in their specifications.

■ Analysis control, which provides performance monitoring and reacts to errors in the operating environment. Problem detection, definition, and reconfiguration are required in a stable, robust operation. The design of problem-detection and -definition procedures must encompass methods for remote execution. Once a problem has been defined, reconfiguration procedures can be used to isolate the malfunction from the operational environment.

■ Registration options maintain environment-wide names and titles. Application processes, protocols, and objects should be members of the registry and be included to support future directory services.

■ Timing and synchronization-service options supply environment-wide time references for all open systems. These services can be used for security, management, and control of time-critical processes.

The basic reference model defines a limited number of management entities at each layer that interact with local and remote management processes. Additional protocols as well as layer-specific functions must be defined and implemented so that management options can be incorporated into the basic structure of an interworking architecture. Addenda Two and Three to the basic OSI reference standard (ISO 7498) begin to address these issues. Agreement on the addenda may be reached late this year, with products appearing thereafter. For the immediate future, though, users are on their own.

Applications

The ultimate aim of users and of OSI itself is the same: to have applications capable of interworking with their counterparts on different computers. Using a seven-layer protocol stack is just a means to an end, although it has received most of the attention so far.

Making computers communicate

Internetworking delivers data between computers attached to different networks. Each network can be chosen to satisfy local needs without restricting future access to other networks and computers. Each autonomous network becomes a subnetwork in an internetwork environment. This makes it possible for local area networks (LANs), metropolitan area networks (MANs), and wide area networks (WANs) to be combined into a single internetworked environment.

Many separate technologies and products are being developed to exploit specialized areas of networking. For example, LANs supply multimegabit exchanges between computers within a small area. In contrast, lower-speed (56-kbit/s) WANs can span a nation or the globe. Specialized technologies such as optical fiber or satellite links can be used to advantage in different situations.

Organizations are discovering the advantages of internetworking. The push to internetworking is fueled by the following factors:

■ The business climate demands internetworking. Many companies, divisions, and groups are being merged, spun off, and grouped into different operational configurations. The new business units often find a set of incompatible networks within a single organization. Overall management and operations now demand that many types of operating units interact quickly.

■ Network-based utilities are growing; many offer a sophisticated range of services, such as stock analysis or specialized database applications. Many organizations need these types of services, yet they cannot afford the costs of creating and maintaining their own. Vendors of these services wish to protect their proprietary products and, at the same time, maximize the number of potential customers. Access through internetworking is attractive to both the users and vendors of such services.

■ Some groups have chosen specialized networking applications, equipment, or technologies that suit their needs. Internetworking must be achieved in ways that respect and protect the specialized interests of the participants. Internetworking will be resisted if it compromises locally optimized operations. Forcing local adaptation leads to a lowest-common-denominator solution, which weakens all participants.

■ Incorporating different technologies allows organizations to extend the life of older equipment while phasing in newer products. Groups can take advantage of future technology advances if the internetworking services is well constructed.

■ Rapidly increasing communications loads are also forcing organizations to investigate different architectures based on internetworking. Large volumes are forcing many network operations to partition traffic so that it can be managed and the costs controlled.

Interworking: The next wave in compatibility

As the number of computers used in business grows, there is an increasing need to share information. To accomplish this end, a means must be developed that facilitates the sharing of data and programs. Interoperation, or interworking, requires an environment that supports process-to-process communications among a set of heterogeneous computers (see figure).

The interworking environment consists of software in each computer as well as an infrastructure of services reached through communications facilities. These facilities can be a single network or an internetworked set of subnetworks.

Interworking enables applications on different computers to perform their tasks without adjusting for specific architectures, operating system services, data-management facilities, or other system-specific limitations. Interworking provides a consistent way for a local process to carry out a set of tasks with partners on a number of different computers.

Many organizations are saddled with incompatible computers and operating systems. Moreover, the number of special-purpose computers is growing as machines designed for artificial intelligence, database management, parallel processing, vector processing, and graphics win acceptance in the marketplace. Many users in organizations that need such special-purpose computers must find a way to spread the cost of special-purpose machines across a large user base. Internetworking provides the basic mechanism to join a special-purpose computer to any network.

An interworking environment is different from most of the single-vendor network products currently available.

Interworking is more difficult than internetworking, since it involves uniting incompatible operating systems. In contrast, a great deal of internetworking occurs outside the computer, particularly within the gateways. The major characteristics of an interworking environment are as follows:

- The interworking environment is separated from communications details. The means of exchanging data between two computers is not of concern at the interworking level; the internetworking environment deals with the delivery details.
- Interworking exhibits distributed control and communications. Computers deal with each other directly rather than communicating through a centralized control point. Patterns of interaction between computers can change rapidly.
- An infrastructure of services supports interworking. For example, the amount of information in an interworking environment may grow very quickly and overwhelm the resources of many computers. Maintaining and updating information in each computer is a large task. Rather than replicate information within each computer, dedicated special-purpose computers maintain the information and distribute it through the network as needed. Computers can keep frequently used information locally and ask a remote service to supply the remainder.
- The scale of the interworking environment must be considered, especially given the number of computers that can become involved. Solutions that are completely appropriate for a few dozen computers may fail badly in the greatly expanded context of interworking. A static environment with a small number of computers could afford

The current thrust of the OSI effort is to define standards for File Transfer, Access, and Management (FTAM), Job Transfer and Manipulation (JTM), Virtual Terminal, Transaction Processing, and Document Interchange. Work on the FTAM specifications has received the most attention, and it has made the fastest progress.

Although an extensive set of services has been defined for FTAM, the initial commercial products will only supply a subset of what is envisioned for the standard. Most products, including FTAM, are expected to unfold in phases over several years. This state of affairs extends to other applications as well.

The delay in rolling out standard products stems from the fact that FTAM and other specifications have a plethora of parameters and features. The diversity permitted under the specification causes interoperability problems among products from different vendors.

The National Bureau of Standards has been a leader in bringing many vendors together to define implementation agreements that specify the features and options of OSI products at each phase of development. Documents describing these agreements are available from the NBS. The NBS effort attempts to increase the likelihood of interoperation between different vendors; the agreements it is based upon are not enforceable.

Many OSI specifications have avoided difficult issues such as network management simply by ignoring them. When the specification does not contain the information necessary to implement an application feature, manufacturers invent their own. With the lack of standardized application support, vendors are free to announce OSI products that really can interoperate only with their own products. Many organizations that have many types of computers are becoming more wary of such "standards."

Interworking applications are a new territory for most designers, and the initial implementations of applications may not be very efficient. As a point of reference, consider the amount of time and effort required to create efficient applications on a single computer, not to mention operation across a variety of networks and computers. Designing with old, centralized assumptions can lead to poor performance and higher costs in this new environment. Many of the important design constraints and approaches will be discovered through painful operational experience, as always. Later generations of each application will incorporate the learning obtained from their predecessors.

to keep a copy of all information in each computer. When the scale moves to thousands of computers and networks, different constraints operate to determine a strategy.

■ The range of resources available in an interworking environment can vary greatly. Each partner's capability and responsibility are defined by the application designer rather than by predefined rules.

■ Virtual resources are used in an interworking environment. When considering heterogeneous hardware and operating systems, the concepts of a file, process, terminal, or other element cannot be tied to any particular implementation. Interworking services must supply a common representation of these types of objects that can be defined and manipulated consistently. Local resources must also be available to transform the virtual resource into an actual representation that can be used by a local process.

■ Interworking boils down to complexity and cost. Different computers have very different operating systems, command languages, services, and data formats. These should be made as transparent as possible. The interworking environment handles these details on behalf of the user processes. The complexity of interworking requires substantial resources and development time.

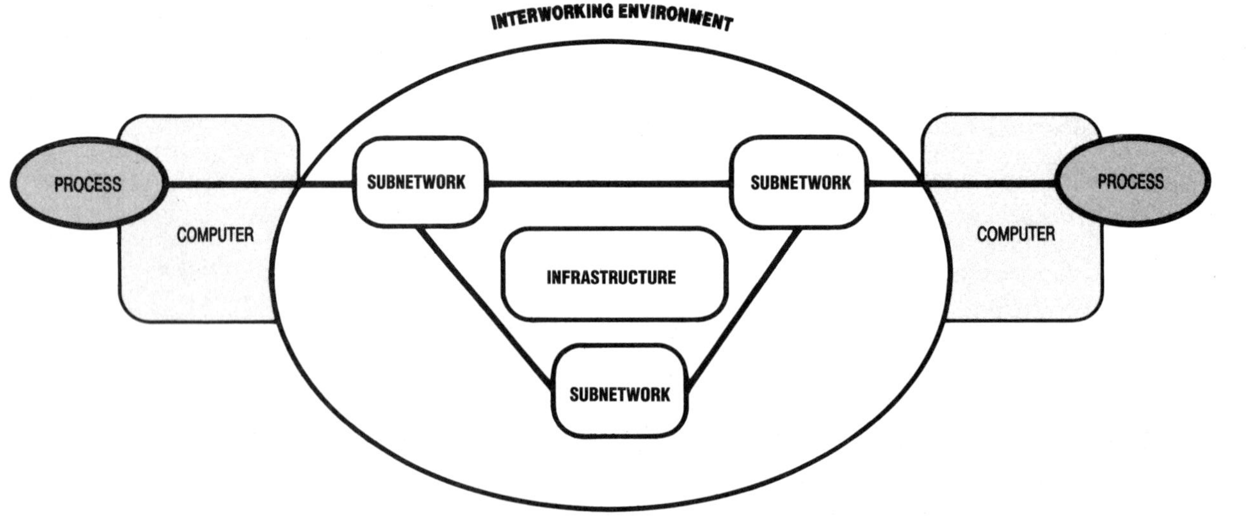

Each OSI layer has at least two specifications: one for the protocol and another for the services provided by that protocol. The protocols have been described in great detail, with messages formatted to the bit level and procedures based upon finite state machine operations. On the other hand, service specifications for each layer have been left at a high level of abstraction. Service definitions have been left at the level of a primitive or a basic unit of service.

The interfaces

The set of primitives used at each interface is defined along with the required and optional parameters. However, there are no definitions of structure, encoding rules, or any other details. There are also no details concerning the mechanisms used to exchange primitives across a layer interface. Defining the details of primitives and their exchange is a delicate area since the OSI services are intimately tied to specific conventions of local operating systems. There may be no common specifications appropriate to the variety of operating systems that may be encountered.

This lack of standard interface definition is causing problems. Proprietary interfaces are being built by vendors that bundle applications into their own seven-layer products. Users become more dependent on the initial vendor when they try to modify another product to use with the proprietary seven-layer product. In the absence of a standard interface, vendors have managed to retain some of the advantages of proprietary products while agreeing to standards. And, as usual, users end up paying more than they expected.

Lack of a standard interface is causing additional problems as software becomes easier to transport to different computers. A user can port a machine-independent OSI application to another machine, only to discover that additional programming is needed because the interface is different.

Several organizations have engaged consultants to define an organization-wide OSI interface for their various computers. A consistent application environment is essential when large numbers of programs must be constructed for an array of computers.

A standard interface should be attractive to users. It should also interest third-party application developers, since it increases the potential market for their products.

Computer vendors would probably be less than enthusiastic about it, since they desire any advantage they can gain while providing open products.

Technical weaknesses

The OSI effort is also hampered by technical weaknesses in the specifications. Some of this should be expected, given that the standards committees are composed of human beings. One aspect of the weakness of design-by-committee is the time involved. Many OSI standards have taken years to develop and refine while the technology and users race ahead. Committees also have constituents with very different interests—government regulators, users, and vendors—so reconciling such different viewpoints into a single specification takes time. On the other hand, committees are inevitable if all parts of the networking community are to be heard and brought into agreement.

Another consideration is that committees dealing with the higher layers—especially above the transport layer—are not necessarily made up of experts in those fields. Few members have had much actual experience building an OSI type of networking environment. Many of the specifications at times reflect old approaches to new issues.

For example, the transport layer suffers from an excess of protocols. Currently, there are five classes of transport protocol with differing degrees of dependence on the underlying internetworking services. The classes are not defined on a strict subset basis, so they are to some extent incompatible with each other. In particular, gateways between such networks must perform transport protocol conversions before relaying the traffic, although the OSI model defines gateways as operating only through the internetwork sublayer. Different transport layers have caused one group, the GOSIP committee, to consider violating other parts of the OSI architecture in order to interconnect computers using different transport-protocol classes.

The initial session-protocol specifications illustrate the application of old, inappropriate thinking to a new environment. The session layer provides different levels of coordinating services for remote processes. The lowest level of coordination is dialogue control. It applies half- or full-duplex operation to the traffic exchanged by a process. Half-duplex operation requires the passing of a data token to indicate a change of direction in the data flow. The next coordination level requires insertion of synchronizing signals in the data stream. These numbered markers can be used to recover from operational errors and to ensure that both partners are at the same point before proceeding. As with half-duplex dialogue, a token must be exchanged to indicate which party is using the synchronization services. The highest level organizes exchanges into activities that can be initiated, suspended, resumed, and terminated.

The problem is that use of the synchronizing services is controlled by ownership of a token. This arrangement creates problems, since both partners cannot mark their data streams at the same time. Application designers are faced with two choices: use full-duplex dialogue for improving the throughput and response while sacrificing simul-

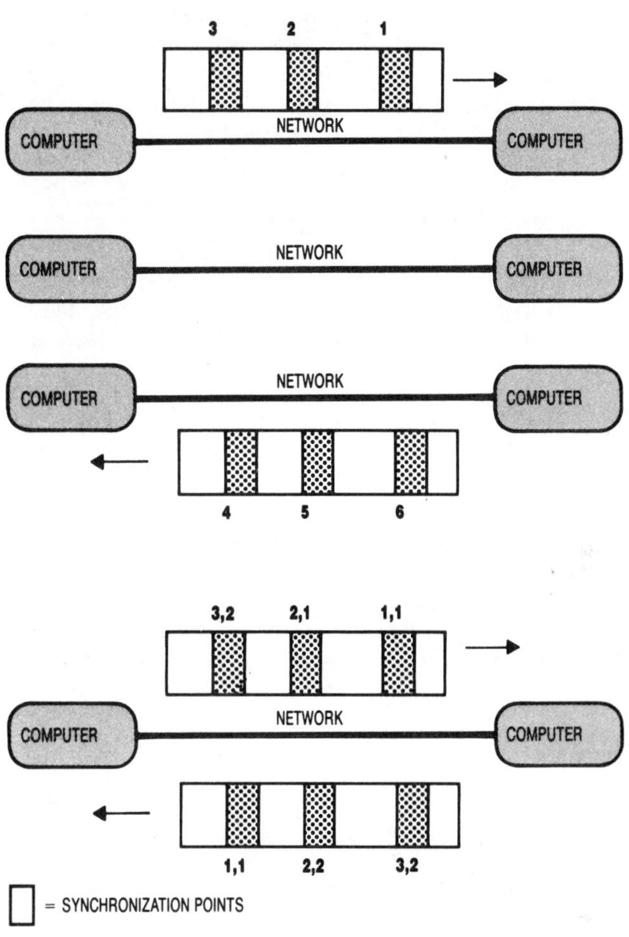

*1. **Session-layer weakness.** When only one computer inserts synchronization points (top), dialogue is reduced. The improved version (bottom) inserts synchronization pairs.*

taneous synchronization, or use of half-duplex dialogue for accurate synchronization while degrading performance (Fig. 1). The first part of the figure shows the current situation, in which the specifications allow only one computer to insert numbered synchronization points in the data stream, reducing dialogue to half duplex. The second part of the figure shows an improvement currently being considered by the committee; both computers use pairs of numbers to mark and report synchronization marks. The two versions are incompatible.

It is ironic that the same committee, which is responsible for both dialogue control and synchronization, chose an approach that causes dialogue control and synchronization to interface so poorly. The half-duplex approach is reminiscent of many older mainframe-to-terminal approaches, but it is inadequate when considering high-performance networks and flexible computers using them.

It is also ironic that the committee did not avail itself of many protocol solutions that have already been demonstrated, such as High-Level Data Link Control (HDLC) and the X.25 Packet Level Protocol. In fact, an addendum similar to HDLC and X.25 is now under study.

Once the addendum is accepted, new products will be offered. Users will pay for the additional development. Moreover, they must be careful when they buy, since the current session protocol and the newer versions will not be completely compatible. This is unfortunate because the delays and expenses are the results of a poor specification-development process. The moral is not to trust a standards committee any more than a vendor. One must evaluate and understand any drawbacks that offset the advantages of adopting a standard.

X.400 Message Handling System

The X.400 Message Handling System is a specification developed by the International Telegraph and Telephone Consultative Committee (CCITT). Application- and presentation-layer services are included with the X.400 specification, while the five lowest layers of the OSI reference model are used to support other services.

As a multipart standard, the X.400 specification defines an application environment for the delivery of many different types of messages between a set of users on different computers. It allows users to construct a message, address it, and specify many different handling and delivery options. Priorities and security levels can be selected, as can certain transformations to accommodate different representations of the messsage contents. Other features allow cross-referencing, distribution of copies, and receipt notifications.

The X.400 standards have some features that weaken them. Some of the weaknesses are consequences of CCITT politics, which is heavily weighted toward European-based government monopolies operating X.25 networks. But some of the problems stem from a misunderstanding of the relationships of the layers to each other.

The session, transport, and network layers defined by X.400 have some undesirable features. First is the exclusive use of X.25 networking facilities. Government monopolies might find it convenient that everyone use X.25, but there are other networking approaches that could supply a standardized X.400 messaging service. For instance, many local area networks (LANs) support comparable messaging facilities without the constraints of X.25 protocol requirements.

Another problem is that only a single class of transport is permitted by the X.400 standard. None of the standard LAN protocols can be used because they are connectionless, and the X.400 transport protocol cannot operate correctly with a datagram transport format.

The session-layer restrictions require half-duplex interchange between X.400 elements. This can increase connection time and reduce throughput when computers are capable of more sophisticated operation. It is ironic that the CCITT mandates half-duplex program communication across a flexible full-duplex X.25 network.

These shortfalls are bound to have a large impact upon many organizations. The X.25 bias and other CCITT-imposed restrictions make it more difficult to incorporate new technology and tend to increase overall communications costs. Moreover, there is no technical reason to forbid the

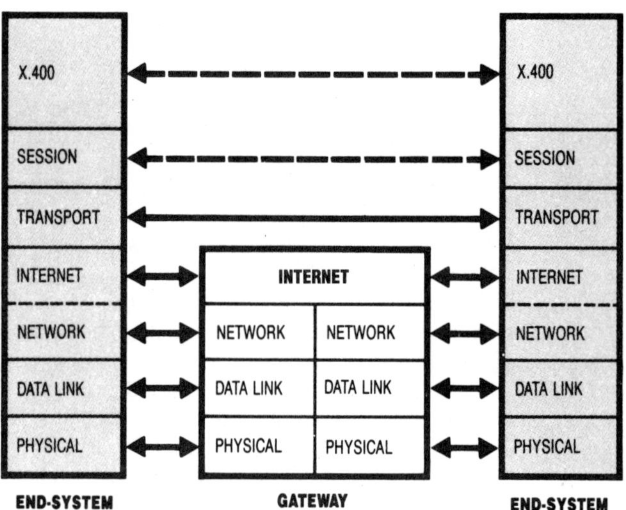

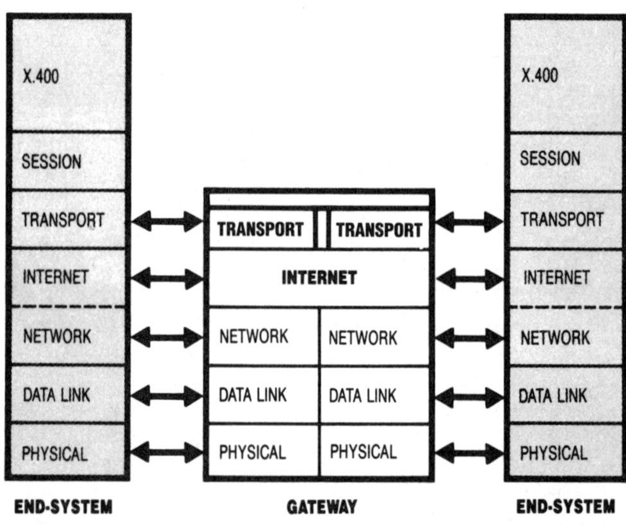

2. Ideal vs. real. X.400 should work with a minimum of overhead according to OSI (top). The CCITT specification (bottom) requires a gateway with an added layer for transport.

use of other session, transport, and network services.

Many organizations, including the U. S. government, are grappling with the use of X.400 in a non-X.25 environment. The GOSIP committee is considering transport protocol or message-relay computers at all interconnection points of heterogeneous networks. This effort and the cost associated with these modifications were caused by the focus of the X.400 committee, which looked only at a relatively static, government-controlled, X.25-based operation.

X.400 should work with a minimum of overhead according to the OSI model shown in the upper portion of Figure 2, but the CCITT specification shown in the lower portion of the figure requires a gateway with an additional layer to handle transport. The added transport requirement increases cost and degrades throughput, but there is a way to reduce the cost of messaging across network boundaries and remain consistent with the OSI model. The Class 4 transport protocol allows any set of subnetworks to be used and makes no distinctions between X.25 and other networks. There is no technical reason why the Class 4 transport protocol cannot be used with an X.25 network. The latest edition of the NBS Implementer's Agreement—which has been signed by vendors and users working together to build OSI-compliant networks—allows a choice of Class 4 with X.400.

There are other portions of the X.400 specifications that are creating problems for implementers and users. The issue of directories of users, mailboxes, distribution lists, and other types of directories have so far been ignored by the committee. This puts the burden on network suppliers to devise their own directory services, or it leaves it to users to devise some means of specifying the information. When different X.400 products are interconnected, the directory services will probably not be compatible with each other, leading to another interoperation problem and additional costs.

The 'all-or-nothing' approach

The OSI model requires that all layers be traversed when communicating with an application or another computer. This creates some problems. Since many operating systems implement the higher layers as separately scheduled processes, moving through each layer takes overhead to manage the internal scheduling and deactivation of internal processes.

These high-layer calls do not necessarily add functionality. For example, the Class 0 transport protocol depends on the underlying networking facilities for its functions. It simply reports any problem to the transport user. It performs no detection and recovery services and does not contribute directly to the transport functions defined in the specification. These extra steps consume computer resources and network connect time, but the added traffic volume has no purpose except to keep the proper number of layers.

There has been discussion of defining a "null" layer, although no specifics have been offered. Designers of an OSI environment should be allowed to choose those layers that are needed, since layers are added only when they increase the functionality of the services for a specific application.

Some layers are redundant for many simple tasks. For example, many applications are not structured according to OSI principles. They may handle session, presentation, and application functions in their own fashion, usually by building them into the application. It is possible that an application may need only a shared transport layer for accurate communication. Mandating the additional layer adds to the communications load as well as the processing load in each computer for no functional reason.

Figure 3 illustrates a more selective use of OSI layers. A shared Class 4 transport protocol supplies a reliable delivery service across all types of networks; the remaining layers are only used as needed. Old applications could be converted in stages as new OSI layers are defined and installed. Applications that are not to be converted could coexist with full OSI operations and avail themselves of whichever common services are appropriate.

Clever use of OSI can reduce costs and improve performance by allowing application designers to select only the layers that add functionality to their operations. A simple extension of the OSI architecture is all that is needed to allow selective layering and maintain the current approach as well. As Figure 2 shows, one possibility is for all computers to share a common Class 4 transport layer. Other layers are used between partners by agreement. This same approach allows different architectures to share some facilities. For instance, OSI and IBM's Systems Network Architecture (SNA) could operate their higher layers independently while sharing an X.25 service. Several large organizations are investigating ways to achieve partial layering within the OSI framework, whether or not it is sanctioned.

The introduction of variable numbers of layers could complicate management and application design. For many organizations, the added complication will not be worth the performance improvement, and they will settle for the consistency of the complete protocol stack. Others will use partial layering as a migration option while OSI products are slowly coming to market. These organizations will attempt to use as much of OSI as quickly as possible without becoming dependent on a complete set of products. Allowing partial layering places the decision back with the users, operators, and owners—with those that have the most accurate understanding of their service needs.

Conformance

Descriptions of protocols can be quite complex. At present, there is no way to determine if a particular protocol conforms to the specifications. The NBS has developed certification tests for X.25 and the transport layer. The Corporation for Open Systems (COS), as well as other groups, are in the process of creating testing facilities where a product can be tested comprehensively. COS announced that delivery of testing products to its members has begun, so conformance testing is beginning to move forward. Products certified by COS as conforming to OSI should be more attractive in the marketplace. However, those with long memories can recall the problems of interoperating products built to conform to a relatively simple RS-232 specification.

OSI costs

The standards committees have ignored how much OSI cost to implement. There are two major areas in which costs must be considered. The first is the cost of implementing a full suite of protocols. The second cost factor is the expenses associated with operating and managing an open-systems environment.

A computer needs a full complement of layer mechanisms as well as the standard protocols for communications with other devices. The entire list of functions specified by OSI is large and complex, and the functions

3. Selective services. By selective violations of the OSI model, services can be built at reduced cost. Shared transport offers reliability to selected upper-layer services.

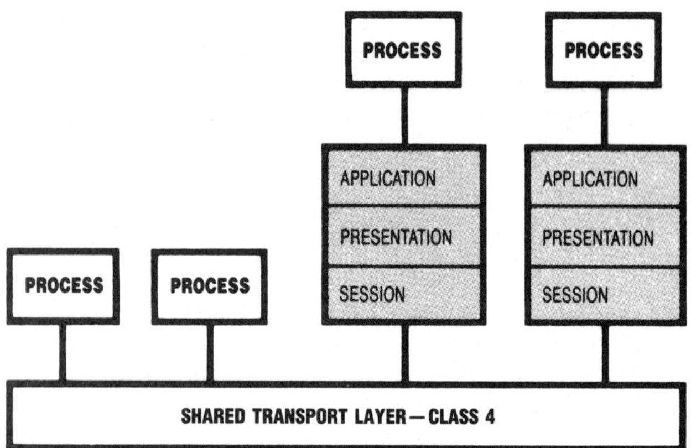

are expensive to build. Costs will also grow as the missing pieces mentioned above become available.

Incorporating OSI functions within a local operating environment also takes some doing. Interworking layers and applications must be integrated with local operating system services. The interworking environment represents many of the common interworking facilities as abstractions. Additional effort is required to create an appropriate mapping between the interworking facilities and the equivalent local service.

OSI's lack of completeness also increases the costs of implementing and testing services. Despite the promises of COS, there still are no formal OSI conformance-testing and certification facilities, so there is no means to run a standardized test on any particular implementation. It may prove difficult to test the interoperation of different products if there is no reference for detecting nonconforming behavior. Organizations may implement OSI products that work with their mix of computers but are incompatible with the actual specifications.

Operational costs can be much greater than the implementation costs. Ongoing, everyday costs of communications facilities, computer overhead, management, and other factors must be evaluated when an OSI strategy is being mapped out.

Networking costs themselves have been ignored in considering the costs of such wide area networking services as X.25 public data networks. In contrast to LANs, charges are based on a combination of connect time and data volume. Any feature that increases these factors also adds to the operational costs. The overhead of nested protocol headers and the additional management traffic for each layer adds to both the data volume and the connection time, especially since all layers are currently mandatory. Additional communications traffic and loads also affect the performance of the applications in each computer.

In an interworking environment, a portion of each computer's resources is used to manage the communications procedures, execute higher-layer protocols, and maintain support information. The manner in which these services are implemented and integrated into the local operating system has a large impact on the cost and performance of all the applications on the computer. Poorly constructed software consumes excessive computer resources and degrades application service. Some vendors, such as IBM, are embedding OSI protocols in their proprietary products. This approach may help bring OSI products to market sooner, but it will keep users dependent on proprietary products and use more computing resources.

Application design

Another major operational concern, especially as interworking matures, is application design. Poorly constructed applications may impose burdens on a computer or cause expensive misuse of networking services. Every design must consider network characteristics, message sizes, and basic protocol operations. For example, just because a network application worked well in a small LAN does not mean it will work properly when extended to an X.25 environment. The application, which worked well with five computers on a single LAN, sent periodic messages to its partners to make sure they were operational. However, when ported to a 500-computer X.25 network, the application's increased message volume resulted in congestion, higher costs, and poorer performance.

Performance benchmarks of OSI networks have proved to be disappointing: Sub-megabit performance has been repeatedly noted on LANs operating at 10 Mbit/s. This is especially worrisome since most measurements were made at the transport layer; adding more layers and then applications will further degrade the measured performance. NASA and other organizations have already held meetings to address this issue.

Effective internetworking and interworking standards are in the user's best interests; vendors will only move in this direction as market pressures dictate. Most user organizations appreciate the advantages of limiting their dependence upon any one vendor. Good standards reduce that dependence, but unquestioning reliance upon standards is risky as well. Each standard must be reviewed for its contribution to a cost-effective solution.

A strategic approach is necessary to achieve internetworking and interworking capability, especially with a diverse set of computers. Most organizations will be migrating toward OSI starting with the equipment they presently use. Conversions have always been costly and disruptive, and this one should not be an exception. There will be pressure for selective violations of the architecture, such as the idea of partial layering, as organizations confront the reality of creating new networking environments. The success of the OSI movement may perhaps be measured by the number of violations and distinct varieties that appear over time. ∎

John McConnell is a vice president at Infonetics Inc., Santa Clara, Calif. He received his B. S. E. E. and an M. S. in computer science from the University of California, Berkeley. McConnell helped develop the Arpanet for the Defense Advanced Research Project Agency.

Thomas J. Routt, contributing editor, DATA COMMUNICATIONS

SNA network management: What makes IBM's Netview tick?

Coping with the nitty-gritty details of IBM's Network Management Architecture.

Most network users intuitively grasp what network management is all about—the processes of planning, implementing, and controlling the diverse physical and logical elements of a network. Any network management package worth the name should ensure a means to deliver, format, present, and interchange appropriate data on a highly available, timely, and cost-effective basis to distributed decision makers.

But managing a network these days takes much more than intuition, especially in the world of IBM's Systems Network Architecture. SNA network topologies have rapidly evolved from centralized, single-host, single-vendor entities into a distributed control, multiprocessor, multivendor, multidata-center processing environment—and the problem of managing it all has increased concomitantly. IBM has continued to upgrade its Network Management Architecture (NMA), also known as Management Services Architecture, to keep pace with the evolution of SNA.

Figure 1 depicts a traditional, hierarchical, single-host SNA network with a simple physical topology. The host computer is channel-attached to a communications controller, which in turn connects a cluster controller over a single link controlled by modems. Terminals and printers are connected to the cluster controller. All interaction with applications is through the host's access method software and database and data communications subsystems. Network control resides in the central host and is cascaded to the communications controller and the cluster controller. All message flows are from the perspective of the host, and, quite important, all message-size, volume, and interarrival distributions are highly predictable. This physical topology is easy to manage by virtue of its limited scope and predictable performance.

Figure 2 is an example of the complex multivendor, multidomain, multinetwork SNA environment of today. The upper half of this figure depicts an SNA network interconnection (SNI) gateway. At the gateway, two multidomain SNA networks are interconnected through Gateway System Services Control Point and Gateway Network Control Program. In SNA, a control point, or CP, controls the functions of a node's resources. Each SNA host is locally and remotely attached to multiple communications controllers and cluster controllers in both multidropped and point-to-point configurations. Hosts can be interconnected through packet-switched data networks or by the Token Ring local area network (LAN). And to top it off, non-IBM subnetworks, such as Digital Equipment Corp. (DEC), Hewlett-Packard, Tandem, Wang, and other environments, are often internetworked through SNA.

Managing a modern SNA network, therefore, involves navigating through a complex of logical and hybrid internetworked environments. An SNA host and communications controller subarea network are shown in Figure 2. The IBM System/36 subnetwork is characterized by the Advanced Peer-to-Peer Networking (APPN) feature, which is based upon Node Type 2.1 Low Entry Networking (LEN). APPN provides distributed, dynamic directories as well as intermediate node functions. The DEC, Hewlett-Packard, Tandem, Wang, and other subnetworks are best characterized as distributed control environments and generally interface into SNA hosts as Physical Unit (PU) Type 2.0 cluster controllers.

SNA's job is to logically manage end-to-end sessions between logical units (LUs) and to physically manage network path control and data link control resources. This was straightforward to accomplish in the hierarchical host environment shown in Figure 1 but became much more difficult in a distributed environment because:

■ Message sizes, volumes, and buffer arrival distributions are not as inherently predictable within distributed topolo-

SNA Network Management Glossary

Advanced Communications Function/Virtual Telecommunications Access Method Version 3 Release 2 (ACF/VTAM V3 R2). Current level of VTAM. Provides VTAM Advanced Program-to-Program Communications application program interface, and supports Logical Unit Type 6.2 and Node Type 2.1.

Advanced Interactive Executive (AIX). Multi-user, multitasking operating system.

Advanced Peer-to-Peer Networking (APPN). A System/36 feature that provides distributed processing through a set of services based on Node Type 2.1 network node and Logical Unit 6.2. These services include connectivity, directory, route selection, session activation, and data transport and provide for distributed, dynamic node resource updates and intermediate, passthrough node capabilities.

Advanced Program-to-Program Communications. Strategic, IBM distributed processing direction that defines Logical Unit Type 6.2 as a general-purpose, interprogram protocol.

Application program interface/communications services (API/CS). On Netview/PC, enables requests from user-written programs and alerts in network management vector transport request unit format to be passed to Netview/PC.

Boundary function (BF). Subset of the SNA subarea that controls non-subarea resources such as PU 2.1, PU 2.0, PU 1, LU, and link resources.

Class-of-service name (COSNAME). The primary logical-unit name provided from a log mode table to a class-of-service table (COSTAB). COSTAB associates COSNAME with a virtual route identifier, which combines a virtual route number and transmission priority number to provide a specific class of service to path control for an LU-to-LU session.

Class-of-service table (COSTAB). ACF/VTAM-resident table containing entries that define virtual routes and transmission priorities to be used for sessions.

Cluster controller. Programmable control-unit device that ports multiple display stations and printers. Can implement Physical Unit Type 2.0 and can support LU Session Types 1, 2, 3, 4, and 7.

Command lists (CLISTs). High-level executive statements that invoke several lines of underlying high-level language or assembler code in order to perform a specific task or set of tasks through nonconditional or conditional execution tests or arguments.

Common storage area (CSA). Virtual storage operating system addressable space below the 16 megabyte line.

Communications controller (COMC). Programmable major Systems Network Architecture node that implements Physical Unit Type 4 and provides global (subarea) SNA transport functions. The 3745, 3720, and 3725 Series support Node Type 2.1 into ACF/VTAM V3 R2.

Configuration report server (CRS). Part of the IBM LAN manager that runs as a Netview/PC application. Forwards LAN configuration change notification to IBM LAN Manager.

Control initiate (CINIT). Formatted Systems Network Architecture request unit sent from system services control point (within a Physical Unit Type 5 Host Node) or control point (within a Physical Unit Type 2.1 Node) to the logical unit that is to be the primary LU for a subsequent LU-to-LU session. Contains the bind image from the SSCP/CP log mode table.

Control-point management services (CPMS). In SNA management services architecture, the control-point component that assists a network operator in problem, performance, accounting, and configuration management. Communicates with physical unit management services over an SSCP-PU control session using network management vector transport request units.

Distributed Data Management (DDM). One of the three SNA Transaction Services Architectures (the others are SNA Distribution Services and Document Interchange Architecture). DDM provides record-oriented, distributed file connectivity, and/or access, and update capabilities to application transaction programs.

Distributed Office Support System (Disoss). A CICS-resident set of transactions that implements SNA distribution services and Document Interchange Architecture.

Distribution Service Unit (DSU). In SNA Distribution Services (SNADS), a SNADS Node, which is a collection of queues and data structures to provide the SNADS general object distribution service.

Entry-sequenced data set (ESDS). A virtual storage access method data set organization that identifies a record for access by specifying the physical byte location of the record's first byte relative to the beginning of the data set.

Explicit route (ER). Assigned by SNA path control (Layer 3). Simplex, physical path between endpoint subarea nodes.

Extended Recovery Facility (XRF). An enhancement to Multiple Virtual Storage/Extended Architecture, Information Management System/Virtual Storage (IMS/VS), Advanced Communications Function/Virtual Telecommunications Access Method, and ACF/Network Control Program that increases availability of IMS/VS Version 2 database/data communications transaction processing as seen by end users with XRF-supported terminals.

Gateway Network Control Program (GW NCP). In SNA network interconnection, requires Advanced Communications Function/Network Control Program Version 3 and later, and enables an ACF/NCP to provide multiple subarea addresses for multiple, interconnected SNA networks. In conjunction with Gateway SSCP, resolves differential network conventions for resource addressing, resource naming, and path control-determined classes of service.

Gateway System Services Control Point (GW SSCP). In SNA network interconnection, requires Advanced Communications Function/Virtual Telecommunications Access Method Version 2 Release 2 and later, and resolves NAU resources on multiple and various SNA networks.

Initiate-self (INIT-SELF). Formatted Systems Network Architecture request unit (RU) sent from the primary LU to the secondary LU to request activation of an LU-to-LU session. Carries the bind image presented to the primary LU from the SSCP/CP Log Mode Table by the control initiate RU.

Initiating LU (ILU). The LU that requests a session with another LU. The ILU propagates the session request to SSCP/CP Log Mode Table within the initiate-self request unit.

Integrated communications adapter (ICA). Provided in several IBM communications products, including the 4361, 9370, System/36, and System/38. On the 4361, supports microcode implementation of Physical Unit Type 4, in the other environments, supports interfaces to IBM Token Ring Network, and CCITT X.25 interfaces to packet-switched data networks.

Key-sequenced data set (KSDS). A virtual storage access method data set organization that identifies a record for access by specifying its key value. The key is an imbedded field that uniquely identifies the record.

Line Attachment Base-C (LAB-C). Hardware base on the 3725/26 Communications Controller to allow attachment to an

IBM Token Ring Network over a Token Ring interface coupler.

Link Problem Determination Aid (LPDA). A subset of the Netview Hardware Monitor (enhanced Network Problem Determination Application) that provides link-level testing of IBM modems.

Local management services (LMS). In SNA management services architecture, the LU component with which physical unit management services communicate.

Low Entry Networking (LEN). Formally, Node Type 2.1 LEN. A distributed extension of SNA that provides the basis for peer-to-peer networking.

Multisystem Networking Facility (MSNF). Advanced Communications Function/Virtual Telecommunications Access Method feature that permits control of multidomain SNA networks.

Netview Distribution Manager (Netview DM). Replaces Distributed Systems Executive for Multiple Virtual Storage and provides change-management functions through centrally controlled data distribution and implementation of software changes within SNA networks.

Network addressable unit (NAU). An addressable and named resource within an SNA network. Includes system services control point, control point, physical unit, and logical unit resources.

Network Communications Control Facility Version 2 Release 2 (NCCF V2 R2). The base Netview product that provides the Netview command facility support for command, message, command list, and other capabilities to ease system and network management.

Network management vector transport (NMVT). NMVT request unit (RU) is the preferred SNA RU to transport network management data over SSCP-PU control sessions between CPMS and PUMS, and is encoded according to a management services major vector scheme, wherein the major vector identifies the management services function provided.

Path table (PATH TAB). Created by the path macro and specified in ACF/VTAM, ACF/NCP, MSNF, and SNI to provide path control connectivity.

Physical unit (PU). An SNA network addressable unit that controls node resources. Physical Unit (PU) Type 5 is a host node, PU Type 4 is a communications controller node, PU Type 2.1 is a network node or an end node, PU Type 2.0 is a cluster controller node, and PU Type 1 is a terminal node.

Physical unit management services (PUMS). In SNA management services architecture, the physical-unit component that is responsible for providing general management services for the node and its associated resources. PUMS communicates with its controlling CPMS using management services request units (generally, NMVT RUs) on an SSCP-PU control session.

Programmable Operator (PROP). The facility that provides an interface to Netview Automation.

Remote console facility (RCF). In Netview/PC, enables one Netview/PC to control another.

Request unit (RU). The fundamental unit of SNA data. Can be constructed by any of SNA Layers 7 through 4.

Reverse explicit route (RER). Assigned by SNA path control (Layer 3). Simplex, physical path between endpoint subarea nodes in the reverse direction of the ER (from the perspective of the virtual route).

Ring error monitor (REM). Within the IBM LAN Manager (as a Netview/PC application), assembles error statistics reported by stations on two rings to which a bridge program is attached.

Ring parameter server (RPS). Within the IBM LAN Manager (as a Netview/PC application), provides a ring number to stations as they insert into rings to which a bridge program is attached.

RU size (RUSIZE). An operand set within the Virtual Telecommunications Access Method build macro that specifies the maximum size in bytes of request units that traverse subareas.

Service point command service (SPCS). Netview R2-generated commands that include LINKPD (link problem determination), LINKTEST (link test), LINKDATA (link data), and RUNCMD (run communication management data). Accepted by Netview/PC and forwarded to the appropriate application.

Session started (SESSST). A field-formatted request (notification) sent over a control session between a primary logical unit and SSCP/CP to notify the SSCP/CP that the primary LU has successfully started a session with another LU.

SNA distribution services (SNADS). One of the three SNA Transaction Services Architectures (along with Document Interchange Architecture and Distributed Data Management). Provides store-and-forward distribution services for generalized objects. Distribution objects can include binary data, files, documents, and downloadable software. Uses Logical Unit Type 6.2 for the underlying SNA session.

SNA network interconnection (SNI). A gateway arrangement to interconnect two or more (theoretically, up to 255) separate SNA networks, each of which contains unique internal naming, addressing, and management agreements. SNI sessions are a special, extended case of cross-domain, same-network sessions. SNI requires ACF/VTAM V2 R2 (and later) and ACF/NCP V3 (and later).

Status monitor (STATMON). In Netview, an enhancement of VTAM Node Control Application that provides domain status at a glance, hierarchical view of network resources, object-action control of network control resources, asynchronous update of the domain status panel, and "critical-message monitor," which is an operator notification mechanism driven by important messages originating from command facility.

Terminal access facility (TAF). Subcomponent of Netview command facility that supports variable terminal screen sizes.

Transmission group. Assigned by SNA path control. Logical collection of data links between adjacent subarea nodes.

Transmission priority (TP). Assigned by SNA path control (Layer 3) as a TP number with a VR number to create a VRID. TPs range from 0 (low) to 1 (medium) to 2 (high).

Unformatted system services table (USSTAB). An SSCP/CP table that accepts character-coded logon requests from initiating LUs and formats and propagates them as INIT-SELF RUs to SSCP/CP Log Mode Table.

Virtual storage access method (VSAM). Facility for processing files that are stored on direct access storage devices.

Virtual Storage Extended (VSE). VSE is a virtual storage operating system that is supported on the IBM 4300 and 9370 processors. Supported by Netview/PC.

VSE/Operator Communication Control Facility (VSE/OCCF). VSE facility that communicates with Netview Automation. Eases the complexity of operating a VSE system by reducing the operator interaction otherwise necessary.

Window size current (WS Cur). Virtual route status display by Netview Session Monitor.

Window size maximum (WS Max). Virtual route status display by Netview Session Monitor.

Window size minimum (WS Min). Virtual route status display by Netview Session Monitor.

gies as they are in classical terminal networks.

- Small computers (such as System/3X, PC, PS/2) can operate as standalone data processing environments, emulate 3270 displays, or perform file transfers. They add elements of unpredictability to network performance.
- LU-to-LU end-to-end session traces used for diagnostics and other purposes must cross gateways. The effectiveness of this operation is a function of the ability of the management of distinct networks and user organizations to cooperate.
- Internal packet-switched data network performance is not normally controllable by users' network management organizations.
- Host domain and communications controller subarea management generally ends at the PU Type 2.0 node.
- Non-IBM environments may locally collect vital network management information but not necessarily be able to notify the SNA hosts.

Host-based

NMA puts the disparate pieces of SNA together. It specifies the management services required to plan, organize, and control functions within SNA networks. But is has some weaknesses. For example, the majority of IBM's NMA products are host- and communications controller-based and reflect a centralized-control philosophy; the centralized-control approach contributes to overhead and reduces throughput. Furthermore, failure of a critical network management host can invalidate the network management and recovery process altogether. It is also true within this centralized-control approach that the very process of attempting to recover from problems can be disruptive to other data traffic in terms of session slowdown and lost or modified data.

Netview, the primary set of NMA implementations, is predicated on System/370 involvement. It is strong as far as it goes but does not address fundamental network management requirements that exist within small SNA networks supporting small system-based (that is, System/36-, System/38-, and PS/2-based) computing. While gateways to System/36 and other environments are a possible solution, the small-system networks do not possess NMA functionality independent of System/370.

It is likely that, one day, IBM will define a standardized set of Netview System/3X capabilities based on Node Type 2.1 LEN functions. Currently, System/36 and System/38 support a communications and systems management feature, which provides change management and distribution as well as problem management and determination. The problem management and determination support is compatible with Netview Command Facility and Hardware Monitor. Change management and distribution support is provided through System/36 Distributed Systems Node Executive, System/38 Distributed System Services, and System/38 SNA-Alert Support. Each is compatible with Netview Distribution Manager. The January 26, 1988, announcements of Advanced Communication Function/Network Control Program (ACF/NCP) Version 5 (V5) Revision 2 (R2) and R2.1 are highly significant in this regard.

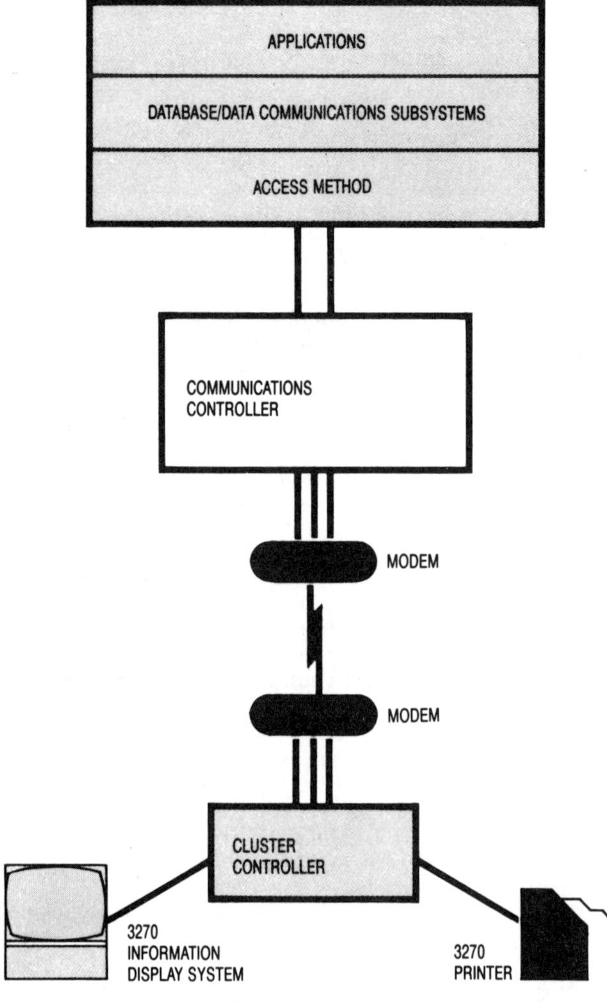

1. Traditional SNA. *The simple physical network control topology is characteristic of early Systems Network Architecture networks.*

And the boundaries between LEN and classical subarea SNA are blurring. In conjunction with the Virtual Telecommunications Access Method (VTAM) Advanced Program-to-Program Communications application program interface provided under ACF/VTAM V3 R2, the Node Type 2.1 LEN architecture is now extended directly into subarea SNA. This makes it highly likely that Netview will be extended so that it participates directly in the management of extended peer-to-peer SNA networks.

In the meantime, existing NMA products are, to a very great extent, interdependent. This raises a major issue within multivendor networks where non-IBM network management setups collect local subnetwork management data and cannot establish native communications with Netview. IBM has developed a set of interfaces that largely resolve this issue, but they require the original equipment manufacturer (OEM) to develop IBM-compatible network management solutions in addition to generalized SNA compatibility.

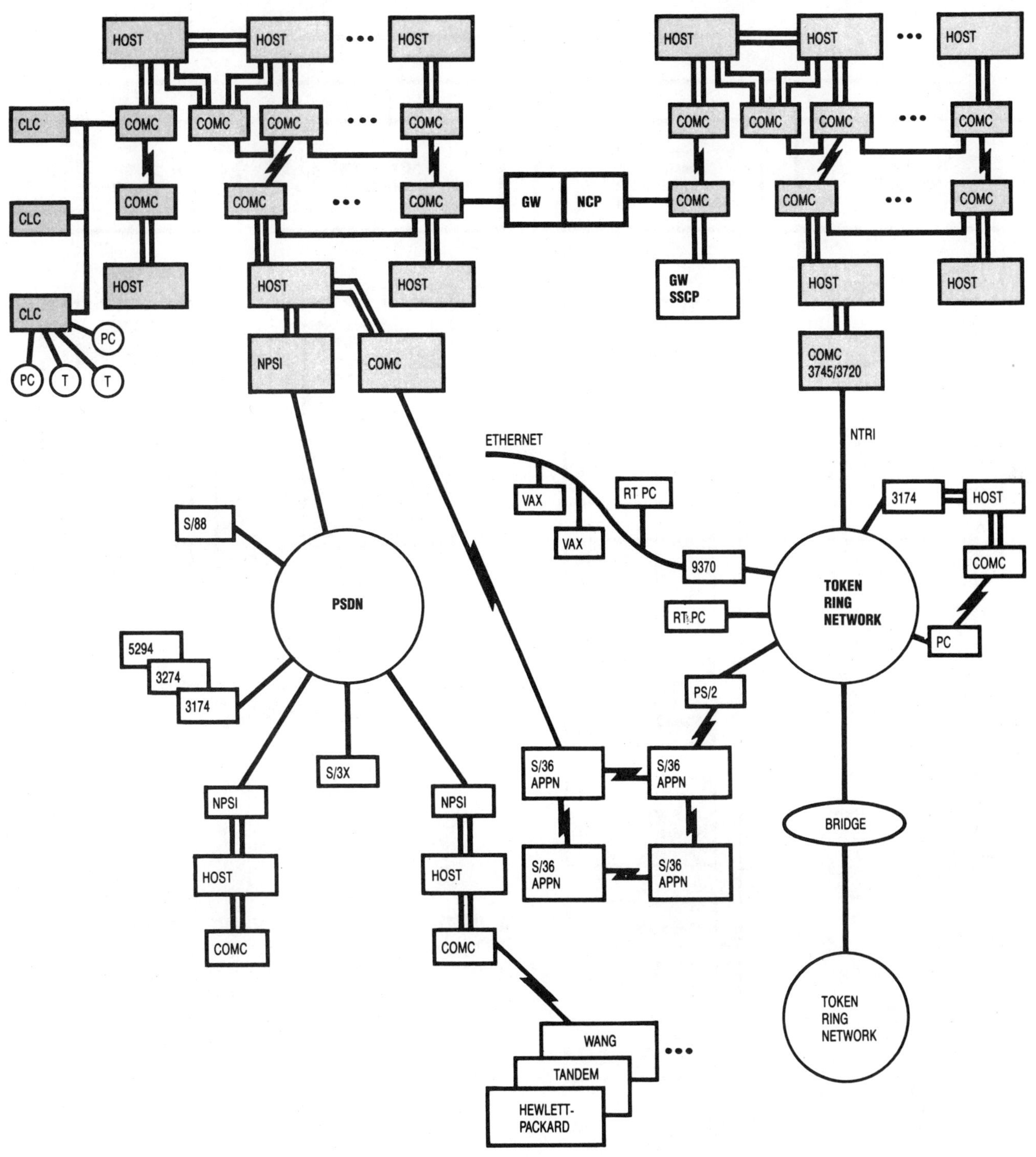

APPN = ADVANCED PEER-TO-PEER NETWORKING
CLC = CLUSTER CONTROLLER
COMC = COMMUNICATIONS CONTROLLER
GW = GATEWAY
NCP = NETWORK CONTROL PROGRAM
NPSI = NCP PACKET-SWITCHED DATA NETWORK
NTRI = NCP TOKEN RING INTERFACE
PC = PERSONAL COMPUTER
PSDN = PACKET-SWITCHED DATA NETWORK
SSCP = SYSTEM SERVICES CONTROL POINT
T = TERMINAL

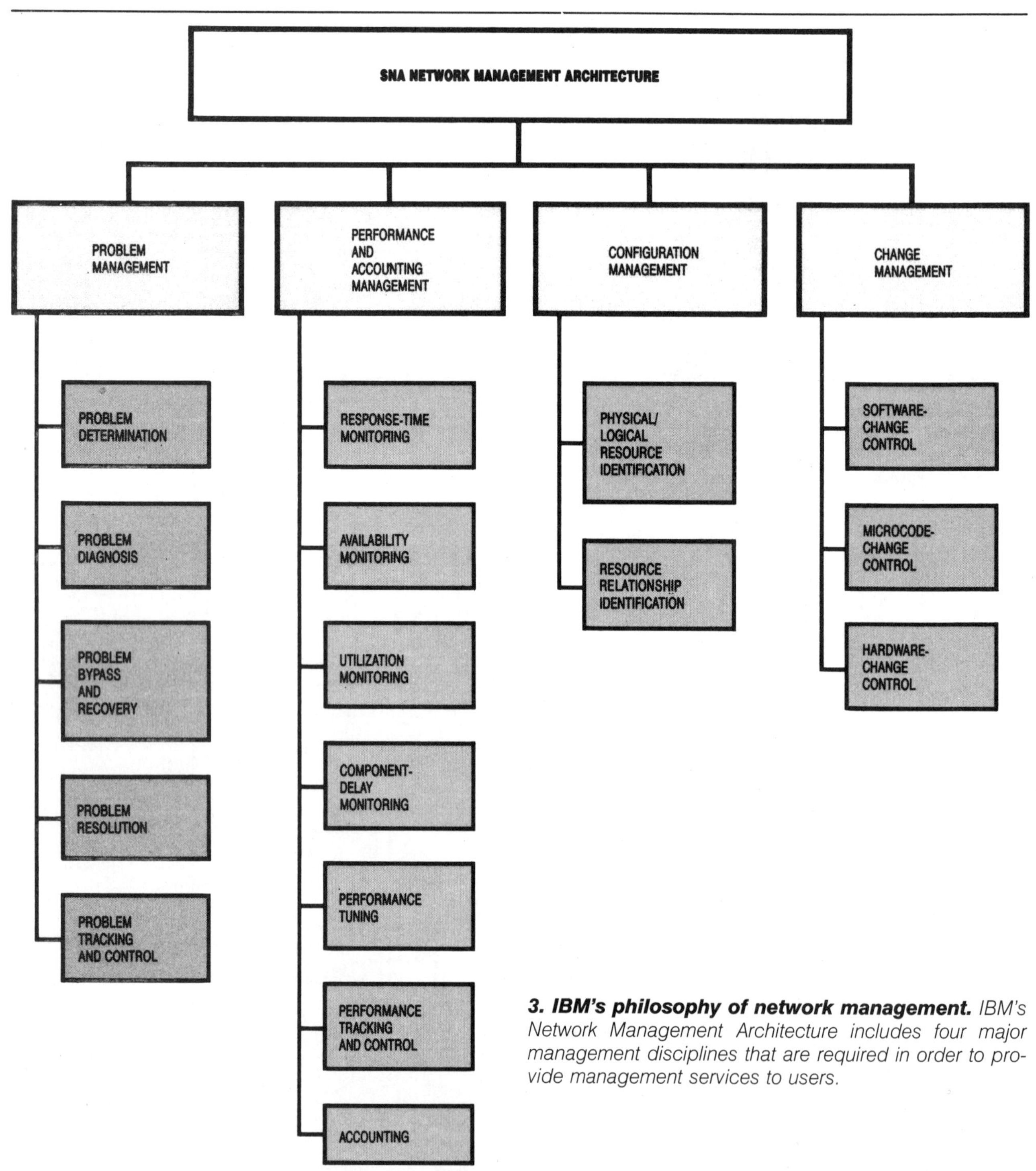

3. IBM's philosophy of network management. *IBM's Network Management Architecture includes four major management disciplines that are required in order to provide management services to users.*

Nevertheless, IBM's willingness to publish its architectural program interfaces indicates a commitment to an open network approach that bodes well for the future. This openness will surely propagate as the OSI network management specifications and protocols evolve and flourish under more and more implementations.

In the world of IBM, NMA specifies the management services required to plan, organize, and control functions within SNA networks. The major components and elements of NMA are presented in Figure 3.

Problem management is the process of managing network problems from initial detection through final resolution. The initial step is problem determination: the automated or manual process that detects a hardware, software, or firmware component problem. Diagnosis determines the problem's cause, while problem bypass and recovery provide either a partial or a complete bypass until final resolution can be enacted. Resolution is the corrective measure taken to eliminate the detected problem or an impending one. Tracking and control is the process of recording the history of the problem.

Performance and accounting management is that part of NMA that quantifies, reports, and controls the utilization and charges associated with network components. Response-time monitoring measures end user session response times and generates problem notifications if predetermined thresholds are exceeded. Availability monitoring reports component availability. Utilization monitoring keeps tabs on network resource-server utilization; it generates unsolicited problem notification if preset threshold values are exceeded. Component-delay monitoring tracks critical component delays; it initiates unsolicited problem notification if predetermined service levels are exceeded. Performance tuning is the process of modifying critical network-performance parameters to improve throughput. Performance tracking and control is the process of recording and tracking performance events or alerts. Accounting records, allocates, and tracks network resources in an effort to properly allocate costs.

Configuration management, according to the philosophy of NMA, is the process of controlling information that is necessary to identify networked resources and their inter-relationships. Physical and logical resource identification records physical network resources. Resources can include such devices as host computers, communications controllers, cluster controllers, modems, multiplexers, concentrators, and protocol converters. Physical and logical resource identification codes each resource by such categories as line types, serial numbers, inventory numbers, telephone numbers, real/virtual memory allocations, and program numbers. It also tracks logical resources by SNA system generation-based information such as system services control point (SSCP), CP, PU, or LU names, addresses, domain statuses, and capabilities. Resource-relationship identification is the process of identifying and recording the physical and logical configuration of network resource topologies.

Change Management is the process of planning and controlling change. It applies to additions, deletions, and modifications to networked hardware, software, and micro-code resources. Software-change control oversees software oscillations such as installation, removal, modifications, and temporary program fixes. Microcode-change control keeps tabs on microcode installation, removal, temporary fixes, engineering changes, or feature changes. Hardware-change control notes the hardware installation, removal, engineering changes, or other updates.

The major elements of NMA—problem management, performance and accounting management, configuration management, and change management—are executed by a network operator. The operator, which can be either human or machine, must be associated with an SNA node with control-point management services (CPMS) and physical unit management services (PUMS).

Figure 4 shows the CPMS in a PU Type 5 host. CPMS

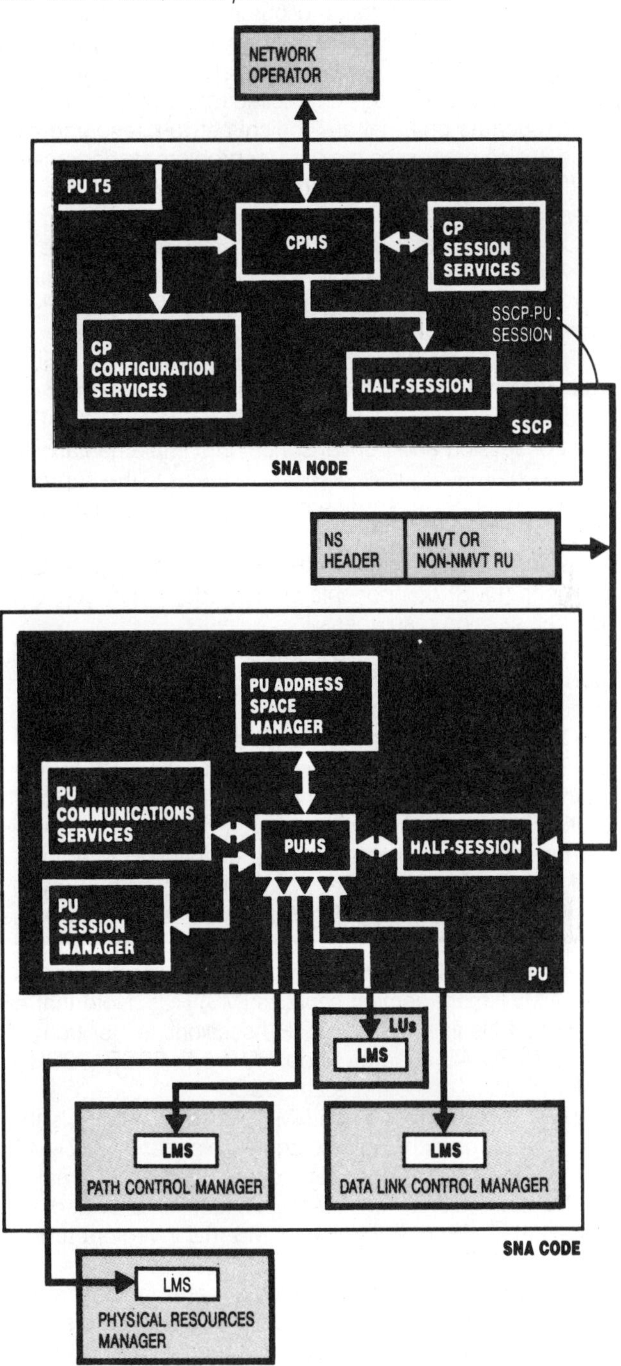

4. Making it work. *Control point and physical unit management services are key management services components that define structured protocol boundaries.*

CPMS = CONTROL POINT MANAGEMENT SERVICES
LU = LOGICAL UNIT
LMS = LOCAL MANAGEMENT SERVICES
NMVT = NETWORK MANAGEMENT VECTOR TRANSPORT
NS = NETWORK SERVICES
PU = PHYSICAL UNIT
PUMS = PHYSICAL UNIT MANAGEMENT SERVICES
RU = REQUEST UNIT
SSCP = SYSTEM SERVICES CONTROL POINT

manages all PUs within its domain through SSCP-PU control sessions. Functionally, the CPMS forwards requests from the network operator to PUs to query status. It also sets parameters and tests resources remotely and solicits management-services data, such as test results, response times, and error and performance statistics. In addition, the CPMS receives and logs unsolicited management services data, such as physical and logical network resource alert data. It also processes the data for problem management, performance and accounting management, configuration management, and change management.

CPMS interacts with CP components, including the network operator, CP configuration services, CP session services, and half-session (for the CPMS-PUMS, SSCP-PU control session) through CPMS protocol boundaries.

The PUMS resides within a PU. It provides node-level management services. PUMS receives management-services request units (RUs) from CPMS over an SSCP-PU control session and converts them into implementation-unique internal requests. It routes requests to the appropriate internal node component and sends CPMS solicited and unsolicited management-services data over SSCP-PU sessions. PUMS also interacts with local management services (LMS) components of the node, which control LU half-session resources.

PUMS interacts with PU components, including PU address-space manager, PU configuration services, PU session manager, and half-session (for the CPMS-PUMS, SSCP-PU control session). PUMS also interacts with the LMS physical resources manager, LMS data link control manager, LMS path control manager, and LMS LU through PUMS protocol boundaries.

The management-services data exchanged over the CPMS-PUMS SSCP-PU session is preambled by 3-byte network services header (Fig. 5). These headers signify the presence of either network management vector transport (NMVT) or non-NMVT RUs. Figure 5 summarizes the 14 non-NMVT management services (MS) RUs. Note that all of these RUs flow over SSCP-PU sessions, either from SSCP-to-PU 4/5 subarea node, PU 4/5-to-SSCP, SSCP-to-PU Type 2, or PU Type 2-to-SSCP.

While NMA supports non-NMVT RU data, NMVT is the preferred approach. Figure 6 depicts a generic NMVT MS RU. NMVT RUs are encoded according to an MS major-vector scheme that identifies the MS function provided. Key values that are set within NMVT MS major vectors are specified in Table 1.

Each MS major vector includes a matrix indicating the subvectors that may be included within it. Subvectors with keys X'80' through X'FE' contain a meaning that is unique to the MS major vector within which they are used. Subvectors with keys X'00' through X'7F' are called common subvectors; their meaning is independent of the MS major vector that contains them.

Figure 7 illustrates a solicited flow of LU response-time monitor (RTM) data. The network operator issues a response-time request for LUs 1 through N associated with a specified SNA node. This request is passed to CPMS and propagates as an RTM data request NMVT RU over

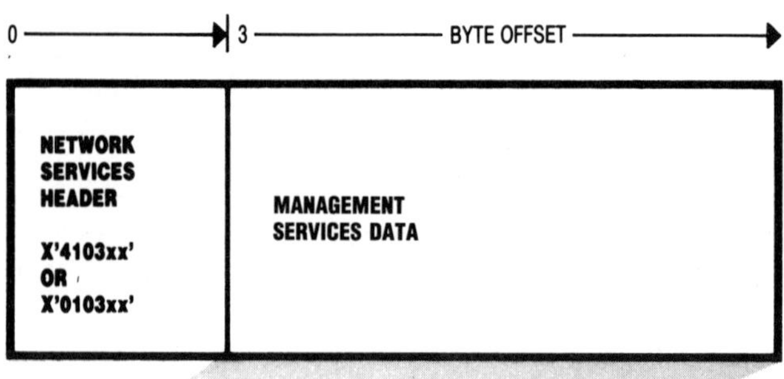

5. SNA hooks. *Nonvector as well as vector management services data can flow over CPMS-PU and SSCP-PU sessions. Vector data is IBM's future direction.*

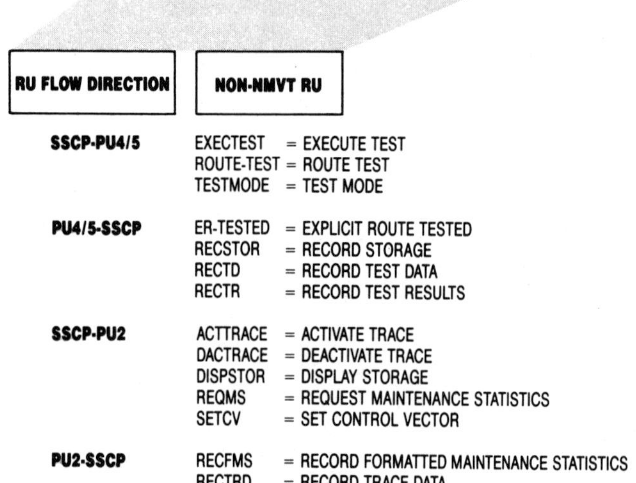

RU FLOW DIRECTION	NON-NMVT RU	
SSCP-PU4/5	EXECTEST	= EXECUTE TEST
	ROUTE-TEST	= ROUTE TEST
	TESTMODE	= TEST MODE
PU4/5-SSCP	ER-TESTED	= EXPLICIT ROUTE TESTED
	RECSTOR	= RECORD STORAGE
	RECTD	= RECORD TEST DATA
	RECTR	= RECORD TEST RESULTS
SSCP-PU2	ACTTRACE	= ACTIVATE TRACE
	DACTRACE	= DEACTIVATE TRACE
	DISPSTOR	= DISPLAY STORAGE
	REQMS	= REQUEST MAINTENANCE STATISTICS
	SETCV	= SET CONTROL VECTOR
PU2-SSCP	RECFMS	= RECORD FORMATTED MAINTENANCE STATISTICS
	RECTRD	= RECORD TRACE DATA

an SSCP-PU control session to PUMS. PUMS then decapsulates the NMVT RU and passes the RTM data request internally to the specified LUs through LMS. The LUs respond with RTM data to PUMS, and PUMS passes this data to CPMS over the SSCP-PU session. CPMS then reads the solicited RTM data RUs and passes the results to the network operator. Unsolicited alerts are passed from PUMS to CPMS when predetermined response-time thresholds are exceeded.

NMA distinguishes between the focal point, entry point, and service point depicted in Figure 8. In the figure, the focal point resides within a System/370 host and makes consolidated network management data available to centralized network management applications. Entry points are locations that provide network management services for themselves and for attached SNA resources and devices. Service points provide management services to support non-IBM SNA and non-SNA access into SNA. In this sense, service points function as network management servers: They collect network management data from non-SNA environments, translate the data into SNA management-services data, and forward the information to a focal point. Service-point communications with non-SNA resources are not governed by SNA protocols.

Netview Release 1, originally announced by IBM on May 20, 1986, is the strategic NMA focal-point implementation. It consolidates several previously disparate host-based network management offerings. On June 16, 1987, IBM announced Netview Release 2 for all major System/370 operating systems, including Multiple Virtual Storage/Extended Architecture (MVS/XA), MVS/370, Virtual Machine (VM), and Virtual Storage Extended (VSE). The major components of Netview Release 2 are shown in Figure 9.

Netview
Working up from the bottom of the figure, the base component of Netview is the command facility, an enhancement of the Network Communications Control Facility V2 R2. NCCF was upgraded to improve its interoperation with other Netview components and to support network products such as IBM 586X/38XX modems, Token Ring Networks, and IBM 3710 Network Controllers.

One subcomponent of the command facility, called the

---

6. SNA shines. *The network management vector transport management-services request units form the basis of SNA communications in Network Management Architecture.*

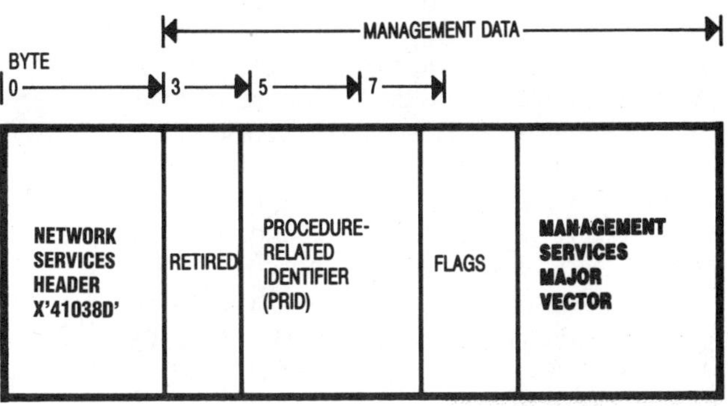

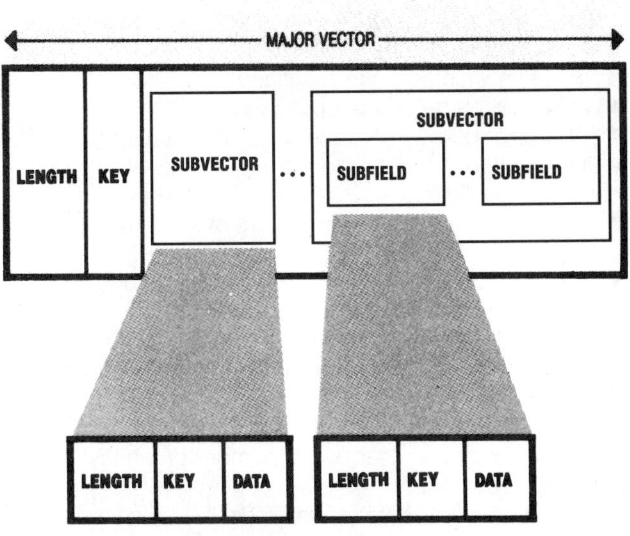

terminal access facility (TAF), presently supports variable terminal screen sizes from 24 rows by 80 columns (1,920 characters; standard 3278-2) to 255 rows by 255 columns (65,025 characters). The latter size accommodates the range available on gas-panel, large-screen devices such as the IBM 3290. Local and remote 586X/38XX modems are configurable from the Netview command facility operator panel to assist in installation as well as load balancing.

The Netview hardware monitor component is an enhancement of Network Problem Determination Application (NPDA) V3 R2. It runs under Netview command facility and provides problem alerts that notify the network operator of error conditions when a preset threshold is exceeded. Alerts can be dynamically displayed on selected operator stations, and statistical data is maintained. The NPDA

NMVT RU MS major vectors

KEY	MS MAJOR VECTOR
0000	UNSOLICITED ALERT
0001	UNSOLICITED LINK EVENT (LINK CONNECTION COMPONENT FAILURE)
0010	TRACE
0020	SOLICITED LINK CONNECTION SUBSYSTEM DIAGNOSTIC
0025	SOLICITED/UNSOLICITED PROBLEM DETERMINATION (PD) STATISTICS. INCLUDES A DATA LINK TRAFFIC COUNTERS SUBVECTOR WITH/WITHOUT A LINK CONNECTION SUBSYSTEM DATA SUBVECTOR, OR AN X.25 DATA LINK CONTROL (DLC) COUNTER SUBVECTOR
0080	RESPONSE-TIME MONITOR (RTM)
0090	REPLY PRODUCT SET IDENTIFIER (ID)
00A0	REPLY LINK RESOURCE CONTROL (REPLY TO MS MAJOR VECTOR X'80A0')
8010	REQUEST TRACE
8020	REQUEST LINK CONNECTION SUBSYSTEM DIAGNOSTIC INFORMATION
8025	REQUEST PD STATISTICS [E.G., REMOTE DATA TERMINAL EQUIPMENT (DTE) INTERFACE STATUS, REMOTE SELF-TEST RESULTS]
8080	REQUEST RTM
8090	REQUEST PRODUCT SET ID
80A0	REQUEST LINK RESOURCE CONTROL (QUERY)

MS = MANAGEMENT SERVICES
NMXT = NETWORK MANAGEMENT VECTOR TRANSPORT
RU = REQUEST UNIT

NMVT RU support is extended to NMVT MS major vectors X'0001', X'00A0', X'8020', and X'80A0' to support alerts from IBM 586X/38XX modems, the Token Ring Network, 37XX Communications Controller, and 3710 Network Controller. NPDA makes use of program-function keys (better known as PF keys), and color and highlighting are used on screen displays.

Link Problem Determination Aid (LPDA) is used in conjunction with the Netview hardware monitor TEST command to test local and remote IBM modems. The 586X modems (5865, 5866, 5868) produce LPDA-2 reports, and the 586X, 3834, and 3864 modems (running in LPDA-1 mode) produce LPDA-1 reports.

The LPDA tests include a check of the remote data terminal equipment (DTE) interface, the link status, and a remote modem self-test. LPDA can also be used to test

7. Calling all data. *Logical unit response time monitor (RTM) data can be requested by a network operator, regardless of whether that operator is human or software.*

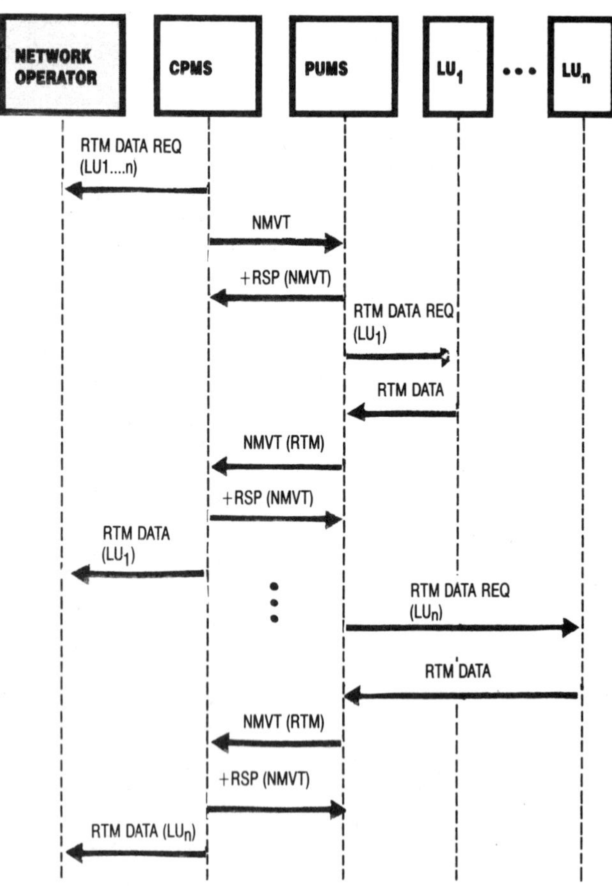

lines for such parameters as signal-to-noise ratio, modem-lines status, and to run a transmit/receive test. This test requests that a modem pair exchange predefined bit patterns over a link, compare them, and report the results.

The hardware monitor also provides LAN support through the 3725 Communications Controller NCP Line Attachment Base Type C Token Ring interface coupler through ACF/NCP V4 R2. The 3745 is supported for all NCP Version 5 levels. This support, called NCP Token Ring interface (NTRI), interprets, logs, and displays unsolicited alert NMVT RUs (X'0000'), link-event NMVT RUs (X'0001'), and problem-determination-statistics NMVT RUs (X'0025').

These NMVTs are forwarded to the host by NTRI. They contain statistical MS subvectors that are logged to the Netview hardware monitor statistical database. Figure 10 summarizes the Netview hardware monitor collection of NMVT RUs from 37XX Communications Controller, 3710 Network Controller, 586X/38XX modems, and Token Ring Network environments.

Reverting to Figure 9, the Netview session monitor is an enhanced version of Network Logical Data Manager (NLDM) V1 R3. Like the Netview hardware monitor, the session monitor runs under Netview command facility.

The session monitor component is designed to provide software problem determination, configuration management, and performance management through SNA LU-to-LU monitoring and trace mechanisms. The NLDM was upgraded for the Netview offering to include automatic detection of extended data-stream terminals for full-color support. It also can invoke the Netview session monitor without a command facility invocation.

Data provided to the session monitor is essential for associating LU-to-LU sessions with SNA path-control components. Also, the session monitor can monitor and trace LU-to-LU session data through single SNA networks or through gateway environments.

The session monitor also supports the Extended Recovery Facility. XRF enhances the solicitation, correlation, and presentation of boundary function trace data, RTM data, and session-awareness data. Session monitor also provides primary, intermediate, secondary, and single-network session configuration data.

Netview's session-monitor configuration data includes the primary or secondary half-session name, as well as subarea and element addresses expressed in hexadecimal. It also includes the domain name, expressed as a Netview identifier, and the local network identifier (NETID), which is the primary half-session network identifier (8-character, alphanumeric). The node type, such as SSCP, PU, LU, link, and cluster controller, and the node name and address and adjacent NETID are also included.

Other session configuration data includes: virtual route number (VRN, 0-7); transmission priority number (TPN, 0-2); explicit route number (ERN, 0-7); reverse explicit route number (RER, 0-7); explicit route inoperative (ER-INOP) status; class-of-service name (COSNAME, assigned by the class-of-service table); and a log mode name (LOGMODE, assigned by the SSCP/CP log mode table).

The session monitor provides VR status through identification of several elements, including:

■ Domain name (Netview identifier).
■ NETID (in which the VR is defined).
■ Name (VR name and endpoint PU).
■ Subarea address, in hexadecimal, of the VR endpoint PU.
■ PU Type (PU Type 5 host node or PU Type 4 communications controller node).
■ VR pool current (the current count of inbound PIUs over the VR).
■ VR pool limit (the maximum number of inbound PIUs allowed over the VR).
■ Status (VR status).
■ bbb . . . bbb (description of the current buffer state at the endpoint PU).
■ Minimum, maximum, and current VR window sizes.
■ Sent and received (sequence number of the last PIUs sent and received).
■ Time (time that VR status was received by session monitor).

8. NMA architectural entities. *NMA implementations in-clude 370-based focal points; entry points based on PU Types; and service points for non-IBM environments.*

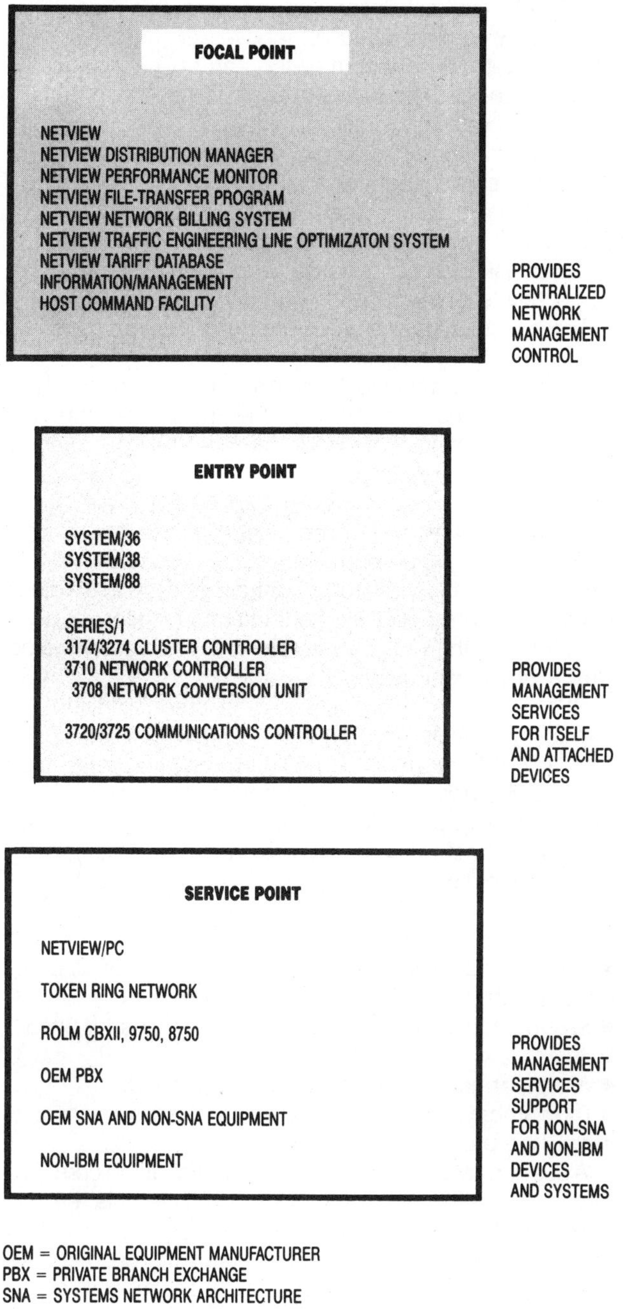

OEM = ORIGINAL EQUIPMENT MANUFACTURER
PBX = PRIVATE BRANCH EXCHANGE
SNA = SYSTEMS NETWORK ARCHITECTURE

■ cccc . . . cccc (description of VR status, such as VR operational, route congestion, VR blocked with NCP, VR, or general congestion, VR blocked—unexpected, or VR transient block).

To provide the software problem determination, config-uration management, and performance management through SNA LU-to-LU monitoring and trace mechanisms, session information must be provided to the Netview session monitor. Figure 11 summarizes the LU-to-LU session information provided to the Netview session monitor. In the figure, an initiating logical unit (ILU) launches a session request to SSCP provided that one or both of the subsequent LU half-sessions reside within a PU Type 5 host node. It can also initiate a request to a CP if the LUs in the session reside within PU Type 2.1 nodes.

The ILU session request is forwarded to the LOGMODE table as an initiate-self (INIT-SELF) formatted system services logon RU. This is called 1A in the figure. It can also be handled by the unformatted system services table (USSTAB) if the logon request does not support formatting into an INIT-SELF RU. This is shown as 1B.1 in the figure. If USSTAB is invoked, it formats the logon request to an INIT-SELF and forwards it to LOGMODE. This is shown as 1B.2.

The INIT-SELF states to LOGMODE the names of the ILU and the targeted LU. The ILU can be either the secondary LU (SLU), primary LU (PLU), or a third-party, such as another PLU or the Netview command facility.

LOGMODE then determines which logical unit is to be PLU and which is to be SLU for the LU-to-LU session. LOGMODE also forwards the PLU name as a class-of-service name (COSNAME) to class-of-service table (COSTAB). This process is depicted as 2 in Figure 11.

COSTAB, upon receipt of a LOGMODE-supplied COSNAME, determines a session class of service as a virtual route identifier (VRID). VRID is a combination of virtual route number (VRN) and the transmission priority number (TPN). COSTAB then forwards the VRID to LOGMODE (3 in Figure 11) and forwards the VRID to path table (PATH TAB), which is depicted as 4 in Figure 11.

The receipt of VRID from COSTAB provides LOGMODE with sufficient information to request the PLU to start an LU-to-LU session. This request is sent as a control initiate (CINIT) to the PLU depicted as 5 in Figure 11. It constitutes the LU-to-LU session bind image.

The PLU then constructs a bind RU and forwards the bind to the SLU shown as 6 in Figure 11. The bind can be up to 256 bytes in length. The bind specifies the PLU/SLU names, the session profiles (protocol sets) at SNA Layers 6, 5, and 4, and the session profile usage at each of these three layers.

If the BIND is positively responded to, the PLU notifies SSCP/CP with a session started (SESSST) request, which is depicted as 7 in Figure 11. Note that all of the prebind RU flows occur over previously established SSCP/CP-LU control sessions.

Netview session monitor is then notified of session status from LOGMODE (8 in Figure 11), of LOGMODE names from LOGMODE (9), and of COSNAME from COSTAB (10). PATH TAB, in conjunction with other SSCP/CP components, provides the session monitor with VRN, TPN, ERN, RERN, and transmission group numbers (11).

ER control (a subset of subarea path control) provides ER and RER status to session monitor (12). VR control (another subarea path-control subset) provides VR status, the minimum window size, the current and maximum windows, as well as sent and received PIUs over the VR status, to session monitor (shown as 13).

9. Netview. Netview is IBM's strategic network manage- ment product implementation. It is System/370-resident, consolidates several previously disparate products.

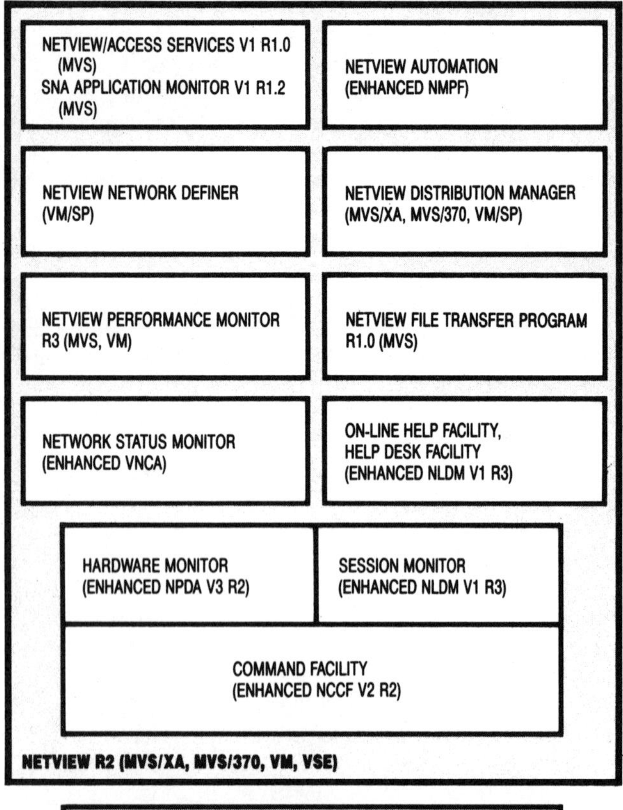

ACF/NCP = ADVANCED COMMUNICATIONS FUNCTION/NETWORK CONTROL PROGRAM
ACF/VTAM = ADVANCED COMMUNICATIONS FUNCTION/VIRTUAL TELECOMMUNICATIONS ACESS METHOD
MVS = MULTIPLE VIRTUAL STORAGE
NCCF = NETWORK COMMUNICATIONS CONTROL FACILITY
NLDM = NETWORK LOGICAL DATA MANAGER
NMPF = NETWORK MANAGEMENT PRODUCTIVITY FACILITY
NPDA = NETWORK PROBLEM DETERMINATION APPLICATION
VM/SP = VIRTUAL MACHINE/SYSTEM PRODUCT
VNCA = VTAM NODE CONTROL APPLICATION
VSE = VIRTUAL STORAGE EXTENDED
XA = EXTENDED ARCHITECTURE

The Netview status monitor (STATMON), noted in Figure 9, is an enhancement of VTAM Node Control Application (VNCA). It provides domain status, a hierarchical view of network resources, and control of network control resources. It also provides asynchronous update of the domain status panel, on-line browse of the Netview log, and an automatic reactivation of failed network resources once they become available. STATMON also has a critical-message monitor, which is an operator-notification mechanism driven by important messages originating from command facility, hardware monitor, VTAM, or TAF.

The Netview on-line help and help-desk facilities shown in Figure 9 are an enhancement of Network Management Productivity Facility (NMPF). The on-line help facility provides simplified installation and customization procedures for Netview command facility, the Netview hardware monitor, Netview session monitor, and STATMON. It also provides on-line help tutorials, a full-screen facility to browse network-descriptive libraries, and command lists (CLISTS) for automating commonly invoked operator functions and network operations. CLISTS are high-level executive statements that invoke several lines of underlying high-level-language or assembler code to perform a specific task or set of tasks through nonconditional or conditional execution tests/arguments.

The help-desk facility is an on-line guide that describes network problem diagnostic procedures. It assists in resolving nonfunctioning terminals, transactions, or applications, slow response time, problems identified through network monitoring, and system message cross-reference.

Netview Performance Monitor R3, shown in Figure 9, was announced by IBM on October 20, 1987. It is a VTAM application that monitors, records, and graphically displays network performance and utilization. It runs under MVS/370, MVS/XA, and VM/Group Control System (GCS) operating environments. Netview Performance Monitor R3 is invoked from the Netview operator console via TAF under Netview command facility.

NPM supports the enhanced session-accounting capability provided within NCP 5.2 (on the 3745/3720) and NCP 4.3 (on the 3725). Given that peripheral node LUs (LU 6.2 with a PU Type 2.1 node) are supported as primary LUs, accounting applications that have classically been host-resident are provided to the non-host PLU to collect byte and PIU counts. This data, as well as session-awareness data, is then reported to NPM R3 in the host and includes:

■ Session accounting for primary, secondary, or all LUs.
■ Immediate or deferred accounting collection.
■ Session-accounting-byte and PIU thresholds for unsolicited data.
■ Whether backup NPM sessions are defined.
■ The number of half-sessions over which session accounting will be provided.

A session-awareness PIU is sent to NPM at the completion of LU-to-LU setup, and byte and PIU counts are updated whenever session traffic flows. If these counts exceed user-specified thresholds, threshold counters are sent to NPM as unsolicited data. In all cases, session-awareness data and the last set of session counters are sent to NPM at session-termination period.

Netview File Transfer Program R1.0 for MVS (Netview FTP MVS, Fig. 9), announced by IBM on October 20, 1987, is the successor program to IBM FTP Version 2.2 for MVS. It is a VTAM application that is positioned as a strategic product for high-performance bulk data transfer within SNA System/370 MVS-, VM/SP- or VSE-based host environments. Netview FTP MVS is provided as both base and Advanced Functions Feature (AFF) products. Both base

__10. Alerts.__ Netview Hardware Monitor runs under command facility and receives and responds to solicited and unsolicited alerts from several classes of devices, including the 37XX Communications Controllers, 3174/3274 Cluster Controllers, 3710 Network Controllers, Token Ring Networks, links, and IBM modems.

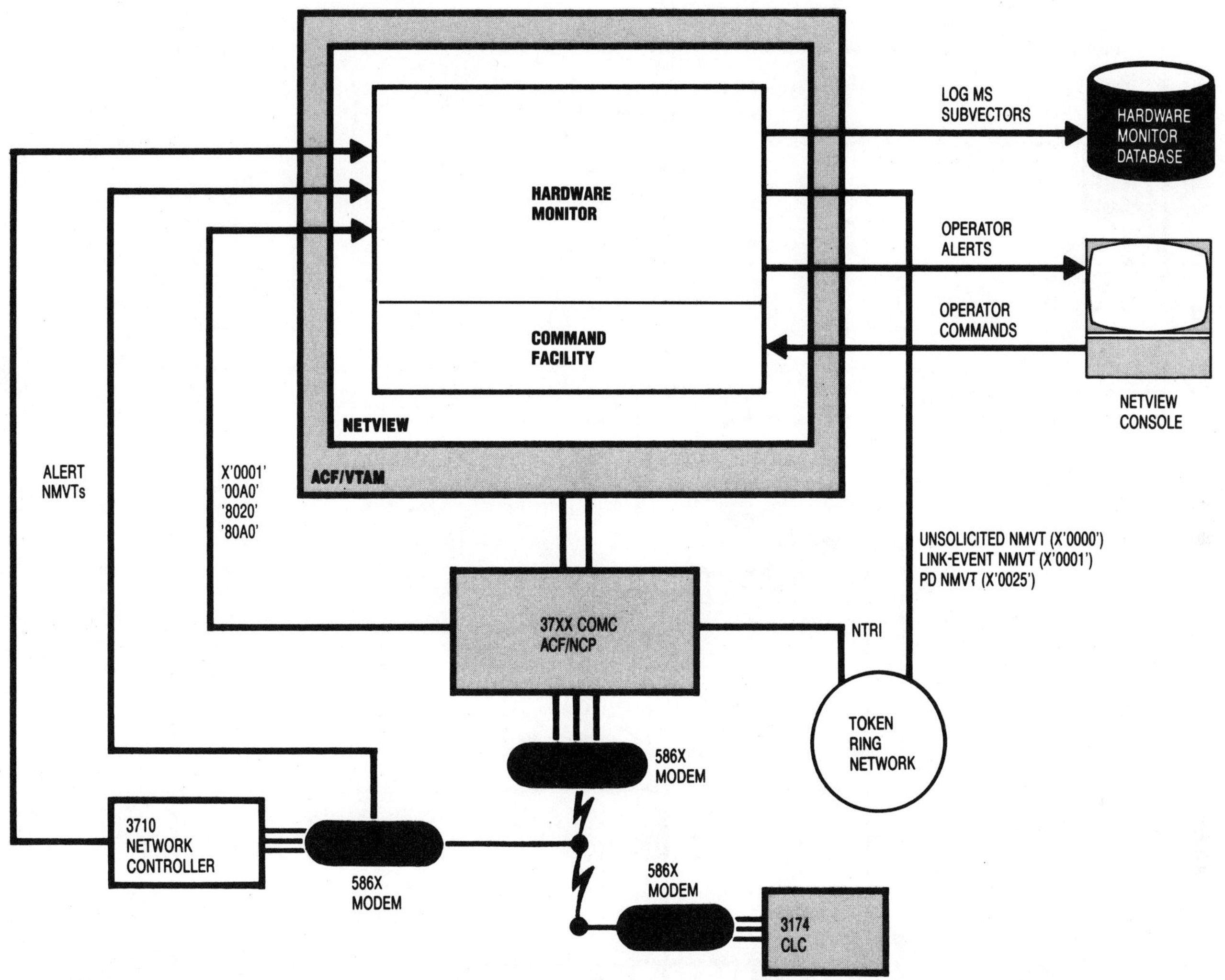

and AFF support the predecessor product (FTP Version 2.2 MVS) features including:

- File-to-file transfer without spooling.
- File handlers for several file methods, including virtual storage access method (VSAM), queued sequential access method (QSAM), entry-sequenced data set, and VSAM key-sequenced data set.
- Checkpoint/restart.
- Data compression.
- RU size (RUSIZE) up to 32 kbytes as a function of NCP buffer capacity.

Netview FTP MVS base has several enhancements, which include a queue handler, server mechanisms, parallel transmissions, Netview operator console commands, and the identification of remote Netview FTP MVS by a set of LU names on the remote node.

Netview FTP MVS AFF contains all the base functions and adds privileged data set (PDS) support and various compression/compaction options. It also supports parallel transmission for up to 99 Netview FTP MVS AFF servers and QSAM support for variable blocked spanned (VBS) records.

The Netview network definer, announced on June 16, 1987, by IBM, runs under VM/SP. It is used to interactively create and update definition tables for VM-based SNA networks, including 9370. It provides configuration management through creation of ACF/VTAM definitions, which support locally attached SNA and non-SNA devices and

11. Netview Session Monitor functions. *Netview Session Monitor, an enhancement of Network Logical Data Manager, provides end-to-end, LU-to-LU logical-session status and reports on all control sessions and Systems Network Architecture path control facilities associated with LU-to-LU sessions.*

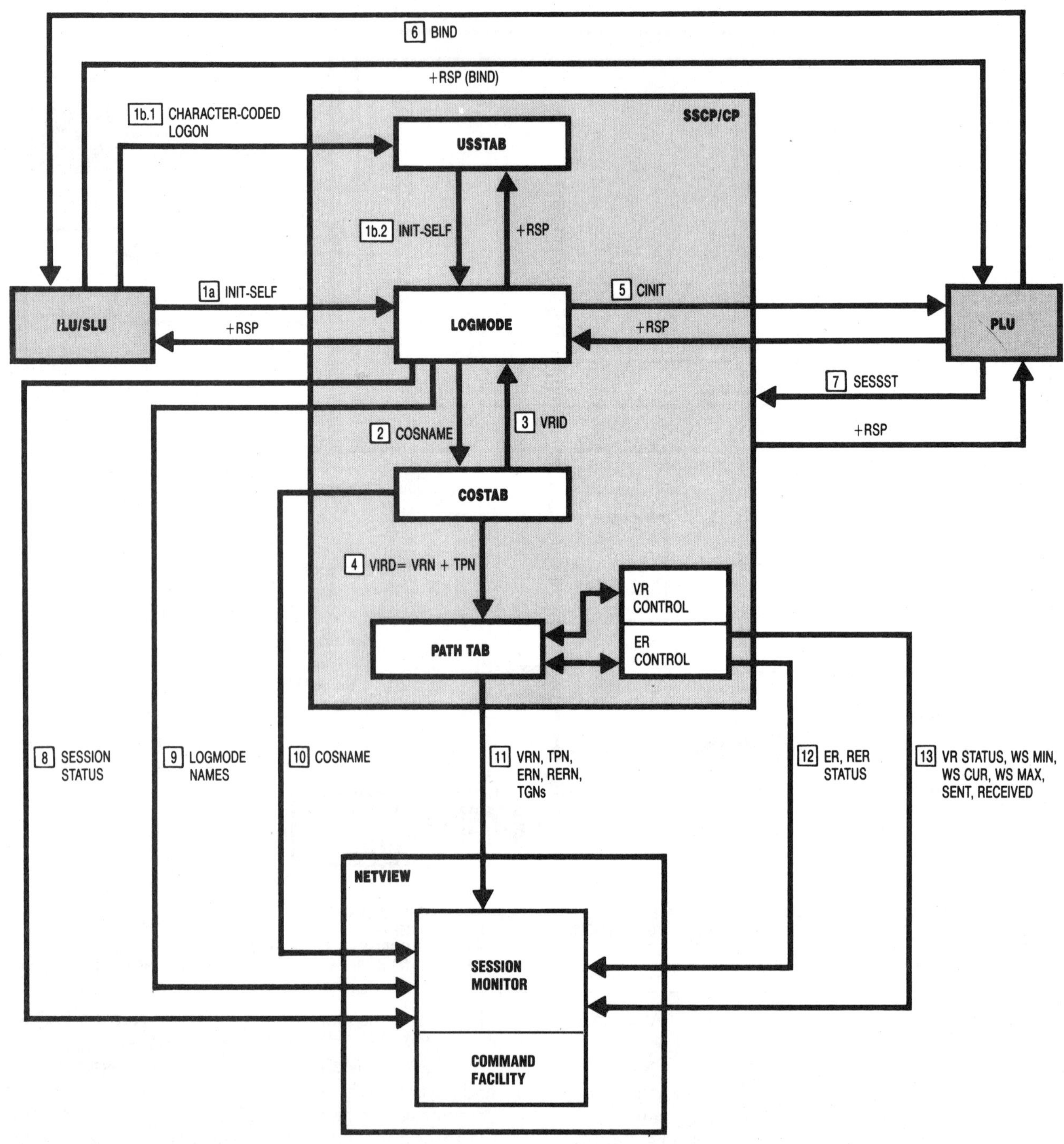

COSNAME = CLASS OF SERVICE NAME	MAX = MAXIMUM	TGN = TRANSMISSION GROUP NUMBER
COSTAB = CLASS OF SERVICE TABLE	MIN = MINIMUM	TPN = TRANSMISSION PRIORITY NUMBER
CP = CONTROL POINT	PATH TAB = PATH TABLE	USSTAB = UNFORMATTED SYSTEM SERVICES TABLE
CUR = CURRENT	PLU = PRIMARY LOGICAL UNIT	VRID = VIRTUAL ROUTE IDENTIFIER
ERN = EXPLICIT ROUTE NUMBER	RERN = REVERSE EXPLICIT ROUTE NUMBER	VRN = VIRTUAL ROUTE NUMBER
ILU = INITIATING LOGICAL UNIT	SESSST = SESSION STARTED	WS = WINDOW SIZE
INIT = INITIATE	SLU = SECONDARY LOGICAL UNIT	
LOGMODE = LOGON MODE TABLE	SSCP = SYSTEM SERVICES CONTROL POINT	

an integrated communications adapter for leased and switched lines. The Netview network definer also supports LOGMODE tables, USSTABS, X.25 communication adapter, and channel-to-channel attachment. The ACF/VTAM definitions can also be used to manage COSTAB, ACF/VTAM attachments to the IBM Token Ring Network, path table definitions, and SNI gateway environments.

The configuration definition, in turn, supports Netview command facility, hardware monitor, session monitor, STATMON, and operators. Thus, the Netview network definer performs change management functions through distribution of the configuration data through VM Remote Spooling Communications Subsystem (RSCS) facilities.

The Netview distribution manager (Netview DM, Fig. 9) was announced by IBM on October 20, 1987, for MVS/XA, MVS/370, and VM/SP operating systems. It replaces the Distributed Systems Executive for MVS and provides change management functions through centrally controlled data distribution and implementation of software changes within SNA networks.

To provide such central-site control, Netview DM implements VM end-node support. It also supports System/36 intermediate network nodes running the APPN feature and PC Disk Operating System (DOS) end nodes connected through a System/36 intermediate node, as well as System/36, VSE, 4680, Series/1, Series/1-PC Connect, 8100, and System/88—all as directly connected end nodes.

SNA change management is supported by:
■ SNA distribution services (SNADS) distributions among customer information control system/virtual storage (CICS/VS)-resident Distributed Office Support System (Disoss), System/36, System/38, and 5520 SNADS distribution service units (DSUs).
■ Distributed Data Management (DDM) file updates among CICS/DDM, System/36 DDM, System/38 DDM, DDM/PC, and Netview/PC DDM implementations.
■ IBM RT PC distributed services program under the Advanced Interactive Executive (AIX) operating system. AIX enables networked RT PCs to share files and application resources.

Netview/Access Services V1 R1.0 (Netview/Access) and SNA Application Monitor (SAMON, Fig. 9) were announced by IBM on June 16, 1987, for MVS. Netview/Access affords access to a number of VTAM applications from a single screen through multiple concurrent sessions. It also automates logon/logoff based on user profiles, permits access to multiple terminal sessions by the same network operator, and interfaces to SAMON. SAMON enables terminals to display the status of all active VTAM applications within an SNA network and to connect the terminal to a VTAM application.

Netview Automation (Fig. 9), announced by IBM on June 16, 1987, as part of Netview R2, provides several functions previously handled by NMPF (under Netview R1). It is defined as a subsystem that automates several key Netview components. The interface to Netview Automation is provided as an MVS subsystem interface (SSI) for MVS environments. This permits Netview Automation to issue MVS system and subsystem commands from any Netview CLIST or operator station in the same or a different domain.

12. Netview Automation. *This offering automates several key Netview components to enable incoming alert-message filtering and responses independent of operator notification.*

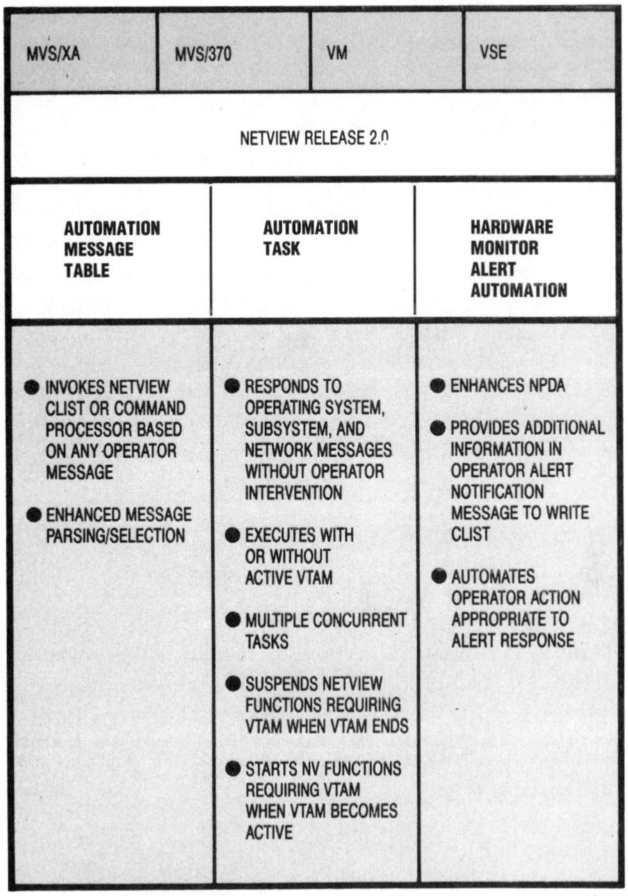

MVS/XA = MULTIPLE VIRTUAL STORAGE/EXTENDED ARCHITECTURE
NPDA = NETWORK PROBLEM DETERMINATION APPLICATION
NV = NETVIEW
VM = VIRTUAL MACHINE
VSE = VIRTUAL STORAGE EXTENDED
VTAM = VIRTUAL TELECOMMUNICATIONS ACCESS METHOD

It also enables the Programmable Operator facility for VM and the VSE/Operator Communication Control Facility (OCCF) for VSE. The MVS SSI under Netview R2 succeeds MVS/OCCF.

Figure 12 illustrates the three principal Netview Automation facilities: the automation message table, automation task, and hardware monitor alert automation. In essence, predefined Netview CLISTs can be activated by automated task functions in addition to classical manual invocations of CLISTS.

Automation message table permits the specification of criteria that cause automated CLIST activation. Automation task enables Netview responses to operating system, subsystem, and network messages in the absence of manual operator intervention. Hardware monitor alert automation enhances Netview hardware monitor. It will begin an automation scenario through activation of predefined CLISTs after receiving network events detected by specific network alert data.

Netview Automation also provides automated console operations through a Netview application called Inter-System Control Facility and a PC program called the Inter-System Control Facility/PC. These enhancements to Netview Automation, announced concurrently with Netview R2, permit operators at a Netview Automation focal point to monitor and control targeted operating system and hardware control consoles with remote initial machine load (IML, warm start) and initial program load (IPL, cold start).

Netview Automation does not presently qualify as a knowledge-based, rule-based inference engine. But the set of functions it invokes clearly indicates a direction. In time, it will become a network management environment with expert system capabilities. This new direction in network management is essential if such complex tasks as message filtering, task inference, and initiation of corrective action are to take place without a human operator overseeing increasingly complex internetworked processing environments.

Netview/PC

Netview/PC is a strategic NMA service point implementation. It acts as an extension to Netview services and is designed to support IBM LANs and Rolm voice networks as well as non-SNA and non-IBM communications devices. Netview/PC V1.1, announced June 16, 1987, supports Netview R2 and non-IBM communications devices through an application program interface/communications services (API/CS) facility. It uses NMVT RUs to send alerts to a host-resident Netview.

Figure 13 depicts the Netview/PC communications environment. Netview/PC can connect, for example, a Token Ring Network to Netview via a PC acting as a gateway, or it can be used to build an asynchronous connection to a Rolm 9750/8750 Business Communications System or CBXII. These Netview/PC connections enable Netview/PC to support voice network management (VNM) products, such as Netview network billing system, Netview network traffic engineering line-optimization system, and Netview tariff database.

The Netview/PC API/CS component communicates with a host Netview using NMVT RUs over an SSCP-PU session. In this environment, Netview interfaces to CPMS, and the Netview/PC API/CS interacts with PUMS. Therefore, the API/CS PUMS half-session behaves as a PU Type 2.0 SNA node. Netview/PC can also communicate with a host CICS/DDM program using an LU Type 6.2 session to transfer, for example, Rolm CBX-generated call detail records (CDRs).

Netview/PC is defined through Base System Services, which is an extension of DOS. Netview/PC's API/CS includes the Netview/PC services, such as communications, help facility, initialization, session manager, dialogue manager, and a database manager. API/CS also includes a remote console facility enabling one Netview/PC to control another; problem determination facilities; and Token Ring Network Manager V1.1, announced by IBM on September 18, 1986,

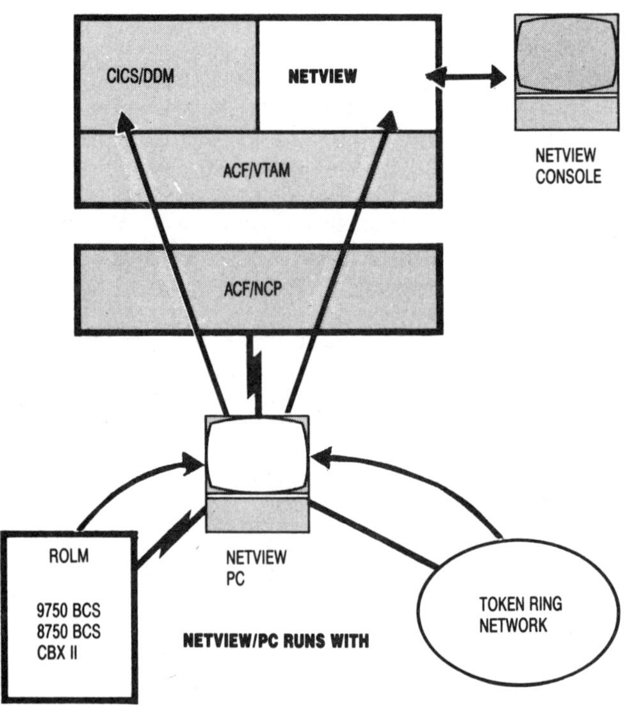

13. Netview/PC service point implementation. *Netview/PC provides NMA service point functions. It works with Token Ring Networks and Rolm environments.*

ACF/NCP = ADVANCED COMMUNICATIONS FUNCTION/NETWORK CONTROL PROGRAM
ACF/VTAM = ADVANCED COMMUNICATIONS FUNCTION/VIRTUAL TELECOMMUNICATIONS
ACCESS METHOD
CICS/DDM = CUSTOMER INFORMATION CONTROL SYSTEM/
DISTRIBUTED DATA MANAGEMENT

which requires a dedicated Netview/PC. netview/PC with OS/2 Extended Edition will also be supported.

Figure 14 depicts the Token Ring Network Manager environment. It is a Netview/PC LAN application with remote-console capabilities. Netview alerts are generated as NMVT RUs. The alerts include a notification when ring-error limits are exceeded and when ring-recovery failures occur. It also provides auto-removal error notification when a multistation access unit fails. Alerts are issued when an adapter is removed, when there is a failure in the adapter microcode, when an adapter fails, or when an abnormal ending occurs.

The IBM LAN Manager Version 1.0, announced on April 2, 1987, also operates as a Netview/PC application. It supports network management capability on both the IBM Token Ring Network and the broadband IBM PC Network. It can be used in concert with the IBM Token Ring Network Bridge Program Version 1.1 (announced April 2, 1987) to manage a multiring Token Ring Network environment.

The Token Ring Bridge program's network management functions include a ring parameter server, which provides ring numbers to stations as they are inserted into rings. The Token Ring Bridge program also has a ring-error monitor function that is used to assemble error statistics reported

14. Token Ring Network Manager. Token Ring Network Manager runs under Netview/PC and notifies the host Netview of ring errors over SSCP-PU sessions.

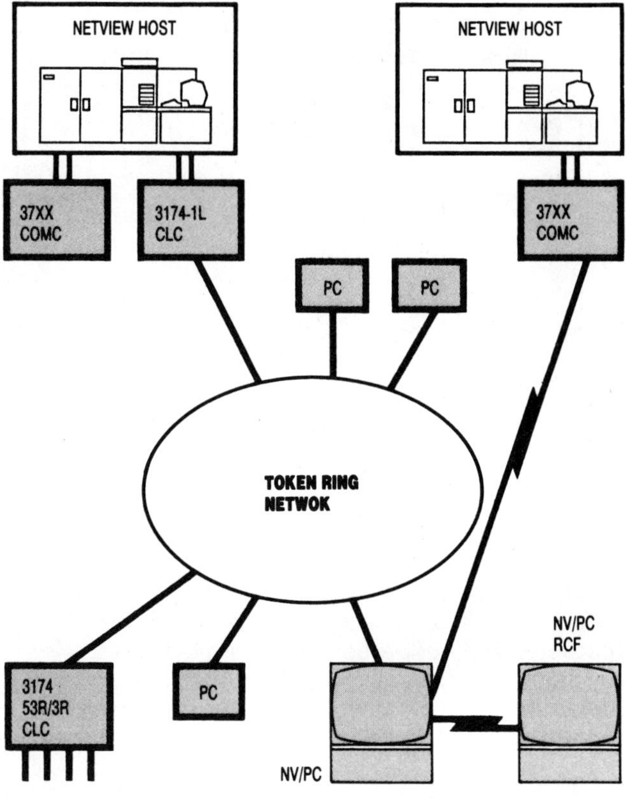

by stations with access to the program. The configuration report server function of the bridge program forwards configuration change notifications to the IBM LAN Manager under Netview/PC.

Netview/PC also accepts Netview R2-generated service point command service (SPCS) commands and forwards these to the appropriate application. The SPCS commands include LINKPD (link problem determination), LINKTEST (link test), LINKDATA (link data), and RUNCMD (run communication management data).

Summary

NMA is significant because it formalizes IBM's long-term approach to management and control of complex SNA networks. It specifies predictable programmatic interfaces between and among network operators, network management applications, and host and nonhost communications. It also specifies the operational sequences needed to control network configurations. Furthermore, NMA addresses end-to-end issues of network management, from application to application and from application to user device.

Netview is the NMA strategic network management product. It is significant for two reasons. For the first time, human and software network operators can pass application data among VTAM network management components.

Netview also makes it possible to communicate across structured protocol boundaries through CPMS and other architected interfaces (Fig. 4).

The PU Type 5 SSCP-resident structured protocol boundaries between CPMS and network operator, CP configuration services, CP session services, and half-session define an API that is architecturally derived and product-independent. Product independence is important to NMA CPMS APIs, since these APIs will foster product life-cycle independence and give the original equipment manufacturer of network management environments a way to communicate with Netview and other IBM NMA implementations.

Major NMA directions include:

- Likely extension of the management-services API to support hybrid subarea/peripheral node peer-to-peer networking based on the Node Type 2.1 LEN architecture.
- Positioning of NMA within IBM's Systems Application Architecture. SAA is a collection of selected software interfaces, conventions, and protocols positioned to provide a standard environment for developing consistent applications across IBM's three major computing environments.
- Likely interfaces between the MS APIs into the developing OSI network standards for resource management, layer management, and system management. ■

Thomas J. Routt is president of Network Systems International, a firm that provides worldwide network architecture consulting to Fortune *1,000 corporations concerned with migration to OSI and SNA. Previously, Routt was manager of Boeing Network Architecture for Boeing Computer Services Company. In this capacity, he managed global network planning, design, and implementation for the Boeing Company. Routt holds an M. B. A. in information systems from Southern Illinois University and a B. S. in environmental science from Western Washington University.*

References:

Systems Network Architecture Format and Protocol Reference Manual: Management Services, IBM, SC30-3346-0.

Netview General Information and Planning, IBM, GC30-3463.

Netview Program Products General Information, IBM, GC30-3350.

Netview Primer, IBM, GG24-3047.

Netview R2.0 Licensed Program Specifications (MVS and VM), IBM, GC30-9589.

Netview Licensed Program Specifications, VSE, IBM, GC30-9602.

Netview R2.0 Installation and Administration Guide, IBM, SC30-3476.

Netview R2.0 Command Lists, IBM, SC30-3423.

Netview/PC, IBM, GG22-9119.

Netview/PC Planning and Operation Guide, IBM, SC30-3408.

Netview/PC Application Program Interface/Communication Services Manual, IBM, SC30-3313.

J. Scott Haugdahl and Carl R. Manson, Architecture Technology Corp., Minneapolis, Minn.

Benchmarking the devices that measure LAN protocols

With LANs becoming more complex, protocol analyzers can help. But picking the right analyzer can involve complex trade-offs.

Increasingly, LANs are becoming more complicated than the easy-linking configurations that many users expected. It's not unheard of these days for the manager of a network to encounter some mysterious occurrence on the LAN, one that requires days—even weeks—of effort to isolate the fault. For that matter, the hardware to be attached and the software to be run on that LAN raise questions. Does software vendor A's implementation of a set of protocols follow the strict rules of the standard? Is that software compatible with vendor B's implementation of the same set of protocols?

Answers to such questions and solutions to many LAN headaches can be found through the use of LAN protocol analyzers. Such devices may be thought of as the ultimate in LAN debugging and testing tools. Other LAN testing tools have capabilities that range from merely scrutinizing the signal on a cable with an oscilloscope to rudimentary devices that count packets and display overall traffic statistics and transmission problems. Analyzers generally are capable of examining all seven LAN protocol layers.

LAN management tools are also available, but in most cases they are unique to a vendor's application and usually "manage" various specific layers from Layer 3 (network) to Layer 7 (application). By contrast, LAN protocol analyzers tend to be general-purpose.

Analyzing the analyzers

To be useful, LAN protocol analyzers must be able to observe all back-to-back packets (including bad packets) that have been transmitted and do so at full LAN transmission rates. However, it isn't necessary to be able to capture every bit of every frame for later observation. With the help of filtering, triggering, and slicing techniques, developers of protocol analyzers have reduced the volume of traffic that needs to be collected.

Most analyzers allow some aspect of the LAN traffic to be viewed as it arrives from the network: packets per second, network utilization, packet distribution, etc. However, events generally occur too quickly to be analyzed as they happen. Therefore, the packets are placed in a capture buffer along with a time stamp and are subject to later analysis. It is this later analysis that distinguishes the various commercially available LAN protocol analyzers.

We shall concentrate on these tools from a benchmarking perspective. Benchmarking has always been controversial, and the potential controversy in benchmarking LAN protocol analyzers is compounded by the virtually infinite ways in which protocol stacks can be assembled. Another complicating factor: Literally millions of bytes of LAN traffic can be collected in a short amount of time. Therefore, we will concentrate on some of the basic capture and analysis features of LAN protocol analyzers such as rates of capturing and filtering raw data.

The LAN chosen as a reference base was Ethernet, since virtually every LAN analyzer supports Ethernet. All LAN analyzers examined were based on the Intel 80286 processor (on clones of the IBM PC/AT), except for the HP 4972A, which is based on a proprietary architecture and uses the Motorola 68010 processor. They also all utilized the Intel 82586 Ethernet controller chip.

First we shall benchmark these devices in terms of their basic performance capability in capturing packets for later examination. Second, we shall examine frame interpretation. There are two methods employed by these LAN protocol analyzers to provide frame interpretation: filtering and decoding (sometimes called parsing). Each method is examined in the latter part of this article.

A number of LAN analyzers are now available from companies such as Hewlett-Packard, Communication Machinery Corporation, Cabletron, Network General,

Excelan, Tandem/Ungermann-Bass, and Spider Systems. Most provide some level of protocol analysis.

We shall examine the protocol analysis performance of four units: the LANalyzer model EX5500 from Excelan; the Sniffer model PA-302 from Network General Corporation; the LAN Protocol Analyzer model HP 4972A from Hewlett-Packard; and the SpiderMonitor model P200 from Spider Systems. During these tests, the LANalyzer was running software version 2.1, the Sniffer version 1.31, the 4972A LAN Protocol Analyzer version B.02.0, and the Spider-Monitor version 2.1.

In order to simulate network traffic on a consistent basis for testing and measuring, we constructed a test bed as shown in Figure 1. The test bed consists of two processors used to generate traffic, the four LAN protocol analyzers, an oscilloscope to calibrate the packet timing of the traffic generators, one LANalyzer, one Sniffer, one SpiderMonitor, and one HP 4972A. Each analyzer was connected by a standard Ethernet cable to a multiport transceiver made by BICC Data Networks. Although we placed each analyzer in the test in receive mode (capture mode), we performed testing to ensure that units did not interfere with each other's operations.

The traffic generators in this test setup will not be identified because differences in generators cannot have bearing on the test results. With equal validity, the traffic could have been generated from virtually any source, from microcomputers to LAN protocol analyzers. The generated traffic simply had to be measurable and consistent.

Benchmark variables
What is a typical LAN? There is no such thing. But to create benchmarks for this test, we examined network traffic from many different configurations of Ethernet LAN. These included pure PC LANs, terminal-to-host hookups, LANs for high-speed workstations, and mixtures of these. Some of the conclusions about the traffic patterns of these LANs were somewhat startling. The majority of packets turn out to be very small—close to the minimum of 60 bytes that standard 802.3 Ethernet requires. And most of the remaining packets are of 1,000 bytes or more, averaging around 1,084 bytes.

This was the case for most of the LANs examined. However, there were a few exceptions. Some networks, such as those using gear made by 3Com, are set up to jam as much data as possible into the largest possible standard Ethernet packet: 1,514 bytes. In this case, longer packets tend to be close to 1,500 bytes.

Another exception to the trend noticed: A few Ethernet network products transmit many packets around the 572-byte size. Broken down by application, terminal-to-host LANs are heavy with 60-byte packets; PC LANs have a fair amount of 1,024-byte packets, which, with overhead, give an average of approximately 1,084 bytes.

The traffic pattern we chose for benchmarking consisted of a mix of the most used configurations: 90 percent

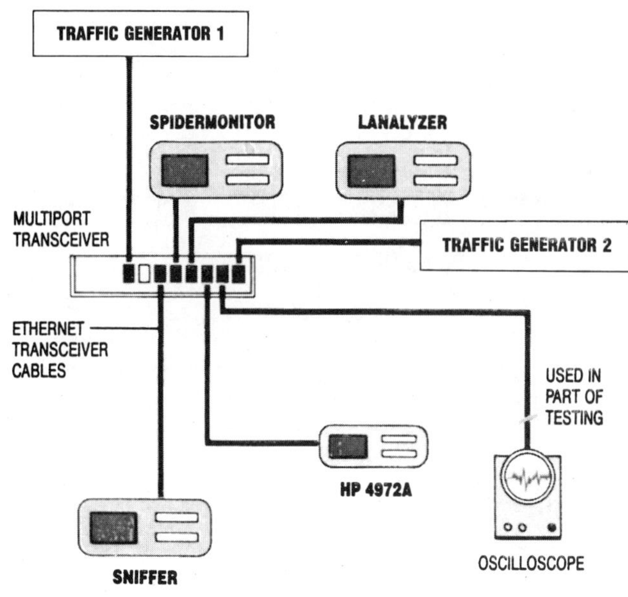

1. Test bed. *The four protocol analyzers were tested with: a multiport transceiver, two processors to generate traffic, and an oscilloscope to calibrate the packet timing.*

60-byte packets, and 10 percent 1,084-byte packets. We chose this sample before the benchmarking began and made no attempt to pick optimal values in order to favor one analyzer or the other.

Typical mix
We used this typical traffic pattern to benchmark the general behavior of the analyzers; specifically, it was used in the maximum steady traffic benchmark and in the save-to-disk benchmark. Other benchmark tests we performed include a count of the maximum number of packets that can be retained in the capture buffer for later analysis and a worst-case maximum traffic burst capture.

For benchmarks that capture all packets, we placed all machines in a promiscuous capture mode. The defaults set up were the same as when the units come from the factory except for the LANalyzer, which was set to a single promiscuous receive channel (multiple receive channels in LANalyzer are analogous to display filters of the Sniffer). We didn't benchmark the display features of the various units; we discuss these briefly near the end of this article.

Particularly important are benchmarks that test LAN analyzer features that work with packet slicing. Since for test purposes the most important data in each packet is usually contained in its header, slicing can minimize processing of long packets. In some cases, a slice can be as little as 20 to 30 bytes, but for benchmarking purposes we chose the 64-byte size so as to cover most sophisticated embedded protocol headers.

Maximum packet buffering
The first benchmark examined—simple in theory but somewhat complex to understand—was the maximum number of packets that can be captured into memory and subsequently displayed. It's a mistake to assume simplistically

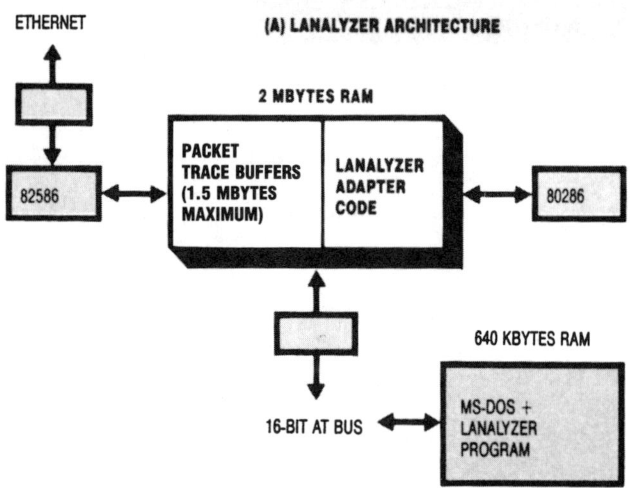

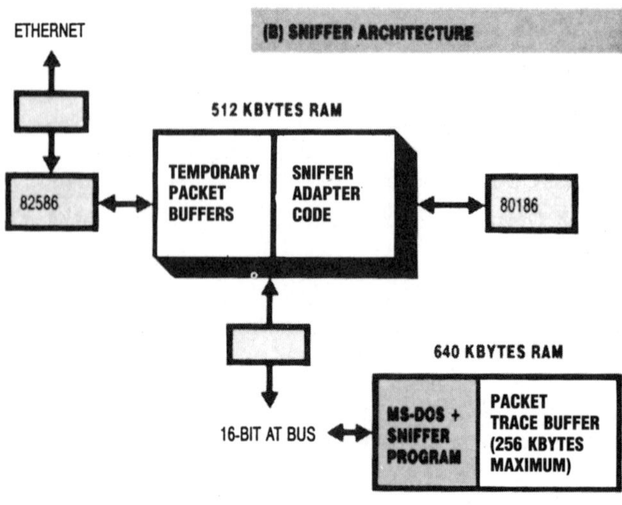

2. The structure of analyzers. *Only two analyzers are detailed here because the basics of the 4972A and Spider-Monitor are very similar to that of the LANalyzer.*

that the larger the packet buffer the greater the number of packets it can hold. This may be true within a single vendor's implementation, but it isn't necessarily true when different vendors' units are compared. The true capability depends on how buffers are managed.

The LANalyzer (Fig. 2A) uses a 1.5-Mbyte buffer on the Ethernet adapter as both a capture and a trace buffer. The Sniffer (Fig. 2B) uses the device's on-board Ethernet adapter memory as a 512-kbyte capture buffer and the unit's internal memory as the trace buffer, which has a maximum size of 256 kbytes. The SpiderMonitor and the 4972A have architectures similar to the LANalyzer's and thus do not require separate illustrations. Since slicing was not available with the supplied software, we didn't compare them in this benchmark.

Because the architectures of the front-ends of the Sniffer and the LANalyzer are so similar (an Ethernet connection, the Intel 82586 Ethernet controller, then a buffer), judging by the buffer size alone might lead one to conclude that

the LANalyzer outperforms the Sniffer by a factor of six (a 1.572-Mbyte buffer compared with 262-kbyte buffer). The results of benchmarking demonstrate, however, that this does not occur in the parameters tested. In many of the sliced-packets-dependent benchmarks we view as critical, Sniffer often outperforms LANalyzer.

Trace buffers
Trace buffers are buffers built to hold LAN packets the user can observe. To perform this buffering, the Sniffer uses the internal memory of its host processor. (By contrast, the other compared analyzers use their on-board adapter memory.) The number of packets that can be held in trace memory depends both on the mode the analyzer is in while capturing and on the received packet sizes (which can be affected by filtering and slicing).

All four units support a display mode with the ongoing activity (such as packet counts, skylines, network utilization, etc.) displayed as is it occurring on the network.

Another mode supported by the LANalyzer and Sniffer is the so-called high-speed mode: All displays of LAN activity are turned off except for the packet count. In high-speed mode, trace buffers are allocated differently than in display mode to ensure that no packets are missed even while receiving full-bandwidth, back-to-back packets. The trade-off is that fewer packets can be stored for later viewing.

This limitation is in part the result of the way in which the Intel 82586 chip chains buffers together while receiving data. Buffer-chaining is used to minimize the amount of memory used. The smaller the buffer, the more efficient the memory allocation—but the greater the processing over-head required. Large buffers are therefore used in high-speed mode.

The 4972A uses large buffers in such a way that even during display mode no packets are dropped. Although the 4972A's buffer size can be adjusted, its technical manual warns that doing so may have adverse effects. We there-fore left the unit's buffer size fixed at its maximum during benchmarking.

Benchmark results
The tests showed that there was indeed a difference between products. Under each unit's normal mode of operation, set to save entire packets in the trace memory, the test results showed that the LANalyzer holds substan-tially more large packets than the Sniffer (Fig. 3A). For 60-byte packets, however, the LANalyzer has only a slight advantage. The capacity for the SpiderMonitor and the 4972A does not vary with packet size and is a fixed 300-packet maximum for the SpiderMonitor and 655 packets for the 4972A.

When slicing is turned on, the amount of partial packets that the Sniffer can hold jumps significantly over that of the other three analyzers benchmarked. Figure 3B shows the two slice-capable machines, LANalyzer and Sniffer, each with slicing set to 64 bytes, with the 0 offset. In this case, the Sniffer can accommodate many more packets, even at modest sizes, than the other protocol analyzers. The Spider Monitor and the 4972A were not shown since neither provides packet slicing.

Surprisingly, the LANalyzer does not appear to take advantage of the sliced packet size to optimize the trace memory, though the user can only view the partial packet. This limitation may be caused by dealing with the 82586 link buffers on the adapter board and not having the flexibility of moving data into the host's internal RAM. Further analysis revealed that LANalyzer allocates buffers 512 bytes at a time so that the overhead is as high for small packets as it is for packet sizes just over the 512-byte boundary.

The capture buffer for the Sniffer is also set to fixed sizes for the benefit of the Intel 82586 chip in its Ethernet controller, but the internal trace buffer is set up as a compacted linked list. During high-speed operation, the Sniffer does not transfer packets off the adapter board. It thus works like LANalyzer, although the units allocate the on-board buffers differently in this mode, as previously discussed.

Figure 4 shows the efficiency of trace buffers' utilization in teams of 1,024 bytes of memory. The red line shows results for the Spider Monitor, the 4972A, and the LANalyzer in high-speed mode, respectively: 0.58; 0.64; and 0.61 packets per kbyte.

Maximum sustained traffic

For this test we used the "typical" traffic pattern—a 10:1 ratio of 60-byte to 1,084-byte packets—and we set the analyzers to capture all frames. In high-speed mode, the LANalyzer and the Sniffer were able to capture both the typical pattern and worst-case, back-to-back packets (60-byte packets sent faster than 14,500 packets per second) on a sustained basis. We used both traffic generators in this test. In normal display mode, the captured number drops because of the overhead in calculations for, and display of, the various counters and statistics.

Using the typical traffic pattern, we increased the frequency in terms of packets per second until the counters no longer accurately reflected the number of packets sent. We sent a total of 100,000 packets each time, in order to simulate a steady-state network for a modest time (a period of merely tens of seconds). Sending more than 100,000 packets did not affect the results of the test.

The 4972A had no problems with frame counts in worst-case scenarios. The LANalyzer and the Sniffer were very close in this test: Both were able to accommodate reliably a steady stream of approximately 25 percent bandwidth. With slicing set to 64, LANalyzer stayed at the same level, while the Sniffer's response increased slightly. The Spider-Monitor faired worst, reliably accommodating only about 12 percent of the bandwidth.

3. A trace of buffer. *In nonslicing mode, LANalyzer generally holds in trace buffer more large packets than the three other analyzers.*

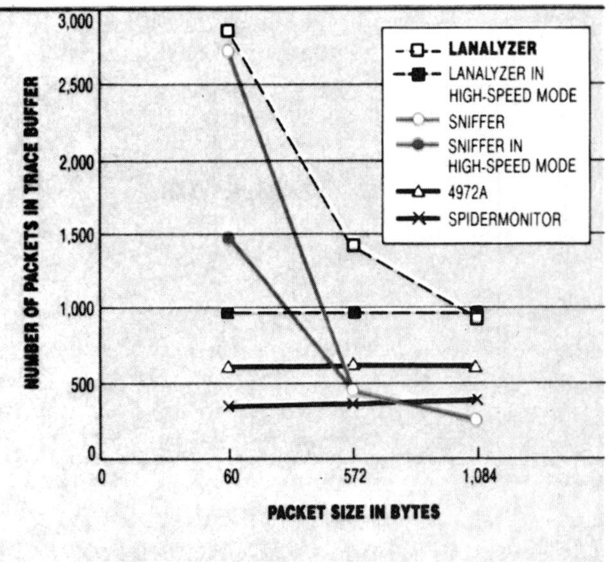

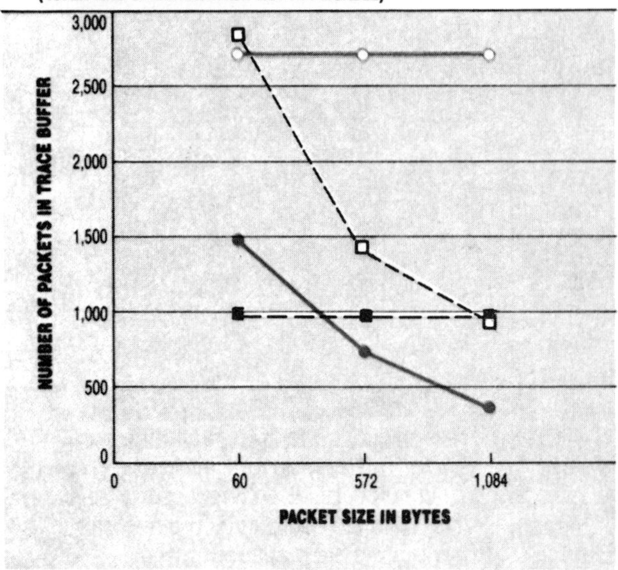

As the tests described thus far have shown, in normal display mode all the tested LAN analyzers could easily capture all the frames transmitted from very short bursts of much higher bandwidth—the question is, exactly what time span this burst can occupy. Unfortunately, its duration turns out to be shorter than could be accurately measured by our test bed. Because the traffic generators are started by pressing a key, making precise short-term measurements is somewhat difficult if both traffic generators must be used.

Our test thus comprised three "burst" benchmarks consisting of 60-, 572-, and 1,084-byte "back-to-back" packets. A single traffic generator could not quite gener-

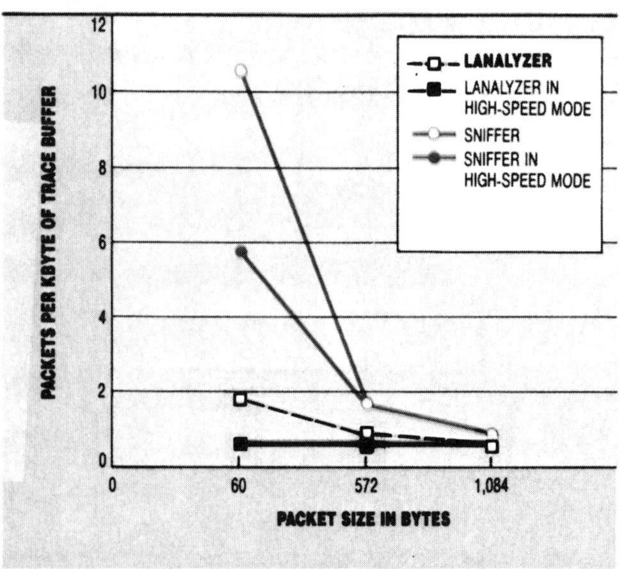

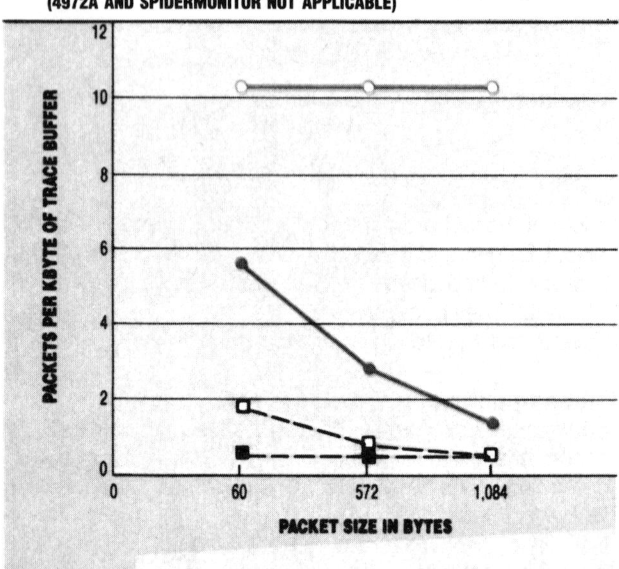

ate packets fast enough to be back-to-back. The approximate packets-per-second rates were as follows: 9,400, 1,940, and 1,081 for the 60-, 572-, and 1,084-byte packets, respectively, with Ethernet utilization of 54.6 percent, 91.3 percent, and 95.5 percent. We also performed this benchmark with the slicing turned on for 64 bytes.

The table below summarizes the results. For medium-to-large packets, only the Sniffer was unable to keep pace. The 4972A could see all packets. For smaller packets, the test results are varied. The SpiderMonitor yielded the most interesting result—indefinite for medium-to-large packets but dropping to 35 for short bursts of 60-byte packets. This was significantly lower than LANalyzer's or Sniffer's results,

meaning that a user might lose packets testing networks with bursty, short packet traffic.

We made another interesting observation concerning the LANalyzer. In another burst test, we allowed the trace buffers of the analyzers to fill, and repeated the test several times to double-check the results. Starting with an empty buffer, the LANalyzer could do a burst of 900 packets. Once the buffer filled, the number dropped sharply, to 260. This was apparently due to the unit's moving packets from the Ethernet adapter memory once it filled. This also explains the numbers for the Sniffer (which is constantly moving packets from the adapter). With slicing set to 64 bytes, the picture changed for the LANalyzer and the Sniffer—the two units with slicing capability. Now, the Sniffer comfortably kept pace when handling medium- to larger-size packets. There was no change with LANalyzer.

Maximum packet bursts

Packet size (bytes)	60	572	1,084
Without slicing			
LANalyzer	260	Indef.	Indef.
Sniffer	350	550	Indef.
SpiderMonitor	35	Indef.	Indef.
4972A	Indef.	Indef.	Indef.
With slicing			
LANalyzer (slice = 64)	260	Indef.	Indef.
Sniffer (slice = 64)	350	Indef.	Indef.

Surprisingly, capturing while filtering station addresses, packet types, pattern matching within the frame, etc., had little or no measurable effect on the capture rates of any of the analyzers. However, in order of filter complexity (number of filters and pattern complexity), the simplest was the Sniffer, followed by the SpiderMonitor, the 4972A, and the LANalyzer. The Sniffer puts sophisticated filtering capabilities at the postcapture point (frame viewing) by allowing the user to select specific protocol levels (802.2, NetWare, etc.) at which to view.

Capturing to hard disk

An interesting feature of the 4972A and the LANalyzer is the claim of each to be able to capture continuously the trace buffer to a hard-disk file for later analysis. The Sniffer and SpiderMonitor require a series of keystrokes to save the trace buffer and then resume operations.

We thought it would be instructive to find out just what the capture rate was for continuous saving to hard disk. For this test, we used our "typical" traffic pattern of the 10:1 ratio of 60-byte to 1,084-byte packets.

The results surprised us. To capture continuously without losing packets, the sustained traffic rate could only be around 5 percent continuous Ethernet utilization. The 4972A had a slight edge here at 6 percent, while the

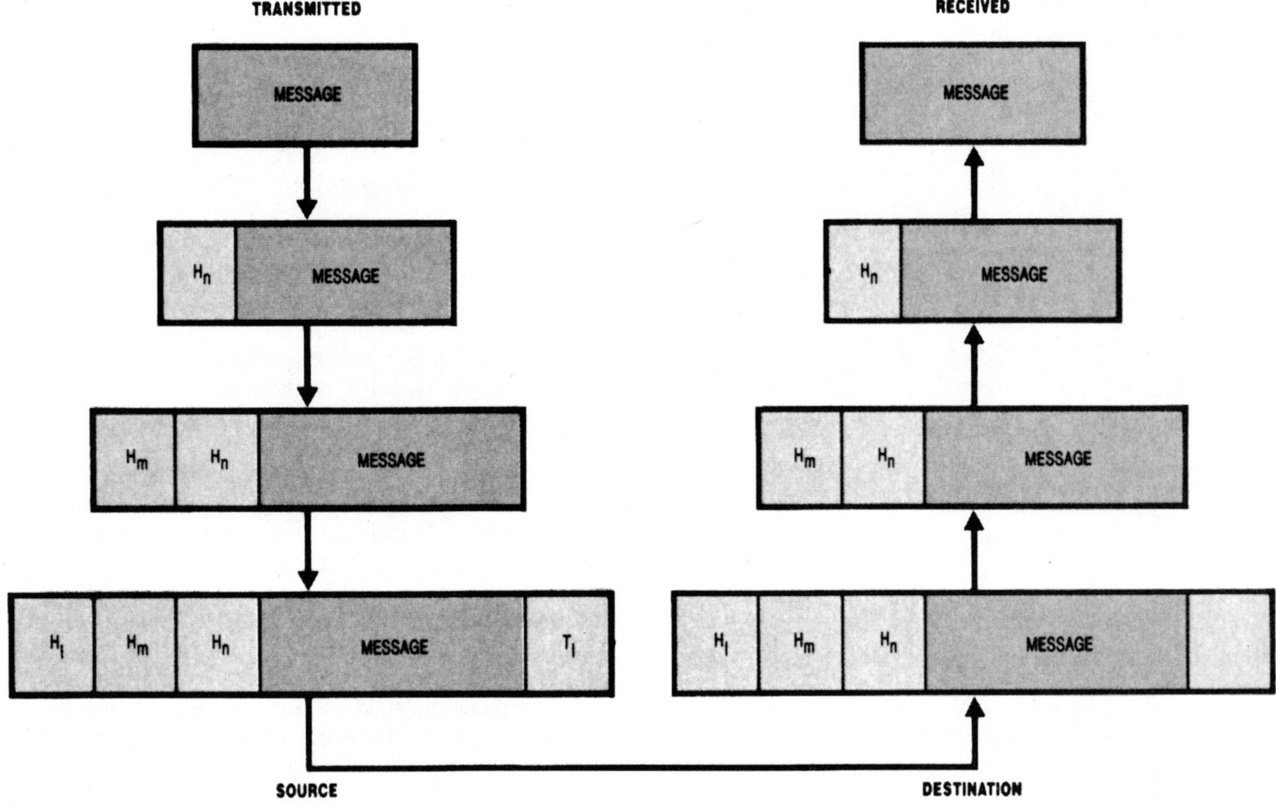

5. How protocol analyzers handle layers. *LAN transmissions involve the assembling and disassembling of packets. When a protocol analyzer uses the decoding method, packets are disassembled as if by a receiving device. Here the message has headers added at levels n, m, and l (H_n, H_m, H_l).*

LANalyzer fell below the 4 percent level.

This brings up the overused argument that the average Ethernet utilization is in the neighborhood of 1 percent over the course of a working day. This is probably true in many office applications. But what about research and development activities, universities, and large networks? Our experience is that networks with dozens of workk stations can keep an Ethernet 20 percent to 40 percent busy for minutes, even hours, at a time. In fact, a single workstation, such as those from Sun Microsystems, can easily chew up 10 percent of Ethernet's bandwidth on a sustained basis.

Protocol decoding

Very important is the capability of these LAN protocol analyzers to interpret a packet (to de-encapsulate and read it) and to convey this information to the user. The capabilities of the several units tested varied greatly. For the Sniffer virtually every popular protocol—including the Transmission Control Protocol/Internet Protocol (TCP/IP), DECnet, IBM's Netbios (Network Basic Input/Output System), and APPC (Advanced Program-to-Program Communications), and Novell's NetWare—was available.

By contrast, the decoding available on the LANalyzer is limited to TCP/IP and DECnet. The SpiderMonitor requires that the protocol, in order to be captured, be identified by the user. Once we had done that, we tested the unit for

some of the ISO protocols, the Internet Protocol of TCP/IP, XNS, DECnet, and hexidecimal. The 4972A filters for TCP/IP and XNS and, according to its specifications, for "some DECnet." The specs also state that "several popular ISO Level 3 and 4 protocols are also provided."

Filtering and decoding

Software is particularly difficult to test for interoperability characteristics. Protocol analyzers perform this test by determining whether various transmissions follow specified formats. One procedure used to test for formats is filtering. If one assumes that packet formats are static in terms of the positions of the fields of interest, it is possible to perform an analysis by applying filters to captured packets. One can create a template of the packet types to be identified. The filter is set in advance to represent the particular packet type (e.g., that of X.25).

Unfortunately, the assumption that packet formats are fixed is not always correct. For example, the International Organization for Standardization (ISO) Transport-layer Protocol Data Unit (TPDU) header has both a fixed and a variable component. Thus, in order to correctly identify allpossible TPDU header combinations, a filter would have to be constructed for each of these combinations. In sum, to identify accurately a network packet's protocol format through filters, filters for all possible combinations of valid packets would have to be constructed. In many cases this

505

6. 4972A's simple response. *For some applications this typical printout is simple, for others perhaps simplistic. The unit requires the user to make the protocol identification.*

is impractical. Using filters to identify packets is relatively simple and fast, but there is a price paid in reduced accuracy and flexibility.

The other method protocol analyzers use is explicit decoding of packets. In network protocols, packets usually contain different levels of information. Figure 5 shows how higher levels are encapsulated by lower-level protocols. Transmissions between communicating devices involve the assembly of packets by sending devices and their disassembly by receiving units. As shown, the message to be transmitted has headers added at Levels n, m, and l (H_n, H_m, H_l). A trailer is added at level l (T_l) prior to the transmission over the network. As a packet is received, this process is reversed, with successive levels stripped, leaving the higher protocols and the message.

When a protocol converter uses the decoding method, packets are disassembled as they would be by a receiving device on a network. To accomplish this, decoding software must identify the upcoming protocol at each level. Since the decoding software can switch protocol stacks while disassembling the packets, combinations of protocols to be identified need not be known in advance. In practice, however, decoding is often more complex. In many common protocols, proper decoding of the fields cannot be done in isolation but rather depends on certain values present in packets that were sent earlier. The analyzer must understand the semantics of the protocols in order to link up related packets, which may be interspersed with other packets that have been captured.

Analyzer testing

We compared the protocol analysis capabilities of the four analyzers by broadcasting various packet examples over the test network. These included "mixed" protocol stacks, or stacks comprising protocols that are not normally considered together. Since the test aimed to determine whether the protocol analyzers could discover

which protocol was transmitted, it was legitimate to make this mix.

We included several protocols in the test. A detailed look at the results provided by each analyzer will be given for a DECnet, TCP/IP, and some of the ISO networking protocols.

We sent a packet with an invalid Ethernet-type field to all the analyzers to see how they handled this invalid packet. We set up all four analyzers to capture all transmitted packets; the network then sent a sampling of packets and, hence, all four units received identical packets. Each unit then tested the packets received.

Test results

As noted, the SpiderMonitor required that the user identify, prior to testing, the protocol to be captured. Hexadecimal was one of the protocol options listed. If hex was selected, however, no decoding was done. If the wrong protocol was selected, there appeared to be no way to determine this from the display. The 4972A also required the user to make protocol identification in advance, even though the unit does no protocol decoding. Even if the user provides the correct protocol selection, the decomposition may be incorrect if he has used the wrong filter for that protocol. Basic filters were provided with the 4972A, but none of these covered all levels at which our test packets were transmitted.

A criticism: The analyzer software provided with the 4972A does not have the status of a Hewlett-Packard-supported product. In fact, HP adds this disclaimer to its documentation: "These tools are UNSUPPORTED and are provided on an as-is basis." A typical display is shown in Figure 6. Because none of the standard filters were set up for all the protocol levels of our test packets, and because the decomposition result depended strictly on the selected filter, the 4972A is not included in the results that follow.

Both the Excelan LANalyzer and the Network General Sniffer provided protocol identification without requiring the user to select the tested protocols in advance. All of the following examples contain protocols extending up through the application layer. The TCP/IP, DECnet, and ISO stacks all included the use of Microsoft's SMB (Server Message Block) protocol, which is the MS-DOS file-service protocol used by most vendors in PC networking products.

Some examples

We selected the TCP/IP example used in the test from a set of packets we gathered from an operating LAN. The test packet consisted of an SMB request made using a Netbios session protocol that, in turn, uses TCP and IP protocols. Of the four units benchmarked, only the Sniffer identified all levels of the protocols, as shown in Figure 7. Testing the LANalyzer (shown in Fig. 8A) showed that the TCP and IP portions of the packet were identified correctly. However, no further decoding of the packet was done. The

```
DLC:  ----- DLC Header -----
DLC:
DLC:  Frame 1 arrived at  00:00:22.1041 ;
      frame size is 91 (005B hex) bytes.
DLC:  Destination: Station 08000200F9A8
DLC:  Source     : Station 08002001A923
DLC:  Ethertype = 0800 (IP)
DLC:
IP:   ----- IP Header -----
IP:
IP:   Version = 4, header length = 20 bytes
IP:   Type of service = 00
IP:        000. .... = routine
IP:        ...0 .... = normal delay
IP:        .... 0... = normal throughput
IP:        .... .0.. = normal reliability
IP:   Total length = 77 bytes
IP:   Identification = 12745
IP:   Flags = 0X
IP:   .0.. .... = may fragment
IP:   ..0. .... = last fragment
IP:   Fragment offset = 0 bytes
IP:   Time to live = 15
IP:   Protocol = 6 (TCP)
IP:   Header checksum = 0062 (correct)
IP:   Source address = [89.9.200.1]
IP:   Destination address = [89.9.255.108]
IP:   No options
IP:
TCP:  ----- TCP header -----
TCP:
TCP:  Source port = 139
TCP:  Destination port = 256
TCP:  Sequence number = 1754362
TCP:  Acknowledgment number = 2024624
TCP:  Data offset = 20
TCP:  Flags = 18
TCP:  ..0. .... = (No urgent pointer)
TCP:  ...1 .... = Acknowledgment
TCP:  .... 1... = Push
TCP:  .... .0.. = (No reset)
TCP:  .... ..0. = (No SYN)
TCP:  .... ...0 = (No FIN)
TCP:  Window = 4096
TCP:  Checksum = 57D1 (correct)
TCP:  No TCP options
TCP:  [37 byte(s) of data]
TCP:
NET:  ----- NetBIOS Session protocol -----
NET:
NET:  [37 more bytes of user data]
NET:
SMB:  ----- SMB Write Byte Range Response -----
SMB:
SMB:  Function = 0B (Write Byte Range)
SMB:  Net path  (NPID) = 0001
SMB:  Process id (PID) = 2FC9
SMB:
SMB:  Return code = 0,0 (OK)
SMB:  Number of bytes written = 33
SMB:
SMB:  [End of "SMB Write Byte Range Response" packet.]
SMB:
```

unit contains filters that match certain SMBs, but they
require that the SMB protocol be present at fixed offsets,
a situation that does not necessarily apply in the case of
TCP (a stream-oriented protocol).

SpiderMonitor results are shown in Figure 8B. The
amount of decoding was similar to that of the LANalyzer.
As noted previously, the HP 4972A decodes according to
the filter selected. In the case of TCP/IP packets, no filters
were available to handle Netbios and/or SMB protocols.
The operation of the 4972A, then, is similar to that of the
SpiderMonitor, except that the 4972A does no decoding at
all—other than applying the selected filter to the captured
packet.

The test of a sample protocol stack based on DECnet's
protocols showed again that only the Sniffer recognized
the SMB protocol. The responses of the LANalyzer and
SpiderMonitor were similar to those generated with the
TCP/IP stack. The HP 4972A provides DECnet filters but,
as in the TCP/IP case, does no decoding of captured
packets.

Reexamination of the analyzers, this time with a focus on
a stack based on the ISO's protocols, showed that again
the Sniffer was able to decode all layers up to and
including the application layer. Of interest was its demonstrated ability to decode two ISO TPDUs within the same
packet, one an acknowledge TPDU and the other user
data.

The LANalyzer did no decoding beyond Layer 2 (802.2
logical link control) and should, therefore, have include the
"03" byte shown in the hex data portion in order to be
correct. Loading a filter from the LANalyzer Application
Library called OSITRANS provided no additional
decoding.

Some additional fields were decoded using a filter
called SINETWK, but the benchmarking showed that the
decoding was not done correctly. The filter apparently
expected an NSAP (Network Service Access Point) address length of less than 16 bytes (the actual length was
16 bytes). As with all filtering schemes, misleading results
are given by the filter if the data is not formatted as
expected.

The SpiderMonitor's response to the ISO stack consti-
tuted a more thorough job than that of the LANalyzer, but
the SpiderMonitor also had some trouble with the NSAP
addresses. The AFI (Authority and Format Indicator) was
not decoded and was presented as part of the address
(the "49" byte at the beginning of each address). The unit
apparently had a bug in its print routine that caused the
alphabetic hex characters to be printed as two-digit decimal values. In sum, in this ISO example, the only analyzer
that provided any protocol identification beyond Layer
3 was the Sniffer, which decoded up through the application layer.

Conclusions

As more LAN products and standards become available,
protocol analysis grows increasingly important in resolving
LAN interoperability problems. Selecting the best LAN
protocol analyzer, however, is not easy. It is much like
buying a new car: There are many price ranges and
options from which to choose. Indeed, the base retail list
prices for the LAN analyzers under discussion range from
$9,950 for module-level products (add your own PC)
to $20,000 or more for complete hardware/software
configurations.

The Sniffer belongs to the class of LAN tools that are
able to decode protocols from Layers 1 through 7 of the
OSI stack and their equivalents in other protocols. The
4972A, SpiderMonitor, and LANalyzer, on the other hand,
fall into the category of tools that decode protocols from

```
(A)

Packet #: 1
Recv Channels: ip          generic
ether: IP      08-00-20-01-a9-23 -> 08-00-02-00-f9-a8    95        0.000       0.000
   ip: TCP     59.09c801 -> 59.09ff6c
  tcp: 139       -> 256         PUSH ACK
  tcp: seq:    1754362  ack:    2024624  win: 4096  len:    37
    0: ff 53 4d 42 0b 00 00 00 00 00 00 00 00 00 00 00    |.SMB............|
   16: 00 00 00 00 00 00 00 00 01 00 c9 2f 00 00 00 00    |............/....|
   32: 01 21 00 00 00                                     |.!...|
```

```
(B)

Packet 1 (91 bytes) at T + 9.5913 secs, Delta t 9.5913 secs
Destination = 08000200F9A8, Source = 08002001A923, Type = 0800
VER/IHL = 45, TOS = 00, Len = 004D, ID = 31C9, FLG/FRG = 0000, TTL = 0F
Prtcl = 06, IP Chksum = 0062, IP Srce = 5909C801, IP Dest = 5909FF6C
Srce Port = 008B, Dest Port = 0100, Seq = 001AC4FA, Ack No. = 001EE4B0
Data Ofst = 5, Flags = ACK,PSH, Window = 1000, TCP Chksum = 57D1
0000: 00 00 FF 53 4D 42 0B 00 00 00 00 00 00 00 00 00      ...SMB..........
0010: 00 00 00 00 00 00 00 00 00 00 01 00 C9 2F 00 00      ............./..
0020: 00 00 01 21 00 00 00                                 ...!...
```

Layers 1 through 4 and that have very limited decoding abilities above that.

Setting prices and protocol decoding capabilities aside, most of the analyzers are comparable in performance, and each has its own strengths. In many cases, these units are equal in performance.

From our perspective, however, protocol analysis involves the capture and decoding of packets on a LAN. This decoding includes an identification of the various protocols within a particular packet. Apparently, this definition of protocol analysis is not universally accepted—at least not by all the manufacturers of LAN protocol analyzers that we benchmarked.

Based on our experiments, the only tested unit that really meets our criteria for LAN protocol analysis is the Network General Sniffer. We've already described the Sniffer's seven-layer decoding abilities. The tested unit consistently decoded more layers than other analyzers tested and provided the results in a more readable form. It did not have problems with mixed protocols, as the other units apparently did.

In our opinion, the Hewlett-Packard 4972A LAN Protocol Analyzer does not provide the capabilities required to perform protocol analysis on a LAN. It will display any packet as containing any protocol without complaint. What is more, it apparently does not provide any automatic identification capability. The burden is on the user: If the user makes a mistake, the 4972A will not catch it. On the other hand, the unit's programming language presents some interesting possibilities for other uses such as traffic simulation. Another good point: The 4972A is the only analyzer with completely accurate frame counts and statistics under worst-case loads.

The Spider Systems SpiderMonitor P200 provides more protocol analysis capabilities than the 4972A but less than the LANalyzer. The unit's major drawback is that, like the 4972A, it provides no automatic packet identification. The user must provide this identification for the P200, an approach not terribly useful for general problem resolution. Indeed, it can be downright unworkable.

The Excelan LANalyzer EX5500 does provide automatic packet identification. Unfortunately, the amount of decoding it does varies greatly from protocol to protocol. The LANalyzer essentially gave no detailed decoding at protocol levels beyond the equivalent of Layer 4 (transport layer). It handles lower levels of DECnet and AppleTalk but does not include DEC's or Apple's standard filing protocols. Another problem is its mishandling of mixed protocols, such as TCP/IP on IEEE 802.2. The tests showed that the LANalyzer failed to handle the mixed protocols and left off identifying the protocols at the 802.2 logical link control layer. It likewise failed to identify the Internet Protocol. Thus, while it provides some protocol-analysis capabilities (under a broad definition of protocol analysis), the LANalyzer also come up short, in our view.

Other factors

In terms of overall ease of use, we found the Sniffer the best, followed, in order of quality, by the SpiderMonitor, the LANalyzer, and finally, the 4972A. Our examination of the written materials provided with the four units led us to the following conclusions. The 4972A's and LANalyzer's documentation was generally good, though poorly organized: We found it difficult to locate the topics we were looking for. The SpiderMonitor's documentation was far too brief, while the Sniffer's was adequate. The Sniffer's was, however, the only documentation we didn't have to refer to in order to figure out the unit's operation.

Summing up the choices: In our opinion, if the user has a thorough technical understanding of protocol operations and bit-level frame interpretation, then LANalyzer might be worth considering. For writing custom analyzer-capture programs in a proprietary language, the 4972A might be worth purchasing. For moderate performance and minimal decoding capabilities, the SpiderMonitor should be considered. And, for the basic question—being able to easily interpret packets, to debug traffic on the network, and to learn about protocol operation—the Sniffer wins by a wide margin.

Our tests benchmarked the units' Ethernet capabilities; there are, however, other LANs with which these protocol

508

analyzers will work. The LANalyzer is also available in a StarLAN configuration. The Sniffer supports StarLAN, the 4-Mbit/s and 16-Mbit/s token rings, and ARCnet. Certain Sniffer combinations are available with dual configurations, giving a choice of any two combinations of LANs.

As we were preparing this article, Network General released the Sniffer's Version 2.0, and 2.1 was about to be released. HP added a TCP/IP application for the 4972A, and HP acquired Eon Systems, maker of the LanProbe for Ethernet. We received no news of enhancements for the LANalyzer or SpiderMonitor.

HP's new TCP/IP application should boost the 4972A's TCP/IP packet-recognition capabilities. The company's acquisition of Eon may have been in direct response to products like the LANalyzer and Sniffer. The Sniffer's Version 2.0 has a major memory upgrade. It supports up to 8 Mbytes of memory under the LIMS (Lotus-Intel Microsoft Specification) 4.0 format, allowing over 60,000 sliced packets to be traced. This ability is due, in part, to the efficient use of memory, as noted in our discussion of Figure 4. The vendor also claims that use of LIMS memory only adds about one percent overhead to the overall performance of the Sniffer. Version 2.1 of the Sniffer will add support for ISO developmental protocols (ISO transport over IP), two-level ISO Abstract Syntax Notation (ASN) decode (ASN is encoded in hex, which in turn has to be decoded to its actual meaning), decode of multiple instances of the same layer within a layer (such as a transport sequence number acknowledgement piggybacked on another transport frame), and support for joining of split frames (where the highest-level protocol information doesn't fit or the implementation does not take advantage of the full packet size available for that network). ∎

Carl Manson is a senior systems engineer with the communications consulting firm Architecture Technology Corp. (Minneapolis, Minn.). He has a Master of Science degree in Computer Science from the University of Minnesota.

J. Scott Haugdahl is a senior systems specialist at Architecture Technology Corp. and is the author of three books: Inside the Token Ring; Inside Netbios; *and* Inside SAA. *He has a Bachelor of Computer Science degree from the University of Minnesota Institute of Technology.*

Kenneth J. Thurber, PhD, Architecture Technology Corp., Minneapolis, Minn.

Getting a handle on FDDI

There's no place to hide when LAN end users suddenly demand high-bandwidth applications. It's coming, and so are cheaper FDDI nodes.

Like most new technologies, FDDI (the 100-Mbit/s fiber distributed data interface) faces the skepticism that greets any novelty. Right now many potential FDDI users are asking: How could my network conceivably have need for 100 Mbit/s?

That's the wrong question. The best way to look at future bandwidth requirements is to see that networks must be able to carry applications, and there will eventually be applications that make even 100 Mbit/s seem slow. For example, with the advent of Reduced Instruction Set Computing and, in time, workstations that do their processing at the speed of 100 million instructions per second, the bandwidth of any communications network to which such a workstation is attached must be dramatically increased.

A number of factors drive up the performance requirements of a communications network: the introduction of new technologies, the improvement and innovative use of existing technologies (including their use in previously untried combinations), and the development of increased user expectations for performance.

One major cause of bottlenecks in future networks will be the expanded use of high-powered microcomputers and workstations. Engineering workstations and computer-aided design/computer-aided engineering devices already incorporate multiple processors, accelerators, smart communications controllers, and Ethernet LANs to increase information throughput. Yet, while the internal backplane of a typical workstation transfers data at approximately 160 Mbit/s for a VME system and 300 Mbit/s (burst rate) for a Multi Bus II processor, Ethernets transfer data at 10 Mbit/s, only a fraction of the internal backplane speed.

FDDI offers the throughput required to fulfill the high-bandwidth demands of: backplane networks for high-speed communications between mainframes and to link processors with high speed storage devices; back-bones to other LANs; and front-end networks used to link workstations.

The FDDI standard is in the process of being drafted by the X3T9 Committee of the Computer and Business Equipment Manufacturers Association, which is an accredited American National Standards Institute (ANSI) committee. In the past, the X3T9 committee has defined only communications schemes and standards for computer channel interfaces. But FDDI supports a variety of front-end, back-end, and backbone networks configured into a variety of topologies.

Beyond FDDI, FDDI-II is being developed to satisfy diverse needs. FDDI-II is intended primarily for voice/data/video capabilities. It is set up to divide the available network bandwidth between voice and data with a time-division multiplexed approach that can create up to 16 separate and equal channels, each using a maximum of 98.304 Mbit/s and each being full duplex.

FDDI Description

The FDDI network is based on dual counter-rotating 100-Mbit/s token rings. The physical layout is two strands of optical fiber powered by light emitting diodes at 1,300 nanometers. FDDI uses the token-passing algorithm to pass packets (which may be no larger than 4,500 bytes) from one active station to the next. Each station generally regenerates and repeats each symbol and serves as the means for attaching one or more devices to the network for the purpose of communicating with other devices on the network.

The method of physical attachment to the FDDI network may vary and is dependent on specific applications. A physical connection consists of the physical layers of two stations that are connected over the transmission medium by both a primary link and a secondary link. Two classes of stations are defined, dual attachment and single attachment. Physical FDDI rings may only be composed of dual stations and these must have two PHY (the physical layer protocol) entitites to accommodate each of the two counter-rotating rings. Concentrators provide additional PHY entities. Because several devices can be hooked to each concentrator—in contrast to a station—it is a relatively inexpensive way to make a number of attachments to the network.

There is, however, a limit on the number of connections. The FDDI standard sets a maximum of 1,000 physical connections, which could be as many as 500 stations.

There is also a relationship between the number of stations and the network's size. According to the formula, fewer connections to the network mean a larger geographic distance that the FDDI LAN can cover. The maximum total perimeter is 200 kilometers, but that's with 500 stations. The maximum distance between two adjacent devices on the FDDI ring can be no more than 2 kilometers. But devices need not be directly attached to the network: They can be connected through fiber optic spurs to the concentrators discussed earlier. Fiber allows a significant increase in their distance from the ring.

Standards status

How close are standard FDDI networks to implementation? How close is a final standard? The answer in both cases is: very close.

Work on the first of the FDDI layers, the Media Access Control, was unanimously approved by X3T9 in February 1986. In the previous year, the FDDI physical layer had been divided into two parts. The lower of these two, the Physical Medium Dependent (see figure), has had a contentious course.

Though a February 1987 X3T9 meeting unanimously approved Physical Media Dependent (PMD) for forwarding to X3, comments received during the public review process raised a bitter dispute over the fiber connector and required some refinements to other specifications, such as a reduction in the loss permitted by the optical bypass switch. The refinements were fairly easy to make, but the connector issue proved difficult. It was finally resolved in a roll call vote in June 1988, with the selection of the fixed-shroud duplex connector footprint. X3T9 has subsequently moved the PMD document to higher committees for further processing, and it is virtually impossible to change it at this time.

PHY was unanimously approved by an X3T9 meeting in August 1987 and has now become an ANSI standard. Thus, three of the four FDDI standards are solid. The only standard that remains to be completed is Station Management (SMT), which may even be a more involved standards effort than PMD because of the complexities of multilayer station management. However, there is a feeling that this task must be accomplished, and I believe that it can be wound up in six to 12 months.

After some initial difficulties with implementing the technology, the early versions of standard FDDI chips are being shipped by Advanced Micro Devices (AMD). Indeed, these

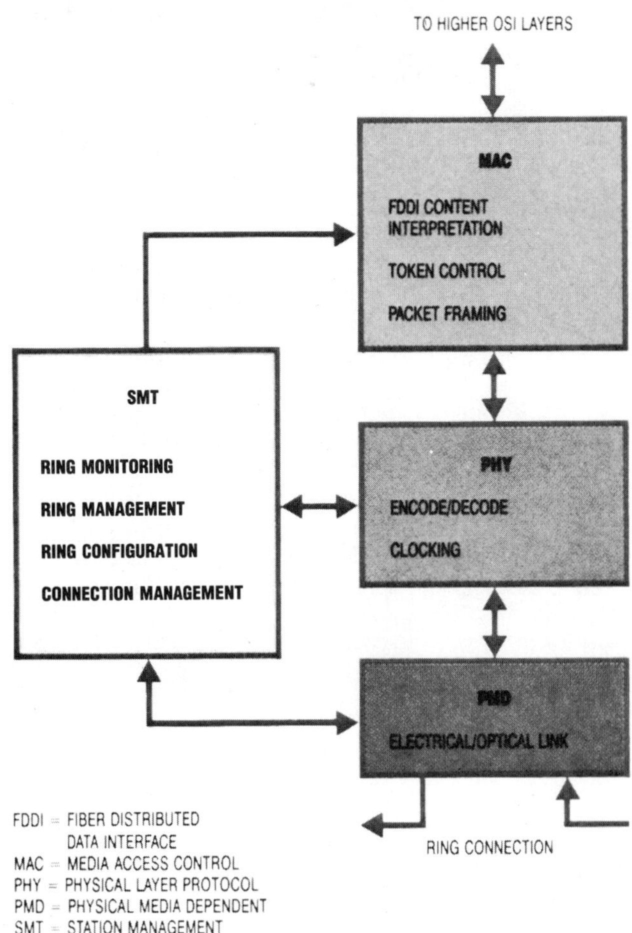

One of four. *Three of the four FDDI protocols are virtually standards. The complex SMT is outstanding, but the X3T9 committee seems committed to swift action.*

chips are likely to be shipped in volume by the end of this year. When these chip sets become generally available, the price of FDDI is likely to plunge. Other chip manufacturers, including National Semiconductor, are working on chip sets.

Costs and availability

Even at a substantial cost, FDDI—the highest performance, standard LAN technology yet available—will find an immediate application niche. In some ways, FDDI is a bargain even at its current high cost. The highest price for an FDDI node is in the $20,000 range for one of the FX family of FDDI nodes from Fibronics International (Hyannis, Mass.). These FDDI products, for example the IBM-Mainframe-to-FDDI Channel-Attached Unit, can be used to replace similar high-speed LAN nodes from Network Systems (the 50-Mbit/s Hyperchannel), which cost around $40,000.

Because of the availability of the AMD chip sets, which are likely to sell for around $800 each, I estimate, based on soundings of the vendors, that the price of FDDI nodes next year will be in the $5,000 $10,000 range. Virtually all

In the long run, FDDI is likely to prove lacking in adequate bandwidth.

the major players have stated—or at least hinted—that they will come into the market. Ungermann-Bass has just announced, and INNET showed FDDI-to-IBM host interfaces at Comnet.

Other board-level products promised or available are from Artel, BICC, Develcon, Ferranti, Fibronics, Network Systems, Raycom, Simple Net Systems, and Siemens. Fibercom and CrossComm have announced FDDI learning bridges, and AT&T, Hewlett-Packard, and ITT have all announced or alluded to other products. I expect IBM to have its FDDI LAN available within 18 months.

In the long run, FDDI, like other LAN technologies, is likely to prove lacking in adequate bandwidth (and already research is being conducted on considerably faster LANs). LAN designers have consistently underestimated the application needs of users and the progress of applications. The designers of FDDI will fare no better than other LAN designers: They too will be criticized for not taking a large enough step.

Also, and importantly, based FDDI's cost, I see room for another increment of performance before 100 Mbit/s. The difference in price between the 16-Mbit/s token ring LAN and FDDI leaves space for a 50-Mbit/s or 64-Mbit/s alternative. I expect some people will move into this market. Finally, it is essential that those who are considering FDDI networks avoid making a decision based on a single technical aspect of a network. If a user focuses on only one part of a configuration—handling links to terminals, for example—an Ethernet may seem like a large available bandwidth. But Ethernet's bandwidth no longer seems high when one considers the requirements of high-performance workstations. In fact, FDDI's 100 Mbit/s may be nowhere near enough bandwidth for some of the applications that are proposed for its use. ■

Kenneth J. Thurber is president of Minneapolis-based Architecture Technology Corporation (ATC), a consulting firm that specializes in LANs. The present article is derived in part from ATC's new FDDI Technology Report.

Dale Neibaur, Novell Inc., Provo, Utah

Understanding XNS: The prototypical internetwork protocol

A leading protocol designer conducts a remarkable guided tour to the little-known fountainhead of modern LAN protocols.

In addition to SNA and DECnet, two architectures have had a major impact on the technical direction of network evolution, and played a seminal role in the development of an international layered architecture. Though they are not as well known as IBM's and DEC's architectures, these protocol suites have had an incalculable impact on the marketplace and both evolved from the same prototype architecture, a university research project called PUP.

One of these two influential architectures was specifically designed to continue delivering packets under battlefield conditions, to survive in the face of extraordinary loss of both user devices and internet switches. The second architecture was optimized for typical office, technical, or university campus environments.

Most would recognize TCP/IP as the battle-ready architecture of choice for our vast military computer networks. It's quieter cousin is Xerox Network Systems (XNS).

The legacy of XNS

XNS was born at the Xerox Palo Alto Research Center (PARC), where scientists began modifying PUP (PARC Universal Packet) to create a more robust product. Once introduced, XNS moved beyond Xerox implementations and was adopted for subsequent customization and modification by the leading LAN designers of the early 1980s.

Such LAN industry leaders as 3Com, Novell, and Ungermann-Bass have all used XNS as the cornerstone of their network product offerings, with subsequent profitable results. The architecture has been an active part of the education and work experience of an entire generation of hardware and software engineers.

XNS's ultimate legacy to the history and progress of network architecture may lie in the international arena. The XNS layered approach is known to have been part of the inspiration for the OSI model's designers in the International Organization for Standardization.

The OSI seven-layer model is in many ways an expanded, more complex version of XNS's basic direction. Since no engineering occurs in a vacuum, many designers who worked on the OSI model's functional requirements had worked extensively with XNS and other existing network architectures and they were naturally influenced by the positive features of XNS's architecture when they were developing the world's future interconnection model.

The XNS approach to networking is well-adapted to most office applications, with clean functional layers, clearly defined protocols, and easy-to-implement features. XNS was adopted in the LAN marketplace primarily because of its simplicity and robust structure.

The key to XNS internetworking is datagram delivery, in which every packet is individually routed on a "best effort" basis. It also includes protocols for quick request and response, more extended conversations, error reporting, route-checking, and the constant updating of routing tables. These latter services work together to turn simple datagram transport into a reliable message delivery system. Reliable delivery of entire messages is, of course, the ultimate user need.

Growing an internetwork

A network architecture does not really have an opportunity to show its power, robustness, and dependability until it must serve a complex internetwork with thousands of devices in hundreds of separate LANs. The evolution from a simple LAN to a demanding internet occurs gradually, in response to changing user needs and the productive ways they find to use their network.

Every workgroup or department reaches a point where it has expanded beyond the floor space that a single Ethernet can handle. The network manager's answer is usually to add a second segment and a *repeater* to link them. Since a repeater simply boosts the electrical signal, the second segment has to be identical to the first.

What happens if the user's needs have changed since the first cable was laid? If users want to add a new unshielded twisted-pair cable plant or if their new applications demand the higher bandwidth of an optical fiber, the network manager will put a *bridge* between the two segments. A bridge can link LANs that differ not only in medium but also in topology (a star linked to a bus, for example) or in transmission method (baseband to broadband).

But as the sophistication and number of network nodes increase, bridges become overloaded and network managers look for different solutions. As the sheer number of devices in a particular building climbs, the need for another type of communication between LANs becomes obvious. Now it is time for *routers* to show their value in the internet.

A router's primary task is to manage traffic loads and alternate routing between LANs. As the number of LANs in the extended network grows, the business need for increased management of the LAN-to-LAN communication increases. In this final stage of the growth of the internet, the network has grown into hundreds or thousands of individual servers, hosts, user devices, and peripherals linked by formerly isolated LANs with bridges, gateways, and routers.

The XNS architecture

Unlike the seven-layer OSI model, XNS developed in four levels, beginning with Level 0 (see Fig. 1). As with the OSI model, each layer provides services to the next higher level.

---

1. OSI and XNS layers. *Though a well-layered architecture, XNS preceded the OSI network model and does not apply the same labels or numbers to its stack components.*

OSI PROTOCOL MODEL		XNS PROTOCOLS	
7	APPLICATION	CLEARINGHOUSE GAP	4
6	PRESENTATION	COURIER	3
5	SESSION		
4	TRANSPORT	SPP PEP RIP	2
3	NETWORK	IDP	1
2	DATA LINK	ETHERNET RS-232 RS-449 X.21	0
1	PHYSICAL		

GAP = GATEWAY ACCESS PROTOCOL
IDP = INTERNETWORK DATAGRAM PROTOCOL   RIP = ROUTING INFORMATION PROTOCOL
PEP = PACKET EXCHANGE PROTOCOL   SPP = SEQUENCED PACKET PROTOCOL

Although XNS could provide a complete architecture from transmission medium to applications support, the most important and unique aspects of the architecture occur at the network and transport layers, which is where we will spend most of our time.

XNS Level 0 corresponds generally with the first and second layers of the OSI model, referred to as the physical and data link layers. Level 0 protocols physically transmit data from one point to another over a transmission medium, just like their OSI counterparts in the physical and data link layers.

The name "Ethernet" is an obvious candidate at this layer, but another XNS-specific protocol, called the Synchronous Point-to-Point Protocol, is also available. The architecture will accept other common transmission protocols, including the X.21, RS-232-C, and RS-449 standards.

XNS Level 1, the core of its router functionality, corresponds to the internetworking aspects of OSI Layer 3 (the network layer). XNS Level 1 protocols determine where the packets go, including internet source and destination addressing. XNS defines only the Internetwork Datagram Protocol (IDP) for this layer.

Level 2 protocols correspond to OSI's fourth, or transport, layer, focusing on message integrity and multiple classes of service. XNS Level 2 specifies five protocols and five corresponding packet types to give structure to a stream of related packets where required and provide for simple request-response service under other circumstances. These protocols ride on top of IDP services and handle retransmission, sequencing, and flow control and determine how routers share information for route-building.

The Level 3 protocols provide services similar to OSI's fifth (session) and sixth (presentation) layers. These protocols control remote procedure interactions and determine conventions for data structuring, allowing users to access remote resources; print, save, and access files; and communicate with a variety of differently formatted display devices.

XNS also has a Level 4 (OSI's application layer) for application protocols that are implemented for specific platforms. Many applications have been developed on this level that use the underlying XNS internetworking protocols.

Addressing and sockets

To understand the operation of routers and other nodes that use XNS protocols, one must first understand internetwork addressing. Every XNS device has a complete address that includes: a network number corresponding to an individual LAN; a device number corresponding to a physical network card (called a host address); and a socket number relating to different application processes in the same node. In OSI terminology, a device number is the data link layer address and the network number is the network layer address. A "host" in this context is any computer on the network.

Within each network device there can be a number of software entities called sockets. A socket is simply a subaddress within the device's memory space that an application process uses as the sender or receiver of data. Using a socket means that the application process is not bogged down with the details of creating, maintaining, or ending connections for every function call it makes. The application process concentrates on its task and delegates the connection-management tasks to the specialist, in this case the socket. A socket that is regularly used for a specific network function, such as file service or print service, is called a well-known socket.

Since understanding internetwork addresses is the key to understanding IDP's functions, let's take a closer look at the structure of an XNS address. Each XNS address has three parts: A 32-bit network number uniquely identifies the subnetwork (LAN) within the internet, logically; a 48-bit device or "host" number identifies the specific device, physically; the 16-bit socket number identifies the socket that is managing the interaction. The device number is identical to the address of the Ethernet, token ring, or other network card. See Figure 2 for these addresses in the context of an XNS packet.

XNS's designers considered it essential to have absolute device numbers in order to identify an individual device independent of the particular network to which it happened to be attached. The combination of absolute device numbers and logical network numbers allows easy moves and changes as well as concurrent attachment by a device to more than one network.

Router revelations

IDP, at the OSI network level, is the workhorse of XNS and all XNS-derived protocols. It resides at the crossroads of the communications stack, where packages of data en route from the application layer are "stamped" with intelligent routing directions and handed to the data link layer for output to the network wire. Understand how IDP and the network layer work and the realm of internetworking will be open to you.

First, an analogy: A router builds routes based on the "next place to send this packet" criterion. Think about how a driver and navigator communicate while en route to an unfamiliar location. The navigator does not give the driver all the landmarks at once . . . the freeway exit, the third light, the left on Main, the right on Second, the railroad tracks, the abandoned farm, and finally, the red house with the white trim. Instead, the driver is told what to do next, and when that landmark is reached, the next one is given.

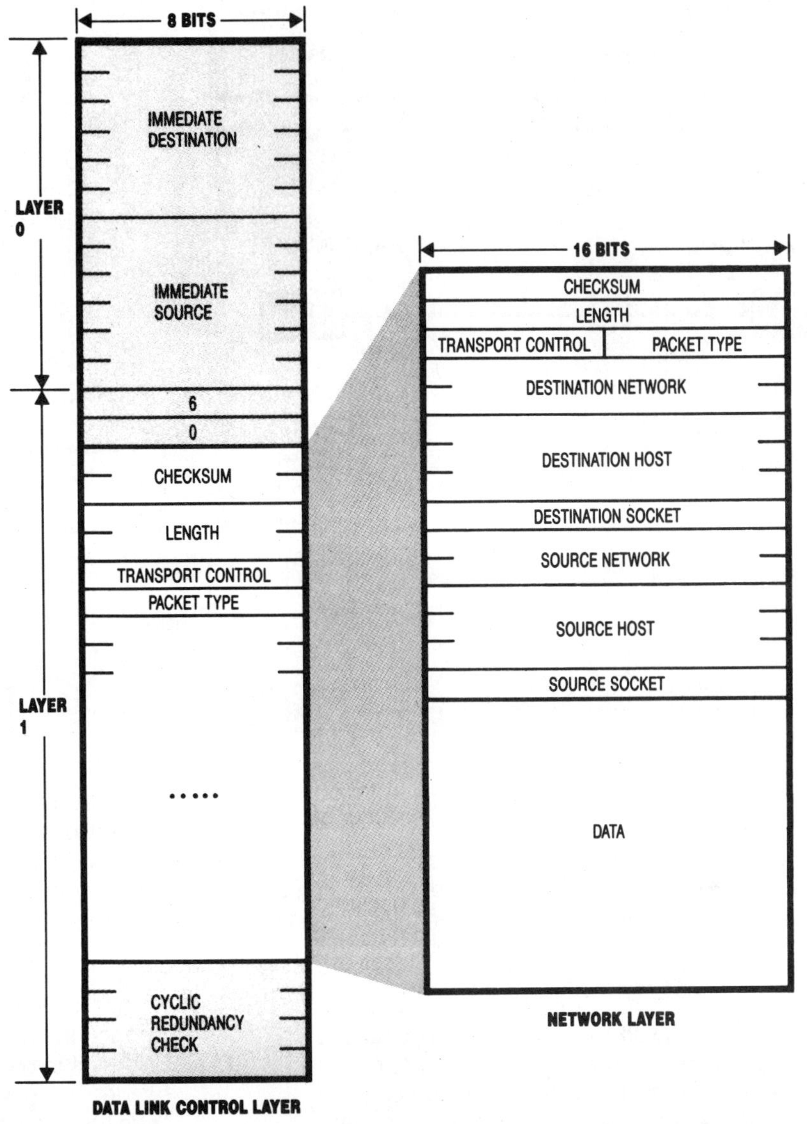

2. An encapsulated packet. *Shown are the IDP fields and their encapsulation by the DLC header and trailer. The DLC layer uses 48-bit devices addresses. Logical network addresses are in the IDP fields of the network layer.*

XNS network routers can only work with each landmark on the particular packet's journey as the previous one is passed.

The process starts when a source node decides to send a packet to a destination node. Before any data is exchanged, the source node must learn the internetwork address of the destination node. The application in the source node most likely knows a high-level symbolic name for the destination node, such as Server5 or VAX23. These names are generally stored in an application table or supplied by the operator. To learn the internetwork address, the source node uses name-service protocols to look up the address in an address directory. Alternatively, the node uses a broadcast facility that can dynamically return the full address of a named network entity, as occurs with Netbios. In either case, this type of name resolution or

3. Hop-along packeting. *Traffic on a single LAN needs only a 48-bit data link layer device address. When a packet hops across multiple LANs, its DLC address is changed by each router it passes through. By looking up the destination network number in its routing table, the router learns the device address of the next router in the path.*

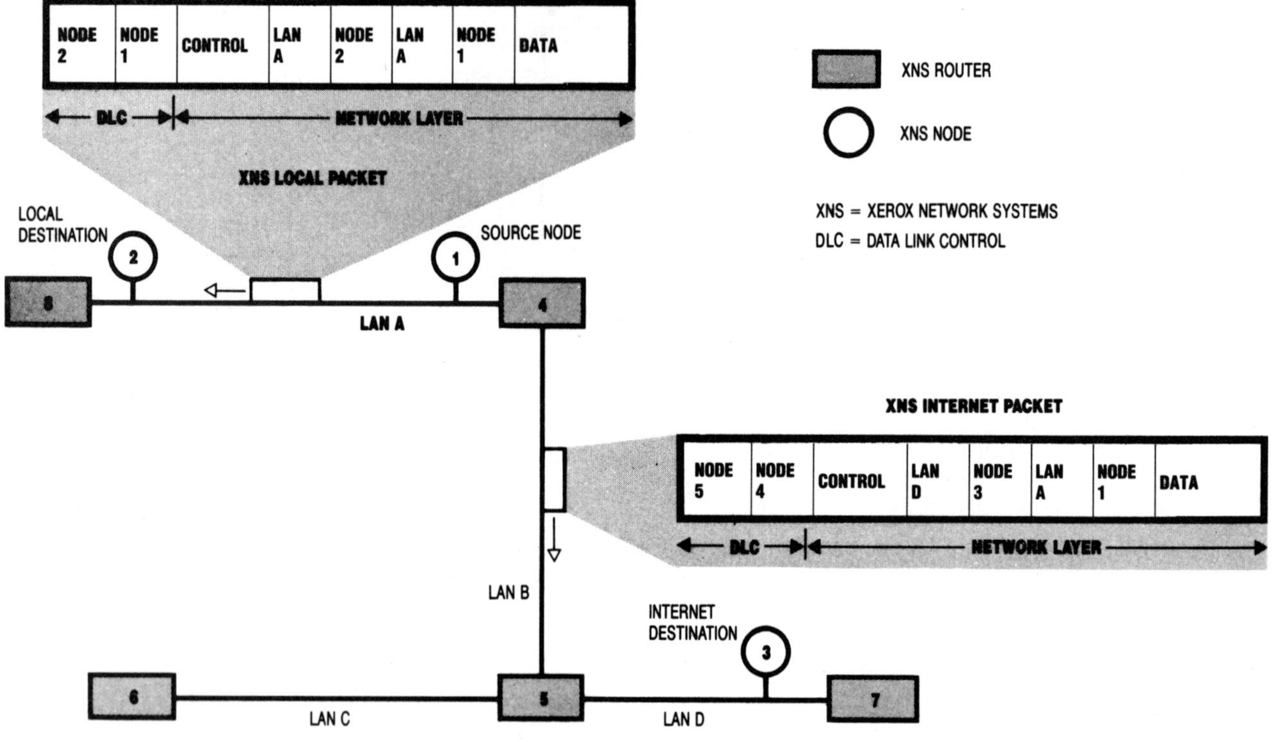

"binding" is above the network layer of IDP, but it must occur before a packet can be sent.

Once the source node has determined the full internetwork address of the destination node, the packet can be sent. IDP, at the network layer, does not understand names, only the network address numbers that it receives, along with the data to be sent, from the higher layers and the application.

Now that the network layer has the user data and an internetwork address, it can make the first routing decision. The network layer software in the source node knows which network (LAN) it is on. If the destination node is on this same network, the source's network layer merely adds its packet header to the user data and hands it to the data link layer with a request to send the packet to the destination node's device number. This is illustrated in the "local packet" example of Figure 3. A simple point-to-point exchange requires no intermediate routing. Much of the traffic on a LAN is this type of local exchange.

Keep in mind that when an internetwork is subdivided by routers, data link layer packets only travel on a single LAN segment that's defined by routers, as with LAN A in Figure 3. Unlike bridges, which pass everything, a router passes only those packets addressed directly to it and that it decides to route.

Now for the internetworking mechanics. When a source node wishes to send to a destination node on another LAN segment, the network layer builds a packet with the destination's full internetwork address inside. But unlike the previous local example, the network layer software tells the data link layer to address the packet to a router's device address, not to the ultimate destination-node device address. The data link layer address is called the immediate address in XNS and is not necessarily the address of the target end node. This is shown in the "internetwork packet" example of Figure 3.

When the addressed router receives the incoming packet, it throws away the immediate address in the DLC header, looks into the packet's destination address field, finds the network number of the target node, and then consults its route tables to decide how best to route the packet.

From its route tables, the router learns the device address of the next router along the best path to the destination node. The device address of this next router is now used for an immediate address, and the packet again is handed to the data link layer for transmission. In this way, a packet may be passed from router to router. Each router in turn strips off the data link layer address and replaces it with the address of the next router along the path to the target node.

Finally, a router on the same LAN segment as the destination node receives the packet and uses the internal destination device address as the immediate DLC address and sends it across the link to the end node.

At this point, the IDP internetwork transmission is complete. If some higher-level software is guaranteeing the transmission, an acknowledgment packet could be sent back to the source node now. But without the higher-layer guarantee, IDP just makes a "best effort" to get the packet there, with no retries and no acknowledgments.

IDP assumes that the packet will have a nominal maximum length of 576 bytes. One of the major ways that vendors have deviated from a pure-XNS implementation of IDP has involved a different maximum packet size. Larger-than-standard packets will require that all routers in the network be aware of the correct packet size because routers will almost always discard aberrant-sized packets.

Rest in peace with RIP

At the transport layer, an XNS network designer has five protocols available to achieve the two basic functions of system management and data transfer. XNS transport layer services use the network layer IDP packet for a basic delivery mechanism.

The XNS system management and control protocols include: Routing Information Protocol (RIP) packets for router-to-router communication; Error Protocol packets for routers to report packet failures; and Echo Protocoi, which tests a path to an unknown device.

The XNS Data Transfer services include: Sequenced Packet Protocol (SPP) and Packet Exchange Protocol (PEP).

For XNS-derived LANs such as Novell's, the two most important of these transport layer protocols are RIP, which allows routers to exchange route data, and SPP, which provides guaranteed services on top of IDP. Novell's Sequenced Packet Exchange (SPX) is a close adaptation of XNS SPP, just as Novell's Internet Packet Exchange (IPX) is largely derived from XNS IDP.

The key to a router's ability to calculate intermediate addresses on an end-to-end route is in its internal routing tables. In XNS, and Novell's IPX and SPX, the protocol that routers use to update and manage route tables is RIP.

Internet routers use RIP and its special packet format to keep each other informed of the network topology. The basic question routers need to answer is: How do I get to Network X, and how close is it to me? RIP allows internet routers to build and maintain routing tables consisting of network numbers, router addresses, and the number of hops to that router.

---

4. XNS routing table. *A routing table doesn't show addresses for all the routers in a path. Instead, it tells only the address of the next router in the path and the hop count.*

SUBNET # 4 BYTES	ROUTER PORT 1 BYTE	NODE # 6 BYTES	HOP COUNT 1 BYTE
68A2	A	169A31	2
C43B	A	C6234B	6
1286	B	6789A2	1
D94C	C	7A7B61	4
672A	A	250311	9
⋮	⋮	⋮	⋮

XNS = XEROX NETWORK SYSTEMS

Routing tables (see Fig. 4) contain an entry for each LAN on the internetwork. For each network's entry, the route table gives the device address of an adjacent router that is the next step toward the target network and the port to which the next router's LAN is connected. Also stored in the routing tables are the total number of routers the packet must pass through to arrive at a given destinaton network. This is referred to as the hop count.

Routers are constantly sharing information about themselves and information they have picked up from listening to other routers. In other words, routers gossip. The self-referential information a router offers is usually true; the data on other routers and LANs is as accrate as gossip usually is. Since routers are working with what is essentially hearsay evidence — except when they are talking about themselves — the databases that they are constantly advertising and sharing are only as accurate as the last broadcast they received.

New information propagates through even a very complex internetwork in a relatively short time because routers listen attentively to each other's gossip. A typical RIP implementation will have routers communicating with each other every 30 or 60 seconds. If a router hears what purports to be new information, it will update its table entry. Each entry in the route table has a timer associated with it. If the timer runs out before a given network's existence is reconfirmed, that entry is deleted from the table. In the Novell version of RIP, this timer is four minutes.

The original XNS version of RIP is adequate when everything is working, but the kind of information that does not propagate quickly is the information that a certain network is no longer reachable. One router may realize that it can no longer get packets to a network, but every other router in the internet may have to try and fail before they all conclude that they can't get packets to the network either. In this sense, routers act like incurable optimists.

Standard XNS implementations insist that routers broadcast their RIP information on all LANs they are connected to, including back to the same network from which they originally received the information. This process can use a substantial amount of network bandwidth and is an area targeted for improvement by router vendors. Some vendors' implementations of RIP have added capabilities to counteract these drawbacks, including the ability of routers to broadcast messages immediately when detecting a change.

Practically every implementation includes some special features, customization, and enhancements. With Novell networks, in an effort to avoid spreading outdated and possibly erroneous information, routers do not advertise down the same LAN segment from which they originally received a certain database item. In standard XNS, of course, a router broadcasts its information everywhere. In addition, routers broadcast their RIP packets every 60 seconds rather than every 30 seconds to avoid using up valuable network bandwidth with excessive router traffic.

Also, the Novell implementation added two extra bytes to the RIP packet for a time-to-net parameter, specifying

5. The SPP packet. *Key to guaranteed service, the fields in the SPP transport layer store sliding window dialogues, packet sequence numbers, and acknowledgment information.*

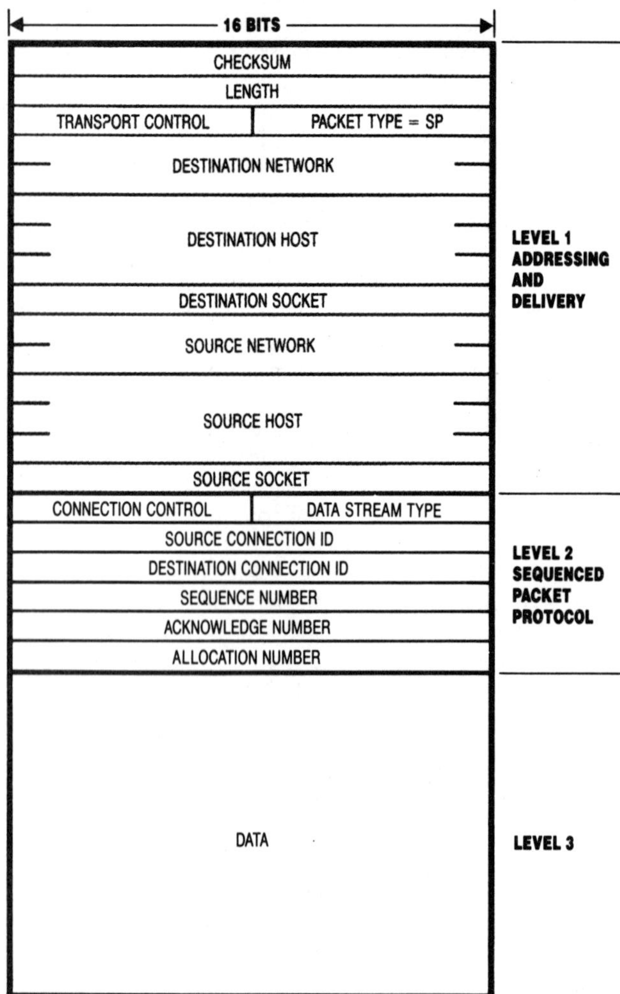

the expected delay to the end station. This allows a sender to determine an accurate delay to the end station, which avoids both timing-out too early and waiting too long for a packet that is genuinely lost.

Sequenced packet protocol

SPP provides a reliability layer above the simple datagram delivery of IDP. This is similar to OSI's transport level virtual-circuit services. The SPP approach to message integrity involves creating a connection between sender and receiver through two sockets that expect a synchronized stream of packets.

Using sliding window techniques, both sockets start with sequence numbers of zero in the first SPP packet that they send to set up the connection. They continue numbering every data packet that they send out during the course of the connection (see Fig. 5). The receiving socket can put the message back together by linking the user data fields of successively numbered packets.

SPP is a robust, full-duplex service that allows a source to send a number of packets to be acknowledged by a

single packet. SPP allows multiple application processes in the same node to simultaneously conduct virtual-circuit sessions with different remote resources.

SSP is key to message integrity in XNS, which becomes an issue in networks because packets can get out of order or be lost entirely. Packets can fail to arrive at their destination for a wide variety of reasons, some of which are application- and network-specific. For instance, when a bridge chokes, it discards frames (packets). Routers using load-balancing algorithms rarely choke, but in a heavily loaded network a momentary buffer overflow with resultant packet loss is possible. Also, if a router finds a checksum error in a packet, it will discard the packet. Finally, the receiver's buffer can overflow, with resultant packet losses.

In addition to these instances of lost packets, some packets are simply delayed and, therefore, out of order because they took a different route from their fellows and encountered longer transmission delays. If they are sufficiently delayed, the sender may time-out on the acknowledgments and generate duplicate packets. In a complex internet with multiple routes available, a network designer can expect that a significant number of packets will arrive out of order and possibly duplicated.

The maximum size of an SPP packet is 576 bytes, the nominal internet packet size, although some vendor implementations vary from this size all the way up to the maximum Ethernet packet size. A pure IDP/SPP implementation is almost impossible to find because of the large number of diffrent vendors who have adopted XNS in their product line.

As user applications evolve in the 1990s, lost and severely delayed packets will become a more significant performance issue in network design. Graphics- and video-intensive workstations are already causing problems on many bridged LANs because of their tendency to hog network bandwidth and clog bridges, locking out other LAN traffic. As digital voice and other time-critical digital applications emerge, these problems will only intensify.

When multitasking, windowing high-performance workstations join their graphics cousins in large numbers in typical LAN installations, the issues of sequencing and message integrity will become a more important part of network protocol design.

Even the best of today's routing and internetwork technologies will not meet the needs of coming LAN applications such as digital voice. Hence, protocol designers must develop new architectures that far exceed the transport capabilities of SPP and similar methods. These future protocols will have to provide classes of service that are suitable for applications that cannot afford the delays.

Other family members

Although IDP, SPP, and RIP are by far the most important XNS protocols, other members of the XNS family have been useful and influential in the evolution of networks.

■ *Packet Exchange Protocol.* PEP was developed to serve transaction-oriented needs in both the general LAN case and the completely connectionless (in OSI terminology) network types. Automated teller machine and credit card verification systems, for example, qualify as entirely transaction-driven, but even the more ordinary LAN environments involve some operations that are exclusively devoted to what XNS calls "request-response."

Since it is designed for simple request-response, the PEP packet has a very simple structure, with only three fields. The ID field lists what action the requester wants, while the Client Type provides a link to a specific transport layer client. The Data field (optional, of course) can have an answer to the request.

For example, a device requests the time of day from a Time of Day server or requests access to a file from an Authentication server. In either case, the server receives a PEP with a request in the ID field and sends back the answer with the same ID and the response in the Data field.

It may be time to rethink the overall design goals of our networks.

■ *Courier*. Subtitled the Remote Procedure Call (RPC) protocol, XNS Courier is similar to session-level services in other architectures. It uses layers below it such as SPP and IDP to provide applications with remote function-execution services. In Courier terms, there is always an active element that is asking for something and a receiving element that is offering a service.

For instance, a client application could use a Courier RPC to make a request to a remote printer, as though the printer was local. To the application, the printer is just a function call away. As with any RPC protocol, Courier takes the local function call, and transfers it to a remote resource (print server, file server, or the like) for execution.

■ *Bulk Data Transfer*. Within Courier's world is the Bulk Data Transfer (BDT) protocol, which allows for the transfer of larger blocks of data than Courier can generally handle. The BDT protocol was designed to accommodate file transfers and mainframe-to-mainframe database transfers with bulk data defined as an arbitrarily long sequence of bytes treated as a single Courier data object.

■ *Clearinghouse*. The Clearinghouse service is an application-level directory service linking the names and aliases of users to the corresponding network and data link addresses.

Xerox specifies that Clearinghouse databases can, and should be, replicated throughout the network, with a Clearinghouse server on each segment if possible. Since the speed with which a user process can access the Clearinghouse database determines how quickly a user can make a connection to the desired resource, Clearinghouse is generally made resident on a dedicated server, along with another service, called the Authentication service. An authentication process allows specific users to access specific resources while barring others.

■ *Error Protocol*. Any device that notices an error in a packet—generally a checksum error, for installation that are still using checksums—and discards it, should send an Error Protocol packet to the sender, specifying the kind of error and the packet that was destroyed. As the underlying hardware becomes more reliable and fewer installations depend on checksums for error control, the Error Protocol is fading from importance in the XNS pantheon. When routers send an Error Protocol packet, they use their well-known router error socket, which does nothing but send and receive error messages.

■ *Other applications*. Xerox uses a Gateway Access Protocol to connect XNS to non-XNS systems. In this way, GAP is like OSI's Virtual Terminal protocol, bringing all types of display devices into communication with each other, performing protocol translation service consistent with a Layer 7 protocol gateway. Other services on the application layer include the Filing service, for file access and management; Print service, for printing to remote printers through the network; Document Interchange service, for translation from one document format to another; and the Mail service, for electronic messaging.

The future of XNS

In the non-SNA marketplace, XNS remains very popular, trailing only DECnet and TCP/IP in popularity. We can expect XNS to remain a popular LAN network architecture through the mid-to-late 1990s when TCP and XNS protocols fade from importance and OSI protocol stacks take their place.

XNS's future will be affected by new technical developments and new market directions sweeping the LAN industry. On the semiconductor side, there has been an almost tenfold increase in the accuracy and reliability of the underlying hardware since XNS was first introduced, rendering some of the original design criteria obsolete. The era of XNS's development was a far cry from the brave new world of very-high-bandwidth media, such as today's 100 and 200 Mbit/s Fiber Distributed Data Interface and tomorrow's 10 Gbit/s successors, as well as desktop devices that have exploded with their own hundredfold increase in processing power. New applications, especially desktop graphics and video, will easily use up the rapidly expanding available bandwidth.

These developments will move the performance bottleneck from the medium—where choke points exist now—to the internet devices. The XNS of the 1990s will need new switching technology and bridges, routers, and gateways operating at two orders of magnitude beyond their present capability. In a world where we must have high-performance delivery systems on this scale, it may be time to rethink the overall design goals of our networks. Contrary to the philosophy that protocols can be developed and then forgotten, each wave of new network applications will drive network designers to recast their protocols in increasingly powerful forms. ■

Dale Neibaur, senior system architect, has been with Novell since 1981. As a programmer and member of the Novell "Superset" programming team, he coauthored such fundamental NetWare components as the bindery, IPX/SPX, and much of the NetWare file system.

Section 4
Standards

Dale Walsh, U. S. Robotics Inc., Chicago, Ill.

V.22*bis* defended: The standard gets some credence

A year after the higher-speed modems hit the streets, positive reports and user enthusiasm counter some initial gloomy predictions.

Last year an article in DATA COMMUNICATIONS written by Ken Krechmer ignited a few flares about the V.22*bis* standard adopted by U. S. manufacturers of the new 2.4-kbit/s modems ("V.22*bis:* The modem specification that's got troubles," April 1985, p. 117). But Krechmer's bleak vision of inevitable compatibility problems appears unfounded.

Actual use indicates the new V.22*bis* 2.4-kbit/s modems, from a number of U. S. manufacturers, are connecting and communicating well on the U. S. network. For example, Tymnet, which has been testing 2.4-kbit/s modems from a number of vendors, reported no compatibility problems (DATA COMMUNICATIONS, January 1985, "2.4-kbit/s modem market is poised to take off," p. 50). This article provides additional evidence of fine performance.

A major reason for the success of the new V.22*bis* modems is that many U. S. manufacturers participated in the writing of the CCITT (International Telegraph and Telephone Consultative Committee) recommendation (see "The birth of V.22*bis*"). The resulting compatibility among the new modems reveals a migration to higher speeds that is unusually orderly and a boon to established users.

One goal of the manufacturers participating in the CCITT deliberations was domestic and international compatibility among the 2.4-kbit/s products. U. S. participants also wanted compatibility with the well-established 1.2-kbit/s modem base. Now that products from several manufacturers are available, it can be said that a U. S.-made 2.4-kbit/s, V.22*bis*-compatible modem is likely to have these characteristics:

■ It operates with any other modem that follows the signaling specifications and calling/answering handshake sequences that are defined in the CCITT V.22*bis* recommendation for 2.4-kbit/s modems.

■ It is Bell 212A signal-compatible at 1.2 kbit/s; optionally, it supports 300-bit/s communications with Bell 103 compatibility.

■ It works with any existing telecommunications software packages and programs a user currently employs at 1.2 kbit/s.

In the article last April, Krechmer was partially correct in saying that the V.22*bis* specification amounts to little more than "a signaling scheme." CCITT recommendations specify what crosses the modem-to-modem, modem-to-network, and modem-to-terminal/computer interfaces. In some cases, they also define certain modem/user functions, such as test modes and options. In general, however, the recommendations do not limit additional options by manufacturers. Nor do they discourage multirate modems that combine more than one recommendation.

This freedom, because it is familiar territory, need not be viewed with alarm. The 1.2-kbit/s environment is a perfect example of such leeway, as a review of that environment's standards makes clear.

There are two 1.2-kbit/s standards, the CCITT V.22 and the U. S. Bell 212A de facto standard. The evolution of these standards was unlike that of V.22*bis*. The Bell 212A scheme was accepted first in this country. The CCITT V.22 recommendation fell in line, providing signal-compatibility with the Bell 212A.

But full compatibility does not exist at 1.2 kbit/s. It is not possible to sell or use a Bell 212A modem in Europe, for example, without modifying it. Operational differences include a. c. power-line voltages, computer/terminal electrical and mechanical specifications, regulatory agency requirements, and incompatibility at the fallback rates, among others. Nevertheless, 212A and V.22 modems communicate perfectly well together at 1.2 kbit/s, across or within national boundaries. As far as I know, only the 1,800-Hz holding tone, a V.22 and V.22*bis* option, causes problems with some 212A modems that do not have adequate filter rejection at 1,800 Hz.

Even within the United States, most 1.2-kbit/s modems are not fully compatible, feature for feature, with the Bell 212A. Most 212A-compatibles do not support synchronous transmission, for example, and there are variations in the RS-232-C pin assignments (DATA COMMUNICATIONS, "What's available in today's async modem marketplace," December 1983, p. 141). Yet most of these modems can call and talk to a Bell 212A—at least in the asynchronous mode.

To say the Bell 212A product, with option switches and test modes, is a standard, as Krechmer does, certainly muddies the waters. The Bell 212A standard is an established signaling scheme, as are the V.22 and V.22*bis* recommendations. But there are many differences among the compatible Bell 212A-type products. If 2.4-kbit/s modems are to evolve smoothly from the 1.2-kbit/s base, then I would expect them to exhibit

a similar variety of options despite their signal compatibility.

Figure 1 summarizes the recent history of dial-up modem standards, with representative manufacturers. The root of the family tree is the Bell 212A. The 1.2-kbit/s generation includes the international standard V.22 modems and two major U. S. groups. One implements the autodial protocol of the Hayes Microcomputer Products AT command set, so called because of its "ATtention" command prefix. This command set is supported by over two dozen 212A-type manufacturers and is generally considered to be the de facto standard for microcomputer autodialing communications. The second 1.2-kbit/s modem group does not support the AT command set and is more akin to the original Bell 212A specification. The same pattern continues in the generation of 2.4-kbit/s modems.

Most of the manufacturers of the new 2.4-kbit/s modems decided to build on their installed base, so users could migrate to the higher speed as easily as possible. Compatibility is a tremendous unifying force among manufacturers of the new 2.4-kbit/s modems,

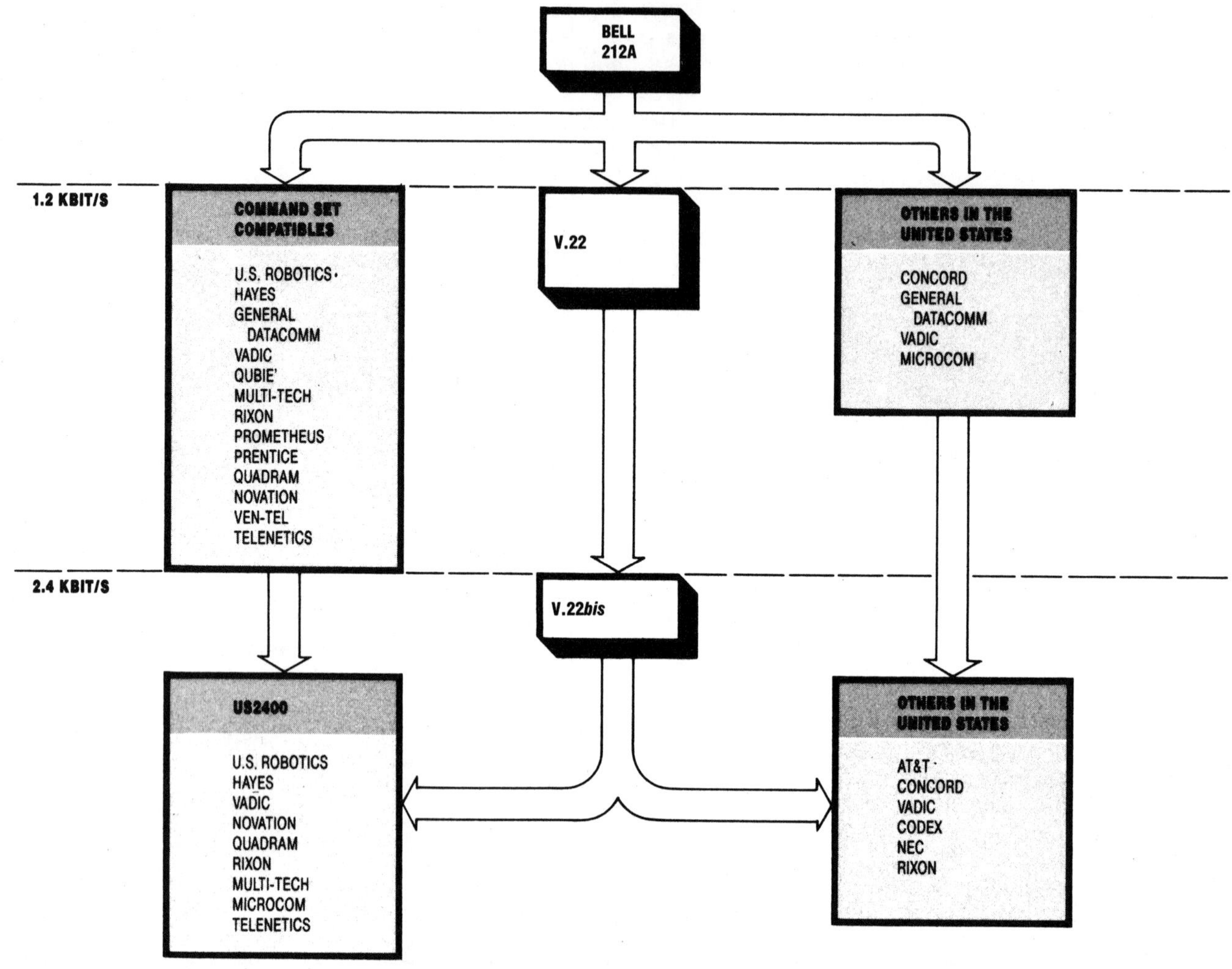

and I expect this modem type to emerge as the de facto U. S. 2.4-kbit/s standard, which is how I will refer to it for the remainder of this article to distinguish it from the international CCITT V.22*bis* recommendation and other Bell 212A-style 2.4-kbit/s modems.

■ **Bell 103 compatibility.** Fallback compatibility to 300 bit/s provides a unique twist to an otherwise fairly straightforward migration to 2.4-kbit/s communications. That the U. S. 2.4-kbit/s standard should include a Bell 103 fallback is without question. (The 600-bit/s fallback in V.22, but not in V.22*bis,* is incompatible with any other modem type, making it essentially a dead end.)

But V.22*bis* does not define automatic fallback to 300 bit/s; its handshake sequences only cover automatic fallback to 1.2 kbit/s. These sequences apply to both originate and answer operations. Thus, a U. S. 2.4-kbit/s standard modem can originate a call at 2.4 kbit/s and, upon detecting a 1.2-kbit/s answering modem, automatically fall back to 1.2 kbit/s. But a U. S. 2.4-kbit/s answering modem automatically falls back to 1.2 kbit/s when a 1.2-kbit/s modem calls.

The 212A-type modems, on the other hand, offer automatic speed switching (between 300 bit/s and 1.2 kbit/s) only at the answer end, not the calling end. As a result, the U. S. 2.4-kbit/s modem is likely to feature automatic three-speed switching — to make it compatible with the 300-bit/s Bell 103 mode at the answer end, while still providing 2.4- to 1.2-kbit/s automatic fallback at the originate end.

Implementation of incoming-call speed indication for three speeds is not the problem, Krechmer maintains. The 2.4-kbit/s to 1.2-kbit/s speed-selection mechanism is part of V.22*bis;* the mechanism for answering 300-bit/s calls is the same as it is in the Bell 212A.

■ **Speed indication.** The U. S. 2.4-kbit/s modem, like the 212A, uses pin 12 of the RS-232-C interface as the incoming-call speed indicator. Currently, the consensus within the modem industry is that "pin 12 high speed" means 2.4 kbit/s, and "pin 12 low speed" covers both 1.2 kbit/s and 300 bit/s.

Some manufacturers use a secondary RS-232-C pin to distinguish 300 bit/s from 1.2 kbit/s. The U. S. 2.4-kbit/s standard has a transmit/receive (TXD/RXD) command-oriented protocol; assignment of 300-bit/s recognition to an additional RS-232-C pin is not necessary. Instead, the modem issues CONNECT, CONNECT 1200, or CONNECT 2400 to the data terminal equipment (DTE), and the terminal software responds accordingly.

■ *The U. S. 2.4-kbit/s command set.* Following the majority of 212A-compatibles, most of the new 2.4-kbit/s modems will adopt the new 2.4-kbit/s modem standard. This means the new higher-speed modems will support the Hayes AT command set. As Krechmer points out, Concord Data and AT&T Information Systems are maintaining their own command sets. I am not aware of other companies that follow suit. It is likely that manufacturers that do not adopt the AT command set will develop 2.4-kbit/s modems compatible with their 1.2-kbit/s modems. On the other hand, recent reports in the press indicate that Concord Data plans to incorporate the AT command set into its offerings, due to market demand.

Product diversity does not seem to be a serious problem for users. Most users are informed enough to select a modem compatible with their software or compatible with the options and front panel of their favorite 1.2-kbit/s modem.

■ *Call waiting.* The U. S. 2.4-kbit/s modem, as Krechmer points out, does not always conform to the V.22*bis* standard of 45-60 msec. as the wait duration following a line interruption before disconnecting. In most cases, a U. S. 2.4-kbit/s has a default 700-msec. "hold-over" before it disconnects. However, an extended hold-over is a common modem feature of many types of modems. In a large number of these products, the time duration is programmable.

As for his concern about automatic speed switching (automatic fallback from 2.4 kbit/s to 1.2 kbit/s during an error-prone connection), I do not see how this is affected by call waiting. A line break caused by a second incoming call does not initiate this speed switching.

A more important issue is the advisability of using call waiting on a data line, since it is bound to result in data errors regardless of hold-over time. Some users do not take the risk. Others may opt to use the "cancel call waiting" code supplied by the local telephone company — an option not available on all lines.

■ *Test modes.* The CCITT 1.2-kbit/s recommendation, V.22, includes remote loopback testing, patterned after the 212A modem. Remote loopback has never been implemented in the Hayes-type U. S. 1.2-kbit/s modems. It is unlikely that the U. S. 2.4-kbit/s modems will implement remote loopback testing.

Figure 2 shows the V.22*bis* handshake sequence, which specifies two answer tones, either 2,250 Hz or 2,225 Hz. (Recommendation V.22 refers to the Bell 212A when it notes that some modems use 2,225 Hz.) Either frequency works quite well, with no compatibility problem. The second answer tone is defined in the V.25 automatic answering sequence and is used on international calls. Any switched network auto-answer modem (V.22*bis*, V.22, Bell 212A) should append this tone on international auto-answer calls.

Krechmer's conclusions about the performance of V.22*bis* modems are easily countered. For instance, most 212A-type modems use a compromise equalizer approach. As a result, the modem's signal-to-noise ratio (SNR), which is its ability to counter noise, varies several decibels (dB) from call to call. The V.22*bis*-compatible U. S. 2.4-kbit/s modem, in contrast, uses an adaptive equalizer that "learns" channel characteristics and removes call-to-call variations. The U. S. 2.4-kbit/s standard sharply focuses the received data signals, which in turn enables it to better distinguish signals from noise.

Furthermore, most 212A designs give up 3 to 4 dB of potential SNR to simplify implementation. Therefore, even though the achievable SNR performance of current Bell 212A-type modems is 7 dB better than that of V.22*bis* modems, in practice the difference is much smaller. Krechmer concludes that the V.22*bis* modem would not perform successfully in originate mode on 50 percent of the 1,450-to-2,900-mile AT&T circuits in the United States. He derives this erroneous conclusion from performance comparisons based almost totally on SNR performance. I disagree both with his analysis and with his conclusion.

First, the margin-of-safety approach he uses applies well to deep space communications, say a Jupiter probe, where background noise is at a fairly constant level. But telephone channel noise varies widely from call to call. Probability of success is more to the point.

Second, Krechmer assumes that a typical V.22*bis* modem's performance is 7 dB worse than theoretical. Three dB is more typical for a well-designed adaptively equalized modem. The 7-dB typical/theoretical ratio is more appropriate for a compromise-equalized 1.2-kbit/s modem. Therefore, an SNR of 17 to 18 dB is needed for successful operation, rather than 21 dB.

Third, random noise is unlikely to limit successful operations. The 1982/83 End Office Connection Study is the most comprehensive summary of the AT&T long-distance network in print (*AT&T Bell Laboratories Technical Journal,* vol. 63, November 1984). Over 6,500 direct-dial connections were tested. The SNR was measured on each connection, along with numerous other impairments, and the results were presented statistically. The measurements were notched noise tests, which measure noise in the presence of a signal. Test results from this method include quantization noise and are more pessimistic than are results from simpler test methods. Ninety-nine percent of the local circuits tested were better than 30 db. Short-haul connections, which represent a larger percentage of calls made, were even better.

The AT&T connection study presents an excellent discussion of impulse noise and correlates impulse magnitudes and frequency of occurrence with different types of end-office switching equipment. Generally, the newer electronic switching equipment produces the least impulse noise, while the older stepping-switch systems produce the most. But the problem of impulse noise does not correlate with call distance. Hence, users frequently have trouble calling the next town, which might be using the old step-by-step switching system, but have no trouble calling a distant city.

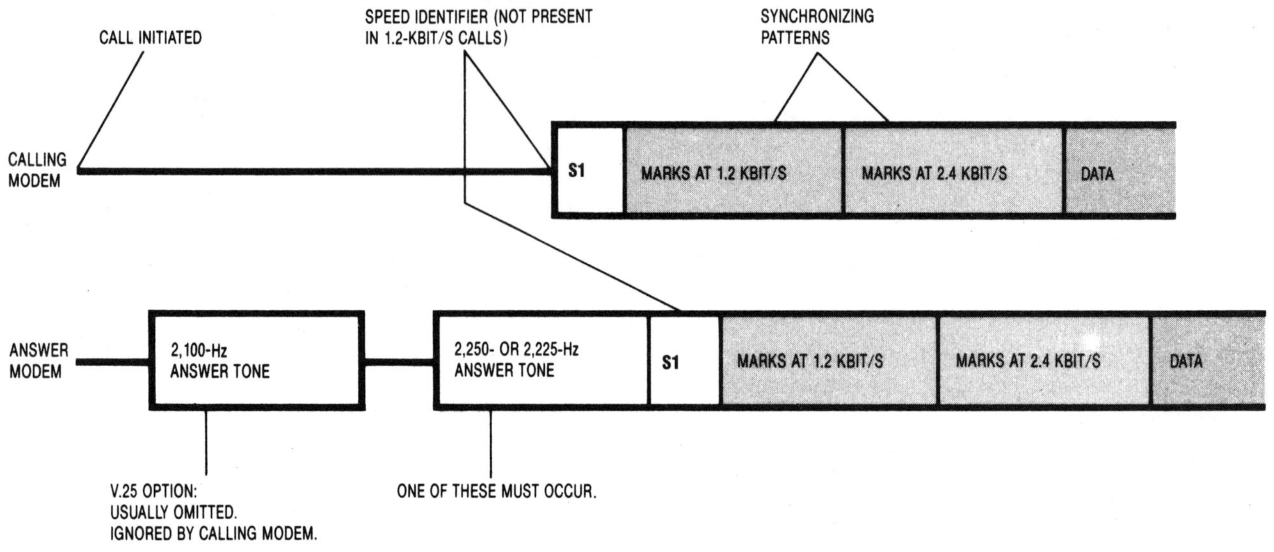

Impulse noise affects all data rates, although higher-speed modems are inherently more susceptible than are lower-speed modems. However, implementation differences in receiver architecture and filter systems play a significant role in reducing the effects of impulse noise. Noise impulses large enough to cause errors at 2.4 kbit/s occur about twice as frequently as larger impulses that would cause 1.2-kbit/s errors, assuming about a 4-dB performance difference between the two speeds. But the 2.4-kbit/s block error rate is approximately the same as that for 1.2 kbit/s—because twice as many good data blocks are transmitted between impulses.

At this time, there are over 250 electronic bulletin boards that offer 2.4-kbit/s service along with their established 1.2-kbit/s service. Operation on a bulletin board is the most demanding challenge a modem faces. Left unattended, the modem fields mixed calls—many of them long distance—at multiple data rates. It is not uncommon for them to be on continuously, 24 hours a day, both responding to calls as well as taking messages.

As yet, no formal study has been made of this broad user base. But an informal survey of 2.4-kbit/s modem users provides additional evidence that the modems are performing quite satisfactorily.

Users who reported performance results were either using or connecting with 2.4-kbit/s modems from the following manufacturers: U. S. Robotics, Hayes, Multi-Tech, Racal-Vadic, Paradyne, Penril, AT&T, Case Rixon. Several users reported that their 2.4-kbit/s connections were better than the same 1.2-kbit/s connections. One user reported fewer block checks at 2.4 kbit/s than at 1.2 kbit/s. Almost all reported overall satisfactory results.

The table, from the AT&T Connection study data, lists five major line impairments. The percentage of successful calls is compared for 1.2-kbit/s and 2.4-kbit/s modems, assuming that each impairment acts separately. A successful call is defined as having fewer than 1 percent block errors. This corresponds roughly to a bit error rate (BER) of less than one error in 105 bits if data block length equals 1,000 bits. The most serious problem is shown to be impulse noise.

But the results of the the connection study reflect the predivestiture network. What about the future? It is speculated that the network, which includes the AT&T network, will degrade for two main reasons: equal-access arrangements, mandated by law, that are now going into place; and the introduction of the 32-kbit/s adaptive delta pulse code modulation (ADPCM) converter.

In most cases, equal access arrangements will cause AT&T long-distance calls to be routed through additional transmission links. It will degrade modem performance somewhat but will not significantly alter the relative performance of one modem type compared with another. However, adaptively equalized modems may be less affected. Certainly the 1.2-kbit/s fallback mode of the U. S. 2.4-kbit/s modem standard—which is Bell 212A modulation—will fare well.

The 32-kbit/s ADPCM converter issue is tougher. The devices will double the number of telephone channels a digital carrier system transmits. These high-density transmission schemes are still in development and are not yet implemented in the U. S. network; if they become widespread, it is expected that dial-up data communications will suffer. While there is no measured data on ADPCM performance, and the ADPCM devices are not generally available, V.22*bis* modulation is not seriously threatened. Data communications at any speed is not going to just suddenly collapse. Rather, the percentage of successful calls will decrease gradually as the network changes.

Successful calls*

TELEPHONE CHANNEL IMPAIRMENT	1.2 KBIT/S	2.4 KBIT/S
RANDOM NOISE	99.75%	99.00%
IMPULSE NOISE	78-79	79-97
PHASE HITS	98.00	98.00
GAIN HITS	100.00	99.75
DROPOUTS	99.10	99.50

*BASED ON THE 1982/83 END OFFICE CONNECTION STUDY, (*AT&T BELL LABORATORIES TECHNICAL JOURNAL,* VOL. 63, NOV. 1984).

Krechmer suggests that V.26*ter*, an alternate recommendation now used primarily in France, may replace V.22*bis* as the preferred 2.4-kbit/s standard. He offers three reasons:
- Better SNR performance (by 4 dB).
- Required echo canceling technique (ECT) will, with technological advances, become more economical.
- Potential compatibility with V.32, a 9.6-kbit/s and 4.8-kbit/s modem recommendation.

V.26*ter* does have an SNR advantage and inherently more impulse noise immunity. But this immunity is less than that of present 1.2-kbit/s modems, so the improved performance in this area is marginal. Further, an echo canceling modem is more susceptible to low-frequency phase jitter and offset frequency. In addition, the echo cancelers of the U. S. network create a problem for ECT modems. CCITT recommendation V.25 was, therefore, recently modified to allow disabling of the network cancelers. It will, however, take some time before the new disabling circuits become widespread.

It is true that technological advances will make the ECT more economical. However, the large semiconductor houses have committed to V.22*bis* chip sets. The economics of this commitment will prove to be greater than any economy gained in ECT technology.

V.26*ter* is not really related to the V.32 recommendation (for 9.6 and 4.8 kbit/s), except that both use ECT technologies. V.32 refers to V.26*ter* "interworking"—a multimodem concept (two modems in one product).

The inclusion of V.26*ter* interworking, and not V.22*bis*, was at the time an extremely sensitive issue. There is currently a movement to change the V.32-modem recommendation to a 9.6-, 4.8-, 2.4-kbit/s recommendation, where the added 2.4-kbit/s mode is not V.26*ter*.

Further, V.26*ter* will have an uphill struggle in achieving workability in the 212A network environment because V.26*ter* does not easily fall back to the existing U. S. standards. The V.22*bis* bandsplitting filters and signaling rates are the same as those for a 212A. This yields tremendous design economies. ■

Dale Walsh is director of advanced design at U. S. Robotics. Walsh has been a delegate to CCITT Study Group XVII and has worked in the modem industry for more than 15 years.

David Anderson, Temple, Barker, and Sloane Inc., Lexington, Mass.

Case studies and implementations of LDI arrangements

This article, second in a series, discusses how many companies have used logistics data interchange in order to reduce costs and make operations more efficient.

As computer and communications technologies advance and become less costly, corporations find new ways to use computer networks to streamline their operations. An emerging application for these technologies is logistics data interchange (LDI) — the use of a computer network to transmit logistics information within a company or to external vendors, transportation carriers, or customers. (LDI is an important subset of the more well-known term: EDI — Electronic Data Interchange, which refers to any type of communications among computers.)

Last month, the motivations behind LDI, its experimental beginnings, and the opportunities it offers for a company's development were discussed. It is clear that data communications executives must prepare for a substantial increase in LDI among a variety of internal and external parties. Further clarifying how LDI schemes actually operate requires a closer look at examples of the way in which several companies have harnassed communications technology to reduce overall logistics costs.

Logistics data interchange is actually a family of related information flows and communications facilities, all focused on monitoring material and product movements from vendors, among company facilities, and to customers. For example, LDI may involve transferring information among only internal company locations or databases, drawing information from or transmitting information to external databases (owned by vendors or transportation carriers), or integrating internal and external data sources on a real-time basis.

As Figure 1 shows, LDI can occur in a variety of normal business situations: material purchasing and vendor monitoring; logistics planning; shipment control; and customer order, verification, and billing. At present, no one scheme is available that performs integrated (companywide) internal or external LDI. Rather, a number of vendor and customized facilities have been or are being developed that will enable a company to engage in selective LDI activities.

LDI linkages between vendors and their customers can use either in-house or third-party communications facilities. Logistics data that is interchanged between companies and their vendors may include material purchase orders, shipment notification and status, order changes and cancellations, and inventory status (either at vendor or company locations). The following case studies illustrate both third-party and in-house LDI options for vendor/company linkages.

The Automotive Industry Action Group (AIAG) communications network is a typical third-party LDI arrangement. Organized in 1981 by all four U. S. automobile manufacturers, AIAG has established standard forms and transmitting instructions for communications between automobile suppliers and their original equipment manufacturers. AIAG has developed its own communications protocols and has adopted American National Standards Institute (ANSI) X.12 standard transaction sets — from bills of lading to purchase-order-acknowledgment documents. The AIAG LDI facility only requires a participating company to have a microcomputer with communications capabilities and a few software programs; because the requirements are so minimal, smaller suppliers are able to access the network. The facility is expected to reduce OEM-to-supplier order-receipt times from weeks to minutes, cut order-processing costs dramatically, and speed up parts movements to vehicle assembly facilities operating in a "just-in-time" environment.

The nine major European automobile makers have formed a similar group, the Organization for Data Exchange by Teletransmission in Europe (ODETTE). The

*1. **Potentials.*** *Most companies have many opportunities to use LDI. The goal is to enhance the operations and planning process with better information.*

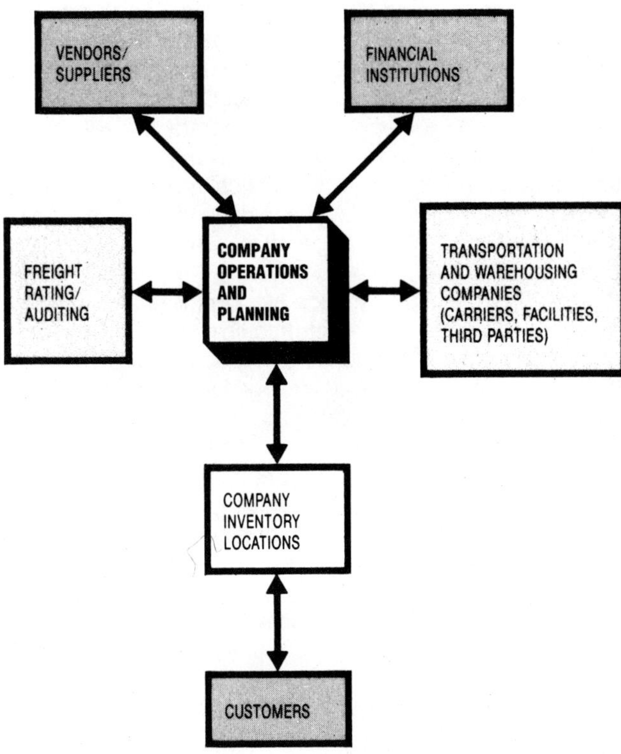

facilities use United Nations-approved electronic transaction standards as a basis for establishing a single European LDI communications network. ODETTE seeks to link automobile manufacturers, suppliers, customs authorities, transportation carriers, and shipping agents across Europe, allowing more rapid and less costly movements of parts and finished vehicles. Plans are under way to expand the ODETTE LDI arrangement to other European industries, including the chemical, electronics, and steel sectors.

Ralph's Grocery Company, one of the oldest grocery businesses in the Western United States, has developed an in-house automated network that automatically links product reorders from company warehouses and vendors to sales data recorded by checkout line product scanners. Ralph's computers are tied to major supplier's computers via direct communications linkages. All purchase order data is exchanged in Uniform Communications Standards (UCS) formats, which have been widely adopted in the U. S. grocery industry. The network allows Ralph's to immediately restock its distribution centers in response to the depletion of products at the stores by electronically linking the company to its product suppliers. This results in lower inventory-holding and product-ordering costs, as well as fewer stockouts of fast-moving items.

RCA, using a third-party LDI network, established an external electronic purchase order facility at a number of its locations in 1983, and it has been expanding the program ever since. A third-party network accepts batch transmissions of RCA purchase orders, then separates and stores the orders by supplier in an electronic mailbox. Suppliers receive the orders after the third-party network has altered the communications protocol to conform to the requirements of individual vendor's computers.

Plans for the future growth of vendor-linked LDI at RCA include expanding the number of suppliers on the network, adding new document types (ANSI currently has over 100 standardized documents for use in LDI), and increasing the number of company facilities tied into the network.

Many companies already use the automated transportation-carrier freight payment programs available from some of the nation's largest banks. In addition to making payments to carriers, these programs can audit freight bills to determine if the correct rate has been charged and can transmit logistics and accounting data (based on summarized carrier freight bill information) back to the company.

A typical freight payment facility is Chase's Transportation Cash Management System (TCMS). Freight bills are transmitted electronically or by magnetic tape from a company to the TCMS facility on a daily or weekly basis (depending on the size of the company). Chase subjects each bill to a pre-audit check prior to payment, arranges an electronic or other payment method with the carrier, and generates logistics-related information from the bills that can be electronically transmitted back to the company for analysis. TCMS also offers an interactive customer inquiry function for status checks on outstanding and paid accounts and can transmit compatible data back to the company's accounting system. Customers can use TCMS to improve cash flow, avoid duplicate carrier payments, and obtain detailed logistics planning information on freight shipments by carrier, traffic lane, and rating class.

Logistics planning and transportation control

A number of companies have developed internal LDI facilities to compile and analyze logistics data from far-flung domestic and foreign operations. The information is directly incorporated into both tactical and strategic physical distribution planning schemes, allowing company logistics facilities to adapt rapidly to changes in external conditions (for example, the marketplace or a particular country's trade policy).

For example, Signode Corporation, which has 10 plants and 11 warehouses, ships over one billion pounds of freight yearly to about 100,000 domestic and international customers. To better plan its myriad freight shipments and to minimize costs, Signode uses an outside transportation management company to organize its worldwide logistics data flows. Carrier freight bills and related information are electronically transmitted to the vendor's computer, where they are organized, sorted, and audited before customized reports are generated and sent back to Signode. Signode continuously tracks transportation costs in its major logistics channels—the shipment path from factory to warehouse to customer—to evaluate whether its existing product movement and storage methods provide

529

the required service at an acceptable cost. Signode uses the data to facilitate carrier rate and service negotiations, identify alternative distribution channels that may prove more cost-effective, and plan improved logistics delivery schemes. Since the Signode LDI network is completely automated and operates on a real-time basis on the vendor's computers, new data is available each day for use in logistics planning and analysis, allowing management to respond rapidly to evolving market needs.

Many companies have set up in-house LDI communications networks to monitor and control inventory holdings and in-transit product flows. For example, Volvo Transport AB of Sweden uses computer-monitoring facilities to control the flow of supplies in various stages of its logistics channels for all Volvo subsidiaries. By closely tracking both materials inbound to plants and products outbound to customers, Volvo estimates that over $28 million in excess inventory stocks is avoided each year. Volvo Transport also has plans to expand its facilities to accommodate nonsubsidiary users. Working with Sweden's state communications group, Televerket, Volvo plans to introduce by early 1986 a computer-switching arrangement that will create an international LDI network capable of linking many different types of computers. Users of the new network will be able to plan, monitor, and document international freight shipments, including arranging for transportation carriers and customs clearances.

To remain competitive in the increasingly deregulated transportation marketplace, facility-based logistics operators, such as ports and public warehouses, are also beginning to offer LDI services to shippers. These facilities vary widely in intent: Some are designed to ease foreign trade bottlenecks by preclearance of freight shipments past the U. S. Customs Service and the Department of Agriculture; others link customers with ocean carriers, brokers and forwarders, and domestic transportation carriers. All these networks attempt to achieve lower inventory costs by expediting shipments from origin to destination and by helping shippers precisely track cargo movements.

For example, a number of U. S. ocean ports (at present, Charleston, Savannah, Portland, and Tacoma) offer a variety of LDI communications capabilities to shippers using their facilities. These automated cargo facilities conform to rules and standards developed by the U. S. Customs Service, which, to lower cargo inspection costs, is adopting customs preclearance procedures that expedite foreign and domestic cargo flow through ports. The Customs Service currently operates the Automated Commercial System and the Automated Brokers Interface System, which are interactive cargo clearance and tracking services available at nominal startup and usage costs to ports, brokers, carriers, and shippers.

Similarly, the Port of Savannah uses one of the nation's first automated information networks for cargo. The service, which began as a cargo-tracking facility, now has fully automated inbound and outbound vessel cargo manifests and data-entry capabilities, provides electronic notification of customs releases to brokers and

carriers, and can electronically generate movement status reports for shippers. Communications is accomplished either via third-party networks or direct customer linkages.

In addition to using third-party LDI networks, some companies have developed a variety of in-house arrangements to improve communications on available product inventories at diverse product warehousing locations. Since a company may operate its own warehouse facilities as well as use public warehouses, difficulties in electronically sharing logistics information among these locations often arise. These difficulties have led to the development of a "cooperative" warehouse LDI procedure.

The Warehouse Information Network System (WINS) establishes a standard electronic link between a company and its own warehouse or a public warehouse through a communications network. Originally organized by the Transportation Data Coordinating Committee, WINS is currently used by some of the nation's largest corporations (General Foods, Beatrice, and Durkee Foods, among others) to electronically handle inventory, shipment, and related information flows on product stocks and availability between their warehouse facilities, corporate headquarters, customers, and transportation carriers. For example, customers wishing to determine shipment status from a vendor's warehouse tied into WINS can dial-up and electronically determine scheduled shipment date, product availability, and related logistics data.

Customer/company linkages

Perhaps the most innovative LDI arrangements being developed today are intimately tied to corporate marketing strategies that attempt to capture customers and their orders by linking them directly to company computers. These arrangements promise to become a major marketing innovation in future years, yielding higher sales and improved customer service.

American Hospital Supply Inc., which distributes products from 8,500 suppliers to over 100,000 healthcare locations, developed a direct electronic order system in the mid-1970s, installing order-taking terminals in the supply rooms of large hospitals. As a result, American Hospital has captured high market shares by allowing customers direct linkages with the vendor. The company can also lower customer prices by using higher order volumes with suppliers.

Inland Steel offers a facility for customers to electronically order steel products and determine pending shipment status. The arrangement has improved customer delivery reliability and reduced excess-inventory costs, allowing Inland to competitively price its products with Japanese steel producers.

Finally, General Foods has a pilot program under way that will allow supermarkets to better match products with demographic profiles of their regional and target markets. The facility plans to combine information collected from bar-code scanning equipment at supermarket checkout counters with economic and demographic data on local markets. The result: customized reports specifying which items a supermarket should stock and in what quantity (like the other information, the report travels over communications links directly to the customer).

Implementation case studies

One of the most sophisticated customer-to-company LDI schemes has been developed by McKesson Corporation. McKesson, a major drug distributor, installed direct computer-ordering facilities in the mid-1970s. Approximately 97 percent of its 15,000 customers (many are local drugstores, for example) use a hand-held order-entry device to order a wide range of products from McKesson. Orders are electronically communicated via dial-up lines and acoustic couplers to IBM and Tandem computers at one of two McKesson data centers, then transmitted via McKesson's own network to one of its 52 distribution centers, where products are prepared for local delivery. In addition, McKesson's LDI arrangement is programmed to contain the purchasing criteria for 60 percent of the 2,000 manufacturers that supply McKesson with products. Knowing delivery timetables and prescribed order quantities, McKesson's computers automatically forward electronic purchase orders to suppliers at the appropriate time. Well over half of McKesson's orders are electronically processed via computer-to-computer linkages with vendors, using order format conversion software.

The unique McKesson customer order procedure can be triggered by electronic data entry scanning of a product bar-code label on a shelf or by entering a product identification number into a keyboard. Thus, McKesson customers can walk the aisles of their drugstores and either scan the shelf labels of products needing restocking or directly enter identification numbers. McKesson estimates that the company's electronic order-entry scheme reduces by 50 to 75 percent the time a typical drugstore spends on ordering.

McKesson's distribution centers are organized by families of products arranged in the same order as they are stocked on customers' retail shelves. Consequently, the electronic order-entry facility can automatically generate order "pick-lists" that correspond to store shelf locations. When the druggists receive their orders, the items can be stocked directly from the shipping containers to the store shelves, wholly avoiding backtracking, a common drawback of random order-pick procedures. Another benefit of McKesson's facility is the significant reduction of inventory requirements—both at stores and at McKesson's distribution centers—because the system is constantly monitoring product-on-hand, product-in-transit, and product-on-order to determine potential shortages, thus minimizing the "safety stock" inventory.

In addition, the McKesson system significantly reduces paperwork flows by explicitly including promotional or trade discounts in each customer's invoice—no matter how complex the discount scheme. The facility, for example, provides for "per-unit" discounts so that drugstores do not have to order a fixed minimum amount (which is generally more than is needed at one time) in order to receive a manufacturer's price break. Finally,

McKesson offers druggists a service called Economost, which provides a detailed report on fast- and slow-moving products.

The McKesson electronic order-entry network, 15 years in development and clearly a competitive advantage in the hotly contested drugstore resupply market, is an excellent example of a dedicated customer-to-company communications linkage. The costs of maintaining and enhancing the network are high—for example, the Sacramento, Calif., data center employs 120 people and is in operation 24 hours per day. Still, McKesson believes that the investment is more than made up for by increased sales and reduced inventories.

It should be noted, however, that the risks are also high. If customers become dissatisfied with McKesson's products, prices, or service, they can simply move to competitors, leaving the company with extensive investments in communications facilities that must then be spread across remaining customers, potentially resulting in higher prices or lower company profits.

One of the most advanced supplier-to-company communications systems has been developed by the Chrysler Corporation. A product of more than two decades of research and development, the Dynamic Inventory Analysis System (DIAS) may be the most sophisticated inbound materials flow-control program in use today in the United States.

Designed to provide real-time information on inbound material movements to Chrysler's 11 vehicle assembly plants, DIAS monitors and controls parts and raw material flows from supplier shipping docks to plant receiving facilities. Every level of the material distribution channel is linked to the automated network—suppliers' production scheduling, purchasing departments, suppliers' shipping points, inbound freight consolidation locations, and Chrysler plant receiving locations. DIAS can track, often with only a few minutes' delay, the progress of a supplier's shipment at each echelon in the logistics chain: as it leaves the supplier dock, in-transit, at the consolidation facility, at the assembly plant protection gate, on the plant receiving dock, and in inventory or on the assembly line.

As Figure 2 indicates, the Chrysler DIAS communications network links all participants in the inbound material flows to vehicle assembly plants. At the beginning of each work week, Chrysler's production scheduling department issues supplier release and authorizations (SRAs) to company authorized suppliers via the DIAS network. The SRA specifies how much of the supplier's raw materials or parts are needed at each assembly plant each day of the coming week.

Upon receipt of the SRA, suppliers have 30 minutes to acknowledge the order using advanced shipping notices (ASNs), which can be sent to DIAS via IBM-compatible terminals, linkages, Telex, or telephone to Chrysler service representatives (who audit the ASNs and directly enter them into DIAS). If the ASN information does not agree with SRA data, DIAS automatically generates a message to the supplier requesting correction or clarification.

2. Chrysler's DIAS. *Chryslers's Dynamic Inventory Analysis System involves a communications link from every stage of the production chain. Because the status of shipments is monitored at every stage, Chrysler has reduced mistakes on orders, improved quality control, and eliminated much paperwork.*

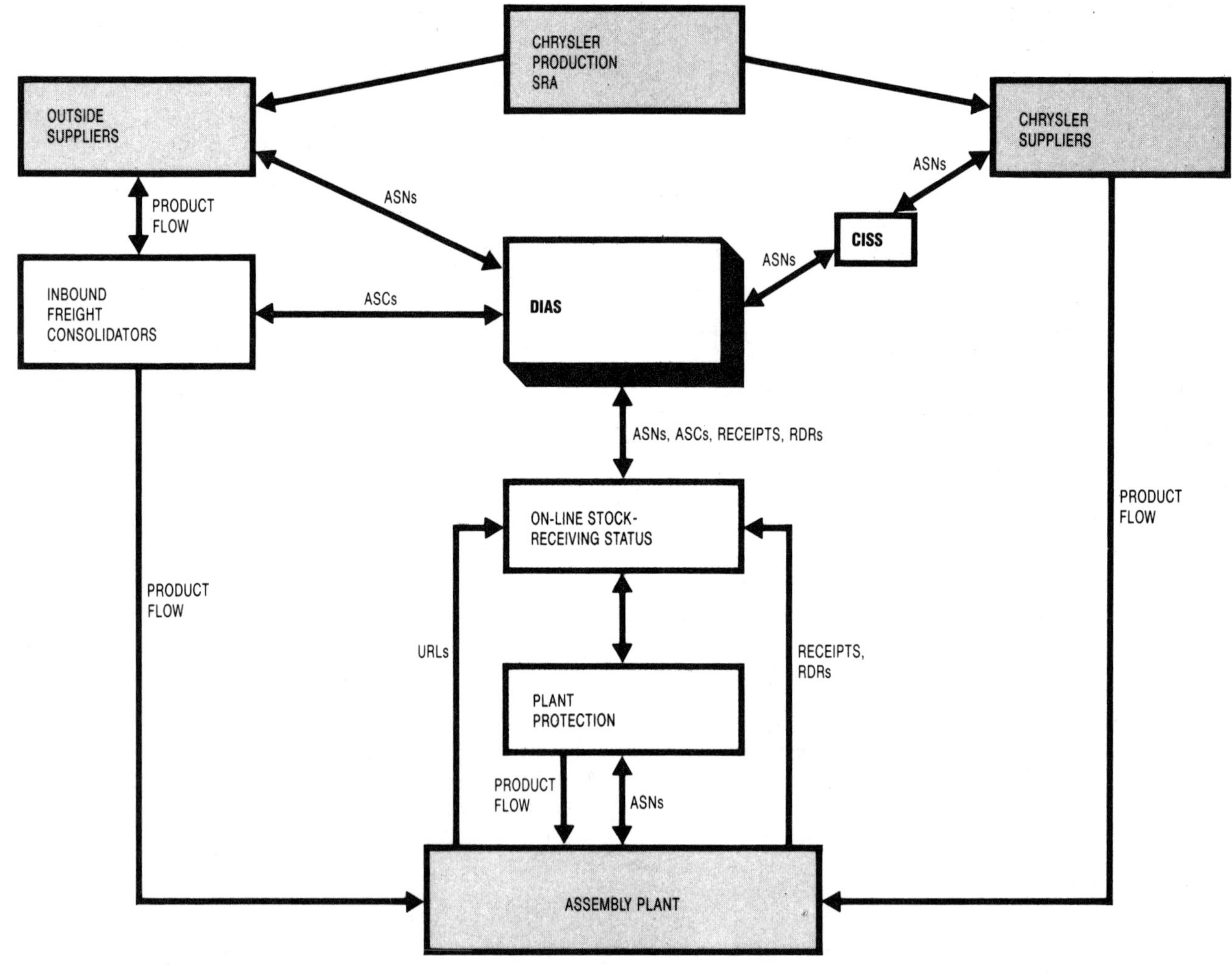

Figure 2 shows that slightly different communications networks are used for captive (in-house) suppliers than for outside suppliers. Outside suppliers normally ship their products via consolidation facilities. The facilities assemble a variety of supplier shipments into a single truckload movement to an assembly plant, thus reducing congestion at the plant and ensuring that all products needed for production arrive at the required time. Once a full trailer load is available at a consolidation facility, an advanced shipping consolidation (ASC) notice is sent via computer, Telex, or telephone to DIAS. The ASC, which contains full bill-of-lading information, is essentially a loading manifest detailing the contents of a trailer.

In addition to outside suppliers, Chrysler fabricates many products at 28 engine and component facilities, most of which are located near assembly plants. The Chrysler interplant shipping system (CISS) computer system controls these material movements and assembles all relevant ASN data for transmission to DIAS.

As material and parts are received at the "protection gates" of each Chrysler assembly plant, a security guard logs in the shipment on DIAS via a remote computer terminal. DIAS then automatically generates documents on each trailer's contents and disposition, which are then transmitted to the plant's receiving dock. Any discrepancies between the shipment receipt (driver's bill of lading) and the ASN data are immediately reported back to DIAS by receiving personnel via a receipt discrepancy report (RDR). In addition, a uniform receipt list (URL) is generated to inform DIAS of the actual material receipt at the facility.

DIAS is mounted on tandem IBM mainframe 3084s located in Detroit, along with CISS and communications system software. A combination of Chrysler-designed and modified IBM packages is used as a basis for DIAS. Under an earlier arrangement — which comprised one of the initial electronic linkages introduced in the late 1970s — suppliers had to mail ASNs to Chrysler, where they were processed by hand. Later, information on material flow tracking was added that included linkages to the purchasing, transportation, and quality control divisions. Full real-time supplier, consolidator, and plant communications and control capabilities were added to DIAS in the early 1980s.

DIAS has generated many benefits for Chrysler over its 20 years of operation. It has allowed just-in-time assembly by maintaining only those materials required for the next few hours' work at the plant, eliminating costly inventories and shortages. In addition, it has helped improve overall material quality, since receiving staff check all inbound shipments against quality standards and immediately notify DIAS of problems. Also, DIAS allows Chrysler to monitor transportation carrier transit times to ensure that material is delivered within specified service requirements. Substantial paperwork and follow-up is also eliminated by the real-time communications capabilities of DIAS. What's more, Chrysler can easily track supplier timeliness and quality by referring to DIAS permanent files. Such information is useful in eliminating suppliers with consistently poor performance.

Future enhancements to DIAS include direct linkages between Chrysler manufacturing and assembly plants (to allow material scheduling further up the channel from the shipping dock), real-time supplier invoice generation (to electronically transmit invoices to and from vendors), tracking capabilities for Chrysler's transportation carriers (to better control in-transit material flows between shipping dock and protection gate), and electronic billing (which would allow transportation carriers to directly bill Chrysler via DIAS).

Although DIAS has not solved all Chrysler's problems with controlling inbound material flows and communicating with suppliers, consolidators, and transportation carriers, the facility has established an industry standard for information accuracy and quality control that few can rival. To constantly update real-time data on material flows requires tremendous cooperation from both in-house and external sources of information, which is often very difficult to achieve. The key to Chrysler's success in developing DIAS is not only its data communications software and hardware (which are clearly state of the art) but also the ability of its people to ensure that the many diverse vendors cooperate as an active part of DIAS under very strict communications protocol conditions. ∎

The next and final article in the series will examine the future of LDI and the role of various communications in advancing the use of LDI.

David Anderson is vice president, logistics practice, at Temple, Barker, and Sloane Inc. Formerly a vice president of Data Resources Inc., Anderson has a Ph. D. in transportion and economics from Boston College.

C. R. Abbruscato, Racal-Milgo, Sunrise, Fla.

Choosing a key management style that suits the application

Message authentication and schemes for encryption range in complexity. If the use warrants the cost, pick the newest high-security protocol.

One of the most difficult aspects of encrypting a data communications network is key management. Poorly done, it can undermine network security. Overdone, it can present an ongoing, burdensome expense. There is no single solution for key management that might apply to all data networks. The chosen method of key management must be consistent with the overall security objectives and the architecture of the network.

When devising a key management scheme, the selection of an encryption algorithm is a relatively easy first decision. For U. S. companies, the choice is usually the Data Encryption Standard (DES), which has been endorsed by the National Bureau of Standards (NBS) and the American National Standards Institute (ANSI). Once that security-related issue has been resolved, questions of physical security must then be addressed. Specifically, the cryptographic equipment needs to be secured against improper handling. Selecting cryptographic equipment and making it secure present an opportunity for cost/security trade-offs. As such, it is also a juncture at which the security of the network itself may inadvertently be undermined.

Physical security becomes a key management issue in cases where the key is stored on a small peripheral module that is not itself physically secured to the cryptographic unit. A bold individual (not necessarily a professional thief) can do more damage to the network's security by "borrowing" the key module for a short period than a cryptanalyst can do with a Cray supercomputer over an extended period. Because of their cost and inconvenience, it is tempting to overlook the need for physical access controls. But they should be considered, for the chain in this instance is truly only as strong as its weakest link.

Before keys can be distributed and used, they must first be created—and they must be random. Keys must be generated so that there is an equal probability of any key or vector in the 2^{56} key space being created. (While DES keys are 64 bits long, 8 of them are parity bits, leaving 56 information bits.) Generating true random numbers can be accomplished in a number of ways. One method uses the inherent noise from a diode as a source. With this approach, the diode noise is amplified and sampled, which sounds simple enough but requires careful design.

For example, if samples are taken at zero crossings of the amplified noise, any voltage offset will create a bias in favor of one polarity producing keys from only a portion of all the theoretical possibilities. Pseudorandom generators are an attractive alternative, but they are just as easy to implement incorrectly as are hardware designs. A simple, practical method for generating random keys is to use the DES algorithm to encrypt a unique, but not necessarily random, seed number. For example, a digital representation of the day, date, and time can be encrypted; the result is then combined with some arbitrarily chosen number and encrypted again under DES. The resultant number has all the characteristics of a randomly produced number.

Key entry

Federal Standard 1027 "Telecommunications: General Security Requirements for Equipment Using the DES" and ANSI X9.17 "Financial Institution Key Management (Wholesale)" both call for dual control during the performance of such manual activities as loading in new keys. The most common method of dual control is via two physical locks on cryptographic equipment. The dual control occurs when the physical keys for the two locks are controlled by two individuals, both of whom must unlock their respective locks to permit any manual key management operations. In this way the network will not be compromised if one individual is compromised.

Manual key entry can also be from printed or written form. Since the security offered by the DES algorithm is no greater than the protection given to the DES keys, special precautions should be taken when working with keys printed out in unencrypted form. When manual key entry into a cryptographic device is from printed form, a technique called split knowledge can be used. Two or more people are given unique full-length key vectors (64 bits) in printed form. They do not show the key vectors to each other. These key vectors are individually entered into the cryptographic gear, where they are combined with binary arithmetic known as exclusive-OR to form the actual key. Again, if the key vector held by one person is compromised, it does not necessarily compromise the network.

Key entry is typically made through a connector on the cryptographic device, although some equipment may have a keypad on each unit to enter keys from printed form. The emerging standard for key entry is a 9-pin connector specified in Federal Standard 1027. This connector is a good choice even for encryption hardware integrated into a computer. Manual key entry from a computer keyboard is not as secure or convenient a method as it first appears to be, mainly because the key should not be displayed on a CRT. The emissions from a CRT can be picked up from outside an unshielded building, and the display can then be reconstructed. Typing in 16 hexadecimal-character keys without a display makes an awkward method of key management even more awkward. Other emissions from the encryption equipment are usually sufficiently low due to compliance with the electromagnetic interference requirement of FCC Code of Federal Regulations No. 47 (CFR47) Part 15J.

The National Security Agency (NSA) supplies DES keys for government use. They produce keys with unimpeachable randomness. However, they provide the keys in printed form or on paper tape. To facilitate key entry from paper tape, the government has a special paper tape reader, called the KOI-18. This manual device is widely used in the government and will soon be made available for some private sector use. Federal Standard 1027 was written with the KOI-18 in mind and specifies its electrical interface requirements for key entry to be compatible. The physical connector on the KOI-18 is different from the 9-pin D-subminiature connector specified in Federal Standard 1027, but the conversion is easily made in the cable linking the KOI-18 with the cryptographic device.

Manual key distribution

Before discussing manual key distribution techniques, an even more primitive method should be mentioned: cryptographic equipment with factory-installed keys. This requires essentially no key management and has very limited applications. For low-risk applications where the users are merely looking for an impediment to intruders, DES encryption units with factory-installed keys may be an adequate, low-cost option to provide

some data security. However, the inability to change keys periodically is such a severe restriction that this method cannot be recommended.

Manual key distribution involves the form in which the keys are prepared and the means to transport the keys to the communicating parties who must share them. Keys can be prepared in printed form, on paper tape, or in electronic form (e.g., random-access memory or EEPROM [Electronically Erasable Programmable ROM]) for transport to the cryptographic devices.

A way of implementing dual control with split knowledge during key transport is to encrypt the keys with a special key that is unknown by the individual transporting the keys. This is easily done for keys that are in an electronic form and are stored and transported in key transport modules. A module containing the security key is manually loaded into the equipment that generates the user keys; it is also manually loaded into the user cryptographic equipment. Before the keys are loaded into the key transport module, they are encrypted under the module security key. The key transport module is taken to the user's cryptographic equipment, where its contents are read into the unit, which then decrypts the keys with the module security key. Knowledge of the module security key by itself does not compromise any user data and possession of the encrypted key transport module by itself does not reveal any secret information.

In regard to key management, NSA has interpreted Federal Standard 1027 to require that keys be manually loaded directly into each cryptographic unit and that those keys be the ones used to encrypt the data. While the federal government requires dual control, it does not require split knowledge for any key entry. Apparently, it is felt that the government's ability to qualify and screen its personnel provides sufficient protection.

Electronic key distribution

The private sector expects and demands a level of convenience and sophistication that is not addressed in Federal Standard 1027. To distribute keys manually every time the data-encrypting key is changed is inconvenient and expensive to the point of being burdensome. Fortunately, there are techniques available that offer more convenience at lower operating cost while still providing for satisfactory security.

Figure 1a shows the one-key method of key management used in Federal Standard 1027. A single key is manually loaded into both ends of the communications line. Since that key is used to encrypt the data going over the line, it is the data key, labeled KD in the figure. To lessen the demands of frequent manual key distribution required by this one-key method, most of the commercial cryptographic equipment provides for a two-key method of key distribution. This is illustrated in Figure 1b. As with the one-key method, there is a data key, KD, to encrypt the data. However, this key is not entered manually into both ends of the line. Instead, the data key is transmitted down the communications link, from one cryptographic unit to the other, encrypted under a key-encrypting key (denoted by KK in the

(A) ONE-KEY METHOD

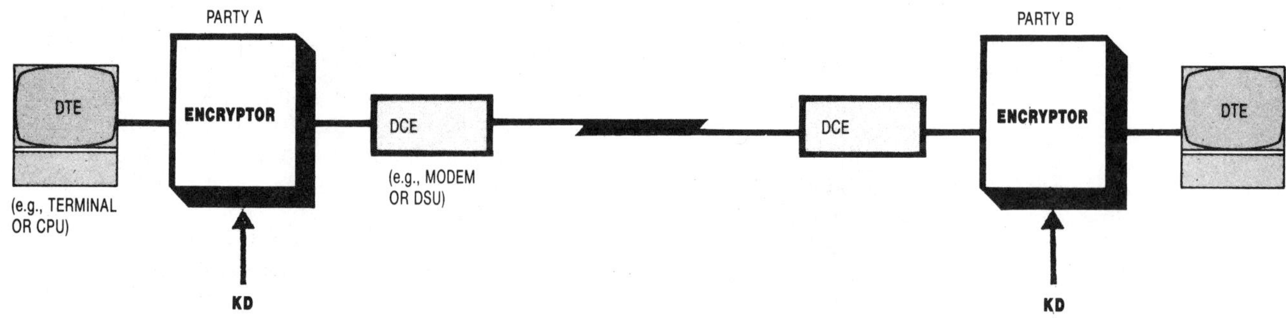

(B) TWO-KEY METHOD

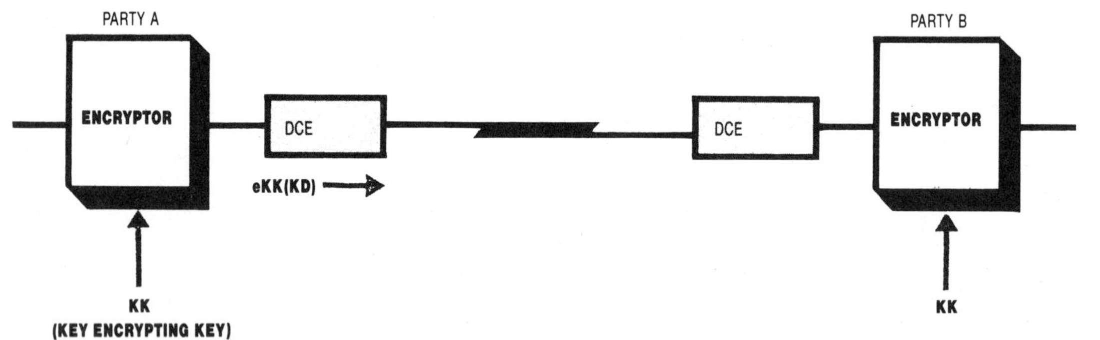

CPU = CENTRAL PROCESSING UNIT

DCE = DATA CIRCUIT-TERMINATING EQUIPMENT

DSU = DATA SERVICE UNIT

DTE = DATA TERMINAL EQUIPMENT

KD = DATA KEY

NOTE: eKK(KD) MEANS THAT KD IS ENCRYPTED UNDER KEY, KK.

figure). This downline loading of data keys permits highly automated key management with relatively little penalty for changing data keys. The automation stops, however, at the point of the key-encrypting key. For the two-key scheme, the key-encrypting key must be entered manually into the cryptographic units at both ends. Since the key-encrypting key's exposure to human contact is relatively brief, it is deemed to have a relatively long crypto-life; even though it must be manually entered, the time between entries is much longer than with the one-key technique. The net result is more frequent automated data key changes with less frequent manual key entries. Typically, one end of the link has responsibility for generating keys, although it is certainly permissible for the data keys to have been loaded manually prior to the downline transfer.

A more automated key management strategy is the three-key method. It uses the public key technique to distribute the initial key-encrypting key electronically. Unlike the DES, which uses the same key for encrypting and decrypting, public key schemes use two different but mathematically related keys: one for encrypting, the other for decrypting. The encrypting key is made public, while the decrypting key is kept secret. Knowledge of the encrypting key alone is insufficient to determine the secret decrypting key except by mathematical brute force, which presents a prohibitive work factor.

Three-key method (public key)

If Party A wishes to send a secret message to Party B, he obtains Party B's public encrypting key, E_B, from the public file; he then uses E_B to encrypt the message. This message can be decrypted only by the decryption key, D_B, which is known only to Party B.

Similarly, Party B uses Party A's public encrypting key, E_A, to send secure messages to Party A. Note that a public key file is not necessarily required. The system can be designed so that each party merely asks the other party to send its public encrypting key over the communications link.

In the three-key scheme, the public key is used to

536

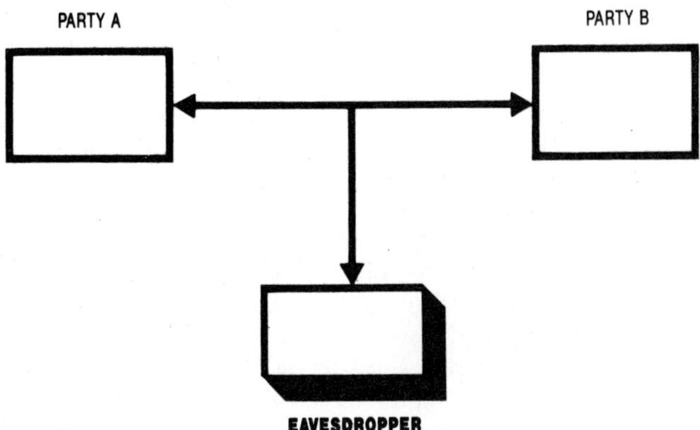

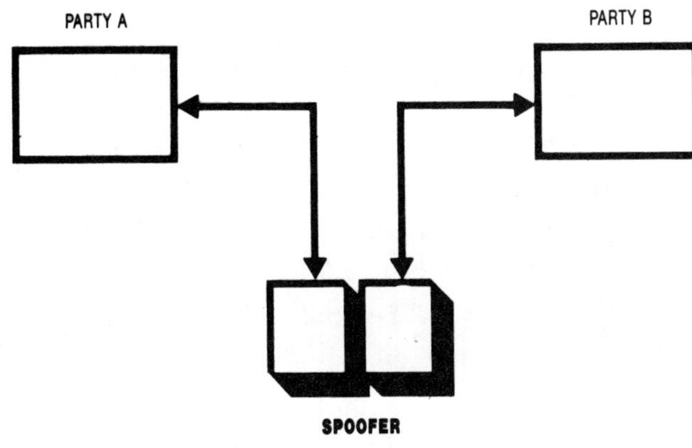

2. Operational threat. *A spoofer would join the communications link and try to imitate the traffic. The parties communicating must have a way to identify each other.*

encrypt a key-encrypting key for downline loading. This eliminates the need for manual distribution of key encrypting keys. As with the two-key method, once a key-encrypting key is shared between the two parties, subsequent data keys can be electronically transferred.

Spoofers

An operational difficulty must be overcome when public key methods are used: the threat of a "spoofer." While an eavesdropper would simply monitor and observe traffic between two cryptographic devices, a spoofer would actually insert himself into the communications link and attempt to imitate the traffic. Thus, while the devices think they are talking to each other, they are actually talking to the spoofer. This can be seen in Figure 2.

In the case of a three-key scheme, how does Party A know that the public key it receives from Party B actually came from Party B and not from a spoofer? Furthermore, how does Party B know that the DES key received from Party A actually came from that location and not from a spoofer?

Clearly, there must be something or some piece of knowledge that Parties A and B share that can be used to identify each to the other. This verification can take many forms and can have varying degrees of practical-

ity. In analyzing these methods, it is important to remember the nature of the threat. In distributing DES keys manually, it is critical that the secrecy of the keys be maintained. With the public key technique, since the encrypting key can be made public, the main threat is from substitution, not from loss of secrecy.

While DES encryption provides secrecy, it also provides inherent protection against substitution. But using a previously distributed DES key to protect the public key seems at first to negate the benefit of the three-key method. During initial installation this is true, but for subsequent key transfers there is an advantage.

The purpose of the original DES key, which will be called here the verification key, is to verify the integrity of the transmission path so that the system cannot be spoofed during the first public transaction (see "Authentication"). Under the protection of the verification key, that transaction transfers a key-encrypting key, which is under the protection of the public key, from the cryptographic equipment at one end of the link to the cryptographic equipment at the other end. Along with the key-encrypting key, a new verification key is transmitted, to be used to protect against substitution on the next public key operation. By creating a chain of verification keys in this manner, the spoofer is effectively shut out. The attacker must break the verification key in real time during the transaction in order to make a substitution. This is impossible with today's technology.

The verification key strategy can still be effective without the chaining. In that case, the same verification key is used continuously. If the verification key is "broken," then a spoofer can perform a public key substitution, so the effective life of the verification key must be established and the key replaced accordingly.

The distribution of the first verification key need not be done in secret prior to the first public key transaction. A nonsecret, default verification key can be used during the first key transaction in combination with a simple manual authentication technique to guard against spoofing. This strategy calls for the computation and display of a message authentication code (MAC). The MAC is computed with the default key using the DES algorithm in the cipher block chaining (CBC) mode of operation. The MAC is the residue of the last DES operation on the message. If any bit is altered in that message, then at the time the MAC is computed at the receive end of the link it will not match the originally computed MAC.

When Party B sends the message containing the public key, he appends the MAC to the message. In addition, he displays the MAC so that it can be read by the installer or operator. When Party A receives the message he also computes the MAC and displays it. Similarly, MACs are computed and displayed for the message containing the key-encrypting key and a new, secret verification key encrypted under the public key from Party A to Party B. If the two parties can verify that the MACs match, then they have verified that they are talking to each other and not to a spoofer; if a spoofer had substituted his own key, then that message would have a different MAC. Even though the default key is

Authentication

One valuable application of the DES (Data Encryption Standard) algorithm is in authenticating, or verifying, the integrity of messages. For this purpose, the DES is used in the cipherblock chaining (CBC) mode of operation (see figure).

To start the process, the first block of 64 bits of data (D_1) is processed through the DES algorithm. The result is exclusive-OR'ed with the second block of 64 bits of data (D_2). The output of the exclusive-OR operation is fed back through the DES algorithm and then combined with the next block of 64 bits of data. This continues until the entire message to be authenticated has gone through this process. Since each pass through the DES computation includes information from the previous block, the residue at the output of the last DES process is a direct function of the

entire message and the key. If any bit of any of those components changes, then the output of the last DES computation will change. The 32 most significant (or left-most) bits of that last computation are called the message authentication code (MAC).

When a message is transmitted, the MAC is calculated and appended to the message. The authorized receiver of that message should have already obtained the correct DES key. Upon receiving the message, the receiver also computes a MAC from the message and compares his computed MAC with the MAC sent with the message. If the MACs are identical, then the message (as well as the key) has not been altered. The procedures for message authentication are described in detail in ANSI X9.9 "Financial Institution Message Authentication (Wholesale)."

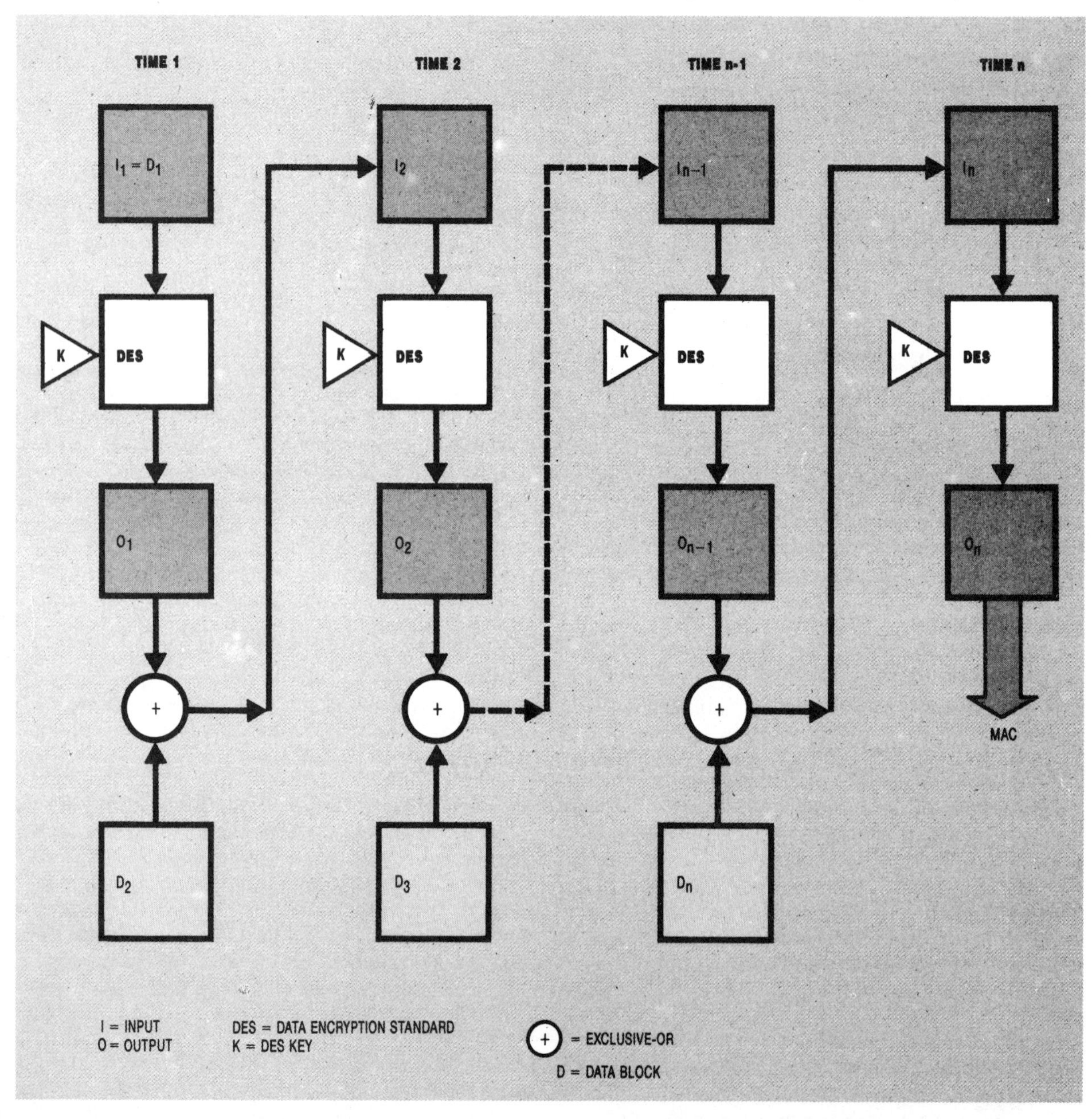

3. Introductions all around. *The Key Translation Center (CKT) allows two or more parties who do not share a key with one another, but who do individually share keys with the CKT, to establish a keying relationship. The asterisk indicates that the keys are double the length of other keys.*

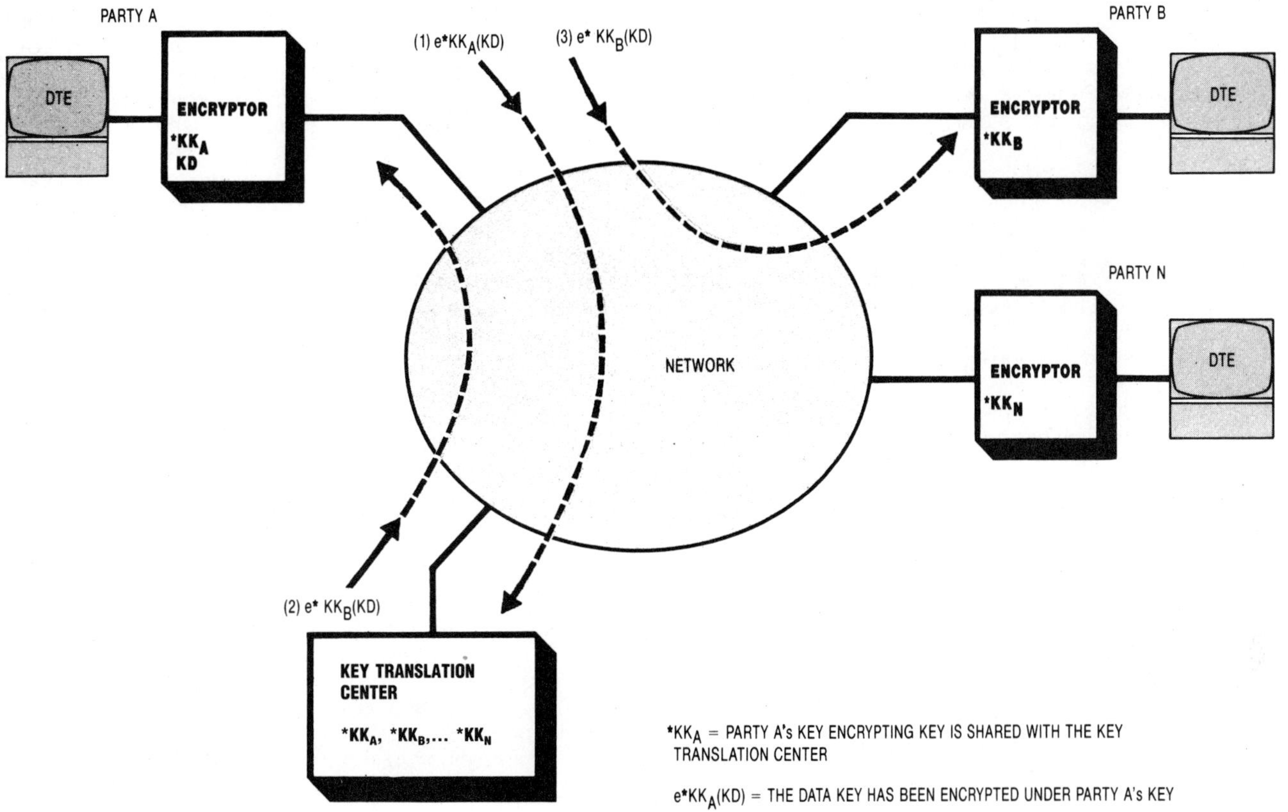

not necessarily kept secret, the authentication of the messages still works.

What remains is figuring out a way for Parties A and B to verify those MACs. The most positive verification method is to have another secured channel between the two sites. This occasionally happens when communications lines are added between established facilities, but is not the norm. For a more typical case, a simple means of verification is by a telephone call between the sites where the operators or installers know each other. If they are strangers, then they can exchange information or phrases previously exchanged by another convenient medium, such as the mail. The bottom line is that there must be some means of verifying the individual parties since if the spoofer can break into one line, he is certainly capable of breaking into a second one. Of course, one piece of information that the two parties can exchange is a DES verification key. Enough methods for ensuring verification exist to permit various levels of security over a range of costs.

Centralized key management

Control, maintenance, and operation of data communications networks are becoming increasingly centralized, with a small cadre of personnel directing the entire network. A continuation of such centralized control can be expected when cryptographic capability (either encryption or authentication) is added. With the April

1985 approval of ANSI X9.17 "Financial Institution Key Management (Wholesale)," that expectation can be fulfilled. X9.17 provides a protocol to permit secure automated key transfers between cryptographic facilities or between devices in a point-to-point configuration or involving a centralized facility. X9.17 describes two types of key centers—a Key Translation Center (CKT) and a Key Distribution Center (CKD).

■ **Key Translation Center.** The CKT allows two parties who do not share a key with one another, but who individually share keys with the CKT, to establish a keying relationship. Figure 3 shows Party A establishing secure communications with Party B. They do not share a key, but Party A shares a key, denoted by *KK_A, with the CKT, and Party B shares a key, denoted by *KK_B, with the CKT. The asterisk indicates that the keys are double-length keys (see "Building blocks for the X9.17 protocol").

Party A, the initiator, generates or acquires a key that will be used with Party B. The figure shows a data key, KD, being used, but translating a key-encrypting key is also permitted. Party A encrypts KD under *KK_A and sends it to the CKT as part of a message that instructs the CKT to encrypt KD under Party B's key, *KK_B. The CKT performs that task and sends the newly encrypted key back to Party A. In that form, only Party B (in addition to the CKT) can decrypt that message to obtain KD. Party A sends the encrypted key to Party B,

Building blocks for the X9.17 protocol

ANSI X9.17 "Financial Institution Key Management (Wholesale)" combines a number of simple techniques to create a secure protocol for key management. Its building blocks include message authentication, key pairs, multiple encryption, offsetting of keys, notarization of keys, and key usage counters. Some convenient notation follows:

- Operators are shown by the lowercase letters:
    "a" for authenticate.
    "e" for electronic code book (ECB) encryption.
    "d" for ECB decryption.
- Exclusive-OR is indicated by " + ".
- Concatenation is indicated by ∥.
- The first letter of a key designator is "K." The second letter denotes the type of key so that:
    "KD" is a data key.
    "KK" is a key-encrypting key.
    "KN" is a notarizing key.
- The third letter further defines the key as follows:
    "o" means the key has been offset.
    "l" means the left key of a key pair.
    "r" means the right key of a key pair.

An asterisk "*" in front of a key character sequence indicates that the key is a DES key pair. "(*)" in front of a key character sequence indicates that the key is a DES key pair.

Keys. A key-encrypting key pair consisting of two 64-bit variables with a left part, l, and a right part, r, is denoted by:
$$*KK = KKl \parallel KKr$$

Encryption and decryption. Encryption and decryption of KD_1, by KKy is shown by:
$$KD_1 \text{ encryption} = e\,KKy\,(KD_1)$$
and
$$KD_1 \text{ decryption} = d\,KKy\,(KD_1)$$
If the encryption and decryption of KD_1 is performed by the key pair *KKy, then that is shown by:
$$KD_1 \text{ encryption} = ede\,{*}KKy\,(KD_1)$$
$$= eKKly\,(dKKry[eKKly(KD_1)])$$
and
$$KD_1 \text{ decryption} = ded\,{*}KKy(KD_1)$$
$$= dKKly\,\{eKKry[dKKly(KD_1)]\}$$
Going a step further, the encryption and decryption of key pair $*KK_1$ by key pair *KKy is:
$$*KK_1 \text{ encryption} = ede\,{*}KKy(*KK_1)$$
$$= eKKly\,\{dKKry[eKKly(KKl_1)]\} \parallel$$
$$eKKly\,\{dKKry[eKKly(KKr_1)]\}$$
and
$$*KK_1 \text{decryption} = ded\,{*}KKy(*KK_1)$$
$$= dKKly\,\{eKKry[dKKly(KKl_1)]\} \parallel$$
$$dKKly\,\{eKKry[dKKly(KKr_1)]\}$$
Note that the key pair algorithm can be used with a single key. In that case:
$$KKly = KKry = KKy \text{ and}$$
$$KD_1 \text{ encryption} = ded\,{*}KKy(KD_1) = eKKy(KD_1)$$
$$KD_1 \text{ decryption} = ded\,{*}KKy(KD_1) = dKKy(KD_1)$$

Authentication. When Cryptographic Service Messages (CSMs) are authenticated in X9.17, the message authentication code (MAC) is computed using the technique defined in ANSI X9.9, Section 4.0, using a data key.
$$MAC = a\,KD(data)$$
A CSM containing a single KD is authenticated using that KD. If two KDs are sent in a CSM, then the key used for the MAC computation is the exclusive-OR of the two data keys.

Counters. Counters are used to indicate the number of times a KK or *KK has been used for encrypting other keys in CSMs. The parties using a particular (*)KK synchronize their counters and use those counters as a means to protect against message replay and for use in offsetting keys. The counters are incremented (never decremented) each time a (*)KK is used. The recipient of a message keeps an expected count and compares that with the actual count received in the message. If the count is a repeat, the message is thrown out and an Error Service Message is sent back to the originator of the message. If the received count matches or is greater than the expected count, then the message is accepted (assuming the MAC checks), and the recipient's expected counter is readjusted to synchronize it with the originator's count.

Offsetting of keys. Since keys are encrypted using the electronic code book mode, it is cryptographically advantageous to include some variable element in the key-encrypting key. This is done by offsetting the (*)KK with a counter. That is, the (*)KK is exclusive-OR'ed with a counter. In X9.17, offsetting is always used to transform a (*)KK prior to encryption of a key by that (*)KK. If CT is the value of the counter, then:
$$KKo = KK + CT$$
and
$$*KKo = (KKl + CT) \parallel (KKr + CT).$$
The exclusive-OR of a 64-bit key KK, with a 56-bit counter, is performed as follows: Combine the first byte of KK formed from the first seven high-order bits of the counter. The eighth bit is the parity bit for that byte and is readjusted to give the byte odd parity. Then the second byte of KK is exclusive-OR'ed with the counter byte formed from the second seven bits of the counter, and so on.

Notarization of keys. Notarization is a method for sealing keys with the identities of the communicating pair. Once sealed, or notarized, keys can only be recovered with knowledge of the key used to perform notarization and the identities of the communicating pair. A KD or a KK can be notarized by encryption with a notarizing key, (*)KN, which is formed by exclusive-OR'ing (*)KK with a notary seal, NS.

Suppose that Party A wants to send a key to Party B. Let $FROM_1$ be the first eight characters of Party A's identity and $FROM_2$ be the second eight characters of Party A's identity. Similarly, let TO_1 and TO_2 represent the first and second halves of Party B's identity. If necessary, the identities are replicated to form 16-character identifiers. For example, if Party A's identity is "PARTYA", then $FROM_1$ is "PARTYAPA" and $FROM_2$ is "RTYAPART". Let *KK be the key to be used to compute the notarizing key. Then
$$*KK = KKl \parallel KKr$$
$$KKl = KKl + FROM_1$$
$$KKr = KKr + TO_1$$
From this we now compute the components of the notary seal, NS, where,
$$NS = NSl + NSr$$
$$NSl = eKKR(TO_2) + CT$$
$$NSr = eKKL(FROM_2) + CT$$
where CT is a counter.
Finally, the notarizing key:
$$*KN = (KKl + NSl) \parallel (KKr + NSr).$$
The above expression is then used to encrypt (or notarize) either a KD or a (*)KK.

Now, if you think this is hard to compute, try breaking it.

4. Dealing out the keys. The sole job of the Key Distribution Center (CKD) is to distribute data keys (A). This is accomplished at the request of the communicating parties or as part of the CKD's own key management program. In (B), the data network is expanded to show transmission lines with link encryption.

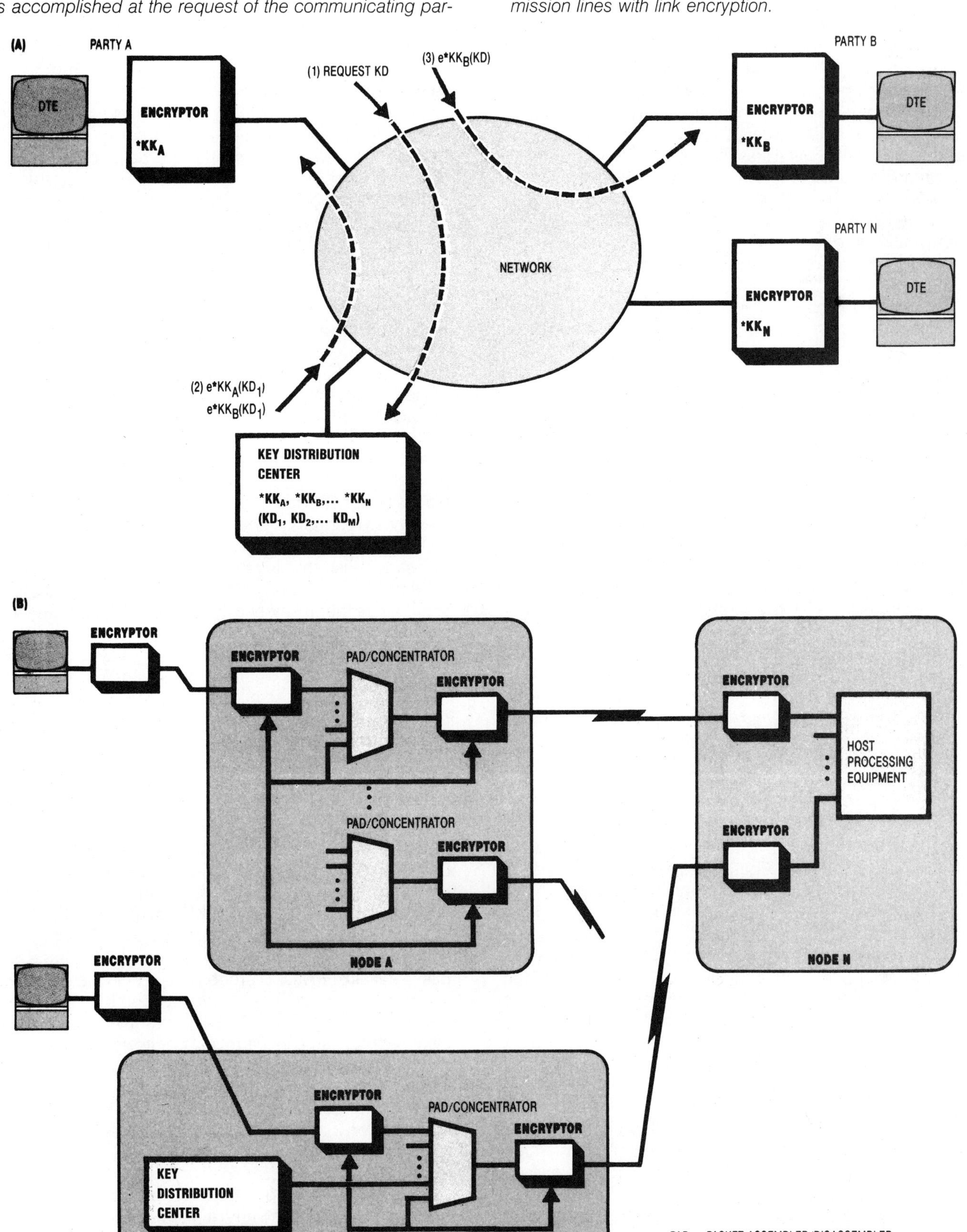

(A)
PARTY A
PARTY B
PARTY N
DTE
ENCRYPTOR *KK_A
ENCRYPTOR *KK_B
ENCRYPTOR *KK_N
DTE
DTE
(1) REQUEST KD
(3) e*KK_B(KD)
NETWORK
(2) e*KK_A(KD_1)
e*KK_B(KD_1)
KEY DISTRIBUTION CENTER
*KK_A, *KK_B,... *KK_N
(KD_1, KD_2,... KD_M)
(B)
ENCRYPTOR
ENCRYPTOR
PAD/CONCENTRATOR
ENCRYPTOR
PAD/CONCENTRATOR
ENCRYPTOR
NODE A
ENCRYPTOR
ENCRYPTOR
HOST PROCESSING EQUIPMENT
NODE N
ENCRYPTOR
ENCRYPTOR
PAD/CONCENTRATOR
ENCRYPTOR
KEY DISTRIBUTION CENTER
NODE M
PAD = PACKET ASSEMBLER/DISASSEMBLER

who decrypts it. Both parties now have KD and can begin data communications using that key. A KK could have been transferred instead. With Parties A and B sharing a key-encrypting key, they can downline load data keys without the involvement of the CKT.

The value of a CKT can be fully appreciated in a switched network, where any party has the capability to talk to any other party. Each possible pair of communicating parties must share a key, but that key must be different from the other keys for all the other possible communicating pairs in the network. Thus, a 10-party network would require each party to store 45 keys, a 100-party network requires 4,950 keys, and a 1,000-party network requires 499,500 keys. This is the number of combinations from n objects taken two at a time. $C(n,2)$ $n(n-1)$P 2. With the CKT, each party need only store one key—the one he shares with the CKT. The CKT must store only as many keys as there are communicating parties in the network. Clearly, without centralized key management even medium-sized switched networks would be unmanageable.

■ *Key Distribution Center.* The CKD can also whittle down the number of keys required in a network, but it operates somewhat differently from the Key Translation Center. The CKD does not generate keys, but it can translate either data keys or key-encrypting keys. The sole job of the CKD is to distribute data keys, either at the request of one of the communicating parties or as part of its own key management program. Figure 4a shows a CKD configuration with Party A initiating a key transaction so that a keying relationship with Party B can be set up. Party A does not send any keys but, rather, requests a new data key. The CKD sends a data key (either generated or acquired by the CKD) in two forms—one encrypted by *KK$_A$ and the other encrypted by *KK$_B$). Party A, receiving the message containing the encrypted data keys, decrypts the one encrypted by *KK$_A$ and sends the one encrypted by *KK$_B$ to Party B—who decrypts the data key and can then encrypt or authenticate data to Party A.

The CKD can be used for key management in other types of data networks including networks employing link-by-link encryption. Figure 4b shows the data network expanded to demonstrate transmission lines having link encryption. The network itself is used to route the CKD messages to the individual encryptors. As shown in the figure, a port off the packet assembler/disassembler (PAD) is connected to the encryptors on at least one end of each link. Since each link can coordinate its own key transfer, only one end of the link need be accessed by the CKD. Figure 4B implies an X.25 packet network, but the concept works just as well if the PAD/concentrators are replaced with multiplexers and modems as in an analog switched network.

In a network like this, it is desirable to control and coordinate key management from a central point. That is where the CKD is located. This arrangement permits all data key generation to be performed by the CKD. In addition to determining what data keys are used, the CKD can determine when key changes are made.

The benefits of electronic key transfers are obvious, but how does one implement those transfers in a secure manner? How does one guard against inadvertent trapdoors in the protocol or against message modification, substitution, deletion, or replay? With ANSI X9.17, the only public standard available dealing with DES key management.

ANSI X9.17 protocol

The security of the X9.17 protocol for electronically transferring keys is predicated on the Cryptographic Service Messages (CSMs) that are defined, the flow of those messages, and, most importantly, the construction of those messages. Together they form a secure protocol that preserves and maintains the high level of security required of keying material. The CSMs for point-to-point key management are:

■ RSI (Request Service Initiation Message). An optional message class that requests that a new keying relationship be initiated. The originator of an RSI might not have a key generation capability.

■ KSM (Key Service Message). A required message class that transfers a key from an originator to a recipient.

■ RSM (Response Service Message). A required message class that provides an authenticated response to a KSM.

■ ESM (Error Service Message). A required message class that reports an error in a CSM.

■ DSM (Disconnect Service Message). An optional message class that is used to discontinue keys.

When using these CSMs, Party A and Party B must first share either a key-encrypting key (KK) or a key-encrypting key pair (*KK). For convenience in this article, (*)KK denotes either a key-encrypting key or key pair. Take a simple case where Party A doesn't have the capability (or permission by the Network Supervisor) to generate or acquire keys but wants to communicate with Party B under a new key. Party B sends an RSI message to Party A requesting that Party A send a key (or keys). If the RSI message has an error in it, Party A returns an ESM to Party B.

Party A sends the requested keys in a KSM. If a (*)KK is sent, it is encrypted under the (*)KK shared with Party B. The accompanying data keys (KDs) in the KSM are encrypted under the new (*)KK sent in that message. If a (*)KK is not sent, then the KDs sent in the KSM are encrypted under the (*)KK shared with Party B. If an encrypted initialization vector (a starting sequence of bits to initialize the DES process) is sent in the message, it is encrypted under the KD (the second KD if two KDs are sent) in that KSM. The KSM is authenticated using the KD or KDs sent in the message. If two KDs are sent, then they are exclusive-OR'ed together with the result used as the authentication key.

Party B responds with an RSM if the KSM is received correctly, or with an ESM if there is an error in the received KSM. If Party A sees an error in the received RSM, he returns an ESM to Party B.

Party A may resend a KSM to Party B an arbitrary number of times, but Party A will not send a new KSM (that is, involving new keys or a new count for the (*)KK specified in the message) until the old KSM is acknowledged by an RSM or an ESM.

Using the DSM requires some special considerations. When either party wishes to terminate a keying relationship, that party sends a DSM. If the DSM is received correctly, the other party returns an RSM; otherwise an ESM is returned. The key named as the authentication key (or the only data key shared by the two parties if no authentication key is explicitly identified) in the DSM is retained to authenticate the subsequent RSM. It is then discontinued. When a (*)KK is discontinued, all keys sent that are encrypted under that (*)KK are also discontinued without being named in the DSM.

So far in this discussion, whenever a CSM has been received in error, an ESM has been sent. However, when an RSM responding to a DSM contains an error, no ESM is sent. The party sending the RSM has discontinued his keys, and manual recovery procedures are required. Besides the CSMs used for point-to-point applications, three more CSMs are used with Key Translation Centers and Key Distribution Centers:

■ RFS (Request for Service Message). A required message class in a Key Translation Center environment that sends keys to a CKT to be translated for the ultimate recipient.

■ RTR (Response to Requester Message). A required message class in either a CKT or CKD environment that responds to an RFS, an ERS, or an RSI to the center. An RTR may be initiated by a Key Distribution Center.

■ ERS (Error Recovery Service Message). A required message class that reports count and key errors to the CKT or CKD and requests resynchronization of the count fields and reinitiation of service.

When a Key Translation Center is used, the Message flow between Parties A and B uses the same CSMs as those used in the point-to-point example, but the messages are constructed somewhat differently. Party A requests a key translation with an RFS message containing new key(s) to be translated and eventually sent to Party B, the ultimate recipient. If a (*)KK is sent, then one KD must be sent. The (*)KK is encrypted under the *KK shared between Party A and the CKT; the KD is encrypted under the (*)KK sent in the message. If a (*)KK is not sent, then at least one and at most two KDs are sent, encrypted under the *KK shared between Party A and the CKT. The RFS message is authenticated using the KD(s) sent in the message. The CKT responds with an RTR if the RFS is received correctly; otherwise, with an ESM.

After receiving the RFS, the CKT decrypts the keys sent in the message. The decrypted keys are then notarized using the *KK shared between the CKT and Party B, the count associated with that *KK, and the identities of Parties A and B. The notarized keys are put into the RTR message, which is sent to Party A. Party A assembles a KSM, which includes the notarized keys as received in the RTR, and sends it to Party B, who responds with an RSM. While the message construction is slightly different, the KSM, RSM, and ESM are handled as in the point-to-point case. The message flow in a CKD environment is similar to that of the CKT except that an RSI is used from Party A to the CKD to initiate service. The CKD provides the KDs for the key exchange. The RTR message from the CKD contains two identical sets of KD(s). One set has the KD notarized with the *KK shared between Party A and the CKD, while the other set has the KD notarized with the *KK shared between Party B and the CKD. This second set is denoted by KDU (U for ultimate recipient) and is passed on to Party B in a KSM. Again, the KSM, RSM, and ESM are handled as they were in the other cases.

Levels of security

How much of this protocol procedure is necessary? The answer is as simple as it is imprecise: It depends. Nothing more definitive can be said unless the question defines the security requirements of the application. Since X9.17 is a standard, it has an obligation to be correct and complete in achieving its objectives. The skeleton of the X9.17 protocol is simple; the complexity enters into it when tailoring the protocol to deal with specific, frequently subtle, issues. This protocol would be used when the security requirements are such that it is not sufficient to guard only against the obvious attacks that can "break" a security arrangement. Attacks that may make breaking the system only slightly easier must also be prevented.

Not every application requires the protection offered by X9.17, which was specifically designed for use in wholesale banking, where a single electronic fund transfer (EFT) can involve millions of dollars. EFT transactions in that dollar range certainly justify substantial protection. But what about EFT transactions for retail banking with only hundreds or thousands of dollars involved? Or what about non-EFT networks where the intent is to provide privacy in corporate or government networks? To answer, the overall security requirements must be known. Even then, the choice of security equipment and features frequently rests with the judgment of a few individuals, and that judgment is typically affected by necessary compromises.

Not very many corporate security officers have the budget to implement the level of security that a rigorous security analysis might dictate. Moreover, the security requirements themselves may defy quantification. The value or worth of maintaining privacy may be difficult to quantify and in the end becomes a business decision based on the available budget. While security officers may not control the security budget, they are expected to implement data communications security consistently. Key management is particularly vulnerable, not only because its importance can be misunderstood, but also because it can be compromised due to inadequate budget or to its operational inconvenience, or to a combination of the two. A reduction in overall security to match the value of that which is being protected and the resource allotted to that protection is the reality facing most security officers. The need to provide an overall consistent level of security, at whatever level they expect to achieve, is their most important and most difficult requirement. ■

Charles Richard Abbruscato is manager of encryption and T1 products at Racal-Milgo. He received a B.S.E.E. from the University of Connecticut and an M.S.E.E. from the Georgia Institute of Technology.

David M. Piscitello, Burroughs Corp., Southeastern, Pa., Alan J. Weissberger, Teledimensions Inc., Santa Clara, Calif., Scott A. Stein, Honeywell Information Systems, Phoenix, Ariz., and A. Lyman Chapin, Data General Corp., Westborough, Mass.

Internetworking in an OSI environment

The authors, who are active in OSI standards groups, provide authoritative information on protocols and connection methods.

Standards bodies concerned with fleshing out the Open Systems Interconnection (OSI) model are also tackling the associated problems of internetworking — that is, communications between an interconnected set of networks. The seven-layer model from the International Organization for Standardization (ISO) has become familiar within the industry. OSI provides a framework for the interaction of users and applications in a distributed data processing environment that may include a wide variety of both computer and terminal equipment as well as many different communications technologies.

The term OSI refers to the seven-layer architectural reference model and to a set of standards that describe how to provide communications among computers and terminals. To examine internetworking, one must understand OSI terminology. For each of the seven layers, a layer service is defined that identifies the set of functions that the layer provides. Layer services in OSI are of two general types: connection-oriented, which allow the service users (entities in the next higher layer) to establish and use logical connections; and connectionless, which allow the service users to exchange information without having to establish a connection (see "Connections vs. connectionless?").

Within each layer, protocols operate to provide the services defined for that layer. As a number of protocol-selection options exist in some layers of the reference model (for example, the Transport Layer defines five distinct connection-oriented protocol classes), conformance requirements are specified by each of the layer-protocol standards. When in compliance with the required suite of standard protocols prescribed for OSI, configurations are considered to be open.

The lowest two layers, Physical and Data Link, provide technology-specific access to the media that is used to interconnect the network equipment. The third layer (Network) performs data routing and relaying.

The fourth layer (Transport) provides for the reliable, error-free, end-to-end delivery of user data. An equally important and often overlooked function of the Transport Layer is to determine the most cost-effective means of providing data-transport service. Given specific quality-of-service (QOS) constraints by the higher layers, the Transport Layer matches a Transport protocol to the Network Layer service provided. (The QOS is defined by the characteristics of a connection-oriented or connectionless transmission as observed between the end points.) Thus the QOS requested is satisfied in the most expedient and cost-effective manner. Note that any meaningful analysis of the problems related to network interconnection often requires consideration of the Transport Layer as well as the Network Layer.

Internetworking is important

To be a successful standard, OSI must provide a homogeneous environment in which information may be accessed and exchanged independent of the immediate network to which corresponding users are attached. Network interconnection, or internetworking, has thus become a most important issue.

The advent of local area network (LAN) technologies has lent new urgency to this effort. Part of the world treats LANs as a sophisticated, multipoint data link; the remainder, as merely one more type of subnetwork (OSI parlance for a network as part of an internetwork) that must be accommodated by OSI. Therefore, it is inevitable that internetworking solutions involving LANs would be similarly divided.

The problem of interconnecting networks to form a single, "global" network is an inevitable consequence of the recent explosion of network technology. Network

designers have investigated and implemented a number of interconnection strategies that attempt to facilitate communications among computers and terminals connected to different networks. While all create a homogeneous networking environment by resolving differences in network technology, access method, address structure, and administration, two appear to be most applicable to an OSI global network.

Strategy 1. In this case, the networks to be connected:

■ Offer predominantly connection-oriented services.
■ Exist where close cooperation among the network administrations can be achieved and enforced.
■ Exist where the extent to which the individual network services differ is limited.

With this approach, connection-oriented internetworking may be achieved by relaying the services of one network directly onto corresponding services of the other networks.

An underlying assumption of this network interconnection strategy is that it is easier to solve the problems associated with subnetwork interconnection when the services that the networks offer are the same than when they are different. Hence, to ensure that the services presented on each side of a relay point are sufficiently similar so that a direct mapping of one set of services onto the other is possible, enhancement of individual networks on a "hop-by-hop" basis (see below) may be necessary. This approach is particularly attractive with public data networks and in countries that centralize provision of network services under a single government-controlled administration, such as a Postal, Telegraph, and Telephone (PTT) organization. In such environments, strong regulatory constraints operate to limit network diversity.

Strategy 2. Here, the networks to be connected offer a mix of connection-oriented and connectionless services and exist where network administration is largely autonomous. The extent to which the individual network services differ cannot be predicted or controlled.

In such configurations, connectionless internetworking preserves individual network autonomy and service characteristics of the networks to be connected. This is achieved by conveying the information necessary to support a uniform network service in an explicit Internetwork Protocol (IP). This protocol makes minimal assumptions about the services available from each of the interconnected networks.

One important observation about these two network interconnection strategies: The service that is ultimately provided to the user at the Transport service boundary is the same in both cases. The only real difference between them is where the end-to-end reliability functions are performed. Hop-by-hop enhancement tries to combine both internetwork routing and end-to-end reliability functions in the Network Layer, thereby making each network connection (hop) a miniature end-to-end transport connection. An internetworking protocol, on the other hand, concentrates on dynamic routing (the proper province of a Network Layer protocol) and leaves to the Transport protocol the responsibility for ensuring end-to-end reliability (the proper province of a Transport Layer protocol).

In practice, hop-by-hop enhancement may provide a reliable Network Layer service. However, the users most concerned with reliability, security, and data integrity — most notably the military and the banking industry — require a Transport service that guarantees those properties from end system to end system. (An end system is defined as a seven-layer configuration. For more detail on this and other OSI topics, see Data Communications, "The status and direction of open

Connections vs. connectionless?

In the earliest work on Open Systems Interconnection, communications was modeled exclusively in terms of connection-based interactions. These interactions proceeded through the three familiar phases of connection establishment, data transfer, and connection release. Traditional monolithic networks — where applications are the users — are the source of this connection model. The classic example is the voice telephone network, which is operated directly by human users who establish connections (call), transfer data (talk), and release connections (hang up the telephone).

An alternative model of connectionless interactions, which begin and end with the transmission of a single self-contained data unit (often called a datagram), was developed as an extension to the OSI architecture. Standards developers, working in today's much more complex multiple-network environment, encountered interconnection scenarios that could not be modeled satisfactorily in entirely connection-oriented terms. Both models have been applied successfully to the specification of OSI layer services and protocols.

The essential difference between these two models is that a connection preserves the state of peer-to-peer communications from one data transfer to the next, storing and distributing information regarding the connection within the service provider; connectionless transmission does not. The components of a connection-oriented network — such as gateways, switches, and interface processors — operate collectively over time to create and maintain state information for each connection that is established between one point on the network and another. (Examples of state information include the locations of the communicating peers, the sequence number of the last data unit forwarded, and the status of peer-to-peer flow control.) This information relates each new data transfer to previous transfers on the same connection, so that the network deals with data units containing shorthand "pointers" to the information base (such as a connection identifier) rather than the information itself (such as a full destination address).

A connectionless network, on the other hand, does not establish or maintain any relationship between individual data transfers. All of the addressing and other information needed to convey data from source to destination is included explicitly in each data unit. Connection-oriented networks recover from errors through global-state resynchronization; connectionless networks, with no state to preserve, use time-outs and retransmissions. Intuitively, connection-oriented networks are "deterministic"; connectionless, "probabilistic."

The obvious question that arises from the existence of two different interaction models in the OSI environment is how to choose between them. Unfortunately, the connections vs. connectionless debate has often been carried on as if the question were simply, "Which model is 'better' " — without regard to the context in which it is applied. Those arguing in such terms would have one believe that because a connection seems to be the best model for a particular application, it must also be the best model for the entire data communications structure that supports the application. Or they argue that because connectionless transmission is the most efficient mode of operation for local area networks that use a particular contention-based access method, it must also be the best model for the operation of all types of networks.

A less dogmatic — and much more practical — approach would consider the individual characteristics of the two types of operation in terms of the applicability of one model or the other to specific interconnection scenarios. This approach recognizes that OSI can be viewed from a number of different perspectives, and that it is often necessary to apply different techniques to the solution of different problems.

In general, when a service that processes a large number of data units in essentially the same way — while keeping track of the data transfer state on behalf of the communicating peers — is desired, the connection model is more useful. When the dynamic flexibility of a service that processes data units independently — or the simplicity of a service that does not maintain state on behalf of the communicating peers — is desired, the connectionless model is more useful. In the real world, of course, there are almost

systems interconnection," February 1985, p. 177.) In any configuration in which end-to-end reliability is important, the most reliable Transport Layer protocol available must be used, and any effort to enhance the subnetworks is largely wasted (although the user, of course, is expected to pay for the enhancement).

Hop-by-hop: For simplicity?

In strategy 1, gateways (Network Layer relays) perform a mapping of the service offered by one network onto another. In general, the gateways do not add services. Rather, they perform the relaying and switching functions necessary to bind the individual subnetworks into a unified or global network. A consequence of this approach is that either all of the subnetworks must inherently provide equivalent services, or each must be enhanced to some common level of service.

The ISO has included this interconnection strategy in its "Internal Organization of the Network Layer" standard (ISO 8648). Called hop-by-hop (subnetwork) enhancement, the approach may be summarized as follows (Fig. 1): All subnetworks that are to be interconnected must provide exactly the Network Layer service (usually, connection-oriented), either directly or through enhancement. Any subnetwork that does not provide this service must be enhanced or modified to do so. Relays are used

always practical trade-offs rather than absolute positions, and they must be evaluated as such.

From the perspective of the OSI user, the only relevant concern is whether the application's operation is connectionless or connection-oriented. From the perspective of the OSI builder, the important issue is the way in which a particular combination of connectionless and connection-oriented layer services and protocols solves the technical, administrative, and economic problems of interconnecting OSI networks. These two perspectives are essentially independent. The user's choice is based on the characteristics of the application. The builder's choices depend on the available network technologies, an overall strategy for achieving network interconnection, and the economic and administrative constraints of a particular operating environment. The clearest illustration of these choices is found in the nature of applications (the ultimate users of OSI) and the different ways in which multiple networks can be interconnected.

Beneficial examples

Some interactions between peer application entities involve the exchange of many related data units. These interactions must be performed in an explicit application context that defines the intent of the entities' exchange. Such applications can benefit from a connection-oriented service. Examples include bulk file transfer (particularly when checkpoint/recovery features are implemented); virtual terminal usage (long-term attachment of a terminal, workstation, or other interactive device to a host computer, for which the security established during an initial log-on procedure is an important part of the context associated with a connection); and access to distributed network components, such as print servers and remote-job-entry stations.

Other application interactions are either entirely self-contained or do not benefit from the context characteristics of a connection. Examples include "inward" data collection (periodic sampling of a large number of data sources, as in a sensor network); "outward" data dissemination (the distribution of a single piece of information to a large number of destinations); broadcast and multicast (group-addressed) communications; and a variety of other request/response applications (such as directory and time-of-day servers) in which a single request is followed by a single response, with no significant relationship between one message and the next.

Interconnection realities

If all networks were of the same type, used for the same purposes, administered by the same organization, and operated under the same tariffs and regulations, interconnecting them would pose few major technical problems. Clearly, not many of these conditions — much less all of them — are met in the real world.

There are excellent reasons for the providers of public network services to prefer that their interactions with users and with each other be connection-based. These service providers must deal with unpredictable and widely fluctuating loads; must limit variations in quality of service to a relatively narrow range, according to the terms of a legal contract; and must charge for their services on a fair and auditable basis in accordance with that contract. Deterministic global resource allocation is of paramount importance. On the other hand, private networks, such as LANs, tend to be owned and used by the same organization. Their operating costs are generally recovered in ways that are only indirectly related to individual instances of use.

Public-network administrators exercise greater global control over their configurations than do private-network administrators, to the extent that public networks are operated (and perceived by their users) as one global network. Private networks, however, usually consist of a number of individual, interconnected smaller networks, forming an internetwork topology in which boundaries persist that are related to administration, local control, and mode of use. The managers of private internetwork topologies are concerned with the flexible and reconfigurable interconnection of a variety of individual networks, and they are correspondingly reluctant to make too many assumptions about the nature of individual underlying services. These networks tend to be connectionless.

to passively map the connection establishment, data transfer, and connection release facilities of one subnetwork onto another whenever network connections cross subnetwork boundaries.

The enhancement of subnetworks that do not provide the OSI network service is usually accomplished in either of two ways: through direct modification of the protocol used to access the subnetwork, as is the case for the 1984 version of CCITT Recommendation X.25, or through the use of what is called a subnetwork dependent convergence protocol (SNDCP). An SNDCP operates on top of a subnetwork access protocol (SNACP), such as X.25, to provide the elements of the OSI network service that are missing from the access protocol. Such a protocol (ISO 8878) has been developed for operation with X.25's 1980 version.

One of the consequences of the hop-by-hop approach is that when a subnetwork administration revises its access protocol to provide the OSI network service, all data terminal equipment (DTE) attached to that subnetwork must often be revised. If the SNACP is modified principally to accommodate internetworking, the user and the DTE manufacturer must absorb the migration expense regardless of whether the DTE is to be used for internetworking or even whether it will be used for OSI at all. Often such a revision does not result in any signif-

1. Enhancing hop-by-hop. *All subnetworks to be interconnected that do not provide the Network Layer service (usually connection-oriented) must be enhanced to do so.* *Gateways are then used to map the connection establishment, data transfer, and connection release facilities of one subnetwork onto another.*

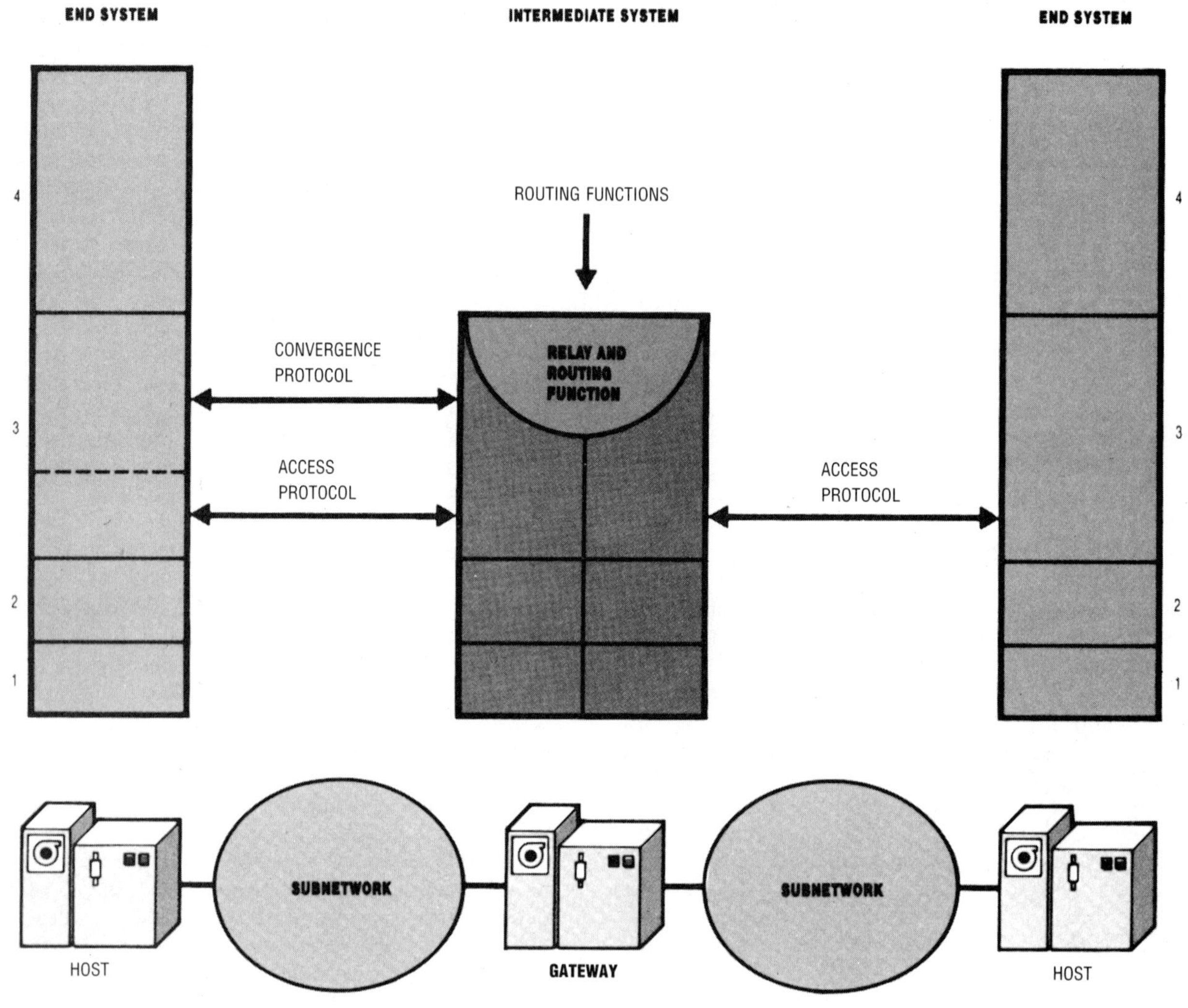

icant improvement in the service provided in the local environment. In fact, accommodations for connection-oriented internetworking often result in lower performance (due to, for example, additional protocol overhead) for local information exchanges.

This is both unreasonable and inefficient. In most subnetworks, local traffic predominates; hence, most subnetwork designs justifiably emphasize efficiency for local traffic. Protocols and addressing are often tailored for the local topology, traffic requirements, and underlying technologies (such as LANs) employed. It should not be necessary to change intranetwork operation—in particular, to modify its access protocol—solely for the purpose of internetworking. The imposition of additional overhead on intranetwork communications just to accommodate the less-frequent instances of internetworking is a poor bargain for most users. Moreover, problems of network interconnection cannot always be resolved by unilaterally imposing a single SNACP on all subnetworks. A more pragmatic approach to internetworking is to examine the interconnection scenarios, then base configuration design on those scenarios that are to be accommodated.

The use of an SNDCP permits existing terminal equipment to coexist in the intranetwork environment with equipment that supports the full OSI network service. However, since an SNDCP is designed to operate in conjunction with a specific SNACP, one must be developed for each subnetwork type to which a particular device may be attached. Such a proliferation of convergence protocols is hardly desirable.

Hop-by-hop subnetwork enhancement, then, is a practicable choice only where the type of service offered by the majority of the subnetworks to be interconnected corresponds very closely to the OSI network service. It is a poor choice for configurations in which the subnetworks provide dissimilar services, provide different or unpredictable qualities of service, or are managed and administered in different ways. In these types of configurations, an alternative method of

2. Connectionless internetworking. *The networks to be connected offer a mix of connection-oriented and connectionless services. The connectionless internetworking strategy is based on the use of a single end-to-end protocol to provide the Network Layer service over any combination of subnetworks.*

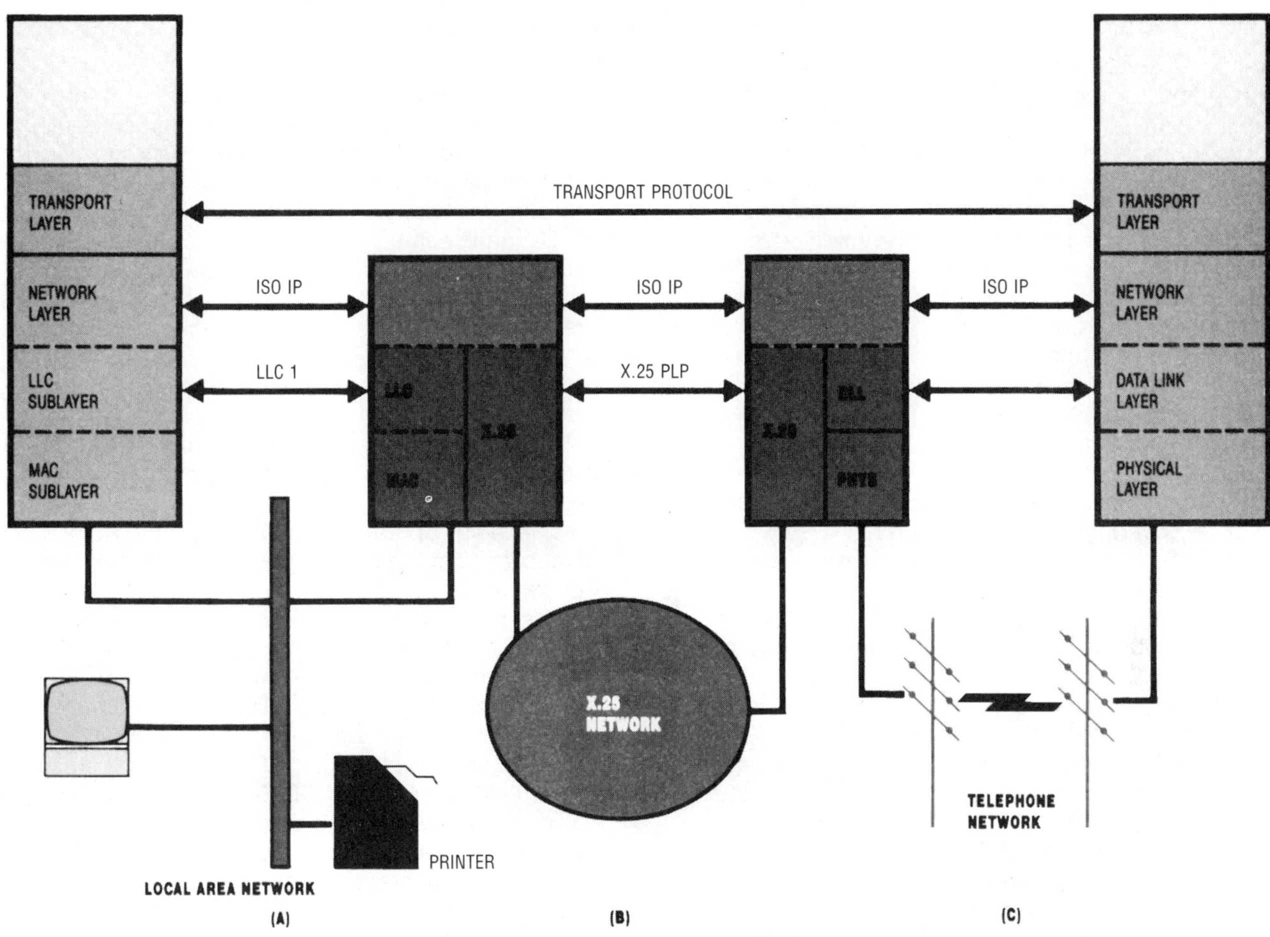

DLL = DATA LINK LAYER
IP = INTERNETWORK PROTOCOL
ISO = INTERNATIONAL ORGANIZATION FOR STANDARDIZATION
LLC = LOGICAL LINK CONTROL PROCEDURE
LLC 1 = LOGICAL LINK CONTROL PROCEDURE, CLASS 1
MAC = MEDIUM-ACCESS COMPONENT
PHYS = PHYSICAL LAYER
PLP = PACKET-LEVEL PROTOCOL

network interconnection should be considered.

Strategy 2 is based on the use of a single end-to-end protocol to provide Network Layer service over any combination of subnetworks (Fig. 2). This IP is operated in a sublayer above the subnetwork-specific protocols in both the hosts and the gateways (see "Protocol relationships"). It performs the addressing and routing functions necessary for end-to-end communications independent of the subnetwork-specific functions operating in each of the interconnected subnetworks. The underlying subnetworks should provide only a data transmission service. No subnetwork enhancement is necessary; an IP can be operated directly over the Data Link Layer.

This second approach to network interconnection was successfully applied by a number of user communities and computer manufacturers long before the ISO began to examine the problems of internetworking. The Defense Data Network (DDN) of the Department of Defense (DOD) and such private networking archi-

Protocol relationships

The relationship of the ISO Internetwork Protocol to the Transport protocol, to others in the Network Layer, and to the Data Link Layer is illustrated in Figure 2 of the accompanying story. The ISO IP may operate (a) over a LAN that uses the IEEE 802.2 LLC (Logical Link Control) Type 1 Class 1 Data Link procedures; (b) over a Public Data Network that uses the X.25 Packet Level Protocol; or (c) directly over a leased or switched telephone line that provides the OSI Data Link service through data link procedures, such as ISO's HDLC or IBM's SDLC. An addendum to the ISO IP, a Draft International Standard, describes how to operate the IP over (a) and (b) above. The U. S. technical subcommittee on the Network Layer (ASC X3S3.3) introduced a description of (c) in April of this year.

tectures as Xerox's XNS (Xerox Network Systems), Burroughs Corporation's BNA (Burroughs Network Architecture), and Digital Equipment's Decnet use internetwork protocols. These protocols provide an efficient and flexible means of interconnecting networks that differ in their types and qualities of service, but they do not impose unnecessary constraints and complexity in the local environment.

The ISO has formalized the second, or internetworking protocol, approach in its "Protocol for Providing the Connectionless-mode Network Service" (ISO 8473). It is designed to operate entirely within the computers (gateways and hosts) and terminal equipment attached to public-switched and private packet data networks, LANs, or other subnetworks. Like forerunners of its kind, the protocol ignores the idiosyncratic characteristics of the individual subnetworks, extracting from each subnetwork a data transmission service with no quality of service or other essential properties. The protocol demands so little from the underlying service (in the subnetwork sublayer or the Data Link Layer) that it may be operated directly over leased and switched telephone lines that provide the OSI Data Link service.

Here is how the ISO IP operates in the OSI environment. Computer and terminal equipment attached to different networks exchange data packets—called Internetwork Protocol Data Units (IPDUs)—in a connectionless (datagram) mode of operation. Each IPDU is routed independently. The route an IPDU takes is determined by the current state of the network links, rather than by the state that existed at some previous connection-establishment time.

Much of the information necessary to determine a route (such as source and destination addresses and quality of service) is conveyed in the protocol control information (PCI) of each IPDU. Additional information, which enables end and intermediate nodes to cooperate dynamically in determining the best route for each IPDU, is distributed and maintained by Network Layer management functions and protocols. In most cases, routing decisions are made independently by each forwarding node. However, the network entity (an active element within the Network Layer) of the end system that generates an IPDU may specify the route the IPDU should take by employing the protocol's optional "source routing" function.

The ISO IP assumes only that each subnetwork traversed is capable of serving as a "data pipe." The IP also harmonizes the service offered by each subnetwork into a uniform connectionless network service. Because subnetworks are required only to provide a data pipe, the mapping of the service required by the IP onto that provided by most SNACPs is extremely simple. For example, in the case of a LAN station operating under the procedures of IEEE 802.2 Type 1 Class 1 (unacknowledged connectionless), the mapping is a relatively trivial one-to-one process.

The ISO IP provides a connectionless network service to the Transport Layer. Unlike a connection-oriented service, a connectionless service dynamically allocates such resources as CPU, buffers, and data link availability on an as-needed basis rather than statically for the duration of a connection. This method of resource allocation is extremely efficient for normally encountered traffic conditions. Coupled with a deterministic or adaptive routing algorithm, it generally results in optimal use of network resources.

It is possible, however, that unusually high traffic volume (involving considerable delay), a temporary shortage of buffer space, the loss of a data link, or some other transient condition will cause an IPDU to be lost. In addition, the Network Layer may not be able to deliver IPDUs in the same order in which they were generated since alternate or parallel routes may be used for the transmission of a particular sequence of IPDUs. (These other routes would be used to enhance throughput or service quality, or in response to changes in the topology or service characteristics of the underlying networks.)

Thus where end-to-end reliability is important, the Transport Layer must provide reliable end-to-end connections that preserve data integrity and sequence. This is achieved by operating a Transport protocol that is able to recover from the loss, duplication, corruption, or reordering of data. In most internetworking configurations, service interruptions such as those mentioned above are relatively infrequent and short-lived. The Transport protocol design must also ensure that any penalty associated with the reliability function is assessed only when the function is invoked. That is, the additional overhead for normal (error-free) operation should be negligible. The ISO Class 4 Transport Protocol (TP 4) was designed precisely for this purpose.

Of the five Transport protocol classes developed by OSI (see Table), Class 4 ensures data integrity and data-transfer reliability when there is a possibility that any of the underlying networks will lose, corrupt, or reorder data. TP 4 utilizes a number of sophisticated error-detection and recovery mechanisms. Detailed below, they include transport protocol data unit (TPDU) numbering, retention of TPDUs until acknowledgment, retransmission of TPDUs following a time-

Comparing transport protocol classes

	CLASS				
FUNCTION	0	1	2	3	4
ERROR RECOVERY	NO	YES	NO	YES	YES
EXPEDITED DATA TRANSFER	NO	YES	YES	YES	YES
EXPLICIT FLOW CONTROL	NO	NO	YES	YES	YES
MULTIPLEXING	NO	NO	YES	YES	YES
DETECTION AND RECOVERY FROM:					
LOST TPDUs	NO	NO	NO	NO	YES
DUPLICATED TPDUs	NO	NO	NO	NO	YES
MISORDERED TPDUs	NO	NO	NO	NO	YES
CORRUPTED TPDUs	NO	NO	NO	NO	YES

TPDU = TRANSPORT PROTOCOL DATA UNIT

out, resequencing of TPDUs, and TPDU checksums. TP 4 provides a reliable, end-to-end transport service no matter what happens in the underlying networks.

All TPDUs that contain user data (DT TPDUs) and are forwarded to a given destination are marked with a sequence number. TPDU sequence numbering is used by flow control, resequencing, and recovery mechanisms to ensure that each transmitted DT TPDU is acknowledged by its destination within a given time interval. If this time interval elapses without receipt of an acknowledgment TPDU, the DT TPDU is retransmitted with the same sequence number as the original transmission. The sending transport entity (an active software element in the Transport Layer) retains a copy of each transmitted DT TPDU until an acknowledgment TPDU is received from the destination transport entity. Once the acknowledgment is received, the resources used to hold the copy are released.

As indicated earlier, misordered (out of sequence) DT TPDUs may occur within the Network Layer. To ensure that data submitted by the source session entity is delivered in sequence to the destination session entity, the receiving transport entity uses the sequence numbers of the DT TPDUs to reconstruct the original user-data sequence. Only TP 4 has this capability.

TP 4 makes use of a checksum mechanism to detect the corruption of TPDUs that are not detected by the Network service. If the receiving transport entity determines that a TPDU has been corrupted, the TPDU is discarded. The retransmission mechanisms described earlier will cause the TPDU to be retransmitted by the sending transport entity.

TP 4 provides explicit flow control. Cooperating transport entities determine a maximum number of outstanding, unacknowledged TPDUs (called the window size) for both communications directions. During the data transfer phase, neither transport entity is permitted to transmit or retransmit more than this number of DT TPDUs until an explicit acknowledgment of previously transmitted DT TPDUs is received. This mechanism, coupled with congestion control procedures in the Network Layer, provides a means of maintaining a uniform service quality for users of the transport service.

Much ado about nothing

One of the most misunderstood features of TP 4 is its extensive use of timers and retransmission mechanisms. These mechanisms are widely recognized to be necessary when a Transport connection is constructed over one or more error-prone subnetworks. However, it is frequently assumed that the presence of the mechanisms results in inefficient operation when the underlying networks are more reliable than the error-prone subnetworks. This is not true. The protocol overhead associated with TP 4 is no greater than that associated with TP 2 and TP 3 during data transfer. In fact, the DT TPDU format is exactly the same for TPs 2, 3, and 4.

From a procedural standpoint, if TP 4's reliability mechanisms are not invoked (that is, TPDUs arrive in sequence, uncorrupted, without loss of data), TP 4 has no more overhead than does any other Transport protocol class. Careful implementation of the protocol and adjustment of the retransmission timers will ensure that no unnecessary delays are introduced during normal operation. When the underlying networks are highly reliable, therefore, the procedural cost of running TP 4 is the same as the cost of running any other Transport protocol class. However, if errors do occur — TPDUs could be lost, duplicated, or corrupted by the underlying networks — then clearly the reliability mechanisms invoked by TP 4 to recover are necessary. This can hardly be classified as overhead.

Proponents of the hop-by-hop approach claim that there will be simplification in Transport protocol operation as a result of the high degree of reliability provided by the enhanced subnetworks. The Transport protocol class of choice in this environment is usually TP 1. However, in the absence of errors, TP 1 and TP 4 operations are essentially equivalent. If an error does occur, the situation is quite different. TP 1 can recover after a failure is correctly signaled by the Network service but cannot detect or recover from errors that are unsignaled or incorrectly signaled, such as corruption of user data. Hence, any user community concerned with data integrity must provide recovery mechanisms at the user application. It is difficult to understand how this can be called simplification.

The protocol's advantages

Because the ISO IP operates in a sublayer above each subnetwork, all the subnetwork sees is data, which is precisely what it saw before there was a need for internetworking. Subnetworks, therefore, are completely unaffected by the presence of the IP (and, for that matter, of OSI). Subnetwork protocols are left intact, and users can continue to employ existing terminal and computer equipment and software. Since the subnetwork protocols continue to be concerned only with efficient operation in the specific environment for which they were optimized, local traffic is not penalized by the introduction of internetworking.

The simple data transmission service required by the ISO IP is readily obtained from the vast majority of subnetworks in existence today. The ISO IP provides segmentation and reassembly mechanisms to accommodate different subnetwork packet sizes. Each subnetwork can continue to use the packet sizes for which it is best suited. Note that the ISO IP was designed specifically to satisfy the OSI connectionless-mode Network service. Therefore, the Transport Layer need not rely upon the quality of service characteristics of any individual subnetwork to provide the QOS requested.

One of the benefits of using the Internetwork Protocol is that the changes required to provide communications beyond the local subnetwork environment are restricted to the terminal equipment and gateways involved in internetworking. In all cases, subnetwork autonomy and local-traffic service characteristics are preserved. Terminal equipment can readily be designed so that the processing overhead associated with internetworking is incurred only when internetworking is actually performed. Routing functions within the Network Layer determine whether the destination is in the local subnetwork. If so, the Inactive Network Layer Protocol (INLP) is used.

The INLP is actually a "null IP subset." It is used strictly to enhance performance, and it serves as an indicator to the destination end system that the complete ISO IP is not present, that the IPDU originator was on the local subnetwork, and that the source and destination subnetwork addresses have been mapped directly onto the corresponding OSI Network addresses for the purpose of expediting the transmission. Contrary to what has been stated in an earlier article (Data Communications, "Of local networks, protocols, and the OSI reference model," November 1984, p. 129), the routing functions that determine when to use the INLP are performed entirely within the Network Layer, and its use is completely transparent to the Transport Layer or to a user.

Finally, from the standpoint of product development, there is one significant advantage of using the ISO IP instead of a hodgepodge of subnetwork dependent convergence protocols. Since the IP can be operated over any subnetwork access or data link protocol, users and DTE manufacturers seeking OSI compatibility can limit the number of convergence protocols they must provide to one.

The tailor-made solution

The nature of most LAN applications ensures that a large proportion of the information exchange takes place within the confines of a single LAN or bridged-LAN topology. For other applications, however, data exchange beyond the local area must be made possible. There is an urgent need for the industry to consider a way to interconnect LANs to other LANs—and to other networks such as packet- or circuit-switched types. Primarily, the impact of providing interconnection of these subnetworks should be minimal. While nonlocal traffic may be generated infrequently, the information exchanged over long (nonlocal) distances is likely to be some of the most important. The ISO IP offers a tailor-made solution to this complex set of LAN interconnection requirements.

Since both the IP and the LLC1 (Logical Link Control Class 1) have relatively simple "state [of operation] machines" (essentially "send" and "idle"), Network Layer design in LAN workstations, as well as in LAN-to-LAN gateways, is quite simple. Each Network Layer service user request-to-send-data results in the generation of one or more IPDUs. The IPDUs are passed to the LLC sublayer along with the destination's LAN station address. The LLC sublayer encapsulates the IPDU into "Unnumbered Information" frames and submits them to the "Medium Access Component [device]" for transmission. When the frame is delivered to the destination LAN station, the receiving LLC sublayer strips the control information from the LLC1 frame and passes the IPDU to the internetwork sublayer for forwarding by the routing function (at a gateway) or for delivery to the transport layer (the "user" of the Network Layer service at the LAN station). The procedures for operating the ISO IP over LLC1 are described

in greater detail in an addendum to the ISO IP: ISO 8473/DAD1.

Gateways between connection-oriented networks (particularly X.25 types) and LANs are the only devices that require the complexity of a connection-oriented state machine. Typical operations involve a call, reset, or disconnect that is pending or awaiting confirmation. However, the complexity is confined to the gateways: End systems on the LANs do not have to operate a connection-oriented state machine at the Network Layer. Also, in many scenarios a wide area network, such as an X.25 type, is but one "hop" among many. Particularly for internetworking scenarios involving many LANs, the number of hops on which the overhead of an additional protocol over a wide area network is incurred is relatively small.

A significant benefit of using the ISO IP is that gateway complexity is greatly reduced because of the way subnetwork connections—in particular, X.25 virtual circuits—are managed. ISO 8473/DAD1 identifies a set of mechanisms and timers for opening and closing X.25 logical channels. This greatly reduces the number of occasions on which state transitions associated with maintaining a connection interfere with the efficient operation of the gateway.

The data transmission service realized through the manipulation of X.25 virtual circuits is essentially the same as that offered by an OSI data link. The establishment and release of X.25 virtual circuits is governed by timer mechanisms. Logical channels are left open (available) to transmit IPDUs for as long as is economically and administratively efficient.

Some concrete examples

The ISO IP should be used where LANs are involved in internetworking; benefits are derived from resource optimization, throughput enhancement (through the use of load-splitting techniques), and redundancy and resiliency (the ability to adapt to redundancy).

The ways in which the ISO IP enables Network service users to get more for their money are considered next.

Resource optimization. Using the hop-by-hop approach (Fig. 3), each LAN station (end system), A, must establish a separate connection to each X.25-network device (end system), B, in order to transfer data. For each connection, resources (such as buffers, a connection-state-information base, and CPU) must be reserved in both end systems as well as in the relay or intermediate system, I_1, for the duration of the call. In particular, I_1 must have ample capacity to maintain all of these connections, even if no traffic is passed. Clearly, if connections remain idle for long periods of time, valuable network resources are wasted.

In contrast, if the ISO IP is used, the sending end system may free resources as soon as the data unit's transmission is completed. Normally, the receiving end system reassembles the IPDU prior to indicating its delivery to the destination Transport entity. I_1 processes each data unit separately, allocating buffer space as required and maintaining a simple state machine (send or idle). Any communicating pair of Network service

3. Hopping between networks. *Using the hop-by-hop approach, each station, A, must establish a separate connection to each X.25-network device, B, in order to transfer data. For each connection, resources must be reserved in both end systems (A and B) as well as in the intermediate system, I_1, for the call's duration.*

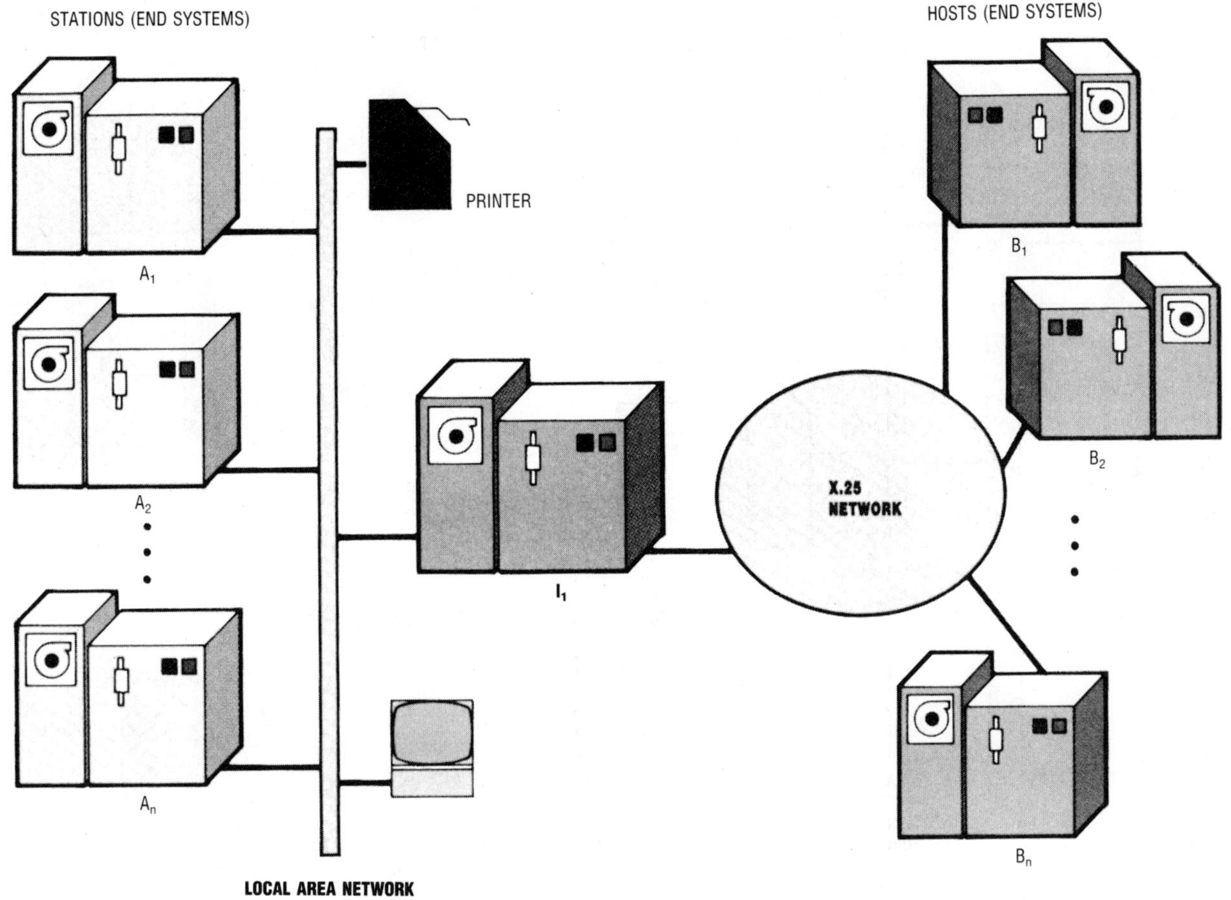

users (hereafter identified as A,B) that has long periods of inactivity between transmissions imposes no overhead. Therefore, the ability of the intermediate system to process transmission requests from any other communicating pair (A,B) remains unaffected. This typically results in highly efficient use of resources.

Throughput enhancement. In many internetworking scenarios, the ability to route IPDUs independently is particularly useful. Data exchanged between hosts attached to one subnetwork can be routed to hosts on a different (remote) subnetwork without the constraint that all data must be routed down the same path (and hence, through the same gateway). Using multiple paths to transmit data to the same destination typically improves throughput and response time.

The ISO IP provides an excellent means of equalizing a potentially vast throughput disparity through the use of load splitting techniques. Consider those configurations (Fig. 4) in which an IEEE 802-compatible LAN (operating at 4, 5, or 10 Mbit/s) must work with a lower-speed wide area network (the maximum throughput of which is normally 48 or 56 kbit/s). In a connection-oriented environment, a separate connection must be established to each network to transfer data. In addition, this separate connection must be relayed

through either I_1 or I_2 relay systems.

A number of constraints can immediately be identified.

■ Some knowledge of which intermediate system (I_1 or I_2) is to be used for which connections—as well as how many connections each intermediate system can maintain—must be known prior to establishing connections, to prevent intermediate-system overloading.

■ Once a connection is established via one intermediate system, the resources of the other cannot be utilized for this connection, as no mechanisms exist for preserving the sequence of data to be transferred if routed via parallel paths.

■ If an intermediate system experiences a failure, all of its connections are broken and must be re-established through a different intermediate system.

In contrast, use of the ISO IP resolves all of the above constraints. Each IPDU contains all of the information necessary to uniquely identify it, and each is processed and routed independent of all other IPDUs. Hence, either or both of the intermediate systems can be used to transmit data between end systems (A,B).

Routing functions performed as part of the ISO IP's operation make it possible to use any available intermediate system to transmit IPDUs This is extremely

553

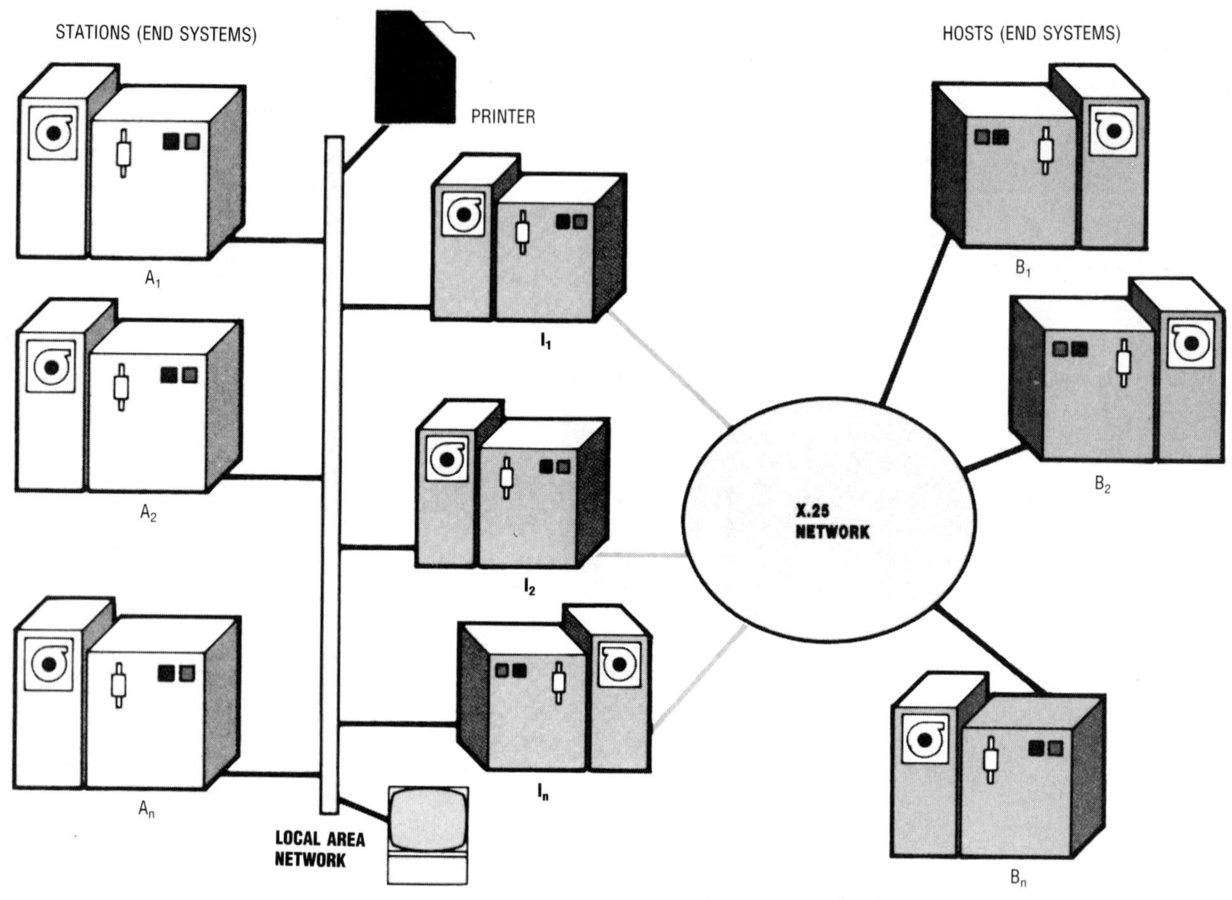

beneficial: Throughput can be effectively improved by a factor n, where n is the number of intermediate systems linking the subnetworks. This technique, called loadsplitting (see "What is load splitting?") is particularly important in internetworking applications.

Consider the case where the subscribed throughput class for a single DTE is 9.6 or 56 kbit/s. Most LAN stations can be expected to operate several orders of magnitude faster. Even if one were to attempt to resolve this throughput disparity through a single DTE using multilink procedures, there would be other problems. One of them: Most data circuit-terminating equipment (DCE) would be unable to respond to such throughput requirements and would impose serious flow control restrictions on the user.

Failure is not final

Another important benefit realized by using the ISO IP is the ability to provide redundancy and timely response to loss or temporary failure of an intermediate system. If an intermediate system fails, or if connectivity to a subnetwork or data link is lost, all communications is not necessarily broken between end systems and other intermediate systems utilizing this intermediate system. In fact, in nearly all routing techniques used in connection-less networks today (and certainly in those anticipated for the OSI environment), traffic can be redirected to other available intermediate systems without a lengthy communications interruption.

If an intermediate system fails, or if connectivity to a subnetwork is lost, most routing algorithms used in connectionless networks today (especially those in the DOD's DDN and in some private networks) respond quickly. Through an exchange of management protocol data units, gateways and end systems are informed of the failure, and traffic is redirected to an alternate available gateway or link. Later, when the failure is corrected, a similar management exchange is used to inform the gateways and end systems.

While the network is responding to such a failure, some IPDUs may be lost. (Upon expiration of a lifetime value encoded in each IPDU, the IPDU is automatically discarded.) Retransmission mechanisms operating in the Transport Layer ensure that no user data is lost or duplicated as a result of the failure.

A similar error-recovery function could be provided in the hop-by-hop approach, in which case the network signals a RESET. Typically, though, such recovery mechanisms are not provided. Normally, a human operator must intervene when calls must be re-estab-

What is load splitting?

One benefit of using a connectionless Network Layer service to support a connection-oriented Transport service is particularly prominent. The functions associated with maintaining user data integrity (sequence preservation, error detection, and error correction) can be separated from functions associated with the exchange of data (routing, Network Layer addressing, and network resource utilization). Networks that use the ISO IP (Internetwork Protocol) are likely to take advantage of this crossover of services by employing load splitting in their routing mechanisms. The reasons: to increase traffic-handling efficiency and to improve overall network performance.

When load-splitting techniques are applied, multiple paths that exist between end systems and gateways are used instead of a single path. IPDUs (Internetwork Protocol Data Units) are routed over these paths in such a way that the traffic load is distributed more evenly throughout the network (see figure).

Load-splitting techniques require participation by Network Layer entities in both end systems and gateways in the routing of IPDUs. This may be perceived as additional overhead. However, the benefits to be had by load splitting substantially outweigh the expense. In the case of a LAN/wide-area-network configuration, significantly higher station-to-station bandwidth may be realized between a LAN station and an X.25 DTE by utilizing more than one DTE (in perhaps more than one gateway) over the slower X.25 network. The same effect could not be accomplished using a multilink procedure under the X.25 packet level protocol. Here, to maintain the sequence of data packets, all traffic must be restricted to the same DTE.

When load-splitting techniques are employed, a higher degree of "resiliency" is also provided. If one of three paths in use suddenly becomes inoperative, the remaining two may support the traffic load. And as a result of a balanced distribution of traffic, individual paths in the network will be less susceptible to overloading. When load splitting is coupled with the flow control features available in TP 4, the network is likely to experience fewer incidents of congestion.

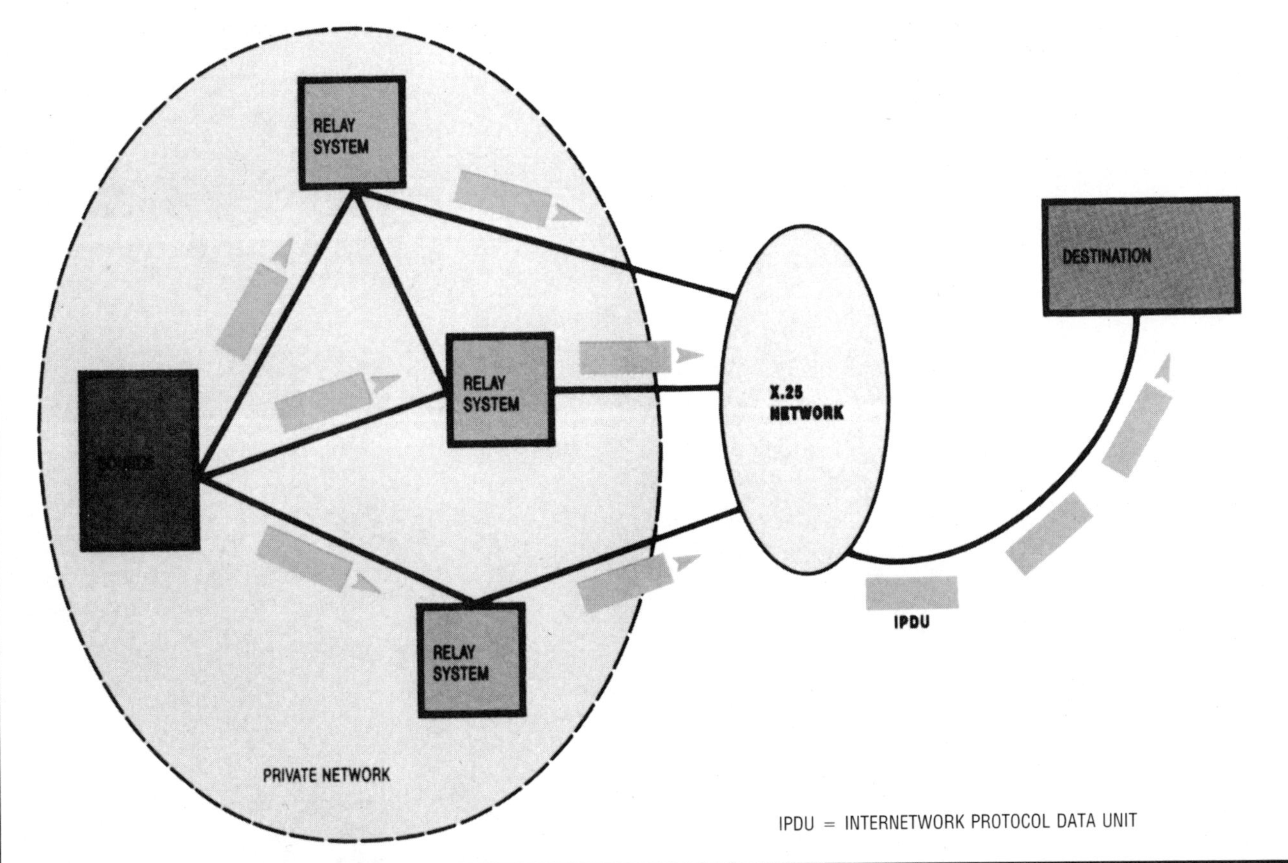

lished to a different DTE as a result of a gateway loss.

The ISO IP standard is in the final publication stage. Enthusiastic support for the protocol and the connectionless internetworking strategy it supports already exists. The European Computer Manufacturers Association (ECMA) has already issued a standard that describes a subset of the protocol suitable for operation over LAN clusters. (These are physically interconnected LANs that offer a uniform service-data-unit size and, hence, do not require the segmentation and reassembly functions defined in the ISO IP.) ECMA intends to reissue its standard, to be fully compatible with the ISO IP.

The National Bureau of Standards (NBS) will issue the

ISO IP as a Federal Information Processing Standard (FIPS). As a FIPS, the IP can be cited in procurement statements by any federal agency.

A significant endorsement for the ISO IP has come from the National Research Council (NRC) of the National Academy of Sciences. Asked by the Defense Communications Agency and the NBS to investigate the suitability of ISO TP 4 and IP in military environments, the NRC conducted a detailed analysis of the ISO protocols. The members unanimously agreed that the DOD should adopt the ISO standards ". . . as costandards with TCP/IP and move toward [their] eventual exclusive use." (TCP/IP is the DOD's Transmission Control Protocol/Internet Protocol).

Support for IP goes beyond the standards arena. General Motors (GM) has selected the ISO IP for its Manufacturing Automation Protocol (MAP) specification. This standard for factory automation is supported by over 50 vendors, including IBM, AT&T, DEC, and Honeywell Information Systems. GM sponsored a demonstration of MAP at the Autofact '85 conference, which included a successful implementation of the ISO IP. GM has installed MAP at its Saginaw Steering Gear's "factory of the future" and intends to continue such installations throughout 1986.

NBS is developing what is hoped to be a worldwide concatenation of public and private networks using OSI protocols, called OSINet. The ISO IP is prominent in its suite of protocols. The purpose of OSINet is to establish continuity of implementations using the OSI protocols. OSINet will undoubtedly encourage users and vendors to adopt the ISO IP as the solution to network interconnection. ∎

David Piscitello is vice chairman of Accredited Standards Committee (ASC) X3S3.3, the task group that oversees the development of OSI Network Layer service and protocol standards. He is involved with network architecture design at Burroughs and holds a B. S. in mathematics from Villanova University. Alan Weissberger participates in ASC and IEEE committees dealing with ISDN, public data networks, and LAN standards. He is a consultant specializing in implementing data communications standards and is an adjunct professor at the University of Santa Clara. Scott Stein participates in ASC and ISO committees that are defining OSI standards. He is a consulting engineer within Honeywell and received a B. S. from the University of Michigan. Lyman Chapin is chairman of ASC's X3S3.3 task group and vice chairman of the ACM SIGComm (Association for Computing Machinery Special Interest Group on Communications). He designs and implements network products at Data General and holds a B. A. in mathematics from Cornell University.

B. Chester Sagaser, GTE Communication Systems Corp., Phoenix, Ariz.

Use integrated PBXs and X.25 in today's networks; don't wait for ISDN

There are benefits to applying existing data communications technologies now. Do so until the standards are sorted out.

As the demand for digital services continues to increase, so too does the need for more efficient, hence more sophisticated, data communications equipment. Particularly, there is a growing demand for networking the devices that handle both data and digitized voice.

The response to the resultant growing device complexity has been the continuing integration of computers and communications. As today's office becomes ever more integrated, there is an increasing emphasis toward office equipment that can itself integrate with, and function in, an environment designed to meet evolving communications needs. This has created a corresponding demand for strong, formal links between various office communications products in order to prevent duplication and maximize integration.

Where PBXs are concerned, this developing interdependence of applications and products presents both a challenge and an opportunity. PBXs can now integrate voice and data (see below). In addition, they have more efficient switching capabilities than ever before. To function most effectively, however, PBXs must be able to work with other types of business information products, supporting everything from local area networks (LANs) and terminal-to-host/terminal-to-terminal connections, to direct access to public and private voice and data networks.

To establish a solid niche in the integrated communications environment, therefore, PBXs must serve as a common interface for integration of communications amidst overlapping technologies. By facilitating the physical transmission between devices, PBXs provide the connections to combine applications, thereby enhancing information exchange.

While voice switching will probably continue to remain a mainstay of PBX applications, it will be to the data side of communications that the PBX will make its most important contribution. Foremost among these contributions is the PBX role of integrating voice and data into a single, multifaceted communications network. The PBX will act as a communications hub for both voice and data interchanges. Moreover, when combined with packet-switching capabilities, the PBX can function as an integrated business communications hub. As such, it is able to handle all types of voice, data, and text information generated by a wide variety of terminals.

A multivendor environment

These new integrated capabilities make the PBX ideally suited to serve as a central data switch in addition to its traditional role as the central voice switch. Growing user acceptance of this fact can be tied to increased awareness as to just where and how the integrated PBX can support multivendor data-device applications, such as:

- Relatively low-speed (operator-keyed) interactive communications.
- Communications between formerly standalone devices (increasingly, these will be microcomputers).
- Terminal-to-host communications.
- The ability to mix and match the above combinations, subject to user needs .
- Elimination of costly multiplexer/port-contention devices by providing multiple data interchanges via a single PBX output port—be it to a host or to a public data network (this in turn provides significant cost reductions in multiplexing applications involving PBX-to-computer interfaces).

On a local basis, the PBX can support a LAN as well as direct communications from the local loop to local-communications or long-haul networks. What's more, in supporting a LAN, the PBX may serve as a parallel or interconnecting network that handles lower-speed (lower than megabit-per-second rates) interactive communications like electronic mail. Or it may be used as an efficient interconnecting device to two or more widely separated LANs.

By using packet-switching technology on the local loop, the integrated PBX can unify many widespread microcomputers into a single network—without the cost of installing coaxial cable or some form of broadband medium between them. In addition, packet switching, with its inherent protocol conversion capabilities, enables the PBX to connect a variety of incompatible devices.

But those local packet networks do much more than provide the connections. Because packet switching simultaneously supports a number of devices, user costs are kept down. Interactive packet switching means that data moves accurately (with error detection and correction) and quickly (in real time) over a packet network to and from the remote device. Thus, local packet networks can provide the most economical transmission medium for a variety of communications applications.

By providing simultaneous virtual connections, packet-switching networks eliminate the need for multiple leased lines and increase the flexibility of connecting a wide range of host computers. Even batch communications could be placed on a dedicated LAN: By reserving higher-speed batch and file transfer traffic for the LAN and lower-speed interactive communications for the PBX, the switch can provide the LAN with even greater capacity and value. And the two can be designed to allow a transfer of traffic between them.

Simplifying network access

Note that packet switching establishes a virtual connection between end points. This means that packet-switching PBXs are capable of putting their data streams directly onto public or private packet-switching networks without requiring any protocol conversion beyond that of the packet assembler/disassembler (PAD) at the user-device location. Also avoided is the data handling required with individual-network PADs or with conversions to circuit-switched transmissions.

The end-to-end use of packet switching eliminates many of the interfaces inherent in transferring data communications from the local loop (with its protocol) to an interconnect link (with *its* protocol) and, finally, to the long-haul network (using still a third protocol, X.25). If the connections are through a standard PBX, this entire protocol sequence must be reversed at the receiving end, resulting in a significantly increased risk of induced bit errors.

Use of X.25-compatible packet-switching protocols on the local loop eliminates much of this redundant processing. For instance, key X.25 functions include establishment of a permanent virtual circuit, setup and supervision of virtual calls, packet sequencing, and flow control of individual virtual calls and permanent virtual circuits. When site networks are X.25 compatible, traditional gateways are no longer necessary.

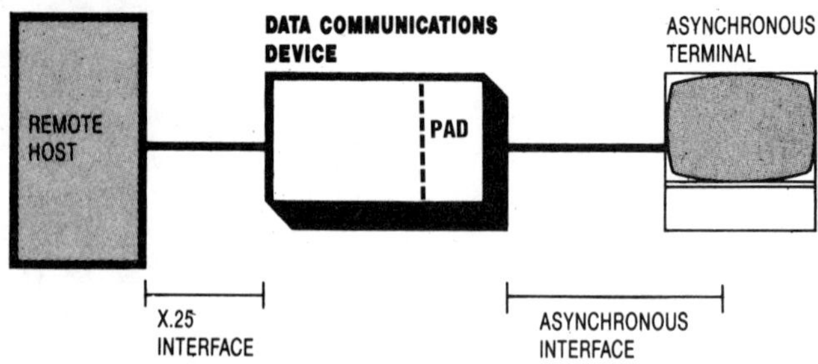

1. Conversion. *In its support of asynchronous terminals, the packet assembler/disassembler provides a form of asynchronous-to-synchronous conversion.*

Note in Figure 1 that the X.25 companion specification X.3 defines the operation and functions of the PAD in support of an asynchronous (start-stop) terminal. The functions performed by the PAD are determined by a set of variables, called parameters (discussed below), internal to the PAD protocol.

An added benefit of packet-switching local loops resides in the ability of a complete X.25 network to provide asynchronous-to-synchronous signal conversion, also shown in Figure 1. That set of rules defined in CCITT Recommendations X.3, X.28, and X.29 ensure efficient call-message interchanges between asynchronous devices and synchro-

X.3 parameters

PARAMETER #	NAME
1	ESCAPE FROM DATA TRANSFER
2	ECHO
3	DATA FORWARDING
4	IDLE TIMER
5	PAD-TO-TERMINAL FLOW CONTROL
6	CONTROL OF SERVICE SIGNALS
7	BREAK HANDLING
8	DISCARD OUTPUT
9	CARRIAGE RETURN PADDING
10	LINE FOLDING
11	COMMUNICATIONS SPEED
12	TERMINAL-TO-PAD FLOW CONTROL
13	LINE-FEED INSERTION
14	LINE-FEED PADDING
15	EDITING (IN DATA TRANSFER)
16	CHARACTER DELETE
17	LINE DELETE
18	LINE DISPLAY

PAD = PACKET ASSEMBLER/DISASSEMBLER

nous hosts, for example.

The 18 X.3 control parameters listed in the table provide terminal users with a command and control structure that less sophisticated protocols cannot. For example, a conventional circuit-switched approach would be hard pressed to provide these control abilities—the 18 parameters—without extensive interference with its data-transfer capacity.

In local-to-long-distance data communications, therefore, the use of a packet-switching PBX serves to eliminate additional equipment and processing between the LAN and long-haul networks, thereby improving data throughput and reducing communications costs. In addition, packet switching permits existing telephone lines to be used for access to the long-haul networks, reducing the number and costs of dedicated lines between the local-loop interface points and the packet-switching network. In this application, a PBX that switches data via internal packet-switching mechanisms has a distinct advantage over those that depend on circuit switching. Public data network and host ports can support multiple virtual connections simultaneously, thus eliminating the need for most contention mechanisms external to the ports.

Hubbing with the local loop

Many major manufacturers of office automation equipment have begun to view the integrated PBX as a communications hub. Much of this acceptance is a direct result of the unit's ability to move data in the local loop on existing twisted-pair telephone wires. Also, more than 200 X.25-certified devices from more than 100 manufacturers are currently registered by the major public packet networks.

The benefits of twisted-pair wire and X.25 compatibility are many. The most obvious is the ability to use the existing installed base of telephone wiring for both data communications and the normal flow of voice traffic. As user acceptance of the PBX as a data switch develops further, PBX manufacturers will begin to implement interfaces for a large portion of the existing coaxial, twinaxial, and shielded twisted-pair installations currently serving terminal-to-host data users.

Coaxial- and fiber-based LANs alone will not meet total short- and long-haul communications needs and can actually generate their own set of interconnection problems. For instance, without X.25, each interconnection would require a conversion in the transition from short- to long-haul transmission. Thus, PBXs that can offer capabilities such as simultaneously connecting hundreds of terminal users over a single 56- or 64-kbit/s channel will become accepted communications adjuncts to existing broadband networks. In fact, the entire spectrum of X.25-compatible technology will become a cost-saving and speed-enhancing service that will be increasingly valuable to the user over time.

Use of the X.25 protocol is significant in that it enables office automation equipment to gain transparent access to national and international packet-switching networks. At the same time, it improves the quality—through inherent error control—of terminal-to-host communications, while allowing users with X.25 mainframe links to reduce their long-distance communications costs. This reduction is brought about because of the economy of local X.25 access.

A growing number of equipment manufacturers are recognizing the utility of the X.25 packet protocol for data switching. As a protocol that allows access to a public packet data network, X.25 is structured to provide users with data communications equipment's full spectrum of capabilities. That is, X.25 serves as the interface between the user device and the network. Additionally, X.25 has been more developed and improved than any de facto standard to date, and it is the most widely accepted protocol with both domestic and international compatibility.

Compelling reasons

The CCITT adopted X.25 as *the* domestic and international standard for connecting user equipment to public packet-switching networks. Besides that fact, there are compelling technical reasons for the use of this protocol as the PBX data standard, such as:

■ There are significant cost reductions in multiplexing applications involving PBX-to-computer interfaces. For example, X.25 interfaces exist today that can replace up to 255 ports on a multiplexer—that is, these interfaces can handle 255 simultaneous asynchronous connections to a single host or front-end processor (FEP) port. In this manner, utilizing the PBX as a controlling hub, with its X.25 port in place of a port contender, very real savings may be realized in the use of high-priced FEP ports—which cost anywhere from four to 100 times that of X.25 ports.

■ Ready connection may be made to outside packet-switching networks via a single, standardized protocol for all communications on the PBX link.

■ This *workable* protocol provides immediate hub benefits. Thus the risks involved in proving a new protocol are avoided—not to mention the expense to manufacturers of providing new protocol conversion equipment for older, current, and future products. This is indeed a critical area since manufacturers are seeking the most workable and economical solution to integrating their LAN and terminal equipment with PBXs. The more difficult it becomes to forge those integrated connections, the greater the cost. As a known and proven standard, X.25 makes it easier to plan, design, and implement economical protocol conversion equipment—such as PADs—for manufacturers' LAN and terminal equipment.

■ A standard X.25 packet-switching interface provides direct PBX access to any LAN and provides such access at no additional equipment cost. This results from the ability of PBX manufacturers to implement the interface during the assembly operation.

■ By packetizing data, X.25 allows the dynamic allocation of bandwidth on standard twisted-pair lines, enabling data to share the same lines with voice. In addition, this dynamic bandwidth allocation, inherent in X.25 packet switching, is responsible for lower PBX equipment costs. (Fewer ports are needed than with circuit switching for the same grade of service. The per-port cost is about $600.) Dynamic bandwidth allocation also substantially reduces leased-line costs—one needs fewer leased lines for the same or better service—as well as the need for more twisted-pair wiring.

■ X.25 gives users tremendous flexibility and resilience. For instance, terminals connected to the network can access remote mainframes via X.25. Moreover, users can "converse" with multiple destinations.

■ A public X.25 network is clearly defined in its interfaces to both the service provided and the organizations requiring that service—the destination and source of a transmission.

■ By eliminating unnecessary links, X.25 allows time-sharing, not only of multiplexer channels, but also of computer ports, modems, and the transmission medium itself—enhancing communications efficiency.

Using the X.25 protocol ensures compatibility in the interconnection of computing devices. Moreover, for those PBXs that employ some form of internal packet switching, this compatibility and interconnectability can be combined with multiple simultaneous connections to single-host or public-data-network ports (Fig. 2).

Maximizing the benefits

Integrated PBXs provide totally digital communications for both voice and data. To eliminate the need for costly rewiring every time functions or features are added, deleted, or modified, these PBXs utilize a building's existing twisted-pair wiring scheme. In addition, if the PBX is a switch with a dual-bus architecture, the voice processing can use pulse code modulation. This allows the data throughput to be greatly expanded—typically to three to four times the previous amount—by using proven packet-switching technology, with no effect on the voice-switching capacity.

A packet switching capability allows dissimilar terminals to communicate with each other or with central computers. It also allows tandem (nodal) switching of data circuits, use of different types of various protocols, and more efficient—because of packet switching—use of available bandwidth. Data may be switched at speeds up to 64 kbit/s synchronous and 19.2 kbit/s asynchronous via a packet-switching PBX.

In creating a parallel local communications network for data, integrated PBXs offer the potential for unnecessarily creating confusion in the data communications industry. The crux of the matter lies in how well the communications industry handles the issue of compatibility, or the standardization of protocols.

Most major PBX and LAN manufacturers have fully accepted the viability of the PBX as a data communications hub. But even though X.25 has received widespread acceptance, it is not the only protocol available. The longer that the marketplace waits for a "final" PBX protocol standard, however, the greater the likelihood that numerous de facto standards will be established—a different one from each PBX manufacturer.

There is currently a controversy over an acceptable standard for PBX-to-computer interfaces, with two opposing factions (see DATA COMMUNICATIONS, "Comparing the two PBX-to-computer specifications," May 1984, p. 215). The eventual merging of the two into the ultimate controlling standard, the Integrated Services Digital

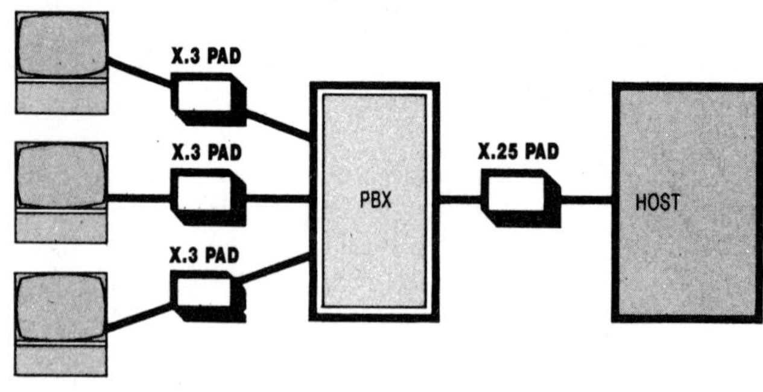

2. Application. *Besides compatibility between connected devices, the packet-switching PBX provides multiple simultaneous connections to X.25 ports.*

Network (ISDN), has focused attention on requirements that will apply later in this decade (see "X.25, ISDN, and the office").

However, users must have assurances that the PBX office-equipment hub can enable communications between existing DTE (data terminal equipment) devices and today's host computers, LANs, and public data networks. Such a PBX, supporting internal packet switching, offers today's data communicator an immediate interface between existing asynchronous terminal equipment and those destination devices required by the user's business needs. Moreover, by providing direct T-carrier connections—which have been offered on modern digital PBXs since 1976—a digital PBX can offer, today, the utilization of multiple simultaneous X.25 connections over a single channel on that T-carrier.

For that future world when both the ISDN network standards and the ISDN terminal standards are agreed upon, the PBX will be able to continue supporting existing devices as "R" (non-ISDN standard) interfaces. With the installation of relatively simple program and hardware modifications, the PBX will provide an ISDN connection and local support of the ISDN standard, as well as of R terminal devices.

What ISDN may mean

Although the production of numerous incompatible protocols may benefit some manufacturers in the short term, in the long run such a dispersed marketplace will probably produce more confusion than advantage. Next-generation standards such as ISDN will parallel and may eventually absorb X.25. But a plethora of manufacturer-based protocols may create extensive and long-lasting confusion in the crucial area of standards. Helping to forestall this eventuality are the most recent CCITT/ISDN-committee recommendations, which have suggested X.25 for the first three layers of ISDN's seven-layer protocol.

When it comes to integrated PBXs and their coexistence in a multidevice environment, the issue of compatibility through a single communications standard is a critical one. Acceptance of a single standard should not curtail development of further improvements to current communications protocols. But the search

X.25, ISDN, and the office

Probably one of the least controversial of the forthcoming data communications offerings insofar as switched network services is concerned is the proposed Integrated Services Digital Network (ISDN). However, this offering has caused, and will continue to cause, a considerable amount of controversy in the area of terminal planning.

ISDN will become a reality. Interested potential suppliers include the nationally owned public telephone administrations in Europe and many other parts of the world, AT&T, the RBOCs (regional Bell operating companies), and the large independent telephone companies in the United States. They see a very real need to establish ISDN to protect against bypass and its erosion of their revenue base. Since these organizations are also determined to cooperate—ultimately—in establishing interface standards, this too will occur.

The controversy, however, arises in the marketplace, that common meeting ground where potential suppliers solicit the cooperation of potential purchasers. By the time ISDN becomes a viable, widespread offering, the North American market will surely contain a considerably greater quantity of terminal equipment than today's sizable numbers. Users of mainframes and minicomputers, smart and not-so-smart terminals, microcomputers, word processors, file servers, graphics devices, and communicating copiers will be encouraged to resist embracing a standard that might require extensive replacement or modification of their existing devices. On the other hand, a large segment of the industry with considerable resources is going to be pushing for the development and introduction of "true-ISDN" terminals.

Until such time as the dictates of the marketplace are more clearly understood, existing, well-defined, protocols and interface rules such as the CCITT Recommendation X.25 would seem to offer the most economically viable solution.

for such enhancements should not be allowed to interfere with the acceptance of a standard *now*, along with the substantial benefits such a standard can provide.

A single standard permits the users *and* the marketplace to continue with their business in an environment of stability and compatibility. Furthermore, it promotes future stability by setting a precedent for agreement among competitors. But most of all, it enables users to gain the greatest benefits from their existing and future communications investments, simply by *not* forcing them to choose among many incompatible options. ∎

Chet Sagaser has been with GTE since 1974, holding positions in marketing, sales, and sales support. He earned a B. S. degree in business administration from Charter Oak College, Hartford, Conn.

Edward H. Lee, Pacific Bell, San Francisco, Calif.

A BOC explains where the bits went

Finally, the straight scoop on the whys and wherefores of missing T1 bits. There's really no skulduggery. It's just a matter of timing and too many zeros.

T1 service is gaining in popularity and will probably form the backbone for future Integrated Services Digital Networks (ISDNs). Yet much confusion remains about which, and how much, data must be used for supervisory and signaling purposes and for general overhead. For example, one consultant was asked to explain why 56 kbit/s per channel rather than 64 kbit/s of clear-channel data was offered in Pacific Bell's private T1 point-to-point service. He responded that the 8-kbit/s difference was needed for supervisory and signaling purposes.

Not so. Pacific Bell's private T1 offering robs one bit out of each 8-bit word and inserts a "1" in its place. This is because the bipolar line-signaling format, used by the public telephone network, loses timing if there are more than eight consecutive zeros. However, this private service can be used by customers on a single point-to-point basis, in which case the signaling format could easily allow for 64-kbit/s clear-channel data.

Traditional T1 digitized-voice format consists of 24 eight-bit words or channels and one framing bit (S-bit), making a total of 193 bits per frame (Fig. 1). Pulse-code modulation (PCM), the entrenched form of voice digitization, requires 8,000 samples per second of the analog voice signal, and each sample consists of one 8-bit word—totaling 64 kbit/s per voice channel. Provided there are 24 time slots, or frames, sent per second, T1 provides a total of 1.536 Mbit/s. By adding the 8,000 extra bits for signaling and control (variously called S and F bits depending on the use) to the total bandwidth, the total becomes 1.544 Mbit/s per T1 frame.

The S-bit is used both to synchronize timing with the channel-bank multiplexer at the telephone company central office and to identify the signaling frame. For the channel-bank multiplexers, the S-bit identifies the loca-

tion of the first time slot of each frame. The series of S-bits sent over time also forms a fixed 12-bit word of its own. This 12-frame format is called the superframe. In binary, the representation of the word is 110111001000. This pattern must be repeated continuously (Fig. 2). When used in the superframe format, the extra bit is called the F-bit. The F-bit circuitry in the telephone company's D-type channel multiplexer bank searches for the pattern (110111001000) in order to synchronize the frames. These superframe bits account for 8 kbit/s missing from the T1 framing format.

Pro forma

The superframe bit pattern is required of T1 circuits terminating at a telephone company's central office for access to the public switched network. However, many customers are using T1 for private data transmission—while never going through the public network. In other words, T1 multiplexers on private networks can use this 12-bit word for more than just framing. Since the pattern is a known sequence, the vendors can rob the sixth bit of every 12-bit superframe for A and B signaling purposes (on-hook, off-hook, lead ground status, and so forth).

For the past few years, AT&T has been advocating that the telecommunications industry adopt its proposed extended superframe format (ESF) in T1 multiplexers. The ESF format is comprised of 24 frames, instead of the standard 12 in the superframe format. If implemented, the ESF frees the least significant bit of every sixth frame, since the A and B signaling is embedded in the framing-bit sequences and not in the information bits (Figs. 3 and 4). Further, ESF allows a 4-bit combination for signaling, thus expanding signaling possibilities from 4 to 16.

Many people believe the use of A and B bit signaling

1. Bits per second. *Data is organized into 24 channels of 8 bits. Each channel represents the equivalent of one dial-up data or one voice connection. Twenty-four chan-* *nels are sent per second, plus an extra bit for supervisory or signaling information. This makes a total of 1.544 Mbit/s.*

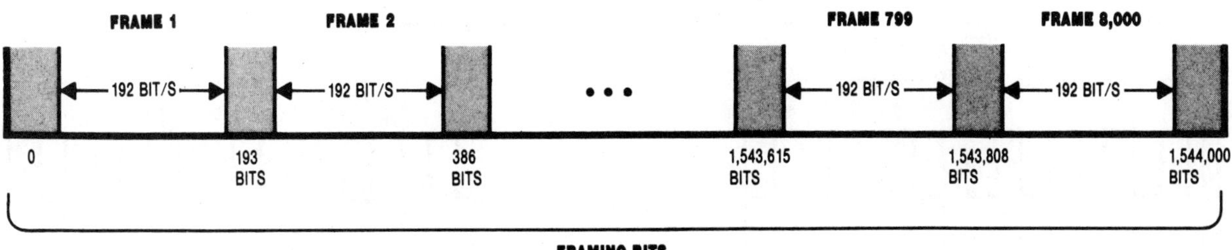

2. Superframe extended. *With the extended superframe, nonswitched T1 link, A and B signaling—which once took place in an information field—can be transmitted using* *the extended superframe format (ESF). The ESF is made up of 24 T1 frames. The A bit would occur every 965 bits, the B bit every 2,123 bits.*

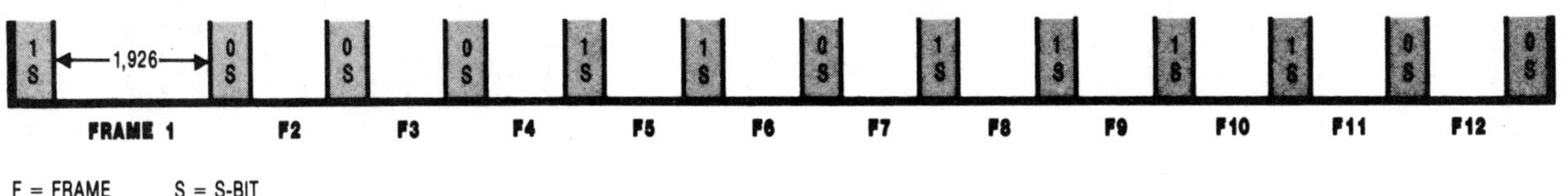

explains the 8 kbit/s lost between a 64-kbit/s voice and 56-kbit/s data transmission. With the superframe format the A and B signaling takes only 1,333 bit/s out of 1.544 Mbit/s. This is far from the 8 kbit/s times 24 channels (192 kbit/s) missed in the T1 data transmission. That is, the difference between the total number of bits required for voice transmission and that required for data is a difference of 192 kbit/s, not 1,333 bit/s. In fact, according to Bell System Technical Reference publication No. 43801, "Digital Channel Bank Requirements and Objectives," the total bandwidth available for usable data is only 56 kbit/s times 23 channels, or

1.288 Mbit/s. The overhead is 256 kbit/s (Fig. 3). So far, only 8 kbit/s for framing and 1,333 bit/s for signaling and information coding and general overhead have been accounted for. There are still 184 kbit/s (23 times 8 kbit/s) unaccounted for.

In the Bell System Practices, Section 314-915-110, the DDS T1WB5 allows the first seven bits in a data byte to transmit data. The eighth bit is designed to transmit status information coding. When the customer's data terminal is sending data, the office channel unit (OCU) inserts a logical one into bit position eight. When the customer's terminal is idle, the OCU inserts

3. Sync pattern. *The synchronization word is made up of a sequence of 12 S-bits (110111001000) that completes itself every 12th frame. The T1 multiplexers at the* *central office continuously search for this sync word to maintain clock synchronization. The S-bit occurs every 193rd bit, at the end of each T1 frame.*

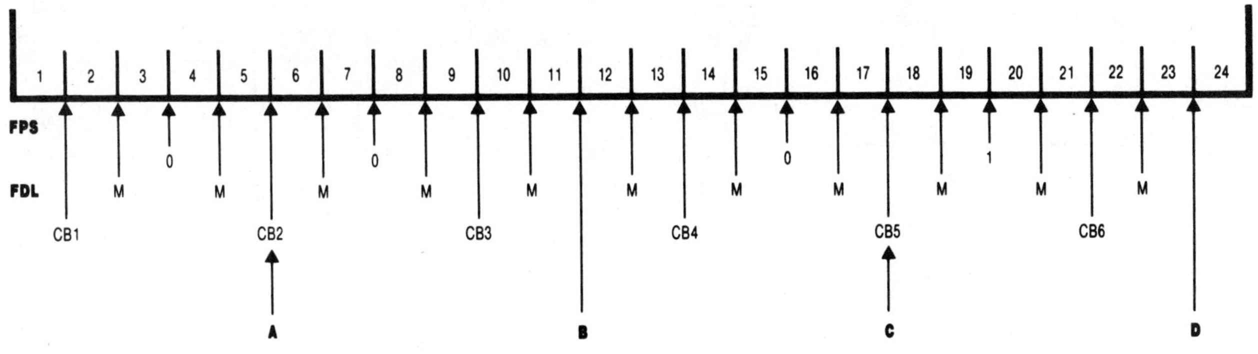

FPS = FRAMING PATTERN SEQUENCE

FDL = FACILITY DATA LINK (M = MESSAGE BITS)

CB = CHECK BIT (PART OF 6-BIT CYCLIC REDUNDANCY CHECK)
     ROBBED-BIT SIGNALING FOR PRESENT DS1 FRAMING FORMAT   A = A   B = B   C = A   D = B

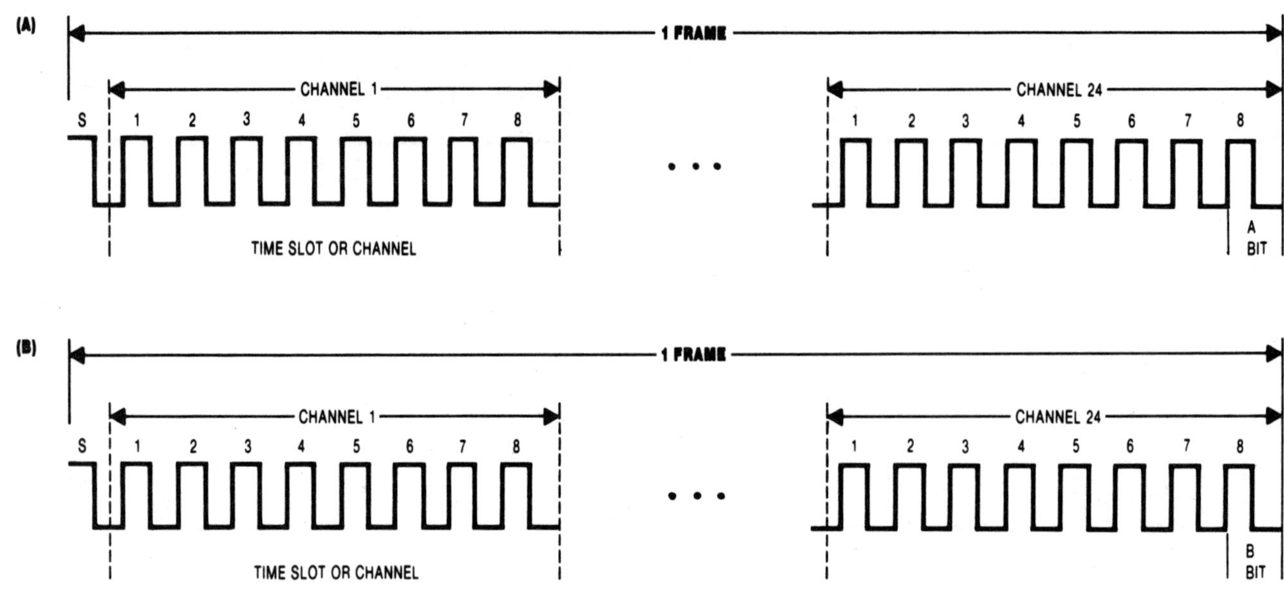

a logical zero into bit position eight and logical ones into bit positions two through seven of that byte. This ensures that the bit stream contains no more than seven consecutive zeros. The requirement for no more than eight consecutive zeros ensures timing recovery by the T1 repeaters throughout the network. This line code constraint is the real culprit in the missing 8 kbit/s in the data transmission format.

As the ISDN environment evolves, the International Telegraph and Telephone Consultative Committee (CCITT) will require a 64-kbit/s clear channel for data transmission. This is in conflict with the current line code restrictions that limit the number of zeros that can be in any given byte. One solution is Bell Laboratory's proposed bipolar with 8 zeros substitution (B8ZS). With B8ZS coding, each block of eight consecutive zeros is replaced by the B8ZS code. For example, if the pulse preceding the inserted code is transmitted as positive, the pulse is

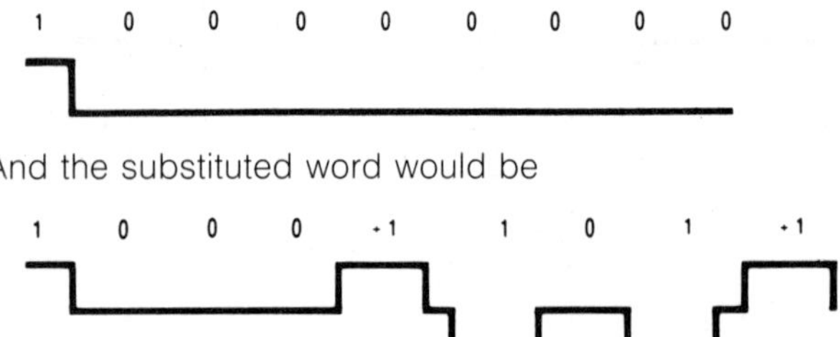

And the substituted word would be

B8ZS creates bipolar violations in the fourth and seventh bit position of the inserted code. If the pulse preceding the inserted code is a negative pulse like this:

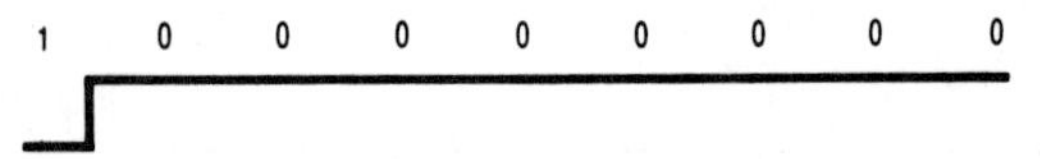

then the B8ZS word would be like this:

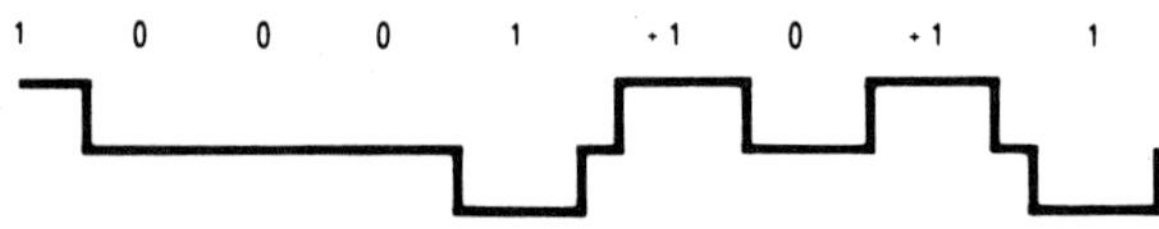

Again, bipolar violations occur in the fourth and seventh bit positions.

Digital signal level 1 (DS1) terminating equipment must be able to monitor the incoming DS1 signals for B8ZS code words. Upon detecting a B8ZS code word, the DS1 terminating equipment should replace it with eight zeros.

While many vendors supplying equipment to the information network market have adopted both bit-robbing techniques and B8ZS coding techniques in their T1 multiplexers, no one since divestiture is setting standards for local operating companies. To replace embedded equipment for this enhanced capability, the local operating companies face a large investment. But there is no incentive for them to make the investment so long as regulatory rules prevent the local operating companies from marketing enhanced services. Even though this regulatory restraint may save the general public some money now, it will definitely slow down the ISDN development process and curtail efforts aimed at moving the United States into a more advanced information exchange era. Consequently, regulators may eventually come to see that this approach is proving foolish. ■

Edward H. Lee earned his B. S. in business administration from Chinese University, Hong Kong. He then received his M. S. in business administration from the University of Denver.

William G. Schmidt, William Schmidt Associates, Gaithersburg, Md.

Can the world agree on the next digital-speech coding algorithm?

Time and technology gain on the 1970s-vintage standard used today, as new methods emerge and fend off controversy.

For more than 20 years, 64-kbit/s companded pulse-code modulation (PCM) has been the only internationally recognized method of coding voiceband signals for digital transmission. The technique, embodied in an international standard known as CCITT Recommendation G.711, was based on the technology of the 1970s and the analog switches of that era. But time and technology are catching up, and a number of new voiceband coding algorithms, more responsive to today's digital networks and to the anticipated ISDN services of the next decade, are appearing.

These new voiceband-coding standardization efforts, however, are mired in controversy—the result of policy differences within the international standards circles as well as legitimate technical concerns. Still, they promise new transmission capabilities and efficiencies—provided the world's standards makers can eventually agree on the details.

Advances in very large-scale integration (VLSI), especially in digital signal processors, are enabling new voiceband signal-processing algorithms—previously thought to be too complex and uneconomical—to be affordably implemented. As a result, quality voice communications can now be achieved at bit rates much lower than 64 kbit/s. And the proliferation of end-to-end digital facilities is also making use of these more efficient coding techniques possible, since the newer algorithms no longer require the built-in performance overdesign to compensate for numerous analog-to-digital conversions, which characterized the hybrid transmission paths of the 1970s and early 1980s.

Recognizing these trends, the International Telegraph and Telephone Consultative Committee (CCITT) began developing a number of new recommendations (as CCITT standards are called), which use these advanced algorithms. The completed and stilldraft specifications are intended both for the provision of future services, as well as for the conservation of existing transmission capacity.

One completed standard, called G.721, is a new voice-coding algorithm that operates at 32 kbit/s. This enables 48 voice channels to be carried where the predecessor 64-kbit/s algorithm (Recommendation G.711) yielded only 24 channels within 1.544-Mbit/s paths. Further, where the 64-kbit/s G.711 has two variants with respect to the type of companding used (one now predominates in North America, the other in Europe), this standard had worldwide acceptance in 1984, and it seemed initially that it would make possible a return to a single-standard world. But acceptance of the 32-kbit/s G.721 seems to be crumbling rapidly, particularly in North American usage.

The CCITT's Study Group XVIII is forging ahead unfettered, however. It plans to initiate "accelerated" procedures to obtain CCITT approval for a wideband (7-kHz) voice-coding algorithm that operates at 64 kbit/s. This will likely be followed in about two years with a 16-kbit/s voiceband coding algorithm designed mainly for mobile telecommunications (see table). In addition, at the 1988 CCITT Plenary meeting, a recommendation on speech/data algorithms, which can provide a fivefold increase in the equivalent capacity of 1.544-Mbit/s links, is expected to be approved.

Turbulent history

In the early 1970s, some of the most heated debates in the history of the CCITT took place over proposed standards addressing the first digital transmission methods, formats, and bit rates. Part of those debates had to do with the voice-coding algorithm. The decision to use pulse-code modulation (PCM) was readily accepted, but agreements on the bit rate and the companding law (which prescribes the digital value assigned to represent an analog-signal sample) were considerably more difficult.

Status of CCITT voiceband coding standards

DATA RATE	STANDARD/DESCRIPTION	COMMENTS
64 KBIT/S	G.711—USES PULSE-CODE MODULATION TO ENCODE 4-KHz VOICE AT 64 KBIT/S.	20 YEARS OLD; CONSIDERED OBSOLETE AND INEFFICIENT.
32 KBIT/S	G.721—USES ADAPTIVE DIFFERENTIAL PCM FOR COMPRESSION OF A G.711-VOICEBAND SIGNAL TO 32 KBIT/S.	ADOPTED IN 1984; LIMITS VOICEBAND DATA TO 4.8 KBIT/S; SOME INCOMPATIBILITY WITH NORTH AMERICAN DIGITAL TRANSMISSION; NOT WIDELY USED.
64 KBIT/S WIDEBAND	DRAFT—USES SUB-BAND ADPCM FOR ANALOG-TO-DIGITAL AT 48, 56, OR 64 KBIT/S.	FOUR MODES OF OPERATION; CAN SUPPORT AN 8- OR 16-KBIT/S AUXILIARY DATA CHANNEL; STANDARD EXPECTED THIS YEAR.
16 KBIT/S	FOR CELLULAR-TELEPHONE, ELECTRONIC MAIL, MARITIME SATELLITE APPLICATIONS.	DRAFT BEING DEVELOPED; STANDARD PERHAPS BY 1988; TO SUPPORT 2.4-KBIT/S MODEM DATA.

The eventual CCITT Recommendation (G.711) specified 64 kbit/s as the bit rate (though others, including 56 kbit/s, were considered), but an irreconcilable difference of opinion on the companding law bred two variants: the mu-law and the A-law options.

An 8-kHz sampling rate and an 8-bit quantization were selected to yield exceptionally high signal-to-quantization-noise (S/Nq) performance at the output of the voice-digitizing code. This was done based on the hypothesis that there would be a significant number of analog-to-digital conversions taking place as the digital signal traversed its connection path. In fact, 12 such conversions were envisaged and, since each such conversion resulted in approximately 3 dB (decibels) of loss of S/Nq, a very high starting value of S/Nq was deemed necessary.

As a result of AT&T's digital implementation, a fully transparent, or "clear" 64-kbit/s channel, upon which much of the ISDN planning currently is based, is not available over North American public networks, nor will it be for some time. And it is for this reason that the ISDN Recommendations refer to "restricted" 64-kbit/s service, which translates to "for North American networks".

Bandwidth efficiency
The same CCITT study group that formulated G.711 became increasingly occupied with planning for a future when all-digital, end-to-end transmission paths would be readily available. This is what led, eventually, to the concept of the Integrated Services Digital Network (ISDN).

Along the way, however, some members of the study group were already viewing the faster-than-expected evolution toward digital networking as an opportunity, if not a mandate, to improve the efficiency and quality of voice communications with new coding algorithms. Indeed, the connections hypothesized for G.711 (with up to a dozen analog-to-digital conversions) were already determined to be unrealistic, outstripped by the introduction of powerful digital switches into public telephone networks.

In the early part of the 1981-84 CCITT study period, proposals were made by a number of telecommunications administrations, including AT&T for the United States, that coding algorithms other than G.711, covering a variety of bit rates and applications, be studied. At a meeting of Study Group XVIII (Digital Networks and ISDN) in June 1982, it was decided to establish an ad hoc working group to study the feasibility of a standard 32-kbit/s coding algorithm.

Top priority was given to the processing of speech at 32 kbit/s, though it was recognized that there were also needs for coding algorithms for other applications. Work on a draft recommendation, based on 32-kbit/s use of adaptive differential PCM (ADPCM), was pursued by a small group of experts from six nations, headed by K. Harrison of British Telecom (of the United Kingdom) and including representatives of Bell Laboratories and COMSAT Laboratories from the United States. Upon CCITT approval in 1984, this algorithm became Recommendation G.721.

But there remained some serious hesitations and concerns about G.721. First, it was acknowledged that it could not support most modem data signals at rates in excess of 4,800 bit/s (a restriction caused by inaccuracies imposed on the signal content by limitations of the on-chip arithmetic processing). Further, the 1.544-Mbits/s transmission facilities in North America require the suppression of all-zero sequences, while the quantization technique specified in G.721 permits such sequences (see "Data problems with ADPCM").

It should be noted that, strictly speaking, G.721 is a transcoding algorithm; that is, it performs a conversion to and from the 64-kbit/s coding format of G.711. It is not designed for the direct conversion of an analog voice signal to digital.

Concerns deferred
When the Speech Processing Working Party of Study Group XVIII convened for its first meetings of the 1985-88 CCITT study period, under the chairmanship of M. Decina of Italy, some of these concerns were voiced. But there was insufficient support among the members to establish a study/testing effort for the revision of G.721.

The group decided that, without adequate resources for developing the required voiceband coding algorithms in parallel, priorities had to be set. And first priority was for a wideband (7-kHz) coding algorithm operating at 64 kbit/s. A 16-kbit/s voice-coding algorithm was to be developed next, and revision or improvement of G.721 was probably not possible in the 1985-88 study period.

However, formulation of a draft recommendation on Digital Circuit Multiplication (DCM) techniques, which involve both low-rate voice coding and speech interpolation algorithms, was proceeding in two major CCITT study groups, XVIII (network aspects) and XV (equipment specification). And because DCM involves the segregation of data from speech, the study of data-optimized 32-kbit/s algorithms has been undertaken within these activities.

Efforts to formulate a wideband speech-encoding algorithm effectively began in November 1983, spurred on primarily by strong interest on the part of the Japanese and the French. The need was recognized for a coding al-

Data problems with 32-kbit/s ADPCM

One of the dominant issues in the ongoing debate over G.721 has been the inability of the algorithm to support modem signals higher than 4,800 bit/s, and in particular those of V.29 (leased line) and V.32 modems. Some say that some existing modem designs can be modified. Others are not so sure.

According to Bell Laboratories, a modification of the existing V.32 modem equalizer would permit their use over G.721-based links. Japan's KDD, however, emphasizes that more than half of Japan's non-voice traffic involves bit rates of 7,200 and 9,600 bit/s, which makes use of G.721 extremely unattractive. In addition, KDD claims there are more than 300,000 CCITT Group 3 facsimile units in Japan, which are V.29-based and also cannot be supported by G.721 coding.

Japanese representatives to the CCITT have detailed four alternate courses of action available to remedy the data problems of G.721:

1. Revise G.721, which appears to be unacceptable to the CCITT at this time.

2. Modify V.32 modems. Even assuming that this could be done, problems would still remain for the V.29 modem population and Group 3 facsimile machines.

3. Adopt a new algorithm, incompatible with G.721, which would replace G.721. The CCITT strongly resists this proposal, mainly due to the shortage of testing resources available to validate the performance of any proposed replacement algorithm.

4. Segregate data from voice and use a data-oriented algorithm for data. This segregation is inherent in digital circuit multiplication (DCM) processing and a new data-optimized algorithm would perhaps involve less testing. What's more, a new data-oriented algorithm could be folded into the draft recommendations now being developed on DCM equipment and technology.

Not only does G.721 have problems with high-speed data, but there have also been reports that it does not perform well for bursty-type, lower-speed, frequency shift-keyed (FSK) modem signaling. It seems that G.721 results in strings of erroneous characters at the beginning of an FSK response after a period of idling.

These reports have been confirmed by a small group of experts working within the T1Y1 Committee of the Exchange Carriers Standards Association. This same group was in the process of circulating for approval a version of the G.721 algorithm for use in North American networks when these reports came to light. The draft North American G.721 stated that a long-term objective of North American networks was to support G.721, but it noted that zero-suppression requirements of domestic networks would make full compliance difficult for a number of years.

G.721's problems with FSK modems have been identified by Bell Laboratories, which developed a software patch for G.721 processing that it says solves the problem. But even so, a change of any kind would mean that the North American version of G.721 would not be compatible with the original G.721 and would be, effectively, a different algorithm.

During the final days of the work on the development of the G.721 standard in 1984, Japan's KDD proposed the use of an algorithm quite different from the one then in the final stages of testing and refinement. Testing of the KDD-proposed algorithm had not been extensive enough at that time, though it gave promise of both meeting speech and non-speech test objectives, and also of supporting 9,600 bit/s modem data. Testing of the Japanese algorithm has proceeded, with a significant amount done at Comsat Laboratories.

According to Henri Suyderhoud of Comsat, there is no question that this algorithm is superior to both the original G.721 as well as the North American modified version. "From my point of view," states Suyderhoud, "the (ECSA) T1Y1 committee has no choice but to consider these two algorithms as independent alternatives to G.721, which is no longer acceptable to North America. We have to select one and then inform the CCITT that North America cannot support G.721."

gorithm for use in teleconferencing (audio conference and video conference audio), for use within the wideband speech channels of ISDN, and for the audio portion of broadcasting systems. Because of the importance many attached to the work, the standardization effort was continued through the interim period between CCITT study periods.

Thinning the herd

Starting from 12 candidate algorithms, the decision was eventually narrowed to a speech-coding algorithm called sub-band adaptive differential pulse-code modulation, or SB-ADPCM. The technique involves splitting the 7-kHz signal spectrum into two sub-bands, each of which is then separately coded via ADPCM. The lower sub-band (0-4,000 Hz) is coded into 48 kbit/s, while the upper sub-band (4,000-8,000 Hz) is coded in an additional 16 kbit/s (see "How Sub-Band ADPCM Works").

An unusual, and some believe highly desirable, feature of this design is that it contains provisions for supporting an auxiliary data channel operating at 8 or 16 kbit/s. Four operating modes for the wideband coding algorithm are identified:

- Mode 0, which codes the speech using the "narrowband," G.711-companded PCM at 64 kbit/s; there is no auxiliary data channel,
- Mode 1, where the full 64-kbit/s sub-band ADPCM capability is applied to the 7-kHz signal; there is no auxiliary data channel.
- Mode 2, which yields 56-kbit/s SB-ADPCM coding for voice and supports an 8-kbit/s auxiliary data channel.
- Mode 3, where, in addition to a 48-kbit/s SB-ADPCM-coded channel, a 16-kbit/s data capability is supported.

To better portray these different modes, the CCITT group of experts has theorized a set of terminals, which would be designed around the wideband capability of the coding algorithm. The most versatile of these would be able to operate in any of the modes; a block diagram for such a terminal is shown in the figure. Note that the terminal has G.711 coding capability and supports a data terminal operating at 8 or 16 kbit/s, in addition to the SB-ADPCM capability. Still to be worked out in future meetings on the draft recommendation are the networking aspects of such terminals: how telephone connections would be set up, controlled, altered, and so on.

Carrying the song

The ability of this algorithm to support the transmission of music is included as a requirement in the standards group's test program, but it is not a major objective of the study effort. In addition, the transport of analog data-modem signals over these links is not anticipated, due mainly to the expected availability of other direct-digital data capabilities and facilities. Therefore, the satisfactory transmission of voiceband modem signals is not included as a requirement in the program set up to test the algorithm.

There are two items of special interest for North American networks in this wideband proposal. First, the algorithm incorporates a 15-level (7-bit) quantizer, on which North American digital coding currently is based, so there is no concern about accommodating the unique zero-suppression requirement. Second, since North American networks are geared to 56 kbit/s, Modes 2 and 3 of the algorithm are important since they can be modified for compatible transmission. However, interworking with fully transparent, ISDN-like, 64-kbit/s channels would still be a problem.

The Japanese were the prime movers in the development of a CCITT recommendation for voiceband coding at 16 kbit/s, though European interest has also now grown. While AT&T has stressed the need for such an algorithm for digital mobile telephony, including for cellular radio, the Japanese telephone administration, KDD, emphasizes a need for 16-kbit/s voice in a digital maritime satellite communications network. Other administrations foresee use of such an algorithm in such applications as voice mail and broadcast services.

The performance requirements associated with such low-rate speech coding include robustness (satisfactory operation) with bit error rates of 1 in 10å bits; low processing delay (about 45-80 milliseconds); the ability to support 2,400-bit/s modem data signals; as well as dual-tone multi-frequency (DTMF) dialing signals; and the provision of speech quality equivalent to 6- or 7-bit PCM coding.

The 16-kbit/s effort is headed by R. Pietroiusti, of Italy, who is currently attempting to more accurately define the network-level requirements for this standardization effort. A Working Party meeting in Geneva this past March was expected to form the framework for that effort.

However, definition of a comparative testing program for 16-kbit/s encoding is not as far along as for the wideband coding standard, and at least another year will probably be required before a draft recommendation is in a form suitable to begin the formal CCITT acceptance procedure. Five algorithms were initially proposed for consideration in this standards effort back in June 1982, and the field of

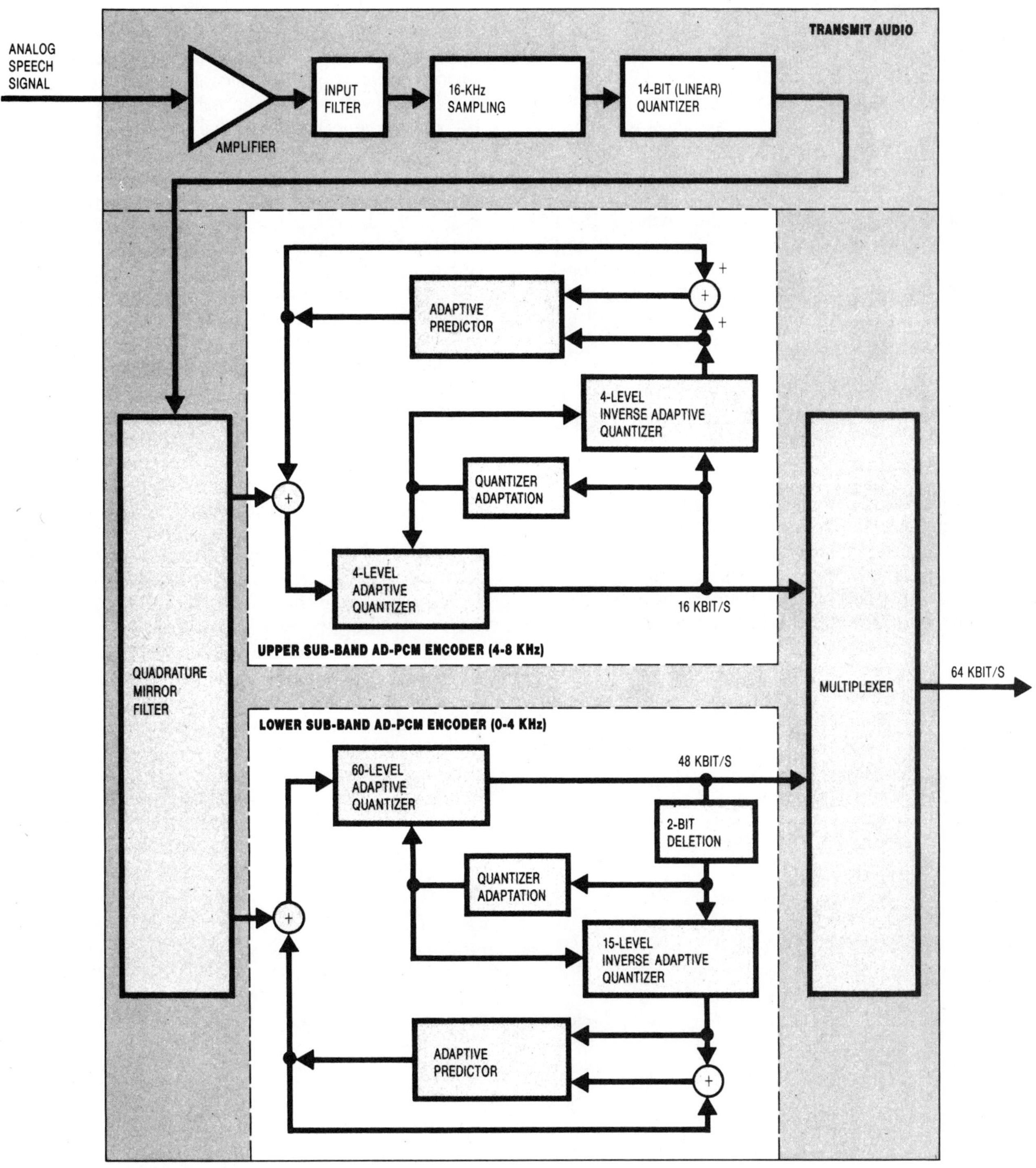

dates can be expected to enlarge. A leading contender at this time is an Adaptive Predictive Coding (APC) algorithm with a fixed bit allocation.

Digital circuit multiplication refers to the use of digital signal-processing techniques to yield greater effective channel capacities than would be available using conventional 64-kbit/s PCM coding. The use of low-rate coding (LRC) is one means of doing this. For example, 32-kbit/s ADPCM permits 48 voice channels to be carried over facilities previously handling only 24 such channels. This is a circuit-multiplication factor of two.

Included in the current activities of CCITT Study Groups XV and XVIII are standardization efforts for DCM. Study Group XV work is directed toward the development of a draft specification for DCM equipment; Study Group XVIII is concentrating on specifying the technology and techniques to be employed in DCM. Both groups are focused on coupling 32-kbit/s coding with another technology called digital speech interpolation, or DSI.

Filling the gaps
DSI uses the pauses in a significant number of voice conversations to insert additional conversations. Depending on speech-activity factors (a typical conversation is active only about 35 to 40 percent of the time, in each direction) and the number of active conversations, circuit multiplication factors of two or more can be achieved using this technique. In the past, this compression technique was called Time Assignment Speech Interpolation, or TASI, and it found considerable application, both in analog and digital transmission, over intercontinental submarine cables and satellite links.

By combining low-rate coding and DSI circuit multiplication, expansion factors of four and five times the non-multiplied channel capacity can be achieved. But key to this is the ability to segregate non-interpolatible signals, such as most data and facsimile signals, from the interpolatible voice signals. Indeed, such segregation is the first step in the DSI process. Once data has been segregated, there is then little need for the data signal to be subjected to a low-rate coding algorithm, which is optimized for very broad voiceband applications.

A data-optimized algorithm could operate effectively in a segregated application (on only data or facsimile, for example), while a voice-optimized algorithm operates separately on the interpolatible (voice) traffic. It is for this reason that, until G.721 is revised or replaced, DCM developments may well be the breeding ground for new and more effective coding algorithms.

Standards outlook
In the months ahead, a wideband (7-kHz) voice-coding algorithm operating at 64 kbit/s will be submitted for "accelerated approval" procedures within the CCITT.

About two years later, approval can be expected of both a 16-kbit/s coding algorithm, as well as a digital circuit multiplication (DCM) equipment specification. The latter may include a non-G.721 coding algorithm, which operates at 32 kbit/s and is capable of supporting 9,600-bit/s voiceband data signals.

Despite its apparent problems, G.721's 32-kbit/s ADPCM transcoding algorithm will probably not be revised during the current study period. Still, work on a direct voice-to-digital coding process may include an internal "gear-shifting" capability so that the type of traffic being sent is recognized, and the optimum algorithm is brought into play. ∎

William Schmidt has nearly 30 years experience in data communications, digital transmission, and network engineering, having worked for Satellite Business Systems and Comsat. Schmidt currently is serving as Special Rapporteur for CCITT Study Group XVIII on the issues of DCM and speech packetization. He holds a bachelor's degree in electrical engineering from Manhattan College and an M.S.E.E. from M.I.T.

Edward E. Stevens and Bonnie Bernstein, Systems Strategies Inc.,
New York, N. Y.

APPC: The future of microcomputer communications within IBM's SNA

This latest major enhancement to SNA should provide multiple benefits to users, as well as to hardware and software vendors.

Until recently corporate communications networks have relied upon mainframes to manage and control all data distribution function across a network. However, the influx of microcomputers into the corporate environment, combined with the need for more capable communications facilities, has necessitated that microcomputers be linked in a more sophisticated manner to mainframes, and to each other.

Advanced Program-to-Program Communications (APPC) is IBM's umbrella term for a new set of facilities that will better facilitate microcomputer to mainframe communications, while allowing the microcomputer to retain full standalone processing capabilities. In addition to freeing microcomputers to function as intelligent workstations on the network, APPC promises to simplify communications and improve data handling and throughput by allowing true peer-to-peer connectivity and program-to-program links.

The architectural base for APPC is contained in enhancements to IBM's Systems Network Architecture (SNA). A brief overview of SNA is therefore pertinent to a discussion of APPC.

As IBM's master plan for communications among its products, SNA defines the structure, formats, rules, and controls for transmitting data through networks, and for managing and operating the network. SNA was conceived in 1974 to implement resource sharing within the communications between mainframe computers and peripherals.

SNA was proffered as a structure upon which all IBM communications could grow, and was intended to be comprehensive, usable, and, most importantly perhaps, extendable. Despite its versatility, the network has often been criticized for being organized around a hierarchical structure. With the rapid growth of microcomputers, superminicomputers, and other specialized equipment such as intelligent communications controllers, connectivity needs have surpassed the capacity available in a central control structure. APPC, the most recent development within SNA, demonstrates the flexibility inherent in the architecture to accommodate new technology and market demands.

In an SNA implementation, Physical Units (PUs) represent network devices, also called nodes. Logical Units (LUs) represent end users, both by providing the interface through which they gain access to network resources, and by managing the information transmitted between them. (In SNA, an "end user" is defined as either a person or an application program).

PUs are defined by the services they provide their associated LUs. Although there are four specific PU types currently defined within SNA, in discussing APPC it is sufficient to note that PU Type 2 (PU2.0) represents a terminal cluster controller, such as the 3274 or 3276, or a batch terminal, such as the 3770; PU Type 1 (PUI.0) represents an individual display terminal or printer. Currently intelligent devices, such as microcomputers, are typically linked to an SNA network through PUI.0 or PU2.0. Consequently, micro-to-mainframe communications primarily occur in the form of the microcomputer emulating a less intelligent 3270-type device.

Users are linked by establishing LU-to-LU sessions; these sessions can only be established between two LUs of the same type. Such sessions are defined by the nature of the services the LUs provide to their programs. Before APPC, the definition of an LU was also intimately related to the type of device in which the LU resided.

APPC is designed to provide enhanced support for distributed transaction processing. Its goal is to provide complete compatibility for interconnection purposes for all the SNA levels below the application level.

The APPC standard is contained in the SNA definitions for Logical Unit Type 6.2 (LU6.2) and Physical Unit Type 2.1 (PU2.1). LU6.2 is an enhanced derivative of LU6.0, which

571

defines a session between two application programs. The enhancements are embodied in a new set of capabilities and services that LU6.2 provides its application programs.

The key difference between LU6.2 and all previous LU types is that LU6.2 was conceived as a single, product-independent LU type. It is this feature of LU6.2 that makes it a true program-to-program interface, capable of providing communications across a broad range of products.

LU6.2 is supported by several PU types, including the new type known as PU2.1. Designed to support the enhanced capabilities of LU6.2, PU2.1 provides extended connectivity capabilities over PU2.0. PU2.1 can connect a node to a mainframe in the traditional hierarchical manner. More significantly, a PU2.1 node can also connect to another PU2.1 node in a peer-to-peer fashion, thereby permitting remote intelligent nodes to connect directly, without mainframe intervention. PU2.1 also improves resource sharing and efficiency by allowing multiple links and supporting parallel sessions.

LU6.2 provides a significant improvement in resource sharing through the use of conversations. Two transaction programs communicate via a conversation, using a session between their associated 6.2 LUs to exchange data. Conversations use time-sliced session segments that share the communications link, creating a very efficient use of the session resource (Fig. 1).

The LU6.2 specifications include a Protocol Boundary, which defines a standardized interface to the SNA network for use by application programs. The Protocol Boundary is rigidly defined and specified by the LU6.2 verbs. These verbs constitute a generic Application Program Interface (API) that facilitates a programmer's task when designing distributed transactions involving different types of products. This API also provides a common specification for hardware designers who want to implement APPC on their products. It is the API approach that allows LU6.2 to have a product-independent nature.

LU6.2 provides parallel session capability, which allows simultaneous connections between many pairs of transaction programs. This capability allows multiple sessions to exist concurrently between LUs, facilitating more efficient use of network resources and increasing overall throughput.

The peer-to-peer nature of LU6.2 communications is supported by the primary LU capability. In order for application programs to communicate without mainframe intervention, both ends of the session must be capable of initiating a session. In SNA, this responsibility lies with the primary LU. Every LU6.2 implementation can assume either the primary or secondary role in any given session.

Another feature of LU6.2, commitment control, allows transactions to synchronize themselves across a network. (This synchronization means that all changes are registered at all relevant databases, even in distributed locations.) The highest level of resource synchronization defined by LU6.2 is called syncpoint in LU6.2 jargon. In addition to synchronization itself, syncpoint also provides error-protection recovery services, known as rollback support.

LU6.2 is the keystone in IBM's long-term office systems communications strategy. It has built-in support for a series of architected services to be implemented at the SNA applications level. These services provide enhanced capabilities for the formatting, interchange, and control of data (such as office documents) across distributed environments. These services currently include Document Interchange Architecture (DIA), Document Content Architecture (DCA), and SNA Distribution Services (SNADS).

DIA and DCA have been developed to overcome the differing commands among diverse operating systems. DIA allows the interchange of documents and other information across a network. Transmitted documents can be in final or revisable form, and can be directed to multiple destinations. DIA also provides access to the processing and distribution services of the Distributed Office Support System (DISOSS).

DCA defines uniform formatting of documents to be interchanged in an office environment, providing document compatibility across the products that support DCA. Formatting controls are included in DCA, including such functions as pagination, highlighting, heading, and centering. As with DIA, documents can be either in draft or final form.

DISOSS is an application subset residing in the host that stores, retrieves, and distributes documents created by IBM products that support APPC. These products currently include the 5520 Administrative System, Scanmaster 1, and Displaywriter, DISOSS allows remote users to access host services, such as the host library.

SNADS is an architecture for asynchronous distribution of information between users. SNADS provides delayed delivery services, allowing information to be forwarded through the network as paths between intermediate nodes become available. This eliminates the need for a complete end-to-end session between the origin and the destination of a transmission.

As of this writing, IBM has announced APPC support for

1. Efficient use of bandwidth. *Conversations use a logical-unit-to-logical-unit session in a serial fashion over time. (Each conversation maps to a Systems Network Architecture bracket.) In this way, logical connections can be established without the overhead of creating an entirely new session for each separate connection.*

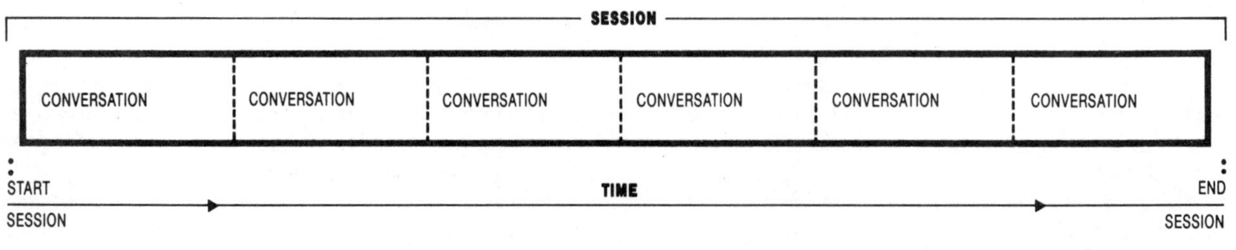

CICS/VS, System/36, System/38, Series/1, the 8100, and the token ring LAN, and has issued a statement of direction indicating future APPC support for the 4700. In a mid-April announcement, IBM detailed a direct link for the token ring network to the System/370 through the 3725 communications controller, a token ring-to-System/36 connection via a PC AT gateway, and a bridge between token ring networks. The company also announced software for the Series/1 that implements links to DISOSS, System/36 and System/38 for its PCs, providing DIA/DCA/SNADS support.

In addition to the IBM products that currently support APPC, IMS/VS support is expected soon, and IBM's new cluster controller is expected to support both standard 3270 and LU 6.2 links to MVS.

PU2.1 capabilities

The major features of PU2.1 — peer-to-peer connectivity, and parallel session support — have been mentioned. In addition to supporting LU6.2 capabilities, PU2.1 yields less obvious benefits. It will standardize the method by which peer-to-peer communications are implemented, simplifying links across many devices and connections of non-IBM equipment to IBM networks.

PU2.1 also greatly reduces the amount of host communications software maintenance required in network implementations. It accomplishes this by offloading certain control functions to the remote intelligent nodes, thus relieving the mainframe of some of the responsibility for communications control.

For example, network control programs operating under host-based ACF/NCP (Advanced Communications Function/Network Control Program) used to keep tabs on the actual physical location of every LU on the network. This meant that if a user moved his terminal, a new system generation was necessary. In token ring 6.2 implementations, the NCP sees the virtual logical units but is transparent to their physical placement on the LAN (Fig. 2).

APPC's effect on users and vendors

With APPC intelligent workstations will no longer need to impersonate 3270 terminals to communicate on the network. When the session involves a link between two intelligent devices other than the mainframe, no host intervention is required. The result will be a net gain in overall network efficiency: improved throughput, more usable computing power, no dormant excess processing power, and more effective handling of peaks.

The definition of the SNA upper layers and the standard program-to-program interface provided by the APPC verbs will result in the "decoupling" of programs and devices. Program-to-program communications become independent of the environments (that is, operating system, programming language, hardware type) of the individual programs.

For example, APPC allows a C language program running on a Unix-based machine to communicate with a Cobol program on an IBM MVS machine. The language, operating system, and physical location of the program are all transparent to the programmer and user. The verbs and syntax specified by APPC will provide a universal "language" for user-written programs. Users can much more

easily configure and maintain large networks and write distributed application programs for those networks.

APPC will allow third-party software developers to enter the market with distributed transaction programs that interface with a common communications protocol, significantly broadening their market potential as APPC becomes more widely implemented. For hardware vendors, the addition of APPC capabilities will grant a competitive edge when selling into the IBM-installed base, as well as against vendors who do not offer the features.

APPC will offer the same lasting use of distributed transaction processing programs that IBM's 360 operating system environment provided for batch processing programs. A vendor's capital investment in software is therefore protected for a longer period of time, and the cost of software maintenance support is reduced.

APPC formalizes the general rules for creating new distributed environments. Consequently, system designers will not have to re-invent application-to-application connections. The cost of design will eventually diminish as less expertise will be needed than is currently required for highly specialized environments.

Hardware vendors will find it easier to provide expandable solutions, since APPC will provide increased flexibility in distributing work across networks. Applications can be written for single or multi-machine environments, and value-added utility programs can be generated for a variety of configurations.

SNA evolution

LU6.2 demonstrates SNA's fluid nature and portends further SNA evolution as the communications environment changes. New network requirements will continue to be formulated and incorporated into the SNA framework. With the more layered approach to SNA that APPC provides, changes can be expected in every layer (physical to presentation) over the next decades.

For example, new Intel 80386-based machines are expected to arrive on the market in approximately two years. Such devices will become even more powerful distributed nodes with new capabilities. An even further enhanced LU type is therefore a distinct possibility.

APPC, along with the advent of the IBM's Low Entry Network (LEN) concept, has brought the PC into the SNA mainstream. A PC configured with APPC PCs can be configured in token-passing rings using broadband, baseband, and twisted-pair cabling. In such configurations, users will be able to move PCs as easily as they move modular-plug telephones today. Eventually such LANs will have extremely powerful distributed processing capabilities (Fig. 2).

With APPC, configuration possibilities have been greatly expanded. Of course, before such configurations can be implemented, the issue of network management and diagnostics clearly needs addressing, and it is no small matter, even for IBM. IBM took the first step in this direction with its late-May announcement of the mainframe-based NetView software, which allows monitoring, control, and reconfiguration of SNA data networks from a single site. NetView offers limited monitor and control functions for the token ring network due to the software's support of the new entry-level members of IBM's 3725 controller family, the

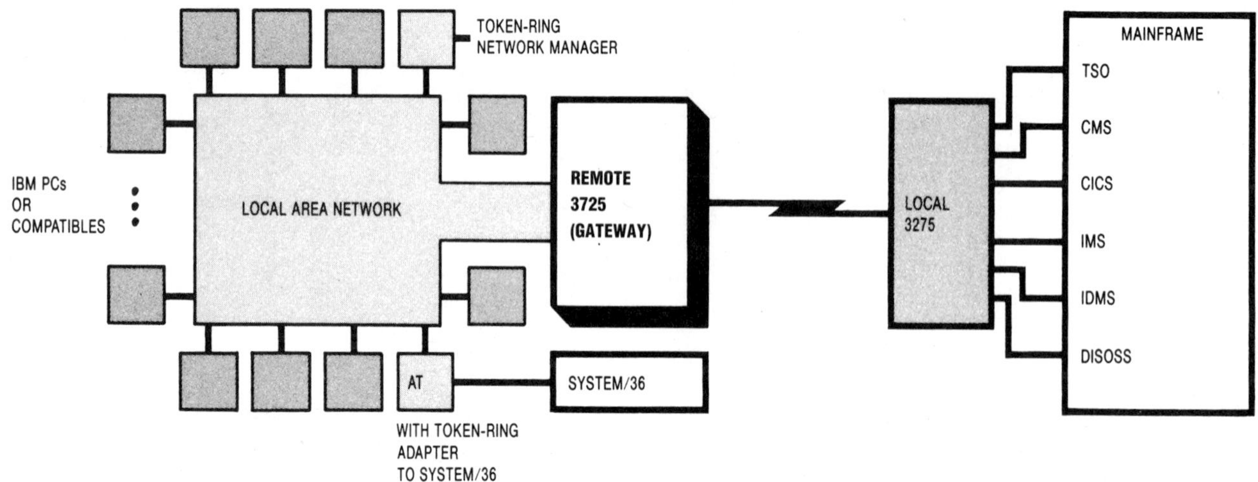

3720 and a related expansion unit, the 3271, which allows support of additional lines.

Like the 3725 controller, the 3720 and 3721 provide an intermediary link between IBM token ring networks and System/370 mainframes, thereby providing a gateway through which NetView can monitor token ring functions.

The non-IBM environment

Despite the defeat of a recent proposal to adopt LU 6.2 as the basis for the presentation level of the OSI, APPC promises to be an important communications standard. Therefore, APPC implementation on non-IBM hardware is a pertinent issue for competitive vendors.

There are already several types of APPC emulation available. As with 3270 emulation, some require that the user purchase additional hardware. Hardware vendors can purchase pre-packaged APPC and device emulation software, port it to their machines, and offer these capabilities as software options. With a properly constructed software product, the SNA and LU6.2 programs are pre-packaged in machine- and operating system-independent modules; to port the package to the host machine, the vendor need only customize the software boundary routines and compile and link the generic code, not endure an entire development effort. The design of such packages simplifies LU6.2 adaptation to diverse operating environments.

For the equipment manufacturer, the benefit of portable software packages is rapid time to market from the point of purchasing decision to field delivery. Furthermore, as the equipment manufacturer broadens the product line, porting to new equipment takes minimal time when compared to the usual development cycle.

Despite the advent of APPC, the need for IBM device emulation will not disappear overnight. With the very large number of current installations, 3270 terminals, remote job entry 3770 workstations, and their associated network configurations are going to be around for a long time. Users must maintain their existing investments and, therefore, the software products to use them. This will promote more demand for emulation as some equipment ends its useful life and requires replacement and as companies expand their terminal networks to accommodate increased requirements. Communications management will not want to buy replacement 3270s or 3770s, and will increasingly turn to emulation.

In addition, System/370s, 380Xs, 4300s, and other large IBM products do not use the same terminals as System/36s. LU6.2 will interconnect them, but a large number of users will continue to have interactive terminal session requirements.

While APPC takes an enormous step toward standardization, the process is far from complete, and even IBM will have variations in LU6.2 implementations from product to product. Competitive vendors will have to test their products in all possible configurations to determine functionality.

Tests will soon be available that exercise LU6.2 functionality on an SNA network in conjunction with the IBM products that currently support APPC. Future test products will be developed as IBM expands its LU6.2 implementations. ■

Edward E. Stevens is the director of software development for Systems Strategies. He has been in the data processing field for over 21 years, and holds bachelor's and master's degrees in electrical engineering from New York University. Bonnie Bernstein is Systems Strategies' director of marketing, and holds bachelor's and master's degrees in communications arts from New York Institute of Technology.

Leonard Magnuson, Intel Corp., Hillsboro, Ore.

Ethernet and MAP, complementary, not competitive

Two LANs have reached prominence as solutions to separate problems. Both will coexist harmoniously.

As enthusiasm spreads, General Motors' Manufacturing Automation Protocol (MAP) is garnering a considerable amount of attention and acclaim. Yet there remains a degree of uncertainty and confusion on the part of some users of local area networks (LANs). For these people, the question is whether Ethernet and MAP will compete with each other in offering networking services within organizations.

But most major companies developing and supporting Ethernet and MAP say the issue is not whether but how they will exist together. Certainly, Ethernet and MAP networks will coexist within an organization, each supported by industrywide standards and each serving the environment for which it was originally designed—Ethernet (IEEE 802.3) in the office and lab, MAP (IEEE 802.4) on the factory floor.

This coexistence means that Ethernet and MAP, in some cases, will be linked together. So rather than choosing between two seemingly competing and incompatible networks, LAN planners will instead have the best of both worlds. They will be able to use a network in the environment for which it was intended, yet still be able to connect it with another network.

Why is Ethernet best suited for the office and MAP for the factory floor? The reasons have to do with their respective features and histories. Briefly, Ethernet works best in the office because it is a data-only, high-performance, cost-sensitive network. MAP is tailor-made for the factory because of the predictable nature of network access under its transmission protocols, and because it handles time-critical data as well as other network services, such as plant security and control (see table).

Both Ethernet and MAP will perform backbone-network functions in their own setting. Networks with lower performance and lower costs, such as IBM's PC Net or AT&T's StarLAN in the office and MAP carrierband in the factory, will be used to link together, for example, a cluster of word processing workstations or a set of robots in one workstation. The following discussion of the major differences between Ethernet and MAP should make clear how they complement each other within an organization.

MAP Version 2.1 is a broadband network. The bandwidth of a MAP line is analogous to that of a home cable-TV cable, which can simultaneously handle dozens of different television signals. The actual LAN messages occupy only two channels of the broadband cable. The rest of the cable can be used by such features as video, plant security, and environmental monitoring and control. Ethernet, by comparison a baseband LAN, transmits nothing but digital network messages on the network.

The ability to transmit many diverse signals is an important feature of a factory LAN and the major reason that MAP, rather than Ethernet, is better suited for the factory. Yet the primary need in an office backbone is for a data-only network like Ethernet. It would be unduly expensive to force an office LAN to deliver more services than were actually necessary.

Cost is another factor that separates the two networks. MAP network connections are expected to be 50 percent more expensive than their Ethernet counterparts. One reason for this is the inherent difference in the two LANs. For example, Ethernet messages are transmitted as serial bits, whereas MAP messages must first be converted into analog signals, necessitating a radio-frequency modem at each node.

This price discrepancy is also due to the relative maturity of Ethernet in the marketplace. Chip manufacturers have had the time to develop Ethernet very large-scale integrated circuits and ship their products in volume, which drastically reduces system costs. While that situation will change as comparable MAP products become available, it is likely that MAP broadband connections will always be more expensive than those for Ethernet.

Access methods

To get on to an Ethernet network—using the now well-known technique carrier-sense multiple-access with collision detection technique—a station listens to hear if the network is being used and sends a message only if the line is clear. If two stations send simultaneous messages, hardware detects the resulting collision, and the stations try again. MAP, on the other hand, uses a token method, in which "permission" to use the network is passed from node to node in a predetermined order.

Ethernet and MAP: A comparison

ETHERNET	MAP
IEEE 802.3	IEEE 802.4
BUS TOPOLOGY	BUS TOPOLOGY
BASEBAND	BROADBAND USUALLY, SOMETIMES BASEBAND
ACCESS: CARRIER SENSE MULTIPLE ACCESS WITH COLLISION DETECTION (CSMA/CD)	**ACCESS:** TOKEN PASSING
CABLE: SHIELDED COAX (50 OHMS)	**CABLE:** CATV-TYPE, WITH HEAD-END REPEATERS, FOR BROADBAND; COAX FOR BASEBAND
DATA RATE: 10 MBIT/S	**DATA RATE:** 10 MBIT/S, 5 MBIT/S
MAXIMUM STATIONS: 1,024	**MAXIMUM STATIONS:** 1,000, DEPENDING ON CONFIGURATION
CONNECTION FROM NODE TO LINE: TWISTED PAIR, UP TO 50 METERS	**CONNECTION FROM NODE TO LINE:** SAME HARDWARE AS USED IN CATV
MAXIMUM DISTANCE BETWEEN NODES WITH REPEATERS: 2.5 KILOMETERS	**MAXIMUM DISTANCE BETWEEN NODES WITH REPEATERS:** 30 KILOMETERS
COST PER NODE: APPROXIMATELY $1,000	**COST PER NODE:** APPROXIMATELY $1,500

MAP is therefore considered to be "deterministic," because it guarantees access to every station within a predictable period. This feature is especially important in the factory, where, for example, a critical gauge reading might need to be reported to a control program without delay. It is hard to imagine a comparable sense of urgency in the office. The guaranteed access of the token netowrk is another reason MAP is identified with industrial settings.

Nevertheless, it should be noted that Ethernet adherents don't make any performance concessions to MAP networks; they believe their LAN can easily handle critical, real-time transmissions. But given the overall LAN trends of the industry, most arguments by now are academic—those arguments that CSMA/CD is better than token passing and vice versa, with the one access method being so much the better that it would obviate the use of the other.

Market history

Because Ethernet was originally conceived for the office and design lab, most of its higher-level software was written with those needs in mind. This is also true for Ethernet user-application software, peripheral devices, and the rest of the Ethernet follow-on market. While MAP is at a much earlier point in its development, this same coalescence is taking place—with MAP products being geared toward the factory floor. If only because it is completely self-fulfilling, this process assures that Ethernet and MAP remain in the application areas for which they were designed.

A good example of the workings of this process is Network File Access (NFA) software, jointly developed by Intel, IBM, and Microsoft. NFA implements the top three layers of the International Organization for Standardization (ISO) model for office and lab settings. For example, the software allows a user at one station to operate directly on a file stored at another station, without first downloading the entire file to the user's terminal. This cuts down on network traffic and allows for tighter data control, since files aren't being duplicated around the network.

Another significant way in which NFA serves the office market is by accommodating multiple operating system environments (initially, Xenix, MS-DOS, and iRMX). The first two are widely used in office settings, while iRMX is designed for real-time applications in the office, factory, and lab. Any viable office or laboratory network must therefore support all three.

While Network File Access is available now, Intel and Westinghouse have co-developed MAPnet, which implements the top three ISO layers as called for by the MAP Version 2.1 standards. Again, MAPnet will be designed in a way to best serve the needs of the factory floor.

While Network File Access and MAPnet will be available as seven-layer network solutions to those wishing to establish Ethernet or MAP networks, customers can also unbundle these packages—for example, combining MAP's top three layers with Ethernet's bottom four layers and ending up with a kind of "office MAP." This is the approach being contemplated by General Motors and Boeing Data Systems in their proposed Technical and Office Protocols network.

These hybrid networks and network interconnections will be important in the many organizations that have a front office and a factory floor. In those situations, LAN routers will play a key role, since they can easily link networks with similar upper-level software by joining them at ISO Layer 3. In the cases where not all networks have the same higher-level protocols, the upper-level software from two or more networks can be stored at each node, allowing that level of software to share data with multiple networks, using multiple protocols.

This network flexibility is possible only with a modularized, standardized, open-system approach to LANs. With this approach, organizations can install an Ethernet network today, yet still link it to future MAP products as they become available. ∎

Leonard Magnuson, OEM communications marketing manager at Intel, has designed automated industrial and business applications involving point-to-point communications between plants. Magnuson has also held positions in sales and marketing management for a variety of communications products, including audio response for packet-switched networks and real-time compressed speech applications for long-haul communications. At Intel he has also had marketing responsibilities for LAN products.

Alan J. Weissberger, Teledimensions Inc., Santa Clara, Calif., and Jay E. Israel, Excelan Inc., San Jose, Calif.

What the new internetworking standards provide

They detail the rules for interconnecting local and wide area networks, both in connection-oriented and connectionless environments.

One of the most challenging aspects of the Open Systems Interconnection (OSI) effort is internetworking. This effort—under the direction of the International Organization for Standardization (ISO)—enables geographically separated computers (and other devices) to communicate effectively, even if the paths between them are complex and involve a diverse collection of transmission entities.

The need for internetworking comes from the fact that there is no one network type that satisfies every computer-communications requirement. Rather, there are several technologies used. Local area networks (LANs) provide high throughput over limited distances; packet-switched data networks (PSDNs) make it relatively easy to connect to a large population of widely separated sites and to conduct several concurrent "conversations"; circuit-switched data networks are more limiting, since each network attachment communicates with only one site at a time. Still more restrictive is a dedicated point-to-point link.

Each of these technologies is geared to a specific set of user needs. Employing one technology assumes that the bulk of a user's traffic has certain characteristics that are most suitable to that choice. But what about the rest of the traffic? Surely it is not desirable to partition computers into categories based on certain characteristics of their predominant traffic, isolating them from computers in other categories. Internetworking's role is to resolve such disparities.

Although the requirement to interconnect diverse networks has long been well known, only recently have international standards emerged to make it possible. Two different approaches are in vogue: connection-oriented and connectionless (see "Internetworking in an OSI environment," DATA COMMUNICATIONS, May 1986, p. 118—hereafter referenced as "Piscitello"). Standards for these two methods have been advanced in both ISO SC6/WG2

(Subcommittee 6/Working Group 2) and IEEE 802.1. These standards use the X.25 packet layer protocol (PLP) and the connectionless Network protocol (CLNP) in the Network Layer in LAN stations and IWUs (internetworking units, such as gateways and Network Layer relays).

With the prevalence of X.25 equipment and the expansion of PSDNs—especially in Europe—it was only natural for the X.25 packet layer to be chosen for connection-oriented internetworking. LAN stations using the X.25 PLP as the Network Layer protocol can communicate with local or remote X.25 hosts through an IWU. The stations can also communicate with each other or with stations of remote LANs that are connected to the local LAN through one or more PSDNs.

Connection-oriented

A LAN station could also act as a packet assembler/disassembler (PAD) to enable attached asynchronous, ASCII terminals to access X.25 hosts. The X.25 PLP provides the OSI connection-oriented Network service (CONS) as specified in ISO 8348. This enables the X.25 PLP to work with future OSI Network Layer protocols over new subnetworks, such as the Integrated Services Digital Network (ISDN).

ISO 8881 is a new standard that specifies how to use X.25 in LAN stations and IWUs for inter- and intra-networking. Implementation of this standard will enable X.25-LAN gateways from different vendors to communicate with each other and with X.25 DTEs (data terminal equipment devices) attached to the LAN or to a PSDN.

Connectionless internetworking offers versatility, efficiency, flexible topologies, load sharing, resistance to failure, and administrative manageability, as spelled out in Piscitello. Originally, connectionless designs for internetworking were the province of proprietary architectures, such as Xerox Network Systems and Digital Equipment

Two internetworking alternatives

An earlier article ("Of local networks, protocols, and the OSI reference model," DATA COMMUNICATIONS, November 1984, p. 129—hereafter referenced as the Burg article) evaluated two alternatives for LAN architecture spanning OSI Layers 1 to 4. Alternative A involved the use of X.25 PLP (packet-layer protocol) and TP 1 (Transport Protocol Class 1) to provide the CONS (connection-oriented Network service); alternative B used the CLNP (connectionless Network protocol) and TP 4 to provide the CLNS (connectionless Network service). The article's conclusion was that alternative A was unquestionably more efficient, simpler, and less costly than alternative B.

A later article ("Internetworking in an OSI environment," DATA COMMUNICATIONS, May 1986, p. 118) examined applications for both connection-oriented and connectionless internetworking, but did not address the X.25 PLP versus CLNP issue. How does a network manager decide which protocol to use in LAN stations to be internetworked?

There is no universal choice. To re-evaluate these two internetworking alternatives, we shall make the following assumptions for alternative A:

A1. The LAN station operates TP 1, X.25 PLP (as per ISO 8881), and LLC (logical link control) 1 for intra- and internetworking.

A2. The LAN side of the IWU (internetworking unit) operates X.25 PLP (as per ISO 8881) over LLC 1. (Several countries believe that LLC 2 should be used instead.) The other subnetwork side operates X.25 PLP (as per ISO 8208) over the Data Link protocol of the subnetwork accessed.

Assumptions for alternative B:

B1. For intra-LAN communications, either the full CLNP or its inactive subset, INLP (inactive Network Layer protocol), may be used over LLC 1. The inactive subset is actually the absence of a Network Layer protocol and is so indicated by a header of one octet of zeros. The Network Layer entity associated with INLP passes service primitives (data and address parameters—a primitive is a description of an interlayer exchange in OSI) to and from the Transport Layer to the Data Link Layer. It translates NSAPs (Network service access points) to logical-link-control/medium-access-control addresses. The source LAN station must know whether the destination station supports INLP in order to make the correct choice of Network Layer protocol.

B2. For off-network communications, CLNP operates over one of three subnetwork dependent convergent functions. The first two are defined in ISO 8473/AD1; the third is a candidate to be added to it: over LLC 1 (ISO 8802/2) in LAN stations, over X.25 PLP (ISO 8208) in IWUs that employ the X.25 PLP for subnetwork access, and over an HDLC-based point-to-point link in an IWU. (HDLC is the ISO's high-level data link control.)

The functions common to intra-LAN and internetworked LAN communications include Network service access point identification, end-to-end flow control, error detection and recovery, and segmentation and reassembly. These were described and the various alternatives compared in the Burg article cited above.

■ *NSAP identification.* The Burg article claims the inactive CLNP subset cannot convey NSAP addresses. That is not the case. For intra-LAN communications, the INLP maps NSAP addresses in the unitdata (a single, self-contained "packet") primitives to and from LLC and medium access control addresses of LAN stations. The domain identifier portion of the NSAP could use the same numbering plan for all LAN stations. (The domain is the subnetwork where the NSAP exists.) This could be X.121—for PSDN (packet-switched data network) internetworking—or a locally administered plan. The domain-specific part would contain the 48-bit MAC address.

In the internetworking case, the CLNP as well as the X.25 PLP convey the NSAP in their headers. With X.25 PLP, the NSAP is completely contained in the address-extension user facility of Call Request and Incoming Call packets. With CLNP, the NSAP is contained in the address field of the CLNP header.

■ *End-to-end flow control and congestion.* In alternative A, flow control is hop-by-hop (per subnetwork, not end-to-end) in LAN stations and IWUs. X.25 PLP, RNR/RR (receive not ready/receive ready) packets, and window rotation is used across each hop in the network. (TP 1 does not provide flow control). Alternative B flow control is via TP 4 in end systems (seven-layer configurations). In addition, CLNP's "congestion-experienced" bit can help defuse any local congestion before Network protocol data units (NPDUs) are discarded in the network.

Because X.25 packet layer flow control is not end-to-end, backpressure techniques (one node's buffer starts to fill, and then the next node is flow-controlled) must be performed by all IWUs and packet-switching nodes to simulate end-to-end flow control. Backpressure flow control must be fast—fast enough to avoid congestion—on an end-to-end basis. Congestion causes packets to be discarded by the network. Subsequent packets would arrive out of sequence, and virtual circuits would be reset, forcing the Transport protocol to resynchronize—to determine the last TPDU (transport protocol data unit) acknowledged—and to retransmit the lost packets (which are TPDUs to the Transport protocol).

The complexity of implementing flow control is also an issue in alternative A. The IWU designer must account for the amount of buffer space required, whether to use static or dynamic allocation of buffers, and must select one or more "high-water marks" to trigger backpressure flow control. If one or more wide-area networks are not X.25 PSDNs, then X.25 packet-layer flow control must be mapped onto the flow control techniques (if any) used on the former network(s). This would require a new *ad hoc* convergence protocol for each such wide-area network transited, and further complicates the IWU.

In alternative B, TP 4 provides end-to-end flow control, which only involves the end systems. This method not only is faster than backpressure flow control but also simplifies the IWUs. Flow control TPDUs between end systems pass transparently over all underlying subnetworks and IWUs. The TP 4 window size can be altered dynamically by means of a credit mechanism (see "A primer: Understanding transport protocols," DATA COMMUNICATIONS, November 1984, p. 201). This mechanism allows more or fewer TPDUs to be outstanding in accordance with receiver capability (X.25 PLP has a fixed window size).

■ *Error detection and recovery.* Alternative A uses the X.25 packet layer and TP 1 to recover from lost packets. Alternative B uses TP 4 for end-to-end error detection and recovery and a CLNP checksum (a numerical error-detection mechanism) in its header. The trade-off here is error-recovery time versus end-to-end reliability. TP 4 end-to-end error recovery will generally take longer than X.25's hop-by-hop. TP 4 uses a no-acknowledgment timer with a time-out value that must be large enough to accommodate two end-to-end propagation delays (one for sending the data and the other for receiving the acknowledgment) over the longest possible path between end stations. X.25 PLP only has to recover over a single hop by sending a DTE-REJECT packet (requesting a retransmission) or a RESET REQUEST (initializing the data transfer state of the virtual circuit).

There is an optional retransmission timer in ISO 8881. If the timer expires, the unacknowledged data packets are resent. TP 1 does not directly recover from lost data, but will resynchronize (upon receipt of a Network Layer reset indication primitive) and resend TPDUs lost during the X.25 packet layer reset procedure.

Reliability depends on the residual error rate (the number of undetected errors) of a given network. With alternative A, there are two instances where the residual error rate might be unacceptable:

1. When the error recovery options chosen are different among communicating LAN stations or the IWU. (A concern expressed in IEEE 802.1 is that—depending on the options selected in ISO 8881 by communicating X.25 PLP entities—error detection and recovery by X.25 PLP may be unreliable).

2. When one or more intermediate subnetworks in an internetwork configuration offer unreliable service, even after hop-by-hop enhancement.

In each of these cases, the Network service is unreliable, and TP 1 is not sufficient to provide a reliable Transport service.

Alternative B assumes an unreliable end-to-end Network service; it employs TP 4 to provide a reliable Transport service. TP 4 is the only TP class that ISO specifies for use on networks where the residual error rate is unacceptable. The ISO Transport service (ISO 8072) states that, for non-negligible residual error rates, TP 4 is necessary for reliable end-to-end data transfer.

There is no appreciable difference in the processing complexity and overhead associated with error detection and recovery for these two alternatives. TP 4 error detection and recovery processing is equivalent to that used in X.25 PLP plus TP 1. Both TP 4 and X.25 PLP use sequence-number detection and retransmission after time-outs to recover from lost or duplicated data. (X.25 PLP can also use the D bit—which confirms delivery—to request an end-to-end acknowledgement of data packets). TP 4 has an optional checksum (seldom used) for end-to-end error detection, while X.25 PLP relies on Data Link-provided error detection. In either case, data received in error is discarded.

■ *Segmentation and reassembly.* In alternative B, this can be done in CLNP or in TP 4. The CLNP can segment and reassemble Network service data units to conform to the user-data field size of the underlying subnetwork. The CLNP can then assign segments to different subnetworks, which will be reassembled at the destination (see the "What is load splitting?" panel—p. 135—in "Internetworking in an OSI environment," DATA COMMUNICATIONS, May 1986, p. 118). TP 4 can block and segment Transport service data units (TSDUs) into TPDUs, which are then sent and received over the same or different Network Layer entities with a marker indicating the last TPDU in the Transport service data unit.

In alternative A, X.25 PLP or TP 1 can handle segmentation and reassembly. However, X.25 PLP segmentation (using the M bit to indicate the presence of one or more data packets in the sequence) must be over the same subnetwork. Therefore, alternative B provides more flexibility for this function. Such flexibility is very important in applications where stations are moved; where topologies, network tariffs, or traffic patterns change; and where it is undesirable to provide every network node with global knowledge of the network.

When internetworking in an environment where the majority of end systems are X.25 DTEs (data terminal equipment devices) or devices attached to PADs (packet assembler/disassemblers), alternative A is preferred. X.25 PLP and TP 1 can be used in LAN stations without any loss of functionality for intraLAN communications. Reliability prevails as long as communicating X.25 packet layer entities on the LAN implement the same error recovery options in ISO 8881—otherwise, TP 4 would be required.

Alternative A is also the better choice when LAN stations are constrained to: support a single Network Layer protocol for both intra- and internetworking; provide a reliable Network service (some European networks would like to use TP 0 for teletex and electronic mail over X.25 PSDNs—this is possible only if the Network service is reliable); use the receipt-confirmation service (via the X.25 PLP D bit) for confirmed Network Layer data transfer; or negotiate packet size, window size, and throughput class (the actual end-to-end data rate, in bit/s) at the Network Layer for better resource management over a private network.

If most subnetworks are not X.25 PSDNs, or if the application is inquiry/response, or it requires a rapid response time, then alternative B should be used. CLNP IWUs do not have to maintain state information on virtual circuits (there are no virtual circuits with CLNP), need not allocate data buffers for NPDU retransmissions (TP 4 in end systems handles retransmissions of TPDUs), and are not responsible for TP 4 flow control.

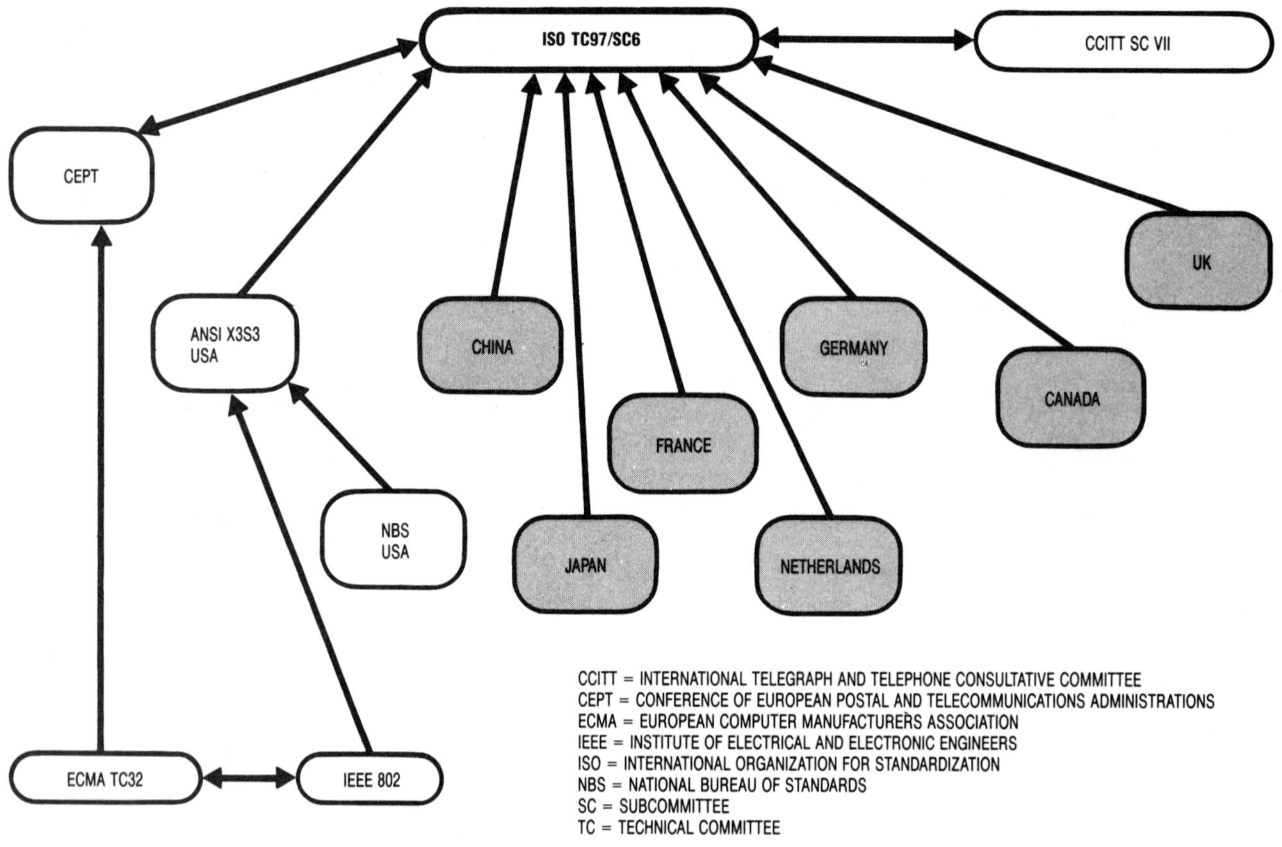

Corp.'s DecNet. The approach was adopted by Arpanet in TCP/IP (Transmission Control Protocol/Internet Protocol), and is used in many networks derived from this technology (see "Two internetworking alternatives").

The connectionless approach is embodied in the ISO 8473 CLNP standard. It is used in MAP (Manufacturing Automation Protocol) and TOP (Technical and Office Protocols) specifications, and was demonstrated by 23 vendors at the Autofact trade show in Detroit in November 1985. An addendum to ISO 8473 specifies its use over LANs and PSDNs. Continuing efforts are under way to detail operation for its use over various other physical networks. CLNP provides the OSI Transport Layer with connectionless Network service (CLNS) as specified in ISO 8348/AD1 (addendum 1).

Resolving technology differences

Internetworking issues dominate design in the OSI reference model's Network Layer. This layer plays a key role because it must resolve the disparities among diverse transmission technologies and network types. These vary dramatically in, for example, the type of service they provide, delay characteristics, reliability, throughput capacity, and geographical coverage.But a uniform image must be presented to the Network Layer's user—the Transport Layer. This image is presented by the Network Layer service providing an end-to-end communications path over any one medium or over combinations of media.

To meet demands on it, the Network Layer has a "rich" internal structure. Most of the intricacy deals with internetworking issues: how to combine subnetworks of similar or dissimilar transmission technologies into an overall network that provides a uniform communications service to its users.

In the Piscitello article, two different approaches to Network Layer design were described. The connection mode works like a telephone call: An end-to-end connection is established for the duration of a session. In the connectionless mode, individual blocks of data (datagrams) are treated independently: Each datagram is routed through the network without the need for permanent end-to-end connections in the Network Layer.

Many applications require sessions that have specific durations. When the Network Layer is connectionless, the notion of a connection can be implemented in the next (Transport) layer, along with such features as end-to-end recovery and flow control. This arrangement conveniently separates the connection-oriented from the connectionless issues, placing the former in the Transport Layer and the latter in the Network Layer.

The debate on whether to use a connectionless- or connection-mode Network Layer will probably go on indefinitely. Different suppliers will be providing capabilities of both types.

The ISO, the formal "arena" for the Network-Layer debate, has representation from various countries, as shown in Figure 1. The organization representing U. S. interests is the American National Standards Institute (ANSI). Ideas that originate within ANSI and in the other national delegations—and those from the IEEE 802 committee via ANSI on LAN-related standards—can advance into the international arena. The concepts that are advanced originate with technical-industry personnel who comprise the standards committees. (Refer to the "Glossary" for some of the standards-related terminology used in this article.)

Internetworking activity

The IEEE 802.1 committee is preparing several standards that will specify LAN interconnections using a single medium-access control (MAC) bridge for LAN-to-LAN communications, a MAC sublayer service common to all LANs, and two types of Network Layer routers for the more general case of LAN-to-any-subnetwork communications. The router document will specify OSI Layers 1 through 3 IWU protocols and Layers 1 through 4 protocols for LAN stations involved in internetworking. It will reference ISO standards at each layer, rather than create new protocols. Three LAN interconnection topologies—called reference configurations—are considered. The X.25 PLP will be the Network Layer protocol used to provide the connection-oriented Network service (CONS), while the connectionless Network protocol (CLNP) will provide the connectionless Network service (CLNS). The three reference configurations are LAN-to-LAN, LAN-to-X.25 wide area network (WAN), and LAN-to-X.25 WAN-to-LAN.

IEEE 802.1 has developed an Internetworking Functional Requirements document to serve as a framework for internetworking. Part of the document identifies what IEEE 802.1 considers the major internetworking functions that have to be performed:

■ *Addressing*—generically, providing the ability to uniquely identify a destination and source LAN/WAN station by a network service access point (NSAP)—the Network Layer address—and/or MAC address.

■ *Buffering*—particularly when stations on dissimilar LANs are communicating directly (or via a WAN) with each other and throughput rates vary significantly.

■ *Error handling*—related to the Data Link and Transport Layers and the separation of functions between LAN stations and IWUs. It includes the ability to control the retransmission of data not correctly received at the designated LAN station. A connection-oriented Transport Layer is assumed.

■ *Flow control*—related to the Data Link, Network, and Transport Layers and the separation of functions between LAN stations and IWUs. It is the ability to prevent overrunning a receiver's buffering capabilities.

■ *Routing*—the selection of an appropriate path or set of paths to transmit data so that a destination station may be reached.

■ *Protocol conversion*—the mapping of elements of one protocol onto another when the two offer similar services, but are dissimilar in protocol composition.

■ *Segmentation and reassembly*—specifically, the ability to resolve a data unit (such as a packet) size disparity between subnetworks. The method includes dividing, at a transmitter LAN station or an IWU, the larger data unit into smaller units that can be managed by the subnetwork, then recombining the smaller data units into the original larger data unit at the receiver.

■ *Congestion control*—or the ability to respond to an overloaded condition within a network. It is usually accommodated by detecting a potential overload and routing around it. If that is insufficient, some data (usually of a low priority) is discarded to free resources for other (higher-priority) data. This is done only as a last resort and should be an exception condition in a properly designed network.

Another part of the Internetworking Functional Requirements document provides illustrations of the three reference topologies: LAN to LAN, LAN to X.25-based WAN, LAN to X.25-based WAN to LAN.

For LAN stations, there are two prime candidate solutions for these topologies:

1. Use of Transport Protocol Class 4, operating over the ISO CLNP, which operates over LLC 1 (logical link control 1—see Piscitello, pp. 125 and 126). This provides a connectionless Network service as well as a connection-oriented Transport service.

2. Use of a Transport Protocol (class to be determined), operating over the X.25 PLP, which operates over LLC 1 or LLC 2. This provides a connection-oriented Network service as well as a connection-oriented Transport service.

For IWUs, there are two three-layer protocol "stacks" for

Glossary

AD	Addendum
CLNP	Connectionless Network protocol (8373)
CLNS	Connectionless Network service (8348/AD1)
CONS	Connection-oriented Network service (8348)
COS	Corporation for Open Systems
INLP	Inactive Network Layer protocol
ISO	International Organization for Standardization
IWU	Internetworking unit (gateway)
LAN	Local area network
LLC	Logical link control (8802/2)
LLP	Lower layer protocol
MAC	Medium access control (8802/3, /4, /5, /6)
MAP	Manufacturing Automation Protocol
NPDU	Network protocol data unit
NSAP	Network service access point
NSDU	Network service data unit
OSI	Open Systems Interconnection
PAD	Packet assembler/disassembler
PLP	Packet layer protocol (8208)
PSDN	Packet-switched data network
SC	Subcommittee
SNDCF	Subnetwork dependent conversion function
TOP	Technical and Office Protocols
TG	Task Group
TP	Transport protocol (8073, 8062)
TPDU	Transport protocol data unit
TSDU	Transport service data unit
ULP	Upper layer protocol
WAN	Wide area network
WG	Working Group

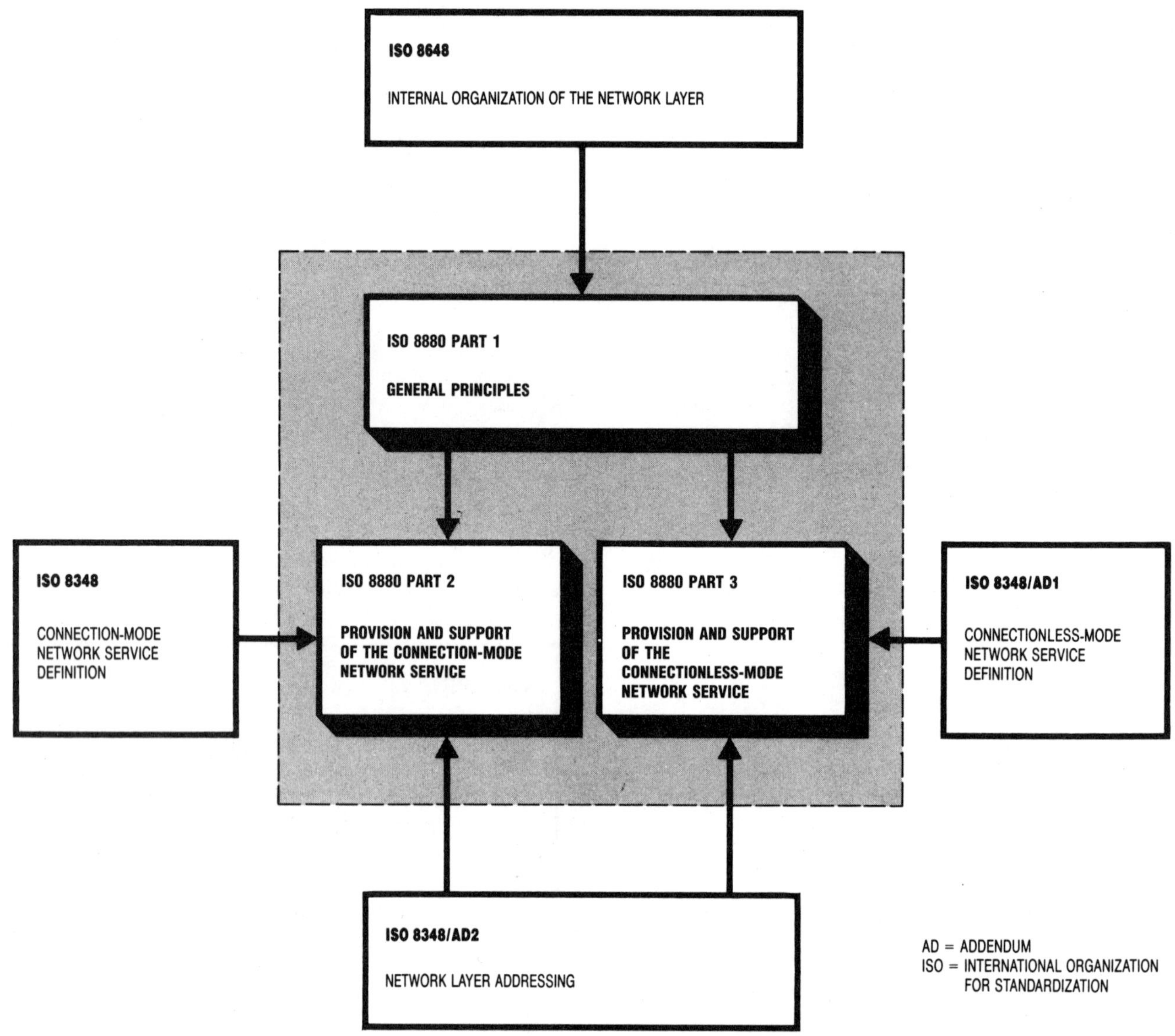

2. Standard using standards. *Shown is how the parts of ISO 8880 relate with the OSI Network service. The ISO 8880 standard specifies how to realize the Network service—using other standards—over a variety of subnetworks and topologies. Implementers of OSI end systems and inter-networking units are guided by these relationships.*

each solution—one for the LAN interface, the other for the subnetwork to be connected. The LAN interface stack is identical to the first three layers of 1 above for CLNS and to 2 above for CONS. The subnetwork stack consists of LAN or X.25 WAN protocols, as appropriate.

Making order is not easy

Since the Network Layer is structurally rich, the standards involved are diverse and scattered. An implementer endeavoring to combine a set of specifications in one of the acceptable ways is faced with a daunting bibliographic quest.

Recognizing the need to facilitate the consistent use of the CLNP and the X.25 PLP over real networks (packet- and circuit-switched networks, LANs, and point-to-point links), ISO SC6/WG2 is developing a new standard which is a "road map" of existing and proposed Network Layer standards, ISO Draft Proposal 8880. This "Specification of Protocols to Provide and Support the OSI NS [Network service]" consists of three parts. Part 1 is on general principles and conformance; part 2 is for CONS via X.25 PLP; part 3 is for CLNS via CLNP (over any subnetwork).

The relationship of the parts of ISO 8880 with the OSI Network service is shown in Figure 2. The ISO 8880 standard specifies how to realize the Network service, using other standards, over a variety of subnetworks and topologies. Such a guide is very much needed by OSI implementers of end systems (seven-layer configurations) and IWUs.

The CONS is specified in ISO 8348; the CLNS, in 8348/AD1. ISO 8648 specifies the internal organization of the Network Layer, segmenting the Layer into three sublayers. It also describes three approaches to internetworking (see "The status and direction of open systems interconnection,"

582

3. ISO 8880/2. *Connection-oriented network service can be provided over various subnetwork types — including local area networks — using the X.25 Packet Layer protocol.*

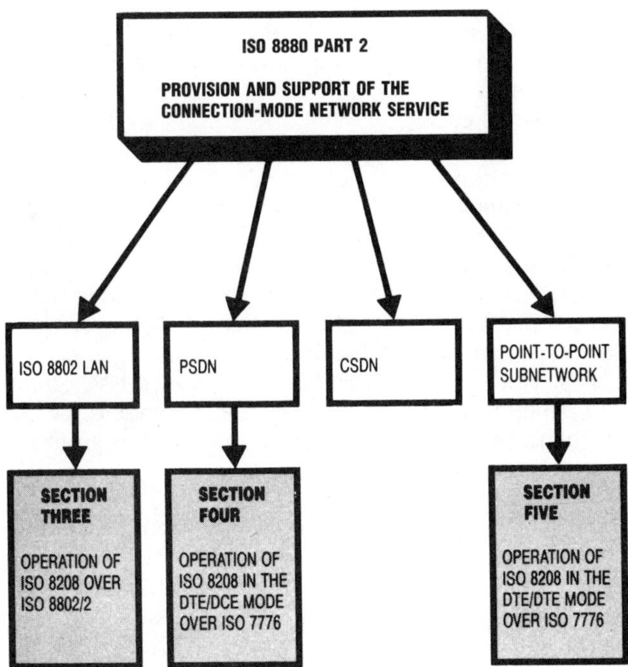

CSDN = CIRCUIT-SWITCHED DATA NETWORK
DCE = DATA CIRCUIT-TERMINATING EQUIPMENT
DTE = DATA TERMINAL EQUIPMENT
ISO = INTERNATIONAL ORGANIZATION FOR STANDARDIZATION
LAN = LOCAL AREA NETWORK
PSDN = PACKET-SWITCHED DATA NETWORK

DATA COMMUNICATIONS, February 1985, p. 177, and the Piscitello article).

The CONS can be provided over various types of sub-networks using the X.25 PLP. Its operation over diverse media is described in ISO 8880/2. Figure 3 illustrates the relationships among the standards involved. For example, an application of the ISO 8208 standard (X.25 PLP for DTEs), ISO 8881, describes how to operate the X.25 PLP over a LAN. Using this method, existing X.25 DTEs attached to a PSDN could operate with LAN stations employing the X.25 PLP. Moreover, X.25 DTEs can be connected to the LAN (through an IWU) without any modification to their hardware or software.

Connectionless operation

The CLNS and its provision by the CLNP over LANs, packet- and circuit-switched data networks, and point-to-point links are of prime concern when internetworking (Fig. 4). As ISO 8880/3 states, CLNP operation over ISO 8802-based LANs and X.25 PSDNs is specified in 8473/AD1 (discussed later). Techniques for CLNS operation over circuit-switched data networks and point-to-point links are not yet standardized, but they are referenced in 8880/3. The choice of HDLC (high-level data link control) procedures for these configurations is currently being investigated (discussed later).

The X.25 PLP provides the following important functions

as the Network Layer protocol in a LAN station:
■ *Addressing* (specific to X.25 PLP), the ability to carry NSAPs in its address fields.
■ *Virtual circuit multiplexing,* for a LAN station that supports multiple data streams, such as a PAD.
■ *Connection setup and release,* for sequenced transfer of data packets.
■ *Segmenting and reassembly,* to divide a data unit into smaller packets, for transfer over a LAN, and to reassemble it into the original data unit.
■ *Explicit flow control,* to prevent receive-buffer overrun and resultant loss of data.
■ *Transfer of expedited data,* to transfer up to 32 octets of high-priority data in an "interrupt" packet, which is not subject to flow control procedures.
■ *Error control,* to detect — and optionally recover from — errors at the packet layer.
■ *Reset,* for procedural-error recovery.
■ *Q-bit* (qualifies a packet as user data for a terminal or as control information for a PAD), for PAD operation, which could support asynchronous, bisynchronous, or synchronous data link control terminals.
■ *Provision of OSI CONS,* for internetworking with other OSI subnetworks.

Why not use CCITT X.25 PLP on a LAN? The need for ISO 8881 arises because CCITT X.25 PLP does not apply to LANs. CCITT X.25 was designed for DTE-to-PSDN operation. It describes the interface almost entirely from the network's viewpoint and leaves open many issues the X.25

---

4. No connection. *ISO 8880/3 is the guide to connectionless Network service and its provision by the connectionless Network protocol for various subnetworks.*

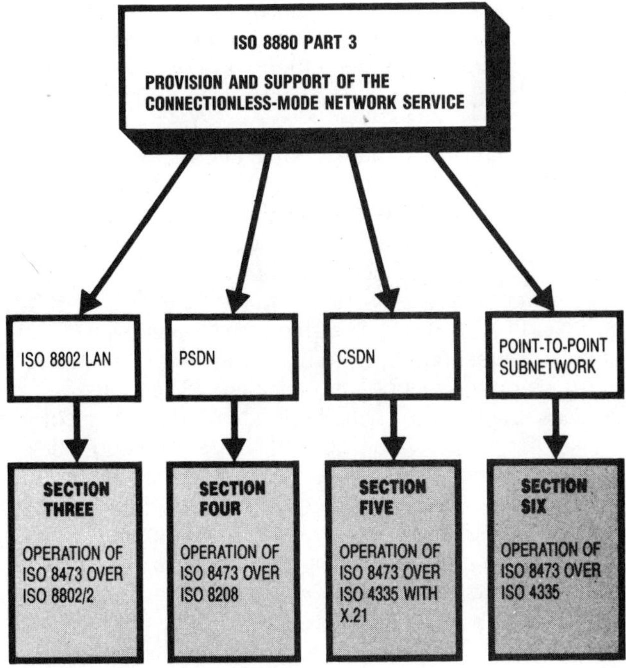

CSDN = CIRCUIT-SWITCHED DATA NETWORK
ISO = INTERNATIONAL ORGANIZATION FOR STANDARDIZATION
LAN = LOCAL AREA NETWORK
PSDN = PACKET-SWITCHED DATA NETWORK

DTE must take into account. These issues include DTE timers, cause and diagnostic codes, and DTE state transitions—for which ISO 8208 (discussed later) was developed. Moreover, there are special considerations needed for the LAN environment. In particular, the CCITT X.25 PLP assumes the following:

■ Asymmetric DTE-to-DCE (data circuit-terminating equipment) procedures. (LAN stations operate in a symmetrical DTE-to-DTE mode.)

■ X.25 LAPB (link access procedure balanced) for Layer 2, which provides a reliable, connection-oriented Data Link Layer service. (Most LAN stations will implement LLC 1, which has no error recovery capability or indication of a Data Link Layer connection.)

■ Packet-layer error recovery by means of DTE-Reject and Reset packets. (Because LLC 1 does not recover from lost data, LAN stations may require data packet retransmission after a time-out, and may want to wait until the packet is sent again when a data packet arrives out of sequence.)

■ One X.25 PLP entity associated with each DTE-to-DCE interface. (LAN stations require one X.25 PLP entity for each destination station or IWU with which they communicate.) Optional user facilities, logical channel numbering, X.25 PLP states—such as call setup, data transfer, and reset—and Diagnostic and Restart packets are applicable to the entire X.25 interface, and therefore require separate X.25 PLP entities for each logical link. (The optional user facilities include packet size, flow-control window size, and reverse-charging. All are attributes of a virtual call.)

■ A logical channel-numbering scheme for virtual circuits based on a DTE-to-DCE point-to-point link. (A LAN is a broadcast medium requiring source- and destination-station addresses for transmissions. Each source-to-destination pairing constitutes a logical link that the stations use for peer-to-peer communications.)

■ X.25 virtual circuits extend from source to destination DTEs, as conveyed by one or more PSDNs. (To create a true end-to-end virtual circuit connection, a virtual circuit between a LAN station and an IWU must be joined with an IWU-to-destination X.25 DTE virtual circuit. The IWU acts as an X.25 PLP relay, similar to a gateway connecting two PSDNs. Typically, there are many LAN stations needing access to a PSDN through a single IWU. The IWU is analogous to an X.25 concentrator that funnels virtual circuits from many LAN stations to the PSDN.)

■ All CCITT X.25 PLP facilities are administered by a PSDN at a single user-network interface. (LAN stations need to administer performance- and resource-related user facilities themselves. These facilities include fast select, packet and window [flow control] size, and throughput class [actual end-to-end data rate in bit/s], and leave global user facilities—such as closed user groups, hunt groups, reverse charging, and network-user I.D.s—to the IWU to administer for all internetworking LAN stations. [Fast select is the ability to send up to 128 octets of data in call setup and clearing packets.])

Providing guidelines

ISO 8881 details how to use the X.25 PLP on a LAN in both LAN stations and IWUs. It is based on ISO 8208 X.25 DTE-to-X.25 DTE operation. One section of 8881 provides guidelines for the LAN-to-WAN relay function needed in an X.25 IWU. Another section discusses alternative restart and clear procedures, to take advantage of the broadcasting capability of a LAN.

LAN stations must use one of two logical link control procedures: LLC 1 or LLC 2. Which should be used as the Data Link Layer below the X.25 PLP?

The X.25 PLP will always work with LLC 2 because the latter provides acknowledgments of Information frames. It will operate effectively with LLC 1 (unacknowledged, connectionless Data Link service) as long as the LAN exhibits acceptable rates of the following: undetected bit errors, packet losses, duplication, and missequencing. In that case, the X.25 PLP error recovery procedures can provide a reliable connection-oriented Network service.

ISO 8881 consists of two parts: one for LLC 2 operation, the other for LLC 1. With LLC 2, inactive links (those not carrying virtual circuits) are disconnected to better utilize LAN station resources. This results in improved efficiency and performance. With LLC 1 operation, no additional mechanisms are required for managing the logical links.

Operation on a LAN

ISO 8881 is actually a specialized version of the X.25 PLP DTE-to-DTE procedures outlined in ISO 8208. The main body of 8881 deals with considerations for using the X.25 PLP on a LAN: between LAN stations or between a LAN station and an IWU. The aspects of packet-layer operation influenced by the LAN environment are detailed in 8881:

■ *Logical channel number management and assignment.* The task of two stations agreeing to the ranges of logical channels available to them as communicating LAN stations (or LAN station and IWU) is difficult, because each station has its own set of requirements regarding the number of simultaneous virtual circuits it can accommodate.

5. Relationships. Each logical link in a LAN station supports a different X.25 PLP entity. Each entity, in turn, has its own set of logical channels to manage.

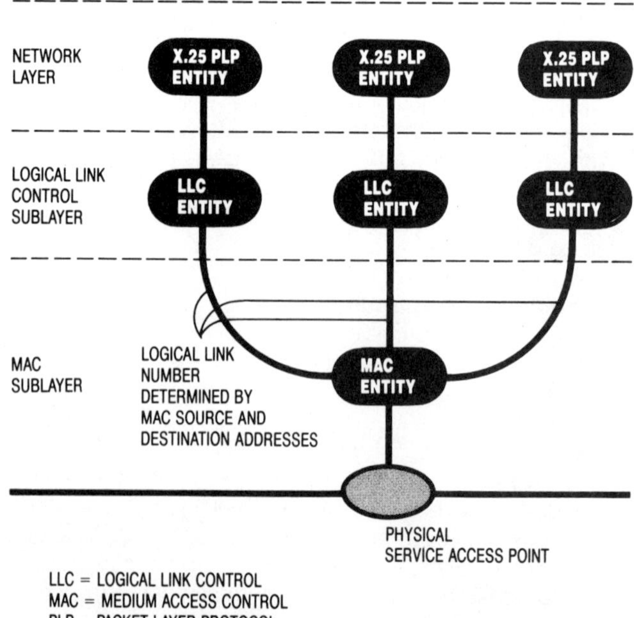

Each logical link in a LAN station supports a different X.25 PLP entity (Fig. 5). Each X.25 PLP entity, in turn, has its own set of logical channels to manage. The large number (realistically 25 to 50) of possible logical channels could tax the resources of a LAN station. If incapable of accepting an incoming-call packet due to lack of logical channel resources, the station should clear the call with a DTE-originated cause code (clearing by DTE rather than by the network) and a diagnostic code indicating "DTE resource constraint."

Two methods are possible for logical channel assignments: 1) One DTE assumes the role of a DCE. (As defined in CCITT X.25, the DCE starts allocation from the lower range of permissible logical channel numbers, the DTE from the higher range.) 2) Use reference numbers that recognize the paired source and destination nature of X.25 packet layer entities on a LAN by allocating a logical channel number for each one (ISO 8208/AD1). The source reference number is chosen by the calling DTE when transmitting a call-request packet. The destination reference number is chosen by the called DTE when transmitting a call-accepted packet.

■ *Network parameters.* While the function of timers and retransmission counters are defined in ISO 8208, the default values for the LAN environment are given in ISO 8881 tables. Of particular interest are the window rotation timer (incrementing of modulo 8 or 128—labeled T25) and data packet retransmission count (R25). These are used to recover from lost data packets and/or lost acknowledgments in a DTE-to-DTE environment. When using LLC 1 (which has no error recovery capability), setting R25 2 (retransmit limit is two) provides a data packet retransmission facility. When the limit is reached, the virtual circuit is reset and the process is repeated. When using LLC 2—which recovers from lost data—R25 should be zero (there is no retransmission of data packets).

■ *Optional user facilities.* A common subset of user facilities should be chosen for all X.25 PLP entities attached to the LAN. In addition, common values of packet size, window size, and throughput class must be agreed upon by each pair of communicating X.25 PLP stations. The maximum packet size will be constrained by the maximum data field of the MAC frame. On-line facility registration (overriding of preset subscribed facilities) can be used to optionally adjust user facilities (except for the reference numbers).

■ *Start-up operation.* A restart procedure is used to determine the DTE/DCE role of each communicating X.25 PLP entity for logical channel allocation and the resolution of virtual-call collisions. Under CCITT X.25, this procedure is not necessary—the roles of the DTE and DCE are fixed. The procedure *is* needed in ISO 8208 for DTE-to-DTE point-to-point communications. Here, a restart request is initiated when the underlying Data Link Layer has established a connection (8208 assumes a connection-oriented Data Link service). When using LLC 1, there is no concept of a Data Link connection, and so another procedure is needed: A count of how many virtual circuits are up is maintained by each LAN station for each X.25 PLP entity with which it will communicate. When the virtual circuit count is zero, the restart request is generated.

■ *Addressing.* X.25 PLP provides for addresses in the address and address-extension fields of call-setup and clearing packets. This results in four possibilities for conveying addressing information: 1) in the address field; 2) in the address extension field; 3) in both fields; 4) no need to carry packet layer addresses.

The addressing method of the LAN determines which of the four methods is used and the contents of the address(es). In order to support the OSI CONS, the network service access point (NSAP) should be entirely contained in the address extension field. The source and destination NSAP would include the numbering plan used and the packet layer, LLC, and MAC addresses.

■ *Operations over LLC 1 using a broadcast capability.* With LLC 1 a packet can be broadcast to more than one destination when reference numbers are used to identify logical channels. The LAN administration defines whether an all-stations or multicast MAC address is used for broadcasting packets to multiple LAN stations. Assume the originator knows the NSAP address—contained in the address extension field—but does not know the MAC (station) address. The LAN station uses the broadcast MAC address to send a call-request packet to multiple destinations. Only one called station will recognize its NSAP and answer the call. Stations receiving such a "global" call-request packet that do not recognize their NSAP will ignore the call. The above function is called a distributed-network directory.

Other packets could also be broadcast. Global restart and clear requests are outlined in Annex B of ISO 8881 (not an integral part of the standard). These specialized packets are used to simultaneously clear all virtual calls for every X.25 PLP DTE-to-DTE interface. The alternative would be to clear all calls on each X.25 PLP DTE-to-DTE interface separately.

■ *X.25 IWU operation.* Annex A of ISO 8881 specifies IWU operation when using the X.25 PLP in LAN stations (Fig. 6). When a LAN station needs to communicate with another station on a subnetwork other than its own, it communicates with the LAN side of the IWU. The IWU relays that communication onto its other subnetwork side. The coupling between these two X.25 PLP entities in the IWU should be of prime concern to X.25-gateway designers.

A new routing scheme
The connectionless Network protocol (CLNP) was extensively described in the Piscitello article. ISO 8473/AD1 is an addendum to the CLNP specification, describing how to operate it over ISO 8802-based LANs and the X.25 PLP. (ISO 8802 is the international designation for IEEE 802.) A new routing protocol to be used in conjunction with 8473 has been circulated for comments, in preparation for draft proposal registration. This protocol permits end systems and intermediate systems (relay systems) to exchange Network Layer configuration and routing information.

It is misleading to hear "Use CLNP over LLC 1" and conclude that this is a complete specification of what an implementer must do. In practice, the situation is far less blissful. When placing an upper-layer protocol (ULP) "on top of" its adjoining lower-layer protocol (LLP), there are many decisions to be made. This was evident for the CONS case above and is equally true in the CLNS case.

The LLP typically contains a variety of features that may

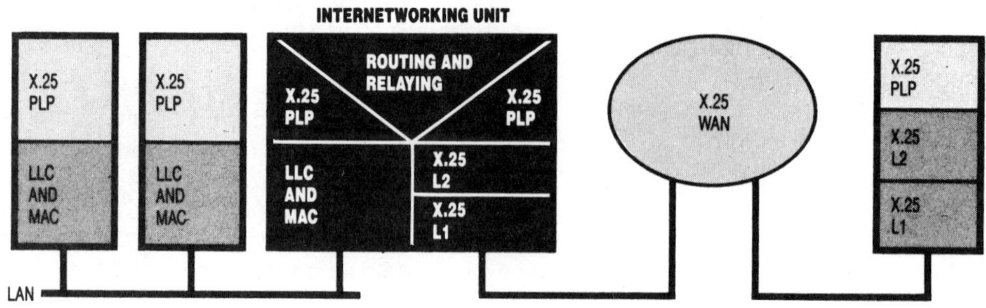

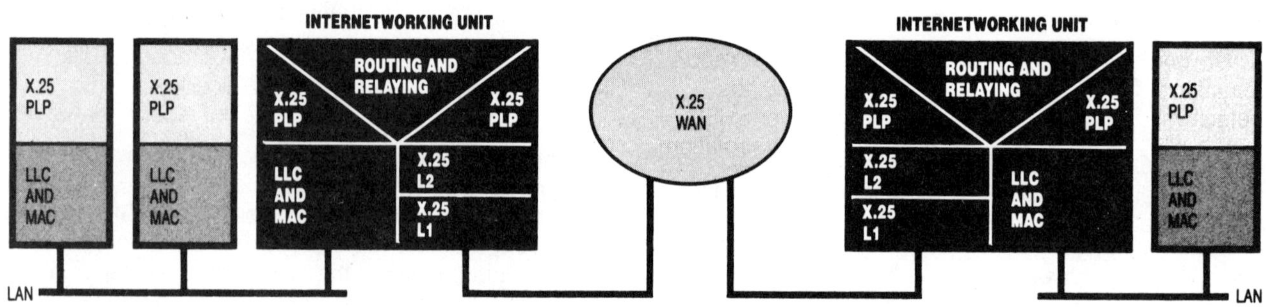

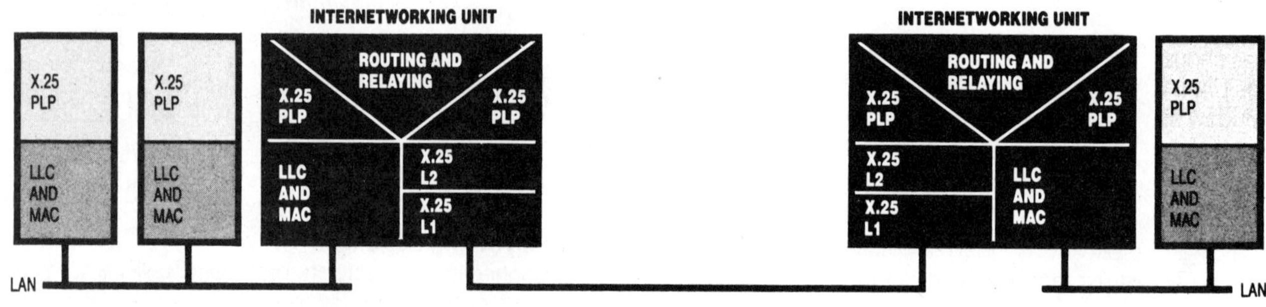

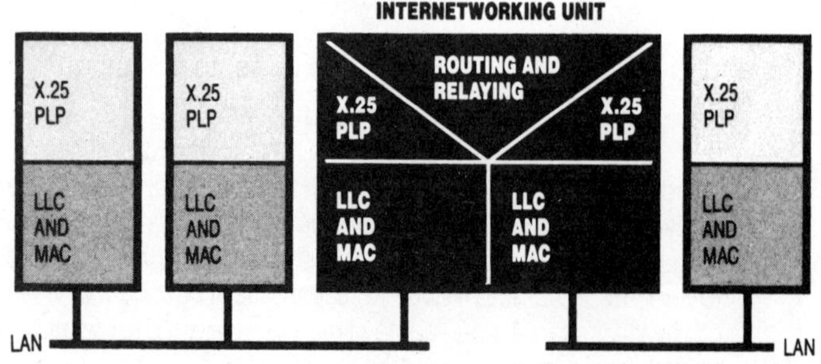

L = LEVEL
LAN = LOCAL AREA NETWORK
LLC = LOGICAL LINK CONTROL
MAC = MEDIUM ACCESS CONTROL
PLP = PACKET LAYER CONTROL
WAN = WIDE-AREA NETWORK

or may not be of use to the ULP being used. The features may include more than one way to accomplish a particular ULP objective. The LLP may have features missing that a particular ULP might need. The specification of how to match the needs of a ULP with the features provided by an LLP is called a convergence function.

In some cases, additional header fields or data interchanges are required at the interface, where the ULP does not provide enough features. In such cases, the convergence function is called a convergence protocol. In simpler cases, a convergence function is a statement of how each ULP requirement matches LLP features. Such a statement is important because, without it, different implementers *could* make different decisions, and their products would not intercommunicate properly.

The unitdata primitive

The CLNP is defined with respect to an underlying connectionless subnetwork service that it expects from below. This subnetwork service consists of a single subnetwork unitdata primitive. (A unitdata is a single, self-contained "packet," analogous to a datagram. A primitive is a description of an interlayer exchange in OSI.) A unitdata request is sent, and a unitdata indication is received. Parameters in this primitive convey the source and destination subnetwork addresses, subnetwork quality of service (detailed later), and user data. The ability to carry at least 512 octets of user data (which is the maximum size of a CLNP-protocol data unit) is assumed.

The connectionless subnetwork service consists of two subnetwork primitives—unitdata request and unitdata indication—and four subnetwork parameters. Each primitive consists of all four of the parameters: destination address, source address, quality of service, and user data.

If the underlying subnetwork does not support connectionless subnetwork service, a subnetwork-dependent convergence function (SNDCF) is needed to map the above primitives and parameters into the appropriate primitives and parameters used by the subnetwork access protocol. When appropriate, the SNDCF specifies how to use the underlying subnetwork protocol in order to work with the CLNP. This is particularly the case for CLNP operation over X.25 PLP. ISO 8473/AD1 specifies the SNDCFs for X.25 PLP and ISO 8802/2-based LANs. The CLNP would operate over the connectionless LLC on a LAN and over the X.25 PLP in an X.25 WAN.

(The convergence function for CLNP over LLC 1 in a LAN station and CLNP over X.25 PLP in an IWU was successfully demonstrated by 23 vendors at the Autofact show in November 1985.)

Connectionless logical link control

The subnetwork service required by the CLNP is precisely that offered by the unacknowledged connectionless service described in ISO 8802/2, with the exception of quality of service.

As described earlier, ISO 8802/2 specifies two classes of logical link control (LLC). LLC Class 1 provides an unacknowledged connectionless service only and should be used to provide the subnetwork service required by ISO 8473. There is a one-to-one mapping of unitdata primitives between CLNP and the connectionless LLC. A 512-octet CLNP data unit must be accommodated in the information field of an unnumbered-information frame for the connectionless LLC.

When CLNP is resident in a LAN station, an X.25 gateway (IWU) uses the CLNP on top of X.25 PLP to access the PSDN. An SNDCF between CLNP and the X.25 PLP must guarantee that an X.25 virtual circuit is made available for the transmission of subnetwork user data following the generation of a subnetwork unitdata request by the CLNP. If a suitable virtual circuit is available, it can be used to carry the subnetwork user data. If not, a new virtual circuit must be created.

The mechanism and timing for creating a virtual circuit is left to the implementer. Strategies include creating one virtual circuit for all LAN stations wishing to access a port on the PSDN, creating several virtual circuits, or using fast select. When a new virtual circuit must be made available, the calling SNDCF performs all X.25 PLP functions associated with establishing a virtual circuit.

Similarly, the clearing of a virtual circuit following the transmission of subnetwork user data is done by the SNDCF, at the prerogative of the implementer. Again, there are many choices possible—such as a no-activity timer that clears the circuit when the time expires.

It is not a requirement that virtual circuits be dynamically created or cleared for the correct operation of the SNDCF. The use of permanent virtual circuits or the maintenance of switched virtual circuits in an available state (from initialization) is also acceptable.

Service quality

The originator-requested quality of service is carried in the CLNP and used along with the address to determine a route for each unitdata-protocol data unit when multiple routes are possible. The routing function in this case is not included in the CLNP. (The CLNP by itself includes a source routing capability where each intermediate destination is specified.) The quality of service appears as a parameter in the unitdata primitive. For each parameter, the SNDCF must be able to obtain information about the service quality that can be expected from the underlying subnetworks.

There are five of these parameters for the connectionless-mode subnetwork service: transit delay, protection against unauthorized access, cost determinants, priority, and residual error probability. The parameters may be mapped onto (or from) the quality of service parameters in the X.25 PLP call request, incoming call, and call confirmation packets.

It was noted earlier that ISO 8880/3 (protocols to provide and support the OSI connectionless Network service) describes how to provide the CLNS using the CLNP over real networks (ISO 8802 LAN, packet- and circuit-switched networks, and point-to-point links). 8880/3 states that data link procedures from HDLC must be defined for CLNP operation over circuit-switched and point-to-point links. In many countries (the United States is one), depending on the application, circuit-switched and dedicated point-to-point links are quite economical, making them a desirable medium for carrying CLNP data units. Those links are also transparent to the actual data transferred, so no additional overhead (such as packet headers) is imposed.

Therefore, an urgent need exists to define point-to-point data link protocols — based on HDLC — for use with CLNP. (One possibility is to use either unnumbered-information frames or X.25 LAPB.) The associated SNDCFs must also be defined. Since HDLC is a catalog of functions (framing, classes of procedures, elements of procedures), one needs to select particular HDLC attributes in order to build a data link protocol. The authors have proposed two such data link protocols and the related SNDCFs, which are being evaluated by the ISO.

The two new data link protocols are identified as Class I and Class II. Class I provides a connectionless data link service; Class II is connection-oriented, with explicit link setup and disconnect states. This is analogous to the ISO 8802/2 logical-link-control procedures.

Both classes are compatible with the HDLC frame format (ISO 3303) with 16-bit CRC (cyclic redundancy check) error detection and are compatible with the OSI Data Link service definition (IS0 8886). A two-octet address identifies source and destination higher-layer entities. Both classes may be used for two-way simultaneous operation on a single link or in a multilink environment (ISO 7478.2 specifies the HDLC multilink procedures). The multilink might be useful for speed matching, load balancing, and/or graceful degradation (reduced capacity) when interconnecting two LANS or other networks.

Class I protocol is connectionless. There are no link setup or disconnect frames exchanged. Instead, Data Link service data units are transparently carried in the information field of unnumbered-information frames. Management-service data units are carried in the information field of exchange-identification frames. Only a single-octet control field is allowed.

Class I provides error detection by means of the HDLC 16-bit CRC. It does not provide flow control, error correction, or protection from lost or duplicated frames (higher layers provide these features). It is intended for situations where the bit error rate and frame-loss rate are acceptably low. Class I advantages are stateless operation, less processing overhead, and economical implementation (resulting from less processing and less line usage). These characteristics and the associated primitives match the simplicity of connectionless Network Layer service.

Class II is equivalent to the balanced asynchronous class of HDLC. It has the basic elements of procedure and HDLC options for the exchange-identification, REJ (request for the retransmission of an information frame), and unnumbered-information frames, and extended address and modulo 128 sequence-number operation. It is better suited to this purpose than X.25 LAPB (ISO 7776) because of its ability to identify higher-layer protocol entities in the address field and do poll/final-bit check-pointing on information frames. (Check-pointing enables the transmission of an information frame that also requests an acknowledgment, which is supplied in the next transmitted information frame response.) For quicker operation, use the unnumbered-information frame for expedited data; use the exchange identification frame for management purposes. (These frames are not available in X.25 LAPB.)

The information field of the exchange identification frame contains management data units. For example, the data link class, timer values, retry counts, window size, and maximum frame size could be parameters negotiated by management entities. Other management functions might include statistics reporting, reading and setting operational parameters, event reporting, connectivity testing, and initial program loading.

Seeking acceptance

While standardization is important to promote multivendor compatibility, efforts in that arena alone do not assure the OSI objective. Industry acceptance is crucial. Progress here has been quite impressive.

General Motors has led the way with its Manufacturing Automation Protocol effort to standardize protocols for factory equipment. More recently, Boeing addressed the office environment with its Technical and Office Protocols effort. The MAP/TOP endeavors now have a combined users' group that is sharing protocol-implementation data. The connectionless Network Layer protocols, as well as the layer's related standards, are specified by both MAP and TOP.

The most tangible evidence of industry acceptance to date occurred in November 1985 at the Autofact trade show. General Motors and Boeing sponsored a multi-vendor demonstration of MAP and TOP. The National Bureau of Standards played a key facilitating role in the issue, with the protocols described in this article featured. Most impressive, this was not merely an exercise in shipping bits from one location to another. Automated equipment built assemblies and kept records. A visitor to the demonstration could enter an order at a terminal and have the automated equipment assemble, test, and deliver a customized product according to the choices made by the visitor.

What is next? Certainly there will be further demonstrations and media events. But more interesting, the National Bureau of Standards is planning an ongoing. multivendor activity called OSINet. This network uses the ISO protocols described here for an international network of about 27 participating companies involved in the advancement of these standards.

Finally, 1986 saw the formulation of the Corporation for Open Systems (COS). This organization is a consortium of U. S. companies devoted to accelerating the introduction of multivendor products that interoperate under OSI. COS is expected to dedicate most of its efforts to the development of testing and validation capabilities. With such facilities scrutinizing products offered in the marketplace, purchasers gain confidence that the diverse computers they acquire do indeed intercommunicate. ∎

Alan Weissberger is an independent consultant specializing in implementing data communications standards. He participates in the activities of standards committees dealing with ISDN, public data networks, and LANs. He is also an adjunct professor at the University of Santa Clara. Jay Israel is manager of software development at Excelan, responsible for ISO protocols. He contributes to internetworking standardization efforts, including those of the Corporation for Open Systems. He holds an undergraduate degree from the University of Pennsylvania and a doctorate from the Massachusetts Institute of Technology. The authors wish to acknowledge the invaluable assistance of Fred M. Burg of AT&T in preparing this article.

Robert A. Heath, NCR Corp., Columbia, S. C.

Integrated PADS unlock Unix end-user services for X.25

Adapting Unix to packet-switched networks is made easy by the addition of X.25 support for two standard Unix utilities.

For the network designer who is adopting packet-switched services, how data streams of existing applications are packaged is an important decision. While the International Telegraph and Telephone Consultative Committee (CCITT) defines the physical, data link control, and packet-level interfaces for public data networks providing packet-switching services in its Recommendation X.25, it defers the contents of the data packets themselves to other standards. The CCITT has standardized the packet assembler/disassembler (PAD) methods for start-stop terminals within an X.25 network as its Recommendations X.3, X.28, and X.29. Together, these latter three recommendations are known less formally as the Interactive Terminal Interface standard. In Unix-based networks, the chief communications protocols are forms of start-stop; therefore, the Interactive Terminal Interface protocols are a natural choice to package Unix's teletype (TTY) data streams. Since X.3, X.28, and X.29 dictate a common data stream within the network, a Unix machine implementing these standards could connect to similar Unix machines as well as to different TTY-oriented equipment.

Unix uses standard TTY hardware and protocols for both terminal-to-host and peer-to-peer communications (Fig. 1). Its applications employ TTY ports in two basic roles: as log-in ports and as dial-out ports. Typical users access Unix through a standard ASCII terminal connected to one of its log-in ports. They then interact with one of its command interpreters, or shells (Fig. 1A). From a shell the user invokes actual applications. The standard shells and basic software tools are based on classic, line-at-a-time Teletype interaction. Later tools, such as the well-known visual editor program, are screen-oriented for use with video display terminals. The screen-oriented approach is gaining popularity as vendors add menu software to shield the user from the command-driven shells. Within the innermost operating system layer, or kernel, the TTY driver assembles the incoming character stream into lines for line-at-a-time applications, but simply passes characters for screen-oriented applications.

Basic networking in Unix

The same TTY driver allows ports to originate outgoing calls as well as to accept incoming log-ins. The standard Unix utility, Call Unix, allows a user to interact with remote equipment through a dial-out port (Fig. 1B). Call Unix is simply a virtual terminal program, routing TTY data between a locally attached terminal and a dial-out port, connecting to the remote device. The remote equipment is called by passing dial digits to a separate auto-dialer port or through the data stream itself to an intelligent dialing modem. Call Unix can also transfer ASCII files but provides neither error checking nor recovery.

For reliable batch file transfer, the standard Unix utility is Unix-to-Unix Copy (Fig. 1C). Besides transferring files, Unix-to-Unix Copy provides such valuable user services as electronic mail, software distribution, network news, remote printer sharing, and store-and-forward capability. These services are actually by-products of its ability to execute a program on a remote machine, giving Unix-to-Unix Copy an open-ended capability of tying into other networking schemes. Unix-to-Unix Copy can be changed and extended by the user, offering a level of accessibility that is only recently being introduced to industry-standard Systems Network Architecture (SNA) in its Logical Unit 6.2. Unix-to-Unix Copy provides peer-to-peer interconnection, using a dial-out port on one computer and a log-in port on the other.

Since Call Unix and Unix-to-Unix Copy share the same physical facilities, these programs also share a common database of node names and dialing information.

At the operating system interface, Unix applications

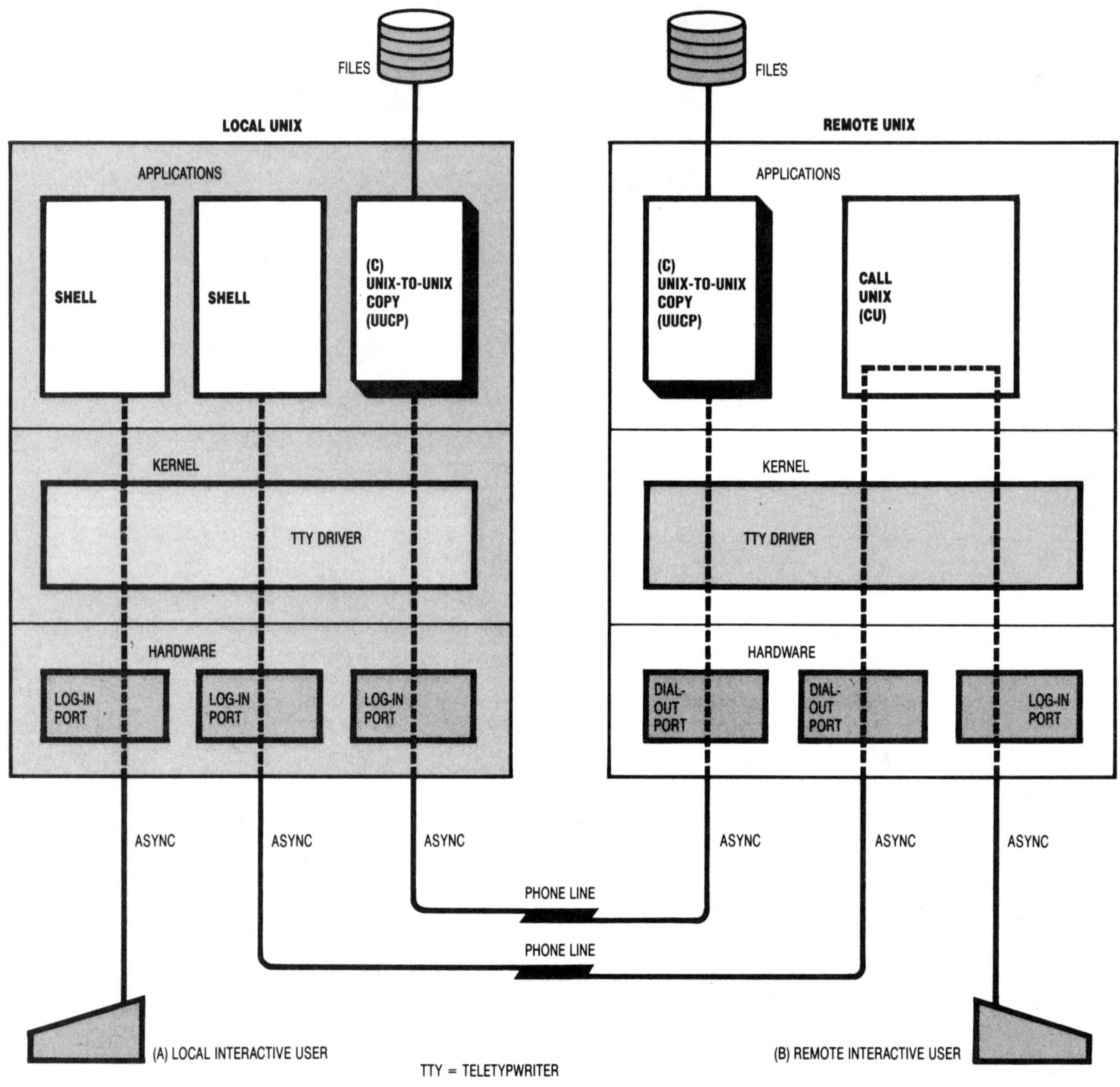

1. Unix ports. *The asynchronous ports serve both batch and interactive processing. In (A) a local user interacts with a shell; in (B), a remove user logs into a local device through the Call Unix utility. In (C) Unix-to-Unix Copy transfers files between Unix computers. The operating system kernel orchestrates the tasks.*

access TTY ports using a standard set of operating system calls, regardless of the hardware involved. Programs that conform to this TTY interface standard can be ported to other mainframes running Unix. There are five calls: open, which establishes a connection; read and write, to pass input and output data; ioctl, the Input/Output Control command, which configures and controls the port; and close, which dissolves a connection. The TTY driver, which implements these operating system calls, provides a rich set of options oriented to start-stop communications, allowing a wide range of standard ASCII terminals to connect to Unix. In fact, there is a strong similarity between the Unix TTY parameters and those of X.3 (see table). This similarity simplifies migration from Unix start-stop communi-

cations to X.25 packet switching, using the Interactive Terminal Interface standards.

For the shell and standard Unix applications (shown in Fig. 2), the TTY driver actually assembles incoming data into lines, echoing and editing data within the typed line. Backspacing and line deletion, when handled at this level, are known in Unix as canonical processing (Fig. 2A). Since X.3 defines similar functions for terminal PADs, X.3 line assembly closely resembles Unix canonical TTY processing. Other similar canonical functions include generating delays for mechanical TTYs, mapping carriage return and line feed sequences, and reacting to break conditions. More sophisticated programs, such as the visual editor and menus, turn off canonical processing (in Fig. 2B), echoing

Equivalence between X.3 pad and unix TTY

X.3 PARAMETER REF. NO.	EQUIVALENT UNIX TTY PARAMETER	X.3 MEANING	INTEGRATED HOST PAD USAGE
1	N/A	PAD RECALL	HOST PAD LEAVES CONTROL TO TERMINAL PAD
2	ECHO	ECHO	HOST PAD TURNS OFF FOR PASSWORD AND SCREEN FUNCTIONS
3	N/A	SELECTION OF DATA FORWARDING CHARACTER	CARRIAGE RETURN IS TYPICAL FORWARDING CHARACTER
4	N/A	SELECTION OF IDLE TIMER DELAY	TRIGGERS FORWARDING DURING SCREEN-ORIENTED FUNCTIONS
5	IXOFF	ANCILLARY DEVICE CONTROL	TERMINAL PAD CONTROLS FLOW OF DATA FROM TERMINAL USING X-ON AND X-OFF
6	N/A	CONTROL OF PAD SERVICE SIGNALS	HOST PAD LEAVES CONTROL TO TERMINAL PAD
7	IGNBRK, BRKINT	BREAK HANDLING	APPLICATION DECIDES WHETHER TO IGNORE BREAK, OR INTERRUPT ON BREAK
8	TCFLSH	DISCARD OUTPUT	APPLICATION FLUSHES OUTPUT USING TCFLSH INTERFACE COMMAND OR DURING BREAK
9	CR0, CR1, CR2, CR3	PADDING AFTER CARRIAGE RETURN	DEFINED DURING UNIX LOG-IN PROCESS
10	N/A	LINE FOLDING	HOST PAD LEAVES FOLDING TO TERMINAL PAD
11	CBAUD	BINARY SPEED	STANDARD UNIX RATES ARE: 50, 75, 110, 134.54, 150, 200, 300, 600 BIT/S, 1.2, 2.4, 4.8, 9.6 KBIT/S
12	IXON	FLOW CONTROL OF THE TERMINAL PAD	TERMINAL USER CONTROLS FLOW OF DATA TO TERMINAL USING X-OFF AND X-ON
13	ICRNL, OCRNL	LINEFEED INSERTION AFTER CARRIAGE RETURN	SET DURING UNIX LOG-IN PROCESS PER TERMINAL TYPE
14	NL0, NL1	PADDING AFTER LINEFEED	UNIX DEFINES NEW-LINE DELAY AS PART OF LOG-IN PARAMETERS
15	N/A	EDITING	HOST OFFLOADS EDITING AT TERMINAL PAD DURING LINE-AT-A-TIME PROCESSING
16	ERASE	CHARACTER DELETE	UNIX STANDARD IS #, BUT VALUE IS CONFIGURABLE
17	KILL	LINE DELETE	UNIX STANDARD IS @, BUT VALUE IS CONFIGURABLE
18	N/A	LINE DISPLAY	LINE DISPLAY REMAINS UNDER CONTROL OF TERMINAL PAD
19	ECHO, ECHOE	EDITING PAD SERVICE SIGNALS	USER DEFINES BACKSPACING FOR TTY OR VDT AT LOG-IN TIME
20	N/A	ECHO MASK	HOST PAD SETS MASK TO ECHO CR AND PRINTABLE GRAPHICS
21	PARINB, PARODD	PARITY TREATMENT	UNIX DEFINES PARITY AT LOG-IN
22	N/A	PAGE WAIT	HOST PAD DEFERS CONTROL TO TERMINAL PAD

N/A = NOT AVAILABLE
PAD = PACKET ASSEMBLY/DISASSEMBLER
TTY = TELETYPEWRITER

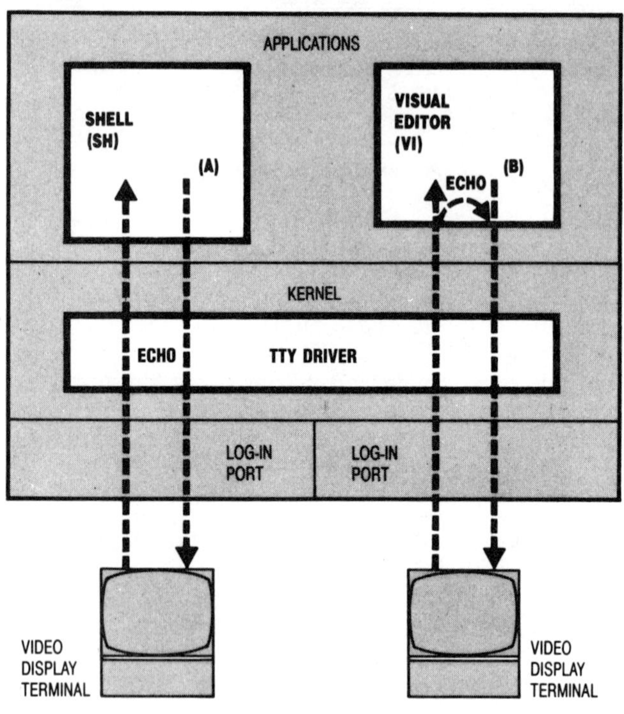

2. Unix TTY. *In (A) the TTY driver performs echo functions for line-at-a-time applications. (B) shows screen-oriented applications echoing directly, in pass-through mode.*

and editing directly from the application level. The Interactive Terminal Interface makes it possible to switch between these two modes of operation without stopping one activity to start another.

What X.25 services does standard Unix provide? In 1983 AT&T released Unix System 5.0, including Bell X.25, which offered a programmatic interface and served as an alternate vehicle for Unix-to-Unix Copy. For general-purpose X.25 interconnection, Unix's Bell X.25 was underfeatured and insufficient. It implemented only permanent virtual circuits, omitting the more popular switched virtual circuits. Further, it did not provide software so that users could log in or call out using an interactive terminal. By mid-1986 the latest release, Unix System 5.3, still had no software support for general X.25 networking; this must be added to upgrade Unix to make it possible to achieve X.25 networking in commercial networks.

What X.25 services are required for Unix? A complete X.25 solution for Unix should encompass the three general services described above: incoming log-ins, outgoing interactive sessions, and machine-to-machine communications. Two conventional solutions are leasing a PAD function within the public data network itself and purchasing a "black box" PAD that resides between the Unix machine and the network. With respect to a Unix computer, these two solutions may be considered external PADs, located outside the physical confines of the machine. An advantage of external PADs is that they can be installed readily with any standard TTY hardware. They have a common limitation in that they require a separate asynchronous port on the Unix computer (and at the PAD itself), because each

interactive session corresponds to a separate virtual circuit in X.25 terms.

How does a PAD work? An external PAD is usually a black box driven by a microprocessor. It resides on the user's site, concentrating the start/stop traffic through a set of asynchronous ports onto a high-speed, synchronous trunk. The trunk leads to a communications processor belonging to the network provider, typically located off-site. In X.25 terms, the black box PAD is known as the data terminal equipment (DTE), and the network provider's communications processor is known as the data circuit-terminating equipment (DCE). If the PAD attaches to start/stop terminals, by definition it provides terminal PAD services. If the PAD front-ends a host processor, by definition it provides host PAD services. Some PAD products implement both services, allowing the user to configure the role on a port-by-port basis.

From the user's point of view, an X.28 terminal PAD operates much like an intelligent dialing modem. The PAD has two modes of operation: command mode, during which the PAD interacts with the local user, and data transfer mode, during which it routes data between the host and the start/stop terminal. The user can toggle between the two modes by entering a specified keyboard character. From command mode, the user initiates a call, clears a call, checks status, displays parameters, and updates parameters. The user's commands to the PAD are known as PAD command signals, and the PAD's messages to the user are known as PAD service signals. The syntax for the X.28 PAD/user dialog is very terse. For this reason, manufacturers and network providers often supplement the standard X.28 repertoire with their own, more descriptive command and message set.

Terminal PAD operation depends upon a set of selectable parameters specified by Recommendation X.3. The 1980 version of X.3 specified 18 parameters; the 1984 version extended that set to 22 (table). The parameters' goal is to accommodate a variety of start/stop terminals as well as a variety of host procedures for using them. The parameters may be set or read locally by the PAD user through the TTY data stream or remotely by the host PAD through the X.25 data stream.

X.29 dictates the mapping of terminal data and control information into packets. Because X.25 traffic consists of blocked packets, packing the randomly arriving TTY characters into a packet introduces a problem. The terminal PAD must optimize the number of characters it accumulates before forwarding a packet against the throughput delay it causes by waiting for more characters. The decision to forward is triggered by a combination of packet size, time-out duration, and detection of end-of-message characters in the data stream. Since the forwarding decision is parametric, the host can change it during the session to forward immediately for screen-oriented programs or to assemble until end-of-message for line-at-a-time applications.

X.29 control messages

This is accomplished through X.29 PAD messages delivered as X.25 qualified data. There are eight control messages:

1. Set Parameters, in which the host PAD lists parameters

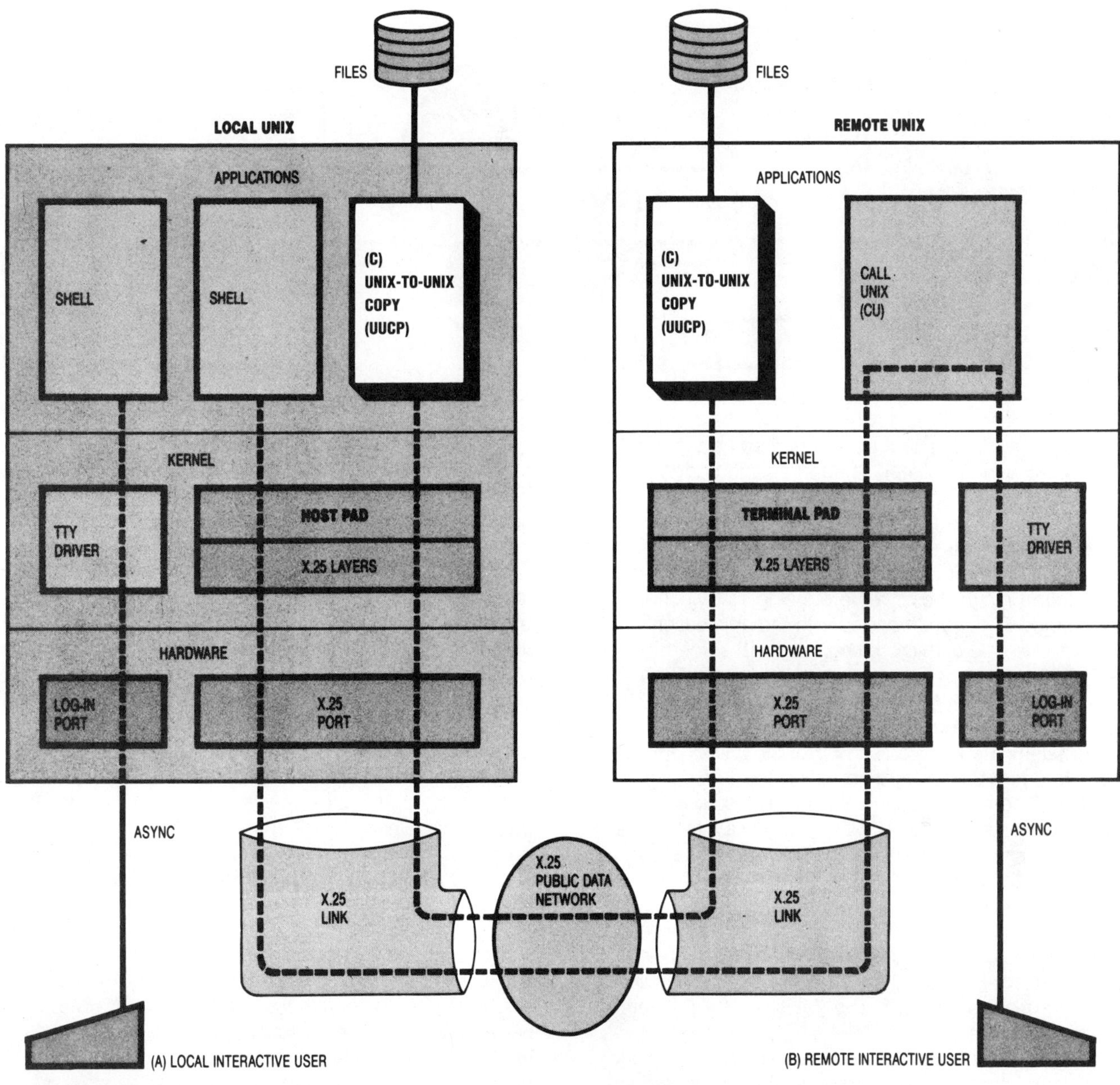

and the values they should take.

2. Read Parameters, in which the host PAD requests the terminal PAD to report the current setting of parameters in the included list.

3. Set and Read Parameters, a combination of the above in which a read operation verifies that the parameters were set properly.

4. Parameters Indication, in which the terminal PAD reports its parameter values.

5. Invitation to Clear, a message from the host that orderly call clearing is now possible.

6. Indication of Break, which can be sent by either the host or the terminal PAD to indicate a break condition.

7. Error, in which the terminal PAD reports errors in messages it received from the host.

8. Reselection, which is sent by the host's directory service so that the PAD clears the existing call, selecting a new destination passed in its data.

Host PADs can be implemented as black boxes, too. Unfortunately, the Interactive Terminal Interface standards do not cover the interaction between a host and its stand-alone PAD for the purpose of originating X.29 command messages. An external host PAD cannot readily sense the host application's shift between line-oriented and screen-oriented operation to generate the proper X.29 messages to keep the terminal PAD in step. Some manufacturers engineer private PAD-to-host or PAD-to-PAD protocols to overcome this. Consequently, external host PADs often

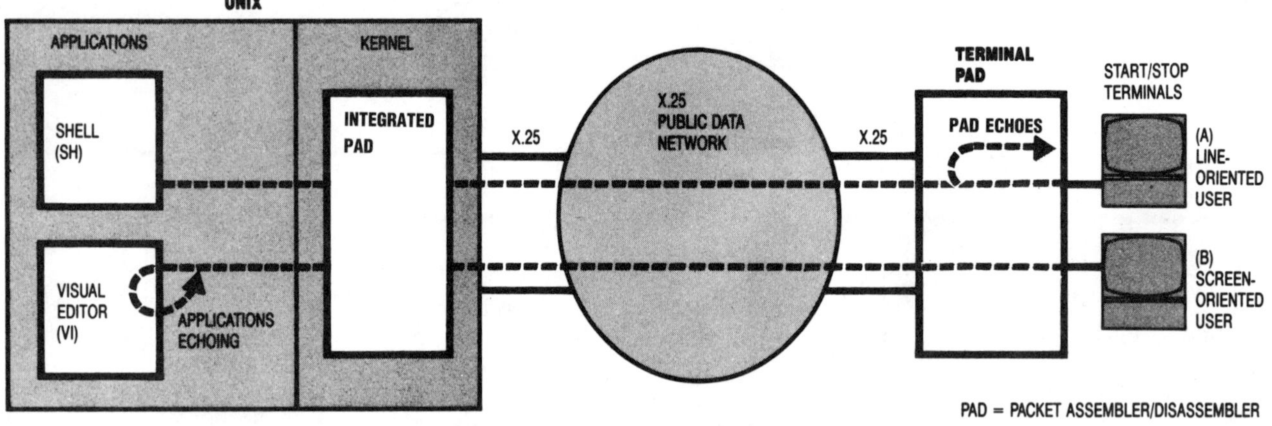

4. Reuse. *The integrated host PAD recycles the Unix TTY interface. The terminal PAD (A) provides local echo for line-oriented applications. The screen-oriented applications in (B) echo through the network. Compare this setup involving the same TTY line assembly shown in Figure 2. This shows the changes that the public data network would bring.*

serve as "byte pipes" into the network, leaving the host processor to perform all echoing and editing under its own steam.

In this situation the terminal PAD user must use the private PAD protocols to control both the terminal PAD and the host PAD. On the other hand, host PAD functions can be integrated into the host itself, producing tightly coupled packet-mode DTE, synchronized with the application's shifts between line-oriented processing and screen-oriented processing.

An alternative to external PADs

An alternate strategy for preserving existing Unix applications is to add X.25 software emulating the TTY driver interface, since it defines the common access point for all existing networking services. By meeting this interface, a new driver can map standard Unix TTY system calls into the data stream defined by X.3, X.28, and X.29 for the benefit of X.25 networking software implemented in lower layers. This scheme results in integrated PAD functions. Unlike the external PAD, an integrated PAD's number of virtual circuits is limited only by memory size, not by the number of physical ports. An integrated PAD also offers performance benefits.

Figure 3 illustrates how the same asynchronous networking services from Figure 1 upgrade to X.25 in just this fashion. An integrated terminal PAD replaces asynchronous dial-out ports, and an integrated host PAD replaces asynchronous log-in ports.

In networks, CCITT Recommendations distribute the line-assembly functions to the terminal (3B) X.3 PAD and presentation functions to the host (3A) X.29 PAD. Figure 4 shows how the same TTY line assembly shown in Figure 2 is redistributed when working across a public data network. This arrangement extends the Unix TTY (3C) subsystems to include the remote terminal PAD. An integrated host PAD controls whether line assembly occurs at the terminal PAD or through the network at the host. The host turns on the more efficient line assembly at the terminal PAD when line-by-line interaction is required (Fig. 4A), and turns it off for screen-oriented processing (Fig. 4B). Line assembly at

the terminal PAD is preferred because it reduces the response time in TTY character echoing. TTY character echoes originating locally at a terminal PAD avoid the noticeable delay which TTY echoes incur when crossing the network from a host PAD.

The Unix applications themselves ultimately decide the required type of interaction. They indicate so by passing parameters to the integrated host PAD, which is a TTY-lookalike at its software interface. The host PAD translates these parameters into an X.29 Set Parameters PAD message packet, which it sends through the X.25 network to define the equivalent X.3 parameter at the network's receiving terminal PAD.

These control packets are generated only at log-ins and at transitions between screen-oriented and line-oriented processing. Since these transitions are not visible in the character stream, an external host PAD cannot detect them to alternate control of line assembly between the host and the terminal PAD.

The host PAD assembles the outbound character stream into packets. Since applications send out characters with no awareness of packet boundaries, the host PAD arbitrarily delimits packet boundaries. It forwards a packet to the network when it either (1) completely fills a packet; (2) receives no additional characters within a given interval; (3) detects an end-of-line character; or (4) receives a read from the application implying a transition from output to input mode. This last feature gives the integrated PAD a performance advantage since an external PAD cannot detect this software event.

On input from the network, the host PAD disassembles data packets into character queues which wait for the application to read them. Since editing within a typed line is offloaded at the terminal PAD, the host PAD does not edit the data before passing it to the application.

Incoming control sequences from the network, such as X.25 Clear Requests or Interrupt packets, are mapped into Unix signals. These asynchronous software events are the standard indication from the TTY driver of disconnections or break conditions. An X.25 Clear Request would occur if the terminal PAD user decides to clear the X.25 call. An

X.25 Interrupt Request could occur if the terminal PAD user hit the terminal's Break key.

Call Unix and Unix-to-Unix Copy can originate X.25 calls to remote log-in ports via an integrated terminal PAD (Fig. 3). When used on the switched telephone network, these programs normally issue dial digits to an autodial device through an autodialer software driver. Since an X.25 network address resembles a telephone number, networking utilities can treat X.25 network addresses like telephone numbers. An autodial virtual device associated with each call-out port can be written in Unix to accept the address digits of the destination X.25 port. This technique reuses the phone number management logic of Call Unix and Unix-to-Unix Copy without modification. Like the host PAD, the terminal PAD assembles the host-bound data into packets. Additionally, it generates a local echo under control of the host PAD.

Unlike external PADs, an integrated terminal PAD does not need to implement the X.28 PAD command signal and PAD service signal set. In an external PAD, this set allows a dialog between the user and the PAD itself to control, configure, and monitor the X.25 call. This interface is unnecessary in the integrated PAD because Call Unix and Unix-to-Unix Copy provide similar services through an existing software connection.

Over X.25, Call Unix reliably transfers legible data and legible files since error recovery is provided by networking protocols. For binary files, though, Unix-to-Unix Copy is required.

A streaming protocol for Unix-to-Unix Copy

On asynchronous links, Unix-to-Unix Copy packetizes data into 64-byte, sequenced packets with checksums, and these must be acknowledged and recovered on a packet basis. Unix-to-Unix Copy overlaps packet transmission with a windowing technique similar to the windowing technique of high-level data link control (HDLC), but the receiving site acknowledges every packet separately. This scheme, which is known as the "g" protocol, is optimized for such error-prone links as telephone circuits. The "g" protocol uses all eight bit positions of a start-stop character to achieve transparency. In some terminal PADs the eighth bit must be used for parity. Therefore, the "g" protocol cannot be considered for X.25.

To adapt Unix-to-Unix Copy to X.25, the "f" protocol was developed. Its coding scheme provides transparency but requires a data path only seven bits wide, so it can be used with standard PADs. It generates larger packets and issues a continuous data stream, requiring end-to-end acknowledgment only on the file basis. This strategy relies upon X.25's basically error-free service to reduce costs, since end-to-end acknowledgment is no longer required on each individual packet. In Unix System V, Unix-to-Unix Copy is configurable on a link basis, so a machine can serve as a batch gateway between an X.25 network using the "f" protocol and switched telephone networks using the "g" protocol.

A sample implementation

In a sample Unix-based computer, X.25 networking software can be distributed between kernel and application processes as shown in Figure 5. An intelligent communica-

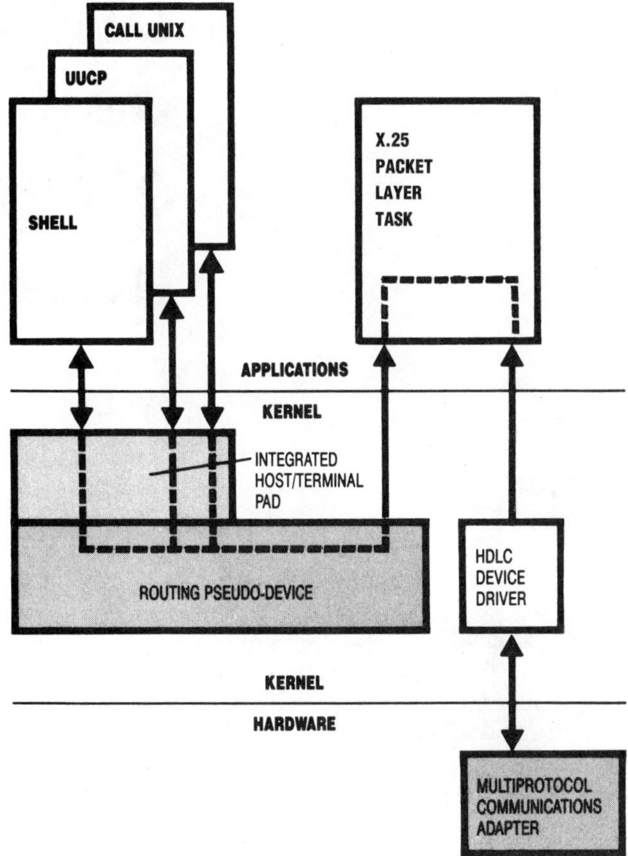

5. X.25 layers. *X.25 layers can be distributed in a sample Unix software application according to speed and memory requirements.*

tions adapter offloads the most time-critical feature of X.25's electrical interface and the HDLC software driver in the Unix kernel implements the slightly less time-critical Link Access Protocol-Balanced, or LAP-B. The packet layer runs as a background task within the applications layer of Unix, where its speed and memory requirements are less demanding. The packet software connects to a kernel virtual device which multiplexes and demultiplexes the X.25's virtual circuits. The host and terminal PADs are actually one software module, serving together as a kernel sublayer between the routing virtual device and the application. User processes, such as the shell or Unix-to-Unix Copy, connect to the PADs, which appear as standard TTY ports to the network.

This approach structures X.25 layers within Unix according to speed and memory requirements. At the same time, it reuses standard TTY connections to preserve the Unix base of networking and user applications. ∎

Consulting analyst Robert Heath has been developing networking software with NCR since 1975. A former member of ANSI committee X3S34, he has edited a number of NCR corporate engineering standards in data communications. He holds a B.A. in electrical engineering (1972) from Georgia Tech and an MSEE from the University of Southern California. Since 1982 he has developed communications software for the NCR Tower.

Daniel R. Ruffalo, Rotelcom, Fairport, N. Y.

Understanding T1 basics: Primer offers picture of networking future

By becoming more familiar with T1, managers can anticipate change in the network before it happens.

Rapid development of digital technology in the early 1960s gave telephone companies the long-sought opportunity to relieve heavy loading on interexchange cables. The foundation of what's turned out to be a great leap forward was pulse code modulation equipment, a new class of central-office gear that converted analog voice signals into a digital format and, in the process, improved network performance.

A cornerstone of the digital revolution in telephony is the channel bank, a device that transmits 24 independent channels over copper cable that had before carried only one voice call. The early channel banks, which acted as multiplexers, were also called T-carriers. The T-carrier is built around two or more channel banks, or D banks, which convert analog signals into a digital format and multiplex them into one digital signal for transmission over a digital trunk facility. The multiplexed digital signal is called the T1 bit stream or the DS-1 signal.

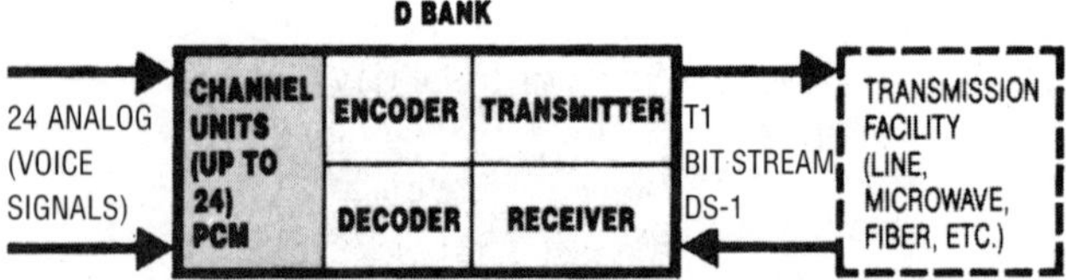

Over the years specifications for the performance of a number of PCM channel banks have evolved. They are generally referred to by the designations first used at Western Electric Co.: D1, D2, D3, and D4. Although D1 and D2 channel banks are no longer being manufactured, many are still used in the telephone network. The D3 and D4 banks are state of the art.

D3 and D4 banks are very similar. The D4 bank is basically two D3 banks in a single chassis; the two share common equipment. The D3 and D4 banks continue to use the T1 bit stream for each set of 24 channels. The D3 bank has a 24-channel capacity using one T1 bit stream, while the D4 bank uses two T1 bit streams for a total capacity of 48 channels.

The T1, or DS-1, bit stream encoded by the D banks in today's time-division multiplexer (TDM) equipment is a high-speed digital stream of ones and zeros that runs at a rate of 1.544 Mbit/s. PCM, or pulse code modulation, is the technique used to transmit analog (voice) signals on D banks. Bipolar, also called AMI, or alternate mark inversion, is the digital form the T1 signal takes once it is passed to the digital trunk facility.

An analog signal is first sampled at preselected, equally distributed time intervals. The resulting analog samples are referred to as pulse amplitude modulation (PAM). Each analog PAM sample is quantized and coded as a digital eight-bit PCM byte. The eight-bit byte can be transmitted on a digital facility to another location where the PCM process is reversed and the information is reconstructed or decoded into its original analog form.

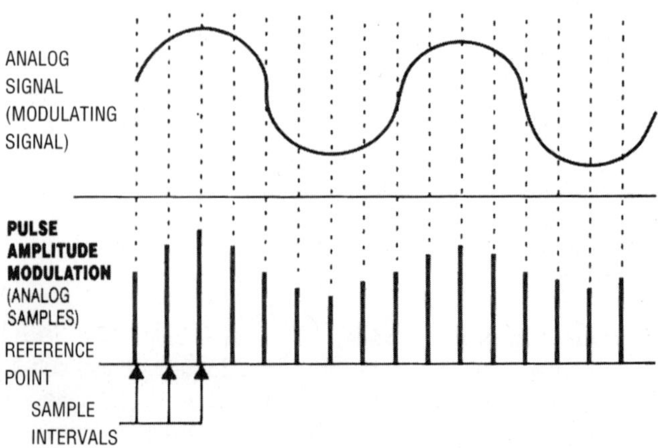

The T1 rate evolves from the sampling rate applied to the analog signal. The Nyquist theorem of information theory states that to encode an analog signal it must be sampled at twice its bandwidth. The telephone industry's voice-grade band runs at about 300 Hz to 3,000 Hz. For various reasons, the upper limit of frequencies on a voice-grade facility is taken as 4,000 Hz. Hence, twice the bandwidth (2 x 4,000 Hz) is 8,000 samples per second. This sampling rate allows reconstruction of the analog signal.

This is an example of a bipolar signal used in a T1 bit stream (DS-1):

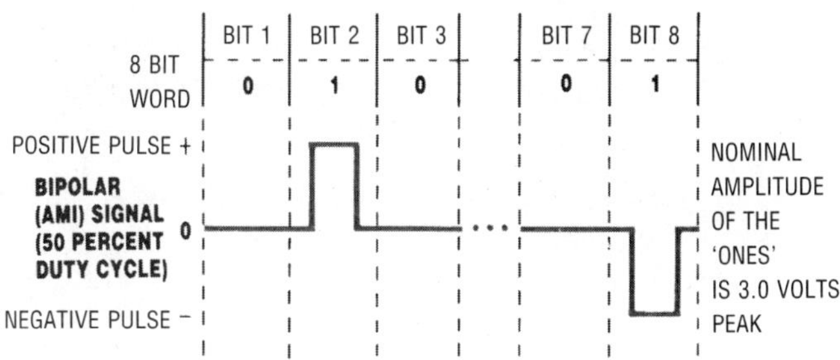

The 0s are at a 0.0 voltage potential, while 1s are produced by a nominal 3.0 volt peak positive or negative going pulse. The 1s pulses have an alternating polarity. If the first 1 is represented by a positive going pulse, the next 1 will be a negative pulse and vice versa. These alternating pulses are called bipolar, or alternate mark inversion. A violation of the bipolar signaling scheme would have occurred if bit 4 had been a positive pulse in relation to bit 2 or if bit 5 had been a negative going pulse in relation to bit 4.

As a fundamental representation of the T1, or DS-1, bit stream transmitted from a D bank or TDM equipment, the 1.544-Mbit/s stream must meet certain basic requirements:

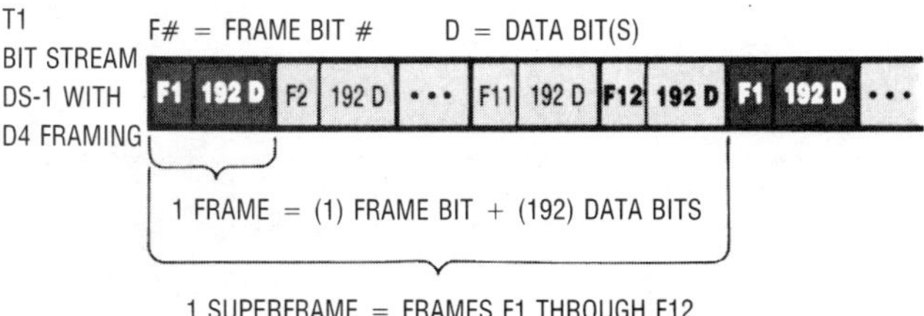

- It is a bipolar AMI, non-return-to-zero signal.
- Each pulse has a 50 percent duty cycle with a nominal voltage of 3.0 volts.
- There can be no more than 15 consecutive "0s" present in the stream.

A D4 framing pattern has been added to the T1 specification. D4 framing has traditionally been used in D banks, although it did not become a requirement in network TDM equipment until early 1985. Prior to that time, suppliers of TDM equipment were required only to comply with the DS-1 specifications.

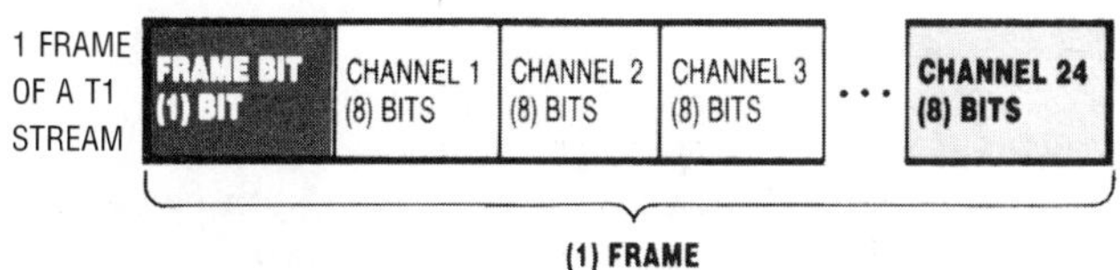

D4 framing in a T1 bit stream begins with a single frame bit (F1) followed by 192 data bits. The F1 is followed by frame bit 2 (F2) and another 192 data bits. Next comes frame bit 3 (F3) followed by its 192 data bits. The sequence continues up through frame bit 12 (F12); each frame bit is followed by 192 data bits. Then the 12-bit frame pattern repeats itself with each frame bit followed by 192 data bits. The 12-bit frame pattern is precise and repeats itself the same each time. This repetition enables the transmission equipment to keep the bit stream in synchronization.

Here a D4 framing pattern is used:

	F1	F2	F3	F4	F5	F6	F7	F8	F9	F10	F11	F12
D4 FRAMING PATTERN (FRAME BITS)	1	0	0	0	1	1	0	1	1	1	0	0

1 FRAME = (1) FRAME BIT + (192) DATA BITS
1 SUPERFRAME = FRAMES F1 THROUGH F12

F1 includes one frame bit followed by 192 data bits for a total of 193 bits in a frame. A superframe includes 12 frame bits, each followed by 192 data bits.

New telephony requirements are being developed for customer equipment. Once again, a new requirement will necessitate that TDM manufacturers upgrade their equipment. Besides having to meet the DS-1 specification and the D4 framing requirement, in the future they will have to meet the D4 formatting requirement as well.

The D4 format consists of 24 consecutive eight-bit words, or "channels," following a framing bit. Much as the D bank transmits and receives 24 voice channels, the D4 framing and formatting will enable customer premises TDM equipment to mimic the separation requirement of the central-office equipment.

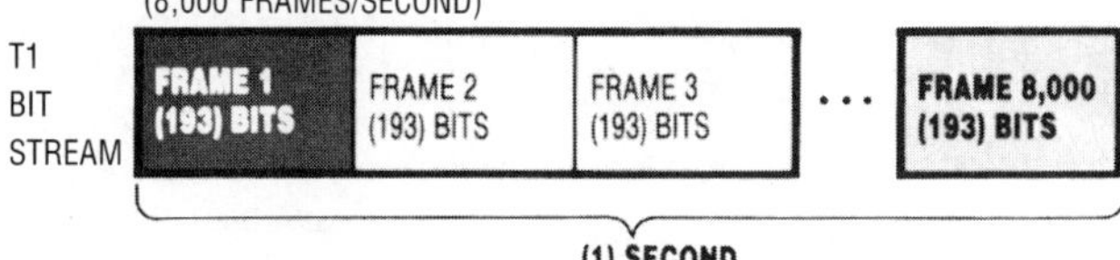

1 FRAME = (1) FRAME BIT + [8 BITS PER CHANNEL × 24 CHANNELS]
1 FRAME = (1) FRAME BIT + [192 CHANNEL BITS OR DATA BITS]
1 FRAME = (193) BITS [FRAME AND DATA]

To summarize: 8,000 samples per second are required to reproduce an analog signal using PCM with each sample represented by an eight-bit byte (channel). There are 24 eight-bit channels following each frame bit in a T1 stream that uses D4 framing and D4 formatting. The frame bit is followed by 24 eight-bit channels yielding 193 bits per frame. These frames are being produced at a rate of 8,000 per second.

1 FRAME INTERVAL (time) = 1/8,000 OF A SECOND (BY VIRTUE OF THE SAMPLING THEOREM)   OR

THERE ARE 8,000 FRAME INTERVALS A SECOND IN A T1 BIT STREAM (8,000 FRAMES/SECOND)

T1 BIT STREAM = 8,000 FRAMES/SECOND
T1 BIT STREAM = 8,000 × (193) BITS/SECOND
T1 BIT STREAM = 1.544 MBIT/S

Thus a total of 1.544 Mbit/s is derived from the 193 bits at a sampling rate of 8,000 bit/s.

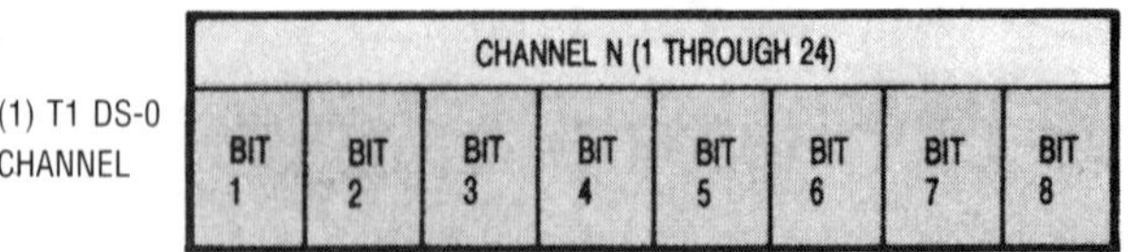

Some basic mathematics will demonstrate that the eight data bits from one of the 24 channels, sampled 8,000 times each second, yields 64,000 bits per second. A single channel from a T1 bit stream yields 64,000 bits per second (64 kbit/s). A channel from the T1 bit stream is referred to as a DS-0. Therefore, there are 24 DS-0s in a T1 bit stream with the D4 format.

Within a DS-0, the eight bits are being sampled 8,000 times a second, thus producing the 64,000 bit/s.

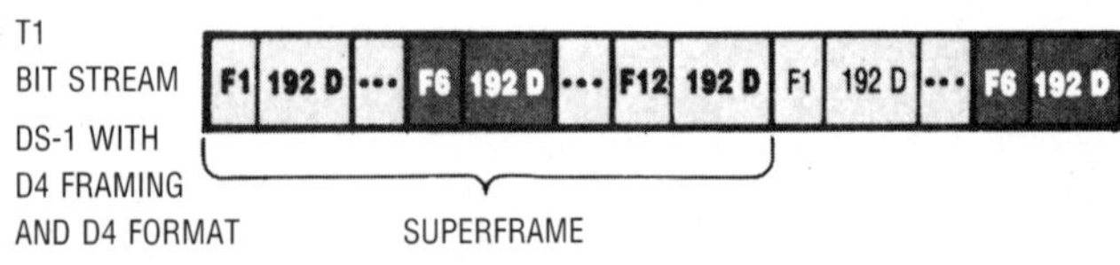

Some restrictions on transmission apply to the T1 bit stream. In voice transmissions, there is a need to transmit not only the voice signal, but also the mechanical signaling information. The D bank at each end must know when the line is "on-hook" or "off-hook," or if there is a battery reversal, and so forth.

Every 6th and 12th frame is used to transmit and receive voice channel signaling information.

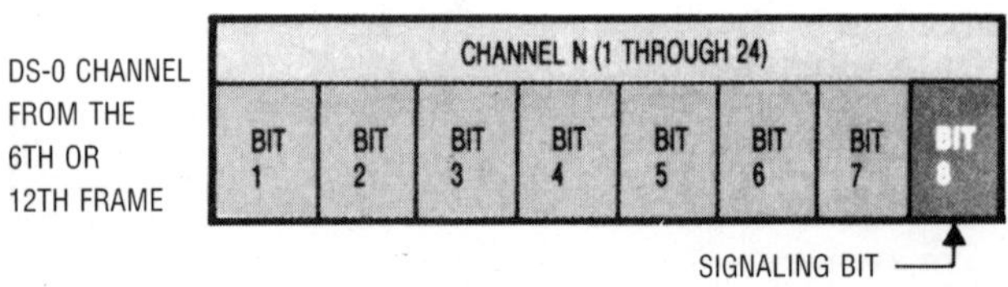

In the 6th and 12th frames, every 8th bit in a voice channel (DS-0) is used for signaling.

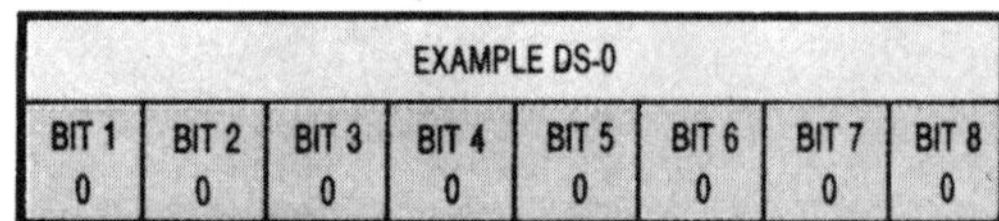

If all 24 DS-0s are used for voice transmission, then there will be 24 signaling bits in every 6th and 12th frame (one bit per channel per signaling frame). This technique is known as bit robbing. The theft of the signaling bits does not interfere with the PCM voice signal.

Those bits taken from the DS-0s during the 6th frame are referred to as the "A" bits, while those taken from the channels during the 12th frame are referred to as the "B" bits. From every superframe there will be one A-and-B bit pair per DS-0 (voice channel). Each pair of A and B bits is used to relay the signaling information for its respective channel between D banks: for example, loop closures, battery reversals, on-hook, off-hook, and so on. Not surprisingly, bit robbing affects data transmissions in the T1 bit stream.

Another T1 requirement that affects the volume of data transmitted in the T1 bit stream is the "1s density" requirement. To keep the telephone company T1 line, repeaters, and channel service units (CSUs) in synchronization, the DS-1 specification calls for no more than 15 consecutive zeros in the bit stream at any one time. This is referred to as 1s density. The telephone company repeaters and CSUs use the 1s pulses like a clock signal to maintain synchronization. Too many 0s (no pulses), and the repeaters and CSUs will drift and lose sync. Though today's equipment may actually be able to handle more than 15 zeros, the standard is set. Private facilities using microwave, fiber optic, and so on may not have a 1s density requirement.

To ensure 1s density in the T1 Bit Stream, the telephone company uses B7 zero code suppression.

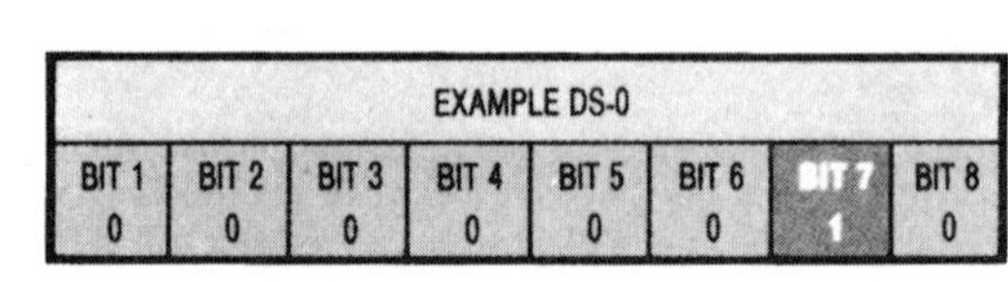

The B7 ensures that if all eight-bit positions in a DS-0 are 0s, than a 1 will be substituted in the Bit 7 position.

Here is a worst-case scenario:

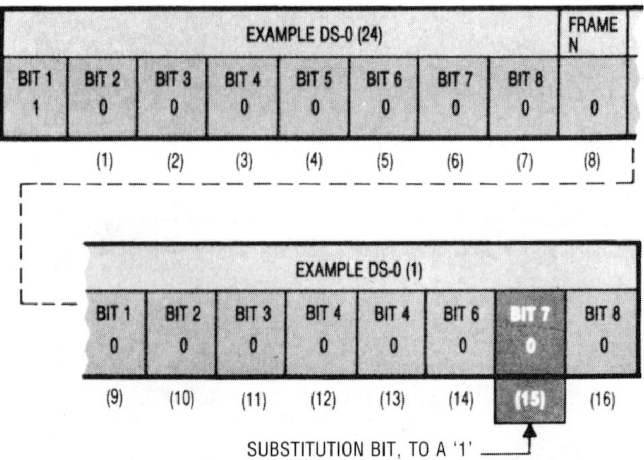

It shows the longest possible string of 0s with B7. Within the T1 bit stream, if Channel 24 were followed by a frame bit "0" and then Channel 1 were all 0s, there would be a total of 16 consecutive 0s. B7 cuts the number of 0s to 14, maintaining the integrity of the DS-1 specification.

How does B7 and bit robbing affect both a voice and data channel at the DS-0 level? Here we have an example of a voice channel (DS-0) in which either the 6th or the 12th frame contains all 0s:

In this example, the original voice channel is losing its Bit 8 to a 0A or 0B signaling bit. A PCM channel can tolerate the loss of the 8th bit to signaling as well as the loss of Bit 7 to the B7 zero code suppression.

There is no need to rob bits in a data channel (DS-0) since no signaling is required. However, having all 0s in the data channel is a possibility. If this occurs, data is corrupted by the B7 zero code suppression. While a voice channel can tolerate this, a data channel cannot. To compensate for this situation, a data channel generally contains only seven usable data bits. One of the eight data bits in the data channel (DS-0) is made a 1. This prevents the data channel from being corrupted by B7 zero code suppression.

This type of arrangement is called a nonclear channel. A nonclear channel is a data channel (DS-0) with seven usable and one unusable data bit.

NON-CLEAR CHANNEL

NON-CLEAR CHANNEL = 7 USABLE DATA BITS (INSTEAD OF 8 BITS) × 8,000 SAMPLES/SECOND IN A T1 STREAM

NON-CLEAR CHANNEL = 7 USABLE DATA BITS × 8,000/SECOND

NON-CLEAR CHANNEL = 56,000 BITS/SECOND (USABLE DATA BITS)

{THERE ARE 8 BITS PER CHANNEL IN A NON-CLEAR CHANNEL (DS-0). ONLY 7 ARE USABLE FOR DATA}

EXAMPLE OF HOW A NON-CLEAR CHANNEL MIGHT LOOK

	DATA CHANNEL (DS-0)						
BIT 1	BIT 2	BIT 3	BIT 4	BIT 5	BIT 6	BIT 7	BIT 8
1			USABLE DATA BITS				

The seven usable data bits yield 56,000 usable bit/s and 8,000 unusable bits. The 56,000 bit/s on a nonclear channel is also referred to as a DS-A.

MORE BASIC T1 MATH MANIPULATION:

IF ALL 24 CHANNELS IN THE BIT STREAM ARE 'NON-CLEAR CHANNELS' THEN:

T1 BIT STREAM = 8,000 FRAME BITS + [64,000 DATA BITS PER CHANNEL × 24 CHANNELS]/SECOND

T1 BIT STREAM = 8,000 FRAME BITS + [(56,000 USABLE DATA BITS + 8,000 UNUSABLE DATA BITS) × 24 CHANNELS]/SECOND

T1 BIT STREAM = 8,000 FRAME BITS + [(1,344,000 USABLE DATA BITS + 192,000 UNUSABLE DATA BITS)]/SECOND

T1 BIT STREAM = 8,000 FRAME BITS + 1,536,000 USABLE AND UNUSABLE DATA BITS/SECOND

T1 BIT STREAM = 1.544 MBIT/S (FRAME AND DATA, BOTH USABLE AND UNUSABLE)

The mathematics shows that in a T1 bit stream in which all channels are considered nonclear, there will be only 1.344 Mbit/s available for data transmission. We have 8,000 frame bits and 192,000 usable data bits that hold to the 1s density requirement in the T1 bit stream. Thus in a T1 bit stream (1.544 Mbit/s) with nonclear channels, fully 200,000 bit/s are needed for framing and 1s density.

Clear channels are available. A clear channel is one in which all 64,000 bits are usable. A medium such as microwave can support clear channels; private microwave links do not require B7 zero code suppression nor do they need 1s insertion. Though there is always a question of losing synchronization if too many consecutive 0s appear on the link, with today's technology the quantity of consecutive 0s can generally run in excess of 15. And just because there are eight consecutive 0s in a particular DS-0 does not mean you will have 15 consecutive 0s in the T1 bit stream.

Clear channel capability can also be obtained on DS-1 telephone company equipment by using bipolar transmission with Binary 8 zero substitution (B8ZS) coding in the T1 bit stream (DS-1). With B8ZS coding each eight consecutive 0s in a byte are removed and the B8ZS code is substituted.

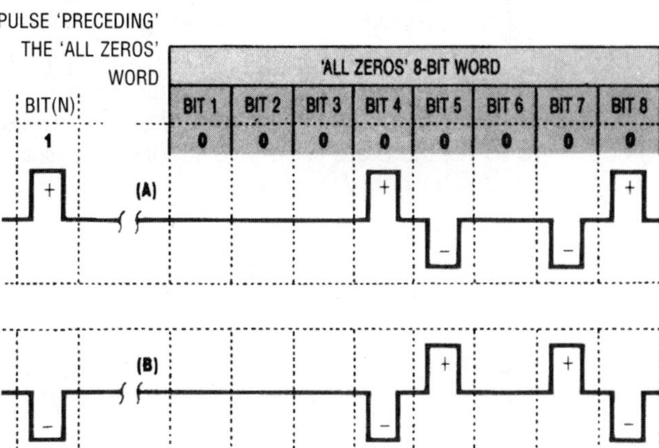

If the pulse preceding the inserted code is transmitted as a positive ($+$) pulse, the inserted code is $0\,0\,0\,+\,-\,0\,-\,+$ (for example, A). If the pulse preceding the inserted code is a negative ($-$) pulse, the inserted code is $0\,0\,0\,-\,+\,0\,+\,-\,0$ (for example, B). In the only two possible examples (A and B), bipolar violations occur in the fourth and seventh bit position. For this operation to work, all the equipment (telephone company and customer) used to transmit the T1 bit stream in the bipolar format must be able to recognize these codes as legitimate signals and not as bipolar violations or errors. Through normal evolution, significant integration of equipment with clear channel capability into the telephone company network is expected in the 1990s. The integrated services digital network will make extensive use of clear channel capability to transmit voice and data and will use a separate out-of-band channel for signaling information.

Another change coming to the network is the Extended Superframe format (ESF), also called the F_e format. ESF redefines the D4 framing pattern. Instead of looking for the resident 12 consecutive bits in the D4 framing, 24 consecutive frame bits are being processed.

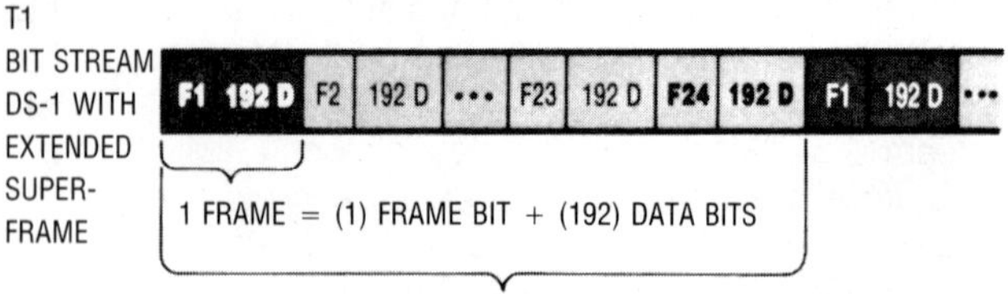

A single ESF frame contains 24 frame bits. Unlike D4 framing, in which the 12 framing bits follow a specific pattern, the ESF is not entirely a specific repeating pattern. The ESF framing pattern always keeps the same format, yet the actual frame bits are broken down into three types of frame bits.

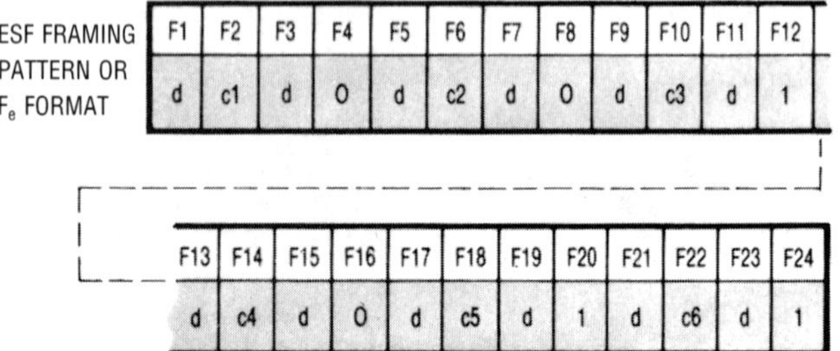

In an ESF frame, the "d" bits appear in frame bit positions 1, 3, 5, 7, 9, 11, 13, 15, 17, 19, 21, and 23. Of the 24 bit positions, the "d" bits use 12 positions or half of the available frame bits. Even though there are now 24 frame bits as opposed to 12, there are still only 8,000 frame bits per second in the T1 stream. Since the "d" bits are using half of the available frame bits, the "d" bits total 4,000 bit/s. The "d" bits will be used by the telephone company to perform network monitoring, alarms, reconfiguration, and so forth.

The remaining bits are split. Frame bit 2, 6, 10, 14, 18, and 22 will be used for a Cyclic Redundancy Check code consuming 2,000 bit/s. The remaining 2,000 bit/s constitute the basic frame pattern. This part of the F_e format is very specific, with a pattern of 0 0 1 0 1 1. The pattern will always appear in frame bits 4, 8, 12, 16, 20, and 24. The ESF, like B8ZS, will be applicable only when the equipment to recognize it is deployed in the network.

Wide implementation of ESF is expected to bring about several improvements in overall network performance. Not the least of these will be the use of the ESF to monitor network performance. With the ESF it is possible to provide continuous performance checking without inhibiting traffic performance. Overall network control and performance measurement will also benefit from the ESF. The ESF makes it possible to use a 4-kbit/s channel to control and report on performance. Another important advantage that will flow from networkwide implementation of the ESF is the elimination of false framing patterns. False framing can lead to serious error conditions going unreported, such as instances when a NAK is mistaken for a network crash. ■

Daniel R. Ruffalo has spent the last eight of his 28 years as a system application engineer at Rotelcom, a subsidiary of Rochester Telephone Corp., Fairport, N. Y. He is a graduate of Auburn Community College in Auburn, N. Y., where he earned an A. A. S. in electronics.

Jay E. Israel, Excelan Inc., San Jose, Calif., and Alan J. Weissberger, Teledimensions Inc., Santa Clara, Calif.

Communicating between heterogeneous networks

Here is the way OSI layers interrelate for both connection-oriented and connectionless approaches.

In an earlier article (What the new internetworking standards provide," DATA COMMUNICATIONS, February, p. 141)—hereafter referred to as Weissberger-Israel—the authors examined the Open Systems Interconnection (OSI) Network Layer to explain why it has received so much attention. It is responsible for resolving the disparities between various transmission technologies and for providing end-to-end service spanning diverse subnetwork types. Both the connectionless and the connection-oriented approaches are making headway in the International Organization for Standardization (ISO) OSI arena.

Here, we take a larger-scale view. While the Weissberger-Israel article looked at a horizontal slice across one OSI layer, this one shows the relationship between OSI layers in a communicating computer—and the methods of combining such computers into heterogeneous networks. As before, we cover both the connectionless and connection-oriented approaches. We also discuss a newly proposed method of providing a measure of compatibility between the two approaches—which were previously considered irreconcilable.

That must multinetwork users consider before implementing either a connectionless or a connection-oriented internetworking operation? Besides being familiar with the Open Systems Interconnection (OSI) seven-layer model, they must understand how to apply connectionless and connection-oriented internetworking.

The Connectionless network protocol (CLNP) is embodied in the ISO (International Organization for Standard-ization) 8473 standard. When the protocol is used between two computers on the same LAN (local area network), the lower-layer protocol exchanges are as shown in Figure 1.

At the Physical Layer (and the lower or MAC—medium access control—sublayer of the Data Link Layer), each LAN end station implements one of the LAN standards in the IEEE standards series. These standards are currently the carrier-sense multiple access with collision detection bus (802.3), token-passing bus (802.4), and token-passing ring (802.5). This configuration of standards is independent of other kinds of subnetworks to which the LAN may be connected via internetworking units (IWUs). Therefore, the topology of the network as a whole does not have to be taken into account in the design of LAN end-station exchanges. (See "Glossary" for some of the standard terminology used in this article.)

Above the MAC sublayer, LLC 1 (logical link control Class 1) is specified, as defined in IEEE 802.2, which is part of the IEEE LAN standards series. LLC 1 provides a uniform Data Link service to the next layer, the Network Layer, so that the latter need not be affected by the distinctions among the different LAN types.

Keeping it simple
LLC 1 was chosen for LAN subnetworks because of its simplicity and speed: It is connectionless (DATA COMMUNI-CATIONS, "Internetworking in an OSI environment," May 1986, p. 120). With LAN technology—featuring reliable multimegabit-per-second transmission—the costs of a more complicated logical link control are not justified.

The lower two layers are involved with the delivery of datagrams (individual blocks of data) between stations within a single LAN segment. The third, or Network, layer is the one that provides end-to-end delivery across several subnetworks, both local and wide area networks. The protocol for the Network Layer is the CLNP, which has been

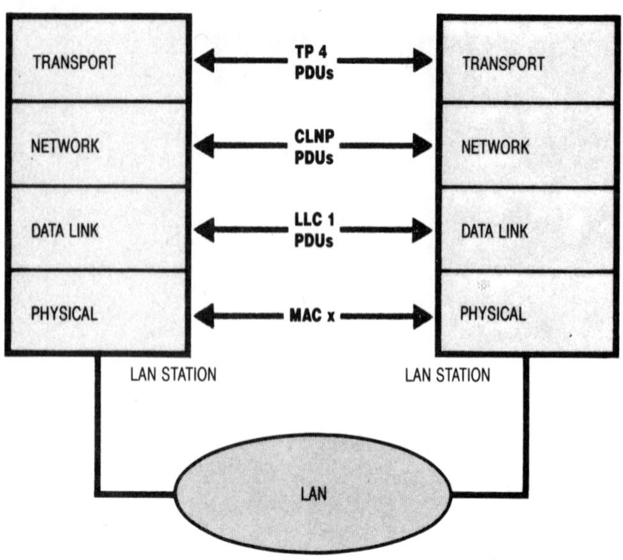

1. LAN protocols. *Shown are the lower-layer protocol exchanges when the connectionless Network protocol is used between two computers on one local area network.*

CLNP = CONNECTIONLESS NETWORK PROTOCOL
LAN = LOCAL AREA NETWORK
MAC = MEDIUM ACCESS CONTROL
PDU = PROTOCOL DATA UNIT
TP = TRANSPORT PROTOCOL

discussed at length in Weissberger-Israel.

In the next, or Transport, layer the ISO Class 4 connection-oriented Transport Protocol—commonly abbreviated TP 4—is prescribed. The standard is ISO 8073. It specifies five protocol classes, numbered 0 through 4. (For more detail about the five TP classes, see DATA COMMUNICATIONS, "Internetworking in an OSI environment," May 1986, p. 126.) The 8073 standard is well known in the industry, and TP 4 is the workhorse Transport Protocol, providing reliable, sequenced, flow-controlled, end-to-end connections.

Less well known is a complementary protocol in the works (ISO 8602) to provide a connectionless Transport. For simple one-time exchanges of information, connectionless operation above the Network Layer has appeal. It is an alternative to TP 4, and it is a natural match to a connectionless Network Layer.

Although the protocol layers above Transport are not illustrated in the figure, they are present in end systems (seven-layer configurations).

Two stacks

An internetworking unit acts as an intermediary for the relay of traffic from one subnetwork to another. On a LAN station, there is a single protocol "stack." With an IWU, there are two stacks: one for each directly connected subnetwork. The two may be the same or different, depending on whether or not the two subnetworks use the same media technology. Several configurations of IWUs can occur in one large network, depending on the various types of subnetworks that are to be connected.

On one side of an IWU, the Data Link Layer and the Physical Layer for a LAN are implemented. On the other side, those of a wide area network (or possibly another LAN of the same or different MAC technology) are implemented. In each IWU, however, the CLNP is the topmost layer, the one that is present end-to-end, providing ultimate delivery to the destination.

The IWU function does not involve anything above the Network Layer, and no physical box or device need be dedicated to the IWU function. There may be other processing taking place in the device, including that of higher protocol layers. Nonetheless, it is convenient to think of the IWU as a well-defined entity and to diagram its internal structure, even though it may be sharing the same computer with other entities, even with other IWUs.

To configure a network containing a variety of different subnetworks, the IWUs are used as building blocks. Each IWU matches two subnetworks to which it is attached. The design of an IWU is affected only by the operation of these directly connected subnetworks, not by that of other subnetworks in place several hops away.

Figure 2 indicates the PDU (protocol data unit) exchanges that are used when interconnecting two LANs. The letters x and y stand for the MAC designators: 802.3, .4, or .5. They may be the same or different. The protocols

Glossary

AD	Addendum
AFI	Authority and format identifier
ASC	Accredited Standards Committee
CLNP	Connectionless Network protocol
CSMA/CD	Carrier-sense multiple access with collision detection
COS	Corporation for Open Systems
DCE	Data circuit-terminating equipment
DSP	Domain specific part
DTE	Data terminal equipment
I	Information (packet)
IDI	Initial domain identifier
ISDN	Integrated Services Digital Network
ISO	International Organization for Standardization
IWU	Internetworking unit (gateway)
LAN	Local area network
LAPB	Link access procedure-balanced
LLC	Logical link control
MAC	Medium access control
NPDU	Network protocol data unit
NSDU	Network service data unit
OSI	Open Systems Interconnection
PDU	Protocol data unit
PLP	Packet layer protocol
PSDN	Packet-switched data network
TCP/IP	Transmission Control Protocol/Internet Protocol
SNA	Systems Network Architecture
TP	Transport protocol
TSDU	Transport service data unit
UI	Unnumbered Information (packet)
WAN	Wide area network

2. Protocols between LANs. *Shown are the protocol data unit exchanges between two interconnected LANs. The letters x and y stand for the medium access control designators: 802.3, .4, or .5. They may be the same or different. The diagram's symmetry results from the fundamental similarity of the two subnetworks.*

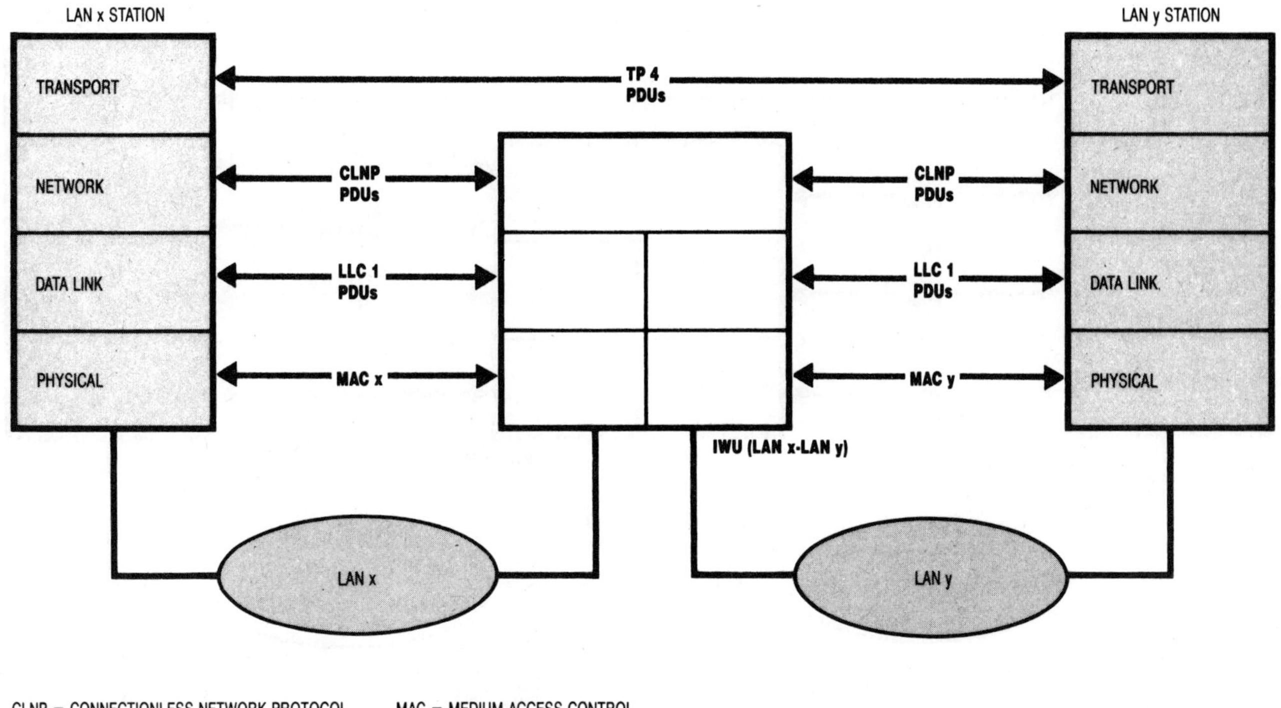

shown are the same as those discussed earlier, but here there are two instances of LLC, MAC, and Physical Layer in the IWU (one for each attached subnetwork). Note the symmetry of the diagram. It results from the fundamental similarity of the two subnetworks.

Below the Network Layer, communications is on a one-hop basis. An entity acts as though it is communicating with its peer entity in the next immediate destination — shown by having the communications-path arrows extend over only a single subnetwork. By contrast, the Transport Layer communication is end-to-end. The Transport entity need consider only the ultimate destination. The Network Layer resolves these two views of the world by implementing end-to-end delivery over a series of subnetworks.

The prevalent X.25

Figure 3 indicates the protocol exchanges for connecting a LAN end station with a WAN (wide area network) end station. On the left are the same LAN Data Link and Physical Layer protocols described above. On the right is the three-layer X.25 protocol for packet-switching data networks. Across the top of both is the CLNP. The X.25 Packet Layer PDUs are employed to encapsulate Network Layer PDUs for conveying over the wide area network.

Still, the LAN end station is unaffected by X.25. Its Network Layer communications with the IWU is the same, whether the next subnetwork is an X.25 WAN, an 802 LAN, or some entirely different technology. As before, once one contemplates the Transport Layer and above, there is no need to consider what precise choice of subnetwork type was made in a previous layer.

Only a minimal subset of the X.25 standard is employed when the WAN is used in this fashion. Specifically, procedures for establishing and clearing a virtual call, data transfer, flow control, and Packet Layer restart are required. This is because CLNP is designed to operate over arbitrary, unenhanced subnetworks, so it does not rely on any subnetwork's specialized features. (These features include X.25's D bit — delivery confirmation — and the interrupt packet, which conveys high-priority data outside the normal X.25 sequence rules.)

Protocols above the Network Layer do not affect IWU operation. In particular, no attempt is made to associate X.25 virtual circuits with Transport Layer connections. This simplifies operation by minimizing the maintenance of state information — because the record of which end systems are involved in traffic that traverses each particular X.25 virtual circuit is not needed — and it provides economical use of virtual circuits.

To build a network out of subnetworks, IWU configurations are applied as building blocks, with the choice of IWUs depending on the pairs of subnetwork types to be connected. For example, Figure 4 shows two LAN end stations using an X.25 WAN to intercommunicate.

Figure 4 is a bit more involved than the previous two figures, but it is assembled from the same components. It shows two LAN stations, remote from each other, that need to communicate. Each is attached only to its LAN.

3. LAN-to-PSDN protocols. *On the right is the three-layer X.25 protocol for packet-switching data networks (PSDNs). Across the top is the ubiquitous connectionless Network protocol. The X.25 packet layer protocol data units (PDUs) are employed to encapsulate Network Layer PDUs for conveying over the wide area network.*

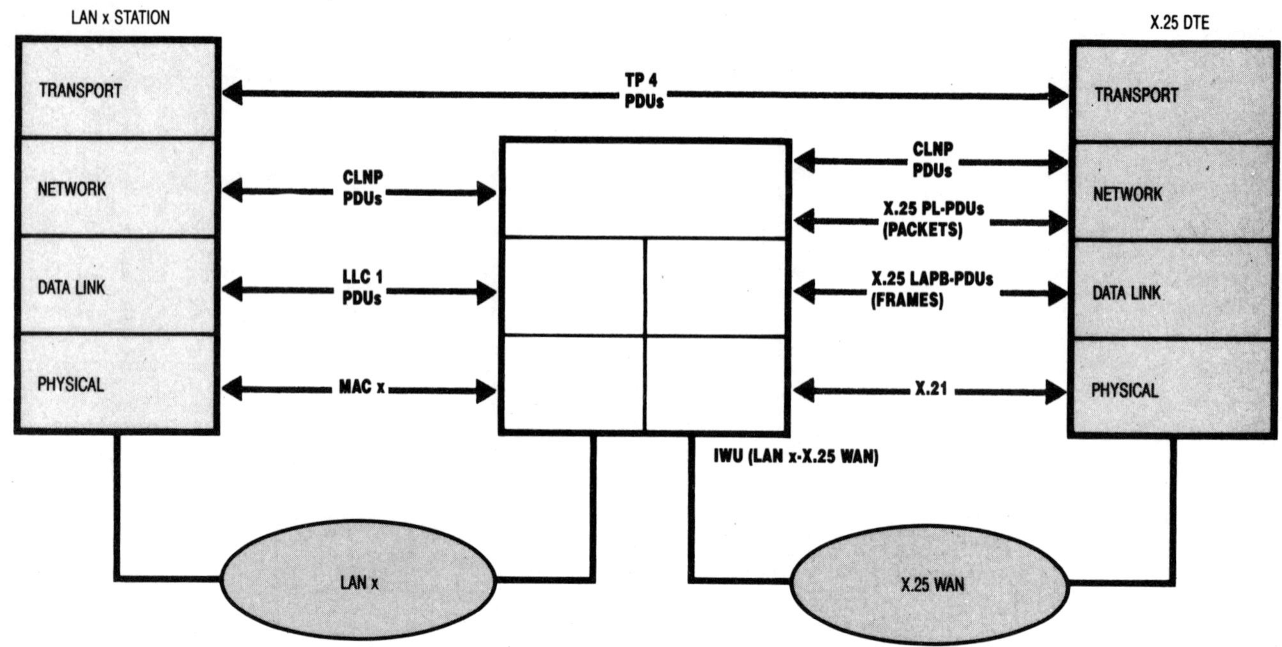

But each LAN also has an IWU attached to an X.25 network. Through the IWUs, end-to-end connectivity is achieved.

Generalizing still further, Figure 5 illustrates a more complex example of a network that a geographically dispersed organization would need. Here, diverse LANs are shown intercommunicating over a variety of WANs. To keep the figure uncluttered, the individual PDU exchanges are not shown. But imagine each IWU as having one of the protocol stack pairs already described, and each subnetwork conveying PDUs as illustrated in the previous figures. All the above descriptions of the Network and Transport Layer roles still apply.

Connectionless internetworking issues

Each specific technology has its own particular design considerations and implementation fine points. Here we discuss some of the issues that pertain to connectionless internetworking.

For any two computers to communicate, there must be an unambiguous way to identify them uniquely. This boils down to designing an addressing plan. People employ names, but a directory reduces a name to a numerical address for automatic processing. The names can be local in context, but the addresses must be globally unique.

Developing an addressing plan for OSI is proving to be controversial. After being considered at length, the outline for uniquely identifying a destination and source LAN/WAN station by a Network service access point has been finalized. Not surprisingly, it is a hierarchical method. The highest level of the hierarchy is an "authority and format identifier" (AF I). It specifies who is responsible for the next level of the hierarchy and how to interpret the rest of the address.

Some of the AF I choices are existing numbering plans: the worldwide telephone network, public data networks, Telex, and Integrated Services Digital Network. Another choice is geographical, based on a country code. Still another is for international organizations to have their own codes. Finally, there is locally administered use in a circumscribed environment.

The second level of the hierarchy is the initial domain identifier (IDI). It is made up of such items as the telephone number, Telex number, or country code. The third level is the domain specific part (DSP). Whoever has authority over a particular IDI also has the prerogative of administering the DSP.

For example, if one has a computer connected to a telephone line, one has authority over those addresses having the corresponding telephone number in their IDI. The decision may be made to have only one address and to leave the DSP empty. Or several DSPs may be assigned to different applications in the computer. More interestingly, the computer may be an IWU attached to a LAN, and one might want to use the DSP to indicate a station on the LAN. Further, instead of a LAN, there may be an elaborate private network of LANs with point-to-point links, placing more demands on the DSP.

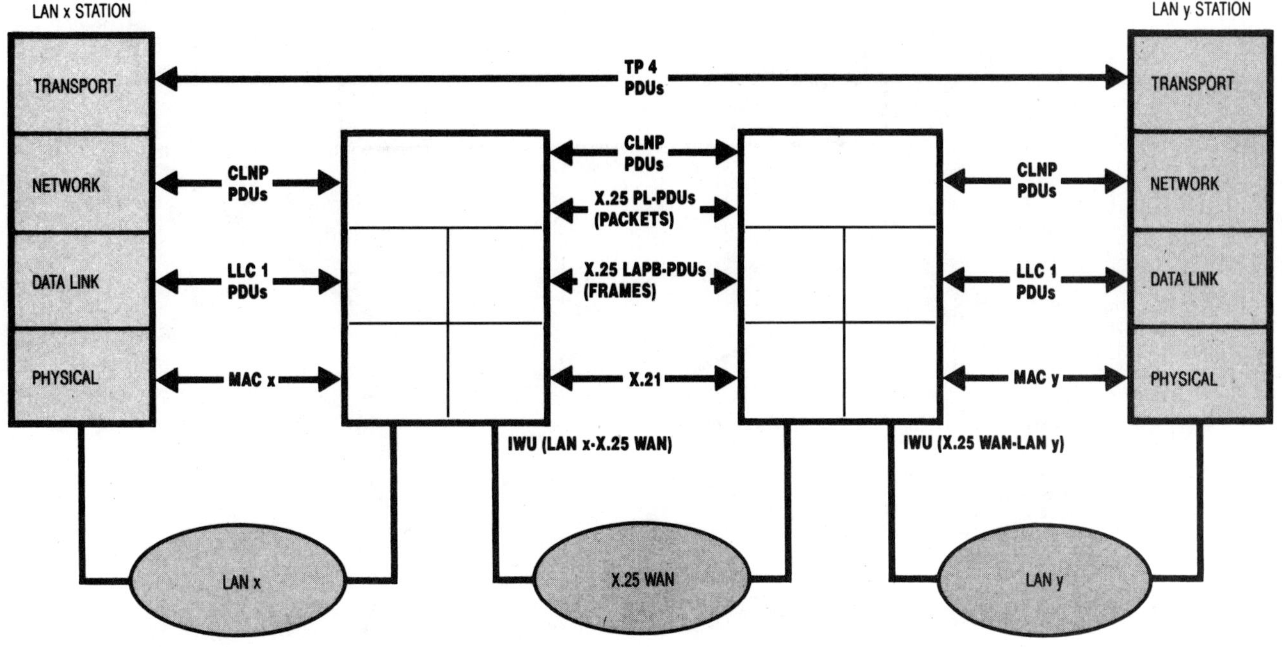

If the private network has several IWUs attached to public networks at several points, one may decide not to base addressing on a telephone number at all but may use one of the other AFI choices. (These choices include the geographic and international-organization codes mentioned previously.) A similar decision may be made with a network that might grow or change, even if it is still small.

The internal structure of the DSP is not standardized. While the expectation is that it will be administered hierarchically, the layout of the address fields is at the discretion of the person who owns a particular IDI. Ramifications of this discretion are discussed below.

Getting the message

End stations and IWUs participate in routing. Before any station transmits an outgoing Network protocol data unit (NPDU), the Network Layer determines the next immediate address in the path of the final destination and then forwards the packet. Routing takes two criteria into account: the address of the final destination and the quality of service prescribed by the originating Network-service user. The attributes of quality of service include transit delay, cost, priority, and residual error probability (the probability of undetected errors). In certain applications, security is a third routing criterion. It limits categories of traffic to specified stations and subnetworks.

As an alternative to these criteria, the source end station may dictate (either completely or partially) the sequence of IWUs to be traversed by an NPDU. This is source routing.

It is useful for various situations: for diagnostic testing, as a fallback when Network Layer-based automatic methods do not apply, and for replying to a query from a previously unknown computer via a reverse path.

CLNP by itself does not solve the complete routing problem. It only specifies source routing. Work is in progress in Accredited Standards Committee (ASC) X3S3.3 to develop a comprehensive routing architecture. One key issue is how much to depend on the structure of the destination address in making routing decisions.

Several different approaches to routing have been advanced. Each imposes some structure on the DSP and uses its substructure as an aid to efficient routing. Each approach deals with an address structure, a way to organize the stations from a routing point of view, and a protocol to exchange information about network connectivity. While some approaches may find acceptance in certain circles, it is unlikely that a single DSP layout will be standardized: The needs of different user communities are too diverse.

The standard for assigning Network Layer addresses places few constraints on the DSP. Different people exploit this flexibility in different ways—such as in hierarchies that have different numbers of levels (for example, three- or two-level hierarchies). For this reason, general-purpose IWUs will doubtless have to embody code for more than one algorithm.

In deciding where to concentrate routing functionality, note that end systems are more numerous than IWUs. Thus

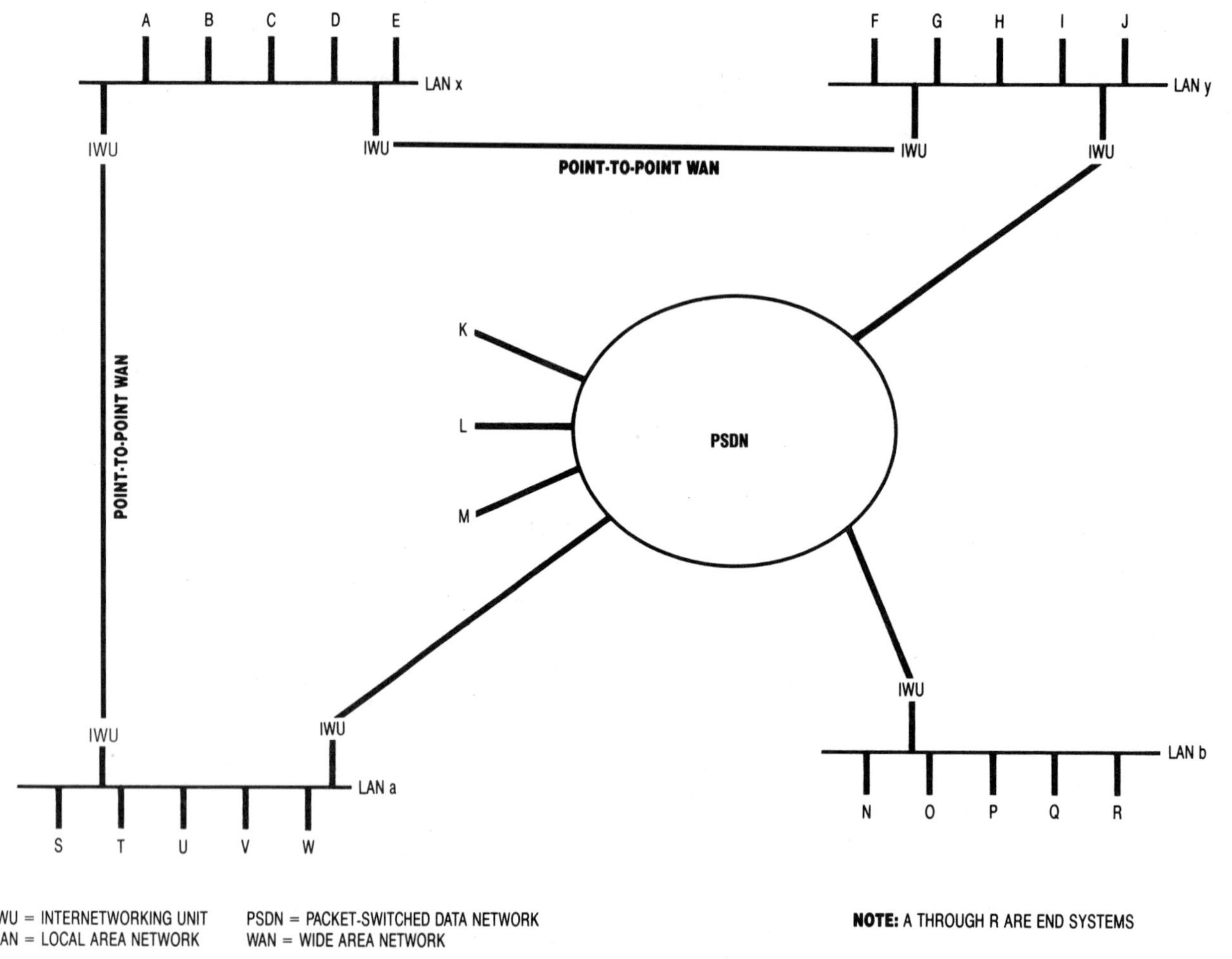

it would be less costly to concentrate the routing functionality in IWUs. The current unfinalized state of routing standards is another factor to consider. When standards are complete, it is desirable for upgrades to be made only to IWUs (revisions made in a minimum number of places). For this reason, one standard protocol is being advanced first by ASC X3S3.3. It would apply to a means for end stations and IWUs to interact so the end stations can play their part in routing. Once this much is settled, the design of end systems will become stable, accommodating most of the computers involved in OSI.

Overload relief

The end systems implement end-to-end flow control by window mechanisms in the Transport protocol Class 4 (see Weissberger-Israel). This helps alleviate traffic overload at end systems and at IWUs, but additional measures are required to address congestion more fully.

For certain kinds of subnetworks, Data Link flow control is a requirement. International Telegraph and Telephone Consultative Committee X.25 LAPB (link access procedure-balanced) on packet data networks is one such case. The imposition of flow control on a single subnetwork does not does not affect the methods employed by the CLNP or by other subnetworks. It is a constraint dictated by the particular technology of the subnetwork.

A mechanism is included in CLNP by which congestion can be controlled. When an IWU detects congestion, it tags traffic that traverses the IWU with a "congestion-experienced" bit. Deciding which particular NPDUs will be tagged this way is done by the IWU. The destination station, sensing the bit, takes measures to reduce the flow of similar traffic. The flow-reduction measures taken are not standardized—they are a local matter. The criterion for setting the congestion-experienced bit is, typically, shortage of buffer space in an IWU.

When CLNP is used, the Transport Layer implements end-to-end error control by acknowledgment and retransmission mechanisms in the Class 4 protocol. This provides reliable, sequenced delivery of data units between Transport users in a pair of communicating end stations.

Since the Class 4 Transport Protocol operates end-to-end, the IWUs need not be concerned with Transport's recovery steps. TP 4 is like a gigantic vacuum cleaner that disposes of all sorts of grime (that is, corrupted or out-of-sequence packets) from lower layers with a single general-purpose tool. It eliminates the need to go over the same ground repeatedly with different specialized cleanup tools: the broom, hose, rake, and sponge that are analogous to Network Layer reliability features.

CLNP does have an optional header checksum. It helps detect processing errors or other failures in the IWUs that relay the traffic. It protects against action being taken on erroneous header information.

Most subnetworks employ a frame check sequence to detect errored incoming Data Link packets. Upon error detection, the Data Link protocol either discards the packet without taking further action or corrects the error via retransmission. (Strictly speaking, it is the next correctly received packet that provokes recovery action because only then does a missing sequence number become apparent.) LLC 1 is an example of the first case (discard); X.25 LAPB, the second (retransmission). The choice of error-control mechanics on a single subnetwork does not affect the methods employed by CLNP or by other subnetworks. It is a consequence of the transmission error rate of the particular subnetwork.

Segmentation and reassembly

Any transmitting computer (either the data source or an IWU) may be required to segment a data unit to convey it over a subnetwork. In the protocols discussed here, there are three places (layers) this segmentation can occur: (a) in X.25 PLP, or packet layer protocol (in the Network Layer), (b) in CLNP, and (c) in a connection-oriented Transport Layer. Segmentation of type (a) can be used only over the X.25 subnetwork portions of a path; segmentation of types (b) and (c) can be employed over any subnetwork.

At the X.25 packet level — type (a) — a data unit can be sent as several packets by using the X.25 M (more data) bit. Such segmenting is only for a single virtual circuit; it is not visible to the CLNP.

When CLNP performs fragmentation — type (b) — it splits a Network service data unit (NSDU), places a Network Layer header on each fragment, and launches it on its way. Each fragment's header carries "offset information" to indicate where the fragment belongs in the complete NSDU. Bear in mind that these fragments may traverse different paths to reach their destination. This implies that fragments may arrive duplicated (a node may resend a fragment if, for example, there is no firm acknowledgment of a transmission) and/or out of order, or not at all. Moreover, fragments may partially overlap one another (fragment sizes may be different over different subnetworks). The reassembly function of the CLNP puts the fragments in proper order to reconstitute the NSDU.

Transport Layer fragmentation and assembly — type (c) — permits a TSDU (Transport service data unit) to be conveyed in multiple NSDUs. This is purely an end-to-end operation, involving none of the intermediate systems in the procedure.

Segmentation can occur in more than one of the three layers, for the same TSDU. In many situations, the originating end system has latitude in deciding where segmentation should actually be performed. (The two determining criteria are the maximum packet sizes permitted by the subnetworks to be traversed and the processing efficiencies of the fragmentation at the different layers.) This

degree of freedom can be exploited to optimize operation, provided that the originator has information about the characteristics of the subnetworks to be traversed.

The segmentation performed by X.25 PLP is for only one subnetwork hop. Its effect is erased by the time the packet reaches the subsequent subnetwork. This is because — unlike CLNP fragmentation — the individual fragments are not self-contained: Fragment headers do not have end-to-end significance independent of the path taken. The X.25 fragments must be recombined immediately in the IWU and handled together, as a unit. In some situations, this makes it more desirable than CLNP fragmentation, where reassembly does not typically occur until the final destination is reached. In other situations (such as a concatenation of diverse subnetworks), doing fragmentation via X.25 PLP results in the same processing being repeated several times.

One complexity of type (b) segmentation is the need to deal with fragments that arrive either out of order or partially overlapping, and the need for reassembly timeouts.

Both (a) and (c) share a simplicity: Reassembly can be applied when incoming data is already in its proper order, and a separate time-out for the reassembly operation is not required. Moreover, if the implementation has knowledge about the maximum packet sizes permitted by the various subnetworks, alternative (c) disposes of segmentation processing for outgoing traffic. If the knowledge is only "highly likely," the benefit is itself highly likely (lower-level fragmentation occurs only on an exception basis).

Procedural strategies

An X.25 virtual circuit is established on demand — that is, when the Network Layer entity must transmit outgoing traffic to a destination not served by an appropriate already-existing virtual circuit. Even if a virtual circuit already exists to the proper next-immediate destination, it might not be appropriate. For example, the new traffic might have quality-of-service requirements (like high throughput or low transit delay) that cannot be satisfied by the circuit already available.

It is possible that two IWUs may attempt to establish virtual circuits to each other simultaneously. Procedures for eliminating one virtual circuit while retaining the other (collision resolution) have been specified. An algebraic comparison of network layer addresses is used to resolve the contention. When more than one virtual circuit between two IWUs is required for throughput, robustness (load-sharing backup), or administrative convenience, a two-octet subnetwork-connection reference number appears in the X.25 call-request for this purpose. In this case, the procedure to eliminate a virtual circuit is not exercised.

An IWU connecting a LAN to a WAN can initiate an X.25 connection when needed, but there is no certain way to determine when the connection is no longer needed. This leaves open the question of when to remove the X.25 virtual circuit. The best the IWU can do is use a time-out to see if usage of the virtual circuit has ceased. During the time-out period, there may be concern that connect charges are accruing unproductively.

The problem can be ameliorated by adapting the time-out value to tariff information. In fact, many carriers charge by traffic generated, but not according to the duration of a virtual call. When using CLNP over X.25, such a policy is ideal, because leaving a virtual circuit idle would not, in this case, be costly.

Performance issues may indicate the need for more than one virtual circuit between the same pair of IWUs. On a given virtual circuit, a typical packet network permits the IWU to send only a limited number (typically less than 10) of Data packets before the IWU must wait for an acknowledgment. This is specified by the packet window size. The waiting time adversely impacts throughput. With an additional virtual circuit, the waiting time can be used for traffic on the second virtual circuit.

Since there is typically a charge for establishing a virtual circuit (the cost of a Call Request packet is typically four to 10 times that of a Data packet), and each virtual circuit requires resources in the IWU, the algorithm for establishing additional virtual circuits should take various factors into account. Among them are: throughput of one virtual circuit, the effective data rate of the X.25 interface to the data network, the quality of service requested by the Network service user, and the desirability of preempting an already existing virtual circuit.

If a release or reset occurs while packets are in transit, these packets may be lost. This sounds severe, but it is actually innocuous, since it is a rare event and Class 4 Transport in the end systems is prepared to recover from it: The originator fails to receive an end-to-end acknowledgment and resends the packet(s).

Connection oriented

Up to now, the discussion has been on connectionless Network Layer design. What follows is a discussion of the connection-oriented Network Layer design. As noted in Weissberger-Israel, ISO 8881 specifies how to use X.25 PLP on a LAN and is an application of ISO 8208. Additional considerations, not necessary in the X.25 DTE-to-PSDN or DTE-to-DTE environments, are needed when using X.25 PLP over a LAN; so 8881 goes beyond the scope of 8208. (DTE is data terminal equipment; PSDN is packet-switching data network.)

There are several reasons for the additional considerations:

■ The LAN is a broadcast medium that supports many logical links and X.25 interfaces (LAN-station-x to LAN-station-y communications). X.25 PLP is meant for a dedicated point-to-point link: DTE-to-PSDN or DTE-to-DTE.

■ Logical Link Control Class 1 does not provide the reliable, connection-mode Data Link service that ISO 8208 expects. There is no error recovery or flow control in LLC 1, on which X.25 PLP relies.

■ When the LAN is connected to an X.25 PSDN, all LAN stations access the PSDN through one (or a small number of) IWU(s). Therefore each IWU must concentrate virtual circuits from various X.25 LAN stations into a single X.25 interface to the PSDN.

■ X.25 user facilities and options (discussed in greater detail later) for LAN stations may differ. The IWU must be made aware of which user facilities are associated with each LAN station and administer those common to all LAN stations. LAN stations must have information on which user facilities they administer and which ones the

---

X.25 error recovery options

Given the possibility of lost packets on a local area network, there are several options that can be exercised to avoid deadlock and to recover lost data. (Deadlock is a condition where each of a communicating pair of stations is waiting for the other to transmit, and neither is aware that the other is waiting.) The X.25 LAN stations and Internetworking units (IWUs) must both choose the same set of error recovery options for each direction of transmission.

1. Either use logical link control (LLC) 1: The X.25 PLP (packet layer protocol) receiver waits after receiving an out-of-sequence Data packet, and the remote transmitter resends Data packet(s) after the expiration of a no-acknowledgment window rotation timer (incrementing of modulo 8 or 128 — labeled T25).

2. Or use LLC 2 for error recovery at the Data Link layer, transmit a DTE (data terminal equipment) reject or reset request packet after detecting an out-of-sequence Data packet, and do not retransmit unacknowledged Data packets. (That would result in duplicates being received.)

There are three X.25 binary variables listed in the table ("X.25 error recovery options for a LAN"), producing six variants, that can be chosen for effective error recovery. If communicating X.25 PLP LAN stations and IWUs don't both implement the same variant, the X.25 PLP will not recover from lost packets, and the Network service will be unreliable. Transport protocol (TP) Class 4 might be necessary for error recovery. The TP class is negotiated by the peer Transport entities, based on the error and loss rate of the network and the need to multiplex several Transport connections into a single Network connection (see Table 2, "TP class selection," of the main story).

X.25 error recovery options for a LAN

TRANSMITTER R25[1]/VALUE:	R25 = 0 (NO RETRANSMISSION)	OR	R25 GREATER THAN 0 (RETRANSMIT UNACKNOWLEDGED PACKETS)
RECEIVER ACTION AFTER DETECTING LOST PACKET:	NONE[2] (WAIT FOR TRANSMITTER TO RESEND PACKET)	OR	RESET REQUEST[3]
TRANSMITTER AND RECEIVER LLC CLASS:	[1](NO DATA LINK ERROR RECOVERY)	OR	[2](DATA LINK ERROR RECOVERY)

1. R25 IS THE NUMBER OF TIMES TO RESEND A DATA PACKET AFTER A T25 NO-ACKNOWLEDGMENT TIME-OUT. IF R25 = 0, X.25 CAN'T RECOVER FROM LOST PACKETS.

2. NOT ALLOWED FOR AN X.25 PSDN INTERFACE.

3. WHEN AN X.25 PACKET LAYER RESET OCCURS, TP 1 OR TP 3 IS NECESSARY TO RESYNCHRONIZE.

LAN = LOCAL AREA NETWORK   PSDN = PACKET-SWITCHED DATA NETWORK
LLC = LOGICAL LINK CONTROL   TP = TRANSPORT PROTOCOL

Table 1: X.25 error recovery options in ISO 8881

TRANSMITTER OPTIONS[1]	RECEIVER OPTIONS		
	DATA TERMINAL EQUIPMENT		
	RESET	REJECT	WAIT
RESEND THE UNACKNOWLEDGED DATA PACKET(S)	RESYNC VIA TP 1 OR TP 3 (RESET INDICATION)	SENDER RECOVERS BY TRANSMITTING DATA PACKETS AFTER RECEIVING 'DTE REJ'	SENDER RECOVERS BY TRANSMITTING DATA PACKETS AFTER TIME-OUT[2] PRIMITIVE
SEND RESET REQUEST PACKET	RESYNC VIA TP 1 OR TP 3 (RESET INDICATION PRIMITIVE)	RESYNC VIA TP 1 OR TP 3	RESYNC VIA TP 1 OR TP 3

1. ON DETECTION OF AN OUT-OF-SEQUENCE DATA PACKET.

2. THIS IS ONLY POSSIBLE IF R25 IS GREATER THAN ZERO (SEE TABLE IN PANEL). IF R25= 0, NO ERROR RECOVERY IS POSSIBLE BECAUSE TRANSMISSION WOULD NOT BE POSSIBLE.

internetworking unit administers for them on a per-call basis.

■ If the LAN is connected to a non-X.25 WAN (such as a satellite network, a circuit-switched public data network, a store-and-forward private network, or another LAN), X.25 packet layer functions must be mapped onto the subnetwork access protocol of the connected network. These functions include flow control, reset, clear, restart, and diagnostics. The mapping requires an ad hoc subnetwork-dependent convergence function in the IWU.

■ Finally, if two packet networks are interconnected, and one uses X.25-1984 while the other uses X.25-1980, a convergence protocol (ISO 8878 Annex 1) is required in the IWU to meet the OSI connection-oriented Network service.

Applicable intercommunications

Within the LAN environment, communications is between X.25 PLP LAN stations. ISO 8208 includes procedures for DTE-to-DTE operation that are applicable on a LAN, since there is no intervening PSDN. In particular, one DTE must act as data circuit-terminating equipment (DCE) for purposes of logical channel assignment and virtual call collision. This decision is based on a restart procedure that is initiated when there are no active virtual circuits on a given logical link. Furthermore, several optional user facilities — such as packet size, window size, and throughput class — must be bilaterally agreed upon prior to initiating communications between X.25 LAN stations.

Because of a multiple logical-link capability, each LAN station requires multiple X.25 PLP entities: one for each destination LAN station or IWU with which it communicates. Each X.25 PLP entity operates over its own logical link and is identified by either the MAC address of the source LAN station or a source reference number.

X.25 PLP error recovery options must be consistent between communicating LAN stations and IWUs. Otherwise, packets will be lost and the Network service will be unreliable. Many Europeans would like to use TP 0 over a reliable X.25 connection-oriented Network service for teletex applications. (TP 1, 3, or 4 could recover from lost packets and an unreliable connection-oriented network service, but they are not used for applications such as teletex and certain electronic-mail implementations.)

A new draft of ISO 8881 will specify error recovery options that must be mutually agreed upon by LAN stations (see "X.25 error recovery options"). The current options when LLC 1 is used are listed in Table 1. The sufficiency of LLC 1 for error recovery is presently controversial, and, for this reason, ISO 8881 has been divided into two parts: one for LLC 1, another for LLC 2. If LLC 2 is used, it will recover from most transmission errors. LLC 2 is connection-oriented itself and includes sequence numbering, flow control, and acknowledgment at the Data Link Layer. The X.25 PLP should then send a Reset Request or DTE Reject packet upon detecting a Data packet out of sequence.

The best way

An X.25 PLP LAN station may need to support inherently connectionless applications, such as inquiry/response or database look-up. The best way to achieve this support with the X.25 PLP is to use Fast Select (the ability to send up to 128 octets of data in Call Setup and Clearing packets). However, the Fast Select user data field's maximum of 128 octets (in the Call Request/Indication and Clear Request/Indication packets) may not be sufficient. If insufficient, one or more Data packets would then be needed to deliver the entire message.

Since an LLC UI (Unnumbered Information) or I (Information) packet may be capable of carrying over 1,000 octets of data, several smaller X.25 Data packets associated with a Fast Select call could be combined and sent in a single UI or I packet. This would substantially improve response time — a prime requirement for inquiry/response types of applications — but it requires a segmentation and reassembly function between the X.25 PLP and the LLC.

An X.25 IWU, or Network Layer router, must concentrate and logically connect several LAN-to-IWU virtual circuits with IWU-to-X.25 PSDN virtual circuits. Therefore, for LAN stations, strategies must be developed to allocate and manage virtual circuits that access the PSDN. This access management is needed to map various packet types between the LAN stations and PSDN. It is also needed to convert a single Restart Indication packet from the PSDN into multiple Clear Indication packets for those LAN stations with PSDN virtual circuits in the data transfer state (virtual circuits between stations on the same LAN would not be cleared).

Permanent virtual circuits, not covered in ISO 8881, also need to be managed. Since there is no Call Request packet, the user facility information that it would contain must be known in advance to the LAN station and IWU.

The IWU must also:

■ Handle X.25 PLP flow control between two X.25 interfaces (the IWU-PSDN and LAN station-IWU).

■ Convey Diagnostic packets from PSDN to the appropriate LAN station.

■ Convey DTE Reject packets from LAN station to PSDN.

■ Notify PSDN of LAN station failure by generating Clear Request packets for all virtual circuits that were up when

that station failed.
■ Generate multiple Reset (or Clear) Indications in response to a single PSDN-generated Reset (or Clear) Indication for all LAN stations sharing a PSDN-IWU virtual circuit.

Another job for the IWU is administration of X.25 user facilities for some or all LAN stations. For example, some of the user facilities that could be requested at call-setup time or fixed at subscription time are:
■ Fast Select.
■ Outgoing/incoming calls barred.
■ One-way outgoing or incoming logical channel.
■ Closed user groups.
■ Call redirection.
■ Transit delay and throughput class negotiation.
■ Charging and local charging prevention.
■ Reverse charging.
■ Network user I.D.
■ Extended packet-sequence numbering (modulo 128).
■ Nonstandard default packet and window sizes.

Charging information, on a departmental or station basis, could be extracted from the optional charging user facility and conveyed to a network management station on the LAN.

Reconciliation?

The connectionless and connection-oriented schools of thought regarding the Network Layer originated in different parts of the data communications industry. Adherents of the connectionless Network Layer approach are typically computer and networking vendors. The most visible technology of this sort is the TCP/IP (Transmission Control Protocol/Internet Protocol) suite of protocols and their applications.

The connectionless Network Layer approach was also followed by proprietary protocols, such as Xerox Network Systems, Decnet (from Digital Equipment Corp.), and Burroughs Network Architecture.

The connection-oriented approach has adherents in telephony. There, the notion of establishing an available channel of communications for a fixed duration of time is the natural thing to do. It is how telephones work—how telephone networks are designed.

This style of operation carried over into the strictly digital world of packet-switching data networks through the CCITT X.25 Recommendation. It deals with virtual Network Layer circuits: establishing them, communicating through them, and clearing them. Another adherent of the connection-oriented approach is IBM, through its Systems Network Architecture communications protocols.

Earlier in this article, diagrams included both X.25 and CLNP. But this was mere coexistence, not cooperation. Consider again Figure 3: Over the WAN, X.25 is used. But X.25 is not the only item in the Network Layer. In this configuration, it is called a subnetwork layer under CLNP. Because that is what PSDNs provide, its use is based on a pragmatic decision. In Figures 3 and 4, CLNP is the end-to-end Network Layer protocol. X.25 is the substratum needed to traverse the WAN. Computers using only X.25-based Network Layer protocols cannot be part of such a network.

Defining Network Layer service

For the two approaches to be reconciled, a way to intercommunicate would be needed. This has been thought by many in the industry to be, in any complete sense, unworkable. Consider two end systems connected

6. Defining Network service. Consider two linked end systems and imagine a Transport Layer entity in each "looking down" at the ruled line separating it from the Network Layer. The services provided at that line—the Network Layer Service Definition—are the aggregate of networking tools available to the two entities.

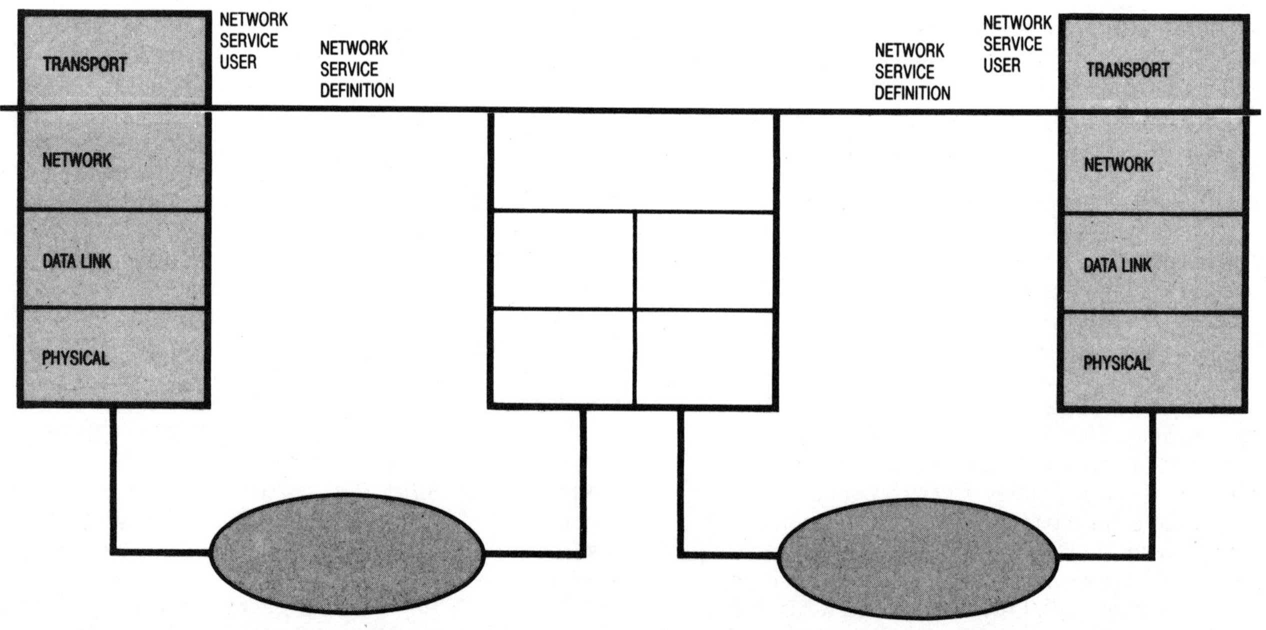

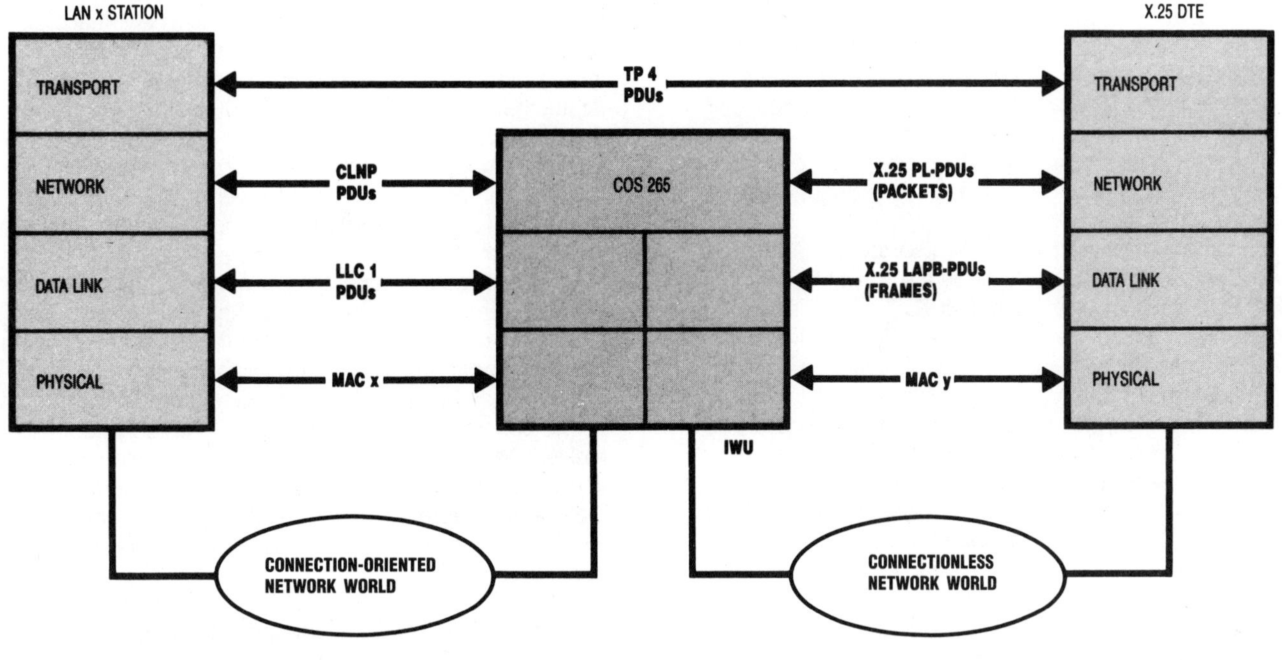

through some collection of links and imagine a Transport Layer entity in each "looking down" at the ruled line separating it from the Network Layer (Fig. 6). The services provided at that line are the networking tools available to the two separated entities. This aggregate of tools is called the Network Layer service definition. The concept is that the Network Layer protocols and all the intervening subnetworks pool their capabilities to provide this service to the two Transport Layer entities (the Network service "users").

Apparently incompatible

ISO has two such service definitions—one for a connectionless Network service and one for connection-oriented. The latter has primitives associated with connection establishment, data transfer, and connection release. The former (connectionless) only has a data transfer primitive. So the two protocol styles would appear to be incompatible. To overcome this apparent incompatibility, one would have to figure out how the Network service users could be provided with different service definitions and still communicate in a coordinated fashion.

The Corporation for Open Systems (COS) was formed in early 1986 as a consortium of companies promoting standards. COS decided not to define standards, but to choose a limited suite of ISO and CCITT standards as a basis for near-term multivendor interoperation. The suite would be supported by vendor participation and by certifi-

cation tests. There were enough adherents to both the connectionless and connection-oriented approaches within COS so that neither approach could be excluded.

The dichotomy between the two Network Layer schools of thought has the effect of splitting the COS community into two halves that cannot communicate with one another. This is at best embarrassing; at worst, it could cast doubt on the credibility of the whole internetworking effort. To deal with this issue, the COS Architecture Committee sought a way to resolve the incompatibility.

Several approaches were considered. It seemed inevitable that the OSI Reference Model would be "bent" in one way or another. The most promising approach now appears to be a particular new sort of IWU operation. Techniques were considered that spanned multiple OSI layers, but the one currently in favor is confined to the Network Layer.

The proposed Network Layer approach calls for a new IWU design, for now called COS 265. The number is the result of a whimsical subtraction of 8208 (the X.25 connection-oriented Network Layer protocol specification) from 8473 (the connectionless Network Layer protocol specification). The "difference" between the two is what the new IWU addresses—hence the subtraction.

The design is illustrated in Figure 7 (a modified version of Figure 3). In concrete terms, one can think of a LAN-WAN interconnection. But COS 265 actually connects any connectionless Network Layer collection of subnetworks on the left with any connection-oriented Network Layer collection of subnetworks on the right. The intent is to implement the COS 265 function in a few carefully chosen points in a network topology to form a bridge between the two dissimilar Network Layer worlds.

The facet of the diagram that provides the reconciliation appears on the connection-oriented side: Notice that the Network Layer consists of X.25 alone—there is no CLNP. X.25 by itself provides the Network Layer service; X.25 is not used as a subnetwork for the conveyance of another Network Layer protocol. This pleases the connection-oriented advocates.

The other salient feature of the diagram is that the Transport Layer is Class 4. This is the most powerful of the five classes included in ISO 8073. Using Class 4 is the opposite half of the compromise. Many connection-oriented advocates prefer one (not always the same one) of the lesser four classes.

The Network Layer in the connection-oriented case deals with error control and flow control; when it detects an abnormal situation (such as a broken network connection), it alerts the Transport Layer to take corrective action. When people choose different Transport Protocol classes, it is based on their perception of how often abnormal situations occur, how much communications disruption is tolerable when an abnormal situation occurs, and the relative cost of implementing and running the various Transport classes. Table 2 indicates how to select the proper Transport class by applying knowledge of the underlying subnetwork characteristics. But with COS 265 in the data path, Class 4 is required; the reason becomes apparent below.

Crossing the boundary
The COS 265 IWU connects the connection-oriented Network Layer world to the connectionless world. This is a fall-back mode of operation invoked only when it is necessary to cross the connection-oriented/connectionless boundary. So the COS 265 function will be packaged in the same IWU with the more conventional IWU operation described at the start of this article.

Conventional operation in both connectionless and connection-oriented cases requires an IWU to make a routing decision, then establish an X.25 virtual circuit to the next (or final) destination. If the virtual circuit is established successfully, conventional operation follows. But if the virtual circuit cannot be established, COS 265 operation is invoked.

Invoking COS 265 means that the virtual circuit will be used in a different way than heretofore (discussed below), informing the next destination that X.25 alone comprises

the Network Layer for the virtual circuit (connectionless-to-connection-oriented case), or that CLNP rides on top of X.25 (connection-oriented-to-connectionless case). If the IWU has been configured with enough topology information in advance, the initial attempt to establish the virtual circuit can be avoided, and the proper mode of operation can be initiated immediately. For example, if one side of the IWU is attached to a LAN on which CLNP only is employed, there is no need to attempt X.25 on that side.

The connection-oriented-to-connectionless direction is easier to implement than the reverse. Each received connection-oriented NPDU is launched independently into the connectionless world. For each virtual circuit, the IWU is programmed to "remember" the ultimate destination's Network service access point (the Network Layer address), since this information does not accompany each incoming connection-oriented NPDU. The usual connectionless load splitting and fragmentation mechanisms can be employed.

The connectionless-to-connection-oriented direction is trickier. Certainly, once the virtual circuit to the next destination is established for a particular final destination, NPDUs may be sent across it after the CLNP header has been stripped. But operating the virtual circuit properly introduces two complications.

The first complication is CLNP's fragmentation. Only complete NPDUs can traverse the connection-oriented side, but CLNP can conceivably split an NPDU and send the fragments over different paths. The fragments might not all arrive at the same IWU, yet they have to be reassembled in one place in order to cross the connectionless-to-connection-oriented threshold. For this reason, COS 265 will place a new demand on the ISO connectionless routing architecture: When fragmentation is employed, there has to be a way to have the fragments all arrive at the same COS 265 IWU for reassembly partway to the final destination.

The second complication deals with the sequence of PDUs. X.25 delivers data in the same order in which it originates; CLNP does not guarantee to do so. This places a demand on the connectionless-to-connection-oriented direction of the COS 265 function. How can the receiving connection-oriented end system cope with the possibility of NPDUs arriving out of order? The answer is in the choice of Transport Layer protocol. Class 4 is perfectly capable of receiving NPDUs in any order and putting them back in the proper sequence. TP 4 is also capable of multiplexing (conveying traffic for several Transport connections over a single Network Layer virtual circuit) and splitting (dividing traffic for a single Transport connection among multiple Network Layer virtual circuits). This makes it ideal for situations where COS 265 might be in use. It is the reason for specifying Class 4 Transport rather than any lesser class in the configuration illustrated in Figure 7.

Limitations
IWUs implementing the COS 265 function cannot be deployed as ubiquitously in the global network as can conventional IWUs. Two reasons for this have already been mentioned: the extra demands on connectionless routing and the constraints on the Transport protocol. There is one more issue: concatenation of paths.

With conventional IWUs, there is considerable latitude in

Table 2: TP class selection

NETWORK TYPE	RESIDUAL ERROR RATE	ACTUAL LOSS RATE	NEED FOR MULTIPLEXING	
			NO	YES
A	ACCEPTABLE	NEGLIGIBLE	TP 0	TP 2
B	ACCEPTABLE	NON-NEGLIGIBLE	TP 1	TP 3
C	NON-NEGLIGIBLE	IMMATERIAL	TP 4	TP 4

(A, B, AND C ARE TYPE LABELS FOR CONVENIENCE)
TP = TRANSPORT PROTOCOL

combining subnetworks via IWUs in complex topologies to build networks. With COS 265 IWUs, there are limitations.

For example, suppose that two connection-oriented end stations are communicating with each other, and that the "conversation" goes from connection-oriented to connectionless and back to connection-oriented. Each end system sees only connection-oriented operation. So if (as permitted by the Transport Layer protocol) they negotiate the Transport Layer class between them on an end-to-end basis, they might choose a class lower than 4. (This choice assumes that the connection-oriented Network Layer is taking care of such necessities as data-order preservation, error control, and flow control.)

But because there is a connectionless hop in the communications path, the assumption is ill-founded. There are several ways to deal with this situation: Somehow prevent more than one COS 265 IWU from being in the path of an NPDU; somehow inform the Transport Layer of the quality of Network Layer service that it is getting through the collection of subnetworks comprising the path for a particular Network connection.

Note that when COS 265 is in use, the two Network service users can see different service definitions. At first, this may seem strange: How can the Transport entities be communications peers, yet see different forms of service? This issue is sidestepped by looking at the situation from the point of view of a protocol, rather than a service definition. COS 265 reconciles two different Network Layer protocols. The same NPDUs are conveyed, in any event. End systems can be organized differently inside, yet still communicate unambiguously. It matters very little whether Transport establishes an X.25 virtual circuit because it has a connection-oriented Network Layer, or whether a Network Layer entity establishes the same X.25 virtual circuit because it is relaying NPDUs. The view from the wire is the same.

One point to bear in mind is that the COS 265 is not as versatile as conventional IWU operation. Its value is that it can functionally bridge the two Network Layer worlds that were previously considered irreconcilable. ∎

Jay Israel is director of software development at Excelan, with responsibility for ISO protocols. He contributes to the internetworking standardization efforts in the IEEE 802 and ASC X3S3.3 committees and the Corporation for Open Systems. He holds a B. A. from the University of Pennsylvania and a Ph. D. from the Massachusetts Institute of Technology. Alan Weissberger is an independent consultant specializing in implementing data communications standards. He participates in the activities of standards committees dealing with ISDN, public data networks, and LANs. He is also an adjunct professor at the University of Santa Clara. Weissberger has a B. S. in mathematics from SUNY-Stony Brook, an M. S. E. E. from Northeastern, and a Ph. D. in electrical engineering from MIT.

Thomas J. Routt, Network Systems Consulting, Seattle, Wash.

From out of the Blue: Interfaces from SNA to X.25

When IBM weaves links to widely used non-SNA lower-layer protocol standards, multivendor networking can take on a whole new meaning.

Of all the technologies available for corporate networking across wide areas, perhaps none has achieved more success than IBM's Systems Network Architecture (SNA) and the X.25 Recommendation adopted long ago by the International Telephone and Telegraph Consultative Committee (CCITT). SNA flourished as the preferred connection among data processing users who also preferred IBM, as most did. X.25 was swept in by the popularity of cost-saving public and private packet-switching networks.

For a long time, however, users seeking the best of both worlds had to devise their own or use third-party solutions, since IBM endorsed mainly synchronous data link control (SDLC) and leased-line networks. Recently, though, IBM has identified major market opportunities to provide gateways between its proprietary SNA and the Open Systems Interconnection (OSI) protocols put forth by the International Organization for Standardization (ISO). IBM has stated its commitment to this approach and announced a series of products that support interchange between SNA and OSI at each of the seven layers of the OSI architectural reference model.

The third layer is known variously as the packet, the network, and the path-control layer; the second provides the link level function; and the lowest offers physical connectivity. X.25 protocols address all three layers. Given the economics of packet switching and IBM's unmistakable move toward support of international standards, even networking managers in pure IBM environments are sure to be affected by X.25 (see "Where X.25 fits in").

The first article in this series ("SNA to OSI: IBM building upper-layer gateways," DATA COMMUNICATIONS, May, p. 120) compared and contrasted the SNA and OSI architectures, analyzed IBM's SNA/OSI gateway approach, and explored IBM interchange products that convert between the upper SNA and OSI architectural layers (OSI layers four through seven). Examined here are IBM's approach to, and products for, interchange between SNA and OSI at the lower three layers of the two architectures.

Layer 3: Packet, network, path control

In May 1980, IBM issued Statements of Direction to define interfaces from SNA to X.25. Figure 1 summarizes those definitions including, clockwise from the top:

■ SNA-to-SNA device connectivity through an X.25 packet-switched data network (PSDN);

■ SNA-to-non-SNA (asynchronous, binary synchronous communications, and so on) device connectivity through an X.25 PSDN;

■ X.25 data terminal equipment (DTE)-to-X.25 DTE connectivity through an SNA network; and

■ X.25 DTE-to-SNA device connectivity through an X.25 PSDN.

Figure 2 depicts the default X.25 (1984 Red Book) packet (X.25), link (Link Access Procedure-Balanced, or LAPB), and physical level (X.21) interfaces from a synchronous DTE operating in the packet mode. Note that these interfaces are defined from DTE to network data circuit-terminating equipment (DCE), which is also associated with a network node (data switching equipment, or DSE). As shown, permanent virtual circuits (which upper-layer SNA views as dedicated lines) and switched virtual circuits (viewed as switched) are defined locally at each DTE/DCE interface but extend logically between DTEs.

The lower layers of SNA do not map precisely to those of X.25. Specifically, X.25's packet level performs SNA Layer 3 (path control) functions as well as some SNA Layer 4 (transmission control) functions. The difference between the two methods is as follows:

■ Packet level X.25 encapsulates end-to-end network addresses defined by CCITT Recommendation X.121. The X.121 address defines an International Data Number as

Where X.25 fits in

X.25 defines a standard interface into packet-switched data networks (PSDNs) from synchronous data terminal equipment (DTE) devices at the packet, frame, and physical levels, as follows:

■ The packet-level definition sets forth procedures and formats to provide such network services as call set-up, data transfer, and selective flow control. Packet-level X.25 utilizes logical channels to multiplex network calls and to optimize bandwidth, and defines up to 4,096 possible logical channel connections through logical channel numbers (LCNs) 0 through 4,095, which can be active concurrently through a single link. Certain synchronous DTEs, principally host computers, can support the entire possible range of LCNs. Other X.25-compliant DTEs, such as synchronous terminals, utilize only one logical channel and do not have the ability to construct multiple virtual calls into the network.

■ The link-level default recommendation for X.25 is Link Access Procedure-Balanced (LAPB), which is a high-level data link control balanced asynchronous class protocol subset. LAPB supports asynchronous balanced mode for modulo 8 sequencing and asynchronous balanced mode extended for modulo 128 sequencing.

■ The physical-level (Level 1) default X.25 recommendation is X.21, which specifies procedures for synchronous DTE interface into a packet-switched digital network.

X.25 was initially approved by the International Telegraph and Telephone Consultative Committee (CCITT) in 1976, as the "Orange Book" version (see "For further reading"). It was updated in 1980 (as the "Yellow Book") and 1984 (the "Red Book"). The Red Book update included the following enhancements over the Yellow Book version:

■ Definition of a hunt group facility to allow connection of several DTEs to the same called address;

■ Call redirection facility, which instructs the network to redirect incoming calls to a selected DTE under user-specified circumstances;

■ Multilink procedure, which allows for multiple links to be defined between a DTE and its attachment node. These links are regarded as a single logical link by the DTE;

■ Definition of the X.25 interface between public and private PSDNs;

■ Alignment of X.25 with the packet-layer protocol defined by the International Organization for Standardization;

■ Definition of dial-in and dial-out PSDN access;

■ Switched DTE identification and authentication to the PSDN through CCITT X.32 procedures;

■ Significant extension of optional user capabilities; and

■ Extension of the allowable packet size range from 16 through 1,024 octets (1980 Yellow Book) to 16 through 4,096 octets (1984 Red Book). The recommended default packet size is 128 octets.

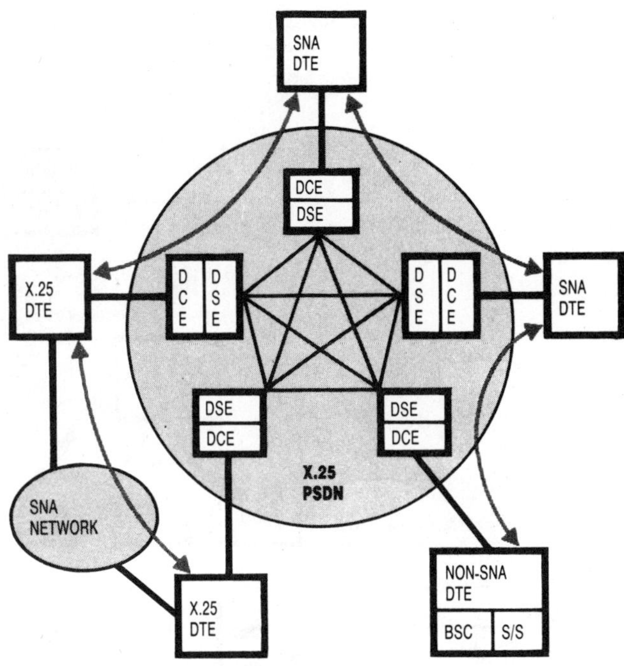

1. Game plan. IBM has proposed linking SNA to SNA, SNA to non-SNA, and SNA to X.25 units through packet networks, and X.25 to X.25 DTEs through SNA networks.

BSC = BINARY SYNCHRONOUS COMMUNICATIONS
DCE = DATA CIRCUIT-TERMINATING EQUIPMENT
DSE = DATA SWITCHING EQUIPMENT
DTE = DATA TERMINAL EQUIPMENT
PSDN = PACKET-SWITCHED DATA NETWORK
SNA = SYSTEMS NETWORK ARCHITECTURE
S/S = START/STOP

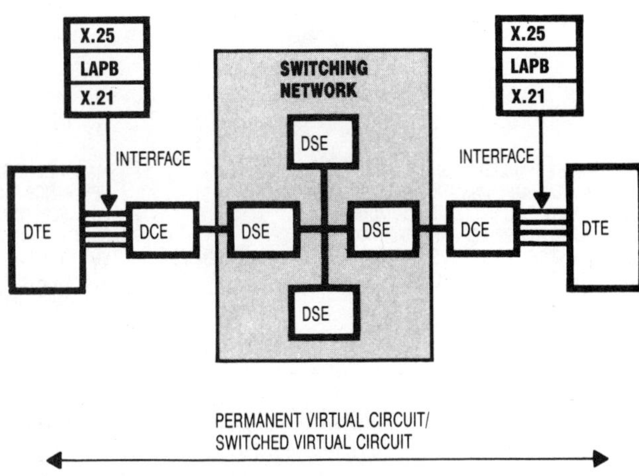

2. X.25 environment. CCITT X.25 defines a standard, three-level interface from synchronous packet data terminal equipment to packet-switched data networks.

DCE = DATA CIRCUIT-TERMINATING EQUIPMENT
DSE = DATA SWITCHING EQUIPMENT
DTE = DATA TERMINAL EQUIPMENT
LAPB = LINK ACCESS PROCEDURE-BALANCED

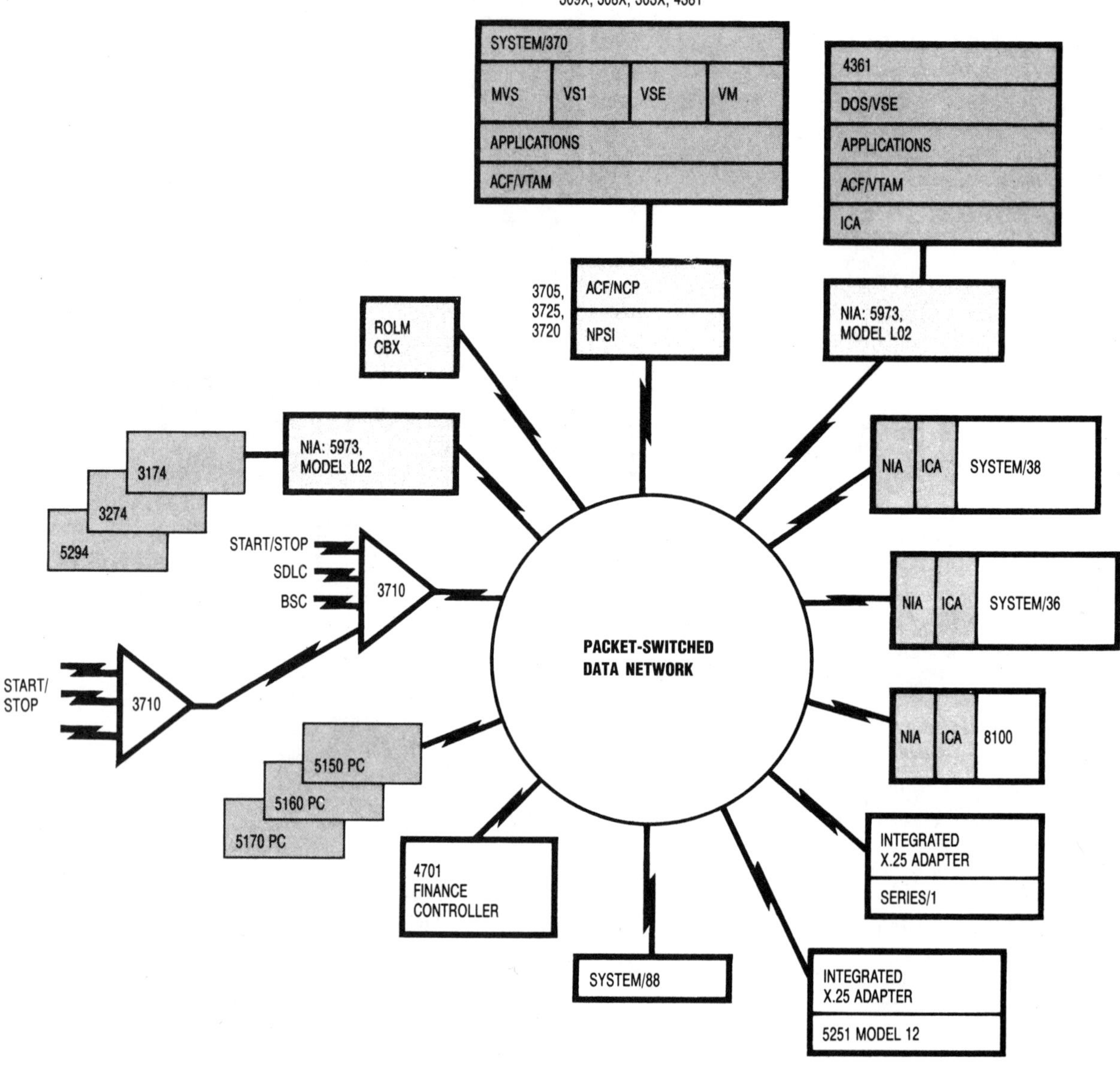

equal to either the Data Network Identification Code plus Network Terminal Number, or the Data Country Code plus National Number. This end-to-end, unique address is defined during the DCE receipt of an incoming call packet (equivalent to sending the DTE call request packet).

■ In SNA, conversely, end-to-end addresses are resolved during session initiation through a virtual route identifier assigned by the session-control sublayer of transmission control (SNA Layer 4). Those end-to-end SNA addresses are extracted from the class of service table under control of ACF/VTAM (Advanced Communications Function/Virtual Telecommunications Access Method), prior to the path control (SNA Layer 3) receipt of a basic information unit (BIU), and subsequent to BIU encapsulation in a Transmission Header Format Identifier, which creates a path information unit (PIU). (For more on the relationship between

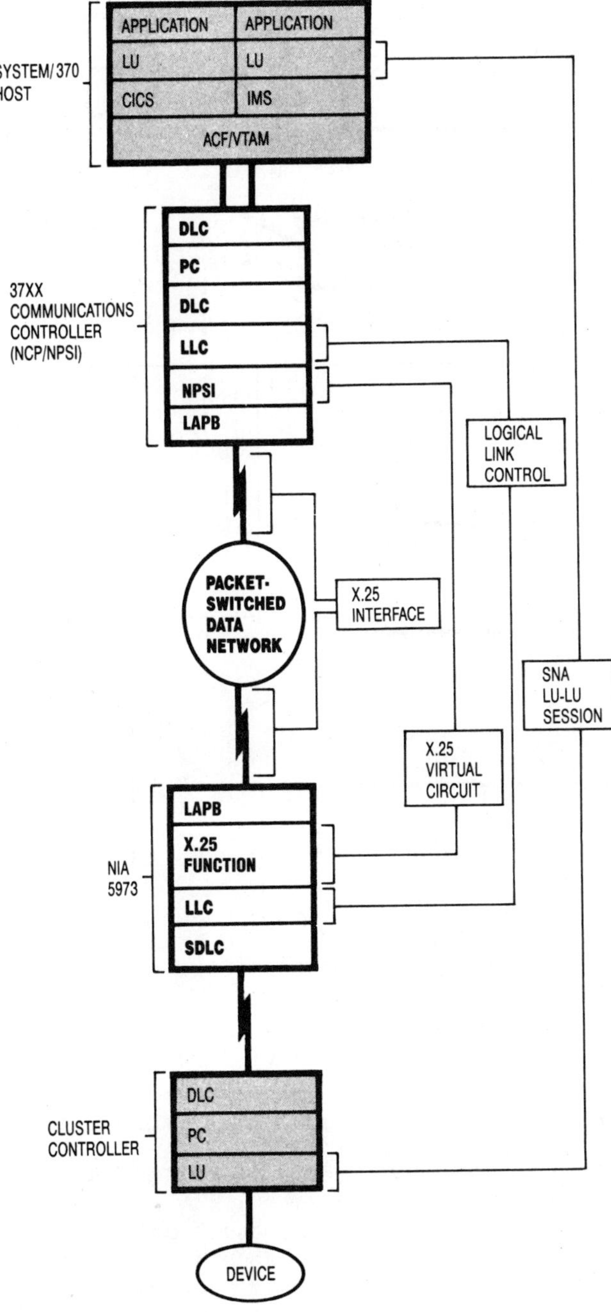

ACF/VTAM = ADVANCED COMMUNICATIONS FUNCTION/
  VIRTUAL TELECOMMUNICATIONS ACCESS METHOD
CICS = CUSTOMER INFORMATION CONTROL SYSTEM
DLC = DATA LINK CONTROL
IMS = INFORMATION MANAGEMENT SYSTEM
LAPB = LINK ACCESS PROCEDURE-BALANCED
LLC = LOGICAL LINK CONTROL
LU = LOGICAL UNIT
NCP = NETWORK CONTROL PROGRAM
NIA = NETWORK INTERFACE ADAPTER
NPSI = NCP PACKET-SWITCHED INTERFACE
PC = PATH CONTROL
SDLC = SYNCHRONOUS DATA LINK CONTROL

SNA message units and the architecture, see "Distributed SNA: A network architecture gets on track," DATA COMMUNICATIONS, February, p. 116.)

Open Communication Architectures

In September 1986, IBM formalized its SNA/X.25 implementation strategy and approach by announcing the Open Communication Architectures (OCAs). OCA is a set of architectures, data streams, and IBM implementations of X.25 and X.21 standards. IBM's OCA is intended to provide reliable and open access among heterogeneous networked environments, and it includes the following:
- Open network management (through network management architecture, Netview, and publication of the Netview architecture and application programming interfaces);
- Node architectures, which incorporate the physical unit 2.1 node architecture;
- Logical unit architecture, which incorporates the logical unit (LU) 6.2 Advanced Program-to-Program Communications (APPC) architecture; and
- Public data network standards, which incorporate SNA product implementation direction into CCITT X.25/X.21 standards. Prior to the OCA announcement, 16 IBM communications products that support interfaces for X.25 networks had been announced.

Where they're found

Figure 3 summarizes the major IBM product implementations that support SNA device interconnection and resource sharing through an X.25 PSDN. The primary approaches, clockwise from the top of the figure, are:
- Network Control Program (NCP) Packet-Switching Interface (NPSI), which operates as an ACF/NCP region within Model 3705, 3725, and 3720 communications controllers;
- Local Network Interface Adapter (NIA): a hardware feature attached to host processors (such as the Model 4361) and to departmental processors (such as the System/38, System/36, and 8100) that contain integrated communications adapters (ICAs);
- Integrated X.25 Adapters (essentially an X.25 packet assembler/disassembler, or PAD) in the Series/1 processor, 5251 Model 12 Display Station Controller, System/88, the 4701 Finance Controller, and Model 5150, 5160, and 5170 Personal Computers;
- Model 3710 Network Controller, a network concentrator and protocol converter;
- Remote NIA: Model 5973 NIA attached to Model 3174, 3274, and 5294 Cluster Controllers; and
- Rolm Computerized Branch Exchange II.

Figure 4 indicates the architectural roles that NPSI and NIA play in defining SNA services to an X.25 PSDN. NPSI and NIA encapsulate and decapsulate SNA message units for transport through X.25-compliant PSDNs. Represented here is a remote Model 5973 associated with an SNA cluster controller, which receives a PIU from the cluster controller, encapsulates it with an X.25 header and LAPB Link Header and Trailer, and forwards it to the PSDN. NPSI receives the LAPB-framed X.25 packet, decapsulates it, and forwards the SNA message unit to ACF/VTAM. The process is performed in reverse for SNA message units traveling in the other direction. Those message units are known as SNA PIUs.

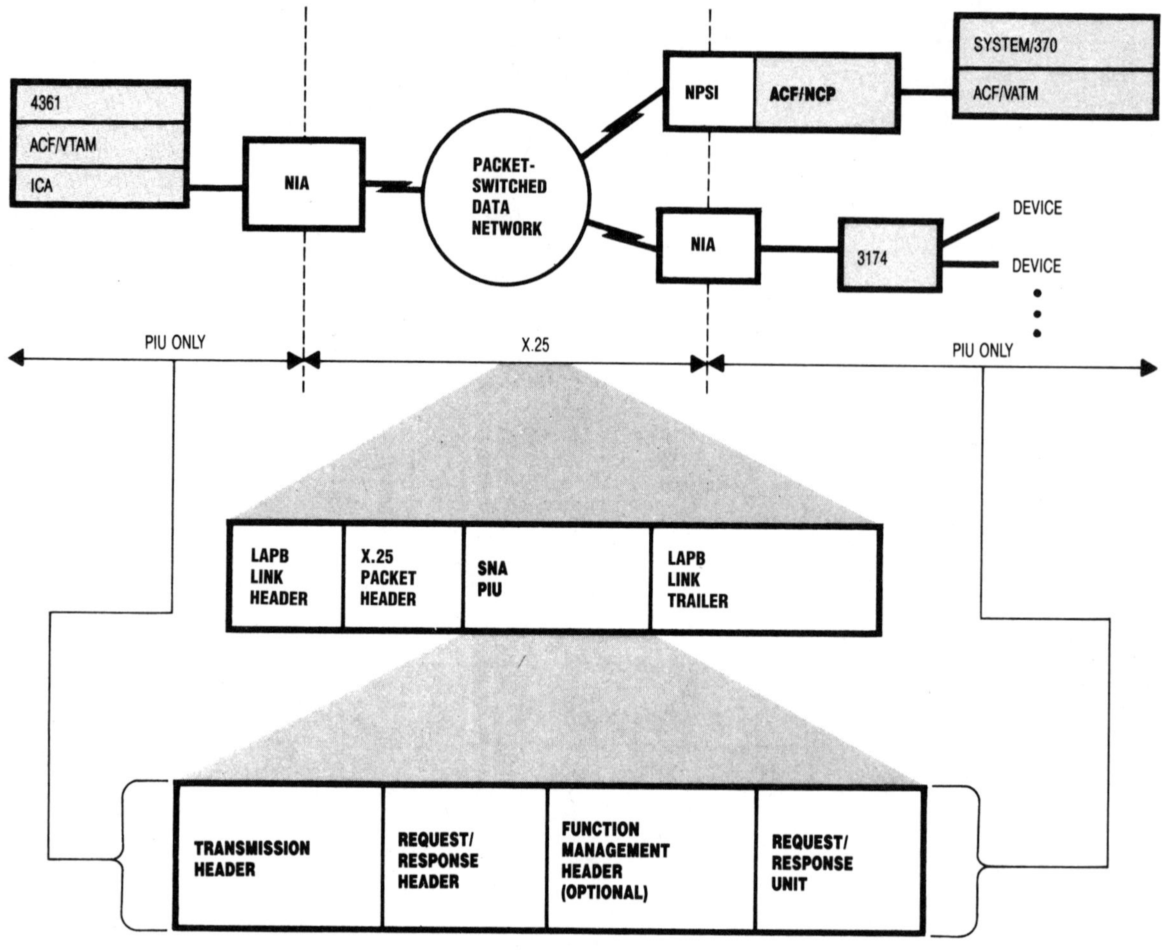

Figure 5 illustrates NPSI and NIA implementations performing a generic encapsulation of a PIU in an X.25 Packet Header and LAPB Link Header and Trailer for transmission through a PSDN.

Figure 6 shows the detail of an X.25 data packet. The packet includes an X.25 Packet Header and an SNA PIU, which is enclosed within the X.25 data packet as user data. Since SNA/X.25 product implementations support both modulo 8 (asynchronous balanced mode, or ABM) and modulo 128 (ABM extended, or ABME) at the link level, and since the X.25 packet-level packet send-and-receive modulus determines the LAPB modulus, Figure 6 illustrates both the ABM and ABME data packet formats.

The price to be paid for extensive packaging can be significant. For example, if the CCITT Red Book's default packet size of 128 octets (eight-bit fields) is supported, the number of PIU bytes (the SNA term for octets) is equal to 128. The path control-assigned Transmission Header may contain six bytes, while the Request/Response Header contains another three. This leaves 119 bytes in the request/response unit. Overhead fields associated with the optional Function Management Header, LU 6.2 record structures, higher-level SNA protocols, and distributed architecture requirements may further reduce data-carrying capacity. Therefore, the net number of user bytes carried in an X.25 Packet Header may easily be reduced to a fraction of the available field, due to overhead imposed by higher-layer protocols.

SNA to non-SNA through X.25
A variety of approaches is provided to support communications between SNA and non-SNA DTEs through PSDNs. Those approaches include the following:
- General Access to X.25 Transport Extension (GATE);
- Dedicated Access to X.25 Transport Extension (DATE);
- Protocol Converter for Non-SNA Equipment (PCNE);

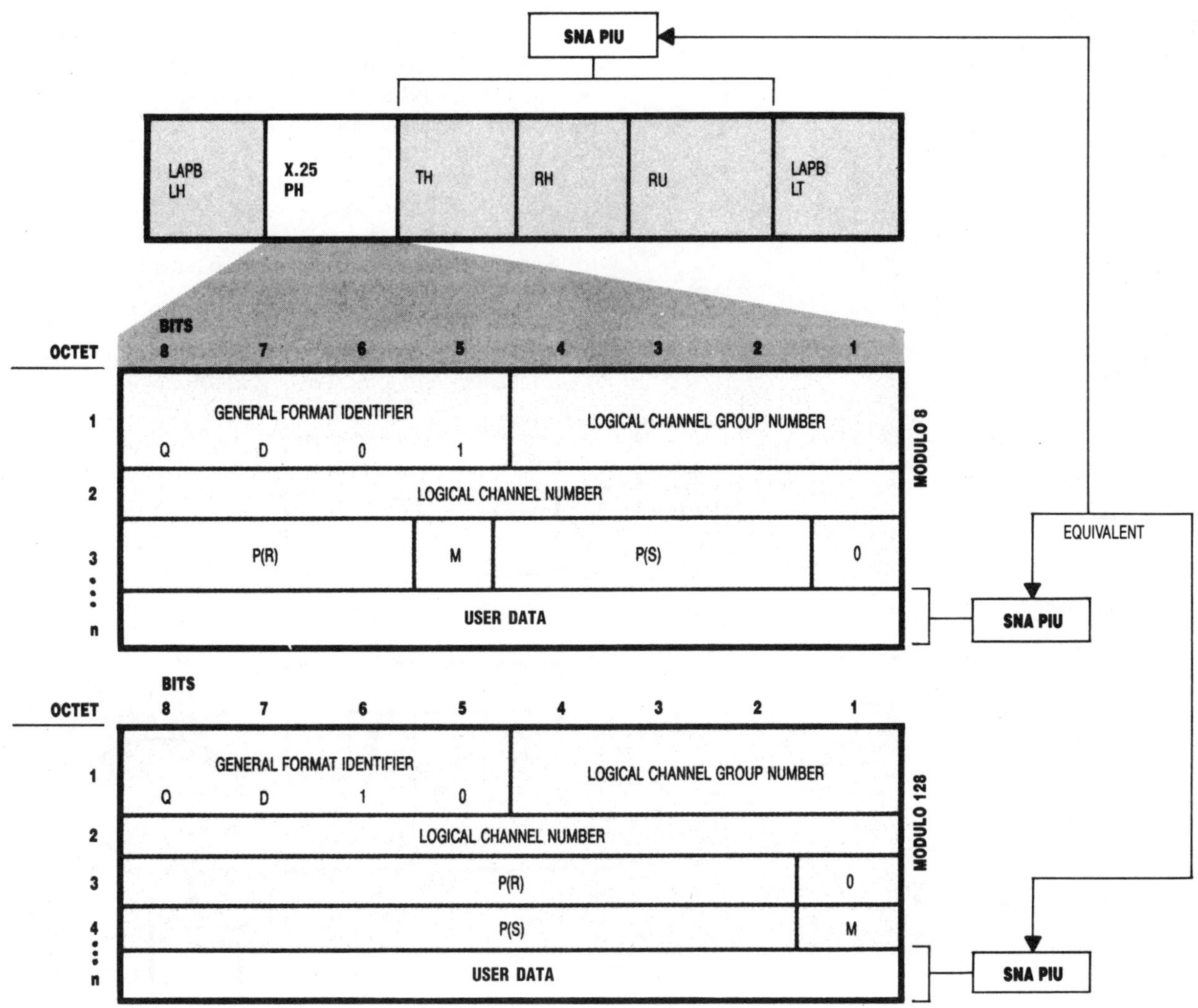

- Integrated Packet Assembler/Disassembler (IPAD); and
- Transparent Packet Assembler/Disassembler (TPAD).

Figure 7 illustrates GATE. A host application program called the Communication and Transmission Control Program (CTCP) can cause NPSI/GATE to assume the task of managing virtual circuits through a PSDN over which CTCP communicates with non-SNA X.25 data terminal equipment. GATE transmits certain types of control packets that activate and deactivate virtual circuits through a packet-switched data network, and enables the host CTCP to send and receive the contents of data packets, qualified data packets, interrupt packets, call setup and clearing packets, and reset packets.

Figure 8 illustrates the DATE NPSI mechanism. DATE allows CTCP to manage packet-switched data network virtual circuits to go to SNA nodes connected through remote NIAs as well as to go to remote non-SNA X.25 data terminal equipment. Through DATE, the host CTCP sends and receives the contents of qualified data packets, interrupt packets, call setup and clearing packets, and reset packets.

Figure 9 illustrates the placement of PCNE in NPSI. PCNE appears to be a Type-One LU (IBM Model 3767 Printer Terminal) to the host. It provides an LU-to-LU session from a non-SNA X.25 DTE to a host LU, supporting conversion of non-SNA X.25 data streams from an X.25 DTE located

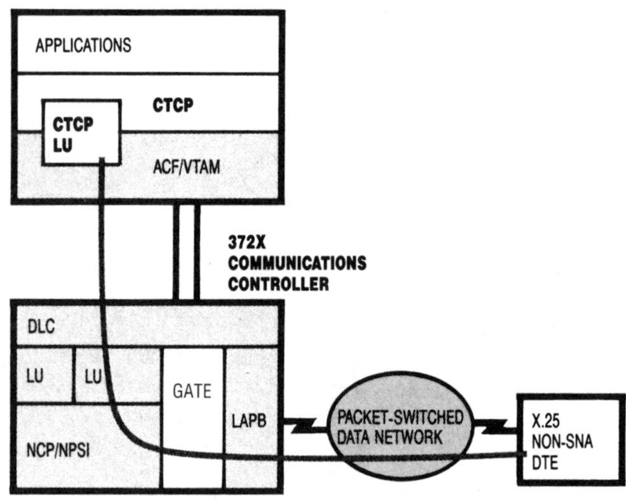

ACF/VTAM = ADVANCED COMMUNICATIONS FUNCTION/
  VIRTUAL TELECOMMUNICATIONS ACCESS METHOD
CTCP = COMMUNICATION AND TRANSMISSION CONTROL PROGRAM
DLC = DATA LINK CONTROL
DTE = DATA TERMINAL EQUIPMENT
GATE = GENERAL ACCESS TO X.25 TRANSPORT EXTENSION
LAPB = LINK ACCESS PROCEDURE-BALANCED
LU = LOGICAL UNIT
NCP = NETWORK CONTROL PROGRAM
NPSI = NCP PACKET-SWITCHING INTERFACE
SNA = SYSTEMS NETWORK ARCHITECTURE

remotely through a packet-switched data network. Figure 9 also indicates the placement of IPAD, which runs under NPSI. IPAD supports communication between an SNA host and an X.28-defined asynchronous DTE. In this sense, IPAD functions as an X.29 host PAD under NPSI and allows the SNA host to communicate with asynchronous devices connected via X.3 PADs.

CCITT Recommendation X.28 defines start-stop (S/S) DTE signaling to an X.3 packet assembler/disassembler. As of the 1984 Red Book, Recommendation X.3 defines 22 PAD parameters that present the S/S data terminal equipment to the PSDN. Recommendation X.29 defines control procedures operative between an X.25 DTE and the X.3 PAD through a packet-switched data network.

In addition, Figure 9 depicts the province of Transparent Packet Assembler/Disassembler, a NPSI region that allows a host-resident application program to control a remote (X.3) PAD associated with a non-SNA DTE. TPAD supports packet assembler/disassembler facilities that are inconsistent with CCITT Recommendations X.3, X.28, and X.29, whereas IPAD supports conformant devices. The host application program communicates with the remote X.3 PAD by sending qualified data packets between TPAD and the X.3 PAD over the packet-switched data network. Qualified data packets set the qualifier bit (Q in Fig. 6) to one. The qualifier bit indicates that the data packet does not contain user data but rather contains command infor-

mation for a control mechanism in the remote PAD. Integrated PAD and Transparent PAD extend the NPSI PCNE function by providing PAD control.

Figure 10 illustrates the use of PCNE in NPSI. PCNE converts X.25 DTE-generated packets into SNA commands and responses, and the reverse.

Figure 11 summarizes the IBM-defined SNA/X.25 virtual circuit (VC) Types 0, 2, 3, 4, and 5, as follows:

■ VC Type 0 is defined through a PSDN between NPSI/PCNE and a remote X.25 DTE;

■ VC Type 2 is defined through a PSDN between Physical Services Header Control and a remote Model 5973 NIA which connects to an SNA cluster controller. (Physical Services Headers were the original support defined from

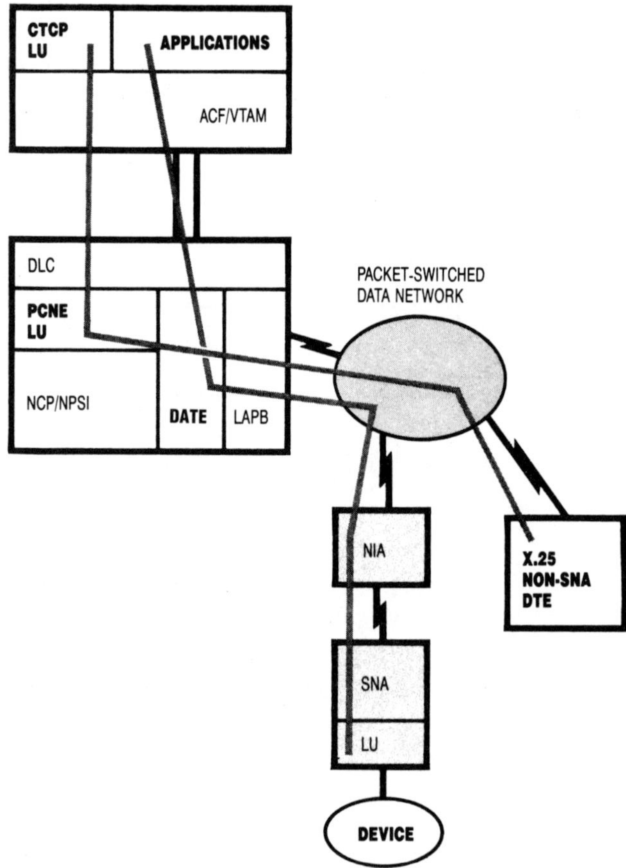

ACF/VTAM = ADVANCED COMMUNICATIONS FUNCTION/
  VIRTUAL TELECOMMUNICATIONS ACCESS METHOD
CTCP = COMMUNICATION AND TRANSMISSION CONTROL PROGRAM
DATE = DEDICATED ACCESS TO X.25 TRANSPORT EXTENSION
DLC = DATA LINK CONTROL
DTE = DATA TERMINAL EQUIPMENT
LAPB = LINK ACCESS PROCEDURE-BALANCED
LU = LOGICAL UNIT
NCP = NETWORK CONTROL PROGRAM
NIA = NETWORK INTERFACE ADAPTER
NPSI = NCP PACKET-SWITCHING INTERFACE
PCNE = PROTOCOL CONVERTER FOR NON-SNA EQUIPMENT
SNA = SYSTEMS NETWORK ARCHITECTURE

9. PCNE, IPAD, TPAD. *Protocol Converter for Non-SNA Equipment and Integrated and Transparent PADs let SNA hosts access non-SNA devices through packet networks.* *PCNE links non-SNA X.25 devices with an SNA host. IPAD links hosts with start-stop DTEs. TPAD lets a host control a PAD not consistent with X.3, X.28, or X.29.*

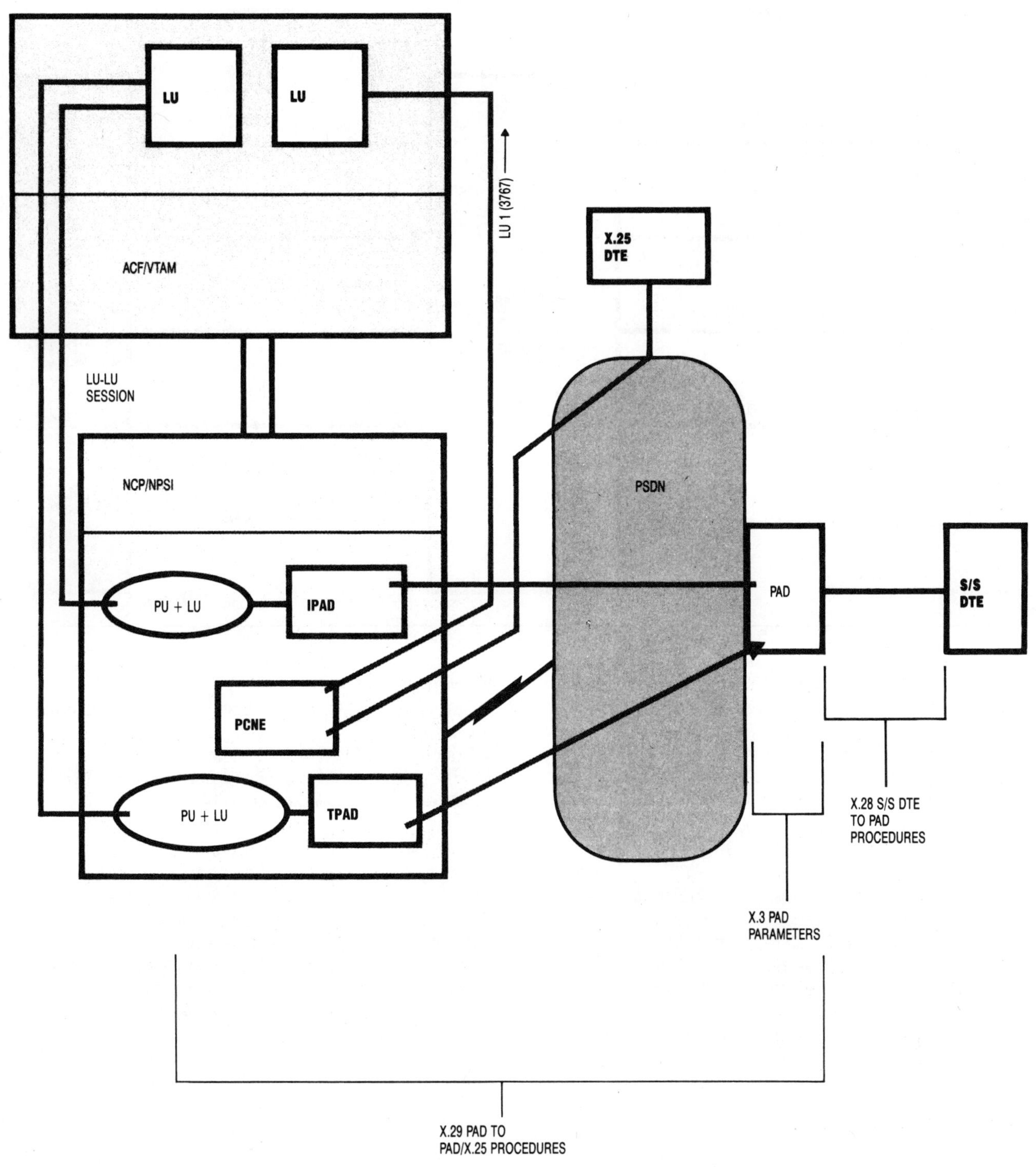

ACF/VTAM = ADVANCED COMMUNICATIONS FUNCTION/ VIRTUAL TELECOMMUNICATIONS ACCESS METHOD
DTE = DATA TERMINAL EQUIPMENT
IPAD = INTEGRATED PAD
LU = LOGICAL UNIT
NCP = NETWORK CONTROL PROGRAM
NPSI = NCP PACKET-SWITCHING INTERFACE

PAD = PACKET ASSEMBLER/DISASSEMBLER
PCNE = PROTOCOL CONVERTER FOR NON-SNA EQUIPMENT
PSDN = PACKET-SWITCHED DATA NETWORK
PU = PHYSICAL UNIT
S/S = START/STOP
TPAD = TRANSPARENT PAD

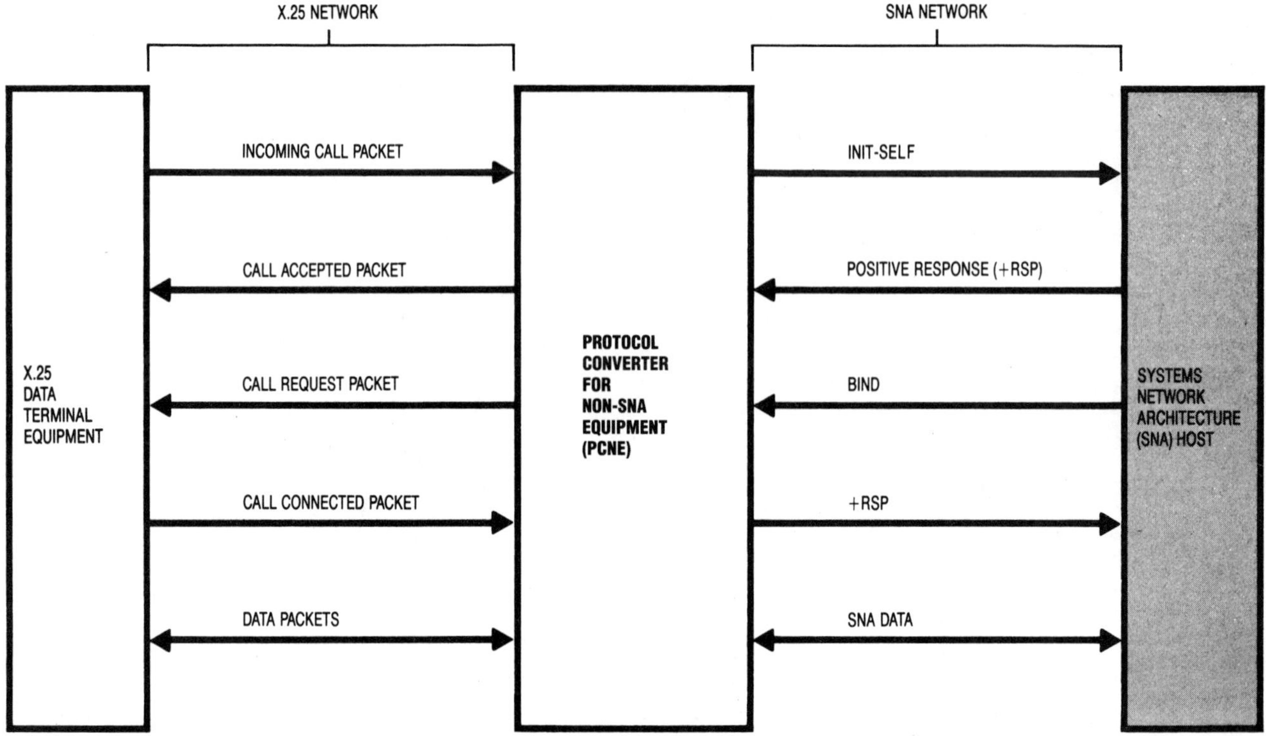

remote NIAs to NPSI.);

■ VC Type 3 is defined through a PSDN between either two NPSIs, two Integrated X.25 Adapters, or a NPSI and an Integrated X.25 Adapter;

■ VC Type 4 is defined through a PSDN between NPSI-resident GATE and a remote, non-SNA X.25 DTE; and

■ VC Type 5 is defined through a PSDN from NPSI-resident PCNE to a remote PAD which supports a start-stop DTE.

First in Europe

X.25 SNA Interconnect (XI) allows X.25 DTE traffic to propagate through SNA transport networks, which conform internationally to the CCITT X.25 recommendations. XI was announced in Europe in June 1985 and in North America in May 1986. The major XI advantage is that it enables X.25 operation over circuits previously reserved for SNA traffic.

Figure 12 illustrates the XI environment. The XI product, which requires ACF/NCP Version 4 Release 2, presents an XI mechanism called Data Exchange Equipment as an X.25 DCE interface to attached X.25 data terminal equipment. X.25 DTE traffic is multiplexed over SNA session traffic and routed between XI environments. The traffic then travels over SNA network links between Model 3725 and/or 3720 Communications Controllers that support XI. The resulting packet is based upon the format specified in CCITT Recommendation X.75, which defines interconnection of distinct X.25 networks.

SNA routing occurs over SDLC links on an XI-established path. Figure 12 depicts four supported XI configurations, which include (from the top of the figure):

■ Connection of two X.25 DTEs through a single 3725 communications controller;

■ Connection of two X.25 DTEs through two XI communications controllers;

■ Connection of two X.25 DTEs through an intermediate Model 3705 Communications Controller, via the two Model 3725 Communications Controllers that support XI; and

■ Connection of a single X.25 DTE to a single host through a single XI communications controller.

Figure 13 illustrates the use of an XI Integrated X.25 Adapter to accomplish local connection of either two System/38s, or one System/38 to one System/36, with no intervening packet-switched data network. The Integrated X.25 Adapter used in this case is an X.25 line connector, which includes external cable (for example, CCITT V.24, V.35, or X.21) and a pair of modems or modem eliminators. This configuration enables the connected System/38 and System/36 departmental processors to support X.25 protocols at the lower three layers.

Layer 2: Logical Link Control

At Layer 2 of SNA, a variety of Data Link Control (DLC) protocols have been implemented to support sessions between network-addressable units residing in SNA nodes. Viable DLC protocols include leased analog circuits, leased digital circuits, Token Ring Network, Logical Link Control/Medium Access Control, and System/370 host data channels. Permanent and switched virtual circuits within PSDNs are also valid Layer 2 DLCs.

Layer 2 SNA/X.25 mechanisms work with the LAPB data

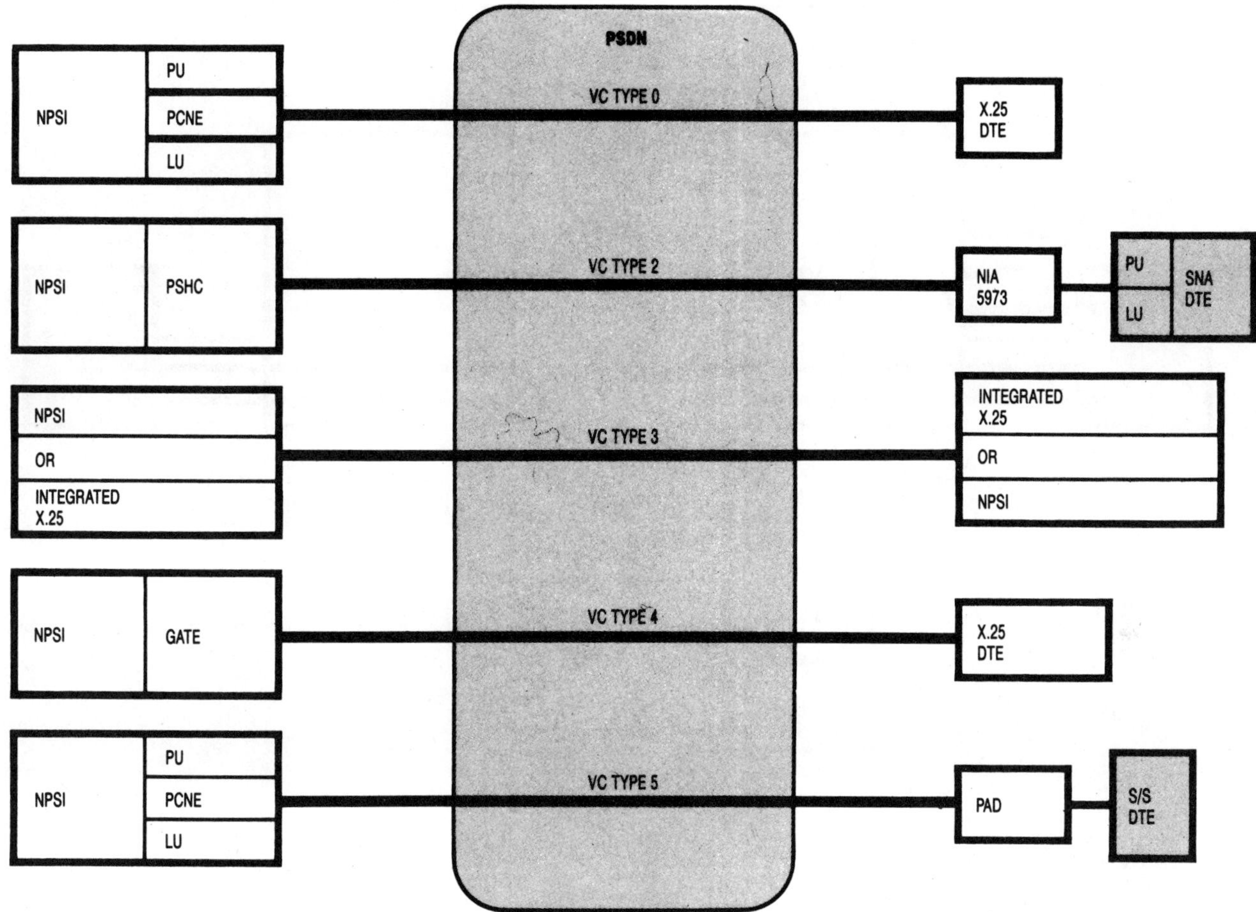

DTE = DATA TERMINAL EQUIPMENT
GATE = GENERAL ACCESS TO X.25 TRANSPORT EXTENSION
LU = LOGICAL UNIT
NIA = NETWORK INTERFACE ADAPTER
NPSI = NCP PACKET-SWITCHING INTERFACE
PAD = PACKET ASSEMBLER/DISASSEMBLER
PCNE = PROTOCOL CONVERTER FOR NON-SNA EQUIPMENT

PSDN = PACKET-SWITCHED DATA NETWORK
PSHC = PHYSICAL SERVICES HEADER CONTROL
PU = PHYSICAL UNIT
SNA = SYSTEMS NETWORK ARCHITECTURE
S/S = START/STOP
VC = VIRTUAL CIRCUIT

link control. Figure 14 indicates the relationship of the LAPB Link Header and Link Trailer that encapsulate the X.25 Packet Header. In the case of SNA-to-SNA session traffic through a PSDN, the header and trailer encapsulate an SNA path information unit as user data within an X.25 Packet Header. The example in Figure 14 depicts the use of NPSI, local NIA (with host Model 4361/4331 ICA), and remote NIA (with cluster controller and device).

Control (nondata) packets transported through a PSDN between SNA devices also support one of three Logical Link Control (akin to SDLC) functions defined by IBM in the X.25 Packet Header. They are as follows:
- Physical Services Header Logical Link Control (PSH LLC);
- Qualified Logical Link Control (QLLC); and
- Enhanced Logical Link Control (ELLC).

Figure 15 illustrates the use of PSH LLC, QLLC, and ELLC. PSH LLC is used strictly between NPSI and a Remote Network Interface Adapter, which connects to an SNA cluster controller with attached devices.

QLLC is used between NPSI and the following:
- Any local NIA (defined as attached to an integrated communications adapter with, for example, Model 4361 host, System/38, System/36, and 8100);
- Integrated X.25 Adapter (with, for example, Series/1 or 5251 Model 12 Cluster Controller for 5250 devices); or
- Model 3710 Network Controller. Both PSH LLC and QLLC support the ABM modulo 8 packet/frame sequencing.

ELLC is supported between any two local NIAs, such as between two System/36s or two System/38s, between a System/36 and a System/38, or between a Model 4361 and a System/36. ELLC is designed to support ABME modulo 128 packet/frame sequencing.

Figure 16 provides an example of a qualified data packet

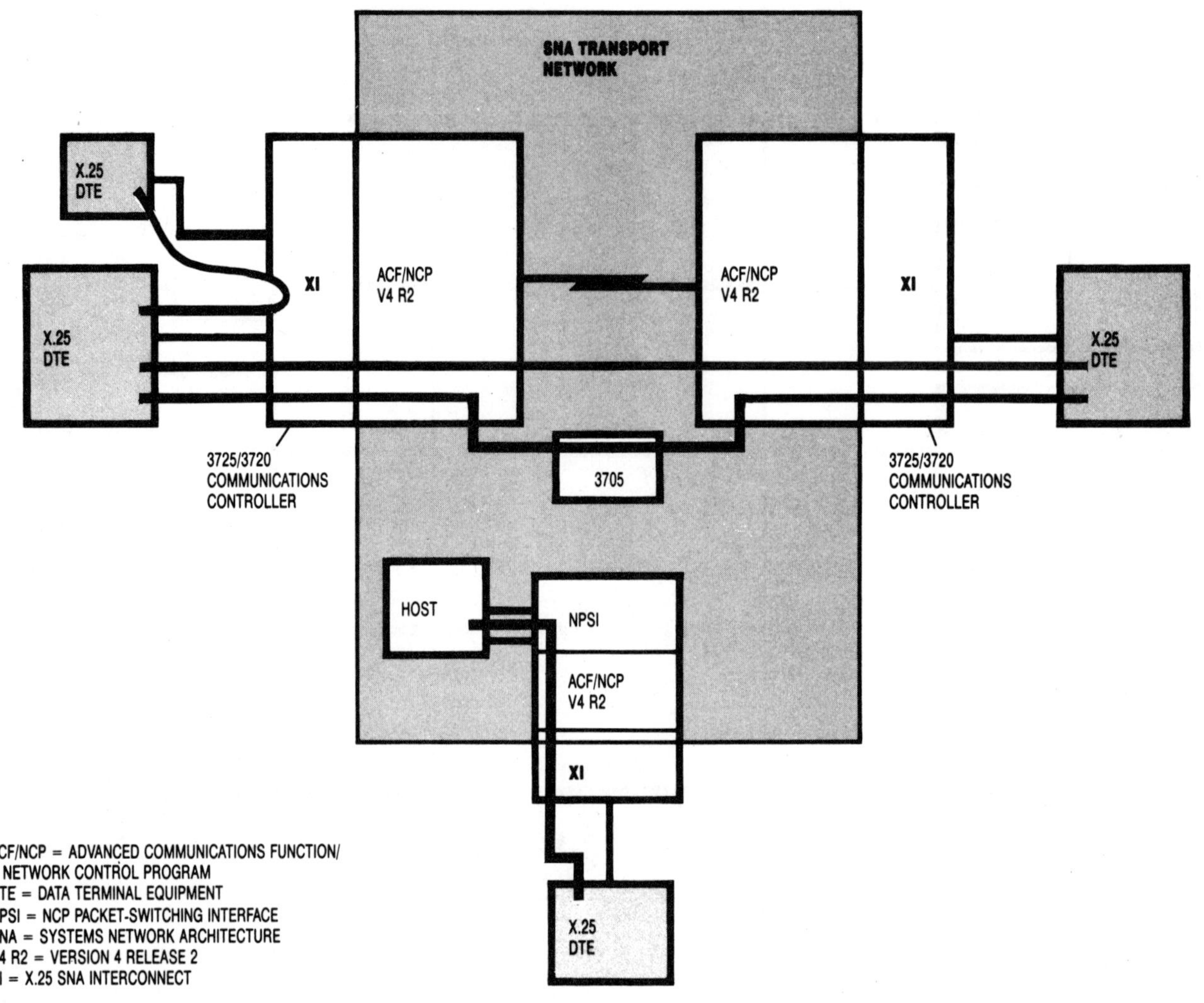

12. X.25 SNA interconnect. *XI allows X.25 DTEs to communicate natively through SNA networks. XI runs on either 3725 or 3720 communications controllers. It supports connections between two X.25 DTEs (directly attached or through a 3705), an X.25 DTE and an SNA host, or two X.25 DTEs, each connected to an XI device.*

using QLLC. QLLC, supported since NPSI Release 3.1, allows synchronous Data Link Control commands, such as Exchange Identification (XID), Test, and Frame Reject (FRMR), to be transmitted in "qualified" data packets. Qualified packets are designated as such by setting the qualifier bit in the general format identifier to one while setting the delivery confirmation bit to zero. Qualified SDLC commands are sent, for example, as qualified XID, qualified Test, and qualified FRMR.

Layer 1: SNA to X.21

In May 1980, IBM issued Statements of Direction to define interfaces from SNA to CCITT Recommendation X.21 and X.21*bis*, as well as to X.25. Figure 17 illustrates the SNA-to-X.21 Statement of Direction, which specifies that SNA and non-SNA data terminal equipment could connect through a circuit-switched, pre-Integrated Services Digital Network (ISDN) by conforming to the CCITT X.21 interface defined in CCITT Recommendation X.21 and by utilizing X.24 interchange circuits (which provide electrical signal interchange between a DTE and a DCE).

Figure 18 indicates the current SNA data terminal equipment X.21 product implementations. In one of the implementations, a Model 4361 host processor and the System/36 and Series/1 departmental processors are physically defined as an X.21 interchange point (IP). Interposed between the DCE and the terminal equipment are Short Hold Mode/Multiple Port Sharing (SHM/MPS) hardware features. The SHM/MPS features permit links to be defined to the network through an X.21 IP, either to a dedicated port or shared among ports. In another SNA X.21 implementation, a Model 3174 Cluster Controller is directly connected through an X.21 IP.

Alternatives

The user requirement for multivendor compatibility is well established. The only alternative to OSI would be to redesign all vendors' operating systems and applications to conform to some other universal standard (an unlikely prospect) or else develop specific gateways between particular vendors (which would require N(N-1)/2 such gateways for N vendor cases). Neither alternative really

13. Integrated X.25 Adapters. *These adapters can directly link System/38s, or one System/38 and one System/36, with no intervening packet-switched network. They* support X.25 packet level, LAPB frame level, and X.21 physical level protocols, or alternative protocols at the physical level (for example, V.24, V.35).

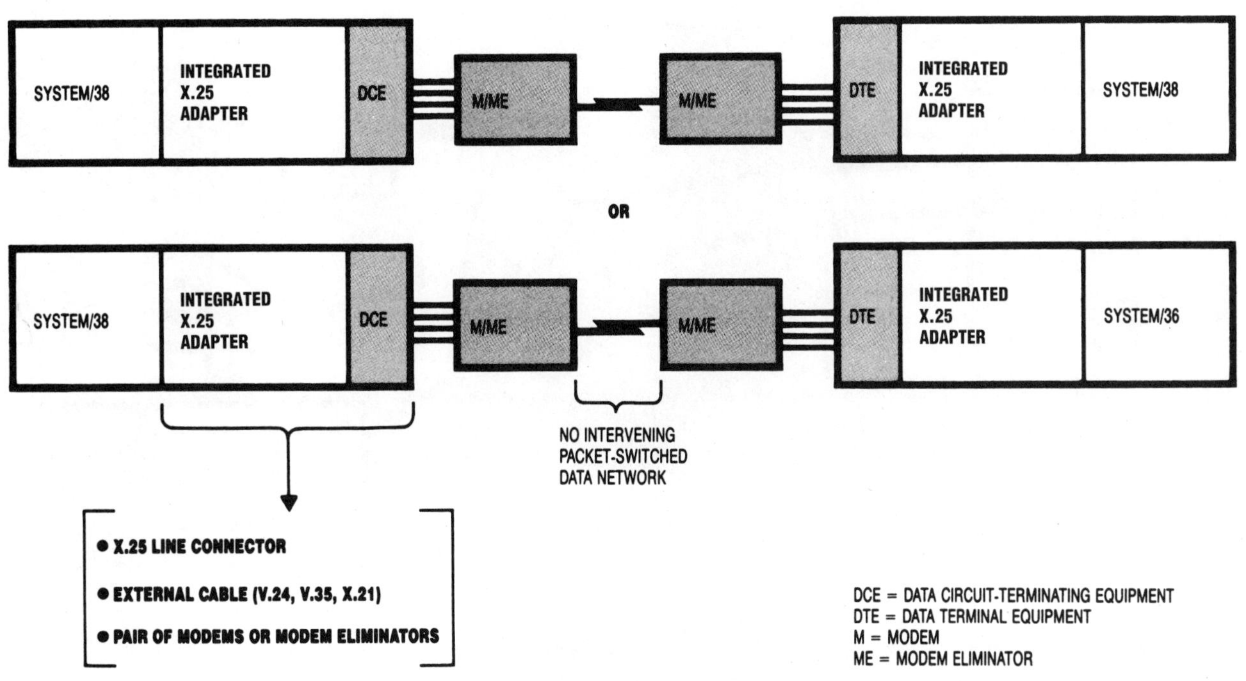

14. Basic link units. *Link Access Procedure-Balanced (LAPB) frames, contained within a header and a trailer, are the basic transfer units for NIAs and NPSI. The LAPB proto-*col defines link level exchanges between balanced link stations, where a primary-secondary link station relationship does not exist.

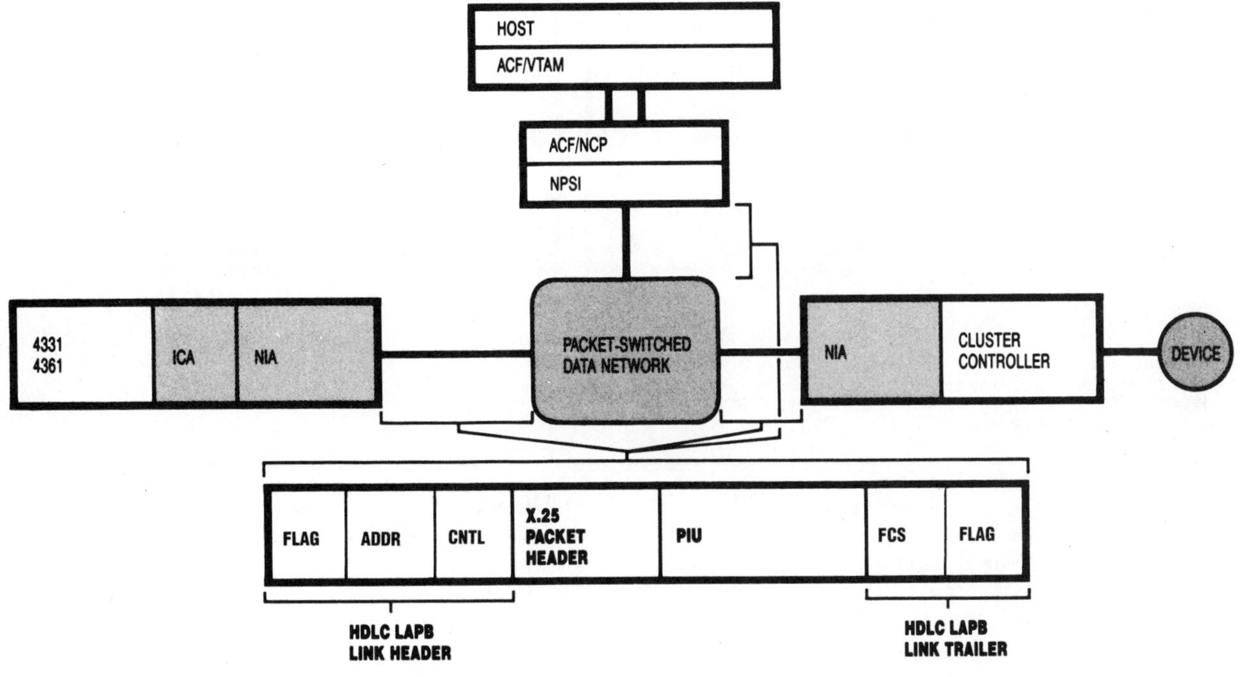

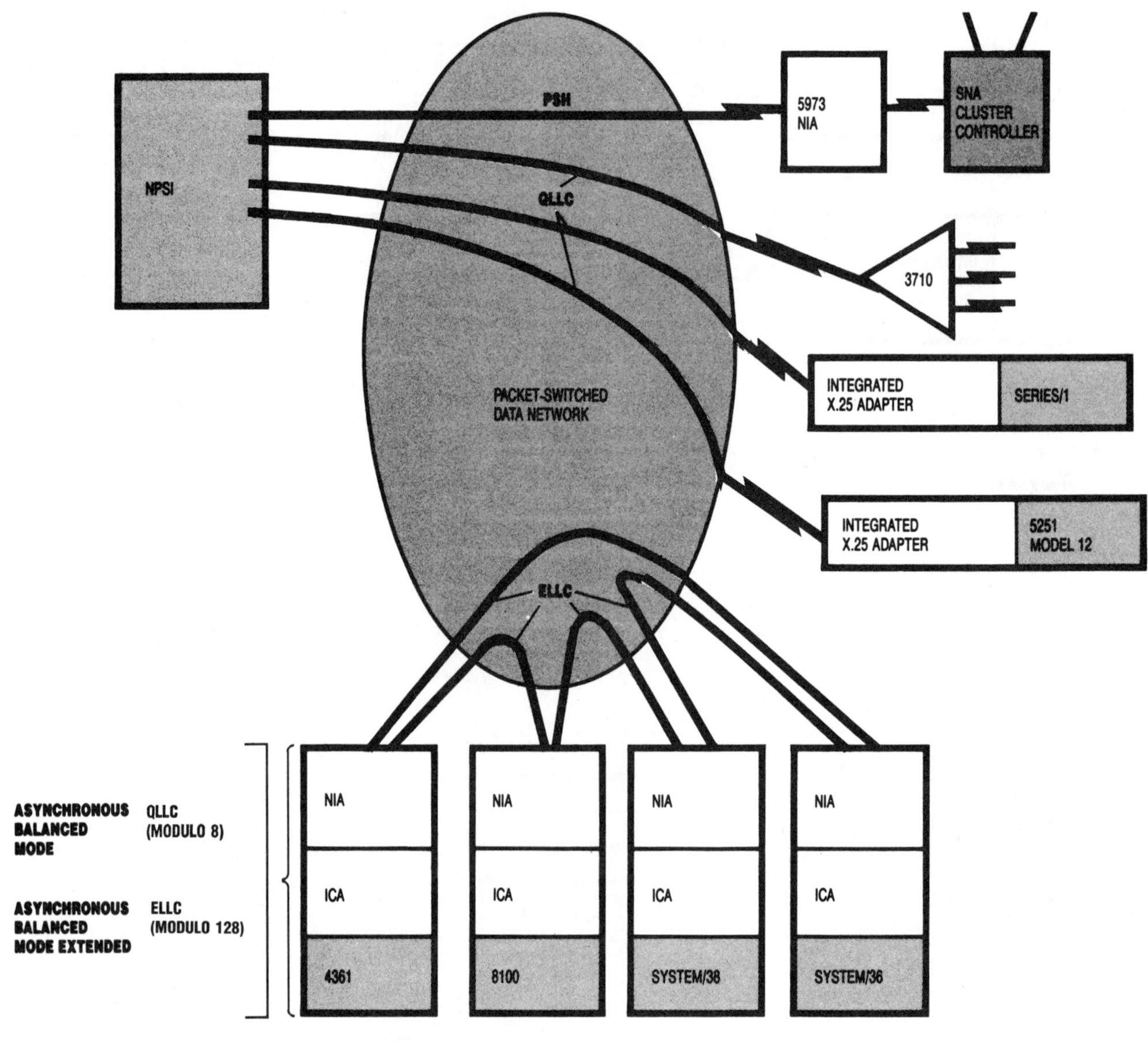

benefits the user.

IBM, for its part, has elected to pursue the ISO-approved OSI protocols and gateway recommendations. IBM's approach is consistent with that of other manufacturers that have opened their architectures to the OSI protocols.

Despite the efforts of IBM and other manufacturers, some concerns about SNA/OSI remain. For example, network performance is degraded with the increased protocol encapsulation and decapsulation at SNA/OSI gateway points. Throughput and response times have been found to be highly variable and unpredictable in hybrid SNA/X.25 networks, due to variable PSDN switched virtual circuit

paths and delays. Moreover, additional overhead associated with SNA/OSI higher-layer conversions introduces increased delays.

The major user objective mentioned last month is for transparent access to targeted applications, regardless of the existence of various vendor architectures, protocols, and products. Given that multivendor networks are the rule, it is imperative that the OSI protocols supported under SNA be from the same set as those supported by all other vendors participating in the Open Systems arena. This issue is resolved to a great extent by the Technical and Office Protocols (TOP) and Manufacturing Automation

16. Qualified format. *Qualified data packets have a qualifier (Q) bit with a binary value of one to indicate the presence of control (that is, nonuser) data.*

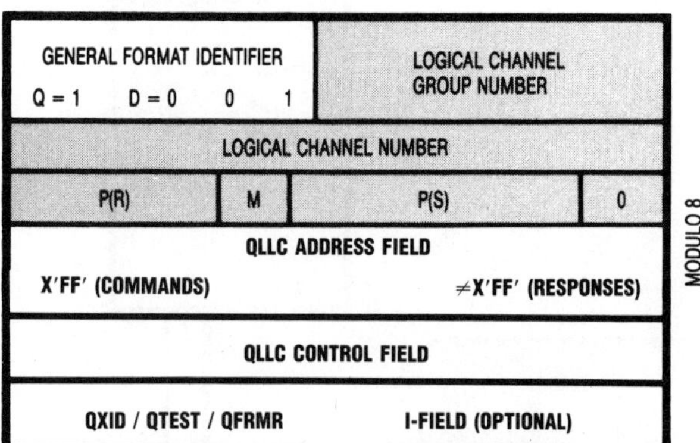

D = DELIVERY CONFIRMATION BIT
I-FIELD = INFORMATION FIELD
M = MORE DATA BIT
P(R) = PACKET RECEIVE SEQUENCE NUMBER
P(S) = PACKET SEND SEQUENCE NUMBER
Q = QUALIFIER BIT
QFRMR = QUALIFIED FRAME REJECT
QLLC = QUALIFIED LOGICAL LINK CONTROL
QTEST = QUALIFIED TEST
QXID = QUALIFIED EXCHANGE IDENTIFICATION
X'FF' = HEXADECIMAL 'FF' (ALL ONES)

Protocols (MAP) definitions of core protocol suites.

Another issue associated with IBM elaboration of SNA-to-OSI products is that the North American marketplace lags behind Europe in SNA/OSI research, development, and implementation.The X.400 products described last month, for example, have been announced only in Europe, and their subsequent testing and verification is, at present, confined to that community. The X.400 OSI test program is based at the IBM European Networking Center in Heidelberg, Germany. Also participating in the program are the University of Zurich; the University of Trondheim, Norway; Catholic University of Nijmegen, the Netherlands; Centre National Universitaire, Montpellier, France; Technical University, Berlin; and CERN, Geneva.

The current direction of this test program (along with that of the OSI verification service based at the IBM European Telecommunications Marketing Center in La Gaude, France, another X.400 OSI test program participant) is to move the European Academic Research Network toward the use of OSI protocols.

OSI protocols are increasingly being accepted and have already found their way into major user architectures, including MAP and TOP. In addition, the Corporation for Open Systems provides an international forum for multivendor and multiuser introduction of interoperable OSI and ISDN products and services. It is evident, therefore, that the North American marketplace represents just as significant an arena for the initial introduction and testing of SNA/OSI products as the European market.

Finally, IBM LU 6.2 was proposed by ICL, Siemens, and Bull to the European Computer Manufacturers Association in 1985 as a base transport mechanism, but the proposal was defeated. During November 1986, a new initiative was begun by IBM, Siemens, and Bull for a transaction processing (TP) standard based on the APPC Application Programming Interface (API) in conjunction with OSI Layer 7 protocols. The ISO/TP specification (which structures a relationship between a TP service user and TP service entities at Layer 7) appears to be semantically compatible with APPC. Therefore, it would be possible to migrate applications written for the APPC API to the ISO/TP Service with only minor modifications. ∎

Thomas J. Routt is president of Network Systems Consulting, which specializes in network migration to SNA and OSI. Previously, Routt was manager of Boeing Network Architecture for Boeing Computer Services Co, in charge of global network planning, design, and implementation. Routt holds an M. B. A. in information systems from Southern Illinois University and a B. S. in environmental science from Western Washington University.

For further reading

CCITT Recommendations:
X.121: *International Numbering Plan for Public Data Networks.*
X.21: *Interface Between Data Terminal Equipment (DTE) and Data Circuit Terminating Equipment (DCE) for Synchronous Operation on Public Data Networks.*
X.24: *List of Definitions for Interchange Circuits Between*

---

17. SNA/X.21 direction. *IBM's Statement of Direction supports the use of X.21 interchange point (IP), X.24 interchange circuits, and 15-pin connectors.*

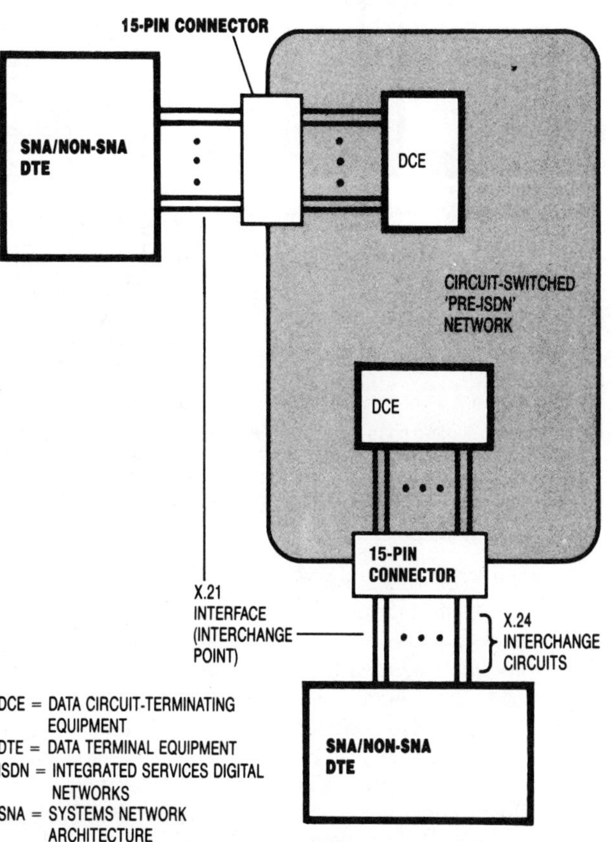

18. SNA to X.21 interfaces. *Current products join the 4361, System/36, and Series/1 through Short Hold Mode/Multiple Port Sharing (SHM/MPS) hardware features,* *which permit a link to be defined to an X.21 interchange point and from the Model 3174 Cluster Controller directly into an X.21 interchange point.*

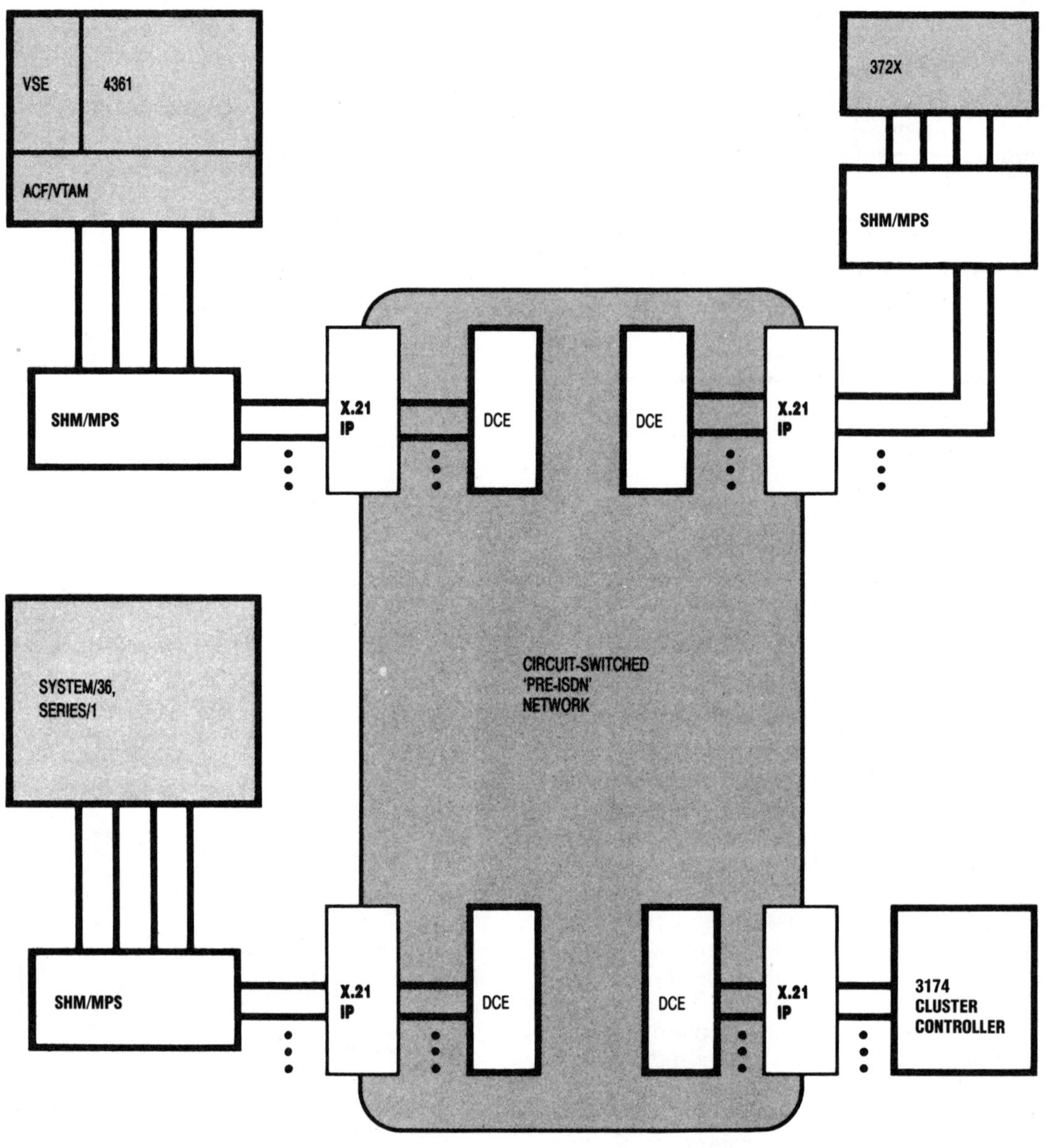

Data Terminal Equipment (DTE) and Data Circuit Terminating Equipment (DCE) on Public Data Networks.

X.25: *Interface Between Data Terminal Equipment (DTE) and Data Circuit Terminating Equipment (DCE) for Terminals Operating in the Packet Mode and Connected to Public Data Networks by Dedicated Circuit.*

Deaton, G. A., Jr., and R. O. Hippert. "X.25 and Related Recommendations in IBM Products." *IBM Systems Journal,* Vol. 22, Nos. 1/2 1983, pp. 11-28.

IBM Document Order No.:

GC30-3189-3: *X.25 NCP Packet Switching Interface General Information,* Fourth Edition, May 1986.

GG24-3052: *Integrating X.25 Function into Systems Network Architecture Networks.*

GA27-3761: *The X.25 1984 Interface for Attaching SNA Nodes to Packet-Switched Data Networks General Information Manual,* First Edition, November 1986.

GA27-3287-2 *IBM Implementation of X.21 Interface General Information Manual,* Third Edition, February 1986.

David Chappell, Cray Research Inc., Mendota Heights, Minn.

Guide to transport-layer interfaces for Unix users

Two types of underlying transport service are now in wide use in the Unix community. How do they differ? Which is best for you?

Transport-layer protocols, which provide transparent end-to-end reliability during data transfer operations regardless of the number or kind of subnetworks being traversed, lie at the heart of modern networking. And Unix—the operating system that has become a de facto standard in many computing environments—owes its widespread acceptance in no small part to a superior communications-handling capability that is predicated on robust transport protocols. However, evolutionary changes in the Unix transport protocols are on the horizon.

Many Unix-based network managers are already familiar with the two most popular transport protocols in Unix: the Transmission Control Protocol (TCP) and the User Datagram Protocol (UDP). Users may be less familiar with the transport protocol, Class 4 (TP4), which has been defined as part of the Open Systems Interconnection (OSI) scheme. While TCP is presently the most widely used Unix transport protocol, that is going to change.

As TP4 becomes more widely available, its popularity is likely to surpass that of TCP. Network managers are beginning to study the relative strengths and weaknesses of TCP and TP4 in order to protect their applications during transition. Both TCP and TP4 are connection-oriented protocols: Two users must establish a connection before they can transfer data.

UDP, on the other hand, is connectionless. In a connectionless protocol, each user sends data to the other without the overhead of establishing and breaking down a connection. These independent data units are sometimes referred to as datagrams. UDP and most other connectionless protocols do not acknowledge received data, and thus cannot guarantee delivery of a user's data. (For a fuller discussion of connection-oriented and connectionless protocols, see DATACOMMUNICATIONS, "Internetworking in an OSI Environment," May 1986, p. 118.)

TCP and TP4 provide very similar services to their users. The most significant difference between the two protocols occurs when a connection ends. When a user requests that a connection be terminated, TCP ensures that all data the user has previously asked to be sent is actually transmitted before closing the connection. This feature is called graceful close or orderly release.

Graceful close is not provided by TP4. (The session layer protocol, immediately above the transport layer, provides this function in OSI networks.) As a result, any user data awaiting transmission within TP4 when a connection is terminated will not be transmitted. Managers must examine their Unix transport options in order to guarantee that all of their data is actually sent before a connection ends.

Transport protocols and Unix

The evolution of transport protocols used in the Unix environment is forcing data communications managers to reexamine the relationship of TCP to TP4. As Unix gained popularity, it underwent enough modification to create two distinct camps within the Unix user community. One camp, which is led by Unix's inventors at AT&T, rallies to the System V banner. The other camp, led by the University of California at Berkeley, is under the BSD banner.

A popular version of Berkeley Unix called 4.2 BSD (for Berkeley Software Distribution) includes implementations of TCP and UDP as well as several higher-layer applications that use TCP and UDP. These include file transfer and support for remote log-in.

To allow these applications the access to the transport protocols that they need, the 4.2 BSD developers defined an interface called a "socket." The socket interface comprises a group of functions which can be called from programs written in the C language. The calls that make up sockets are system calls, that is, they are direct calls to an operating system permitting an application program to

Streams

The Unix operating system was designed before the widespread use of computer networks. As a result, Unix provides no direct support for the special demands of networking software. While flexibility and ease of implementation were possible via protocols running as user processes, achieving acceptable performance usually required implementation within Unix itself—in the operating system kernel.

As in other areas, the two major Unix versions have taken different approaches. The Berkeley Unix TCP/IP additions are supported in the kernel by a set of routines providing such things as generalized buffer and queueing mechanisms. AT&T, the official guardian (and proponent) of Unix System V, decided against that approach, and instead created Streams.

Orginally conceived by Dennis Ritchie, one of the original designers of Unix, Streams allows protocol modules to be implemented within the kernel in a flexible, modular way. Like the Berkeley kernel protocol support, Streams provides various generic services for implementations of protocols, and is intended to provide support for all types of Unix networking.

A Stream (written in mixed case) is a processing and data transfer path between a Unix user process and a device driver in the Unix kernel. A Stream, which exists entirely within the kernel, consists of a Stream head, zero or more modules, and a device driver. A module is a piece of software, which might typically be an implementation of a specific protocol such as TP4. A Stream, then, may include several different protocols, each of which is passed through in succession. If the modules between the Stream head and the driver are written to conform to a standard kernel interface (to use only a well-defined set of kernel services, for example), then they are called protocol modules.

The facilty called Streams (written entirely in upper case) refers to the group of system calls and kernel services which can create and manipulate Streams. The system calls form an interface to user processes, the interface on which the TLI library routines depend.

User processes may use these system calls to dynamically add modules to and delete modules from a Stream. An example group of protocol modules which might be present in a typical Stream is TP4, the OSI Internetwork Protocol, and the IEEE 802.2 data link protocol. A second example might include TCP, the Arpanet Internet protocol, and a packet switching network-layer protocol such as X.25.

Each individual protocol could be implemented in its own protocol module, allowing a user process to build a Stream made up of exactly those protocols required for its application.

Streams provides support for modern protocol architectures. For example, a service interface in Streams is defined as a set of messages together with the rules governing legal sequences of those messages. It exists between each pair of protocol modules. This maps well to the abstract service interfaces defined between the layers of OSI.

access the services provided by the TCP and the UDP.

Unix System V Release 3, introduced by AT&T in mid-1986, also includes an interface to the transport layer, called Transport Layer Interface (TLI). Like the socket interface, TLI is defined as a group of functions that can be called from programs written in C.

Unlike the socket interface, however, TLI is intended to support access to several different transport protocols, including TCP, TP4, and UDP. No transport protocol was automatically bundled into the System V Release as was the case with 4.2 BSD. TLI is based on the transport layer services defined in the International Organization for Standardization's Standard 8072, the OSI Transport Service Specification with extensions that allow access to non-OSI transport protocols.

TLI provides functions very similar to Berkeley Unix's sockets. It is somewhat more general, however, enabling it to cover a larger set of transport protocols. TLI is implemented as a set of library routines, that is, routines that are linked with a user's program. These libraries rely ultimately on several system calls that are provided as part of Streams, a new feature of Unix System V, Release 3 (see "Streams").

Sockets and TLI

Anyone using either TLI or sockets must perform a similar sequence of events to use the underlying transport protocol services. First, the user initiates a logical process called the user process. That process, in turn, creates a common point of reference called an end point. The end point is known both to the user process and to the actual software which implements the protocol.

The end point is used by both the user's process and the protocol implementation to identify a particular connection. Once the end point is established, the user can bind, or assign, an address to the newly created end point (see "Connections and end points").

At that stage, the user of a connection-oriented transport protocol builds a connection before he or she sends and receives data. A person using a connectionless transport protocol simply begins transmitting. Once two users have completed their interaction, any connection that had been established must be released. Finally, the user process removes the end point, a step that may be combined with connection release.

The steps required for connection establishment are different in the user process initiating the connection (the client) and the process responding to the connection (the server). The client attempts to establish a connection by sending a connection request to the server. The server, after binding its address to its end point, must listen at that address for incoming connection indications from clients. When one arrives, the server may accept or reject the request. If the connection is accepted, the server may either handle the connection itself or create another process to handle it. Once the connection is accepted, data transfer between client and server may begin.

Sockets and TLI both provide routines allowing users to perform each of these steps. The major routines used by each interface are summarized in Table 1. The functions (and even the names) of the routines used during each phase of communication are very similar.

The end point that identifies a transport service user to a transport service provider is called a socket in Berkeley Unix and a transport end point in System V. Both are special file descriptors, or small integers used to index a table of open files. A **socket** call returns socket identifiers to the service user while a **t__ open** returns to the transport end point in TLI. In either case, an end point must be created prior to establishing a connection or transferring any data. This end point is then passed as a parameter on all subsequent calls, identifying a particular connection.

Getting specific

When the socket is created, the user must specify a domain, or a general class of protocols, to be used with the socket. The type of data transfer that will take place over the socket must also be specified—either connection-oriented or connectionless. Both choices are specified by parameters on the socket call. Within a domain, a specific protocol such as TCP may also be chosen.

With TLI, the user specifies either the type of service required (such as connectionless, connection-oriented with orderly release, or connection-oriented without orderly release) or a particular protocol by opening a file. If only a type of service is chosen, the user may be unaware of exactly which transport protocol is being used.

Both sockets and TLI transport end points must have addresses bound to them. In the Berkeley 4.2 BSD environment, the address structure used to bind addresses to end points varies according to the domain specified by the socket call. Rather than having a variety of addressing structures, TLI uses a single basic structure for all addresses. The functions **t__ alloc** and **t__free** are used to dynamically allocate and free these address structures. Based on the transport end point identifier (passed as a parameter), **t__alloc** can determine which transport protocol is in use and allocate exactly the space required for that protocol's address needs.

A server must specify the address it wishes to bind to an end point. If this were not done, clients would have no way to connect to a specified server. Most clients, however, don't care what their address is, since no other process will try to connect to them. With sockets, a client typically does not bother calling a bind. A TLI client, on the other hand, must call **t__bind** and explicity specify a null address. In both cases, the transport provider chooses an address and assigns it to the end point.

Making connections

Clearly, the steps required for connection establishment differ in clients and servers. Clients simply issue a connection request using the **connect** system call—in sockets in a 4.2 BSD environment—or the **t__ connect**—in a TLI System V environment. Based on the call's return value, the client can determine whether a connection has been established.

Servers must perform more than one step. After an address has been bound to an end point, the server process must listen on that end point. The socket routine for this is **listen,** the TLI routine **t__listen**. With sockets, **listen** simply marks the socket as listening and returns immediately; the server must then call **accept** to be notified of an incoming connection. The **accept** routine

Connections and end points

The OSI reference model defines a service access point (SAP) as the interface between a service user and a service provider. Each SAP has an address, and communicating with a specific service user on a remote machine requires learning the address of that user's SAP before exchanging information via the service provider.

A transport service provider, then, must be told the remote address with which a user wishes to communicate. It may also need to be told the local address on which its user will be listening for incoming connection requests or for incoming data. Several connections can exist between the same pair of addresses.

The OSI reference model also defines a terminator called a connection end point (CEP), which is located within a particular SAP at one end of a connection. The CEP is a local identifier used to associate a specific service user with a particular connection. While many connections can terminate at the same address (within the same SAP, for example), each of those connections has a unique end point.

By definition, CEPs exist only after a connection has been established. In an actual implementation, however, an end point may be created and bound to an address (that is, associated with an SAP) before connection establishment or, in connectionless communications, before data transfer begins.

For example, a file server may have a single well-known address. Several remote clients, each having their own (possibly shared) addresses and (locally unique) end points, may access that server. Assuming the server protocol is connection oriented, a connection will be established between each client and the server. Each of those connections is assigned a unique end point within the server, which is then used to respond to each client's request.

blocks transmission until a connect indication arrives; when the call returns, a connection has been established. If the server does not wish to handle this particular connection, it must close it after acceptance.

With TLI, the sequence of events is slightly different. The **t__listen** call normally blocks transmission, returning only when a **connect** indication arrives. The server may call **t__accept** to accept the connection or **t__snddis** to reject it.

A TLI client's **t__connect** call may return an indication of connection refusal. With sockets, however, a call to **connect** cannot indicate refusal of a connection by the server. Instead, the connection must first be established, then terminated. Connection establishment using both sockets and TLI is summarized in Table 2.

In the Unix environment one process is frequently designated as a master server. It listens on a particular end point at a specific address. All incoming connection requests are handled by this process, which then creates a new process to serve each connection. The new process must have its own end point identifier, distinct from that of the master server, to uniquely identify the new connection.

Table 1: Major calls

SOCKETS	TRANSPORT LAYER INTERFACE (TLI)	FUNCTION
socket	t_open	CREATE AN END POINT
bind	t_bind	ASSOCIATE AN ADDRESSS WITH AN END POINT
connect	t_connect	REQUEST ESTABLISHMENT OF A CONNECTION
listen	t_listen	LISTEN FOR AN INCOMING CONNECTION REQUEST
accept	t_accept	ACCEPT AN INCOMING CONNECTION REQUEST
read	read*	
write	write*	
send	t_snd	SEND AND RECEIVE DATA OVER A CONNECTION
recv	t_rcv	
sendmsg		
recvmsg		
sendto	t_sndudata	SEND AND RECEIVE DATA WITHOUT A CONNECTION
recvfrom	t_rcvudata	
select	poll	WAIT FOR AN EVENT
close, shutdown	t_sndrel, t_snddis, t_close, close	RELEASE A CONNECTION AND DESTROY AN END POINT
unlink	t_unbind	

*REQUIRES SPECIAL STREAMS HANDLING WITH TLI

The new identifiers are handled in sockets by having the accept call return a new end point (socket) each time a connect indication arrives. That socket is then typically given to a newly created process, spawned specifically to handle the new connection, while the master server goes

Table 2: Making connections

CONNECTION ESTABLISHMENT USING SOCKETS

CLIENT	SERVER
ep = socket(...);	ep = socket(...); bind(ep,<server address>); listen(ep,...);
connect(ep,<server address>);	new_ep = accept(ep,...);

CONNECTION ESTABLISHMENT USING THE TRANSPORT LAYER INTERFACE

CLIENT	SERVER
ep = t_open(...); t_bind(ep,<null address>); t_connect(ep,<server address>);	ep = t_open(...); t_bind(ep,<server address>); t_listen(ep,...); new_ep = t_open(...); t_bind(new_ep,<null address>); t_accept(ep,new_ep,...);

back to listening on the original end point.

TLI-based servers handle the problem differently. When **t_listen** returns with a connect indication, the server uses **t_open** and **t_bind** to create a new end point. This end point and the original listening end point are both specified as parameters to **t_accept**, which accepts the incoming connection on the new end point. This end point may then be given to a newly created server process.

The TP4 transport protocol allows user data to be transferred during connection establishment, while TCP does not. The socket interface doesn't allow data exchange during connection establishment, a reflection of TCP orientation. A TLI option supports this feature.

Both the socket and TLI interfaces provide routines for connection-oriented and connectionless data transfer. The basic connection-oriented routines for sockets are the standard Unix system calls **read** and **write**—the same calls that are used to read and write to ordinary disk files. Users may also call **send** and **recv,** or **sendmsg** and **recvmsg,** all of which provide various enhancements to the basic data transfer service. In TLI, the basic connection-oriented routines are **t_snd** and **t_rcv**. The standard system calls **read** and **write** may also be used, but require use of a special Streams mechanism.

Connectionless data transfer is supported over sockets by the **sendto** and **recvfrom** calls. The corresponding TLI routines are **t sndundata** and **t rcvundata**. Both interfaces require the requisite end points with addresses bound to them, though no connection is established.

Orderly release of connections is generally assumed by socket users. A process communicating via a socket calls **close** (a standard Unix system call) when its communication is complete. The transport provider will still attempt to deliver any data previously sent by the user via that socket. If a process does not require orderly connection release, it may call **shutdown** before calling **close,** which may result in some data being lost.

TLI users can explicitly specify which type of connection-oriented transport protocol is being used. Thus if the underlying transport protocol is TP4, for example, orderly release is not available. A **t_snddis** call always results in an abortive connection release, which can result in a possible loss of data. A **t_sndrel** call provides for an orderly release.

Addresses are unbound from end points, and end points can be destroyed. These functions, together with connections release, are subsumed in the socket **close** call. A TLI user, on the other hand, may specifically disassociate an end point from its currently assigned address by calling **t_unbind,** then reuse the end point. If an end point will not be reused, either **t_close** or the standard system call **close** can be used to both release any existing connection and destroy the end point.

Sockets are simple to use and provide worthwhile functions for TCP users. Though TLI is slightly more complex, it accommodates a greater variety of transport service providers than the 4.2 BSD socket interface. Both interfaces will be widely used, and both will be widely supported by Unix vendors. ∎

David Chappell, a Unix senior software developer at Cray Research, is involved in OSI standards activities. He has an M. S. in computer science from the University of Wisconsin.

Shukri Wakid, National Bureau of Standards, Gaithersburg, Md., and Paul Brusil and Lee LaBarre, Mitre Corp., Bedford, Mass.

Coming to OSI: Network resource management and global reachability

Transition strategies are being developed to permit operation between proprietary protocols and the new OSI standard ones.

The need to share information and processing resources knows no bounds. Indeed, the resources may be distributed both within the local environment as well as across several other "islands" of workers and computers. The need to share distributed information and processing is being effectively satisfied by interconnecting computers via communications networks, which increasingly are composed of concatenated LAN (local area network) and WAN (wide-area network) subnetworks. (See "Glossary" for the spelling out of the acronyms used in this article.)

Many problems can arise when creating such networks. The various end systems (computers with communications protocols) and subnetworks may each be supplied independently by different vendors using different proprietary technologies. The subnetworks may operate on different media, use different internal architectures, and provide different capabilities. Furthermore, as subnetworks become larger, more complex, more highly interconnected, and more heavily utilized, automated, non-labor-intensive management of network resources becomes more crucial. This automated management is needed to ensure interoperability and information sharing among processing resources. The networks must be managed to provide connectivity and reachability among devices, availability of resources, quality of services, and an appropriate level of performance.

Such networking considerations can be substantially ignored in the heterogeneous, multivendor environment by agreeing on a standard suite of communications protocols and a standard framework for managing those protocols. As shown below, the ISO's (International Organization for Standardization's) OSI (Open Systems Interconnection) protocol suite effectively addresses user needs for distributed processing support tools.

Commercial products based on OSI protocols are emerging. On the other hand, the work by several standards bodies of developing management specifications for the protocols has not yet reached total fruition. Some work is beginning to reach early phases of international standardization. Only a few OSI-based products are beginning to reach the nonstandard proprietary marketplace.

User requirements for distributed processing support tools are many. Explicitly, users have to be able to transfer, access, and manipulate both files and processes, either locally or remotely. They need to exchange messages and uniformly access multivendor resources across concatenated networks.

Specifically, multiple distributed application programs need to communicate with each other. Two subordinate problems arise: determining the physical locations of, and routes between, the communicating processes; and disseminating a consistent picture of this information to interested parties. In addition, copies of any distributed databases must remain current and consistent.

While such direct communications and data processing (DP) support capabilities are mandatory, mechanisms are needed to monitor, control, maintain, and administer the various distributed networking resources that are cooperating to provide these capabilities.

The instantaneous configuration and status of network components and media segments must be able to be assessed and controlled so that alternate communications paths can be created. Performance associated with alternate configurations must be predicted. Actual nodal and network-traffic and performance trends need to be monitored and analyzed. This is to predict performance optimization and alleviate performance bottlenecks (such as response time). This can be effected via changes in protocol parameters and resources and by balancing traffic loads across multiple channels.

Resources need to be identified unambiguously, and

Glossary

ACSE: Application Common Service Element
ASC: American Standards Committee
ASN: Abstract Syntax Notation
CASE: Common application service elements
CMIP: Common Management Information Protocol
CMIS: Common Management Information Service
CSA: Client Service Agent
DAP: Directory Access Protocol
DASE: Directory Access Service Element
DCE: Data circuit-terminating equipment
DOD: Department of Defense
DP: Data processing
DSA: Directory System Agent
DSP: Directory System Protocol
DSSE: Directory System Service Element
DTE: Data terminal equipment
ECMA: European Computer Manufacturers Association
ES: End system
FDDI: Fiber Distributed Data Interface
IP: Internetwork Protocol
IS: Intermediate system
ISDN: Integrated Services Digital Network
ISO: International Organization for Standardization
LAN: Local area network
LLC: Logical Link Control
LME: Layer Management Entity
MAP: Manufacturing Automation Protocol
MIB: Management Information Base
NBS: National Bureau of Standards
NSAP: Network service access point
OSI: Open Systems Interconnection
PDU: Protocol data unit
SASE: Special application service elements
SMAE: System management application entity
SMAP: System Management Application Process
SMIS: Specific management information-passing service
SNA: Systems Network Architecture
VLSI: Very large-scale integration
WAN: Wide-area network

such identifications (names) may need to be disseminated to internetworked users and processes. Both real-time and historical operational behavior of network components and media need to be monitored and analyzed to predict, detect, isolate, and circumvent or correct subtle as well as hard faults. (Subtle faults cause, for example, out-of-specification indications; hard faults cause full outages.)

Traffic and resource-utilization information needs to be collected, correlated, and analyzed for purposes of billing, productivity analysis, and configuration analysis.

For certain organizations, security of management information as well as control of the access to shared information and application processes is paramount. Of concern is that compromise of network-resource-management information and creation of bogus management directives can lead to incorrect management decisions. These decisions may have consequences as disastrous as physical damage to network resources. For example, believing that all communications links are down can be as disruptive to networking as actual tampering with or destruction of links.

OSI support for the various distributed processing requirements is provided in one of three ways. The three are: by functions performed by the protocols themselves; by entities managing specific protocol layers; or by applications managing the entire stack of protocols, protocol-layer managers, and subnetworks.

The new architecture

The OSI protocol suite emerging from integration of efforts by the CCITT (X.25, ISDN [Integrated Services Digital Network], X.400), IEEE 802, ASC (Accredited Standards Committee) X3T9.5, and ISO is shown in Figure 1. The various common and special application service elements—CASE (common application service elements) and SASE (special application service elements), respectively—at the application layer directly provide the explicit distributed processing support tools described earlier. These service elements use the underlying services provided by other layers of the protocol suite.

A family of network technologies is available for selection at the lowest protocol layers to provide flexibility. This flexibility is adequate for satisfying specific needs (such as WAN distances between users) or specific user traffic characteristics (such as bursty, interactive messages) or performance requirements (such as a guaranteed maximum delay). The IEEE and FDDI (Fiber Distributed Data Interface) standards family apply to LANs, whereas X.25 and ISDN more typically have WAN applications.

Thus, a variety of subnetwork solutions is available to use within and between islands of distributed processing users. For example, LANs chosen to suit specific local environments and communications needs can be interconnected with processing elements of a data processing center and with ISDN interfaces such as PBXs via a high-capacity (100 Mbit/s) FDDI network.

The maturity of the protocols and the technology-independence of several OSI layers (Fig. 1) suggest potential, near-term VLSI (very large-scale integration) implementations. Nearly all applicable protocols are either international standards or nearly so. All the various SASE use the protocol stack at CASE and below. While the lowest layers are dependent on underlying network-media technologies, the technology independence of LLC (Logical Link Control) up through CASE suggests these layers are ripe for VLSI.

OSI management

The protocol suite provides direct communications and distributed processing support capabilities and permits each protocol layer to monitor and control a single instance of communications within the layer. Meanwhile, an ancillary management mechanism is needed to monitor, control, supervise, and administer the entirety of the OSI resources that provide the communications and support capabilities. This mechanism must also establish and maintain the conditions (such as flow control) that permit effective communications to occur.

ISO has charged the ASC X3T5.4 to develop the OSI management standard. Related activities, mentioned

1. Emerging. *The integration of efforts by standards groups is supplying the various common and special application service elements at the application layer, which provide explicit distributed processing support tools. These service elements use the underlying services provided by other layers of the protocol suite.*

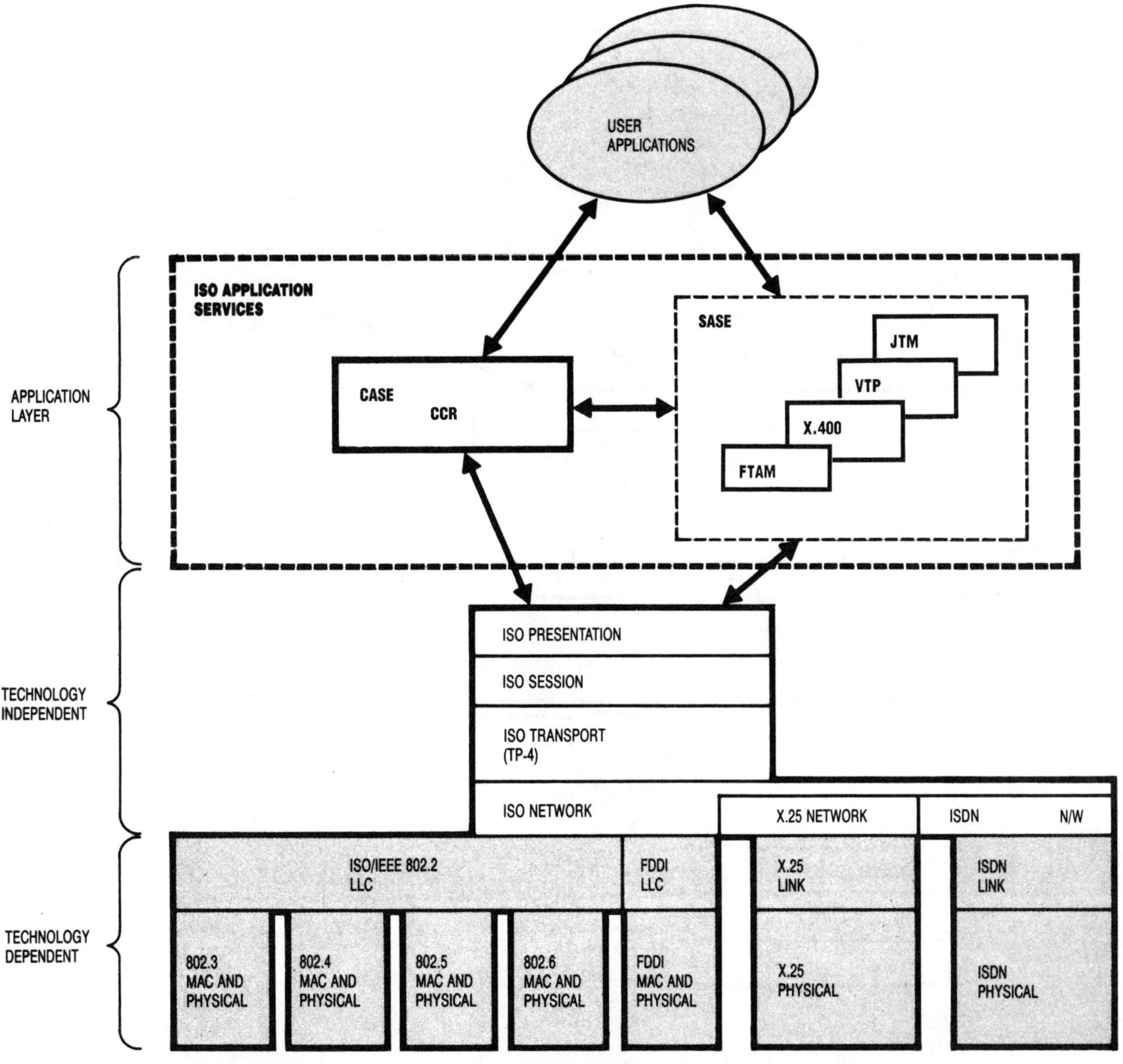

below, are also occurring in other standards bodies and are being coordinated with X3T5.4. The conceptual management framework has reached the first phase of international standardization.

The framework model accommodates three levels of OSI resource management: protocol management, layer management, and system management. Protocol management consists of those protocol-internal mechanisms within any one of the seven protocol layers needed to control a particular communications instance. An example is flow control windows on a particular transport layer connection.

Protocol management is described within the standards describing each layer's protocol and services. Layer management can affect multiple communications instances. It consists of those activities needed to manage all OSI resources associated with a particular protocol layer

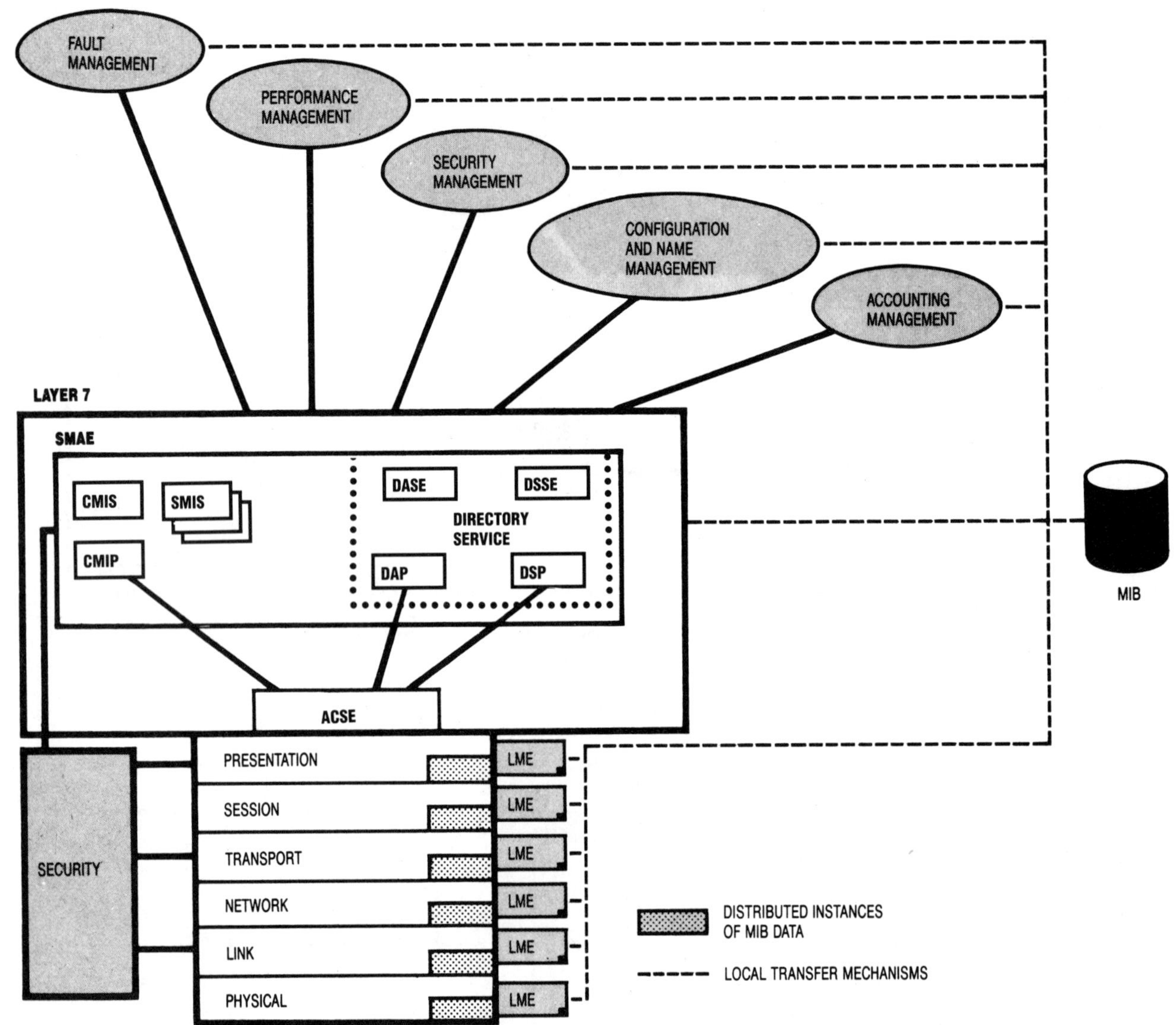

(such as network layer routing mechanisms). System management consists of those activities needed to manage the totality of OSI resources associated with any or all protocol layers within open systems.

Layer management is affected by Layer Management Entities (LMEs). One LME is associated with each protocol layer, into which it probes. The LME permits observation of layer-specific information, such as state variables, protocol operations, events (errors, thresholds, state changes), and performance. (A state is a layer condition, such as waiting or transmitting.) The LME also permits protocol parameters and resources to be loaded, controlled, or set.

An LME permits layer-specific decision making based on protocol observations made either locally (by itself) or remotely by other LMEs associated with other instances of the layer being managed. Communications between LMEs at a given layer is primarily intended to occur via Layer 7 (application) system management protocols, which use all seven layers of the underlying communications protocols. However, a layer-specific management protocol may be employed where all seven layers do not exist.

System management is supported by system management application entities (SMAEs), resident in Layer 7. The SMAE is a "tool box" of management services and protocols for management information between open systems. One SMAE is associated with each aggregate state of the seven-layer protocol stack.

The SMAEs communicate with each other via system management protocols. ASC X3T5.4 is developing this protocol specification (Common Management Information Protocol or CMIP) and its accompanying service definition (Common Management Information Service or CMIS). Additional specific management information-passing services (SMISs) that use CMIP are also being developed by X3T5.4 to support the five "system" management functional areas described below. The CMIP uses the services and protocols provided by the rest of the protocol stack (Fig. 2).

The decision making used to manage an entire OSI system (seven-layer stack) is effected through a set of centralized- or distributed-management processes. These processes (Fig. 2) are applications that reside above Layer 7—therefore outside the scope of OSI standardization.

The management application processes may include management of faults, accounting, configuration, performance, security, and names (a subset of configuration management). These management processes receive inputs from local administrative personnel and/or automated software agents, and from local and remote SMAEs and LMEs. Decisions made by the management application processes are either effected by local mechanisms on local OSI communications resources or communicated to remote OSI resources via their associated SMAEs and LMEs. Working drafts of the SMAE's services (SMISs) supporting these management processes exist.

In the case of name management, distribution of name-related information may be assisted by SMAE-resident directory services (DASE: Directory Access Service Element; DSSE: Directory System Service Element) and protocols (DAP: Directory Access Protocol; DSP: Directory System Protocol). These services and protocols are being standardized by ASC X3T5.4 with the collaboration of the CCITT. Work is under way to ascertain whether some of the directory services and protocols can actually be provided by CMIS and CMIP.

The logically distributed set of resource data (Fig. 2) that is used by OSI management functions is called the Management Information Base (MIB). This data may reside within each protocol layer and LME state and within one or more logical databases supporting the system management application processes. The MIB's data elements are being standardized by ASC X3S3.4/IEEE 802 for Layer 2 and ASC X3S3.3 for the transport and network layers. Soon X3T5.5 will initiate similar efforts for layers above transport.

Specs as subsets

The MAP (Manufacturing Automation Protocol) 3.0 network management task force, needing a complete MIB definition earlier than possible from ISO bodies, has developed MIB specifications for MAP 3.0. These specifications are being provided to the ISO bodies and will likely emerge as major subsets of the eventual ISO/MIB standards.

SMAEs and LMEs communicate this management data—or changes thereto—among open systems, as needed. The syntax (format) for management information exchange is being standardized by the ISO via the Abstract Syntax Notation One (ASN.1). A working draft document describes the MIB's structure by defining the abstract model of MIB data relationships and characteristics. It guides layer standards groups in designing layer-specific MIB elements, defines the syntax of this information, while each layer standard defines the semantics.

For LANs that have efficient, connectionless, data link layer broadcast facilities, and that support nodes that implement less than the full seven-layer protocol stack (such as bridges and network routers), the IEEE 802.1 group is developing a resource management model comparable to that in development by ISO (Fig. 3). IEEE's SMAP (System Management Application Process) is the process that executes IEEE 802 system management functions. It interfaces the data link layer LMEs and communicates with other SMAPs via an 802.1 systems management protocol executed between SMAEs in different 802 nodes. The 802 SMAEs communicate using the services provided by the 802.2 LLC protocol.

A mapper (protocol translator) maps the communications services required by the 802.1 systems management protocol to those provided by LLC. Uncertainty exists in trying to interpret the management reference model in situations where an implementer feels that both X3T5.4 and 802 management functions have to coexist in a LAN. For this situation the MAP 3.0 network management task force has taken the approach that a MAP manager (software) will be able to manage concurrently both nodes with either full or partial OSI stacks. The X3T5.4 SMAE in the manager will thus be interfaced both to the presentation layer (for managing full-stack nodes) and to the LLC layer via a thin (subset), null-layers protocol stack (for managing partial-stack nodes).

When deemed necessary, the exchange of management information among SMEs or LMEs can be protected by the various encryption levels (link, end-to-end, and process-to-process) provided by ISO's security framework. Implementation is by security modules at the link/network, transport, and presentation/application layers, respectively (Fig. 2). In addition, access control can be provided to MIB management information as well as to encryption key management information within the security module(s).

Identifying OSI resources

Name registration facilitates generation of unique, unambiguous names to be used to identify OSI resources. Name management actually identifies OSI resources by associating OSI names (such as protocol layer identifiers) to them. Address and route management ensures that a given application name, pertinent to a process in an end system (ES), can be bound to an NSAP (network service access point), then to a physical address, and finally to a route. This translation would prevail, potentially, through an internetwork environment consisting of multiple concatenated subnetworks joined by intermediate systems (ISs), such as IP (Internetwork Protocol) gateways. To accomplish these tasks, the name management application process needs to integrate and coordinate functionality provided by directory services as well as the network layer LME.

Directory services facilitate the dynamic binding of application layer names to various name attributes (such as the name's location) as well as to other names or groups of

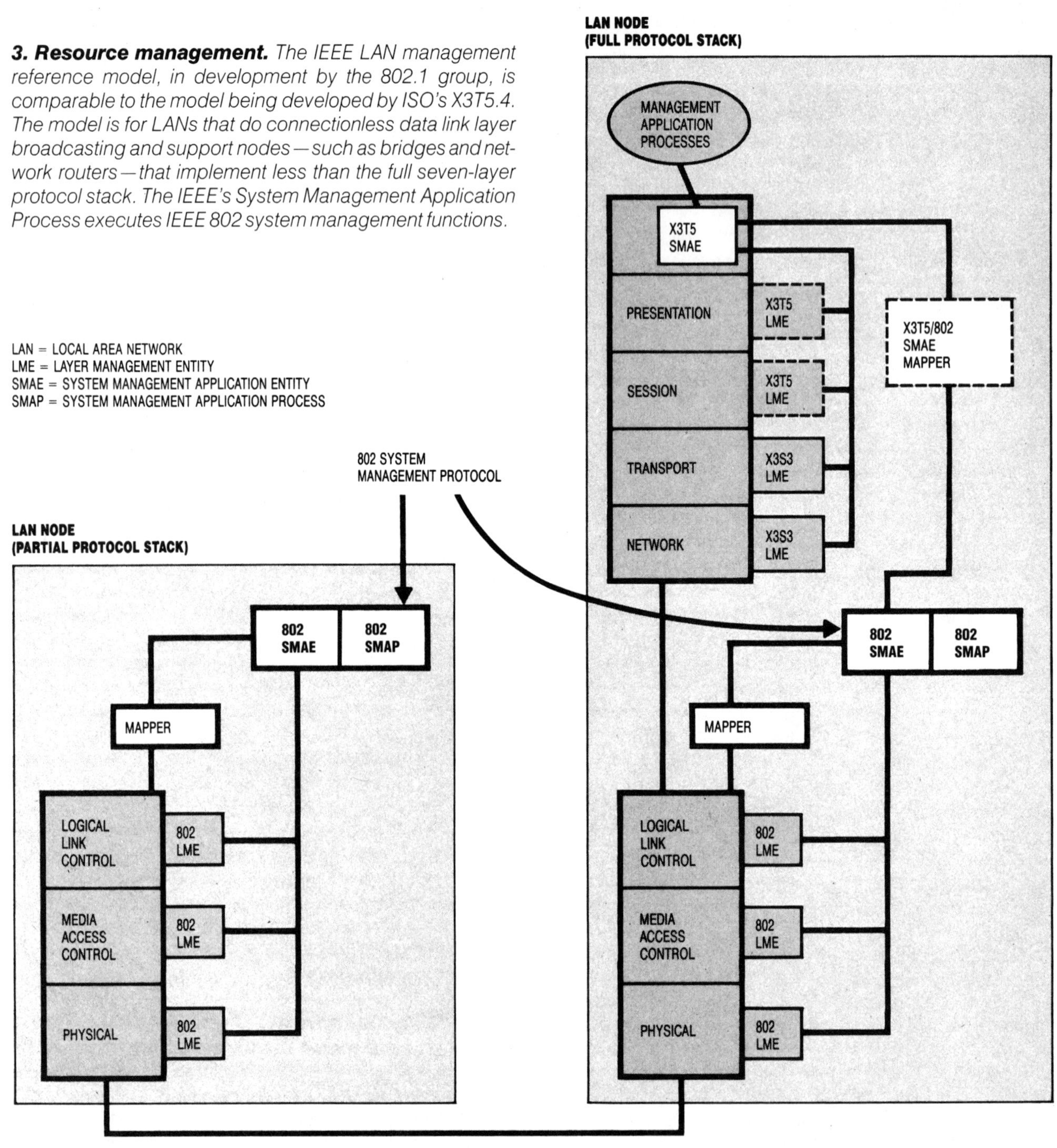

names. This CCITT definition may be extended to include relational (table-like) coupling of attributes and matching patterns in a schema (logical data structure). ISO is developing a general model where directory services apply to various attributes at various layers and are not necessarily restricted to application layer names. Directory services are needed, for example, to support the interprocess communications mechanism in the session layer and the mapping of NSAPs to physical addresses and routes in the network layer. Directory services may evolve to support system management functions as an integrated repository of various relevant layers' data (Fig. 2).

This directory service facilitates interrogation of a distributed database pertinent to various aspects (such as user addresses and file names) of communications. Therefore, a protocol is in the process of being defined between a user agent, called a Client Service Agent (CSA), and a Directory System Agent (DSA). A particular DSA may "own" only a portion of the global database, but it has the ability to network with other DSAs, if needed, for a proper response to the CSA's query.

Hence, an additional protocol, using CMIS protocols and services, is needed between various DSAs for the purpose of constructing a complete answer to the CSA's query, as well as building and maintaining the various databases into a transparent entity for the CSA/user. The aggregate set of cooperating DSAs forms the directory system. The DSA-to-DSA protocol must provide features such as chaining (forwarding) and may use the shadowing technique (copying of various databases at each DSA) as a means of establishing transparency.

What does it mean?

CCITT, ISO (ASC X3T5.4), and ECMA (European Computer Manufacturers Association) are currently developing a definition of the Directory Service Protocol. CCITT has defined access to the distributed database via a tree-like structure with nodes designating countries, organizations within countries, names within organizations, and respective attributes. This access, together with alias (name) management, authentication, exploration (random search), basic kernel services (such as the address associated with a name), query listing (a listing of all possible searches), object (attribute) management, and shadowing, forms the set of functions that define the protocol.

In some environments, the OSI name management application process may need to utilize and coordinate functions performed by the network layer LME. Consider an OSI environment that is comprised of concatenated subnetworks with multivendor products using different technologies and controlled by various administrations. Such an environment contains a superset of ISs—called an Internet—which is the aggregate of all gateways. The Internet is partitioned into multiple routing areas contained within administrative domains, each consisting of a set of concatenated subnetworks that is dynamically coupled to a given cluster of NSAPs. These NSAPs are typically mapped to end systems, and the concatenated subnetworks are connected by intermediate systems.

An ES-IS protocol, as part of the network layer's LME, is being developed for ISO by ASC X3S3.3. The purpose is to allow ESs on a subnetwork to determine the condition of the ISs attached to that subnetwork and, hence, forward an IP datagram through one such IS. These ISs in turn determine the condition of their assigned ESs and deliver datagrams arriving from the external gateways (ISs). The Internet traffic is forwarded through the subnetworks by the IP. The IP calls on the services of the routing algorithm, which examines the reachability (routing) tables to make routing decisions based on reachability metrics. (Examples of reachability metrics are distance vectors [number of hops between ISs], or the more recently used link state [connectivity matrix], cost of link, and reliability of a link for a given destination IS.)

The correctness, consistency, and comprehensibility of these tables are essential to proper routing. The network layer's LME protocol that builds and maintains these tables is the IS-IS protocol and is essential for the propagation of ES-ES datagrams. To maintain the routing tables, the IS-IS protocol uses the unreliable (datagram) services of the IP to transmit updates. The Internet complexity justifies having consistent tables throughout the Internet.

Various problems may arise in attempting to maintain consistent tables in a timely manner. One problem could be caused by various bandwidth capacities in the connectivity of the Internet and the possibility that certain ISs will

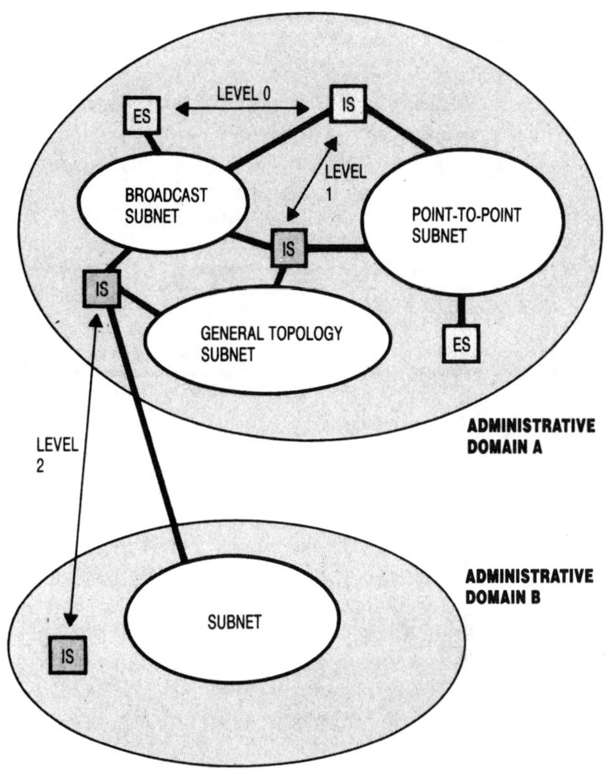

4. Routing architecture. *The intermediate system/intermediate system protocol may be defined at two levels. A third is the end system/intermediate system protocol.*

either malfunction or be out of service during the propagation of table updates. Race (out-of-sequence transmission) and loopback (circular transmission, where the message returns to the sender) conditions are known to occur. False reachability metrics may be maliciously propagated. To solve this last problem, one may partition the ISO Internet into administrative domains, each of which consists of routing areas. A set of ISs within an administrative domain is then designated to communicate with peer ISs in other domains, each of which consists of routing areas.

Due to issues of trust and the requirements for "firewalls" among various domains, one may expect the IS-IS protocol to be defined at two levels, intra- and interadministrative domain. These levels, together with ES-IS protocol, form an integrated three-level architecture that is being considered by ASC X3S3.3 and ECMA (Fig. 4). Some intradomain routing techniques and reachability metrics are likely to remain proprietary (at least for some time), while interdomain exchange of reachability data is a candidate for standardization.

To ensure global reachability and a manageable-size routing table, a naming-and-addressing scheme needs to be defined to enable accessing naming authorities and directories whenever physical addresses are unknown. Hierarchical structures are likely to be imposed on the Internet to restrict the size of routing tables employed by ISs and to manage the inter-IS information traffic for reach-

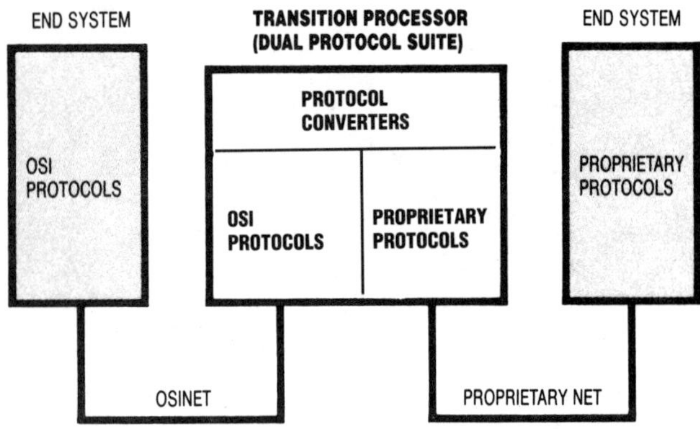

5. Gateway development. *An application layer protocol converter has an OSI end system operating with a proprietary-protocol end system via two subnetworks.*

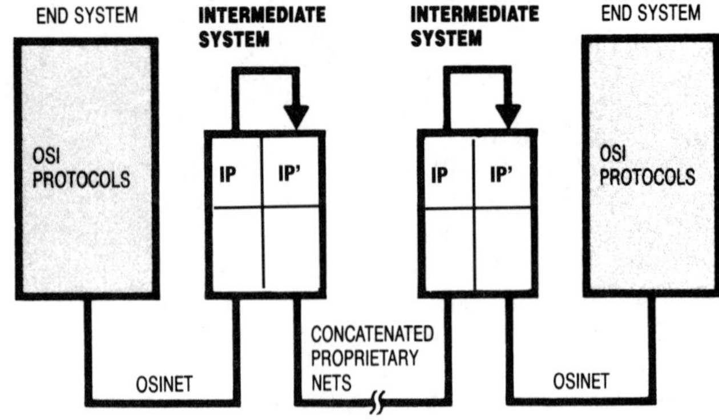

6. Network layer conversion. *OSI and proprietary protocols coexist where two OSI end systems interoperate via an encapsulated proprietary subnetwork.*

ability, quality of service, and update traffic.

Using a service—such as a virtual circuit—more reliable than the IP datagram to update routing tables helps maintain the consistency of the reachability data. Also needed: understanding the dynamics and stability of adjustments to congestion and error problems, flow control by adaptive selection of routes as user demands change, congestion avoidance algorithms, error monitoring, and security.

The technical problems common to both the IS-IS protocol and the Distributed Directory Services are those of concurrency control—how consistent the tables are at any instant, including update and shadowing—and routing in distributed databases. The IS-IS protocol, however, deals with much smaller databases (routing tables) and may have more stringent requirements on the total time needed to update all tables. The number of databases in the IS-IS environment is expected to be much larger than those of Distributed Directory Services. The algorithmic solutions to both problems may, therefore, be different.

Transition guidelines

To capitalize on OSI's capabilities of distributed processing support and network resource management, several networking users—such as DOD (Department of Defense)—that currently depend on non-OSI protocols are planning to migrate totally to OSI networks. Two possible transition strategies are: (a) emulating TP-4 (Transport Protocol Class 4—refer to "Internetworking in an OSI environment," DATA COMMUNICATIONS, May 1986, p. 126) on top of TCP (Transmission Control Protocol) and use ISO upper-layer protocols throughout; (b) concatenating protocol suites.

In the interim, OSI subnetworks are likely to be deployed in concatenated environments that, in part, consist of various proprietary protocols. Examples are SNA (IBM's Systems Network Architecture), Decnet (from Digital Equipment Corp.), and Arpanet (DOD's Advanced Research Projects Agency network). Two cases of concatenated environments are considered: an OSI end system interoperating with a proprietary protocol end system via two concatenated subnetworks (Fig. 5), and two OSI end

systems interoperating via an encapsulated proprietary subnetwork (Fig. 6). (The mention of proprietary product names does not imply an NBS [National Bureau of Standards] or Mitre Corp. endorsement of such products.)

In the first case, an application layer gateway (protocol converter) can perform the transformation function by mapping the respective PDUs (protocol data units) of file transfer, messaging, and virtual terminal (an end system that is programmed to appear as a terminal) to their respective counterparts. This mapping process—at least between Arpanet's application layer protocols and OSI's—appears simple because of the similarity of the protocol functions offered by the respective protocols. However, a performance penalty may occur since protocols below the application layers must be executed in both protocol suites. The NBS is currently developing such a protocol converter for the OSI and Arpanet protocol suites.

When application layer protocol mapping is not possible or feasible, OSI and proprietary protocols can coexist even though the protocol suites cannot interoperate. In this case (the second transition strategy cited above), protocol conversion is only needed at the third (network) layer to ensure proper delivery of network layer PDUs. A translation (mapping of PDUs) is, therefore, needed between respective IP layers. This ensures the propagation of datagrams through concatenated proprietary networks as well as OSI concatenated networks. Since the IP uses tables built and maintained by routing-table protocols, such as the IS-IS protocol, a mapping between these dissimilar protocols may only be necessary to preserve the quality of reachability on an end-to-end basis. ■

Shukri Wakid is chief of the Advanced Systems Division of the National Bureau of Standards. He holds a Ph.D. in atomic physics from Louisiana State University. Paul Brusil is group leader of performance and standards in the Secure Distributed Systems Department at Mitre-Bedford. He holds a Ph.D. in systems analysis from Harvard University. Lee LaBarre is a senior member of the technical staff in the Secure Distributed Systems Department at Mitre-Bedford. He is a Ph.D. candidate in computer sciences at Clarkson College of Technology (Potsdam, N. Y.).

John L. Hullett, QPSX Communications Pty. Ltd., Western Australia, and
Peter Evans, Telecom Australia Research Laboratories, Western Australia

New proposal extends the reach of metro area nets

IEEE 802.6 committee adopts Telecom Australia plan for 'dual bus' scheme; said to work faster and farther than ring architectures

The metropolitan area network, an evolutionary step beyond the local area network, promises high-speed communications at distances greater than any LAN can handle. But in another sense, the MAN is what standards groups will make it. Just what standards will define a MAN is being hammered out by the 802.6 committee of the Institute of Electrical and Electronic Engineers (IEEE).

A good standard is crucial to MAN development, since interoperability between computer and telecommunications networks is a prerequisite to a successful launch of the new technology. Several key requirements for MANs have already been fashioned by 802.6. These include employing a shared medium capable of operating over areas of at least 50 kilometers in diameter, providing high-speed packet data transmission and voice capability as well as other services requiring guaranteed bandwidth and constrained delay.

The large area envisioned for MANs, as well as the ability to handle voice, places the MAN squarely in the arena of such public network providers as the Postal, Telegraph, and Telephone agencies (PTTs) and the Bell operating companies (BOCs). They welcome that position and are taking an active role in its development.

In addition to its being a highly versatile customer-access network, telephone companies see the MAN as meeting the market for multimegabit data services. The types of services envisioned for such bit rates include computer-to-computer communications and image transfers. For example, graphics-intensive applications such as computer-aided design, computer-aided manufacturing, and medical imaging require data rates up to 150 Mbit/s or more.

The need to make the MAN compatible with the public network environment was brought into sharp focus at a recent meeting of the 802.6 committee. The committee adopted these goals for a MAN standard:

■ It should accommodate fast and robust signaling schemes for MANs.
■ It should guarantee security and privacy and permit establishment of virtual private networks within MANs.
■ It must ensure high network reliability, availability, and maintainability.
■ It should promote efficient performance for MANs regardless of their size.

The Queued Packet and Synchronous Switch (QPSX) dual bus MAN proposal sponsored by Telecom Australia was adopted in November 1987 by the 802.6 committee because it meets or exceeds those requirements. Figure 1 illustrates how LAN standards and the proposed dual bus MAN standard relate to the Open Systems Interconnection (OSI) model. The dual bus network can operate with any synchronous transmission interface including DS-3, CCITT G.703, and Sonet.

A dual bus MAN employing the QPSX access protocol is the ideal networking technology for a MAN operating in the public network. It performs more reliably and efficiently than other protocols that were proposed. This is because its signaling, multilevel priority structure, synchronization, and signaling are unaffected by congestion.

The dual bus architecture of QPSX is shown in Figure 2. It consists of two lines, or buses, which carry traffic in opposite directions. Each node, with connections to both buses, has read and unidirectional write capability. Every node can communicate to every other node sending information on one bus and receiving it on the other.

In contrast to ring architecture, data does not pass through each node. Nodes on the bus read the addresses of passing packets and copy data if there is an address match between the node and the destination address within the packet.

By way of comparison, ring architectures are being used in the Fiber Distributed Data Interface (FDDI), the multi-

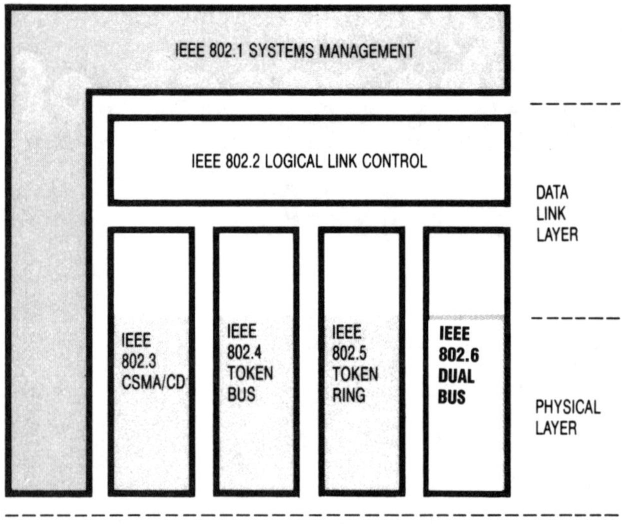

1. OSI relationship. *The queued packet and synchronous switch dual bus proposal, sponsored by Telecom Australia, fits neatly into the Open Systems Interconnection model.*

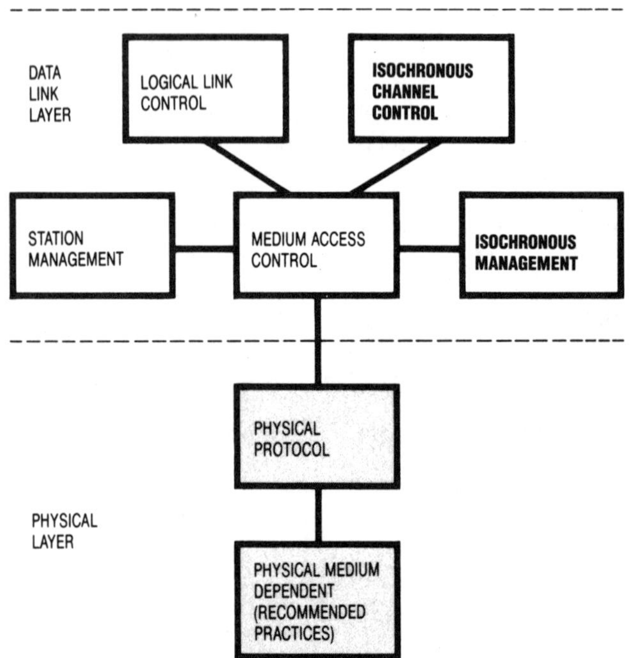

plexed slotted and token (MST) network, and the Cambridge Ring. Nodes in ring architectures are serially connected on a single line. Each node receives and retransmits or repeats the messages in turn. Messages are generally removed by the source node. The bus architecture offers several significant advantages over the ring in terms of robustness and reliability.

In the dual bus architecture, the unidirectional reading and writing to each bus is implemented electronically using simple OR gates and shift registers, as shown in Figure 3. Writing is accomplished by transmitting a logical OR onto

a synchronized and formatted time structure generated by the frame generator at the head of each bus.

It is possible to loop the dual buses, a configuration shown in Figure 4. Its similarity to the ring architecture is in form only, since the looped bus can use a master clock located, for example, in the telephone network.

Ticka ticka timing

Time on each bus is divided into fixed-length slots with a fixed number of slots allocated to each 125-microsecond frame. The arrangement is depicted in Figure 5. The actual number of slots in each frame depends on the bit rate on the buses. The bit rate depends on the particular transport adopted for the physical medium-dependent sublayer.

In North America, the slot size would be 45 octets, although size can be varied once broadband ISDN standards emerge. The overhead in logically linking packet segments in QPSX is only about 7 percent.

Each node may engage in packet- or channel-switched (asynchronous or synchronous) communications. Slots not reserved for synchronous traffic use are available for packet switching. The allocation of bandwidth between synchronous and packet use is dynamically controlled according to demand.

Because the information flow on the buses is unidirectional, all nodes on the bus may be synchronized without regard to distance. Slots used for packet switching are accessed using the distributed queuing protocol. The distributed queuing protocol's efficiency is unaffected by distance. As a consequence, QPSX bus networks can be arbitrarily extended. The medium used for the buses is also arbitrary, but in most cases it would be optical fiber. Cable TV technology could operate as a variant of QPSX distributed queuing (see "Networking for greater metropolitan areas," in this issue).

Reliability built in

The reliability of QPSX stems both from its architecture and its distributed queuing medium-access control (MAC) protocol. There are two reasons for the inherent reliability of the bus architecture. First, the network nodes are logically adjacent to the bus, not serially and logically con-

2. Dual bus. *In the QPSX dual bus, every node can communicate to every other node by sending information on one bus and receiving it on the other.*

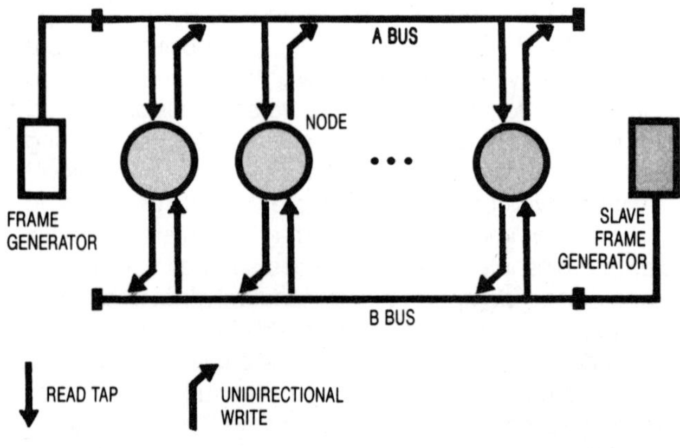

3. Write stuff. *Unidirectional reading and writing to each bus is implemented electronically, using OR gates and shift registers. Writing is accomplished by transmitting a logical* OR *onto a synchronized and formatted time structure generated by a frame generator located adjacent to the head end of each queued packet and synchronous switch bus.*

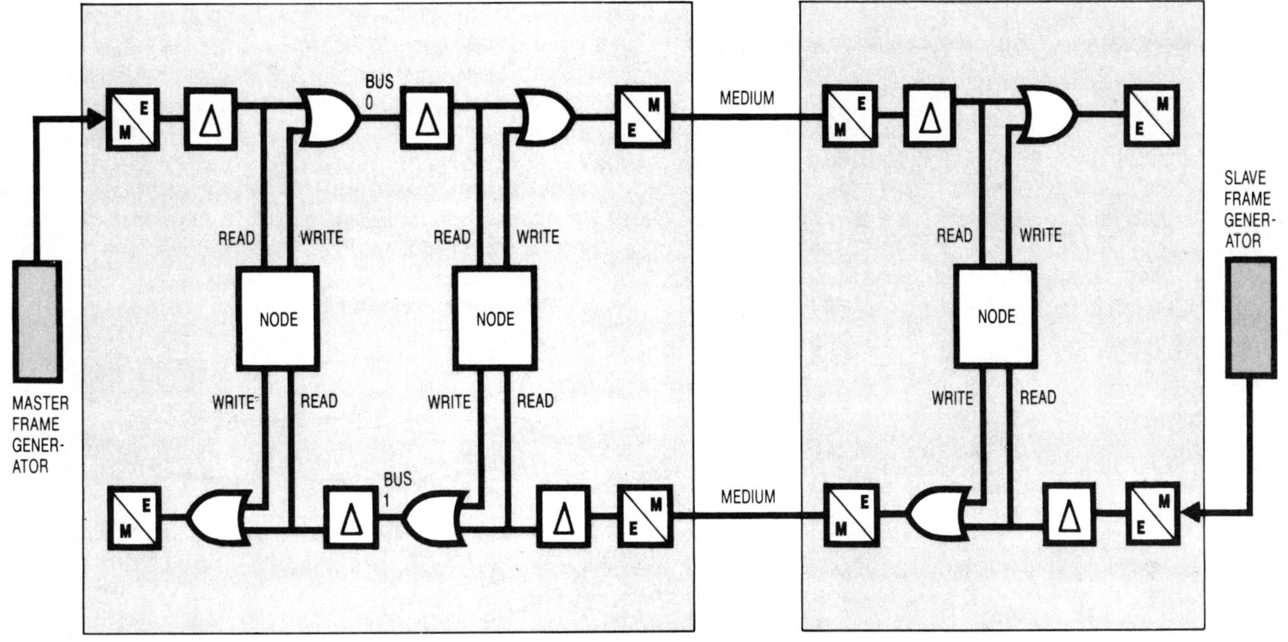

nected as in a ring. Thus, data does not pass through the nodes, and passive MAC failures have no effect. Second, because the node's writing function is by logical OR (that is, without overwrites), active MAC failures and bus failures are easily detected by input-to-output coincidence checking (Fig. 6). Any failures that occur are bypassed at the node. The operation can be totally hardware-based with immediate response, no loss of synchronization, and minimal network disruption. With QPSX, no node monitoring functions are required to check the MAC.

In ring-based networks, active- and passive-node MAC failures are catastrophic. This is because both types of failure must invoke healing mechanisms associated with their redundant rings. Healing involves considerable network disruption because it entails a reconfiguration, which causes a loss of synchronization. Any additional node failure can then produce isolated network islands.

QPSX architecture node failures do not invoke any network healing mechanism that requires reconfiguration of the network. Faulty nodes are easily bypassed. Failures in the physical transport, however, do involve reconfiguration. But once the healing is completed, the network captures the same synchronization, so disruption is minimal. Physical faults or line breaks are healed by repositioning the natural break in the loop to the position of the break.

There is no loss of network capacity involved in this type of network reconfiguration. This contrasts sharply with ring-type networks. If a ring network carries traffic on a

4. Looped bus. *Though the looped bus looks similar to the ring architecture, its fault-healing and synchronization is superior. Its master clock is located in the telephone network.*

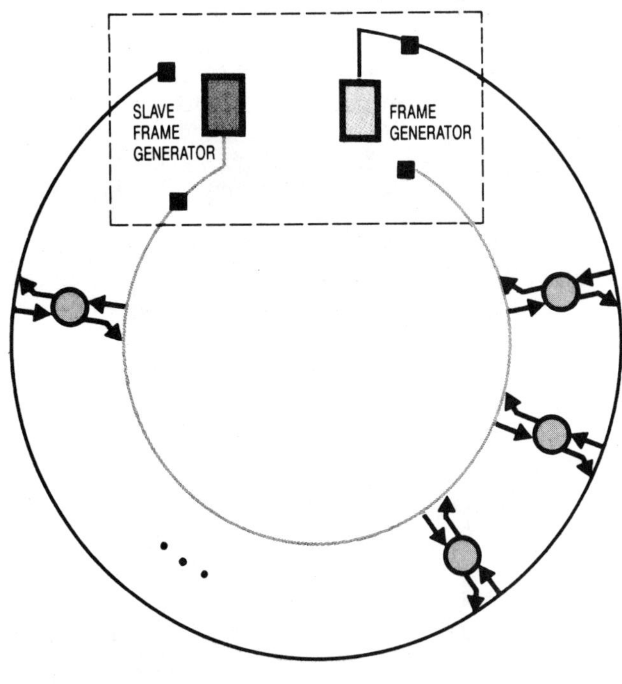

5. Timing. *Fixed-length slots with a fixed number of slots allocated to each frame are used to keep time across the bus. In North America, slot size is 45 octets.*

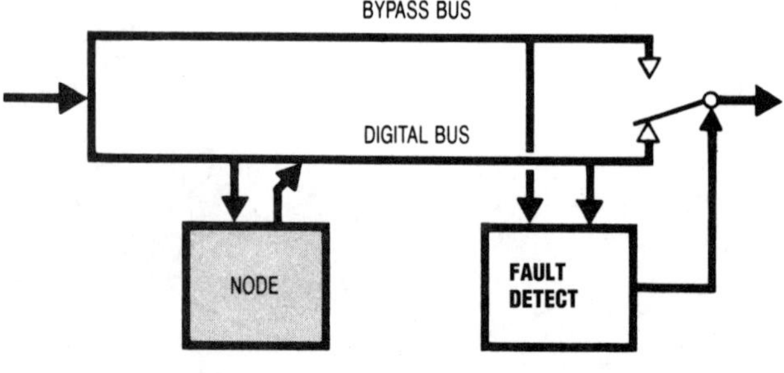

backup ring, then network reconfiguration due to either node or transport failure introduces a 50 percent reduction in packet data capacity. Alternatively, if the backup ring carries no data traffic, there is always a 50 percent inefficiency factor relative to the QPSX bus network.

QPSX invokes healing only after a real disaster, such as a backhoe through physical transport. Node failures do not invoke reconfiguration in QPSX, since faulty nodes are excised using simple low-cost hardware.

Speedy access

The distributed queuing data-access protocol of QPSX enables looped bus networks to operate at maximum efficiency at very high speeds and over unlimited distance. Here is how it works.

The operation is fundamentally different from all existing LAN packet-access protocols. In all random- or controlled-access protocols, each station has no record of network loading. Only when a station has a packet for transmission does it ascertain, either explicitly or implicitly, the information required for scheduling access.

By contrast, each distributed queuing node keeps a current-state record of the number of packet segments across the network awaiting access. When a station has a packet for transmission, it uses this count to determine its position in the distributed queue. If no packet segments are waiting, access is immediate. Otherwise, deference is given to those packets that are queued first.

With this arrangement, capacity is never wasted, and minimum access delay at all levels of loading is guaranteed right up to 100 percent utilization of the bus. This performance is achieved with negligible control overhead (less than 1 percent), and it is effectively independent of the bit rate and physical extent of the network. Access is uniform across the network, so there is no possibility of network hogging.

6. Reliability. *Because network nodes are logically adjacent to the bus, not serially and logically connected as in a ring, data will not be lost with a node failure.*

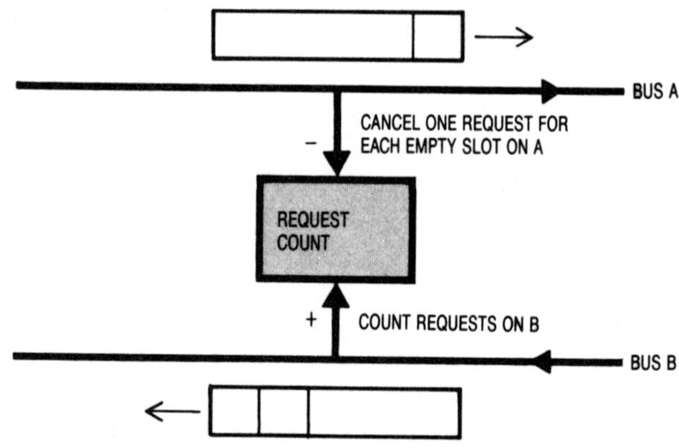

The distributed queuing access control is completely distributed. It requires only simple logic hardware at each station. The only shared function is the frame timing generation that must be at the head of the bus.

The queuing protocol uses just two bits of control overhead in the access control field of each packet. The Busy and Request Control bits order the access of packets to the bus. The Busy bit indicates that a packet is filled with data, so it is not available for access. The Request Control bit is used to indicate that a node has a packet queued for transmission.

7. Distributed queuing. *A position in the distributed queuing access control is signified by a sequence number. A station uses this count to determine its position in the queue.*

(A) QUEUE FORMATION ON BUS A

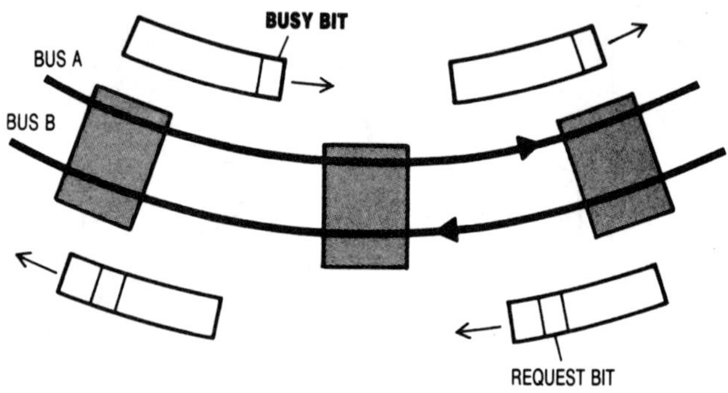

(B) NODE NOT QUEUED TO SEND

How does the distributed queue operate? In Figure 7A, a queue is formed in relation to nodes using bus A, which flows to the right. The position in the queue is signified by a sequence number. At a node on the network, the sequence number is held in a request counter. When that node has no packet to send on line A, the request counter tracks the Request Control bits sent on line B. Line B request signaling is used for line A access and vice versa. The counter is incremented for each Request Control bit received on line B and decremented for each empty packet slot passing on line A (Fig. 7B). Decrementing the count recognizes that the passing empty packet will serve a node queued downstream.

When a node has a packet ready for transmission, it obtains its position in the queue by reading its request counter. The request counter is reset, and the count is transferred to a countdown counter. In the countdown state, when a node is awaiting access, passing an empty packet slot decrements the countdown counter, while new requests increment the request counter. The situation is shown in Figure 8. When the countdown count is zero, the node may access the bus using the next non-busy packet. If the node has another packet for the distributed queuing protocol, the process is repeated using the current request count.

The QPSX distributed queuing protocol can be used to assign priority to packets. By operating separate distributed queues for each level of priority, queued packets with high priority gain access to the bus before lower-priority packets. In the MAN, the highest priority would be reserved for signaling, control, and fault configuration. Even when the network is highly loaded, with many nodes simultaneously transmitting large, 8-kbyte packets, high-priority access will be immediate.

In this context it is worth noting that the packet segmentation used in QPSX offers a near-immediate response to sharing of network capacity or changes in loading. A similar situation in terms of processing capacity exists in time-shared computing. In the computing environment, queued jobs cyclically receive a quantum of service each. Token rings use nonsegmented access that is analogous to batch processing.

Performance

By using request counters, the distributed queuing protocol provides ideal ordered-access characteristics. If the queue size is zero, a packet will gain immediate access, but if the queue size is anything other than zero, the packet waits only while those queued ahead of it access the bus. Thus, in contrast to all existing media-access protocols, there

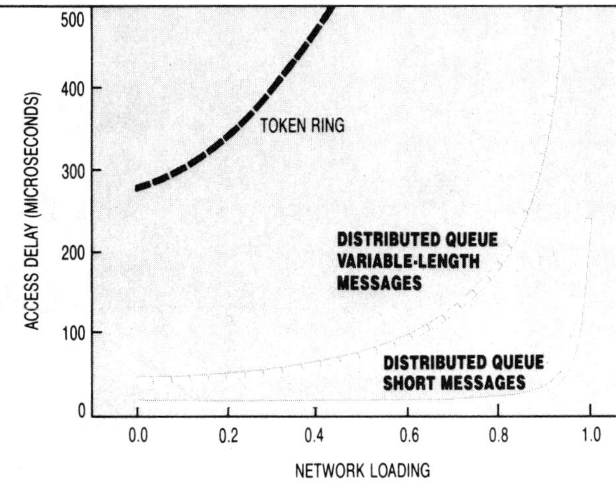

9. No token. *Distributed queuing has a shorter access delay than token ring access since there is no overhead waiting for a token to transfer.*

is never any wasted capacitywith distributed queuing.

The ideal access characteristics of distributed queuing are illustrated by comparing its expected transmission delay with that of a token ring (Fig. 9). In the example, a network of 50 stations is shown operating at 100 Mbit/s over a loop length of 100 kilometers. The average packet size is 100 bytes. The figure also shows a graph of the delay for short packets (acknowledgment or control packets).

Distributed queuing provides two clear advantages over the token ring. First, it has a shorter access delay since there is no overhead waiting for a token to transfer. Access can be immediate if no other packets are queued. Second, fair treatment is given in the distributed queue to short messages, providing all the advantages of time-shared processors. The big problem with the token ring is the delay in token transfers: It takes an average access delay of at least half of the ring latency—even when the network is lightly loaded. This delay increases with the network size and eventually limits the physical size of the network.

Public network architecture

Since the QPSX can be used in either a dual bus or a looped configuration, many network architecture variations can be considered. It can be used in a looped-network hierarchy or a star-network hierarchy based on dual buses. Or a topology of loops and stars can be combined.

Considerable savings can be made in transmission and switch resources by running multiple dual bus connections in conjunction with a single looped bus return. By creating a number of virtual looped buses, reliability and global healing of the looped bus can be achieved at lower cost. This achitecture may suit many applications, particularly on intercity routes. ∎

Peter Evans, a senior engineer with the local-access section of Telecom Australia, received a B. S. E. E. from the University of Adelaide, Southern Australia. John L. Hullett received his Ph.D. in electrical engineering from the University of Western Australia in 1970. He worked for Telecom Australia before joining QPSX as its technical director.

8. Countdown. *When a node has a packet ready for transmission, it obtains its position in the queue by reading its request counter.*

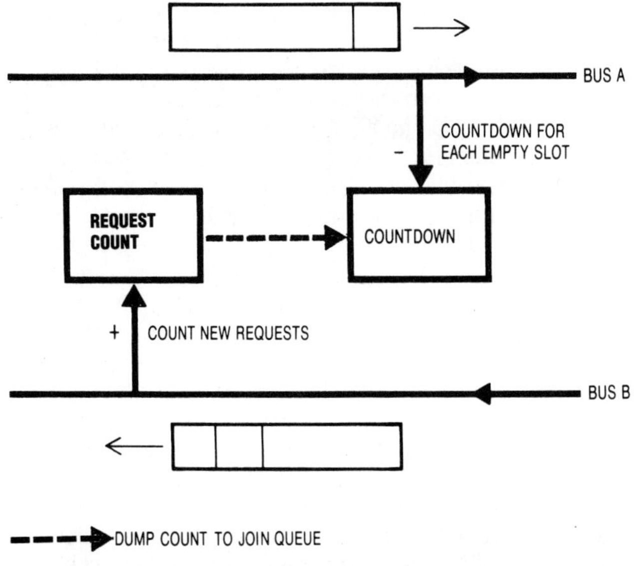

Lemont Southworth, Lemont Southworth Consulting, Simi Valley, Calif.

Preparing for the new electronic funds transfer message standards

Though standards are being created for retail transactions, there's no surefire way to ensure compatibility across all networks.

Electronic funds transfers for retail financial transactions have flourished despite the fact that the setups were often proprietary and unique to each pair of participating institutions. However, demand for these services has led to an explosion in the number of firms that want to offer them. As soon as more than two institutions attempted to intercommunicate using EFT, there was the beginning of the need for a standard. The early standards that arose to meet that need are yielding to more sophisticated transaction-processing standards.

In 1980, the American National Standards Institute published a document called ANSI X9.2—1980, Interchange Message Specification for Debit and Credit Card Message Exchange Among Financial Institutions. This small (28-page) document established a minimum level of information for the exchange of financial transactions. It not only provided the basis for standardization within the United States but also became the springboard for the development of an international standard.

Soon, the path will run full circle. The international standard was approved for publication in 1986 and has returned to stimulate an update of ANSI X9.2. The revised X9.2 standard is expected to be published in late 1988. Basically, the industry has outgrown the old standard because of the growth of automated teller machine (ATM) activity; the addition of point-of-sale (POS) services; and the publication of ISO 8583 (Bank Card Originated Messages—Interchange Message Specifications—Content for Financial Transactions), the international equivalent of X9.2.

If EFT providers are to survive in an increasingly international marketplace, they will have to upgrade to an internationally compatible standard, either the new ANSI X9.2 or ISO 8583.

Existing implementations of the original ANSI X9.2—1980 contain many anomalies that make them incompatible with each other. Some implementations have taken liberties with the format and content of specific data elements so that, for example, the account number may be right-justified in one implementation and left-justified in another. Others have modified the format and values of essential data elements, such as the processing code that defines the transaction and type of accounts affected by the transaction. While many of these variations may have resulted from ignorance of the standard, others were most likely deliberate deviations made to accommodate existing proprietary software.

The single-institution ATMs of the mid-1970s gave way to shared networks where several institutions jointly operated a number of ATMs. Regional networks further expanded interchange within a common market area, and the development of national and international networks now gives EFT cardholders access to funds at tens of thousands of locations worldwide.

The EFT industry has grown to include third-party service providers and merchants; financial institutions such as banks, savings and loans, and credit unions; and nationwide ATM networks, such as Cirrus, Plus, Nationet, Master Teller, and Electron. This industry has expanded from single institutions through proprietary and shared networks to regional, national, and international networks, and the need to standardize the interchange of financial transactions has increased. Figure 1 illustrates this problem.

Today, there are many EFT networks using a variety of interchange message formats. As one sign of response to the proliferation of formats, major national and international EFT networks, such as those operated by Visa and Master-Card, will soon require their affiliates to conform to new message standards based on ISO 8583. The American Bankers Association is developing an Implementation Guideline for POS applications that is also based on ISO

8583 and features of the new ANSI X9.2. The guideline, which will provide one interpretation of the standards, is intended to encompass the requirements of only the POS segment of EFT but will probably influence future ATM interchange as well.

Ultimately, the need to meet international standards will be passed on to the lowest-level processor of EFT communications. Such processors include operators of the terminal networks that acquire the transactions, operators of the switches that provide interconnection among the networks, and financial institutions that issue the credit and debit cards. Thus, unless an institution maintains a pure iso-

---

1. Complex internetwork relationships. *An EFT service provider may have multiple paths to a single card issuer and each path may have a different interchange format.*

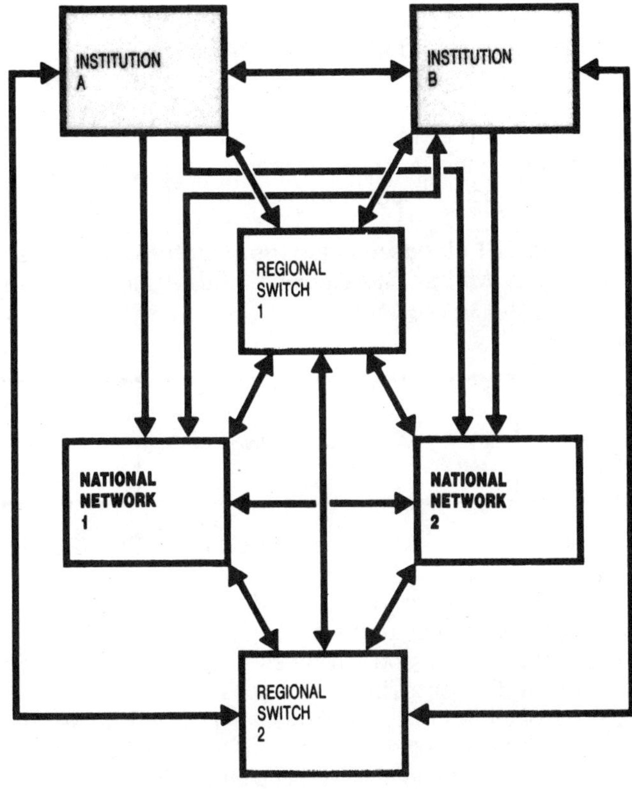

lationist EFT policy, virtually all participants in retail EFT will be affected—from the processors or service providers who operate ATMs and retail merchant terminals for the regional and national networks all the way to the credit card-issuing institutions. Eventually, the new standards will touch the lives of all EFT processors.

To remain competitive in the growing retail EFT market, processors must begin now to prepare for the new standards. For many, the change will be great; for some, it will be overwhelming. Much will depend on the existing interchange setups within an institution—how they were designed, how they fit together, and how well they can accommodate change. Even more will depend on the unique

business requirements of each organization.

The ANSI subcommittee authors of the revised X9.2 struggled in vain for many months to develop a universal implementation guide for X9.2. They found that too much depends upon the business practices and policies of the participants to create a single implementation that will satisfy all the needs of all users. While some aspects of EFT message standards were universally recognized, others, such as error recovery, exception handling, and fee processing, were not.

Many of these issues constitute legitimate competitive differences among the services offered by different EFT networks, so they could not be precluded by the message standard. In fact, the standard was designed to accommodate such differences. That leaves it up to each organization, institution, or network to develop its own implementation of the standard that will fulfill its business and technical requirements. The top technical manager at one of the leading national EFT networks has said that there are fewer than a dozen individuals in the entire United States who understand the EFT standards well enough to implement them. Nonetheless, communications managers would do well to understand some of the issues involved.

When an organization is required to make connections to several different networks, its design must accommodate all the requirements of all the different interfaces it must support. With the additional difficulty of migrating from existing interfaces to new ones and having to maintain and operate both sets of interfaces for some period of time, the task becomes even more ominous and complex. Neither the ISO standard nor the new ANSI X9.2 specification was designed to facilitate migration from the old ANSI standard.

It would have been inappropriate for the authors of the international standards to restrict ISO 8583 to being compatible with the original version of X9.2 developed in 1980 (called, logically enough, ANSI X9.2—1980). Even within the United States, the needs of contemporary networks that combine ATM and POS are far more complex than were the needs of the fledgling ATM industry that existed when X9.2—1980 was developed. In the long run, compatibility with the international standard is more important to an ever-widening EFT industry than easy coexistence with outdated implementations.

The new ANSI X9.2 is designed to provide a standard framework to ensure that sufficient data in a compatible format is available to all parties participating in an interchange, yet to provide enough flexibility to meet the needs of a wide variety of businesses. The new ANSI standard, in general, will be a superset of the international standard. That is, it will contain all the data required by the international standard and will further define standard data elements for use within the United States. However, ANSI X9.2 is still in draft form and no processor should undertake a development based on any draft standard.

A cautionary tale: One POS network developed an interchange specification based on an intermediate draft of the ISO standard and now, with the final standard approved, finds that its implementation is out of compliance. Consequently, custom programming is necessary for many who wish to connect to that network. Such programming delays implementation and increases costs.

If an EFT service provider has immediate need for a new interchange format and cannot wait for the publication of the revised X9.2, ISO 8583 should be used. A well-designed implementation of ISO 8583 should be easily adaptable to any additional requirements in ANSI X9.2.

The new standards represent more than just a change in message format—there is also a change in message content. The new standards require processing of additional data that is not found in existing standards and is unlikely to be available in any proprietary network. The new standards require more detailed information regarding transaction and fee amounts, conditions at the point of service, and identification of intermediate network facilities through which transactions are routed. Many existing implementations will have to be entirely rewritten to support the new message standards.

Basics

The basic principles of both the ANSI and ISO interchange standards are the data-element list and the bit map. The data-element list is a set of all data items from which messages can be constructed. Each data element is assigned a number by which it is identified. Each message contains a bit map that defines which data elements are present in that message (Fig. 2.). Bits in the bit map correspond to specific items from the data-element list.

Both X9.2 and 8583 messages are made up of fields selected from a list of data elements, often called the data dictionary. The specific data elements that make a particular message are designated by way of a bit map that appears as the second field in a message. Each bit represented in the bit map represents a data element in the data dictionary. A value of 1 for a bit in the bit map indicates that the corresponding data element from the data dictionary is present in the message. The X9.2 data dictionary and bit map constructs have also been adopted in the international standard, ISO 8583, Bank Card Originated Messages—Interchange Message Specifications—Content for Financial Transactions.

The ANSI/ISO bit-map technique provides a method in which dynamic or variable format messages can be constructed that contain only the information required to perform the function of the message. This reduces transmission of unused or unnecessary data while retaining the flexibility needed to accommodate the ever-increasing complexity of contemporary EFT transactions. Each individual message can be constructed to contain only those data elements required to fulfill its intended function, regardless of additional data requirements of other, similar messages.

The advent of POS has introduced transaction considerations previously unknown in ATM transactions. POS installations often accept alternate methods of cardholder verification, such as signature, in lieu of entering the personal identification number at the POS terminal. Off-line backup procedures may include manual entry of trans-

actions captured through paper draft. Each of these situations requires that a unique set of data elements be transmitted to the card issuer. This increased complexity in the number and type of transactions being processed demands more variation in message content.

Not only are the transactions more complex but response times also become increasingly critical in POS networks, making reduced transmission time an extremely important factor. The flexibility of variable-length, bit map-driven messages allows transmission of only those items required for a given transaction, eliminating unnecessary communications and processing time taken by unused fields in fixed-format configurations. Bit map-driven messages also simplify the addition of new data elements as changing business functions or regulations demand.

Existing interchange methods may use message formats that range from the strange and wonderful forms developed within a closed proprietary network to those that claim to be standard X9.2 implementations. While the problems of upgrading nonstandard interfaces are obvious, even so-called standard interfaces are not immune to difficulty. It is doubtful that any two standard X9.2 implementations in the United States today could communicate with each other without some modification. The evolution to

---

2. Basic EFT standard message structure. *The bit map specifies only those data elements required for a particular transaction need be present.*

MESSAGE

TYPE	BIT MAP	DATA ELEMENTS

---

compatibility with the upcoming revision to ANSI X9.2 and ISO 8583 will present even more challenges.

One of the first steps in planning for migration to the new standards is to analyze the existing arrangement to determine what level of modification and migration support will be required. Existing implementations may be described as one of the following: proprietary interface, "quick-and-dirty" standard implementation, modified standard implementation, or true standard implementation (Fig. 3).

Analyze what exists

■ *Proprietary interface.* A proprietary network uses an interchange interface that does not conform to any currently recognized national or international standard. Such an interface may work perfectly well in its intended universe but will not lend itself to the support of standards. If any proprietary interfaces remain in use, they are likely to have been developed early in the EFT lifetime to serve a single purpose and probably will not be used for connection to any regional or national network. It is unlikely that the software developed for a proprietary interface can be easily modified to support standard message formats and processing requirements.

■ *"Quick-and-dirty" standard implementation.* An implementation falls into this category if message formats, transaction codes, response codes, and/or transaction routing are hard-coded. These conditions are likely to exist if changes to message formats, transaction codes, response codes, transaction routing, or other processing options require program changes, recompilations, or a new system generation.

A quick-and-dirty implementation claims to use the ANSI standard but may be limited to a narrow subset of the standard. It is usually hard-coded to process a minimal number of messages whose fixed formats may resemble ANSI or ISO standard messages. Like the proprietary implementation, it probably functions well in the limited world for which it was intended. However, since the only real constant in the EFT world is change, such an implementation severely limits the opportunities for growth.

Hard-coded implementations are difficult to maintain and even more difficult to enhance. The addition of a single field to a single message can sometimes trigger extensive program changes. The wise processor will avoid acquiring or creating any new quick-and-dirty implementations and work to phase out those already in place. Such programs lack the flexibility to keep pace with today's EFT market.

■ *Modified standard implementation.* This situation is a little more difficult to detect. The interface may be represented as an implementation of the standard. It may require detailed analysis of the actual message formats and data elements to determine if they are consistent with published standards. In some cases, even making this determination may be extremely difficult due to the many different interpretations of the same standard. A really thorough analysis may require delving into the actual program code to determine whether the implementation actually supports the features of the standard or merely mimics a limited set.

Some of the easier clues that identify an implementation of modified standards are the misuse of messages for purposes other than those defined by the standard, the misuse of standard data elements through modified formats or for purposes other than those defined by the standard, or the omission of data elements that are defined as mandatory by the standard. Implementations of modified standards may be adaptable to the new message formats. They may work well in the present but could contain hidden obstacles to progress. Due to inadequate understanding of the ANSI standards, many proprietary modifications are out of compliance with both the letter and the intent of the standard. Proprietary modifications often misuse or redefine standard data elements instead of employing private-use or installation-specific fields. Each departure from the standard, even a good enhancement for valid reasons, will prove to be an impediment to compatibility, especially if it has not been implemented within the capabilities for enhancements provided by the standard.

While a modified implementation may have some of the elements necessary to support the development of versions of current standards, the effort required for conversion may be greater than for the development of an entirely new implementation.

3. Implementation flavors. *The addition of proprietary features and innovative services should be accommodated through legitimate enhancements.*

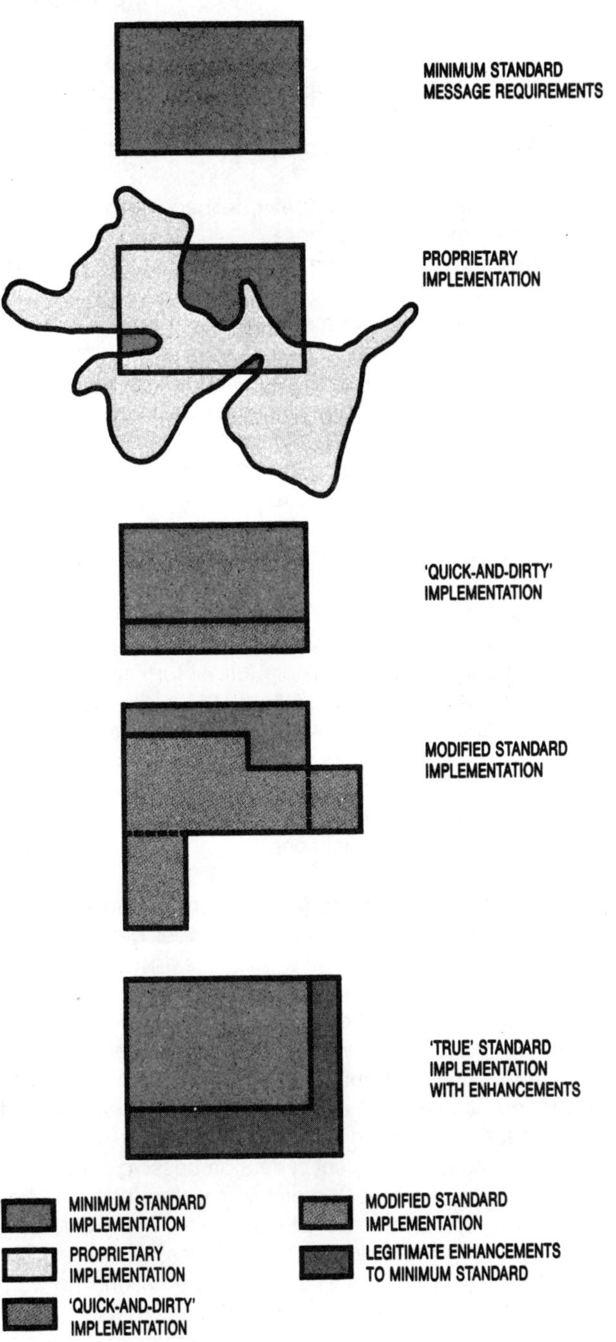

■ *True standard implementation.* Finding an implementation that fits into this category may be much like Diogenes's search for an honest man—it is theoretically possible to find such a man but, like the human beings who create the products, all implementations contain some flaws.

The first impediment to the implementation of a true standard is in defining what a true standard is. Until recently, the only published standard in the United States for the exchange of retail EFT transactions was ANSI X9.2—1980, which has been interpreted hundreds of ways. Some tests that might be applied to determine if an implementation is capable of supporting a true standard are as follows:

■ Message types are used only as defined in the standard.
■ All mandatory data elements are present in each message.
■ The format of all data elements conforms to the standard.
■ All enhancements are properly defined within private-use data elements and codes.
■ Variations in message format as defined by the bit map are supported.

An implementation that meets the above criteria may be sufficiently flexible to accommodate the new standard. Most interchange packages on the market today support only a single, fixed-format implementation of each message in the ANSI X9.2 standard, and many have modified field definitions to accommodate their proprietary considerations. Those that support multiple formats have usually accomplished this through the use of multiple, hard-coded interfaces. Few are capable of processing true variable-format messages under bit-map control.

Most computer programs and programmers deal largely with fixed-format messages. Thus, for most implementations, it is easier to pick a single format for interchange messages than to develop software to handle bit map-driven variable-format messages. However, the genius of the X9.2 bit map-driven design rapidly becomes apparent when one EFT service provider needs to interconnect to a number of different networks having very different interchange message specifications.

Planning an interchange for today and tomorrow
One of the most critical elements in proper planning is a thorough understanding of the business and philosophy that the network will support. Business requirements must be translated into technical specifications to develop or evaluate a product that will fulfill the requirements. Too often, a business will purchase a product on the strength of how well it worked in another situation, only to find that it fails in the required context. A business that is rigid and stable creates a different set of data processing conditions than one that is dynamic and growing, just as the technical needs of a regional switch that ties together many different computers and gateways with various interchange requirements differ from those of a national or international network that dictates an interface format to its participants.

The EFT industry is certainly more fluid than rigid. Computer software supporting such a business climate must be designed to accommodate the functions rather than the specific details of individual interchange agreements. Adherence to industry standards and flexibility to meet the rapidly changing needs of today's EFT marketplace will be critical.

Once the technical requirements supporting the intended business problem have been defined, criteria for evaluating the alternatives must be established. The evalu-ation criteria should include the relative importance of main-tainability, performance, portability, reliability, and cost.

There will be thousands of individual decisions made at all levels during the acquisition or development and mainte-nance of a major EFT setup. Criteria that are well-defined and well-understood by all members of the project team will help to ensure that the final product and its life-cycle modifications will meet management goals. Without such criteria, each analyst or programmer is left to make deci-sions based on his or her own individual preferences, prejudices, and interpretations. Too often, this results in an elegant solution to an individual segment of the problem that turns out to be limited in scope, inconsistent with the rest of the program and with management goals, and impossible to maintain.

The high cost of software maintenance together with the need for rapid response to an ever-changing environment make maintainability a crucial factor. Reliability will proba-bly come next, along with performance. Cost is usually a significant factor to the user. Portability may or may not be of major concern, depending on the rigidity of vendor selection within an installation. Each of these factors is considered below:

■ *Maintainability.* This can be regarded as more important than reliability and performance. If the EFT interface cannot be maintained, reliability and performance cannot be guaranteed. On the other hand, a network that can be easily maintained can be tuned to improve reliability and performance if these fall below acceptable levels.

There are several milestones of maintainability. Stan-dardized design and programming procedures should be employed, using good, structured techniques. Source code should be organized into functional modules. Each module should have one function, and each function should exist in only one source module. On-line documen-tation should be contained within source code modules. High-level language should be used for volatile code that is most likely to require modification as the business and regulatory requirements change, with low-level coding reserved for routines with relatively high use and low modification. Implementation should not depend on esoteric computer language tricks. (Implementations written in assembler or C programming language are particularly vulnerable.) Lastly, code must never rely on side effects of the compiler or operating system.

■ *Reliability.* It is not enough to establish reliability require-ments. The design team must also provide a methodology for measuring reliability.

Traditional time-based reliability measurements may not be appropriate for transaction processing. Instead of mean-time-between-failure rates, perhaps mean trans-actions between failures would be more useful. Overall reliability will depend on hardware and telecommunications reliability as well as software stability. Reliability measure-ments must include parameters for monitoring hardware and telecommunications failures separately from software errors. Tools for monitoring and measuring reliability should be designed from the outset. Well-designed EFT software should include collection of data for real-time evaluation of reliability measures and should alert operations staff when error rates exceed predefined levels.

■ *Performance.* Performance requirements will greatly depend on the business needs. The performance required for a single institution to authorize its own EFT transactions on-line will be much less than that needed by a regional network that may be driving thousands of terminals and communicating with hundreds of institutions. Performance criteria should include response time, overall capacity, and throughput measurements.

Like reliability, performance requirements must be accompanied by criteria for measuring performance and should be built into the overall design. Here again, what the on-line software needs to collect will vary depending on contractual and business concerns. Typically, the software should include measures of response time, peak transaction rates, average transaction rates, and message-error rates. It should also monitor the rate of successful and denied transactions.

■ *Cost.* Acceptable cost will vary greatly from organization to organization, depending on business needs, performance requirements, funds available for development or acquisition, and marketing strategies.

Cost factors include initial cost of acquisition, implementation and integrations, maintenance, operation, and upgrade expenses. Comparing the costs of different setups with varying configurations and capabilities can pose a difficult problem. Reducing the costs of all configurations under consideration to a common denominator (such as cost per transaction over the expected lifetime) will simplify the task. Often, the acquisition cost is erroneously judged to be the major cost consideration when, in reality, it may be insignificant compared to long-term operating and maintenance costs.

■ *Portability.* This may or may not be a significant factor depending on the overall data processing policy. Portability is of little concern to an installation that has a long-term commitment and investment in existing hardware. In more volatile situations, portability may be essential.

An off-the-shelf package designed to work on multiple vendors' hardware is obviously an easy solution when portability is a factor. Portability of in-house or single-vendor hardware configurations can only be ascertained by careful control and evaluation of the source language and actual code. Suffice it to say that portability should be a factor in the current, extremely dynamic data processing milieu.

Design considerations for future growth

Existing and future requirements that can be identified must be provided for. In order to provide maximum protection against unforeseen future requirements, the implementation should be easy to modify and maintain and independent of specific external message formats and data-element values.

The EFT world will not change to the new ANSI or ISO formats instantaneously. Therefore, it will be necessary to continue to support existing formats for some time. One way to accomplish this is to simply continue to run the old versions in parallel until all interfaces have been converted to the new. However, the cost of operating and maintaining parallel formats for any length of time is likely to be prohibitive and can create a logistical nightmare. Parallel operation may also require the additional cost of implementing a connection between the new and old setups.

A better solution may be to develop a new version that can continue to support the old formats while converting to the new. The data dictionary/bit map approach makes it possible to economically support old interfaces on the new software during the transition period, as well as allow the new interfaces to be installed with a minimum of effort.

Having a national or international standard does not guarantee that everything that should follow the standard will do so or that the standard will be implemented in exactly the same way from vendor to vendor. The standard itself is designed to accommodate different requirements generated by unique business needs and product differentiation. A successful implementation will have to accommodate many different variations of the standard as well as offer a migration path from the old to the new.

To accomplish these rather lofty goals, the implementation must be designed with the flexibility to adapt message formats and message flows for each interchange interface. In the past, this has often been done by cloning a

The EFT world will not change to the new ANSI or ISO formats instantaneously.

foundation program and modifying it for each unique interface. The trouble with this approach is that it can quickly multiply the maintenance efforts and costs in a multi-interface situation.

A better solution is to design the new core EFT software to be independent of the external message formats and data-element representations and provide a simple way to define external messages to the EFT program. Using this approach, multiple interface formats for both old and new interchanges can be accommodated with minimum effort.

The necessary tools

ANSI X9.2 provides two of the key elements for constructing such software: the data-element list and the bit map. Together, they allow messages to be dynamically configured for individual transactions. A well-designed program created around a data-element list and bit-map structure can be easily adapted to almost any external message format. The approach can even be used to process fixed-format messages that do not contain bit maps by prestoring the bit maps on the host for each message type.

Each variation of an ANSI or ISO data-element list can be implemented as a data dictionary for a particular interface, allowing additional flexibility as needed. The use of data dictionaries to define the messages and data elements allows the software to be independent of external message formats and data representations. Data dictionaries can be used to define the library of message types to be supported, the format of each message, the format, content, and editing rules for each data element, and the translation rules for converting each data element from its external format and location into a standard internal format.

The data dictionaries equate external message types and transaction codes to internal functions. They should be entirely external to the programs to provide the greatest amount of configuration flexibility. It is essential to provide appropriate tools to build and maintain the data dictionaries. Since the entire interchange interface depends upon the accuracy of these files, the data-entry tools must perform careful edits and consistency checks before any data is released into the production environment. In the ideal implementation, with the right data-entry and edit tools, data dictionary entries can be modified on-line in real time to allow for uninterrupted processing.

The software itself must be designed from a functional point of view. Functions common to all transactions should be separated from those peculiar to a specific type of transaction. Each software module should perform a specific function, which should be performed in only one module for quality control and efficient maintenance.

More than just theory

The practical interchange described above is more than just a theoretical ideal — it has actually been implemented in a switch connecting more than two dozen interchanges using more than a dozen different interchange messages formats, including a completely proprietary interface that does not conform to any national or international interchange standard (Fig. 4). The switch forms the heart of the Instant Teller Network, originally developed and operated by City National Bank (Los Angeles, Calif.). It was purchased last year by Automatic Data Processing Inc. (ADP) of Clifton, N. J. The CNB network on which the recommendations presented above are based so impressed ADP that it contracted to adapt CNB's original Hewlett-Packard implementation to run on ADP's Tandem equipment.

The network provides for dynamic transaction routing, wherein transactions are routed depending upon the acquirer or source of the transaction, the transaction type, and the card issuer. Transactions originated by the same ATM card at different locations on the network may be routed differently depending on the internetwork participation specified in the switch-parameter files. Messages are automatically converted from the acquirer (the institution that drives the ATM or POS terminal) to the format required by the card issuer.

All switch-message formatting is accomplished using a single program, which provides simultaneous support to multiple interchange processors with transaction response times well under one second. All message format and processing customization is accomplished through the data dictionary, bit maps, and switch parameter tables, which are external to the processing programs. Implemen-

tation of most new switch interfaces has been reduced from months to a few days.

To remain competitive in the rapidly advancing retail EFT industry, it is no longer sufficient to implement a simplified program using a fixed-format message merely based on an ANSI standard. Instead, full support of the new national and international standards is required — not only for growth but perhaps even for survival. ■

---

4. Sample network. *All the interfaces are processed through a single data dictionary/bit map-driven switch program. A new implementation takes only a few days.*

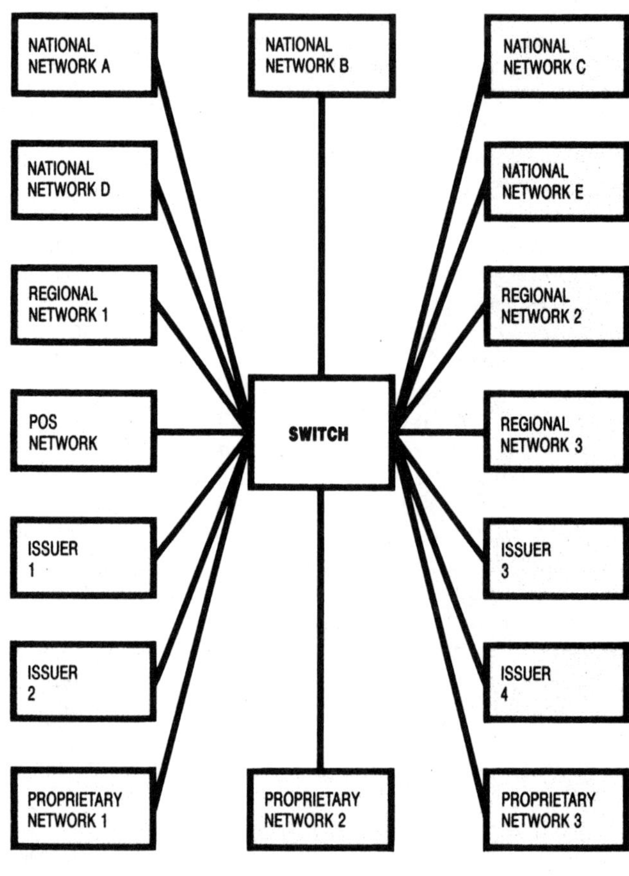

Lemont Southworth has more than 20 years of experience in data processing and has been an EFT consultant for more than eight years. Among other projects, he designed, developed, and implemented the first EFT transaction processing setup connecting the Instant Teller Network to American Express. The network enabled American Express cardholders to use bank ATMs and allowed bank customers to use American Express traveler's check dispensers. In 1986, Southworth was appointed recording secretary of ANSI X9A after serving on the committee and the X9.2 working group since 1984. He has also served on the ABA's Banker Task Force preparing the Implementation Guidelines for Debit Card Systems at the Point of Sale.

Bryan F. Gearing, Digital Equipment Corp., Merrimack, N. H.

Coming soon: A cabling standard for buildings

Finally! After a three-year wait, users are about to get a standard for fiber and copper cabling in commercial buildings.

If your company is planning to build a new facility, the question you have probably already been asked is: What's the best way to wire it for voice and data? Well, there will soon be a definitive answer: A new standard for fiber optic and copper cabling in commercial building wiring is almost finished. The Electronic Industries Association (EIA) TR-41.8.1 Ad-Hoc Working Group on Building Wiring, after laboring for three years with dozens of vendors and users, is recommending that 62.5/125-micron multimode fiber become the standard for data and voice backbone applications in commercial buildings and campus-size local area networks.

Final approval by the EIA and the American National Standards Institute (ANSI) could come at any time. Once the standard is approved, it will have a far-reaching effect: Architects and engineers will likely start specifying the new standard fiber optic medium whenever local area data distribution systems are called for. What kind of an impact could such a standard have in the real world? Look at the case of unshielded twisted pair: The RJ connector has become ubiquitous in the office and in the home as well.

No single answer

From a user's perspective, the ideal wiring standard would specify a single medium with a standard connector. But the EIA committee discovered it could not limit its work to fiber; it found a role for unshielded and shielded twisted pair, as well as thin coaxial cable, in building wiring.

The important issues addressed by the fiber and copper wiring standard—media, topology, distances, number of cross connects, and connector loss—ultimately affects the operation and performance of the communications network. It is in the realm of operation and performance that fiber shows its superiority over copper.

The standard targets the commercial office building. The building's internal data-transport wiring is broken down into several elements, including the office, horizontal, backbone, and administration wiring elements. When combined, these elements make up the total office network (Fig. 1).

The office element is the wiring from the workstation to the wall outlet and consists primarily of the line cord. This element is not part of the standard because it is not permanent building wiring.

The horizontal element represents the wiring connection between the serving closet and the outlet on the wall of the office. The length of these cable runs is estimated to be a maximum of 295 feet in commercial offices. Each user requires a separate horizontal element.

The backbone element represents the connection between the local wiring closet and the building closet (building backbone) or between buildings (the campus backbone). The building and campus backbones are functionally the same, though the type of cable used can vary, depending on whether an indoor or outdoor application is envisioned.

The administration element addresses the moves, changes, and rearrangements that invariably take place in a network. It consists of the hardware, labeling, and documentation needed to manage the individual connections. Since the wiring in a commercial building has to accommodate a large number of variables, the creation of a single standard to satisfy the entire user community was difficult to achieve. Building codes, construction materials, and office styles have an impact on the types of cable that can be used and the cable paths. Building styles and dimensions, along with the use of the building, also affect where closets can be placed and the lengths of cable runs.

The star topology works best with the fiber optic standard (Fig. 2). A physical star is versatile: It can be configured in a wiring closet to perform as a logical ring,

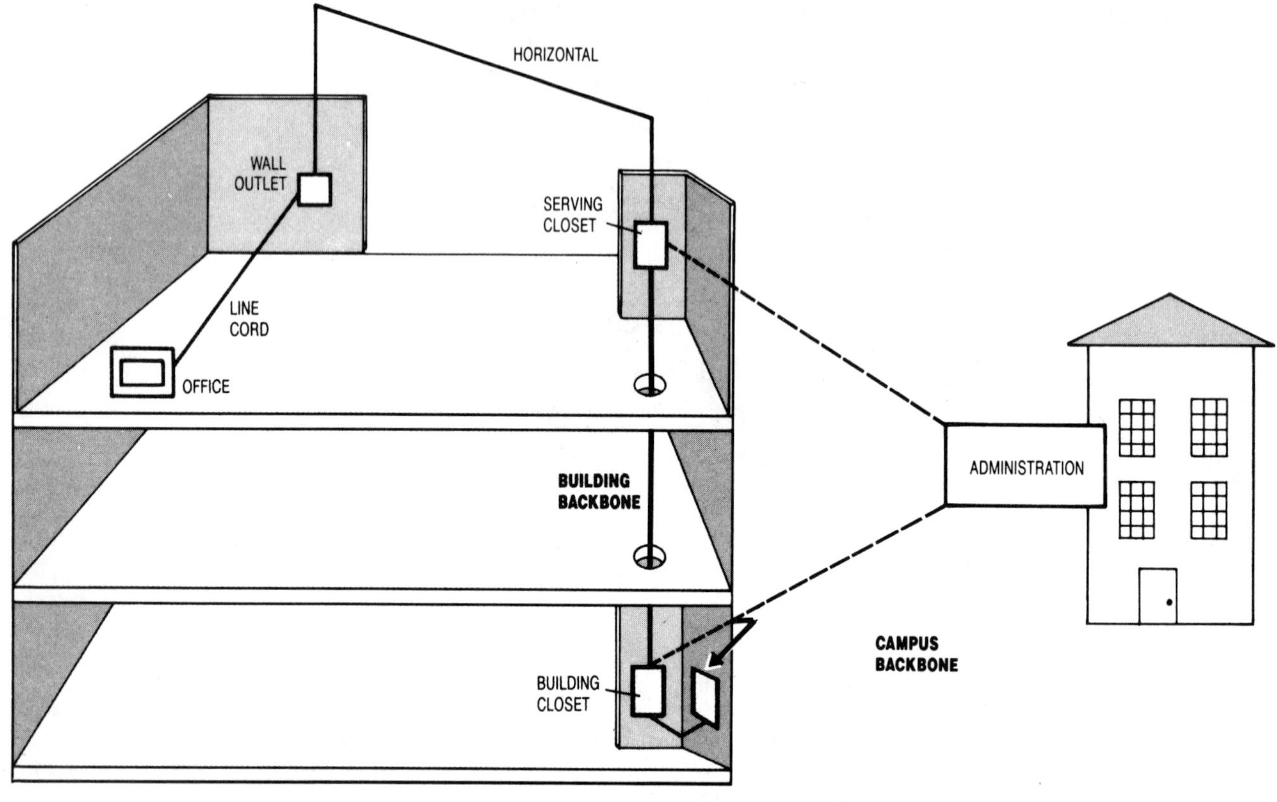

1. Wiring elements. *The proposed Electronic Industries Association's standard for commercial office building wiring identifies the internal office, horizontal, backbone, and ad-ministration wiring elements. When combined, these elements make up the total office network. The standard presupposes the coexistance of copper with fiber.*

a logical bus, or a logical tree in either a centralized or distributed communications network. In addition, the star has other advantages: It provides central reconfiguration points, for example, which come in handy for maintenance, traffic balancing, or when new technology is introduced.

The flexibility provided by the star topology supports the longevity requirement for building wiring, as well as product and vendor independence. It is also application-independent. This means that the same closets can be used for housing active and passive equipment for many voice, data, and video applications.

Some copper-based products may have distance constraints that conflict with the hierarchical star topology. This is true, for example, of the coaxial backbone for Ethernet—today's most extensively installed local area network (LAN). Not so the fiber-based products. For example, the proposed internode distance for the Fiber Distributed Data Interface (FDDI) is 6,560 feet. This distance is unlikely to affect intrabuilding cable plant requirements and will satisfy most interbuilding requirements.

The two predominant types of media used in wiring today are optical fiber and copper. The optical fiber medium has several intrinsic advantages over copper: It is immune to ground potential differences and to electrical overloads. In addition, its small diameter means it can be threaded into existing ducting, cable trays, and risers—thus avoiding disruptive and expensive installation procedures.

Fiber connections, which include connectors as well as the splices, are still expensive and labor-intensive compared to copper. But this is a dynamic area where significant cost reductions can be expected. For example, a move from ceramic to plastic connectors is already under way, and considerable research is being undertaken to find a way to mate fiber ends without significant polishing. If both efforts succeed, the parts counts and the labor costs associated with installing fiber will drop.

Moreover, light-emitting diode-driven multimode fiber backbones are inexpensive enough to compete with copper. Fiber can be shared by many users, and its distance and bandwidth are superior to copper.

In new installations, fiber generally wins out over copper because of its intrinsic benefits and its future performance potential. At 295 feet, rates on the order of 500 Mbit/s can be achieved using baseband schemes—and multiplexing extends the information-carrying capacity of the cable into the gigabit-per-second transmission range.

If multiplexing cannot provide enough capacity, multimode fiber backbones can be upgraded to single-mode fiber. The cost of replacing multimode with a single-mode backbone to get the added performance can be justified since the bulk of the building cable plant cost remains fixed

654

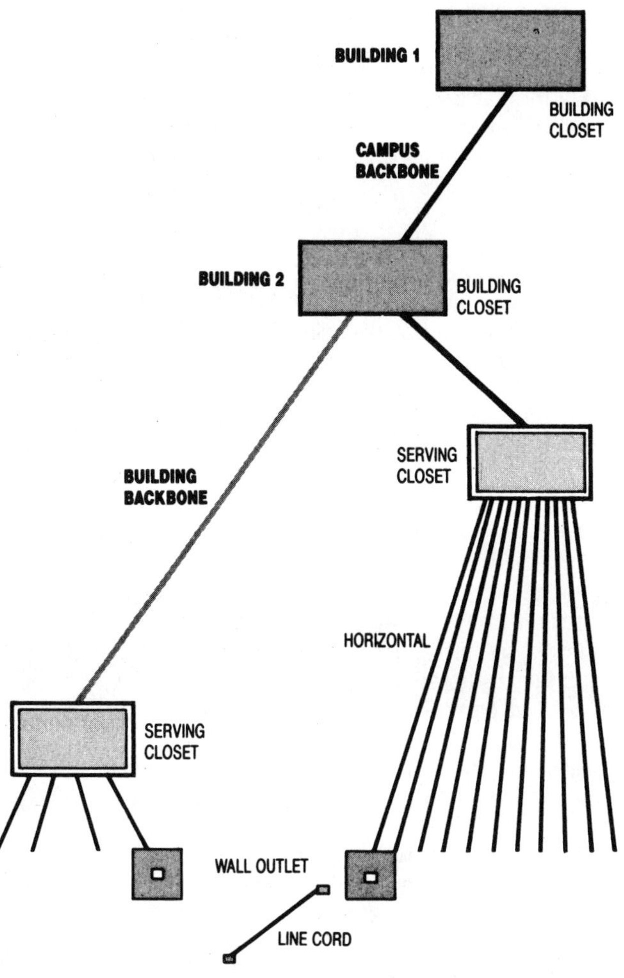

in the horizontal, multimode-fiber plant.

LAN installations in commercial buildings have gone hand in hand with deployment of shielded twisted pair and inexpensive coaxial cable in the office. Three of the major office-automation suppliers have a big stake in copper media:

- AT&T's 1-Mbit/s and 10-Mbit/s Starlan use 100-ohm unshielded twisted pair.
- IBM designed its 4-Mbit/s Token Ring around a 150-ohm shielded twisted pair.
- DEC's 10-Mbit/s Ethernet uses an inexpensive thin coaxial cable.

The standard recognizes each type of medium:

- 100-ohm unshielded twisted pair in four-pair cable.
- 150-ohm shielded twisted pair in two-pair cable.
- 50-ohm thin coaxial cable.
- 62.5/125-micron "dual window" multimode fiber.

The standard provides users with guidance in selecting from among the different media. If a standard that specifies many kinds of media seems far from the ideal, at least it may halt proliferation of different wiring schemes in commercial buildings. The unshielded twisted-pair wiring satisfies current and future voice requirements of the Integrated Services Digital Network (ISDN) and it can be used with most LANs. Coaxial cable compares favorably with unshielded twisted-pair wires in size and flexibility, and it has a standard connector. Though fiber as a horizontal element in building wiring is still rare, in time it likely will supplant copper.

Picking the fiber

The performance characteristics of different fiber proposals were not significant enough to determine the standard fiber size. A proposal for 100/140-micron fiber was eliminated because it did not conform to the commonly accepted external diameter. Nearly all multimode and single-mode fiber cables have an external diameter of 125 microns. An alternative, adopting an 85/125 fiber, was rejected because it has seen little use, and a 50/125-micron proposal was turned back because the 62.5/125 proposal has superior coupling characteristics.

How was the committee able to settle on just one standard size? It was timing. Since none of the major equipment vendors were sufficiently committed to a particular size, they were open to change. The 62.5/125 proposal prevailed.

The copper connectors at the wall outlets and in the cross connects have also been standardized (Table 1). However, the fiber connector is currently undecided. The FDDI committee is standardizing on an ST-based duplex connector; it is polarized and is keyed for the different classes of connection. A smaller duplex connector, which is polarized and unkeyed, will likely be adopted for commercial building wiring at some later date.

All two-wire transmission schemes require a crossover, or a lead transposition, so that transmit at one end of the link goes to receive at the other end. One way to achieve this is by using a crossover in the equipment (Fig. 3). This

Table 1: Commercial building cabling standards

MEDIUM	OUTLET	CROSS CONNECT
100-OHM UNSHIELDED TWISTED PAIR	8-PIN MODULAR; ISDN OUTLET	PUNCH-DOWN OR OUTLET CONNECTOR
150-OHM SHIELDED TWISTED PAIR	IBM CONNECTOR	IBM CONNECTOR
50-OHM THIN COAXIAL	STANDARD BNC	STANDARD BNC
50-OHM THICK COAXIAL	NONINTRUSIVE TAP	?
62.5/125-MICRON MULTIMODE FIBER	?	?

ISDN = INTEGRATED SERVICES DIGITAL NETWORK

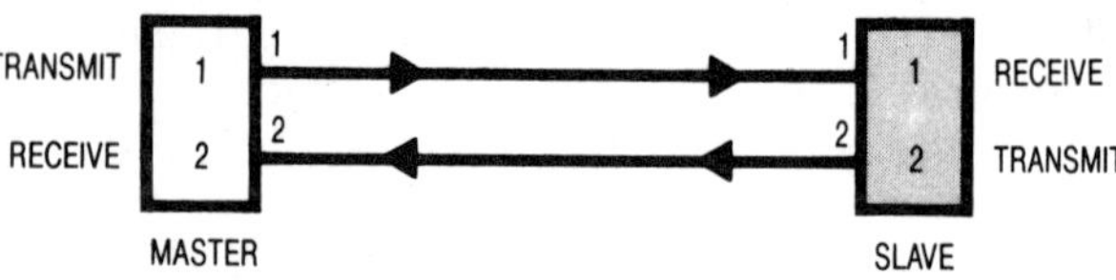

3. Crossover simplified. *An equipment-based lead transposition makes it possible to assign the same pin numbers to equipment on both ends of the link.*

makes it possible to assign the same pin numbers to equipment on both ends of the link. Doing so satisfies cases that define equipment as from and to, but it does not satisfy peer connections—connections between identical equipment that uses the same pin numbers.

In peer-to-peer communications, crossover wiring is needed. If the equipment pin numbers are the same at both ends of the link, simple crossover wiring will suffice (Fig. 4).

When the crossover wiring and extension cables are used, an odd total of crossovers is required to ensure an overall end-to-end crossover. That can be achieved transparently by using couplers that have crossovers built in (Fig. 5). Such an arrangement makes it possible to extend a wiring run by adding couplers and a cable—provided it results in an odd total of crossovers. In this approach, all cables are the same and have the same connector at both ends.

In a building, straight-through cabling is easiest to install and maintain. But the crossover approach is clearly superior for point-to-point interconnections between equipment. With the crossover approach, a single cable type can be used for all wiring, and the user need have no knowledge of lead transpositions.

The crossover wiring poses some minor management concerns, however, since connectors have to be installed in opposition to each other at each end of the cable. This means that knowledge of the remote end is required to install the near end. One way to overcome that is by using directional indicators or arrows along the individual fibers. It simplifies installations, and the arrows on the connectors solve the maintenance and administration problems. At installation time, just line up the arrows on a cable with the arrows on a connector—no pin numbers are needed (Fig. 6).

This solution presupposes adoption of a crossover standard for commercial building multimode cable. If such a standard were finally accepted, it would encourage system designers to follow the crossover concept.

Currently, simplex fiber connectors are used nearly everywhere. This leaves end-to-end crossovers in the hands of the installer. But the FDDI standard calls for a duplex connector with crossover in the wiring, so there is a precedent for the crossover approach. This may help it win acceptance for the fiber commercial building standard as well. However, where straight connections in building wiring are the norm, it is unlikely that a crossover scheme will be adopted for copper.

When planning a new building, the standard should be consulted for medium specifications, topology, distances, and connection losses. Fiber optic cables should meet the published specification; using cables below the specification limitations may work in the initial installation, but when the wiring is reconfigured or a new communications system is added, problems are likely to occur.

By the same token, there are no benefits to installing cables that offer better performance than the specification because future communications systems will not be designed to utilize your cable's superior performance characteristics.

The highs and the lows

The runaway adoption of unshielded twisted-pair wiring presents another potential class of problems—and another reason to consult the standard. Heavy user pressure to operate many established communications networks over unshielded twisted pair has led to the appearance of dozens of kinds of adapters in the marketplace. The picture is further complicated by a large variation in the types of cables being offered.

Amid such confusion, the low-bandwidth applications tend to be very forgiving. However, the high-bandwidth applications may exhibit poor performance if they are not specified for the correct cable. If unshielded twisted-pair wiring is specified incorrectly, it may unfavorably affect such factors as error rate, distance, and the number of nodes that can be put on the network. Also, under certain conditions, unshielded twisted pair does not allow daisy-chaining. Understanding these limitations is important. When the medium is being extended to its limit, operating margins are in jeopardy.

In the horizontal wiring elements of a building, the recommendation calls for two separate cables: one cable of four pairs of unshielded twisted copper and either an additional four-pair unshielded or a two-pair shielded or thin coax is recommended. Mixing signaling schemes within a cable sheath should be avoided in the horizontal runs, since crosstalk can become a problem.

Recommendations for backbone wiring tend to be application-dependent. If telephone traffic is envisioned, 50 pair or more of copper is acceptable. If an Ethernet LAN backbone will run up through the building risers, thick coaxial cable can be specified. Shielded twisted pair works fine for a Token Ring LAN backbone.

But fiber may be the best option. Though cost tradeoffs between copper and fiber must be evaluated, fiber

---

4. Peer crossover. *In peer-to-peer communications, crossover wiring is usually required. If pin numbers are the same at both ends, crossover wiring will suffice.*

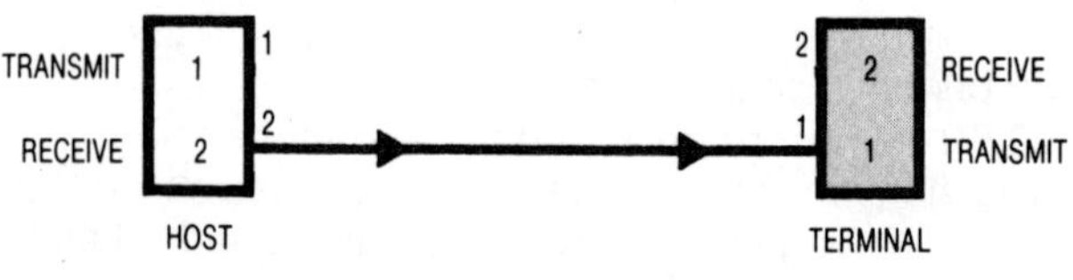

5. Crossover extensions. *Using couplers with built-in crossovers and extension cable will extend a wiring run, though an odd number of crossovers is needed.*

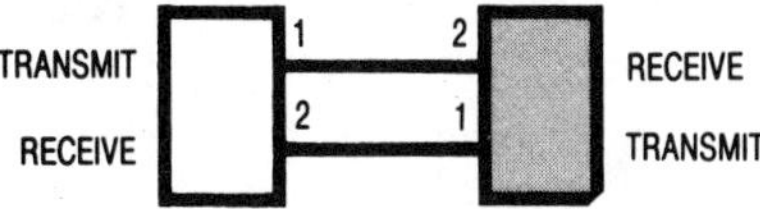

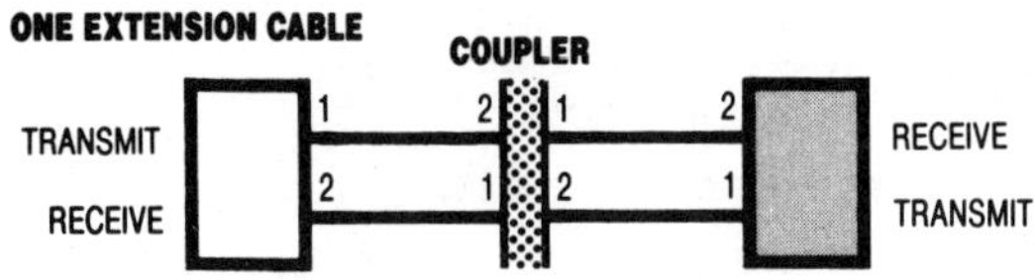

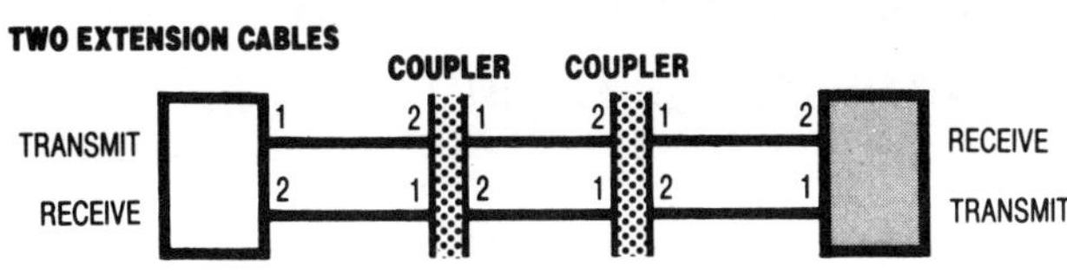

has great potential. And the existence of a standard for fiber will minimize any future risks involved with installing fiber today.

Fiber has the ability to become the first true universal communications utility, and the 62.5/125 size is expected to become the formal North American standard in the near future. The performance parameters of the dual-window fiber cable are shown in Table 2. But adding a fiber into a cable can increase the attenuation, so parameters must always be checked for the entire cable, and not just for each fiber.

To minimize risks and maximize the longevity of the cabling installed in a commercial building, all optical media should:

■ Conform to the specification for dual-window 62.5/125 fiber.

■ Use a hierarchical star topology with two levels of cross connects. The loss of a connector pair is about 1 dB. Thus, a cross connect uses up 2 dB of the link budget.

Generally, the backbone cables between intrabuilding closets should not exceed 1,640 feet and should contain six or more fibers. The distance between closets is dependent on system internode distance and is affected by the number of passive closets between nodes. The suggested distance of 1,640 feet is offered as a con-

6. Cable marking. *Directional indicators or arrows applied directly to the fibers simplify installation, maintenance, and administration problems.*

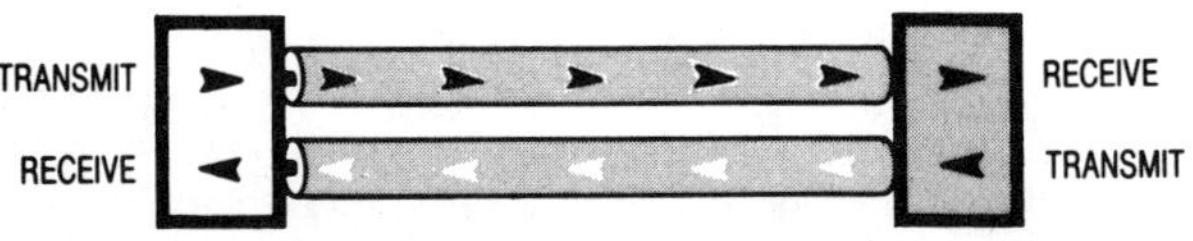

Table 2: Performance parameters of dual window fiber cable

WINDOW	MODAL BANDWIDTH (PER KILOMETER)	ATTENUATION (MAXIMUM PER KILOMETER)
850 NANOMETERS	160 MHz	4.5 dB
1,300 NANOMETERS	400 MHz	2.0 dB

servative number that is unlikely to be exceeded in most buildings.

A dual-ring network topology requires four fibers. But there are other factors to consider when determining the number of fibers in a cable: Will systems not presently sharing the media be added during the life of the cable plant; are there several of the same kinds of equipment in a given closet; and are there enough spare fibers in the cable to replace failed fibers?

Extra fibers should generally be installed because the cost of the cable sheath and the cost of pulling additional cable are offset by putting in spare capacity. The number of fibers should be higher between buildings to provide a more flexible cable plant.

Where the backbone cables between buildings exceed the internode distances of the network, repeaters can be used to extend the distance, provided an appropriate place to house and power them is available.

Horizontal element runs should be a maximum of 295 feet long and contain two fibers. The cost of installing the horizontal plant is orders of magnitude higher than installing the backbone plant, so providing an additional fiber per drop now saves installation costs later.

Upgrading a backbone cable is a far less costly affair. Pulling high-fiber-count cables today, or including single-mode fibers in a backbone, will minimize the need to add capacity in the future.

Adding connectors to a run should always be avoided. Connectors are expensive, they add loss, and they reduce reliability. They should be installed only when there is an application for the cable. Though there is no specific recommendation for connectors today, the ST, in both its simplex and duplex configurations, is becoming a de facto standard.

Deciding which medium to pull to wire a building poses difficult choices. Commercial construction is now in transition from copper to fiber media—though copper will retain a major position for many years to come, especially in the horizontal plant. Fiber is the technology of tomorrow, however, since it makes available the high data rates needed for voice, video, and high-speed data in an office environment. ■

Bryan F. Gearing is a principal engineer in the Network Systems Group at Digital Equipment Corp.'s Merrimack, N. H., facility. He is a member of the Electronic Industries Association's Ad-Hoc Working Group on Building Wiring and holds several patents in telephone switching systems.

H. Kim Lew and Cyndi Jung, 3Com, Mountain View, Calif.

Getting there from here: Mapping from TCP/IP to OSI

A technical overview, straight from the NBS Implementors' Workshop, detailing the mapping of TCP/IP-based virtual terminal functions onto their Open Systems Interconnection equivalents.

With the network and computer community's movement toward Open Systems Interconnection, files previously transferred between devices using TCP/IP's File Transfer Protocol will reach their intended destination with File Transfer, Access, and Management; electronic mail will circle the globe in Message Handling System envelopes instead of with Simple Mail Transfer Protocol; and OSI's Virtual Terminal Protocol will replace TCP/IP's Telnet in providing remote terminal access to a multitude of hosts, regardless of physical distance.

Though TCP/IP (Transmission Control Protocol/Internet Protocol) has received high praise as the protocol of choice for solving contemporary internetworking problems, many network managers view it as a stopgap solution, in part because of its limited addressing scheme and large communications overhead. For these reasons, OSI is likely to eclipse the venerable TCP/IP over the next few years as the preferred multivendor conduit. Even now, both the U. S. and foreign governments dictate official use of the OSI protocols. But with the large and growing population of TCP/IP networks, prospects for overnight conversion to the OSI stack seem remote.

The International Organization for Standardization's OSI protocol suite is finally gaining momentum and may well be standardized throughout most of the ISO's own seven-layer model during 1988 (see "ISO's slow motion"). When it finally does clear the draft and rewrite process, an onslaught of OSI-based networking products from both network and computer vendors will no doubt follow.

The great migration

ISO's Virtual Terminal Protocol (VTP) provides a flexible set of functions that aids in this transition from homegrown protocols to international standards. Its flexibility allows for the mapping of TCP/IP to an OSI virtual terminal gateway.

This gateway will enable terminals to access all resources within the mixed TCP/IP-OSI network, independent of the communications protocols themselves.

Network strategists planning for the migration from TCP/IP to OSI must make provisions for the concurrent operation of both protocol suites and for the interoperation of equipment using both protocols. The resulting hybrid networks will support a wide array of functionally diverse terminal types. Implementation issues will revolve around managing the migration and the phasing in of the OSI protocol suite.

During the transition period, gateways (Layer 7 Intermediate Systems) will be required to map between File Transfer, Access, and Management (FTAM) and File Transfer Protocol (FTP), Message Handling System (MHS) and Simple Mail Transfer Protocol (SMTP), and ISO VTP and Telnet, respectively. These gateways will provide the glue to interconnect TCP/IP networks with those networks running OSI. Initially, most networks will continue to run the TCP/IP protocols, but as networking becomes more and more global (and TCP/IP runs out of addresses), OSI networks will survive and become the dominant networking standard.

Application layer gateways must map each functional element from one TCP/IP application layer protocol to its OSI counterpart and vice versa, thereby providing protocol transparency to the user. When there is no equivalent function, the gateway must perform the work of the OSI End System (endpoint of network connection) in addition to Intermediate System activities, so that it may satisfy the requirements of its protocol peer. In terms of creating an OSI-to-TCP/IP gateway, ISO VTP offers developers some genuine advantages. With the right negotiation (the method of creating a common ground for communications), ISO VTP can mimic nearly any other virtual terminal protocol

OSI's slow motion

The International Organization for Standardization's standards-development cycle consists of four stages: working paper, Draft Proposal (DP), Draft International Standard (DIS), and International Standard (IS). Once a working paper matures to the point that its technical content is well-developed, it is registered as a DP. Registration is either by a vote at a meeting of the appropriate ISO subcommittee or by letter ballot of the member bodies. After registration, the DP is distributed for a 90-day ballot. Multiple ballots, each followed by an editing meeting, may be required. Successful passage advances the DP to the DIS level. As a DIS, the document is usually considered sufficiently stable technically to serve as the basis of initial implementations. Once at the DIS level, a document is distributed for a 180-day ballot. As with a DP, a DIS may require multiple editing/balloting meetings. A successful ballot elevates the DIS to the level of IS and completes ISO's work on the standard. It is then up to users and vendors to put the standard into useful practice.

The process of standardizing ISO's Open Systems Interconnection (OSI) protocol suite has been arduous. It has taken so long that two independent, albeit related, protocols have emerged as complementary (and, to a degree, competing) communications standards: the Manufacturing Automation Protocol (MAP) and the Technical and Office Protocols (TOP). All three are part of an industry-wide implementation demonstration at Baltimore's Enterprise Networking Event '88 International.

ISO's protocols are fairly stable through Layer 5 (session) of the OSI model. In addition, several Layer 7 (application) standards have reached either IS or DIS status. The File Transfer, Access, and Management (FTAM) family of standards was voted to IS status in Tokyo last summer; ISO's electronic mail standard, dubbed Message Oriented Text-Interchange System (MOTIS) has reached DIS and is expected to converge with the CCITT's 1984 X.400 specifications sometime during 1988; and ISO's

Virtual Terminal Protocol has reached DIS status.

Unfortunately, serious issues remain to be resolved in other upper-layer standards-writing efforts, and some of these upper-layer issues may have an impact on lower-layer standards. One of the most conspicuous and controversial application layer standards projects involves OSI network management. The OSI network management standardization efforts aim to provide the ability to monitor and control OSI resources within an OSI network. OSI network management considers several broad categories of management objectives: performance management, fault management, configuration management, security management, and accounting management. Several groups are producing standards for OSI network management. These include ISO, the American National Standards Institute (ANSI), the Institute of Electrical and Electronic Engineers (IEEE), the International Consultative Committee for Telephone and Telegraph (CCITT), and the European Computer Manufacturers Association (ECMA). The primary responsibility for developing OSI management standards in the United States rests with ANSI's Accredited Standards Committee (ASC) X3T5.4. A key accomplishment of the X3T5.4 subcommittee during the past year was participation in formulating the OSI Management Framework Overview document. At the Tokyo meetings, held in July 1987, a DIS was proposed for this element of the network management standard. Unless significant disagreements arise, the Management Framework Overview document should be voted to DIS status in 1988.

In an National Bureau of Standards report issued last year (March 1987), analysts cited six areas of concern as risks for the network management standards. These issues still influence the direction of network management standards activities as well as the prospects for completing standards according to the tentative schedule. The issues are as follows:

■ *MAP activity* — The General Motors-led MAP specifica-

(such as CCITT X.3/X.29 Packet Assembler/Disassembler [PAD], IBM 3270, or Telnet).

Figure 1 illustrates the most general form of the virtual terminal model. The translation of addressing operations is mapped to actual escape sequences necessary to move a cursor on a screen. In the figure, B performs a local mapping between VT services and an application, providing the same interface that the application uses for terminals directly attached to it. From this model, ISO Draft International Standards (DIS) 9040 and 9041 were developed (see "Glossary"). These draft standards define the Basic Class Virtual Terminal (VT) service and protocol residing at the application layer of the OSI Basic Reference Model. Basic Class VTP is intended to support character-oriented devices, including both synchronous (IBM 3270-type) and asynchronous ASCII (DEC VT-100-type) terminals. ISO VTP specifies the ways a virtual terminal can be

tailored to fit individual requirements. This flexibility is essential, since an application may demand that virtual terminals take on different characteristics — for example, behaving like an IBM 3270 terminal at one moment and like a DEC VT-100 at another.

In contrast, other applications can adapt to a physical terminal. One example is the Unix operating system's TTY terminal device driver aided by the Termcap file. Termcap, which stands for terminal capabilities, is a file containing entries for all terminals on a network. The entries are compact codes describing characteristics such as cursor movement and numbers of lines per screen.

Three key concepts provide a framework for understanding the ISO VTP model. These are association, negotiation, and the VTP profile, as follows:

■ *Association* — The terminal and the application engage each other in communications by establishing a VT assocition-writing process placed a high priority on developing network management standards for inclusion in release 3.0 of MAP last year. This issue was considered a significant potential problem. Critics believed that the creation of a competing network management specification, if adopted by enough vendors, might dilute the effectiveness of ISO's OSI network management effort. However, no network management specifications were included in release 3.0. With MAP 3.0, each device or end node on a network has an agent capability for collecting data in a device. MAP currently leaves it to the vendor network management implementation to find that data on the device and extract a report. It now seems more likely that MAP, TOP, and OSI will all adopt a single set of network management standards, and hopefully save network managers from many headaches in the future.

■ *Resource attributes*—A second potential risk lies in possible delay in the specification of resource attributes to be managed. At each layer, resources exist that must be monitored and controlled in order to manage that layer. Because of the unique nature of each resource and its attributes, specific and equally unique actions may be defined for it. The process of identifying resources and attributes, as well as allowed actions on those resources and attributes, has been slow to begin.

■ *Connection-oriented versus connectionless*—The current set of standards defines a connection-oriented (CO) remote operation service (ROS) to support the Common Management Information Protocol (CMIP). There is a group of organizations supporting a connectionless (CL) ROS for the CMIP. The CO versus CL argument has cropped up in nearly every OSI standards-writing effort, particularly in the Layer 3 (network) standards work. It typically pits U. S. vendors and users (favoring CL ROS) against their European counterparts. This argument has slowed other OSI standards efforts and may slow network management standards development as well. It is a controversy that has dogged data communications theorists for years.

Another ROS issue involves the selection of an appropriate class of ROS functions to support CMIP. Currently, CMIP assumes that a supporting ROS implements the general class of functions available. However, the ROS now defined provides a minimal class of functions. To complicate matters, a number of organizations have questioned whether CMIP should use ROS services at all. The uncertainty associated with ROS specifications, which CMIP relies upon, results in CMIP uncertainty.

■ *Incomplete stacks*—A fourth problem area concerns the definition of network management operations for network nodes with fewer than seven protocol layers. Examples are intermediate systems, mini-MAP nodes, and media access control (MAC)-layer bridges. The current OSI network management standards assume that all nodes contain a full seven layers of protocols. This is an unrealistic assumption; it is likely that OSI's network management standards will accommodate incomplete stacks, although such an accommodation will again lead to delays in completing standards.

■ *Implementation-dependent resources*—The current network management standards permit monitoring and control of interoperable OSI resources but not of implementation-dependent resources. Monitoring and controlling these resources is essential to optimizing OSI performance. If the standards are modified to enable control of implementation-dependent resources, significant difficulty could almost certainly be encountered in identifying resources that should be subject to control.

■ *Security*—Little in the way of security has been defined for the OSI protocols. This is especially true for local area networks. Because LANs operate in a broadcast mode, they are sensitive to problems associated with ensuring data transfer security. Thus, the development of standards for OSI security management are dependent upon the definition of the OSI security standards.

ation, usually initiated by the communications device to which the terminal is directly attached. The initiator proposes a Virtual Terminal Environment (VTE), which may be expressed as a complete list of objects, comprising the VTE (display objects, device objects, and control objects, all generalized variables that the protocol refers to in its dialogue) or by referencing by name a registered profile containing a consistent list of such objects.

■ *Negotiation*—The initiator's counterpart at the other end of the communications link, called the acceptor, may agree to the proposed VTE or may reject it, in which case the initiator and acceptor enter a state of VTE negotiation. The degree to which the negotiation can modify the proposed VTE is determined by the set of functional units selected by the initiator. These functional units have also been described as subsets: subset A allows no negotiation; subset B allows only a complete switch to a new profile; and subset C allows an explicit listing of objects. Under subset C, dialogue can go on until a consistent and mutually desirable VTE has been achieved. This third, and most complex, negotiation option is called Multiple Interaction Negotiation.

■ *Profiles*—VT profiles, which are consistent sets of physical and logical characteristics, are extremely important in creating the VT environment. With profiles, users can make VT-to-VT connections in one operation. Development of profiles is not considered part of the ISO standards effort. Profiles may be registered publicly or kept private. Originally, in the first ISO DIS of the VTP Protocol Specification, a text string was used during association establishment to identify the profile. When the concept of object identifier was unveiled as the preferred way at once to classify, to name, and to encode the reference to any OSI object, the second DIS of the protocol specification changed the

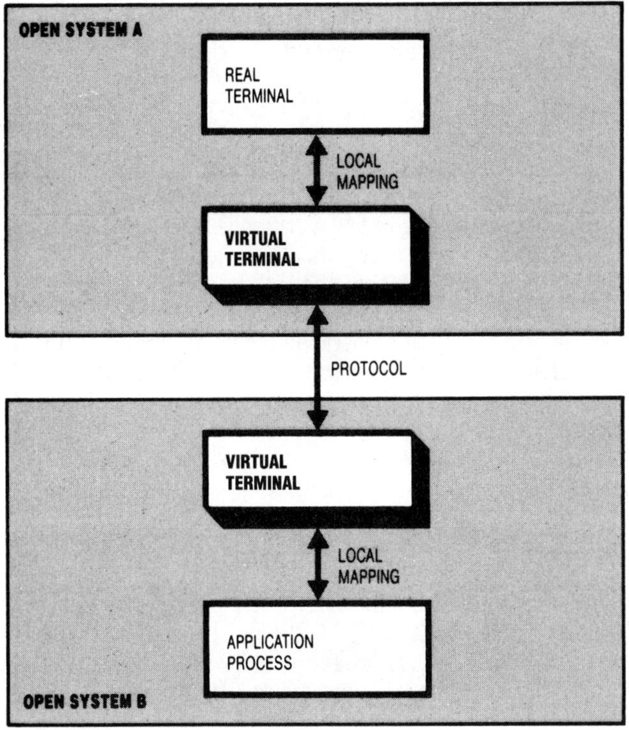

1. Two open systems. *(A) and (B) are joined by an active VTP association. (A) performs a local mapping between VT services and the physical terminal.*

profile name to be one of these object identifiers. Before a profile can become registered, a registration authority must be established. This authority is recognized internationally and assumes the responsibility for assigning an object identifier to each profile. Currently, there is no internationally recognized registration authority for ISO VTP profiles. The National Bureau of Standards (NBS) has acted as an interim registration authority for object identifiers required for FTAM implementations, and will probably intercede as the de facto registration authority for U. S. implementations of ISO VTP.

The importance of profiles

The Virtual Terminal Special Interest Group (VTSIG) of the NBS Workshop for Implementors of OSI is chartered with the development of several essential profiles. The current list of profiles under consideration includes the Telnet and X.3 and X.29 PAD profiles as well as the transparent, scroll, forms, and page profiles. The first three profiles were primarily selected to support migration from their namesakes to OSI. Both the Telnet and the X.3/X.29 profiles can provide a smooth transition to OSI for existing applications that expect the services available in the real Telnet or X.3/X.29 protocols. The transparent profile replaces the direct wire between a terminal and a host computer.

The last three profiles—scroll (supports scrolling terminals), forms (applications that operate with fixed forms such as spreadsheets), and page (terminals or applications that function a page at a time)—are targeted to support these three operational modes of modern terminals. Future applications that directly use these profiles will finally be freed from dealing with the nuances of each terminal type—they will only need to know how virtual terminals behave.

The Telnet profile lies at the heart of the Internet community's migration strategy for ISO VTP. The Telnet profile is the first profile on the NBS's VTSIG list entered into the Implementor Agreements, a document produced by the OSI workshop. The Internet Telnet specification allows for extended operations, but what the implementations have in common remains small. This is the secret to Telnet's wide interoperability. The ISO VTP Telnet profile is restricted to a minimal, but proven, set of functions that includes echo control, character-set-selection control, terminal signaling, line editing, and line termination.

The ISO VTP Service Definition includes a profile equivalent to CCITT's X.3/X.29 services. This profile was developed because most contemporary computers have communications interfaces for direct attachment to wide area networks that use protocols described in the CCITT recommendations. In fact, a large portion of the Internet community actually uses X.25 as a subnetwork protocol over which to pass IP packets. In addition, several computer vendors in the United States (and many more in Europe) have applications that expect the level of service provided by the X.29 recommendation. This level of service includes virtual circuit establishment and clearing (disconnecting) as well as remote manipulation of the X.3 parameters used to configure terminal-attachment PADs.

Besides giving the existing applications their accustomed service, both the Telnet and X.3/X.29 profiles facilitate development of gateways. The X.3/X.29 profile promotes the building of a gateway between ISO VTP and the X.29 protocol operating on a wide area network (CCITT-type PAD service), while the Telnet profile allows for the relatively simple development of a gateway function between the Telnet of TCP/IP and ISO VTP.

VTEs and profiles consist primarily of detailed descriptions of each of three kinds of abstract objects: display objects, control objects, and device objects. These objects are organized within a logical construct referred to as the Conceptual Communications Area (CCA). Both sides of a VT association reflect the same state of the CCA, and exchanges of data or control information between VT-user peers are expressed by the Virtual Terminal Protocol Machine (VTPM) as updates to these objects (control-object updates and display-object updates). Device objects are not subject to direct updates. Instead, device objects contain links to one display object and one or more control objects. When a display or control object is updated, updates are mapped onto the real devices represented by the linked device objects.

Figure 2 illustrates the general relationships between the OSI architecture, VTPMs, and the shared CCA. Clients in both open systems are provided with local mappings to the physical terminal and application. VTPMs, as peers, exchange information concerning the CCA using VTP. Note

Glossary

Access rights. Each object of a complete Virtual Terminal Environment (VTE) has an access-right parameter. The value of this parameter indicates whether or not access to the object is restricted and, if it is restricted, which VT user peer in the VT association is allowed to access the object. The list of access rights is: not subject to access control; write access controlled by initiator (WACI); write access controlled by acceptor (WACA); and write access variable (WAVAR). The WACA and WACI access rights are assigned at the beginning of an association and cannot be changed. The WAVAR access right is assigned initially to one of the two peer VT users and is reassigned according to conditions and events described in the profile of the VTE. For example, a network operator presses the carriage return key and the WAVAR is passed to the application.

DIS 9040. The ISO number assigned to the Draft International Standard for Virtual Terminal Service Definition. This document defines the service interface that an implementation of ISO Virtual Terminal Protocol must provide to its clients.

DIS 9041. The ISO number assigned to the Draft International Standard for Virtual Terminal Protocol Specification. This document specifies the Virtual Terminal Protocol Machine (VTPM) as an event-driven state machine and describes the information content of the packets exchanged between VTPMs.

Display pointer. The VTE always contains one or two display objects, which are one-, two-, or three-dimensional character box arrays. The display pointer always points to the next character box element to be assigned a character value at the next update of that display object. The VT Service provides explicit control of the display pointer through addressing operations. Each dimension of the display object has parameters that define the valid addressing operations. For example, in the x-dimension, there are the parameters x-bound, x-addressing, x-absolute, and x-window.

Object identifiers. Elements of a classification schema subscribed to by ISO and CCITT. The schema is hierarchical and may be graphically depicted by an inverted tree with three arcs emanating from the root node, dividing all objects into one of three classes: CCITT, ISO, and joint ISO/CCITT. Each arc is then the root-node for the classification of all objects that fall under the broader class assigned to the arc. Each arc is assigned a number, and the object identifier associated with an object in the tree is found by concatenating (chaining) the entire sequence of numbers from the root to the leaf that identifies the object.

Protocol peer. Protocol peers are same-layer complementary protocol functions existing in two physically separate locations engaged in communications. They always reside in the same layer of the basic ISO reference model and provide the same level of service to their respective clients, which are also in relative peer relationships with their counterparts. In the ISO Basic Reference Model for OSI, each of the seven OSI protocol layers has direct communications across the network to its protocol peer.

Virtual Terminal Protocol Machine (VTPM). The portion of the VT Service Elements that maintains the state of the association and follows the protocol rules delineated by DIS 9041.

VT user. An application process that uses the VT service for communications with another VT user.

---

that the CCA intervenes between the two different protocols. Figure 3 is an expanded view of the elements that make up the CCA. Each real device is represented inside the CCA by a device object, each with links to the control and display objects that can have actual effects on a device. The Access Control Store contains the current assignment of write-access control (discussed below) for all objects in the CCA that are subject to access control. The Data Structure Definition contains definitions of all display, control, and device objects plus parameters that define the VTE. The Conceptual Data Store contains one or two display objects, depending on the mode parameter selected. The Control, Signaling, and Status Store contains two or more control objects.

Display objects are descriptions of one-, two-, or three-dimensional character box arrays, in which each element could be defined either as a position on a terminal screen or as a page within a set of pages. They can be assigned primary attributes (character values from a selected repertoire) and secondary attributes, which may include emphasis (underline, blinking, bold, and so forth), color (foreground and background colors are separately assign-

able), and font type. Various addressing operations can be performed on these array elements by manipulating a display pointer in software, although a particular profile may choose to disallow these display pointer updates. The display-object definition also indicates whether or not the display object may be erased and what access rights have been assigned to it (that is, which VT user is allowed to update it).

Control objects are used for any form of exchange between VT users that does not directly affect the contents of a display object. The standard is quite liberal in terms of defining how a control object can be used. A control object can be exclusively linked to a device object, shared by more than one device object, or unasociated with any device object of the CCA. A control-object definition indicates with which level of service an update is sent (normal or urgent) and the type of access rights assigned to it (including "not subject to access control").

Each device object has at least one control object linked to it—its own default control object—consisting of eight booleans (true-false control flags), one of which is used to indicate whether the device is on or off. Another control-ob-

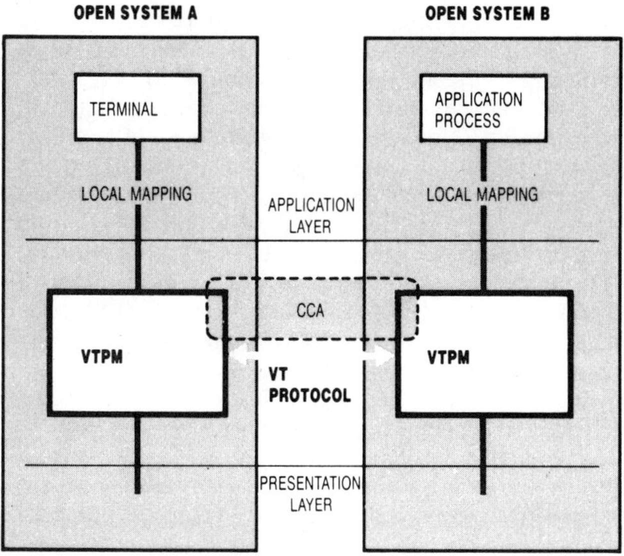

ject parameter selects a trigger, which causes any buffered display-object updates to be delivered when the control object is updated. The control-object definition also gives the category and size of the control-object update values. Its possible categories are integer, boolean, or character, and the associated sizes indicate the maximum integer value, number of booleans, or number of characters. If the control object has been registered with a recognized authority, the assigned identifier is also contained in the definition. All control objects have unique text-string names.

Device objects represent real devices, and their definitions give some guidance as to how updates to the display objects and control objects linked to device objects affect the real device. The device object has repertoire, font, emphasis, and color assignments that may be different from those assigned in the linked display object. As an example of how the contents of the display object can be mapped onto the capabilities of the real device, consider a single display object that has color capability with eight possible colors. In the same VTE, there may be two device objects, each with a link to the display object, with one representing a terminal and the other representing a printer. The terminal can display all eight colors assignable to array elements in the display object, but the printer can print only one color. The actual sizes of x, y, and z are dimensions of the real device as stated in the device object. Details are provided concerning those events generated by the real device that constitute a termination event. Termination events cause the input collected at one end of a connection to be delivered at the other end as a

display-object update. Each device object has a unique name assigned to it that takes the form of a text string.

Along with the objects of the VTE, there are also a number of important parameters found in the CCA. ISO VTP defines two modes, A-mode ("asynchronous") and S-mode ("synchronous"), characterized by the kinds of access rights that may be assigned to display and control objects. There are three kinds of access rights associated with the objects of the CCA: write access controlled by the initiator (WACI); write access controlled by the acceptor (WACA); and write access variable (WAVAR), where control alternates between the initiator and the acceptor.

The WAVAR access right is available only in S-mode, which employs the half-duplex functional unit of the session layer to control dialogue in a two-way alternating mode. The session layer data token is exchanged between the two endpoints; only the user with the data token gets to send data. There is only one display object in an S-mode profile, and the only VT user allowed to update it at any particular time is the one that possesses the session data token.

The other two kinds of access rights, WACI and WACA, are available only in A-mode. These access rights are non-reassignable, mandating the existence of two display objects, one for the initiator to update and one for the acceptor. Dialogue control in A-mode uses the full-duplex functional unit of the session layer, which allows either VT user to send updates to the other in a two-way simultaneous mode.

Originally, European contributors to ISO VTP standards work only considered the S-mode of operation relevant. However, the American ISO VTP contingent has, for several years, advocated A-mode's two-way simultaneous dialogue because it recognizes a need for type-ahead capability. A compromise was made by creating VTE mode parameter.

The fact that S-mode and A-mode are sometimes called synchronous-mode and asynchronous-mode results in a certain amount of confusion, even within the standards-creating committee itself. There is no relationship between these logical modes and the characteristics of the physical line connecting a real terminal to a physical computer. It is a more general and flexible notion of synchronization between the initiating and accepting VT users. The locked keyboard of an IBM 3270 (which prevents any action unless the host dictates to the terminal that it is ready to accept keyboard-input data from the terminal) can be supported with an S-mode profile, but this aspect of dialogue control can be employed with a terminal that uses an asynchronous physical attachment to the terminal as well. Similarly, the half-duplex operation provided by the session layer is logical rather than physical—the physical line connecting the device may be capable of carrying character data in both directions, but the application will not send it until it has been given the session layer data token.

The type of delivery control to be used is also a VTE parameter. This parameter determines whether no delivery control, simple delivery control, or quarantined delivery control can be used in issuing updates to display objects

3. CCA. *Various objects and parameters in the CCA support the physical components of a virtual terminal. CCA contains numerous objects and parameters.*

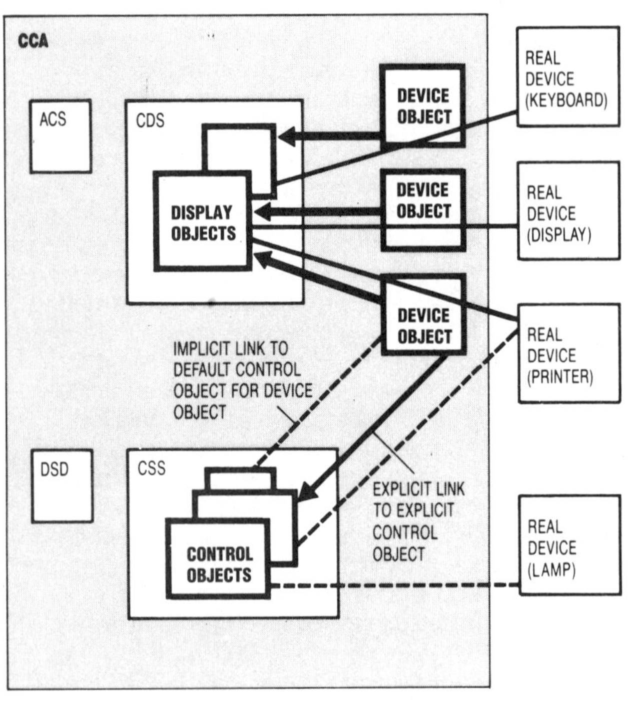

and control objects that have been assigned normal update priority.

"No delivery control" means that the VT user has no control over when updates are delivered: It is entirely up to the VTPM. With simple delivery control, the VT user can force delivery of updates to be sent by issuing a VT DELIVER request to the VTPM. Quarantined delivery control provides the additional control to the VT user. This last type of delivery control allows for the possibility of "net-effecting," whereby updates that undo each other can be consolidated into any resulting update. No matter which type of delivery control is in effect, some events implicitly signal the delivery of any queued updates, as follows: entry into negotiation; release of an association; and, in S-mode only, relinquishing of the WAVAR access right.

Telnet profile

To model Telnet behavior with an ISO VTP profile, the basic functional elements of Telnet must first be identified and then mapped onto the equivalent objects and mechanisms provided by the VT model. The display objects and device objects are quite generic and map relatively directly, while the control objects are created specifically to produce Telnet behavior in the ISO VTP environment.

■ *Telnet display objects*—Mode selection has a profound effect on a profile. To model TCP/IP Telent behavior, A-mode is selected for the ISO VTP Telnet profile. Simple delivery control is selected, providing a function similar to the TCP PUSH (a signal to the local TCP module to send all of its data). The only access rights in A-mode are WACA and WACT, necessitating two display objects to represent the display and the keyboard. These are identified by the text strings D and K, respectively. Access rights assigned to D give the acceptor update control (WACA), and access rights for the K are assigned to be WACI, giving the initiator control of that display object. This separation of keyboard and display maps well onto the Network Virtual Terminal (NVT) model of the TCP/IP Telnet, since NVT is described as a bidirectional character device, possessing a printer and a keyboard.

Both display objects are two-dimensional, which allows VT users to explicitly convey the notion of a new line (a carriage return followed by a line feed) in an application- and device-independent way: The addressing operation "next x-array" indicates that the next character is to be placed in the first column of the next row in the character-box array that represents the screen. (An x-array represents a line of text; a set of x-arrays constitutes a y-array, which represents an entire page.) All aspects of the x and y dimensions are identical in the two display objects (they were defined that way to match the Telnet functionality). Erasure is allowed in the x-array only, either a single character at a time using the relative addressing operation "$x = x - 1$" or, for the full current x-array, the absolute addressing operation "$x = 1$." Telnet accomplishes these two forms of erasure with the Telnet special commands Erase Character (EC) and Erase Line (EL).

Two profile parameters may be used to customize the display objects: line width and repertoire assignment. Line width is self-explanatory. The repertoire assignment parameter selects the default character sets. When the binary repertoire, which is always available, is selected, no addressing operations are used. This effect parallels the Telnet Transmit Binary option, which also eliminates these mappings in Telnet connections.

■ *Telnet device objects*—Each display object is linked to a separate device object, which shares the access right of the associated display object. The device object representing the keyboard is known by the text string "KEYBOARD-DEVICE," while the device object representing the screen is named "DISPLAY-DEVICE."

■ *Telnet control objects*—The choice of control objects for the ISO VTP Telnet profile completes the VTE. A concise set of control functions is provided by the TCP/IP Telnet to provide signaling between the two ends of the NVT connection. These signals are BREAK, Interrupt Process (IP), Abort Output (AO), Are You There (AYT), and the Telnet Sync.

Although more typically issued from the terminal side, the BREAK, AO, AYT, and IP signals may be sent in either direction to support the TCP/IP Telnet symmetry. To ac-

664

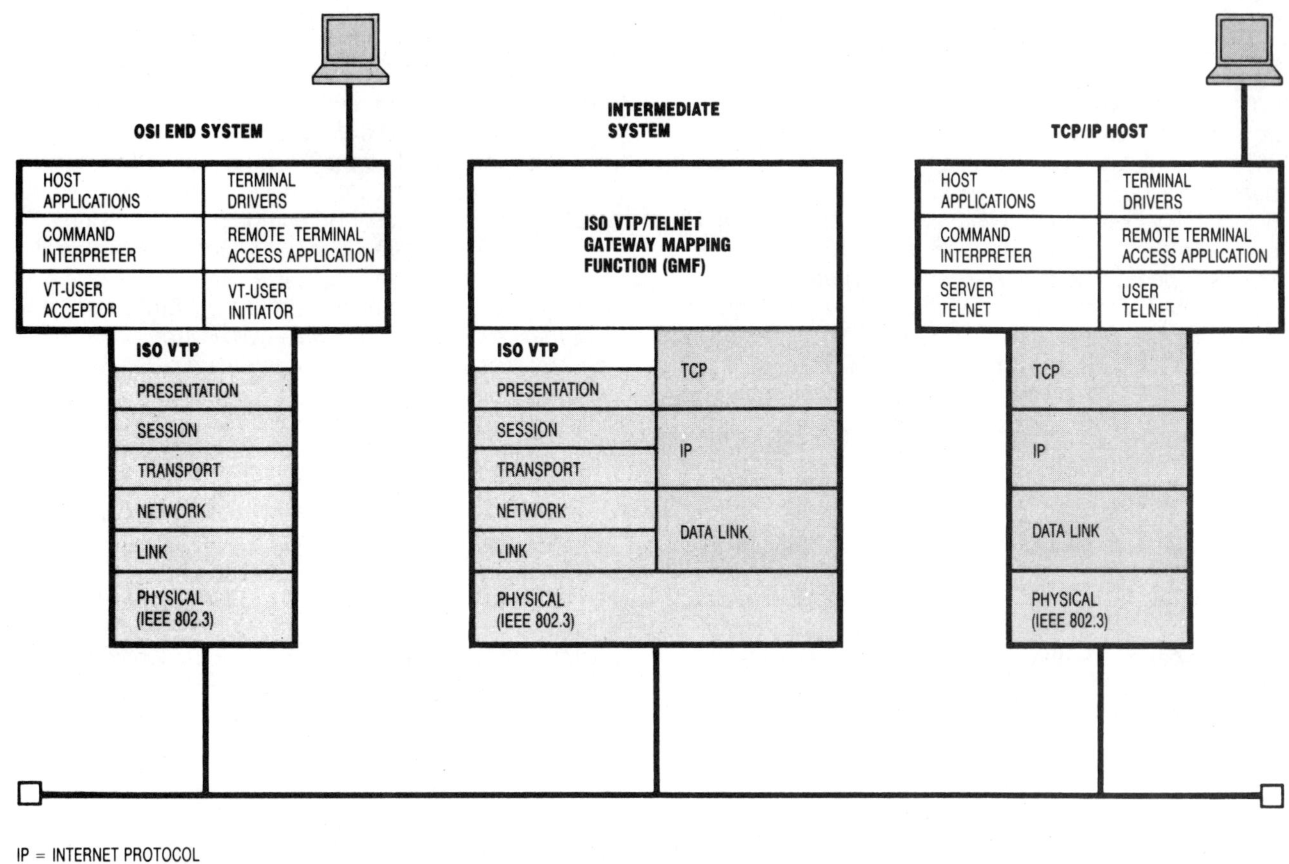

4. OSI meets TCP/IP. *Remote terminal connections in mixed TCP/IP-OSI network are made through a VT gateway. For the sake of simplification, all three devices are attached* *on a common IEEE 802.3 cable, although another topology might feature separate physical networks with the Intermediate System attached to each.*

complish this, two control objects—identified with the text strings DI (display) and KB (keyboard)—are used to provide all these signals, with the appropriate access rights inherited from their respective device objects (WACA and WACI).

Each object has five boolean switches that allow the VT user to convey these signals to its peer. The Sync signal uses a boolean in these two control objects to represent the Telnet Data Mark (DM) in addition to a separate control object, SY. The SY control object is sent on the presentation layer Expedited Data service ahead of the DM to ensure that it gets through any queued-up data. The VT user receiving the SY control object must flush all updates from its peer until it receives the DM, which terminates the Sync. ISO VTP supplies an additional service called VT-BREAK, which flushes the updates in both directions.

the negotiation of Telnet options—a mandatory part of any TCP/IP Telnet connection. The ISO VTP Telnet profile is limited to supporting the negotiation capability of only the most common of the Telnet options: Echo, Suppress Go-Ahead, and Transmit Binary. Any option negotiation beyond these three basic types merits a switch to a new ISO VTP profile.

To negotiate the states of these options, the Telnet profile has a pair of control objects called NI (negotiation-by-initiator) and NA (negotiation-by-acceptor). NI is linked to the keyboard and NA is linked to the display. This pair of control objects provides a complete modeling of the symmetric nature of TCP/IP Telnet option negotiation and its confirmation/rejection capabilities. Either side may initiate a change in option status: If both sides attempt a negotiation at the same time, there is no collision.

The initial values of the Echo and Go-Ahead options in TCP/IP Telnet assign Echo responsibility to the initiator (terminal side) and select the Go-Ahead to control which side sends data to the NVT printer. The ISO VTP Telnet profile uses the same initial conditions for the corresponding NI and NA control objects: Echo responsibility is provided by the initiator and the Go-Ahead option is selected. When Go-Ahead use is selected, another control object (identified as GA) may be updated to convey Telnet Go-Ahead. The effect is to enable the keyboard when a GA control object is updated, allowing the next line of keyboard input to be read. Although the access rights associated with this optional object are not subject to access control, the use of the GA control object is very similar to the exchange of WAVAR with an S-mode display object, which changes the entire character of the essentially A-mode-oriented Telnet profile. This renders it unsuitable for interactive applications but ideal for line-oriented ones.

OSI Telnet gateway function

There are functional mappings associated with an OSI-to-TCP/IP gateway. Each gateway mapping link must join a VT user and a Telnet client, keeping state information for both connection halves. Moreover, each must behave in a prescribed way in response to all events indicated by the End System peers. The gateway never originates events but simply maps them from one virtual terminal onto the other. Figure 4 illustrates how an OSI-to-TCP/IP gateway (Intermediate System) would fit into a mixed protocol network. ISO VTF GMF chains a TCP/IP connection to a VT association; the GMF is at the same time a protocol peer to the VT user in an OSI End System and to the Telnet server or user on a TCP/IP host. The Intermediate System provides two independent protocol stacks, one OSI and one TCP/IP, each matching layer for layer the protocol stacks of the two incompatible single-stack setups. While both TCP/IP Telnet and ISO VTP virtual terminals illustrated in Figure 4 may be generally viewed as symmetric, terminals differ in behavior in the ways they access their applications. In a gateway function, it is thus critical to ask the following question: Who started this, or from which protocol family did this linkage originate? In other words, was the requested linkage initiated by a terminal on the OSI or the Internet side of the Intermediate System? In an Internet-originated gateway mapping, the Telnet half of the Gateway Mapping Function (GMF) behaves in the Server Telnet role, while the OSI half of the GMF acts as the initiator of the VT Association. The OSI VTP standards provide well-defined guidelines for handling remote interactive access within hybrid protocol networks. When making the change to OSI networks, users will find profile development critical to the smooth transition from older terminal connection protocols to ISO VTP. The National Bureau of Standards' Virtual Terminal Special Interest Group will continue to develop implementation agreements and a set of profiles for key applications, with the Telnet profile most prominent. ■

H. Kim Lew is a technical writer with Bridge Communications. He received a B. A. in journalism from San Jose State University. Lew has worked as a freelance technology writer, as an editor for the now-defunct technical trade journal, Military Electronics/Countermeasures, *and as a technical writer for a number of Silicon Valley firms.*

Cyndi Jung is a senior project manager at Bridge. Her primary responsibility is the direction of Bridge's OSI-based product development. She received a B. S. in mathematics from the California Institute of Technology and an M. A. in mathematics from the University of California, Berkeley. Jung is an active participant in the NBS-sponsored Virtual Terminal Special Interest Group, an extention of the OSI Implementor's Workshop.

Paul R. Strauss, DATACOMMUNICATIONS

The standards deluge: A sound foundation or a Tower of Babel?

The Year of Standards is upon us. Hundreds have already been unleashed, and many more—such as FDDI and MAC Bridge—will affect users for years.

Standards that impact networking make up but a tiny part of the thousands of standards promulgated every year. The American National Standards Institute (ANSI), for example, includes among its members the American Ladder Institute, the Automotive Lift Institute, the International Carwash Association, and the Insect Screening Weavers Association. While sharing the limelight with such distinguished and flamboyant activities, information networking is increasingly in the spotlight and, as a result, has become among the most heated standards arenas today.

Within the world of networking standards, new specifications have been pouring out of the standards bodies at an extraordinary pace. During the 1960s and '70s, specifications on an occasional new connector would be big news. But in the past 12 months, there have been hundreds of new standards, some of them unusually well-researched and innovative. It was a year in which the vital nature of standards became manifest.

And these days, new standards are often on the cutting edge of technology: The upcoming 100-Mbit/s Fiber Distributed Data Interface (FDDI) is a good example. "When I first became involved with standards in 1974," recalls Ivor N. Knight, chairman of the ANSI T1 Committee, which was organized in February 1984 by the Exchange Carriers Standards Association, "every standard was selected from existing technology. Now, at times, the work that we do goes hand in hand with the work in the laboratories."

It has also been a year of unusual standards diversity. Documents affecting networking are being issued in such different areas as keyboards, facsimile, wiring, and transmission quality. Various industries and professional fields are seeking or upgrading networking standards. Some examples: A Standard Field Bus (twisted pair, Manchester encoding, and an access technique similar to AT&T's Datakit data PBX) is being put together by the Instrument Society of America. A self-configuring medical bus/LAN is discussed below.

Also, an error-correcting standard for Group 3 facsimile is emerging from the Electronic Industries Association (EIA) TR-29 Committee. (The protocol requires coding each line so that redundancy checks can be performed and the line retransmitted. Error-correcting fax can be compatible with Group 3 fax issued prior to the standard because a handshaking protocol has been set to determine whether the error codes are to be transmitted.)

This year's spate of standards was largely caused by a tidal wave of documents related to Open Systems Interconnection (OSI, see Fig. 1) and to the Integrated Services Digital Network (ISDN).

This flood crested so rapidly because a deadline looms: the upcoming quadrennial CCITT (International Consultative Committee for Telephone and Telegraph) plenary session, which convenes in Melbourne, Australia, in November. By latest count, that session—which perhaps 300 or more delegates from 50 or more nations are expected to attend—will be acting on somewhere between 900 and 1,000 different standards.

That a deluge of new standards has fallen upon the world is, by itself, not all that important. What does matter is that many of those standards are likely to have significant impact on users. They offer the potential for new products, and indeed, many standards-related products are on the way.

The past 12 months were also a period of ferment among standards bodies. The most notable creation was the first Joint Technical Committee of the ISO and International Electrotechnical Commission (IEC), ISO/IEC JTC-1, which held its first meeting in Tokyo last November. JTC-1 was a restructuring of the international standards process. Prior to its creation, the ISO and IEC cooperated, but standards

X12
ISIS
TIA
JTC-1
CEPT
NEMA
SG
SPAG
IEEE
X3
MA
CCITT
EIA
ISO
OSI
FORUM
ECMA
BSI
ECSA
MAP
80
ETSI
CSA
CEN
CAM
RIA
CENELEC
XO
OP
K. Gengler © 1988

1. OSI matures. *The Open System Interconnection's layered structure is getting crowded, especially at the top. Standards within the OSI model, which is a decade old this year, are drawing increasing attention around the world. Products are appearing, and plans for functional profiles and international standard profiles are being laid.*

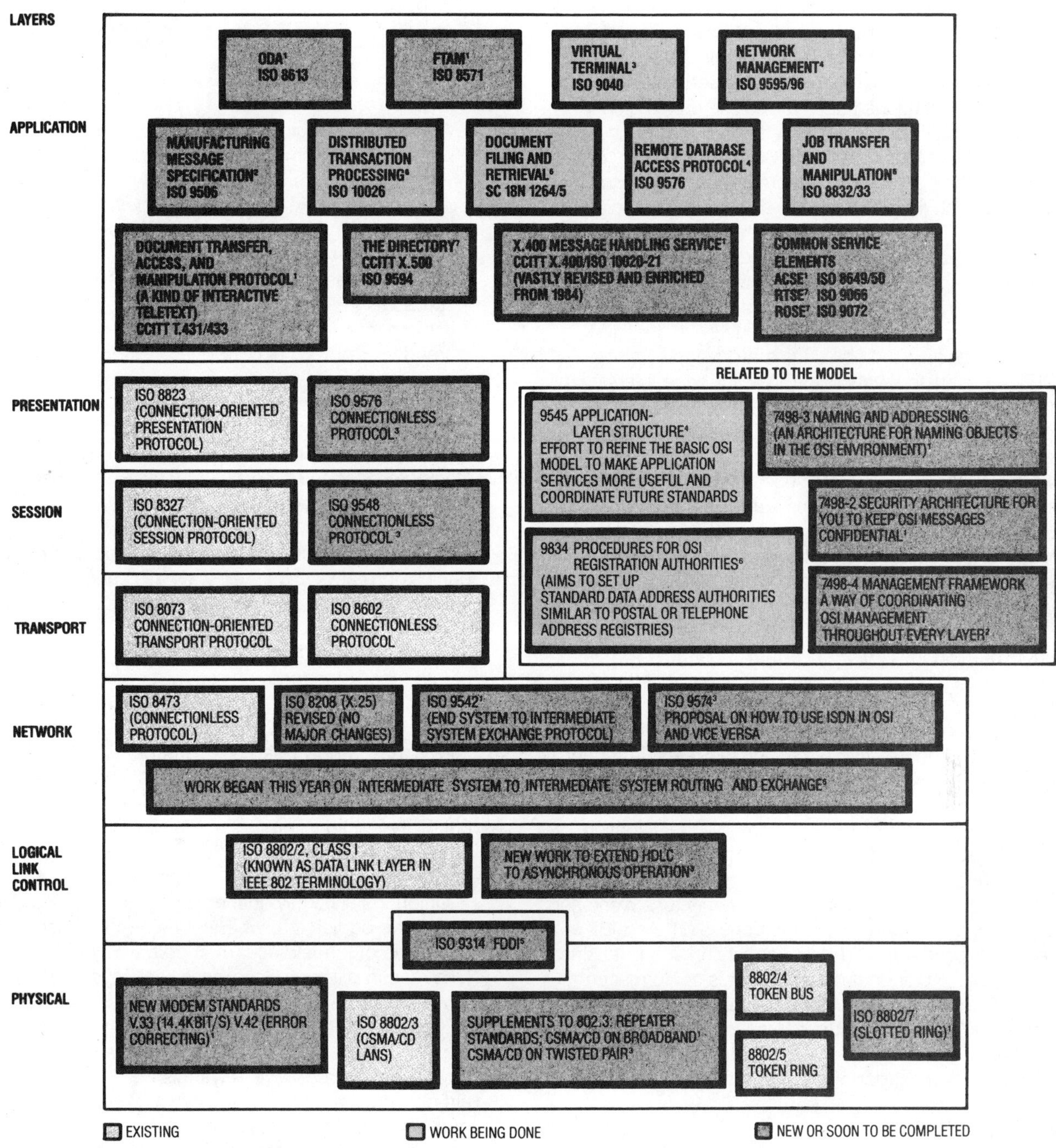

1. COMPLETED BETWEEN JULY 1987 AND SEPTEMBER 1988 (FOR CCITT STANDARDS, COUNTS STUDY GROUP ACTION AS FINAL).   2. EXPECTED 1988.   3. EXPECTED 1989.
4. EXPECTED 1990.   5. WORK NEARLY COMPLETED.   6. COMPLETION DATE UNCLEAR.   7. PASSED CCITT STUDY GROUP; ISO APPROVAL NEXT YEAR.

CSMA/CD = CARRIER-SENSE MULTIPLE ACCESS WITH COLLISION DETECTION
CCITT = INTERNATIONAL CONSULTATIVE COMMITTEE FOR TELEPHONE AND TELEGRAPH
ODIF = OFFICE DOCUMENT ARCHITECTURE AND INTERCHANGE FORMAT
FDDI = FIBER DISTRIBUTED DATA INTERFACE
FTAM = FILE TRANSFER, ACCESS, AND MANAGEMENT
HDLC = HIGH-LEVEL DATA LINK CONTROL

ISDN = INTEGRATED SERVICES DIGITAL NETWORK
ISO = INTERNATIONAL ORGANIZATION FOR STANDARDIZATION
OSI = OPEN SYSTEMS INTERCONNECTION
LAN = LOCAL AREA NETWORK
ACSE = ASSOCIATION CONTROL SERVICE ELEMENTS
RTSE = RELIABLE TRANSFER SERVICE ELEMENTS
ROSE = REMOTE OPERATIONS SERVICE ELEMENTS

SOURCES: RETIX, SANTA MONICA, CALIF.; OMNICOM INC., VIENNA, VA

had to be portioned out between them or at times dealt with in parallel bodies.

Another important new body is ETSI, the European Telecommunications Standards Institute, formed this spring, which officially began work at its headquarters near Nice, France, this May. ETSI is a spin-off of the Geneva-based European Conference of Postal and Telecommunications Administrations (CEPT), long the only regional telecommunications standards-setter in Europe and still partially involved in standards. ETSI is designed for "voluntary standards," said its new secretary general, Diodato Gagliardi, in an interview. However, a CEPT subsidiary body, called TRAC (Technical Recommendations Applications Committee), retains the power to act on ETSI's recommendations about whether standards should be made mandatory for European governments, he said.

Another standards change that may be in the wind, though opposition is mobilizing, is a drive to eliminate CCITT's present four-year cycle, in which final titular action on every standard is taken by a plenary session. The proposal is to put the CCITT on a perpetual standards-creation basis similar to that of the ISO.

CCITT Secretary General Theodor Irmer has been pressing for this, he said in an interview. If his move is approved, 1992 likely would not have the deluge of standards that has characterized 1988. (Approval of the measure would require a vote not at the upcoming plenary but at an even bigger meeting, called an International Telecommunications Union Plenipotentiary Session, which is scheduled to be held in Nice, France, next spring.)

Stress on standards seems to be having its effects on vendors. IBM has been quietly telling consultants and big users that some of its OSI products, long available in Europe, will soon be sold in the United States. In recent years, top IBM executives have stressed how much they are committed to promoting standards and linking the IBM world to them. In terms of prominent IBM participation among standards-writers, this is certainly true. IBM staffers currently head three out of 10 special interest groups of the National Bureau of Standards OSI Implementor's Workshop (no other firm heads up more than one SIG). And IBM's director of standards and data security, L. John Rankine, chairs JTC-1. Another important trend is conformance testing. The Corporation for Open Systems will have a trial "COS-mark" testing program to issue a seal of proven conformity, under way by the end of the year, says Jan E. G. Aminoff, manager of the program.

The why of it all

Why do standards committee members, engineers who could be turning out useful products, spend days or weeks every month flying off to different committee meetings around the country and around the world? Is it the lure of exotic places? CCITT meetings have been held recently in Brasilia, Brazil; Seoul, South Korea; and on the English Channel island of Guernsey. By contrast, many U. S. meetings have more humdrum sites. "Hardly glamour spots," says Knight, who, in addition to his ANSI T1 Committee job, works for the Communications Satellite Corp.

"We hold them in airports: Fly in, work, and fly out."

"It takes a lot of time, a couple of weeks a month," says Arthur K. Reilly, T1's vice chairman and an executive at Bell Communications Research. "I spend two weeks a month away from home." Rankine says he finds the process "personally rewarding," but he believes that "anyone who participates has a vested interest." That interest could be as broad as the creation of standards, he says. Others think it is often more narrow.

Vendor or government motives boil down to "political issues, economic issues, regulatory issues, and just plain public relations issues—vendors don't want to seem as though they do not support standards," asserts John J. Berg, an editor of the Dutch-published quarterly journal *Computer Standards and Interfaces*. But an academic student of the standards process, Marvin R. Sirbu, an associate professor of engineering and public policy at Carnegie-Mellon University, says he finds that big companies don't always get their way. "It's not a purely technical process or just one of size. It's a political process—and a very human one," he says.

Standards have figured in international and legal issues of late (see "Standards at issue: Countries, courts involved"). By contrast, a more quiet trend has been user participation in the standards arena. So far, the mechanism for this has largely been user groups. One is the newly created North American ISDN Users' Forum (NIU-Forum), which had its first meeting in June. NIU-Forum aims to turn out ISDN functional profiles similar to OSI functional profiles of the National Bureau of Standards' OSI Implementors Workshop (see "Standards of standards," below).

Unfortunately, individual users can rarely be found in standards bodies that were not founded as user groups, say some of the few user members who regularly attend. One reason is the expense, says Joel Snyder, a University of Arizona graduate student who represents Decus, the DEC user group, on several of the X3 standards committees. "It costs about $1,000 for each U. S. meeting I attend," says Snyder, who says this includes hotels and airfare. Snyder contributes his own time but has his expenses payed by Decus. "And it costs about $2,000 for each international meeting."

What does Decus get for its money? "The main thing is information. Standards are what our members will be working with. They've got to know where standards are heading."For that matter, Snyder doesn't mind saying that some of the committees he has attended would, at times, forget the user perspective—unless users were attending.

Another user who participates in U. S. and international telecommunications committees is Michael E. Varassi, who bears the unusual title of Technical Administrator for CCITT

670

Standards at issue: Countries, courts involved

Everyone knows that standards are important, but many data networkers may not know that they are also, at times, the source of considerable friction between normally friendly nations.

Standards help promote the interworking of networks and equipment, so how can anybody not encourage and support them? Every vendor supports standards these days, or at least gives them lip service. For that matter, the U. S. Government supports standards through its soon-to-be-published Government OSI Profile, GOSIP (see main story). Why then should not France, Japan, and the United Kingdom support the same standards within their networks?

The position of the United States in recent years has been that some standards are merely hidden trade barriers. "Many countries use the old AT&T concept of 'danger to the network,'" says Diana Lady Dougan, former State Department coordinator for international communications and information policy. "The CCITT process is supposed to arrive at recommendations and not requirements," she told DATA COMMUNICATIONS, "but some countries regard that as law."

Nations also vie with each other within international standards bodies. The issues are usually the economic health of each country's public carriers or ways of hurting or promoting particular equipment vendors.

Here, for example, is part of a U. S. State Department cable sent after the final meeting of CCITT Study Group I (Operations of Telematic Services) in Geneva in May: "In the area of charging and accounting for telegram services, the U. S. [delegation], in conjunction with others, rejected a proposal that could have been a substantial revenue threat to U. S. carriers, along with administrative requirements that would have been costly to implement."

No negative votes on standards are expected at the upcoming Melbourne, Australia, CCITT plenary session, say members of the U. S. delegation's preparatory group. But there still are some open issues. For example, the United States is dissatisfied with the way CCITT committees have structured work on broadband ISDN during the next study period. The topic has been broken up between too many committees for quality work to be done, says Ivor N. Knight, the chairman of the T1 standards committee, who has been attending meetings of the U. S. delegation to the upcoming plenary.

A subsequent conference in Melbourne will handle a trickier political issue over standards: Can the international "recommendations" somehow be barred from being transformed into government regulations? That is on the agenda at the late-November meeting of the World Administrative Telegraph and Telephone Conference (WATTC).

What worries the United States about WATTC, says Dougan, is that there are moves afoot to make CCITT standards more like international law. At issue is a phrase in an article in the WATTC treaty document stating that "any entity" that provides international telecommunications service must obey the regulations of the CCITT's parent body, the International Telecommunications Union (ITU), she says. ITU regulations deal mainly with the division of tariff funds, but many countries think they also embrace CCITT standards, Dougan says.

■ **To the highest court.** Speaking of competition, a standards-versus-competition issue arose this year at the U. S. Supreme Court. The case was important for a number of reasons. For one, many of the standards bodies regarded the decision as "chilling" to their work in the future.

The court's conclusion wasn't a new legal interpretation, but it restressed that members of standards committees are not protected from legal action by disgruntled firms that view a particular standards action as hindering their business (see "Companies can be sued for their standards activities," DATA COMMUNICATIONS, August, p. 25).

This issue is likely to arise increasingly as "standards of standards"—specific implementation subsets of much larger, multi-option standards (also called functional standards)—are promulgated. After all, the presence of numerous options within many standards have long allowed many vendors to claim their products are standard or standards-compatible. As these options are pared down, many agree, the chances for legal action against committees and their members increases.

In the recent Supreme Court case, Indian Head Corp., a manufacturer of plastic tubing, won an antitrust judgement (which, with treble damages, is worth more than $11 million, says Henry D. Levine, a partner with the Washington, D. C., law firm Morrison & Foerster who specializes in telecommunications law) against Allied Tube, a maker of steel conduit pipe.

The alleged fire-retardant qualities of steel over plastic was the standards issue that led to the case. But a lower court had ruled that whatever the qualities of the two conduit materials, the standards committee that made the decision had been "packed" by Allied. As a result, the standard was not related to fire at all, but merely a way of keeping a competitor out of a market, the court said.

The Supreme Court's action, backing that ruling, should remind standards committees and committee members that they are working in a vulnerable area, say Levine and James S. Blaszak, who represents the Ad Hoc Telecommunications Users Association. "You have to have a record that shows that the meeting was fair," says Levine. "A representative of one of the affected parties cannot be the chairman of the committee. Votes have got to go out to all the members; all the members have to be notified—that kind of stuff."—*P. R. S.*

Affairs for the overnight package-delivery service Federal Express. Both information from the standards committee and participation in making actual regulations are important to Federal Express, he says. "We need to know upcoming standards so that our equipment can be compatible, so that we will not be locked into a proprietary solution, but we have also got to participate in standards."

The year in standards

To better see what has been happening, a selection of the recent standards follows. The list covers some of the many different types of standards that have emerged of late — software standards, hardware standards, modem standards, wire-installation standards, telephone network quality standards, etc. — as an overview of what has been evolving. Listings were arbitrarily limited to standards that have emerged within the past year, or more accurately, the past 13 months (a slight aberration caused by the time involved in the selection process).

A few standards were included in the compilation that have not been formally ratified, but only when a committee member commented that they were, in his or her view, within six months of final committee approval.

OSI upper levels

■ *ISO 8613-1/8: Information Processing—Text and Office Systems—Office Document Architecture (ODA) and Interchange Format.* Considered highly important in Europe and Japan, ODA has rarely been discussed in the United States, a significant oversight. ODA has a lot going for it. For example, the Interchange Format of ODA is embraced in TOP (Technical and Office Protocols) of the MAP/TOP 3.0 specification (see below); it is also slated to be inserted into an upcoming version of GOSIP (Government OSI Profile, see below). Work on ODA began in the European Computer Manufacturers Association (ECMA), which has its own ODA version (ECMA-101, passed September 1985). European and Japanese vendors see ODA as a quick way to pass beyond U. S. dominance in word processing, financial spreadsheets, and graphics. Several big U. S. vendors have ODA-compatible products coming soon, say ISO sources. The ODA specification has details of word processing in final-form text as well as revisable text and allows graphics to be inserted in the text. It has enough linking information to build subsequent ODA standards for categories not yet written—spreadsheets, for example. ECMA this year also published TR/41, a compatible language for writing ODA programs. Status: ODA passed ISO/IEC Joint Technical Committee 1, Study Committee 18, in mid-July.

■ *ISO 9595/96: Information Processing Systems—Open Systems Interconnection—Management Information Service.* A much agonized-over standard. A complete version of network management may be two years from conclusion. However, a vital portion of 9595 was stabilized at an editors' meeting in July, and that section is likely to go to draft international standard status in the fall. This part of 9595 is known as CMIS/CMIP for Common Management Information Services/Common Management Information Protocol. CMIS/CMIP is useful outside OSI because it has been

selected to be the network management protocol of TCP/IP (Transmisson Control Protocol/Internet Protocol, see below). It is also likely to be used by the newly formed OSI/Network Management Forum, a specialized standards-promotion group, in some kind of internetworking demonstration, tentatively scheduled for April 1990. The MAP/TOP Users Group chose an early version of 9595 to be displayed at the Enterprise Networking Event in June and wrote it into MAP/TOP 3.0 (which cannot be changed for six years). The result was a working ENE display. A side effect, however, is that it isn't clear whether the two OSI network management versions will work together without expensive software to toggle back and forth.

Layer 7 services

■ *Global Electronic Data Interchange. ISO 9735. Syntax Language for Edifact (Electronic Data Interchange for Administration, Commerce, and Transport).* A worldwide standard for passing electronic forms, such as orders for goods and demands for payment, between different businesses or businesses and government bodies. Worked on for more than a decade by the United Nations Working Party on the Facilitation of International Trade Procedures (which reports to the U. N. Commission for Europe). Incompatibilities between European and U. S. EDI (X12, see below) have long existed, and major efforts are under way to align them. ISO 9735, passed in September 1987, spells out the structuring of EDI messages and how they relate to lower-level standards (such as X.400).

■ *U. S. Electronic Data Interchange. ASCX12B/87/001: Version 2, Release 1 of X12 Standard.* Extensive revision and additional functions added to X12, the sole ANSI-accredited Electronic Data Interchange standard, which specifies methods for electronically passing business documents. Version 2 adds shipping notices and payment-remittance advance forms to existing specified documents. Some upgrades are not compatible with previous versions. U. S. EDI standards for specific industries—trucking or petroleum, for example—are voted on by committees within their industrial associations (such as the Association of American Railroads). These standards are published and maintained by the Transportation Data Coordinating Committee/Electronic Data Interchange Association, a non-ANSI group. Status of X12 V2: passed November 1987. Committee: X12 of Data Interchange Standards Association.

Computer graphics/windowing protocols

■ *High-level windowing. X Windows Version 11. A current de facto standard; official U. S. status being sought.* Version 11 of the M.I.T.-developed windowing-graphics protocol began shipping in September. Much-increased

functionality includes tiling as well as overlapping windows. Three-dimensional graphics, two-way image processing, and—for the truly advanced—such video applications as videoconferencing inside of windows, are all being researched. X Windows is supported by virtually all major computer vendors, including DEC and IBM. It operates mainly on Unix systems, but DEC's Decnet implementation is planned soon, committee sources say. Current standards body: X Window Consortium at M.I.T. Official status sought through X3H3.6. The first vote on an official version is expected in October.

■ *Standard file format for graphics.* ISO 8632 (Parts 1-4): Information Processing Systems Computer Graphics— Metafile for the Storage and Transfer of Picture-Descriptive Information. CGM Is the first official broad-based graphics standard for storing user information (some similar videotex standards exist but do not allow for two-way passing of graphics or for the details of CGM). 8632 spells out a binary file format that permits passing images between different types of computers through CGM interpreters. CGM was one of the applications demonstrated at the Enterprise Networking Event in June. Embraced in the TOP specification. Status: international standard, published August 1987.

Computer access hardware and software

■ *1-2-3 beats 7-8-9.* ISO DIS 9995: Keyboard Layouts for Text and Office Systems. In an unusually visible cooperative effort between CCITT and ISO, the world's standards bodies selected as a preferred configuration the numbering format used on keypad telephones (a block of 10 number keys, nine in a block, 1-2-3 across the top line, 0 centered at the bottom, see Fig. 2A) over the common computer keyboard numeric pad format (7-8-9 across the top, 0 at the left of the bottom line, see Fig. 2B) to be the standard for communicating computers in the future. For decades, computers and adding machines followed the 7-8-9 format, which must have been created in the days of mechanical adding machines. Apparently, ISDN drove the 1-2-3 vs. 7-8-9 confrontation. After all, computers that dial numbers are likely to use the same keypad for dialing and adding. So far, the standard does not require * and # symbols on the computer keyboard. But blank keys must be at the left and right of the 0 to do *ing and #ing, if needed. U. S./European debate continues about placing letters on the keys. Status: ISO draft international standard, passage likely within eight months. Committees involved: CCITT SG II, WP 2; ANSI X3V1.9; ISO/IEC JTC-1 SC 18 WG 9.

■ *Better viewscreens, keyboards.* ANSI/HFS 100-1988: American National Standard for Human Factors Engineering of Visual Display Terminal Workstations. Though much of ANSI 100 deals with the physical construction of worksta- tions to decrease back stress, much also deals with future viewscreens and keyboards. (There's no section on mice.) Likely to directly affect network management terminals are the standard's recommended practices on color use: Blue on a dark background should be avoided because of eye stress, red because it is less noticeable by color-blind people. When multiple color codes are used, ANSI 100 recommends the minimum spacing between colors should be at least 40 units on the standard CIE chromaticity chart, which the standard says will make available at least seven to 10 different colors. Status: American National Standard, adopted February 1988.

De facto standard/standard operating systems

■ *New Blue OS/2.* Operating System 2, OS/2, jointly developed by IBM and Microsoft, seems to be the only obvious de facto standard that has arisen during the past 365 days. There have been significant upgrades to other de facto standards during the period, however. One of these is IBM's new Version 2 of of its relational database, DB2. Another IBM de facto standard is the database-writing language SQL, which is also an ANSI standard (an unusually powerful combination). Looming as de facto standards are IBM's Systems Application Architecture (SAA) and Presentation Manager user interface. IBM's new operating system was designed to take advantage of the fast speed and multitasking capabilities of the Intel 80286 chip, running with the IBM Personal System 2 Microchannel bus. OS/2 offers 16 megabytes of addressable memory and is compatible with MS-DOS applications that were created for 8088-based IBM PCs and PC/XTs.

■ *Posix coming soon.* IEEE 1003. With attention focused on the Open Software Foundation and its unstated controversy with the AT&T/Sun Microsystems axis over the future of Unix (see "Behind the scenes at the great Unix revolt," DATA COMMUNICATIONS, June, p. 16), it has been overlooked that an official Unix-related standard is nearing completion. Posix, the Portable Operating Systems for Computer Environments, passed its final draft version at the IEEE Technical Committee on Operating Systems Standards Subcommittee in July, and now it is before the Revision Committee of the IEEE Standards Board, where a letter ballot was scheduled to end in August. If the vote goes well, and it is likely to, the committee will immediately apply for ANSI and ISO status. Related work on Unix standards—particularly a user interface—is being done at X-Open, a consortium of vendors that IBM joined in early August.

ISDN

■ *The way it works.* I.451/Q.931: ISDN User-Network Interface Layer 3 Specification. Of the scores of ISDN standards, some are outstanding because they are innovative. Most are important simply because they will make ISDN work. Of the latter standards, which are the nitty-gritty components of ISDN, I.451/Q.931 could be featured as a kind of unknown soldier for the rest. The "B" channel, "D" channel, "U" interface, and so forth, have been discussed at length; I.451 hasn't. It is a good example of what makes ISDN different from POTS (plain old telephone service), however. I.451 is the standard that will change the user signaling technology, for example, the tonal signals of a punch-pad telephone, into the digital codes of ISDN. Status: I.451/Q.931 passed Study Group XI in May. Passage at the CCITT November plenary session is certain.

■ **Broadband ISDN.** *G.707-709: New Synchronous Digital Hierarchy.* The first format for broadband ISDN. It includes Sonet, the 150-odd-Mbit/s Synchronous Optical Network that was the cause of disputes between European and U. S. standards bodies. 707/709 is a notable compromise. Contrast its universal speeds with the present differences over T1: 1.544 Mbit/s in the United States, 2.048 Mbit/s in Europe and Japan. To get that amity, U. S. negotiators had to give up a lot, however. Sources close to the negotiations say that U. S. vendors were ready to roll out U. S. Sonet (T1X9.4)-based products perhaps a year ahead of the rest of the world. 707/709 is a hierarchy of super-fast digital speeds, starting at 150 Mbit/s (which is allowed to be broken down into 50-Mbit/s chunks) and running up to 600 Mbit/s (and higher, theoretically, though nothing that fast is yet listed). Status: Passed by SG XVIII in June; certain to pass November plenum. A related standard, 1.121: Broadband Aspects of ISDN, discusses the Asynchronous Transfer Mode, one approach to high-speed packet services.

Non-ISDN interfaces and tests

■ **Testing conformance to Part 68 rules.** *PN 1925: FCC Part 68 Test and Measurement Guide.* Updates long-outdated Federal Communications Commission test procedures for equipment compatible with its Part 68 rules for switched and dedicated digital network attachments. Equipment makers currently use various diverse tests for same specifications. Provides grid of 60 rules classified by 17 types of equipment and specifies simple test procedures for each. Covers signal power, digital and analog line balance, billing protection, and hazardous voltage tests. Most tests are already well known, but a new procedure for longitudinal balance may be devised. It will likely be accepted by the FCC and proposed as an ANSI standard. Status: likely to go to EIA ballot by the end of the year.

Fire! Fire!

■ **NFPA versus CBEMA.** *National Electrical Code, Articles 725-38 (b) 1,2,3; 800-3 (b) 1,2,3; and 770-6 (a), (b), and (c).* The speed at which cable insulation burns isn't usually considered a data communications standard. Yet the new provisions of the National Electrical Code show that standards designed for quite another purpose can have an odd impact on networking. In this case, one noticeable result is some thick cables. Another is a spat between two standards bodies. On July 1, major revisions to the NEC went into effect, imposing much stiffer requirements on data communications cables running under the floor or in the walls. (Cables in suspended ceilings were already subject to tougher standards, which have not been changed.) One of two newly required tests, for example, specified that a flame at least as hot as 527,000 British Thermal Units (BTUs) per hour be applied to a test cable for 20 minutes to half an hour. This compares with an old test: 3,000 BTUs applied for 75 seconds. CBEMA, the

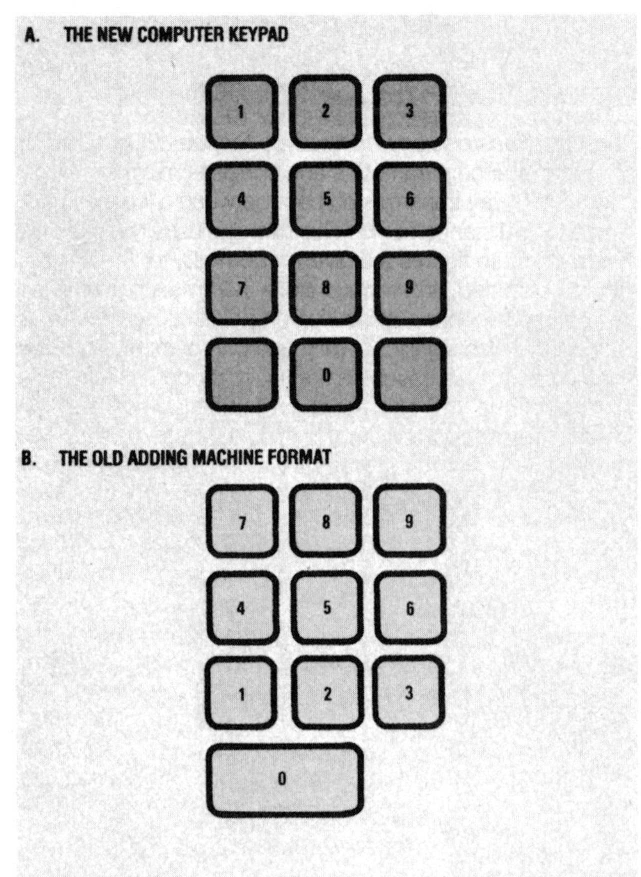

Computer and Business Equipment Manufacturers Association (itself a standards body as parent of the X3 Committee) begged NFPA for a delay before letting the new rules come into effect, saying that many of its vendor members hadn't time to comply. But NFPA disagreed, and the code provisions are now in force—though CBEMA is continuing to appeal within the NFPA structure. The new fire requirements have made cable vendors find slower-burning insulation materials. There hasn't been an increase in cable costs with the new insulation, say Jay E. Thomas, director of the Black Box catalog for Black Box Inc., a Pittsburg, Pa., subsidiary of Micom Systems, and Al Harnish, executive vice president of Glasgal Communications, in Northvale, N. J.—both firms sell wire along with other gear. Some new cables aren't as good as before. Thomas says he has seen new coax with a diameter roughly twice that of older cables. Wider cables reduce the number of cables that can be pulled through a conduit.

Telephone service quality

■ **Exchange carrier-to-interexchange carrier standards.** *No number, in T1.Q1 Subcommittee: Draft of American National Standard for Telecommunications, Network Performance Standards, Switched Exchange Access*

Network Transmission Performance Standard. Defines analog performance parameters and specifies minimum quality for the two-way transmission path between a local carrier and a long-distance carrier. This circuit is usually digital these days, so figures are given in both dB, for the analog signals encoded, and various digital parameters. Designed to improve telephone quality for long-distance calls. The standard is also significant because part of its quality methodology was based on tests with modems. For example: "The V.29 test results revealed that the EIA criteria represented a threshold of satisfactory performance. Based on this, it was concluded that any further increase in impairment levels would result in unsatisfactory performance." Status: successful T1Q1 letter ballot expected by August; then it enters T1 letter ballot.

LANs and MANs

■ *100-Mbit/s fiber LAN.* *X3.139-187, X3.148-1988, X3.166-198X. Fiber Distributed Data Interface Media Access Control, FDDI Physical Layer Protocol, and FDDI Physical Medium-Dependent Layer.* Together make up FDDI, a 100-Mbit/s Token Ring standard that is nearing completion. X3.139 passed the X3T9 committee and full X3 ballot last year; X3.148 is in second public review and is expected to be completed late this year. X3.166 was forwarded for public review in late June. With conclusion of these specifications, the only work remaining on FDDI is for specific applications and some protocols of FDDI-II. The committee has already heard a tentative proposal to launch work on a 1.2-Gbit/s standard.

■ *Standard inter-LAN bridge.* *802.1D (5)88/36: MAC Bridge.* Creates a standard bridge between 802.3 (CSMA/CD), 802.4 (token bus), and 802.5 (Token Ring) networks or a configuration of large numbers of different 802 networks, and other access procedures (apparently including MAN and FDDI) are under consideration. It is not a protocol conversion for messages on the upper layers, but it specifies an architecture and provides a protocol for passing packets on the physical and data link layers. Works through individual MAC (Media Access Control) nodes on each network and a central node. More complex configurations can be handled with the spanning-tree algorithm, which is capable of searching for the best route between LANs. Status: likely to go out for final letter ballot in 802.1 later this year or early 1989.

■ *Metropolitan area network.* *IEEE 802.6: Distributed Queue Double Bus (DQDB).* Sole Metropolitan Area Network standard, formerly known as QPSX (Queued Packet and Synchronous Exchange). The name was changed because the Australian group that promoted the standard subsequently set up a firm with the QPSX name to sell

product. Competing protocol MST (Multiplexed Slot and Token) was withdrawn as draft standard and is being sold as a proprietary network. (For details of DQDB, see "Networking for greater metropolitan areas," DATA COMMUNICATIONS, February, p. 114). Status: passed 802.6; out for 802 letter ballot. Passage considered certain. Committee: IEEE 802.6, IEEE Communications Society.

■ *Medical LAN.* *IEEE 1073: Medical Information Bus.* Sets specifications for a two-stage network for hospitals. The first stage, which is the close-to-the-patient stage, is an EIA RS-485-based dumb terminal emulation network in star configuration using twisted pair for bedside-to-local-processor applications. Other links, such as between the local processor and central processors, ride on a standard Ethernet-type bus. Much innovation has been done on an easy-to-use set-up interface. Standards-makers decided that a node must be automatically configured and a patient file created any time a nurse plugs a bedside device (monitor, fluid pump, etc.) into the lower-layer network. IEEE 1073 also sets a standard language for local medical devices. The maximum LAN speed of a bedside link is 357 kbit/s. Status: After five years of work, the first part of the document, 1073.2, passed committee. Other portions are expected to pass later this year. Committee: Medical Information Bus Committee of IEEE Engineering in Medicine and Biology Society.

Standardized interfaces to de facto standards

■ *TCP/IP to Netbios.* *RFC 1001 and 1002: Protocol Standard for a Netbios Service in a TCP/IP Transport.* Though it has been around so long that most users consider it a formal standard, TCP/IP, the Transmission Control Protocol/Internet Protocol, has never been numbered in the catalogs of ISO or ANSI. Modifications to TCP/IP standards are approved by about 15 members, known as the Internet Activities Board and composed mainly of government users. IAB's latest move was approval of a standard interface between IBM's LAN environment, Netbios, itself a de facto standard, and TCP/IP. After a conference on the subject early last year, IAB approved the standard in December. Work is being done on a network management specification for TCP/IP, which is likely to follow a salient part of the OSI network management standard (see "OSI upper layers," above).

■ *TOP to Netbios.* A working party of the MAP/TOP Users Group is hard at work on a standard interface between TOP, the Technical and Office Protocols, and IBM's Netbios. Status: The document is in draft form but is thought likely to be completed this year or early next.

Modems/modem interfaces

■ *Error-correcting modems.* *V.42: Error-Correcting Procedures for DCEs using Asynchronous-to-Synchronous Conversion.* This is the first modem error-correction standard (see "Much to gain from V.42 standard, but some problems likely at first," DATA COMMUNICATIONS, July, p. 74). Status: passed CCITT SG XVII in April.

■ *A simple substitute for RS-232-C.* *PN-1890: Simple-Eight-Position Non-Synchronous Interface between Data*

Terminal Equipment and Data Circuit-Terminating Equipment Employing a Serial Binary Data Interchange. PN-1890 creates a cheaper computer-to-modem interface for applications not requiring full RS-232-C functionality. It is electronically compatible with RS-232-C, permitting the use of the same chip sets. But instead of the RS-232-C connector, the standard uses an eight-pin RJ-13-like connector (see Fig. 3). In order to reduce pin numbers, the interface sacrifices some test capability. It has no secondary channel or data-rate select. All other functionality is present, however. Work is nearly complete on an asynchronous version; some work has been done on a synchronous model. Status: likely to be submitted for final EIA vote by end of 1988. Committee: TR 30.2.

■ *A pre-ISDN, ISDN-compatible modem interface.*
V.230: New Interface for Modems and DTEs. Today's microcomputer-to-modem connections inevitably use RS-232-C connectors. What will be the standard connector during the interim period during which analog networks wane and ISDNs wax? Possibly V.230. It sets the physical specifications and electrical characteristics for a computer-to-modem interface that could replace RS-232-C. It is an eight-pin modular plug/jack identical to the RJ-13 connector and to ISDN's CPE interface I.430 (see Fig. 3). The standard's aim is to create a computer-to-modem interface that can be replaced by a computer-to-ISDN interface once ISDN arrives. Further work is required to determine a rate-adaptation standard. Status: Physical specifications passed CCITT SG XVII in March; work on rate-adaptation continues in EIA TR 30.2.

Standards on . . . standards
■ *First from the "feeder forums."* NBS Special Publica-*tion 500-150: Stable Implementation Agreements for Open Systems Interconnection Protocols, V1.* No more influential standards document has been unveiled with less fanfare than 500-150. Published last December, it is the first

"functional profile" (FP, that's newly coined standards jargon for a standard of standards). In time, there will be a formal, trilateral arrangement of high-level standards bodies (see "ISO plans cure for incompatible versions of OSI standards: ISPs," DATA COMMUNICATIONS, August 1987, p. 68) to produce continental FPs. Though 500-150 has no formal status under ANSI or ISO, it has already been selected as the basis for conformance tests by the Corporation for Open Systems (COS), and Europe's Standards Promotion and Application Group (SPAG), and it is the basis for both the U. S. and U. K. Government OSI Profiles (GOSIP, see below). What makes 500-150 so important is that it cuts through the snarl of OSI functionality, selecting just a few options from OSI's bouquet. For example, it selects X.25 Transport Classes 0 and 4 (eliminating 1, 2, and 3), and it sets as the medium-access addressing specification 48-bit addressing (throwing out 16-bit addressing). As an entity, 500-150 must be "stable," which means that all future amendments must be compatible with V1. However, upgrades are planned annually, and the December 1988 agreement (which will include ODA) is currently being prepared. Whether NBS will participate in planned tricontinental functional forums with ETSI and the Asian and Oceanean Workshop on OSI is a question, however. The three members of the three profile-seeking organizations are being called "feeder forums," notes Roger Gibbons, who heads the European operations of Omnicom, a consulting firm that summarizes many of the ISO and CCITT standards. European members of the planned three-way alliance say that they are not satisfied that the NBS workshop can join their club. Their view is that the NBS workshop is not a government body, and the planned forums aren't supposed to be linked to governments. Plans call for a single international stan-

dard of these standards of standards, a so-called ISP, or International Standardization Profile to be consummated at one of JTC-1's subcommittees.

■ *The two GOSIPs.* Strictly speaking, a government specification for the equipment it purchases is not a standard; it is merely the requirements of a single large user. In the world of standards, however, the two GOSIPs—the U. S. and U. K. Government OSI Profiles—play a complex and powerful role. U. S. GOSIP was completed early this year and is slated for publication in the Federal Register in late August or September. When published, GOSIP becomes a FIPS, a Federal Information Processing Specification, binding on member-government bodies—just about every bureaucracy from the Agriculture Department through the Department of Transportation—in late 1990. But there are plenty of exceptions within GOSIP that allow TCP/IP networks to be grandfathered. The U. K. GOSIP differs from its American counterpart in supporting the connection-oriented mode of transmission (the United States supports the connectionless). U. K. GOSIP also encourages users to delve into products that work with OSI's security architecture, ISO 7498-2, which was finalized early this year but is not a full standard.

MAP/TOP and other factory networks

■ *Manufacturing Automation Protocol Version 3.0/Technical and Office Protocols Version 3.0.* Counted as a completed specification from its demonstration at the Enterprise Networking Event in Baltimore in June, MAP/TOP 3.0 could also be dated from the time of its publication, which was expected in August. MAP 3.0 includes a revised presentation layer and adds the Manufacturing Message Specification (see below) to the application layer. On that level, too, is FTAM, and X.400. There have been some refinements to the "Mini Map" (MAP Carrier Band) specifications. FTAM and X.400 were also added to TOP 3.0, as was the Office Document Interchange Format of ODA (see above), and the Product Definition Interchange Format, a high-level graphics application that can pass details of the materials used. Both MAP and TOP added an early version of ISO 9595, a standard network management specification.

■ *Broadband frequencies and quality control. MAP/TOP Broadband Specification.* Broadband LANs are attractive to some users because they allow several types of communications to occur simultaneously, each transmission passing another without interfering because each is on a different frequency. But a survey conducted by the MAP/TOP Media Committee prior to writing this document showed that vendors often transmit on the same frequen-

cies. The result: chaos. The MAP/TOP Broadband Specification doesn't tell vendors which frequencies to use. But it does make strong recommendations about spacing frequencies, particularly a method of allotting signals sent from, and returning to, the LAN head end. Most useful, it also tells users how to retune their networks to avoid frequency traffic jams. The document's main purpose is sweeping: "to specify the minimum acceptable requirements for the design, installation, acceptance, service, and support of a broadband coaxial system implementation." It tackles the quality problem head-on. For example: "The path loss design tolerance attributable to specified characteristics of cable systems components shall be ±3 dB . . . The path loss acceptance tolerance shall be ±2 dB greater than the design tolerance. . . . The acceptance path loss tolerance of ±5 dB shall be achieved at the time of cable system acceptance."

Factory automation and CAD/CAM

■ *A syntax for the factory. ISO/DIS 9506: Manufacturing Message Specification, Parts 1 and 2; ISO/TC 184/SC 5/ WG 2 Draft Technical Report: Introduction to the Manufacturing Message Specification. Application*-layer software for monitoring and controlling factory devices. Outlines a standard structured language of factory automation, MMS (Manufacturing Message Specification), to be conveyed over a standard LAN. References more specific manufacturing instruction sets prepared by EIA, NEMA (National Electrical Manufacturers Association), and RIA (Robotic Industries Association). Sets criteria for subsidiary instruction sets, known as companion standards. The volume of standards work completed in this area and its substantial acceptance by vying manufacturers sets the stage for significant increases in factory automation installations in the near future. Status: Out of ISO committee and submitted as draft; final ISO approval was scheduled by late August; also expected to be EIA and ANSI standard.

■ *A language for coordinate measuring. Dimensional Measuring Interface Specification V.2.* There are users of factory automation who think the DMIS standard will do for coordinate measuring devices—factory-floor gear that checks the fit of parts, the size and shape of gears, and so forth—what standard factory languages for cutting tools did in the late 1960s and into the '70s—a new spurt of factory automation. Unlike MMS, which is a grammar to convey messages, DMIS is the actual language and a tool for writing that language. It is intended to be the interface between a proprietary language that the measuring device may speak and some other language spoken by a computer that is running a CAD/CAM program. As such, it is a protocol converter, but it can also be the language spoken by both the shop-floor device and the processor, and some vendors are starting to make straight DMIS products. Computer-Aided Manufacturing International Inc. (CAM-I), an Arlington, Tex., consortium of factory automation vendors, completed work on the standard last year and passed it on for ANSI accreditation in April. ■

Daniel R. Seligman, Codex Corp., Mansfield, Mass.

Mastering SS7 takes a special vocabulary

Forget the computer jargon, SS7 has its own terminology. Concepts familiar in a computer communications environment are often disguised in the SS7 lexicon.

For someone with a computer background, one of the most confusing aspects of Signaling System 7 (SS7) is its terminology. And concepts that are familiar to someone with a computer communications background are often disguised in the SS7 lexicon by unfamiliar names. Here's a handy translation.

In SS7, a network node is referred to as a *signaling point.* There are three types of signaling points. A *service control point* (SCP) supports applications that provide services such as 800 number service. A *service switching point* (SSP) is the point of origin of a request for services. And a *signaling transfer point* (STP) is, for all intents and purposes, a packet switch, capable of accepting a packet on an incoming channel and transmitting it on the appropriate outgoing channel.

The SS7 term most closely associated with a communications line is a *signaling link.* Strictly speaking, *signaling data link* refers to the physical properties of the communications line, while signaling link is reserved for a communications line capable of reliable message exchange between two adjacent signaling points. In general, multiple signaling links connect the same two signaling points for performance and reliability purposes. These multiple signaling links are referred to as a *link set* and correspond roughly to an SNA transmission group.

Similarly, a sequence of signaling points between the origin and destination of a message is referred to as a *signaling route,* and the collection of all routes between the origin and destination, a *signaling route set.*

Protocol Levels

SS7 consists of four layers, or levels, somewhat analogous to the Open Systems Interconnection (OSI) model layers as shown in the table. However, the terminology and the functions of the levels are not strictly in accord with the OSI model. Moreover, the venerable architectural rules that underpin the OSI model are often broken.

Signaling data link functions (Level 1) are concerned with providing a bidirectional communications path between two adjacent signaling points. This level corresponds directly to the OSI physical layer.

Signaling link functions (Level 2) support reliable delivery of messages between two adjacent signaling points and correspond rather closely to the OSI data link layer. Indeed, the signaling link protocol is quite similar to high-level data link control or synchronous data link control protocols. The signaling link functions are often called, collectively, the *link control function.*

Signaling network functions (Level 3) enable data messages and control information concerning outages and congestion to be exchanged between nonadjacent signaling points, corresponding more or less to the OSI network layer. Level 3 is also called the *common transfer function.*

The *signaling connection control part* (Level 4) supports several categories of connectionless and connection-oriented service as well as the addressing of individual applications on a signaling point. Such features are commonly associated with the OSI transport and higher layers.

The lowest three layers of SS7 are collectively called the *message transfer part* (MTP), a carryover from a time when these layers were thought to be sufficient to deliver user data between two remote signaling points. The MTP provides a datagram service between two signaling points.

The signaling connection control part (SCCP) was developed only as it became apparent that SS7 would have to support more than signaling and needed more explicit addressing and more sophisticated services between remote signaling points. The MTP and the SCCP are collectively referred to as the *network services part.*

The choice of SCCP as a name is unfortunate, since

SCCP is invariably confused with SSCP, even though the SNA System Services Control Point bears very little resemblance in function to the SS7 concept.

While SS7 does show the OSI influence, SS7 is characterized by a less than strict adherence to OSI principles. The signaling data link and signaling link functions correspond directly to the OSI physical link and data link layers. But the one-to-one correspondence ends at the link layer.

The signaling network functions are divided into two major categories: *signaling message handling* and the *signaling network management.* The signaling message handling is concerned with routing messages to their appropriate destinations—either to local applications or remote signaling points. It is consistent with the network layer functions of the OSI model. However, the signaling network management manifests some differences, both in terminology and in function, from what experience with computer communications would suggest.

In computer communications, network management is usually a feature that enables a user or an application program to monitor, control, and troubleshoot a network. But in SS7 parlance, the term signaling network management is used to describe how a signaling network functions. It refers to the signaling network's ability to: divert traffic from one signaling link to an alternative *(signaling traffic management);* manage the state of an individual signaling link *(signaling link management);* and exchange control messages to permit the network to adapt to outages and congestion *(signaling route management).*

Signaling link management is concerned with such link-oriented activities as activation, deactivation, and restoration of signaling links. In a conventional computer

SS7 architecture and the Open Systems Interconnection model

ORIGINAL SIGNALING SYSTEM 7 LEVELS	OPEN SYSTEMS INTERCONNECTION LAYERS	REVISED SIGNALING SYSTEM 7 LEVELS
USER AND APPLICATION SERVICE PARTS	APPLICATION	USER AND APPLICATION SERVICE PARTS
	PRESENTATION	
	SESSION	
	TRANSPORT	SIGNALING CONNECTION CONTROL PART
SIGNALING CONNECTION CONTROL PART	NETWORK	SIGNALING NETWORK
SIGNALING NETWORK		
SIGNALING LINK	DATA LINK	SIGNALING LINK
SIGNALING DATA LINK	PHYSICAL	SIGNALING DATA LINK

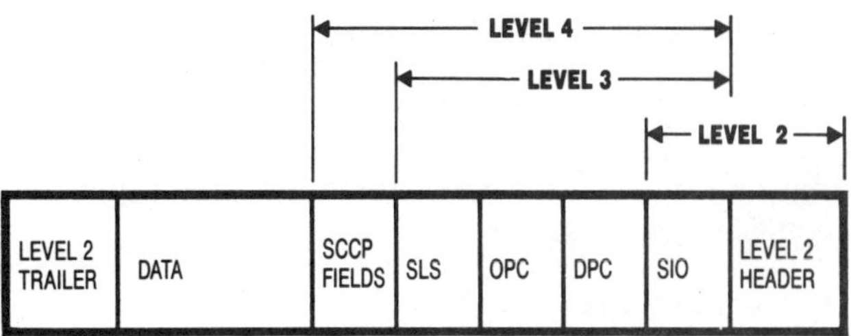

1. Message signal unit. *Certain fields in an SS7 packet are shared among different levels. This adds efficiency but makes it impossible to replace one protocol with another.*

DPC = DESTINATION POINT CODE
OPC = ORIGINATING POINT CODE
SCCP = SIGNALING CONNECTION CONTROL PART
SIO = SERVICE INFORMATION OCTET
SLS = SIGNALING LINK SELECTION

context, these features are more likely to be associated with the data link layer than the network layer.

The SCCP is analogous to the upper half of OSI's network layer, while the signaling network functions comprise the lower half. SCCP is intended to support basic and sequenced connectionless services and three classes of connection-oriented services: basic, flow control, and error recovery with flow control. All grades of service are built upon the datagram service provided by the signaling network level. In one sense, such services seem more characteristic of OSI transport than the network layer.

Another unique feature of SS7 concerns its treatment of the fields in the message headers associated with the communications protocols at the various layers. If SS7 were handling communications in a computer communications context, its use of the fields would be suspect because fields are shared among different protocol levels. This violates the rigid separation characteristic of most computer communications protocols.

Figure 1 shows an example of an SS7 data packet or *message signal unit.* The fields corresponding to the various protocol levels are indicated.

The *service information octet* (SIO) identifies the type of message, its priority level (for congestion control), whether the SS7 network is domestic or international, and a limited address for the MTP user concerned with the message. The very presence of the field is necessary for the signaling link functions to distinguish the message signal unit from other types of signal units; the congestion and message type information is used by the signaling network functions; and the address is needed by SCCP or any other user of the MTP. Thus, a single field is used by three layers.

Routing is handled by the *routing label.* The routing label is made up of the destination address, or the *destination point code,* the source address, called the *originating point code*, and the *signaling link selection* field. The signaling link selection field is a bit configuration that permits load sharing among redundant signaling links. Both the SCCP and signaling network functions utilize the routing label. This is an example of three fields used by two different layers.

Common access to a single field makes it impossible to replace one level with a corresponding level without perturbing other levels. For example, DEC's replacement of its wide area network data link protocol with a protocol more suitable for an Ethernet would be impossible in SS7 without affecting other layers. The rigid structure of SS7 reflects its origins as a self-contained signaling architecture, which was developed prior to general acceptance of OSI layering and OSI principles.

Reliability issues

SS7 is characterized by a pronounced emphasis on reliability. In a computer communications environment, inaccessibility of services or inordinately long response times are occasionally acceptable. In a telephone service environment, on the other hand, major losses in revenue can result from even a few minutes of downtime. As a result, SS7 has highly developed reliability features.

Signaling links between adjacent nodes are generally deployed in groups of as many as eight. SCPs are laid out as mated pairs; identical service nodes are used in different geographic locations. STPs are also deployed in pairs. Numerous alternative routes typically connect SCPs with remote SSPs. The signaling network functions are designed to handle these redundancies. In addition, an elaborate exchange of SCCP messages between an SCP and its mate is required before an application can be taken out of service.

SS7 adapts to degradations and failures by propagating messages designating intermediate signaling points as *transfer-allowed, transfer-prohibited,* or *transfer-restricted* with respect to a given destination. The allowed and prohibited states indicate whether the signaling point is capable of routing traffic to the destination or whether an alternative route must be sought. This type of behavior is rather typical of computer communications environments. The restricted state, however, represents a refinement of this concept and indicates that the signaling point in question is still capable of routing traffic to the destination but the route is in some fashion degraded and that an alternative route should be used if possible. A restricted or prohibited signaling point is tested periodically for changes by an inquiry and response procedure called a *signaling-route-set test.*

SS7 supports a relatively advanced scheme for adaptation to congestion situations, as depicted in Figure 2. Each message is assigned a priority level. Congestion status is determined by the number of occupied transmit buffers associated with an outgoing signaling link. Three congestion statuses are defined for each signaling link, each characterized by three thresholds: *congestion onset, congestion abatement,* and *congestion discard.* Congestion abatement and congestion discard thresholds for a given congestion status are set respectively below and above the corresponding congestion onset threshold.

At congestion onset, warning messages are sent to appropriate signaling points. If the congestion situation does not improve, the number of occupied transmit buffers increases. When the congestion discard threshold is crossed, messages with priorities less than the congestion status are discarded. If the congestion situation improves, the number of occupied transmit buffers decreases, the congestion abatement threshold is crossed, and the congestion status is dropped to the next lower level. The congestion status of a congested signaling route set is periodically tested via an inquiry and response procedure similar to the signaling-route-set test called a *signaling-route-set-congestion test.*

---

2. Signaling link congestion. SS7 *supports a sophisticated scheme for congestion management. For each signaling link, three congestion statuses are defined.*

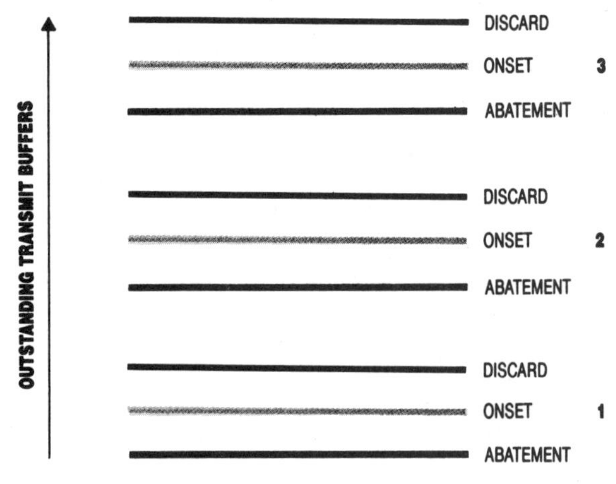

This scheme is far more complex than congestion control procedures in the more common network architectures. Contrast this scheme with, say, DECnet Phase IV where preference is given to messages routed through a node over messages originating at the node. In DECnet Phase IV, outgoing messages are simply discarded when predetermined buffer thresholds are reached. No messages are sent to neighboring nodes to indicate a congested situation.

SS7 remains uncomfortably poised between its telecommunications antecedents and its computer communications future. To the users in the computer world who will inherit it, SS7 presents the challenge of a different worldview and an emphasis on different capabilities than the more conventional computer network architectures. The first step toward mastering it is to understand SS7 terminology. ∎

Daniel R. Seligman is a consulting engineer at Codex Corp. Until recently, he was a senior consultant at Technology Concepts Inc., Sudbury, Mass. He has authored several papers on computer network analysis and design and lectured on various data communications topics. Seligman received his Ph.D. in physics from Yale University in 1976.

Paul R. Strauss, special to DATA COMMUNICATIONS

An update on U.S. services and standards

With 60,000 U. S. ISDN lines in place, users seek to link 'pseudo' ISDN products while standards makers ponder profiles.

Where does ISDN stand eight months before the start of the 1990s? As might be expected from such a complex and vast undertaking, the Integrated Services Digital Network has had both encouraging factors and troubling obstacles.

Some would list as good news that 60,000-odd ISDN circuits have been sold in the United States. (AT&T claims that more than 200,000 ISDN line cards have been sold to the local operating companies, but it does not know how many are really in service.) In the main, these were provided as part of the more than 50 well-publicized ISDN trials. In Canada, about 50 lines are involved in external trials.

Virtually all the U. S. regional Bell operating companies (RBOCs) now sell ISDN on a special-construction basis. Illinois Bell has tariffed a basic-rate service for a price of about 1.3 times the cost of a similar analog centrex service, says James Devine, director of ISDN marketing for Ameritech Services. He refused to disclose the number of ISDN users under the tariff, but says Illinois Bell expects 16,000 ISDN lines by June, when AT&T Bell Laboratories (Napierville, Ill.) adds its 5,000 centrex lines to the ISDN count. AT&T won't reveal how many customers it has for its primary-rate interface (PRI) service.

But remember, in these frontier days of ISDN, much that has been labeled ISDN doesn't follow all the ISDN standards. AT&T's PRI isn't yet ISDN, since it cannot convey a 64-kbit/s clear-channel signal. On the basic-rate side, only several hundred of the 60,000 lines are, strictly speaking, ISDN-conformant.

So much for the bad news. The good is that ISDN standards have moved rapidly in the last two years and are virtually completed, with two exceptions: There is as yet no compatibility in Q.931 signaling, and the specifics of the Q.932 special services standard remain to be worked out. Equally important, there is a wellspring of user interest—the largest and most active of which is the U. S. Government—pressing for standard implementations, or functional profiles, of the existing standards. A spate of recent ISDN demonstrations and a giant upcoming international ISDN display are likely to further accelerate interest. In addition, there are plans for intercarrier ISDN trials, which DATA COMMUNICATIONS has learned will take place early next year.

Impelled by all this attention, the rate of ISDN installation is expected to increase geometrically (see Table 1). Yet this should be put in perspective. The ISDN access lines in 1992 will make up considerably less than 1 percent of the total 145 million or so lines that access telephone company offices in the United States.

The need for ISDN clarity

"ISDN-compatible" has become a kind of touchstone. Vendors don't necessarily care what ISDN is; they just know that it sells gear. A short definition, therefore, is in order: ISDN is simply a standard way to replace local analog circuits with local digital circuits and to provide certain services. There are specifications for basic rate (two clear-channel 64-kbit/s circuits and a packet-switched signaling/data channel) and the primary rate (23 clear-channel 64-kbit/s circuits and a 64-kbit/s signaling channel).

The foregoing, of course, refers only to first-stage ISDN. Broadband ISDN (which the standards bodies have defined as circuits of 150 Mbit/s and up, but others interpret more loosely as any bandwidth above 1.544 Mbit/s) consists of an effort to create standard local and long-distance

| Table 1: Slow road to ISDN | | | | | | |
| (THOUSANDS OF U.S. ISDN ACCESS LINES IN SERVICE AT YEAR-END, EXCEPT AS NOTED) | | | | | | |
	1988	MAY 1989	1989	1990	1991	1992
BASIC RATE[1]	50	60	250	470	770	1,170
PRIMARY RATE[2]	0.5	N.E.	2	5	9	15

1. INCLUDES SOME 1B+D CIRCUITS AS BASIC RATE, NO FIGURES AVAILABLE AS TO HOW MANY.
2. INCLUDES AS PRIMARY RATE SOME NONCLEAR-CHANNEL 23B+D SERVICES, NO FIGURES AVAILABLE AS TO HOW MANY.

N.E.=NO ESTIMATE AVAILABLE

Source: Dataquest Inc.

transmissions in the hundreds of Mbit/s. There may or may not ever be widespread broadband ISDN. It depends on the future installation costs of fiber and on the appearance of ISDN applications for residential users such as high-definition television.

One reason the overall development of ISDN seems to lag: It just isn't an easy technology to grapple with. "There are levels of complexity in ISDN vastly more complex than OSI [the Open Systems Interconnection model]," says George Craft, manager of ISDN standardization at the National Institute of Science and Technology (NIST). "OSI usually deals with a simple bit stream between two workstations. This is a transmission between two points, as well as communications with the intelligence of the network itself."

2B1Q, or not 2B1Q?

There is, to be sure, another reason why ISDN hasn't moved as fast as some expected. Not all the standards are completed, and some that are finished require something close to leading-edge technology. An example of the former: Until the Q.931 standards are firm, all the ISDN switches are using proprietary call-processing signals. Thus, there is no guarantee that AT&T ISDN telephones or PCs set to work with AT&T switches will work with Northern Telecom, Siemens, or NEC central office switches. "It'll take at least two years for all the switches to be compatible in Q.931 messaging," says Tibor G. Szekeres, vice president of engineering at Teleos Communications. The Q.932 standard, still being worked on, explains how switches can do complicated functions together: things such as call forwarding and conferencing.

As always in networking, when processors fail to communicate, outsiders find ways to do the translation. At the International Communications Association (ICA) conference in Dallas, Teleos demonstrated that its already-introduced product, the IAP6000—normally used to create multiple basic-rate channels out of primary-rate channels—can work as a protocol converter to pass signaling between a DMS-100 and a 5ESS. The protocols converted here are from AT&T's versions of Q.931 to Northern's versions of Q.931—and vice versa. Without this conversion, the two do not pass calling-number identification, say sources at the ICA show, where interswitch links were tried out.

An example of where ISDN is near the leading edge of technology: the development of the 2B1Q line code, which is specified for North America (other countries have adopted different coding techniques). A line code is the electrical representation of digital signaling, the actual stuff carried across the wire that forms the "1s" and "0s" transmitted. To this pattern of pulses, 2B1Q adds adaptive digital signal processing—which can smooth out interference on a line—to create the capability of using ordinary twisted pair for distances up to 18,000 feet (5,486 meters).

The 2B1Q technique was picked at a T1D1.3 meeting on August 29, 1986. But not until early this year were the first 2B1Q chips, a two-chip set made by AT&T Technologies, put on public display at the IEEE International Solid State Circuits Conference in New York City and two months later put on sale. However, the switch vendors have not said when they will bring 2B1Q to their products. Until they do, each switch uses its company's own line code. AT&T's is called Alternate Mark Inversion (AMI).

To some potential users, such differences will be insignificant. In many cases PCs can plug into terminators for AMI or 2B1Q circuits with no visible difference. However, users getting both AMI and 2B1Q circuits would have to keep track of the difference because mixing up terminating units could prove to be embarrassing. And big users would have to maintain stockpiles of the various terminators.

Virtually all the important ISDN standards were wrapped up in the CCITT (International Telegraph and Telephone Consultative Committee) at its November plenary session in Melbourne, Australia. However, the standards makers have allowed enough national divergence between standards to put ISDN's envisioned world of universal, portable attachment in doubt. In Germany, for example, the electrical power for an ISDN line must be provided by the telephone company; in most other countries, ISDN gear must be powered by the user.

Other important standards are emerging rapidly. One such is the North American physical level, primary-rate ISDN standard, which was frozen at a T1E1.2 meeting in April and is set for committee vote next month. Unfortunately, where standards and products intersect, there is perennial confusion. For example, if T1E1.2 is not final, how can true ISDN-compatible PBXs be sold in North America?

The paradox arises from a standards ambiguity: It is possible to be compatible with the relevant CCITT documents without obeying the North American specifications.

However, the T1E1.2 specs are likely to be quite different from CCITT's in electrical characteristics, says William Buckley, T1E1.2 chairman.

To make ISDN gear and services work together, more than just standards are needed. Standards allow options, so NIST, the newly created North American ISDN Users Forum (which goes by the acronym NIU), and the Corporation for Open Systems (COS) are hard at work on "implementation" agreements. These are, in effect, standards of standards or functional profiles of existing ISDN standards (see Table 2). Products that comply with these profiles will be shown as "red line" ISDN implementations at NIU's planned ISDN showcase in 1991, says the NIU's user workshop chairman, James Kendricks.

The cachet of fielding a red-line product at ISDN's biggest expo may encourage some vendors to eschew proprietary implementations. But the big incentive for conversion from proprietary implementations of the standards to the envisioned standards of standards lies in potential sales.

Here Uncle Sam is likely to play a big role. NIST sources say that the latest version of GOSIP, the Government OSI Profile, virtually mandates ISDN in any potential area in which it can be used. The General Services Administration's top administrator for the multibillion-dollar FTS-2000 project, Deputy Commissioner Michael L. Corrigan, says that he has been strongly pushing ISDN.

However, he is concerned about interoperability. "You can buy ISDN, or a pseudo-ISDN, or what some say is ISDN, and it'll work all right—so long as you buy all the same vendor's switches or CPE [customer premises equipment]. But when you want a multivendor world, then it gets more difficult."

To make sure that ISDN products really obey the standards, conformance testing is needed. AT&T and Bellcore are already at work on ISDN testing (see "Testing to see if ISDN products make the grade," DATA COMMUNICATIONS, December 1987, p. 55.).

The costs of conforming

AT&T is making money by doing testing. "We charge $15,000 to start testing and $3,000 per day of testing," says Mike Bearov, a venture manager in the Development Relations Group, who is in charge of AT&T's primary-rate testing program. Such tests usually take about 10 working

Table 2: Unresolved ISDN standards issues

QUESTIONS FACING THE NORTH AMERICAN ISDN USERS FORUM:	AT THE ISDN USER INTERFACE	AT THE ISDN CENTRAL OFFICE SWITCH
USE THE CCITT'S RED BOOK (1984) OR BLUE BOOK (1988) SPECIFICATIONS?	X	X
USE CCITT SPECIFICATIONS PURELY, OR ENDORSE ANSI'S? (THERE ARE SIGNIFICANT INCOMPATIBLE DIFFERENCES)	X	X
SHOULD PACKET CONNECTIONS USE X.25 OR Q.931 SPECIFICATION OVER D CHANNEL?	X	
SHOULD PACKET COMMUNICATIONS VIA ISDN BE CONNECTION-ORIENTED OR CONNECTIONLESS, OR BOTH?	X	
FOR CIRCUIT-SWITCHED DATA, USE V.110 OR V.120 RATE ADAPTION?	X	
ARE U.S. STANDARDS NEEDED FOR AN 'R' INTERFACE (ISDN-TO-EXISTING DATA EQUIPMENT)?	X	
AT PHYSICAL LAYER, ARE THERE TOO MANY OPTIONS FOR THE PROVISION OF ELECTRICAL POWER?	X	
AT WHAT MINIMUM DATA RATE SHOULD SWITCHES SUPPORT PACKET DATA—19.2 KBIT/S, 64 KBIT/S, HIGHER?		X
HOW TO MERGE, OR WHETHER TO MERGE, PROPRIETARY IMPLEMENTATIONS OF Q.931 SIGNALING?		X
WHETHER TO PASS DIALING INFORMATION NUMBER BY NUMBER OR IN BLOCK FORM (CCITT ALLOWS BOTH), OR TOGGLE BETWEEN FORMATS?		X
EMBRACE AT&T'S OR BELLCORE'S SPECIFICATIONS FOR ISDN MANAGEMENT, OR WAIT FOR COMPLETED OSI STANDARD?		X
HOW TO USE U-INTERFACE CONTROL CHANNEL (16-KBIT/S CHANNEL DIFFERENCE BETWEEN 144-KBIT/S BASIC RATE AND 160-KBIT/S SIGNALING RATE).		X

days. For the basic rate, AT&T's charges somewhat less: $6,000 for each terminal or device tested and $5,000 for the first day of tests.

Since Bearov and McDonald stress that their tests are for conformance to "AT&T's ISDN specification," another body may be needed to test non-AT&T ISDN conformance. Indeed, AT&T's and other vendors' efforts to establish their ISDN specs as de facto standards have not been greeted with delight in standards bodies, say NIST sources who asked not to be identified for fear of political repercussions.

Two organizations are preparing for ISDN conformance testing. NIST will write ISDN test suites based on standards that have been stripped of their options by NIU, and the Corporation for Open Systems will then launch an ISDN testing service, says COS head of ISDN conformance testing Jayant G. Gadre, whose official title is manager of advanced studies.

Big Four

What is the status of ISDN from a service-availability standpoint? Better than expected, say many observers. For example, this month's ICA conference in Dallas is to demonstrate ISDN call interconnection of four central office switches: an AT&T 5ESS (running 5E4.2 software), a Northern Telecom DMS-100, a Siemens EWSD, and a NEC NEAX 61E.

There are as yet no interLATA ISDN services in the United States. But the good news is that US Sprint's and MCI Communications's Signaling System No. 7 networks are now in operation (Sprint's late last year and MCI's announced in March), though neither carrier has announced an ISDN service. AT&T has given no expected completion date for its ISDN signaling network.

The first U. S. trials of connections between local ISDNs and long-distance carriers are scheduled for the first quarter of 1990, as are the first trials of connections between AT&T and Northern Telecom central office switches, says Ken Goodgold, area manager for advanced technology of Southwestern Bell, where some of the trials will take place.

Some customer premises gear that is said to be ISDN is beginning to emerge. Of course, there was gear that was said to be ISDN in 1986. Much of that comprised proprietary versions of ISDN that have by now disappeared.

Still, gear relevant to ISDN is starting to emerge more rapidly. For example, at the recent shows, data products were demonstrated by IBM, Advanced Micro Devices, Codex, General DataComm, Harris Corp., Hayes Microcomputer, Gandalf, ICL, Lachman Associates, Microcom, Progressive Computing, and Telrad—to give a sampling.

Much ISDN gear consists of testers for determining whether other gear is ISDN-compatible. Several products would use ISDN B channels to link LAN remote bridges or routers. Naturally, there are B-channel PC boards. And rearing their heads again are IVDTs (integrated voice-data terminals)—similar to the PC clones with telephones attached that flopped a few years ago. (But they used four wires. ISDN needs only a single twisted pair.)

Some of the more interesting ways of using ISDN are coming from the NIU, where the User Workshop has been proposing applications after which vendors field teams to try to meet the need. Work is under way on using ISDN to bridge Manufacturing Automation Protocol networks and/or Technical and Office Protocols networks, on a way to use the same telephone numbers for incoming voice and data calls but to route each to either a voice or data internal processing unit by use of the incoming call's transmitted number (thus saving on a telephone line). A similar arrangement is being worked on to make distinctions between incoming synchronous and asynchronous transmissions.

The NIU projects are seeking future products and services, the results of which may not be seen for years. But users already have had a taste of ISDN, mainly in trials. Based on such experience, a sampling of ISDN users gave generally favorable results. But in some cases, users reported odd disparities—such as ISDN terminals that passed data down the B channel at a top speed of 19.2 kbit/s.

There are those who have tried ISDN out, compared it to LANs, and found ISDN wanting. They consider its 64 kbit/s or even 144 kbit/s of bandwidth potentially limiting. "It's not as good as a LAN, not in terms of bandwidth, anyway. But, in many applications, it's very useful," says Franklin Fung, project leader for ISDN at Chevron Information Technology Corp. "We are discussing with the terminal adapter makers the upgrade of 19.2-kbit/s terminals to full 64 kbit/s."

"We have our own X.25 network, and we want to get messages from our teller machines and automatic teller machines over the D channel onto that network," says Earl C. Voght, manager of the telecommunications service department of US Bank of Oregon. (Such a hookup is intriguing since it could be considered a private ISDN.)

And there are those who say that ISDN software is still primitive. "ISDN, so far, is a switch and not a total solution," says Lt. Col. Anthony T. Cira, program director for the SC4 Project (Systems for Command, Control, Communications, and Computers) at Mather Air Force Base, Sacramento, Calif. (The Mather project is assessing ISDN's utility for the Air Force.) However, he adds: "Though ISDN has not been developed as fast as we had expected, perhaps our expectations were too high. Now we have to roll up our sleeves and develop it."

Passions aroused

The ISDN idea arouses passions. Apple Computer's guru on the subject, David Gilbert, a software engineering manager in the Communications Tools Group, extolls ISDN as a potential universal information utility. Others have doubts that ISDN will even work as expected. "Have ISDN switches been tried out for high data usage?" asks Harold W. Lockhart Jr., a senior consultant with Technology Concepts Inc., a Sudbury, Mass., consulting firm. IBM's top ISDN expert, Toby Terrill, manager of the ISDN systems management office, voices similar concern about the data rates ISDN switches can deliver: "There must be work on the true performance we can expect from existing and future systems." But, by and large, the effort spent on ISDN seems to have been worthwhile. ■

Lee Mantelman, DATA COMMUNICATIONS INTERNATIONAL

Taking your SNA network abroad

Customs is not the problem when crossing borders with your SNA data. It's how to interconnect and administer a multinational network.

As the business world continues to compress into a single global economy, the effect on data networks—many multinational firms are finding—is just the opposite. To exploit the changing international social and economic landscape, businesses are expanding across national boundaries, oceans, and continents with unprecedented fervor. And it is corporate communications management that is tasked with linking these newly established, or newly acquired, foreign manufacturing and marketing activities into a seamless global network.

Many of these networks are built on IBM mainframes held together with SNA. According to IBM figures, by the end of 1988, users around the world were using SNA to support nearly 40,000 System/370 hosts—more than half of which are outside the United States.

But many pitfalls, as well as potential benefits, await networks that cross familiar national borders. The various PTTs can seem very strange indeed. So network managers should pack the following guidebook of suggestions, offered by users, consultants, and IBM, when planning to "go abroad" with their SNA networks (or with any private networks, for that matter).

Guided tour

■ *Consider granting national autonomy.* On one hand, corporations want to control their network resources. On the other, organizations in different countries often seek some measure of autonomy. Clearly, a compromise is needed.

Like other large IBM users, IBM itself faced a number of technical and managerial problems in building a network that now has more than 3,000 attached mainframes around the world.

"We decided that the best approach was a confederation of networks," says Ray Reardon, head of international networks integration with IBM Europe. Each country manages its own network, with gateways to international networks and applications.

"The trick is, how do you accept sufficient rules to make it all work without cutting across national autonomy?" asks Reardon. One way is for network overseers to set up rules but leave local issues to national data centers. Those rules might include naming conventions, service-level agreements, and when each country will be up and running.

■ *Break out the service center.* Those people in a user organization who fund an international service may not be the ones who benefit from it. To avoid budget battles, Reardon suggests that users establish a service subsidiary to provide and operate international telecommunications.

More simply, this role can be made the mission of one of the country organizations. Of course, users can also opt to turn to a value-added network (VAN) or international managed data network services (MDNS) provider.

"I'm pretty lucky; I've got a critical mass that's enabled me to put together a pretty cohesive international network," says Reardon. "Not all companies have that, which is why there's a VAN/MDNS business."

■ *Explore the role of SNI.* "The main thing about international SNA networking is the number of terminals you're trying to support," says John Wishney, London-based chief executive of communications business development with Electronic Data Systems, another firm with a large multinational SNA network. "As you expand geographically, you tend to add more terminals, and when you get 30,000 or more, you run into severe technical problems."

Time zones can also make life difficult. In a network with Pacific, European, and U.S. hosts, downtime for repair and maintenance is limited. "You'd be busy trying to get the network down and back up again by the time people come

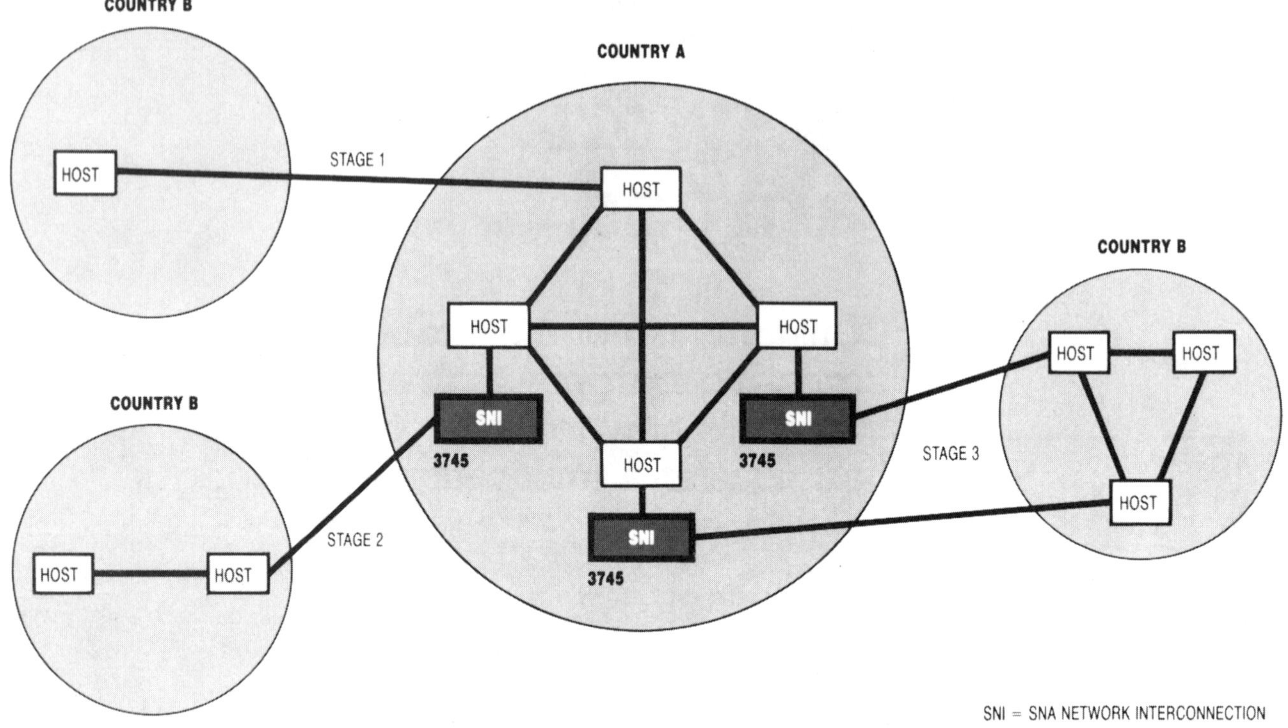

1. Three-step process. *No SNI is needed when a remote country only has a single host, but it is useful when there are two or more. Multiple SNI links provide redundancy. Mapping from the original host in the remote country can be translated directly into the SNI tables. In general, the sooner the user deploys SNI, the better.*

to work in Japan," says Wishney.

The problem here lies in the SNA system generation (sysgen) tables, which have to be coordinated, synchronized, and loaded throughout an SNA network for any change (such as moving a terminal). "IBM would say, 'You don't have to take the whole network down, just sysgen more devices than are actually active. Then, when new ones come in, activate a spare,' " says Wishney. "But it burns resources to carry all those extra definitions."

One IBM tool can make coping with complex international networks a lot easier: SNA Network Interconnection. SNI, an off-the-shelf software package for the 3745 communications controller, segments a large SNA network into more manageable subnetworks.

SNI functions by separating the address space of one SNI subnetwork from that of another. This requires devices within the subnetworks to be given aliases if they are to be addressed across the SNI gateway.

Originally developed by IBM for its Information Network, "SNI is probably one of the most stable products IBM has ever produced, in that it worked on day one," says Richard Lavender, senior consultant with Logica Financial Systems Ltd., London.

With an SNI gateway in each country, users can localize network administration. "Even with SNI, problems are still there, but you can deal with them on a country-by-country basis rather than struggling with the whole thing," says Wishney.

One disadvantage of SNI might be performance, according to David Welch, senior consultant with BIS Applied Systems in Birmingham, England. "There are limits to the amount of traffic you can handle on an SNI. If traffic between the networks grows, it can cause response times to increase, especially for interactive transmissions," he says.

■ *Plan an orderly growth.* Using SNI also adds a degree of complexity to the administrative task. While two national networks can use the SNI, someone has to administer it and make sure network definitions and route mapping are done and maintained properly.

Welch advises growing the SNI configuration in three stages (see Fig. 1). Each stage calls for local administration (to obtain and manage lines, modems, and multiplexers) and user support (for the local community).

Stage 1—for single-processor sites in foreign countries: Treat the remote hosts as simple extensions to the home network by bringing them into that network's addressing regime. Make sure all procedures used to install and maintain operating software are well documented at the central site and implemented as a management responsibility at the remote sites.

Stage 2—where there is more than one processor in a foreign country: Keep the original network addresses and addressing scheme, but implement them on an SNI and use them as aliases for the new remote network being built. Give the SNI the same address as the original processor.

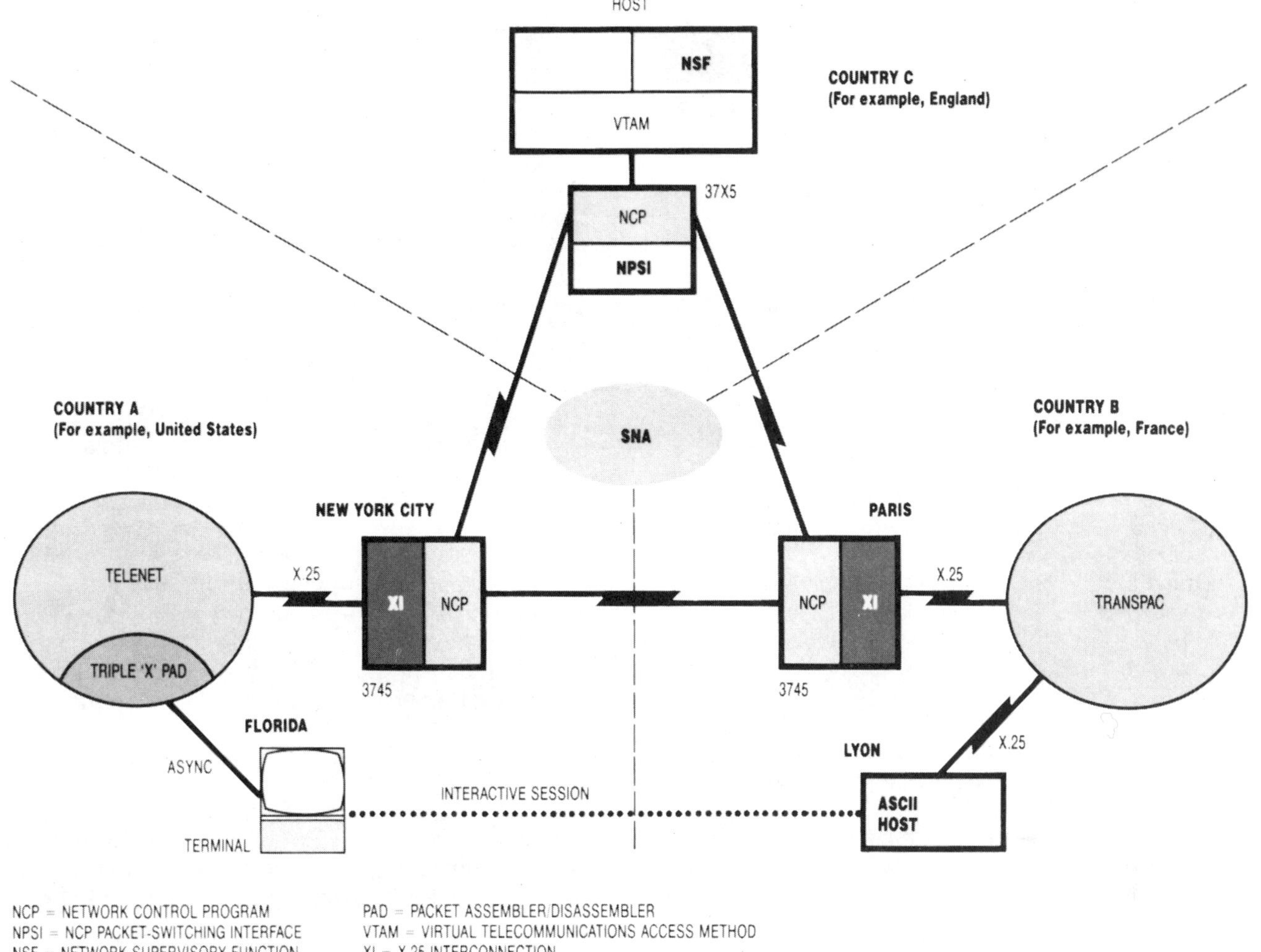

Don't hire armies of software people in each country, just enough for administration and user support.

Stage 3—when the remote network grows and exchanges more traffic with the home network: Install additional SNIs to ensure performance and reliability.

■ *Rationalize software distribution.* With five or more satellite countries, Welch suggests, the network manager might consider providing each remote site with a complete "envelope" of software, including operating system, database management, communications—and possibly even applications—based on the local configuration and requirements. To update a site, then, simply modify a central copy of the envelope and send it out.

This approach is efficient: It's much less effort to generate an envelope and install it in a number of locations than to have each site do its own. Also, the central controlling site then knows what software all the others are using. Standardizing the hardware platform used in the various countries can improve efficiency even more, though this may be politically difficult.

However, Lavender notes, an envelope of compiled code could be a lot of data to transfer over an SNA network, perhaps several Mbytes per node. Rather than generating these load modules at the central site, it might be better to transmit the SNA network definition statements, just a few kbytes, and have the code generated locally. Though this requires the remote-site staff to have some skill, this approach could work for companies with centralized network decision-making.

■ *Let your network do double duty.* Users may not be aware of the potential to send non-SNA data (such as asynchronous ASCII files) over international SNA backbone networks via X.25. This technique, suggested by Logica's Lavender, can save users money and avoid the well-known performance problems of international public packet-switching networks.

The secret ingredient is XI, IBM's X.25 Interconnection product (Fig. 2). XI, which translates information carried in

X.25 packets into an SNA-compatible format, lets users link packet networks using their own SNA backbone as an international transport medium for non-SNA data. In this way, a terminal user only has to pay for a local call to access a host in another country.

Figure 2 shows XI software running on IBM 3745 communications controllers in two countries that are to be connected. Each 3745 is linked either to its local public X.25 network, or directly to an X.25 terminal or packet assembler/disassembler.

This setup also requires the Network Supervisory Function, a NetView subtask, in one of the network hosts to manage the XI nodes and the NCP Packet-Switching Interface that is loaded in that host's 37X5 communications controller.

"Although all the people I know who are doing this are using it within their own companies," says Lavender, "you could almost resell this bandwidth to third parties and no one would be the wiser."

Since the traffic crosses international boundaries, the PTTs could view this as a value-added service if it connected people in different organizations. But, Lavender says, "I'm sure the PTTs don't have a hold of this, because they can't get a hold of it."

■ *Get your staff in sync.* According to Wishney, several staffing issues arise from the vagaries of Europe's telecommunications—and its distance from IBM's U.S. heartland. SNA programmers outside the United States have to accept the fact that they don't have access to the same telecommunications facilities, quality, or availability as their American counterparts.

Generally, whenever something goes wrong in the physical SNA network, it has an impact on the logical SNA network—the realm of IBM's Virtual Telecommunications Access Method (VTAM) and Network Control Program. For this reason, it's important that telecommunications staffers and SNA programmers coordinate closely. "Most human-error problems will come from a breakdown in communications between those two groups," Wishney says.

Another problem is that software release levels may be slightly behind those in the States. IBM-provided patches for software may not always be available. "The problem may be new for Europe but already fixed in the U.S., so it may take longer to find the fix," says Wishney.

■ *Favor multinational vendors.* IBM makes sure that all its offered equipment (communications controllers, modems, multiplexers) is approved in each country in which it is sold. But buying pure Blue is not always possible.

"I can't afford to use IBM everywhere, even if I wanted to," says one user who requested anonymity. "So I stick with larger companies with an international presence, such as Codex, Racal, and Timeplex. We stay with IBM in front-end processors, but NCR Comten should be okay." He adds that smaller, entrepreneurial suppliers, while

adequate in one country, might not offer international support. "You might not be able to buy it in another country, and I don't want to mix products in the network." Other users, however, are more loyal to Big Blue.

"IBM will hold people's hands if that's what's needed," says Roger Cornish, European communications manager with Texas Instruments Ltd. in Bedford, England. "They're always very willing to guide their customers."

But users should not be lulled into an international sense of security. "What's remarkable is the variability of support that people get from IBM in various countries," says Ray Northcott, the London director of networking practice with Butler Cox and Partners Ltd.

"I can think of at least one case within the last three years where a customer was poorly served by IBM in one country in Europe but well served in the U.K.," Northcott says, "and requests to IBM U.K. didn't appear to do much in the other country." The reason for this variation, he explains, may be that the user was bigger in England than in the other country.

■ *Bring in the brass.* Users working in, say, Timbuktu want the same service from IBM that they get in London. And IBM, just like many other vendors, may claim to provide a uniform level of service. "You'll always get reassurance. Every supplier can do everything everywhere," says Northcott, "but words are cheap. You have to get senior management involved."

One user company took an approach that others could also benefit from. It brought in top IBM people to meet with its senior management, who said, "Here's what we want to do, we have these problems, and we want to know what you're going to do about them." The users didn't focus on such technical details as what NetView could do for them today and tomorrow but rather emphasized the commercial and management issues.

"The old adage of no one getting fired for buying IBM has a lot of weight and is a substantial credit to IBM," says Northcott.

■ *Be patient with IBM's central support.* Outside the United States, Northcott says, "IBM seems like a company of national units rather than an international company. So if you put up an SNA network across Europe, it's difficult to get a single point of support."

To address this concern, IBM set up the Global Networking Support Office, a supranational group based in La Gaude, France. GNSO, which has only been active for several months, has offices in France, the United States, Canada, and Japan. Its aim is to help large account teams understand and get answers to such issues as international network design, PTT tariffs, and service availability.

The centralized support group "comes out of user demand for pan-European networking in the 1992 era," says Patrick Abbott, network consultant with the GNSO. Northcott agrees. "For some time, IBM has been asked for

> # Users working in Timbuktu want the same service from IBM that they get in London.

and expected to provide this global support. Customers like ICI, Exxon, and Ford operate worldwide."

But it may be too soon to judge GNSO's effectiveness. "The good will and support have been spilling out of IBM verbally, but don't appear to have been established on the ground," says Northcott.

■ *Keep abreast of standards.* Though SNA has been a credible strategy for building international networks, it faces stiffening competition from standardized architectures such as the OSI model.

"Europe has always been very strongly for OSI. As governments start to dictate an OSI strategy, I think they're forcing the issue," says Texas Instruments' Cornish. Wishney adds: "Every man and his brother is now after you to implement standards, and SNA is not an international standard, X.25 is."

Private users now running IBM hosts and SNA networking, Wishney says, "should probably stay SNA when they go international, but I expect to make a different recommendation in about 12 months time" "I wouldn't disagree with that," says Cornish.

One advantage of OSI over SNA in international networks is that there could, in time, be a broader market of people around the world with OSI experience. Wishney says, "VTAM programmers are a fairly esoteric bunch of people. The industry is faced with a serious-enough skills shortage as it is. I can only expect an equal or more acute shortage of SNA people."

But IBM stresses that SNA and OSI are not conflicting approaches. "If you want to connect two SNA networks, use SNI. If you want to connect two dissimilar networks, use the appropriate OSI standard. That's what OSI is supposed to be," says IBM's Reardon.

Though all the users agree that OSI is on its way to becoming more of an international requirement, they bristle at any potential attempt governments might make to mandate its use. "If you're a private user, you should be able to do whatever you like," says Wishney. That includes sticking with a proprietary architecture like SNA, where innovations can be deployed much more quickly. "Remember, standards are a leveling-down process. You could standardize to a point where you start stifling things," he says.

IBM's international database

With all these suggestions firmly in hand, users may decide to plunge right into an international network design, or they may prefer to farm the job out to a consultant. In either case, the designer should take account of service differences between countries.

IBM's Centre d'Etudes et Recherches (CER), in La Gaude, has highlighted 10 such differences (see Table). The ones shown in the table are only examples and illustrations. IBM can, however, provide a specific country-by-country breakdown of each parameter.

"That source is a real database and a real asset, because lots of people would like to know what you can do in this domain," says Etienne P. Gorog, CER's telecommunications center director.

According to Gorog, the reason for discrepancies is that each PTT has been optimizing its services in its own country. Even if several PTTs are also offering international services, they are not necessarily compatible.

Some services provided within a country may not be available between countries. And international facilities that are available may differ in options provided by each country (as with X.25) or in the type of lines available for switching data (only digital lines in

International service variations

PARAMETER	EXAMPLE/EXPLANATION
AVAILABILITY — SPEED: — TYPE: — CONFIGURATION: — TECHNOLOGY:	2.048 MBIT/S IN U.K., 1.920 MBIT/S IN FRANCE ANALOG-FOR-DATA NOT AVAILABLE IN GERMANY DIFFERENT OPTIONS FOR SUCH SERVICES AS X.25 ISDN STATUS VARIES AROUND EUROPE
CONSTRAINTS ON USAGE	VOICE COMPRESSION NOT ALLOWED IN GERMANY BUT PERMITTED (WITH RESTRICTIONS) IN U.K.
CONSTRAINTS ON USER (SINGLE/ MULTIPLE)	BANDWIDTH RESALE FORBIDDEN IN MANY COUNTRIES; SWITCHED-TO-LEASED MAY BE FORBIDDEN (ITALY)
TARIFFS	NOT PUBLISHED FOR ALL AVAILABLE SERVICES; TARIFF MAY DIFFER IN COUNTRIES AT EITHER END OF AN INTERNATIONAL SERVICE
LOCAL AVAILABILITY AND DELAYS TO OBTAIN FACILITIES	PTT MAY PROVIDE INTERNATIONAL SERVICE ONLY FROM SPECIFIC NATIONAL LOCATIONS; MAY TAKE SOME TIME TO PROVIDE SERVICE IN AREA WHERE NOT PREVIOUSLY AVAILABLE
EQUIPMENT — APPROVED: — MANDATORY:	PTTs APPROVE NETWORK-ATTACHED EQUIPMENT SOME ALLOW ONLY PTT-PROVIDED EQUIPMENT
COMPATIBILITY OF EQUIPMENT	VERIFICATION TESTS NEEDED TO CHECK SAME INTERPRETATION OF STANDARD AT EACH END
PERFORMANCE OF PTT FACILITIES (RELIABILITY, AVAILABILITY, AND SERVICEABILITY)	NOT ALL PTTS GUARANTEE QUALITY OF SERVICE; INTERNATIONAL LINKS MAY DEGRADE THE PERFORMANCE ACHIEVED AT EACH END
MAINTENANCE	NO AUTOMATED MAINTENANCE INTERNATIONALLY; EACH PTT HAS OWN APPROACH OR IMPLEMENTATION
BILLING	SAME AS MAINTENANCE; ONE-STOP-SHOPPING FOR UNIFIED INTERNATIONAL BILLING AND MAINTENANCE NOT YET AVAILABLE

Source: IBM Centre D'Études et Recherches, La Gaude, France

Germany but switched analog lines as well in the United Kingdom, France, and Italy).

Differences in speed may be due to use of the channel or slot by the PTT for billing or signaling. The PTT may also restrict what the user can do with a given service or who may be allowed to use it. In Switzerland, for example, the monthly cost for a line may vary by two to three times, depending on its use. In Italy, a service that is to be shared among different users must be accessed through switched, and not leased, facilities. Some countries allow no resale at all, while the United Kingdom allows resale of most data facilities, but not voice.

Besides different rates based on local versus long-distance and switched versus leased-line, there's little rhyme or reason to the structure of international tariffs. "There's no case where one country has the same tariff as another," says Gorog. One end of a connection often costs much more than the other. Leased-line tariffs can have ratios as high as one to three.

"Network designers may choose countries as node sites based on these differences," notes Gorog.

Also, not all tariffs are published, especially for high-speed services. In many cases, a PTT has no published tariff for, say, a 2-Mbit/s service, but it can still be obtained. "Just knowing that a service can be or has been negotiated can be critical," says Gorog.

Paying premiums

Another twist is varying transborder premiums. For example, the U.K. tariff to cross the English channel via a leased line can be more than double the cost of covering the same distance within England. France Telecom's cross-channel tariff is about 30 percent more than the French domestic charge (which is itself higher than its English counterpart).

Even if an international service exists in both countries, it may not be available from point A in country X to point B in country Y. If the desired end points are outside the two countries' business centers, "maybe you can't get a link, or you have to wait three years," Gorog says. Planners would be well-advised to get a current local map from each PTT showing precisely where service is available.

The approval process can also be daunting. Each country will approve only certain products for connection to its network. Network planners have to determine whether a PTT requires the use of network-access standards, either voluntary (such as X.25) or mandatory ones (such as specific modulation schemes).

The more countries in a network design, the fewer the designer's equipment options. "We haven't gotten IBM modems approved in Germany because we weren't allowed to," says Gorog. "But in every country where we're allowed, our modems have been approved. Other modem suppliers may be approved in, say, only three out of seven European countries, which is not bad, but you have to be everywhere to respond to an international network," he says. And there may be few international vendors with IBM's clout and perseverence to get its products approved.

"It costs IBM an arm and a leg to get its stuff approved across Europe," confirms Jim Norton, director of industry studies with Butler Cox and Partners Ltd.

Indeed, equipment not only has to be approved (say, a Siemens box in Germany and a Bull machine in France), it also has to be compatible. And even if it works well across the room, the link may perform erratically across an international connection.

> The more countries in a network design, the fewer the designer's equipment options.

Getting quality

Another variable is the performance and quality level of PTT facilities, which some countries guarantee and other don't. France is a good case: Its PTT guarantees performance of the switched network at 9.6 kbit/s, while other countries may guarantee it only to a rate of 1.2 kbit/s.

Alternate-routed leased lines and exchange connection may or may not be available in a given country. For example, the PTT may offer high-reliability service customers, for a fairly small charge, an additional link into the local exchange as a hot standby. Such PTT offerings in the Netherlands, the United Kingdom, and France are very worthwhile, according to Abbott.

Crossing a border also makes a big difference here. For example, X.25 connections in the United Kingdom and France each attain a certain level of performance, but that level degrades over the international link.

Finger-pointing can also be a problem in transborder link maintenance. When a line drops, the user normally has to go to both sides to fix the problem. Though several individual countries offer automated network maintenance schemes, not one is the same as or compatible with any other.

Billing problems are as prevalent as maintenance problems: there is no coordination from the two sides of an international line. And users are growing more vocal in demanding a simpler, more modular way of billing. This is an aim of the PTT plan for one-stop shopping and billing called Managed Data Network Service, but, Gorog says, "we don't see that materializing."

Though on a somewhat different level, the services available from value-added suppliers also differ from country to country, as do order-to-install times and the quality of lines and adapters.

Users can try to deal with all these variable themselves, or they can turn to a consultant for help. But with its own experience and the detailed database it has already assembled, IBM should certainly be on users' lists of resources to draw upon in building international SNA networks. ■

SNA
CW

Uyless Black, Information Engineering Institute Inc., Falls Church, Va.

A user's guide to the CCITT's V-series modem recommendations

It's true. ISDN is coming. But until then, the rich and growing repertoire of international modem standards will rule the stage.

The Integrated Services Digital Network (ISDN) will eventually lead to the changing of the familiar physical connectors and interfaces now found in many user devices and data communications equipment. For the foreseeable future, however, most data transmissions will continue to use the analog telephone lines or other lines engineered to similar specifications.

During the past decade, the CCITT V-series recommendations have become prominent specifications for defining physical level interfaces. The V series defines the interfaces and signaling procedures between user equipment (DTEs, or data terminal equipment) and modems, multiplexers, and digital service units (DCEs, or data circuit-terminating equipment).

Specifications for the physical level operations of modems, digital service units, and other DCE-type components with DTE devices are also published by the Electronic Industries Association (EIA), the Institute of Electrical and Electronic Engineers (IEEE), and others. In addition, the International Standards Organizaton (ISO) publishes standards for the dimensions of the mechanical connectors that join the DCEs with DTEs. In North America, Bell specifications have become de facto standards; in the past few years, Hayes modems have taken the lion's share of the market with their microcomputer-based modem product line. It is noteworthy that most vendors have aligned their products, including the recent Bell modems and the Hayes modem family, with the V series.

Although the CCITT V-series conventions are used worldwide, the reader is cautioned that some vendors' "CCITT-aligned" products may be at variance with a specific recommendation. For example, the European and North American products sometimes use different originate and answer signals on certain modems. When in doubt, as the saying goes, read the directions.

The V series is published as part of the 1984 Red Book, Volume VIII-Fascicle VIII.1: "Data Communication over the Telephone Network." The 1984 document is intended to be a reference, not a tutorial. As such, it assumes the reader's familiarity with the many terms and concepts used therein. (Several key changes to the V-series specifications were made in the latest round of CCITT standards activity. For highlights of these changes see "Latest changes to V series.")

The V-series recommendations can be somewhat confusing to the uninitiated because a V-series specification may describe a specific type of modem or, alternatively, a convention that is used within the modem. For purposes of compatibility and simplicity, the V modems include a set of foundation V-series specifications and then use specific techniques unique to the modem itself to achieve the actual data encoding and modulation.

The entire V-series recommendations are broadly classified as:
- The foundation recommendations
- Voiceband modems
- Wideband modems
- Error-control and transmission-quality conventions
- Internetworking with other networks.

The foundation V series

These recommendations are used in many of the V-series voiceband and wideband modems (see "V-series recommendations"). They provide conventions for the electrical interfaces, the signaling rates in bits per second, definitions of the interchange circuits (pins), and procedures for dial-and-answer operations.

The V.28 and V.24 recommendations are examples of two foundation specifications that are used extensively in North America. They are found in the RS-232-C and EIA-

232-D standards. Most modem and multiplexer manufacturers stipulate the use of V.28 and a subset of V.24 in their specification sheets and marketing material.

V.28 is applied to almost all interchange circuits operating below the limit of 20 kbit/s. On a general level, the signals must conform to the following characteristics. For data interchange circuits, the signal is in the binary 1 condition when the voltage on the circuit is more negative than -3 volts. The signal is in the binary 0 condition when the voltage is more positive than $+3$ volts. For control and timing interchange circuits, the circuit is on when the voltage on the interchange circuit is more positive than $+3$ volts and is off when the voltage is more negative than -3 volts.

V.24 defines the functions of the connecting interchange circuits (pins) between the DTE and DCE. Many devices also use V.24 for direct DTE-to-DTE or DCE-to-DCE interfaces. The V-series voiceband and wideband modems typically use V.24, as do standards such as RS-232-C and EIA-232-D, although the EIA standards use different designations for the circuits.

The reader should be aware that a device may use V.24 and be incompatible with another device that also uses V.24. One reason is that V.24 is what might be called a superset standard. That is to say, V.24 provides descriptions of the functions of 43 pins, and most of the modem manufacturers then choose the appropriate circuits for their interface.

The voiceband modems

The presence of the V series may be no more noticeable than in the area of voiceband modems. A modem vendor's specification for medium (2.4-kbit/s) to high-speed (9.6-kbit/s) data transfer rates, for example, may say something like ". . . compatible with V.22*bis*, V.32 . . .," and so on.

Unless one is tenacious enough to read through myriad detailed V specifications, it is quite difficult to gain an overall understanding of these protocols. The principal characteristics of the V-series voiceband modems are summarized in Table 1, and each column entry is briefly explained below.

A V-series modem type shown in Column 1 may be listed in the table more than once. For example, V.29 has three entries. These multiple entries do not mean the series is published in more than one recommendation. Rather, it means that the modem type has more than one possible option for its implementation (usually, but not always, variations in speed).

The modems operate either with alternate two-way transmission (half duplex) or simultaneous two-way transmission (full duplex), as shown in Column 3. To achieve this, the V modem uses one of three techniques, shown in Column 4, to achieve channel separation:
- Frequency division
- Four-wire circuit
- Echo cancellation.

With frequency division, at least two signals are used, one for each direction of transmission. For example, a signal of 1,080 hertz (Hz) can be used to carry the data in one direction of transmission and a 1,750-Hz signal is used for the other direction. These carrier signals are listed in Column 5.

Another approach for achieving channel separation is through the use of a four-wire circuit. The two pairs of wires are used for the signals, a signal in each direction on each of the wire pairs. The newer V-series recommendations stipulate the use of echo cancellation, which uses the modem's receiver circuitry to cancel the transmitted signal. This provides full-duplex operations (see "V.32 modems are breaking through the echo barrier, DATA COMMUNICATIONS, April 1988, p. 187).

The chart also notes the modulation technique of each modem. The following methods are employed:
- Frequency shift
- Frequency modulation
- Phase shift
- Quadrature amplitude modulation
- Trellis-coded modulation.

The earlier recommendations stipulate the use of frequency shifting, where a carrier signal is modulated by the binary data stream by shifting a basic carrier signal by $+100$ Hz to represent a binary 1 or -100 Hz to represent a binary 0. For example, consider the V.21 modem. Its

<table>
<tr><td>

Latest changes to V series

The 1989 CCITT Blue Books, to be released later this year, contain several changes and additions to the V-series recommendations published in the 1984 Red Books. Perhaps the most interest has focused on the addition of V.42, which specifies the use of error-correcting modems. These modems also perform asynchronous-to-synchronous conversion between the host machine (data terminal equipment, or DTE) and the modem (data circuit-terminating equipment, or DCE). Consequently, the DTE can operate with conventional asynchronous protocols (as found in most personal computers).

The V.42 modem converts the transmission to a synchronous stream for transmission over the communications circuit. It also contains a link-level protocol, called Link Access Procedure for Modems (LAPM) for error correction, which is derived from high-level data link control.

Another new recommendation of interest is V.33, which describes the operations for 14.4-bit/s modems over four-wire leased circuits.

The Blue Books also include other V-series recommendations on simulated carrier control (V.13), asynchronous-to-synchronous conversion (V.14), ISDN, and V-series interfaces (V.120 and V.230).

The major modifications to existing V-series recommendations have occurred to V.25*bis* (automatic calling/answering modems), and another ISDN-to-V series interface (V.110). Both recommendations contain enhancements to the 1984 versions, and have been edited to improve their clarity.

</td></tr>
</table>

10	11	12	13	14	15	16	17
BACKWARD CHANNEL	SWITCHED LINES	LEASED LINES	USE OF V.26	ISO PIN CONNECTOR	EQUALIZATION	SCRAMBLER	USE OF V.54
ND	YES	NO	YES	2110	ND	ND	ND
ND	YES	POINT-TO-POINT, 2 WIRE	YES	2110	FIXED	YES	YES
ND	YES	POINT-TO-POINT, 2 WIRE	YES	2110	FIXED	YES	YES
ND	YES	POINT-TO-POINT, 2 WIRE	YES	2110	FIXED/ADAPTIVE	YES	YES
ND	YES	POINT-TO-POINT, 2 WIRE	YES	2110	FIXED/ADAPTIVE	YES	YES
YES	YES	NO	YES	2110	ND	ND	ND
YES	YES	NO	YES	2110	ND	ND	ND
YES	NO	POINT-TO-POINT, MULTIPOINT, 4 WIRE	YES	2110	ND	ND	ND
YES	YES	NO	YES	2110	FIXED	ND	ND
YES	YES	NO	YES	2110	FIXED	ND	ND
ND	YES	POINT-TO-POINT, 2 WIRE	YES	2110	EITHER	YES	YES
ND	YES	POINT-TO-POINT, 2 WIRE	YES	2110	EITHER	YES	YES
YES	NO	YES[3]	YES	2110	MANUAL	YES	ND
YES	NO	2 WIRE, 4 WIRE	YES	2110	ADAPTIVE	YES	ND
YES	NO	2 WIRE, 4 WIRE	YES	2110	ADAPTIVE	YES	ND
YES	YES	NO	YES	2110	ADAPTIVE	YES	ND
YES	YES	NO	YES	2110	ADAPTIVE	YES	ND
NO	NO	POINT-TO-POINT, 4 WIRE	YES	2110	ADAPTIVE	YES	ND
ND	NO	POINT-TO-POINT, 4 WIRE	YES	2110	ADAPTIVE	YES	ND
ND	NO	POINT-TO-POINT, 4 WIRE	YES	2110	ADAPTIVE	YES	ND
ND	YES	POINT-TO-POINT, 2 WIRE	YES	2110	ADAPTIVE	YES	YES
ND	YES	POINT-TO-POINT, 2 WIRE	YES	2110	ADAPTIVE	YES	YES
ND	YES	POINT-TO-POINT, 2 WIRE	YES	2110	ADAPTIVE	YES	YES

KBIT/S = KILOBITS PER SECOND (THOUSAND BITS PER SECOND)
KHz = KILOHERTZ (THOUSAND CYCLES PER SECOND)

NA = NOT APPLICABLE
ND = NOT DEFINED (I.E., NOT SPECIFIED IN THE RECOMMENDATION)

carriers of 1,080 Hz and 1,750 Hz are shifted by 100 Hz to represent binary 0s and 1s.

Phase-shift modulation is used on several of the medium-speed modems. This technique alters the carrier's signal by shifting its phase at precise degree markings. Table 2 provides more detail for the interested reader.

Quadrature amplitude modulation (QAM) is stipulated for the higher-speed modems (9.6 kbit/s) and the widely used V.22*bis* recommendation. QAM allows the carrier amplitude values and phase markings to be changed to represent the binary data stream.

The V-series modems that use combined amplitude modulation (AM) and phase-shift (PS) modulation still differ in the bit-encoding structure they use:

■ V.22*bis,* operating at 2.4 kbit/s, encodes four consecutive bits (quadbits); the first two bits are encoded relative to the quadrant of the previous signal element, the last two bits are associated with the new quadrant.

■ V.22*bis*, operating at 1.2 kbit/s, encodes two consecutive bits (dibits); the dibits are encoded as a change relative to the previous signal element.

■ V.29, operating at 9.6 kbit/s, encodes four consecutive bits (quadbits); the first bit determines the amplitude, the last three bits use the encoding scheme of V.27.

■ V.29, operating at 7.2 kbit/s, encodes three consecutive bits (tribits); the three bits are determined as in V.29 operation at 9.6 kbit/s.

■ V.29, operating at 4.8 kbit/s, encodes two consecutive bits (dibits); amplitude is constant and phase changes are the same as V.26.

■ V.32, operating at 9.6 kbit/s, encodes four consecutive bits (quadbits); the bits are mapped to a QAM signal.

■ V.32, operating at 9.6 kbit/s with Trellis-coded modulation (TCM), encodes four consecutive bits, two of which are used to generate a fifth bit; the bits are mapped to a QAM signal.

■ V.32, operating at 4.8 kbit/s, encodes two consecutive bits (dibits), which are mapped to a QAM signal.

Trellis-coded modulation is employed as one option of the V.32 modem for the purposes of forward error correction (see "Trellis Coded Modulation: What it is and how it affects data transmission," DATA COMMUNICATIONS, May 1985, p. 143). TCM actually uses QAM modulation techniques, but adds 1 bit to every 4 bits to aid in the error-correcting process at the receiving modem.

The modulation rate, shown in Column 7, is the rate of signaling change of the carrier(s). It is measured in the number of changes per second and is more commonly known as baud. Thus, the modulation rate of the V.29 modem is 2,400 baud. In the case of lower-speed modems, the line speed (in bits per second) is the same as the modulation rate (in baud). In the case of the medium- and higher-speed modems, bit/s and baud are not the same. Unfortunately, many people use these terms as if they were synonymous.

To analyze this seeming discrepancy, look at Column 8. The values there express the number of bits encoded per one signal change (that is, per baud). It is possible to encode multiple bits per baud. As an example, the V.26 modem encodes two bits per baud. The reader need only multiply the value in Column 8 by the value in Column 7 (modulation rate) to reveal the value in Column 2 (speed).

This simple equation holds true for all the entries except the V.32 TCM. It uses a 5:1 encoding ratio but achieves a bit rate of 9.6 kbit/s. Its actual throughput is 12,000 bits (5 × 2,400 = 12,000) but 2,400 bits are extra (redundant) bits used for forward error correction and do not contribute to the syntax of the user data stream.

V series recommendations

V.1—Definitions of key terms for binary symbol notation, such as binary 0 = space, binary 1 = mark.

V.2 (1)—Specification of power levels for data transmission over telephone line.

V.4—Definition of the order of bit transmission, the use of a parity bit, and the use of start/stop bits for asynchronous transmission.

V.5—Specification of data-signaling rates (bit/s) for synchronous transmission in the switched telephone network.

V.6—Specification of data signaling rates (bit/s) for synchronous transmission on leased telephone circuits.

V.7—Definitions of other key terms used in the V-series recommendations.

V.10—Description of an unbalanced physical level interchange circuit (unbalanced means one active wire between transmitter and receiver with ground providing the return).

V.11—Description of a balanced physical level interchange circuit (balanced means two wires between the transmitter and receiver with both wires' signals constant with respect to Earth).

V.15—Description of use of acoustic couplers for data transmission.

V.16—Description of the transmission of ECG (electrocardiogram) signals on the telephone channel.

V.19—Description of one-way parallel transmission modems using push-button telephone sets.

V.20—Description of one-way parallel transmission modems, excluding push-button telephone sets.

V.24—Definition of the interchange circuit pins between DTEs (data terminal equipment) and DCEs (data circuit-terminating equipment).

V.25 (2)—Specifications for automatic-answering equipment.

V.25*bis* (2)—Specifications for automatic-answering equipment.

V.28—Description of unbalanced interchange circuits operating below 20 kbit/s.

V.31—Description of low-speed interchange circuits (up to 75 bit/s).

V.31*bis*—Description of low-speed interchange circuits (up to 1.2 kbit/s).

Note: In the United States, EIA RS-496 specifies these measurements and RS-366 specifies these procedures.

Table 2: Modems using phase-shift modulation

(Entries represent bit(s) encoded with the phase changes)

SERIES NUMBER	SPEED (BIT/S)	PHASE CHANGE							
		0°	45°	90°	135°	180°	225°	270°	315°
V.22	1,200	01		00		10		11	
V.22	600			0				1	
V.26	2,400	00		01		11		10	
V.26*bis*	2,400		00		01		11		10
V.26*bis*	1,200			0				1	
V.26*ter*	2,400	00		01		11		10	
V.26*ter*	1,200	0				1			
V.27	4,800	001	000	010	011	111	110	100	101
V.27*bis*	4,800	001	000	010	011	111	110	100	101
V.27*bis*	2,400	00		01		11		10	
V.27*ter*	4,800	001	000	010	011	111	110	100	101
V.27*ter*	2,400	00		01		11		10	

NOTE: A FEW OTHER ENCODING OPTIONS ARE AVAILABLE FOR SEVERAL OF THE MODEMS.

Column 9 states whether the modem supports asynchronous or synchronous transmission. Several of the V-series modems can be configured to support either convention. The new recommendations specify only synchronous transmission. The asynchronous modems use timing signals between the modem and user device called start/stop bits. They are placed around each character. Synchronous transmission requires the use of a timing circuit between the devices to achieve synchronization (interchange circuit numbers 113, 114, and 128).

Column 10 indicates whether the V series uses a backward channel (also known as reverse channel). Several of the medium-speed V-series modems provide this channel. It is of limited capacity (typically, 75 baud with 390 Hz representing a 1 and 450 Hz representing a 0).

The channel is often used to obtain a return channel for diagnostic data or acknowledgments of the data transmitted over the primary circuit. It can also be used to send a limited amount of data. The use of a reverse channel does not preclude the simultaneous use of two primary full-duplex channels, but the V series defines this channel only for half-duplex modems using two-wire circuits or full-duplex modems using four-wire circuits.

The V-series modems provide several options for the use of switched or leased lines. These options are shown in Columns 11 and 12 of Table 1.

The inclusion of Columns 13 and 14 may seem somewhat superfluous since all the V-series voiceband modems use the V.28 electrical specification and the ISO 2110 mechanical connector. They are included to emphasize how certain foundation standards are used in the other standards.

Column 15 shows whether the modem uses equalization techniques. (Equalization is used to compensate for the attenuation associated with certain frequencies.)

Column 16 notes whether the modem uses a scrambler and descrambler to create self-sychronizing signals between the two modems' transmitters and receivers.

If the modem uses the V.54 loopback procedures, it is listed in Column 17. Fault location can be facilitated with the use of a looping procedure. In its simplest form, signals are generated at the transmitter and returned (looped back) to the transmitter to be checked for accuracy.

The wideband modems

The V-series recommendations also include specifications for wideband modems (Table 3). V.35 is widely used in North America. However, the North American implementation does not use the 48-kbit/s speed. The majority of implementations use the familiar 56-kbit/s digital data rate known to data communications users.

The V-series wideband modems operate within the 60- to 180-kHz bandwidth. They can be used for the transmission of data at rates from 58 kbit/s to 168 kbit/s. They also have options for the transmission of voice pulse-code modulation signals.

In January 1987, the EIA revised the RS-232-C standard and renamed it EIA-232-D. EIA-232-D includes:
- Specification for the 25-pin interface connector
- Addition of local loopback (pin 18), remote loopback (pin 21, which was named Signal Quality Detector in RS-232-C), and test-mode (pin 25) interchange circuits
- Addition of shield
- Redefinition of Protective Ground
- Terms of data communications equipment and data set defined as DCE
- Driver renamed Generator
- Terminator renamed Receiver.

The changes bring the standard into conformance with the following CCITT and ISO standards:
- Electrical: CCITT V.28
- Circuit definitions: CCITT V.24
- Mechanical connector: ISO 2110.

Bell modems (data sets) are widely used throughout the

Table 3: Wideband modems

SERIES NUMBER	LINE SPEED (KBIT/S)	FULL DUPLEX OR HALF DUPLEX	CARRIER FREQUENCY (KHz)	MODULATION TECHNIQUE	USE OF V.28	USE OF V.24	SCRAMBLER	BANDWIDTH (KHz)	LEASED LINES
V.35	48	FULL DUPLEX	100	SINGLE-SIDEBAND AMPLITUDE MODULATION	YES[3]	YES	YES	60-108	YES
V.36	48[1]	FULL DUPLEX	100	SINGLE-SIDEBAND AMPLITUDE MODULATION	NO[4,5]	YES	YES	60-108	YES
V.37	72[2]	FULL DUPLEX	100	SINGLE-SIDEBAND AMPLITUDE MODULATION	NO[4]	YES	YES	60-108	YES

1. RATE MAY ALSO BE 56, 64, AND 72 KBIT/S.
2. RECOMMENDED RATES ARE 96, 112, 128, 144, 168 KBIT/S.
3. EXCEPT THE DATA CIRCUITS (V.24 103, AND 104) AND TIMING CIRCUITS (V.24 114, AND 115) ARE BALANCED.
4. INTERCHANGE CIRCUITS USE A MIX OF V.10 AND V.11 RECOMMENDATIONS
5. FOR AN INTERIM PERIOD, V.35 INTERFACE AND ISO 2593 (34-PIN CONNECTION) CAN BE USED. 4902 IS A 37- OR 9-PIN CONNECTOR.

United States and other parts of the world. The physical level interfaces in North America have been largely dictated by the former Bell System specifications. For example, the vast majority of vendors base their automatic dial-and-answer DCEs on the Bell 103/212A specifications, and the Bell 103, 113, 201C, 208A/B, 212A specifications are used by many vendors as a basis for their modem designs.

The Bell modems

The term "Bell modem" has been associated with those modems manufactured by AT&T/Bell/Western Electric before divestiture. For convenience, the term is still widely used. The newer CCITT V-series modem specifications are increasingly used in North America, especially since divestiture, when AT&T relinquished its role as North American modem-specification writer and standards setter.

As noted in this section, the Bell modems and the self-styled CCITT counterparts are not always compatible.

Generally speaking, the Bell modems use the RS-232-C recommendation as it is defined by the EIA. However, exceptions exist. For example, the Bell 212A DCE defines pin 12 differently than does the EIA. A careful review of the vendors' specifications is quite important.

The Bell modems are categorized as follows:
- 100 series: Narrowband
- 200 series: Voiceband
- 300 series: Broadband
- 400 series: Voiceband parallel.

The more recent Bell modems use microprocessor-based synchronous protocols. These modems also provide adaptive equalizers and extensive diagnostic capabilities. They continuously monitor themselves and analyze the quality of the received signal. If necessary, they identify problems and report them to diagnostic control devices. Generally, the trouble reporting is provided over the reverse channel.

As with most modems today, the Bell modems provide the user with test menus and command menus, which allow the isolation and diagnosis of problems.

Recognizing that existing installed devices will need an interface to ISDN (probably for a considerable period of time), the CCITT has defined the physical level interface between the ISDN terminal adapter (TA) and a V-series device. This information is available in CCITT V.110.

V series interfaces with an ISDN

The TA provides the electrical/mechanical interface signal conversion and bit-rate adaptation between the non-ISDN user device, TE2 (terminal equipment 2). The TA also provides synchronization and automatic dial-and-answer functions as well as manual call-control functions for either voice or data circuit-switched services.

One principal task for the TA is to adapt the V-series bit rate to the ISDN 64-kbit/s, B-channel rate. This function is performed by 2-bit rate adapters (RA) located inside the TA. The first adapter, RA1 converts the V-series voiceband bit rate to an intermediate rate of either 8 kbit/s, 16 kbit/s, or 32 kbit/s. RA2 takes the intermediate rate or the V-series wideband modem rate and converts this rate to 64 kbit/s. The TA also provides adaptation of an incoming 64-kbit/s B channel to the appropriate V-series interface.

The CCITT V-series recommendations have provided a cohesive foundation for vendors to build compatible products. The user is the winner with this approach. It is anticipated that the ISDN physical level standards will provide a similar foundation for the emerging all-digital communications facility. ■

Uyless Black is president of Information Engineering Institute Inc., a consulting firm in Falls Church, Va. The author of numerous articles, he has just completed two books: Physical Level Interfaces and Protocols, IEEE Computer Society Press (Washington D.C., 1988), and Data Networks: Concepts, Theory and Practice, Prentice-Hall Inc. (Englewood Cliffs, N.J., 1988). He holds a BS in industrial psychology from the University of New Mexico, Albuquerque, an MS in Computer Systems from American University, Washington, D.C., and a graduate degree in banking and finance from Stonier Graduate School of Banking at Rutgers University, New Brunswick, N.J.

Lee Mantelman, DATA COMMUNICATIONS INTERNATIONAL

OSI unifies West German networks

An ambitious proposal by Siemens and Nixdorf for their largest user knocks down networking walls wit OSI, ISDN, and X/Open-style Unix.

For European computer vendors, the transition from proprietary network architectures to those offering broad support of OSI is still very much in the future tense. Many promise to provide comprehensive OSI products in five to 10 years.

In the meantime, vendors are willing to tie together incompatible networks via custom OSI solutions for the right user at the right price. One such user is the Bundesanstalt für Arbeit (BA), West Germany's employment agency and the largest user of both Siemens and Nixdorf computers. The OSI solution proposed by these vendors, although not yet accepted by the BA, shows the practical problems of implementing these new protocol stacks. It also sheds light on the way the German vendors' incompatible architectures may use OSI as the networking glue of the future.

A networked job bank

The BA is voyaging from the old world of terminal-attached host processors to the brave new world of servers and clients. These PCs and minicomputers will be running Unix System V Release 3, which complies with the Unix Portability Guide published by X/Open Company Ltd. (San Francisco, and Reading, England). By 1991, they will be linked over LANs based on communications software that conforms to Layers 1 through 4 of the OSI standard. By 1994, data lines linking these LANs will share long-distance ISDN links with voice traffic.

Currently, labor offices around West Germany use computers and local terminals to track job openings in their areas. The BA's goal is to enable a job seeker to enter any of its offices in any city and access any BA job-listings database in any other city. In this way, an unemployed person in Stuttgart could look for a job in Munich or Hamburg without having to leave town or spend a lot of time making long-distance telephone calls.

In fact, with the increase in workers' mobility—which can only be accelerated by Europe's 1992 project—the BA's ambitious plans could one day reach beyond West Germany. "They have in the back of their head that this should work Europe-wide in the long-term future," says Erich Eisner, product manager for the Data Systems group of Siemens AG (Munich). Use of international standards such as OSI and ISDN may improve the BA's chances of success.

The BA itself is modest about its leading-edge long-term project at this point. In fact, it's not saying a word. "We can't comment, because that would make our decision more difficult," says Arthur Decker, director of BA's information and communication technology division. At press time, the employment agency was nearing a decision about the final shape of its plans.

However, Siemens and Nixdorf Computer AG (Paderborn) felt that the BA, their largest joint customer, would agree to their proposal. "I'm pretty sure they're going to accept it without major changes," says Josef Offermann, Nuremburg-based head of Nixdorf's software development group for the BA.

Labor of love

The BA comprises 146 labor offices scattered around West Germany and a headquarters in Nuremburg. About 10 years ago, the BA began installing Nixdorf 8850 data entry minicomputers in the labor offices to keep track of job listings and administrative information. As many as seven computers might be needed to handle the large amounts of data in a large office.

At some sites, demand for computer power soon overwhelmed these early machines. So the BA decided to install Siemens 7.5XX mainframes in the 46 largest offices,

1. Today. In the BA's current setup, the labor offices send and receive messages via a central mainframe, which also distributes programs to the field hosts. They cannot exchange messages directly, and as a result, inquiries about job openings from one office can take several days to be answered by another.

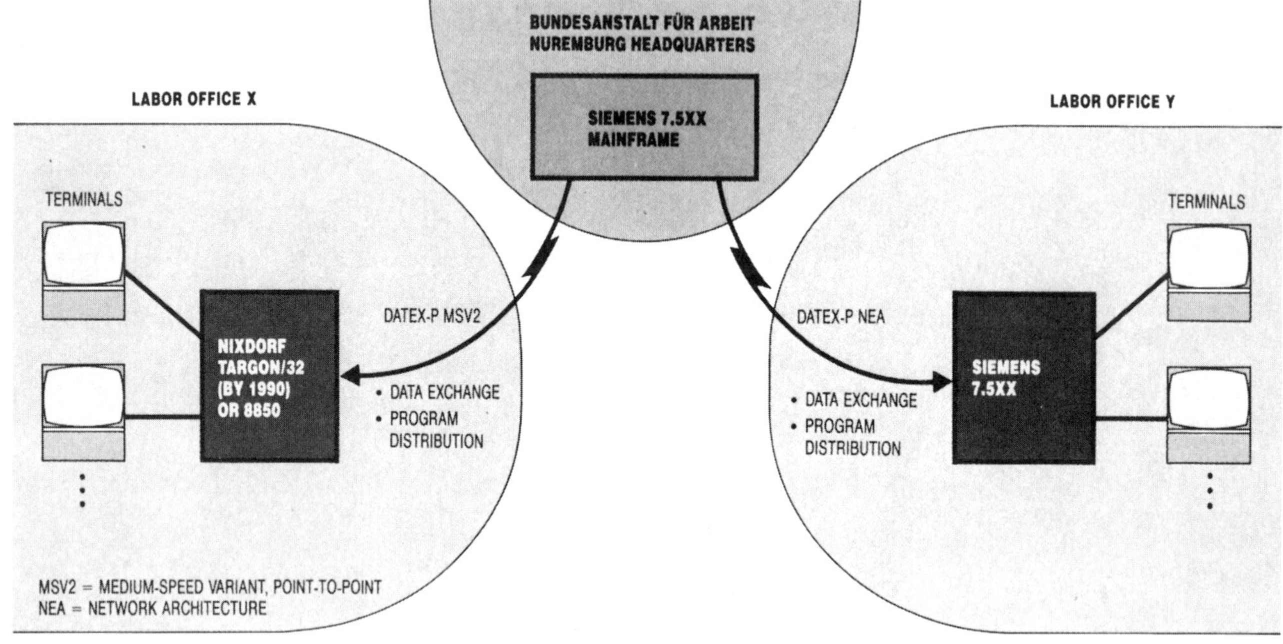

running a Siemens database called Sesam.

About five years ago, the agency started a pilot with Nixdorf Targon/32 Unix minicomputers performing the same applications as the Siemens machines. Ninety labor offices are due to receive Targons by the end of 1989. More than half of these sites have already been installed. By 1990, the Unix machines should have completely replaced the 8850s.

Currently, two BA offices cannot exchange job bank data directly. Instead, a large central Siemens host in the BA's Nuremburg headquarters contacts each of the 146 labor offices at night via the Deutsche Bundespost's (DBP) Datex-P packet network or another DBP public network (see Fig. 1). The mainframe picks up and delivers data and distributes the updates to each job database in each city. Thus, it can take several days for a job inquiry from one office to reach the database of listings and receive an answer.

Service included

A year and a half ago, the BA asked the Frankfurt-based consultancy Diebold Deutschland GmbH to help it decide whether to link all the labor offices and, if so, how. Diebold and the vendors came up with a client-server scenario in which the latest Nixdorf and Siemens microcomputers share programs with each other and are able to send directory files out over the network to other micros and the central mainframe.

The solution was to use the following machines as either clients or servers in each office: Nixdorf's Intel 80386-based Targon microcomputers running SCO Unix (from the Santa Cruz Operation, Santa Cruz, Calif., which is based on the System V Version 3 Unix) and Siemens's 80386-like National Semiconductor X20 micros running System V.3 Unix. The user interface and dialogue manager runs on client microcomputers while database and text server software runs on those micros that act as servers.

The BA decided to use the standard OSI seven-layer protocols to link the servers wherever possible. It selected Siemens to supply the higher-layer OSI software for wide area networking, even though Siemens offers no such code at the moment (see "Proprietary vs. standard solutions").

"The BA wants OSI, and they'll get it, but in a year or two," says Siemens's Eisner.

Today, the Siemens machines talk to each other using the vendor's proprietary Network Architecture (NEA) protocols. The BA's Nixdorf-Siemens communications use a Siemens data-exchange procedure called Medium-Speed Variant, Point-to-Point (MSV2). MVS2 is a file-transfer protocol used to exchange files between headquarters and the labor offices.

The central mainframe will not be able to support OSI protocols. Instead, the MSV2 exchanges will be replaced by a connection from a Siemens Unix server, dedicated to host communications, that will be added to all the labor offices. This host server will distribute programs to the other local servers or microcomputer-based clients. It will be needed to talk to both the old Siemens Transdata protocols with the large Siemens central host and OSI with the new equipment.

"The migration steps are very important," says

Nixdorf's Offermann. Nixdorf is proposing that the BA first replace all its terminals with microcomputers, which Offermann estimates will take about two years. During this time, Nixdorf will only be supplying Layer 1 through 4 OSI functionality.

"In the first step, it's not so important to have clean OSI, but it's important that programs can run on a client-server architecture," says Offermann. "In the second, we can move to full OSI to have the [benefit of its] communications power."

Trying to see ISDN-to-ISDN
From the outset, the BA was inclined to use the DBP's ISDN service to connect the labor offices.

"We're proposing a packet server and ISO CSMA/CD [carrier-sense multiple access with collision detection] LAN, but the BA wants a LAN for local communications only, with ISDN to each server," says Offermann (see Fig.

2). A packet server is a combination packet switch and protocol converter for connecting an ISDN wide area network (WAN) with an OSI LAN. Offermann says the X.25 packet-switched data will be transferred over the D channel of the basic-rate (two 64-kbit/s B channels and a 16-kbit/s D channel) connections. The problem with the BA's scenario, according to Offermann, is that each server must then be able to support ISDN protocols.

"Nixdorf's packet server idea makes sense, but so does the other, where all servers are ISDN-compatible," says Eisner. "It depends on the traffic patterns." The question is how often people at client workstations will want to access local as opposed to remote servers.

For instance, if most Stuttgart job seekers are looking primarily for jobs in Stuttgart—those listed in the local server—they will go out only occasionally into the WAN to look for jobs in, say, Hamburg. In that case, says Eisner, the packet server will probably suffice. But if a majority of

__2. Tomorrow?__ In the future, mainframe links will only be used for program distribution. Field offices, equipped with LAN-connected Unix machines serving users and applications, will communicate directly using ISDN. (Siemens and Nixdorf propose a packet server for ISDN-to-server traffic, though the user favors direct links.)

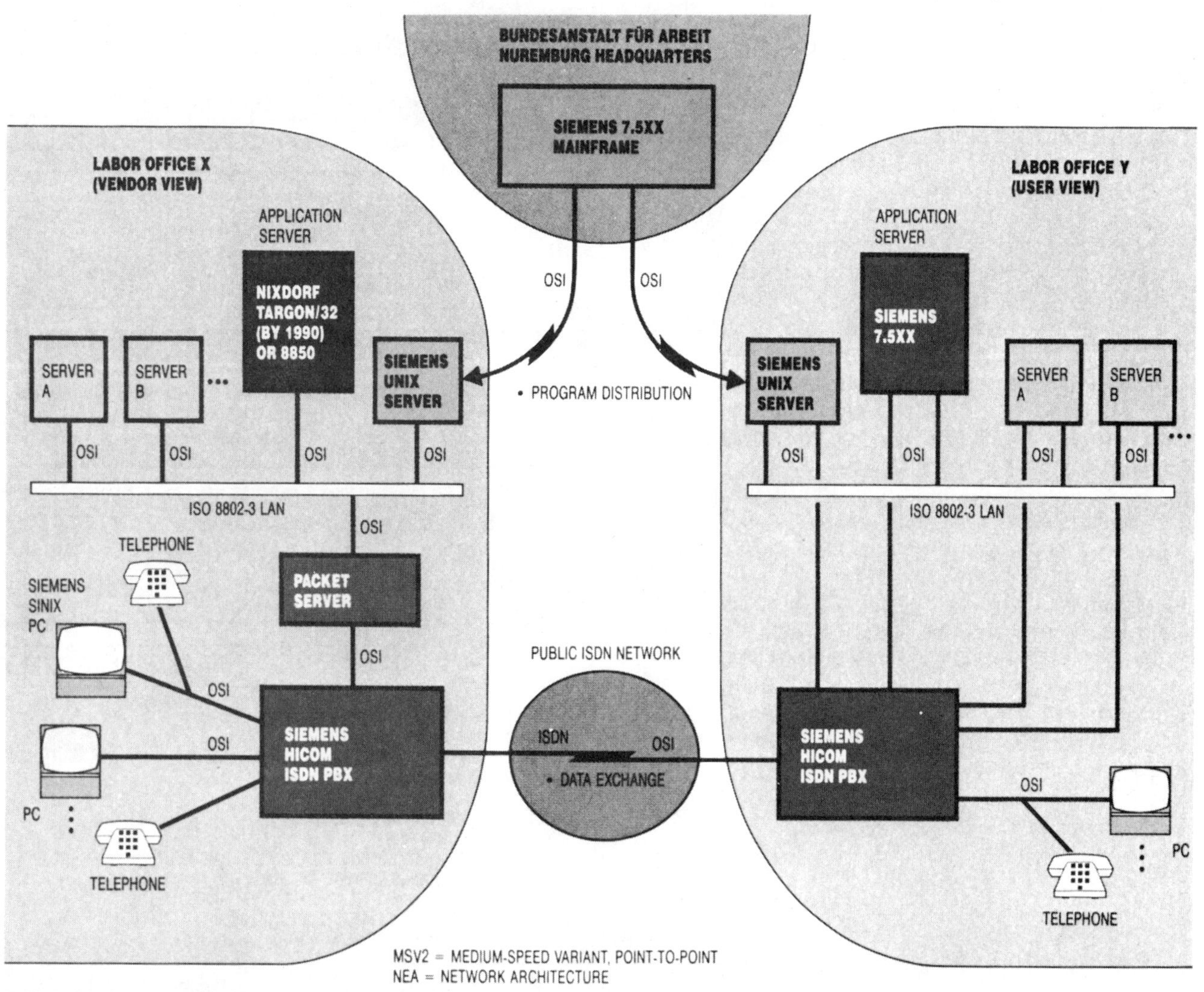

Siemens's proprietary products vs. Nixdorf's support of standards

Siemens, which claims to be Europe's largest indigenous computer vendor and number two behind IBM in the European market, is following several intertwined paths to the future. It offers two main operating systems for its computers, a third for its communications devices, and three major protocol suites on its mainframes, of which two are part of its network architecture.

The following is an attempt to untangle these strands (see figure):

■ Siemens calls its network architecture Transdata, which comprises OSI protocols for LANs (available, except for Layer 3) and WANs (Layers 1 through 4 expected by the end of 1989), as well as a set of proprietary protocols called NEA (from the German for Network Input and Output).

■ The Siemens operating system, BS2000, runs on its entire range of computers, including the largest processors. BS2000 gives Siemens a natural base for networking (as VMS does for Digital Equipment Corp.).

■ The Program System for Data Processing and Network Control (PDN) operating system is common to all Siemens communications processors.

■ Siemens's third major operating system, Sinix (Siemens Unix), is also included in the architecture because of Sinix modules that support NEA protocols. However, Sinix does not run on the older Siemens hosts used by many of its larger users.

■ While a Siemens host can understand both proprietary and OSI protocols, the communications controllers (such as front-end processors [FEPs]) cannot, though they will with the next release of PDN (due at the end of 1989). In addition, it can talk TCP/IP local area networking.

A typical Siemens network has at least one host running a BS2000. A channel-connected FEP runs PDN, as do optional remote FEPs (RFEPs), which can be beyond the channel's 30-meter limitation.

Users build networks out of FEPs, RFEPs, and terminal controllers (TCs). Since it also uses PDN, the TC can run applications programs, an early example of moving processing power nearer to the terminal user. A cluster controller handles terminals but without PDN software, only firmware, so it offers no application support. Finally, Siemens also offers a local channel-attached cluster controller.

These elements combine under the Transdata network architecture, which has been on the market since 1972. In many ways, it resembles IBM's SNA, but is more peer-to-peer and less reliant on a host-based control point that brings all its sessions down if it fails. In Transdata, each processor runs a session controller.

Transdata began as three layers: a port service (corresponding to OSI Layers 1 and 2), transport service (OSI Layers 3 and 4), and user service (OSI Layers 5 and 6). Siemens thought of Layer 7 as belonging to the realm of applications. Around 1979, the layers were broken out

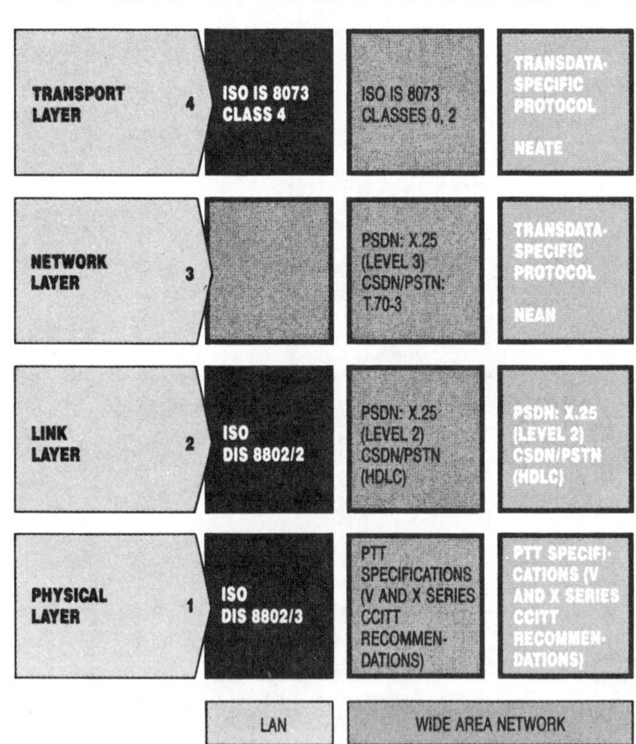

ISO 7-LAYER MODEL		TRANSDATA (ISO PROTOCOLS)		TRANSDATA (NEA PROTOCOLS)
APPLICATION LAYER	7	OFFICE SERVICES (FOR EXAMPLE, ELECTRONIC MAIL AS PER X.400)	TELEMATIC SERVICES (FOR EXAMPLE, TELETEX)	TRANSDATA-SPECIFIC PROTOCOLS NEAB FAMILY
PRESENTATION LAYER	6	X.409/X.410 REMOTE OPERATION	TELEMATIC SERVICES	
SESSION LAYER	5	ISO IS 8327 BSS/BCS		
TRANSPORT LAYER	4	ISO IS 8073 CLASS 4	ISO IS 8073 CLASSES 0, 2	TRANSDATA-SPECIFIC PROTOCOL NEATE
NETWORK LAYER	3		PSDN: X.25 (LEVEL 3) CSDN/PSTN: T.70-3	TRANSDATA-SPECIFIC PROTOCOL NEAN
LINK LAYER	2	ISO DIS 8802/2	PSDN: X.25 (LEVEL 2) CSDN/PSTN (HDLC)	PSDN: X.25 (LEVEL 2) CSDN/PSTN (HDLC)
PHYSICAL LAYER	1	ISO DIS 8802/3	PTT SPECIFICATIONS (V AND X SERIES CCITT RECOMMENDATIONS)	PTT SPECIFICATIONS (V AND X SERIES CCITT RECOMMENDATIONS)

LAN	WIDE AREA NETWORK

BCS = BASIC COMBINED SUBSET
BSS = BASIC SYNCHRONIZED SUBSET
CSDN = CIRCUIT-SWITCHED DATA NETWORK
DIS = DRAFT INTERNATIONAL STANDARD
HDLC = HIGH-LEVEL DATA LINK CONTROL
IS = INTERNATIONAL STANDARD
NEAB = USER SERVICE LAYER PROTOCOL FOR FILE/JOB TRANSFER, BATCH MODE, TIMESHARING MODE, OTHERS
NEAN = NETWORK ARCHITECTURE, NETWORK LAYER PROTOCOL
NEATE = NETWORK ARCHITECTURE, TRANSPORT PROTOCOL
PSDN = PACKET-SWITCHED DATA NETWORK
PSTN = PUBLIC SWITCHED TELEPHONE NETWORK

into a six-layer model, mimicking that of OSI.

For wide area networking, "OSI is still in planning mode," says Erich Eisner, product manager for the Siemens Data Systems Group. "If users demand OSI protocols, they'll get a prerelease version, but it's not 100 percent ready or finished with quality testing," he says.

Direct host-to-host communications can use OSI protocols, but FEPs and TCs don't yet support OSI, precluding OSI networks. So, at present, if an application in one host wanted to talk OSI to a remote counterpart, the FEP would wrap the OSI packets in an NEA envelope.

This could get even more complicated with a packet network, such as Datex-P, in between. Then, the NEA envelope containing the OSI packet would itself be put into an X.25 envelope. "At Layers 1 through 3, it would be like having NEA between two slices of OSI," says Eisner. No users are doing this, because "this is a performance problem, which is why users are against the gateway approach."

Siemens hopes to stop selling its non-OSI protocols in about five years, depending on the demands of its users. "We want to stop as fast as possible, but our users with old machines continue to want upgrades," says Eisner. So Siemens will continue its strategy of supporting both proprietary and standard stacks: "In the meantime, we'll stand on two legs for a lot of years," he says.

Unlike Siemens, Nixdorf has never had a proprietary architecture. Rather, it uses existing international and industry standards to link its computers, such as the following:

- High-Level Data Link Control;
- TCP/IP in LANs of Unix machines;
- X.25 in WANs; and
- The ISO TP Class 2 over X.25.

Before ISO defined its transport protocol, Nixdorf used one defined by the West German government to make applications independent of the underlying network.

At the upper layers, the vendor uses proprietary protocols, such as file transfer protocols, that run on all Nixdorf computers. This application layer protocol is independent of the transport layer, a design that matches Nixdorf's approach to network architecture.

"We proposed building applications atop the ISO transport interface, but not many people follow us," says Karl Bidlingmaier, Nixdorf's head of network software development for Targon systems.

However, Nixdorf supports such upper-layer OSI protocols as FTAM and X.400. In addition, "if an application uses, say, ACSE or ROSE, we'll support that," says Bidlingmaier.

Nixdorf connects to other vendors, including Bull, Siemens, and ICL, at the terminal-emulation level. The firm offers 3270 emulation and Remote Job Entry as *well as Physical Units 2 and 2.1.* —*L.M.*

the Stuttgarters want to look for jobs in other cities, then ISDN-compatible servers make better sense.

At first, the agency did not agree with the idea of using LANs, but "at the moment, the BA is LAN-minded," Eisner says. Also, since the BA wants the same configuration in all offices, it would not accept a LAN in one place and some other setup in another.

"The LAN issue is a political matter," says Eisner. "One specialist in the BA is an ISDN champion. If you have 20 to 30 servers, it's cheaper to have a LAN than to have all ISDN connections."

Both Nixdorf and Siemens have submitted bids to provide the packet servers.

Portable OSI under Unix

For a time, the BA will have three hardware platforms, the 7.5XX, 8850, and Targon/32 machines. To avoid triplicating its application software development efforts, the labor agency told both vendors it wanted only Unix machines in the future.

However, because Siemens has no mainframe Unix offerings, the plan is to use the 7.5XX as a database server with Unix micros in the role of intelligent workstations.

Other Unix machines can be added in the future as servers for text editing and other functions.

For the sake of compatibility, the BA decided to migrate all its offices to Nixdorf's DDB4 database management package, which runs under Unix. So DDB4 will be used on the BA's Targons, on microcomputers, and on Siemens's old 7.5XXs. The kernel of DDB4 is written in Pascal and has previously been ported to many machines, including the Siemens hardware.

Beyond its use in hardware-independent applications, Unix also allows one vendor's set of OSI communications protocol software—in this case Siemens's Remote Operation System code for OSI Layers 5 and 6 (with some application layer commands)—to be ported to different machines as a sort of application running under Unix. The BA didn't feel comfortable relying on both Nixdorf and Siemens for the full OSI stack.

"If they chose, say, an FTAM [File Transfer, Access, and Management] from Siemens and an FTAM from Nixdorf, how would they know which was correct if the two implementations didn't fit together?" says Karl Bidlingmaier, Nixdorf's head of network software development for Targon systems.

The BA wanted to make life easier for its programmers and to ensure that programs could be ported to future computers. So it told its vendors to follow the X/Open Unix guidelines in those areas that were specified. In other areas, interim approaches would be acceptable until a standard is agreed on—they will have to be changed to comply.

But X/Open has not yet defined interfaces for Unix programs to allow it to access OSI at the application layer. This posed a dilemma for the BA, which wanted to develop its own applications using OSI services and protocols. If it used a nonstandard interface from one supplier of OSI software, it would be dependent on that supplier. To

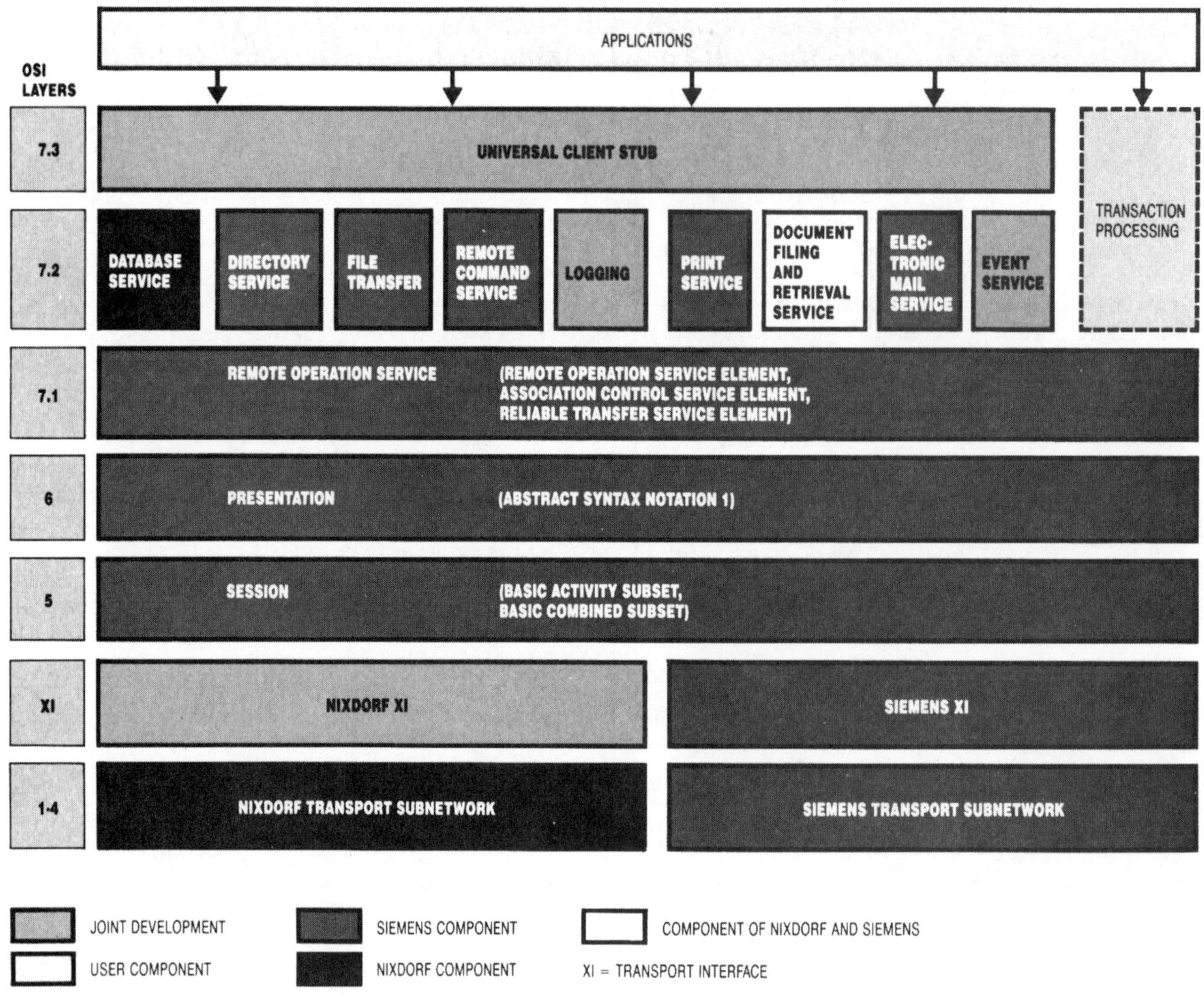

3. Integrated stack. *Nixdorf plans to provide the BA with the lower four layers of OSI on its machines. The plan would have Siemens providing its own seven layers of OSI on top of Nixdorf's stack. The two vendors would work together on other components, including Nixdorf's transport interface to Siemens's upper layers.*

change to another vendor, the BA would have to rewrite its applications.

Instead, the BA decided to define its own application programming interface, which OSI vendors could map to their proprietary interfaces. At the BA's request and approval, Nixdorf and Siemens specially devised the Universal Client Stub (UCS), which is an application access method (Fig. 3).

The UCS will allow BA programmers to access OSI services with only a handful of programming steps. "The interface is similar to the X/Open Transport Interface [XTI], but on the level of ACSE [Association Control Service Element] or ROSE [Remote Operation Service Element]," says Bidlingmaier.

(ACSE and ROSE are OSI Layer 7 elements that support application processes. Like XTI, the UCS provides its clients with services in the form of primitives. The UCS primitives are: connection establish and release, and send and receive data.

In the future, could such interfaces be developed that would unite other vendors' computer architectures? Offermann points out that UCS is a solution unique to the BA. "Paderborn [Nixdorf headquarters] doesn't accept this as a general solution. Perhaps it will in the future, but not yet."

Currently, Nixdorf uses a proprietary socket interface or X/Open's XTI. However, the nascent OSI Transaction Processing (TP) standard could, if it arrives in time, render this point moot. OSI TP would serve the same purpose as UCS, providing a set of program calls for applications to access OSI services. OSI TP became a draft proposal in March 1988. It is expected to reach draft international standard status in October of this year and become a full international standard by November 1990. ∎

704

H. Kim Lew and Jim Robertson, 3Com Corp., Mountain View, Calif.

TCP/IP network management with an eye toward OSI

The Internet community is actively working on network management techniques that will help control existing nets and make upcoming ISO protocols easier to work with.

Building multivendor networks without universal standards for network management products can be an exercise in futility.

But some relief may be on the way. A recently completed Internet standards-setting effort tackled the network management requirements of networks running TCP/IP. The resulting standards and agreements are expected to enable the Internet community to make a smooth migration to the OSI protocol stack.

Despite the standardization of electronic mail, file transfer, and remote connection applications, standards for network management functions on the Internet's TCP/IP-based networks have been slow to materialize. One problem has been the mismatch between TCP/IP's Simple Network Management Protocol (SNMP) and the International Organization for Standardization's (ISO) Common Management Information Protocol (CMIP) over TCP/IP, known as CMOT (see "Network management on TCP/IP: When experts can't agree," Data Communications, Newsfront, November 1988). This is changing, however, and the recently completed Internet standards are likely to yield results during the next several years both in the Internet community and in commercial networks running TCP/IP protocols.

Internet's strategy

The Internet (consisting of the Defense Department's Arpanet and academic and research networks distributed throughout North America and Europe) grew out of the first packet-switched, store-and-forward, host-to-host digital computer network. Named for the Internet Protocol (IP) on which it relies, the Internet provides access to several hundred LANs, as well as to public and private data networks.

The Internet Activities Board (IAB), the Internet's govern-ing body for both operational and research and development issues, has developed both long- and short-term solutions to help bridge the gap between today's network management requirements and those of tomorrow's worldwide, interoperable nets. With one eye on the progress of OSI network management standards and the other on its own immediate needs, the IAB adopted a network management strategy last year for the increasingly popular TCP/IP protocol suite. That strategy is expected to encourage the development of management tools capable of handling multivendor networks.

With the release of Request for Comment (RFC) 1067, the board approved the Simple Network Management Protocol as the platform for a short-term solution. SNMP, formerly referred to as the Simple Gateway Management Protocol (SGMP), incorporates a number of extensions to the original specification's list of capabilities.

SNMP operates above the transport layer in the OSI seven-layer model and is intended to provide management data concerning hosts, routers, and other network devices. SGMP was originally proposed for use by the Internet community in 1987, and is documented in RFC 1028. It was developed in response to the proliferation of Internet networks linked together through gateways and the requirement that those gateways be monitored and managed.

As a long-term solution, the board decided to model the Internet network management tools after ISO's CMOT and its two main elements—Common Management Information Protocol (CMIP), the basic OSI protocol for network management, and Common Management Information Service (CMIS), the programming definition used by applications to access OSI network management functions.

Another key decision was an agreement to implement a common Management Information Base (MIB, the list of objects that can be managed) and Structure of Management Information (SMI) approach for both SNMP and the ISO's CMOT. (SMI defines the rules used to define managed objects.) By establishing this fundamental commonality between the two, IAB protocol developers allowed SNMP activity to proceed immediately while leaving a path for implementation of OSI's CMIP strategy. CMIP, in its current iteration, is defined in ISO draft international standard (DIS) 9596/2.

The IAB's strategy may prove to be an important step in making heterogenous networks more manageable, especially as communications and computer manufacturers incorporate TCP/IP into their Unix-based systems. Clearly, the IAB strategy also creates a path for TCP/IP-based networks to migrate to the OSI stack once ISO's standards replace TCP/IP in the networking community.

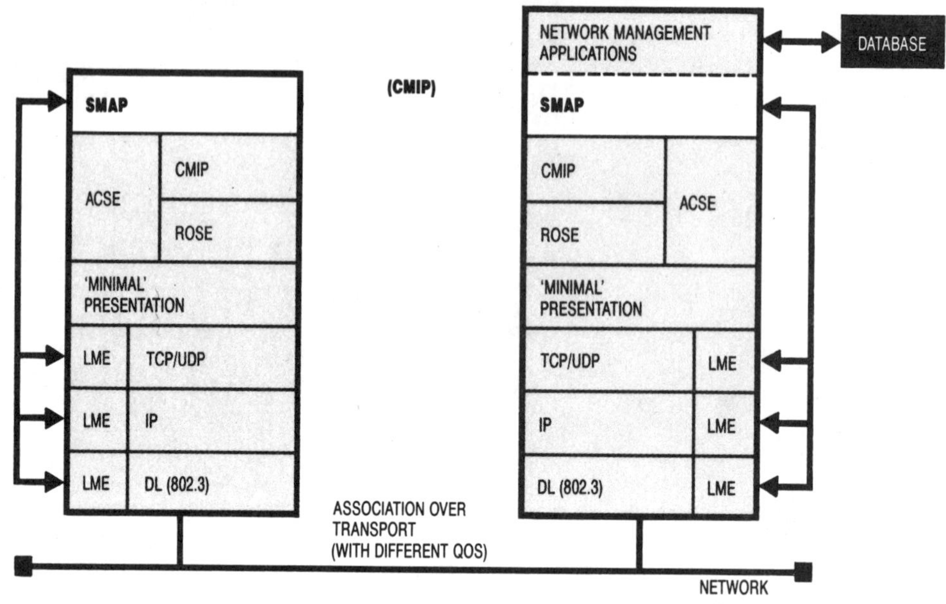

1. CMIP. Defined within OSI standards, this protocol provides the transaction-oriented monitor and control services required by the System Management Application Process (SMAP). Associations can be accomplished over either TCP or UDP.

The driving force behind this OSI-based approach was a working group formed under the IAB's Internet Engineering Task Force (IETF), which consists of vendors, users, and researchers.

The working group, dubbed the Network Management Working Group, chose CMOT as an elegant interim interoperable network management solution because, by providing a comprehensive network management capability for TCP/IP, it will allow a smooth transition to the OSI stack.

Unlike SGMP/SNMP, which maximizes the benefits of running over the User Datagram Protocol (UDP) transport (the simple connectionless packet/message delivery transport protocol), CMOT fully exploits network management standards developed by ISO over either TCP/IP's Transmission Control Protocol or UDP transport services.

Despite the differences between TCP/IP and OSI, many protocols and services associated with them are functionally analogous. By adopting a common management services specification to which network management applications can connect, migration from TCP/IP to OSI network management is simplified.

These services are carried via the CMIP and Remote Operations Service Element (ROSE)—the OSI standard for remote procedure calls—protocols. Relying on CMIP and ROSE facilitates the management of OSI and TCP/IP nodes in a mixed network. The structure of management information for CMOT will be made to track OSI forms or templates that have been defined for managed objects.

To accommodate the operation of the OSI network management scheme over TCP or UDP transport protocols, the Netman Group identified several mandatory delivery requirements:
■ specifying an architecture and model;
■ identifying applicable ISO documents and using them as references for and to help create tools for the CMOT RFCs;
■ establishing a universal MIB and SMI;
■ developing implementers agreements (the essence of the CMOT RFC); and
■ specifying the glue pieces needed to run over TCP/IP's transport protocols.

Network management and model of operation

The CMOT Network Management System (NMS), a collection of entities using CMOT to run the network, is hierarchical. Its model of operation is tailored after ISO's Management Framework specification, DIS 7498/4. It does not, however, implement OSI standards defined for presentation, session, transport, or network layers.

Within this context, a network can be split into domains of management, with each domain having a master manager (or group of managers) capable of controlling a specific domain or group of domains. Those domains may overlap, work cooperatively, or operate under hierarchical constraints. The CMOT model currently only addresses the operations and characteristics of a single domain of management. This could be a problem because actual network management often requires handling more than one domain at a time.

A management domain can be split into a collection of managed entities; each managed entity can then be further split into one or more managed objects. A management entity, as defined by OSI and CMOT, is an application process within a management domain which implements monitoring and control functions on managed objects via their associated managed entities. A managed object (in real-world terms, a T1 line card or an Ethernet interface card) is a resource that is monitored and controlled by one or more management systems. Managed objects are located within managed systems and may be embedded within other managed objects. A managed entity could be a host or router or whatever has managed objects under its sovereignty.

In general, each managed node on a network must include an embedded network management system. The network management system contains the application layer software and necessary transport layer software to facilitate intermachine communication and, ultimately, interoperable device management.

Each NMS is independent and capable of interacting with other NMSs, accepting or initiating commands, and sending information. Each NMS in a relationship with another NMS assumes the role of either agent or manager. In the role of agent, the NMS collects information and reports to the peer NMS in the manager role. An NMS in the manager role runs management applications, collects network data generated by agents, and issues commands to agents on the network. In general, a manager NMS is associated with the human network manager. Figure 1 illustrates the basic model of interaction between an agent and a manager.

Agents constitute the lowest hierarchical level of network management. They can exist in every IP-addressable device of a network—terminals, terminal servers, micro-computers, hosts, bridges, routers, and gateways. However, the managed objects are not necessarily restricted to those objects residing within a given device. Agents can also provide access to objects associated with devices that are not IP-addressable. In this case, the agent acts as a proxy to provide access to those objects.

Each agent reports to, and is controlled by, a manager station. The association between agent and a manager is not fixed and can be configured by a network administrator or operator. The number of manager stations, and the number of agents per manager, depends on the network configuration and the processing power of a manager station.

If multiple manager stations have been created, it is possible to bundle them in a tree structure with a single manager station at the top of the inverted tree. Such a station is expected to be the central management station, where management for the entire network occurs. The number of stations reporting to higher levels of the network management hierarchy is not fixed either, and is largely contingent on issues of performance and network con-

figuration. Manager-to-manager interactions are not addressed by the initial Netman effort.

Agents include modules associated with each of the communications layers of ISO's model. These modules are known as Layer Management Entities (LMEs). LMEs facilitate layer management functions that ensure the integrity of the layer protocols and allow the changing of layer parameters to accommodate changing technical conditions and user needs. These modules communicate with other LMEs and are coordinated inside the agent by a management entity that accepts information from, and delivers information to, the LMEs. This entity is referred to as the System Management Application Process (SMAP). The SMAP is a local process responsible for executing management functions. In addition, it is responsible for communication over the management protocol.

A manager has the same basic structure, allowing management communication between SMAPs. The model does not assume that an association is opened by one SMAP or the other, neither does it specify the direction of management relative to the initiator of the association. To create management relations between an agent and a manager, the two must associate with each other. In this respect, the mechanisms provided are fully symmetrical between the manager and the agents.

Association is accomplished via the services provided by the ISO-defined Application Control Service Entity (ACSE), a link analogous to the TCP/IP connection. This association can occur over a reliable or unreliable transport (TCP or UDP), depending on the quality-of-service instructions established by the initiator of the association. It is during this phase of association that the manager-agent relationship is established and agreement on the scope of the relationship is negotiated. Network management applications also rely on the ROSE protocol to provide the transaction-oriented services required by the SMAP.

Another element of the CMOT model is the implementation of OSI's management services. In general, these services fall into three categories: data manipulation services; event reporting services; and direct control services. The CMIS definition (ISO DIS 9595/2) provides the specific services for each of these general functions. The Netman Group implemented a subset of the services defined in that document.

Managed information

Network management requires a large and comprehensive database and associated data manipulation tools. Such a database must store information concerning network and computer configurations, performance and problem logs, security data, and accounting specifics.

The OSI Management Framework, the model upon which CMOT's information model is based, specifies that all this information reside in the MIB. Under the CMOT standard, conventions for locating and identifying MIB information allow the MIB to be referenced within the management protocols for the purpose of extracting or modifying it.

The structure of management information and the specification of the MIB employed in CMOT are defined in RFC 1065 and RFC 1066, respectively. These RFCs were produced in a joint effort between the SNMP and Netman groups under the direction of the IAB.

This joint development activity ensures that the transition from SNMP to CMOT will be minimized with a common definition for the SMI and MIB. The protocol-specific issues regarding the SMI for the Netman proposal are documented in RFC 1095. These issues deal with mapping the Internet SMI, defined in RFC 1065, to the ISO SMI, which allows greater flexibility in specifying the containment relationship between object classes.

In general, management information describes managed objects and takes the form of attributes, actions, and events associated with each object. A collection of managed objects with similar or related properties represents an "object class."

Each object class is uniquely identified by an administrative name. The name is hierarchical in nature and easily represented by the ASN.1 type object identifier. An object identifier is a sequence of integers that traverse a global tree, in this case the Management Information Tree (MIT) for the TCP/IP internetworks.

The name of a given object class is the accumulation of the arcs (a set of branches through a MIB tree) traversed from the root of the MIT to the object type. Each arc has associated with it a label composed of two elements: an integer and descriptive text for that arc. The descriptive text of the labels in the MIT identify the organization or document responsible for assigning offspring arcs.

The following criteria were used in the selection of objects:

■ An object must be useful for either fault or configuration management.

■ Only weak control objects can be permitted (weak means that limited damage can occur if the object is misused). Netman Working Group members believe that the current management protocols are insufficient in secure access control mechanisms.

■ Evidence of current use and utility is necessary.

■ The number of objects should be limited to about 100 to simplify implementation.

■ To avoid redundant variables, no objects should be included that can be derived from others in the MIB.

■ Implementation-specific objects, such as those for BSD (Berkeley System Development) Unix, should be excluded.

■ Excessively specifying managed objects for critical sections of implementations should be avoided. As a result, a general guideline of one counter per critical section per layer was specified. A critical section of an implementation is considered a section that significantly affects performance if overloaded with management tasks.

Conventions in RFC 1066, RFC 1065, and RFC 1095 allow the descriptions of managed objects to be encoded and transferred using CMIP. Currently, the SMI specified by RFC 1065 does not define any action or event object types. A commonly implemented set of semantic rules for operation will help to create consistency in the meaning of the structure of management information and ultimately management NMS interoperability.

Names for objects and their respective attributes, actions, and events are arranged into a hierarchical Manage-ment Information Tree (MIT). This hierarchy, as specified in RFC 1066 and used by SNMP, reflects the decomposition hierarchy of the managed objects, in other words, how managed objects contain managed objects. In order to align with the ISO SMI, RFC 1095 interprets the MIT as strictly a registration hierarchy used to uniquely identify objects, and then provides a containment hierarchy to reveal containing relationships between objects. The containment relationship groups objects of similar characteristics to form an object class.

The Internet management object classes (that is, the MIT) are elements of a subtree of the universal object-class tree to be defined through ISO's OSI effort. In order to ensure a common naming scheme, all object classes must occur in a single, universally managed object-class tree. Managed object-class names will be represented by a path in the object-class tree. By identifying and classifying objects and other entities in the same way as the OSI specification, CMOT leaves the door open for inter-operation and migration.

Quality of transport

CMOT addresses two protocols defining the quality of service for the underlying transport required by network management applications. Depending on the situation, either of the two TCP/IP transport protocols available, UDP or TCP, may be better suited to specific situations.

There are advantages and disadvantages to each approach. The Datagram-based UDP is simple, requires minimal code space to implement, and can operate under conditions where interactive connection is not possible. However, a connection-oriented approach, such as TCP, offers reliability of data and provides guaranteed, consistent service to the network management application process—at the expense of establishing and maintaining a connection.

CMOT is neutral on the subject of selecting one protocol or the other. It allows for both services and interfaces to an application, enabling that application to select the transport type required. The selection of the underlying protocol is determined during association and is established by setting the quality-of-service parameter to indicate TCP or UDP.

In addition, UDP and TCP can be used in a variety of combinations. Specific implementations might depend on the type of information being transferred between manager and agent. The simplest association might involve the transfer of special events updates from the agent to the manager. UDP would probably be adequate for this kind of communication.

An extension of this basic association might allow the manager to solicit information from the agent. In contrast, a third scenario might involve a situation where the manager and agent each retrieve information from one another, as well as report exceptions to each other. The manager might also be able to set variables in the agent and instruct the agent to perform specific actions. These added options require the use of TCP, with its reliable transport services.

In OSI network management, and by implication TCP/IP network management, every device that wants to participate in the exchange of management information must implement software that supports that information and the underlying

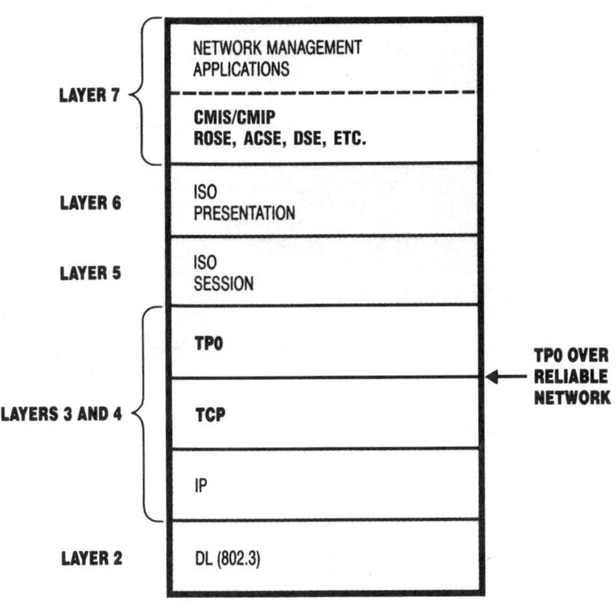

ACSE = APPLICATION CONTROL SERVICE ENTITY
CMIP = COMMON MANAGEMENT INFORMATION PROTOCOL
CMIS = COMMON MANAGEMENT INFORMATION SERVICE
DL = DATA LINK
DSE = DIRECTORY SERVICE ELEMENT
IP = INTERNET PROTOCOL
ISO = INTERNATIONAL ORGANIZATION FOR STANDARDIZATION
ROSE = REMOTE OPERATIONS SERVICE ELEMENT
TCP = TRANSMISSION CONTROL PROTOCOL
TP = TRANSPORT PROTOCOL

network management architecture and model, such as TCP/IP protocols, CMIP, LMEs, and SMAP. In many potential limited devices it may be unwieldy or impractical to implement a complete NMS. (A limited device is one that cannot meet all the basic criteria for implementing an underlying architecture or model. For instance, a bridge may not inherently have an Internet address, while the memory limitations of a microcomputer may make it unsuitable for implementation of a complete network management device.)

To include such devices in the managed network, the Netman Group adopted a "management by proxy" approach. Under this arrangement, the proxy is an open system—one that supports the TCP/IP protocol stack. It has a network address, is capable of exchanging management information, and has been designated to act on behalf of limited devices as their agent for exchange of management information.

Management information intended for a limited device, such as a Media Access Control (MAC)-layer bridge, is first passed to its proxy. The proxy then conveys or retrieves information to or from the limited device, and passes any pertinent results to a management peer. The entire process is transparent to the management peer (typically a manager station). From the management peer's point of view, informa-

tion is exchanged directly with the limited device.

The type of information exchanged between a proxy and a limited device depends on the nature of the limited device, and is generally beyond the scope of the NMS definitions. Limited devices may use standard or proprietary mechanisms available at their level of operation. For instance, a MAC-layer bridge may use IEEE 802.1 data link layer management between itself and the proxy.

Each proxy might support several limited devices, in addition to supporting management functions for its own operation. The various devices managed by a proxy are differentiated by specifying a valve for a distinguishing attribute of an object class. This selection of information is carried in the object instance field of the CMIP protocol.

A manager entity can establish multiple, concurrent associations with the proxy using different presentation selectors, each relating to a different system. During data transfer, the proxy system uses the association information to distinguish between the different limited systems it supports. The mapping between a specific presentation selector and an actual limited system is considered a local matter and is not likely to be addressed by the NMS RFCs.

Protocol architecture

CMOT tracks the OSI model at the application layer and the Internet model in the transport layer. However, that leaves a protocol gap in the intervening two layers, presentation and session. Two approaches for filling the gap were considered in the process of defining the NMS protocol.

One proposal, offered in Internet RFC 1006 (ISO De-

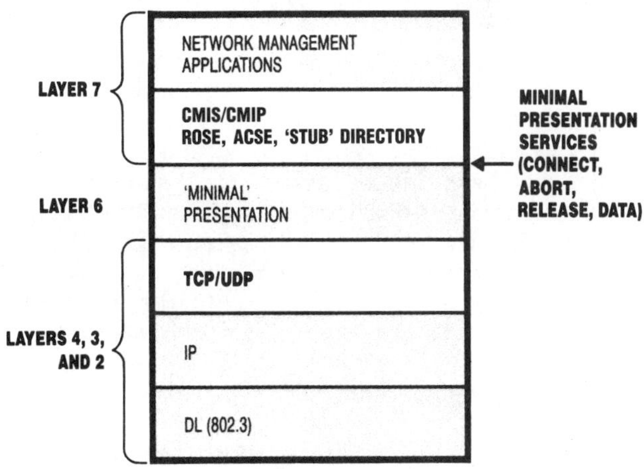

ACSE = APPLICATION CONTROL SERVICE ENTITY
CMIP = COMMON MANAGEMENT INFORMATION PROTOCOL
CMIS = COMMON MANAGEMENT INFORMATION SERVICE
DL = DATA LINK
IP = INTERNET PROTOCOL
ROSE = REMOTE OPERATIONS SERVICE ELEMENT
TCP = TRANSMISSION CONTROL PROTOCOL
UDP = USER DATAGRAM PROTOCOL

velopment Environment, or ISODE), suggested extending the specifications of one layer to the point that it fills the functional gap. Figure 2 illustrates how the protocol stack would look for a device based on such a model. This approach enables a device to run standard OSI applications over TCP regardless of its service requirements. In this case, all services are provided and network management would simply be another application. The downside of such an approach is that it would require developers to incur high development costs—both in engineering resources and machine memory—because of the vendor-specific nature of each implementation and the overhead required to implement complete OSI layers.

The competing proposal—and the one adopted by the IETF—is considerably less ambitious in scope. This strategy suggests a new filler layer between the application and transport layers. Figure 3 illustrates how the various elements of this minimal presentation layer fit together. Such a solution requires that the filler be both simple and compact. The Netman Group intends that the filler layer support the application layer entities with no changes in expected presentation services, and that they provide interfacing capabilities to other elements of the protocol stack (ROSE, ACSE, and Directory Services).

This approach is premised on the following architectural subtleties:
■ TCP is a stream-oriented transport protocol.
■ ASN.1 (Abstract Syntax Notation.1) objects, when represented as a stream of octets, are self-delimiting.
■ The ISO presentation service permits the exchange of ASN.1 objects.

ACSE and ROSE require the following presentation facilities: Connection Establishment Facility, Connection Terminal Facility, and Information Transfer Facility. The majority of parameters used by the services that provide these facilities can be hard-wired to avoid negotiation.

In principle, these characteristics point to a cheap emulation (in code size and processing efficiency) of the ISO presentation services that can be implemented by serializing ASN.1 objects over a TCP connection.

According to this proposal, each client and server box implementing this minimal protocol contains three modules:
■ A dispatch module provides the presentation services interface.
■ A serialization module takes an ASN.1 object and applies the encoding rules defined in ISO's Specification of Basic Encoding Rules for Abstract Syntax Notation (IS 8825) to produce a stream of octets. A deserializer performs the reverse operation.
■ A network module manages TCP connections.

Implementer's agreements
The software architecture used to model a network entity using the approach defined in RFC 1085 is illustrated in Figure 4. In general, the OSI presentation layer is primarily used to negotiate transfer syntaxes, in addition to transforming to and from transfer syntax. With the minimal mechanism, no negotiation component is employed.

Implementation of an interoperable Netman product will

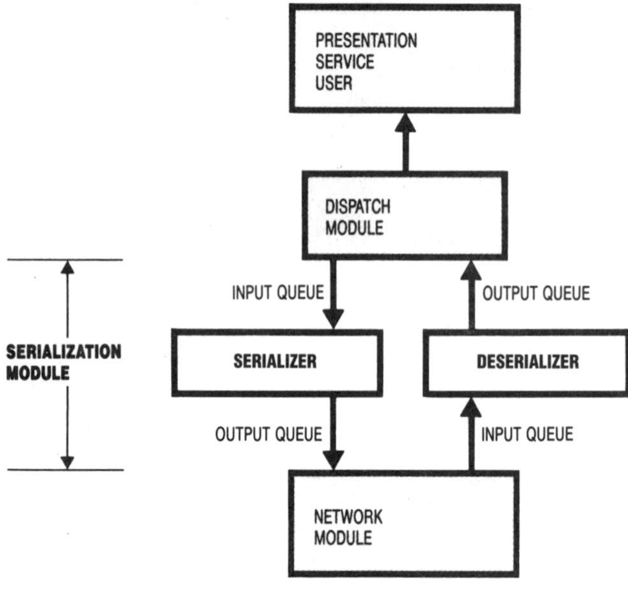

4. RFC 1085. *Client and server boxes implement the minimal protocol described in RFC 1085. Each box contains three modules: for dispatch, serialization, and networking.*

not be a matter of simply reading ISO standards, studying the Internet RFCs, and then pounding out some code. ISO standards define the overall framework and the set of services and protocols applicable to management of network devices and layered protocols. The RFCs describe mechanisms that allow OSI services and protocols to operate over a TCP/IP network and define management information for the lower protocol layers.

These standards and RFCs consist of procedures, parameters, and parameter values that are left to the individual vendors and implementers to specify. Such a situation might lead to many implementations that conform to CMOT with none capable of participating in interoperable network management.

To ensure interoperability, the participating CMOT implementers have established a profile of accepted procedures and parameters and a set of parameter values. These "implementer's agreements" are embodied in RFC 1095. This RFC identifies ISO CMIS/CMIP, ACSE, and ROSE standards as central elements of the commonly adopted Netman profile. ■

H. Kim Lew is a marketing specialist for 3Com's Enterprise Systems Division (formerly Bridge Communications). He has worked as a freelance writer, an editor for a technical trade journal, and a technical writer for a number of Silicon Valley firms. He has a BA in journalism from San Jose State University and is currently pursuing an MBA at Santa Clara University.

Jim Robertson is department manager for network management with 3Com's Enterprise Systems Division. He represented 3Com on the IETF's TCP/IP Netman Working Group since its inception in May 1987. He received a BSEE from the University of Florida (Gainesville).

Michael Lefkowitz, Larse Corp., Santa Clara, Calif.

A tale of two standards—the T1 ESF (r)evolution

Nondisruptive monitoring via ESF is critical to the management of T1 networks. However, ESF comes two ways: an AT&T version and a recently adopted ANSI standard.

The growth of T1-based networks has been a startling phenomenon of the data communications industry and user community. The proliferation of these networks reflects a growing corporate dependence on fast, reliable information transfer. But any disruption of a corporation's T1 (1.544-Mbit/s) network can severely restrict its ability to do business. Efficient network management is more critical here than with lower-speed networks.

As a measure of T1's network popularity, from a start of less than $100 million in 1984, the T1 equipment market is forecast to grow beyond $2 *billion* by 1993. Efforts to keep the resultant networks fully operational has fostered the development and deployment of the extended superframe format. As a monitoring and diagnostic aid, ESF has major ramifications for network management (see "The hidden treasures of ESF," DATA COMMUNICATIONS, September 1986, p. 204).

Now, a sea change in ESF standards is significantly affecting how T1 networks are being planned and implemented. Network managers must understand the impact of this change and know the right questions to ask their service and equipment vendors.

The ESF standard is a critical one since it provides, for the first time on digital facilities, a method of nondisruptive full-time monitoring for both logic and format errors (see "T1 network management"). This capability provides for more rapid trouble isolation, resulting in reduced downtime. Considering how much of a typical corporation's success is riding on its digital backbone network, taking advantage of ESF is a must for any network manager.

Similar, but not the same

The two ESF standards, AT&T's PUB 54016 and ANSI's T1.403-1989 (T1E1), have many similarities. They also have several important differences. Both can be seen in an examination of salient aspects of the standards (see table).

Monitored parameters. PUB 54016 calls for two parameters to be monitored: CRC-6 errors, where the calculated CRC-6 does not equal the received CRC-6; and Out-of-Frame (OOF), defined as two out of four or five consecutive framing bits in error.

The T1E1 standard specifies five error events, two mandatory and three optional. Error events that *must* be detected—called Severely Errored Framing in T1E1—are the same as in 54016: CRC-6 errors and OOF. Error events whose detection is optional are Controlled Slip (duplication or deletion of an entire frame), Framing Error (a single framing bit in error), and Bipolar Violation (BPV, where a mark or space has the same—not opposite—polarity as the previous mark or space).

Derived parameters. PUB 54016 specifies three types of problem seconds:

■ Errored Second (ES): a second having one or more CRC-6 errors and/or an OOF state.

■ Severely Errored Second (SES): a second having 320 or more CRC-6 errors and/or an OOF state. (A total of 320 CRC-6 errors corresponds to a bit error rate of one in 10^3, a good-quality threshold for voice lines but not for data. Some carriers have contracted to provide T1 service with SES defined to correspond to more stringent bit error rates, such as one in 10^5.)

■ Failed Second (FS): a second during which a failed signal state is in effect. A failed signal state is declared after 10 consecutive SESs and cleared after 10 consecutive non-SESs. (FS is so defined to distinguish between error bursts—which are typical of digital facilities—and failure states.)

These derived parameters are organized into performance registers that may be accessed over the data link by monitoring equipment in the central office.

The T1E1 standard does not call for any processed parameters. Instead, a performance report is transmitted over the data link every second. No historical data is kept beyond three seconds.

Performance Reports. In PUB 54016, derived parameters are organized into 24-hour and one-hour registers of Errored Seconds and Failed Seconds. Each register is organized into 15-minute increments. In addition, all ESF errors (CRC-6 and OOF) are counted and stored in the ESF Error Counter. The four registers and the ESF Error Counter are accessed by data link commands using the Telemetry Asynchronous Block Serial (TABS) protocol, a modified X.25 Level 2 AT&T standard.

Typically, registers are read once a day and then reset.

Central office equipment stores this information and processes it to create other performance reports used by the carrier.

In contrast, the T1E1 standard specifies a single performance report formatted to conform to the Q.921/LAPD (Link Access Procedure-D) protocol and broadcast via the data link. (Other message-oriented signals and reports may be added to the standard in the future.) The performance report, consisting of 112 bits, contains performance information about the current second and the three previous seconds. The report is transmitted every second by equipment (such as a channel service unit, or CSU) located on the

---

T1 network management

There are several factors that contribute to the difficulty of T1 network management:

■ The high volume of traffic carried by a single T1 line means that line degradations and failures have a much greater impact on the network.

■ The complexity of services and equipment increases the ways in which things can go wrong, making troubleshooting more complicated.

■ The multivendor networks make rapid isolation and restoral more difficult.

■ Last, but certainly not least, there is a shortage of trained personnel to manage this T1 complexity.

With the extended superframe format, real-time performance data is gathered at various network sites and promptly made available at a central location. With this data, the management team rapidly pinpoints, diagnoses, and corrects a problem, thus keeping downtime to a minimum. Degradations are identified and dealt with before they seriously affect operation. Historical data is used for trend analysis and performance documenting. And because the carrier and user have access to the same performance data, finger-pointing is greatly reduced.

■ **Historical perspective.** In 1981, driven by the need to provide better maintenance for the Dataphone Digital Service network and the then-planned High Capacity Terrestrial Service (the precursor of Accunet T1.5), AT&T developed the ESF format. ESF is basically an enhancement of the D4, or superframe, format. In both D4 and ESF, the digital bit stream is organized into frames consisting of 192 information bits and one framing bit. The 1.544-Mbit/s bit stream is thus divided into 1.536 Mbit/s of data and 8 kbit/s of overhead.

The D4 format employs a superframe of 12 frames, with all 12 framing bits providing a specified pattern for framing synchronization. ESF employs an extended superframe of 24 frames, with six of the framing bits used for framing synchronization and 18 bits available for other monitoring and maintenance functions. Specifically, the ESF format divides the 8 kbit/s of framing information into three data streams as follows:

■ 2 kbit/s for framing;

■ 2 kbit/s for a CRC-6 logic check (CRC-6 is a cyclic redundancy check that uses six frame bits, those in frames 2, 6, 10, 14, 18, and 22); and

■ 4 kbit/s for a data link, used for transmission of performance information and control signals.

When AT&T published the ESF Technical Reference, PUB 54016, in late 1984, the only unresolved issue was if and how users could access the data link for their own applications. In early 1985, AT&T started testing ESF equipment for the central office, and also encouraging manufacturers to design and market ESF equipment for the customer premises.

At the same time, AT&T submitted PUB 54016 to the newly created Exchange Carriers Standards Association committee T1C1.

Things were sailing along smoothly in T1C1.2, the working group responsible for the DS-1 interface standard, until August 1985, when Bellcore introduced a new proposal. Under this scheme, the 4-kbit/s data link would be split into four channels so that each stakeholder (the user, local exchange carrier, interexchange carrier, and equipment vendor) would have its own link for maintenance purposes. This proposal, considered at Bell Labs prior to 1981, had some interesting merits, but was rejected by AT&T. (The merits included: notification to the sending end of an error detected at the receiving end and a designated channel portion for each carrier involved and for the user.)

After many long and sometimes heated debates, a compromise was reached. It was agreed to retain the data link as a single 4-kbit/s channel and to use a message-oriented (Q.921/LAPD [Link Access Procedure-D]) protocol for performance information. A number of bit-oriented data link maintenance messages were defined, such as Yellow Signal (indicating loss of synchronization), loopback commands, and protection switching commands that can activate standby circuits.

In early 1988, the T1 standards committees were reorganized and T1E1 was charged with the DS-1 interface standard. This standard was recently issued by ANSI as T1.403-1989.

During the deliberation and approval processes, AT&T continued to deploy central office equipment compatible with the PUB 54016 version of ESF. In addition, many users deployed customer premises equipment compatible with PUB 54016, creating something of a dilemma. To what extent are the two standards compatible? And how do we make the transition from one to the other?—*M.L.*

customer premises at the network interface. Transmitting data four times for each second helps ensure the accuracy of the performance reports to the receiving network devices.

The following information is provided for each second:
- Range of CRC-6 errors: one, two to five, six to 10, 11 to 100, 101 to 319, 320+;
- Severely Errored Framing (same as OOF), occurrence equal to or greater than one;
- Frame bit errors, equal to or greater than one;
- BPVs equal to or greater than one;
- Slip event equal to or greater than one; and
- Payload loopback (where only information bits are looped) activated.

There are three bits reserved for future applications, such as synchronization.

Maintenance messages. In addition to performance reports, the data link transmits maintenance messages that, in the D4 (superframe) format, are transmitted in-band. Three maintenance messages are defined in both PUB 54016 and T1E1: Yellow Signal, Line Loopback, and Payload Loopback. The maintenance messages are either identical or very similar in the two standards.

Data link operation. The main difference between the two standards is in the operation of the data link. Besides using different protocols (TABS versus Q.921/LAPD), the standards differ in basic maintenance philosophy (see the figure).

As specified in PUB 54016, the data link operates on an inquiry-response basis, depending on the premises equipment (CSU) to store 24 hours of performance data. On receipt of a valid command from the network's central office, the CSU transmits the contents of the appropriate performance register(s).

Under the T1E1 standard, performance messages are broadcast every second on the data link. These performance reports apply to the direction opposite to that in which they are transmitted. For example, performance data for the link from A to B is broadcast from B toward A. T1E1 performance reports can be monitored anywhere along the T1 network.

Bridged performance monitors, located in the central office, monitor the data stream for performance parameters such as CRC-6 errors and OOF conditions. In addition, they extract performance data for the direction of transmission opposite from the data link's. Collected data is organized into reports and forwarded to an Operations Support System (OSS), which is used to isolate network problems and provide historical performance information for ongoing studies, such as trend analysis. (As shown in the figure, as

Summary of features, AT&T PUB 54016 versus T1E1

ATTRIBUTE	AT&T PUB 54016	T1E1 (ANSI T1.403)
ALLOCATION OF 8 KBIT/S OF OVERHEAD	2 KBIT/S FRAMING 2 KBIT/S CRC-6 ERROR CHECKING 4 KBIT/S DATA LINK (DL)	SAME AS PUB 54016
MONITORED PARAMETERS	CRC-6 ERRORS OUT OF FRAME (OOF)	CRC-6 ERRORS SEVERELY ERRORED FRAMING (= OOF) CONTROL SLIP (OPTIONAL) FRAMING BIT ERROR (OPTIONAL) BIPOLAR VIOLATION (OPTIONAL)
DERIVED PARAMETERS	ERRORED SECOND (ES) SEVERELY ERRORED SECOND (SES) FAILED SECOND (FS)	RANGE OF CRC-6 ERRORS
MONITORING EQUIPMENT (CARRIER)	READ AND WRITE ON DATA LINK	READ DATA LINK
DATA LINK PROTOCOL	TABS	Q921/LAPD
MAINTENANCE PHILOSOPHY	IN-LINE INQUIRY-RESPONSE	BROADCAST TO BRIDGED MONITORS
MAINTENANCE MESSAGES	YELLOW SIGNAL PAYLOAD LOOPBACK LINE LOOPBACK	YELLOW SIGNAL PAYLOAD LOOPBACK LINE LOOPBACK PROTECTION SWITCHING (RESERVED) SYNCHRONIZATION (RESERVED)
HISTORICAL PERFORMANCE DATA	24 HOURS	NONE

CRC = CYCLIC REDUNDANCY CHECK
LAPD = LINK ACCESS PROCEDURE-D

many as three OSS units may be present on a single T1 configuration.)

From the carrier's point of view, T1E1 is more efficient to implement. First, T1E1 is less expensive because the performance monitor in the central office is bridged—that is, it reads the data link but does not write on it as required under PUB 54016. Second, a bridged monitor is not a potential point of failure in the T1 network, as a 54016 in-line performance monitor would be.

From the user's point of view, access to historical performance data is the critical issue. Currently, where only AT&T PUB 54016 has been implemented, users have access to the same 24-hour performance registers as the carrier. In addition, some CSU manufacturers build in more extensive, user-accessible performance registers. Under T1E1, users would have to add performance data storage external to the CSU or be able to access information from the carrier's OSS. In fact, some carriers are planning to allow customers to access their own performance data; others are evaluating the possibility of doing so.

The good news

At first glance, things look pretty bleak for the user in the ESF world. There are key differences between the two ESF standards. On one hand, AT&T has made a big investment

Data link operation. *The two ESF standards differ in basic maintenance philosophy. Under AT&T PUB 54016, the data link operates on an inquiry-response basis, where the network retrieves 24 hours of performance data from the T1 CPE. Under the T1E1 standard, performance messages are broadcast to the network once every second.*

AT&T PUB 54016: Inquiry/response

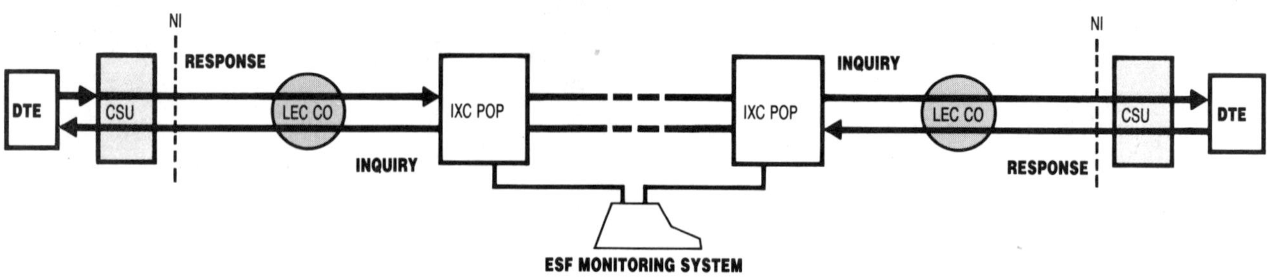

T1E1: Broadcast

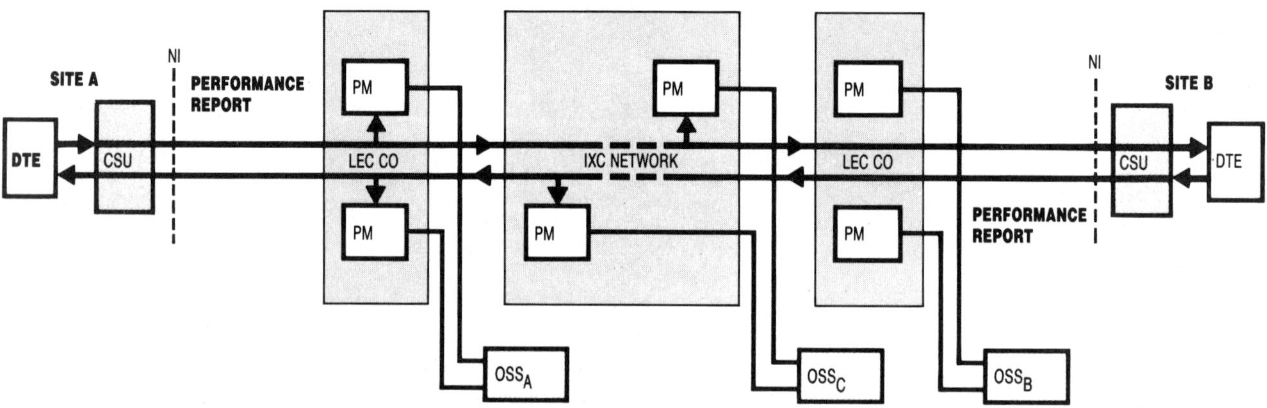

CO = CENTRAL OFFICE
CSU = CHANNEL SERVICE UNIT
DTE = DATA TERMINAL EQUIPMENT
ESF = EXTENDED SUPERFRAME FORMAT
IXC = INTERLATA CARRIER
LEC = LOCAL EXCHANGE CARRIER
NI = NETWORK INTERFACE
OSS = OPERATIONS SUPPORT SYSTEM
PM = PERFORMANCE MONITOR
POP = POINT OF PRESENCE

in deploying equipment based on PUB 54016. And on the other, most of the regional BOCs and other interLATA carriers are either planning or are likely to implement T1E1. What's the user to do today?

In spite of the fact that some observers are calling the two standards completely incompatible, the good news for users is that the two standards can coexist. The main factor making this possible is the brevity of the T1E1 performance report, which takes only 112 bit/s of the 4-kbit/s data link (or only 28 milliseconds of each second on the data link). With proper flow control, this leaves more than enough bandwidth for PUB 54016 messages. Furthermore, since maintenance messages such as Yellow Signal and loop-back commands take priority over other messages, a CSU or other ESF terminating device can wait until these preemptive messages are transmitted over the network. The devices can then resume responding to and generating the proper messages for both standards. The CSU can even store historical performance data for access by the user.

The possibility of coexistence is good news because the transition between PUB 54016 and T1E1 standards will take time. While AT&T is the only carrier that invested heavily in PUB 54016 ESF equipment, most vendors of T1 customer premises equipment have also implemented PUB 54016, either directly or through separate CSU equipment.

There is a substantial amount of ESF equipment on customer premises today that is compatible with PUB 54016. Once the RBOCs and other local exchange carriers begin to implement T1E1, this equipment will, in all likelihood, have to be upgraded. If AT&T is the interLATA carrier, the equipment may have to meet both standards.

The transition can be accomplished with minimum disruption to the corporate network if the CSU or other ESF terminating device can add T1E1 capability through downline-loadable software. Otherwise, CSUs or PROMs (programmable ROMs) must be physically swapped at every network site, a process both disruptive and expensive.

The key to a smooth transition is planning. Users should be made aware of the likely evolution to T1E1 by their network carriers. To respond to evolving conditions, users should choose CSUs and other network equipment that meet both standards or that can be readily upgraded through downline-loadable software.

The not-so-good news

From a user's point of view, no discussion of ESF is complete without considering its limitations. First of all, both ESF standards are carrier-oriented; they provide one-way information from the customer premises to the network. Neither has a provision for user access to the performance data residing in the carrier's network or at the far end of the user's network.

The second limitation is that use of the data link is restricted to the carrier. Currently, there is no provision for user applications such as reconfiguration and far-end performance-data retrieval. Responsibility for this shortcoming thus far rests—at least in part—with the users. As stakeholders, users need to take an active role in the standards process. Since T1E1.2 has an open project to define alternative applications of the data link, there is still time for users to become involved in setting the standards for their applications.

The third limitation of the current ESF standards is that neither supports the capturing of all major events at the customer premises. For example, Loss of Signal, Yellow Signal, Alarm Indication Signal, and other performance problems are not captured. Bipolar Violations are a good indicator of performance degradations on metallic circuits (they are not a factor with other media), yet neither standard makes use of BPV rates.

Finally, neither standard—except for one item in PUB 54016—defines user-oriented performance thresholds. The lone exception is the Severely Errored Second in PUB 54016, which corresponds to a bit error rate of one in 10^3 bits. This is considered a good threshold for voice circuits, but it is much too poor for data or integrated voice/data T1 circuits. ESF standards need to define performance thresholds that more accurately indicate line availability. Optimally, thresholds should not be set solely by the carrier but jointly with the user. This is another area of standards development in which users should get involved—for their own protection. ∎

Michael Lefkowitz earned a BSEE from Cooper Union (New York City) and an MSEE from New York University. He spent six years at AT&T Bell Laboratories designing data communications networks and nine years at AT&T in a variety of technical and marketing positions. He joined Larse in 1984, where he is director of business development.

Lee Mantelman, DATA COMMUNICATIONS INTERNATIONAL

The birth of OSI TP: A new way to link OLTP networks

An OSI TP standard is coming. But it's still a long way from the maturity and penetration of such proprietary techniques as Logical Unit 6.2

A new standard protocol for linking proprietary transaction processing methods has lots of vendors hopping and many users scratching their heads. On July 28, representatives of national standards bodies at an editing meeting in London unanimously agreed to recommend that the OSI Transaction Processing (OSI TP) protocol become a Draft International Standard (DIS).

It's up to ISO Subcommittee 21 to decide in November whether to move the standard, currently a second Draft Proposal (DP), to a DIS or kick it back to a third DP.

The distinction is crucial: Vendors often regard a DIS, but not a DP, as stable enough to begin working on implementations. But whether to go DIS or stay DP could be a difficult choice: "We're caught between a rock and a hard place," says Peter Rich, an OSI TP group member and consulting systems engineer for Bank of America. "There's enormous pressure to move forward and equally enormous pressure to get it right."

Not surprising, since OSI TP might be the only way for vendors to compete with IBM for share in an increasingly important market. An International Data Corp. report estimates that the on-line transaction processing (OLTP) industry has a "50 percent or more domination by IBM, primarily through its 370 architecture products."

And that market could grow rapidly. "Up to 80 percent of user application programs will be based on transaction processing by the early 1990s," forecasts John Neumann, principal consultant for Open Strategies, a Vienna, Va., consulting firm and rapporteur for the standard.

OSI TP is "the first real OSI application protocol from the user's point of view," says Neumann. "I'm not disparaging X.400, X.500, or FTAM [File Transfer, Access, and Management], but they're not solving real application problems. OSI TP can be used by any application requiring interprocess or reliable communications," he says.

But some observers think the new standard faces a tough fight against the IBM equivalents to OSI TP—LU6.2 and its Application Program Interface (API), Advanced Program-to-Program Communications (APPC).

"LU6.2 has been around for years, it's a proven system implemented on many machines, but OSI TP is not there yet," says Clive Partridge, director of Data Connection Ltd., a software engineering company in Enfield, U.K. "There are no OSI TP products you can buy from a manufacturer. If OSI TP is to succeed, it has to be significantly better than LU6.2."

TP in the world of IBM

Historically, transaction processing in the IBM world has not been based on LU6.2 at all. "If you want the highest-performance OLTP system, it will be the mainframe software TPF (Transaction Processing Facility) that IBM sells to airlines," says Partridge.

Helmut Wrubel, Siemens AG's system architect and one of OSI TP's developers, agrees that "IBM's centralized transaction-processing systems are used all over the world, but they're getting old. The current OSI TP offers a lot more functionality than LU6.2."

Mitchell R. Wiggins, an OSI TP working group member from IBM communication standards development, says that "some features of OSI TP go beyond the present capabilities of LU6.2." However, he adds, "proprietary approaches look at things outside the scope of OSI."

One is an API, which provides hooks for programmers to access the protocol over a service interface. LU6.2 provides an API called APPC. "OSI TP needs standardized interfaces like X/Open is doing for Unix," says Wrubel.

Such interfaces would make it easier to implement applications that use the protocol. "OSI TP must do more at the service interface to bring it to the same level of usability that APPC has," says Partridge. His company recently implemented an APPC-to-OSI TP mapping based on the first DP for a major U.K. financial institution.

To those who see OSI TP as the only real multivendor approach, Partridge answers, "LU6.2 is multivendor as well. IBM is hoping everyone will just use LU6.2."

Indeed, many vendors do provide APPC connections. But OSI TP could be better for them in the long run. "LU6.2 is an SNA protocol that uses concepts and technology proprietary to IBM," says Anthony Fletcher, member of the OSI TP group from British Telecom. "Vendors have to pay IBM royalties. A lot of people did LU6.2 implementations without paying and IBM's legal department came after them.

Besides, says Fletcher, "IBM can change LU6.2 when it suits them and put everyone else out of step."

Clamor for OSI TP

The controversy can only get hotter—many vendors want OSI TP now. According to Wrubel, two types of vendors need the standard: those with a transaction-processing product in the market today and those without one. The former want to satisfy customer demands for product enhancements with extensions that move the product closer to a standard, rather than pouring more resources into a proprietary cul-de-sac.

And vendors without such product want something to bring to market. If it takes too long to agree on the OSI standard, these vendors would have to implement their own approach and then reimplement the standard. A few companies can afford to implement different incompatible stacks and do the same thing twice," says Wrubel.

IBM has also taken a keen interest in OSI TP. Wrubel estimates that a quarter or more of the OSI TP standards people work for IBM. "It means that IBM is interested in every country where it has premises," he says. But Partridge thinks that IBM is putting the work into OSI TP "because they always hedge their bets."

---

1. TP tree. *Transactions take place over tree structures. Here, a travel agent's computer contacts others to put together a fly-drive-bed package.*

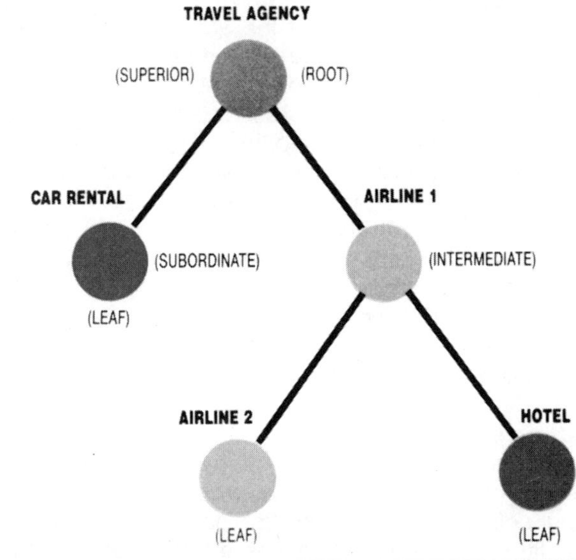

"OSI TP has the same opportunity for being a general platform as LU6.2 but in an OSI environment. We envision a world in which customers will have the choice to use either," says Matthew L. Hess, manager of IBM communication standards development in Raleigh, N.C.

Hess agrees that OSI TP can be used to support existing software. "LU6.2 applications could access their communication partners with the same calls, using OSI TP," he says.

It could be quite a bet to hedge. Besides governments, which are beginning to put muscle behind their OSI procurement schemes, "users have an urgent need for OSI TP in booking, banking, and wholesale," says Wrubel. Manufacturing outfits could also use OLTP, he says, for their real-time production robots and just-in-time inventory control.

So far, the main users of OLTP have been financial service firms and the travel industry, particularly the airlines. In fact, their applications reflect the growth of the technology.

Transacting business

To cope with such transactions as flight reservations and funds transfers, vendors introduced transaction monitors (TMs) about a decade ago. A TM ran on a single machine (usually a mainframe) and encompassed a database and output onto a peripheral, such as a printer.

For each transaction, the TM ensured both timeliness, so that the check or airline ticket would be printed out right away if the funds withdrawal or booking succeeded, and consistency, so that printing would not take place if the transaction failed. Thus, the transaction had to be "atomic," which is an all-or-nothing-at-all affair.

These TMs were originally centralized, but distributed access soon became possible. For example, in the past passengers could only book their seats with one airline at an airline counter, but now they can book at any travel agency and have the flight confirmed immediately.

What's needed next is a way to link TMs from different vendors. Currently, "centralized systems can exchange some information between them, but not in an atomic way," says Wrubel.

The problem is that vendors tend to use their own protocols between OLTP machines. Moreover, they split those protocols into layers based on different models, in the way that Digital Equipment Corp. (DEC) and IBM layer their architectures differently. And even the definition of a transaction can vary from vendor to vendor, an obvious reason for a standard (see "OSI TP fundamentals").

If vendors agreed on a protocol for OLTP, as well as an OLTP model (such as what transactions are, the structures in which they occur, and how to handle recovery) and service (the abstract way in which users of the protocol can access it), new applications could be spurred.

For example, say a customer in a travel agency wanted to stay in a posh hotel on a remote island for two weeks and drive around exploring. Today, the agent might have to log a number of separate requests for the components of this holiday. It could take several days to complete all the inquiries and, if all the elements are available, to book them.

But if the providers of these services and the travel agency all used computers compatible with OSI TP, the

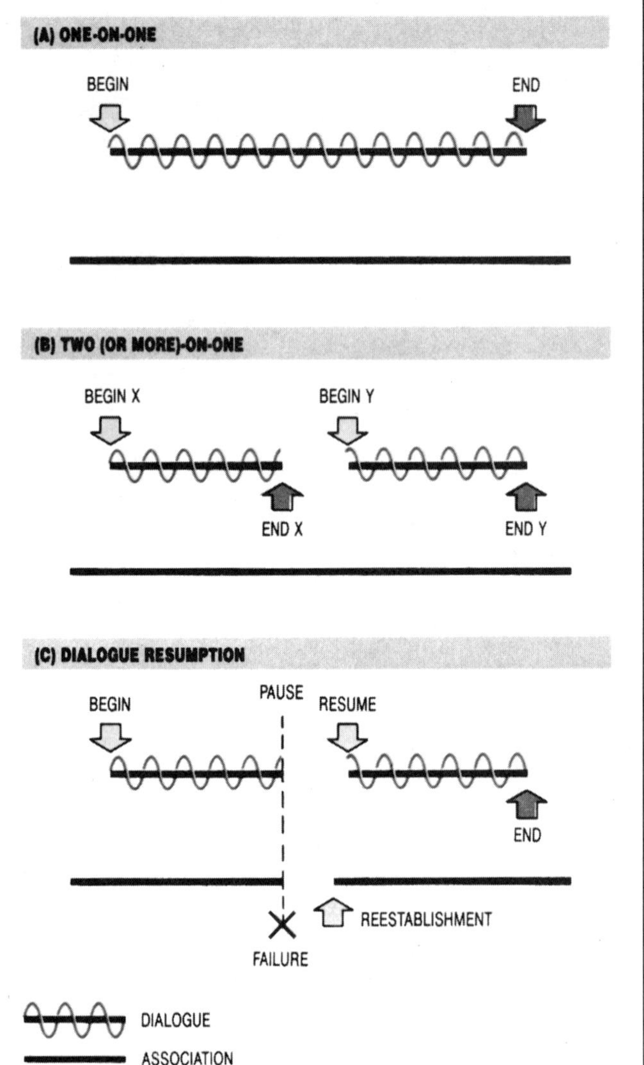

transaction would be carried out over a tree structure like that shown in Figure 1. Bookings would be made during the search of the tree. If any element was unavailable, all the bookings would be canceled. But if everything was available, and the customer agreed to the package, all the bookings could be confirmed.

The transaction would proceed as follows: First, the agency's computer would contact the computers of a car rental firm with a branch on the island and an airline known to serve the area. That airline might offer a package in conjunction with a smaller carrier and a hotel chain.

So the airline's computer contacts its partners to see if the right flights and rooms are available. If they are, and the major airline itself has an appropriate flight, it reports the package to the agency's computer. If a car is also available, the agent's computer reports the package to the agent, who could confirm all the bookings at once. But a nonavailability in any computer would be sent to the travel agent's machine and cause it to tell all the others to cancel their bookings.

Is this scenario, versions of which are bandied about in standards meetings, viable in the world of real users? It's hard to say, because few users have had any input into OSI TP so far. "Standards people at their meetings tend to act like carriers of the faith and seeds of the future, and not once do you hear a mention of the user," says Partridge.

"We've had almost no other nonvendor participation," agrees Rich. Bank of America is one of the few user organizations involved in creating OSI TP. "That's part of the problem," he says. "If we users don't get our requirements in now, we have no reason to complain if the standards don't fulfill those requirements. Not all the vendors have enough experience in transaction processing to understand users' view of it."

Getting involved

Users don't get involved and learn what's going on, so they have no control over what vendors do and can't evaluate vendor offerings to know whether they adhere to the standard. "What usually happens is that vendors come in like car salesmen and try to persuade you, rather than you saying, 'these are our requirements,'" says Rich.

And the current standard might not meet those requirements. "It's not complete enough for us to make use of it," Rich adds. "There are architectural things in the current system that we feel will limit its proliferation and restrict the environment you can implement in."

For example, the standard has not yet begun to deal with transaction routing, which chooses the logical path a transaction will follow if there's no logically adjacent node. "If the association is through intermediaries, we need transaction routing to get there," says Rich.

But proprietary solutions to transaction routing already exist. According to Partridge, IBM's Advanced Peer-to-Peer Networking nodes can exchange topological and resource information, providing a directory service to correctly route transactions through a peer network.

Further, OSI TP invokes other protocols to perform specific actions. Lacking a data-transfer mechanism of its own, it uses existing protocols such as FTAM, remote database access, or the presentation layer to transfer data. But Rich says plugging such data transfer mechanisms into TP protocols spells trouble. "Users could run into contention problems and problems of coordinating commitment."

Partridge says he experienced just that. His company's implementation of OSI TP "had a real problem figuring out who should have the token at the end of a dialogue." Though the implementation was based on OSI TP's first DP, Rich saw the problem continuing into the second.

Partridge says that the snag, caused by the token mechanism in OSI's session layer, might not have arisen using LU6.2, which works on a contention basis. If both ends want to start a dialogue at the same time, one side wins the contention.

In addition, Rich thinks the naming and addressing mechanisms are not sufficient to deal with thousands of users. "The standard assumes we will use X.500, but that area hasn't been dealt with extensively," he says.

LU6.2 could have the edge in this area as well. "SNA addressing is significantly simpler than OSI addressing," says Partridge. "Also, it's well defined and people have been using it in things like VTAM [Virtual Terminal Access Method] generations for years. People know how to make big networks out of it."

Out of the Blue

But users should not write off OSI TP in favor of IBM's proprietary OLTP mechanism, actually its progenitor.

LU6.2 played a key role in the development of OSI TP, and today's standard "still has a strong flavor of LU6.2," says Barry Rubinson, a member of the OSI TP working group and DEC senior consulting software engineer.

A closer look at the OSI TP protocol (see "Protocol flow") shows that "the resemblance [to LU6.2] is uncanny," says Partridge. "There's a one-to-one correspondence between the message in the two protocols."

"The semantics are identical," explains Neumann, that is, every concept in LU6.2 maps to one in OSI TP. Conversations in the former equate to dialogues in the latter, sessions

Protocol flow

In the current OSI TP standard, all the nodes involved in a transaction must form a tree structure, like that shown in Figure 1 in the text. Don't be confused by the different levels: transactions, which the current standard says must take place in a tree pattern; dialogue trees, all or part of which may support a transaction tree, depending on the application's requirements; and associations that support dialogues, which are not now limited to a tree structure.

One node, which is called the root, initiates a task by establishing dialogues with subordinate nodes. If these nodes are not able to respond to the root's requests entirely on their own, they may initiate dialogues with other nodes in the dialogue tree, becoming superiors to the new subordinate nodes. All these nodes are then partners in the transaction.

To remain in step, all the nodes can either commit (complete) or roll back (abort) a transaction. If they roll back, they return all their bound data (data that might have been changed during the transaction) to its previous state. To do this, they should have put the initial values of the bound data into stable store (for example, on disk), from where it could be recovered after a failure (such as a node crash).

The figure shows how OSI TP would be used between two nodes, a superior and a subordinate. The first exchange in the establishment phase starts the dialogue, the second begins a transaction.

When the action phase begins, the initial state of any bound data, along with a transaction identifier, is recorded in stable store. (The transaction ID is a tag that marks the bound data and ties the log to that data.) Then the nodes exchange data to further the TP application.

The superior node signals the end of the action phase and the beginning of the two-phase commitment protocol by sending a "prepare-to-commit" message. Up to this point, either side could have backed out of the transaction by issuing a "roll back request."

After receiving "prepare-to-commit," the subordinate can either roll back, to undo all the actions, or declare itself ready to commit or to roll back (if some other node issues a roll back request).

First, though, the subordinate must ensure that it has both initial and final versions of all bound data in stable store. It must also write a "ready log," which records the fact that it has said "ready to commit," the transaction

equate to associations, and verbs can be mapped to service primitives (see Fig. 2).

Both protocols offer what OSI TP calls a "service definition," namely a specification of what information is needed to use the protocol. For example, to establish a dialogue, an application must specify addressing information, functional units to be used, and other parameters.

Interestingly, according to Neumann, APPC or any other OLTP interface can be slid on top of the OSI TP stack with relatively simple mapping software. For example, the interface primitive "give me a session with A, B, and C

identifier, and the identity of its superior (addressing information).

The subordinate then says, "I'm ready to commit." (An intermediate node cannot reply "ready" until it has received "ready" from all subordinates and is ready itself.) If all other branches of this transaction have sent the same message, the superior records a "commit log" (including the decision to order commitment, transaction ID, and identity of each subordinate).

The superior can now start the "commit" portion of the two-phase protocol by commiting its own data and sending a "commit" message. The subordinate then commits the final state of its data and discards the initial state. It deletes its ready log and responds to the superior that it has committed. On receipt of "I've committed," and if it has finished its own commitment sequence, the superior deletes its commit log.

To increase the efficiency of the protocol, certain messages may be concatenated with others. For instance, a new transaction may begin by piggybacking onto the "commit" message, thus providing a chained (or continuous) transaction service. Likewise, the transaction- and dialogue-begin message may be collapsed into a single exchange.

Although any node can request a rollback of the whole transaction, only the root can presently initiate the "prepare-to-commit" and "commit" messages, which are then propagated along all the tree branches from superiors to subordinates.

However, future enhancements are likely to allow a nonroot node to initiate these prepare and commit sequences. They will make use of the fact that, if you shake a tree, it's still a tree: Topologically, any node on a tree can be taken as the root.

— *A.M.F.*

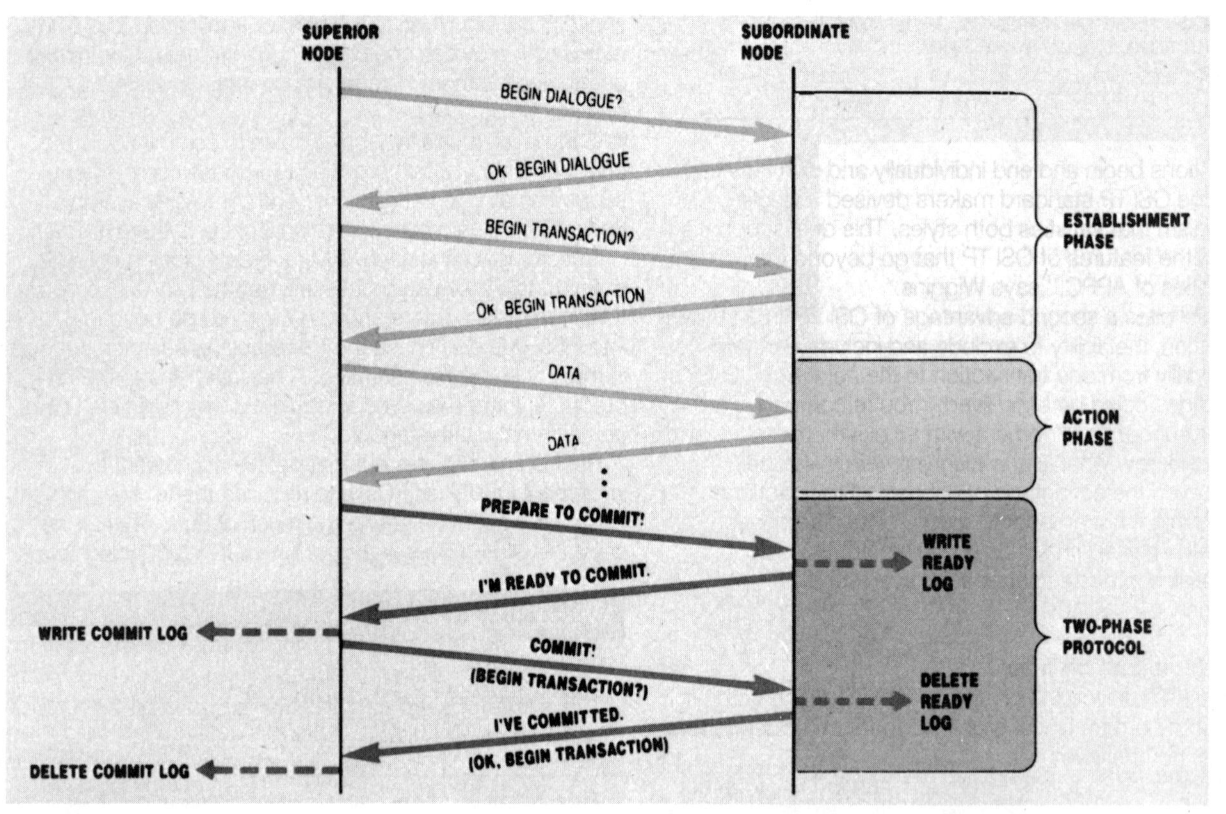

parameters" in LU6.2 becomes "begin a dialogue with X, Y, and Z parameters" in OSI TP.

This "mappability" protects the user's networking investment because it allows vendors to quickly migrate their own OLTP schemes to the standard or easily provide OLTP—if they don't already.

It also means that applications written to run with LU6.2, or any other form of OLTP, don't have to be rewritten, at least if they are "well-behaved" (do not bypass the API).

"With a mapping, programs work interchangeably, so people are keen on having an APPC adapter module that eases migration," according to Partridge.

The two protocols may be similar, but they're not identical. LU6.2 includes hooks for managing a proprietary environment that would be too vendor-specific for OSI.

And LU6.2 requires transactions to be chained, that is, the end of one coincides with the beginning of another. The figure in the panel "Protocol flow" illustrates this where a "Commit" message can also carry "Begin transaction" and "I've committed" can carry "OK, begin transaction."

In fact, most OLTP implementations handle only one style of transaction, either chained or unchained. Unchained

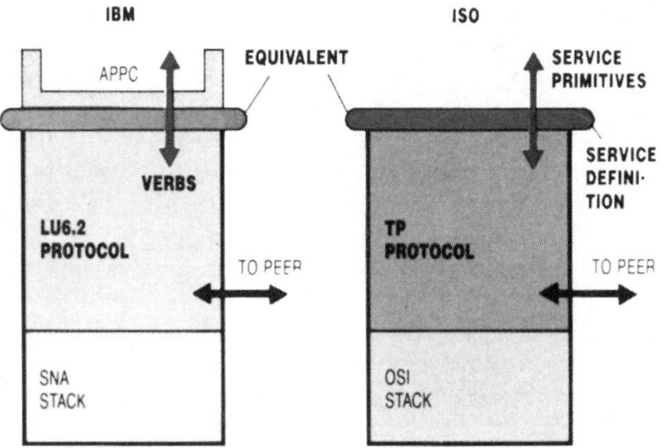

APPC = ADVANCED PROGRAM-TO-PROGRAM COMMUNICATIONS
ISO = INTERNATIONAL ORGANIZATION FOR STANDARDIZATION
LU = LOGICAL UNIT
TP = TRANSACTION PROCESSING

transactions begin and end individually and don't overlap.

But the OSI TP standard makers devised a single mechanism that satisfies both styles. This dual support is "one of the features of OSI TP that go beyond the present capabilities of APPC," says Wiggins.

Wrubel cites a second advantage of OSI TP: in a chained transaction, the ability to exclude and include partners dynamically from one transaction to the next. But OSI TP's advantages could be short-lived: "You're comparing a standard under development with an existing product, and one can't know what IBM is planning," says Wrubel.

And even the advantage of unchained transactions support might not amount to much. "The differences [between chained and unchained] are subtle, historic," says Rubinson. "The user doesn't even see the difference."

Hard decisions on hold

While OSI TP solved the chained-unchained dichotomy, it left a lot of hard technical problems to future addenda (see "What's not there yet").

One decision that was made, and that is likely to affect users, concerns the question of what it means to conform to OSI TP. Before agreement was reached, Rubinson called the conformance clause "possibly the only important remaining battle." The goal was to find some subset of the standard's capabilities required for an implementation to be called minimally conformant.

The group faced a menu of features called functional units (see table). Each FU provides a piece of what's required to perform the different types of transaction processing. Everyone agreed that the kernel and either polarized or shared FUs were necessary.

However, some of the members also thought these were not sufficient without the commit and, possibly, the un-

chained FUs, so that the application would not have to supply the atomicity, consistency, isolation, and durability (ACID) properties at the core of TP.

So the group compromised on three separate classes of TP that vendors could claim conformance to:
- Basic FUs: kernel and either polarized or shared. With only these, the application itself must take care of commitment.
- The basic plus commit FUs. This covers chained transactions, so that when one transaction ends, either another begins or the dialogue ends.
- The basic plus the commit FUs in the unchained MODE, supporting unchained OLTP implementations.

But such variations are not unknown even within proprietary TP schemes. For example, IBM's LU6.2 supports three modes:
- "Sync level equals none," equivalent to the OSI TP kernel FU, simply provides dialogue support. This level offers no commitment.
- "Sync level equals confirm," which includes the handshake FU, leaves it up to the user or application to provide recovery. It provides one-phase commitment ("Commit/I've committed" without "Prepare to commit/I'm ready to commit").
- "Sync level equals syncpoint," akin to commit FU, is the only form of LU6.2 that provides two-phase commitment supporting atomic transactions. And this is only available under IBM's Customer Information Control System (CICS).

According to Rubinson, IBM favored including only the ability to talk between processes, not the full ACID properties, in minimal conformance. "When you go beyond 370s into PCs, you don't have the full reliable transaction support in most LU6.2 implementations," he says. "In most of the products, there's no syncpoint. That's why IBM didn't want commitment in the standard."

But Neumann points out that people might want to implement OSI TP on PCs, and requiring the full commitment capabilities might be asking too much of PCs. After all, he says, the 640-Kbyte limitation of MS-DOS is not going away.

What TP offers

FUNCTIONAL UNIT	SERVICES OFFERED
KERNEL	DIALOGUE CONTROL, ERROR HANDLING
SHARED CONTROL	ALLOWS BOTH PARTNERS TO SIMULTANEOUSLY INVOKE SERVICES
OR POLARIZED CONTROL	ALLOWS ONLY CERTAIN PRIMITIVES TO BE ISSUED SIMULTANEOUSLY; ONE SIDE USUALLY OWNS CONTROL (SUCH AS FOR DATA TRANSFER)
HANDSHAKE	SYNCHRONIZE PARTNERS, SET UP CHECKPOINTS
COMMIT	USED TO COMMIT OR ROLL BACK A TRANSACTION
UNCHAINED TRANSACTIONS	OVERRIDES THE DEFAULT CHAINED MODE, WHEREBY ONE TRANSACTION BEGINS AS SOON AS A PREVIOUS TRANSACTION ENDS

What's not there yet

Coping with failure is the whole point of OSI TP, the logs, the two-phase protocol, and the ACID properties. But a transaction can encounter some problems that the standard cannot yet fully handle, in the following areas:

■ *Heuristic decisions.* If a node has signaled that it is ready but has had to wait too long for its liking (say, longer than an application-determined time-out period) before being ordered to commit or roll back, it may make its own decision.

Such moves can lead to the resources affected by the transaction ending up in an inconsistent state. For example, the root may have ordered commitment, while further down the tree a node that makes the heuristic decision to roll back is out of step with the rest of the tree.

OSI TP currently defers all action on heuristic support to a future addendum, except for the ability of a node to tell its superior that an inconsistent heuristic decision has been (or might have been) made.

■ *Deadlock.* Two or more transactions may be unable to proceed because each owns resources that the other needs to proceed. The standard now recommends the simple expedient of setting a local timer and rolling back any transaction that cannot be given the resources it requires within a given time period. No recommendations are made on how to determine an appropriate time period.

However, certain versions of this algorithm do not work well on a network basis. Consider, for instance, two nodes that each start a transaction with the other one. Neither can proceed because each needs resources already allocated to that node's own transaction. Both use the same deterministic time-out period and roll the incoming transaction back. Both then use the same deterministic time period to try their transactions again. The result is "livelock," a repeated impasse, until one or both give up. Some international agreement on the algorithm and any time-out periods appears to be needed.

■ *Recovery.* OSI TP is designed to aid recovery, but the success of the recovery procedures will depend primarily on design of the participating systems and the precise nature of the failure.

There are three major phases of recovery. Phase 1 deals with fault detection and containment. Many types of failure are envisaged, including communications failure, full or partial system crashes, and loss of bound data. This phase includes automatic and manual attempts to restore the failed systems or communication paths.

Phase 2 recovery attempts to rescue interrupted transactions and to place their bound data into a consistent state or to report inconsistencies. It makes use of special channels between the TP protocol modules, similar to the dialogues between applications.

For Phase 3 an attempt is made to gracefully terminate each dialogue affected by a failure or to allow its active continuation. Although transactions can be recovered in the present standard, dialogues cannot.

■ *Security.* Users like financial companies, who could make extensive use of OSI TP, will look for such security features as access control and authentication. As OSI security is still under discussion, these aspects of OSI TP have been deferred. However, the protocol is designed to carry user information, which can include security.

Other candidates for future addenda to the initial standards include the following:

■ The ability to deliberately suspend and later resume a dialogue;

■ Further performance optimizations, such as the transfer of comrnit coordination to the node best suited to the task;

■ Enhancements to the transaction model, such as sub-transactions, where portions of the transaction can be executed or rolled back separately but committed as a whole; and

■ Guidance on writing application-specific protocols that *can be used with OSI TP.* —*A.M.F.*

Partridge thinks users may not be ready for the most advanced forms of OSI TP or LU6.2. "It's clear IBM doesn't perceive syncpoint as a fundamental market requirement, because only CICS provides it."

"The full commit protocol presumes a complex network of nodes participating in a transaction, but in most real cases, the network is simple, such as a requester and a server [an automatic teller machine transacting with a bank's central mainframe]. In that case, a two-phase commit protocol gives no more security than a one-phase version," says Partridge. With more than one node, though, the first phase is helpful because it limits the extent to which nodes can be out of phase.

"Users don't implement syncpoint because it's too complicated. Commitment doubles or triples the complexity of LU6.2," says Partridge. "It's too code- and resource-intensive to be worthwhile in anything smaller than a mainframe."

Moreover, he says, people who have to run and manage networks these days are much more worried about utilization of resources. Do they want two-phase commit protocols running over their lines? No. Do they want quick response times? Yes. "It's all very well to define theoretical standards, but they don't address the needs of people who are running large enterprise networks," says Partridge.

Even users of proprietary schemes are often more concerned with squeezing the most out of them and less with their bells and whistles. "I've seen people build large SNA networks and then not use any of their features, such as pacing, to maximize resources and minimize costs," says Partridge. "Ninety percent of users just won't want to get involved with the complex forms of OSI TP."

Point for point, OSI TP and LU6.2 provide just about the same services. In the end, says Partridge, "the choice of which to use has to do with what network you have. A business with an SNA network will want APPC, and one with an OSI network will want OSI TP. Most users have SNA, so OSI TP has a lot of work to do. ■

Index

Page references in this index are to the first pages of the articles in which the subjects appear, or to special sections devoted to those subjects.